Child, Family, and State

E. Allan Farnsworth
On January 31, 2005, Aspen Publishers lost a great author, colleague, and friend with the death of E. Allan Farnsworth, the Alfred McCormack Professor of Law at Columbia Law School and author of the seminal student treatise, Contracts, Fourth Edition, by Aspen Publishers.

Child, Family, and State

Problems and Materials on Children and the Law

Fifth Edition

Robert H. Mnookin
Samuel Williston Professor of Law
Harvard University

D. Kelly Weisberg
Professor of Law
Hastings College of the Law
University of California

111 Eighth Avenue, New York, NY 10011
www.aspenpublishers.com

Aspen Publishers
Attn: Permissions Department
111 Eighth Avenue, 7th Floor
New York, NY 10011-5201

Printed in the United States of America.

1 2 3 4 5 6 7 8 9 0

ISBN 0-7355-4060-8

Library of Congress Cataloging-in-Publication Data

Mnookin, Robert H.
   Child, family, and state : problems and materials on children and the law / c Robert H. Mnookin, D. Kelly Weisberg.– 5th ed.
      p. cm.
   Includes index.
   ISBN 0-7355-4060-8 (hardcover : alk. paper)
   1. Children—Legal status, laws, etc.—United States—Cases. 2. Parent and child (Law)—United States—Cases. 3. Child abuse—Law and legislation—United States. 4. Custody of children—Law and legislation—United States. I. Weisberg, D. Kelly. II. Title.

KF479.A7M56 2005
346.7301'35—dc22   2005013346

About Aspen Publishers

Aspen Publishers, headquartered in New York City, is a leading information provider for attorneys, business professionals, and law students. Written by preeminent authorities, our products consist of analytical and practical information covering both U.S. and international topics. We publish in the full range of formats, including updated manuals, books, periodicals, CDs, and online products.

Our proprietary content is complemented by 2,500 legal databases, containing over 11 million documents, available through our Loislaw division. Aspen Publishers also offers a wide range of topical legal and business databases linked to Loislaw's primary material. Our mission is to provide accurate, timely, and authoritative content in easily accessible formats, supported by unmatched customer care.

To order any Aspen Publishers title, go to *www.aspenpublishers.com* or call 1-800-638-8437.

To reinstate your manual update service, call 1-800-638-8437.

For more information on Loislaw products, go to *www.loislaw.com* or call 1-800-364-2512.

For Customer Care issues, e-mail CustomerCare@aspenpublishers.com; call 1-800-234-1660; or fax 1-800-901-9075.

Aspen Publishers
A Wolters Kluwer Company

In memory of I. J. Mnookin, whose parental love illumined a
sovereignty the law must reflect.
—*R. H. M.*

To my husband, George, and my children, Aaron and Sarah.
—*D. K. W.*

SUMMARY OF CONTENTS

CONTENTS

PREFACE

A single overarching question lies at the core of this fifth edition, as in the previous editions: Who decides on behalf of the child? More precisely, how does law allocate power and responsibility for children in our society, and how should it do so? This question reflects the belief that the primary function of law in relation to children is to outline a framework for the distribution of decisional power among the child, the family, and various agencies of the state. Thus, the title of the book.

What makes the study of children and the law particularly intriguing is the fact that as children grow up they acquire an increasing capacity for making decisions for themselves. Babies and very young children are incapable of making decisions about many important questions affecting their lives. It is not simply unwise to emancipate a two-and-a-half-year-old; it is impossible. Therefore, for the very young, the question is not whether the child should decide, but rather which adult should decide on behalf of the child. As the child grows older, however, it becomes increasingly possible for the child to assume responsibility. Consequently, a critical issue that recurs in many contexts throughout the book concerns the degree to which law should recognize the autonomy of older children — that is, the extent to which the law gives power to children to decide for themselves.

Another core issue explored in various contexts throughout the book concerns the appropriate role of government vis-à-vis children and their families. The parens patriae tradition reflects a deep-rooted notion that government has a special responsibility to protect children even from their parents. Delineating the scope of the government's role necessarily poses profound questions of political and moral philosophy concerning the proper relationship of children to their family and of the family to the state.

Note on the Fifth Edition. This fifth edition of the casebook continues the basic design and emphasis of the former editions. At the same time, this edition takes into account many timely and fascinating changes in the law.

Chapter 1 provides a discussion of legal developments wrought by the Internet, including federal and state regulation of sexually explicit content (Ashcroft v. ACLU (*Ashcroft II*)), child pornography, and student library access to the Internet (United States v. American Library Assn.). The chapter also explores the legal ramifications of the school violence epidemic, including the movement to restrict minors' access to violent materials in movies, television, music, and video games; mandatory dress codes aimed at preventing school violence; and the extension of zero-tolerance policies to include a wider variety of behaviors and harsher sanctions.

In addition, Chapter 1 explores many contemporary educational issues that involve state and federal regulation of the family, such as home schooling, school vouchers, proposed "parental rights" legislation that permits increased authority over children, and parental disputes about the religious education of children (i.e., Elk Grove Unified School District v. Newdow). Finally, the chapter includes the latest developments on abortion (i.e., parental notification requirements, partial-birth abortion bans, violence at abortion clinics), regulation of research on embryos, and legal protection of the fetus in a variety of novel contexts (e.g., fetal homicide legislation and the imposition of criminal liability on pregnant substance abusers).

Chapter 2 includes an update on federal welfare reform legislation, as well as legal developments regarding the parental obligation for necessaries, state and federal enforcement of child support obligations, postmajority support, the legal status of nonmarital children, and stepparent support obligations. Cutting-edge topics include the legal status of children born of assisted reproduction, including disputes involving same-sex couples (T.F. v. B.L.), as well as the posthumous child's right to government survivorship benefits (Gillett-Netting v. Barnhart).

Chapter 3 covers updates on the parental privilege to discipline children, central registries, corporal punishment in the schools and at home (including international developments), the clergy sex abuse scandal, evidentiary concerns involving the child sexual abuse victim as a witness (including the implications of Crawford v. Washington), and termination of parental rights. The chapter also highlights developments regarding foster care, including foster parents' rights, the problems raised by exit from foster care for older children (Occean v. Kearney), and foster care reform.

Chapter 4 incorporates a discussion of current developments regarding state-imposed health requirements applicable to all children, mandatory HIV testing of newborns, and the resolution of disputes about the medical treatment of infants with severe physical and mental impairments. This chapter features many new topics. In particular, it explores the issue of parents' refusal of treatment in the context of a severely premature newborn whose prognosis is uncertain (Miller ex rel. Miller v. HCA). The chapter also examines the issue of whether parents may consent to nontherapeutic medical procedures for their children (Grimes v. Kennedy Krieger Institute, Inc.). The chapter concludes with a new section highlighting some of the legal issues that are implicated in the context of adolescent health (e.g., suicide and obesity).

Chapter 5 addresses legal developments in the custody and visitation rights of stepparents, grandparents (Troxel v. Granville), lesbian mothers, and unwed fathers; the child's preference in custody decision making; legal representation for children (including discussion of the ABA Standards of Practice for Lawyers Representing Children in Custody Cases); relocation disputes, and child custody jurisdiction and enforcement (including discussion of the Uniform Child Custody Jurisdiction and Enforcement Act); and alternative dispute resolution (including a new discussion of collaborative law techniques). The chapter also covers updates on the topics of assisted reproduction, such as post-dissolution disputes over "ownership" of embryos, surrogate parenting (including international developments), and the use of reproductive technology by gays and lesbians. A new section addresses the relevance of sexual orientation in adoption (Lofton v. Secretary of the Department of Children and Family Services), and a new case focuses on the relevance of race in adoption (Adoption of Vito). Finally, the chapter includes a comprehensive discussion of the ALI Principles of Family Dissolution and the recently revised

Uniform Parentage Act, particularly the latter's significance for maternity/paternity establishment and gestational surrogacy agreements.

Revisions to Chapter 6 include updates on state regulation of juvenile drivers (regarding employment, substance abuse, and graduated licenses); sex education in the schools (i.e., abstinence-based sex education programs); teen contraception; a new case on juvenile curfews (Hodgkins v. Peterson (*Hodgkins II*)); status offenders (i.e., changes in the standard of proof, entitlement to counsel, and developments in the re-institutionalization movement to detain status offenders in secure facilities); and emancipation (i.e., juveniles "divorcing" their parents).

Finally, Chapter 7 explores several major legal developments in juvenile justice. Significantly expanded sections focus on the law of search and seizure (Board of Education v. Earls), the voluntariness of juvenile confessions (Yarborough v. Alvarado), the right to jury trial, anti-gang legislation, *Miranda* rights for juveniles, and the juvenile death penalty (Roper v. Simmons). The chapter also highlights developments and criticisms regarding the practice of judicial waiver to adult court. Finally, the chapter explores suggestions for reform of the juvenile justice system.

Like the previous editions, this fifth edition places considerable emphasis on empirical psychological and sociological research. This edition highlights data on minors' exercise of abortion rights; corporal punishment; the effects of divorce on children; the changing foster care population; gay and lesbian parenting; state compliance with deinstitutionalization requirements for status offenders and runaways; juvenile drinking and driving; teenage sexual activity (rates of intercourse and pregnancy) and contraceptive practices; juvenile curfews; differential treatment of male and female status offenders; juvenile crime rates; transfer to adult criminal court; juvenile capacity and maturity in the contexts of confessions and the juvenile death penalty; and the legal representation of juveniles in the delinquency context.

Note on the First Edition. This book is designed for a law school course on children and the law. The first edition grew out of a conviction that critical questions relating to children could not be adequately addressed in the traditional family law or juvenile justice course and that there were intellectual and pedagogical advantages in a more systematic examination of the legal treatment of childhood. Juvenile law courses typically concentrate on the juvenile court — its jurisdiction and its procedures. Family law courses, on the other hand, are primarily concerned with questions relating to marriage and divorce. Existing casebooks for such courses seemed either too narrow or too broad to allow a systematic examination of what it means to be a child for purposes of the law.

In approaching the task of writing this book, it was obvious that an extraordinarily broad range of law might affect or be relevant to children. It was decided that the primary objective would be to write a book that would provide students with the opportunity of learning how to think about children and the law and how to develop a framework that might then prove useful in exploring a broad variety of issues, including many that are not touched on in the book.

Note to Instructors. Because the book is designed for law school teaching, a few paragraphs addressed primarily to law school instructors are in order. The Questions and Problems sections in each chapter are the heart of the book. More questions are included than could possibly be discussed with any thoroughness in the available class time. It is hoped, however, that questions not discussed in class may nonetheless stimulate student thought, be useful to generate student research that can result in law review notes and comments, and encourage scholarship by lawyers and nonlawyers alike.

In addition to the Questions, there are a number of Problems. In fact, this fifth edition includes many more Problems than did the fourth edition. These Problems can serve either as vehicles for classroom discussion or as written exercises for students; in our teaching we use them for both. The Problems exhibit considerable variety not only in subject areas but also in terms of the lawyering skills required.

Some background in psychology, human development, and sociology is extremely helpful in the study of children and the law. Instructors may wish to assign background reading concerning children and families at the beginning of the course. In this respect we would like to recommend Arlene S. Skolnick's *The Intimate Environment: Exploring Marriage and the Family* (6th ed. 1996) and Arlene S. Skolnick and Jerome Skolnick's *The Family in Transition: Rethinking Marriage, Sexuality, Child Rearing and Family Organization* (12th ed. 2002). These books provide a lucid introduction to and summary of a great deal of theoretical and empirical research relating to the social context of childhood, the psychology of socialization, child development, and the child's social relationships within the family. Other excellent areas for background reading are the history of childhood and the history of the family. Recommended sources include the chapter on "Inducting Children into the Social Order" in Carl N. Degler's *At Odds: Women and the Family in America from the Revolution to the Present* (1980) and the introductory chapter on "The Evolution of Childhood" in *The History of Childhood* (Lloyd deMause ed., 1974). For more recent works, see Paula S. Fass and Mary Ann Mason eds., *Childhood in America* (2000) and Steven Mintz, *Huck's Raft: A History of American Childhood* (2004). Several collections of materials relating to the history of childhood merit special mention, including Robert H. Bremner ed., *Children and Youth in America: A Documentary History* (3 vols., 1970-1974) and Paula S. Fass ed., *Encyclopedia of Children and Childhood in History and Society* (3 vols., 2003).

Many students will undoubtedly wish to do outside reading on the questions, problems, and cases presented in the book. For this purpose, we have included references to helpful articles and books. Several additional collections of essays are particularly useful: Margaret K. Rosenheim et al. eds., *A Century of Juvenile Justice* (2001), S. Randall Humm et al. eds., *Child, Parent, and State: Law and Policy Reader* (1994), and the journals in the series "The Future of Children" (on such topics as adoption, child abuse, divorce, firearms, foster care, health care, and the juvenile court), published by the David and Lucile Packard Foundation, Center for the Future of Children, Los Altos, California. Finally, a number of recent law review symposia have focused on interesting issues relevant to children. See Symposium, Caring for Our Children: Delivery of Mental Health Services to Children and Adolescents, 25 J. Legal Med. 1 (2004); Symposium, Defending Childhood, 14 U. Fla. J.L. & Pub. Pol'y 125 (2003); Symposium: The Relationship Rights of Children, 11 Wm. & Mary Bill Rts. J. 843 (2003); Symposium, Therapeutic Jurisprudence and Research, 71 U. Cin. L. Rev. 13 (2002); Symposium, Research with Children: The New Legal and Policy Landscape, 6 J. Health Care L. & Pol'y 1 (2002).

This edition of the casebook continues to allow instructors considerable flexibility in designing courses or seminars of varying lengths and emphasis. The book as a whole is intended for a one-semester course that meets three hours a week. The book also could be used, however, for shorter courses such as in-depth seminars. For example, a seminar might focus on the juvenile justice system, emphasizing Chapters 3, 6, and 7. For law schools that offer a separate course in juvenile delinquency or in which delinquency issues are covered in criminal law courses, the instructor might use Chapters 1 through 6 and omit Chapter 7. Particular chapters will also provide a focus for specialized seminars. Chapters 3, 4, and 5 certainly could form the core materials for in-depth seminars: Chapter 3 on child abuse and neglect, Chapter 4 on medical treatment of children, and Chapter 5 on custody law. Apart from the first chapter — which introduces major themes that are explored in the remainder of the book — the chapters may be rearranged to suit the needs of the instructor.

Editorial Matters. This fifth edition incorporates significant editorial revisions. Judicial opinions often tend to be long and redundant. Instructors will note that many of the cases and excerpts in previous editions have been shortened markedly for the sake of brevity and clarity. Throughout the book, deletions are indicated by ellipses, with the following exceptions: citations have been modified or eliminated, footnotes have been eliminated, and paragraphs have been modified to make edited excerpts coherent without indication. When retained, footnotes in reprinted materials have the original footnote numbers. Our own footnotes are indicated by footnote numbers in brackets. These bracketed footnotes are numbered consecutively throughout each chapter. Additions to reprinted materials are indicated by brackets as well.

Acknowledgments for the Fifth Edition. We would like particularly to acknowledge the valuable research assistance provided by the following students: Jennifer Cannistra and Karen Tenenbaum of Harvard Law School; and Christopher Bell, Kathryn Kaufman, Michelle Leung, Benjamin Lillien, and Josh Sugnet of Hastings College of the Law. Thanks are due also to Dean Mary Crossley for her helpful suggestions on Chapter 4; John Borden of Hastings College of the Law for his excellent library reference assistance; and to Barbara Rappaport, Barbara Roth, and Carmen Corral-Reid of Aspen Publishers for their superb editorial assistance.

Robert H. Mnookin
Harvard Law School

D. Kelly Weisberg
Hastings College of the Law

May 2005

ACKNOWLEDGMENTS

We wish to thank the authors and copyright holders of the following works who permitted their inclusion in this book:

ABA, Model Code of Professional Responsibility (1986). Reprinted with permission of the American Bar Association. Copies of ABA *Model Code of Professional Responsibilty* are available from Service Center, American Bar Association, 321 North Clark Street, Chicago, IL 60610, 1-800-285-2221.

ABA, Institute of Judicial Administration, Juvenile Justice Standards. Copyright 1980, Ballinger Publishing Company.

American Law Institute, Model Penal Code §3.08 (Tent. Draft No. 8). Copyright 1958 by the American Law Institute. Reprinted with permission. All rights reserved.

American Law Institute, Restatement (Second) of Torts, §§147, 150-155 (1965). Copyright 1965 by the American Law Institute. Reprinted with permission. All rights reserved.

Andrews, R. Hale, Jr. & Andrew H. Cohn, Note, Ungovernability: The Unjustifiable Jurisdiction, 83 Yale L.J. 1383 (1974). Reprinted by permission of The Yale Law Journal Company and Fred B. Rothman & Company.

Annas, George J., Mandatory PKU Screening: The Other Side of the Looking Glass, 72 Am. J. Public Health 1401 (1986). Reprinted with permission of the author.

Arthur, Lindsay G., Child Sexual Abuse: Improving the System's Response, 37 Juv. & Fam. Ct. J. (No. 2) 1-14 (1986). Reprinted with permission of the author and the National Council of Juvenile and Family Court Judges, Reno, NV.

Bartholet, Elizabeth, The Challenge of Children's Rights Advocacy: Problems and Progress in the Area of Child Abuse and Neglect, 3 Whittier J. Child & Fam. Advoc. 215, 218-221 (2004). Used by permission of Whittier Journal of Child and Family Advocacy.

Bass, Sandra, et al., Children, Families and Foster Care: Analysis and Recommendations, The Future of Children, v. 14 no. 1 (Winter 2004), pp. 6-8. From The Future of Children, a publication of the David and Lucile Packard Foundation.

Belgum, Eunice, Book Review, 89 Harv. L. Rev. 823. Copyright © 1976 by Harvard Law Review Association.

Bennett, Robert, Allocation of Child Medical Decision-Making Authority: A Suggested Interest Analysis, 62 Va. L. Rev. 285 (1976). Reprinted with permission of Fred B. Rothman & Company.

Besharov, Douglas, J., Child Abuse Realities: Over-Reporting and Poverty, 8 Va. J. Soc. Pol'y & L. 165, 188-192, 196-203 (2000).

Bishop, Jerry, Limited Tests Are Conducted on Children Needing Special Diet for Genetic Defect, Wall St. J., Dec. 1, 1975, 10, col. 2. Reprinted with permission of the Wall Street Journal, © Dow Jones & Company, Inc. 1976. All Rights Reserved.

Bodenheimer, Brigitte M., New Trends and Requirements in Adoption Law and Proposals for Legislative Change, 49 S. Cal. L. Rev. 10 (1975).

Bremner, Robert H., ed., Children and Youth in America: A Documentary History, Volumes II-III. Reprinted by permission of Harvard University Press, Copyright © 1971, 1974 by the American Public Health Association.

Calabresi, Guido, Reflections on Medical Experimentation, 98 Daedalus (No. 2) 387 (1969). Reprinted by permission of Daedalus: American Academy of Arts and Sciences.

Capron, Alexander, Legal Considerations Affecting Pharmacological Studies in Children, 21 Clinical Res. 141 (1973).

Chambers, David L., Rethinking the Substantive Rules for Custody Disputes in Divorce, 83 Mich. L. Rev. 477 (1984).

Chambers, David L, & Michael S. Wald, "Smith v. OFFER," in In the Interest of Children (Robert H. Mnookin ed. 1985). Copyright © 1985 by W. H. Freeman and Company.

Collier, Susan A., Comment, Reporting Child Abuse: When Moral Obligations Fail, 15 Pac. L.J. 189 (1983).

Coons, John E., Law and the Sovereigns of Childhood, 58 Phi Delta Kappan (No. 1) 19 (Sept. 1976).

DeFrancis, Vincent, Child Abuse Legislation in the 1970's 2-13 (Am. Humane Assn. 1974).

Duff, Raymond S. & August B. Campbell, Moral and Ethical Dilemmas in the Special-Care Nursery, 289 N. Eng. J. Med. 890 (1973). Reprinted by permission from the New England Journal of Medicine.

Emerson, Thomas I., The System of Freedom of Expression (1970). Copyright © 1970 by Thomas I. Emerson. Used by permission of Random House, Inc.

English, Diana J., The Extent and Consequences of Child Maltreatment, The Future of Children, v. 8, no. 1 (Spring 1998), 40-42, 45-48. From The Future of Children, a publication of the David and Lucile Packard Foundation.

Faust, Frederic L. & Paul J. Brantingham (eds.). The Invention of the Juvenile Court, in Juvenile Justice Philosophy: Readings, Cases and Comments. Copyright © 1974, West Publishing Company. All rights reserved.

Feld, Barry C., The Transformation of the Juvenile Court, 75 Minn. L. Rev. 691 (1991).

Foot, Philippa, Euthanasia, in 6 Phil. and Pub. Aff. (No. 2) 85-97, 109-112. © 1977 by Philippa Foot. Reprinted by permission of the author and Princeton University Press.

Garrison, Marsha, Why Terminate Parental Rights?, 35 Stan. L. Rev. 423 (1983). Reprinted with permission of the Stanford Law Review and Fred B. Rothman Company, Copyright 1983 by the Board of Trustees of the Leland Stanford Junior University.

Grisso, Thomas, Juveniles' Waiver of Rights, 34 Juv. & Fam. Ct. J. 49 (1983-1984).

Hafen, Bruce C., Children's Liberation and the New Egalitarianism: Some Reservations about Abandoning Youth to Their "Rights", 1976 B.Y.U. L. Rev. (No. 3) 605. Copyright 1976 by the Brigham Young University Law Review. Reprinted by permission.

Hawkins-León, Cynthia G., & Carla Bradley, Race and Transracial Adoption: The Answer Is Neither Simply Black or White Nor Right or Wrong, 51 Cath. U. L. Rev. 1227, 1255-1267 (2002). Work used with permission of Catholic University Law Review. Excerpts from Carla Bradley & Cynthia Hawkins-León, The Transracial Adoption Debate: Counseling and Legal Implications, Journal of Counseling & Development, 80(4), 433-440 (2002). ACA. Reprinted with permission. No further reproduction authorized without written permission from the American Counseling Association.

Hetherington, E. Mavis, & John Kelly, For Better or For Worse: Divorce Reconsidered, W.W. Norton & Co., 228-229 (2002). Copyright © 2002 by E. Mavis Hetherington and John Kelly. Used by permission of W.W. Norton & Company, Inc.

Kandel, Randy Frances, & Anne Griffiths, Reconfiguring Personhood: From Ungovernability to Parent Adolescent Autonomy Conflict Actions, 53 Syracuse L. Rev. 995, 1002-1003, 1032-1042, 1059-1063 (2003).

Keith-Spiegel, Patricia C., Children and Consent to Participate in Research, in Children's Competence to Consent (G. Melton et al. eds., 1983).

Kempe, C. Henry & Ray E. Helfer, eds., Helping the Battered Child and His Family (1972).

Krugman, Richard D., The Coming Decade: Unfinished Tasks and New Frontiers, 9 Child Abuse & Neglect 119 (1985). Copyright 1985, Pergamon Press.

Langer, Dennis H., Medical Research Involving Children: Some Legal and Ethical Issues, 36 Baylor L. Rev, 1, 11-16 (1984).

Levine, Robert J., Ethics and Regulation of Clinical Research 239-241 (2d ed. 1986). Copyright 1986 Urban and Schwarzenberg, Baltimore-Munich.

Maccoby, Eleanor E. & Robert H. Mnookin, Dividing the Child: Social and Legal Dilemmas of Custody 274-275 (1992). Reprinted by permission of Harvard University Press. Copyright © 1992 by the President and Fellows of Harvard College.

Maccoby, Eleanor E. et al., Custody of Children Following Divorce, in The Impact of Divorce, Single-Parenting and Step-Parenting on Children (E. Mavis Hetherington & Josephine D. Arasteh eds., 1988).

McIntire, Roger W., Parenthood Training or Mandatory Birth Control: Take Your Choice, Psychology Today 34 (Oct. 1973). Reprinted from Psychology Today Magazine, © 1973 Sussex Publishers, Inc.

McIvor, Greg, Human Rights: Swedish Parents Demand Right to Smack Children, Inter Press Service, Feb. 5, 1993. Inter Press Service, available from Global Information Network, NY, NY.

Mitchell, Ross G., The Child and Experimental Medicine, 1 Brit. Med. J. 721-722 (1964). Published by permission of British Medical Journal.

Mnookin, Robert H., Child-Custody Adjudication: Judicial Functions in the Face of Indeterminacy, 39 Law & Contemp. Probs. (No. 3) 226 (Summer 1975).

Mnookin, Robert H., Foster Care — In Whose Best Interest? 43 Harv. Ed. Rev. 4 (Nov. 1973). Copyright © 1973 by President and Fellows of Harvard College.

Mnookin, Robert H., Two Puzzles, 1984 Arizona State Law Journal 667, 668-671, 677-679.

Mnookin, Robert H., The Guardianship of Phillip B.: Jay Spears' Achievement, 40 Stan. L. Rev. 841 (1988). Copyright 1988 by the Board of Trustees of the Leland Stanford Junior University.

Mnookin, Robert H. & Lewis Kornhauser, Bargaining in the Shadow of the Law: The Case of Divorce, 88 Yale L.J. 950 (1979).

Mosher, James, The History of Youthful-Drinking Laws: Implications for Public Policy, in Minimum-Drinking-Age Laws: An Evaluation (Henry Wechsler ed., 1980). Reprinted by permission of the author.

National Research Council, Risking the Future: Adolescent Sexuality, Pregnancy, and Childbearing, vol. 1 (1986). Copyright 1986 by the National Academy of Sciences.

Nelson, F. Kirk & Joel E. Bernstein, Consent in Pediatric Medical Experimentation, 3 J. Legal Med. 15 (March 1975).

Olson, Dennis Alan, Comment, The Swedish Ban of Corporal Punishment, 1984 B.Y.U. L, Rev. 447.

O'Malley, Patrick M. & Alexander C. Wagenaar, Effects of Minimum Age Drinking Laws, 52 J. Stud. Alcohol 478-491 (1991). Reprinted with permission from Journal of Studies on Alcohol. Copyright by Alcohol Research Documentation, Inc., Rutgers Center of Alcohol Studies, Piscataway, NJ 08855.

Pearson, Jessica & Nancy Thoennes, The Denial of Visitation Rights: A Preliminary Look at Its Incidence, Correlates, Antecedents and Consequences, 10 Law and Policy (No. 4) 363-380 (1988).

Posner, Richard A., The Regulation of the Market in Adoptions, 67 B.U. L. Rev. 59 (1987).

President's Commission for the Study of Ethical Problems in Medicine and Biomedical and Behavioral Research: Deciding to Forgo Life-Sustaining Treatment (Pub. No. 83-17978) 197-204, 217-223 (1983).

President's Commission for the Study of Ethical Problems in Medicine and Biomedical and Behavioral Research: Screening and Counseling for Genetic Conditions 12-15 (1983).

President's Commission on Law Enforcement and Administration of Justice, Task Force Report: Juvenile Delinquency and Youth Crime 4-6 (1967).

Ramsey, Paul, A Reply to Richard McCormick: The Enforcement of Morals: Nontherapeutic Research on Children, 6 Hastings Center Rep. (No. 4) 21 (Aug. 1976). © Institute of Society, Ethics and the Life Sciences, 360 Broadway, Hastings-on-Hudson, NY 10706.

Roberts, Dorothy E., Is There Justice in Children's Rights?: The Critique of Federal Family Preservation Policy, 2 U.PA. J. Const. L. 112, 118-138 (1999).

Robertson, John A., Involuntary Euthanasia of Defective Newborns: A Legal Analysis, 27 Stan. L. Rev. 213 (1975). Copyright 1975 by the Board of Trustees of the Leland Stanford Junior University.

Ryan, Ann E., Comment, Protecting the Rights of Pediatric Research Subjects in the International Conference of Harmonisation of Technical Requirements for Registration of Pharmaceuticals for Human Use, 23 Fordham Int'l L.J. 848, 855-857 (2000).

Saposnek, Donald T., Mediating Child Custody Disputes 7-16 (rev. ed. 1998).

Schultz, J. Lawrence & Fred Cohen, Isolationism in Juvenile Court Jurisprudence, in Pursuing Justice for the Child (Margaret Kenney Rosenheim ed. 1976). © The University of Chicago 1976. All rights reserved.

Schwartz, Harold L. & Arthur Hirsh, Child Abuse and Neglect: A Survey of the Law, 28 Medical Trial Technique Quarterly 293, 306-308 (1982). Reprinted with permission from Clark Boardman Callaghan, 50 Broad Street East, Rochester, NY 14694.

Simpson, Anna Louise, Comment, Rehabilitation as the Justification of a Separate Juvenile Justice System, 64 Cal. L. Rev. 984 (1976). Copyright © California Law Review, Inc. Reprinted by permission.

Smith, Steven R., Disabled Newborns and the Federal Child Abuse Amendments: Tenuous Protection, 37 Hastings L.J. 765-825 (1986). Copyright 1986 Hastings College of the Law. Reprinted with permission.

Snyder, Howard, Juvenile Arrests 2001, Juvenile Justice Bulletin, Office of Juvenile Justice and Delinquency Prevention. (Dec. 2003), pp. 1, 4, 5, 7-10. From The Future of Children, a publication of the David and Lucile Packard Foundation.

Steinman, Susan, Joint Custody: What We Know, What We Have Yet to Learn, and the Judicial and Legislative Impact, 16 U.C. Davis L. Rev. 739 (1983). Copyright 1983 by The Regents of the University of California. Reprinted with permission.

Strauss, Andrew R., Note, Losing Sight of the Utilitarian Forest for the Retributivist Trees: An Analysis of the Role of Public Opinion in a Utilitarian Model of Punishment, 23 Cardozo L. Rev. 1549, 1571-1581 (2002).

ten Bensel, Robert W., The Scope of the Problem, 35 Juv. & Fam. Ct. J. 1 (Winter 1984). Reprinted with permission of the author and the National Council of Juvenile and Family Court Judges.

UCLA Medicine and Society Forum, Would It Have Been Ethical to Give Swine Flu Vaccine to Children Without Prior Testing? (Jan. 27, 1977).

Uniform Parentage Act, §§201, 204, 301, 302, 402, 403, 404, 405. Copyright © 2002 by National Conference of Commissioners on Uniform State Laws.

Wagenaar, Alexander C., Alcohol, Young Drivers and Traffic Accidents (1983). Reprinted by permission of Lexington Books, Lexington, MA. Copyright 1983 D.C. Health and Company.

Wald, Michael S. et al., Protecting Abused and Neglected Children 9-12 (1988). Reprinted with the permission of the publishers, Stanford University Press. Copyright © 1988 by the Board of Trustees of the Leland Stanford Jr. University.

Wallerstein, Judith S., Children of Divorce: An Overview, 4 Behav. Sci. & L. 105-116 (1986). Reproduced by permission of John Wiley & Sons Limited.

Weir, Robert F., Life-and-Death Decisions in the Midst of Uncertainty, in Compelled Compassion: Government Intervention in the Treatment of Critically Ill Newborns 25-29 (Arthur L. Caplan et al. eds., 1992).

Weisberg, D. Kelly, The "Discovery" of Sexual Abuse: Experts' Role in Legal Policy Formulation, 18 U.C. Davis L. Rev. 1 (1984). Copyright 1984 by the Regents of the University of California. Reprinted with permission.

Child, Family, and State

CHAPTER **1**

The Child, the Family, and the State

A. *INTRODUCTION*

Over a century ago, John Stuart Mill observed that "[t]he existing generation is master both of the training and the entire experience of the generation to come."[1] Mill thought this to be true and proper. Our generation appears to be the first in which Mill's proposition will encounter serious challenge in what may prove a long intellectual and ultimately legal and political campaign.

The idea that adults "master" the "training and the entire experience" of children seems empirically wrong, both from the perspective of the child's individual psychology and as a matter of social roles. While an infant obviously comes into the world dependent for its survival upon adults, experimental psychologists suggest that even the very young child selectively perceives and interprets situations and events.[2] There is no way for adults to make sure that children will receive or accept a particular message because children contribute to what they experience.[3] For this reason, and because environmental events and cultural determinants beyond the purposeful control of adults bear so heavily on the child's experience, the notion that adults somehow control the socialization of the next generation seems dubious. Arguably, the present-day social reality in America would be as accurately described by turning Mill's assertion on its head — children and youth may dominate the experience of their elders. The victims of intergenerational confrontation may include adults as well as children. In all events, Mill's description is strangely one-sided: the older and younger generations seem in fact inextricably intertwined in a reciprocal relationship in which the unique experience of each affects the other.

---

[1] John Stuart Mill, On Liberty 77 (David Spitz ed. 1975). This part of the introduction has been adapted from Robert H. Mnookin, Foreword — Symposium on Children and the Law, 39 Law & Contemp. Probs. (No. 3) 1–3 (1975).

[2] See H. Rudolph Schaffer, The Growth of Sociability (1971).

[3] See Arlene S. Skolnick, The Intimate Environment 372–374 (4th ed. 1987).

Apart from the accuracy of Mill's description, could it possibly describe a just relationship among human beings? For children, Mill explicitly rejected his own principle of individual liberty on a variety of grounds, the most important of which related to the notion that the child was incapable of self-improvement by means of rational discussion.[4] Limiting the freedom of children was therefore, by his lights, necessary both to protect children against "their own actions as well as against external injury"[5] and to protect society from the untutored.[6] Mill rejected, however, the prevalent nineteenth-century notion that parents should have unfettered dominion over their children. He instead thought that the state was justified in using law to limit parental liberty when necessary for the good of the child or society.[7]

How the family and the state dominate the lives of children and whether they should are questions that provide a useful starting point for an examination of children and the law. Law outlines a framework for the distribution of decisional power among the child, the family, and various agencies of the state. While the pattern of the law is complex, it seems plain that children generally have less liberty than adults and are often less accountable. Within the family, parents have legal power to make a wide range of important decisions that affect the life of the child, but the state holds them responsible for the child's care and support.[8] Children have the special power to avoid contractual obligations[9] but are not normally entitled to their own earnings[10] and cannot manage their own property.[11] Moreover, in accordance with age-based lines, persons younger than certain statutory limits are not allowed to vote,[12] hold public office,[13] work in various occupations,[14] drive a car,[15] buy liquor,[16] or be sold certain kinds of reading material,[17] quite apart from what they or their parents may wish.

Because of such legally imposed limitations on the child's power to decide, some reformers suggest that a children's liberation movement should follow the trail blazed by the civil rights and women's movements.[18] At the core of these

---

[4] See Mill, supra note 1, at 11.

[5] Id. See also id. at 75.

[6] See id. at 100.

[7] See id. at 96-101.

[8] See Chapters 2 and 3.

[9] See Chapter 6, p. 659.

[10] See Chapter 2, p. 153.

[11] See Chapter 2, p. 210.

[12] See, e.g., Cal. Const. art. II, §2 (West 2002); cf. Oregon v. Mitchell. 400 U.S. 112 (1970) (upholding congressional power to lower voting age from 21 to 18 for federal but not for state elections).

[13] See, e.g., Cal. Govt. Code §1020 (West 1995) ("A person is incapable of holding a civil office if at the time of his election or appointment he is not 18 years of age.").

[14] See, e.g., Fair Labor Standards Act, 29 U.S.C. §212 (2000); Cal. Lab. Code §§1285-1312 (West 2003 & Supp. 2004). See generally Chapter 6, section B.

[15] See Chapter 6, p. 648.

[16] See, e.g., Cal. Const. art. XX, §22 (West 1996); Cal. Bus. & Prof. Code §§25658-65 (West 1997 & Supp. 2004). See Chapter 6, p. 661.

[17] See Ginsberg v. New York, p. 81 infra.

[18] See, e.g., Virginia Coigney, Children Are People Too (1975); Richard E. Farson, Birthrights (1974).

other movements, however, is the rather straightforward notion that a person's legal autonomy should not be made dependent upon race or sex, at least without some compelling justification. Any broad assertion that age is also irrelevant to legal autonomy inescapably collides with certain biological and economic realities.[19]

Because the young are necessarily dependent for some period after birth, the relevant question often is which adult should have the power to decide on behalf of the child. That an element of domination of children by adults is inevitable gives no license to ignore the moral dimension implicit in the advocates' challenge. Moreover, for older children, the emancipators' rhetoric has raised questions worthy of serious examination: in what circumstances should the law give children the power to decide certain things for themselves and to be responsible for their own actions? Are some of the age-based lines drawn too high? What are the advantages and disadvantages of arbitrary lines as opposed to more flexible alternatives? In addressing all these questions, it must be recognized that the legal system reflects at least as much as it shapes the social context in which children grow up. The law's assignment of roles and authority for children of various ages gives expression to society's perception of the child's humanity and importance as an individual.

John E. Coons, Law and the Sovereigns of Childhood
58 Phi Delta Kappan (No. 1) 19 (Sept. 1976)

The common law and statutory structures that affect childhood come in three styles which can be labeled rules, minimums, and sovereignties. Rules are more or less specific standards of conduct and may take a positive or negative form. Thus children under 15 are forbidden to drive automobiles or work in factories and are commanded to attend school. Parents are limited in their choice of punishments and are commanded to provide adequate nourishment. Minimums are legal devices which in various ways assure that the level of goods and services necessary to the child's protection, control, and preparation for adult life will not fall below some floor. For example, where the family is unable to supply the basics of nutrition, protection, dress, or housing, law provides money, goods, or services sufficient to raise its performance to the standard; if the family's failure is beyond the help of material resources, law places the child in a foster family for which it provides a modest subsidy. And, recognizing the child's need for a substantial period of formal education and the family's frequent incapacity to provide it by itself, law also supplies a school meeting at least some basic criteria. Here we see that minimums and rules often become indistinguishable; the rule that a child must be a student for 180 days a year is part of the guarantee that he will enjoy the social minimum of education.

blur btw. rules & minimums

---

[19] See generally Martin Guggenheim, What's Wrong with Children's Rights (forthcoming 2005) (exploring the ways in which the children's rights movement has been invoked in such contexts as abortion, adoption, custody, and foster care).

However, by far the law's most significant intervention is of the third type, one which occupies and pre-empts that vast area of child rearing which is above the guaranteed minimum and not covered by specific rules. Here the law's way is to recognize in someone or some institution a residual authority and discretion to protect, control, and prepare the child. Law, in short, ordains the petty sovereignties of childhood.

But petty only in the sense that each of these infant hegemonies is itself subject in theory to substantial regulation by the overarching government; the actual scope of its authority often is anything but petty. . . .

B. IS A FETUS A CHILD?

Roe v. Wade
410 U.S. 113 (1973)

Mr. Justice BLACKMUN delivered the opinion of the Court. . . .

I

The Texas statutes that concern us here are Arts. 1191–1194 and 1196 of the State's Penal Code,[1] Vernon's Ann. P.C. These make it a crime to "procure an abortion," as therein defined, or to attempt one, except with respect to "an abortion procured

---

[1]**Article 1191. Abortion**

If any person shall designedly administer to a pregnant woman or knowingly procure to be administered with her consent any drug or medicine, or shall use towards her any violence or means whatever externally or internally applied, and thereby procure an abortion, he shall be confined in the penitentiary not less than two nor more than five years; if it be done without her consent, the punishment shall be doubled. By 'abortion' is meant that the life of the fetus or embryo shall be destroyed in the woman's womb or that a premature birth thereof be caused.

Art. 1192. Furnishing the means

Whoever furnishes the means for procuring an abortion knowing the purpose intended is guilty as an accomplice. . . . [Article 1193 punishes attempted abortion.]

Art. 1194. Murder in producing abortion

If the death of the mother is occasioned by an abortion so produced or by an attempt to effect the same, it is murder.

Art. 1196. By medical advice

Nothing in this chapter applies to an abortion procured or attempted by medical advice for the purpose of saving the life of the mother. . . .

or attempted by medical advice for the purpose of saving the life of the mother."
Similar statutes are in existence in a majority of the States. . . .

II

Jane Roe, a single woman who was residing in Dallas County, Texas, instituted this
federal action in March 1970 against the District Attorney of the county. She sought
a declaratory judgment that the Texas criminal abortion statutes were unconstitutional on their face, and an injunction restraining the defendant from enforcing the
statutes.

Roe alleged that she was unmarried and pregnant; that she wished to terminate her pregnancy by an abortion "performed by a competent, licensed physician,
under safe, clinical conditions"; that she was unable to get a "legal" abortion in
Texas because her life did not appear to be threatened by the continuation of her
pregnancy; and that she could not afford to travel to another jurisdiction in order to
secure a legal abortion under safe conditions. She claimed that the Texas statutes
were unconstitutionally vague and that they abridged her right of personal privacy,
protected by the First, Fourth, Fifth, Ninth, and Fourteenth Amendments. By an
amendment to her complaint Roe purported to sue "on behalf of herself and all other
women" similarly situated. [The district court held that the Ninth and Fourteenth
Amendments protected the fundamental right of single women and married persons to choose to have children, and that the Texas abortion legislation was vague
and overbroad. The Supreme Court concurred with the district court that Jane Roe
had standing and that the case was not rendered moot by the termination of her
pregnancy prior to its decision.] *State-level decisions in Roe's favor*

V

The principal thrust of appellant's attack on the Texas statutes is that they improperly invade a right, said to be possessed by the pregnant woman, to choose to
terminate her pregnancy. Appellant would discover this right in the concept of personal "liberty" embodied in the Fourteenth Amendment's Due Process Clause; or
in personal, marital, familial, and sexual privacy said to be protected by the Bill
of Rights or its penumbras, see *Griswold v. Connecticut,* 381 U.S. 479 (1965);
Eisenstadt v. Baird, 405 U.S. 438 (1972) (White, J., concurring); or among those
rights reserved to the people by the Ninth Amendment, Griswold v. Connecticut,
381 U.S., at 486 (Goldberg, J., concurring), Before addressing this claim, we feel
it desirable briefly to survey, in several aspects, the history of abortion, for such
insight as that history may afford us, and then to examine the state purposes and
interests behind the criminal abortion laws.

VI

It perhaps is not generally appreciated that the restrictive criminal abortion laws in
effect in a majority of States today are of relatively recent vintage. [T]hey derive
from statutory changes effected, for the most part, in the latter half of the 19th
century. . . .

VII

Three reasons have been advanced to explain historically the enactment of criminal abortion laws in the 19th century and to justify their continued existence.

It has been argued occasionally that these laws were the product of a Victorian social concern to discourage illicit sexual conduct. Texas, however, does not advance this justification in the present case, and it appears that no court or commentator has taken the argument seriously. . . .

A second reason is concerned with abortion as a medical procedure. When most criminal abortion laws were first enacted, the procedure was a hazardous one for the woman. . . . Thus it has been argued that a State's real concern in enacting a criminal abortion law was to protect the pregnant woman, that is, to restrain her from submitting to a procedure that placed her life in serious jeopardy.

Modern medical techniques have altered this situation. Appellants and various amici refer to medical data indicating that abortion in early pregnancy that is, prior to the end of first trimester, although not without its risk, is now relatively safe. Mortality rates for women undergoing early abortions, where the procedure is legal, appear to be as low as or lower than the rates for normal childbirth. Consequently, any interest of the State in protecting the woman from an inherently hazardous procedure, except when it would be equally dangerous for her to forgo it, has largely disappeared. Of course, important state interests in the area of health and medical standards do remain. The State has a legitimate interest in seeing to it that abortion, like any other medical procedure, is performed under circumstances that insure maximum safety for the patient. This interest obviously extends at least to the performing physician and his staff, to the facilities involved, to the availability of after-care, and to adequate provision for any complication or emergency that might arise. The prevalence of high mortality rates at illegal "abortion mills" strengthens, rather than weakens, the State's interest in regulating the conditions under which abortions are performed. Moreover, the risk to the woman increases as her pregnancy continues. Thus the State retains a definite interest in protecting the woman's own health and safety when an abortion is proposed at a late stage of pregnancy.

The third reason is the State's interest — some phrase it in terms of duty — in protecting prenatal life. Some of the argument for this justification rests on the theory that a new human life is present from the moment of conception. The State's interest and general obligation to protect life then extends, it is argued, to prenatal life. Only when the life of the pregnant mother herself is at stake, balanced against the life she carries within her, should the interest of the embryo or fetus not prevail. Logically, of course, a legitimate state interest in this area need not stand or fall on acceptance of the belief that life begins at conception or at some other point prior to live birth. In assessing the State's interest, recognition may be given to the less rigid claim that as long as at least *potential* life is involved, the State may assert interests beyond the protection of the pregnant woman alone.

Parties challenging state abortion laws have sharply disputed in some courts the contention that a purpose of these laws, when enacted, was to protect prenatal life. Pointing to the absence of legislative history to support the contention, they claim that most state laws were designed solely to protect the woman. Because medical advances have lessened this concern, at least with respect to abortion in early pregnancy, they argue that with respect to such abortions the laws can no longer be justified by any state interest. There is some scholarly support for this view of original purpose. The few state courts called upon to interpret their laws in the late 19th and early 20th centuries did focus on the State's interest in protecting the woman's health rather than in preserving the embryo and fetus. Proponents of this view point out that in many States, including Texas, by statute or judicial interpretation, the pregnant woman herself could not be prosecuted for self-abortion or for cooperating in an abortion performed upon her by another. They claim that adoption of the "quickening" distinction through received common law and state statutes tacitly recognizes the greater health hazards inherent in late abortion and impliedly repudiates the theory that life begins at conception.

It is with these interests, and the weight to be attached to them, that this case is concerned.

VIII

The Constitution does not explicitly mention any right of privacy. In a line of decisions, however, going back perhaps as far as Union Pacific R. Co. v. Botsford, 141 U.S. 250, 251 (1891), the Court has recognized that a right of personal privacy, or a guarantee of certain areas or zones of privacy, does exist under the Constitution. In varying contexts the Court or individual Justices have indeed found at least the roots of that right in the First Amendment, . . . in the Fourth and Fifth Amendments, . . . in the penumbras of the Bill of Rights, Griswold v. Connecticut, 381 U.S. 479, 484-485 (1965); in the Ninth Amendment, id., at 486 (Goldberg, J., concurring); or in the concept of liberty guaranteed by the first section of the Fourteenth Amendment, see Meyer v. Nebraska, 262 U.S. 390, 399 (1923). These decisions make it clear that only personal rights that can be deemed "fundamental" or "implicit in the concept of ordered liberty" are included in this guarantee of personal privacy. They also make it clear that the right has some extension to activities relating to marriage, Loving v. Virginia, 388 U.S. 1, 12 (1967), procreation, Skinner v. Oklahoma, 316 U.S. 535, 541-542 (1942), contraception, Eisenstadt v. Baird, 405 U.S. 438, 453-454 (1972); id., at 460, 463-465 (White, J., concurring), family relationships, Prince v. Massachusetts, 321 U.S. 158, 166 (1944), and child rearing and education, Pierce v. Society of Sisters, 268 U.S. 510, 535 (1925), Meyer v. Nebraska, supra.

This right of privacy, whether it be founded in the Fourteenth Amendment's concept of personal liberty and restrictions upon state action, as we feel it is, or, as the District Court determined, in the Ninth Amendment's reservation of rights to the people, is broad enough to encompass a woman's decision whether or not to terminate her pregnancy. The detriment that the State would impose upon the pregnant woman by denying this choice altogether is apparent. Specific and direct harm medically diagnosable even in early pregnancy may be involved. Maternity, or additional offspring, may force upon the woman a distressful life and future. Psychological harm may be imminent. Mental and physical health may be taxed by child care. There is also the distress, for all concerned, associated with the unwanted child, and there is the problem of bringing a child into a family already

[handwritten margin note: privacy guaranteed by precedent more than text]

unable, psychologically and otherwise, to care for it. In other cases, as in this one, the additional difficulties and continuing stigma of unwed motherhood may be involved. All these are factors the woman and her responsible physician necessarily will consider in consultation.

On the basis of elements such as these, appellants and some amici argue that the woman's right is absolute and that she is entitled to terminate her pregnancy at whatever time, in whatever way, and for whatever reason she alone chooses. With this we do not agree. Appellants' arguments that Texas either has no valid interest at all in regulating the abortion decision, or no interest strong enough to support any limitation upon the woman's sole determination, is unpersuasive. The Court's decisions recognizing a right of privacy also acknowledge that some state regulation in areas protected by that right is appropriate. As noted above, a state may properly assert important interests in safeguarding health, in maintaining medical standards, and in protecting potential life. At some point in pregnancy, these respective interests become sufficiently compelling to sustain regulation of the factors that govern the abortion decision. The privacy right involved, therefore, cannot be said to be absolute. In fact, it is not clear to us that the claim asserted by some amici that one has an unlimited right to do with one's body as one pleases bears a close relationship to the right of privacy previously articulated in the Court's decisions. The Court has refused to recognize an unlimited right of this kind in the past. Jacobson v. Massachusetts, 197 U.S. 11 (1905) (vaccination); Buck v. Bell, 274 U.S. 200 (1927) (sterilization).

We therefore conclude that the right of personal privacy includes the abortion decision, but that this right is not unqualified and must be considered against important state interests in regulation. . . .

Where certain "fundamental rights" are involved, the Court has held that regulation limiting these rights may be justified only by a "compelling state interest," and that the legislative enactments must be narrowly drawn to express only the legitimate state interests at stake. . . .

IX

The District Court held that the appellee failed to meet his burden of demonstrating that the Texas statute's infringement upon Roe's rights was necessary to support a compelling state interest, and that, although the defendant presented "several compelling justifications for state presence in the area of abortions," the statutes outstripped these justifications and swept "far beyond any areas of compelling state interest." 314 F. Supp., at 1222-1223. Appellant and appellee both contest that holding. Appellant, as has been indicated, claims an absolute right that bars any state imposition of criminal penalties in the area. Appellee argues that the State's determination to recognize and protect prenatal life from and after conception constitutes a compelling state interest. As noted above, we do not agree fully with either formulation.

A

The appellee and certain amici argue that the fetus is a "person" within the language and meaning of the Fourteenth Amendment. In support of this they outline at length and in detail the well-known facts of fetal development. If this suggestion of personhood is established, the appellant's case, of course, collapses, for the fetus' right to life is then guaranteed specifically by the Amendment. . . .

The Constitution does not define "person" in so many words. Section I of the Fourteenth Amendment contains three references to "person." The first, in defining "citizens," speaks of "persons born or naturalized in the United States." The word also appears both in the Due Process Clause and in the Equal Protection Clause. "Person" is used in other places in the Constitution: in the listing of qualifications for representatives and senators, Art. I, §2, cl. 2, and §3, cl. 3; in the Apportionment Clause, Art. I, §2, cl. 3;[53] in the Migration and Importation provision, Art. I, §9, cl. 1; in the Emolument Clause, Art. I, §9, cl. 8; in the Electors provisions, Art. II, §1, cl. 2, and the superseded cl. 3; in the provision outlining qualifications for the office of President, Art. II, §1, cl. 5; in the Extradition provisions, Art. IV, §2, cl. 2, and the superseded Fugitive Slave Clause 3; and in the Fifth, Twelfth, and Twenty-second Amendments as well as in §§2 and 3 of the Fourteenth Amendment. But in nearly all these instances, the use of the word is such that it has application only postnatally. None indicates, with any assurance, that it has any possible prenatal application.[54]

All this, together with our observation, supra, that throughout the major portion of the 19th century prevailing legal abortion practices were far freer than they are today, persuades us that the word "person," as used in the Fourteenth Amendment, does not include the unborn. . . .

This conclusion, however, does not of itself fully answer the contentions raised by Texas, and we pass on to other considerations.

B

The pregnant woman cannot be isolated in her privacy. She carries an embryo and, later, a fetus. . . . The situation therefore is inherently different from marital intimacy, or bedroom possession of obscene material, or marriage, or procreation, or education, with which *Eisenstadt, Griswold, Stanley, Loving, Skinner, Pierce,* and *Meyer* were respectively concerned. As we have intimated above, it is reasonable and appropriate for a State to decide that at some point in time another interest, that of health of the mother or that of potential human life, becomes significantly

---

[53] We are not aware that in the taking of any census under this clause, a fetus has ever been counted.

[54] When Texas urges that a fetus is entitled to Fourteenth Amendment protection as a person, it faces a dilemma. Neither in Texas nor in any other State are all abortions prohibited. Despite broad proscription, an exception [exists] for an abortion procured or attempted by medical advice for the purpose of saving the life of the mother. . . . But if the fetus is a person who is not to be deprived of life without due process of law, and if the mother's condition is the sole determinant, does not the Texas exception appear to be out of line with the Amendment's command?

There are other inconsistencies between Fourteenth Amendment status and the typical abortion statute. It has already been pointed out, supra, that in Texas the woman is not a principal or an accomplice with respect to an abortion upon her. If the fetus is a person, why is the woman not a principal or an accomplice? Further, the penalty for criminal abortion . . . is significantly less than the maximum penalty for murder. . . . If the fetus is a person, may the penalties be different?

involved. The woman's privacy is no longer sole and any right of privacy she possesses must be measured accordingly.

Texas urges that, apart from the Fourteenth Amendment, life begins at conception and is present throughout pregnancy, and that, therefore, the State has a compelling interest in protecting that life from and after conception. We need not resolve the difficult question of when life begins. When those trained in the respective disciplines of medicine, philosophy, and theology are unable to arrive at any consensus, the judiciary, at this point in the development of man's knowledge, is not in a position to speculate as to the answer.

It should be sufficient to note briefly the wide divergence of thinking on this most sensitive and difficult question. There has always been strong support for the view that life does not begin until live birth. This was the belief of the Stoics. It appears to be the predominant, though not the unanimous, attitude of the Jewish faith. It may be taken to represent also the position of a large segment of the Protestant community, . . . As we have noted, the common law found greater significance in quickening. Physicians and their scientific colleagues have regarded that event with less interest and have tended to focus either upon conception or upon live birth or upon the interim point at which the fetus becomes "viable," that is, potentially able to live outside the mother's womb, albeit with artificial aid. Viability is usually placed at about seven months (28 weeks) but may occur earlier, even at 24 weeks. The Aristotelian theory of "mediate animation," that held sway throughout the Middle Ages and the Renaissance in Europe, continued to be official Roman Catholic dogma until the 19th century, despite opposition to this "ensoulment" theory from those in the Church who would recognize the existence of life from the moment of conception. The latter is now, of course, the official belief of the Catholic Church [and] is a view strongly held by many non-Catholics as well and by many physicians. Substantial problems for precise definition of this view are posed, however, by new embryological data that purport to indicate that conception is a "process" over time, rather than an event, and by new medical techniques such as menstrual extraction, the "morning-after" pill, implantation of embryos, artificial insemination, and even artificial wombs.

In areas other than criminal abortion the law has been reluctant to endorse any theory that life, as we recognize it, begins before live birth or to accord legal rights to the unborn except in narrowly defined situations and except when the rights are contingent upon live birth. For example, the traditional rule of tort law had denied recovery for prenatal injuries even though the child was born alive. That rule has been changed in almost every jurisdiction. In most States recovery is said to be permitted only if the fetus was viable. . . . In a recent development, generally opposed by the commentators, some States permit the parents of a stillborn child to maintain an action for wrongful death because of prenatal injuries. Such an action, however, would appear to be one to vindicate the parents' interest and is thus consistent with the view that the fetus, at most, represents only the potentiality of life. Similarly, unborn children have been recognized as acquiring rights or interests by way of inheritance or other devolution of property, and have been represented by guardians ad litem. Perfection of the interests involved, again, has generally been contingent upon live birth. In short, the unborn have never been recognized in the law as persons in the whole sense.

X

In view of all this, we do not agree that, by adopting one theory of life, Texas may override the rights of the pregnant woman that are at stake. We repeat, however, that the State does have an important and legitimate interest in preserving and protecting the health of the pregnant woman, whether she be a resident of the State or a nonresident who seeks medical consultation and treatment there, and that it has still *another* important and legitimate interest in protecting the potentiality of human life. These interests are separate and distinct. Each grows in substantiality as the woman approaches term and, at a point during pregnancy, each becomes "compelling."

With respect to the State's important and legitimate interest in the health of the mother, the "compelling" point, in the light of present medical knowledge, is at approximately the end of the first trimester. This is so because of the now established medical fact . . . that until the end of the first trimester mortality in abortion is less than mortality in normal childbirth. It follows that, from and after this point, a State may regulate the abortion procedure to the extent that the regulation reasonably relates to the preservation and protection of maternal health. Examples of permissible state regulation in this area are requirements as to the qualifications of the person who is to perform the abortion; as to the licensure of that person; as to the facility in which the procedure is to be performed, that is, whether it must be a hospital or may be a clinic or some other place of less-than-hospital status; as to the licensing of the facility; and the like.

This means, on the other hand, that, for the period of pregnancy prior to this "compelling" point, the attending physician, in consultation with his patient, is free to determine, without regulation by the State, that in his medical judgment the patient's pregnancy should be terminated. If that decision is reached, the judgment may be effectuated by an abortion free of interference by the State.

With respect to the State's important and legitimate interest in potential life, the "compelling" point is at viability. This is so because the fetus then presumably has the capability of meaningful life outside the mother's womb. State regulation protective of fetal life after viability thus has both logical and biological justifications. If the State is interested in protecting fetal life after viability, it may go so far as to proscribe abortion during that period except when it is necessary to preserve the life or health of the mother.

Measured against these standards, Art. 1196 of the Texas Penal Code, in restricting legal abortions to those "procured or attempted by medical advice for the purpose of saving the life of the mother," sweeps too broadly. The statute makes no distinction between abortions performed early in pregnancy and those performed later, and it limits to a single reason, "saving" the mother's life, the legal justification for the procedure. The statute, therefore, cannot survive the constitutional attack made upon it here.

This conclusion makes it unnecessary for us to consider the additional challenge to the Texas statute asserted on grounds of vagueness.

XI

To summarize and to repeat:

1. A state criminal abortion statute of the current Texas type, that excepts from criminality only a *life saving* procedure on behalf of the mother, without regard to pregnancy stage and without recognition of the other interests involved, is violative of the Due Process Clause of the Fourteenth Amendment.

(a) For the stage prior to approximately the end of the first trimester, the abortion decision and its effectuation must be left to the medical judgment of the pregnant woman's attending physician.

(b) For the stage subsequent to approximately the end of the first trimester, the State, in promoting its interest in the health of the mother, may, if it chooses, regulate the abortion procedure in ways that are reasonably related to maternal health.

(c) For the stage subsequent to viability the State, in promoting its interest in the potentiality of human life, may, if it chooses, regulate, and even proscribe, abortion except where it is necessary, in appropriate medical judgment, for the preservation of the life or health of the mother.

2. The State may define the term "physician," . . . to mean only a physician currently licensed by the State, and may proscribe any abortion by a person who is not a physician as so defined.

In Doe v. Bolton, [410 U.S. 179 (1973)], procedural requirements contained in one of the modern abortion statutes are considered. That opinion and this one, of course, are to be read together.[20]

This holding, we feel, is consistent with the relative weights of the respective interests involved, with the lessons and example of medical and legal history, with the lenity of the common law, and with the demands of the profound problems of the present day. The decision leaves the State free to place increasing restrictions on abortion as the period of pregnancy lengthens, so long as those restrictions are tailored to the recognized state interests. The decision vindicates the right of the physician to administer medical treatment according to his professional judgment up to the points where important state interests provide compelling justifications for intervention. Up to those points the abortion decision in all its aspects is inherently, and primarily, a medical decision, and basic responsibility for it must rest with the physician. . . .

NOTE: DISSENTERS' VIEWS IN *ROE*

Justices Rehnquist and White, dissenting in both *Roe* and its companion Doe v. Bolton, criticized the Court for usurping the function of the legislature. According

---

[20] Doe v. Bolton, a companion case to *Roe*, invalidated Georgia's statute (inspired by the American Law Institute's Model Penal Code provision permitting abortion in limited cases), including its procedural requirements of hospitalization in an accredited facility, committee approval, two-doctor concurrence, and state residency.

to Justice White, "The Court . . . values the convenience of the pregnant mother more than the continued existence and development of the life or potential life that she carries. . . . I find no constitutional warrant for imposing such an order of priorities on the people and legislatures of the States." 410 U.S. at 222.

Justice Rehnquist did not think the right of privacy was involved in the abortion cases. He stated, however, that freedom from "unwanted state regulation of consensual transactions" is a form of liberty recognized in earlier Supreme Court decisions; moreover, "[t]he Due Process Clause of the Fourteenth Amendment undoubtedly does place a limit, albeit a broad one, on legislative power to enact laws such as this. If the Texas statute were to prohibit abortion even where the mother's life is in jeopardy, I have little doubt that such a statute would lack a rational relation to a valid state objective." 410 U.S. at 172-173.

Stenberg v. Carhart   *partial birth abortion*
530 U.S. 914 (2000)

Justice BREYER delivered the opinion of the Court.

We again consider the right to an abortion. We understand the controversial nature of the problem. Millions of Americans believe that life begins at conception and consequently that an abortion is akin to causing the death of an innocent child; they recoil at the thought of a law that would permit it. Other millions fear that a law that forbids abortion would condemn many American women to lives that lack dignity, depriving them of equal liberty and leading those with least resources to undergo illegal abortions with the attendant risks of death and suffering. Taking account of these virtually irreconcilable points of view, aware that constitutional law must govern a society whose different members sincerely hold directly opposing views, and considering the matter in light of the Constitution's guarantees of fundamental individual liberty, this Court, in the course of a generation, has determined and then redetermined that the Constitution offers basic protection to the woman's right to choose. Roe v. Wade, 410 U.S. 113 (1973); Planned Parenthood of Southeastern Pa. v. Casey, 505 U.S. 833 (1992). . . .

Three established principles determine the issue before us. We shall set them forth in the language of the joint opinion in *Casey.* First, before "viability . . . the woman has a right to choose to terminate her pregnancy." Id., at 870 (plurality opinion).

Second, "a law designed to further the State's interest in fetal life which imposes an undue burden on the woman's decision before fetal viability" is unconstitutional. Id., at 877. An "undue burden is . . . shorthand for the conclusion that a state regulation has the purpose or effect of placing a substantial obstacle in the path of a woman seeking an abortion of a nonviable fetus." Ibid.

Third, " 'subsequent to viability, the State in promoting its interest in the potentiality of human life may, if it chooses, regulate, and even proscribe, abortion except where it is necessary, in appropriate medical judgment, for the preservation of the life or health of the mother.' " Id., at 879 (quoting Roe v. Wade, supra, at 164-165).

We apply these principles to a Nebraska law banning "partial birth abortion." The statute reads as follows:

> No partial birth abortion shall be performed in this state, unless such procedure is necessary to save the life of the mother whose life is endangered by a physical disorder, physical illness, or physical injury, including a life-endangering physical condition caused by or arising from the pregnancy itself. Neb. Rev. Stat. Ann. §28-328(1) (Supp. 1999).

The statute defines "partial birth abortion" as:

> an abortion procedure in which the person performing the abortion partially delivers vaginally a living unborn child before killing the unborn child and completing the delivery. §28-326(9).

It further defines "partially delivers vaginally a living unborn child before killing the unborn child" to mean

> deliberately and intentionally delivering into the vagina a living unborn child, or a substantial portion thereof, for the purpose of performing a procedure that the person performing such procedure knows will kill the unborn child and does kill the unborn child. Ibid.

The law classifies violation of the statute as a "Class III felony" carrying a prison term of up to 20 years, and a fine of up to $25,000. It also provides for the automatic revocation of a doctor's license to practice medicine in Nebraska. We hold that this statute violates the Constitution.

I

Dr. Leroy Carhart is a Nebraska physician who performs abortions in a clinical setting. He brought this lawsuit in Federal District Court seeking a declaration that the Nebraska statute violates the Federal Constitution, and asking for an injunction forbidding its enforcement. [The District Court held the law unconstitutional, and the Court of Appeals affirmed.]

Because Nebraska law seeks to ban one method of aborting a pregnancy, we must describe and then discuss several different abortion procedures. . . . The evidence before the trial court, as supported or supplemented in the literature, indicates the following:

1. About 90% of all abortions performed in the United States take place during the first trimester of pregnancy, before 12 weeks of gestational age. During the first trimester, the predominant abortion method is "vacuum aspiration," which involves insertion of a vacuum tube (cannula) into the uterus to evacuate the contents. Such an abortion is typically performed on an outpatient basis under local anesthesia. Vacuum aspiration is considered particularly safe. As the fetus grows in size, however, the vacuum aspiration method becomes increasingly difficult to use.

2. Approximately 10% of all abortions are performed during the second trimester of pregnancy (12 to 24 weeks). In the early 1970s, inducing labor through

the injection of saline into the uterus was the predominant method of second trimester abortion. Today, however, the medical profession has switched from medical induction of labor to surgical procedures for most second trimester abortions. The most commonly used procedure is called "~~dilation and evacua~~tion" (D & E). That procedure (together with a modified form of vacuum aspiration used in the early second trimester) accounts for about 95% of all abortions performed from 12 to 20 weeks of gestational age.

3. [D & E generally involves:] (1) dilation of the cervix; (2) removal of at least some fetal tissue using nonvacuum instruments; and (3) (after the 15th week) the potential need for instrumental disarticulation or dismemberment of the fetus or the collapse of fetal parts to facilitate evacuation from the uterus.

4. When instrumental disarticulation incident to D & E is necessary, it typically occurs as the doctor pulls a portion of the fetus through the cervix into the birth canal. . . .

6. [A variation of the D & E procedure, referred to as an "intact D & E" also] begins with induced dilation of the cervix. The procedure then involves removing the fetus from the uterus through the cervix "intact," i.e., in one pass, rather than in several passes. It is used after 16 weeks at the earliest, as vacuum aspiration becomes ineffective and the fetal skull becomes too large to pass through the cervix. The intact D & E proceeds in one of two ways, depending on the presentation of the fetus. If the fetus presents head first (a vertex presentation), the doctor collapses the skull; and the doctor then extracts the entire fetus through the cervix. If the fetus presents feet first (a breech presentation), the doctor pulls the fetal body through the cervix, collapses the skull, and extracts the fetus through the cervix. The breech extraction version of the intact D & E is also known commonly as "dilation and extraction," or D & X. . . .

9. Dr. Carhart testified he attempts to use the intact D & E procedure during weeks 16 to 20 because (1) it reduces the dangers from sharp bone fragments passing through the cervix, (2) minimizes the number of instrument passes needed for extraction and lessens the likelihood of uterine perforations caused by those instruments, (3) reduces the likelihood of leaving infection-causing fetal and placental tissue in the uterus, and (4) could help to prevent potentially fatal absorption of fetal tissue into the maternal circulation. . . .

10. The materials presented at trial referred to the potential benefits of the D & X procedure in circumstances involving nonviable fetuses, such as fetuses with abnormal fluid accumulation in the brain (hydrocephaly). Others have emphasized its potential for women with prior uterine scars, or for women for whom induction of labor would be particularly dangerous.

11. There are no reliable data on the number of D & X abortions performed annually. Estimates have ranged between 640 and 5,000 per year. . . .

II

The question before us is whether Nebraska's statute, making criminal the performance of a "partial birth abortion," violates the Federal Constitution, as interpreted in Planned Parenthood of Southeastern Pa. v. Casey, 505 U.S. 833 (1992), and Roe v. Wade, 410 U.S. 113 (1973). We conclude that it does for at least two independent reasons. First, the law lacks any exception " 'for the preservation of the . . . health of the mother.' " *Casey*, 505 U.S., at 879 (plurality opinion). Second, it "imposes an undue burden on a woman's ability" to choose a D & E abortion, thereby unduly burdening the right to choose abortion itself. Id. at 874. We shall discuss each of these reasons in turn.

The *Casey* plurality opinion reiterated what the Court held in *Roe*; that " 'subsequent to viability, the State in promoting its interest in the potentiality of human life may, if it chooses, regulate, and even proscribe, abortion *except where it is necessary, in appropriate medical judgment, for the preservation of the life or health of the mother.*' "

The fact that Nebraska's law applies both previability and postviability aggravates the constitutional problem presented. The State's interest in regulating abortion previability is considerably weaker than postviability. See *Casey*, supra, at 870. Since the law requires a health exception in order to validate even a postviability abortion regulation, it at a minimum requires the same in respect to previability regulation.

The quoted standard also depends on the state regulations "promoting [the State's] interest in the potentiality of human life." The Nebraska law, of course, does not directly further an interest "in the potentiality of human life" by saving the fetus in question from destruction, as it regulates only a *method* of performing abortion. Nebraska describes its interests differently. It says the law " 'show[s] concern for the life of the unborn,' " "prevent[s] cruelty to partially born children," and "preserve[s] the integrity of the medical profession." But we cannot see how the interest-related differences could make any difference to the question at hand, namely, the application of the "health" requirement. [T]his Court has made clear that a State may promote but not endanger a woman's health when it regulates the methods of abortion.

Nebraska responds that the law does not require a health exception unless there is a need for such an exception. And here there is no such need, it says. It argues that "safe alternatives remain available" and "a ban on partial-birth abortion/D & X would create no risk to the health of women." The problem for Nebraska is that the parties strongly contested this factual question in the trial court below; and the findings and evidence support Dr. Carhart. The State fails to demonstrate that banning D & X without a health exception may not create significant health risks for women, because the record shows that significant medical authority supports the proposition that in some circumstances, D & X would be the safest procedure.

We shall reiterate in summary form the relevant findings and evidence. On the basis of medical testimony the District Court concluded that "Carhart's D & X procedure is . . . safer tha[n] the D & E and other abortion procedures used during the relevant gestational period in the 10 to 20 cases a year that present to Dr. Carhart." . . .

We find the [state's] arguments insufficient to demonstrate that Nebraska's law needs no health exception. For one thing, certain of the arguments are beside the point. The D & X procedure's relative rarity . . . is not highly relevant. The D & X is an infrequently used abortion procedure; but the health exception question is whether protecting women's health requires an exception for those infrequent occasions. . . . Nor can we know whether the fact that only a "handful" of doctors use the procedure . . . reflects the comparative rarity of late second term abortions, the procedure's recent development, the controversy surrounding it, or, as Nebraska suggests, the procedure's lack of utility. . . .

The word "necessary" in *Casey*'s phrase "necessary, in appropriate medical judgment, for the preservation of the life or health of the mother," cannot refer to an absolute necessity or to absolute proof. Medical treatments and procedures are often considered appropriate (or inappropriate) in light of estimated comparative health risks (and health benefits) in particular cases. Neither can that phrase require unanimity of medical opinion. Doctors often differ in their estimation of comparative health risks and appropriate treatment. [T]he division of medical opinion about the matter at most means uncertainty, a factor that signals the presence of risk, not its absence. . . .

In sum, Nebraska has not convinced us that a health exception is "never necessary to preserve the health of women." Rather, a statute that altogether forbids D & X creates a significant health risk. The statute consequently must contain a health exception. . . .

B

The Eighth Circuit found the Nebraska statute unconstitutional because, in *Casey*'s words, it has the "effect of placing a substantial obstacle in the path of a woman seeking an abortion of a nonviable fetus." [505 U.S. at 877.] It thereby places an "undue burden" upon a woman's right to terminate her pregnancy before viability. Nebraska does not deny that the statute imposes an "undue burden" *if* it applies to the more commonly used D & E procedure as well as to D & X. And we agree with the Eighth Circuit that it does so apply.

Our earlier discussion of the D & E procedure shows that it falls within the statutory prohibition. The statute forbids "deliberately and intentionally delivering into the vagina a living unborn child, or a substantial portion thereof, for the purpose of performing a procedure that the person performing such procedure knows will kill the unborn child." We do not understand how one could distinguish, using this language, between D & E (where a foot or arm is drawn through the cervix) and D & X (where the body up to the head is drawn through the cervix). Evidence before the trial court makes clear that D & E will often involve a physician pulling a "substantial portion" of a still living fetus, say, an arm or leg, into the vagina prior to the death of the fetus. . . .

Even if the statute's basic aim is to ban D & X, its language makes clear that it also covers a much broader category of procedures. The language does not track the medical differences between D & E and D & X—though it would have been a simple matter, for example, to provide an exception for the performance of D & E and other abortion procedures. Nor does the statute anywhere suggest that its application turns on whether a portion of the fetus' body is drawn into the vagina as part of a process to extract an intact fetus after collapsing the head as opposed to a process that would dismember the fetus. . . .

The Nebraska State Attorney General argues that the statute does differentiate between the two procedures. He says that the statutory words "substantial portion" mean "the child up to the head." He consequently denies the statute's application where the physician introduces into the birth canal a fetal arm or leg or anything less than the entire fetal body. He argues further that we must defer to his views about the meaning of the state statute. We cannot accept the Attorney General's narrowing interpretation of the Nebraska statute. [T]wo lower courts have both rejected the Attorney General's narrowing interpretation. . . .

In sum, using this law some present prosecutors and future Attorneys General may choose to pursue physicians who use D & E procedures, the most commonly used method for performing previability second trimester abortions. All those who perform abortion procedures using that method must fear prosecution, conviction, and imprisonment. The result is an undue burden upon a woman's right to make an abortion decision. We must consequently find the statute unconstitutional. . . .

Justice GINSBURG, with whom Justice STEVENS joins, concurring.

I write separately only to stress that amidst all the emotional uproar caused by an abortion case, we should not lose sight of the character of Nebraska's "partial birth abortion" law. As the Court observes, this law does not save any fetus from destruction, for it targets only "a *method* of performing abortion." Nor does the statute seek to protect the lives or health of pregnant women. Moreover, as Justice Stevens points out, ante, at 2617 (concurring opinion), the most common method of performing previability second trimester abortions is no less distressing or susceptible to gruesome description. [As Seventh Circuit] Chief Judge Posner commented, the law prohibits the procedure because the state legislators seek to chip away at the private choice shielded by Roe v. Wade, even as modified by *Casey*. . . .

A state regulation that "has the purpose or effect of placing a substantial obstacle in the path of a woman seeking an abortion of a nonviable fetus" violates the Constitution. *Casey*, 505 U.S., at 877 (plurality opinion). Such an obstacle exists if the State stops a woman from choosing the procedure her doctor "reasonably believes will best protect the woman in [the] exercise of [her] constitutional liberty." Ante, at 2617 (Stevens, J., concurring). Again as stated by Chief Judge Posner, "if a statute burdens constitutional rights and all that can be said on its behalf is that it is the vehicle that legislators have chosen for expressing their hostility to those rights, the burden is undue." [Hope Clinic v. Ryan, 195 F.3d 857, 881 (7th Cir. 1999).]

Justice SCALIA, dissenting.

I am optimistic enough to believe that, one day, Stenberg v. Carhart will be assigned its rightful place in the history of this Court's jurisprudence beside *Korematsu* and *Dred Scott.*. The method of killing a human child — one cannot even accurately say an entirely unborn human child — proscribed by this statute is so horrible that the most clinical description of it evokes a shudder of revulsion. And the Court must know (as most state legislatures banning this procedure have concluded) that demanding a "health exception" — which requires the abortionist to assure himself that, in his expert medical judgment, this method is, in the case at hand, marginally safer than others (how can one prove the contrary beyond a reasonable doubt?) — is to give live-birth abortion free rein. The notion that the Constitution of the United States, designed, among other things, "to establish Justice, insure domestic Tranquility, . . . and secure the Blessings of Liberty to ourselves and our

Posterity," prohibits the States from simply banning this visibly brutal means of eliminating our half-born posterity is quite simply absurd. . . .

In my dissent in *Casey,* I wrote that the "undue burden" test made law by the joint opinion created a standard that was "as doubtful in application as it is unprincipled in origin," "hopelessly unworkable in practice," "ultimately standardless." Today's decision is the proof. As long as we are debating this issue of necessity for a health-of-the-mother exception on the basis of *Casey,* it is really quite impossible for us dissenters to contend that the majority is *wrong* on the law — any more than it could be said that one is *wrong in law* to support or oppose the death penalty, or to support or oppose mandatory minimum sentences. The most that we can honestly say is that we disagree with the majority on their policy-judgment-couched-as-law. And those who believe that a 5-to-4 vote on a policy matter by unelected lawyers should not overcome the judgment of 30 state legislatures have a problem, not with the *application* of *Casey,* but with its *existence. Casey* must be overruled.

While I am in an I-told-you-so mood, I must recall my bemusement, in *Casey,* at the majority opinion's expressed belief that Roe v. Wade had "call[ed] the contending sides of a national controversy to end their national division by accepting a common mandate rooted in the Constitution," *Casey,* 505 U.S., at 867, and that the decision in *Casey* would ratify that happy truce. . . . I cannot understand why those who *acknowledge* that, in the opening words of Justice O'Connor's concurrence, "[t]he issue of abortion is one of the most contentious and controversial in contemporary American society," persist in the belief that this Court, armed with neither constitutional text nor accepted tradition, can resolve that contention and controversy rather than be consumed by it. If only for the sake of its own preservation, the Court should return this matter to the people — where the Constitution, *but Const. is silent on* by its silence on the subject, left it — and let *them* decide, State by State, whether *many things —* this practice should be allowed. . . . *dnt keep us from making Const'al judgments/rulings*

Justice KENNEDY, with whom The CHIEF JUSTICE joins, dissenting. *Rehnquist*

The Court's failure to accord any weight to Nebraska's interest in prohibiting partial-birth abortion is erroneous and undermines its discussion and holding. . . . The majority views the procedures from the perspective of the abortionist, rather than from the perspective of a society shocked when confronted with a new method of ending human life. . . .

Casey is premised on the States having an important constitutional role in defining their interests in the abortion debate. It is only with this principle in mind that Nebraska's interests can be given proper weight. The State's brief describes its interests as including concern for the life of the unborn and "for the partially-born," in preserving the integrity of the medical profession, and in "erecting a barrier to infanticide." A review of *Casey* demonstrates the legitimacy of these policies. The Court should say so.

States may take sides in the abortion debate and come down on the side of life, even life in the unborn. . . . States also have an interest in forbidding medical procedures which, in the State's reasonable determination, might cause the medical profession or society as a whole to become insensitive, even disdainful, to life, including life in the human fetus. Abortion, *Casey* held, has consequences beyond the woman and her fetus. The States' interests in regulating are of concomitant extension. . . .

Nebraska was entitled to find the existence of a consequential moral difference between the procedures. . . . The D & X differs from the D & E because in the D & X the fetus is "killed *outside* of the womb" where the fetus has "an autonomy which separates it from the right of the woman to choose treatments for her own body." . . . D & X's stronger resemblance to infanticide means Nebraska could conclude the procedure presents a greater risk of disrespect for life and a consequent greater risk to the profession and society, which depend for their sustenance upon reciprocal recognition of dignity and respect. The Court is without authority to second-guess this conclusion. . . .

The holding of *Casey*, allowing a woman to elect abortion in defined circumstances, is not in question here. Nebraska, however, was entitled to conclude that its ban, while advancing important interests regarding the sanctity of life, deprived no woman of a safe abortion and therefore did not impose a substantial obstacle on the rights of any woman. . . .

Courts are ill-equipped to evaluate the relative worth of particular surgical procedures. The legislatures of the several States have superior factfinding capabilities in this regard. . . .

In deferring to the physician's judgment [in requiring a health exception], the Court turns back to cases decided in the wake of *Roe*, cases which gave a physician's treatment decisions controlling weight. Rather than exalting the right of a physician to practice medicine with unfettered discretion, *Casey* recognized: "Whatever constitutional status the doctor-patient relation may have as a general matter, in the present context it is derivative of the woman's position." 505 U.S. at 884 (joint opinion of O'Connor, Kennedy, and Souter, JJ.). . . .

The Court fails to acknowledge substantial authority allowing the State to take sides in a medical debate, even when fundamental liberty interests are at stake and even when leading members of the profession disagree with the conclusions drawn by the legislature. . . .

[The separate concurring opinions of Justices Stevens and O'Connor, as well as the separate dissenting opinions of Chief Justice Rehnquist and Justice Thomas, are omitted.]

NOTES AND QUESTIONS: *ROE* AND *STENBERG*

(1) Background. In Roe v. Wade, what are the three reasons described by Justice Blackmun that were advanced historically to justify criminal abortion laws?

(2) Conflict of Interests. On what grounds does Justice Blackmun conclude that a woman's right to privacy "is broad enough to encompass a woman's decision whether or not to terminate her pregnancy" (supra p. 7)? The Court determines that the right of personal privacy included in the abortion decision is not absolute and must be considered against important state interests. What are these state interests? How does *Roe* accommodate these interests? Does Justice Blackmun recognize that the state has a legitimate interest in protecting "potential life," or does he assume that the state may only protect the life of a child after birth? Does he assume that the interest of a pregnant woman and the interest of the fetus coincide? If not, who

speaks for the interest of the fetus? If you had been the trial judge in *Roe*, would you have appointed a guardian ad litem to represent unborn fetuses?

(3) Fetal Personhood. Why does Justice Blackmun reject the contention that the fetus is a "person" for purposes of the Fourteenth Amendment? What difference does it make if a fetus were a "person" for these purposes? *"born"*

(4) How does Justice Blackmun determine when the state's interest in protecting prenatal life becomes a compelling interest? Do you think that the state's interest in protecting prenatal life grows "substantially as the woman approaches term"? What justification does Blackmun give for concluding that it does? Does the state have a more compelling interest in protecting older rather than younger children?

(5) Viability as the Standard. On what ground does Justice Blackmun determine that the "compelling" point is at viability? How long will an infant born at full term be "viable" without human intervention and help? What is the legal and moral significance of viability?

Many commentators criticized the Court's adoption of viability as a benchmark. Compare John H. Ely, The Wages of Crying Wolf: A Comment on Roe v. Wade, 82 Yale L.J. 920, 924 n.1 (1973) (suggesting that the Court has mistaken "a definition for a syllogism"), with Patricia A. King, The Juridical Status of the Fetus: A Proposal for Legal Protection of the Unborn, 77 Mich. L.J. 1647, 1677 (1979) (defending the Court's selection of viability because technological advances permit the capacity for independent existence to occur earlier than birth).

Why should the capacity to live independently be a reason to force a woman to allow the fetus's continued dependency on her? Cf. Judith J. Thomson, A Defense of Abortion, 1 Phil. & Pub. Aff. 47 (1971) (arguing that abortion is morally permissible because the right of bodily autonomy legitimizes the right to deny another the continued and traumatic use of one's body for a nine-month period).

(6) Assuming, as the Supreme Court did, that viability is a relevant standard, what is the definition of "viability"? In Planned Parenthood of Central Missouri v. Danforth, 428 U.S. 52 (1976) (holding that a spousal consent requirement for abortion was unconstitutional) (discussed infra p. 38), the Court unanimously upheld a Missouri statutory definition of "viability" as "that stage of fetal development when the life of the unborn may be continued indefinitely outside the womb by natural or artificial life-supportive systems," and thus rejected plaintiff's contention that the definition must be fixed at a specific gestational time.

> [I]t is not the proper function of the legislature or the courts to place viability, which essentially is a medical concept, at a specific point in the gestation period. The time when viability is achieved may vary with each pregnancy, and the determination of whether a particular fetus is viable is, and must be, a matter for the judgment of the responsible attending physician. [428 U.S. at 64.]

(7) How is viability measured? Physicians who perform and report abortions typically measure fetal age differently than embryologists do. Embryologists use the direct observation of "defined cells or early structures" to pinpoint the moment of fertilization. On the other hand, physicians generally use the first day of the last menstrual period as a basis for measuring gestational age (thereby including the two weeks that precede fertilization). Barbara Santee & Stanley K. Henshaw, The

Abortion Debate: Measuring Gestational Age, 24 Fam. Plan. Persp. 172 (1992). Because abortion statistics are based on physicians' estimates of fetal age, such data overstate the number of abortions occurring after 20 weeks. Id. Currently, only 1.4 percent of abortions occur after 20 weeks. Centers for Disease Control and Prevention, "Abortion Surveillance — United States 2000," Morbidity & Mortality Weekly Report (Nov. 28, 2003), at 52.

(8) Consideration of the impact of technological advances on the stage at which a state may prohibit abortions serves to sharpen the concern over the relevance of viability. As technology permits increasingly premature babies to be saved, must the time necessarily shrink during which a mother is permitted to have an abortion? In City of Akron v. Akron Center for Reproductive Health, 462 U.S. 416 (1983), Justice O'Connor (in a dissenting opinion) predicted that as technology advances, the time in which abortions would be available might shrink to perhaps as early as the first trimester, leading to the conclusion that Roe's trimester scheme is "clearly on a collision course with itself." Id. at 458. O'Connor's concern that fetuses might become viable in the first trimester in the not too distant future seems to be exaggerated. The actual changes in viability in over two decades appear to be modest. At the time of Roe v. Wade, viability occurred at approximately 28 weeks. By the time of Planned Parenthood of Southeastern Pennsylvania v. Casey, 500 U.S. 833 (1992) (discussed infra), viability occurred at 23 to 24 weeks. Id. at 860. Physicians currently set viability at 23 weeks. See Bill Would Establish Fetus Viability at 20 Weeks, Fort Wayne News Sentinel, Feb. 18, 2005, at L3 (criticizing pending Indiana legislation that sets viability at 20 weeks as creating a standard lower than "medical science's ability to sustain a fetus" and pointing to survival rates for babies at 23 weeks of gestation from 11 to 30 percent).

One technological innovation that facilitates abortion is mifepristone, also known as RU 486, for termination of early pregnancies. The Food and Drug Administration (FDA) approved RU 486 for general use as a method of medical abortion in 2000. How does the availability of an abortion pill change the debate over abortion? See Lawrence Lader, A Private Matter: RU 486 and the Abortion Crisis (1995).

(9) Sex Discrimination.   Abortion regulation raises obvious questions of sex discrimination. Only women get pregnant, and only women seek abortion.

> Laws restricting abortion so dramatically shape the lives of women, and only of women, that their denial of equality hardly needs detailed elaboration. While men retain the right to sexual and reproductive autonomy, restrictions on abortion deny that autonomy to women. Laws restricting access to abortion thereby place a real and substantial burden on women's ability to participate in society as equals. Even a woman who is not pregnant is inevitably affected by her knowledge of the power relationships created by a ban on abortion. [Laurence H. Tribe, Abortion: The Clash of Absolutes 105 (1990)].

Does equal protection doctrine provide a better rationale than privacy doctrine for the right to an abortion? See Ruth Bader Ginsburg, Some Thoughts on Autonomy and Equality in Relation to Roe v. Wade, 63 N.C. L. Rev. 375, 386 (1985); Catharine A. MacKinnon, Privacy v. Equality: Beyond Roe v. Wade, in Feminism Unmodified: Discourses on Life and Law 93, 97 (1987); Elizabeth M. Schneider, The Synergy of Equality and Privacy in Women's Rights, 2002 U. Chi. Legal F. 137 (2002).

(10) Post-*Roe *Abortion Regulation. Roe v. Wade produced a variety of hostile reactions, including efforts to enact constitutional amendments to prohibit abortion. See Tribe, supra, at 162. Although abortion foes were unsuccessful in overturning *Roe*, they enjoyed more success in attempts to place restrictions on abortion. Congress and a number of states enacted numerous laws (discussed infra) regulating abortion rights. Many of these statutes have been challenged in litigation.

a. Public Abortion Funding. If a woman lacks funds for an abortion, must a state provide one free? Apparently not, according to a trilogy of cases decided by the Supreme Court. In Beal v. Doe, 432 U.S. 438 (1977), the Court interpreted Title XIX of the Social Security Act, 42 U.S.C. §1396 (2000) (establishing the Medicaid Program to provide federal and state funds for medical care), not to require states to fund nontherapeutic abortions as a condition of participation. That same year, in Maher v. Roe, 432 U.S. 464 (1977), the Court determined that the Constitution does not require a state to pay for nontherapeutic abortions (reasoning that the Equal Protection Clause was not violated if a state participating in the Medicaid program chose to subsidize medical expenses incident to childbirth but not nontherapeutic abortion). Finally, in Harris v. McRae, 448 U.S. 297 (1980), the Court sustained the Hyde Amendment, a federal statute prohibiting the expenditure of federal Medicaid money for abortions except to preserve the woman's life. See also Webster v. Reproductive Health Servs., 492 U.S. 490 (1989) (relying on Harris v. McRae to uphold a statute prohibiting the use of public hospitals and medical staff in the performance of abortions).

Subsequently, in 1993 Congress amended the Hyde Amendment to permit abortion services when a pregnancy resulted from rape or incest. More than one-third of the states refused to comply with that legislation. Federal courts ordered 11 states into compliance. National Abortion and Reproductive Rights Action League (NARAL), Fact Sheet: The Appropriations Process and Discriminatory Abortion Funding Restrictions 3 (Jan. 1, 2004). Currently, 27 states fund abortions for Medicaid recipients only when the woman's life is endangered or the pregnancy results from rape or incest. NARAL, Who Decides: A State-by-State Review of Abortion and Reproductive Rights, Overview of State Reproductive Rights Laws 3 (2004). Compare New Mexico Rights to Choose/NARAL v. Johnson, 975 P.2d 841 (N.M. 1998) (holding that restrictions on state funding of abortions for Medicaid-eligible women violate state constitutional provisions) with Bell v. Low Income Women of Texas, 95 S.W.3d 253 (Tex. 2002) (holding that funding restrictions do not violate the Texas Constitution's Equal Rights Amendment, Equal Protection Clause, or right to privacy).

In 1997, Congress applied the Hyde Amendment to Medicaid recipients enrolled in managed care plans and, the following year, to ban publicly funded abortions for the disabled (under the Medicare Program) except to preserve the life of the mother or in cases of rape or incest. NARAL Fact Sheet, supra, at 2-3. Similar funding restrictions currently apply to Native American women on reservations, military personnel (prohibiting even services paid for by private funds at military facilities overseas), and federal inmates. Id. at 4-6.

After Roe v. Wade and until 1976, all legal abortions performed annually at public hospitals were funded by Medicaid. Tribe, supra, at 151. By withdrawing Medicaid funding and permitting prohibitions on abortion in public hospitals, has the state effectively deprived indigent women of the right to terminate a pregnancy? For indigent women, are these restrictions any different in effect from an outright prohibition?

b. Speech: Restrictions on Abortion Counseling. Title X of the Public Health Service Act, 42 U.S.C. §§300-300a-6 (2000) provides subsidies to family planning clinics that serve low-income clients. As enacted, the legislation prohibited funding of abortion but was silent with respect to abortion counseling and referral. In 1988, the Secretary of Health and Human Services promulgated regulations prohibiting service providers from providing abortion counseling and referral services (a so-called gag rule). In Rust v. Sullivan, 500 U.S. 173 (1991), the Supreme Court upheld the challenged regulations, rejecting claims that the regulations violated petitioners' (i.e., Title X grantees' and physicians') First Amendment rights. In response to plaintiffs' argument that the gag rule infringed on the fundamental right to abortion, the Court relied on the principle announced in *Maher, McRae,* and *Webster* to reiterate that there is no right to public funds to secure access to a particular benefit even if the right to such benefit is protected by the government. President Bill Clinton rescinded the so-called gag rule upon taking office. See Memorandum on the Title X "Gag Rule," 29 Weekly Comp. Pres. Doc. 87 (Jan. 22, 1993).

These cases set the stage for Stenberg v. Carhart, supra.

(11) Partial-Birth Abortion Bans. In invalidating a state abortion restriction, Stenberg v. Carhart relies to some extent on Planned Parenthood of Southeastern Pa. v. Casey, 505 U.S. 833 (1992), a challenge to a Pennsylvania statute, including a detailed informed consent (requiring the physician's provision of certain information about fetal development, abortion risks, and alternatives), a 24-hour waiting period, spousal consent, parental consent, and record keeping and reporting requirements. *Casey* upheld all the challenged provisions except the spousal notification requirement (discussed infra p. 40). To what extent does *Stenberg* (and *Casey*) reaffirm Roe v. Wade and to what extent does it depart from it? Is abortion still a "fundamental right"? If so, is the right still based on the right to privacy? Does the Court retain the importance of viability? Under *Roe*'s trimester framework, virtually no regulation was permitted during the first trimester; regulations designed to protect the woman's health were permitted during the second trimester; and regulations designed to protect the potential life of the fetus were permitted only in the third trimester. Is that still true after *Stenberg*? At what point in pregnancy does the state develop a substantial interest in protecting potential life, according to *Stenberg*?

Currently, more than half the states have partial-birth abortion bans. See Guttmacher Institute, State Policies in Brief: Bans on "Partial-Birth" Abortion 1 (Feb. 1, 2005) (pointing to 31 states with bans that apply either throughout pregnancy or after viability; of these 31 bans, 27 state bans do not contain a health exception). In *Stenberg*, Justice Breyer found that the Nebraska ban was unconstitutional for two reasons: (1) the law lacked a health exception for the mother, and (2) the banned procedure was described so vaguely as to apply to other permissible methods of abortion and thus constituted an undue burden on the right to choose to have an abortion. Why did the Court reject the state's arguments that the absence of a health exception was permissible because of a lack of need for the prohibited procedure? Why did the Court hold that the ban was vague and overbroad?

Some states responded to *Stenberg* and other similar decisions by redrafting their statutes to include a maternal health exception and to prohibit only the D & X procedure (not the more common D & E procedure). Do such narrow statutes pass constitutional muster? See Women's Professional Medical Corp. v. Taft, 353 F.3d 436 (6th Cir. 2003) (upholding the constitutionality of an Ohio prohibition on partial-birth abortions).

(12) Undue Burden Standard.   How does the undue burden test, derived by *Stenberg* from *Casey*, differ from *Roe*'s strict scrutiny test? After *Stenberg* and *Casey*, only those regulations that impose an "undue burden" on the woman's right to an abortion will be invalidated. According to the Court, what constitutes an "undue burden"? Is the adoption of this standard likely to help states draft regulations that are constitutionally permissible or to open the door to more litigation?

How does a requirement of mandatory pre-abortion counseling and a 24-hour waiting period (the challenged provisions in *Casey*) *not* constitute an undue burden on a woman's right to an abortion? What are the effects of mandatory waiting periods? By mandating a 24-hour waiting period, is a woman required to make two trips to the abortion facility? Does this regulation impose an undue burden on a woman who must travel from another county or state to find an abortion provider? On a woman with limited funds? On battered women or women who do not wish their family members to discover the pregnancy? See Ruth Colker, Abortion and Violence, 1 Wm. & Mary J. Women & L. 93 (1994).

An empirical study in one jurisdiction with waiting periods found that pregnant women are more likely to travel to neighboring states to evade restrictions and also to delay having abortions performed. Ted Joyce & Robert Kaestner, The Impact of Mississippi's Mandatory Delay Law on the Timing of Abortion, 32 Fam. Plan. Persp. 4 (2000). Currently, 27 states require abortion counseling and 21 states mandate a waiting period before a woman may obtain an abortion. Rachel Benson Gold, Key Reproductive Health-Related Developments in the States: 2003, The Guttmacher Report, Dec. 2003, at 11.

Recall Rust v. Sullivan, supra, which upheld regulations prohibiting service providers from providing abortion counseling and referral services. Compare *Rust* with *Casey*, which requires staff at such clinics to discuss certain aspects of abortion, such as fetal development. Consider the following:

> I must have missed something. Let's see, if you come into a family-planning clinic asking for information about abortion, you can't get it. If you go to an abortion clinic . . . but wait a second, this time you're not asking for *information* — you just want the operation. But now you have to listen to me say that I think abortion is horribly risky; I'll show you gross pictures of mushed-up fetuses and tell you that you're a shameless, baby-murdering hussy. You have to listen up — or no abortion. I guess the way it works is: You can only get information when you really don't want it. [Susan Faludi, Forum, She's Come for an Abortion, What Do You Say?, Harper's, Nov. 1992, at 47.]

Note that the Supreme Court previously invalidated a detailed list of abortion warnings because of their interference with the physician-patient relationship and anti-abortion motivation. See City of Akron v. Akron Ctr. for Reproductive

Health, 462 U.S. 416, 442-449 (1983); Thornburgh v. American College of Obstetricians & Gynecologists, 476 U.S. 747, 759-765 (1986). Are detailed informed consent requirements that apply to abortion paternalistic?

(13) How does the Court in *Roe* and *Stenberg* regard the role of the physician in the woman's decision to have an abortion? What should be the role of the physician in such an important decision?

(14) Sex Selection. The state abortion restriction in *Casey* contained another regulation not challenged by the petitioners: a ban on abortions procured for the purpose of terminating a fetus of an unwanted gender. Should sex-selection abortions be prohibited? Suppose the abortion is sought for medical, rather than psychological, reasons? Do such bans constitute an "undue burden" on a woman's right to choose? Because the "wrong" gender is often female, is sex-selection abortion a form of gender-based discrimination? See generally Lynne Marie Kohn, Sex Selection Abortion and the Boomerang Effect of a Woman's Right to Choose: A Paradox of the Skeptics, 4 Wm. & Mary J. Women & L. 91 (1997); Rachel E. Remaley, Note, "The Original Sexist Sin": Regulating Preconception Sex Selection Technology, 10 Health Matrix 249 (2000).

(15) Morality. Philosophers and moralists have long debated the morality of abortion and the legitimacy of state intervention to protect prenatal life. Compare John T. Noonan, A Private Choice (1979) (arguing that a fetus, as a human organism, should be accorded full moral status from conception) with Michael Tooley, Abortion and Infanticide, 2 Phil. & Pub. Aff. 37 (1972) (arguing that the moral significance of personhood lies in conscious experience, a stance that makes abortion (and infanticide) morally permissible). What should be the role of morality in the abortion decision? In Lawrence v. Texas, 539 U.S. 558 (2003), the Supreme Court invalidated a state sodomy statute by holding that substantive due process protects the right to make decisions about private sexual conduct. In so doing, the Court asserted that "this Court's obligation is to define the liberty of all, not to mandate its own moral code" and cited *Casey*, 505 U.S. at 850. Who should decide moral issues such as those about abortion and sexuality: the family, legislature, or courts?

(16) Problem. Alison and Andrew Rowbotham, a British couple, travel to an American fertility clinic after British authorities deny them permission to create and screen embryos to engineer a "designer baby" free of the rare genetic blood disease that afflicts their two-year-old, Anna. After the birth, the Rowbothams plan a transplant from the infant's umbilical cord blood to Anna. Their healthy embryos that are not selected will be discarded. According to Richard Doerflinger of the U.S. Conference of Catholic Bishops, "[t]his [is] a search-and-destroy mission." Cited in Lindsey Tanner, "Creating a Baby to Save a Sibling," S.F. Chron., May 5, 2004, at A2.

After *Roe* and *Stenberg*, may the state prohibit a woman from participating in such a medical procedure? Could the state intervene to protect the fetus if the woman desires instead to abort the fetus in order to provide fetal stem cells for an older sibling, or to abort the fetus after participating in medical experimentation that would create grave risks for the fetus in utero, or to sell the aborted fetus to a laboratory for experimentation that would involve maintaining the life of the fetus for a short period?[21] See generally Janet L. Dolgin, Embryonic Discourse: Abortion, Stem Cells and Cloning, 19 Issues L. & Med. 203 (2004) (suggesting that embryos have different representations in abortion discourse compared to rhetoric about stem cell research and therapeutic cloning).

(17) Fetal Rights Legislation. In *Roe*, Blackmun points out that the "unborn have never been recognized by the law as persons in the whole sense" (supra p. 9). The federal government in various legislation recently recognized the unborn as persons. In 2004, Congress passed the Unborn Victims of Violence Act, Pub. L. No. 108-212, 118 Stat. 568 (codified at 18 U.S.C. §1841), criminalizing the act of killing or injuring an unborn child (at any period of gestation) during the commission of a federal crime involving a pregnant woman (i.e., recognizing two victims of the crime). The federal government also conferred legal rights on a fetus by recent revisions to the State Children's Health Insurance Program (SCHIP), 67 Fed. Reg. 61,956 (Oct. 2, 2002) (codified at 42 C.F.R. pt. 457). SCHIP provides health insurance coverage to states for uninsured children whose families are at the poverty level. New regulations redefine "child" to include all children, from conception until age 19, regardless of the pregnant woman's immigration status. What are the implications of such legislation for abortion? See also the discussion of fetal homicide, infra p. 44.

(18) Epilogue to Stenberg: *Federal Partial-Birth-Abortion Legislation.* Three years after *Stenberg*, Congress enacted the Partial-Birth Abortion Ban Act of 2003, 18 U.S.C.A. §1531 (West Supp. 2004), which holds any physician criminally and civilly liable "who, in or affecting interstate or foreign commerce, knowingly performs a partial-birth abortion." Id. at §1531(a). "Partial-birth abortion" is defined as "an overt act . . . that kills the partially delivered living fetus" during a vaginal delivery in which "the entire fetal head is outside the body of the mother . . . or any part of the fetal trunk past the navel is outside the body of the mother." Id. at §1531(b)(1)(A), (B). Abortion rights advocates filed challenges to enjoin its enforcement. Subsequently, three federal district courts ruled the Act unconstitutional. See Planned Parenthood Federation of America v. Ashcroft, 320 F. Supp. 2d 957 (N.D. Cal. 2004) (finding the Act an undue burden, unconstitutionally vague, and lacking a maternal health exception); Carhart v. Ashcroft, 331 F. Supp. 2d 805 (D. Neb. 2004) (same); National Abortion Federation v. Ashcroft, 330 F. Supp. 2d 436 (S.D.N.Y. 2004) (holding that Congress violated the due process rights of physicians and patients when it passed statute barring partial-birth abortions without providing a maternal health exception).

---

[21] Legislation currently prohibits federal funding of research that uses the fetus as an experimental object before, during, or after an abortion. 45 C.F.R. §46.201.211 (2000). Stem cells hold considerable promise for the treatment of diabetes, Parkinson's and Alzheimer's diseases, and brain and spinal injuries. Stem cells, extracted from days-old embryos, can be grown into any type of cell in the body. However, because extraction results in destruction of the embryo, some persons oppose such research. President George W. Bush opposed federal funding for embryonic stem cell research in 2000, but by an executive order in August 2001, he permitted federal funds to be used for research on then-existing stem cell lines. Critics contend that this policy has only limited potential for research because few embryonic stem cell lines continue to exist and many have been contaminated. See generally Bryn E. Floyd, Comment, Regulation of Stem Cell Research: A Recommendation That the United States Adopt the Australian Approach, 13 Pacific Rim L. & Pol'y 31(2004).

During litigation on the constitutionality of the federal ban, the Department of Justice (DOJ) subpoenaed records of abortion providers, contending that the records were central to plaintiffs' claims that the banned procedure is medically necessary. In Northwestern Memorial Hospital v. Ashcroft, 362 F.3d 923 (7th Cir. 2004), the Seventh Circuit Court of Appeals held that the subpoena imposed an undue burden on abortion providers when the limited probative value of the records was weighed against patients' privacy. See also Planned Parenthood Federation v. Ashcroft, No. C 03-4872, 2004 WL 432222 (N.D. Cal. 2004) (denying defendant's motion to compel discovery seeking similar medical records from health care providers). The DOJ subsequently abandoned its effort to seek the patients' medical records.

(19) Clinic Violence.   Clinic violence also affects access to abortion. Since 1993, anti-abortion protests have resulted in the deaths of three doctors, two clinic employees, a clinic escort, and a security guard; since 1991 such protests resulted in 17 attempted murders; and finally, since 1977 there have been 4,100 reported acts of violence against abortion providers (i.e., bombings, arsons, death threats, kidnappings, and assaults) and 80,600 reported acts of disruption (i.e., bomb threats and harassing phone calls). NARAL, Fact Sheet: Clinic Violence and Intimidation 1 (Jan. 1, 2004).

In response to such violence, Congress enacted the Freedom of Access to Clinic Entrances Act of 1994 (FACE), 18 U.S.C. §248 (2000), which bars force, threat of force, or physical obstruction aimed at injuring, intimidating, or interfering with any patients or providers of reproductive health services. Violators face criminal and civil penalties. States also have enacted legislation modelled after the federal act. NARAL, Fact Sheet, supra (listing 15 states and the District of Columbia).

In Planned Parenthood of the Columbia/Willamette, Inc. v. American Coalition of Life Activists, 290 F.3d 1058 (9th Cir. 2002), *cert. denied*, 539 U.S. 958 (2003), a federal court of appeals upheld a permanent injunction enjoining the posting by "wanted posters" on the Internet, listing personal information (i.e., addresses, license plates) of health care providers. The court determined that the posters constituted "true threats" in light of prior incidents when physicians identified on the Web site were murdered. In addition, the court upheld a jury verdict ordering the creators of the Web site to pay compensatory damages to the abortion providers. See Adam Liptak, Posters by Abortion Foes Posed Threat, Court Rules, N.Y. Times, May 17, 2002, at A20.

Several federal appellate courts have upheld the constitutionality of FACE. See, e.g., Norton v. Ashcroft, 298 F.3d 547 (6th Cir. 2002) (holding that the Act did not violate the First Amendment, was not unconstitutionally vague or overbroad, did not violate the equal protection rights of activists, and that Congress acted validly pursuant to its authority under Commerce Clause); American Life League, Inc. v. Reno, 47 F.3d 642 (4th Cir. 1995) (holding that FACE did not violate the First Amendment, Tenth Amendment or the Religious Freedom Restoration Act). But cf. United States v. Bird, 279 F. Supp. 827 (S.D. Tex. 2003) (holding that Congress lacked authority under the Commerce Clause to enact FACE since the targeted activity was intrastate and had, at most, an attenuated effect on interstate commerce).

The Supreme Court has addressed clinic violence. See Scheidler v. National Organization for Women, 537 U.S. 393 (2003) (holding that pro-life activities aimed at disrupting clinic access, although unlawful, did not amount to extortion, a predicate offense for liability under the Racketeer Influenced and Corrupt Organizations Act, 18 U.S.C. §1961 (2000)); Bray v. Alexandria Women's Health Clinic, 506 U.S. 263 (1993) (holding that pro-life blockades do not constitute gender discrimination for purposes of evoking protection under the federal civil rights law, Ku Klux Klan Act, 42 U.S.C. §1985(3) (2000)).

Also, the Court has permitted various "buffer zones" to permit peaceful protest while concomitantly protecting patients and providers outside clinic entrances. Compare Madsen v. Women's Health Center, 512 U.S. 753 (1994) (upholding an injunction preventing protests within 36 feet of a clinic entrance to accomplish the governmental interest in protecting access); Hill v. Colorado, 530 U.S. 703 (2000) (upholding the constitutionality of a restriction on protestors to more than eight feet from any person near a health care facility, absent consent, as a permissible content-neutral regulation) with Schenck v. Pro-Choice Network, 519 U.S. 357 (1997) (invalidating a 15-foot "floating" buffer zone around any person or vehicle seeking access to or leaving a clinic as an excessive burden on free speech but upholding a 15-foot fixed buffer zone around doorways, driveways, and parking lot entrances as necessary to ensure individual and vehicular access).

(20) Restrictions on Physicians as Providers.   The number of abortion service providers is dwindling. Currently, 87 percent of American counties lack abortion providers. Lawrence B. Finer & Stanley K. Henshaw, The Accessibility of Abortion Services in the United States in 2001, 35 Perspectives on Sexual and Reproductive Health 16, 22 (2003). Some states impose restrictions on professionals who provide abortion services, such as requirements that only physicians (and not licensed physician assistants) may perform abortions. See Mazurek v. Armstrong, 520 U.S. 968 (1997) (holding that such requirements are constitutional and do not create a substantial obstacle to women's access to an abortion). However, such physician-only requirements may violate state constitutions. See, e.g., Armstrong v. State, 989 P.2d 364 (Mont. 1999).

(21) Epilogue.   Norma McCorvey (identified as "Jane Roe" in Roe v. Wade), later announced that she had joined opponents of legalized abortion. See "Jane Roe" Joins Anti-Abortion Group, N.Y. Times, Aug. 11, 1995, at A12. In McCorvey v. Hill, 385 F.3d 846 (5th Cir. 2004), McCorvey filed a motion for relief from judgment in which she sought to have the district court revisit the United States Supreme Court's decision based on "new" scientific knowledge that abortion harms women. The district court denied her motion. The Fifth Circuit Court of Appeals affirmed, finding that the plaintiff lacked standing because the case is moot. The Supreme Court deemed certiorari. 125 S. Ct. 1387 (2005).

Abortion regulation also is relevant to other issues of reproductive control. For a discussion of minors' contraceptive rights, see Chapter 6, and new reproductive technologies, see Chapter 5.

Legal Paternalism: Forcing Medical Treatment on Pregnant Women

The Supreme Court, in *Roe, Casey,* and *Stenberg,* recognizes that the state has an interest in protecting potential life during pregnancy. To what extent should the state be able to assert its interest in protecting potential life as a justification for influencing the behavior of a mother during pregnancy? Should the state be able to compel the pregnant woman to take actions thought necessary to protect the health, present and future, of the unborn child? Even before the point of viability?

Jefferson v. Griffin Spalding County Hospital Authority
274 S.E.2d 457 (Ga. 1981)

PER CURIAM.

On Thursday, January 22, 1981, the Griffin Spalding County Hospital Authority petitioned the Superior Court of Butts County, as a court of equity, for an order authorizing it to perform a caesarean section and any necessary blood transfusions upon the defendant . . . in the event she presented herself to the hospital for delivery of her unborn child, which was due on or about Monday, January 26. The superior court conducted an emergency hearing on Thursday, January 22, and entered the following order:

Defendant is in the thirty-ninth week of pregnancy. In the past few weeks she has presented herself to Griffin Spalding County Hospital for pre-natal care. The examining physician has found and defendant has been advised that she has a complete placenta previa; that the afterbirth is between the baby and the birth canal; that it is virtually impossible that this condition will correct itself prior to delivery; and that it is a 99% certainty that the child cannot survive natural childbirth (vaginal delivery). The chances of defendant surviving vaginal delivery are no better than 50%.

The examining physician is of the opinion that a delivery by cesarean section prior to labor beginning would have an almost 100% chance of preserving the life of the child, along with that of defendant.

On the basis of religious beliefs, defendant has advised the Hospital that she does not need surgical removal of the child and will not submit to it. Further, she refuses to take any transfusion of blood.

The Hospital is required by its own policies to treat any patient seeking emergency treatment. It seeks authority of the Court to administer medical treatment to defendant to save the life of herself and her unborn child.

The child is, as a matter of fact, viable and fully capable of sustaining life independent of the mother (defendant). The issue is whether this unborn child has any legal right to the protection of the Court. . . .

Because the life of defendant and of the unborn child are, at the moment, inseparable, the Court deems it appropriate to infringe upon the wishes of the mother to the extent it is necessary to give the child an opportunity to live.

Accordingly, the plaintiff hospitals are hereby authorized to administer to defendant all medical procedures deemed necessary by the attending physician to preserve the life of defendant's unborn child. This authority shall be effective only if defendant voluntarily seeks admission to either of plaintiff's hospitals for the emergency delivery of the child.

The Court has been requested to order defendant to submit to surgery before the natural childbirth process (labor) begins. The Court is reluctant to grant this request and does not do so at this time. However, should some agency of the State seek such relief through intervention in this suit or in a separate proceeding, the Court will promptly consider such request.

On Friday, January 23, the Georgia Department of Human Resources, acting through the Butts County Department of Family and Children Services, petitioned the Juvenile Court of Butts County for temporary custody of the unborn child, alleging that the child was a deprived child without proper parental care necessary for his or her physical health (see Code Ann. §24A-401(h)(1)), and praying for an order requiring the mother to submit to a caesarean section. After appointing counsel for the parents and for the child, the court conducted a joint hearing in both the superior court and juvenile court cases and entered the following order on the afternoon of January 23:

> At the proceeding held today, Jessie Mae Jefferson and her husband, John W. Jefferson were present and represented by counsel, Hugh Glidewell, Jr. Richard Milam, Attorney at Law, represented the interests of the unborn child.
>
> Based on the evidence presented, the Court finds that Jessie Mae Jefferson is due to begin labor at any moment. There is a 99 to 100 percent certainty that the unborn child will die if she attempts to have the child by vaginal delivery. . . . There is a 50 percent chance that Mrs. Jefferson herself will die if vaginal delivery is attempted. There is an almost 100 percent chance that [the baby and] Mrs. Jefferson will survive if a delivery by Caesarean section is done prior to the beginning of labor. . . .
>
> Mrs. Jefferson and her husband have refused and continue to refuse to give consent to a Caesarean section. This refusal is based entirely on the religious beliefs of Mr. and Mrs. Jefferson. They are of the view that the Lord has healed her body and that whatever happens to the child will be the Lord's will.
>
> Based on these findings, the Court concludes and finds as a matter of law that this child is a viable human being and entitled to the protection of the Juvenile Court Code of Georgia. The Court concludes that this child is without the proper parental care and subsistence necessary for his or her physical life and health.
>
> Temporary custody of the unborn child is hereby granted to the State of Georgia Department of Human Resources and the Butts County Department of Family and Children Services. The Department shall have full authority to make all decisions, including giving consent to the surgical delivery appertaining to the birth of this child. The temporary custody of the Department shall terminate when the child has been successfully brought from its mother's body into the world or until the child dies, whichever shall happen.
>
> Because of the unique nature of these cases, the powers of the Superior Court of Butts County are invoked and the defendant, Jessie Mae Jefferson, is hereby Ordered to submit to a sonogram (ultrasound). . . . Should said sonogram indicate to the attending physician that the complete placenta previa is still blocking the child's passage into this world, Jessie Mae Jefferson, is Ordered to submit to a Caesarean section and related procedures. . . .
>
> The Court finds that the State has an interest in the life of this unborn, living human being. The Court finds that the intrusion involved into the life of Jessie Mae Jefferson and her husband, John W. Jefferson, is outweighed by the duty of the State to protect a living, unborn human being from meeting his or her death before being given the opportunity to live.
>
> This Order shall be effective at 10:00 a.m. on Saturday, January 24, 1981, unless a stay is granted by the Supreme Court of Georgia or some other Court having the authority to stay an Order of this Court.

[The parents filed a motion for a stay, which was denied.]

HILL, Presiding Justice, concurring.

The power of a court to order a competent adult to submit to surgery is exceedingly limited. Indeed, until this unique case arose, I would have thought such power to be nonexistent. Research shows that the courts generally have held that a competent adult has the right to refuse necessary lifesaving surgery and medical treatment (i.e., has the right to die) where no state interest other than saving the life of the patient is involved. Anno. Patient's Right to Refuse Treatment, 93 A.L.R.3d 67, §3 (1979).

On the other hand, one court has held that an expectant mother in the last weeks of pregnancy lacks the right to refuse necessary life saving surgery and medical treatment where the life of the unborn child is at stake. Raleigh Fitkin-Paul Morgan Memorial Hospital v. Anderson, [201 A.2d 537 (N.J. 1964)]; see also Re Melideo, 88 Misc.2d 974, 390 N.Y.S.2d 523 (1976); Re Yetter, 62 Pa. D. & C.2d 619, 623 (1973).

The Supreme Court has recognized that the state has an interest in protecting the lives of unborn, viable children (viability usually occuring at about 7 months, or 28 weeks). Roe v. Wade, 410 U.S. 113, 160, 164-165 (1973). . . .

In denying the stay of the trial court's order and thereby clearing the way for immediate reexamination by sonogram and probably for surgery, we weighed the right of the mother to practice her religion and to refuse surgery on herself, against her unborn child's right to live. We found in favor of her child's right to live.

Although we are not called upon here to decide whether the intervention of the juvenile court was necessary, I for one approve the trial court's action in exercising jurisdiction over the unborn child as juvenile judge and over the mother as judge of a court of equity. According to the testimony, this child was facing almost certain death, and was being deprived of the opportunity to live. For this reason, Code Ann. §24A-401(h) (5) is inapplicable.[1] . . .

SMITH, Justice, concurring.

The free exercise of religion is, of course, one of our most precious freedoms. . . . The courts have, however, drawn a distinction between the free exercise of religious belief which is constitutionally protected against any infringement and religious practices that are inimical or detrimental to public health or welfare which are not. . . .

In the instant case, it appears that there is no less burdensome alternative for preserving the life of a fully developed fetus than requiring its mother to undergo surgery against her religious convictions. Such an intrusion by the state would be extraordinary, presenting some medical risk to both the mother and the fetus. However, the state's compelling interest in preserving the life of this fetus is beyond dispute. See Roe v. Wade, supra; Code §26-1202 et seq. Moreover, the medical evidence indicates that the risk to the fetus and the mother presented by a Caesarean section would be minimal, whereas, in the absence of surgery, the fetus would almost certainly die and the mother's chance of survival would be no better than 50 per

[1] According to newspaper reports, "a third ultrasound test performed Friday night showed the placenta had moved — a most unusual occurrence . . . " Atlanta Journal/Constitution, January 25, 1981.

cent. Under these circumstances, I must conclude that the trial court's order is not violative of the First Amendment, notwithstanding that it may require the mother to submit to surgery against her religious beliefs. See Raleigh Fitkin-Paul Memorial Hospital v. Anderson, supra; see also Green v. Green, 448 Pa. 338, 292 A.2d 387 (1972).

We deal here with an apparent life and death emergency; questions relating to the jurisdiction of the lower court are not our primary concern.

Code §24A-301 sets forth the jurisdiction of the juvenile courts. It provides in pertinent part: "(a) The court shall have exclusive original jurisdiction over *juvenile* matters and shall be the sole court for initiating action: (1) Concerning any *child* . . . (C) Who is alleged to be deprived . . . " (Emphasis supplied.). Code §24A-401 defines the term "child" as "any individual under the age of 17 years." I believe the legislature intended that the juvenile courts exercise jurisdiction only where a child has seen the light of day. I am aware of no "child deprivation" proceeding wherein the "child" was unborn.

This is a case of first impression, and the trial court, in an attempt to cover all possible ground, rendered its judgment "both as a Juvenile Court and under the broad powers of the Superior Court of Butts County." As the trial court's action was a proper exercise of its equitable jurisdiction with respect to both the mother and the fetus and its decision on the merits a correct one, I fully concur in the denial of appellant's motion for stay. . . .

QUESTIONS ON INTERVENTION DURING PREGNANCY

(1) Epilogue. A few days after the Georgia Supreme Court's order, Ms. Jefferson delivered a healthy baby without any need for surgical intervention. The "99% certainty that the child cannot survive natural childbirth" was probably an inaccurate estimate. See George J. Annas, Forced Cesareans: The Most Unkindest Cut of All, Hastings Center Rep. 16 (June 1982) (also citing another case where the woman was forced to undergo a cesarean because a fetal monitor indicated signs of fetal distress which turned out in fact to be significantly overstated). If it is difficult to predict the risks to the woman and the fetus, should physicians (and courts) defer to the woman's preference?

How is a judge, faced with an emergency request for an order compelling a cesarean section, to evaluate the physician's claims of benefits and risks? See generally Joel J. Finer, Toward Guidelines for Compelling Cesarean Surgery: Of Rights, Responsibility, and Decisional Authenticity, 76 Minn. L. Rev. 239 (1991) (proposing guidelines for compulsory cesarean sections balancing the mother's decision, the net gain or loss in human life, bodily integrity, and privacy rights).

(2) Justifications for Intervention. Is a state justified in requiring a cesarean section, or in regulating abortion, to protect a woman's health if she is prepared to accept the risks? As Justice Hill's concurring opinion indicates, ordinarily a state cannot compel a competent adult to accept medical treatment. See, e.g., Cruzan v. Director, Missouri Dept. of Health, 497 U.S. 261, 262 (1990) ("a competent person has a liberty interest under the Due Process Clause in refusing unwanted medical treatment"). Should it matter that a woman is pregnant?

Can you think of other examples of legal paternalism (i.e., where the state prohibits individuals from engaging in conduct that is harmful only to themselves or that requires individuals to take self-protective measures)? For example, some states require motorists to wear seat belts and compel motorcyclists to wear helmets. See, e.g., Ohio Rev. Code Ann. §4513.263 (West 1999) (seat belts); N.Y. Veh. & Traf. §381 (McKinney 1996); Wash. Rev. Code Ann. §46.37.530 (West 2001 & Supp. 2004) (helmets). Although arguably the state's interest in preserving life is even greater than its interest in protecting health and safety, the underlying justifications for the religious objection cases (of which *Jefferson* is an example) are unclear. While there are numerous cases in which courts have compelled unwilling patients to submit to medical treatment, the decisions often rely not on a compelling state interest to protect the health or life of the individual but on a desire to protect others. Courts have intervened typically "only when the lives of third parties were jeopardized or when the patient was not competent to refuse care." Barry Nobel, Religious Healing in the Courts: The Liberties and Liabilities of Patients, Parents, and Healers, 16 U. Puget Sound L. Rev. 599, 617 (1993). Does this suggest that there are few situations where a course of action only affects the actor? Or that legal paternalism is an accepted justification for state action, John Stuart Mill notwithstanding?[22]

(3) Problem. Simmone Ikerd pleads guilty to welfare fraud. Simmone is a drug addict who is 11 weeks pregnant and is undergoing treatment at a methadone clinic. She is sentenced to five years' probation, conditioned upon completion of drug treatment. Subsequently, she appears in court for a probation violation, i.e., failure to appear for a drug test (she claims she had to leave the test site to take an older child to the doctor). Believing that the only place where Simmone's addiction and the health of her fetus could be addressed is a correctional facility, the judge sentences her to prison for the duration of her pregnancy. The judge explains that if Simmone loses the baby, he will reconsider the sentence. She appeals. What result? See State v. Ikerd, 850 A.2d 516 (N.J. Super. Ct. App. Div. 2004). See generally Jean Reith Schroedel & Pamela Fiber, Punitive Versus Public Health Oriented Responses to Drug Use by Pregnant Women, 1 Yale J. Health Pol'y L. & Ethics 217 (2001).

Given the important influence of prenatal care, consider the range of ways that conduct during pregnancy may affect the baby's well-being. Could a state require prenatal care for all pregnant women? Even during the first six months? Regulate the diet of pregnant women or prohibit them from using certain drugs (e.g., caffeine) not otherwise illegal? Make it a criminal offense to smoke or drink alcohol? Compel a diabetic to accept insulin to protect the fetus? Make public health benefits contingent on a pregnant woman's submission to physical examination or abstention from drugs or alcohol? What guidance do *Roe* and *Casey* provide?

Suppose that surgery on the fetus before birth could correct a severe birth defect. Could a state order a pregnant woman to undergo fetal surgery? See Krista L. Newkirk, Note, State-Compelled Fetal Surgery: The Viability Test Is Not Viable, 4 Wm. & Mary J. Women & L. 467 (1997). Could a state compel prenatal genetic testing of a pregnant woman at risk of giving birth to a child with a defect? See Wendy E. Roop, Note, Not in My Womb: Compelled Prenatal Genetic Testing,

---

[22] For two classic articles analyzing the philosophical justifications for legal paternalism, see Joel Feinberg, Legal Paternalism, 1 Canadian J. Phil. 105 (1971); Gerald Dworkin, Paternalism, in Morality and the Law (Richard A. Wasserstrom ed. 1971).

27 Hastings Const. L.Q. 397 (2000). Similarly, could a state force a pregnant woman who is HIV-positive to take medicine that would protect her unborn fetus? See Andrea Marsh, Testing Pregnant Women and Newborns for HIV: Legal and Ethical Responses to Public Health Efforts to Prevent Pediatric AIDS, 13 Yale J.L. & Feminism 195 (2001).

Should a court be able to appoint a guardian ad litem to represent the interests of the unborn child if the mother is unable to provide proper prenatal care or to make decisions to protect the fetus's health? See In re Guardianship of J.D.S. v. Department of Children and Families, 864 So. 2d 534 (Fla. Dist. Ct. App. 2004) (concluding that the state guardianship statute did not cover fetuses and adequate safeguards existed to ensure that J.D.S.'s guardian did not "act capriciously or cavalierly when considering the health of the incapacitated mother and fetus"). Id. at 539.

(4) Benefit vs. Risk. In *Jefferson*, the court believed that requiring a caesarean in the circumstances would save the baby and reduce a perceived risk to the mother's life. The intervention was seen, in other words, as benefiting both the mother and the child. Suppose a mother refused a caesarean in circumstances where her refusal created no risks to her own life or health but grave risks for the unborn child. In such circumstances, would it be appropriate to require a caesarean, which itself creates some risk for the mother?

In Baby Boy Doe v. Mother Doe, 632 N.E.2d 326 (Ill. App. Ct. 1994), a pregnant woman refused, on religious grounds, a caesarean section that was recommended because the placenta of her 35-week fetus was receiving insufficient oxygen. The Illinois appellate court denied the state's request to order the forced caesarean. Refusing to balance fetal rights versus the woman's rights, the court held that a woman's competent choice to refuse "medical treatment as invasive as a cesarean" must be honored, even in circumstances where the choice may be harmful to her fetus. Id. at 330.

Baby Boy Doe, supra, left open the question whether blood transfusions (considerably less invasive than caesarean sections) could be ordered for a pregnant woman. In In re Fetus Brown, 689 N.E.2d 397 (Ill. App. Ct. 1997), a woman who was 34 weeks' pregnant lost more blood than anticipated during an operation, posing a life-threatening risk to the patient and her fetus. The patient refused, on religious grounds, the recommended transfusion. The circuit court ordered the blood transfusion. The appellate court reversed. Applying *Baby Boy Doe*, the appellate court reiterated that the state may not balance interests and may not override a competent woman's treatment decision to save the life of her viable fetus. These cases may signify a change in judicial attitudes toward legal intevention for pregnant women.

See also David M. Caruso, Childbirth Choices Debated, L.A. Times, May 30, 2004, at A19 (citing a survey by University of Chicago researchers in 2002 finding that 4% of directors of maternal-fetal medicine fellowship programs believe pregnant women should be required to undergo Caesareans for the sake of their fetuses compared to 47% in 1987). But cf. Pemberton v. Tallahassee Regional Med. Ctr., 66 F. Supp. 2d 1247 (N.D. Fla. 1999) (holding that mother's constitutional rights were not violated by court-ordered Caesarean when she insisted on vaginal delivery against medical advice).

(5) Religious Justification. Reported cases suggest that the most common reason for refusal of treatment by pregnant women is religious belief. See, e.g.,

Jefferson, supra; Taft v. Taft, 446 N.E.2d 395 (Mass. 1983); Raleigh Fitkin-Paul Morgan Memorial Hosp. v. Anderson, 201 A.2d 537 (N.J. 1964), *cert. denied*, 377 U.S. 985 (1964). Should the religious beliefs of a pregnant woman matter when the survival of the fetus is at risk? See generally April L. Cherry, The Free Exercise Rights of Pregnant Women Who Refuse Medical Treatment, 69 Tenn. L. Rev. 563 (2002). Should it be easier to intervene if the woman's justification is not religious? Or if she refuses to give a reason? See Caruso, supra (citing case of hospital that obtained a court order to compel a Caesarean for a woman with a normal history of delivering large babies who chose natural childbirth).

(6) Applicable Standard.   By what standard should a court consider and balance the risks and benefits for the mother and child in deciding whether to intervene? May the state then intervene solely on the fetus's behalf without regard to the mother? Or order a procedure that creates a serious risk to the mother's life in order to save the child? In In re A.C., 533 A.2d 611 (D.C. 1987), *reh'g granted, vacated*, 539 A.2d 203 (D.C. 1988), a judge ordered a Caesarean section on a terminally ill woman, A.C., who was 26 weeks pregnant, without her consent and despite the objections of her family, physicians, and the hospital obstetric staff. The baby died almost immediately, and two days later A.C. died. The surgery was listed as a contributing cause of her death. On appeal, a three-judge panel of the District of Columbia Court of Appeals held that in the constitutionally mandated balancing test between the life of the women and the life of the fetus, a pregnant women's wishes may be overridden if she is not in "good health," stating that the "Caesarean section would not significantly affect A.C.'s condition because she had, at best, two days left. . . . " 533 A.2d at 617.

Vacating the earlier opinion and granting a rehearing en banc, the Court of Appeals held that a terminally ill pregnant woman has the right to determine the course of her own medical treatment unless she is incompetent or unable to provide informed consent, in which case her decision must be ascertained via substituted judgment. In re A.C., 573 A.2d 1235 (D.C. 1990).

(7) Autonomy vs. Equality.   What implication does recognition of fetal rights, and thereby overriding the pregnant woman's autonomy to control her life during her pregnancy, have for women's equality? An empirical study of 21 court-ordered obstetrical procedures reveals that orders are obtained in 86 percent of the cases (most frequently in cases involving minority women in teaching hospitals or on public assistance). The authors conclude: "Clearly court orders force women to assume medical risks and forfeit their legal autonomy in a manner not required of competent men or non-pregnant women. . . . " Veronica B. Kolder et al., Court-Ordered Obstetrical Interventions, 316 N. Eng. J. Med. 1192, 1194 (May 7, 1987). Also, what is the implication of framing the issue as a "maternal-fetal" conflict? See April L. Cherry, *Roe*'s Legacy: The Nonconsensual Medical Treatment of Pregnant Women and Implications for Female Citizenship, 6 U. Pa. J. Const. L. 723 (2004) (suggesting that compelled medical treatment of pregnant women subordinates women to their reproductive capacity and state-sanctioned mothering roles); Michelle Oberman, Mothers and Doctors' Orders: Unmasking the Doctor's Fiduciary Role in Maternal-Fetal Conflicts, 94 Nw. U. L. Rev. 451 (2000) (arguing that this paradigm ignores the role played by doctors in undermining the autonomy rights of their pregnant patients).

A related problem is the inability of pregnant women to execute living wills. All 50 states and the District of Columbia authorize the use of either living wills or power of attorney (or both) for incompetent patients. However, 34 states prohibit the withdrawal of life support in cases of pregnancy. See Amy Lynn Jerdee, Note, Breaking Through the Silence: Minnesota's Pregnancy Presumption and the Right to Refuse Medical Treatment, 84 Minn. L. Rev. 971 (2000) (derived from author's state-by-state survey). Does the state's interest in protecting the unborn child justify limiting the mother's exercise of her "right to die"? Are such limits constitutional?

(8) Discriminatory Application?   There is some evidence to suggest that physicians are more likely to intervene to compel Caesareans and other invasive procedures if the mother is a woman of color or a member of a lower socioeconomic class. See Deborah J. Krauss, Regulating Women's Bodies: The Adverse Effect of Fetal Rights Theory on Childbirth Decisions and Women of Color, 26 Harv. C.R.-C.L. L. Rev. 523 (1991). As Krauss reports:

> Physicians seek court-ordered obstetrical interventions most often when the pregnant woman is a member of a racial minority or disadvantaged socioeconomic group. A national study found that in eighty-one percent of the court-ordered obstetrical interventions reported (including Caesarean sections, hospital detentions and intrauterine transfusions), the woman was African-American, Asian-American or Latina. One-quarter of the women ordered to undergo unwanted treatment did not speak English as their primary language. Specifically in cases of court-ordered Caesarean sections, eighty percent of the patients were members of minority groups, and twenty-seven percent were not native English speakers. Every request for a court order involved a woman who was a patient at a teaching hospital or who received public assistance. None of the patients in the study were deemed incompetent by a psychiatrist. [Id. at 531.]

See also Dorothy Roberts, Killing the Black Body: Race, Reproduction, and the Meaning of Liberty (1997).

(9) Imposition of Criminal Sanctions. After the fact, should the state ever be able to impose criminal sanctions on a mother if her child dies or is severely harmed because of the mother's failure to protect the "child" during the pregnancy? In State v. McKnight, 576 S.E.2d 168 (S.C. 2003), Regina McKnight was convicted of homicide by child abuse after giving birth to a stillborn girl with cocaine in her system. The South Carolina Supreme Court held that the prosecution did not violate due process or the right to privacy and that the 20-year sentence was not cruel and unusual punishment. *McKnight* represents the minority approach to the imposition of criminal liability on pregnant substance abusers.

Two years before *McKnight*, the United States Supreme Court addressed the constitutionality of a hospital policy of testing pregnant women for the purpose of fetal protection. In Ferguson v. City of Charleston, 532 U.S. 67 (2001), a state hospital developed a policy of testing pregnant patients suspected of substance abuse without their knowledge or consent. Patients who tested positive were arrested. When patients challenged the policy as a violation of the Fourth Amendment, the United States Supreme Court held that the tests constituted unreasonable searches absent consent, in view of the policy's law enforcement purpose. *McKnight* distinguished *Ferguson* by contending that the South Carolina policy was not developed in conjunction with law enforcement and the taking of the urine sample was consensual.

See also News, Mom in Caesarean Case Gets Probation, Chi. Trib., Apr. 30, 2004, at 18 (describing case of substance abuser who was sentenced to probation for child endangerment for refusing to have a Caesarean). See generally Lisa Eckenwiler, Why Not Retribution? The Particularized Imagination and Justice for Pregnant Addicts, 32 J.L. Med. & Ethics 89 (2004); Lynn M. Paltrow, The War on Drugs and the War on Abortion: Some Initial Thoughts on the Connections, Intersections and the Effects, 28 S.U. L. Rev. 201 (2001).

(10) Fetal Protection Policies. Should concern for the unborn child justify barring pregnant women or women of child-bearing age from employment that exposes a woman to toxic agents with mutagenic or teratogenic effects? In International Union, UAW v. Johnson Controls, 499 U.S. 187 (1991), a lead battery manufacturer adopted a fetal protection policy barring *all* female employees except those who could document infertility from working in jobs with potential lead exposure in excess of OSHA standards. The United States Supreme Court held that the policy was facially discriminatory under Title VII because it barred only female employees, despite evidence showing the debilitating effects of lead exposure on the male reproductive system as well. On the legacy of *Johnson Controls*, see Elaine Draper, Reproductive Hazards and Fetal Exclusion Policies After *Johnson Controls*, 12 Stan. L. & Pol'y Rev. 117 (2001).

Spousal Consent

So far the analysis has centered on the extent to which the state is justified in interfering with the pregnant woman's decision, in order to protect the woman or to preserve the life or well-being of the fetus. This involves the allocation of decisional power between the state, on the one hand, and the woman, on the other. But what about the interest of the father? There is, of course, the possibility that the mother and father of the fetus may not agree. In that case there remains the issue of which private individual shall have the power to decide on an abortion: the mother acting alone? Or only if the father consents as well? Should it make any difference if the mother and father are married?

In the wake of *Roe*, several states passed abortion statutes that conditioned abortion by a married woman on spousal consent. Such provisions were challenged on constitutional grounds in a number of cases. The Supreme Court decided this question, as well as a number of others, in the *Danforth* case, an extract from which follows.

Planned Parenthood of Central Missouri v. Danforth[23]
428 U.S. 52 (1976)

BLACKMUN, J. delivered the opinion of the Court.

[Physicians challenge a number of provisions of the Missouri abortion statute enacted after *Roe* and *Doe*.]

---

[23] That portion of the *Danforth* opinion relating to Missouri's parental consent requirement for an abortion by a minor is discussed at pp. 136-138, infra.

. . . Section 3(3) [of Missouri House Bill No. 1211] requires the prior written consent of the spouse of the woman seeking an abortion during the first 12 weeks of pregnancy, unless "the abortion is certified by a licensed physician to be necessary in order to preserve the life of the mother."

The appellees defend §3(3) on the ground that it was enacted in the light of the General Assembly's "perception of marriage as an institution," and that any major change in family status is a decision to be made jointly by the marriage partners. Reference is made to an abortion's possible effect on the woman's childbearing potential. [Reference is made to . . . Missouri's general requirement that for an *adoption* adoption of a child born in wedlock the consent of both parents is necessary; to *comparison* similar joint consent requirements imposed by a number of States with respect to artificial insemination and the legitimacy of children so conceived; to the laws of two States requiring spousal consent for voluntary sterilization; and to the long-established requirement of spousal consent for the effective disposition of an interest in real property. It is argued that "[r]ecognizing that the consent of both parties is generally necessary . . . to begin a family, the legislature has determined that a change in the family structure set in motion by mutual consent should be terminated only by mutual consent," and that what the legislature did was to exercise its inherent policymaking power "for what was believed to be in the best interests of all people of Missouri."

The appellants, on the other hand, contend that §3(3) obviously is designed to afford the husband the right unilaterally to prevent or veto an abortion, whether or not he is the father of the fetus, and that this not only violates *Roe* and *Doe* but is also in conflict with other decided cases . . . . They also refer to the situation where the husband's consent cannot be obtained because he cannot be located. And they assert that §3(3) is vague and overbroad. . . .

We now hold that the State may not constitutionally require the consent of the spouse . . . as a condition for abortion during the first 12 weeks of pregnancy. [T]he State cannot "delegate to a spouse a veto power which the state itself is absolutely and totally prohibited from exercising during the first trimester of pregnancy." 392 F. Supp., at 1375. Clearly, since the State cannot regulate or proscribe abortion during the first stage, when the physician and his patient make that decision, the State cannot delegate authority to any particular person, even the spouse, to prevent abortion during that same period. . . . [11]

----

[11] As the Court recognized in Eisenstadt v. Baird, "the marital couple is not an independent entity with a mind and heart of its own, but an association of two individuals each with a separate intellectual and emotional makeup. If the right of privacy means anything, it is the right of the *individual*, married or single, to be free from unwarranted governmental intrusion into matters so fundamentally affecting a person as the decision whether to bear or beget a child." 405 U.S., at 453 (emphasis in original).

The dissenting opinion of our Brother White appears to overlook the implications of this statement upon the issue whether §3(3) is constitutional. This section does much more than insure that the husband participate in the decision whether his wife should have an abortion. The State, instead, has determined that the husband's interest in continuing the pregnancy of his wife always outweighs any interest on her part in terminating it irrespective of the condition of their marriage. The State, accordingly, has granted him the right to prevent unilaterally, and for whatever reason, the effectuation of his wife's and her physician's decision to terminate her pregnancy. This state determination not only may discourage the consultation that might normally be expected to precede a major decision

It seems manifest that, ideally, the decision to terminate a pregnancy should be one concurred in by both the wife and her husband. No marriage may be viewed as harmonious or successful if the marriage partners are fundamentally divided on so important and vital an issue. But it is difficult to believe that the goal of fostering mutuality and trust in a marriage, and of strengthening the marital relationship and the marriage institution, will be achieved by giving the husband a veto power exercisable for any reason whatsoever or for no reason at all. . . .

We recognize, of course, that when a woman, with the approval of her physician but without the approval of her husband, decides to terminate her pregnancy, it could be said that she is acting unilaterally. The obvious fact is that when the wife and the husband disagree on this decision, the view of only one of the two marriage partners can prevail. Since it is the woman who physically bears the child and who is the more directly and immediately affected by the pregnancy, as between the two, the balance weighs in her favor. Cf. Roe v. Wade, 410 U.S., at 153.

We conclude that §3(3) of the Missouri Act is inconsistent with the standards enunciated in Roe v. Wade, 410 U.S., at 164-165, and is unconstitutional. . . .

Mr. Justice WHITE, joined by The Chief Justice and Mr. Justice REHNQUIST dissenting:

. . . Section 3(3) of the Act provides that a married woman may not obtain an abortion without her husband's consent. The Court strikes down this statute in one sentence. It says that "since the State cannot . . . proscribe abortion . . . the State cannot delegate authority to any particular person, even the spouse, to prevent abortion. . . . " Ante, at 15. But the State is not — under §3(3) — delegating to the husband the power to vindicate the *State's* interest in the future life of the fetus. It is instead recognizing that the husband has an interest of his own in the life of the fetus which should not be extinguished by the unilateral decision of the wife. . . . A father's interest in having a child — perhaps his only child — may be unmatched by any other interest in his life. See Stanley v. Illinois, 405 U.S. 645, 651 [infra p. 483], and cases there cited. It is truly surprising that the majority finds in the United States Constitution, as it must in order to justify the result it reaches, a rule that the State must assign a greater value to a mother's decision to cut off a potential human life by abortion than to a father's decision to let it mature into a live child. . . . These are matters which a State should be able to decide free from the suffocating power of the federal judge, purporting to act in the name of the Constitution. . . .

QUESTIONS ON SPOUSAL CONSENT

(1) Spousal Consent vs. Spousal Notification.   In *Danforth*, the Court invalidated Missouri's spousal *consent* requirement. Would the Court uphold a spousal *notification* requirement? In Planned Parenthood of Southeastern Pennsylvania v. Casey, 500 U.S. 833 (1992), the Supreme Court considered the constitutionality of §3209 of Pennsylvania's abortion law requiring that a married woman provide

affecting the marital couple but also, and more importantly, the State has interposed an absolute obstacle to a woman's decision that *Roe* held to be constitutionally protected from such interference.

her physician with a signed statement certifying that she had notified her husband of her abortion plans. Notification was not required if (1) the husband was not the father; (2) the husband could not be located; (3) the pregnancy was the result of spousal sexual assault that she had reported; or (4) the woman believed notification would cause her bodily injury. Relying on *Danforth*, the woman's liberty interest in her body, and empirical evidence revealing that this provision would prevent many battered wives from procuring abortions, the Supreme Court found that §3209 constituted an undue burden. The Court in *Casey* stated:

Casey

> . . . In well-functioning marriages, spouses discuss important intimate decisions such as whether to bear a child. But there are millions of women in this country who are the victims of regular physical and psychological abuse at the hands of their husbands. Should these women become pregnant, they may have very good reasons for not wishing to inform their husbands of their decision to obtain an abortion. Many may have justifiable fears of physical abuse. . . . Many may have a reasonable fear that notifying their husbands will provoke further instances of child abuse; these women are not exempt from §3209's notification requirement. Many may fear devastating forms of psychological abuse from their husbands, including verbal harassment, threats of future violence, the destruction of possessions, physical confinement to the home, the withdrawal of financial support, or the disclosure of the abortion to family and friends. These methods of psychological abuse may act as even more of a deterrent to notification than the possibility of physical violence. . . . And many women . . . will be unable to avail themselves of the exception for spousal sexual assault, §3209(b) (3), because the exception requires that the woman have notified law enforcement authorities within 90 days of the assault, and her husband will be notified of her report once an investigation begins. . . .
>
> Statute assumes marriage is well-functioning
>
> The spousal notification requirement is thus likely to prevent a significant number of women from obtaining an abortion. It does not merely make abortions a little more difficult or expensive to obtain; for many women, it will impose a substantial obstacle. We must not blind ourselves to the fact that the significant number of women who fear for their safety and the safety of their children are likely to be deterred from procuring an abortion as surely as if the Commonwealth had outlawed abortion in all cases.
>
> undue burden
>
> Respondents attempt to avoid the conclusion that §3209 is invalid by pointing out that it imposes almost no burden at all for the vast majority of women seeking abortions. They begin by noting that only about 20 percent of the women who obtain abortions are married. They then note that of these women about 95 percent notify their husbands of their own volition. Thus, respondents argue, the effects of §3209 are felt by only one percent of the women who obtain abortions. Respondents argue that since some of these women will be able to notify their husbands without adverse consequences or will qualify for one of the exceptions, the statute affects fewer than one percent of women seeking abortions. For this reason, it is asserted, the statute cannot be invalid on its face. . . .
>
> The analysis does not end with the one percent of women upon whom the statute operates; it begins there. . . . The proper focus of constitutional inquiry is the group for whom the law is a restriction, not the group for whom the law is irrelevant. . . . The unfortunate yet persisting conditions we document above will mean that in a large fraction of the cases in which §3209 is relevant, it will operate as a substantial obstacle to a woman's choice to undergo an abortion. It is an undue burden, and therefore invalid. . . .

We recognize that a husband has a "deep and proper concern and interest . . . in his wife's pregnancy and in the growth and development of the fetus she is carrying." *Danforth*, 428 U.S. at 69. With regard to the children he has fathered and raised, the Court has recognized his "cognizable and substantial" interest in their custody. Stanley v. Illinois, 405 U.S. 645, 651-652 (1972); . . .

Before birth, however, the issue takes on a very different cast. It is an inescapable biological fact that state regulation with respect to the child a woman is carrying will have a far greater impact on the mother's liberty than on the father's. . . .

. . . In keeping with our rejection of the common-law understanding of a woman's role within the family, the Court held in *Danforth* that the Constitution does not permit a State to require a married woman to obtain her husband's consent before undergoing an abortion. 428 U.S., at 69. The principles that guided the Court in *Danforth* should be our guides today. . . .

The husband's interest in the life of the child his wife is carrying does not permit the State to empower him with this troubling degree of authority over his wife. The contrary view leads to consequences reminiscent of the common law. A husband has no enforceable right to require a wife to advise him before she exercises her personal choices. If a husband's interest in the potential life of the child outweighs a wife's liberty, the State could require a married woman to notify her husband before she uses a postfertilization contraceptive. Perhaps next in line would be a statute requiring pregnant married women to notify their husbands before engaging in conduct causing risks to the fetus. After all, if the husband's interest in the fetus' safety is a sufficient predicate for state regulation, the State could reasonably conclude that pregnant wives should notify their husbands before drinking alcohol or smoking. Perhaps married women should notify their husbands before using contraceptives or before undergoing any type of surgery that may have complications affecting the husband's interest in his wife's reproductive organs. And if a husband's interest justifies notice in any of these cases, one might reasonably argue that it justifies exactly what the *Danforth* Court held it did not justify — a requirement of the husband's consent as well. A State may not give to a man the kind of dominion over his wife that parents exercise over their children.

Section 3209 embodies a view of marriage consonant with the common-law status of married women but repugnant to our present understanding of marriage and of the nature of the rights secured by the Constitution. Women do not lose their constitutionally protected liberty when they marry. The Constitution protects all individuals, male or female, married or unmarried, from the abuse of governmental power, even where that power is employed for the supposed benefit of a member of the individual's family. These considerations confirm our conclusion that §3209 is invalid. . . . [505 U.S. at 892-899.]

(2) Father's Interests.   After *Danforth* and *Casey*, does the father possess any legal interest in decisions regarding the unborn child? Does the father's interest grow as the mother approaches term? Is it reasonable to allow the state, but not the father, to intervene on behalf of the unborn child to prohibit postviability abortions?

(3) Empirical Data.   Data from abortion clinics reveal that as many as 86 percent of women inform their male partners about their abortion plans. Married women are as likely as single women to inform the biological father. Marcelle Christian Holmes, Reconsidering a "Woman's Issue:" Psychotherapy and One Man's Postabortion Experiences, 58 Am. J. Psychotherapy 103 (Jan. 1, 2004). For an

empirical study of men's role in the abortion decision, see Arthur B. Shostak, The Role of Unwed Fathers in the Abortion Decision, in Young Unwed Fathers, Changing Roles and Emerging Policies 292 (Robert I. Lerman & Theodora J. Ooms eds., 1995).

(4) Undue Burden Test. Under the undue burden test, is it clear that Pennsylvania's statute requiring a woman to sign a statement of notification is so burdensome? What course of action do you suppose most women would take if they did not desire to notify their husbands?

(5) What reasons does the Court give for suggesting that the requirement constitutes an undue burden? Are those reasons persuasive? Recall, for example, Justice O'Connor's statement that "The unfortunate yet persisting condition we document above will mean that in a large fraction of the cases in which §3209 is relevant, it will operate as a substantial burden. . . . " 505 U.S. at 895. What data support this "large fraction"? If you were advising a Pennsylvania legislator, how would you suggest the statute be changed to address the Court's objections?

(6) Does the portion of *Casey* cited above signify that a state could require a mother to notify the father before providing a "living child" with necessary medical care? Before allowing a child to enroll in private school? Before consenting to a daughter's abortion?

(7) Compelling Fetal Surgery. Suppose a couple discovers that the viable fetus which the wife is carrying has a serious birth defect. The problem is correctable by fetal surgery. Does the husband have any right to compel the wife to undergo the surgery? How is the husband's right similar to, or different from, his right in the abortion context? See David C. Blickenstaff, Comment, Defining the Boundaries of Personal Privacy: Is There a Paternal Interest in Compelling Therapeutic Fetal Surgery?, 88 Nw. U. L. Rev. 1157 (1994).

(8) It is now possible to transplant an embryo from a pregnant woman to a carrier who can bear the child. If the transplant involves no more substantial risk to the mother than an abortion, would the state have the right to compel a transplant rather than allow an abortion? Would the father have the right to insist on the transplant if he were willing to care for and support the child without the mother's help? Should the scope of the father's rights be affected by his duty of support? See Chapter 2.

(9) Comatose Pregnant Wife. How should a court balance a pregnant woman's interests against the father's interests if the woman is severely disabled? Marie Henderson, when six and one-half months pregnant, was put on life support due to a brain tumor. Her parents asked the physicians to remove her from the equipment that was keeping her and her fetus alive. The father of the unborn child, who was Ms. Henderson's fiancé, obtained a court order naming him the fetus's guardian and directing the hospital not to remove the equipment. Almost two months later, a healthy and apparently normal child was delivered by Caesarean section, and physicians disconnected Ms. Henderson's life support system. See San Jose Mercury News, June 13, 1986, at 1A; June 22, 1986, at 1A; Aug. 1, 1986, at 1B; and Aug. 5, 1986, at 1B.

See also Matter of Klein, 538 N.Y.S.2d 274 (App. Div. 1989) (appointing husband of comatose pregnant woman to be her guardian in order to sign informed consent abortion authorization forms), *appeal denied*, 536 N.E.2d 627 (N.Y. 1989), *stay denied sub nom.* Short v. Klein, 489 U.S. 1003 (1989). On the moral and legal aspects of maintaining a brain-dead woman on life support for the successful delivery of her fetus, see Daniel Sperling, Maternal Brain Death, 30 Am. J.L. & Med. 453 (2004).

(10) Fathers' Claims.   Much of the litigation concerning father's rights in the abortion context took place in the years following *Roe* when fathers tried to enjoin their wives and/or their wives' doctors from undertaking abortions. Occasional cases arose subsequently in which potential fathers sought injunctions or damages. See, e.g., Coe v. Cook County, No. 96C2636, 1997 WL 797662 (N.D. Ill. Dec. 24, 1997) (dismissing father's claims against health professionals for damages for violation of his right to equal protection based on his girlfriend's abortion). See generally Melanie G. McCulley, The Male Abortion: The Putative Father's Right to Terminate His Interests in and Obligations to the Unborn Child, 7 J.L. & Pol'y 1 (1998).

(11) Standing to Intervene to Challenge Ban.   Do the husbands of pregnant women have standing to intervene as parties to challenge a state ban on partial-birth abortions? See Planned Parenthood of Wisconsin v. Doyle, 162 F.3d 463 (7th Cir. 1998) (holding that plaintiff-husbands have no significant interest in the litigation other than an ideological one, which is not an adequate basis for standing).

(12) Husband's Support Obligation.   Should a woman's right to decide whether to have an abortion affect a man's obligation to support the child if the woman chooses instead to have the baby? Suppose the man asks that she have a first trimester abortion which he offers to pay for? See Erika M. Hiester, Note, Child Support Statutes and the Father's Right Not to Procreate, 2 Ave Maria L. Rev. 213 (2004).

The Legal Treatment of a Fetus

(1) At common law, it appears that it was not a crime to abort or kill a fetus prior to quickening. The abortion or killing of a "quick" fetus was a crime, but the commentators were split over whether it was a felony or instead some lesser crime. Bracton, writing in the thirteenth century, took the position that it was a homicide "if the foetus is already formed or quickened." Henry de Bracton, 2 On the Laws and Customs of England 341 (Thorne ed. 1968). According to Coke, the abortion of a woman "quick with childe" was "a great misprision and no murder." 3 Coke Institutes 50 (1648). Blackstone suggested that at ancient common law the abortion of a quickened fetus had been considered homicide or manslaughter. 1 William Blackstone, Commentaries 129-130 (1765). In an omitted portion of the *Roe* opinion, Justice Blackmun wrote that in America, "it now appear[s] doubtful that abortion was ever firmly established as a common-law crime even with respect to the destruction of a quick fetus." 410 U.S. at 136.

(2) Fetal Homicide Legislation.   The courts of several states have wrestled with whether the killing of an unborn fetus is homicide. A majority of states have enacted fetal homicide laws imposing criminal liability for harm committed to the fetus. See Lisa Eckenwiler, Why Not Retribution? The Particularized Imagination and Justice for Pregnant Addicts, 32 J.L. Med. & Ethics 89, 96 (2004) (citing a survey listing 28 states with such laws). States vary in terms of the degree of

protection and the stage of pregnancy at which criminal liability attaches. On the different approaches, see Sandra L. Smith, Note, Fetal Homicide: Woman or Fetus as Victim? A Survey of Current State Approaches and Recommendations for Future State Application, 41 Wm. & Mary L. Rev. 1845 (2000).

In March 2004, Congress passed the Unborn Victims of Violence Act, Pub. L. No. 108-212, 118 Stat. 568 (to be codified at 18 U.S.C. §1841). The Act was dubbed "Laci and Conner's Law" in memory of a California woman who was murdered when she was eight months pregnant. The Act creates a criminal offense for killing or injuring an unborn child (at any period of gestation) during the commission of a federal crime involving a pregnant woman (i.e., recognizing two victims of the crime). What will be the impact of such legislation on abortion rights? See generally Alison Tsao, Fetal Homicide Laws: Shield Against Domestic Violence or Sword to Pierce Abortion Rights?, 25 Const. L.Q. 457 (1998).

The federal government also conferred legal rights on a fetus by means of recent revisions to the State Children's Health Insurance Program (SCHIP), 67 Fed. Reg. 61,956 (Oct. 2, 2002) (codified at 42 C.F.R. pt. 457) redefining "child" to include the unborn. SCHIP provides health insurance coverage to states for uninsured children whose families are at the poverty level. New regulations redefine "child" to include all children, from conception until age 19, regardless of the pregnant woman's immigration status. See generally Elisabeth H. Sperow, Redefining Child Abuse Under the State Children's Health Insurance Program: Capable of Repetition, Yet Evading Results, 12 Am. U.J. Gender Soc. Pol'y & L. 137, 138 (2004) (criticizing the legislation as "a step toward overturning Roe v. Wade without providing any substantial benefits to pregnant low income and immigrant women").

(3) Postpartum Psychosis Defense.   In England, the Infanticide Act, 1938, 1 & 2 Geo. 6, ch. 36, provides that if a woman kills her baby within one year of birth while disturbed by the effects of giving birth, she shall be charged with manslaughter, not murder. Postpartum psychosis has been used as a defense in American courts, such as in the much publicized trial of Andrea Yates, a mother who drowned her five children in the bathtub. A Texas jury recommended a life sentence. Jim Yardley, Mother Who Drowned 5 Children in Tub Avoids a Death Sentence, N.Y. Times, Mar. 16, 2002, at A1. See generally Sheri L. Bienstock, Mothers Who Kill Their Children and Postpartum Psychosis, 32 Sw. U. L. Rev. 451 (2003); Michelle Oberman, "Lady Madonna, Children at Your Feet": Tragedies at the Intersection of Motherhood, Mental Illness and the Law, 10 Wm. & Mary J. Women & L. 33 (2003).

(4) Tort Law: Wrongful Death.   For purposes of tort law, if a child was not born alive because of injuries inflicted during the pregnancy, the traditional rule refused to permit recovery on behalf of the fetus because the fetus was considered part of the mother — only the mother could sue for injuries to herself. Dietrich v. Northampton, 138 Mass. 14 (1884). The "born-alive" rule developed at common law because of the inability of early medical science to determine if a fetus was alive. The majority rule now permits recovery under state wrongful death statutes for prenatal injuries even if a child is stillborn. Sperow, supra, at 145.

(5) Tort Actions Against Parents for Prenatal Injuries.   The "born-alive" rule permitted a child to recover damages from *third parties* for prenatal injuries. Should a child have an action against a *parent* for a prenatal injury? Jurisdictions are split on

this issue. Compare Remy v. MacDonald, 801 N.E.2d 260 (Mass. 2004) (rejecting plaintiff's negligence suit against her mother for prenatal injuries sustained during an automobile accident) with National Cas. Co. v. Northern Trust Bank of Florida, 807 So. 2d 86 (Fla. 2001) (permitting a suit in similar circumstances). Should such suits be permitted? What are the implications of this expansion of liability? Should it matter whether the prenatal injury is caused by the mother's negligence or intentional infliction of prenatal injuries (e.g., stemming from substance abuse during the pregnancy)?

(6) Additional Birth-Related Torts: Wrongful Life, Wrongful Birth. Wrongful life claims are asserted by a *child* who suffers from birth defects, claiming that the physician's negligence in failing to inform the mother of potential birth defects deprived the mother of the option of avoiding conception or terminating the pregnancy (i.e., but for the defendant's negligence, the child would not have been born). Claims for wrongful birth and wrongful pregnancy are pursued by *parents* to recover damages for expenses and emotional distress resulting from the birth of a disabled or unwanted child, respectively. Deana A. Pollard, Wrongful Analysis in Wrongful Life Jurisprudence, 55 Ala. L. Rev. 327, 327-328 (2004). Whereas only a few jurisdictions recognize wrongful life or wrongful pregnancy actions, most jurisdictions allow parents' wrongful birth claims. Id. at 328 n. 8.

An obstacle to recovery in some jurisdictions are statutes that bar wrongful life or wrongful birth (stemming from anti-abortion sentiment) if the woman would have obtained an abortion but for the negligent act or omission. Do such statutes constitute an undue burden on a woman's right to an abortion? See Christine Intromasso, Reproductive Self-Determination in the Third Circuit: The Statutory Proscription of Wrongful Birth and Wrongful Life Claims as an Unconstitutional Violation of Planned Parenthood v. Casey's Undue Burden Standard, 24 Women's Rts. L. Rep. 101 (2003) (so arguing).

(7) Both at common law and under modern statutes, an infant *en ventre sa mère* who is subsequently born alive is regarded as a life in being for purposes of inheritance. California Civil Code §43.1 (West Supp. 2004) provides that "(a) child conceived, but not yet born, is deemed an existing person, so far as necessary for the child's interests in the event of the child's subsequent birth." Many states today have statutes regulating inheritance by posthumous children. E.g., Mass. Gen. Laws Ann. ch. 190 §8 (West 2004); N.Y. Est., Powers & Trusts §4-1.1(c) (McKinney 1998); Ohio Rev. Code Ann. §2-101 (Anderson 1994). See also Uniform Probate Code §2–108 which provides "relatives of the decedent conceived before his death but born thereafter inherit as if they had been born in the lifetime of the decedent."

(8) A father's duty of support extends to a "child conceived but not yet born." Cal. Penal Code §270 (West 1999) (child conceived but not yet born deemed an existing person); In re Clarke, 309 P.2d 142 (Cal. Ct. App. 1957) (affirming criminal nonsupport conviction of a father who willfully failed to provide support for unborn child by refusing to furnish "indirect necessities" to the mother).

With the advent of the new reproductive technology, children can be born more than nine months after the death of a biological father. Do such children have inheritance rights? See Gillett-Netting v. Barnhart, infra p. 203. See generally Kristine S. Knaplund, Postmortem Conception and a Father's Last Will, 46 Ariz. L. Rev. 91 (2004); Margaret Ward Scott, Comment, A Look at the Rights and Entitlements of Posthumously Conceived Children: No Surefire Way to Tame the Reproductive Wild West, 52 Emory L.J. 963 (2003). Child support issues are considered more generally in Chapter 2.

(9) Is a fetus a "child" for purposes of civil child abuse and neglect statutes? There are a number of cases, like *Jefferson*, supra, in which state officials have sought to use such statutes to protect unborn children by intervening in the life of a pregnant woman. See, e.g., Arkansas Dept. of Human Servs. v. Collier, 95 S.W.3d 772 (Ark. 2003); Angela M.W. v. Kruzicki, 561 N.W.2d 729 (Wis. 1997) (both holding that state child abuse and neglect statutes are inapplicable to unborn children). See generally Lynn M. Paltrow, Pregnant Drug Users, Fetal Persons, and the Threat to Roe v. Wade, 62 Alb. L. Rev. 999, 1045-1049 (1999) (discussing these developments). For further discussion of child abuse and neglect, see Chapter 3.

C. THE JUDICIAL ALLOCATION OF POWER BETWEEN PARENTS AND THE STATE

Meyer v. Nebraska
262 U.S. 390 (1923)

Mr. Justice MCREYNOLDS delivered the opinion of the Court.

Plaintiff in error was tried and convicted . . . under an information which charged that on May 25, 1920, while an instructor in Zion Parochial School, he unlawfully taught the subject of reading in the German language to Raymond Parpart, a child of ten years, who had not attained and successfully passed the eighth grade. The information is based upon "An act relating to the teaching of foreign languages in the State of Nebraska," approved April 9, 1919, which follows [Laws 1919, c. 249]:

> Section 1. No person, individually or as a teacher, shall, in any private, denomi-national, parochial or public school, teach any subject to any person in any language other than the English language.
>
> Sec. 2. Languages, other than the English language, may be taught as languages only after a pupil shall have attained and successfully passed the eighth grade as evidenced by a certificate of graduation issued by the county superintendent of the county in which the child resides.
>
> Sec. 3. Any person who violates any of the provisions of this act shall be deemed guilty of a misdemeanor and upon conviction, shall be subject to a fine of not less than twenty-five dollars ($25), nor more than one hundred dollars ($100) or be confined in the county jail for any period not exceeding thirty days for each offense.
>
> Sec. 4. Whereas, an emergency exists, this act shall be in force from and after its passage and approval.   *sup Ct rules there's no emergency*

The Supreme Court of the State affirmed the judgment of conviction. It declared the offense charged and established was "the direct and intentional teaching of the German language as a distinct subject to a child who had not passed the eighth grade," in the parochial school maintained by Zion Evangelical Lutheran Congregation, a collection of Biblical stories being used therefor. . . .

The problem for our determination is whether the statute as construed and applied unreasonably infringes the liberty guaranteed to the plaintiff in error by the Fourteenth Amendment. "No State shall . . . deprive any person of life, liberty, or property, without due process of law."

While this Court has not attempted to define with exactness the liberty thus guaranteed, the term has received much consideration. . . . Without doubt, it denotes not merely freedom from bodily restraint but also the right of the individual to contract, to engage in any of the common occupations of life, to acquire useful knowledge, to marry, establish a home and bring up children, to worship God according to the dictates of his own conscience, and generally to enjoy those privileges long recognized at common law as essential to the orderly pursuit of happiness by free men. The established doctrine is that this liberty may not be interfered with, under the guise of protecting the public interest, by legislative action which is arbitrary or without reasonable relation to some purpose within the competency of the State to effect. Determination by the legislature of what constitutes proper exercise of police power is not final or conclusive but is subject to supervision by the courts.

The American people have always regarded education and acquisition of knowledge as matters of supreme importance which should be diligently promoted. . . . Corresponding to the right of control, it is the natural duty of the parent to give his children education suitable to their station in life; and nearly all the States, including Nebraska, enforce this obligation by compulsory laws.

Practically, education of the young is only possible in schools conducted by especially qualified persons who devote themselves thereto. The calling always has been regarded as useful and honorable, essential, indeed, to the public welfare. Mere knowledge of the German language cannot reasonably be regarded as harmful. Heretofore it has been commonly looked upon as helpful and desirable. Plaintiff in error taught this language in school as part of his occupation. His right thus to teach and the right of parents to engage him so to instruct their children, we think, are within the liberty of the Amendment. . . .

It is said the purpose of the legislation was to promote civic development by inhibiting training and education of the immature in foreign tongues and ideals before they could learn English and acquire American ideals. . . . It is also affirmed that the foreign born population is very large, that certain communities commonly . . . move in a foreign atmosphere, and that the children are thereby hindered from becoming citizens of the most useful type and the public safety is imperiled.

That the State may do much, go very far, indeed, in order to improve the quality of its citizens, physically, mentally and morally, is clear; but the individual has certain fundamental rights which must be respected. The protection of the Constitution extends to all, to those who speak other languages as well as to those born with English on the tongue. Perhaps it would be highly advantageous if all had ready understanding of our ordinary speech, but this cannot be coerced by methods which conflict with the Constitution — a desirable end cannot be promoted by prohibited means. . . .

The desire of the legislature to foster a homogeneous people with American ideals prepared readily to understand current discussions of civic matters is easy to appreciate. Unfortunate experiences during the late war and aversion toward every characteristic of truculent adversaries were certainly enough to quicken that aspiration. But the means adopted, we think, exceed the limitations upon the power of the State and conflict with rights assured to plaintiff. . . . No emergency has arisen which renders knowledge by a child of some language other than English so clearly harmful as to justify its inhibition with the consequent infringement of rights long freely enjoyed. We are constrained to conclude that the statute as applied is arbitrary and without reasonable relation to any end within the competency of the State.

As the statute undertakes to interfere only with teaching which involves a modern language, leaving complete freedom as to other matters, there seems no adequate foundation for the suggestion that the purpose was to protect the child's health by limiting his mental activities. It is well known that proficiency in a foreign language seldom comes to one not instructed at an early age, and experience shows that this is not injurious to the health, morals or understanding of the ordinary child.

The judgment of the court below must be reversed. . . .

Pierce v. Society of Sisters
268 U.S. 510 (1925)

Mr. Justice MCREYNOLDS delivered the opinion of the Court.

These appeals are from decrees . . . which granted preliminary orders restraining appellants from threatening or attempting to enforce the Compulsory Education Act. . . .

The challenged Act, effective September 1, 1926, requires every parent, guardian or other person having control or charge or custody of a child between eight and sixteen years to send him "to a public school for the period of time a public school shall be held during the current year" in the district where the child resides; and failure so to do is declared a misdemeanor. There are exemptions — not specially important here — for children who are not normal, or who have completed the eighth grade, or who reside at considerable distances from any public school, or whose parents or guardians hold special permits from the County Superintendent. The manifest purpose is to compel general attendance at public schools by normal children, between eight and sixteen, who have not completed the eighth grade. And without doubt enforcement of the statute would seriously impair, perhaps destroy, the profitable features of appellees' business and greatly diminish the value of their property.

Appellee, the Society of Sisters, is an Oregon corporation, organized in 1880, with power to care for orphans, educate and instruct the youth, establish and maintain academies or schools, and acquire necessary real and personal property. It has long devoted its property and effort to the secular and religious education and care of children, and has acquired the valuable good will of many parents and guardians. . . . The Compulsory Education Act of 1922 has already caused the withdrawal from its schools of children who would otherwise continue, and their income has steadily declined. . . .

[T]he Society's bill alleges that the enactment conflicts with the right of parents to choose schools where their children will receive appropriate mental and religious training, the right of the child to influence the parents' choice of a school, the right of schools and teachers therein to engage in a useful business or profession, and is accordingly repugnant to the Constitution and void. And, further, that unless enforcement of the measure is enjoined the corporation's business and property will suffer irreparable injury.

Appellee, Hill Military Academy, is a private corporation organized in 1908 under the laws of Oregon, engaged in owning, operating and conducting for profit an elementary, college preparatory and military training school for boys between the ages of five and twenty-one years. . . . By reason of the statute and threat of enforcement appellee's business is being destroyed and its property depreciated; parents and guardians are refusing to make contracts for the future instruction of their sons, and some are being withdrawn.

[The Academy alleges that the Act violates its Fourteenth Amendment rights and seeks an injunction.]

[The matter was heard] by three judges on motions for preliminary injunctions. . . . The court ruled that the Fourteenth Amendment guaranteed appellees against the deprivation of their property without due process of law consequent upon the unlawful interference by appellants with the free choice of patrons, present and prospective. It declared the right to conduct schools was property and that parents and guardians, as a part of their liberty, might direct the education of children by selecting reputable teachers and places. Also, that these schools were not unfit or harmful to the public, and that enforcement of the challenged statute would unlawfully deprive them of patronage and thereby destroy their owners' business and property. . . .

No question is raised concerning the power of the State reasonably to regulate all schools, to inspect, supervise and examine them, their teachers and pupils; to require that all children of proper age attend some school, that teachers shall be of good moral character and patriotic disposition, that certain studies plainly essential to good citizenship must be taught, and that nothing be taught which is manifestly inimical to the public welfare.

The inevitable practical result of enforcing the Act under consideration would be destruction of appellees' primary schools, and perhaps all other private primary schools for normal children within the State of Oregon. These parties are engaged in a kind of undertaking not inherently harmful, but long regarded as useful and meritorious. Certainly there is nothing in the present records to indicate that they have failed to discharge their obligations to patrons, students or the State. And there are no peculiar circumstances or present emergencies which demand extraordinary measures relative to primary education. *precedent*

Under the doctrine of Meyer v. Nebraska, 262 U.S. 390, we think it entirely plain that the Act of 1922 unreasonably interferes with the liberty of parents and guardians to direct the upbringing and education of children under their control. As often heretofore pointed out, rights guaranteed by the Constitution may not be abridged by legislation which has no reasonable relation to some purpose within the competency of the State. The fundamental theory of liberty upon which all governments in this Union repose excludes any general power of the State to standardize its children by forcing them to accept instruction from public teachers only. The child is not the mere creature of the State; those who nurture him and direct his destiny have the right, coupled with the high duty, to recognize and prepare him for additional obligations.

(handwritten margin note: defines what child's rel. to state isnt)

The decrees below are affirmed.

NOTES AND QUESTIONS ON *MEYER* AND *PIERCE:* A CONSTITUTIONAL FRAMEWORK FOR EDUCATION

(1) Whose Rights are Vindicated?   The constitutional importance of *Meyer* and *Pierce*, especially in establishing the constitutional framework for American education, would be difficult to exaggerate. Both opinions are opaque, however, and subject to various interpretations. Whose rights are being vindicated? In *Meyer*, is the Court concerned with the liberty of the teacher, the child, or the child's parents? In *Pierce*, is the concern with the private school's proprietary rights or parents' rights to rear their children or both?

(2) In her "revisionist" account of *Meyer* and *Pierce*, Barbara Woodhouse claims that the right vindicated in both cases is the right of parents to control their children, which the Court finds protected by the "liberty" clause of the Fourteenth Amendment. Barbara B. Woodhouse, Who Owns the Child?: *Meyer* and *Pierce* and the Child as Property, 33 Wm. & Mary L. Rev. 995 (1992). Woodhouse argues that it only makes sense to locate the right to control children in the liberty clause if children are viewed as parental property:

> Ironically, the Court in *Meyer* and *Pierce* chose to hang parental control of children on the branch of Fourteenth Amendment "liberty." Courts before *Meyer* had generally been slow to extend Fourteenth Amendment protection to the parent's rights over the child. Pierce himself observed that "it is a strange perversion of the word 'liberty' to apply it to a right to control the conduct of others." Yet adopt, for a moment, the perspective that children are patriarchal property. Suddenly, the right of parental control in *Meyer* and *Pierce* — authored and joined by the court's most inflexible laissez-faire conservatives and grounded on economic substantive due process precedents — acquires a logical framework. Property and ownership were indeed a powerful subtext of parental rights rhetoric in the era of *Pierce* and *Meyer.* [Id. at 1041-1042.]

Given our long history of treating children as the property of their parents (usually of their father), do you find this view compelling? Or, do you think that if the Court viewed children as parental property, it would have located the parents' right to control children in the Fourteenth Amendment's "property" clause, rather than in its "liberty" clause?

(3) Principle of Family Autonomy.   *Meyer* and *Pierce* establish broad liberal principles of family autonomy in the face of government intervention. Subsequently, the U.S. Supreme Court reaffirmed parents' fundamental liberty interest in childrearing in Troxel v. Granville, 530 U.S. 57 (2000). *Troxel*, relying on *Meyer* and *Pierce,*

held that a court order compelling visitation between children and their grandparents violated a mother's due process rights to control the upbringing of her children by failing to give sufficient deference to the mother's wishes. (*Troxel* is reprinted infra p. 79).

Are there any negative implications for children by virtue of the recognition of broad principles of family autonomy? See Barbara Bennett Woodhouse, Child Abuse, the Constitution, and the Legacy of Pierce v. Society of Sisters, 78 U. Det. Mercy L. Rev. 479, 489 (2001) (suggesting that *Pierce* presents two "faces": protection of children via principles of liberty, family privacy, and pluralism versus endangerment of those children who are "held hostage in the child welfare system by a distorted vision of the family and of the Constitution").

(4) Historical Background.   The legislation at issue in both *Meyer* and *Pierce* stemmed from anti-Bolshevist and xenophobic fears. No state other than Oregon had a requirement that children attend only *public* schools. The Oregon legislature adopted the provision following a referendum campaign promoted by the Ku Klux Klan and the Scottish Rite Masons, who claimed to want to "Americanize" the schools, with the support of public school teachers who feared a negative vote would hurt public education. For historical background, see Paula Abrams, The Little Red Schoolhouse: *Pierce*, State Monopoly of Education and the Politics of Intolerance, 20 Const. Comment. 61, 66-70 (2003); Woodhouse, Who Owns the Child, supra, at p. 51.

(5) Pluralism.   Several commentators characterize *Pierce* as a triumph of pluralism both in terms of family values and educational decisionmaking. See, e.g., Peggy Cooper Davis, Contested Images of Family Values: The Role of the State, 107 Harv. L. Rev. 1348, 1363 (1994); Martha Minow, Before and After *Pierce*, A Colloquium on Parents, Children, Religion and Schools, 78 U. Det. Mercy L. Rev. 407, 408-409 (2001).

Does pluralism in education promote children's interests? What justifications exist for a public school monopoly? Might not a common public education best ensure critical common values? At the other extreme, what would the world look like if there were no compulsory education? What reasons would parents have to invest in their children's education? What public or state interests exist to justify compelling parents who would choose not to provide for their children's education? Does *Pierce* represent a workable compromise between these two extremes? Does *Pierce* strike an appropriate balance among the competing interests of the child, family, private schools, and the state? See Barbara Bennett Woodhouse, Speaking Truth to Power: Challenging "The Power of Parents to Control the Education of Their Own," 11 Cornell J.L. & Pub. Pol'y 481 (2002) (questioning the deference given to parents' educational choices).

(6) Could the state, after Meyer v. Nebraska, prohibit parents from sending their children to a private school where *all* instruction was in a foreign language? Put another way, could a state constitutionally require a school to offer some English instruction? Could "too much" foreign language instruction interfere with the child's ability to learn English?

(7) What if parents claim that substantial foreign language instruction is essential to preserve their children's ethnic heritage? Cf. Wisconsin v. Yoder, infra, p. 60. Are there circumstances in which the state should be under an affirmative obligation to offer instruction in a foreign language? Cf. Lau v. Nichols, 414 U.S. 563 (1974)

(failure of San Francisco school system to provide English language instruction to students of Chinese ancestry who did not speak English denied them a meaningful opportunity to participate in the public educational program, in violation of §601 of the Civil Rights Act of 1964).

(8) After *Pierce*, would it be possible for the state to require the registration of children at birth and the compulsory placement of children in state-controlled day care and nursery schools?

(9) Home schooling is the education of children in the home as opposed to in an institutional setting such as a public or private school. Do *Meyer* and *Pierce* guarantee the right of parents to educate their children at home? (Home schooling is also discussed infra p. 65-66.)

(10) Who should decide whether and where a child should go to school? Who should pay for a child's education? If the principle of *Pierce* is that the state cannot compel parents to send their children to state schools, what does this imply for the rights of parents who lack the funds to send their children to private schools? Is the *Pierce* principle only important for those who can afford private school alternatives?

(11) School Vouchers.   Can you imagine a school system where parents have the right to choose public or private education for their children — and their choice would be funded by the state? The "parental choice" movement has been gaining in popularity. Stemming from intense criticism of the public school system, parents increasingly have been advocating passage of legislation that provides "vouchers" or "school choice grants." Under such legislation, parents receive state financial assistance to fund the tuition costs of their children's attendance at sectarian schools. Several publicly funded voucher programs exist across the country.

The "parental choice" movement met with its first success at the federal level in 2004 when President George W. Bush signed an appropriations bill creating a federally financed school voucher program in the District of Columbia. Consolidated Appropriations Act, 2004, Pub. L. No. 108-199, 118 Stat. 3 (2004). In addition, several municipalities have implemented voucher programs. In 1999, Florida became the first state to enact a statewide voucher law. See Florida Signs Private Voucher Law, Detroit News, June 22, 1999, at A5.

Do such programs violate the Establishment Clause? In Zelman v. Simmons-Harris, 536 U.S. 639 (2002), the U.S. Supreme Court addressed the constitutionality of a school voucher program established by the state of Ohio. The program provided tuition aid to students residing within failing school districts. Parents of eligible students received tuition aid to send their children to a public or private school of their choosing within the district. The majority of students participating in the program enrolled in sectarian schools. A group of Ohio taxpayers sought to enjoin the program, claiming that it violated the Establishment Clause. The Supreme Court disagreed:

> In sum, the Ohio program is entirely neutral with respect to religion. It provides benefits directly to a wide spectrum of individuals, defined only by financial need and residence in a particular school district. It permits such individuals to exercise genuine choice among options public and private, secular and religious. Id. at 662.

See also Locke v. Davey, 540 U.S. 712 (2004) (holding that prohibition on state aid to students pursuing devotional theology degrees did not violate Free Exercise

Clause); Mitchell v. Helms, 530 U.S. 793 (2000) (holding that program under which local school districts may use federal funds to provide equipment to private schools, including religious schools, did not violate the Establishment Clause).

Some commentators speculated that *Zelman* would have a profound impact on the relationship between education and religion. See, e.g., Klint Alexander, The Road to Vouchers: The Supreme Court's Compliance and the Crumbling of the Wall of Separation Between Church and State in American Education, 92 Ky. L.J. 439 (2003/2004). In fact, *Zelman* triggered a rash of lawsuits focusing on the validity of state constitutional and statutory bans against public aid for sectarian education. Such provisions, called Blaine Amendments, exist in 37 states. They consist of two different types: prohibitions on public aid to any religious institution (including religious schools) and prohibitions on aid to any nonpublic educational institution. Tresa Baldas, School Voucher Suits Hitting States, Natl. L.J., Dec. 13, 2003, at A1. See, e.g., Owens v. Colorado Cong. of Parents, Teachers, and Students, 92 P.3d 933 (Colo. 2004) (finding Colorado's voucher program unconstitutional for violating the state constitution by stripping local school boards of their control over education); Bush v. Holmes, 867 So. 2d 1270 (Fla. Dist. Ct. App. 2004) (declaring Florida's voucher program a violation of state constitutional ban on use of public funds for sectarian schools). For discussion of the Blaine Amendments, see Mark Edward DeForrest, An Overview and Evaluation of State Blaine Amendments: Origins, Scope and First Amendment Concerns, 26 Harv. J.L. & Pub. Pol'y 551 (2003).

Criticisms of public education also led to major reform legislation, No Child Left Behind Act (NCLB) of 2001, Pub. L. No. 107-110, 115 Stat. 1425 (2002) (codified at 20 U.S.C. §§6301-7941). NCLB attempts to increase accountability for student performance by rewarding states and schools that improve educational achievement and requiring all children to reach proficiency in state educational standards. For commentary on the Act, see James E. Ryan, The Perverse Incentives of the No Child Left Behind Act, 79 N.Y.U. L. Rev. 932 (2004); Amy M. Reichbach, Note, The Power Behind the Promise: Enforcing No Child Let Behind to Improve Education, 45 B.C. L. Rev. 667 (2004).

(12) Public Duty to Educate.   Consider whether a state has the constitutional duty to provide the opportunity for free public education, at least for children whose parents could not otherwise afford to send them to school. For example, could a state close its public schools or charge tuition?

In the United States, history and custom have created the expectation that all children, regardless of parental resources, are entitled to an education. Every state provides for free public education, typically through high school. Many state constitutions require as much. See, e.g., Mich. Const. Art. VIII, §2. The Supreme Court observed in Brown v. Board of Education, 347 U.S. 483, 493 (1954), that "education is perhaps the most important function of state and local governments." Nevertheless, the Supreme Court held that education is not a "fundamental" right, i.e., the right to education is not explictly or implicitly guaranteed for purposes of requiring strict judicial scrutiny under the Equal Protection Clause. See San Antonio Indep. Sch. Dist. v. Rodriguez, 411 U.S. 1 (1973). The Court left open in *Rodriguez*, however, the possibility that a state would violate equal protection if it adopted a system that absolutely denied all educational opportunities to any of its children. See 411 U.S. at 36-37.

This issue was squarely faced by the Court in Plyler v. Doe, 457 U.S. 202 (1982) (holding unconstitutional a Texas statute that denied funds for a free education of undocumented school-age alien children). In *Plyler*, the Court reaffirmed its position that "[p]ublic education is not a 'right' granted to individuals by the Constitution." But, the Court went on to point out, "neither is it merely some governmental 'benefit' indistinguishable from other forms of social welfare legislation." Id. at 220. Noting the lifetime hardship and stigma connected with illiteracy, the Court found that the statute denied to a discrete class of children (illegal aliens) a basic education, and by so doing, "foreclosed any realistic possibility that they will contribute in even the smallest way to the progress of our Nation" Id. at 223.

(13) Problem.   Recently, a nationwide "parental rights" movement has been gaining momentum to persuade legislators to amend state constitutions or to enact legislation to provide increased parental authority over children's education and discipline. The movement stems in part from concerns about controlling the teaching of sex education, AIDS, and homosexuality. In the late 1990s, proponents of parental rights introduced legislation in 28 states as well as in Congress. Linda L. Lane, Comment, Parental Rights Movement, 69 U. Colo. L. Rev. 825, 833 (1998).

You are a legislator in a state legislature that is considering passage of the following state constitutional amendment:

> Be It Resolved by the Legislature of Our State that the amendment proposed herein shall appear on the ballot as follows: Section 26 of Article 1 of the State Constitution shall provide that parents have a fundamental right to raise, educate, and care for their children; require the Legislature to protect parental rights by appropriate legislation; and exclude application of the new section to minors emancipated by general law or laws protecting minors from neglect, abuse, or criminal wrongdoing.

Hypothetical

The amendment addresses the relative rights of parents and children when such rights come into legal conflict, specifically by providing that parental rights supesede children's rights, including any rights claimed by minors under the privacy provision of the state constitution. This would allow the legislature to protect parental rights in all matters affecting their children, including, but not limited to, the decision of a minor to obtain an abortion. Minors would retain all of the rights guaranteed under the U.S. Constitution.

What arguments would you make in favor of the proposed legislation? Against? Does such legislation merely reaffirm *Meyer* and *Pierce* or does it grant parents additional rights?

Prince v. Massachusetts
321 U.S. 158 (1944)

Mr. Justice RUTLEDGE delivered the opinion of the Court.

The case brings for review another episode in the conflict between Jehovah's Witnesses and state authority. This time Sarah Prince appeals from convictions for violating Massachusetts' child labor laws, by acts said to be a rightful exercise of her religious convictions.

[T]he only questions for our decision [are] whether §§80 and 81 [of chapter 149, Gen. Laws of Mass.], as applied, contravene the Fourteenth Amendment by denying or abridging appellant's freedom of religion and by denying to her the equal protection of the laws.

Sections 80 and 81 form parts of Massachusetts' comprehensive child labor law. They provide methods for enforcing the prohibitions of §69, which is as follows:

> No boy under twelve and no girl under eighteen shall sell, expose or offer for sale any newspapers, magazines, periodicals or any other articles of merchandise of any description, or exercise the trade of bootblack or scavenger, or any other trade, in any street or public place.

Sections 80 and 81, so far as pertinent, read:

> Whoever furnishes or sells to any minor any article of any description with the knowledge that the minor intends to sell such article in violation of any provision of sections sixty-nine to seventy-three, inclusive, or after having received written notice to this effect from any officer charged with the enforcement thereof, or knowingly procures or encourages any minor to violate any provisions of said sections, shall be punished by a fine of not less than ten nor more than two hundred dollars or by imprisonment for not more than two months, or both.
>
> Any parent, guardian or custodian having a minor under his control who compels or permits such minor to work in violation of any provision of sections sixty to seventy-four, inclusive, . . . shall for a first offense be punished by a fine of not less than two nor more than ten dollars or by imprisonment for not more than five days, or both; . . .

. . . Mrs. Prince, living in Brockton, is the mother of two young sons. She also has legal custody of Betty Simmons [a niece, age 9], who lives with them. The children too are Jehovah's Witnesses and both Mrs. Prince and Betty testified they were ordained ministers. The former was accustomed to go each week on the streets of Brockton to distribute "Watchtower" and "Consolation," according to the usual plan. She had permitted the children to engage in this activity previously, and had been warned against doing so by the school attendance officer, Mr. Perkins. But, until December 18, 1941, she generally did not take them with her at night.

That evening, as Mrs. Prince was preparing to leave her home, the children asked to go. She at first refused. Childlike, they resorted to tears; and, motherlike, she yielded. Arriving downtown, Mrs. Prince permitted the children "to engage in the preaching work with her upon the sidewalks." That is, with specific reference to Betty, she and Mrs. Prince took positions about twenty feet apart near a street intersection. Betty held up in her hand, for passers-by to see, copies of "Watchtower" and "Consolation." From her shoulders hung the usual canvas magazine bag on which was printed: "Watchtower and Consolation 5cts. per copy." No one accepted a copy from Betty that evening and she received no money. Nor did her aunt. But on other occasions, Betty had received funds and given out copies.

Mrs. Prince and Betty remained until 8:45 P.M. A few minutes before this, Mr. Perkins approached Mrs. Prince. A discussion ensued. He inquired and she refused to give Betty's name. However, she stated the child attended the Shaw School.

Mr. Perkins referred to his previous warnings and said he would allow five minutes for them to get off the street. Mrs. Prince admitted she supplied Betty with the magazines and said, "[N]either you nor anybody else can stop me. . . . This child is exercising her God-given right and her constitutional right to preach the gospel, and no creature has a right to interfere with God's commands." However, Mrs. Prince and Betty departed. She remarked as she went, "I'm not going through this any more. We've been through it time and time again. I'm going home and put the little girl to bed." It may be added that testimony, by Betty, her aunt and others, was offered at the trials, and was excluded, to show that Betty believed it was her religious duty to perform this work and failure would bring condemnation "to everlasting destruction at Armageddon."

[T]he questions are no longer open whether what the child did was a "sale" or an "offer to sell" within §69 or was "work" within §81. . . . The only question remaining therefore is whether, as construed and applied, the statute is valid. . . .

[Appellant's argument] rests squarely on freedom of religion under the First Amendment, applied by the Fourteenth to the states. She buttresses this foundation, however, with a claim of parental right as secured by the due process clause of the latter Amendment. Cf. Meyer v. Nebraska, 262 U.S. 390. These guaranties, she thinks, guard alike herself and the child in what they have done. Thus, two claimed liberties are at stake. One is the parent's, to bring up the child in the way he should go, which for appellant means to teach him the tenets and the practices of their faith. The other freedom is the child's, to observe these; and among them is "to preach the gospel . . . by public distribution" of "Watchtower" and "Consolation," in conformity with the scripture: "A little child shall lead them." . . .

To make accommodation between these freedoms and an exercise of state authority always is delicate. . . . On one side is the obviously earnest claim for freedom of conscience and religious practice. With it is allied the parent's claim to authority in her own household and in the rearing of her children. The parent's conflict with the state over control of the child and his training is serious enough when only secular matters are concerned. It becomes the more so when an element of religious conviction enters. Against these sacred private interests, basic in a democracy, stand the interests of society to protect the welfare of children, and the state's assertion of authority to that end, made here in a manner conceded valid if only secular things were involved. . . . It is the interest of youth itself, and of the whole community, that children be both safeguarded from abuses and given opportunities for growth into free and independent well-developed men and citizens. . . .

The rights of children to exercise their religion, and of parents to give them religious training and to encourage them in the practice of religious belief, as against preponderant sentiment and assertion of state power voicing it, have had recognition here, most recently in West Virginia State Board of Education v. Barnette, 319 U.S. 624 [(1943)].[24] Previously in Pierce v. Society of Sisters, 268 U.S. 510, this Court

[24] In West Virginia Board of Education v. Barnette, the Supreme Court upheld an injunction restraining the enforcement against Jehovah's Witnesses of a regulation requiring public school students to recite the Pledge of Allegiance under pain of expulsion. The Court based its decision on the First Amendment free speech guarantee which prohibited a compulsory rite "touching matters of

had sustained the parent's authority to provide religious with secular schooling, and the child's right to receive it, as against the state's requirement of attendance at public schools. And in Meyer v. Nebraska, 262 U.S. 390, children's rights to receive teaching in languages other than the nation's common tongue were guarded against the state's encroachment. It is cardinal with us that the custody, care and nurture of the child reside first in the parents, whose primary function and freedom include preparation for obligations the state can neither supply nor hinder. Pierce v. Society of Sisters, supra. And it is in recognition of this that these decisions have respected the private realm of family life which the state cannot enter.

But the family itself is not beyond regulation in the public interest, as against a claim of religious liberty. Reynolds v. United States, 98 U.S. 145 [(1878)]; Davis v. Beason, 133 U.S. 333 [(1890)]. And neither rights of religion nor rights of parenthood are beyond limitation. Acting to guard the general interest in youth's well being, the state as parens patriae may restrict the parent's control by requiring school attendance, regulating or prohibiting the child's labor and in many other ways. Its authority is not nullified merely because the parent grounds his claim to control the child's course of conduct on religion or conscience. Thus, he cannot claim freedom from compulsory vaccination for the child more than for himself on religious grounds. [Jacobson v. Massachusetts, 197 U.S. 11 (1905).] The right to practice religion freely does not include liberty to expose the community or the child to communicable disease or the latter to ill health or death. The catalogue . . . is sufficient to show what indeed appellant hardly disputes, that the state has a wide range of power for limiting parental freedom and authority in things affecting the child's welfare; and that this includes, to some extent, matters of conscience and religious conviction.

But it is said the state cannot do so here. This, first, because when state action impinges upon a claimed religious freedom, it must fall unless shown to be necessary for or conducive to the child's protection against some clear and present danger, and, it is added, there was no such showing here. The child's presence on the street, with her guardian, distributing or offering to distribute the magazines, it is urged, was in no way harmful to her, nor in any event more so than the presence of many other children at the same time and place, engaged in shopping and other activities not prohibited. Accordingly, in view of the preferred position the freedoms of the First Article occupy, the statute in its present application must fall. . . . And, finally, it is said, the statute is, as to children, an absolute prohibition, not merely a reasonable regulation, of the denounced activity.

Concededly a statute or ordinance identical in terms with §69, except that it is applicable to adults or all persons generally, would be invalid. But the mere fact a state could not wholly prohibit this form of adult activity, whether characterized locally as a "sale" or otherwise, does not mean it cannot do so for children. . . .

The state's authority over children's activities is broader than over like actions of adults. This is peculiarly true of public activities and in matters of employment.

---

opinion and political attitude," 319 U.S. at 636, although the plaintiffs were Jehovah's Witnesses parents bringing suit for themselves, their children, and others for whom the salute and pledge offended religious beliefs. Cf. Elk Grove Unified Sch. Dist. v. Newdow, 542 U.S. 1 (2004) (ruling that a noncustodial father lacked standing to challenge recitation of the Pledge of Allegiance).

A democratic society rests, for its continuance, upon the healthy, well-rounded growth of young people into full maturity as citizens, with all that implies. It may secure this against impeding restraints and dangers within a broad range of selection. Among evils most appropriate for such action are the crippling effects of child employment, more especially in public places, and the possible harms arising from other activities subject to all the diverse influences of the street. It is too late now to doubt that legislation appropriately designed to reach such evils is within the state's police power, whether against the parent's claim to control of the child or one that religious scruples dictate contrary action.

It is true children have rights, in common with older people, in the primary use of highways. But even in such use streets afford dangers for them not affecting adults. And in other uses, whether in work or in other things, this difference may be magnified. This is so not only when children are unaccompanied but certainly to some extent when they are with their parents. What may be wholly permissible for adults therefore may not be so for children, either with or without their parents' presence.

[T]he validity of [the street preaching] prohibition applied to children not accompanied by an older person hardly would seem open to question. The case reduces itself therefore to the question whether the presence of the child's guardian puts a limit to the state's power. That fact may lessen the likelihood that some evils the legislation seeks to avert will occur. But it cannot forestall all of them. The zealous though lawful exercise of the right to engage in propagandizing the community, whether in religious, political or other matters, may and at times does create situations difficult enough for adults to cope with and wholly inappropriate for children, especially of tender years, to face.... Parents may be free to become martyrs themselves. But it does not follow they are free, in identical circumstances, to make martyrs of their children before they have reached the age of full and legal discretion when they can make that choice for themselves. Massachusetts has determined that an absolute prohibition, though one limited to streets and public places and to the incidental uses proscribed, is necessary to accomplish its legitimate objectives. Its power to attain them is broad enough to reach these peripheral instances in which the parent's supervision may reduce but cannot eliminate entirely the ill effects of the prohibited conduct. We think that with reference to the public proclaiming of religion, upon the streets and in other similar public places, the power of the state to control the conduct of children reaches beyond the scope of its authority over adults, as is true in the case of other freedoms, and the rightful boundary of its power has not been crossed in this case.

In so ruling we dispose also of appellant's argument founded upon denial of equal protection. [T]he contention is that the street, for Jehovah's Witnesses and their children, is their church ... and to deny them access to it for religious purposes as was done here has the same effect as excluding altar boys, youthful choristers, and other children from the edifices in which they practice their religious beliefs and worship.... However Jehovah's Witnesses may conceive them, the public highways have not become their religious property merely by their assertion. And there is no denial of equal protection in excluding their children from doing there what no other children may do....

The judgment is affirmed.

[handwritten margin notes: " martyrs argument. nearly quoted"; "refutes = protection argument"]*

QUESTIONS ON PRINCE V. MASSACHUSETTS

(1) State's Power.   The Court states that a child labor prohibition, such as §69 applied in *Prince*, would not be constitutional if applied to adult Jehovah's Witnesses, and the cases cited by the Court support that conclusion. Why should the state's power be greater vis-à-vis children? What reasons does the Court give for its conclusion that the "validity of such a prohibition applied to children not accompanied by an older person hardly would seem open to question" (supra p. 59)? Do you agree with the conclusion? What reasons can you give? Do these reasons apply if the child is accompanied by an adult? A parent or guardian?

(2) Actual Harm.   Was there a showing in *Prince* of actual risk or harm to this particular child? Do the justifications for preventing child labor apply to the facts of this case? See Chapter 6. Is there any harm on the facts of *Prince* to any substantial state interest?

making martyr of child(?)

(3) Limits of State's Power.   Does the Court in *Prince* define the outer limits of the state's power to constrict parental freedom because of the state's interest in protecting the child? What do you think those limits are?

Wisconsin v. Yoder
406 U.S. 205 (1972)

Mr. Chief Justice BURGER delivered the opinion of the Court. . . .

. . . Respondents Jonas Yoder and Adin Yutzy are members of the Old Order Amish Religion, and respondent Wallace Miller is a member of the Conservative Amish Mennonite Church. . . . Wisconsin's compulsory school attendance law required them to cause their children to attend public or private school until reaching age 16 but the respondents declined to send their children, ages 14 and 15, to public school after completing the eighth grade. The children were not enrolled in any private school, or within any recognized exception to the compulsory attendance law, and they are conceded to be subject to the Wisconsin statute.

On complaint of the school district administrator for the public schools, respondents were charged, tried, and convicted of violating the compulsory attendance law in Green County Court and were fined the sum of $5 each. Respondents defended on the ground that the application of the compulsory attendance law violated their rights under the First and Fourteenth Amendments. . . .

In support of their position, respondents presented as expert witnesses scholars on religion and education [who] expressed their opinions on the relationship of the Amish belief concerning school attendance to the more general tenets of their religion, and described the impact that compulsory high school attendance could have on the continued survival of Amish communities. . . . The history of the Amish sect was given in some detail, beginning with the Swiss Anabaptists of the 16th century who rejected institutionalized churches and sought to return to the early, simple, Christian life de-emphasizing material success, rejecting the competitive spirit, and seeking to insulate themselves from the modern world. As a result of their common heritage, Old Order Amish communities today are characterized by a fundamental belief that salvation requires life in a church community separate and apart from the world and worldly influence. This concept of life aloof from the world and its values is central to their faith.

A related feature of Old Order Amish communities is their devotion to a life in harmony with nature and the soil, as exemplified by the simple life of the early Christian era which continued in America during much of our early national life. Amish beliefs require members of the community to make their living by farming or closely related activities. . . .

Amish objection to formal education beyond the eighth grade is firmly grounded in these central religious concepts. They object to the high school and higher education generally because the values it teaches are in marked variance with Amish values and the Amish way of life; they view secondary school education as an impermissible exposure of their children to a "worldly" influence in conflict with their beliefs. . . .

Formal high school education beyond the eighth grade is contrary to Amish beliefs not only because it places Amish children in an environment hostile to Amish beliefs with increasing emphasis on competition in class work and sports and with pressure to conform to the styles, manners and ways of the peer group, but because it takes them away from their community, physically and emotionally, during the crucial and formative adolescent period of life. [H]igh school attendance with teachers who are not of the Amish faith — and may even be hostile to it — interposes a serious barrier to the integration of the Amish child into the Amish religious community. . . .

The Amish do not object to elementary education through the first eight grades as a general proposition because they agree that their children must have basic skills in the "three R's" in order to read the Bible, to be good farmers and citizens and to be able to deal with non-Amish people when necessary in the course of daily affairs.

[However, as Dr. John Hostetler, an expert on Amish society, testified,] compulsory high school attendance could not only result in great psychological harm to Amish children, because of the conflicts it would produce, but would, in his opinion, ultimately result in the destruction of the Old Order Amish church community as it exists in the United States today. The testimony of Dr. Donald A. Erickson, an expert witness on education, also showed that the Amish succeed in preparing their high school age children to be productive members of the Amish community. He described their system of learning- through-doing the skills directly relevant to their adult roles in the Amish community as "ideal" and perhaps superior to ordinary high school education. . . .

In sum, the unchallenged testimony of acknowledged experts in education and religious history, almost 300 years of consistent practice, and strong evidence of a sustained faith pervading and regulating respondents' entire mode of life support the claim that enforcement of the State's requirement of compulsory formal education after the eighth grade would gravely endanger if not destroy the free exercise of respondents' religious beliefs.

III . . .

We turn then to the State's broader contention that its interest in its system of compulsory education is so compelling that even the established religious practices of the Amish must give way. . . .

The State advances two primary arguments in support of its system of compulsory education. It notes, as Thomas Jefferson pointed out early in our history, that some degree of education is necessary to prepare citizens to participate effectively and intelligently in our open political system if we are to preserve freedom and independence. Further, education prepares individuals to be self-reliant and self-sufficient participants in society. We accept these propositions.

However, the evidence adduced by the Amish in this case is persuasively to the effect that an additional one or two years of formal high school for Amish children in place of their long established program of informal vocational education would do little to serve those interests. . . . It is one thing to say that compulsory education for a year or two beyond the eighth grade may be necessary when its goal is the preparation of the child for life in modern society as the majority live, but it is quite another if the goal of education be viewed as the preparation of the child for life in the separated agrarian community that is the keystone of the Amish faith.

The State attacks respondents' position as one fostering "ignorance" from which the child must be protected by the State. No one can question the State's duty to protect children from ignorance but this argument does not square with the facts disclosed in the record. [T]he Amish community has been a highly successful social unit within our society even if apart from the conventional "mainstream." Its members are productive and very law-abiding members of society; they reject public welfare in any of its usual modern forms. . . .

The State, however, supports its interest in providing an additional one or two years of compulsory high school education to Amish children because of the possibility that some such children will choose to leave the Amish community, and that if this occurs they will be ill-equipped for life. [T]hat argument is highly speculative. There is no specific evidence of the loss of Amish adherents by attrition, nor is there any showing that upon leaving the Amish community Amish children, with their practical agricultural training and habits of industry and self-reliance would become burdens on society because of educational shortcomings. . . .

The requirement of compulsory schooling to age 16 must therefore be viewed as aimed not merely at providing educational opportunities for children, but as an alternative to the equally undesirable consequence of unhealthful child labor displacing adult workers, or, on the other hand, forced idleness. The two kinds of statutes — compulsory school attendance and child labor laws — tend to keep children of certain ages off the labor market and in school; this in turn provides opportunity to prepare for a livelihood of a higher order than that children could perform without education and protects their health in adolescence.

In these terms, Wisconsin's interest in compelling the school attendance of Amish children to age 16 emerges as somewhat less substantial than requiring such attendance for children generally. For, while agricultural employment is not totally outside the legitimate concerns of the child labor laws, employment of children under parental guidance and on the family farm from age 14 to age 16 is an ancient tradition which lies at the at the periphery of the objectives of such laws.[19] There

---

[19] . . . The Federal Fair Labor Standards Act of 1938 excludes from its definition of "oppressive child labor" employment of a child under age 16 by "a parent . . . employing his own child . . . in an occupation other than manufacturing or mining or an occupation found by the Secretary of Labor

is no intimation that the Amish employment of their children on family farms is in any way deleterious to their health or that Amish parents exploit children at tender years. . . . Moreover, employment of Amish children on the family farm does not present the undesirable economic aspects of eliminating jobs which might otherwise be held by adults.

IV

— State uses precedent

Finally, the State, on authority of Prince v. Massachusetts, argues that a decision exempting Amish children from the State's requirement fails to recognize the substantive right of the Amish child to a secondary education, and fails to give due regard to the power of the State as parens patriae to extend the benefit of secondary education to children regardless of the wishes of their parents. Taken at its broadest sweep, the Court's language in *Prince*, might be read to give support to the State's position. However, the Court was not confronted in *Prince* with a situation comparable to that of the Amish as revealed in this record; this is shown by the Court's severe characterization of the evils which it thought the legislature could legitimately associate with child labor, even when performed in the company of an adult. 321 U.S., at 169–170. . . .

State's arg.

This case, of course, is not one in which any harm to the physical or mental health of the child or to the public safety, peace, order, or welfare has been demonstrated. The record is to the contrary, and any reliance on that theory would find no support in the evidence. . . .

[O]ur holding today in no degree depends on the assertion of the religious interest of the child as contrasted with that of the parents. It is the parents who are subject to prosecution here for failing to cause their children to attend school, and it is their right of free exercise, not that of their children, that must determine Wisconsin's power to impose criminal penalties on the parent. The dissent argues that a child who expresses a desire to attend public high school in conflict with the wishes of his parents should not be prevented from doing so. There is no reason for the Court to consider that point since it is not an issue in the case. The children are not parties to this litigation. The State has at no point tried this case on the theory that respondents were preventing their children from attending school against their expressed desires, and indeed the record is to the contrary.[21] The State's position from the outset has been that it is empowered to apply its compulsory attendance law to Amish parents in the same manner as to other parents — that is, without regard to the wishes of the child. That is the claim we reject today.

— Kids' wishes not up for consideration here

Our holding in no way determines the proper resolution of possible competing interests of parents, children, and the State in an appropriate state court proceeding in which the power of the State is asserted on the theory that Amish parents are

---

to be particularly hazardous for the employment of children between the ages of sixteen and eighteen years or detrimental to their health or well-being." 29 U.S.C. §203(1).

[21] The only relevant testimony in the record is to the effect that the wishes of the one child who testified corresponded with those of her parents. Testimony of Frieda Yoder, Tr. 92-94, to the effect that her personal religious beliefs guided her decision to discontinue school attendance after the 8th grade. The other children were not called by either side.

preventing their minor children from attending high school despite their expressed desires to the contrary. Recognition of the claim of the State in such a proceeding would, of course, call into question traditional concepts of parental control over the religious upbringing and education of their minor children recognized in this Court's past decisions. It is clear that such an intrusion by a State into family decisions in the area of religious training would give rise to grave questions of religious freedom comparable to those raised here and those presented in Pierce v. Society of Sisters. On this record we neither reach nor decide those issues. . . .

However read, the Court's holding in *Pierce* stands as a charter of the rights of parents to direct the religious upbringing of their children. And, when the interests of parenthood are combined with a free exercise claim of the nature revealed by this record, more than merely a "reasonable relation to some purpose within the competency of the state" is required to sustain the validity of the State's requirement under the First Amendment. To be sure, the power of the parent, even when linked to a free exercise claim, may be subject to limitation under *Prince* if it appears that parental decisions will jeopardize the health or safety of the child, or have a potential for significant social burdens. But in this case, the Amish have introduced persuasive evidence undermining the arguments the State has advanced to support its claims in terms of the welfare of the child and society as a whole. . . .

For the reasons stated we hold, with the Supreme Court of Wisconsin, that the First and Fourteenth Amendments prevent the State from compelling respondents to cause their children to attend formal high school to age 16. . . . Nothing we hold is intended to undermine the general applicability of the State's compulsory school attendance statutes. . . .

Affirmed.

Mr. Justice POWELL and Mr. Justice REHNQUIST took no part in the consideration or decision of this case.

Mr. Justice STEWART, with whom Mr. Justice BRENNAN joins, concurring. . . .

This case in no way involves any questions regarding the right of the children of Amish parents to attend public high schools, or any other institutions of learning, if they wish to do so. As the Court points out, there is no suggestion whatever in the record that the religious beliefs of the children here concerned differ in any way from those of their parents. Only one of the children testified. The last two questions and answers on her cross-examination accurately sum up her testimony.

> Q. So I take it then, Frieda, the only reason you are not going to school, and did not go to school since last September, is because of *your* religion?
> A. Yes.
> Q. That is the only reason?
> A. *Yes.* (Emphasis supplied.)

It is clear to me, therefore, that this record simply does not present the interesting and important issue discussed in Part II of the dissenting opinion of Mr. Justice Douglas. With this observation, I join the opinion and the judgment of the Court. [Justice Douglas' dissenting opinion is at p. 76 infra.]

NOTES AND QUESTIONS

(1) Justification.   Does *Yoder* overrule *Prince?* How is *Prince* characterized and distinguished in *Yoder?* Does absence from public school risk "harm" to the "health" of the child, "public safety, peace, order or welfare"? If not, what then is the justification for compulsory secondary education?

(2) Conflict of Interests.   Unlike *Pierce, Yoder* poses the question of whether there are constitutional interests of children and parents that outweigh the state's interest in compelling all children to attend school. What is at stake for (1) the Amish community; (2) Amish parents; (3) the state; and (4) the child?

Yoder presumes that the parents are in agreement about the child's religious and educational upbringing. Suppose that the parents disagree. How should such conflicts be resolved? In Elk Grove Unified School Dist. v. Newdow, 542 U.S. 1 (2004), the United States Supreme Court ruled that a *noncustodial* father lacked standing to challenge under the Free Exercise and Establishment Clauses the required daily recitation at his daughter's public school of the phrase "under God" in the Pledge of Allegiance. The Court also rejected the father's argument that the Pledge recitation impaired his own right to instruct his daughter in his religious views. But cf. Circle Schools v. Pappert, 381 F.3d 172 (3d Cir. 2004) (holding that requirement that school students recite Pledge of Allegiance or national anthem at beginning of school day violated First Amendment and that parental notification clause, requiring parental notification of students who declined to recite pledge or refrained from saluting flag, constituted viewpoint discrimination in violation of First Amendment).

(3) State's Interest.   Does the state have a legitimate interest in "seeking to develop the latent talents of its children" and "in seeking to prepare them for the life style that they may *later choose,*" as Justice White, in an omitted concurring opinion, suggests (406 U.S. at 240)? Does an Amish child with only an eighth grade education have a real chance to "later choose" to live outside the Amish community? Does the majority deal with this issue? The Wisconsin Supreme Court squarely decided that to "force a worldly education on all Amish children, the majority of whom do not want or need it, in order to confer a dubious benefit on the few who might later reject their religion is not a compelling interest." State v. Yoder, 182 N.W.2d 539 (Wis. 1971).

(4) *Yoder* can be seen as a case in which there is a conflict between the state and the Amish parents over how the children would be socialized. Are eight years of schooling sufficient to satisfy the two interests advanced by the state to justify compulsory education: the need to prepare children for citizenship and economic self-reliance? Will two years matter?

(5) Home Schooling.   Suppose parents have sincere religious or academic objections to sending their children to public school but they are not part of a self-contained and self-sufficient religious community for which an eighth-grade education and on-the-job training will suffice. Should they be allowed to educate their children at home?

Over the past several decades, more parents have opted to educate their children at home. Currently, 34 states have statutes directly pertaining to home schooling. Brad Colwell & Brian D. Schwartz, Implications for Public Schools: Legal Aspects of Home Schools, 173 Educ. L. Rep. 381, 393 (2003). State and federal courts have upheld parents' right to home school. However, states retain the power to regulate home schooling, including the qualifications of the instructor, curriculum, number of days of instruction, standardized tests that must be administered, and parental reporting obligations. See, e.g., Mass. Gen. Laws Ann. ch. 76, §1 (West 1996 & Supp. 2004); Mich. Comp. Laws Ann. §1 (West 1997 & Supp. 2004). Although many parents have challenged the constitutionality of these state regulations, most courts have rejected their challenges.

In Blackwelder v. Safnauer, 689 F. Supp. 106 (N.D.N.Y. 1988), for example, a New York district court considered a free exercise challenge to New York Education Law §3204(2) (McKinney 2001), providing that nonpublic schools should be "at least substantially equivalent to the instruction given to minors of like age and attainments at the public schools" and should be provided by "competent" instructors. The court recognized that " . . . Yoder, especially when read in conjunction with Pierce v. Society of Sisters, offers strong support for plaintiffs' contention that they have a right protected by the Constitution to teach their children at home. . . . " 689 F. Supp. at 132. However, the court also recognized that the state has the ability to take necessary action to ensure that education meets certain minimal standards. In rejecting the parents' free exercise challenge, the court limited Yoder to its facts.

Some parents who home school would like limited access to the public schools — e.g., for advanced math or science courses or for extracurricular activities. Do parents who have chosen home schooling have the right to force public schools to accept their children on a part-time basis? See Swanson v. Guthrie Indep. Sch. Dist. No. I-L, 153 F.3d 694 (10th Cir. 1998) (holding that school policy prohibiting part-time attendance did not violate home schooler's free exercise rights). See generally Darryl C. Wilson, Home Field Disadvantage: The Negative Impact of Allowing Home Schoolers to Participate in Mainstream Sports, 3 Va. J. Sports & L. 1 (2001).

(6) Special Public School District.   Should self-contained, self-sufficient religious communities be able to establish their own public school districts if they are opposed, for religious reasons, to their children attending regular public schools? In Kiryas Joel Village School District v. Grumet, 512 U.S. 687 (1994), a public school district was created by special legislative act in an exclusive Hasidic community. The religious group, adherents of a strict sect of Judaism, had plenary authority over education in the district. The Supreme Court held that the creation of such a district violated the Establishment Clause.

Immediately after the decision, the New York state legislature abolished the special district and enacted a new law attempting to re-establish the district under more religiously neutral grounds. That statute and another subsequent statute re-establishing the special school district were declared unconstitutional. Grumet v. Cuomo, 625 N.Y.S.2d 1000 (N.Y. Sup. Ct. 1995), *rev'd*, 647 N.Y.2d 565 (N.Y. App. Div. 1996), *aff'd*, 681 N.E.2d 340 (N.Y. 1997). See also Grumet v. Pataki, 675 N.Y.S.2d 662 (N.Y. App. Div. 1998); *motion to vacate denied*, 702 N.E.2d 837 (N.Y. 1998), *aff'd*, 720 N.E.2d 66 (N.Y. 1999), *stay granted*, 527 U.S. 1019 (1999), *cert. denied*, 528 U.S 946 (1999). However, the fourth attempt of the state legislature was upheld, thus ending the 12-year effort to create a separate school district for the community. See Tamar Lewin, Controversy Over, Enclave Joins School Board Group, N.Y. Times, Apr. 20, 2002, at B4.

(7) Federal Legislation.   Subsequent to *Yoder*, the Supreme Court decided Employment Division v. Smith, 494 U.S. 872 (1990), in which two employees were terminated for smoking peyote, a ritual of their Native American religion. They claimed that their termination constituted a violation of their right to free exercise of their religion. Rejecting this argument, the Court held that free exercise can bar application of a generally applicable law only when joined with a violation of some other constitutional protection, such as freedom of speech or press, or a parental right (citing *Yoder*). In 1993, Congress rejected this interpretation and enacted the Religious Freedom Restoration Act (RFRA), 42 U.S.C. §2000bb (1994), requiring states to provide religious exemptions from generally applicable laws. In City of Boerne v. Flores, 521 U.S. 507 (1997), the Supreme Court ruled RFRA unconstitutional on the ground that it exceeded Congress's enforcement powers under the Fourteenth Amendment. Three years later, Congress enacted a narrower version of the RFRA. The Religious Land Use and Institutionalized Persons Act of 2000, Pub. L. No. 106-274, 114 Stat. 803 (2000), exempts religious institutions from regulations that impose a "substantial burden" on religious exercise.

(8) Epilogue.   Economic pressures and the scarcity of farmland have contributed to a transformation in the nature of Amish labor from farming to sawmills and woodworking. See Joe Milicia, Outside World Touches Amish; Many Have Left Farming and Operate Small Businesses. Farm Machinery and Telephones Have Become Part of Their Lives, L.A. Times, May 16, 2004, at A26; S. 974, 108th Cong. (2003) (remarks of Sen. Specter (R.-Pa.)) As a result, the Amish have incurred fines for violating the Fair Labor Standards Act of 1938, 29 U.S.C. §213(c) (2000), which gives the U.S. Department of Labor the authority to set child labor standards to prohibit children from working in hazardous occupations.

In January 2004, to address the issue of Amish labor, Congress enacted an amendment to the Fair Labor Standards Act exempting a minor from child labor restrictions if the minor is "supervised by an adult relative of the entrant or is supervised by an adult member of the same religious sect or division as the entrant" and does not himself operate the woodworking machinery. See Consolidated Appropriations Act, 2004; Pub. L. No. 108-199, §108, 118 Stat. 3, 236 (2004). Senator Joseph Pitts (R.-Pa.), one of the architects of the amendment, hailed its passage as a "victory for the Amish, for religious liberty, and for diversity in America." 150 Cong. Rec. H255-07 (daily ed. Feb. 3, 2004). Critics have pointed out that the fatality rate for the lumber and wood products industry is five times the national average. See H.R. 4257, 105th Cong. (1998) (remarks of Rep. Bill Clay (D.-Mo.)). Does such legislation violate the Establishment Clause?

In other developments in the Amish community, federal agents arrested two Amish men for selling cocaine to other young Amish in Lancaster County, Pennsylvania, as part of the "Pagan" motorcycle gang's narcotics operation. See David L. Greene, Amish Alarmed by Teen Drug Use, Baltimore Sun, July 9, 1998, at 1A. Do these developments (regarding vocational training and drug use) call for a reevaluation of *Yoder*?

For historical background concerning the conflict between Amish communities and the government, see John Andrew Hostetler, Amish Society (4th ed. 1993); The Amish and the State (Donald B. Kraybill ed., 2d ed. 2003).

Roger W. McIntire, Parenthood Training or Mandatory Birth Control: Take Your Choice
Psychology Today 34 (Oct. 1973)

Few parents like to be told how to raise their children, and even fewer will like the idea of someone telling them whether they can have children in the first place. But that's exactly what I'm proposing—the licensing of parenthood. Of course, civil libertarians and other liberals will claim this would infringe the parents' rights to freedom of choice and equal opportunity. But what about the rights of children? Surely the parents' competence will influence their children's freedom and opportunity. Today, any couple has the right to try parenting, regardless of how incompetent they might be. No one seems to worry about the unfortunate subjects of their experimenting.

The idea of licensing parenthood is hardly new. But until recently, our ignorance of environmental effects, our ignorance of contraception, and our selfish bias against the rights of children have inhibited public discussion of the topic. In recent years, however, psychologists have taught us just how crucial the effect of the home environment can be, and current research on contraception appears promising.

Contraception by Capsule

Successful control of parenthood will require a contraceptive that remains in effect until it is removed or counteracted by the administration of a second drug. . . .

The Child Victim

Clearly, we will soon have the technology necessary to carry out a parenthood licensing program, and history tells us that whenever we develop a technology, we inevitably use it. We should now be concerned with developing the criteria for good parenthood. In some extreme cases we already have legal and social definitions. We obviously consider child abuse wrong, and look upon those who physically mistreat their children as bad parents. In some states the courts remove children from the custody of parents convicted of child abuse.

In a recent review of studies of child-abusing parents, John J. Spinetta and David Rigler concluded that such people are generally ignorant of proper child-rearing practices. They also noted that many child-abusing parents had been victims of abuse and neglect in their own youth. Thus our lack of control over who can be parents magnifies the problem with each generation.

In the case of child-abusing parents, the state attempts to prevent the most obvious physical mistreatment of children. At this extreme, our culture does demand that parents prove their ability to provide for the physical well-being of their children. But our culture makes almost no demands when it comes to the children's psychological well-being and development. Any fool can now raise a child anyway he or she pleases, and it's none of our business. The child becomes the unprotected victim of whoever gives birth to him.

Ironically, the only institutions that do attempt to screen potential parents are the adoption agencies, although their screening can hardly be called scientific. Curiously enough, those who oppose a parent-licensing law usually do not oppose the discriminating policies practiced by the adoption agencies. It seems that our society cares more about the selection of a child's second set of parents than it does about his original parents. In other words, our culture insists on insuring a certain quality of parenthood for adopted children, but if you want to have one of your own, feel free.

Screening and selecting potential parents by no means guarantees that they will in fact be good parents. Yet today we have almost no means of insuring proper child-rearing methods. The indiscriminate "right to parent" enables everyone, however ill-equipped, to practice any parental behavior they please. Often their behavior would be illegal if applied to any group other than children. But because of our prejudice against the rights of children, we protect them only when the most savage and brutal parental behavior can be proved in court. Consider the following example:

Supermarket Scenario

A mother and daughter enter a supermarket. An accident occurs when the daughter pulls the wrong orange from the pile and 37 oranges are given their freedom. The mother grabs the daughter, shakes her vigorously, and slaps her. What is your reaction? Do you ignore the incident? Do you consider it a family squabble and none of your business? Or do you go over and advise the mother not to hit her child? If the mother rejects your advice, do you physically restrain her? If she persists, do you call the police? Think about your answers for a moment.

Now let me change one detail. *The girl was not that mother's daughter.* Do you feel different? Would you act differently? Why? Do "real" parents have the right to abuse their children because they "own" them? Now let me change another detail. Suppose the daughter was 25 years old, and yelled, "Help me! Help me!" Calling the police sounded silly when I first suggested it. How does it sound with a mere change in the age of the victim?

Now let's go back to the original scene where we were dealing with a small child. Were you about to advise the mother or insist? Were you going to say she shouldn't or couldn't? It depends on whose rights you're going to consider. If you think about the mother's right to mother as she sees fit, then you advise; but if you think about the child's right as a human being to be protected from the physical assault of this woman, then you insist. The whole issue is obviously tangled in a web of beliefs about individual rights, parental rights, and children's rights. We tend to think children deserve what they get, or at least must suffer it. Assault and battery, verbal abuse, and even forced imprisonment become legal if the victims are children.

When I think about the issue of children's rights, and the current development of new contraceptives, I see a change coming in this country. I'm tempted to make the following prediction in the form of a science-fiction story:

Hypothetical

Motherhood in the [Future]

"Lock" was developed as a kind of semipermanent contraceptive. . . . One dose of Lock and a woman became incapable of ovulation until the antidote "Unlock" was administered. As with most contraceptives, Lock required a prescription, with sales limited by the usual criteria of age and marital status.

Gradually, however, a subtle but significant distinction became apparent. Other contraceptives merely allowed a woman to protect herself against pregnancy at her own discretion. Once Lock was administered, however, the prescription for Unlock required an active decision to allow the *possibility* of pregnancy.

[Soon,] the two drugs were being prescribed simultaneously, leaving the Unlock decision in the hands of the potential mother. Of course, problems arose. Mothers smuggled Lock to their daughters and the daughters later asked for Unlock. Women misplaced the Unlock and had to ask for more. Faced with the threat of a black market, the state set up a network of special dispensaries for the contraceptive and its antidote. When the first dispensaries opened . . . , they dispensed Lock rather freely, since they could always regulate the use of Unlock. But it soon became apparent that special local committees would be necessary to screen applicants for Unlock. "After all," the dispensary officials asked themselves, "how would you like to be responsible for this person becoming a parent?"

Protect Our Children

That same year, [when the dispensaries opened], brought the school-population riots. Overcrowding had forced state education officials to take some action. Thanks to more efficient educational techniques, they were able to consider reducing the number of years of required schooling. This, however, would have thrown millions of teenagers out onto the already overcrowded job market, which would make the unions unhappy. Thus, rather than shortening the entire educational process, the officials decided to shorten the school day into two half-day shifts. That led to the trouble.

Until then, people had assumed that schools existed primarily for the purpose of education. But the decision to shorten the school day exposed the dependence of the nation's parents on the school as the great baby sitter of their offspring. Having won the long struggle for daycare centers, and freedom from diapers and bottles, mothers were horrified at the prospect of a few more hours of responsibility every day until their children reached 18 or 21. They took to the streets.

In Richmond, Virginia, a neighborhood protest over the shortened school day turned into a riot. One of the demonstrators picked up a traffic sign near the school that cautioned drivers to "Protect Our Children," and found herself leading the march toward city hall. Within a week that sign became the national slogan for the protesters, as well as for the Lock movement. It came to mean not only protecting our children from overcrowding and lack of supervision, but also protecting them from pregnancy.

Because of the school-population riots, distribution of Lock took on the characteristics of an immunization program under the threat of an epidemic. With immunization completed, the state could control the birth rate like a water faucet by the distribution of Unlock. However, this did not solve the problem of deciding who should bear the nation's children.

Congress Takes Over

To settle the issue, Congress appointed a special blue-ribbon commission of psychologists, psychiatrists, educators, and clergymen to come up with acceptable criteria for parenthood, and a plan for a licensing program. The commission issued its report. . . . Based upon its recommendations, Congress set up a Federal regulatory agency to administer a national parenthood-licensing program similar to driver-training and licensing procedures.

The agency now issues study guides for the courses, and sets the required standards of child-rearing knowledge. Of course, the standards vary for parents, teachers, and childcare professionals, depending upon the degree of responsibility involved. The courses and exams are conducted by local community colleges, under the supervision of the Federal agency. Only upon passing the exams can prospective parents receive a prescription for Unlock.

Distribution of Lock and Unlock is now strictly regulated by the Federal agency's local commissions. Since the records of distribution are stored in Federal computer banks, identification of illegitimate pregnancies (those made possible by the unauthorized use of Unlock) has become a simple matter. Parents convicted of this crime are fined, and required to begin an intensive parenthood-training program immediately. If they do not qualify by the time their child is born, the child goes to a community childcare program until they do.

Drawing the Battle Lines

As might be expected, the parent-licensing program has come under attack from those who complain about the loss of their freedom to create and raise children according to their own choice and beliefs. To such critics, the protect-our-children or Lock faction argues: "It's absurd to require education and license to drive a car, but allow anybody to raise our most precious possession or to add to the burden of this possession without demonstrating an ability to parent."

"But the creation of life is in the hands of God," says the freedom-and-right-to-parent-faction (referred to by their opposition as the "far-right-people").

"Nonsense," say the Lock people. "Control over life creation was acquired with the first contraceptive. The question is whether we use it with intelligence or not."

"But that question is for each potential parent to answer as an individual," say the far-right-people.

The Lock people answer: "Those parents ask the selfish question of whether they want a child or not. We want to know if the child will be adequately cared for — by them and by the culture."

The far right respond, "God gave us bodies and all their functions. We have a right to the use of those functions. Unlock should be there for the asking. Why should the Government have a say in whether I have a child?"

"Because the last century has shown that the Government will be saddled with most of the burden of raising your child," say the Lock people. "The schools, the medical programs, the youth programs, the crime-prevention programs, the colleges, the park and planning commissions — they will be burdened with your child. That's why the Government should have a say. The extent of the Government's burden depends on your ability to raise your child. If you screw it up, the society *and* Government will suffer. That's why they should screen potential parents."

From the right again: "The decision of my spouse and myself is sacred. It's none of their damn business."

But the Locks argue: "If you raised your child in the wilderness and the child's malfunctions punished no one but yourselves, it would be none of their damn business. But if your child is to live with us, be educated by us, suffered by us, add to the crowd of us, we should have a say."

Face of the Future

I can understand how some people might find this story either far-fetched or frightening, but I don't think any prediction in it is too far in the future. Carl Djerassi suggested the possibility of a semipermanent contraceptive such as "Lock" and "Unlock" (although he didn't use those brand names) as early as 1969, in an article in Science. [O]ther scientists are currently making significant strides in contraceptive research.

Throughout history, as knowledge has eroded away superstition about conception and birth, humans have taken increasing control over the birth of their offspring. Religious practices, arranged marriages, mechanical and biochemical contraception have all played a role in this regulation of procreation. Until now, however, such regulation has dealt only with the presence or absence of children, leaving their development to cultural superstitions. Anyone with normal biology may still produce another child, and, within the broadest limits, treat it anyway he or she chooses.

We have taken a long time in coming to grips with this problem because our society as a whole has had no demonstrably better ideas about child-rearing than any individual parent. And until now, people couldn't be stopped from having children because we haven't had the technology that would enable us to control individual fertility.

How to Rear a Child

The times are changing. With the population problem now upon us, we can no longer afford the luxury of allowing any two fools to add to our numbers whenever they please. We do have, or soon will have, the technology to control individual procreation. And, most important, psychology and related sciences have by now established some child-rearing principles that should be part of every parent's knowledge. An objective study of these principles need not involve the prying, subjective investigation now used by adoption agencies. It would merely insure that potential parents would be familiar with the principles of sound child-rearing. Examinations and practical demonstrations would test their knowledge. Without having state agents check every home (and of course, we would never accept such "Big Brother" tactics) there could be no way to enforce the use of that knowledge.

But insistence on the knowledge would itself save a great deal of suffering by the children.

The following list suggests a few of the topics with which every parent should be familiar:

1. Principles of sound nutrition and diet.
2. Changes in nutritional requirements with age.
3. Principles of general hygiene and health.
4. Principles of behavioral development: normal range of ages at which behavioral capabilities might be expected, etc.
5. Principles of learning and language acquisition.
6. Principles of immediacy and consistency that govern parents' reactions to children's behavior.
7. Principles of modeling and imitation: how children learn from and copy their parents' behavior.
8. Principles of reinforcement: how parent and peer reactions reward a child's behavior, and which rewards should be used.
9. Principles of punishment: how parents' reactions can be used to punish or discourage bad behavior.
10. Response-cost concept: how to "raise the cost" or create unpleasant consequences in order to make undesirable behavior more "expensive" or difficult.
11. Extinction procedures and adjunctive behavior: if rewards for good behavior cease, children may "act up" just to fill the time.
12. Stimulus-control generalization: children may act up in some situations, and not in others, because of different payoffs. For example, Mommy may give the child candy to stop a tantrum, whereas Daddy may ignore it or strike the child.

Most of us have some familiarity with the principles at the beginning of this list, but many parents have little knowledge of the other topics. Some psychologists would obviously find my list biased toward behavior modification, but their revisions or additions to the list only strengthen my argument that our science has a great deal to teach that would be relevant to a parenthood-licensing program.

Misplaced Priorities

Of course the word licensing suggests that the impersonal hand of Government may control individual lives, and that more civil servants will be paid to meddle in our personal affairs. But consider for a moment that for our safety and well-being we already license pilots, salesmen, scuba divers, plumbers, electricians, teachers, veterinarians, cab drivers, soil testers and television repairmen. To protect pedestrians, we accept restrictions on the speed with which we drive our cars. Why, then, do we encourage such commotion, chest thumping, and cries of oppression when we try to protect the well-being of children by controlling the most crucial determiner of that well-being, the competence of their parents? Are our TV sets and toilets more important to us than our children? Can you imagine the public outcry that would occur if adoption agencies offered their children on a first-come-first-served basis, with no screening process for applicants? Imagine some drunk stumbling up and saying, "I'll take that cute little blond-haired girl over there."

We require appropriate education for most trades and professions, yet stop short at parenthood because it would be an infringement on the individual freedom of the parent. The foolishness of this position will become increasingly apparent the more confident we become in our knowledge about child-rearing.

The first step toward a parenthood law will probably occur when child-abuse offenders will be asked or required to take "Lock" as an alternative to, or in addition to, being tried in court. Or the courts may also offer the child abuser the alternative of a remedial training program such as the traffic courts now use. The next step may be the broadening of the term "child abuse" to include ignorant mistreatment of a psychological nature. Some communities may add educational programs to marriage-license requirements, while others may add parenthood training to existing courses in baby care.

When the Government gets around to setting criteria for proper childrearing, these must be based upon a very specific set of principles of nutrition, hygiene, and behavior control. They cannot be based on bias and hearsay. Some of the criteria now used by adoption agencies, such as references from neighbors and friends, cannot be considered objective. We don't interview your neighbors when you apply for a driver's license, and it shouldn't be done for a parent's license either. But just as a citizen must now demonstrate knowledge and competence to drive a car, so ought he to demonstrate his ability to parent as well. Proof of exposure to education is not enough. We are not satisfied merely with driver training courses, but demand a driver's test as well. We should require the same standards of parents.

We can hope that as progress occurs in the technology of contraception and the knowledge of child-rearing principles, the current "right to parent" will be re-evaluated by our society. Perhaps we can construct a society that will also consider the rights that children have to a humane and beneficial upbringing.

PROBLEM: SHOULD THE GOVERNMENT LICENSE PARENTS?

Assume it is the year 2020, and you are legislative counsel to a United States Senator. A bill has been drafted setting up a federal regulatory agency to administer a national parenthood-licensing program incorporating the ideas put forward in the McIntire article. Would such a bill be constitutional in light of *Roe, Pierce, Prince*, and *Yoder*? If not, which provisions are invalid? As applied to whom? What changes would make the bill valid? Could there be compulsory contraception? Compulsory adult education in parenting? Would either make sense in terms of policy?

With the benefit of hindsight, do McIntire's predictions seem so outlandish? Consider the following:

(1) The fictional "Lock" was intended as a semipermanent contraceptive, requiring a prescription. Once "Lock" was administered, a prescription for "Unlock"

necessitated an affirmative decision to procreate. Do we now possess the technology to implement a parenthood-licensing program? Various semipermanent contraceptives (e.g., implantable as well as injectable methods) currently provide effective birth control for periods ranging from three months to five years. Are these contraceptives the nonfictional equivalents of "Lock"?

(2) McIntire also suggests that the "first step toward a parenthood law" would occur with the imposition of "Lock" as an alternative to trial. In In re Bobbijean P., No. NN 03626-03, 2005 WL 127048 (N.Y. Fam. Ct. Jan. 10, 2005), a family court judge ordered two parents, after a finding of neglect, not to conceive additional children until the parents were able to obtain custody of their children currently in foster care. The court did not mandate a particular birth control method, pointing instead to the variety of methods (including injections, Norplant, and the patch, among others). The family court judge subsequently denied plantiffs' motion to vacate the restriction on procreation. Does *Bobbijean* suggest that we have taken "the first step toward a parenthood law"?

Several states have considered legislation mandating use of the implantable contraceptive Norplant by convicted child abusers. Other states have considered legislation to make Norplant mandatory for female drug addicts or welfare recipients. Are such measures sound policy? Are they constitutional? See generally Kimberly A. Smith, Note, Conceivable Sterilization: A Constitutional Analysis of a Norplant/Depo-Provera Welfare Condition, 77 Ind. L.J. 389 (2002).

In August 2002, the manufacturer of Norplant suspended sales of the contraceptive after settling the claims of 30,000 women who claimed that they had not been warned adequately about the drug's side effects. Andrew Harris, Ruling Finishes Off Norplant Suits, Natl. L.J., Sept. 30, 2002, at B6.

McIntire also suggests that another "next step" will be broadening of the term "child abuse" to include psychological abuse. Since his article, many states have expanded the definition in this manner. See, e.g., Alaska Stat. §47.17.0101 (2002) (definition includes mental injury); 23 Pa. Cons. Stat. §6303 (West 2001 & Supp. 2004). Issues of child abuse are explored further in Chapter 3. For thought-provoking essays about parental licensing, see Claudia Mangel, Licensing Parents: How Feasible?, 22 Fam. L.Q. 17 (1988); Michael J. Sandmire & Michael S. Wald, Licensing Parents: A Response to Claudia Mangel's Proposal, 24 Fam. L.Q. 53 (1990). See also Jack C. Westman, Licensing Parents: Can We Prevent Child Abuse and Neglect? (2001).

D. WHAT VOICE FOR THE CHILD?

The majority in *Yoder* sidestepped analyzing the possible conflict between the views of the Amish children and the views of their parents about the children's best interests. Should the majority have sought to identify the independent interests of the children? How? Should the children have been separately represented in the litigation? Are there disadvantages to this sort of inquiry? Consider the approach advocated by Justice Douglas in his dissenting opinion in *Yoder*, which follows.

Wisconsin v. Yoder *Cont'd.*
406 U.S. 205, 241 (1972)

... Mr. Justice DOUGLAS, dissenting in part:

I

I agree with the Court that the religious scruples of the Amish are opposed to the education of their children beyond the grade schools, yet I disagree with the Court's conclusion that the matter is within the dispensation of parents alone. The Court's analysis assumes that the only interests at stake in the case are those of the Amish parents on the one hand, and those of the State on the other. The difficulty with this approach is that, despite the Court's claim, the parents are seeking to vindicate not only their own free exercise claims, but also those of their high-school-age children.

It is argued that the right of the Amish children to religious freedom is not presented by the facts of the case, as the issue before the Court involves only the Amish parents' religious freedom to defy a state criminal statute imposing upon them an affirmative duty to cause their children to attend high school.

First, respondents' motion to dismiss in the trial court expressly asserts, not only the religious liberty of the adults, but also that of the children, as a defense to the prosecutions. It is, of course, beyond question that the parents have standing as defendants in a criminal prosecution to assert the religious interests of their children as a defense.[1] Although the lower courts and the majority in this Court assume an identity of interest between parent and child, it is clear that they have treated the religious interest of the child as a factor in the analysis.

Second, it is essential to reach the question to decide the case not only because the question was squarely raised in the motion to dismiss, but also because no analysis of religious liberty claims can take place in a vacuum. If the parents in this case are allowed a religious exemption, the inevitable effect is to impose the parents' notions of religious duty upon their children. Where the child is mature enough to express potentially conflicting desires, it would be an invasion of the child's rights to permit such an imposition without canvassing his views. As in *Prince*, it is an imposition resulting from this very litigation. As the child has no other effective forum, it is in this litigation that his rights should be considered. And, if an Amish child desires to attend high school, and is mature enough to have that desire respected, the State may well be able to override the parents' religiously motivated objections.

---

[1] Thus, in Prince v. Massachusetts, 321 U.S. 158, a Jehovah's Witness was convicted for having violated a state child labor law by allowing her nine-year-old niece and ward to circulate religious literature on the public streets. There, as here, the narrow question was the religious liberty of the adult. There, as here, the Court analyzed the problem from the point of view of the State's conflicting interest in the welfare of the child. But, as Mr. Justice Brennan, speaking for the Court, has so recently pointed out, "The Court [in *Prince*] implicitly held that the custodian had standing to assert alleged freedom of religion . . . rights of the child that were threatened in the very litigation before the Court and that the child had no effective way of asserting herself." Eisenstadt v. Baird, 405 U.S. 446, n. 6. Here, as in *Prince*, the children have no effective alternate means to vindicate their rights. The question, therefore, is squarely before us.

Religion is an individual experience. It is not necessary, nor even appropriate, for every Amish child to express his views on the subject in a prosecution of a single adult. Crucial, however, are the views of the child whose parent is the subject of the suit. Frieda Yoder has in fact testified that her own religious views are opposed to high-school education. I therefore join the judgment of the Court as to respondent Jonas Yoder. But Frieda Yoder's views may not be those of Vernon Yutzy or Barbara Miller. I must dissent, therefore, as to respondents Adin Yutzy and Wallace Miller as their motion to dismiss also raised the question of their children's religious liberty.

II

This issue has never been squarely presented before today. Our opinions are full of talk about the power of the parents over the child's education. See Pierce v. Society of Sisters, 268 U.S. 510; Meyer v. Nebraska, 262 U.S. 390. And we have in the past analyzed similar conflicts between parent and State with little regard for the views of the child. See Prince v. Massachusetts, 321 U.S. 158. Recent cases, however, have clearly held that the children themselves have constitutionally protective interests.

These children are "persons" within the meaning of the Bill of Rights. We have so held over and over again. . . .

On this important and vital matter of education, I think the children should be entitled to be heard. While the parents, absent dissent, normally speak for the entire family, the education of the child is a matter on which the child will often have decided views. He may want to be a pianist or an astronaut or an ocean geographer. To do so he will have to break from the Amish tradition.[2]

It is the future of the student, not the future of the parents, that is imperilled in today's decision. If a parent keeps his child out of school beyond the grade school, then the child will be forever barred from entry into the new and amazing world of diversity that we have today. The child may decide that that is the preferred course, or he may rebel. It is the student's judgment, not his parent's, that is essential if we are to give full meaning to what we have said about the Bill of Rights and of the right of students to be masters of their own destiny.[3] If he is harnessed to the Amish

[2] A significant number of Amish children do leave the Old Order. Professor Hostetler notes that "the loss of members is very limited in some Amish districts and considerable in others." Amish Society, 210. In one Pennsylvania church, he observed a defection rate of 30%. Id. Rates up to 50% have been reported by others. Casad, Compulsory High School Attendance and the Old Order Amish: A Commentary on State v. Garber, 16 Kan. L. Rev. 423, 434 n.51 (1968).

[3] The court below brushed aside the students' interests with the off-hand comment that "when a child reaches the age of judgment, he can choose for himself his religion." 49 Wis. 2d 430, 182 N.W.2d 549. But there is nothing in this record to indicate that the moral and intellectual judgment demanded of the student by the question in this case is beyond his capacity. Children far younger than the 14- and 15-year-olds involved here are regularly permitted to testify in custody and other proceedings. Indeed, the failure to call the affected child in a custody hearing is often reversible error. See, e.g., Callicott v. Callicott, 364 S.W.2d 455 (Tex. Civ. App. 1963) (reversible error for trial judge to refuse to hear testimony of eight-year-old in custody battle). Moreover, there is substantial agreement among child psychologists and sociologists that the moral and intellectual maturity of the fourteen-year-old approaches that of the adult. See, e.g., J. Piaget, The Moral Judgment of the Child (1948); Elkind, Children and Adolescents 75-80 (1970); L. Kohlberg, Moral Education in the Schools: A Developmental View, in R. Muuss, Adolescent Behavior and Society 199-200 (1971); W. Kay, Moral

way of life by those in authority over him and if his education is truncated, his entire life may be stunted and deformed. The child, therefore, should be given an opportunity to be heard before the State gives the exemption which we honor today.

The views of the two children in question were not canvassed by the Wisconsin courts. The matter should be explicitly reserved so that new hearings can be held on remand of the case.[4] . . .

QUESTIONS ON *YODER* DISSENT

(1) Is Justice Douglas correct that the children's rights are necessarily implicated in this case? If the parent is being criminally prosecuted, why are the religious views of the child "crucial"? On the other hand, under the majority opinion, how would a child who disagreed with his parents' views vindicate his rights? If the parent kept the child home after eighth grade, would the child bring suit against his parents? Who would pay for the suit? Who would be guardian ad litem? Is Douglas correct that if the children's views are not canvassed in this suit against their Amish parents, "the children have no effective alternate means to vindicate their rights"? See n. 1 of Douglas' dissent, p. 76 supra.

(2) If the denial of a high school education can, as Douglas asserts, lead to a "stunted and deformed" life, why is not the state's interest in requiring *all* children to stay in school past eighth grade a compelling one?

(3) Justice Douglas asserts that "where the child is mature enough to express potentially conflicting desires, it would be an invasion of the child's rights to permit . . . an imposition" of parents' notions of religious duty "without canvassing [the child's] views." When is the child "mature enough"? Is the child "mature enough" by definition if able "to express" disagreement? Or does Justice Douglas have in mind an independent evaluation, perhaps case-by-case, of each Amish child's maturity? See n. 4 of Douglas' dissent, below.

(4) If an Amish child were to express disagreement with parental notions of religious duty, what would Douglas' view require the lower court to do? Do as the child wants? Apply the Wisconsin compulsory education statute? Or have the court evaluate what is best for the child? What if the parents said they would not want the child living at home if he were to attend a secular high school?

(5) Compare the approach to the identification of the children's interests of the majority and dissent in *Yoder* with Justice Stevens' dissent in Troxel v. Granville, which follows. In *Troxel*, the United States Supreme Court found unconstitutional a broad Washington state statute (allowing any person to petition for visitation at any time based on the child's best interests) as a violation of substantive due process when applied to a mother's decision to limit the visitation rights of grandparents

---

Development 172-183 (1968); A. Gesell & F. Ilg, Youth: The Years From Ten to Sixteen 175-182 (1956). The maturity of Amish youth, who identify with and assume adult roles from early childhood, see M. Goodman, The Culture of Childhood 92-94 (1970), is certainly not less than that of children in the general population.

[4] Canvassing the views of all school-age Amish children in the State of Wisconsin would not present insurmountable difficulties. A 1968 survey indicated that there were at that time only 256 such children in the entire State. Comment, 1971 Wis. L. Rev. 832, 852 n. 132 (1971).

following the death of her children's father. (Justice Stevens, dissenting, would have denied certiorari.) The plurality opinion in *Troxel* is reprinted at page 595 in Chapter 5. (Issues concerning religion also arise in connection with custody and adoption. See Chapter 5, sections B and C.)

Troxel v. Granville
530 U.S. 57, 86-91 (2000)

. . . Justice STEVENS, dissenting.

. . . The presumption that parental decisions generally serve the best interests of their children is sound, and clearly in the normal case the parent's interest is paramount. But even a fit parent is capable of treating a child like a mere possession.

Cases like this do not present a bipolar struggle between the parents and the State over who has final authority to determine what is in a child's best interests. There is at a minimum a third individual, whose interests are implicated in every case to which the statute applies — the child. . . .

A parent's rights with respect to her child have thus never been regarded as absolute, but rather are limited by the existence of an actual, developed relationship with a child, and are tied to the presence or absence of some embodiment of family. These limitations have arisen, not simply out of the definition of parenthood itself, but because of this Court's assumption that a parent's interests in a child must be balanced against the State's long-recognized interests as parens patriae, and, critically, the child's own complementary interest in preserving relationships that serve her welfare and protection.

While this Court has not yet had occasion to elucidate the nature of a child's liberty interests in preserving established familial or family-like bonds, it seems to me extremely likely that, to the extent parents and families have fundamental liberty interests in preserving such intimate relationships, so, too, do children have these interests, and so, too, must their interests be balanced in the equation. At a minimum, our prior cases recognizing that children are, generally speaking, constitutionally protected actors require that this Court reject any suggestion that when it comes to parental rights, children are so much chattel. . . .

This is not, of course, to suggest that a child's liberty interest in maintaining contact with a particular individual is to be treated invariably as on a par with that child's parents' contrary interests. Because our substantive due process case law includes a strong presumption that a parent will act in the best interest of her child, it would be necessary, were the state appellate courts actually to confront a challenge to the statute as applied, to consider whether the trial court's assessment of the "best interest of the child" incorporated that presumption. . . .

But presumptions notwithstanding, we should recognize that there may be circumstances in which a child has a stronger interest at stake than mere protection from serious harm caused by the termination of visitation by a "person" other than a parent. The almost infinite variety of family relationships that pervade our ever-changing society strongly counsel against the creation by this Court of a constitutional rule that treats a biological parent's liberty interest in the care and supervision of her child as an isolated right that may be exercised arbitrarily. It is indisputably the business of the States, rather than a federal court employing a national standard, to assess in the first instance the relative importance of the conflicting interests that give rise to disputes such as this. Far from guaranteeing that parents' interests will be trammeled in the sweep of cases arising under the statute, the Washington law merely gives an individual — with whom a child may have an established relationship — the procedural right to ask the State to act as arbiter, through the entirely well-known best-interests standard, between the parent's protected interests and the child's. It seems clear to me that the Due Process Clause of the Fourteenth Amendment leaves room for States to consider the impact on a child of possibly arbitrary parental decisions that neither serve nor are motivated by the best interests of the child. . . .

NOTE ON JUVENILE COURT JURISDICTION

As explained above, Justice Douglas in his *Yoder* dissent does not clarify how a child who disagreed with parental views could vindicate his or her rights. Because various sorts of juvenile proceedings are considered throughout this book, it is useful at this point to identify the typical juvenile court proceedings.

(1) Child Neglect or Abuse: Dependency Jurisdiction. Every state has as part of its jurisdictional statute a provision allowing the court to assume jurisdiction over children who are thought to be endangered because of parental neglect or abuse. Once jurisdiction is established, the court is empowered to remove the child from parental custody or take other steps to protect the child. Typically these statutory standards are broad and vague. The question of when it is appropriate for the state to intervene coercively in the family in order to protect children is analyzed in various contexts later in the book. The physical abuse of children and the general issues of when the state should remove children from parental custody and what should happen to such children are considered in Chapter 3, infra. In all events, neglect or abuse cases focus primarily on the parents, not on the child's conduct. Problems of neglect in connection with the medical treatment of children are considered in Chapter 4.

(2) Delinquency Jurisdiction. Courts may also take jurisdiction over a young person who is shown to have violated criminal law — i.e., to have committed an act, which, for an adult, would have been a crime. A variety of questions relating to delinquency are considered in Chapter 7.

(3) Noncriminal Misbehavior of Minors: Children in Need of Supervision. Juvenile courts may also hear claims that a young person is "unruly" or "in need of supervision" or is engaged in vaguely defined types of conduct regarded as improper or quasi-criminal — e.g., truancy, refusal to obey parental commands, or hanging around in places that are thought inappropriate for young persons. A number of modern juvenile statutes have a separate jurisdictional heading for such young people, who are determined to be "Persons In Need of Supervision" (PINS) or "Children In Need of Supervision" (CHINS). See p. 704 infra. Older statutes simply include such noncriminal misbehavior within the definition of delinquency. In all events, these "offenses" are sometimes called "status offenses" or "crimes for

children alone," for they typically permit a court to assume jurisdiction over a young person in circumstances where there could be no state intervention in the life of an adult. These aspects of juvenile court jurisdiction are considered in Chapter 6, which deals generally with various state-imposed constraints on the liberties of young people.

Ginsberg v. New York
390 U.S. 629 (1968)

Mr. Justice BRENNAN delivered the opinion of the Court.

This case presents the question of the constitutionality on its face of a New York criminal obscenity statute which prohibits the sale to minors under 17 years of age of material defined to be obscene on the basis of its appeal to them whether or not it would be obscene to adults.

Appellant and his wife operate "Sam's Stationery and Luncheonette" in Bellmore, Long Island. They have a lunch counter, and, among other things, also sell magazines including some so-called "girlie" magazines. Appellant was prosecuted under two informations, each in two counts, which charged that he personally sold a 16-year-old boy two "girlie" magazines on each of two dates in October 1965, in violation of §484-h of the New York Penal Law, McKinney's Consol. Laws, c. 40. He was . . . found guilty on both counts. The judge found (1) that the magazines contained pictures which depicted female "nudity" in a manner defined in subsection 1(b), that is "the showing of . . . female . . . buttocks with less than a full opaque covering, or the showing of the female breast with less than a fully opaque covering of any portion thereof below the top of the nipple . . . ," and (2) that the pictures were "harmful to minors" in that they had, within the meaning of subsection 1(f) "that quality of . . . representation . . . of nudity . . . [which] . . . (i) predominantly appeals to the prurient, shameful or morbid interest of minors, and (ii) is patently offensive to prevailing standards in the adult community as a whole with respect to what is suitable material for minors, and (iii) is utterly without redeeming social importance for minors." He held that both sales to the 16-year-old boy therefore constituted the violation under §484-h of "knowingly to sell . . . to a minor" under 17 of "(a) any picture . . . which depicts nudity . . . and which is harmful to minors," and "(b) any . . . magazine . . . which contains . . . [such pictures] . . . and which, taken as a whole, is harmful to minors." . . . We affirm.

I

The "girlie" picture magazines involved in the sales here are not obscene for adults. . . . Section 484-h does not bar the appellant from stocking the magazines and selling them to persons 17 years of age or older, and therefore the conviction is not invalid under our decision in Butler v. State of Michigan, 352 U.S. 380.

Obscenity is not within the area of protected speech or press. Roth v. United States, 354 U.S. 476, 485. The three-pronged test of subsection I(f) for judging the obscenity of material sold to minors under 17 is a variable from the formulation for determining obscenity under *Roth.* . . . Appellant's primary attack upon §484-h is leveled at the power of the State to adapt this . . . formulation to define the material's obscenity on the basis of its appeal to minors, and thus exclude material so defined from the area of protected expression. He makes no argument that the magazines are not "harmful to minors" within the definition in subsection I(f). Thus "[n]o issue is presented . . . concerning the obscenity of the material involved." *Roth*, 354 U.S., at 481.

The New York Court of Appeals "upheld the Legislature's power to employ variable concepts of obscenity"[4] in a case in which the same challenge to state power to enact such a law was also addressed to §484-h. Bookcase, Inc. v. Broderick, 18 N.Y.2d 71, 271 N.Y.S.2d 947, 218 N.E.2d 668, appeal dismissed for want of a properly presented federal question, *sub nom.* Bookcase, Inc. v. Leary, 385 U.S. 12. In sustaining state power to enact the law, the Court of Appeals said, Bookcase, Inc. v. Broderick, 18 N.Y.2d, p. 75, 271 N.Y.S.2d, p. 952, 218 N.E.2d, p. 671:

> [M]aterial which is protected for distribution to adults is not necessarily consti-tutionally protected from restriction upon its dissemination to children. In other words, the concept of obscenity or of unprotected matter may vary according to the group to whom the questionable material is directed or from whom it is quaran-tined. Because of the State's exigent interest in preventing distribution to children of objectionable material, it can exercise its power to protect the health, safety, welfare and morals of its community by barring the distribution to children of books recognized to be suitable for adults.

Appellant's attack is not that New York was without power to draw the line at age 17. Rather, his contention is the broad proposition that the scope of the constitutional freedom of expression secured to a citizen to read or see material concerned with sex cannot be made to depend upon whether the citizen is an adult or a minor. He accordingly insists that the denial to minors under 17 of access to material condemned by §484-h, insofar as that material is not obscene for persons 17 years of age or older, constitutes an unconstitutional deprivation of protected liberty.

We have no occasion in this case to consider the impact of the guarantees of freedom of expression upon the totality of the relationship of the minor and the State. It is enough for the purposes of this case that we inquire whether it was constitutionally impermissible for New York, insofar as §484-h does so, to accord minors under 17 a more restricted right than that assured to adults. . . . We conclude that we cannot say that the statute invades the area of freedom of expression constitutionally secured to minors.

---

[4] People v. Tannenbaum, 18 N.Y.2d 268, 270, 274 N.Y.S.2d 131, 133, 220 N.E.2d 783, 785, dismissed as moot, 388 U.S. 439. The concept of variable obscenity is developed in Lockhart & McClure, Censorship of Obscenity: The Developing Constitutional Standards, 45 Minn. L. Rev. 5 (1960). At 85 the authors state:

> Variable obscenity . . . furnishes a useful analytical tool for dealing with the problem of denying adolescents access to material aimed at a primary audience of sexually mature adults. For variable obscenity focuses attention upon the make-up of primary and periph-eral audiences in varying circumstances, and provides a reasonably satisfactory means for delineating the obscene in each circumstance.

Appellant argues that there is an invasion of protected rights under §484-h constitutionally indistinguishable from the invasions under the Nebraska statute forbidding children to study German, which was struck down in Meyer v. State of Nebraska, 262 U.S. 390; the Oregon statute interfering with children's attendance at private and parochial schools, which was struck down in Pierce v. Society of Sisters of the Holy Names of Jesus and Mary, 268 U.S. 510; and the statute compelling children against their religious scruples to give the flag salute, which was struck down in West Virginia State Board of Education v. Barnette, 319 U.S. 624. We reject that argument. We do not regard New York's regulation in defining obscenity on the basis of its appeal to minors under 17 as involving an invasion of such minors' constitutionally protected freedoms. Rather §484-h simply adjusts the definition of obscenity "to social realities by permitting the appeal of this type of material to be assessed in term of the sexual interests . . . " of such minors. Mishkin v. State of New York, 383 U.S. 502, 509; Bookcase, Inc. v. Broderick, supra, 18 N.Y.2d, at 75, 271 N.Y.S.2d, at 951, 218 N.E.2d, at 671. That the State has power to make that adjustment seems clear, for we have recognized that even where there is an invasion of protected freedoms "the power of the state to control the conduct of children reaches beyond the scope of its authority over adults. . . . " Prince v. Commonwealth of Massachusetts, 321 U.S. 158, 170.[6] . . .

[T]wo interests justify the limitations in §484-h upon the availability of sex material to minors under 17, at least if it was rational for the legislature to find that the minors' exposure to such material might be harmful. First of all, constitutional interpretation has consistently recognized that the parents' claim to authority in their own household to direct the rearing of their children is basic in the structure of our society. "It is cardinal with us that the custody, care and nurture of the child reside first in the parents, whose primary function and freedom include preparation for obligations the state can neither supply nor hinder." Prince v. Commonwealth of Massachusetts, supra, at 166. The legislature could properly conclude that parents and others, teachers for example, who have this primary responsibility for children's well-being are entitled to the support of laws designed to aid discharge of that

---

[6] Many commentators, including many committed to the proposition that "[n]o general restriction on expression in terms of 'obscenity' can . . . be reconciled with the first amendment," recognize that "the power of the state to control the conduct of children reaches beyond the scope of its authority over adults," and accordingly acknowledge a supervening state interest in the regulation of literature sold to children, Emerson, Toward a General Theory of the First Amendment, 72 Yale L.J. 877, 938, 939 (1963):

> Different factors come into play, also, where the interest at stake is the effect of erotic expression upon children. The world of children is not strictly part of the adult realm of free expression. The factor of immaturity, and perhaps other considerations, impose different rules. Without attempting here to formulate the principles relevant to freedom of expression for children, it suffices to say that regulations of communication addressed to them need not conform to the requirements of the first amendment in the same way as those applicable to adults.

. . . Prince v. Commonwealth of Massachusetts is urged to be constitutional authority for such regulation. See, e.g., [R. Kuh, Foolish Figleaves? 258-260 (1967)]; Comment, Exclusion of Children from Violent Movies, 67 Col. L. Rev. 1149, 1159-1160 (1967); Note, Constitutional Problems in Obscenity Legislation Protecting Children, 54 Geo. L.J. 1379 (1966).

responsibility. . . . Moreover, the prohibition against sales to minors does not bar parents who so desire from purchasing the magazines for their children.

The State also has an independent interest in the well-being of its youth. . . . Judge Fuld . . . emphasized its significance in the earlier case of People v. Kahan, 15 N.Y.2d 311, 258 N.Y.S.2d 391, 206 N.E.2d 333, which had struck down the first version of §484-h on grounds of vagueness. In his concurring opinion, 15 N.Y.2d, at 312, 258 N.Y.S.2d, at 392, 206 N.E.2d, at 334, he said:

> While the supervision of children's reading may best be left to their parents, the knowledge that parental control or guidance cannot always be provided — and society's transcendent interest in protecting the welfare of children justify reasonable regulation of the sale of material to them. It is, therefore, altogether fitting and proper for a state to include in a statute designed to regulate the sale of pornography to children special standards, broader than those embodied in legislation aimed at controlling dissemination of such material to adults.

In Prince v. Commonwealth of Massachusetts, supra, 321 U.S., at 165, this Court, too, recognized that the State has an interest "to protect the welfare of children" and to see that they are "safeguarded from abuses." . . . The only question remaining, therefore, is whether the New York Legislature might rationally conclude, as it has, the exposure to the materials proscribed by §484-h constitutes such an "abuse."

Section 484-e of the law states a legislative finding that the material condemned by §484-h is "a basic factor in impairing the ethical and moral development of our youth and a clear and present danger to the people of the state." It is very doubtful that this finding expresses an accepted scientific fact. But obscenity is not protected expression and may be suppressed without a showing of the circumstances which lie behind the "clear and present danger" in its application to protected speech. Roth v. United States, supra, 354 U.S., at 486-487.[9] To sustain state power to exclude material defined as obscenity by §484-h requires only that we be able to say that it was not irrational for the legislature to find that exposure to material condemned by the statute is harmful to minors. In Meyer v. State of Nebraska, supra, 262 U.S., at 400, we were able to say that children's knowledge of the German language "cannot reasonably be regarded as harmful." That cannot be said by us of minors' reading and seeing sex material. To be sure, there is no lack of "studies" which purport to demonstrate that obscenity is or is not "a basic factor in impairing the ethical and moral development of . . . youth and a clear and present danger to the people of the state." But the growing consensus of commentators is that "while these studies all agree that a causal link has not been demonstrated, they are equally agreed that a causal link has not been disproved either."[10] We do not demand of legislatures

---

[9] Our conclusion in *Roth*, 354 U.S., at 486-487, that the clear and present danger test was irrelevant to the determination of obscenity made it unnecessary in that case to consider the debate among the authorities whether exposure to pornography caused antisocial consequences.

[10] Magrath, [The Obscenity Cases: Grapes of *Roth*, 1966 Sup. Ct. Rev. 1, 52]. See, e.g., id., at 49-56; Dibble, Obscenity: A State Quarantine to Protect Children, 39 So. Cal. L. Rev. 345 (1966); Wall, Obscenity and Youth: The Problem and a Possible Solution, Crim. L. Bull., Vol. 1, No. 8, pp. 28, 30 (1965); Note, 55 Cal. L. Rev. 926, 934 (1967); Comment, 34 Ford. L. Rev. 692, 694 (1966).

"scientifically certain criteria of legislation." Noble State Bank v. Haskell, 219 U.S. 104, 110. We therefore cannot say that §484-h, in defining the obscenity of material on the basis of its appeal to minors under 17, has no rational relation to the objective of safeguarding such minors from harm.

[The Court also rejected appellant's claims that subsections (f) and (g) of §484-h were void for vagueness, and that the statute lacked a sufficient scienter requirement.]

Affirmed.

Mr. Justice STEWART, concurring in the result.

A doctrinaire, knee-jerk application of the First Amendment would, of course, dictate the nullification of this New York statute. But that result is not required, I think, if we bear in mind what it is that the First Amendment protects.

The First Amendment guarantees liberty of human expression in order to preserve in our Nation what Mr. Justice Holmes called a "free trade in ideas." To that end, the Constitution protects more than just a man's freedom to say or write or publish what he wants. It secures as well the liberty of each man to decide for himself what he will read and to what he will listen. The Constitution guarantees, in short, a society of free choice. Such a society presupposes the capacity of its members to choose.

When expression occurs in a setting where the capacity to make a choice is absent, government regulation of that expression may co-exist with and even implement First Amendment guarantees. . . .

I think a State may permissibly determine that, at least in some precisely delineated areas, a child — like someone in a captive audience — is not possessed of

---

See also J. Paul & M. Schwartz, Federal Censorship: Obscenity in the Mail 191-192; Blakey, Book Review, 41 Notre Dame Law. 1055, 1060, n.46 (1966); Green, Obscenity, Censorship, and Juvenile Delinquency, 14 U. Toronto L. Rev. 229, 249 (1962); Lockhart & McClure, Literature, The Law of Obscenity, and the Constitution, 38 Minn. L. Rev. 295, 373-385 (1954); Note, 52 Ky. L.J. 429, 447 (1964). But despite the vigor of the ongoing controversy whether obscene material will perceptibly create a danger of antisocial conduct, or will probably induce its recipients to such conduct, a medical practitioner recently suggested that the possibility of harmful effects to youth cannot be dismissed as frivolous. Dr. Gaylin of the Columbia University Psychoanalytic Clinic, reporting on the views of some psychiatrists in 77 Yale L.J., at 592-593, said:

> It is in the period of growth [of youth] when these patterns of behavior are laid down, when environmental stimuli of all sorts must be integrated into a workable sense of self, when sensuality is being defined and fears elaborated, when pleasure confronts security and impulse encounters control — it is in this period, undramatically and with time, that legalized pornography may conceivably be damaging.

Dr. Gaylin emphasizes that a child might not be as well prepared as an adult to make an intelligent choice as to the material he chooses to read:

> [P]sychiatrists . . . made a distinction between the reading of pornography, as unlikely to be per se harmful, and the permitting of the reading of pornography, which was conceived as potentially destructive. The child is protected in his reading of pornography by the knowledge that it is pornographic, i.e., disapproved. It is outside of parental standards and not a part of his identification processes. To openly permit implies parental approval and even suggests seductive encouragement. If this is so of parental approval, it is equally so of societal approval — another potent influence on the developing ego. Id., at 594.

that full capacity for individual choice which is the presupposition of First Amendment guarantees. It is only upon such a premise, I should suppose, that a State may deprive children of other rights — the right to marry, for example, or the right to vote — deprivations that would be constitutionally intolerable for adults.

I cannot hold that this state law, on its face, violates the First and Fourteenth Amendments.

Mr. Justice FORTAS dissenting.

This is a criminal prosecution. Sam Ginsberg and his wife operate a luncheonette at which magazines are offered for sale. A 16-year-old boy was enlisted by his mother to go the luncheonette and buy some "girlie" magazines so that Ginsberg could be prosecuted. He went there, picked two magazines from a display case, paid for them, and walked out. Ginsberg's offense was duly reported. . . . Ginsberg was prosecuted and convicted. The court imposed only a suspended sentence. But as the majority here points out, under New York law this conviction may mean that Ginsberg will lose the license necessary to operate his luncheonette.

The two magazines that the 16-year-old boy selected are vulgar "girlie" periodicals. However tasteless and tawdry they may be, we have ruled (as the Court acknowledges) that magazines indistinguishable from them in content and offensiveness are not "obscene" within the constitutional standards heretofore applied. These rulings have been in cases involving adults.

The Court avoids facing the problem whether the magazines in the present case are "obscene" when viewed by a 16-year-old boy, although not "obscene" when viewed by someone 17 years of age or older. It says that Ginsberg's lawyer did not choose to challenge the conviction on the ground that the magazines are not "obscene." He chose only to attack the statute on its face. Therefore, the Court reasons, we need not look at the magazines and determine whether they may be excluded from the ambit of the First Amendment as "obscene" for purposes of this case. . . .

In my judgment, the Court cannot properly avoid its fundamental duty to define "obscenity" for purposes of censorship of material sold to youths, merely because of counsel's position. By so doing the Court avoids the essence of the problem; for if the State's power to censor freed from the prohibitions of the First Amendment depends upon obscenity, and if obscenity turns on the specific content of the publication, how can we sustain the conviction here without deciding whether the particular magazines in question are obscene?

The Court certainly cannot mean that the States and cities and counties and villages have unlimited power to withhold anything and everything that is written or pictorial from younger people. But it here justifies the conviction of Sam Ginsberg because the impact of the Constitution, it says, is variable, and what is not obscene for an adult may be obscene for a child. This it calls "variable obscenity." I do not disagree with this, but I insist that to assess the principle — certainly to apply it — the Court must define it. We must know the extent to which literature or pictures may be less offensive than *Roth* requires in order to be "obscene" for purposes of a statute confined to youth. See Roth v. United States, 354 U.S. 476 (1957).

I agree that the State in the exercise of its police power — even in the First Amendment domain — may make proper and careful differentiation between adults and children. But I do not agree that this power may be used on an arbitrary, free-wheeling basis. This is not a case where, on any standard enunciated by the Court, the magazines are obscene, nor one where the seller is at fault. . . .

The conviction of Ginsberg on the present facts is a serious invasion of freedom. To sustain the conviction without inquiry as to whether the material is "obscene" . . . in face of this Court's asserted solicitude for First Amendment values is to give the State a role in the rearing of children which is contrary to our traditions and to our conception of family responsibility. It begs the question to present this undefined, unlimited censorship as an aid to parents in the rearing of their children. This decision does not merely protect children from activities which all sensible parents would condemn. Rather, its undefined and unlimited approval of state censorship in this area denies to children free access to books and works of art to which many parents may wish their children to have uninhibited access. For denial of access to these magazines, without any standard or definition of their allegedly distinguishing characteristics, is also denial of access to great works of art and literature. . . .

[Justice Douglas, joined by Justice Black, dissented in an opinion that is omitted.]

Ashcroft v. American Civil Liberties Union (*Ashcroft II*)
124 S. Ct. 2783 (2004)

Justice KENNEDY delivered the opinion of the Court.

This case presents a challenge to a statute enacted by Congress to protect minors from exposure to sexually explicit materials on the Internet, the Child Online Protection Act (COPA). 112 Stat. 2681-736, codified at 47 U.S.C. §231. We must decide whether the Court of Appeals was correct to affirm a ruling by the District Court that enforcement of COPA should be enjoined because the statute likely violates the First Amendment. . . .

COPA is the second attempt by Congress to make the Internet safe for minors by criminalizing certain Internet speech. The first attempt was the Communications Decency Act of 1996, Pub.L. 104-104, §502, 110 Stat. 133, 47 U.S.C. §223 (1994 ed., Supp. II). The Court held the CDA unconstitutional because it was not narrowly tailored to serve a compelling governmental interest and because less restrictive alternatives were available [Reno v. American Civil Liberties Union, 521 U.S. 844 (1997)]. In response to the Court's decision in *Reno*, Congress passed COPA. COPA imposes criminal penalties of a $50,000 fine and six months in prison for the knowing posting, for "commercial purposes," of World Wide Web content that is "harmful to minors." §231(a)(1). Material that is "harmful to minors" is defined as:

> "any communication, picture, image, graphic image file, article, recording, writing, or other matter of any kind that is obscene or that—
>
>> "(A) the average person, applying contemporary community standards, would find, taking the material as a whole and with respect to minors, is designed to appeal to, or is designed to pander to, the prurient interest;"
>>
>> "(B) depicts, describes, or represents, in a manner patently offensive with respect to minors, an actual or simulated sexual act or sexual contact, an actual

or simulated normal or perverted sexual act, or a lewd exhibition of the genitals or post-pubescent female breast; and

"(C) taken as a whole, lacks serious literary, artistic, political, or scientific value for minors." §231(e)(6).

"Minors" are defined as "any person under 17 years of age." §231(e)(7). A person acts for "commercial purposes only if such person is engaged in the business of making such communications." "Engaged in the business," in turn,

"means that the person who makes a communication, or offers to make a communication, by means of the World Wide Web, that includes any material that is harmful to minors, devotes time, attention, or labor to such activities, as a regular course of such person's trade or business, with the objective of earning a profit as a result of such activities (although it is not necessary that the person make a profit or that the making or offering to make such communications be the person's sole or principal business or source of income)." §231(e)(2).

While the statute labels all speech that falls within these definitions as criminal speech, it also provides an affirmative defense to those who employ specified means to prevent minors from gaining access to the prohibited materials on their Web site. A person may escape conviction under the statute by demonstrating that he

"has restricted access by minors to material that is harmful to minors —

"(A) by requiring use of a credit card, debit account, adult access code, or adult personal identification number;

"(B) by accepting a digital certificate that verifies age, or

"(C) by any other reasonable measures that are feasible under available technology." §231(c)(1). . . .

[Respondents, Internet content providers, and others concerned with protecting the freedom of speech filed suit in federal district court seeking a preliminary injunction against enforcement of the statute. The District Court granted the injunction, holding that the statute would burden some protected speech and concluding that respondents were likely to prevail because there were less restrictive alternatives to the statute. The Court of Appeals affirmed but on a different ground, concluding that the "community standards" language in COPA rendered the statute unconstitutionally overbroad. The United States Supreme Court reversed, holding that the community-standards language did not, standing alone, make the statute unconstitutionally overbroad. Ashcroft v. American Civil Liberties Union, 535 U.S. 564, 585 (2002) (*Ashcroft I*). The Court remanded the case to the Court of Appeals to reconsider whether the District Court had been correct to grant the preliminary injunction. On remand, the Court of Appeals again affirmed, concluding that the statute was not narrowly tailored to serve a compelling government interest, was overbroad, and was not the least restrictive means available for the government to serve the interest of preventing minors from using the Internet to gain access to materials that are harmful to them. 322 F.3d 240 (2003). The government again sought review, and the Supreme Court again granted certiorari.]

[W]e agree with the Court of Appeals that the District Court did not abuse its discretion in entering the preliminary injunction. Our reasoning in support of this conclusion, however, is based on a narrower, more specific grounds than the rationale the Court of Appeals adopted. . . . Because we affirm the District Court's decision to grant the preliminary injunction for the reasons relied on by the District

Court, we decline to consider the correctness of the other arguments relied on by the Court of Appeals. . . .

In considering [a challenge to a content-based speech restriction], a court assumes that certain protected speech may be regulated, and then asks what is the least restrictive alternative that can be used to achieve that goal. The purpose of the test is not to consider whether the challenged restriction has some effect in achieving Congress' goal, regardless of the restriction it imposes. The purpose of the test is to ensure that speech is restricted no further than necessary to achieve the goal, for it is important to assure that legitimate speech is not chilled or punished. . . .

In deciding whether to grant a preliminary injunction stage, a district court must consider whether the plaintiffs have demonstrated that they are likely to prevail on the merits. . . . As the Government bears the burden of proof on the ultimate question of COPA's constitutionality, respondents must be deemed likely to prevail unless the Government has shown that respondents' proposed less restrictive alternatives are less effective than COPA. Applying that analysis, the District Court concluded that respondents were likely to prevail. That conclusion was not an abuse of discretion, because on this record there are a number of plausible, less restrictive alternatives to the statute.

The primary alternative considered by the District Court was blocking and filtering software. Blocking and filtering software is an alternative that is less restrictive than COPA, and, in addition, likely more effective as a means of restricting children's access to materials harmful to them. The District Court, in granting the preliminary injunction, did so primarily because the plaintiffs had proposed that filters are a less restrictive alternative to COPA and the Government had not shown it would be likely to disprove the plaintiffs' contention at trial.

Filters are less restrictive than COPA. They impose selective restrictions on speech at the receiving end, not universal restrictions at the source. Under a filtering regime, adults without children may gain access to speech they have a right to see without having to identify themselves or provide their credit card information. Even adults with children may obtain access to the same speech on the same terms simply by turning off the filter on their home computers. Above all, promoting the use of filters does not condemn as criminal any category of speech, and so the potential chilling effect is eliminated, or at least much diminished. All of these things are true, moreover, regardless of how broadly or narrowly the definitions in COPA are construed.

Filters also may well be more effective than COPA. First, a filter can prevent minors from seeing all pornography, not just pornography posted to the Web from America. The District Court noted in its factfindings that one witness estimated that 40% of harmful-to-minors content comes from overseas [31 F. Supp. 2d at 484]. COPA does not prevent minors from having access to those foreign harmful materials. That alone makes it possible that filtering software might be more effective in serving Congress' goals. Effectiveness is likely to diminish even further if COPA is upheld, because the providers of the materials that would be covered by the statute simply can move their operations overseas. It is not an answer to say that COPA reaches some amount of materials that are harmful to minors; the question is whether it would reach more of them than less restrictive alternatives. In addition, the District Court found that verification systems may be subject to evasion and circumvention, for example by minors who have their own credit cards. See id., at 484, 496-497. Finally, filters also may be more effective because they can be applied to all forms of Internet communication, including e-mail, not just communications available via the World Wide Web.

That filtering software may well be more effective than COPA is confirmed by the findings of the Commission on Child Online Protection, a blue-ribbon commission created by Congress in COPA itself. Congress directed the Commission to evaluate the relative merits of different means of restricting minors' ability to gain access to harmful materials on the Internet. Note following 47 U.S.C. §231. It unambiguously found that filters are more effective than age-verification requirements. See Commission on Child Online Protection (COPA), Report to Congress, at 19-21, 23-25, 27 (Oct. 20, 2000) (assigning a score for "Effectiveness" of 7.4 for server-based filters and 6.5 for client-based filters, as compared to 5.9 for independent adult-id verification, and 5.5 for credit card verification). Thus, not only has the Government failed to carry its burden of showing the District Court that the proposed alternative is less effective, but also a Government Commission appointed to consider the question has concluded just the opposite. That finding supports our conclusion that the District Court did not abuse its discretion in enjoining the statute.

Filtering software, of course, is not a perfect solution to the problem of children gaining access to harmful-to-minors materials. It may block some materials that are not harmful to minors and fail to catch some that are. Whatever the deficiencies of filters, however, the Government failed to introduce specific evidence proving that existing technologies are less effective than the restrictions in COPA. The District Court made a specific factfinding that "[n]o evidence was presented to the Court as to the percentage of time that blocking and filtering technology is over- or underinclusive." Ibid. In the absence of a showing as to the relative effectiveness of COPA and the alternatives proposed by respondents, it was not an abuse of discretion for the District Court to grant the preliminary injunction. The Government's burden is not merely to show that a proposed less restrictive alternative has some flaws; its burden is to show that it is less effective. *Reno*, 521 U.S., at 874. It is not enough for the Government to show that COPA has some effect. Nor do respondents bear a burden to introduce, or offer to introduce, evidence that their proposed alternatives are more effective. The Government has the burden to show they are less so. The Government having failed to carry its burden, it was not an abuse of discretion for the District Court to grant the preliminary injunction.

One argument to the contrary is worth mentioning — the argument that filtering software is not an available alternative because Congress may not require it to be used. That argument carries little weight, because Congress undoubtedly may act to encourage the use of filters. We have held that Congress can give strong incentives to schools and libraries to use them. United States v. American Library Assn., Inc., 539 U.S. 194 (2003). It could also take steps to promote their development by industry, and their use by parents. It is incorrect, for that reason, to say that filters are part of the current regulatory status quo. The need for parental cooperation does not automatically disqualify a proposed less restrictive alternative. [United States v. Playboy Entertainment Group, 529 U.S. 803, 824 (2000) ("A court should not assume a plausible, less restrictive alternative would be ineffective; and a court should not presume parents, given full information, will fail to act").] In enacting

COPA, Congress said its goal was to prevent the "widespread availability of the Internet" from providing "opportunities for minors to access materials through the World Wide Web in a manner that can frustrate parental supervision or control." Congressional Findings, note following 47 U.S.C. §231 (quoting Pub.L. 105-277, Tit. XIV, §1402(1), 112 Stat. 2681-736). COPA presumes that parents lack the ability, not the will, to monitor what their children see. By enacting programs to promote use of filtering software, Congress could give parents that ability without subjecting protected speech to severe penalties.

The closest precedent on the general point is our decision in *Playboy Entertainment Group* [529 U.S. 803, 824 (2000)]. *Playboy Entertainment Group*, like this case, involved a content-based restriction designed to protect minors from viewing harmful materials. The choice was between a blanket speech restriction and a more specific technological solution that was available to parents who chose to implement it. Absent a showing that the proposed less restrictive alternative would not be as effective, we concluded, the more restrictive option preferred by Congress could not survive strict scrutiny. Id., at 826 (reversing because "[t]he record is silent as to the comparative effectiveness of the two alternatives"). In the instant case, too, the Government has failed to show, at this point, that the proposed less restrictive alternative will be less effective. The reasoning of *Playboy Entertainment Group*, and the holdings and force of our precedents require us to affirm the preliminary injunction. To do otherwise would be to do less than the First Amendment commands. "The starch in our constitutional standards cannot be sacrificed to accommodate the enforcement choices of the Government." Id., at 830 (Thomas, J., concurring).

There are also important practical reasons to let the injunction stand pending a full trial on the merits. First, the potential harms from reversing the injunction outweigh those of leaving it in place by mistake. Where a prosecution is a likely possibility, yet only an affirmative defense is available, speakers may self-censor rather than risk the perils of trial. There is a potential for extraordinary harm and a serious chill upon protected speech. Cf. id., at 817 ("Error in marking that line exacts an extraordinary cost"). The harm done from letting the injunction stand pending a trial on the merits, in contrast, will not be extensive. No prosecutions have yet been undertaken under the law, so none will be disrupted if the injunction stands. Further, if the injunction is upheld, the Government in the interim can enforce obscenity laws already on the books.

Second, there are substantial factual disputes remaining in the case. As mentioned above, there is a serious gap in the evidence as to the effectiveness of filtering software. For us to assume, without proof, that filters are less effective than COPA would usurp the District Court's factfinding role. By allowing the preliminary injunction to stand and remanding for trial, we require the Government to shoulder its full constitutional burden of proof respecting the less restrictive alternative argument, rather than excuse it from doing so.

Third, and on a related point, the factual record does not reflect current technological reality — a serious flaw in any case involving the Internet. The technology of the Internet evolves at a rapid pace. Yet the factfindings of the District Court were entered in February 1999, over five years ago. Since then, certain facts about the Internet are known to have changed. Compare, e.g., 31 F. Supp. 2d, at 481 (36.7 million Internet hosts as of July 1998) with Internet Systems Consortium,

Internet Domain Survey, Jan. 2004, *http://www.isc.org/index.pl?/ops/ds* (as visited June 22, 2004, and available in the Clerk of Court's case file) (233.1 million hosts as of Jan. 2004). It is reasonable to assume that other technological developments important to the First Amendment analysis have also occurred during that time. More and better filtering alternatives may exist than when the District Court entered its findings. Indeed, we know that after the District Court entered its factfindings, a congressionally appointed commission issued a report that found that filters are more effective than verification screens. See supra, at 8.

Delay between the time that a district court makes factfindings and the time that a case reaches this Court is inevitable, with the necessary consequence that there will be some discrepancy between the facts as found and the facts at the time the appellate court takes up the question. . . . [Here] the usual gap has doubled because the case has been through the Court of Appeals twice. The additional two years might make a difference. By affirming the preliminary injunction and remanding for trial, we allow the parties to update and supplement the factual record to reflect current technological realities.

Remand will also permit the District Court to take account of a changed legal landscape. Since the District Court made its factfindings, Congress has passed at least two further statutes that might qualify as less restrictive alternatives to COPA — a prohibition on misleading domain names, and a statute creating a minors-safe "Dot Kids" domain. Remanding for trial will allow the District Court to take into account those additional potential alternatives.

On a final point, it is important to note that this opinion does not hold that Congress is incapable of enacting any regulation of the Internet designed to prevent minors from gaining access to harmful materials. The parties, because of the conclusion of the Court of Appeals that the statute's definitions rendered it unconstitutional, did not devote their attention to the question whether further evidence might be introduced on the relative restrictiveness and effectiveness of alternatives to the statute. On remand, however, the parties will be able to introduce further evidence on this point. This opinion does not foreclose the District Court from concluding, upon a proper showing by the Government that meets the Government's constitutional burden as defined in this opinion, that COPA is the least restrictive alternative available to accomplish Congress' goal.

On this record, the Government has not shown that the less restrictive alternatives proposed by respondents should be disregarded. . . . The judgment of the Court of Appeals is affirmed, and the case is remanded for proceedings consistent with this opinion. . . .

NOTE: U.S. COMMISSION ON OBSCENITY AND PORNOGRAPHY, REPORT: DRAFT OF PROPOSED LEGISLATION — SALE AND DISPLAY OF EXPLICIT SEXUAL MATERIAL TO YOUNG PERSONS (1970)[25]

The purpose of the Commission's proposed legislation is "to regulate the direct commercial distribution of certain explicit sexual materials to young persons in

---

[25] The federal government established two commissions to study pornography and issue recommendations. In 1967 President Lyndon Johnson created the U.S. Commission on Obscenity and

order to aid parents in supervising and controlling the access of children to such materials. The legislature finds that whatever social value such material may have for young persons can adequately be served by its availability to young persons through their parents." Id. at 66.

The proposed statute prohibits the knowing distribution or display for sale of "explicit sexual material" to young persons. However, if the material has "artistic, literacy, historical, scientific, medical, educational or other similar social values for adults," it is not prohibited. The statute covers pictorial or three-dimensional material including but not limited to books, magazines, films, photographs and statuary, but it does not include broadcasts or telecasts by facilities licensed under the Federal Communications Act, 47 U.S.C. §§30 et seq. Distribution with a parent's consent or to a married young person is not prohibited. Id. at 66-67.

In its Report, the Commission limited its obscenity regulation to "young persons" because of the lack of empirical proof that a causal relationship exists between adult exposure to sexual material and crime or emotional abnormalities. Id. at 52. Due to the serious ethical problems involved in experimentally exposing children to sexual materials, no such conclusion can be reached in regard to children. Also, the Commission was influenced, to a considerable degree, by its finding that a large majority of Americans believe that children should not be exposed to certain sexual materials. Therefore, the Commission leaves the ultimate decision to parents as to whether their children should be exposed to sexual material. Id. at 57.

The proposed legislation is limited to pictorial material because of the existence of many textual works which are explicit, yet valuable to young people. The Commission believes it could not create a clear legal distinction between harmful text and valuable text. Further, commercial distributors and dealers might seriously curtail their distribution for fear of violating a vague law. Id. at 58. "The speculative risk of harm to juveniles from some textual material does not justify these dangers," said the Commission. Id. at 60.

DISCUSSION OF *GINSBERG* AND *ASHCROFT II*: STATE REGULATION OF SEXUALLY EXPLICIT MATERIALS

(1) The Role of the State

a. A Different Standard for Children?   Why does *Ginsberg* uphold a statute regulating minors' access to sexually explicit materials (permitting a variable standard for obscenity) whereas *Ashcroft II* enjoins enforcement of such a statute? What rationale does the majority in *Ginsberg* offer to explain why the standard for obscenity should be different for adults and children? Why does *Ashcroft II* find that the statute with its variable standard would likely violate the First Amendment?

Pornography (sometimes termed the "Lockhart Commission" after its chairperson, constitutional scholar William Lockhart). In 1985 President Ronald Reagan requested the Attorney General to establish a second commission — the U.S. Attorney General's Commission on Pornography (commonly referred to as the "Meese Commission" after then-Attorney General Edwin Meese). For a discussion of these commissions, see generally Gordon Hawkins & Franklin E. Zimring, Pornography in a Free Society (1988).

The U.S. Commission on Obscenity and Pornography (supra pp. 92-93) in 1970 also advocated different standards for adults and children. What rationale does the Commission offer for its "two-tier" proposals — the repeal of all obscenity laws for adults but some limitations for children? Are you persuaded by the Commission's justification?

Compare the following theories about a variable standard. Professor Thomas Emerson, who wrote extensively on the First Amendment, suggests that for adults there should be no governmental restriction of expression on grounds of obscenity. As footnote 6 of the *Ginsberg* opinion indicates, however, Professor Emerson thought differently with regard to children. He subsequently elaborated:

> A system of freedom of expression . . . cannot and does not treat children on the same basis as adults. The world of children is not the same as the world of adults, so far as a guarantee of untrammeled freedom of the mind is concerned. The reason for this is, as Justice Stewart said in *Ginsberg*, that a child "is not possessed of that full capacity for individual choice which is the presupposition of the First Amendment guarantees." He is not permitted that measure of independence, or able to exercise that maturity of judgment, which a system of free expression rests upon. This does not mean that the First Amendment extends no protection to children; it does mean that children are governed by different rules. This differentiation concerns one of the most delicate aspects of the obscenity problem and embodies a key concept for dealing with that problem. . . . [Thomas Emerson, The System of Freedom of Expression 496-497 (1970).]

On the other hand, why should the "world of children" not be included fully in the system of free expression? Is it so clear that immaturity requires the imposition of different rules? Consider the following:

> If one of the core purposes of the First Amendment is to prevent the government from using censorship to impose its own political and moral values on the population, then entirely exempting children from that protection would create a gaping hole in that purpose, since after all, most people's values, beliefs, and world views are formed during childhood. Permitting the State to completely control "the ethical and moral development" of minors threatens to produce the worst kind of tyranny — a point made by Judge Posner [in American Amusement Mach. Assn. v. Kendrick, 244 F.3d 572, 576-577 (7th Cir. 2001) (enjoining the enforcement of a municipal ordinance limiting minors' access to violent video games)] using the example of the Hitler Jugend during World War II. [Ashutosh Bhagwat, What If I Want My Kids to Watch Pornography? Protecting Children from "Indecent" Speech, 11 Wm. & Mary Bill Rts. J. 671, 690 (2003).]

Beginning in 1996, Congress enacted several statutes to protect children from harmful material on the Internet. The Child Online Protection Act (COPA), at issue herein, addressed the constitutional infirmities of its predecessor statute (Communications Decency Act of 1996 or CDA) in several ways: targeting only commercial pornographers (rather than both commercial and noncommercial Web site publishers), applying only to Web-based communications (rather than to all Internet communications including e-mails and chat rooms), and defining essential terms (e.g., "by means of the World Wide Web," "commercial purposes," "engaged in business" and limiting the definition of "minor" to those 17 and under). Finally,

COPA narrowed the vague "indecent" and "patently offensive" standard of the CDA to a "harmful to minors" community-based standard incorporating the three-prong Miller v. California test [413 U.S. 15 (1973)] (i.e., appealing to the prurient interest of minors; patently offensive to minors; and lacking serious literary, artistic, political, or scientific value for minors). Susan Hanley Kosse, Try, Try Again: Will Congress Ever Get It Right? A Summary of Internet Pornography Laws Protecting Children and Possible Solutions, 38 U. Rich. L. Rev. 721, 731 (2004).

The difficulty of defining "harmful to minors" has been a shortcoming of both COPA and its predecessor, CDA. Is COPA's standard an improvement compared to the CDA standard? What do the terms "prurient interest," "patently offensive," and "lacking serious literary, artistic, political, or scientific value" mean *with respect to minors*? How does one determine what is "patently offensive" to a 6-year-old as opposed to a 14-year-old? To a 12-year-old girl as opposed to a 16-year-old boy? As one commentator notes:

> It is not clear whether COPA prohibits material that lacks value for all minors, for some minors, or for some variation of the "average" or "reasonable" sixteen-year-old. It is unclear whether minors of a certain age can discern any "value," whether social, political, or literary, in certain materials. A speaker who attempts to satisfy COPA's "harmful to minors" standard may be assigned the hopelessly difficult task of determining whether its content contains "value" for an eight-year-old. . . . [Timothy Zick, Congress, The Internet, and the Intractable Pornography Problem: The Child Online Protection Act of 1998, 32 Creighton L. Rev. 1147, 1194-1195 (1999).]

Based on *Ashcroft II*, would the Supreme Court be likely to uphold a standard incorporating a variable standard for harmful materials on the Internet? Could a sufficiently narrow statute be drafted to surmount a challenge on the ground of vagueness? What should such a statute encompass? Who will determine what material is harmful to minors? Would material be harmful to any minor or only those below a certain age? Would the Court be likely to uphold a standard that varies according to both the age and gender of the minor?

The Supreme Court in Miller v. California, supra (establishing constitutional standards for obscenity) permitted community standards to govern the determination of obscenity. If community standards are relevant in the determination of materials that are harmful to minors, which "community" would apply to the Internet? See Justice Stevens' omitted concurring opinion (in which he is joined by Justice Ginsburg) in *Ashcroft II* (identifying "community standards" as a constitutional deficiency that permits the least tolerant community to determine Internet content). [124 S. Ct. at 2796.]

Ginsberg and *Ashcroft II* address different media and different rules. Is such different context-specific regulation justifiable in an age when the forms of communication are converging? For example, personal computers now have sound and graphic capabilities to display video games, music, and movies. Internet access is possible via modems attached to television cables. What are the implications of this convergence in terms of the standard to be applied to minors' access to sexually explicit materials? Note that broadcasting has received the most limited First Amendment protection. See, e.g., FCC v. Pacifica Foundation, 438 U.S. 726

(1978) (holding that the broadcast of a monologue featuring "Filthy Words" could be subject to administrative sanctions because of its use in an afternoon broadcast when children were in the audience). If sexually explicit materials from the Internet are accessible at any time of day, does that dictate a different result in *Ashcroft II*? See also Reno v. ACLU, 521 U.S. 844, 868-870 (1997) (distinguishing the Internet from broadcasting by suggesting that the former is not invasive).

b. The State's Dual Interests: Effects on Children.   According to *Ginsberg*, two interests justify limitation on the availability of sexually explicit materials to minors: (1) the importance of the parental role in the rearing of their children and (2) the state's "independent interest in the well-being of its youth," specifically youth's "ethical and moral development." In terms of the second interest, did the Court in *Ginsberg* and/or *Ashcroft II* actually find that exposure to sexually explicit materials is harmful to minors? What evidence of harm was considered by the Court in the respective cases? Might such exposure have positive impact? Did the Court in *Ginsberg* and/or *Ashcroft II* presume that the protection of minors was a compelling interest? Or did the Court merely decide that it was rational for the legislature to find such exposure harmful?

Does the government have an appropriate role in protecting the well-being of its youth in terms of inculcating moral and ethical values? Subsequent to *Ginsberg*, the Supreme Court again addressed the government's "independent interest" in protecting children from the harmful influences of sexually explicit material. United States v. Playboy Entertainment Group, 529 U.S. 803 (2000), explored the constitutionality of Section 505 of the Telecommunications Act of 1996 that required cable television operators carrying channels devoted to sexually oriented programs either to block such channels so that no "signal bleed" occurred (i.e., enabling viewers to see fleeting images) or to limit transmission to nighttime hours between 10 P.M. and 6 P.M., when youths presumably would not constitute a significant number of viewers. The Court held that the statutory provision violated the First Amendment absent a showing by the government that the infringement was the least restrictive means of achieving the goal of protecting children (because another provision of the Act provided a less restrictive means for achieving the same end by requiring cable operators to block channels *upon request* by a customer). In reaching its decision, the majority (in an opinion by Justice Kennedy) expressed some skepticism about the existence of a independent governmental interest in protecting children from sexually explicit material. "Even upon the assumption that the Government has an interest in substituting itself for informed and empowered parents, its interest is not sufficiently compelling to justify this widespread restriction on speech." Id. at 825. Cf. Action for Children's Television v. FCC, 58 F.3d 654 (D.C. Cir. 1995) (en banc) (upholding radio and television broadcasting of indecent materials to nighttime hours on the ground that it survived strict scrutiny by being narrowly tailored to advance the government's twin goals of facilitating the parental role and protecting children's ethical and moral development). What are the implications of finding that the government has an "independent interest" in protecting children from sexually explicit material?

The Effects Panel of the first U.S. Commission on Obscenity and Pornography summarized its findings regarding the evidence on the relationship between erotic materials and antisocial behavior as follows:

In its assignment to the Commission "to study the effect of obscenity and pornography upon the public," Congress added for emphasis "and particularly minors, and its relationship to crime and other antisocial behavior" (P.L. 90-100). This emphasis reflects: (a) a long-standing concern that has been voiced by many officials and (b) the state of scientific knowledge at the time the Commission was established.

The paucity of research information regarding the effects of pornography on the antisocial behavior of adults and youth is partly a function of a general sensitivity about the scientific study of private behavior — especially sexual behavior and specifically as it concerns children. The Commission was not immune to social forces restricting research in this area nor to the logistical and methodological difficulties inherent in pioneering efforts. Research that the Commission initiated is, therefore, somewhat more restricted in quantity and in the quality of rigor than that required for unequivocal conclusions. . . .

Two important findings emerge from the studies reviewed:

(a) experience with erotic materials is widespread among American youth; and (b) the experiences of delinquent and nondelinquent youth, thought not identical, are generally similar. The small differences which appear to be in the amount of exposure and the reactions to it, seem to be attributable to age and subcultural variables. Taken together, these data provide no particular support for the thesis that experience with sexual materials is a significant factor in the causation of juvenile delinquency.

There is some evidence that both juvenile misbehavior and certain dimensions of experience with erotic materials may be explained by the subcultural and social processes operative in the home, neighborhood, and school peer groups. . . .

. . . Available research concerning the effects of erotic material upon juveniles has not included experimental studies in which the direction of relationships is more systematically assessed. Continuing fears about the consequences of controlled exposure studies have precluded the accumulation of strong evidence. The generally wide experience of adolescents with sexual materials, however, suggests that concerns about detrimental effects of experimentation may well be unwarranted. . . .

The subsequent Commission on Pornography (established in 1985) also addressed the issue of the effects of pornography. After extensive study, the Meese Commission reported several general findings: (1) extended exposure to pornography increases the belief that less common sexual practices are common; (2) pornography that portrays sexual aggression as pleasurable for the victim increases the acceptance of coercive sexual practices; (3) acceptance of coercive sexuality appears to be related to sexual aggression; and (4) exposure to violent pornography, at least in the laboratory setting, increases punitive behavior toward women. Michael J. McManus, Introduction, Final Report of the Attorney General's Commission on Pornography xviii (1986).

What explains the difference in the findings of the two Commissions? Does the evidence of harm to minors found by the Commission(s) justify proposed restrictions? The first commission draws a distinction between pictorial materials and written materials, in terms of both enforcement and harm. Are these distinctions justified? Are they distinctions of constitutional dimension? Given that exposure to violent pornography appears to foster harmful behavior toward women, do such materials violate women's right to equal protection? See generally Catharine A. MacKinnon, Only Words (1993).

Considering the relevance of the uncertain state of the social science evidence to the questions facing the Supreme Court in *Ginsberg* and *Ashcroft II*, does uncertainty justify a separate standard for children? Or does such a question "miss the point" because it "fail[s] to address the true question: whether the State has a legitimate or compelling interest in inculcating moral and ethical values in children by controlling their access to indecent materials as a step towards creating a morally virtuous citizenry." Bhagwat, supra, at 685. Who should decide whether children should be exposed to sexually explicit materials — parents, children, the legislature, the courts?

(2) The Role of Parents

a. The State versus Parental Role.   As explained above, *Ginsberg* recognizes that the state has a legitimate interest in the regulation of indecent speech in order to support the parental role in childrearing. Does the Court's suggestion in *Ginsberg* that "constitutional interpretation" has consistently recognized the parent's claim to authority in childrearing place *Ginsberg* in the *Pierce-Yoder* tradition that parents decide for children? Or does the suggestion that the state has an independent interest in the well-being of its youth align *Ginsberg* with *Prince* in asserting the power of the state to protect children even over parental opposition?

May the state intervene to prevent a child's access to such materials when: The parents deliberately provide the child with "objectionable" reading? Leave such reading matter lying around the house? Accompany the child to buy such material selected by the child? Give the child a note addressed to a store clerk, saying that the child has their permission to buy sexually oriented reading? Purchase, but fail to install, blocking and filtering software on the home computer? Should any of the above situations provide grounds for a child neglect proceeding? See Chapter 3. Could such parental conduct be made criminal? Suppose the parents' permissive conduct was discovered because the child was selling (or downloading and distributing) the objectionable materials to classmates? Are criminal sanctions an appropriate method of protecting minors from the harm of exposure to sexually explicit materials?

b. Protection of Parents' Rights.   Under the New York statute in *Ginsberg*, parents have the power to permit access to soft-core magazines for their children. Under COPA, children are able to access pornographic and sexually explicit sites and images on the Internet with parental consent. Does such parental power create an inevitable conflict between parents who wish their children to be free to choose and parents who want to protect their children from sexual materials? Effective protection for parents who do not want their children to be exposed might require a flat prohibition on minors' possession of, and Internet access to, objectionable material: children might otherwise show the material to each other. On the other hand, allowing parents to buy material for their children, or to install blocking/filtering software, does not enable permissive parents to allow *the child* free choice to decide what material is of interest. Children may be inhibited from revealing to the permissive parent their interest in material because of embarrassment or fear of parental disapproval. Compare *Ginsberg*'s resolution with the recommendation of the first United States Commission on Obscenity and Pornography.

c. Is Parental Regulation Effective? In *Ashcroft II*, the Supreme Court favors blocking and filtering software as less restrictive alternatives than COPA to regulate speech. Is reliance on parental control and supervision justified to regulate minors' access to sexually explicit materials on the Internet? To what extent should the state assume that parents are capable and/or willing to regulate children's access to inappropriate materials on the Internet? In an omitted dissent, Justice Breyer (joined by Chief Justice Rehnquist and Justice O'Connor) highlights problems with filtering software: It allows some pornographic material to pass through; it costs money (more than age verification); it lacks precision by blocking considerable valuable material; and it depends on parents' willingness to reach a decision about children's access and parents' ability to enforce their decision. 124 S. Ct. at 2802-2803. If the state can demonstrate that parents who are aware of their children's exposure to sexually explicit materials are failing to act, may the state nonetheless regulate such materials in the interests of child protection? See Bhagwat, supra, at 683 (suggesting that the Supreme Court in *Playboy* "leave[s] the door open to [this] possibility").

Can parental or state regulation ever be effective? The first Commission on Pornography found widespread violation of *Ginsberg*-type laws. As long as sexually explicit materials are available to adults (and indeed are constitutionally protected), is it possible to control effectively children's access? Children can be refused admission to movies, but denial of access to books, printed matter, and the Internet is obviously more difficult. Indeed, a system that is so restrictive that bookstore owners tend not to carry books that are banned for children would probably violate Butler v. Michigan, 352 U.S. 380, 383 (1957), where the Supreme Court unanimously invalidated a Michigan law that prohibited the distribution to the general public of material "tending to incite minors to violent or depraved or immoral acts, manifestly tending to the corruption of the morals of youth." Justice Frankfurter characterized the legislation as "quarantining the general reading public against books not too rugged for grown men and women in order to shield juvenile innocence." Id. at 383. This would result, he suggested, in reducing "the adult population of Michigan to reading only what is fit for children." Id.

Is it legitimate to adopt legislation that will probably be ineffective in controlling the access of youth, but that will nevertheless express social disapproval? See Lawrence v. Texas, 539 U.S 558, 571 (2003) (finding unconstitutional as a violation of substantive due process a state sodomy statute, reasoning that the Court's obligation is to "define the liberty of all, not to mandate our own moral code").

What are the appropriate roles of parents and the state in regulating children's access to the Internet? Consider the following view:

[T]he widespread availability of [indecent] material in the larger society makes it virtually impossible for parents to act effectively on their own. Instead, if parents are to have meaningful rights in this area, the community must have the power to regulate the manner in which such material is distributed. . . . Although liberalism presumes that adults are sufficiently autonomous to resist harmful social and cultural influences, this assumption cannot be made with respect to children.

[Steven J. Heyman, Ideological Conflict and the First Amendment, 78 Chi.-Kent
L. Rev. 531, 608-609 (2003).]

Do you agree? Compare Nadine Strossen, William O. Douglas Lecture: Current
Challenges to the First Amendment, 36 Gonz. L. Rev. 279 (2000-01) (opposing gov-
ernmental regulation of the Internet) with Emily Vander Wilt, Considering COPA:
A Look at Congress's Second Attempt to Regulate Indecency on the Internet, 11
Va. J. Soc. Pol'y & L. 373 (2004) (favoring regulation).

Alternatively, should the industry (the content providers and/or service
providers) regulate itself? Is cyberspace "so different from other communication
media that it will, or should, resist all government regulation"? Jack L. Goldsmith,
Against Cyberanarchy, 65 U. Chi. L. Rev. 1199 (1998) (arguing that it is not). What
are the advantages and disadvantages of parental, state, and industry regulation? If
the state facilitates parental control, should it also facilitate the control of those in
loco parentis, such as teachers? For example, should it require public schools and
libraries to use filtering software on their computers to prevent children's access to
sexually explicit materials? See the discussion at p. 128.

(3) The Role of the Child.   Regarding both *Ginsberg* and *Ashcroft II*, to what
extent does a minor's own First Amendment rights constrain the state's power
to limit access to sexually explicit materials? Minors might desire "girlie" magazines for entertainment purposes; however, children access the Internet not only
for entertainment but also for research purposes. Sexually explicit materials on
anatomy that are posted on the Internet, for example, might serve as a resource for
biology students.

Because of the nature of the respective challenges in *Ginsberg* and *Ashcroft II*,
the Supreme Court did not concern itself with this issue. Several decades ago, however, the Court conceded that minors might possess such an interest. In Erznoznik v.
Jacksonville, 422 U.S. 205 (1975), the Court invalidated a Jacksonville, Florida,
ordinance making it illegal for drive-in movies to show films containing nudity.
Rejecting the city's argument that the ordinance was for the protection of children,
the Court indicated that minors do have a "significant measure (id. at 212) of First
Amendment protection. See id. at 214 ("In most circumstances, the values protected
by the First Amendment are no less applicable when government seeks to control
the flow of information to minors.")

More recently, a federal district court in Michigan affirmed that view in
Cyberspace, Communications, Inc. v. Engler, 55 F. Supp. 2d 737 (E.D. Mich. 1999)
(enjoining enforcement of amendments to a state statute that criminalized use of
computers or the Internet to disseminate sexually explicit materials to minors). In
holding that the amendments would have had an adverse effect on public policy
by stifling discussions and were not narrowly tailored, Judge Tarnow vigorously
defended the rights of children to information:

> The Defendants failed to satisfy that the Act will further a compelling interest
> of the State. Plaintiffs though did submit testimony and documentation that such
> an Act could produce a result contrary to the desires of society. The free flow
> of information on the Internet enables a teenager to ask about premarital sex or

sexually transmitted diseases with anonymity. Plaintiffs at the hearing read into the record an example of a teenager asking Dr. Marty Klein, a sex therapist in California and plaintiff in this case, who operates a website entitled "Ask Me Anything", about an encounter with her boyfriend that she incorrectly reasoned was not sexual intercourse. Other examples offered at the hearing include submitted transcripts of chat room discussions concerning contraceptives and abstention. Sometimes words were utilized in these discussions which could be construed as "sexually explicit" and "harmful to a minor", which theoretically could subject the disseminator to criminal prosecution.

This would have an adverse effect on public policy. With all Internet participants fearful of criminal prosecution if certain terminology is utilized, the discussions would be stifled to the point that a teenager seeking answers to curious questions concerning a subject foremost on their mind, could not find answers via this medium. Without open discussion of how to prevent being raped or birth control or abstention, there would quite possibly be greater numbers of teenage pregnancy or sexually transmitted diseases. This would be contrary to the interests of the State. [Id. at 749.]

See also American Amusement Machine Assn. v. Kendrick, 244 F.3d 572 (7th Cir. 2001) (Posner, J.) (enjoining a municipal ordinance that limited minors' access to violent video games by pointing out that children must be provided access to the world of ideas and opinions). For further discussion of minors' access to violent materials, see infra p. 103.

PROBLEM

Congress recently enacted the Family Movie Act (FMA), H.R. 4586, 109th Cong. 1st Sess. (2005), as part of the Family Entertainment and Copyright Act (FECA) (to be codified at 15 U.S.C. §1114), which inter alia protects technology that filters sex, violence, and profanity on DVD movies by exempting such technology from federal copyright laws. The legislation permits technology companies to sell DVD players for home use that produce "sanitized" versions of DVD's that delete or mute sexually explicit and violent audio/video content that some persons find objectionable. Several major movie studios, civil liberties associations, and parents' groups challenge the FMA as unconstitutional. What result? Does the FMA create a variable standard of obscenity that would be constitutional based on Ginsberg and/or Ashcroft II?

NOTE: PROTECTION OF CHILDREN FROM SEXUAL EXPLOITATION: CHILD PORNOGRAPHY

Both Congress and the Supreme Court have upheld the government's right to protect minors from such forms of sexual exploitation as child pornography. Congress first enacted the Protection of Children Against Sexual Exploitation Act of 1977, 18 U.S.C. §§2251-2257 (2000), prohibiting any person from "knowingly" transporting, shipping, receiving, or distributing material in interstate commerce that shows minors engaged in sexually explicit conduct. Id. at §2252(a). The Act was designed to remedy gaps in existing federal legislation and to provide more efficient enforcement among the various federal agencies (i.e., Department of Justice, FBI, postal and custom services).

In New York v. Ferber, 458 U.S. 747 (1982), the United States Supreme Court upheld a New York statute prohibiting distribution of materials that depict a sexual performance of a child under age 17. The Court held that child pornography, even if not technically obscene, falls outside First Amendment protection for several reasons. The Court found a compelling state interest in protecting the children's physical and psychological welfare by preventing their use in making pornography and also reasoned that the distribution of child pornography is directly linked to the sexual abuse of children because it provides a record of the abuse and encourages the production of such materials. *Ferber* limited the application of child pornography statutes to depictions of *live performances* and required that any ban on the material must have a *scienter* requirement.

Both the Protection of Children Against Sexual Exploitation Act and *Ferber*, supra, addressed *distribution* of pornographic materials. In Osborne v. Ohio, 495 U.S. 103 (1990), the United States Supreme Court upheld a state statute prohibiting the *possession* of child pornography. Relying on a policy rationale similar to that of *Ferber*, the Court reasoned that prohibiting possession of child pornography would reduce supply and demand.

The scienter requirement in the Protection of Children Against Sexual Exploitation Act was at issue in United States v. X-Citement Video, 982 F.2d 1285 (9th Cir. 1992). A defendant argued that the statute violated the First Amendment because it lacked the necessary element of knowledge regarding the minority of the performer. Disagreeing, the Ninth Circuit held (based on legislative intent) that the scienter requirement applied to both the knowledge of the performer's minority and the nature of its contents.

In 1986, Congress enacted the Child Sexual Abuse and Pornography Act, Pub. L. No. 99-628, 100 Stat. 3510 (codified as 18 U.S.C. §§2251, 2255-2256, 2421-2423 (2000)). That legislation banned the production and use of advertisements for child pornography and clarified the term "visual depiction" to include undeveloped film and videotape.

The development of computer networks capable of transmitting child pornography to a worldwide audience resulted in the passage of additional federal legislation. Congress amended the Protection of Children Against Sexual Exploitation Act with the Child Protection and Obscenity and Enforcement Act of 1988, 18 U.S.C. §§2251-2256 (2000), to make it a federal crime to transmit computerized advertisements for or visual depictions of child pornography. Congress again amended the Protection of Children Against Sexual Exploitation Act in 1996 with the Child Pornography Prevention Act (CPPA), 18 U.S.C. §2252(A) (2000), to criminalize computer-generated child pornography. Prior to the CPPA, a work was considered pornographic if it depicted an *actual* minor, under age 18, engaging in actual or simulated sexually explicit conduct. (Recall that *Ferber*, supra, limited First Amendment protection to conduct involving *live* performances.) However, advances in computer technology necessitated broadening the definition of "child pornography" to include virtual pornography — pictures that *appear* to be of minors engaging in sexually explicit conduct that are virtually indistinguishable from pictures of actual children. In Ashcroft v. Free Speech Coalition, 535 U.S. 234 (2002), the United States Supreme Court declared key provisions of the CPPA unconstitutionally overbroad. The Court reasoned that the CPPA banned protected speech because of its prohibition on speech that recorded no crime and created no victims in its production.

Congress next enacted the Protection of Children Against Sexual Predators Act of 1998, 18 U.S.C. §1470 (2000), to punish sex offenders who lure children by means of the Internet. The Act permits sentence enhancements for the use of computers in the sexual exploitation of children, creates liability on Internet service providers to report violations of federal child pornography laws to law enforcement, and directs the U.S. Sentencing Commission to review sentencing guidelines to ensure that penalties for acts of sexual child exploitation are consistent and reflective of congressional intent to punish child sex offenders severely. Finally, in 1998, Congress passed the Child Online Privacy Protection Act (COPPA), 15 U.S.C. §6501 (2000), to protect children's safety online by placing restrictions on the solicitation of personal information from children online without parental consent. On international efforts to combat child sexual exploitation, see Mike Keyser, The Council of Europe Convention on Cybercrime, 12 J. Transnatl. L. & Pol'y 287 (2003).

NOTE: RESTRICTING MINORS' ACCESS TO OTHER MATERIALS IN THE MODERN ERA

The second governmental commission on pornography (the Meese Commission) was formed in 1985 to determine the "nature, extent, and impact" of pornography and to make recommendations concerning more effective enforcement. Final Report of the Attorney General's Commission on Pornography 3 (1986). In issuing its report, the Meese Commission explained the need for such a study of pornography by pointing to technological changes affecting society. "Nor have the changes been solely technological," stated the report.

> In sixteen years [since the first commission] there have been numerous changes in the social, political, legal, cultural, and religious portrait of the United States, and many of these changes have undeniably involved both sexuality and the public portrayal of sexuality. With reference to the question of pornography, therefore, there can be no doubt that we confront a different world than that confronted by the 1970 Commission. [Final Report of the Attorney General's Commission on Pornography 6-7 (1986).]

Another aspect of this "different world" is an increasingly violent youth culture. Beginning in 1997, several incidents of school violence erupted in schools across the country.[26] Youth violence, once limited to inner cities, spread to rural areas and affluent suburbs.

[26] In 1997, in Pearl, Mississippi, a 16-year old killed his mother and two classmates, and wounded seven others; and in West Paducah, Kentucky, a 14-year old killed three students and wounded

The most serious incident took place in April 1999 at Columbine High School in the upper-middle-class Denver suburb of Littleton, Colorado. Two students dressed in black trench coats killed 17 students and a teacher, and wounded 23 other students. Shortly afterwards, reports emerged in the media about the gunmen's fascination with violent movies, heavy-metal music, and violent video games.[27] Some attributed the violence to the influence of the Internet.[28] In response to the massacre, the public demanded increasing regulation of violence in the entertainment industry and stricter gun control regulation.[29]

Consider the implications of *Ginsberg* and *Ashcroft II* for other forms of sexually explicit materials as well as materials that are violent (rather than sexually explicit). Historically, regulation of minors' access to sexually explicit and violent materials has focused on several areas, including:

(1) Dial-a-Porn. "Dial-a-porn," or "phone sex," is the telephonic transmission of pornography. Dial-a-porn became nationally available in 1983. There are two types of dial-a-porn: either the customer converses with a live paid performer who talks in a sexually explicit manner or, alternatively, the customer listens to a sexually explicit prerecorded message. In either case, the customer incurs substantial telephone or credit-card bills. In 1988, Congress placed a complete ban on the transmission of obscene and indecent messages by telephone by means of an amendment to the Communications Act of 1934, 47 U.S.C. §223 (as amended).

In Sable Communications, Inc. v. FCC, 492 U.S. 115 (1989), a dial-a-porn provider challenged the constitutionality of the ban. The United States Supreme Court held that Congress could prohibit the transmission of obscene but not indecent telephone messages because the latter are protected by the First Amendment. The Court reasoned that, although Congress had a compelling interest in child protection, the statute was overbroad because the FCC could limit minors' access to indecent dial-a-porn messages by less restrictive means (e.g., by regulatory methods that had been proposed by the FCC such as credit cards, access codes, and scrambled messages). Further, the Court ruled that a total ban on indecent, sexually explicit messages would impermissibly restrict adults' access to such materials:

> Under our precedents, §223(b), in its present form, has the invalid effect of limiting the content of adult telephone conversations to that which is suitable for children to hear. It is another case of "burn[ing] up the house to roast the pig." [Id. at 130-131.]

---

five others. In 1998, in Jonesboro, Arkansas, two boys, ages 11 and 13, called in a false fire alarm and then killed four girls and a teacher and wounded ten others; and in Springfield, Oregon, a 15-year old first killed his parents and then two students, and wounded 22 others in a high school cafeteria. See Valerie Richardson, A Massacre in Colorado, Students Killed, Injured in Blood Bath, Wash. Times, Apr. 21, 1999, at A1. In the most recent school shooting, a 16-year-old boy killed nine people and wounded 14 others in Redlake, Minnesota. Amanda Paulson et al., School Shooting: Familiar Echoes, New Concerns, Christian Sci. Monitor, Mar. 23, 2005, at 1.

[27] See Ellen Barry, Games Feared as Violent Youths' Basic Training, Boston Globe, Apr. 29, 1999, at A1; Richard Corliss, Bang, You're Dead, Time Magazine, May 3, 1999, at 49; Marilyn Manson's Music Blamed in Colorado Shooting (NBC television broadcast, Apr. 29, 1999).

[28] Do Not Enter, PC Mag., June 22, 1999 (comments of former Vice President Al Gore).

[29] Jeffrey Taylor, House GOP Tries to Curb Violent Fare, Wall St. J., June 8, 1999, at A20.

In response to *Sable*, Congress again attempted to regulate the dial-a-porn industry with the Helms Amendment, 47 U.S.C. §223(c)(2) (2000), requiring telephone companies to block access to dial-a-porn services unless customers affirmatively requested access in writing. The Second and Ninth Circuits upheld these opt-in restrictions in Dial Information Servs. v. Thornburgh, 938 F.2d 1535 (2d Cir. 1991), and Information Providers' Coalition v. FCC, 928 F.2d 866 (9th Cir. 1991), on the basis that the restrictions did not amount to a complete ban. See generally Paul R. Abramson et al., Sexual Rights in America: The Ninth Amendment and the Pursuit of Happiness (2003) (arguing that the Ninth Amendment should be interpreted to protect a range of sexual freedom including dial-a-porn services).

(2) Movie Ratings. In the 1960s, films began reflecting pervasive societal changes in sexual mores that were triggered by the women's liberation movement, the greater availability of contraceptives, and criticisms of the institution of marriage. As films displayed more nudity and sex, the public voiced increasing demands for regulation.

The city of Dallas in 1965 enacted the first ordinance aimed at protecting children. That ordinance, which served as a model for other municipalities, authorized an administrative board to classify films as "suitable" for children under age 16. Statutory grounds for classification as "not suitable" included portrayal of "sexual promiscuity [so as] to incite or encourage delinquency or sexual promiscuity on the part of young persons or to appeal to their prurient interests." Revised Code of Civil and Criminal Ordinance of the City of Dallas, 1960, Ch. 46A-1 (cited in Interstate v. Dallas, 390 U.S. 676, 681 (1968)). The board could consider a film "likely to incite or encourage" such conduct if the film created "the impression on young persons that such conduct is profitable, desirable, acceptable, respectable, praiseworthy or commonly accepted." Id.

The Supreme Court invalidated the Dallas ordinance on grounds of vagueness. The majority opinion, authored by Justice Marshall, stated that vagueness in the standards for regulation of expression was not excused by the "salutary purpose of protecting children" (id. at 689), and further, that constitutional standards for vagueness did not vary according to the age of the persons protected by a statute. However, recognizing the dangers of motion pictures, particularly for youth, the Court (citing *Ginsberg*) affirmed the desirability of age classifications in regulating the dissemination to minors of objectionable material. Id. at 690.

Fearing a rash of legislative reform in response to Interstate v. Dallas, officials in the Motion Picture Association of America (MPAA) moved quickly to regulate the movie industry themselves. The resultant MPAA rating system, adopted in 1968, still forms the basis for movie-viewing standards.

The MPAA system has four rating categories: "G" for general audiences (all ages admitted); "PG" for "parental guidance suggested"; "R" for "restricted" (those under age 16 must be accompanied by a parent or guardian); and "X" for "X-rated" (no one under age 17 admitted).[30] The MPAA subsequently added a "PG-13"

---

[30] Originally, MPAA President Jack Valenti urged that the industry adopt only three categories, ending in "R" ratings. "It was my view that a parent ought to have the right to accompany children to any movie the parent chose without the movie industry or the government denying that right." Swopes v. Lubbers, 560 F. Supp. 1328, 1336-1337 (W.D. Mich. 1983) (citing background statement).

category (parental guidance suggested for those under age 13), in reaction to protests over violence contained in "Indiana Jones and the Temple of Doom." Further, the MPAA later substituted the term "NC-17" for the "X" rating to signify that no children under 17 will be admitted. (Thus, ratings for "X-rated" movies currently are applied by other organizations and not the MPAA.) On the history of movie regulation, see Angela J. Campbell, Self-Regulation and the Media, 51 Fed. Comm. L.J. 711, 750-752 (1999); Swopes v. Lubbers, 560 F. Supp. 1328, 1335-1337 (W.D. Mich. 1983) (background statement by MPAA President Jack Valenti).

The MPAA failed to copyright its rating system, so the producers of porno-graphic films were able to commandeer the "X" rating for use in their movies. Because the "X" rating came to be associated with pornographic films, which many theaters refused to play and many publications refused to advertise, a nonpornographic adult movie that received a rating of "X", rather than "R", suffered severe economic losses.

In 1990, the producers of one such film, "Tie Me Up! Tie Me Down!," filed suit against the MPAA to compel a change in the film's rating from "X" to "R." Miramax Films Corp. v. Motion Picture Assn. of America, 560 N.Y.S.2d 730 (Sup. Ct. 1990). The Supreme Court of New York County refused to grant the film-makers' request. The opinion, however, is noteworthy for its candid expression of reservations regarding the MPAA rating system:

> Although each of the categories which the rating system uses is cloaked in terms which suggest that they are fashioned to protect America's children, the inference of concern for the welfare of children is not borne out by any scrutiny of the standard and the guidance given to the rating board members. The standard is not scientific. There are no physicians, child psychiatrists or child care professionals on the board, nor is any professional guidance sought to advise the board members regarding any relative harm to minor children. Id. at 733.

The court continued:

> If the MPAA chooses to rate films for the benefit of children, it is its duty to do so with standards that have a rational and professional basis. . . . The respondent is strongly advised either to consider proposals for a revised rating system that permits of a professional basis for rating films or to cease the practice altogether. Id. at 736.

Do you agree with the *Miramax* court's assessment? Should the MPAA hire psychologists or other experts to rate movies? Or should the MPAA "cease the practice altogether"?

If a 16-year-old desires to see an "X-rated" movie, or an "NC-17"-rated movie (no children under 17), who should decide whether the child views the film? By prohibiting minors under the age of 17 from attending "NC-17"-rated movies, does the MPAA infringe upon the rights of the child to choose? Does the MPAA infringe upon the rights of parents under *Meyer, Pierce*, and *Yoder* to raise that child as they

---

However, the movie exhibitor organization advocated the X rating, stemming from fear of possible legal repercussions, and Valenti acquiesced.

see fit? If someone other than the child or parents makes decisions about the child's movie attendance, should it be a private organization such as the MPAA? Would your answers differ if the MPAA rated novels rather than movies?

Does the state have a role to play in regulating minors' movie viewing? How effective is the rating system? How easy is it for minors to evade the rating system? Two common ways to evade such restrictions, of course, are the rental of videotapes (rather than viewing films in movie theaters) and viewing of airline movies.

In Video Software Dealers Assn. v. Webster, 773 F. Supp. 1275 (W.D. Mo. 1991), *aff'd*, 982 F.2d 684 (8th Cir. 1992), the Eighth Circuit Court of Appeals declared unconstitutional, as overbroad, a state statute that prohibited the sale or rental of violent videotapes to minors under 17 years of age. And, in response to parental complaints to the airline industry regarding sex and violence in airline movies, some airlines have responded by showing less violent and sexually explicit films. See Joe Garofoli, The Film-Unfriendly Skies; Major Airlines Struggle to Find Good Movies That Are Appropriate for Passengers of All Ages, S.F. Chron., Aug. 26, 2001, at 48.

Congressional concern about the impact of television violence on children dates to the dawn of television. Despite numerous hearings from 1952-1985, Congress has adopted only two legislative proposals addressing the problem. In the Television Program Improvement Act of 1990, 47 U.S.C. §303c (2000), Congress provided for an antitrust exemption to allow (but not require) the industry to hold discussions or formulate agreements to limit violent material on television. That exemption expired in 1993 with little effect, except for influencing broadcast and cable networks to air parental advisories before programs with violent content.

Next, as part of the Telecommunications Act of 1996, 47 U.S.C. §303(x) (2000), Congress authorized the V-chip, a set of internal controls that can read ratings transmitted by television networks in order to block programming with violence and sexually explicit content. The legislation mandated a "voluntary" television rating system that was similar to movie ratings and also required all television sets with a screen 13 inches or greater to be equipped with the device. The V-chip enables parents to block programs or entire channels. As a result of V-chip legislation, many broadcast and cable networks formulated policies to rate programs by age and contents. Is the V-chip constitutional? See Denver Area Telecomms. Consortium, Inc. v. FCC, 518 U.S. 727, 756 (1996) (suggesting in dicta that it is). How effective, do you think, is the approach of parental monitoring in this context? See Joel Timmer, Incrementalism and Policymaking on Television Violence, 9 Comm. L. & Pol'y 351, 379 (2004).

The Supreme Court addressed the constitutionality of another provision of the Telecommunications Act (§505) (limiting sexually explicit adult cable television programming to nighttime hours) in United States v. Playboy Entertainment Group, 529 U.S. 803 (2000). Invalidating the legislation as a violation of the First Amendment, the Court reasoned that a different provision of the Telecommunications Act provided a less restrictive means for achieving the same end by requiring cable operators to block channels *upon request* by a customer.

Congress again devoted attention to the subject of television violence with congressional hearings following the shootings at Columbine High School in 1999. This time, attention was focused on the marketing of violent entertainment to children in several different media — music lyrics, movies, video games, and the Internet. Congress considered, but never adopted, various legislative proposals to restrict the marketing of violent entertainment to children. Proposals included: a requirement that the FCC establish a toll-free number and a Web site to log complaints about television violence; a "safe harbor proposal" to require airing violent programming when children were least likely to watch; the establishment of a national commission to determine the causes of youth violence; a permanent antitrust exemption for the industry to develop voluntary guidelines on television violence; criminalizing the sale of extremely violent movies, video games, and books to minors; and a requirement that the industry develop a universal labeling system for violent television programs, movies, video games, and records. Timmer, supra, at 370-372. Also, then-President Clinton called on the movie industry itself to regulate the violence in films and broadcasts. Clinton Challenges Hollywood to Curb Violence in Movies and on Television (CNN television broadcast, May 16, 1999). Subsequently, the National Association of Theatre Owners (representing two-thirds of the nation's movie screens) announced that they would require teenage viewers to present photo identification when they show up without an adult to see an R-rated film. David E. Rosenbaum, Theaters Will Ask to See Photo ID's for R-Rated Films: A Response to Violence, N.Y. Times, June 9, 1999, at A1.

Congress recently enacted the Family Entertainment and Copyright Act (FECA), S. 167, 109th Cong. 1st Sess. (2005). One section of FECA is the Family Movie Act, H.R. 4586 (to be codified at 15 U.S.C. §1114) which legalizes electronic filtering technology designed to modify DVDs by "sanitizing" (i.e., skipping or muting) their sexually explicit or violent audio/video content. The legislation exempts both the filtering technology and the resultant "sanitized" DVDs from federal copyright laws provided the filtering software and resultant DVDs are for home use. See Jon Healey, Anti-Piracy Legislation Also Has a Bitter Pill for Studios, L.A. Times, Apr. 19, 2005; Richard Simon, Push to Allow DVD's to be 'Sanitized' Alarms Studios; As the Senate Acts on Broadcast Decency, A Bill to Allow Technology to Filter Screens Looms, L.A. Times, July 23, 2004, at C1.

What do you think of the various proposals above to regulate minors' access to sexually explicit and violent materials? Why do you suppose Congress has faced such difficulty enacting any of these proposals?

(3) Music Labels. Efforts to censor music in the interests of child protection began in the 1980s. In 1984, the National Parent Teachers Association of America (NPTA) requested that the Recording Industry Association of America (RIAA) adopt a voluntary rating system similar to that of the movie industry. The RIAA, however, delayed until an influential citizen group led by Tipper Gore (wife of former Vice President Al Gore) and other politicians' wives formed the Parents' Music Resource Center (PMRC) to lobby the music industry. Specifically, the PMRC urged a rating system to inform parents of objectionable content in albums (i.e., violence, sex, references to drugs and alcohol, etc.); lyrics and ratings on album covers; and ratings for music concerts. See Deborah Cazan, Concerts: Rated or Raided? First Amendment Implications of Concert-Rating, 2 Vand. J. Ent. L. & Prac. 170, 171 (2000) (tracing history of regulation).

The PMRC took its concerns to Congress; and the Senate Committee on Commerce, Science, and Transportation held hearings. See Contents of Music and Lyrics of Records: Hearings Before the Senate Comm. on Commerce, Science and Transportation, 99th Cong., 1st Sess. (1985). The PMRC's lobbying efforts netted two results: the RIAA finally agreed to place a voluntary warning label on all albums containing sexually explicit lyrics or violent imagery (saying "Explicit Lyrics — Parental Advisory"), and several state legislatures initiated measures to require parental advisory labels.

Stemming from similar concerns, the Washington state legislature enacted a statute that subjected distributors of music sound recordings to civil and criminal penalties for distribution of "erotic" sound recordings to minors. In Soundgarden v. Eikenberry, 871 P.2d 1050 (Wash. 1994), the Washington Supreme Court held the statute unconstitutional. Although the court concluded that the statutory definition of "erotic material" satisfied the *Ginsberg* test of variable obscenity, the court nonetheless held that the statute was overbroad and a violation of due process as a prior restraint on protected speech and for lack of proper notice to distributors before subjecting them to sanctions.

Two decades after the voluntary adoption of warning labels, critics of the music industry continue to maintain that it has not done enough to protect children from objectionable lyrics. In 2001, the Federal Trade Commission released a report (discussed infra at p. 110) castigating the music recording industry for its marketing tactics to children of albums with sexually explicit and violent lyrics. Although the industry had made some progress in self-regulation, according to the report, it continued to promote to children irresponsibly such music on television, radio, the Internet and teen magazines. Congressional hearings in 2001 and 2002 examined the entertainment industry's self-regulatory efforts. Kyonzte Hughes, Rating and Labeling Entertainment, available at *www.firstamendmentcenter.org/speech/arts* (last visited Aug. 28, 2004). Legislators criticized the music recording industry for refusing to use more descriptive parental advisory labels. Id. Recent industry reforms, effective April 1, 2002, introduce a label saying "Edited Version" to identify albums with modified versions of albums that contain parental advisories as well as the label "Edited Version Also Available" to alert consumers of the availability of a modified version of an album. Id. See also Lynette Holloway, Industry Is Resisting Tougher Label Standards, N.Y. Times, Oct. 21, 2002, at C7. Many state legislatures also have proposed another regulatory measure originally proposed by the PMRC — rating concerts for sexually explicit and violent lyrics. See generally Cazan, supra.

Yet another approach to limiting minors' access to recordings that advocate violence is through the imposition of tort liability on record manufacturers and/or performers. Several parents initiated such suits unsuccessfully after their children's suicides or homicidal acts. See, e.g., Davidson v. Time Warner, Inc., No. Civ.A. V-94-006, 1997 WL 405907 (S.D. Tex. Mar. 31, 1997); Waller v. Osbourne, 958 F.2d 1084 (11th Cir. 1992); Vance v. Judas Priest, Nos. 86-5844, 86-3939, 1990 WL 130920 (Nev. Dist. Ct. Aug. 24, 1990). Should the first Amendment be a defense to tort liability? See generally Justine Wellstood, Note, Tort Liability of the Media, 15 St. John's J. Legal Comment. 187 (2000); Peter A. Block, Comment, Modern-Day Sirens: Rock Music and the First Amendment, 63 S. Cal. L. Rev. 777 (1990).

(4) Video Games. Video games (played on home video game systems, portable hand-sized machines, personal computers, and coin-operated machines

in arcades and stores) comprise a major component of the entertainment industry. Originally targeted to children, the games' audience now includes large numbers of adults as well. In 2004, sales of video games constituted a $14 billion industry. Michael McCarthy, Media Giants Suit Up to Take on Video Games; TV Viewers Play Rather Than Watch, USA Today, Aug. 27, 2004, at B5.

Congress first became concerned about violent video games in 1993 after the launch of the popular "Mortal Kombat" (featuring a tournament in which players kill their opponents to yells of "Finish him!" and the sight of spurting blood). Following congressional hearings, Senators Joseph Lieberman (D.-Conn.) and Herb Kohl (D.-Wis.) introduced the Video Game Rating Act of 1994, S. 1823, 103rd Cong. (1994), which proposed the establishment of a commission to create a rating system for video games. To avert the possibility of governmental regulation, the Interactive Digital Software Association used the MPAA ratings to establish the Entertainment Software Rating Board in 1994 that created letter ratings for video games (EC for Early Childhood (ages 3 and older), E for Everyone, T for Teen (suitable for ages 13 and older), M for Mature (ages 17 and older), AO for Adults Only, and RP for Rating Pending). In March 2005, the video game industry adopted a new category of "E10$^+$" for games rated between "E" and "T" to designate games that are slightly more violent and mature for children approaching their teens. The Board also uses content descriptors to reveal the presence of violence, strong sexual content or strong language, mature sexual themes, use of drugs, or other potentially offensive content. The American Amusement Machine Association drafted similar ratings for coin-operated video arcade machines.

Video games came under increasing scrutiny following the school violence at Littleton, Colorado, in April 1999. Media reports highlighted the teen gunmen's fascination with the violent video games "Quake" and "Doom." Shortly thereafter, then-President Bill Clinton announced the initiation of a federal study into the marketing strategies of the movie, music, and video game industries. Betty Streisand & Angie Cannon, Lawyers, Guns, Money, Hollywood, Under New Probe, May Have a Lot to Hide, U.S. News & World Report, June 14, 1999, at 56. After an 18-month study, the Federal Trade Commission released a report, "Marketing Violent Entertainment to Children: A Review of Self-Regulation and Industry Practices in the Motion Picture, Music Recording and Electronic Game Industries," available at *www.ftc.gov/opa/2000/09/youthviol* (last visited Aug. 30, 2004). The report finds that companies in the motion picture, music recording, and electronic game industries routinely target children under 17 in their marketing of products that their own rating systems deem inappropriate or that warrant parental caution due to violent content and also that retailers make little effort to restrict youths' access to violent material. Rather than suggest specific legislative proposals, the FTC recommended additional self-regulation by the industry, including: (1) the improvement of the usefulness of the movie, music, and video game industries' ratings and labels by the establishment or expansion of codes that prohibit target marketing to children under 17; an increase in compliance at the retail level by checking identification or requiring parental permission; and an effort to increase parental understanding about the meanings of the ratings and labels.

Since 2003, legislators in various states have introduced 16 anti-video-game bills. Lillian R. BeVier, Controlling Communications that Teach or Demonstrate

Violence: "The Movie Made Them Do It," 32 J.L. Med. & Ethics 47, 47 (2004). Video game manufacturers have filed suit to enjoin enforcement of some of the resulting legislation. To date, no regulation has passed constitutional muster. See, e.g., Video Software Dealers Assn. v. Maleng, 325 F. Supp. 2d 1180 (W.D. Wash. 2004); Interactive Digital Software Assn. v. St. Louis Cty., 329 F.3d 954 (8th Cir. 2003); American Amusement Mach. Assn. v. Kenrick, 244 F.3d 572 (7th Cir. 2001).

Suits seeking to establish tort liability based on harm to children and others resulting from dissemination of violent video games have similarly been unsuccessful. See, e.g., James v. Meow Media, Inc., 300 F.3d 683 (6th Cir. 2002); Sanders v. Acclaim Entertainment, Inc., 188 F. Supp. 2d 1264 (D. Colo. 2002). See generally William Li, Unbaking the Adolescent Cake: The Constitutional Implications of Imposing Tort Liability on Publishers of Violent Video Games, 45 Ariz. L. Rev. 467 (2003).

Congress is currently considering legislation, Protect Children from Video Game Sex and Violence Act of 2003, H.R. 669, 108th Cong. (2003), introduced by Representative Joe Baca (D.-Cal.), prohibiting the sale or rental of adult video games to minors. Retail stores would be subject to increasing fines for selling or renting, or attempting to sell or rent, "to a minor any video game that depicts nudity, sexual conduct, or other content harmful to minors." Id.

Why have reformers focused so much attention on the threat to youth from video games? Is the interactive nature of the media a factor? The portability of the game machines? Are movies and television, in fact, more harmful to minors? Or, as some cynics suggest, is the attention attributable to the fact that the video game industry has no lobby in Washington and fails to provide significant campaign contributions? See Jeffrey Taylor & Bob Davis, Clinton Picks an Easy Target for His Campaign Against Youth Violence: Makers of Video Games, Wall St. J., June 3, 1999, at A28. See generally Patrick M. Garry, Defining Speech in an Entertainment Age: The Case of First Amendment Protection for Video Games, 57 SMU L. Rev. 139 (2004); Kevin W. Saunders, Regulating Youth Access to Violent Video Games: Three Responses to First Amendment Concerns, 2003 Mich. St. DCL L. Rev. 51.

Tinker v. Des Moines Independent Community School District
393 U.S. 503 (1969)

Mr. Justice FORTAS delivered the opinion of the Court.

Petitioner John F. Tinker, 15 years old, and petitioner Christopher Eckhardt, 16 years old, attended high schools in Des Moines, Iowa. Petitioner Mary Beth Tinker, John's sister, was a 13-year-old student in junior high school.

In December 1965, a group of adults and students in Des Moines held a meeting at the Eckhardt home. The group determined to publicize their objections to the hostilities in Vietnam and their support for a truce by wearing black armbands during the holiday season and by fasting on December 16 and New Year's Eve. Petitioners and their parents had previously engaged in similar activities, and they decided to participate in the program.

The principals of the Des Moines schools became aware of the plan to wear armbands. On December 14, 1965, they met and adopted a policy that any student wearing an armband to school would be asked to remove it, and if he refused he would be suspended until he returned without the armband. Petitioners were aware of the regulation that the school authorities adopted.

On December 16, Mary Beth and Christopher wore black armbands to their schools. John Tinker wore his armband the next day. They were all sent home and suspended from school until they would come back without their armbands. They did not return to school until after the planned period for wearing armbands had expired — that is, until after New Year's Day.

This complaint was filed in the United States District Court by petitioners, through their fathers, under §1983 of Title 42 of the United States Code. It prayed for an injunction restraining the respondent school officials and the respondent members of the board of directors of the school district from disciplining the petitioners, and it sought nominal damages. After an evidentiary hearing the District Court dismissed the complaint. It upheld the constitutionality of the school authorities' action on the ground that it was reasonable in order to prevent disturbance of school discipline. 258 F. Supp. 971 (1966). The court referred to but expressly declined to follow the Fifth Circuit's holding in a similar case [forbidding students to wear freedom buttons] that the wearing of symbols like the armbands cannot be prohibited unless it "materially and substantially interfere[s] with the requirements of appropriate discipline in the operation of the school." Burnside v. Byars, 363 F.2d 744, 749 (1966).

[The Court of Appeals for the Eighth Circuit affirmed. 383 F.2d 988 (1967).]

The District Court recognized that the wearing of an armband for the purpose of expressing certain views is the type of symbolic act that is within the Free Speech Clause of the First Amendment. . . . As we shall discuss, the wearing of armbands in the circumstances of this case was entirely divorced from actually or potentially disruptive conduct by those participating in it. It was closely akin to "pure speech" which, we have repeatedly held, is entitled to comprehensive protection under the First Amendment.

First Amendment rights, applied in light of the special characteristics of the school environment, are available to teachers and students. It can hardly be argued that either students or teachers shed their constitutional rights to freedom of speech or expression at the schoolhouse gate. This has been the unmistakable holding of this Court for almost 50 years. . . .

On the other hand, the Court has repeatedly emphasized the need for affirming the comprehensive authority of the States and of school officials, consistent with fundamental constitutional safeguards, to prescribe and control conduct in the schools. Our problem lies in the area where students in the exercise of First Amendment rights collide with the rules of the school authorities.

The problem posed by the present case does not relate to regulation of the length of skirts or the type of clothing, to hair style, or deportment. Cf. Ferrell v. Dallas Independent School District, 392 F.2d 697 (C.A. 5th Cir. 1968); Pugsley v. Sellmeyer, 158 Ark. 247, 250 S.W. 538, 30 A.L.R. 1212 (1923). It does not concern aggressive, disruptive action or even group demonstrations. Our problem involves direct, primary First Amendment rights akin to "pure speech."

The school officials banned and sought to punish petitioners for a silent, passive expression of opinion, unaccompanied by any disorder or disturbance on the part of petitioners. There is here no evidence whatever of petitioners' interference, actual or nascent, with the schools' work or of collision with the rights of other students to be secure and to be let alone. Accordingly, this case does not concern speech or action that intrudes upon the work of the schools or the rights of other students.

Only a few of the 18,000 students in the school system wore the black armbands. Only five students were suspended for wearing them. There is no indication that the work of the schools or any class was disrupted. Outside the classrooms, a few students made hostile remarks to the children wearing armbands, but there were no threats or acts of violence on school premises.

The District Court concluded that the action of the school authorities was reasonable because it was based upon their fear of a disturbance from the wearing of the armbands. But, in our system, undifferentiated fear or apprehension of disturbance is not enough to overcome the right to freedom of expression. Any departure from absolute regimentation may cause trouble. Any variation from the majority's opinion may inspire fear. Any word spoken, in class, in the lunchroom, or on the campus, that deviates from the views of another person may start an argument or cause a disturbance. But our Constitution says we must take this risk, and our history says that it is this sort of hazardous freedom — this kind of openness — that is the basis of our national strength and of the independence and vigor of Americans who grow up and live in this relatively permissive, often disputatious, society.

In order for the State in the person of school officials to justify prohibition of a particular expression of opinion, it must be able to show that its action was caused by something more than a mere desire to avoid the discomfort and unpleasantness that always accompany an unpopular viewpoint. Certainly where there is no finding and no showing that engaging in the forbidden conduct would "materially and substantially interfere with the requirements of appropriate discipline in the operation of the school," the prohibition cannot be sustained. Burnside v. Byars, supra, 363 F.2d at 749.

In the present case, the District Court made no such finding, and our independent examination of the record fails to yield evidence that the school authorities had reason to anticipate that the wearing of the armbands would substantially interfere with the work of the school or impinge upon the rights of other students. Even an official memorandum prepared after the suspension that listed the reasons for the ban on wearing the armbands made no reference to the anticipation of such disruption.

On the contrary, the action of the school authorities appears to have been based upon an urgent wish to avoid the controversy which might result from the expression, even by the silent symbol of armbands, of opposition to this Nation's part in the conflagration in Vietnam. It is revealing, in this respect, that the meeting at which the school principals decided to issue the contested regulation was called in response to a student's statement to the journalism teacher in one of the schools that he wanted to write an article on Vietnam and have it published in the school paper. (The student was dissuaded.)

It is also relevant that the school authorities did not purport to prohibit the wearing of all symbols of political or controversial significance. The record shows that students in some of the schools wore buttons relating to national political campaigns, and some even wore the Iron Cross, traditionally a symbol of Nazism. The order prohibiting the wearing of armbands did not extend to these. Instead, a particular symbol — black armbands worn to exhibit opposition to this Nation's involvement in Vietnam — was singled out for prohibition. Clearly, the prohibition of expression of one particular opinion, at least without evidence that it is necessary to avoid material and substantial interference with schoolwork or discipline, is not constitutionally permissible.

In our system, state-operated schools may not be enclaves of totalitarianism. School officials do not possess absolute authority over their students. Students in school as well as out of school are "persons" under our Constitution. They are possessed of fundamental rights which the State must respect, just as they themselves must respect their obligations to the State. In our system, students may not be regarded as closed-circuit recipients of only that which the State chooses to communicate. They may not be confined to the expression of those sentiments that are officially approved. In the absence of a specific showing of constitutionally valid reasons to regulate their speech, students are entitled to freedom of expression of their views. . . .

The classroom is peculiarly the "marketplace of ideas." The Nation's future depends upon leaders trained through wide exposure to that robust exchange of ideas which discovers truth "out of a multitude of tongues, [rather] than through any kind of authoritative selection."

The principle of these cases is not confined to the supervised and ordained discussion which takes place in the classroom. The principal use to which the schools are dedicated is to accommodate students during prescribed hours for the purpose of certain types of activities. Among those activities is personal intercommunication among the students. This is not only an inevitable part of the process of attending school; it is also an important part of the educational process. A student's rights, therefore, do not embrace merely the classroom hours. When he is in the cafeteria, or on the playing field, or on the campus during the authorized hours, he may express his opinions, even on controversial subjects like the conflict in Vietnam, if he does so without "materially and substantially interfer[ing] with the requirements of appropriate discipline in the operation of the school" and without colliding with the rights of others. Burnside v. Byars, supra, 363 F.2d at 749. But conduct by the student, in class or out of it, which for any reason — whether it stems from time, place, or type of behavior — materially disrupts classwork or involves substantial disorder or invasion of the rights of others is, of course, not immunized by the constitutional guarantee of freedom of speech. . . .

As we have discussed, the record does not demonstrate any facts which might reasonably have led school authorities to forecast substantial disruption of or material interference with school activities, and no disturbances or disorders on the school premises in fact occurred. These petitioners merely went about their ordained rounds in school. Their deviation consisted only in wearing on their sleeve a band of black cloth, not more than two inches wide. They wore it to exhibit their disapproval of the Vietnam hostilities and their advocacy of a truce, to make their views known, and, by their example, to influence others to adopt them. They neither interrupted school activities nor sought to intrude in the school affairs or the lives of others. They caused discussion outside of the classrooms, but no interference with work and no disorder. In the circumstances, our Constitution does not permit officials of the State to deny their form of expression. . . .

Reversed and remanded.

[Concurring opinions of Justice Stewart and Justice White omitted.]

Mr. Justice BLACK, dissenting.

The Court's holding in this case ushers in what I deem to be an entirely new era in which the power to control pupils by the elected "officials of state supported public schools . . . " in the United States is in ultimate effect transferred to the Supreme Court. The Court brought this particular case here on a petition for certiorari urging that the First and Fourteenth Amendments protect the right of school pupils to express their political views all the way "from kindergarten through high school." . . .

Assuming that the Court is correct in holding that the conduct of wearing armbands for the purpose of conveying political ideas is protected by the First Amendment, the crucial remaining questions are whether students and teachers may use the schools at their whim as a platform for the exercise of free speech — "symbolic" or "pure" — and whether the courts will allocate to themselves the function of deciding how the pupils' school day will be spent. . . .

While the record does not show that any of these armband students shouted, used profane language, or were violent in any manner, detailed testimony by some of them shows their armbands caused comments, warnings by other students, the poking of fun at them, and a warning by an older football player that other, non-protesting students had better let them alone. There is also evidence that a teacher of mathematics had his lesson period practically "wrecked" chiefly by disputes with Mary Beth Tinker, who wore her armband for her "demonstration." Even a casual reading of the record shows that this armband did divert students' minds from their regular lessons, and that talk, comments, etc., made John Tinker "self-conscious" in attending school with his armband. While the absence of obscene remarks or boisterous and loud disorder perhaps justifies the Court's statement that the few armband students did not actually "disrupt" the classwork, I think the record overwhelmingly shows that the armbands did exactly what the elected school officials and principals foresaw they would, that is, took the students' minds off their classwork and diverted them to thoughts about the highly emotional subject of the Vietnam war. [I]f the time has come when pupils of state-supported schools, kindergartens, grammar schools, or high school, can defy and flout orders of school officials to keep their minds on their own schoolwork, it is the beginning of a new revolutionary era of permissiveness in this country fostered by the judiciary. . . .

I deny, therefore, that it has been the "unmistakable holding of this Court for almost 50 years" that "students" and "teachers" take with them into the "schoolhouse gate" constitutional rights to "freedom of speech or expression." Even *Meyer* did not hold that.

. . . In my view, teachers in state-controlled public schools are hired to teach there. [C]ertainly a teacher is not paid to go into school and teach subjects the State does not hire him to teach as a part of its selected curriculum. Nor are public school students sent to the schools at public expense to broadcast political or any other views to educate and inform the public. The original idea of schools, which I do not believe is yet abandoned as worthless or out of date, was that children had not yet reached the point of experience and wisdom which enabled them to teach all of their elders. It may be that the Nation has outworn the old-fashioned slogan that "children are to be seen not heard," but one may, I hope, be permitted to harbor the thought that taxpayers send children to school on the premise that at their age they need to learn, not teach.

[M]embers of this Court like all other citizens, know, without being told, that the disputes over the wisdom of the Vietnam war have disrupted and divided this country as few other issues ever have. Of course students, like other people, cannot concentrate on lesser issues when black armbands are being ostentatiously displayed in their presence to call attention to the wounded and dead of the war, some of the wounded and dead being their friends and neighbors. It was, of course, to distract the attention of other students that some students insisted up to the very point of their own suspension from school that they were determined to sit in school with their symbolic armbands.

. . . We cannot close our eyes to the fact that some of the country's greatest problems are crimes committed by the youth, too many of school age. School discipline, like parental discipline, is an integral and important part of training our children to be good citizens — to be better citizens. Here a very small number of students have crisply and summarily refused to obey a school order designed to give pupils who want to learn the opportunity to do so. One does not need to be a prophet or the son of a prophet to know that after the Court's holding today some students in Iowa schools and indeed in all schools will be ready, able, and willing to defy their teachers on practically all orders. . . .

. . . Turned loose with lawsuits for damages and injunctions against their teachers as they are here, it is nothing but wishful thinking to imagine that young, immature students will not soon believe it is their right to control the schools rather than the right of the States that collect the taxes to hire the teachers for the benefit of the pupils. This case, therefore, wholly without constitutional reasons in my judgment, subjects all the public schools in the country to the whims and caprices of their loudest-mouthed, but maybe not their brightest, students. I, for one, am not fully persuaded that school pupils are wise enough, even with this Court's expert help from Washington, to run the 23,390 public school systems in our 50 States. I wish, therefore, wholly to disclaim any purpose on my part to hold that the Federal Constitution compels the teachers, parents, and elected school officials to surrender control of the American public school system to public school students. I dissent.

Hazelwood School District v. Kuhlmeier
484 U.S. 260 (1998)

Justice WHITE delivered the opinion of the Court. . . .

I

Petitioners are the Hazelwood School District in St. Louis County, Missouri; various school officials; Robert Eugene Reynolds, the principal of Hazelwood East High School, and Howard Emerson, a teacher in the school district. Respondents are three former Hazelwood East students who were staff members of *Spectrum*, the school newspaper. They contend that school officials violated their First Amendment rights by deleting two pages of articles from the May 13, 1983, issue of Spectrum.

Spectrum was written and edited by the Journalism II class at Hazelwood East. The newspaper was published every three weeks or so during the 1982-1983 school year. More than 4,500 copies of the newspaper were distributed during that year to students, school personnel, and members of the community.

The Board of Education allocated funds from its annual budget for the printing of Spectrum. These funds were supplemented by proceeds from sales of the newspaper. . . . The other costs associated with the newspaper — such as supplies, textbooks, and a portion of the journalism teacher's salary — were borne entirely by the Board. . . .

The practice at Hazelwood East during the spring 1983 semester was for the journalism teacher to submit page proofs of each Spectrum issue to Principal Reynolds for his review prior to publication. On May 10, Emerson delivered the proofs of the May 13 edition to Reynolds, who objected to two of the articles. . . . One of the stories described three Hazelwood East students' experiences with pregnancy; the other discussed the impact of divorce on students at the school.

Reynolds was concerned that, although the pregnancy story used false names "to keep the identity of these girls a secret," the pregnant students still might be identifiable from the text. He also believed that the article's references to sexual activity and birth control were inappropriate for some of the younger students at the school. In addition, Reynolds was concerned that a student identified by name in the divorce story had complained that her father "wasn't spending enough time with my mom, my sister and I" prior to the divorce, "was always out of town on business or out late playing cards with the guys," and "always argued about everything" with her mother. Reynolds believed that the student's parents should have been given an opportunity to respond to these remarks or to consent to their publication. He was unaware that Emerson had deleted the student's name from the final version of the article.

Reynolds believed that there was no time to make the necessary changes in the stories before the scheduled press run. . . . Accordingly, he directed Emerson to withhold from publication the two pages containing the stories on pregnancy and divorce. . . .

[Respondents sought injunctive relief and nominal damages. The District Court held that the school officials' action was reasonable and did not violate the First Amendment. The Eighth Circuit Court of Appeals reversed. Applying *Tinker*, the court of appeals found no evidence that the articles would have materially disrupted classwork, given rise to substantial disruption, or resulted in tort liability for libel or invasion of privacy.]

We granted certiorari, and we now reverse.

II

Students in the public schools do not "shed their constitutional rights to freedom of speech or expression at the schoolhouse gate." *Tinker*, supra, 393 U.S., at 506. They cannot be punished merely for expressing their personal views on the school premises — whether "in the cafeteria, or on the playing field, or on the campus during the authorized hours," unless school authorities have reason to believe that such expression will "substantially interfere with the work of the school or impinge upon the rights of other students."

We have nonetheless recognized that the First Amendment right of students in the public schools "are not automatically coextensive with the rights of adults in other settings," Bethel School District v. Fraser, 478 U.S. 675, 682 (1986), and must be "applied in light of the special characteristics of the school environment." A school need not tolerate student speech that is inconsistent with its "basic educational mission," even though the government could not censor similar speech outside the school. Accordingly, we held in *Fraser* that a student could be disciplined for having delivered a speech that was "sexually explicit" but not legally obscene at an official school assembly, because the school was entitled to "disassociate itself" from the speech in a manner that would demonstrate to others that such vulgarity is "wholly inconsistent with the 'fundamental values' of public school education." We thus recognized that "[t]he determination of what manner of speech in the classroom or in school assembly is inappropriate properly rests with the school board," rather than with the federal courts. It is in this context that respondents' First Amendment claims must be considered.

A

We deal first with the question whether Spectrum may appropriately be characterized as a forum for public expression. The public schools do not possess all of the attributes of streets, parks, and other traditional public forums that "time out of mind, have been used for purposes of assembly, communicating thoughts between citizens, and discussing public questions." Hence, school facilities may be deemed to be public forums only if school authorities have "by policy or by practice" opened those facilities "for indiscriminate use by the general public," or by some segment of the public, such as student organizations. If the facilities have instead been reserved for other intended purposes, "communicative or otherwise," then no public forum has been created, and school officials may impose reasonable restrictions on the speech of students, teachers, and other members of the school community. . . .

The policy of school officials toward Spectrum was reflected in Hazelwood School Board Policy 348.51 and the Hazelwood East Curriculum Guide. Board Policy 348.51 provided that "[s]chool sponsored publications are developed within the adopted curriculum and its educational implications in regular classroom activities." The Hazelwood East Curriculum Guide described the Journalism II course as a "laboratory situation in which the students publish the school newspaper applying skills they have learned in Journalism I." The lessons that were to be learned from the Journalism II course, according to the Curriculum Guide, included development of journalistic skills under deadline pressure, "the legal, moral, and ethical community," and "responsibility and acceptance of criticism for articles of opinion." Journalism II was taught by a faculty member during regular class hours [who selected editors, scheduled publications, determined the number of pages, assigned story ideas, edited stories, and dealt with the printer]. Students received grades and academic credit for their performance in the course.

The evidence relied upon by the Court of Appeals in finding Spectrum to be a public forum is equivocal at best. For example, Board Policy 348.51, which stated in part that "[s]chool sponsored student publications will not restrict free expression or diverse viewpoints within the rules of responsible journalism," also stated that such publications were "developed within the adopted curriculum and its educational implications." One might reasonably infer from the full text of Policy 348.51 that school officials retained ultimate control over what constituted "responsible journalism" in a school-sponsored newspaper. Although the Statement of Policy published in the September 14, 1982, issue of Spectrum declared that "Spectrum, as a student-press publication, accepts all rights implied by the First Amendment," this statement, understood in the context of the paper's role in the school's curriculum, suggests at most that the administration will not interfere with the students' exercise of those First Amendment rights that attend the publication of a school-sponsored newspaper. It does not reflect an intent to expand those rights by converting a curricular newspaper into a public forum. Finally, that students were permitted to exercise some authority over the contents of Spectrum was fully consistent with the Curriculum Guide objective of teaching the Journalism II students "leadership responsibilities as issue and page editors." . . . School officials did not evince either "by policy or by practice," any intent to open the pages of Spectrum to "indiscriminate use," by its student reporters and editors, or by the student body generally. Instead, they "reserve[d] the forum for its intended purpos[e]," as a supervised learning experience for journalism students. Accordingly, school officials were entitled to regulate the contents of Spectrum in any reasonable manner. It is this standard, rather than our decision in *Tinker*, that governs this case.

B

The question whether the First Amendment requires a school to tolerate particular student speech — the question that we addressed in *Tinker* — is different from the question whether the First Amendment requires a school affirmatively to promote particular student speech. The former question addresses educators' ability to silence a student's personal expression that happens to occur on the school premises. The latter question concerns educators' authority over school-sponsored publications, theatrical productions, and other expressive activities that students, parents, and members of the public might reasonably perceive to bear the imprimatur of the school. These activities may fairly be characterized as part of the school curriculum, whether or not they occur in a traditional classroom setting, so long as they are supervised by faculty members and designed to impart particular knowledge or skills to student participants and audiences.

Educators are entitled to exercise greater control over this second form of student expression to assure that participants learn whatever lessons the activity is designed to teach, that readers or listeners are not exposed to material that may be inappropriate for their level of maturity, and that the views of the individual speaker are not erroneously attributed to the school. Hence, a school may in its capacity as publisher of a school newspaper or producer of a school play "disassociate itself," not only from speech that is, for example, ungrammatical, poorly written, inadequately researched, biased or prejudiced, vulgar or profane, or unsuitable for immature audiences. A school must be able to set high standards for the student speech that is disseminated under its auspices — standards that may be higher than those demanded by some newspaper publishers or theatrical producers in the "real" world — and may refuse to disseminate student speech that does not meet those standards. In addition, a school must be able to take into account the emotional maturity of the intended audience in determining whether to disseminate student speech on potentially sensitive topics, which might range from the existence of Santa Claus in an elementary school setting to the particulars of teenage sexual activity in a high school setting. A school must also retain the authority to refuse to sponsor student speech that might reasonably be perceived to advocate drug or alcohol use, irresponsible sex, or conduct otherwise inconsistent with "the shared values of a civilized social order," or to associate the school with any position other than neutrality on matters of political controversy. Otherwise, the schools would be unduly constrained from fulfilling their role as "a principal instrument in awakening the child to cultural values, in preparing him for later professional training, and in helping him to adjust normally to his environment."

Accordingly, we conclude that the standard articulated in *Tinker* for determining when a school may punish student expression need not also be the standard for determining when a school may refuse to lend its name and resources to the dissemination of student expression. Instead, we hold that educators do not offend the First Amendment by exercising editorial control over the style and content of student speech in school-sponsored expressive activities so long as their actions are reasonably related to legitimate pedagogical concerns.

This standard is consistent with our oft-expressed view that the education of the Nation's youth is primarily the responsibility of parents, teachers, and state and local school officials, and not of federal judges. It is only when the decision to censor a school-sponsored publication, theatrical production, or other vehicle of student expression has no valid educational purpose that the First Amendment is so "directly and sharply implicate[d]," as to require judicial intervention to protect students' constitutional rights.

III

We also conclude that Principal Reynolds acted reasonably in requiring the deletion from the May 13 issue of Spectrum of the pregnancy article, the divorce article, and the remaining articles that were to appear on the same pages of the newspaper. . . . [The] principal's decision to delete two pages of Spectrum, rather than to delete only the offending articles or to require that they be modified, was reasonable under the circumstances as he understood them. Accordingly, no violation of First Amendment rights occurred.

Justice BRENNAN, with whom Justice MARSHALL and Justice BLACKMUN join, dissenting.

When the young men and women of Hazelwood East High School registered for Journalism II, they expected a civics lesson. Spectrum, the newspaper they were to publish, "was not just a class exercise in which students learned to prepare papers and hone writing skills, it was a . . . forum established to give students an opportunity to express their views while gaining an appreciation of their rights and responsibilities under the First Amendment to the United States Constitution. . . . "

"[A]t the beginning of each school year," the student journalists published a State-ment of Policy — tacitly approved each year by school authorities — announcing their expectation that "Spectrum, as a student-press publication, accepts all rights implied by the First Amendment. . . . Only speech that 'materially and substantially interferes with the requirements of appropriate discipline' can be found unaccept-able and therefore prohibited." The school board itself affirmatively guaranteed the students of Journalism II an atmosphere conducive to fostering such an apprecia-tion and exercising the full panoply of rights associated with a free student press. "School sponsored student publications," it vowed, "will not restrict free expres-sion or diverse viewpoints within the rules of responsible journalism." (Board Policy §348.51).

This case arose when the Hazelwood East administration breached its own promise, dashing its students' expectations. The school principal, without prior consultation or explanation, excised six articles — comprising two full pages — of the May 13, 1983, issue of Spectrum. He did so not because any of the articles would "materially and substantially interfere with the requirements of appropri-ate discipline," but simply because he considered two of the six "inappropriate, personal, sensitive, and unsuitable" for student consumption.

In my view the principal broke more than just a promise. He violated the First Amendment's prohibitions against censorship of any student expression that neither disrupts classwork nor invades the rights of others, and against any censorship that is not narrowly tailored to serve its purpose.

Public education serves vital national interests in preparing the Nation's youth for life in our increasingly complex society and for the duties of citizenship in our democratic Republic. . . .

Free student expression undoubtedly sometimes interferes with the effective-ness of the school's pedagogical functions. Some brands of student expression do so by directly preventing the school from pursuing its pedagogical mission: The young polemic who stands on a soapbox during calculus class to deliver an eloquent polit-ical diatribe interferes with the legitimate teaching of calculus. . . . Other student speech, however, frustrates the school's legitimate pedagogical purposes merely by expressing a message that conflicts with the school's, without directly interfering with the school's expression of its message. . . .

If mere incompatibility with the school's pedagogical message were a con-stitutionally sufficient justification for the suppression of student speech, school officials could censor . . . students or student organizations . . . . converting our public schools into "enclaves of totalitarianism," that "strangle the free mind at its source." The First Amendment permits no such blanket censorship authority. While the "constitutional rights of students in public school are not automatically coextensive with the rights of adults in other settings," *Fraser*, students in the public schools do not "shed their constitutional rights to freedom of speech or expression at the schoolhouse gate," *Tinker* . . . .

In *Tinker*, this Court struck the balance. We held that official censorship of student expression — there the suspension of several students until they removed their armbands protesting the Vietnam war — is unconstitutional unless the speech "materially disrupts classwork or involves substantial disorder or invasion of the rights of others. . . . " [393 U.S. at 513.] School officials may not suppress "silent, passive expression of opinion, unaccompanied by any disorder or disturbance on the part of" the speaker. Id. at 508. The "mere desire to avoid the discomfort and unpleasantness that always accompany an unpopular viewpoint," id., at 509, or an unsavory subject, *Fraser*, supra, 478 U.S. at 688-689 (Brennan J., concurring in judgment), does not justify official suppression of student speech in the high school. . . .

. . . The Court today casts no doubt on *Tinker*'s vitality. Instead it erects a taxonomy of school censorship, concluding that *Tinker* applies to one category and not another. On the one hand is censorship "to silence a student's personal expression that happens to occur on the school premises." On the other hand is censorship of expression that arises in the context of "school-sponsored . . . expressive activities that students, parents, and members of the public might reasonably perceive to bear the imprimatur of the school."

The Court does not, for it cannot, purport to discern from our precedents the distinction it creates. . . . Nor has this Court ever intimated a distinction between personal and school-sponsored speech in any other context. . . .

Even if we were writing on a clean slate, I would reject the Court's rationale for abandoning *Tinker* in this case. The Court offers no more than an obscure tangle of three excuses to afford educators "greater control" over school-sponsored speech than the *Tinker* test would permit: the public educator's prerogative to control curriculum; the pedagogical interest in shielding the high school audience from objectionable viewpoints and sensitive topics; and the school's need to dissociate itself from student expression. None of the excuses, once disentangled, supports the distinction that the Court draws. *Tinker* fully addresses the first concern; the second is illegitimate; and the third is readily achieveable through less oppressive means.

[T]he Court attempts to justify censorship of the article on teenage pregnancy on the basis of the principal's judgment that (1) "the [pregnant] students' anonymity was not adequately protected," despite the article's use of aliases; and (2) the judgment "that the article was not sufficiently sensitive to the privacy interests of the students' boyfriends and parents. . . . " Similarly, the Court finds in the principal's decision to censor the divorce article a journalistic lesson that the author should have given the father of one student an "opportunity to defend himself" against her charge. . . .

But the principal never consulted the students before censoring their work. "[T]hey learned of the deletions when the paper was released. . . . " Further, he explained the deletions only in the broadest of generalities. In one meeting called at the behest of seven protesting Spectrum staff members (presumably a fraction of the full class), he characterized the articles as " 'too sensitive' for 'our immature audience of readers,' " and in a later meeting he deemed them simply "inappropriate, personal, sensitive and unsuitable for the newspaper." The Court's supposition that the principal intended (or the protesters understood) those generalities as a lesson on the nuances of journalistic responsibility is utterly incredible. If he did, a fact that neither the District Court nor the Court of Appeals found, the lesson was lost on all but the psychic Spectrum staffer.

The Court's second excuse for deviating from precedent is the school's interest in shielding an impressionable high school audience from material whose substance is "unsuitable for immature audiences." . . .

Tinker teaches us that the state educator's undeniable, and undeniably vital, mandate to inculcate moral and political values is not a general warrant to act as "thought police" stifling discussion of all but state-approved topics and advocacy of all but the official position. . . .

The mere fact of school sponsorship does not, as the Court suggests, license such thought control in the high school, whether through school suppression of disfavored viewpoints or through official assessment of topic sensitivity. The former would constitute unabashed and unconstitutional viewpoint discrimination. . . .

Official censorship of student speech on the ground that it addresses "potentially sensitive topics" is, for related reasons, equally impermissible. "[P]otential topic sensitivity" is a vaporous nonstandard . . . that invites manipulation to achieve ends that cannot permissibly be achieved through blatant viewpoint discrimination and chills student speech to which school officials might not object. . . .

The case before us aptly illustrates how readily school officials (and courts) can camouflage viewpoint discrimination as the "mere" protection of students from sensitive topics. . . .

The sole concomitant of school sponsorship that might conceivably justify the distinction that the Court draws between sponsored and nonsponsored student expression is the risk "that the views of the individual speaker [might be] erroneously attributed to the school." . . . Dissociative means short of censorship are available to the school. It could, for example, require the student activity to publish a disclaimer. . . .

Since the censorship served no legitimate pedagogical purpose, it cannot by any stretch of the imagination have been designed to prevent "materia[l] disruption of] classwork." Nor did the censorship fall within the category that *Tinker* described as necessary to prevent student expression from "inva[ding] the rights of others," ibid. If that term is to have any content, it must be limited to rights that are protected by law. . . . And, as the Court of Appeals correctly reasoned, whatever journalistic impropriety these articles may have contained, they could not conceivably be tortious, much less criminal.

Finally, even if the majority were correct that the principal could constitutionally have censored the objectionable material, I would emphatically object to the brutal manner in which he did so. Where "[t]he separation of legitimate from illegitimate speech calls for more sensitive tools," the principal used a paper shredder. He objected to some material in two articles, but excised six entire articles. He did not so much as inquire into obvious alternatives, such as precise deletions or additions (one of which had already been made), rearranging the layout, or delaying publication. Such unthinking contempt for individual rights is intolerable from any state official. It is particularly insidious from one to whom the public entrusts the task of inculcating in its youth an appreciation for the cherished democratic liberties that our Constitution guarantees.

The Court opens its analysis in this case by purporting to reaffirm *Tinker's* time-tested proposition that public school students " 'do not shed their constitutional rights to freedom of speech or expression at the schoolhouse gate.' " That is an ironic introduction to an opinion that denudes high school students of much of the First Amendment protection that *Tinker* itself prescribed. Instead of "teach[ing] children to respect the diversity of ideas that is fundamental to the American system," and "that our Constitution is a living reality, not parchment preserved under glass," the Court today "teach[es] youth to discount important principles of our government as mere platitudes." The young men and women of Hazelwood East expected a civics lesson, but not the one the Court teaches them today. . . .

QUESTIONS ON *TINKER* AND *HAZELWOOD*

(1) Are *Ginsberg* and *Tinker* consistent? *Ginsberg* expressly adopts a notion of "variable" First Amendment rights and upholds the legitimacy of a different legal standard of obscenity for young people. Does *Tinker* hold that students have the same First Amendment rights as adults?

Do *Tinker* and *Hazelwood* suggest that the public secondary school students and state university students have the same First Amendment rights? See Hosty v. Carter, 325 F.3d 945 (7th Cir. 2003), *reh'g en banc granted, vacated*; Kincaid v. Gibson, 236 F.3d 342 (6th Cir. 2001). See generally Richard J. Peltz, Censorship Tsunami Spares College Media: To Protect Free Expression on Public Campuses, Lessons from the "College *Hazelwood*" Case, 68 Tenn. L. Rev. 481 (2001); Karyl Roberts Martin, Note, Demoted to High School: Are College Students' Free Speech Rights the Same as Those of High School Students?, 45 B.C. L. Rev. 173 (2003).

(2) Tinker Test.   According to *Tinker*, schools may not restrict student speech unless necessary to avoid a material and substantial interference with the work of the school or discipline. The applicability of *Tinker* depends in large part on the definition of these terms. What is meant by "the work of the school"? "Disruption"? "Material and substantial" interference? What do you think the public school's educational mission is? What should it be? One commentator contrasts the majority and dissent's views of "school work," by pointing out that the majority (Justice Fortas) defines the term narrowly (i.e., teaching), whereas the dissent (Justice Black) believes that schools are instruments of socialization. Mark Yudof, *Tinker* Tailored: Good Faith, Civility, and Student Expression, 69 St. John's L. Rev. 365 (1995) (symposium on the 25th anniversary of *Tinker*).

How relevant in the determination of "disruption" is the reaction of the recipient of the derogatory speech? Suppose the recipient is so upset by the student's expressive activity that she or he is unable to complete the school year? See J.S. ex rel. H.S. v. Bethlehem Area Sch. Dist., 807 A.2d 847 (Pa. 2002). Is peer harassment a basis for regulation of speech? See Davis v. Monroe Cty. Bd. of Educ., 526 U.S. 629 (1999) (holding that schools incur liability if they are aware of peer sexual harassment and fail to respond). Is the First Amendment a defense to peer harassment? Must the "disruption" be actual or only potential?

(3) Parental Role.   What power does a parent have to punish or constrain a child in activities that might be constitutionally protected from state intrusion? Would the result in *Tinker* have been different if the children's parents had told the children *not* to wear armbands and had asked the school to punish the children if in defiance of parental wishes they insisted on wearing them?

(4) In *Tinker*, the youngest protestor, Paul Tinker, was eight years old. As Justice Black noted in an omitted portion of his dissent, the Tinkers' father was "a Methodist minister without a church . . . paid a salary by the American Friends

Service Committee," and Christopher Eckhardt's mother was "an official in the Women's International League for Peace and Freedom." (393 U.S. at 516.) What role did these parents play in the minors' decision to wear armbands? As Professor Robert Burt has queried: "From this record, is it crystal clear whose political expression rights were being protected—the children's or their parents'?" Robert Burt, Developing Constitutional Rights of, in, and for Children, 39 Law & Contemp. Probs. (No. 3) 118, 122 (1975). Burt adds:

> *Tinker*, from this perspective, is no different from the parental-rights cases [*Yoder* and *Prince*] considered earlier. In general, it is false psychology to portray a dispute between children and the state without acknowledging the direct—implicit or explicit—role of parents in that dispute. Id. at 123.

(5) Political Speech. Does *Tinker* turn in important part on the fact that the school prohibited some but not all symbolic speech that involved political expression? May a school ban student displays of the Confederate flag? Would a student's display of that flag be likely to lead to a material and substantial disruption of school discipline under *Tinker*? See Scott v. School Bd. of Alachua Cty., 324 F.3d 1246 (11th Cir. 2003), *cert. denied*, 540 U.S. 824 (2003).

(6) Public Forum. Why does *Hazelwood* determine that *Tinker* is inapplicable? According to the Court, since "Spectrum" is an integral part of the school curriculum, the principal's actions need only be reasonable. Were they reasonable according to the Court? In your opinion? Was "Spectrum" a public forum according to the Court? What factors are relevant to the determination? Why was the Court's determination of whether "Spectrum" constitutes a public forum so critical? After *Hazelwood*, what type of student forum would be entitled to First Amendment protection?

(7) Viewpoint Discrimination. According to constitutional doctrine, speech restrictions must be made without regard to the viewpoint expressed in the speech (i.e., viewpoint discrimination is constitutionally impermissible). *Hazelwood* left open the question of whether viewpoint discrimination is permissible for student school-sponsored speech. Contrast the opinion of the majority and dissent on this issue. In the wake of *Hazelwood*, the federal circuit courts have split on whether the Supreme Court created a constitutional exception to viewpoint restrictions on student expression. See Susannah Barton Tobin, Note, Divining *Hazelwood*: The Need for a Viewpoint Neutrality Requirement in School Speech Cases, 39 Harv. C.R.-C.L. L. Rev. 217, 231-238 (2004) (pointing out that the First, Third, and Tenth Circuits read *Hazelwood* to permit viewpoint restrictions of school-sponsored speech, whereas the Sixth, Ninth, and Eleventh Circuits read *Hazelwood* to require viewpoint neutrality). What is the appropriate role of schools in dictating the viewpoints students may express?

(8) Tinker's Invasion of Rights Test. What does the "invasion of rights of others" prong of the *Tinker* case mean? Note that *Hazelwood*, by holding *Tinker* inapplicable, avoids clarifying this aspect of *Tinker*. The Eight Circuit opinion in *Hazelwood* interpreted the invasion-of-rights standard to signify only a tortious act. 795 F.2d 1368, 1376 (8th Cir. 1986). If the invasion-of-rights standard refers to

potential tort liability, does this require school officials to be cognizable of tort law to decide whether student expression would result in tort liability to the school?

(9) Limits of **Hazelwood.**   What are the limits of *Hazelwood*? Is it limited to school-sponsored publications? How important is the on-campus/off-campus distinction — i.e., is *Hazelwood* restricted to speech produced only on campus? What does "school sponsorship" mean? Could the school ban an underground newspaper published and distributed off campus? What if the same publication is distributed off campus at an official school function (such as at a senior class barbecue)? See Burch v. Barker, 861 F.2d 1149 (9th Cir. 1988).

How do *Tinker*, *Fraser*, and *Hazelwood* apply to speech that students place on the Internet, such as derogatory speech about a student, a teacher, or the school that is created on a home computer (such as on a personal Web site) but that can be accessed at school? See J.S. ex rel. H.S. v. Bethlehem Area Sch. Dist., 807 A.2d 847 (Pa. 2002); Beussink v. Woodland R-IV Sch. Dist., 30 F. Supp. 2d 1175 (E.D. Mo. 1998). Should it matter if the creator of the speech e-mails it to a friend and the friend then distributes it at school? See Killion v. Franklin Regional Sch. Dist., 136 F. Supp. 2d 446 (W.D. Pa. 2001). See generally Thomas E. Wheeler II, Slamming in Cyberspace: The Boundaries of Student First Amendment Rights, 21 Computer & Internet L. 14, 17 (2004). See also M. Bradford Grabowski, Student Drops Appeal Over Offensive Song, Providence Journal-Bulletin, Aug. 30, 2001, at B1.

(10) Is a high school student's sexual orientation within the sphere of protected expression? See Fricke v. Lynch, 491 F. Supp. 381 (D.R.I. 1980) (student challenged school's decision to prevent gay high school students from attending a senior prom together on the ground that it violated plaintiff's First Amendment rights). See also Deb Price, Opinion, Utah Student Reinforces Gay Youth Rights, Detroit News, Apr. 26, 2004, at A9 (discussing the impact of *Fricke*).

(11) Who Should Decide?   In *Hazelwood*, the Court states that schools rather than the federal courts should decide such issues. Do you agree that courts should defer to school authorities when constitutional rights are at stake? How should the tension be resolved between student's expressive rights and the interests of schools as educators of youth?

(12) Effect of **Hazelwood.**   What do you think is the effect of *Hazelwood*? Some survey data suggest that censorship of the student press rose after *Hazel-wood*. Rosemary C. Salomone, Free Speech and School Governance in the Wake of *Hazelwood*, 26 Ga. L. Rev. 253, 306-325 (1992). Moreover, the number of journalism classes and journalism students appears to have decreased after *Hazelwood*. Peter Fimrite, High School Journalism Classes May Be Eliminated, S.F. Chron., May 21, 2003, at A1 (noting 10% drop in journalism classes and students in California at a time when overall student enrollment was increasing, and attributing the decrease to censorship and funding cuts). The problems of censorship and budget cuts are not unrelated. The executive director of the Student Press Law Center, Mark Goodman, notes: "[W]hen schools are beleaguered because of funding issues," they become especially concerned about their image and hence, more likely to engage in censorship. Id.

On the other hand, some states already had or did enact protective legislation following *Hazelwood*. Salomone, supra, at 302-306. See also Student Press Law Center, State Student Free Expression Laws, *http://www.splc.org/stateantihazlaws.asp*

(last visited Sept. 5, 2004) (pointing out that Arkansas, California, Colorado, Iowa, Kansas, and Massachusetts have laws "sometimes called anti-*Hazelwood* laws" and that Pennsylvania and Washington have state administrative code provisions that protect student free expression rights).

(13) Problems. Public schools, increasingly, are establishing dress codes. Some schools ban certain types of clothing; others prohibit the wearing of gang apparel. Are the types of student conduct in the examples below expressive speech? If so, are the following regulations constitutional? Are *Tinker, Fraser,* and/or *Hazelwood* applicable? Do the following regulations serve legitimate pedagogical objectives?

a. A high school student is asked to turn inside-out his T-shirt portraying a three-faced Jesus with the wording "See No Truth, Hear No Truth, Speak No Truth" and "Marilyn Manson" printed on the front. The word "Believe," emphasizing the letters "l-i-e," is printed on the back. The rock band Marilyn Manson promotes violence and pro-drug views in their lyrics. The school dress and grooming policy forbids "clothing with offensive illustrations, drug, alcohol, or tobacco slogans." See Boroff v. Van Wert City Bd. of Educ., 220 F.3d 465 (6th Cir. 2000).

b. A student is asked to remove his T-shirt displaying a picture of President George W. Bush with the phrase "international terrorist" printed on the front. Barber ex rel. Barber v. Dearborn Pub. Sch., 286 F. Supp. 2d 847 (E.D. Mich. 2003).

c. A student is asked to remove her pin of the Palestinian flag. Tamar Lewin, High School Tells Student to Remove Antiwar Shirt, N.Y. Times, Feb. 26, 2003, at A12.

d. A school bans the wearing of Muslim head scarves by female students. Derek H. Davis, Reacting to France's Ban: Headscarves and Other Religious Attire in American Public Schools, 46 J. Church & State 221 (2004).

e. A school prohibits a transsexual high school student from wearing clothes and accessories that are consistent with her gender identity. See Doe ex rel. Doe v. Yunits, No. 001060A, 2000 WL 33162199 (Mass. Super. Ct. Oct. 11, 2000).

f. A school regulates hair length of male students. See Alabama & Coushatta Tribes of Texas v. Trustees of Big Sandy Indep. Sch. Dist., 817 F. Supp. 1319 (E.D. Tex. 1993). Or the school prohibits the wearing of "sagging pants." See Bivens ex rel. Green v. Albuquerque Pub. Sch., 899 F. Supp. 556 (D.N.M. 1995), *aff'd without opinion*, 131 F.3d 151 (10th Cir. 1997).

See generally Todd A. DeMitchell et al., Dress Codes in the Public Schools: Principals, Policies, and Precepts, 29 J.L. & Educ. 31 (2000); Rob Killen, Note, The Achilles' Heel of Dress Codes: The Definition of Proper Attire in Public Schools, 36 Tulsa L.J. 459 (2000).

NOTE: STUDENTS' RIGHT TO INFORMATION — SCHOOLBOOKS AND THE INTERNET

First Amendment issues concerning the censorship of school libraries and texts have been the focus of controversy since *Tinker.* The Supreme Court first addressed censorship of public school libraries in Board of Education v. Pico, 457 U.S. 853

(1982). In *Pico*, a local school board removed nine books (including Kurt Von-negut's *Slaughterhouse Five*, Langston Hughes' *Best Short Stories of Negro Writers* and the anonymous memoir of a young addict, *Go Ask Alice*) from the high school and junior high school libraries on the ground that the books were "anti-American, anti-Christian, anti-Semitic, and just plain filthy." Id. at 857 (quoting the Board's press release). In response to the students' suit challenging the constitutionality of the school board's policy, the Supreme Court held that the First Amendment imposes limitations upon a local school board's ability to censor information. Although local school boards have a legitimate role in the determination of school library content, they may not remove books from school libraries merely because they dislike the ideas contained therein.

After *Pico*, school libraries broadened student access to information by the installation of computers. In 1994, Congress enacted legislation to provide sectarian and nonsectarian schools with the necessary funds to do so. Improving America's Schools Act of 1994, Pub. L. No. 103-382, 108 Stat. 3518 (codified at 20 U.S.C. §§7351(a), (b)) (2000 & Supp. 2001). In 2000, Congress responded to calls for child protection from harmful material on the Internet by the passage of the Children's Internet Protection Act (CIPA), Pub. L. No. 106-554, 114 Stat. 2763A-335 (2000) (codified as amended in 47 U.S.C. §254 and scattered sections of 20 U.S.C.). CIPA conditions federal Internet access subsidies to elementary and secondary schools and libraries upon the installation of filtering technology to prevent minors from obtaining access to harmful material.

When a group of public libraries, library associations, library patrons, and Web site publishers challenged the constitutionality of CIPA, the Supreme Court held that CIPA did not impose an impermissible condition in violation of the First Amendment. According to Chief Justice Rehnquist (with three Justices concur-ring and two Justices concurring in result), federal subsidies were intended to help libraries fulfill their traditional role of obtaining material of appropriate quality for educational purposes, and Congress could validly insist that public funds be spent for the purposes for which they were authorized, even though filtering software tended to erroneously block some constitutionally protected speech. United States v. American Library Assn., 539 U.S. 194 (2003). See generally Steven D. Hinckley, Your Money or Your Speech: The Children's Internet Protection Act and the Con-gressional Assault on the First Amendment in Public Libraries, 80 Wash. U. L.Q. 1025, 1099 (2002) (criticizing CIPA as an attempt to "end-run constitutional roadblocks" to content-based regulation by means of the spending power).

NOTE: PROCEDURAL RIGHTS AND THE PUNISHMENT OF STUDENTS FOR EXPRESSIVE ACTIVITY

Following *Tinker*, there was some question as to whether *Tinker* applied not only to prior restraints of student speech but also to subsequent punishment of students for expressive activity. The Supreme Court addressed the latter issue in Bethel v. Fraser, 478 U.S. 675 (1986).

In *Bethel*, a high school student, Matthew Fraser, gave a nominating speech for a fellow student at a school assembly. Although the speech contained no patently offensive language, it referred to the candidate in an elaborate sexual metaphor. Charged with violating a school disciplinary rule for disruptive conduct, Fraser was suspended for three days and his name was removed from the graduation speaker list. Fraser alleged that the discipline violated the First and Fourteenth Amendments. The Ninth Circuit Court of Appeals affirmed the district court ruling in Fraser's favor, holding that the school district failed to establish the requisite disruption under *Tinker.*

Reversing, the Supreme Court refused to apply *Tinker*, reasoning that *Tinker* applied only to political speech. According to the Court, the compelling interest of school officials in inculcating appropriate values and maintaining a proper educational environment outweighed Fraser's right to free speech. The Court also rejected the argument that the disciplinary action violated Fraser's right to procedural due process. The Court held that the brief three-day suspension did not give rise to full due process rights. Earlier, the Supreme Court had held that minimum procedural due process requirements apply (i.e., notice of the charges, an explanation of the evidence against him and an opportunity to present his side of the case) when a high school student is subject to a ten-day suspension. Goss v. Lopez, 419 U.S. 565, 581 (1975). *Goss* determined that the ten-day suspension implicated both the "property" and "liberty" interests of high school students. Expulsion might require even more formal procedures, according to the majority. Id. at 584. In contrast, the dissent criticized that "No one can foresee the ultimate frontiers of the new 'thicket' the Court now enters" by constitutionally imposing procedural requirements on the day-to-day operation of schools. Id. at 597. See also American Bar Association, Juvenile Justice Standards, Standards Relating to Schools and Education (1982) (proposing substantial formal safeguards for suspensions of one month or more).

In the late 1980s and early 1990s, states adopted a stricter approach to school discipline, known as a "zero tolerance policy," in response to perceptions of increasing school violence. Alicia C. Insley, Comment, Suspending and Expelling Children From Educational Opportunity: Time to Reevaluate Zero Tolerance Policies, 50 Am. U. L. Rev. 1039 (2001). Zero-tolerance policies received approbation at the federal level when Congress enacted the Gun-Free Schools Act of 1994, 20 U.S.C. §8921(b), which conditioned federal funding on enactment of state laws imposing at least a one-year expulsion on any student who brings a firearm to school and requiring referrals of such students to law enforcement. The Supreme Court subsequently held the Act unconstitutional in United States v. Lopez, 514 U.S. 549 (1995) (concluding that the Act exceeded congressional authority under the Commerce Clause because possession of a gun in a local school zone is not an economic activity that substantially affects interstate commerce), and Congress repealed the Act in subsequent legislation (No Child Left Behind Act of 2001, Pub. L. No. 107-110, 115 Stat. 1425). Nonetheless, all states had enacted zero-tolerance laws in compliance with federal law and continued to enforce them.

Schools extended zero-tolerance policies far beyond the federal requirements. "In acknowledgment of the intensifying public pressure, school administrators began expanding the federal mandates surrounding weapons policies to include a wider variety of behaviors and harsher sanctions." Christina L. Anderson, Comment, Double Jeopardy: The Modern Dilemma for Juvenile Justice, 152 U. Pa. L. Rev. 1181, 1185 (2004). The number of students who were subject to suspension and expulsion "exploded." Id. at 1192. Schools sanctioned a variety of allegedly disruptive expressions, including those that are written, verbal, artistic, gestural, fashion-related, and Internet-based. Louis P. Nappen, School Safety v. Free Speech: The Seesawing Tolerance Standards for Students' Sexual and Violent Expressions, 9 Tex. J. on C.L. & C.R. 93, 101-114 (2003). See, e.g., In re George T., 16 Cal. Rptr.3d 61 (Cal. 2004) (exploring whether a high school student's dark poetry, along with circumstances surrounding its dissemination, established that poem as a criminal threat).

In the post-Columbine era, these policies led to strict punishments for verbal expression that was even slightly threatening. For example, (1) a Louisiana middle school student served two weeks in a juvenile detention center for saying to another student in the lunch line, "If you take all the potatoes, I'm gonna get you"; (2) a Massachusetts student was suspended indefinitely for telling a boy that the latter was "on his list" (he meant to say "shit list" but refrained from profanity because of a teacher's presence); (3) an Oklahoma student received a 15-day suspension for casting a magic spell that caused a teacher to become sick; and (4) a Nevada girl received a ten-day suspension for compiling a list of classmates with whom she was "frustrated." Nappen, supra, at 108. In fact, schools punished violent expressions more severely than sexual expressions. "To contrast, delivering a speech with sexual innuendos to an entire student body in 1988 results in a suspension for three days (*Bethel*); whereas, reading a violent story to a creative writing class in 2001 may result in mandatory suspension or expulsion." Id. at 109.

Cases examining the constitutionality of punishment for Internet-based expressive activity have proliferated. The Pennsylvania Supreme Court recently applied both *Tinker* and *Fraser* to determine whether a school district could expel a student for derogatory and threatening comments regarding a teacher that were on the student's personal Web site. In J.S. ex rel. H.S.v. Bethlehem Area School District, 807 A.2d 847 (Pa. 2002), the court adopted a two-prong analysis, first considering whether the student's Web site (describing his math teacher in obscene terms, including pictures of her decapitation, and a solicitation for funds to hire a hit man to kill her) constituted a "true threat" that was outside First Amendment protection.

The "true threat" doctrine is derived from Watts v. United States, 394 U.S. 705, 708 (1969) (per curiam) (holding that a particular threat against the president was not a true threat but only a "crude offensive method of stating a political opposition"). In *Watts*, the Court failed to develop a bright-line test to define "true threats," merely suggesting some relevant factors (e.g., the context and conditional nature of the statement as well as the reaction of listeners). In response, federal courts wrestled with establishing criteria for threatening speech and have adopted either an objective speaker-based test or a subjective recipient-based test. Compare Lovell By and Through Lovell v. Poway Unified Sch. Dist., 90 F.3d 367 (9th Cir. 1996) (applying an objective speaker-based test of whether a reasonable person would foresee that his or her statement would be interpreted as a serious expression of intent to harm) with Doe v. Pulaski Cty. Special Sch. Dist., 306 F.3d 616 (8th Cir. 2002) (adopting a subjective recipient-based test of whether a reasonable recipient would interpret the statement as a serious expression of intent to harm).

Many courts have explored whether students' expressive activities constitute "true threats." In *J.S.*, supra, the Pennsylvania Supreme Court found that the student's personal Web site was not a true threat because of several factors, including the "sophomoric, crude" characters, the school's lack of immediate disciplinary reaction, the student viewers' benign reactions, the fact that the statements were indirectly conveyed to the teacher by other students and an administrator (in fact, the student designed the Web site to preclude access by school officials), and the student had never threatened the teacher before or shown any propensity for violence. Despite this finding, the court applied *Fraser* and *Tinker* to find the school district's disciplinary action constitutional. Applying *Fraser*, the court held that the student's derogatory, threatening speech on his Web site was just as offensive as the speech disciplined in *Fraser* and similarly undermined the basic function of a public school. Applying *Tinker*, the court found that the Web site was on-campus speech (because it could be accessed on campus) and also resulted in significant interference with the work of the school. The requisite level of interference consisted of the teacher's being so distressed that she took a leave of absence, and the need to hire three different substitute teachers to replace her — which had a demoralizing effect on the school and severely disrupted the educational process. *J.S.*, 807 A.2d at 869.

Litigation challenging zero-tolerance policies generally has proven unsuccessful. Anderson, supra, at 1199. Courts have held that the zero-tolerance sanctions of suspension and expulsion comport with due process requirements. Id. One commentator explains that procedural due process challenges are futile because most schools currently provide notice and some form of a hearing. She adds that substantive due process challenges, similarly, have not met with much success because of the high standard (an "extraordinary departure from established norms" that is "wholly arbitrary") as well as judicial deference to local school systems regarding disciplinary decisions. Insley, supra, at 1056. "In conclusion, both procedural and substantive due process challenges are likely to be successful only in cases of blatant omissions of minimum procedures or extreme policies that present no rational connection [with pedagogical purposes]." Id. at 1057.

SOME QUERIES: CORPORAL PUNISHMENT IN SCHOOLS

Many schools have traditionally used corporal punishment to discipline students. Should parents have the power to prohibit use of corporal punishment on their child in a public school? What do the cases considered in this chapter imply? See Baker v. Owen, p. 236, infra. From the child's perspective, could corporal punishment ever offend the constitutional prohibition against cruel and unusual punishment? If corporal punishment is permitted, does the Due Process Clause (particularly in light of Goss v. Lopez) require some sort of hearing before punishment is imposed? See Note on Ingraham v. Wright, p. 242, infra. Chapter 3 considers generally the parental right to discipline children and legal limitations on the physical mistreatment of children. Corporal punishment in schools is considered in that context. See pp. 235-242, infra.

North Florida Women's Health & Counseling Servs. v. State
866 So. 2d 612 (2003)

SHAW, Senior Justice.

. . . Under the Parental Notice Act [Fla. Stat. Ann. §390.01115 (1999)], prior to undergoing an abortion, a minor must notify a parent of her decision or, alternatively, must convince a court that she is sufficiently mature to make the decision herself, or that, if she is immature, the abortion nevertheless is in her best interests. . . . When the Parental Notice Act became effective on July 1, 1999, several women's clinics, women's rights groups, and physicians filed suit in circuit court seeking injunctive and declaratory relief to block its enforcement, claiming that the Act violates a minor's constitutional rights under our earlier decision in [In re T.W., 551 So. 2d 1186 (Fla. 1989) (holding a parental *consent* statute unconstitutional)]. . . .

[W]e first consider the source and nature of the right of privacy asserted by petitioners. The text of the Florida Constitution begins with the Declaration of Rights [which was amended in 1980] to include an express, freestanding Right of Privacy Clause [Art. I, §23, Fla. Const.]. . . . By amending the constitution to contain this Clause, the electors opted to create a broader, more protective right than that which had existed theretofore. . . . The Right of Privacy Clause has been implicated in a wide range of matters dealing with personal privacy.

The seminal Florida case in this area is In re T.W., 551 So. 2d 1186 (Fla. 1989), wherein this Court held that section 390.001(4)(a), Florida Statutes (Supp. 1988), i.e., the Parental Consent for Abortion Act, violated the Right of Privacy Clause. [Based on the strict scrutiny test], [t]he Court determined that a woman has a reasonable expectation of privacy in deciding whether to continue her pregnancy, more so than in virtually any other decision, and that the right of privacy is implicated in the decision. Significantly, the Court held that both the expectation and right apply to pregnant minors. . . .

In evaluating the present trial court's decision, . . . we focus on two key questions addressed by the court. (1) Does the Parental Notice Act impose a significant restriction on a minor's right of privacy? And if so, (2) does the Act further a compelling State interest through the least intrusive means?

As to whether the Parental Notice Act imposes a significant restriction on a minor's right of privacy, the trial court addressed this matter as follows:

> The State argues, alternatively, that the Parental Notification Statute is essentially different in character and effect than a Parental Consent Statute, such as was struck down in *T.W.* After all, the minor is still free to choose an abortion. There is no veto power by the parent over the minor's decision. Thus, the State argues, the Act is an insignificant intrusion on a woman's right of privacy and should be permissible. The State cites federal case authority in support of this argument. I am unpersuaded. . . .
>
> [T]he argument that a statute requiring notice to parents is not a significant intrusion on a minor's right of privacy ignores the realities of the intended and expected effect of the Act. While the requirement of notification is certainly less restrictive than the requirement of parental consent, it is by no means insignificant. The stated, obvious, and intended purpose of the law is to allow the parents an opportunity to exert parental authority and influence over their child, to provide care, comfort and guidance. And, the ability of parents, for better or worse, to

persuade, influence, coerce, intimidate, and otherwise affect the decisions and conduct of their children is tremendous. Further, what parent would not do all he or she could; including seeking relief in court, to prevent their child from doing something they felt was not in her best interest.

Even under the best of conditions, there will be some delay and thus increased risk to the minor child in having the abortion performed. Having to speak to a guardian ad litem and/or attorney, coming up before a judge and other court personnel can be embarrassing and intimidating. The chance of a breach in the confidentiality requirement is a real possibility, especially in small communities. Some minors, fearful that a judge will deny their petition, or that their parents will find out anyway, will delay their decision long enough that termination of the pregnancy will no longer be an option. Some children, without doubt, will seek at all cost to avoid telling their parents, including going to other states, having illegal abortions, or self-inducing abortions. Some physicians, unsure of their potential for liability, will be more cautious and less likely to perform an abortion for a minor if there is any question as to proper notification. . . .

Our review of the record shows that the trial court's ruling on this point must be sustained. First, the court's main finding — that the notification requirement is similar to the consent requirement in that it constitutes a significant intrusion on a minor's right of privacy — is supported by competent substantial evidence in the record. As noted above, few decisions are more private and properly protected from government intrusion than a woman's decision whether to continue her pregnancy, and yet the Act's notification requirement prohibits a pregnant minor from keeping this matter private. And second, the court's ultimate conclusion — that the Act can meet constitutional muster only if it furthers a compelling State interest through the least restrictive means — comports with the applicable law as articulated in *T.W.* and other decisions of this Court.

As to whether the Parental Notice Act furthers a compelling State interest, the trial court addressed this matter thusly:

> 5. The State may be able to establish a compelling state interest justifying intrusion upon a minor's right of privacy that would not justify the intrusion into the privacy interest of an adult. . . .

—some things are different for minors

> 7. The State's interests in protecting an immature minor and fostering the integrity of the family, while important and worthy, do not justify restricting a minor's right to choose abortion where similar restrictions are not imposed on comparable choices or decisions. . . .

> One of the key holdings of *T.W.* as it pertains to the present case, is Number 7. You can't say that our interest in protecting immature minors and preserving family unity is so compelling that it justifies interfering with a minor's choice to have an abortion, where those interests are not deemed sufficiently compelling to justify interference with comparable decisions. It is not enough for the state to say that an interest is compelling. It must be demonstrated through comprehensive and consistent legislative treatment.

In support of this last point, the court cited section 743.065, Florida Statutes (1999), which was the same statutory section we relied on in *T.W.* The trial court then quoted the following passage from *T.W.*:

> Under [section 743.065], a minor may consent, without parental approval, to any medical procedure involving her pregnancy or her existing child — no matter how

dire the possible consequences — except abortion. Under In re Guardianship of Barry, 445 So. 2d 365 (Fla. 2d DCA 1984) (parents permitted to authorize removal of life support system from infant in permanent coma), this could include authority in certain circumstances to order life support discontinued for a comatose child. In light of this wide authority that the state grants an unwed minor to make life-or-death decisions concerning herself or an existing child without parental consent, we are unable to discern a special compelling interest on the part of the state under Florida law in protecting the minor only where abortion is concerned. We fail to see the qualitative difference in terms of impact on the well-being of the minor between allowing the life of an existing child to come to an end and terminating a pregnancy, or between undergoing a highly dangerous medical procedure on oneself and undergoing a far less dangerous procedure to end one's pregnancy. If any qualitative difference exists, it certainly is insufficient in terms of state interest. [*T.W.*, 551 So. 2d at 1195.]

Critical to the trial court's decision — and to our decision today — is the fact that nothing whatsoever has changed in this statutory scheme since *T.W.* was decided. . . .

The State claims that, despite the ruling of the trial court below, we should find the Parental Notice Act constitutional because the United States Supreme Court has approved similar parental notification statutes under the federal constitution. Further, the State relies on the United States Supreme Court decision in Planned Parenthood v. Casey, 505 U.S. 833 (1992), wherein a plurality of the Court abandoned the "strict" scrutiny standard in favor of the less stringent "undue burden" standard. The State urges this Court to recede from *T.W.* and adopt the same "undue burden" standard in Florida. We decline to do so.

First, any comparison between the federal and Florida rights of privacy is inapposite in light of the fact that *there is no express federal right of privacy clause.* Florida is one of only a handful of states wherein the state constitution includes an independent, freestanding Right of Privacy Clause. [S]econd, it is settled in Florida that each of the personal liberties enumerated in the Declaration of Rights is a fundamental right. Legislation intruding on a fundamental right is presumptively invalid and, where the right of privacy is concerned, must meet the "strict" scrutiny standard. Florida courts consistently have applied the "strict" scrutiny standard whenever the Right of Privacy Clause was implicated, regardless of the nature of the activity. The "undue burden" standard, on the other hand, is an inherently ambiguous standard and has no basis in Florida's Right of Privacy Clause. . . .

The State in effect is asking this Court to recede from *T.W.* because it was wrongly decided. We decline to do so. . . . We cannot forsake the doctrine of stare decisis and recede from our own controlling precedent when the only change in this area has been in the membership of this Court. . . .

We approve the trial court's decision permanently enjoining enforcement of the Parental Notice Act. We expressly decide this case on state law grounds and cite federal precedent only to the extent that it illuminates Florida law. . . .

WELLS, J., dissenting.

I dissent from the decision of the majority. . . . My first and fundamental reason is that I simply recognize that there is a very real difference between parental consent, which was the subject of this Court's decision in In re T.W., 551 So. 2d 1186 (Fla.1989), and parental notification, which is the subject of the statute in the present case. . . .

[I]t is simply logical to me that the community, acting through the State, has an exceedingly compelling interest in having parents parent their children. Thus, the State has established a compelling interest in requiring parental responsibility for providing medical care, guidance, and counseling, particularly when a parent's child is in crisis. It is illogical to me, if the State has such a compelling interest in parental responsibility, to conclude that there is not a compelling interest in "notifying" the parent when the child is in a crisis situation. How can a parent be expected to act responsibly without notice? . . .

I believe that it is this Court's obligation in ruling upon what the majority recognizes are "the most gut wrenching, emotion-laden issues of our day" in which there are "well-intentioned, civic-minded individuals on both sides of the debate," majority op. at 639, not to allow constitutional review to become a vehicle for substituting the judicial branch's judgment as to policy questions for the judgment of the legislative branch. . . .

In the present case, the Legislature has acted in a narrow way, and this Court should follow its precedent and give the proper deference to the Legislature's decision in enacting this statute. Upholding the Legislature's decision here does not conflict with In re T.W. because of the plain distinction between parental consent and parental notification as recognized by sound legal authority. . . .

[A] majority of this Court has recognized that minors do not have the same level of privacy rights that adults possess. [Jones v. State, 640 So. 2d 1084 (Fla. 1994) (Kogan, J., concurring) (holding that statutory rape provision was constitutional).] In respect to parental notification, the analysis of a minor's right to privacy should, in accord with this precedent, begin with the question of whether a minor has a reasonable expectation to keep knowledge of medical information from a parent. The legislative determination was that there is no such reasonable expectation to keep such information from a parent. That determination simply is not clearly erroneous, nor was it found to be by the trial court, nor could it be because it is plainly in keeping with common sense and experience. . . .

It appears to me that a more logical constitutional analysis of legislation regarding minors' rights in respect to their parents would be to accept that the State has a compelling interest in the health and welfare of minors. This Court should then use the analysis provided by [Planned Parenthood of Southeastern Pennsylvania v. Casey, 505 U.S. 833 (1992)], which was released three years after In re T.W. In Casey, 505 U.S. at 876, they recognized that the strict scrutiny test (which is almost always fatal in fact) was not the appropriate standard for addressing regulation of the right to abortion: The very notion that the State has a substantial interest in potential life leads to the conclusion that not all regulations must be deemed unwarranted. Not all burdens on the right to decide whether to terminate a pregnancy will be undue. In our view, the undue burden standard is the appropriate means of reconciling the State's interest with the woman's constitutionally protected liberty.

. . . Using this analysis rather than the rigid "compelling state interest" standard not only eliminates the inherent problems with the judiciary using legislative inconsistency as a basis for holding a statute unconstitutional, but this analysis logically addresses the real constitutional question, which is whether the Legislature by its statute unduly burdened a minor's right to privacy. When this analysis is used, the answer is plain that a statute requiring notice to a parent cannot be an undue burden on the minor's right to privacy, given the fact that a minor has at most a limited reasonable expectation of privacy in respect to the minor's parent and the fact that a parent has a fundamental right in parenting the child. . . .

QUESTIONS: PRIVACY RIGHTS OF MINORS

(1) Epilogue.   As the principal case reveals, the Florida Supreme Court twice invalidated laws mandating parental involvement (both parental consent and parental notification) in minors' abortion decision making. However, in November 2004, Florida voters overwhelmingly approved an amendment to the state constitution that exempts parental notification for purposes of abortion from the state constitutional right to privacy. Subsequently, the state supreme court dismissed an appeal by pro-choice organizations contending that the summary of the ballot measure was misleading, thereby paving the way for the state legislature to enact parental notification legislation, Jackie Hallifax, Court Tosses Appeal Over Abortion Measure, Tallahassee Democrat. Jan. 14, 2005. at B2.

(2) Different Treatment of Minors' Abortion Rights.   The United States Supreme Court permits greater regulation of minors' abortion rights compared to those of adults. The juvenile abortion cases are fascinating because they involve a conflict between the juvenile's own privacy interests (which are entitled to at least some constitutional protection) and parents' interests in childrearing (which *Pierce* and *Yoder* suggest are also constitutionally protected from state intrusion). What should the state's role be?

The Court in Bellotti v. Baird (*Bellotti II*), 443 U.S. 622 (1979) (discussed infra), explains the differences between adults and teenagers that allow states to regulate minors' abortion decisions to an extent that would be impermissible if applied to adults: "the peculiar vulnerability of children; their inability to make critical decisions in an informed, mature manner; and the importance of the parental role in child rearing." Id. at 634.

a. With respect to vulnerability, is the Supreme Court's assumption correct that the psychological effects of abortion are more severe for teenagers than adults? Psychological evidence refutes that assumption: studies reveal that few women or adolescents experience severe psychological problems after abortion. See Wendy J. Quinton et al., Adolescents and Adjustment to Abortion: Are Minors at Greater Risk?, 7 Psychol. Pub. Pol'y & L. 491 (2001) (presenting empirical findings that minors do not experience greater adjustment difficulties following abortion in either the short or long term).

b. Are adolescents less able to make informed, mature decisions? What does an informed and mature abortion decision entail? Studies that have examined decision-making processes of adolescents and adults find few, if any, differences in cognitive abilities, at least for adolescents who are age 14 and older. J. Shoshanna Ehrlich, Grounded in the Reality of Their Lives: Listening to Teens Who Make the Abortion Decision Without Involving Their Parents, 18 Berkeley Women's L.J. 61, 150

(2003). See also Preston A. Britner et al., Psychology and the Law: Evaluating Juveniles' Competence to Make Abortion Decisions: How Social Science Can Inform the Law, 5 U. Chi. L. Sch. Roundtable 35 (1998).

c. Consider the importance of the parental role. How might involvement of parents be helpful? How should the parents' and minors' rights be accommodated, according to the majority and dissent in *North Florida Women's Health Center*? In your opinion?

(3) Parental Role Generally. Currently, a majority of states require parental involvement in a minor's decision to have an abortion. Eighteen states require parental consent and 14 states require parental notification. Guttmacher Institute, State Policies in Brief: Parental Involvement in Minors' Abortion (as of Sept. 1, 2004), *www.agi-usa.org* (last visited Sept. 10, 2004). A few strict states require consent or notification of *both* parents. However, most states require consent or notification of only one parent. The most liberal states allow *other adult relatives* to substitute for parental consent. Many states with parental involvement laws make exceptions in cases of a medical emergency and/or abuse, assault, incest, or neglect. Id.

What interests are promoted by parental involvement requirements? Do they promote family unity? Parental control? Result in more informed decisions by the minor? Result in actual consultation with parents and an exploration of all available options? Suppose the parents disagree about permitting the minor to have the abortion. How is such disagreement to be resolved? See, e.g., S.H. v. D.H., 796 N.E.2d 1243 (Ind. Ct. App. 2003) (holding that mother's consent alone was sufficient).

(4) Federal Protection of Parental Rights: Child Custody Protection Act. The Supreme Court, in *Bellotti II*, emphasized the importance of the parental role in childbearing, especially the parents' ability to help their daughter make critical decisions. May states mandate that this counseling function be fulfilled only by parents? Data reveal that virtually all minors who refuse to involve their parents do consult at least one adult (relatives, boyfriends' parents, foster parents, or health care professionals). Ehrlich, Grounded in the Reality, supra, at 98-100.

Does the involvement of other adults in a minor's abortion decision interfere with parental control? Proposed federal legislation, the Child Custody Protection Act, H.R. 1755, 108th Cong., 1st Sess. (2003), introduced by Rep. Ros-Lehtinen (R.-Fla.) would make it a federal offense for a non-parent to knowingly transport a minor across a state line with the intent that she obtain an abortion, in circumvention of a state's parental consent or notification law. Re-introduced as the Child Interstate Abortion Notification Act, H.R. 748, 110th Cong., 1st Sess. (2005), the bill would also subject physicians to criminal liability for failure to notify parents.

What is the purpose of such legislation? To strengthen the family by protecting parental rights to custody? To make abortion more difficult to obtain? If such a law — No were enacted, what would be its effect? To decrease teenage sexual activity? To lower the abortion rate? To promote better communication among family members? Would such legislation be constitutional? Does the prohibited conduct fall within Congress' constitutional authority to regulate the transportation of individuals in interstate commerce? Does it interfere with the constitutionally protected right to travel? See Joanna S. Liebman, Note, The Underage, the "Unborn," and the

Unconstitutional: An Analysis of the Child Custody Protection Act, 11 Colum. J. Gender & L. 407 (2002).

(5) Parental Consent.   The United States Supreme Court has delivered several pronouncements on parental involvement laws. In *Planned Parenthood of Central Missouri v. Danforth,* 428 U.S. 52(1976), the Court invalidated a Missouri blanket parental consent requirement that would have required all minors to involve their parents in abortion decision making unless a physician certified that the abortion was necessary to preserve the mother's life. In *Bellotti II,* supra, the Court invalidated a Massachusetts blanket-consent statute that lacked an effective alternative procedure for minors who elected not to seek parental consent and that permitted withholding of judicial authorization for a minor who was determined to be mature by a court. However, in *Planned Parenthood of Southeastern Pennsylvania v. Casey,* 505 U.S. 833 (1992), the Court upheld a one-parent consent requirement with a judicial bypass procedure, reasoning that the provision was consistent with prior case law and furthered the state's legitimate interest "in the welfare of its young citizens, whose immaturity, inexperience, and lack of judgment may sometimes impair their ability to exercise their rights wisely." Id. at 970-971 (citing Hodgson v. Minnesota, 497 U.S. 417, 444 (1990)).

(6) Parental Notification.   The Supreme Court has examined the constitutionality of parental notification statutes as well. See, e.g., Lambert v. Wicklund, 520 U.S. 292 (1997) (upholding a one-parent notification statute with judicial bypass allowing waiver when notification was not in minor's best interests); Hodgson v. Minnesota, supra (upholding a two-parent notification requirement because of the presence of a judicial bypass procedure); Akron v. Akron Center for Reproductive Health (*Akron II*), 462 U.S. 416 (1983) (upholding a one-parent notification statute containing a judicial bypass provision because it satisfied the *Bellotti II* criteria for parental consent statutes). Although the United States Supreme Court has not explicitly required a judicial bypass proceeding for notification statutes, the Court has held that the presence of such a provision guaranteeing this proceeding renders parental notification statutes constitutional.

Are notification and consent requirements distinguishable where minors are concerned? Compare the views of the majority and dissent in *North Florida Women's Health Center.* Whose view is more persuasive?

(7) Bypass Procedure.

a. Burden of Proof.   Virtually all states with parental involvement laws (except Utah) require bypass proceedings to enable minors to obtain an abortion without parental consent. Guttmacher, State Policies in Brief: Parental Involvement in Minors' Abortions, *www.agi-usa.org* (last visited Sept. 10, 2004). According to *Bellotti II,* supra, the minor has the burden of showing that she is sufficiently mature to make the abortion decision or, if not, that an abortion nonetheless would be in her best interests.

Data suggest that courts in many jurisdictions grant virtually all petitions by minors who seek judicial authorization for abortions. Margaret C. Crosby & Abigail English, Mandatory Parental Involvement/Judicial Bypass Laws: Do They Promote Adolescent Health?, 12 J. Adolescent Health 143 (1991); Robert H. Mnookin, Bellotti v. Baird: A Hard Case, in In the Interest of Children 242 (1985).

b. Determination of Maturity.   The Supreme Court has not clarified the meaning of "maturity." How is a trial court to make such a determination? How relevant are factors such as grades, school attendance, extracurricular activities, employment history, future plans, financial situation, prior court involvement, health, history of substance abuse, prior contraceptive history, future plans to use contraception, and prior consultation with health professionals? How relevant is the minor's composure (or lack thereof) during her testimony? See, e.g., Ex parte Anonymous, 812 So. 2d 1234 (Ala. 2001) (affirming finding of immaturity based on minor's lack of emotion and "rehearsed" testimony). See Suellyn Scarnecchia & Julie Kunce Field, Judging Girls: Decision Making in Parental Consent to Abortion Cases, 3 Mich. J. Gender & L. 75, 99-112 (1995) (suggesting relevant areas of inquiry for the trial court). Should the Supreme Court articulate maturity guidelines?

Given the difficulties in determining maturity on a case-by-case basis, could a state adopt an age-based line and provide that a girl below that age is presumed immature and requires parental consent? See *Akron II*, supra, at 440 (invalidating a blanket determination that all minors under the age of 15 are too immature to make the abortion decision).

c. Evidentiary Standard. What should be the evidentiary standard for proof of maturity — clear and convincing evidence? A preponderance? See, e.g., In re B.S., 74 P.3d 285 (Ariz. Ct. App. 2003) (holding that minor bears burden of proving entitlement to abortion by clear and convincing evidence). Does a clear-and-convincing standard constitute an undue burden under *Casey*?

d. Judicial Role. Do judges have the requisite expertise to assess maturity and competence? Should judges delegate this duty to mental health personnel? To what extent is the judgment about maturity shaped by the judge's ideology and values? See Ex Parte Anonymous, 806 So. 2d 1269 (Ala. 2001) (upholding denial of petition by high school junior who was physicians' daughter; had A average, part-time job, and college plans; researched the abortion procedure on the Internet and spoke with abortion counselors). Will a liberal or conservative judge think it mature or immature for a young woman to become pregnant? Not to want to talk to her parents? To choose to assume responsibility herself? What other value judgments may be influential? See Nanette Dembitz, The Supreme Court and a Minor's Abortion Decision, 80 Colum. L. Rev. 1251, 1255-1256 (1980) (arguing that the minor's very decision to seek an abortion shows deliberation and responsibility).

If the judge decides that a teenager is not mature but that an abortion is nonetheless in her best interests, may the judge still require the minor to consult with her parent(s)? See In re Moe, 423 N.E.2d 1038, 1042 (Mass. App. Ct. 1981) (determining that once the judge decides that an abortion is in the minor's best interests, the judge may not decide it would be "in her even better interest" to consult with one or both parents).

e. Representation in Bypass Proceedings. In some bypass proceedings, judges have the option to appoint a guardian ad litem for the fetus. Are such guardianship appointments constitutional? Do they constitute an undue burden on the minor's right to an abortion? See Helena Silverstein, In the Matter of Anonymous, A Minor: Fetal Representation in Hearings to Waive Parental Consent for Abortion, 11 Cornell J.L. & Pub. Pol'y 69 (2001) (arguing that such appointments are a constitutionally permissible regulation of a minor's abortion right).

Some states permit the appointment of independent counsel on behalf of a minor in judicial bypass proceedings. Are such rules constitutional? Do they unduly burden the minor's rights? How does the appointment of a guardian ad litem in bypass proceedings accord with the traditional role of a guardian ad litem in litigation generally? See Elizabeth Susan Graybill, Note, Assisting Minors Seeking Abortions in Judicial Bypass Proceedings: A Guardian Ad Litem Is No Substitute for an Attorney, 55 Vand. L. Rev. 581 (2002).

(8) Physician's Role.   What should be the role of the physician in the minor's abortion decision? Should judges delegate the determination of maturity to the physicians who perform the abortions? Would this create a conflict of interest?

Should physicians be subject to tort liability for negligence for failing to verify the age of a minor? Recently, a Texas woman and her father filed suit against an abortion clinic, alleging that the physician who performed the woman's abortion was negligent and violated the Texas parental notification statute by accepting a grocery card as proof that the minor was old enough to have the abortion without parental consent. The jury allocated liability 90 percent to the minor and 10 percent to the physician but awarded zero damages. Subsequently, the Texas Department of Health established stricter guidelines about the requisite forms of identification that abortion clinics can accept. Scott E. Williams, Plaintiffs Take Nothing in Suit Against Doctor Who Performed Abortion, Tex. Law., Apr. 19, 2004, at 10.

Should physicians be required to give medical records of minors who have had abortions to law enforcement officials on the basis that such records may provide evidence of rape or statutory rape? Or would disclosure of such records violate minors' right to privacy? See Ron Sylvester, Kansas Seeks Abortion Patient IDs; Attorney General Says the Records May Reveal Crimes, Bradenton Herald, Feb. 25, 2005, at 6.

(9) Vision of the Family.   What is the vision of the family reflected in parental consent and notification statutes? How is that vision articulated in the majority and dissent in *North Florida Women's Health Center*? See generally Anne C. Dailey, Constitutional Privacy and the Just Family, 67 Tul. L. Rev. 955 (1993).

(10) State Constitutional Right to Abortion.   Why have plaintiffs been more successful in securing abortion rights under state constitutions? What light is shed on this question by *North Florida Women's Health Center*? See also Planned Parenthood of Central N.J. v. Farmer, 762 A.2d 620 (N.J. 2000) (holding that requirement of parental notification absent judicial waiver for abortion, without imposing a corresponding limitation on minor who seeks medical and surgical care otherwise related to her pregnancy, violates state constitution's equal protection provision); American Academy of Pediatrics v. Lungren, 940 P.2d 797 (Cal. 1997) (declaring parental consent statute an unconstitutional invasion of minor's right to privacy under California constitution). Note the different treatment by the majority and dissent in *North Florida Women's Health Center* of the minor's right to privacy and equal protection under the state constitution. See also J. Shoshanna Ehrlich, Minors as Medical Decision Makers: The Pretextual Reasoning of the Court in the Abortion Cases, 7 Mich. J. Gender & L. 65 (2000) (criticizing the Supreme Court for ignoring the equal protection argument that minors possess significant self-consent rights in medical contexts other than abortion).

(11) Empirical Data.

a. Reasons for Nondisclosure.   For what reasons would a teenager not wish to notify her parents of her pending abortion? Ehrlich points out that minors have multiple reasons for nondisclosure. They fear that their parents would be extremely upset or have a severe adverse reaction (leading to ejecting the minor from the home, inflicting physical harm, or other abuse); anticipate parental opposition to abortion or parental pressure to have the baby or get married; and anticipate problematic family dynamics. Ehrlich, Grounded in the Reality, supra, at 94-95. Of minors living with one or both parents, 30 percent feared a severe adverse reaction, such as abuse. Id. at 95. Would a statute providing for a bypass procedure only for abused and neglected minors (whose abuse/neglect has been documented and reported) be constitutional? See Planned Parenthood, Sioux Falls Clinic v. Miller, 63 F.3d 1452 (8th Cir. 1995) (invalidating such a statute because it failed to consider the mature-minor and best-interests test). See also Planned Parenthood of Blue Ridge v. Camblos, 155 F.3d 352 (4th Cir. 1998) (holding that judicial bypass was not required in all notification statutes if the statute contained appropriate exceptions, such as for minors who are victims of parental abuse or neglect).

   b. Reasons for Choosing Abortion.   According to Ehrlich, minors also gave multiple reasons for choosing to have an abortion. Their responses included not being ready for motherhood (feelings of not being sufficiently mature to raise a child); interference with future plans (desire to complete education); difficult life circumstances (such as already having a child or children, not having a place to live, or health problems); concerns about the child's well-being (being unable to support the child); and issues related to pregnancy, abortion, and adoption. Ehrlich, Grounded in Reality, supra, at 97.

   c. Consequences of Parental Involvement Laws.   What are the consequences of parental involvement laws? Some research suggests that parental involvement laws negatively impact minors' health by causing delays in medical care — i.e., increasing the incidence of abortions late in pregnancy. Jennifer Blasdell, Mother, May I? Ramifications for Parental Involvement Laws for Minors Seeking Abortion Services, 10 Am. U. J. Gender Soc. Pol'y & L. 287, 288-290 (2002) (reviewing data). Other research suggests that parental involvement laws decrease birth rates and abortion rates. James L. Rogers et al., Impact of the Minnesota Parental Notification Law on Abortion and Birth, 81 Am. J. Pub. Health 294 (1991). Can you think of an alternative explanation for the decrease in birth rates and abortion rates in a given jurisdiction (e.g., forum shopping)?

   (12) Medical Emergencies.   Some states provide that parental consent or notification is not required in cases of a medical emergency. According to *Roe, Casey*, and *Carhart*, regulations must contain adequate provision for abortion if the pregnancy poses a threat to the mother's life or health. Courts recently have addressed the constitutionality of the medical emergency exception. See, e.g., Planned Parenthood of Idaho, Inc. v. Wasden, 376 F.3d 908 (9th Cir. 2004) (invalidating state statute because the definition of "medical emergency" was so narrow as to preclude invocation of exception by minors with conditions that, while medically necessitating an abortion, were not "sudden, unexpected," and "abnormal"); Planned Parenthood of Northern New England v. Heed, 390 F.3d 53(1st Cir. 2004) (holding that exception to statute's notification requirement to prevent *death* of a minor was unconstitutionally narrow), *cert. granted sub nom.* Ayotte v. Planned Parenthood of Northern New England, No. 04-1144, 2005 WL 483164 (U.S. May 23, 2005).

(13) Problem.   Jane Doe is 15 years old and 11 weeks pregnant. She maintains a C grade-point average. After graduation, she plans to attend a trade school. She has a part-time job doing general office work in a family-run business. Jane has discussed available options with her gynecologist. She also consulted her mother, her boyfriend, and his family. Jane's mother, although she supports Jane's decision to have an abortion, will not give her consent for fear that Jane's father will be upset. Jane petitions the juvenile court for a waiver of the jurisdiction's parental consent requirement. According to state statute, a juvenile court shall grant a petition for a waiver of parental consent to an abortion if it finds either (1) that the minor is mature and well-informed enough to make the abortion decision on her own; or (2) that performance of the abortion would be in the best interest of the minor.

After a hearing, the juvenile court judge makes the following factual findings:

"(a) The minor's demeanor, coupled with her young age, evidence an immaturity for making decisions with significant consequences."

"(b) The minor's C average in school evidences her immaturity and her lack of ability to make a well-reasoned decision."

"(c) The minor has never engaged in employment on her own other than in her family business, which constitutes a lack of decision-making experience."

"(d) Based on the totality of the evidence and the court's personal observation of the witness, the Court is of the opinion that the minor is not mature enough to make the decision on her own."

Jane appeals from the order denying her petition for waiver of parental consent to abortion. What result? In re Anonymous, 888 So. 2d 1265 (Ala. Civ. App. 2004).

For a discussion of minor's access to contraceptives and issues of sex education, see Chapter 6.

CHAPTER 2

The Legal Framework
for a Child's Economic
Relationship Within
the Family

This chapter explores the legal framework for the child's economic relationship to the family. Its primary focus is the parental support obligation, and the state's role to enforce this obligation. It also briefly examines the state's role in supplementing the family's income where the parents lack adequate resources to care for the child. The extract from Blackstone's Commentaries highlights the common law background. After you have finished this chapter, reread the Blackstone extract and ask yourself how the law has changed, and perhaps more interestingly, what doctrinal relics still remain, and how our present-day law reflects its historical antecedents.

In studying the material in this chapter, keep the following questions in mind. To what extent is the duty to support children a legal obligation? A moral one? Who has the legal duty of support? To whom is the duty owed? What is included in support and how is it determined? What are the legal mechanisms for enforcing a support obligation? What are the sanctions? Who may sue? Are the child's economic claims affected by the marital status of its parents? What is the parents' support obligation to children who are born via assisted reproduction? What role should law and courts have in allocating resources within the ongoing family? If the parents should separate or divorce? If a parent dies? When does (and should) the state provide the resources for the support of children?

A. COMMON LAW BACKGROUND

William Blackstone, Commentaries on the Laws of England
Vol. 1, 446-454

The next, and the most universal relation in nature, is immediately derived from the preceding, being that between parent and child.

Children are of two sorts; legitimate and spurious, or bastards; each of which we shall consider in their order; and, first of legitimate children.

Legitimate Children

A legitimate child is he that is born in lawful wedlock, or within a competent time afterwards. *"Pater est quem nuptiae demonstrant,"* [The nuptials show who the father is.] is the rule of the civil law; and this holds with the civilians, whether the nuptials happen before, or after, the birth of the child. With us in England the rule is narrowed, for the nuptials must be precedent to the birth; of which more will be said when we come to consider the case of bastardy. At present let us inquire into, 1. The legal duties of parents to their legitimate children. 2. Their power over them. 3. The duties of such children to their parents.

And, first, the duties of parents to legitimate children: which principally consist in three particulars; their maintenance, their protection, and their education.

Duty to Support

The duty of parents to provide for the *maintenance* of their children, is a principle of natural law: an obligation, says Puffendorf, laid on them not only by nature herself, but by their own proper act, in bringing them into the world: for they would be in the highest manner injurious to their issue, if they only gave their children life, that they might afterwards see them perish. By begetting them, therefore, they have entered into a voluntary obligation, to endeavour, as far as in them lies, that the life which they have bestowed shall be supported and preserved. And thus the children will have a perfect *right* of receiving maintenance from their parents. And the president Montesquieu has a very just observation upon his head: that the establishment of marriage in all civilized states is built on this natural obligation of the father to provide for his children: for that ascertains and makes known the person who is bound to fulfil this obligation: whereas, in promiscuous and illicit conjunctions, the father is unknown; and the mother finds a thousand obstacles in her way; — shame, remorse, the constraint of her sex, and the rigour of laws; — that stifle her inclinations to perform this duty; and besides, she generally wants ability.

The municipal laws in all well-regulated states have taken care to enforce this duty though Providence has done it more effectually than any laws, by implanting in the breast of every parent that natural $\sigma \tau o \rho \gamma \eta$ or insuperable degree of affection, which not even the deformity of person or mind, not even the wickedness, ingratitude, and rebellion of children can totally suppress or extinguish.

The civil law obliges the parent to provide maintenance for his child: and, if he refuses, *"judex de ea re cognoscet."* [The judge shall take cognizance of the matter.] Nay, it carries this matter so far, that it will not suffer a parent at his death totally to disinherit his child, without expressly giving his reason for so doing; and there are fourteen such reasons reckoned up, which may justify such disinherison. If the parent alleged no reason, or a bad, or a false one, the child might set the will aside, *tanquam testamentum inofficiosum*, [as an undutiful will] a testament contrary to the natural duty of the parent. And it is remarkable under what colour the children were to move for relief in such a case; by suggesting that the parent had lost the use of his reason, when he made the *inofficious* testament. And this, as Puffendorf observes, was not to bring into dispute the testator's power of disinheriting his own offspring; but to examine the motives upon which he did it: and, if they were found defective in reason, then to set them aside. But perhaps this is going rather too far; every man has, or ought to have, by the laws of society, a power over his own property: and, as Grotius very well distinguishes, natural right obliges to give a *necessary* maintenance to children; but what is more than that they have no other right to, than as it is given them by the favour of their parents, or the positive constitutions of the municipal law. [See p. 207 infra, for present-day limitations on parental power to disinherit minor children in civil law countries as well as the United States.]

Let us next see what provisions our own laws have made for this natural duty. It is a principle of law, that there is an obligation on every man to provide for those descended from his loins; and the manner, in which this obligation shall be performed, is thus pointed out. The father and mother, grandfather and grand-mother of poor impotent persons shall maintain them at their own charges, if of sufficient ability, according as the quarter session shall direct: and if a parent runs away, and leaves his children, the church-wardens and overseers of the parish shall seize his rents, goods, and chattels, and dispose of them toward their relief.[1] By the interpretations which the courts of law have made upon these statutes, if a mother or grandmother marries again, and was before such second marriage of sufficient ability to keep the child, the husband shall be charged to maintain it for this being a debt of hers, when single, shall like others extend to charge the hus-band. But at her death, the relation being dissolved, the husband is under no farther obligation.

No person is bound to provide a maintenance for his issue, unless where the children are impotent and unable to work, either through infancy, disease, or acci-dent; and then is only obliged to find them with necessaries, the penalty on refusal being no more than 20*s*. a month. For the policy of our laws, which are ever watchful to promote industry, did not mean to compel a father to maintain his idle and lazy children in ease and indolence: but thought it unjust to oblige the parent against his will to provide them with superfluities, and other indulgences of fortune; imagining they might trust to the impulse of nature, if the children were deserving of such favours. . . .

Our law has made no provision to prevent the disinheriting of children by will: leaving every man's property in his own disposal, upon a principle of liberty in this, as well as every other action; though perhaps it had not been amiss, if the parent had been bound to leave them at the least a necessary subsistence. Indeed, among persons of any rank or fortune, a competence is generally provided for younger children, and the bulk of the estate settled upon the eldest, by the marriage-articles. Heirs also and children are favourites of our courts of justice, and cannot be disinherited by any dubious or ambiguous words; there being required the utmost certainty of the testator's intentions to take away the right of an heir.

---

[1] [In support of this proposition, Blackstone cited the Poor Laws, 43 Eliz., c. 2 (Poor Relief, 1601) described further at p. 151 infra.]

Duty to Protect

From the duty of maintenance we may easily pass to that of *protection*, which is also a natural duty, but rather permitted than enjoined by any municipal laws: nature, in this respect, working so strongly as to need rather a check than a spur. . . .

Duty to Educate

The last duty of parents to their children is that of giving them an *education* suitable to their station in life; a duty pointed out by reason, and of far the greatest importance of any. For, as Puffendorf very well observes, it is not easy to imagine or allow, that a parent has conferred any considerable benefit upon his child by bringing him into the world, if he afterwards entirely neglects his culture and education, and suffers him to grow up like a mere beast, to lead a life useless to others, and shameful to himself. Yet the municipal laws of most countries seem to be defective in this point, by not constraining the parent to bestow a proper education upon his children. Perhaps they thought it punishment enough to leave the parent, who neglects the instruction of his family, to labour under those griefs and inconveniences, which his family, so uninstructed, will be sure to bring upon him. Our laws, though their defects in this particular cannot be denied, have, in one instance made a wise provision for breeding up the rising generation; since the poor and laborious part of the community, when past the age of nurture, are taken out of the hands of their parents, by the statutes for apprenticing poor children; and are placed out by the public in such a manner, as may render their abilities, in their several stations, of the greatest advantage to the commonwealth. The rich indeed are left at their own option, whether they will breed up their children to be ornaments or disgraces to their family. . . .

Parental Power

The *power* of parents over their children is derived from the former consideration, their duty: this authority being given them, partly to enable the parent more effectually to perform his duty, and partly as a recompence for his care and trouble in the faithful discharge of it. And upon this score the municipal laws of some nations have given a much larger authority to the parents than others. The ancient Roman laws gave the father a power of life and death over his children; upon this principle, that he who gave had also the power of taking away. But the rigour of these laws was softened by subsequent constitutions; so that we find a father banished by the emperor Hadrian for killing his son, though he had committed a very heinous crime, upon this maxim, that *"patria potestas in pietate debet, non in atrocitate, consistere."* [Paternal power shall consist of kindness, not cruelty.] But still they maintained to the last a very large and absolute authority: for a son could not acquire any property of his own during the life of his father; but all his acquisitions belonged to the father, or at least the profits of them for his life.

The power of a parent by our English laws is much more moderate; but still sufficient to keep the child in order and obedience. He may lawfully correct his child, being under age, in a reasonable manner; for this is for the benefit of his education.

The consent or concurrence of the parent to the marriage of his child under age was also *directed* by our ancient law to be obtained: but now it is absolutely *necessary;* for without it the contract is void. And this also is another means, which the law has put into the parent's hands, in order the better to discharge his duty; first, or protecting his children from the snares of artful and designing persons: and next, of settling them properly in life, by preventing the ill consequences of too early and precipitate marriages. A father has no other power over his son's *estate*, than as his trustee or guardian; for though he may receive the profits during the child's minority, yet he must account for them when he comes of age. He may indeed have the benefit of his children's labour while they live with him, and are maintained by him; but this is no more than he is entitled to from his apprentices or servants. The legal power of a father (for a mother, as such, is entitled to no power, but only to reverence and respect), the power of a father, I say, over the persons of his children ceases at the age of twenty-one: for they are then enfranchised by arriving at years of discretion, or that point which the law has established (as some must necessarily be established), when the empire of the father, or other guardian, gives place to the empire of reason. Yet, till that age arrives, this empire of the father continues even after his death; for he may by his will appoint a guardian to his children. He may also delegate part of his parental authority, during his life, to the tutor or schoolmaster of his child; who is then *in loco parentis*, and has such a portion of the power of the parent committed to his charge, viz. that of restraint and correction, as may be necessary to answer the purposes for which he is employed.

Duties of Children

The *duties* of children to their parents arise from a principle of natural justice and retribution. For to those who gave us existence, we naturally owe subjection and obedience during our minority, and honour and reverence ever after: they, who protected the weakness of our infancy, are entitled to our protection in the infirmity of their age; they, who by sustenance and education have enabled their offspring to prosper, ought in return to be supported by that offspring in case they stand in need of assistance. Upon this principle proceed all the duties of children to their parents which are enjoined by positive laws. And the Athenian laws carried this principle into practice with a scrupulous kind of nicety; obliging all children to provide for their father, when fallen into poverty; with an exception to spurious children, to those whose chastity has been prostituted by consent of the father, and to those whom he had not put in any way of gaining a livelihood. The legislature, says baron Montesquieu, considered, that in the first case the father, being uncertain, had rendered the natural obligation precarious; that in the second case, he had sullied the life he had given, and done his children the greatest of injuries, in depriving them of their reputation; and that in the third case he had rendered their life (so far as in him lay) an insupportable burden, by furnishing them with no means of subsistence.

Our laws agree with those of Athens with regard to the first only of these particulars, the case of spurious issue. In the other cases the law does not hold the tie of nature to be dissolved by any misbehaviour of the parent; and therefore a child is equally justifiable in defending the person, or maintaining the cause or suit of a bad parent, as a good one; and is equally compellable, if of sufficient ability, to maintain and provide for a wicked and unnatural progenitor, as for one who has shewn the greatest tenderness and parental piety.

Yale Diagnostic Radiology v. Estate of Fountain
838 A.2d 179 (Conn. 2004)

BORDEN, J.

The sole issue in this appeal is whether a medical service provider that has provided emergency medical services to a minor may collect for those services from the minor when the minor's parents refuse or are unable to make payment. . . .

The following facts and procedural history are undisputed. In March, 1996, [Harun Fountain, a 13-year-old unemancipated minor] was shot in the back of the head at point-blank range by a playmate. As a result of his injuries, including the loss of his right eye, Fountain required extensive lifesaving medical services from a variety of medical services providers, including the plaintiff. The expense of the services rendered by the plaintiff to Fountain totaled $17,694. The plaintiff billed Tucker, who was Fountain's mother,[2] but the bill went unpaid and, in 1999, the plaintiff obtained a collection judgment against her. In January, 2001, however, all of Tucker's debts were discharged pursuant to an order of the Bankruptcy Court for the District of Connecticut. Among the discharged debts was the judgment in favor of the plaintiff against Tucker.

During the time between the rendering of medical services and the bankruptcy filing, Tucker, as Fountain's next friend, initiated a tort action against the boy who had shot him. Among the damages claimed were "substantial sums of money [expended] on medical care and treatment. . . . " A settlement was reached, and funds were placed in the estate established on Fountain's behalf under the supervision of the Probate Court. Tucker was designated the fiduciary of that estate. Neither Fountain nor his estate was involved in Tucker's subsequent bankruptcy proceeding.

Following the discharge of Tucker's debts, the plaintiff moved the Probate Court for payment of the $17,694 from the estate. The Probate Court denied the motion, reasoning that, pursuant to General Statutes §46b-37(b),[3] parents are liable for medical services rendered to their minor children, and that a parent's refusal or inability to pay for those services does not render the minor child liable. The Probate Court further ruled that minor children are incapable of entering into a

---

[2] There is no reference to Fountain's father in the record or briefs of either party. We therefore assume that he is not available as a viable source of payment of the plaintiff's bill for services rendered to Fountain.

[3] General Statutes §46b-37(b) provides: "Notwithstanding the provisions of subsection (a) of this section, it shall be the joint duty of each spouse to support his or her family, and both shall be liable for: (1) The reasonable and necessary services of a physician or dentist; (2) hospital expenses rendered the husband or wife or minor child while residing in the family of his or her parents; (3) the rental of any dwelling unit actually occupied by the husband and wife as a residence and reasonably necessary to them for that purpose; and (4) any article purchased by either which has in fact gone to the support of the family, or for the joint benefit of both." . . .

legally binding contract or consenting, in the absence of parental consent, to medical treatment. The Probate Court held, therefore, that the plaintiff was barred from seeking payment from the estate. [On appeal, the superior court reversed and entered judgment for the plaintiff-provider.]

. . . Connecticut has long recognized the common-law rule that a minor child's contracts are voidable. Under this rule, a minor may, upon reaching majority, choose either to ratify or to avoid contractual obligations entered into during his minority. See 4 S. Williston, Contracts (4th Ed.1992) §8:14, pp. 271-72. The traditional reasoning behind this rule is based on the well established common-law principles that the law should protect children from the detrimental consequences of their youthful and improvident acts, and that children should be able to emerge into adulthood unencumbered by financial obligations incurred during the course of their minority. The rule is further supported by a policy of protecting children from unscrupulous individuals seeking to profit from their youth and inexperience.

The rule that a minor's contracts are voidable, however, is not absolute. An exception to this rule, eponymously known as the doctrine of necessaries, is that a minor may not avoid a contract for goods or services necessary for his health and sustenance. See 5 S. Williston, Contracts (4th Ed.1993) §9:18, pp. 149-57. Such contracts are binding even if entered into during minority, and a minor, upon reaching majority, may not, as a matter of law, disaffirm them. Id.

The parties do not dispute the fact that the medical services rendered to Fountain were necessaries; rather, their dispute centers on whether Connecticut recognizes the doctrine of necessaries. As evidenced by the following history, the doctrine of necessaries has long been a part of Connecticut jurisprudence.

In Strong v. Foote, [42 Conn. 203, 205 (1875)], this court affirmed a judgment in favor of a dentist against a minor for services rendered to the minor, who had an estate and who was an orphan for whom a guardian had been appointed. This court stated: "In suits against minors, instituted by persons who have rendered services or supplied articles to them, the term 'necessaries' is not invariably used in its strictest sense, nor is it limited to that which is requisite to sustain life, but includes whatever is proper and suitable in the case of each individual, having reference to his circumstances and condition in life." Id. The court further noted that the services were "within the legal limitations of the word 'necessaries,' " and that the plaintiff was not required to inquire as to the minor's guardianship before rendering the services because the services were "necessary to meet an unsupplied want." Id.

Furthermore, from 1907 to 1959, statutory law regarding minors and the doctrine of necessaries remained unchanged. General Statutes §42-2 [codified] the common law doctrine of necessaries. We recognize that §42-2 was repealed in 1959, when Connecticut adopted the Uniform Commercial Code. That repeal was not intended, however, to eliminate the doctrine because the statute was replaced by General Statutes §42a-1-103, which contemplated that the Uniform Commercial Code would continue to be supplemented by the general principles of contract law regarding minors.

In light of these precedents, we conclude that Connecticut recognizes the doctrine of necessaries. We further conclude that, pursuant to the doctrine, the defendants are liable for payment to the plaintiff for the services rendered to Fountain.

We have not heretofore articulated the particular legal theory underlying the doctrine of necessaries. We therefore take this occasion to do so, and we conclude that the most apt theory is that of an implied in law contract, also sometimes referred to as a quasi-contract. We further conclude that based on this theory, the defendants are liable.

[W]hen a medical service provider renders necessary medical care to an injured minor, two contracts arise: the primary contract between the provider and the minor's parents; and an implied in law contract between the provider and the minor himself. The primary contract between the provider and the parents is based on the parents' duty to pay for their children's necessary expenses, under both common law and statute. Such contracts, where not express, may be implied in fact and generally arise both from the parties' conduct and their reasonable expectations. The primacy of this contract means that the provider of necessaries must make all reasonable efforts to collect from the parents before resorting to the secondary, implied in law contract with the minor.

The secondary implied in law contract between the medical services provider and the minor arises from equitable considerations, including the law's disfavor of unjust enrichment. Therefore, where necessary medical services are rendered to a minor whose parents do not pay for them, equity and justice demand that a secondary implied in law contract arise between the medical services provider and the minor who has received the benefits of those services. These principles compel the conclusion that, in the circumstances of the present case, the defendants are liable to the plaintiff, under the common-law doctrine of necessaries, for the services rendered by the plaintiff to Fountain.

The present case illustrates the inequity that would arise if no implied in law contract arose between Fountain and the plaintiff. Fountain was shot in the head at close range and required emergency medical care. Under such circumstances, a medical services provider cannot stop to consider how the bills will be paid or by whom. Although the plaintiff undoubtedly presumed that Fountain's parent would pay for his care and was obligated to make reasonable efforts to collect from Tucker before seeking payment from Fountain, the direct benefit of the services, nonetheless, was conferred upon Fountain. Having received the benefit of necessary services, Fountain should be liable for payment for those necessaries in the event that his parents do not pay.

Furthermore, in the present case, we note, as did the trial court, that Fountain received, through a settlement with the boy who caused his injuries, funds that were calculated, at least in part, on the costs of the medical services provided to him by the plaintiff in the wake of those injuries. Fountain, through Tucker, brought an action against the tortfeasor and, in his complaint, cited "substantial sums of money [expended] on medical care and treatment. . . . " This fact further supports a determination of an implied in law contract under the circumstances of the case.

The defendants claim, however, that the doctrine of necessaries has been legislatively abrogated by §46b-37(b)(2). We disagree. Section 46b-37(b)(2) governs the joint liability of parents for the support and maintenance of their family, and, in doing so, merely codifies the common-law principle, long recognized in Connecticut, that both parents are primarily responsible for providing necessary goods and services to their children. Section 46b-37(b)(2), however, is silent as to a child's secondary liability. That statute neither promotes nor prohibits a determination of secondary liability on the part of a minor when the minor has received emergency medical services and the parents are either unwilling or unable to pay for those services. . . . Nothing in either the language or the purpose of §46b-37(b)(2) indicates an intent on the part of the legislature to absolve minors of their secondary common-law liability for necessaries.

To the contrary, the purposes behind the statutory rule that parents are primarily liable and the common-law rule, pursuant to the doctrine of necessaries, that a minor is secondarily liable, when read together, serve to encourage payment on contracts for necessaries. Those purposes are (1) to reinforce parents' obligation to support their children, and (2) to provide a mechanism for collection by creditors when, nonetheless, the parents either refuse or are unable to discharge that obligation.

The defendants further contended, at oral argument before this court, that, even if we were to conclude that the doctrine of necessaries is applicable, the defendants are not liable to the plaintiff because there has been no showing that Tucker was unwilling or unable to provide necessaries to Fountain. . . . We disagree.

The undisputed facts show that Tucker had four years to pay the plaintiff's bill for the services rendered to Fountain. She did not pay that bill even when the plaintiff pursued a collection action against her. These facts are sufficient to show that Tucker was unwilling or unable to pay for Fountain's necessary medical services. . . . The judgment is affirmed.

NOTES AND COMMENTS: COMMON LAW

(1) Moral or Legal Obligation?   Early English cases, such as Mortimore v. Wright, 151 Eng. Rep. 502 (Exch. Ch. 1840), suggest that there was a moral but not a legal obligation on the part of parents to support their children. What does this mean? That the child had no power to sue the parent for support? That a creditor could not recover from the parent the cost of providing goods or services to a child even if they were "necessaries"? That there would be no legal sanctions brought against a father who failed to support his child?

(2) Elizabethan Poor Laws.   The Elizabethan "Poor Laws" did in effect create a legal obligation to exhaust parental resources for the support of a child before the local parish was obligated to provide relief.

The Act for Relief of the Poor, 43 Eliz., c. 2, §1 (1601) provided:

> [T]hat the church wardens of every parish, and four . . . substantial householders there . . . shall be called overseers of the poor of the same parish; and they . . . shall take order from time to time, by and with the consent of two or more . . . justices of peace . . . for setting to work all such persons, married or unmarried, having no means to maintain them, and use no ordinary and daily trade of life to get their living by: and also to raise . . . by taxation of every inhabitant . . . and every occupier of lands, houses . . . or salable underwoods in the same parish . . . a convenient stock of flax, hemp, wool, thread, iron and other necessary ware and stuff, to set the poor on work: and also competent sums of money towards the necessary relief of the lame, impotent, old, blind, and such others among them, being poor and not able to work, and also for the putting out of such children to be apprentices. . . .

Section 7 of the same act made it plain that primary responsibility for the indigent was with the family, not the state:

> That the father and grandfather, mother and the grandmother, and the children of every poor, old, blind, and impotent person, or other poor person not able to work, being of a sufficient ability, shall at their own charges relieve and maintain every such person. . . .

It was only when the family was unable to support the child that the local parish was called upon to provide assistance. The statute contemplated that if a parent was a recipient of aid, their children would be apprenticed or indentured to some other person in order to provide the child with a trade. As Blackstone suggests, however, where the child was able to work, a father had no support obligation under the poor laws. See supra p. 145.

(3) Parental Right to a Minor's Services and Earnings.   While the parental support obligation at common law was not well established, a parent's common law right to a child's services was clear. This meant that the parent could take the earnings of an unemancipated child. See Blackstone p. 147 supra. This common law tradition remains part of the law today and is incorporated in the statutory provisions of most states. See, e.g., Cal. Fam. Code §7500 (West 2004).

At common law "emancipation denoted the release of a minor from parental control, and the acquisition by the minor of the right to dispose of his own earnings." 5 Chester Garfield Vernier, American Family Laws §282 (1938). Emancipation was normally thought to require parental consent, or assent (which sometimes would be implied), and this too is also reflected in present-day statutes. "The parent, whether solvent or insolvent, may relinquish to the child the right of controlling the child and receiving the child's earnings. Abandonment by the parent is presumptive evidence of that relinquishment." Cal. Fam. Code §7504 (West 2004).

(4) "Necessaries" Doctrine.   At common law, a husband had an obligation to provide support for his wife and children. Related to that support obligation was the necessaries doctrine — the husband's duty to provide *necessary goods and services* to his wife and children, and if he failed to do so, the creditor's ability to sue the husband to recover the cost. This gender-based common law doctrine largely has been abrogated based on the Equal Protection Clause and state equal rights amendments. Many jurisdictions render each spouse liable for expenses incurred by the other spouse. (Sometimes, one spouse is primarily liable and the other is secondarily liable.) Similarly, many jurisdictions have held, by case law or statute, that both parents have equal obligations to contribute to their children's support.

Yale Diagnostic illustrates current American law regarding parents' obligation to provide necessaries to their children. In most jurisdictions today, both parents are liable for "necessaries" purchased by unemancipated minors living with the family. Minors ordinarily may disaffirm their own contracts prior to, or within, a reasonable time after reaching majority. However, an exception to this rule exists for necessaries. As *Yale Diagnostic* explains: "a minor may not avoid a contract for goods or services necessary for his health and sustenance." Also, the necessaries doctrine in effect permits self-help, for the parents' credit or the minor's own credit may be used by the minor to purchase essential goods and services.

The most frequently litigated issue is: were the goods or services "necessaries"? If not, the doctrine does not apply. Also, was the minor emancipated at the time of the purchase? If so, the parents are not responsible.

Yale Diagnostic, in announcing principles of primary (parents') and secondary (minors') liability for the costs of necessary medical treatment of minors, is consistent with the trend in recent case law. See, e.g., Williams v. Baptist Health Systems, Inc., 857 So. 2d 149 (Ala Civ. App. 2003); Layton Phys. Therapy Co. v. Palozzi, 777 N.E.2d 306 (Ohio Ct. App. 2002). See also American Law Institute, Restatement (Third) of the Law of Restitution & Unjust Enrichment, §20 (Illustration 2) (Tentative Draft No. 2, 2002 (accord).

(5) Changes in the Child's Economic Contributions to the Family — Some Broader Issues.   Until the late nineteenth century, young people often assumed adult work roles and contributed to the family's support. The twentieth century has seen, however, a substantial increase in the period of dependence of youth on their families. It is now difficult for a minor either to contribute substantially to the family's economic well-being, or to be economically self-sufficient. Indeed, many young people are now economically dependent upon their parents for a number of years after they reach the age of majority.

These historical changes in the work role of children are described in David Stern et al., How Children Used to Work, 39 Law & Contemp. Probs. (No. 3) 93 (1975). This article suggests that in the past, children were economic assets to their parents: young people could work and thus contribute to family support. Grown children frequently contributed to the support of their elderly parents. Now these economic benefits to parents have largely disappeared.[2] While parents still have the legal right to the earnings of their minor children, few children can have earnings that substantially contribute to the family pot, given the constraints imposed by compulsory education, child labor prohibitions (see Chapter 6 infra), and the increased specialization of work roles. Moreover, social security and pension funds appear to be displacing the family as the primary source of old age assistance.

Consider the broader implications of these changes. Thomas Hobbes asserted that "there is not reason why any man should desire to have children or to take care to nourish them if afterwards to have no other benefit from them than from other men." Leviathan 329 (William Molesworth ed. 1939-1945). The disappearance of these economic benefits poses difficult questions. In an age when the economic benefits to parents of having children are largely gone, should society bear a larger share of the cost of child raising? Are parents as a group more trustworthy, given the absence of opportunities for economic exploitation of their children and the primacy of noneconomic motivation to have them in the first place? Or must the state assume a more active role because of the diminution of an economic motive for parents themselves to "invest" in their own children?

---

[2] The exception is filial support legislation in many jurisdictions that imposes a duty on adult children to support *indigent* elderly parents. See generally Seymour Moskowitz, Filial Responsibility Statutes: Legal and Social Policy Considerations, 9 J.L. & Pol'y 709 (2001).

William Blackstone, Commentaries on the Laws of England
Vol. 1, 454-459

Illegitimate Children

We are next to consider the case of illegitimate children, or bastards; with regard to whom let us inquire, 1. Who are bastards. 2. The legal duties of the parents towards a bastard child. 3. The rights and incapacities attending such bastard children.

Who Are Bastards

A bastard, by our English laws, is one that is not only begotten, but born, out of lawful matrimony. The civil and canon laws do not allow a child to remain a bastard, if the parents afterwards intermarry: and herein they differ most materially from our law; which, though not so strict as to require that the child shall be *begotten*, yet makes it an indispensable condition that it shall be *born*, after lawful wedlock. And the reason of our English law is surely much superior to that of the Roman, if we consider the principal end and design of establishing the contract of marriage, taken in a civil light; abstractedly from any religious view, which has nothing to do with the legitimacy or illegitimacy of the children. The main end and design of marriage, therefore, being to ascertain and fix upon some certain person, to whom the care, the protection, the maintenance, and the education of the children should belong; . . .

Children born during wedlock may in some circumstances be bastards. As if the husband be out of the kingdom of England (or, as the law somewhat loosely phrases it, *extra quatuor maria* — beyond the four seas), for above nine months, so that no access to his wife can be presumed, her issue during that period shall be bastards. But, generally, during the coverture access of the husband shall be presumed, unless the contrary can be shown; which is such a negative as can only be proved by showing him to be elsewhere: for the general rule is, *praesumitur pro legitimatione* [the presumption is in favor of legitimacy].

Support of Bastards

Let us next see the duty of parents to their bastard children, by our law; which is principally that of maintenance. For, though bastards are not looked upon as children to any civil purposes, yet the ties of nature, of which maintenance is one, are not so easily dissolved: and they hold indeed as to many other intentions; as, particularly, that a man shall not marry his bastard sister or daughter. The civil law, therefore, when it denied maintenance to bastards begotten under certain atrocious circumstances, was neither consonant to nature, nor reason; however profligate and wicked the parents might justly be esteemed.

The method in which the English law provides maintenance for them is as follows: When a woman is delivered, or declares herself with child, of a bastard, and will by oath before a justice of peace charge any person having got her with child, the justice shall cause such person to be apprehended, and commit him till he gives security, either to maintain the child, or appear at the next quarter sessions to dispute and try the fact. But if the woman dies, or is married before delivery, or miscarries, or proves not to have been with child, the person shall be discharged: otherwise the sessions, or two justices out of sessions, upon original application to them, may take order for the keeping of the bastard, by charging the mother or the reputed father with the payment of money or other sustentation for that purpose. And if such putative father, or lewd mother, run away from the parish, the overseers by direction of two justices may seize their rents, goods, and chattels, in order to bring up the said bastard child. Yet such is the humanity of our laws, that no woman can be compulsively questioned concerning the father of her child, till one month after her delivery: which indulgence is, however, very frequently a hardship upon parishes, by giving the parents opportunity to escape.

The Rights and Incapacities of Bastards

I proceed next to the rights and incapacities which appertain to a bastard. . . .

The incapacity of a bastard consists principally in this, that he cannot be heir to anyone, neither can be have heirs, but of his own body; for, being *nullius filius*, he is therefore of kin to nobody, and has no ancestor from whom any inheritable blood can be derived. A bastard was also, in strictness, incapable of holy orders; and, though that were dispensed with, yet he was utterly disqualified from holding any dignity in the church: but this doctrine seems now obsolete; and in all other respects, there is no distinction between a bastard and another man. And really any other distinction, but that of not inheriting, which civil policy renders necessary, would, with regard to the innocent offspring of his parents' crimes, be odious, unjust, and cruel to the last degree, and yet the civil law, so boasted of for its equitable decisions, made bastards in some cases incapable even of a gift from their parents. A bastard may, lastly, be made legitimate and capable of inheriting, by the transcendent power of an act of parliament, and not otherwise, as was done in the case of John of Gaunt's bastard children, by a statute of Richard the Second.

Michael H. v. Gerald D.
491 U.S. 110 (1989)

Justice SCALIA announced the judgment of the Court and delivered an opinion, in which The Chief Justice joins, and in all but note 6 of which Justice O'CONNOR and Justice KENNEDY join.

Under California law, a child born to a married woman living with her husband is presumed to be a child of the marriage. Cal. Evid. Code Ann. §621 (West Supp. 1989). The presumption of legitimacy may be rebutted only by the husband or wife, and then only in limited circumstances. The instant appeal presents the claim that this presumption infringes upon the due process rights of a man who wishes to establish his paternity of a child born to the wife of another man, and the claim that it infringes upon the constitutional right of the child to maintain a relationship with her natural father.

The facts of this case are, we must hope, extraordinary. On May 9, 1976, in Las Vegas, Nevada, Carole D., an international model, and Gerald D., a top executive in a French oil company, were married. The couple established a home in Playa del Rey, California, in which they resided as husband and wife when one or the other was not out of the country on business. In the summer of 1978, Carole became involved in an adulterous affair with a neighbor, Michael H. In September 1980, she conceived a child, Victoria D., who was born on May 11, 1981. Gerald was listed as father on the birth certificate and has always held Victoria out to the world as his daughter. Soon after delivery of the child, however, Carole informed Michael that she believed he might be the father.

In the first three years of her life, Victoria remained always with Carole, but found herself within a variety of quasi-family units. In October 1981, Gerald moved to New York City to pursue his business interests, but Carole chose to remain in California. At the end of that month, Carole and Michael had blood tests of themselves and Victoria, which showed a 98.07% probability that Michael was Victoria's father. In January 1982, Carole visited Michael in St. Thomas, where his primary business interests were based. There Michael held Victoria out as his child. In March, however, Carole left Michael and returned to California, where she took up residence with yet another man, Scott K. Later that spring, and again in the summer, Carole and Victoria spent time with Gerald in New York City, as well as on vacation in Europe. In the fall, they returned to Scott in California.

In November 1982, rebuffed in his attempts to visit Victoria, Michael filed a filiation action in California Superior Court to establish his paternity and right to visitation. In March 1983, the court appointed an attorney and guardian ad litem to represent Victoria's interests. Victoria [through her guardian ad litem] then filed a cross-complaint asserting that if she had more than one psychological or de facto father, she was entitled to maintain her filial relationship, with all of the attendant rights, duties, and obligations, with both. In May 1983, Carole filed a motion for summary judgment. During this period, from March through July 1983, Carole was again living with Gerald in New York. In August, however, she returned to California, became involved once again with Michael, and instructed her attorneys to remove the summary judgment motion from the calendar.

For the ensuing eight months, when Michael was not in St. Thomas he lived with Carole and Victoria in Carole's apartment in Los Angeles and held Victoria out as his daughter. In April 1984, Carole and Michael signed a stipulation that Michael was Victoria's natural father. Carole left Michael the next month, however, and instructed her attorneys not to file the stipulation. In June 1984, Carole reconciled with Gerald and joined him in New York, where they now live with Victoria and two other children since born into the marriage.

In May 1984, Michael and Victoria, through her guardian ad litem, sought visitation rights for Michael *pendente lite*. To assist in determining whether visitation would be in Victoria's best interests, the Superior Court appointed a psychologist to evaluate Victoria, Gerald, Michael, and Carole. The psychologist recommended that Carole retain sole custody, but that Michael be allowed continued contact with Victoria pursuant to a restricted visitation schedule. The court concurred and ordered that Michael be provided with limited visitation privileges *pendente lite.*

On October 19, 1984, Gerald, who had intervened in the action, moved for summary judgment on the ground that under Cal. Evid. Code §621 there were no triable issues of fact as to Victoria's paternity. This law provides that "the issue of a wife cohabiting with her husband, who is not impotent or sterile, is conclusively presumed to be a child of the marriage." Cal. Evid. Code Ann. §621(a) (West Supp. 1989). The presumption may be rebutted by blood tests, but only if a motion for such tests is made, within two years from the date of the child's birth, either by the husband or, if the natural father has filed an affidavit acknowledging paternity, by the wife. §621(c) and (d).

On January 28, 1985, having found that affidavits submitted by Carole and Gerald sufficed to demonstrate that the two were cohabiting at conception and birth and that Gerald was neither sterile nor impotent, the Superior Court granted Gerald's motion for summary judgment, rejecting Michael's and Victoria's challenges to the constitutionality of §621. The court also denied their motions for continued visitation pending the appeal under Cal. Civ. Code §4601, which provides that a court may, in its discretion, grant "reasonable visitation rights . . . to any . . . person having an interest in the welfare of the child." Cal. Civ. Code Ann. §4601 (West Supp. 1989). It found that allowing such visitation would "violat[e] the intention of the Legislature by impugning the integrity of the family unit." Supp. App. to Juris. Statement A-91.

On appeal, Michael asserted, inter alia, that the Superior Court's application of §621 had violated his procedural and substantive due process rights. Victoria also raised a due process challenge to the statute, seeking to preserve her de facto relationship with Michael as well as with Gerald. She contended, in addition, that as §621 allows the husband and, at least to a limited extent, the mother, but not the child, to rebut the presumption of legitimacy, it violates the child's right to equal protection. Finally, she asserted a right to continued visitation with Michael under §4601. After submission of briefs and a hearing, the California Court of Appeal affirmed the judgment of the Superior Court and upheld the constitutionality of the statute. . . .

The Court of Appeal denied Michael's and Victoria's petitions for rehearing, and, . . . the California Supreme Court denied discretionary review. [W]e noted probable jurisdiction of the present appeal. 485 U.S. 903. Before us, Michael and Victoria both raise equal protection and due process challenges. We do not reach Michael's equal protection claim, however, as it was neither raised nor passed upon below. . . .

We address first the claims of Michael. At the outset, it is necessary to clarify what he sought and what he was denied. California law, like nature itself, makes no provision for dual fatherhood. Michael was seeking to be declared the father of Victoria. The immediate benefit he evidently sought to obtain from that status was visitation rights. . . . But if Michael were successful in being declared the father, other rights would follow — most importantly, the right to be considered as the parent who should have custody, Cal. Civ. Code Ann. §4600 (West 1983), a status which "embrace[s] the sum of parental rights with respect to the rearing of a child, including the child's care; the right to the child's services and earnings; the right to direct the child's activities; the right to make decisions regarding the control, education, and health of the child; and the right, as well as the duty, to prepare the child for additional obligations, which includes the teaching of moral standards, religious beliefs, and elements of good citizenship." 4 California Family Law §60.02[l][b] (C. Markey ed. 1987) (footnotes omitted). All parental rights, including visitation, were automatically denied by denying Michael status as the father. . . .

Michael contends as a matter of substantive due process that, because he has established a parental relationship with Victoria, protection of Gerald's and Carole's marital union is an insufficient state interest to support termination of that relationship. This argument is, of course, predicated on the assertion that Michael has a constitutionally protected liberty interest in his relationship with Victoria. . . .

In an attempt to limit and guide interpretation of the [Due Process] Clause, we have insisted not merely that the interest denominated as a "liberty" be "fundamental" (a concept that, in isolation, is hard to objectify), but also that it be an interest traditionally protected by our society. As we have put it, the Due Process Clause affords only those protections "so rooted in the traditions and conscience of our people as to be ranked as fundamental." Snyder v. Massachusetts, 291 U.S. 97 (1934) (Cardozo, J.). . . .

This insistence that the asserted liberty interest be rooted in history and tradition is evident, as elsewhere, in our cases according constitutional protection to certain parental rights. Michael reads the landmark case of Stanley v. Illinois, 405 U.S. 645 (1972), and the subsequent cases of Quilloin v. Walcott, 434 U.S. 246 (1978), Caban v. Mohammed, 441 U.S. 380 (1979), and Lehr v. Robertson, 463 U.S. 248 (1983), as establishing that a liberty interest is created by biological fatherhood plus an established parental relationship — factors that exist in the present case as well. We think that distorts the rationale of those cases. As we view them, they rest not upon such isolated factors but upon the historic respect — indeed, sanctity would not be too strong a term — traditionally accorded to the relationships that develop within the unitary family.[3] . . .

Thus, the legal issue in the present case reduces to whether the relationship between persons in the situation of Michael and Victoria has been treated as a protected family unit under the historic practices of our society, or whether on any other basis it has been accorded special protection. We think it impossible to find that it has. In fact, quite to the contrary, our traditions have protected the marital family (Gerald, Carole, and the child they acknowledge to be theirs) against the sort of claim Michael asserts.[4]

---

[3] Justice Brennan asserts that only "a pinched conception of 'the family' " would exclude Michael, Carole, and Victoria from protection. We disagree. The family unit accorded traditional respect in our society, which we have referred to as the "unitary family," is typified, of course, by the marital family, but also includes the household of unmarried parents and their children. Perhaps the concept can be expanded even beyond this, but it will bear no resemblance to traditionally respected relationships — and will thus cease to have any constitutional significance — if it is stretched so far as to include the relationship established between a married woman, her lover, and their child, during a 3-month sojourn in St. Thomas, or during a subsequent 8-month period when, if he happened to be in Los Angeles, he stayed with her and the child.

[4] Justice Brennan insists that in determining whether a liberty interest exists we must look at Michael's relationship with Victoria in isolation, without reference to the circumstance that Victoria's mother was married to someone else when the child was conceived, and that that woman and her husband wish to raise the child as their own. We cannot imagine what compels this strange procedure of looking at the act which is assertedly the subject of a liberty interest in isolation from its effect upon other people — rather like inquiring whether there is a liberty interest in firing a gun where the case at hand happens to involve its discharge into another person's body. The logic of Justice Brennan's

The presumption of legitimacy was a fundamental principle of the common law. Traditionally, that presumption could be rebutted only by proof that a husband was incapable of procreation or had had no access to his wife during the relevant period. As explained by Blackstone, nonaccess could only be proved "if the husband be out of the kingdom of England (or, as the law somewhat loosely phrases it, *extra quatuor maria* [beyond the four seas]) for above nine months. . . . " I Blackstone's Commentaries 456 (J. Chitty ed. 1826). And, under the common law both in England and here, "neither husband nor wife [could] be a witness to prove access or nonaccess." J. Schouler, Law of the Domestic Relations §225, p. 306 (3d ed. 1882); R. Graveson & F. Crane, A Century of Family Law: 1857-1957, p. 158 (1957). The primary policy rationale underlying the common law's severe restrictions on rebuttal of the presumption appears to have been an aversion to declaring children illegitimate, thereby depriving them of rights of inheritance and succession, 2 J. Kent, Commentaries on American Law *175, and likely making them wards of the state. A secondary policy concern was the interest in promoting the "peace and tranquillity of States and families," Schouler, supra, §225, at 304, quoting Boullenois, Traite des Status, bk. 1, p. 62, a goal that is obviously impaired by facilitating suits against husband and wife asserting that their children are illegitimate. . . .

We have found nothing in the older sources, nor in the older cases, addressing specifically the power of the natural father to assert parental rights over a child born into a woman's existing marriage with another man. Since it is Michael's burden to establish that such a power (at least where the natural father has established a relationship with the child) is so deeply embedded within our traditions as to be a fundamental right, the lack of evidence alone might defeat his case. But the evidence shows that even in modern times — when, as we have noted, the rigid protection of the marital family has in other respects been relaxed — the ability of a person in Michael's position to claim paternity has not been generally acknowledged. . . .

Moreover, even if it were clear that one in Michael's position generally possesses, and has generally always possessed, standing to challenge the marital child's legitimacy, that would still not establish Michael's case. As noted earlier, what is at issue here is not entitlement to a state pronouncement that Victoria was begotten by Michael. It is no conceivable denial of constitutional right for a State to decline to declare facts unless some legal consequence hinges upon the requested declaration. What Michael asserts here is a right to have himself declared the natural father *and thereby to obtain parental prerogatives.* What he must establish, therefore, is not that our society has traditionally allowed a natural father in his circumstances to establish paternity, but that it has traditionally accorded such a father parental rights, or at least has not traditionally denied them. Even if the law in all States had always been that the entire world could challenge the marital presumption and obtain a declaration as to who was the natural father, that would not advance Michael's claim. Thus, it is ultimately irrelevant, even for purposes of determining current social attitudes towards the alleged substantive right Michael asserts, that the present law in a number of States appears to allow the natural father — including the natural father who has not established a relationship with the child — the

_____

position leads to the conclusion that if Michael had begotten Victoria by rape, that fact would in no way affect his possession of a liberty interest in his relationship with her.

theoretical power to rebut the marital presumption, see Note, Rebutting the Marital Presumption: A Developed Relationship Test, 88 Colum. L. Rev. 369, 373 (1988). What counts is whether the States in fact award substantive parental rights to the natural father of a child conceived within, and born into, an extant marital union that wishes to embrace the child. We are not aware of a single case, old or new, that has done so. This is not the stuff of which fundamental rights qualifying as liberty interests are made.[6] . . .

We do not accept Justice Brennan's criticism that this result "squashes" the liberty that consists of "the freedom not to conform." It seems to us that reflects the erroneous view that there is only one side to this controversy — that one disposition can expand a "liberty" of sorts without contracting an equivalent "liberty" on the other side. Such a happy choice is rarely available. Here, to provide protection to an adulterous natural father is to deny protection to a marital father, and vice versa. If Michael has a "freedom not to conform" (whatever that means), Gerald must equivalently have a "freedom to conform." One of them will pay a price for asserting that "freedom" — Michael by being unable to act as father of the child he has adulterously begotten, or Gerald by being unable to preserve the integrity of the traditional family unit he and Victoria have established. Our disposition does not choose between these two "freedoms," but leaves that to the people of California. Justice Brennan's approach chooses one of them as the constitutional imperative, on no apparent basis except that the unconventional is to be preferred.

We have never had occasion to decide whether a child has a liberty interest, symmetrical with that of her parent, in maintaining her filial relationship. We need not do so here because, even assuming that such a right exists, Victoria's claim must fail. Victoria's due process challenge is, if anything, weaker than Michael's. Her basic claim is not that California has erred in preventing her from establishing that Michael, not Gerald, should stand as her legal father. Rather, she claims a due process right to maintain filial relationships with both Michael and Gerald. This assertion merits little discussion, for, whatever the merits of the guardian ad litem's belief that such an arrangement can be of great psychological benefit to a child, the claim that a State must recognize multiple fatherhood has no support in the history or traditions of this country. Moreover, even if we were to construe Victoria's argument as forwarding the lesser proposition that, whatever her status vis-à-vis Gerald, she has a liberty interest in maintaining a filial relationship with her

---

[6] Justice Brennan criticizes our methodology in using historical traditions specifically relating to the rights of an adulterous natural father, rather than inquiring more generally "whether parenthood is an interest that historically has received our attention and protection." . . . We do not understand why, having rejected our focus upon the societal tradition regarding the natural father's rights vis-à-vis a child whose mother is married to another man. Justice Brennan would choose to focus instead upon "parenthood." Why should the relevant category not be even more general — perhaps "family relationships"; or "personal relationships"; or even "emotional attachments in general"? Though the dissent has no basis for the level of generality it would select, we do: We refer to the most specific level at which a relevant tradition protecting, or denying protection to, the asserted right can be identified. If, for example, there were no societal tradition, either way, regarding the rights of the natural father of a child adulterously conceived, we would have to consult, and (if possible) reason from, the traditions regarding natural fathers in general. But there is such a more specific tradition, and it unqualifiedly denies protection to such a parent. . . .

natural father, Michael, we find that, at best, her claim is the obverse of Michael's and fails for the same reasons.

Victoria claims in addition that her equal protection rights have been violated because, unlike her mother and presumed father, she had no opportunity to rebut the presumption of her legitimacy. We find this argument wholly without merit. We reject, at the outset, Victoria's suggestion that her equal protection challenge must be assessed under a standard of strict scrutiny because, in denying her the right to maintain a filial relationship with Michael, the State is discriminating against her on the basis of her illegitimacy. See Gomez v. Perez, 409 U.S. 535, 538 (1973). Illegitimacy is a legal construct, not a natural trait. Under California law, Victoria is not illegitimate, and she is treated in the same manner as all other legitimate children: she is entitled to maintain a filial relationship with her legal parents.

[A]llowing a claim of illegitimacy to be pressed by the child — or, more accurately, by a court-appointed guardian ad litem — may well disrupt an otherwise peaceful union. Since it pursues a legitimate end by rational means, California's decision to treat Victoria differently from her parents is not a denial of equal protection.

The judgment of the California Court of Appeal is affirmed.

[The separate concurring opinions of Justices O'Connor and Stevens are omitted, as is the dissenting opinion by Justice Brennan, in which Justices Marshall and Blackman joined].

NOTE: NONMARITAL CHILDREN

(1) Introduction: English Common Law Backdrop. Should a child's support or inheritance rights be affected by whether his or her parents were married when the child was born? The common law answer to this question in England was harsh and reasonably clear cut. A child born "out-of-wedlock" (now termed a "nonmarital child") was illegitimate; that status affected both inheritance and support rights.

The most clear-cut consequence at common law of birth "out-of-wedlock" was the denial of all inheritance rights. Sometimes called "filius nullius" (nobody's child), the child could not be the lawful heir of either the mother or father.[3] Support rights were less clear. Such a child was said not to have a legally enforceable common law right to support from either its mother or its father. Nevertheless, it appears that both parents might be held economically responsible for the child by the local parish under the Poor Laws.[4] Moreover, even before the enactment of the Poor Laws in the seventeenth century, there is historical evidence that the courts of the Church of England enforced support obligations against fathers of such children.[5]

Although the common law treatment of the nonmarital child in England was comparatively straightforward, the status of nonmarital children is more complicated in the United States today. This is true for several reasons. First,

---

[3] Ralph C. Brashier, Inheritance Law and the Evolving Family 125 (2004).

[4] R.H. Helmholz, Support Orders, Church Courts, and the Rule of *Filius Nullius:* A Reassessment of the Common Law, 63 Va. L. Rev. 431, 432 (1977).

[5] Id.

state and federal law gradually have eliminated distinctions between nonmarital and marital children. Second, it is now possible to have legal recognition of a nonmarital child's relationship with a father subsequent to the child's birth (until the child's 18th birthday). In contrast, at common law, the status of illegitimacy could *not* be affected by parental actions after the child's birth — an act of Parliament was required to legitimize the child and thus make the child capable of inheritance.[6] Finally, recent federal law as well as the revised Uniform Parentage Act (discussed infra) have established new frameworks for legal recognition of nonmarital children's relationships with their fathers.

What follows is only a brief introduction to the complicated subject of how being born outside marriage affects a child's legal rights concerning various economic issues. Marital status of a child's parents may also affect questions relating to custody and adoption. These issues are considered in Chapter 5.

(2) Contemporary Definitions: What Is a "Nonmarital Child"?

a. Presumption of Legitimacy in Marriage.   For children both begotten and born in wedlock, biology makes it easy to determine who the child's mother is, and there usually is not much difficulty in determining whether she is married at the time the child is born. But how can one ever be sure who the father is? As *Michael H.* reveals, there is a long-standing presumption that treats a child born to a married woman as the offspring of the woman and her husband. In some states this presumption is irrebuttable. Other states reach the same result by applying "Lord Mansfield's Rule," which denies the spouses the right to testify concerning the illegitimacy of a child born during the marriage. In some states the presumption is rebuttable upon clear and convincing evidence to the contrary. State laws typically provide that a child is considered born within a marriage if born within a certain period (usually ten months or 300 days) following divorce. E.g., Kan. Stat. Ann. §38-1114(a)(1), (b) (2000); Mass Gen. Laws Ann. ch. 209C §6(a)(1) (West 1998). See also Unif. Parentage Act §204(a), 9B U.L.A. 14 (Supp. 2002) reprinted infra p. 489.

Do the stated policy rationales in *Michael H.* continue to justify the presumption of legitimacy? How relevant to the continued vitality of the presumption are the increased accuracy of genetic testing and the decreasing stigma of illegitimacy? Are presumptions of paternity necessary or should they be discarded in favor of case-by-case determinations of paternity? How should courts resolve conflicting presumptions of paternity?

Increasingly, jurisdictions are undertaking case-by-case determinations. In some jurisdictions, courts determine putative fathers' claims to paternity based on either the best-interests-of-the-child standard or the substantial relationship test. See, e.g., Evans v. Wilson, 856 A.2d 679 (Md. 2004) (finding that alleged biological father had not overcome the statutorily imposed presumption of legitimacy and that ordering genetic testing was not in the child's best interests); N.A.H. v. S.L.S., 9 P.3d 354, 357 (Colo. 2000) ("best interest of the child must be considered as part of the policy and logic analysis used to decide legal fatherhood"); Randy A.J. v. Norma I.J., 677 N.W.2d 630 (Wis. 2004) (putative father was unable to establish

---

[6] 1 William Blackstone, Commentaries *459.

paternity in part because he failed to establish that he had a substantial relationship with child).

Because *Michael H.* was based in large part on judicial reluctance to disrupt an intact marriage, should the presumption be applicable if the married couple has separated or divorced when the putative father makes a claim? See, e.g., Fish v. Behers, 741 A.2d 721 (Pa. 1999) (holding that presumption of paternity does not apply where husband and wife have divorced, as the underlying policy rationale is not advanced).

Reaction to *Michael H.* has been mixed.[7] Some jurisdictions follow *Michael H.* and hold that statutes denying rights to a putative father are constitutional under state or federal constitutions. See, e.g., S.B. v. D.H., 736 So. 2d 766 (Fla. Dist. Ct. App. 1999); Aichele v. Hodge, 673 N.W.2d 452 (Mich. Ct. App. 2003); In re Adoption of Baby Girl H., 635 N.W.2d 256 (Neb. 2001). Other jurisdictions hold that such statutes violate state constitutions. See, e.g., Callender v. Skiles, 591 N.W.2d 182 (Iowa 1996) (statute denied putative father due process rights under state constitution); In re J.W.T., 872 S.W.2d 189 (Tex. 1994) (same) (superseded by Tex. Fam. Code Ann. §160.101(a)(3) (West 2002) (replaced with the revised Uniform Parentage Act permitting biological father to contest a claim by presumed father).

Similarly, the legislature and judiciary in California (where *Michael H.* arose) have not been completely receptive to the operation of the presumption. Indeed, several California state courts refused to follow *Michael H.* See, e.g., Steven W. v. Matthew S., 39 Cal. Rptr. 2d 535 (Ct. App. 1995); Comino v. Kelly, 30 Cal. Rptr. 2d 728 (Ct. App. 1994); Brian C. v. Ginger K., 92 Cal. Rptr. 2d 294 (Ct. App. 2000). But cf. In re Jesusa V., 10 Cal. Rptr. 3d 205 (Cal. 2004) (holding that factors supporting husband's claim to be presumed father outweighed those of biological father); Dawn D. v. Superior Court, 71 Cal. Rptr. 2d 871 (Cal. 1998) (relying on *Michael H.* to reject putative father's claim as against husband on the basis that alleged father's "mere desire" to establish parental relationship does not constitute a protected interest).

Also, dissatisfaction with *Michael H.* led the California legislature to amend the conclusive presumption of legitimacy to allow a putative father in some cases (i.e., if the man who is not the husband has received the child into his home and openly held out the child as his child) to move for blood tests within two years of birth (Cal. Fam. Code §7541(b), enacted by Stats. 1992, c. 162 (A.B. 2650), §10, amending former Cal. Evid. Code §621). Currently, the California legislature is considering adoption of the revised Uniform Parentage Act (A.B. 2380, introduced by Assemblyman Tom Harman, Feb. 19, 2004). Four states (Delaware, Texas, Washington, and Wyoming, have already adopted the new UPA.[8] (The new UPA incorporates the two-year limitation on the putative father's ability to request blood tests, subject to estoppel

---

[7] Following the Supreme Court decision, plaintiff Michael Hirschensohn formed an advocacy group for unmarried fathers (Equality Nationwide for Unwed Fathers, or ENUF) and successfully lobbied to change California law. Then, at age 47, Hirschensohn enrolled at the University of West Los Angeles School of Law. Marcia Coyle, After the Gavel Comes Down, Natl. L.J., Feb 25, 1991, at 1.

[8] UPA, Legislative Fact Sheet, *http://www.nccusl.org/Update/uniformact_factsheets/uniformacts-fs-upa.asp* (last visited Mar. 5, 2005).

principles that operate to preserve the child's ties to a non-biological father who held the child out as his. U.P.A. §608.)

On California paternity law, see Anthony Miller, Baseline, Bright-Line, Best Interests: A Pragmatic Approach for California to Provide Certainty in Determining Parentage, 34 McGeorge L. Rev. 637 (2003). On unwed fathers' rights generally, see Genetic Ties and the Future of the Family: The Impact of Paternity Testing on Parents and Children (Mark A. Rothstein et al. eds., 2005); Elizabeth Bartholet, Guiding Principles for Picking Parents, 27 Harv. Women's L.J. 323 (2004); Nancy E. Dowd, From Genes, Marriage and Money to Nurture: Redefining Fatherhood, 10 Cardozo Women's L.J. 132 (2003); Theresa Glennon, Somebody's Child: Evaluating the Erosion of the Marital Presumption of Paternity, 102 W. Va. L. Rev. 547 (2000); Jeffrey A. Parness, Old-Fashioned Pregnancy, Newly-Fashioned Paternity, 53 Syracuse L. Rev. 57 (2003).

b. Assisted Reproduction.   Traditionally, if a married woman became pregnant via artificial insemination, statutes provided that the child was treated as the legitimate offspring of the marriage, especially if the artificial insemination occurred with the husband's knowledge or consent. See, e.g., Unif. Parentage Act §5, 9B U.L.A. 301 (1973). New UPA provisions apply to nonmarital as well as marital children who are born via assisted reproductive techniques. Specifically, a man is the father of a child created by assisted reproduction if the man "provides sperm for, or consent to, assisted reproduction by a woman with the intent to be the parent of her child." Unif. Parentage Act, §703, 9B U.L.A. 16 (Supp. 2002). The man must consent in writing "in a record signed by the woman and the man." Id. at §704(a). Failure to provide written consent will not necessarily preclude a finding of paternity, provided that the man resided together in the same household with the woman and child during the first two years of the child's life and the couple openly held out the child as theirs. Id. at §704(b). Thus, the evidentiary fact of "holding out" substitutes for the written consent.

According to the new UPA, a husband who does *not* consent to assisted reproduction before or after the child's birth may challenge paternity. Such a challenge is permitted within two years of the husband's discovery of the child's birth. Id. at §705(a). An exception ("at any time") is permitted to this two-year rule in several circumstances: if the husband did not provide the sperm, the couple has not cohabited since the use of assisted reproduction, and the husband never openly held out the child as his. Id. at §705(b).

Occasionally, an ex-wife may proceed with assisted reproduction *following a divorce.* In such a case, the former husband is not the father of the resulting child unless the man previously provided written consent to post-divorce assisted reproduction. Id. at §706(a). In addition, both a woman and a man have the ability to withdraw consent by so stating in writing. Id. at §706(b). Presumably, such a writing would be filed with the fertility laboratory. Id. (cmt.). The new UPA envisions, therefore, that a child may be without a legally recognized father if the woman's husband establishes nonpaternity by proof of lack of consent to assisted reproduction, if he fails to authorize post-divorce assisted reproduction, or withdraws his consent before placement of eggs, sperm, or embryos.

c. Legitimation.   Although the practice was unknown at common law, states provide mechanisms for a child to be "legitimated" subsequent to birth. Historically, the "legitimated" nonmarital child was placed on an equal legal footing with the marital child. Requirements for legitimation vary from state to state (e.g., marriage after the birth; acknowledgment, etc.).

Beginning in the late 1960s, the United States Supreme Court invalidated state legislation that discriminated against nonmarital children or their parents by denying them benefits granted to legitimate children and their parents.[9] In response, states began abrogating distinctions between illegitimate and legitimate children. See, e.g., N.C. Gen. Stat. §49-15 (2001) (enacted in 1967) ("[A]fter the establishment of paternity of an illegitimate child . . . , the rights, duties, and obligations of the mother and the father so established, with regard to support and custody of the child, shall be the same . . . as if the child were the legitimate child").

Influenced by the original Uniform Parentage Act of 1973, many states adopted rebuttable "presumptions of paternity." That is, presumptions of paternity arose if the child's mother and father married subsequent to the birth (even if the attempted marriage is invalid) (UPA §4(1), (2), (3)); if formal written acknowledgment was properly filed and not disputed by the child's mother within a reasonable time (UPA §4(5)); or based on the father's conduct (i.e., taking the child into his home and holding out the child as his) (UPA §4(4)). (The new UPA of 2000, as amended in 2002, revises these methods by requiring a time frame for establishment of paternity by conduct — the reception and holding out must be during the first two years of the child's life (UPA §204(a)(5)) — and by eliminating the acknowledgment requirement because it conflicts with a subsequent UPA provision (Article 3 on Voluntary Acknowledgment of Paternity), under which a valid acknowledgment establishes paternity rather than a presumption of paternity.)

Such changes blurred the lines between establishment of paternity (i.e., the biological relationship) and legitimacy (i.e., the legal relationship of father and child). Many state statutes establishing legal rights between nonmarital children and their biological fathers applied even when a father acknowledged paternity but failed to have his child legitimated judicially or to seek a judicial determination of paternity. As a result, "by acknowledging paternity, without legitimation, a father and child currently are entitled to receive parental rights and benefits once reserved for 'the legitimate.' " Bartina L. Edwards, Casenote, The Established Standard for Fathers Who Have Acknowledged Paternity and Are Seeking Custody of Their Illegitimate Children: Rosero v. Blake, 357 N.C. 193 (2003), 26 N.C. Cent. L.J. 116, 128 (2004). Because law reform effectuated similarities in the effects of paternity acknowledgment, judicial determination of paternity, and legitimation proceedings, most distinctions regarding the consequences of paternity establishment versus legitimation (in terms of such legal rights as custody, inheritance, support, and notice for adoption, for example) have been eliminated.

(3) Births of Nonmarital Children in the United States: Demographics. In 2002, there were 4,021,726 live births registered in the United States. Of these

---

[9] See, e.g., Glona v. American Guarantee & Liability Ins. Co., 391 U.S. 73 (1968) (holding unconstitutional a statute under which the mother of an illegitimate child was not permitted to recover for her child's wrongful death); Levy v. Louisiana, 391 U.S. 68 (1968) (holding unconstitutional a statute under which illegitimate children were denied the right to recover for the wrongful death of their mother).

live births, 34 percent were to unmarried women. The percentage of live births to unmarried women has increased significantly from 1980, when it was 18.4 percent.[10]

The ratio of births of nonmarital children differs markedly for white and African-American children. In 2002, 28.5 percent of white children were born to unmarried women, compared with 68.2 percent of African-American children born to unmarried women.[11] In comparison, in 1980, 11 percent of white children were born to unmarried women, compared with 55 percent of African-American children born to unmarried women.[12]

(4) Support of Nonmarital Children in the United States. In the United States, absent a statute to the contrary, the mother but not the father was traditionally said to have a common law duty of support for nonmarital children. Allen v. Hunnicut, 52 S.E.2d 18 (N.C. 1949); Baugh v. Maddox, 95 So. 2d 268 (Ala. 1957). The Supreme Court established in Gomez v. Perez, 409 U.S. 535 (1973), that a state cannot grant children born within marriage a statutory right to paternal support and maintenance while denying this right to nonmarital children. Today, every state has statutes under which both parents can be compelled to contribute directly to the support of nonmarital children.

(5) Inheritance Rights Involving Nonmarital Children in the United States.
a. The Nonmarital Child's Right to Inherit from a Father. The laws in most states traditionally provided that a nonmarital child occupied the same position as a child born within marriage with regard to inheritance rights vis-à-vis the child's *mother.*[13] However, while a father could include a nonmarital child as a named beneficiary in a will, the child would receive nothing if the father died intestate (without a will). The nonmarital child's right to inherit intestate from the biological father was problematic because of concerns about proof of paternity.

In the late 1970s, the United States Supreme Court began examining whether states could impose a higher standard of proof or require particular kinds of proof in order for nonmarital children to inherit via intestate succession from their fathers. The Court held that, in order for a nonmarital child to inherit from a noncustodial biological father, a state could require a higher level of proof in the form of a judicial declaration of paternity (Lalli v. Lalli, 439 U.S. 259 (1978)), but could not require that the child's parents subsequently marry after the child's birth (Trimble v. Gordon, 430 U.S. 762 (1977)).

Today, an increasing number of jurisdictions have expanded the inheritance rights of nonmarital children. Many states have done so by adopting the original UPA, declaring equal treatment for all children without regard to the marital status of their parents so long as the father can be identified by presumptions of parentage. When the Uniform Probate Code underwent substantial revision in 1990, it adopted similar language. UPC §2-114(a). The new UPA, as amended in 2002, reaffirms the original policy of equality of treatment (providing that "A child born to parents

---

[10] National Center for Health Statistics, National Vital Statistics Report, vol. 52, no. 10, Dec. 17, 2003, at 10 (Table C).

[11] Id. at 49 (Table 13).

[12] National Center for Health Statistics, National Vital Statistics Report, vol. 47, no. 18, Apr. 29, 1999, at 43 (Table 18).

[13] See generally Brashier, supra note [3], at 125.

who are not married to each other has the same rights under the law as a child born to parents who are married to each other." UPA §202. See generally Ralph C. Brashier, Inheritance Law and the Evolving Family 125-147 (2004).

  b. The Parent's Right to Inherit from a Nonmarital Child. At common law, parents could not inherit *from* their nonmarital children. Because a nonmarital child was *filius nullius* (a child of no one), the child was deemed to have no heirs if the child died without issue. Today, many jurisdictions have liberalized this rule. However, in some states, whereas mothers can inherit from a nonmarital child, fathers must prove that they have supported and acknowledged a nonmarital child in order to inherit from the child. Do statutes conditioning a father's ability to inherit from his nonmarital child violate the Equal Protection Clause? See Rainey v. Cheever, 510 S.E.2d 823 (Ga. 1999) (so holding), *cert. denied*, 527 U.S. 1044 (1999). See generally Eleanor Mixon, Note, Deadbeat Dads: Undeserving of the Right to Inherit from Their Illegitimate Children and Undeserving of Equal Protection, 34 Ga. L. Rev. 1773, 1775-1776 (2000).

  (6) Identifying the Father: Paternity Proceedings. For support purposes, and sometimes for inheritance purposes, it is important to identify the child's biological father. We have seen that, according to traditional law, there is a presumption applicable to a marital child — in some states irrebuttable — that the mother's husband is the child's father. Now, in a majority of states, the presumption is rebuttable.[14] Paula Roberts, Truth and Consequences: Part I. Disestablishing the Paternity of Non-Marital Children, 37 Fam. L.Q. 35, 36 n.5 (2003). On the other hand, for a child whose mother is not married, the father can be legally identified and made subject to a support obligation through a paternity proceeding.

  Paternity actions, rooted in the English bastardy proceeding, historically were quasi-criminal proceedings characterized by short statutes of limitations, proof beyond a reasonable doubt, and trial by jury. Increasing social awareness on the federal level of the problems of child support enforcement prompted a reformulation of these elements. In the 1980s, the United States Supreme Court invalidated several state statutes of limitations on paternity suits. See Clark v. Jeter, 486 U.S. 456 (1988) (six-year statute); Pickett v. Brown, 462 U.S. 1 (1983) (two-year statute); Mills v. Habluetzel, 456 U.S. 91 (1982) (one-year statute). Under federal welfare reform legislation enacted in 1996 (the Personal Responsibility and Work Opportunity Reconciliation Act or PRWORA), states now must allow paternity suits to be brought at any time before the child attains 18 years of age. 42 U.S.C.A. §666(a)(5)(A) (West Supp. 2002).

  Historically, states justified short statutory periods in order to prevent the filing of stale claims and discourage fraud. Concerns about blackmail and fraudulent claims of paternity have been eliminated, however, by advances in scientific proof of paternity. Formerly, test results were admitted into evidence to exclude a putative father, i.e., the human leukocyte antigens (HLA) blood-test system produced a 97.3 percent exclusion rate. Today, scientific advances in DNA testing yield a 99 percent probability that a given man is the child's father. Roberts, supra, at 37 n. 16.

---

[14] Federal child support legislation currently gives states the option of making the presumption rebuttable or conclusive depending on genetic testing results' indicating a threshold probability that the alleged father is the father of the child. 42 U.S.C.A. §666(5)(G) (West Supp. 2002).

Inroads have also been made on several other quasi-criminal elements of paternity establishment. By 1990, many jurisdictions began lowering the standard of proof in determinations of paternity. See, e.g., Rivera v. Minnich, 483 U.S. 574 (1987) (holding that due process was satisfied by a standard of preponderance of the evidence to establish paternity). In addition, new federal legislation (explained infra) provides that the parties in paternity procedures are not entitled to a trial by jury. States now commonly view paternity actions as civil proceedings.

Recent federal legislation establishes new procedures for paternity establishment. According to PRWORA, states must adopt new paternity provisions in order to receive federal funds for child support enforcement programs and welfare programs. Paternity can be established by: (1) either parent bringing a paternity suit; (2) both parents in a voluntary acknowledgment of paternity.

a. Paternity Suits and Genetic Testing.   According to federal law (42 U.S.C. §§654(20) and 602(a)(2)), either parent may bring a paternity suit at any time until the child attains 18 years of age. Id. at §666(a)(5)(A). Upon either parent's request (provided that the request is supported by a sworn statement "establishing a reasonable possibility of the requisite sexual contact between the parties") (id. at §666(a)(5)(B)(I)(1), a court must order genetic tests. Paternity is established on the basis of these tests. (If one party refuses to undergo such tests, a court will establish paternity based on other evidence or by default.) Once paternity is established, the court enters an appropriate order that often includes an award of child support. These paternity establishment procedures may create either a rebuttable or a conclusive presumption of paternity (at the state's option). Id. at §666(a)(5)(G).

b. Voluntary Paternity Establishment.   A significant development in paternity establishment is the transformation from judicial proceedings to voluntary affidavits. Beginning in 1992, a few states adopted voluntary programs that targeted mothers at birthing facilities, providing that in-hospital affidavits established a rebuttable presumption of paternity. These programs were so successful that Congress included a requirement in the Omnibus Budget Reconciliation Act of 1993, 42 U.S.C. §666(a)(5)(C) (2000), that all states adopt voluntary paternity establishment programs. PRWORA in 1996 expanded the scope of these programs by providing that (1) a valid, unrescinded, unchallenged acknowledgment of paternity is equivalent to a judicial determination of paternity (rather than merely a presumption of paternity) and is entitled to full faith and credit; (2) parents must be advised of the legal consequences before signing a voluntary acknowledgment; and (3) either parent has the option to rescind within 60 days, but may challenge the voluntary acknowledgment thereafter only judicially and only on limited grounds (fraud, duress, or material mistake of fact). Id. at §666(a)(5). If a parent desires a support order, he or she must petition in a separate proceeding. See Paul K. Legler, The Coming Revolution in Child Support Policy: Implications of the 1996 Welfare Act, 30 Fam. L.Q. 519, 532-534 (1996). The revised UPA of 2002 also complies with the federal mandate by providing for voluntary establishment of paternity and specifies that voluntary affidavits serve as judgments for enforcement purposes. UPA, Article 3 (cmt).

c. Paternity Establishment By Conduct.   Under the original version of the Uniform Parentage Act, paternity could also be established by conduct — i.e., a man's receiving the child (during the child's minority) into his home and openly holding out the child as his own child. UPA §4(a)(4), 9B U.L.A. 295 (2001). Provided that this presumption was not challenged, the man achieved presumed fatherhood status.

Occasionally, a man's conduct might give rise to conflicting presumptions of paternity under the original UPA. For example, whereas one man might enjoy a presumption of paternity arising from having accepted the child into his home and having held the child out as his own, another man might enjoy a presumption of paternity arising from the child's being born during marriage or from genetic testing revealing that he is the child's biological father. The original UPA provided that in the case of competing presumptions, "the presumption which on the facts is founded on the weightier considerations of policy and logic controls." UPA §4(b).

The revised UPA eliminates this manner of resolution of competing presumptions. According to the Prefatory Note to the new UPA: "Nowadays the existence of modern genetic testing obviates this old approach to the problem of conflicting presumptions when a court is to determine paternity." However, under the new UPA, courts may deny requests for genetic testing based on estoppel principles "in the interests of preserving a child's ties to the presumed or acknowledged father who openly held himself out as the child's father regardless of whether he is in fact the genetic father." UPA §608.

d. Interstate Paternity Establishment. Historically, establishing paternity was difficult when the mother and father resided in different states. Personal jurisdiction could be obtained under a long-arm statute only if the child's father had "minimum contacts" within the state of the mother's residence. In the most recent effort to address this problem, the National Conference of Commissioners on Uniform State Laws promulgated the Uniform Interstate Family Support Act (UIFSA), 9 U.L.A. (pt. IB), 235 (1999), in 1992. UIFSA replaced two previous uniform interstate support acts, the Uniform Reciprocal Enforcement of Support Act (URESA), and the Revised Uniform Reciprocal Enforcement of Support Act (RURESA). UIFSA facilitates interstate enforcement by utilizing long-arm jurisdiction without the necessity for the intervention of a court or agency in the obligor's state (abrogating the reciprocity requirement that was the hallmark of previous legislation), eliminates the possibility of conflicting support orders, and extends recognition to support orders entered by administrative agencies. Federal welfare legislation (PRWORA, discussed infra, pp. 217-221), enacted in 1996, mandated that all states adopt UIFSA as a condition of state eligibility for federal funding of child support enforcement. By 1998 all jurisdictions had complied with the federal mandate. John J. Sampson & Barry J. Brooks, Uniform Interstate Family Support Act (2001) with Prefatory Note and Comments (With Still More Unofficial Annotations), 36 Fam. L.Q. 329, 338 (2002).

UIFSA was amended in 2001. The most important amendments recognize that jurisdictions may extend comity to foreign support orders and, in addition, clarify jurisdictional rules regarding modification of support orders (e.g., providing that nonresident parties may voluntarily agree, even if the parties and child have moved from the issuing state, that the original forum will continue to exercise exclusive jurisdiction in order to avoid relitigating issues).

Do paternity statutes violate equal protection by permitting a man to be adjudged a father and ordered to pay child support without according him the same parental rights that automatically inure to the mother of that child? See Palmer v.

Bertrand, 541 S.E.2d 360 (Ga. 2001) (holding that paternity statutes do not violate the right to equal protection because fathers and mothers of nonmarital children are not similarly situated).

e. Paternity Disestablishment. Some jurisdictions, by either case law or statute, now recognize the disestablishment of paternity, generally on grounds of paternity fraud. Increasingly, former husbands and unwed fathers are seeking to disestablish paternity in order to avoid child support obligations after genetic testing reveals that their "children" are not biologically related to them. Some states require that the man act within a prescribed time. A few states impose criminal penalties for those who intentionally establish the paternity of the wrong man. Paula Roberts, Part III, Who Pays When Paternity Is Disestablished?, 37 Fam. L.Q. 69, 69 (2003). Are these approaches sound policy?

Should a father be permitted to disestablish paternity if he has *already* assumed the role of the child's father? Courts sometimes deny a parent's disestablishment claim based on principles of equitable estoppel. See, e.g., Hubbard v. Hubbard, 44 P.3d 153 (Alaska 2002). Other courts bar paternity disestablishment based on res judicata principles — i.e., the divorce decree or child support order establishing paternity is regarded as a final judgment. See, e.g., State v. R.L.C., 47 P.3d 327 (Colo. 2002); In re Marriage/Children of Betty L.W. v. William E.W., 569 S.E.2d 77, 88 (W. Va. 2002). See also Paula Roberts, Part II: Questioning the Paternity of Marital Children, 37 Fam. L.Q. 55 (2003).

If a father is permitted to disestablish paternity, who becomes responsible for child support? The biological father? The state? What is the likely effect on the parent-child relationship of the disestablishment of paternity? Should that consequence deter a court from permitting paternity disestablishment? See B.E.B. v. R.L.B., 979 P.2d 514 (Alaska 1999) (holding that risk of emotional harm inherent in severing father-child relationship cannot suffice as a basis for invoking the doctrine of paternity by estoppel).

Although disestablishment of paternity terminates the current obligation to pay child support, some jurisdictions are reluctant to discharge *child support arrearages.* Roberts, Part III, supra, at 73. Compare In re T.S.R., No. W2003-01321-COA-R3-JV, 2004 WL 1361359 (Tenn. Ct. App. June 17, 2004) (requiring payment of arrearages) with Walter v. Gunter, 788 A.2d 609 (Md. 2002) (relieving father of arrearages). What policy reasons support such judicial reluctance?

Should a father be able to *recover* past child support payments that were based on the mother's fraudulent representation of paternity? See Bouchard v. Frost, 840 A.2d 109 (Me. 2004) (holding that sovereign immunity barred recovery of support payments made to state agency). See generally Andrew S. Epstein, Note, The Parent Trap: Should a Man Be Allowed to Recoup Child Support Payments If He Discovers He Is Not the Biological Father of the Child?, 42 Brandeis L.J. 655 (2004).

(7) Nonmarital Children and Other Dependency Benefits. In a variety of contexts, benefits may be available to a child because the decedent is the parent. For example, dependency benefits may be available to a child under a pension plan, or a governmental program (e.g., the Social Security Act, 42 U.S.C. §§301-1397f (2000 & Supp. 2004)), or a statute (e.g., as the Copyright Act, 17 U.S.C. §§101-1101 (2000). Thus, in a variety of areas it is important to determine whether a

young person is a "child" or a "dependent" of a particular adult. These issues can be particularly troublesome for nonmarital children, as illustrated below:

a. May a nonmarital child recover for the wrongful death of the father under a state wrongful death statute? Does barring a nonmarital child from recovery violate equal protection? See Levy v. Louisiana, 391 U.S. 68 (1968); Brookbank v. Gray, 658 N.E.2d 724 (Ohio 1996) (so holding). Conversely, should parents of a nonmarital child be able to recover for the wrongful death of the child? Does barring such a parent from recovery violate the right to equal protection? See Glona v. American Guarantee & Liability Ins. Co., 391 U.S. 73 (1968) (so holding).

b. May a nonmarital child recover under a state workers' compensation act? Does barring a nonmarital child from recovery violate equal protection? See Weber v. Aetna Casualty & Surety Co., 406 U.S. 164 (1972) (so holding); Findaya W., by and through Theresa W. v. A.-T.E.A.M. Co., 546 N.W.2d 61 (Neb. 1996) (holding that requiring nonmarital children to prove actual dependency on decedent while presuming dependency for legitimate children violates the right to equal protection).

c. May a mother of a nonmarital child be denied "mother's insurance benefits" because she was never married to the wage earner on whom her claim is based? Would a denial of these benefits violate equal protection? See Califano v. Boles, 443 U.S. 282 (1979) (holding constitutional a Social Security Act provision granting "mother's benefits" to a widow or divorced wife but not to the mother of the deceased's nonmarital child because Congress could reasonably conclude that the mother of the nonmarital child was less likely to be a dependent).

d. The Social Security Act provides death benefits for minor dependents of a decedent wage earner. For children born within the marriage, the Act simply assumes the requisite dependency. However, benefits are available to nonmarital children: (1) who would be entitled to take an intestate share of the deceased's property under the laws of the state in which the decedent resided at death; (2) who have been acknowledged in writing; (3) where the insured was subject to a child support order; or (4) where there is sufficient evidence to demonstrate that the father was living with the child or contributing to the child's support. 42 U.S.C. §§416(h)(2), (3) (2000). Do such provisions violate the nonmarital child's right to equal protection? See, e.g., Mathews v. Lucas, 427 U.S. 495 (1976) (upholding differential treatment of nonmarital children against an equal protection attack based on rational basis review).

On the issue of whether posthumous children who are conceived after the father's death qualify for Social Security survivor's benefits, see Gillett-Netting v. Barnhart, infra, p. 203.

(8) Nonmarital Children and Immigration Status. Nonmarital children merit special treatment in immigration law. In Nguyen v. INS, 533 U.S. 53 (2001), a nonmarital child (Nguyen) born to a Vietnamese mother and American father faced deportation following a criminal conviction for sexual assault. His deportation order was pursuant to an immigration provision (8 U.S.C. §1409) that specified different requirements for the acquisition of citizenship by nonmarital children born to an alien mother and a citizen father compared to nonmarital children born to an alien father and citizen mother. Nguyen and his father alleged that the provision violated the Equal Protection Clause by imposing stricter requirements for nonmarital children with citizen fathers. The Supreme Court rejected their argument, reasoning that

the stricter provisions for establishment of citizenship in cases involving a citizen father served important governmental interests (i.e., facilitating the identification of a parent-child relationship and ensuring that parent and child have the opportunity to develop a significant relationship). See generally Laura Weinrib, Note, Protecting Sex: Sexual Disincentives and Sex-Based Discrimination in Nguyen v. INS, 12 Colum. J. Gender & L. 222 (2003).

B.   THE PARENTAL SUPPORT OBLIGATION

The introductory materials suggest that at common law in England there was some question whether there was a legal (as opposed to a moral) obligation to support minor children. Today, the legal nature of the parental support obligation is plain. Statutes in every jurisdiction impose a duty of support upon *both* parents to support their minor children.

Disputes relating to child support arise in a variety of circumstances and in many different legal contexts. A parent who is not living with a child (typically the father) may be ordered by a court to make periodic payments (typically to the mother) in order to defer the costs of supporting the child. The parents may or may not have ever been married, or even lived together. The absent parent may have deserted the child or may be apart because of parental divorce or separation not of his or her choosing. Both civil and criminal sanctions may be imposed on a noncustodial parent in a variety of proceedings for the failure to make required child support payments.

Today, imposition of the duty of child support is complicated by the rise of diverse family forms as well as the increasing use of assisted reproduction. The cases in this chapter highlight the variety of proceedings and contexts as they relate to child support. *Yale Diagnostic*, supra, involves the common law "necessaries" doctrine and a creditor's claim against the parents. T.F. v. B.L. and *Harmon*, infra, are cases in which a child support issue arose in the context of dissolution of the parental relationship (a same-sex relationship in one case versus a marital relationship in the other). Wallis v. Smith explores the issue of a father's obligation to pay child support when the mother has committed contraceptive fraud. *Gillett-Netting*, infra, raises the issue of the inheritance rights of children who were conceived and born after their father's death.

1.   Who Has the Legal Duty of Support?

T.F. v. B.L.
813 N.E.2d 1244 (Mass. 2004)

COWIN, J.

The plaintiff, T.F., and the defendant, B.L., are two women who lived together from 1996 to 2000. During this time, the plaintiff became pregnant through artificial insemination, and in July, 2000, after the couple had separated, she gave birth to a child. [Soon after the couple's commitment ceremony, the plaintiff communicated her longstanding desire to have a child. The defendant, who was initially reluctant, eventually agreed in order to preserve the relationship. The birth followed the dissolution of the couple's relationship. Although the defendant visited the mother and child in the hospital, she subsequently notified the plaintiff that she desired no further contact with her or the child.] In January, 2001, the plaintiff filed a complaint in the Probate and Family Court Department. Based on theories of promissory estoppel and breach of an oral contract, she requested that the defendant be ordered to pay child support under the child support guidelines. . . .

The plaintiff's argument for imposing a child support obligation on the defendant is essentially two pronged. First, she claims that the defendant entered into an enforceable implied contract with her to coparent a child, or at least that she impliedly promised to support the child, and is now estopped from denying that support. The defendant's refusal to pay child support, the argument goes, is therefore a breach of contract. Second, the plaintiff asserts that an order of child support in the present situation would be consistent with oft-expressed legislative policies as manifested in related statutes, and that the "broad and flexible" equity powers of the Probate Court can and should be invoked to implement said polices. We discuss these arguments in turn.

A. "Parenthood by contract." The plaintiff does not contend that there was any express written agreement between the parties,[3] but rather that the defendant's initial statement, in the summer of 1999, that she wished to discuss having a child, followed by her course of conduct, reflect an implied contract to create a child. In the absence of an express agreement, an implied contract may be inferred from (1) the conduct of the parties and (2) the relationship of the parties. An implied contract requires proof that there was a benefit to the defendant, that the plaintiff expected the defendant to pay for that benefit, and that the defendant expected, or a reasonable person should have expected, that he or she would have to pay for that benefit. When the defendant was, or should have been, aware of the plaintiff's expectations in this regard, the defendant's failure to object can create a contract. The defendant's subjective intent is irrelevant when she knows or has reason to know that her objective actions manifest the existence of an agreement. See Restatement (Second) of Contracts §19 (1981).

In this case, the evidence warranted the judge's finding that there was an agreement by the defendant to undertake the responsibilities of a parent in consideration of the plaintiff's conceiving and bearing a child. Although the defendant claims that the plaintiff should not have relied on her passive silence, the judge reasonably concluded that the circumstances and relations of the parties, as stated in her findings, told a different story. The parties cohabited for several years as a couple, pooling all their financial resources. After the 1999 conversation, the plaintiff agreed to

---

[3] The clinic "consent form" is not a written contract between the plaintiff and the defendant, for its primary purposes were to explain the risks of the insemination procedure and to define the couple's legal relationship as a unit with the clinic. See A.Z. v. B.Z., 431 Mass. 150, 158, 725 N.E.2d 1051 (2000). That form does not state, nor does the record show, that the parties intended it to act as, or be a part of, any binding agreement between them. See id.

conceive and give birth to a child. Following this agreement, the defendant not only did not object, but actively participated in medical decisions and procedures, and in discussions about the child's future and the finances related to the conception and raising of the child. Furthermore, the judge found that the defendant intentionally manifested an outward desire to have a child in order to maintain her relationship with the plaintiff. A finding of an implied contract based on these facts, while not compelled, was certainly permissible.

The conclusion does not end our analysis; the question remains whether the court can enforce this contract. Contracts between unmarried cohabitants regarding property, finance, and other matters are normally enforceable. Such contracts may concern the welfare and support of children, provided they do not contravene the best interests of the child. Contracts between unmarried same-sex couples concerning the welfare and support of a child stand on the same footing as any other agreement between unmarried cohabitants. However, when a contract violates or conflicts with public policy, we treat it as void and will not enforce it. This is such a contract.

In A.Z. v. B.Z., [725 N.E.2d 1051 (Mass. 2000)], we refused to enforce an agreement that compelled a party "to become a parent against his or her will." In that case, the plaintiff successfully prevented his estranged wife from using his own sperm (which had been frozen and stored by an in vitro fertilization clinic) to create a child. "[F]orced procreation," we concluded, "is not an area amenable to judicial enforcement." [Id. at 1058.]

The principles expressed by this court in A.Z. v. B.Z., supra, are applicable, and of like force, in the present case. The decision to become, or not to become, a parent is a personal right of "such delicate and intimate character that direct enforcement . . . by any process of the court should never be attempted." Id., quoting Kenyon v. Chicopee, 320 Mass. 528, 534, 70 N.E.2d 241 (1946). "Parenthood by contract" is not the law in Massachusetts, and, to the extent the plaintiff and the defendant entered into an agreement, express or implied, to coparent a child, that agreement is unenforceable.[8]

The dissent acknowledges that the agreement to create a child was unenforceable, but insists that this agreement "includes" an enforceable promise to pay child support. . . . Nothing in the record gives substance or meaning to any specific promise to provide child support separate and apart from the implied agreement to create a child; support was, as the [Probate Court] judge stated, one of the inherent consequences of parenthood. . . . Therefore, any implied promise that the defendant made respecting child support is inextricably linked to her unenforceable promise to coparent the child, and is similarly unenforceable.[10]

---

[8] Concluding, as we do, that there was an implied contract to create a child but that it was unenforceable, we need not address the plaintiff's promissory estoppel argument. The same public policy considerations apply to this alternative theory of recovery.

[10] The dissent's conclusion that "parenthood by contract" is not the law, yet that a separate support obligation may nevertheless be imposed on a nonparent, is conspicuously silent on the possible ramifications of such a conclusion. Given the unprecedented nature of imposing a long-lasting support obligation independent of parenthood, we have no recognized legal principles for determining the defendant's status. For example, although the defendant voluntarily ceased visitation, would she have visitation rights, or some right to resume contact with the child, that she could seek to enforce? While presumably not having a right to custody, would she have any say in some aspects of the child's care, or at least in those aspects that would profoundly affect her own financial obligations (e.g., the decision

B. Equity power of the Probate and Family Court. The plaintiff and the dissenting Justices do not rely exclusively on contract theory, but also invoke the equity powers of the Probate and Family Court, arguing, as the dissent puts it, that "[t]he existence of an agreement to support on the part of the defendant, buttressed by society's interests (as expressed through our statutes and our case law) and the best interests of the child standard, requires relief here." . . . This argument, however informed by genuinely good intentions, misapprehends the extent and purpose of the Probate and Family Court's equity powers. The equity powers conferred by the Legislature on the Probate and Family Court are intended to enable that court to provide remedies to enforce existing obligations; they are not intended to empower the court to create new obligations.

The duty to support a minor child is statutory. See, e.g., G.L. c. 208, §28; G.L. c. 209, §37; G.L. c. 209C, §9. A parent's duty to support his child financially has existed by statute in some form since as early as 1692. Over time, the Legislature has created a comprehensive statutory scheme governing child support, imposing that duty on a person who acknowledges paternity or is adjudicated the father. . . .

The Legislature has identified those persons who are liable as parents to support their children. See, e.g., G.L. c. 209C, §1 (a person who is adjudicated the father of a child born out of wedlock); G.L. c. 210, §6 (a person who adopts a child). In addition, G.L. c. 46, §4B, provides that, if the spouse of a woman who undergoes artificial insemination consents to the procedure, that spouse is considered the legitimate parent of a resulting child, and is thus obligated to pay child support. But the Legislature has not addressed the situation, present in this case, where a nonmarital cohabitant consents to such a procedure. This absence of legislative action is not a nod in our direction.

Here, the defendant is not a parent of the child under any statutory provision. She has not become a "de facto" parent by virtue of a long-term relationship with the child. Contrast E.N.O. v. L.M.M., 429 Mass. 824, 830, 711 N.E.2d 886 (1999); Youmans v. Ramos, 429 Mass. 774, 776, 711 N.E.2d 165 (1999).[12] Apart from the unenforceable contractual obligation found by the Probate Court judge, the defendant is legally a stranger to the child. Because the defendant is not a parent under any of the statutory provisions enacted to establish parenthood, she has no duty to support the child financially, and she may not be ordered to pay child support.

. . . Equitable principles cannot be used to create a duty to pay child support where the law does not recognize a legally cognizable parent-child relationship. Similarly, we cannot infer that a void in the comprehensive statutory scheme that imposes an obligation of child support on parents authorizes us to fill that void by legislating an outcome that suits us.[13] Equity is not an all-purpose judicial tool by

---

to send the child to private as opposed to public school)? What if the plaintiff marries and her spouse wants to adopt the child? With an adoptive second parent to provide support, would there still be a basis for continuing the defendant's obligation? What if the plaintiff dies, or becomes incapable of caring for the child? Would the defendant then have the obligation (or the right) of full custody? . . .

[12] To date, we have not considered whether a "de facto" parent has an obligation to support a child, and we express no opinion on that issue. We merely point out that the defendant had no relationship with the child and would not qualify as a "de facto" parent.

[13] The dissent cites to the American Law Institute's Principles of the Law of Family Dissolution: Analysis and Recommendations §3.03(1) (2000), which recommend imposing parental obligations by

which the "right thing to do" can be fashioned into a legal obligation possessing the legitimacy of legislative enactment.

Similarly, the "best interests of the child" is not a free-floating concept that empowers probate judges to impose legal obligations on people who have no legal obligations to begin with. The Legislature has specifically defined when the "best interests of the child" standard is to be applied and has tailored the factors to be considered, depending on the nature of the proceeding. See, e.g., G.L. c. 210, §3(c) (granting a petition for adoption without requiring parental consent in certain circumstances); G.L. c. 208, §28 (care, custody, and maintenance of child after divorce); G.L. c. 119, §23 (foster care).

It may be the case that a child is better off with two persons responsible for providing support than with only one such person, and that it will always be in the child's "best interest" to impose a support order on some second person. But that second person may not be imposed on, by way of equity or the "best interests" standard, until and unless the Legislature establishes that he or she is among a class of persons who have a legal obligation to the child. . . .

Wallis v. Smith

22 P.3d 682 (N.M. Ct. App. 2001)

BOSSON, Judge.

. . . [Peter] Wallis and [Kellie Rae] Smith began an intimate, sexual relationship some time before April 1997. They discussed contraceptive techniques and agreed that Smith would use birth control pills. Wallis and Smith further agreed that their sexual intimacy would last only as long as Smith continued to take birth control pills because Wallis made it clear that he did not want to father a child. Wallis participated in contraception only passively; he relied on Smith to use birth control and took no precautions himself.

As time went by, Smith changed her mind. She chose to stop taking birth control pills, but never informed Wallis of her decision. Wallis continued their intimate relationship, and Smith became pregnant. Smith carried the fetus to term and gave birth to a normal, healthy girl on November 27, 1998. [Wallis sued Smith for money damages, asserting four causes of action — fraud, breach of contract, conversion, and prima facie tort. The district court dismissed for failure to state a claim upon which relief may be granted. Wallis appealed.]

Wallis alleges that he has suffered, and will continue to suffer, substantial economic injury as a proximate result of his unintended fatherhood because New Mexico law requires him to pay child support for the next eighteen years. See NMSA 1978, §40-11-15 (1997). Due to his statutory obligations, Wallis asserts that he has

---

agreement even where the person may not be a parent under State law. While §3.03(1) would provide some definition limiting the types of persons who could potentially be subject to an order of support, the articulation of the factors to be considered concludes with the open-ended invitation to base a support order on "any other facts that may relate to the equity of imposing a parental support duty on the person." Id. at §3.03(2)(d), at 415. Given the elusive nature of this definition, and the magnitude of the obligations being imposed, the task is better left to the Legislature and not to individual judges.

been injured by Smith's conduct, and requests compensatory and punitive damages from her. The district court determined that public policy prohibited the relief sought by Wallis, and dismissed the case with prejudice.

Contraceptive Fraud

. . . At the onset of our discussion it is important to distinguish the factual allegations of this case from other kinds of related lawsuits, and thus underscore the limited reach of this opinion. Wallis's complaint is not about sexually-transmitted disease, e.g., McPherson v. McPherson, 712 A.2d 1043 (Me. 1998), nor does it concern the damages arising from an unwanted pregnancy that led to an abortion, e.g., Alice D. v. William M., 450 N.Y.S.2d 350 (Civ. Ct. 1982), or an undesired pregnancy resulting in medical complications, e.g., Barbara A. v. John G., 193 Cal. Rptr. 422 (Ct. App. 1983). This case is not even brought to recover the expense of giving birth. E.g., Chrystal R.M. v. Charlie A.L., 459 S.E.2d 415, 417 (W. Va. 1995); see also §40-11-15(C) (providing recovery for the "reasonable expenses of the mother's pregnancy, birth and confinement"). Wallis's complaint is limited to compensatory damages for the "economic injury" of supporting a normal, healthy child.

Although Wallis insists that he is not attempting to circumvent his child support obligations, we cannot agree. It is self-evident that he seeks to recover for the very financial loss caused him by the statutory obligation to pay child support. At oral argument when pressed by the Court to clarify what damages Wallis was seeking, his counsel stated that Wallis was seeking not punitive, but compensatory damages measured by his "out of pocket loss." Therefore, this case boils down to whether sound public policy would permit our courts to require Smith to indemnify Wallis for child support under the circumstances of this case.

Our legislature has spoken to the public policy that governs the economic consequences of sexual relationships that produce children, and that policy is reflected in New Mexico child support laws. See NMSA 1978, §§40-11-1 to -23 (1986, as amended through 1997). In 1986, our legislature adopted, with minor revisions, the Uniform Parentage Act (UPA), which outlines the legal procedure to establish a parent-child relationship and the corresponding obligation of child support. See 1986 N.M. Laws, ch. 47, §§1-23; Unif. Parentage Act §§1-30, 9B U.L.A. 287 (West 1987). The UPA imposes a form of strict liability for child support, without regard to which parent bears the greater responsibility for the child's being.

Making each parent financially responsible for the conception and birth of children also illuminates a strong public policy that makes paramount the interests of the child. Our jurisprudence has abandoned the notion that the father of an "illegitimate" child could decline to accept the financial responsibility of raising that child. . . . Placing a duty of support on each parent has the added benefit of insulating the state from the possibility of bearing the financial burden for a child. In our view, it is difficult to harmonize the legislative concern for the child, reflected in the immutable duty of parental support, with Wallis's effort in this lawsuit to shift financial responsibility for his child solely to the mother.

New Mexico is not alone in its view of parental responsibility and the conflict created by lawsuits such as this. To our knowledge, no jurisdiction recognizes contraceptive fraud or breach of promise to practice birth control as a ground for adjusting a natural parent's obligation to pay child support. . . .

Some courts have dismissed contraceptive fraud cases on the ground that the claims tread too far into the realm of an individual's privacy interests. [Stephen K. v. Roni L., 164 Cal. Rptr. 618 (Ct. App. 1980).] We agree that individuals are entitled a sphere of privacy into which courts should not tread. A person's choice whether or not to use contraceptives understandably fits into this sphere. We also believe that the "privacy interests involved . . . require a cautious approach," and therefore we elect to rely primarily on the prevailing public policy of child support, while at the same time recognizing the serious privacy concerns implicated and threatened by the underlying lawsuit.

Wallis's attempt to apply traditional contract and tort principles to his contraceptive agreement is unconvincing and, in the end, futile. The contract analogy fails because children, the persons for whose benefit child support guidelines are enacted, have the same needs regardless of whether their conception violated a promise between the parents. Further, a parent being sued for causing the conception and birth of a child is no ordinary tortfeasor; a defendant under these circumstances is legally entitled to collect financial support on behalf of the child. We will not re-enter the jurisprudence of illegitimacy by allowing a parent to opt out of the financial consequences of his or her sexual relationships just because they were unintended. Nor will we recognize a cause of action that trivializes one's personal responsibility in sexual relationships. Indeed, permitting "such actions while simultaneously encouraging paternity actions for support flies in the face of all reason." [Welzenbach v. Powers, 660 A.2d 1133 (N.H. 1995).] We also observe that if Wallis did not desire children, he was free and able to practice contraceptive techniques on his own.

Wallis tries to make the basis for liability not so much the birth of the child, but the fact that Smith lied, and perpetrated a fraud on him. But not all misrepresentations are actionable. . . . Finally, Wallis argues that our courts have recognized tort claims which measure damages by the economic injury of supporting an unwanted child. See Lovelace Med. Ctr. v. Mendez, 111 N.M. 336, 345, 805 P.2d 603, 612 (1991) [holding that a couple who sought to protect their financial resources by limiting the size of their family through sterilization could sue a negligent physician for economic damages measured by the cost of raising an additional child to the age of majority]. Because *Lovelace* does not speak to the issue of inter-parental liability, which is the crux of Wallis's appeal, it has no bearing on our decision.

Accordingly, we hold that the actions asserted here cannot be used to recoup the financial obligations of raising a child. . . .

Harmon v. Department of Social Services
951 P.2d 770 (Wash. 1998)

GUY, Justice.

. . . Appellant Edward Harmon married Darlene Dooley in 1985. At that time Darlene was the custodial parent of two daughters, ages eight and nine years old, who were born during her marriage to Tom Dooley. After living with their mother and stepfather for almost seven years, both children left the Harmon home in February 1992 and moved into the home of their father and stepmother, Tom and Linda Dooley.

On March 31, 1992, the superior court modified custody of the children, ordering the primary residential placement of the children be changed from the mother's home to the father's home. The modification order did not address child support. In April 1992, the children's father requested the Department of Social and Health Services (hereafter Department) to calculate and collect support payments for the children. . . . The Administrative Law Judge (ALJ) determined the mother was permanently disabled and had no ability to earn income. Based on this state's child support schedule, RCW 26.19.020, the ALJ ordered the mother to pay $25 per child per month. Shortly after the proceeding against the mother was concluded, the Department served the stepfather, Appellant Edward Harmon, with a "Notice and Finding of Financial Responsibility."

[B]ased on the net incomes of the stepfather and father, the ALJ computed the stepfather's total monthly support obligation (should he be found to be liable on appeal) to be $486.10. The stepfather is disabled and unemployed. His monthly net income of $1,320.20 is received from Department of Labor and Industries and Social Security Administration disability payments. [The stepfather appealed.]

Does RCW 26.16.205 impose an obligation upon a stepparent which is equal to that of the natural mother and father for the purpose of calculating and paying child support for stepchildren who have moved from the stepparent's home?

[RCW 26.16.205, the family expense statute that dates from 1881] was enacted in derogation of the common law, under which a husband was primarily responsible and a wife only secondarily responsible for the expenses of the family. Under this statute, a mother and a father were equally obligated for the necessary expenses of child rearing, and this obligation survived the termination of the marriage. [The statute] remained unchanged for nearly 90 years, until 1969, when, at the request of the Department of Public Assistance, the law was amended as follows:

> The expenses of the family and the education of the children, *including stepchildren*, are chargeable upon the property of both husband and wife, or either of them, and in relation thereto they may be sued jointly or separately: *PROVIDED, That with regard to stepchildren, the obligation shall cease upon the termination of the relationship of husband and wife.*

The Department explained to the Legislature that the purpose of the [amendment] was to comply with federal regulations governing allocation of federal public assistance funds to the State. In determining eligibility for public assistance, the Department treated a child who lived with a stepparent and one of his or her parents in the same manner as it treated a child who lived with both natural parents. [F]ederal regulations required that all stepparents, not just those on public assistance, be treated the same, under a law of general application. . . .

The Legislature again amended RCW 26.16.205 in 1990. [The amended statute provides:]

> The expenses of the family and the education of the children, including stepchildren, are chargeable upon the property of both husband and wife, or either of them, and they may be sued jointly or separately. When a petition for dissolution of marriage or a petition for legal separation is filed, the court may, upon motion of the

stepparent, terminate the obligation to support the stepchildren. The obligation to support stepchildren shall cease upon the entry of a decree of dissolution, decree of legal separation, or death.

. . . In the present case, the Court of Appeals held that while RCW 26.16.205 does not, in clear and unambiguous language, set forth a new rule redefining how the stepparent's duty of support arises, "the statute does, in clear and unambiguous language, redefine the events that terminate the duty of support once it has arisen: 'entry of a decree of dissolution, decree of legal separation, or death.' " [Harmon v. Dept. of Soc. & Health Servs., 922 P.2d 201 (Wash. Ct. App. 1996)].

With this background in mind, we begin our analysis of the issue before us. . . . One of the overriding policies and a standard of the statewide child support schedule is that the obligation to support a child should be equitably apportioned between the parents of the child. Another aim of the law is to provide uniformity throughout the state for calculating support obligations. To that end, the law requires worksheets and instructions that must be used in every case. . . . The basic child support obligation is determined under Part I and is based on the monthly incomes of the parents of the child whose support is being determined. Once the combined net monthly income is determined pursuant to RCW 26.19.071, a presumptive amount of child support is calculated, based on the child support economic table contained in RCW 26.19.020.

RCW 26.19.071(1) sets the standard for determining the income, upon which the basic child support obligation is based, as follows: All income and resources of each parent's household shall be disclosed and considered by the court when the court determines the child support obligation of each parent. *Only the income of the parents of the children whose support is at issue shall be calculated for purposes of calculating the basic support obligation. Income and resources of any other person shall not be included in calculating the basic support obligation.* (Emphasis added.)

A new spouse's, or stepparent's, income must be listed under Part VI (Additional Factors for Consideration) but may not be used to calculate the presumptive basic support obligation. In the present case, under the child support statute, only the mother's income and the father's income should have been used to determine the presumptive basic support obligation.

A court may deviate from the presumptive amount, but deviations are the exception to the rule and should not be used routinely. Additionally, the income of a new spouse is not, by itself, a sufficient reason for deviation. RCW 26.19.075(1)(a)(i).

In making its recommendation to the Legislature, the Child Support Schedule Commission considered the use of the support schedule in families involving stepparents. The Commission reported to the Legislature that it was guided in part by the principle that the child support schedule "should not create extraneous negative effects on the major life decisions of either parent. The schedule should avoid creating economic disincentives for remarriage. . . . " Report at 8. . . . In a special report on the use of the schedule for blended families, the Commission recommended that the "income of spouses [of the child's parents] should be disregarded in any formula approach." Washington State Child Support Schedule Comm'n Rep. On Use of Support Schedule for Blended Families 3 (Dec. 1989). [The Legislature accepted the Commission's recommendations.]

Two questions are considered in our analysis. The first is whether the statute imposes a child support obligation on a stepparent that is equal to that of the child's parents. The second is whether the statute provides the only means of ending whatever obligation is created by RCW 26.16.205. We answer both questions in the negative.

First, to interpret the family expense statute in a manner that makes stepparents equally responsible, with parents, for child support would require us to disregard the language and the impact of our child support schedule and to judicially create an exception to RCW 26.19. We cannot construe RCW 26.16.205 to conflict with the language or the purposes of RCW 26.19.

The family expense statute is not a child support statute but, rather, a statute that makes both parties to a marriage equally responsible for the necessary expenses of the family. The family includes stepchildren who are part of the family unit, who reside in the family home, or who are in the residential care of one of the adults in this family unit. It does not include children who are in the primary residential care of the other parent.

With respect to the language regarding termination of a stepparent's obligation under the family expense statute, we believe the Legislature intended only to distinguish between parents and stepparents to the extent that the obligation, once assumed, would not continue for stepparents beyond the termination of the marriage. The parent's obligation for the support of a child continues and is not dependent on the continuation of the marital relationship. The provision for terminating a stepparent's obligation under the statute is not the exclusive means for terminating the obligation. Notwithstanding the statute's specific and limiting language, any support obligation for a child may terminate when the child reaches the age of majority, is married, emancipated or otherwise no longer dependent. Because we hold the stepfather in this appeal was not primarily liable for the support of his wife's children after the court ordered the placement of the children be changed to their father, we do not determine what other ways the obligations that arise under the family expense statute might terminate. . . .

NOTES AND QUESTIONS: WHO SHOULD HAVE THE SUPPORT OBLIGATION?

(1) Biological or Social Relationship as the Basis for Child Support.   Children of same-sex couples challenge traditional notions of child support obligations based on biological relationships. Historically, the legal obligation to pay child support was entwined with paternity establishment. For a nonmarital child, a court order establishes paternity as well as child support. Alternatively, paternity of a nonmarital child can be established through voluntary acknowledgment (and child support orders sometimes follow). For a marital child, both parents have the duty of support during the marriage; upon dissolution, the divorce court generally awards child support. As we have seen, competing claims of paternity may arise (*Michael H.*, supra). Increasingly, competing claims of maternity are emerging. Competing claims of either paternity or maternity have implications for child support obligations.

Should the child support obligation be based on an adult's biological or social relationship to the child? Should either relationship alone be enough? Should the child support obligation be based on the parties' relationship (i.e., marriage or domestic partnership)? A few states (e.g., California, Hawaii, New Jersey, and Vermont) now confer legal rights on domestic partners provided that the couple registers as such. Should registration be a prerequisite to the imposition of liability for child support for a same-sex couple? See Grace Ganz Blumberg, Legal Recognition of Same-Sex Conjugal Relationships: The 2003 California Domestic Partner Rights and Responsibilities Act in Comparative Civil Rights and Family Law Perspective, 51 UCLA L. Rev. 1555 (2004) (arguing that same-sex couples would be better served by a system that recognizes both registered and stable unregistered cohabitation).

Should a biological father who had sexual intercourse with the child's mother only once and never had any relationship with the child have a legal obligation to support the child? If so, why shouldn't the same-sex partner in the principal case — who participated in medical decisions and procedures — be legally obligated to support the child?

Massachusetts (the jurisdiction of the principal case) became the first state to permit same-sex marriage in May 2004. See Goodridge v. Department of Pub. Health, 798 N.E.2d 941 (Mass. 2003). If the couple in the principal case, T.F. and B.L., had been married, how would that fact have altered the result?

As the principal case reveals, courts increasingly are wrestling with resolution of disputes involving child support (as well as custody and visitation) upon dissolution of same-sex relationships. Some courts (like that in the principal case) refuse to mandate support from a domestic partner who is neither a biological nor an adoptive parent. See also D.R.M. v. Wood, 34 P.3d 887 (Wash. Ct. App. 2001). Other courts, however, apply equitable principles to hold that the same-sex partner is estopped from denying child support responsibilities. See, e.g., L.S.K. v. H.A.N., 813 A.2d 872 (Pa. Super. Ct. 2002). For discussion of custody and visitation issues involving same-sex couples, see Chapter 5.

(2) Mother's Refusal to Enforce Support.   Suppose a mother does not choose to enforce the support obligation against the father (or her partner, as the case may be). Does the child have a right to child support from that party nonetheless? Should it matter whether the mother would otherwise require public assistance to support the child? Does it alter your opinion regarding B.L.'s support obligation to learn that T.F.'s baby, who was premature, required considerable medical assistance?

(3) Child Support Obligations of Gamete Donors.   The original Uniform Parentage Act (§5b) provided that a sperm donor was not considered the child's natural father (and therefore was relieved of parental obligations such as child support liability) if he donated sperm to a licensed physician for purposes of insemination of a married woman who was not the donor's wife. The revised UPA of 2002 (§702) flatly provides that "A donor is not a parent of a child conceived by means of assisted reproduction." The new provision thereby eliminates the requirements that the sperm donation be made to a licensed physician and inseminated in a married woman (because of concerns about protecting the procreative rights of the unmarried). Further, intent to be a parent under the revised UPA is determinative: the father-child relationship is established if a man provides sperm for, or consents to, assisted reproduction by a woman with the *intent to be the parent* of her child (§703). See also Steven S. v. Deborah D., 25 Cal. Rptr.3d 482 (Ct. App. 2005) (rejecting a claim of parental relationship by a known sperm donor who provided semen to

a licensed physician to inseminate an intimate partner who was not his wife); In re Parentage of J.M.K. 89 P.3d 309 (Wash. App. Ct. 2004) (holding that father's failure to consent by complying with writing requirement of artificial insemination statute precluded finding of paternity and liability for child support).

Cases involving disputed maternity sometimes also arise. For example, suppose one same-sex partner serves as the egg donor but the other partner carries the resulting embryo. When the child is born, who is (are) the child's mother(s)? Which parent or parents bear(s) responsibility for child support? What light on this issue is shed by new UPA §106: "Provisions of this [Act] relating to determination of paternity apply to determinations of maternity"?

See also K.M. v. E.G., 13 Cal. Rptr. 3d 136 (Ct. App. 2004) (holding that egg donor had standing to bring action to determine parentage under Uniform Parentage Act but evidence supported finding that she waived her parental rights by signing egg donor consent form); *petition for review granted*, 18 Cal. Rptr. 3d 667 (Cal. 2004). See generally Laurence C. Nolan, Legal Strangers and the Duty of Support: Beyond the Biological Tie — But How Far Beyond the Marital Tie?, 41 Santa Clara L. Rev. 1 (2000).

(4) Contraceptive Fraud. Should a father's child support obligations be affected by the fact that the mother deceived him about her use of birth control? *Wallis* illustrates the general rule that the mother's contraceptive fraud does not serve as a defense to a father's support obligation. See also L. Pamela P. v. Frank S., 449 N.E.2d 713 (N.Y. Ct. App. 1983). Should the father be permitted to maintain a tort action for fraud or infliction of emotional distress instead? See Day v. Heller, 653 N.W.2d 475 (Neb. 2002) (rejecting husband's suit). Should support obligations in cases of fraud, if not dismissed, at least be reduced?

Should the mother's wrongful conduct *ever* relieve the father of liability for child support? That is, should the general rule apply when the woman acquires the "purloined sperm" from (a) a man who is unconscious? See, e.g., S.F. v. State ex rel. T.M., 695 So. 2d 1186 (Ala. Civ. App. 1996); (b) a male who is a victim of statutory rape? See, e.g., State ex rel. Hermesmann v. Seyer, 847 P.2d 1273 (Kan. 1993); (c) a fertility clinic (from deposited sperm intended for an earlier use), but long after the couple's intimate relationship terminates? See, e.g., In re Parentage of J.M.K., supra.

See generally Donald C. Hubin, Daddy Dilemmas: Untangling the Puzzles of Paternity, 13 Cornell J.L. & Pub. Pol'y 29, 52-62 (2003) (discussing "purloined sperm" cases); Laura W. Morgan, It's Ten O'Clock: Do You Know Where Your Sperm Are? Toward a Strict Liability Theory of Parentage, 11 Divorce Litig. 1 (1999); Ellen London, Comment, A Critique of the Strict Liability Standard for Determining Child Support in Cases of Male Victims of Sexual Assault and Statutory Rape, 152 U. Pa. L. Rev. 1957 (2004); Brenda Saiz, Note, Tort Law: Tort Liability When Fraudulent Misrepresentation Regarding Birth Control Results in the Birth of a Healthy Child — Wallis v. Smith, 32 N.M. L. Rev. 549 (2002).

(5) Support Obligations of Stepparents. Suppose a child's mother remarries after a divorce or after the father dies. If her new husband adopts the child, he clearly has a legal support obligation. What financial responsibility does he have if he does not adopt the child? As a matter of policy, should a stepparent have a legal support obligation? Suppose the natural father is alive, as in the *Harmon* case. Should the child support obligation be apportioned between the two fathers?

How should the obligation be affected if the stepfather and mother later separate or divorce? Should any other circumstances terminate the stepparent's financial obligation — for example, if the children leave the stepparent's household, as in *Harmon*? Faced with the fact that approximately one-fourth of all children will live with a stepparent before the age of majority, many courts and legislatures have reformulated the rules affecting stepparent support obligations. Mary Ann Mason & Nicole Zayac, Rethinking Stepparent Rights: Has the ALI Found a Better Definition?, 36 Fam. L.Q. 227, 227 (2002).

    a. Stepparent Obligation During the Marriage.   Most states follow the common law rule that stepparents have no obligation to support their stepchildren during the stepparent's marriage to the child's custodial parent. This general rule is subject to two exceptions. In a few jurisdictions, *stepparent support statutes* impose a duty on stepparents (although sometimes only if the stepchildren are, or will be, likely to become public charges). John C. Mayoue, Stepping In to Parent, 25 Fam. Advoc. 36, 42 (2002) (listing 16 states with stepparent support statutes). In addition, some jurisdictions impose a duty based on the "in loco parentis" doctrine (i.e., the stepparent has voluntarily taken the child into the home and assumed parental obligations). Id., at 38.

    b. Stepparent Obligation Post-Divorce.   A stepparent has no legal duty to support a former stepchild after the termination of the stepparent's marriage to the child's custodial parent. Thus, none of the stepparent support statutes continue the obligation post-divorce. Id. Moreover, the in loco parentis doctrine does not apply after divorce, even if the stepparent continues his or her relationship with the stepchild (for example, by visitation). Id. However, in limited cases, courts may impose a post-divorce duty of support on stepparents by means of the equitable estoppel doctrine or principles of implied contract. Id. at 39. Equitable estoppel might arise, for example, if a stepparent interferes with a biological parent's efforts to visit or provide support to a child.

    c. New Mate Income Excluded.   Are a stepparent's financial resources taken into account in determining the custodial or noncustodial parent's support obligation? Some states explicitly exclude the stepparent's resources from such consideration. See, e.g., Cal. Fam. Code §4057.5 (West 2004) (excluding income of a subsequent spouse or nonmarital partner except in cases of "extreme and severe hardship" to the child).

    d. Federal Legislation.   Federal treatment of stepparents' support obligations lacks consistency, although "there is more coherence in federal than state law." Mason & Zayac, supra, at 231. For example, eligibility for purposes of Social Security survivor benefits is based on the child's "dependency" on the stepparent (defined by percentage of support and duration of co-residence). See generally Mary Ann Mason & David Simon, The Ambiguous Stepparent: Federal Legislation in Search of a Model, 29 Fam. L.Q. 445 (1995).

    e. ALI Principles.   The American Law Institute (ALI), an influential group of lawyers, law professors and judges, recently completed a decade-long project to promote uniformity in family law. See ALI, Principles of the Law of Family Dissolution: Analysis and Recommendations (2002). The ALI Principles, although they recognize two new types of parents (parents by estoppel and de facto parents) for purposes of custody and visitation rights, do not significantly alter the rules regarding stepparent support obligations. Mason & Zayac, supra, at 246. Thus, for example, the ALI Principles (§3.12) provide that the income of a stepparent (or steppartner) should not be considered in calculating the custodial parent's support obligation post-divorce. Custody and visitation rights are discussed in Chapter 5.

(6) Relative Responsibility. A majority of states have statutes that for some purposes extend support obligations beyond the traditional obligations of parents to support their minor children. (As noted in Blackstone, above, the Elizabethan Poor Laws themselves made grandparents responsible.) "Family expense statutes" generally provide that the expenses of the family are chargeable against the property of both spouses. (Such statutes are similar to, but broader than, the common law doctrine of necessaries.) In addition, some state "filial responsibility laws" make adult children responsible for the support of elderly parents in some circumstances, thereby relieving governmental authorities from the burden of doing so. See Seymour Moskowitz, Adult Children and Indigent Parents: Intergenerational Responsibilities in International Perspective, 86 Marq. L. Rev. 401, 422 (2002) (finding that 30 states have filial responsibility laws).

Filial responsibility statutes differ in scope and duration of liability, responsible relatives, and penalties. Standing is accorded to different persons or institutions, such as the indigent parent, a public agency, the welfare authority, or creditors furnishing necessaries. Id. at 425-426. The laws, however, are similar in terms of imposing financial responsibility only for the benefit of relatives who are indigent and only when the responsible adult has adequate resources for his or her own spouse and dependents. Relative responsibility laws have withstood constitutional challenges. See, e.g., Americana Healthcare v. Randall, 513 N.W.2d 566 (S.D. 1994). However, such laws are rarely enforced.

Filial responsibility laws are highly controversial. Supporters argue that such laws help achieve the goal of ensuring adequate income and care to the elderly, express familistic values, and save public dollars that may be better spent for general social obligations. Moskowitz, supra, at 430-435. As a matter of public policy, to what extent should relatives be held financially responsible for one another's support? See generally Shannon Frank Edelstone, Filial Responsibility: Can the Legal Duty to Support Our Parents Be Effectively Enforced?, 36 Fam. L.Q. 501 (2002); Seymour Moskowitz, Filial Responsibility Statutes: Legal and Policy Considerations, 9 J.L. & Pol'y 709 (2001).

2. The Scope of the Parental Support Obligation

INTRODUCTORY PROBLEM

Ann Wriggins graduated from Berkeley High this past June at the age of 16 because she accumulated extra credits by taking summer school courses. She has been admitted to junior college for this fall, but her father claims that she would learn more by going to work. Ann is willing to continue living at home but wants to go to junior college. Because her parents are unwilling to pay her fees, she will not be able to attend college even if she lives at home. The fees amount to $4,500 per year, and her parents (whose annual income is $90,000 per year) acknowledge that they could afford the cost. Should Ann be able to sue her parents for nonsupport? How long should Ann's parents be required to support her? Until she reaches 18? She obtains a bachelor's degree? If she decides to attend law school? Suppose Ann's parents divorce. Are her chances of obtaining educational support better?

Suppose that Ann's father finally agrees to pay for her college expenses, and Ann enrolls in the junior college. Then Ann decides she prefers living with her boyfriend rather than at home. Can her father condition his educational support on Ann's continuing to live at home? After Ann completes her education, at age 22, she becomes completely incapacitated in an automobile accident. Do her parents have an obligation to continue to pay for her support?

Waddell v. Waddell
No. 2020219, 2004 WL 2128630 (Ala. Civ. App. Sept. 24, 2004)

MURDOCK, Judge.

This case was commenced by the filing of a petition by Holayne Lester Waddell seeking a modification of a 1995 judgment divorcing her from Edward Lee Waddell, Jr. Among other things, the mother's petition sought an award of postminority educational support for the benefit of the parties' two sons. . . .

The mother and the father were married in 1979. The parties had two minor sons at the time of the divorce in 1995. Based on his annual income of $65,000 at the time of the divorce, the father was ordered to pay child support in the amount of $464 biweekly, as well as a portion of his sons' medical expenses. The trial court did not award the mother any alimony at the time of the divorce, but it reserved the right to do so in the future.

Following the divorce, the father moved to Missouri and married a woman with whom he had been having an adulterous relationship that had led to the divorce. Subsequently, in 1997, the father petitioned to modify his child-support obligation on the ground that his annual income had decreased from $65,000 at the time of the divorce to only $20,000 at the time he filed the petition. The trial court denied the petition; neither party appealed from that judgment.

In April 2001, when the parties' older son was 18 years old and the younger son was 16 years old, the mother filed her petition requesting postminority educational support for the benefit of each of the parties' sons. [The trial court terminated the father's obligation to pay child support for the older child, set the father's child-support obligation at $298 per month for the younger child until majority, and required the father to pay one-half of the college expenses for both sons. The father appeals.]

I. Postminority-Support Issues

In Ex parte Bayliss, 550 So. 2d 986 (Ala. 1989), our Supreme Court held that the trial court has discretion whether to order postminority educational support at all, and that, in exercising that discretion, the trial court shall consider

"all relevant factors that shall appear reasonable and necessary, including *primarily* the financial resources of the parents and the child and the child's commitment to, and aptitude for, the requested education." [Ex parte Bayliss, 550 So.2d at 987 (emphasis in original)].

In addition, the trial court may consider

"the standard of living that the child would have enjoyed if the marriage had not been dissolved and the family unit had been preserved and the child's relationship with his parents and responsiveness to parental advice and guidance." [Id. at 987]

After he graduated from high school, the parties' older son attended Shoals Community College for two years on a tuition scholarship. The mother paid the older son's college-related expenses other than tuition, which totaled $1,199.04 for both years. In 2002, following his sophomore year, the older son transferred to the University of North Alabama ("UNA"), where the parties' younger son also enrolled as a freshman. The mother paid the Fall 2002 tuition and enrollment fees for both sons, which she testified totaled $4,252.68.

There is no dispute that both of the parties' sons have the aptitude for and commitment to continuing their college educations. There is also no dispute that the father has sufficient financial resources to pay for the sons' educations. At the time of the divorce, the father had already established a brokerage account specifically intended to pay for the sons' college expenses. At the time of the divorce, the account had a value of $27,000; as of the August 2002 hearing, according to the father's testimony, the account's value had grown to approximately $165,000.

A. The Effect of the Relationship of the Father and His Sons on the Award of Postminority Support

The father first contends that the trial court has wrongly required him to provide postminority support when the parties' sons do not respect him and are not responsive to his parental advice and guidance. The father testified that his sons refuse to visit him or to communicate with him and that he was not even invited to the younger son's high-school graduation. The mother testified that she had discussed with the sons their obligation to communicate with their father but that the father no longer called them. With the approval of both parties, the trial judge met with both sons in chambers before issuing his original judgment; however, there is no transcript of their discussion.

The Alabama Supreme Court held in Ex parte Bayliss, 550 So. 2d 986 (Ala.1989), that a trial court "may" consider "the child's relationship with his parents and responsiveness to parental advice and guidance" in deciding whether and to what extent a noncustodial parent should be obligated to provide postminority educational support for his or her children following a divorce. 550 So. 2d at 987. [I]n the absence of a transcript of the in camera interview of the children, we assume that the trial court's interview of the parties' sons supports the trial court's judgment.

Although the relationship between the father and his sons may be strained, the trial court concluded that this was at least partially the result of the father's adulterous conduct that led to the divorce. Based on our review of the record and the judgment of the trial court, we cannot conclude that the trial court abused its discretion in awarding postminority support in this case.

B. The Temporal Limitations on the Award of Postminority Support

The father next argues that the trial court should have limited the father's duty to provide postminority support to a definite period of time. The portion of the trial court's judgment awarding postminority support reads as follows:

> "There exists a 'College Fund' that was specifically set up by the father/defendant to pay the college expenses for the two sons. Therefore, *all* college expenses that directly relate to room, board, books, tuition and fees are to be paid from this 'fund.' Further, *this charge shall continue until the sons finish college within a reasonable period of time*, maintain at least a 'C' average, and are full time students. Additionally, room and board costs are to be determined by the rates established by the University of North Alabama as it pertains to a student living on campus and sharing a room with one roommate." (Second emphasis added.)

. . . In general, a trial-court judgment that prescribes a definite duration for a noncustodial parent's obligation to provide postminority financial support to a child better allows that parent to make plans for the payment of that support. Moreover, if the specific duration of the postminority-support obligation is unknown, the non-custodial parent may be unable to measure, or "make the case" for, the degree of hardship that ultimately will be caused by that award.

In the present case, the trial court's use of the term "reasonable period of time" in its judgment will mean, at best, that the judgment will be open to interpretation by the trial court at some future date and that the father will be hard-pressed to obtain a critical appellate review of whatever interpretation the trial court may place on that term at that time. At worst, it might be argued that the fact that the judgment leaves the parties with an issue to determine on their own prevents that judgment from being a final judgment.

In light of the foregoing, we hold that an award of postminority educational support for a "reasonable period of time" lacks sufficient certainty. . . . Upon remand, the trial court should modify its judgment to more specifically state the period during which the father is obligated to provide such support.

C. Expenses for Room and Board

The father further argues that the trial court erred by requiring that his postminority-support obligation include an amount equivalent to the cost of room and board at UNA, even though both of the parties' sons continue to live at home with their mother. Although the language of the judgment is not entirely clear, it does appear that the trial court's judgment requires the father to pay the equivalent of room and board expenses to the mother for both sons while they are attending college. [W]e conclude that it was error for the trial court's judgment to require the father to pay room and board costs when no such costs are actually expended.

D. The Overlap of Child Support and "Postminority" Educational Support

The father also argues that the trial court erred by requiring him to pay college-related expenses for the younger son while the younger son is a minor and the father is still paying child support for that son's benefit. . . . To the extent the father contests the overlap in his child-support obligation with the requirement that he pay for tuition and fees associated with the younger son's college education, we conclude that his argument is not well-taken. In essence, the father argues that, although a parent may have an obligation under Ex parte Bayliss to pay for a child's college or other postsecondary educational expenses after the child reaches the age of majority, no such obligation is to be imposed upon a parent so long as the child remains a minor. Our Supreme Court rejected this very notion in Ogle v. Ogle, 156 So. 2d 345 (Ala. 1963). Indeed, the Supreme Court's reaffirmation in Ex parte Bayliss of its view on this issue laid the foundation for its holding in that case as to postminority educational support:

> "This Court in deciding this issue in Ogle v. Ogle, 156 So. 2d 345, 348 (Ala. 1963), wrote: " 'While there are divergent views on the question, it seems to us that the cases from other jurisdictions holding that a father may be required to contribute toward the college education of his minor child, who is in his mother's custody pursuant to a divorce decree, are supported by the better reasoning.'
>
> "[The son] was born March 5, 1969. If the age of majority had remained 21 years, as it was from 1852 to 1975, [the son] would have been entitled to have his father contribute toward his college education, at least until [the son turned 21 years of age]." [Ex parte Bayliss, 550 So. 2d at 990-91.]

We therefore reject the argument that the trial court erred in requiring the father to pay the cost of tuition, books, and fees associated with the younger son's postsecondary education merely because some of those costs would be incurred during the son's minority.

E. Postminority Health Insurance

The father also argues that the trial court erred by requiring him to provide health-insurance coverage for the sons after they reach the age of majority and while they are attending college. [W]e see no principled, material distinction between an award of health-insurance costs and an award of other educational expenses, such as room and board. As a practical matter, the former often may be just as necessary as the latter to enable children of divorced parents to devote themselves to the pursuit of college educations. [R]eason compels the conclusion that a child should not be required to run the risk of incurring a serious or even catastrophic injury without the ability to afford medical care in order to obtain that education, at least where the child's parents can afford to, and in the absence of a divorce would have, removed that risk for the child.

The justness of maintaining children in as near as possible the same position they would have been in absent a divorce was central to our Supreme Court's reasoning in Ex parte Bayliss. As the Court explained,

" '[W]e are living today in an age of keen competition, and if the children of today . . . are to take their rightful place in a complex order of society and government, and discharge the duties of citizenship as well as meet with success the responsibilities devolving upon them in their relations with their fellow man, the church, the state and nation, it must be recognized that their parents owe them the duty to the extent of their financial capacity to provide for them the training and education which will be of such benefit to them in the discharge of the responsibilities of citizenship. It is a duty which the parent not only owes to his child, but to the state as well, since the stability of our government must depend upon a well-equipped, a well-trained, and well-educated citizenship. We can see no good reason why this duty should not extend to a college education. Our statutes do not prohibit it, but they are rather susceptible of an interpretation to allow it. The fact is that the importance of a college education is being more and more recognized in matters of commerce, society, government, and all human relations, and the college graduate is being more and more preferred over those who are not so fortunate. No parent should subject his worthy child to this disadvantage if he has the financial capacity to avoid it.' "

"This is the public policy of our State. Since the normal age for attending college extends beyond the age of 19 years [the age of majority under Ala. Code §30-3-1], courts have the right to assure that the children of divorced parents, who are minors at the time of the divorce, are given the same right to a college education before and after they reach the age of 19 years that they probably would have had if their parents had not divorced." [Ex parte Bayliss, 550 So. 2d at 994-95.]

. . . Given the financial ability of the father and the needs of the children in the present case, we affirm the judgment of the trial court insofar as it requires the father to maintain health insurance for the benefit of his sons while they are attending college. . . .

DISCUSSION: CHILD SUPPORT AFTER DIVORCE

(1) The Transformation from Discretion to Guidelines.   When granting a divorce, courts establish whether the noncustodial parent should pay child support, and if so, the amount. In making this determination, the trial court considers the financial resources of each parent and the family's prior standard of living. Until comparatively recently, courts accomplished this discretionary determination using imprecise statutory standards. For example, the Uniform Marriage and Divorce Act (UMDA) §309, 9A U.L.A. (pt. 1) 159 (1998 & Supp. 2004), provides:

In a proceeding for dissolution of marriage, legal separation, maintenance, or child support, the court may order either or both parents owing a duty of support to a child of the marriage to pay an amount reasonable or necessary for his support, without regard to marital misconduct, after considering all relevant factors including:
(1) the financial resources of the child;
(2) the financial resources of the custodial parent;
(3) the standard of living the child would have enjoyed had the marriage not been dissolved;

(4) the physical and emotional condition of the child and his educational needs; and

(5) the financial resources and needs of the noncustodial parent.

However, beginning in the late 1960s, Congress became increasingly involved in child support enforcement (see discussion of historical background pp.199-203, infra). Initially, federal involvement was confined to welfare cases, but subsequently expanded to all child support cases. As a consequence of federal legislative reform, the former regime of discretionary standards gave way to enforcement by guidelines. In the Child Support Enforcement Amendments of 1984, 42 U.S.C. §§651 et seq. (2000), Congress mandated that states establish definite numerical formulas ("child support guidelines") to assist courts in determining child support. States were required to have these guidelines in place by 1987 or risk losing a percentage of federal welfare (i.e., Aid to Dependent Children) funds. Subsequent federal legislation (the Family Support Act of 1988, 42 U.S.C. §667 (2000)) specified that states must use these guidelines as a rebuttable presumption *in all cases* and required states to update their guidelines regularly. The intent of these federal laws was to remedy several shortcomings: the inadequacy of awards compared to the actual cost of child rearing, inconsistent orders among those parents with similar economic circumstances, and delays in processing.[15]

The federal mandate did not require that states adopt any particular model for the calculation of child support. As a result, states implemented the guidelines according to three models: (1) the most popular Income Shares Model (adopted by approximately three-fourths of the states), which relies on the combined income of both parents on the assumption that a child should receive the same proportion of parental income as if the family had remained intact; (2) the Percentage-of-Income Approach (adopted by approximately ten states), which bases support on a percentage of the noncustodial parent's income (i.e., the obligor's income alone); and (3) the Melson Formula (now virtually abandoned), which is based on the idea that parents should keep income for their basic needs first, and then additional income should flow to the child. Jo Michelle Beld & Len Biernat, Federal Intent for State Child Support Guidelines: Income Shares, Cost Shares, and the Realities of Shared Parenting, 37 Fam. L.Q. 165, 167 (2003).

This variation in treatment has resulted in considerable statewide rules regarding

> [t]he income basis for the determination of support; the estimates of spending on children upon which the guidelines are based; the treatment of child care costs; the treatment of medical insurance and out-of-pocket expenditures for medical care; provisions for other children to whom the parent owes a duty of support; adjustments for parenting time; and provisions for adjusting support when the obligor is low-income. [Id. at 166.]

Was Congress wise to require the establishment of child support schedules? What are the advantages and disadvantages of the new system, compared with the

---

[15] Nancy Thoennes et al., The Impact of Child Support Guidelines on Award Adequacy, Award Variability, and Case Processing Efficiency, 25 Fam. L.Q. (No. 3) 325, 326 (1991).

former practice of allowing courts to exercise discretion on a case-by-case basis? How effective do you think the models are in meeting the needs of contemporary families and accomplishing the above goals? For example, is the percentage-of-income model "based on outdated assumptions about parental roles and resources"? Id. at 200. Should more generous adjustments take into account the noncustodial parent's visitation expenses? William V. Fabricius & Sanford L. Braver, Non-Child Support Expenditures on Children by Nonresidential Divorced Fathers, 41 Fam. Ct. Rev. 321 (2003) (so arguing). But cf. Irwin Garfinkel et al., Visitation and Child Support Guidelines: A Comment on Fabricius & Braver, 42 Fam. Ct. Rev. 342 (2004) (rebuttal). See also Marygold S. Melli, Guideline Review: The Search for an Equitable Child Support Formula, in Child Support: The New Frontier 113-127 (J. Thomas Oldham & Marygold S. Melli eds., 2000) (critiquing state guideline reviews as inadequate).

Empirical evidence has explored the effectiveness of the guidelines in accomplishing their objectives. One recent study (of award rates, award levels, variation in awards and deviations from guidelines formulas) concludes: (1) guidelines increase the probability of obtaining an award for many women who previously would not have received an award, especially for mothers of nonmarital children; (2) guidelines may also increase the size of the awards for these particular mothers; (3) guidelines do appear to achieve greater uniformity of treatment — primarily by eliminating extreme awards — but have not resulted in identical awards for families with similar circumstances; and (4) deviations from the guidelines occur in a significant percent of the awards.[16] See also Andrea H. Beller & John W. Graham, Small Change: The Economics of Child Support (1993) (finding little improvement in child support enforcement in states with guidelines, based on a study conducted prior to the most recent federal support legislation of 1996).

(2) Postmajority Support for Education.   *Waddell* illustrates the problem of whether a parent is liable for support after the child reaches majority. Traditionally, a parent's duty of support ceased upon the child's reaching the age of majority (or upon emancipation, discussed infra). Although the age of majority used to be 21, most states now have lowered the age to 18. This development has given rise to the issue whether a noncustodial parent is liable for postmajority child support for college expenses.

Jurisdictions have responded to this issue in several ways. Some states rigidly enforce the statutory age limitation (18 years) and refuse to award postmajority educational support. Other states permit such support by either statute or case law. See, e.g., Conn. Gen. Stat. §46b-56c (West 1997) (authorizing educational support orders for four years of higher education for any child who has not attained age 23); In re Breault, 821 A.2d 1118 (N.H. 2003) (court has broad discretion in interpreting child support statute to order postmajority educational support). Some states also extend eligibility for postmajority support to children who reach the age of majority

---

[16] Laura M. Argys et al., Can the Family Support Act Put Some Life Back into Deadbeat Dads? An Analysis of Child Support Guidelines, Award Rates, and Levels, 36 J. Hum. Resources 250-251 (2001).

while still enrolled in high school. Ariz Rev. Stat. §25-501A (West 2000) (permitting educational support only until age 19).

Some jurisdictions (like that in *Waddell*) require that children's eligibility for postmajority educational support depends on their maintenance of at least a "C" average and full-time student status. Occasionally, a statute has an additional reporting requirement (e.g., the student must submit documentation of grades and credit to the parent each semester) for continued eligibility. See, e.g., Spencer v. Spencer, 126 S.W.3d 770 (Mo. Ct. App. 2004) (finding that child's noncompliance with statute caused by grandmother's mailing transcripts to child's father did not disqualify child from support).

a. Constitutionality. Do statutes requiring divorced parents to pay for post-majority educational support violate equal protection? Most courts reject attacks on the constitutionality of statutes requiring divorced parents to provide postmajority educational support for their children, reasoning that such statutes further a legitimate governmental objective. See, e.g., Johnson v. Louis, 654 N.W.2d 886 (Iowa 2002); Kohring v. Snodgrass, 999 S.W.2d 228 (Mo. 1999); In re Crocker, 22 P.3d 759 (Ore. 2001). But cf. Curtis v. Kline, 666 A.2d 265 (Pa. 1995).

b. Definition of "Educational Expenses." If noncustodial fathers are required to pay for "educational expenses," it becomes important to know what is included in the term. Is the term limited to tuition and books? Does it include living expenses? Extracurricular activities? Entertainment? Transportation costs (i.e., a car)? Clothing? Laundry? A cash allowance? What light does *Waddell* shed on the matter? Compare In re Gilmore, 803 A.2d 601 (N.H. 2002), with In re Vannausdle, 668 N.W.2d 885 (Iowa 2003).

Suppose the statute (or marital agreement) provides for postmajority education support for "reasonable" expenses. Can the father be ordered to pay tuition at a college of the child's choice? Or is "reasonable" limited by the payor's circumstances? If the latter, are circumstances measured at the time of the divorce or the child's enrollment in college? The majority view requires determining whether the child's choice of college is "reasonable" (for settlement agreements with no explicit limitation) in consideration of both the child's needs and the parent's ability to pay at the time of the divorce. Hathaway v. Hathaway, 98 S.W.3d 675, 680 (Tenn. Ct. App. 2002) (adopting majority view). See generally Linda J. Ravdin, Prenups to Protect Children, 24 Fam. Advoc. 33 (2002) (urging that parents' agreements better define the term "college expenses").

c. Conditioning Postmajority Educational Support on Conduct. May a parent condition continuance of the support obligation on the student's conduct? How does *Waddell* respond? According to the general rule, parents do not have financial responsibility for children who are emancipated. At common law, emancipation could occur by marriage or military service (or today, pursuant to statute). Some courts find that a minor may "constructively emancipate" himself or herself (and thereby end the parents' support duty) by withdrawing from parental control and supervision without cause. See, e.g., Matter of Roe v. Doe, 272 N.E.2d 567 (N.Y. 1971) (father no longer had support obligation for daughter who refused to live in dorm against father's wishes). Alternatively, constructive emancipation might occur if the child abandons the noncustodial parent by refusing all contact without justification. See, e.g., Chambers v. Chambers, 742 N.Y.S.2d 725 (App. Div. 2002) (daughter became emancipated, thereby forfeiting support, when she chose to defy father's wishes and leave home to evade his rules about dating).

How much control should a noncustodial parent be allowed to exert over an adult child's lifestyle when the parent is contributing to the child's financial support? Should the answer depend on a determination of the reasonableness of the parent's conduct? The minor's conduct? Or a judicial assessment of comparative fault? See generally Leslie J. Harris et al., Making and Breaking Connections Between Parents' Duty to Support and Right to Control Their Children, 69 Or. L. Rev. 689 (1990). Emancipation is discussed further in Chapter 6.

d. Separation Agreements Requiring Postmajority Educational Support. Spouses can obligate themselves to pay for child support for longer than a jurisdiction requires. Courts have more latitude to permit postmajority support if the parties provide for that eventuality in a separation agreement. See, e.g., Wood v. Wood, 667 N.W.2d 235 (Neb. 2003) (holding that court has authority to order postmajority support where support was included in approved settlement agreement). What rights does a child as a third-party beneficiary have to enforce the parents' separation agreement? See Chen v. Chen, 840 A.2d 335 (Pa. Super. Ct. 2003) (permitting theory).

e. ALI Principles.   The ALI Principles (§3.16) suggest that postmajority educational support be determined on a case-by-case basis. That judicial determination should depend on the availability of parental resources and the likelihood of such support had the parents remained together. See also Burkett v. Gresham, 888 So. 2d 505 (Ala. Civ. App. 2004) (discussing factors for courts to consider in making awards of postmajority educational support).

f. Empirical Research.   For policy purposes, it would be useful to learn how frequently noncustodial fathers voluntarily contribute toward their children's college expenses. Although empirical research is limited, one study that followed 49 children in Marin County, California, found that after high school, many middle-class fathers ceased financial support, maintained it at minimal levels, or attached burdensome strings. Judith S. Wallerstein & Shauna B. Corbin, Father-Child Relationships After Divorce: Child Support and Educational Opportunity, 20 Fam. L.Q. (No. 2) 109 (1986). A more recent study found that mothers and fathers voluntarily contribute a similar proportion of their financial resources to their children's college education, but fathers with joint legal custody provide more voluntary assistance than fathers without custody. See William V. Fabricius et al., Divorced Parent's Financial Support of their Children's College Expenses, 41 Fam. Ct. Rev. 224 (2003) (study of 368 college students measuring the amount that both divorced parents contributed to college education).

(3) Postmajority Support for Adult Disabled Children.   Most jurisdictions recognize another exception to the common law rule (that the parental support obligation terminates at majority) for a disabled child who has reached majority but is unable to become self-supporting. However, courts are divided about financial liability for a child who becomes disabled *after* majority. Although the common law did not impose a parental support obligation in the latter case, many courts currently do so. Compare Riggs v. Riggs, 578 S.E.2d 3 (S.C. 2003) with In re Jacobson, 842 A.2d 77 (N.H. 2004).

3.   Modification of Child Support Decrees and Enforcement Problems

INTRODUCTORY PROBLEM — MODIFICATION AND ENFORCEMENT

In May 2000 Mary Jones and Thomas Jones were divorced. At that time Thomas earned $46,000 a year, Mary did not work, and they had one child, age three. Their divorce decree provided that Thomas was to pay Mary $250 a month for spousal support for a period of three years (until she could complete her nursing degree and be self-supporting), and $350 a month for child support. Thomas paid Mary the $600 a month at the beginning of every month from May of 2000 until September of 2003, when Thomas married Evelyn, who has a child by an earlier marriage.

(1) What effect should Thomas's remarriage have on his child support payments?

(2) What remedies are available to Mary to collect support if Thomas simply stops making payments?

(3) Suppose Thomas and Evelyn are about to move to Ohio from California, where Mary lives. What would you recommend to Mary in terms of insuring payment of support? After the move, if she were to sue, how would she enforce the support order?

(4) Suppose Thomas and Evelyn move away and leave no forwarding address. How can Mary find out where Thomas now lives?

NOTE: MODIFICATION OF CHILD SUPPORT AFTER DIVORCE

It is generally recognized that provisions for child support in divorce decrees are modifiable on a showing of changed circumstances. The primary concern in making the order is the welfare of the child. Most courts allow modification to provide for support, even though the original decree contained neither a provision for child support nor a reservation of the power to include one.

Jurisdictions vary on the degree of change necessary to justify modification. The majority require that the change be substantial and permanent, while at the same time allowing a good deal of discretion to the trial judge to determine whether that standard has been met. The Uniform Marriage and Divorce Act §316, 9A U.L.A. (pt. ii) 102 (1998 & Supp. 2004), does not allow for modification of child support provisions unless there is a showing of "changed circumstances so substantial and continuing as to make the terms unconscionable."

Many of the grounds for modification can be classified under the general heading of changes in the financial condition or needs of the parent or the child. A reduction in the income of a father paying support is usually grounds for reducing the obligation, unless the reduction was "voluntary." Suppose the ex-husband-father is a tax lawyer earning $200,000 a year. Should his decision to give up his practice and work for a legal aid clinic for $60,000 a year be sufficient grounds to authorize reduction of his child support obligation? Or suppose the father decides to quit his full-time job and go to law school? See Little v. Little, 975 P.2d 108 (Ariz. 1999).

Several jurisdictions have considered the effect on child support obligations of a parent's voluntary decision to forgo employment. Courts apply one of three tests to determine modification in such circumstances: (1) the good faith test (whether the obligor acted in good faith and not to evade support); (2) the strict rule test, which considers the obligor's earning capacity; and (3) a balancing test that weighs various factors. Lewis Becker, Spousal and Child Support and the "Voluntary Reduction of Income" Doctrine, 29 Conn. L. Rev. 647, 658 (1997).

An increase in the income of the obligor may also be grounds for modification, particularly where the needs of the child have also increased. E.g., In re Marriage of Ellis, No. H024506, 2003 WL 1558071 (Cal. Ct. App. Mar. 25, 2003).

Another obvious ground for a modification is a change in the needs of the child. Most of the cases involve increased needs, the strongest ones for increase being increased educational or medical costs. DeArriba v. DeArriba, 100 S.W.3d 134 (Mo. Ct. App. 2003) (education); In re Marriage of Ford, 100 Cal. Rptr. 817 (Ct. App. 1972) (medical).

Remarriage of an obligor and the birth of additional children are often rejected as a ground for reduction of support. See, e.g., In re Marriage of Potts, 696 N.E.2d 1263 (Ill. App. Ct. 1998). Similarly, remarriage of an obligee-wife is not normally an adequate ground for modification. (Note that if the obligee-wife's new husband adopts the children, then he assumes the duty of support.) Some states specifically exclude from consideration, for child support purposes, the obligor's or obligee's subsequent spouses. See, e.g., Cal. Fam. Code §4057.5 (West 2004).

An agreement between the husband and wife to change support payments will usually be accepted as a ground for modification, but the court will examine the agreement to determine whether it is consistent with the child's welfare. In re Marriage of Adamson, No. E031472, 2003 WL 1849343 (Cal. Ct. App. Apr. 10, 2003).

A number of circumstances result in termination of a parent's support duty, including the child's reaching the age of majority, emancipation, the child's adoption by a stepparent, or paternity disestablishment. In addition, at common law the duty of support terminated upon the obligor's death unless the obligor bound himself or herself contractually to continue child support payments after death. Therefore, courts generally do not have the power to make a support order against an obligor's estate. Benson v. Patterson, 830 A.2d 966 (Pa. 2003). But cf. L.W.K. v. E.R.C., 735 N.E.2d 359 (Mass. 2000) (holding that assets of an inter vivos trust established by the father could be reached to satisfy his child support obligations).

Can support orders be modified retroactively? The majority rule is that a court is not authorized to increase or decrease child support payments retroactively, on the theory that the right to support payments is vested as payments become due. See, e.g., Aguero v. Aguero, 976 P.2d 1088 (Okla. Ct. App. 1999) (holding that trial court erred when it allowed father to assert equitable defenses of laches, waiver, and estoppel to mother's claim for child support arrearages). See generally Susan L. Thomas, Death of Obligor Parent As Affecting Decree for Support of Child, 14 A.L.R.5th 557 (1993).

(1) The Problem: Policy Perspectives. Existing studies indicate that a high percentage of fathers fail to make child support payments. According to recent census data, of custodial mothers who are awarded child support, 74.1 percent

receive some payment, but only 45.4 percent receive the full amount due.[17] The finding that only about half of women who are due child support receive full payment is confirmed by earlier studies.[18] One recent study of single mothers points out that despite improvement in child support enforcement over the last two decades, the proportion overall of those mothers who receive child support has remained largely unchanged.[19] However, the study does find that some *subgroups* of single mothers (comparing the never-married with those who were married, separated, divorced, and widowed) have experienced dramatic gains in receipt of child support — that is, never-married mothers experienced a four-fold increase in receipt rate from 1976 to 1997.[20] The study concludes that a considerable percentage of the rise in receipt rates can be traced to specific enforcement tools as well as to the overall expansion of the child support enforcement programs.[21] The specific enforcement tools are discussed infra, pp. 200-203.

(2) Remedies for Enforcement of Child Support.

a. Money Judgments: Sequestration, Attachment of Property. The economic obligation imposed by the divorce decree can be enforced as a money judgment. If the wife can get personal jurisdiction over the husband, then the decree can be enforced like any other money judgment. Traditionally, state statutes also provide various remedies even without personal jurisdiction over the obligor. For example, attachment and sequestration of the husband's money or property within a state may provide the wife with remedies even if the husband is no longer in the state.

b. Contempt Power. When a child support order arises out of divorce, the courts have broad equitable enforcement powers; most important is the contempt power. By holding in contempt a father who fails to pay support, a court may send the father to jail until he pays or agrees to pay. Studies reveal increased rates of compliance for delinquent noncustodial parents who are exposed to the possibility of jail time.[22]

Some limitations exist on the ability to use the contempt power. A distinction is normally made between spousal support and child support, on the one hand, and property settlements, on the other. Property settlements, often included in the decree of divorce, may not normally be enforced by contempt proceedings. See Danielson v. Evans, 36 P.3d 749 (Ariz. Ct. App. 2001); Christopher H. Hall, Annotation, Divorce: Propriety of Using Contempt Proceeding to Enforce Property Settlement Award or Order, 72 A.L.R. 4th 298 (1989).

---

[17] Census Bureau, Custodial Mothers and Fathers and Their Child Support: 2001, Table A ("Comparison of Custodial Parent Population and Those with Child Support Awarded, Due and Received: 1994-2002").

[18] Andrea H. Beller & John W. Graham, Small Change: The Economics of Child Support 18, 41 (1993).

[19] Elaine Sorensen & Ariel Halpern, Child Support Enforcement Is Working Better Than We Think, Urban Institute, New Federalism Series, No. A-31 (Mar. 1999), at 1.

[20] Id.

[21] Id. at 5.

[22] David Chambers, Making Fathers Pay: The Enforcement of Child Support Enforcement (1979); Drew A. Swank, The National Child Non-Support Epidemic, 2003 Mich. St. DCL L. Rev. 357, 375.

c. Criminal Nonsupport Proceedings.   The most drastic sanction available to enforce support is a criminal proceeding. This can often be a powerful weapon, because in some jurisdictions a criminal nonsupport claim filed by a wife can lead to the immediate police arrest of the husband. There are sometimes limitations that make this remedy unavailable. Some courts will not entertain a criminal complaint if the husband makes any support payments at all, no matter how inadequate. Moreover, the pendency of a contempt enforcement provision is sometimes used to decline jurisdiction. Unlike civil contempt, if a husband is in prison, payment does not lead to automatic release. Often, however, the husband is put on probation if he keeps up support payments.

(3) Problems with the Enforcement of Child Support: Interstate Enforcement. There are basically three reasons child support is difficult to enforce. First, the father may not have the resources to make the payments. Second, the mother may have great difficulty in locating the father. Third, even if the father can be located, if he now resides in a state different from that where the mother and child are found, there may be substantial difficulties relating to interstate enforcement.

The United States Supreme Court has interpreted the scope of the Full Faith and Credit Clause very narrowly as it applies to the enforcement of spousal support and child support. The Court has held that the constitutional obligation of full faith and credit is limited to *final* as distinguished from modifiable decrees. Consequently, a spousal support or child support decree, which is subject to modification in the future by the court that rendered it, need *not* be given full faith and credit. . . . See Sistare v. Sistare, 218 U.S. 1 (1910); Barber v. Barber, 323 U.S. 77 (1944). Full faith and credit can apply, however, with regard to the amount that has been reduced to judgment for sums past due.

It was not until the National Conference of Commissioners on Uniform State Laws (NCCUSL) promulgated the Uniform Reciprocal Enforcement of Support Act (URESA), 9B U.L.A. 273 (2001), in 1950 that there was a widely adopted solution to the enforcement of child support decrees in sister states. URESA provided an effective two-step process to reach nonresident obligors, allowing the filing of a complaint in the *obligee's home state* that could be heard, processed, and collected in the *obligor's home state.* URESA also contained criminal provisions and a method of permanently registering a foreign support order in the state where the obligor resided.

Nonetheless, URESA and its 1968 successor, the Revised Uniform Reciprocal Enforcement of Support Act (RURESA), 9B U.L.A. 81 (2001), had significant shortcomings, specifically the potential to create multiple support orders in varying amounts in different jurisdictions. In part, the lack of uniformity among states (in terms of their adoption of the different versions) complicated the enforcement process. The acts also were dependent upon the courts for enforcement, rather than taking advantage of administrative procedures such as wage withholding. In response to these and other problems, NCCUSL replaced the earlier models with the Uniform Interstate Family Support Act (UIFSA), 9 U.L.A. (pt. 1B) 235 (1999 & Supp. 2004), in 1992. Although based on URESA and RURESA, UIFSA contains new procedures for establishing, enforcing, and modifying support orders.

UIFSA replaces the former two-state approach (under URESA and RURESA) with a one-state proceeding under which a tribunal in one state only may issue or modify a support order. UIFSA provides uniform rules for child support enforcement by setting basic jurisdictional standards, by requiring that one state exercise continuing exclusive jurisdiction, by establishing rules for determining which state issues the controlling order in the event of multistate proceedings, and by providing rules for modifying or refusing to modify another state's child support order. UIFSA's eight bases for expanded long-arm jurisdiction over absent obligors include when the individual resided with the child in the state, the child resides in the state "as the result of acts or directives of the individual," the individual engaged in intercourse in the state and the child may have been conceived therefrom, and there is any other basis consistent with the Constitution for the exercise of personal jurisdiction. 9 U.L.A. (pt. 1B) 275 (1999 & Supp. 2004).

Amendments to UIFSA in 2001 clarify jurisdictional rules limiting modification in the non-issuing state (e.g., all parties and the child must have left the issuing state and the petitioner must be a nonresident of the state where modification is sought). The amendments explain that UIFSA is not the exclusive method of establishing or enforcing a support order (i.e., a nonresident may voluntarily submit to jurisdiction). The amendments explain in greater specificity how a controlling order is to be determined and reconciled if multiple orders are issued. The amendments also provide that a party who submits to jurisdiction for support purposes does not automatically submit to jurisdiction for custody or visitation purposes, specify the applicability of the local law of a responding state with regard to enforcement procedures and remedies, and fix the duration of a support order to that required under the law of the issuing state (i.e., a second state cannot modify an order to extend support to age 21 if the issuing state limits support to age 18). Finally, the amendments expand UIFSA to include coverage of support orders from foreign countries.

To ensure acceptance by the states, Congress made enactment of UIFSA a condition for federal funding for child support enforcement under PRWORA, 42 U.S.C. §666(f) (2000). PRWORA is discussed infra.

(3) Federal Child Support Enforcement Efforts.

a. Background: AFDC. The early 1970s were marked by a recognition of the relationship between high welfare costs and the inadequacy of child support. By 1973, the federal Aid for Dependent Children program, or AFDC, was costing taxpayers $7.6 billion a year. A large percentage of this money went to support children who should have been covered by child support. Although many delinquent fathers could afford to pay, they evaded responsibility because state welfare agencies were lax in collection efforts. Congress responded by passing the Child Support Enforcement Act of 1974, 42 U.S.C. §§651-669 (2000 & Supp. 2001), which added Part D (Child Support and Establishment of Paternity) to Title IV of the Social Security Act (Public Law 93-647), and which marked the first federal involvement in a matter that had formerly been left to the states. Title IV-D created a cooperative state and federal program (Office of Child Support Enforcement or OCSE) to locate wayward fathers and collect child support money due to AFDC recipients.

During 1976, the program's first full year of operation, IV-D agencies throughout the United States collected over $600 million in child support.[23] After that time, the amount of money collected under the program increased each year, reaching $7

[23] Beller & Graham, supra note [18], at 4, 163; Joseph I. Lieberman, Child Support in America 6 (1986).

billion in 1991.[24] Federal child support enforcement efforts resulted in over $18 billion in total collections by 2002.[25] Nonetheless, increases in collection were marked by the ever-increasing number of women with children who were in need of support. Whereas in 1979, 7 million women were eligible for child support, by 1999 the number had grown to nearly 11.5 million.[26]

b. Child Support Enforcement Amendments of 1984.   The Child Support Enforcement Amendments of 1984, Pub. L. No. 98-378, 98 Stat. 1305 (1984) (codified as amended in scattered sections of 42 U.S.C.), amended Title IV-D to make child support enforcement services available to all families, not merely to those on welfare. The core provisions of the legislation were mandatory wage attachment and an extension of the tax intercept program created in 1982. The 1984 bill required all support orders to include a conditional order for wage withholding. Withholding was to begin when payments were one month in arrears or when a noncustodial parent voluntarily requested that payments be withheld. The legislation specifically provided for the interception of federal and state tax refunds of non-welfare obligors. Prior to this enactment, tax refund withholding was allowed only for families receiving welfare.

The 1984 Amendments encouraged the imposition of liens against property and the posting of bonds to guarantee overdue payment, and extend provisions for bonds and liens to out-of-state orders. States were required to provide information on past-due child support to consumer credit agencies, and might impose late-payment penalties on overdue support payments. In addition, the amendments required states to establish specific nonbinding guidelines for child support awards. The amendments also required states, as a condition for receipt of federal funds, to extend their statutes of limitations to permit paternity establishment until 18 years post-birth.

The legislation provided the noncustodial parent with procedural protection. The parent was to be notified in advance if either wage withholding or a tax refund offset was to go into effect. The obligor was then given an opportunity to prove that his support obligations had been fulfilled.

c. Family Support Act of 1988.   In 1988 Congress enacted the Family Support Act (FSA), Pub. L. No. 103-485, 102 Stat. 2343 (codified in scattered sections of titles 5, 26, and 42 U.S.C.). The FSA addressed child support awards and enforcement mechanisms. The Act provided that the standardized guidelines that states were required to adopt by the Child Support Enforcement Amendments of 1984 should serve as a rebuttable presumption. In addition, the FSA provided for periodic review and adjustment of child support awards under Title IV-D, state review of guidelines every four years, mandatory wage withholding for all child support orders, and time limits within which state child support enforcement agencies must take various actions. Wage withholding was to be instituted absent a judicial finding

[24] Lieberman, supra note [23], at 8.

[25] Census Bureau, Statistical Abstract of the United States 2003, Table 567 ("Child Support Enforcement Program — Caseload and Collections: 1990-2002").

[26] Census Bureau, Custodial Mothers and Fathers and Their Child Support 1999, Table A ("Comparison of Custodial Parent Population and Those with Child Support Awarded, Due, and Received: 1993, 1995, 1997, 1999").

of good cause or a parental agreement to a different effect. The FSA also enacted reforms regarding paternity establishment (discussed infra).

    d. Child Support Recovery Act and the Full Faith and Credit for Child Support Orders Act.   Congress enacted the Child Support Recovery Act (CSRA) of 1992, Pub. L. No. 102-521, 106 Stat. 3403 (codified in scattered sections of 18 U.S.C. and 42 U.S.C.). CSRA created a new federal remedy for interstate child support enforcement by criminalizing the willful failure to pay child support owed to a child in another state. The Supreme Court's decision in United States v. Lopez, 514 U.S. 549 (1995) (holding unconstitutional the Gun Free School Zone Act for exceeding Congress' power to regulate interstate commerce), subsequently raised questions about congressional regulation of matters (such as child support) that were traditionally regulated by the states. Almost all of the federal courts that considered challenges to the CSRA on this basis later determined the CSRA to be constitutional. See, e.g., United States v. King, 276 F.3d 109 (2d Cir. 2002); United States v. Crawford, 115 F.3d 1397 (8th Cir. 1997), *cert. denied*, 522 U.S. 934 (1997). But cf. United States v. Faase, 227 F.3d 660 (6th Cir. 2000).

    In 1994, Congress enacted the Full Faith and Credit for Child Support Orders Act (FFCCSOA), 28 U.S.C. §1738B (2000), based on Article IV (the Full Faith and Credit Clause) of the Constitution. FFCCSOA requires states to recognize those child support orders of other states (including those decrees of the District of Columbia, Puerto Rico, U.S. possessions and territories, but not including foreign jurisdictions), and prohibits states from modifying such orders. Congress passed the FFCCSOA to promote uniformity in the face of the proliferation of conflicting child support orders in different states. On the background of FFCCSOA, see Margaret Campbell Haynes, Federal Full Faith and Credit for Child Support Orders Act, 14 Del. Law. 26 (1996). See also Patricia Wick Hatamyar, Critical Applications and Proposals for Improvement of the Uniform Interstate Family Support Act and the Full Faith and Creditor for Child Support Orders Act, 71 St. John's L. Rev. 1 (1997).

    More recently, Congress passed the Deadbeat Parents Punishment Act (DPPA) of 1998, 18 U.S.C. §228 (2000). Aimed at strengthening the CSRA, DPPA provides that any person can be charged with a felony who (1) travels across state lines with the intent to evade a child support obligation over $5,000 or one that has remained unpaid for longer than one year, or (2) willfully fails to pay support for a child living in a different state if that obligation is greater than $10,000 or if the obligation remains unpaid for more than two years.

    Critics charged that DPPA, like CSRA, constituted an invalid congressional attempt to regulate interstate commerce. The Supreme Court renewed the debate in United States v. Morrison, 529 U.S. 598 (2000) (holding unconstitutional, as an overextension of congressional powers under the Commerce Clause, a provision of the Violence Against Women Act which provided a federal remedy for victims of gender-motivated violence). Recently, however, in United States v. King, 276 F.3d 109 (2d Cir. 2002), the Second Circuit Court of Appeals upheld the DPPA as a legitimate exercise of congressional power under the Commerce Clause.

    e. Personal Responsibility and Work Opportunity Reconciliation Act (PRWORA) and Child Support Enforcement.   In 1996 Congress enacted PRWORA, Pub. L. No. 104-193, 110 Stat. 2105 (codified in scattered sections of

42 U.S.C. and 8 U.S.C.). Several of PRWORA's provisions address child support enforcement.

By January 1, 1998, PRWORA §321 required all states to adopt the Uniform Interstate Family Support Act (UIFSA) to facilitate interstate child support enforcement. PRWORA improves full faith and credit for child support orders by revising procedural guidelines for courts to follow in determining which order to recognize when multiple orders have been issued. For example, the Act defines a child's "home state" as the place where a child has lived with a parent for six consecutive months preceding the time of petitioning for support. The support order from the home state is given preference in determining continuing and exclusive jurisdiction for purposes of modification and enforcement of the support order (§322).

PRWORA requires the establishment and maintenance of statewide case registries for collection and disbursement of support payments (§312). Specifically, PRWORA expands the Federal Parent Locator Service to require states to maintain automated case registries containing records of all cases in which the state provides services pertaining to collection or modification of child support payments, and for recording any support order established or modified after October 1, 1998. Among other things, the registries are to be used for transmitting orders or notices regarding income withholding (one of the child support enforcement mechanisms authorized by the Act).

PRWORA also requires states to adopt certain methods for child support enforcement, specifically procedures for automated directories for new hires (§313) and mandatory income withholding (§314). That is, states must maintain automated directories containing information on all newly hired employees. This directory of new hires may be used for locating parents who owe support, verifying eligibility for programs, and administering employment security or worker's compensation programs. States may impose monetary fines on employers who fail to comply with these requirements (§316).

PRWORA requires states to have procedures for mandatory income withholding to collect support payments subject to state enforcement, and specifies that income withholding will also apply to support arrearages on orders issued prior to October 1, 1996, without need for a judicial or administrative hearing. Income is defined as any periodic payment to an individual and includes worker's compensation, disability payments, or interest. PRWORA revises the procedural guidelines for income withholding, primarily ensuring that it is carried out in compliance with due process requirements. Further, PRWORA insulates employers from liability for complying with a notice for withholding that appears regular on its face (§314).

In addition, the Act authorizes recording of the social security numbers of all applicants for professional or occupational licenses, drivers' licenses, and marriage licenses for the purpose of tracking those individuals owing support (§317). PRWORA permits restricting these licenses for individuals owing support arrearages, and provides that states must have plans in place to provide for liens against property for such individuals (§365). The Act amends bankruptcy laws so that debts for child support are nondischargeable. Also PRWORA requires states to prescribe procedures for child support orders relating to children of minor parents to be enforceable against grandparents (§§300-375). Other provisions of PRWORA (regarding work requirements, paternity establishment, and unwed teenage mothers) are discussed infra pp. 217-219.

(4) Proposed Federal Legislation: "Responsible Fatherhood" Bill. In 1999, Congress introduced the Father's Count Act, H.R. 3073, 106th Cong. (1999), to amend the Social Security Act (Title IV, Part A) to provide for grants to public and private organizations to promote "responsible fatherhood." The proposed legislation was designed to encourage young fathers to marry the mothers of their children and become financially responsible. The bill would have provided $150 million in grants to promote marriage and successful parenting, and to supply assistance to fathers and their families to avoid or leave welfare. Critics questioned the need for the bill, claiming that the majority of men owing child support are financially stable and do not need government assistance. They also questioned the policy of encouraging marriage in all cases, contending that the bill provided no protection for victims of domestic violence. The bill passed the House but not the Senate. Congress renewed efforts to pass the legislation in 2003, when the Responsible Fatherhood Act, S.B. 604, 108th Cong. (2003), was introduced in the Senate to achieve approximately the same goals as the Father's Count Act. See generally Jocelyn Elise Crowley, The Politics of Child Support in America 160-193 (2003).

C. A CHILD'S INHERITANCE RIGHTS

Gillett-Netting v. Barnhart
371 F.3d 593 (9th Cir. 2004)

Betty FLETCHER, Circuit Judge:

Plaintiff-Appellant Rhonda Gillett-Netting, on her own behalf and on behalf of her minor children Juliet O. Netting and Piers W. Netting, appeals the district court's grant of summary judgment for the Commissioner of Social Security. The district court affirmed the Commissioner's decision holding that Juliet and Piers are not entitled to child's insurance benefits based on the earnings of their deceased father, Robert Netting. . . . [1]

In December 1994, Netting was diagnosed with cancer. At the time, he and his wife, Gillett-Netting, were trying to have a baby together, but Gillett-Netting suffered from fertility problems that had caused her to miscarry twice. Because doctors advised Netting that chemotherapy might render him sterile, he delayed the start of his treatment for several days so that he could deposit his semen at the University of Arizona Health Sciences Center, where it was frozen and stored for later use by his wife. Netting quickly lost his battle with cancer. He died on February 4, 1995, before his wife was able to conceive. Earlier, Netting confirmed that he wanted Gillett-Netting to have their child after his death using his frozen sperm.

---

[1] Gillett-Netting also argues that applying the Act to preclude the award of child's insurance benefits to posthumously conceived children violates the children's right to equal protection of the laws. Because we conclude that Juliet and Piers are entitled to benefits under the Act, we do not reach Gillett-Netting's equal protection claim.

In-vitro fertilization of Gillett-Netting's eggs with Netting's sperm was undertaken successfully on December 19, 1995. . . . Juliet and Piers Netting were born on August 6, 1996.

On August 19, 1996, Gillett-Netting filed an application on behalf of Juliet and Piers for Social Security child's insurance benefits based on Netting's earnings. The Social Security Administration (SSA) denied the claim initially and upon reconsideration, and Gillett-Netting timely filed a request for a hearing before an Administrative Law Judge (ALJ) [who also denied her claim].

Developing reproductive technology has outpaced federal and state laws, which currently do not address directly the legal issues created by posthumous conception. Neither the Social Security Act nor the Arizona family law that is relevant to determining whether Juliet and Piers have a right to child's insurance benefits makes clear the rights of children conceived posthumously. Our task is to determine whether Juliet and Piers have a right to child's insurance benefits under the law as currently formulated.

Under the Act, every child is entitled to benefits if the claimant is the child, as defined in 42 U.S.C. §416(e), of an individual who dies fully or currently insured; the child or the child's representative files an application for benefits; the child is unmarried and a minor (or meets disability requirements) at the time of application; and the child was dependent on the insured wage earner at the time of his death. 42 U.S.C. §402(d)(1). It is undisputed that Netting was fully insured under the Act when he died, that Juliet and Piers are his biological children and are unmarried minors, and that Gillett-Netting filed an application for child's insurance benefits on their behalf. . . .

The Act defines "child" broadly to include any "child or legally adopted child of an individual," as well as a stepchild who was the insured person's stepchild for at least nine months before the insured person died, and a grandchild or stepgrandchild of the insured person under certain circumstances. *See* 42 U.S.C. §416(e). Courts and the SSA have interpreted the word "child" used in the definition of "child" to mean the natural, or biological, child of the insured.

The Commissioner argues and the district court held that "child" is further defined by 42 U.S.C. §§416(h)(2), (3) [set forth infra], and that Juliet and Piers cannot be considered the children of Netting unless they meet the requirements of one of these provisions. These sections were added to the Act to provide various ways in which children could be entitled to benefits even if their parents were not married or their parentage was in dispute. They have no relevance to the issue before us. . . .

Under the current version of §416(h), a claimant whose parentage is disputed is deemed to be the child of an insured individual if: (1) the child would be entitled to take an intestate share of the individual's property under the laws of the state in which the individual resided at death; (2) the child's parents went through a marriage ceremony resulting in a purported marriage between them that, but for a legal impediment unknown to them at the time, would have been a valid marriage; (3) the deceased wage earner acknowledged the claimant as his or her child in writing; (4) the deceased wage earner, before dying, had been decreed by a court to be the parent of the claimant; (5) the deceased wage earner, before dying, had been ordered by a court to contribute to the support of the claimant because the claimant was his or her child; or (6) the insured individual is shown by evidence satisfactory to the Commissioner to have been the parent of the claimant and to have been living with or contributing to the support of the claimant at the time that he died. See U.S.C. §§416(h)(2), (3).

Although these provisions offer means of "determining whether an applicant is the child . . . of a fully or currently insured individual," id. at §416(h)(2)(A), when parentage is disputed, nothing in the statute suggests that a child must prove parentage under §416(h) if it is not disputed. We conclude that these provisions do not come into play for the purposes of determining whether a claimant is the "child" of a deceased wage earner unless parentage is disputed. In this case, the Commissioner concedes that Juliet and Piers are Netting's biological children. Therefore, we conclude that the district court erred by holding that Juliet and Piers are not Netting's children for the purposes of the Act.

. . . The only remaining issue is whether Juliet and Piers, the undisputed biological children of a deceased, insured individual, are statutorily deemed dependent on Netting without proof of actual dependency.

Under the Act, a claimant must show dependency on an insured wage earner in order to be entitled to child's insurance benefits. 42 U.S.C. §402(d)(1). However, the Act statutorily deems broad categories of children to have been dependent on a deceased, insured parent without demonstrating actual dependency. It is well-settled that all legitimate children automatically are considered to have been dependent on the insured individual, absent narrow circumstances not present in this case.

Similarly, "illegitimate" children who prove parentage under 42 U.S.C. §§416(h)(2), (3) are "deemed to be the legitimate child of such individual" and, therefore, are deemed to have been dependent on the insured wage earner. 42 U.S.C. §402(d)(3). Thus, the provisions of §416(h) described above typically come into play to prove dependency rather than parentage. . . .

. . . Dependency is a broad concept under the Act, whereby the vast majority of children are statutorily deemed dependent on their deceased parents, and only completely unacknowledged, illegitimate children must prove actual dependency in order to be entitled to child's insurance benefits. Moreover, the Act is construed liberally to ensure that children are provided for financially after the death of a parent.

Juliet and Piers are indisputably Netting's legitimate children under the law of the state in which they reside. "Arizona has eliminated the status of illegitimacy[.]" State v. Mejia, 97 Ariz. 215, 399 P.2d 116 (1965). In Arizona, "[e]very child is the legitimate child of its natural parents and is entitled to support and education as if born in lawful wedlock." Ariz. Rev. Stat. §8-601. "It has long been the policy of th[e] state to protect innocent children from the omissions of their parents" by abolishing legal distinctions based on legitimacy. Hurt v. Superior Court, 124 Ariz. 45, 601 P.2d 1329, 1331 (1979). Under Arizona law, Netting would be treated as the natural parent of Juliet and Piers and would have a legal obligation to support them if he were alive, although they were conceived using in-vitro fertilization, because he is their biological father and was married to the mother of the children. See Ariz. Rev. Stat. §25-501(providing that children have a right to support from their natural parents; the biological father of a child born using artificial insemination is considered a natural parent if the father is married to the mother). Although Arizona law does not deal specifically with posthumously-conceived children, *every* child in Arizona, which necessarily includes Juliet and Piers, is the legitimate child of her or his natural parents.[7]

The Commissioner nevertheless argues that Juliet and Piers do not satisfy the "legitimate child" requirement, and therefore cannot be deemed dependent under §402(d)(3), unless they also are able to inherit from Netting under state intestacy laws or meet one of the other provisions of §416(h). This is not the case. Legitimacy in §402(d)(3) is determined in accordance with state law. See Jimenez v. Weinberger, 417 U.S. 628, 635-36 (1974) (noting that children who are considered legitimate under state law are entitled to child's insurance benefits without proving dependency). While §416(h) provides alternative avenues for children to be deemed legitimate, nothing in the Act suggests that a child who is legitimate under state law separately must prove legitimacy under the Act. It would make little sense to require a child whose parents were married to demonstrate legitimacy by showing she meets a test set forth in §416(h), for example by showing that her parent acknowledged her in writing or that a court determined her parentage prior to the parent's death.[8]

Because Juliet and Piers are Netting's legitimate children under Arizona law, they are deemed dependent under §402(d)(3), and need not demonstrate actual dependency nor deemed dependency under the provisions of §416(h). As Netting's legitimate children, Juliet and Piers are conclusively deemed dependent on Netting under the Act and are entitled to child's insurance benefits based on his earnings. . . .

DISCUSSION: THE INHERITANCE RIGHTS OF CHILDREN

(1) Intestate Share for a Child. If parents die without a will, legislation in every state provides for an intestate share for the child. For example, the Illinois statute provides:

(a) If there is a surviving spouse and also a descendant of the decedent: ½ of the entire estate to the surviving spouse and ½ to the decedent's descendants per stirpes.

(b) If there is no surviving spouse but a descendant of the decedent: the entire estate to the decedent's descendants per stirpes. 755 Ill. Comp. Stat. Ann. 5/2-1 (West 1992 & Supp. 2004).

---

[7] This is not to say that every posthumously-conceived child in Arizona would be eligible for survivorship benefits on the basis of the earnings of the deceased sperm donor. If the sperm donor had not been married to the mother, Arizona would not treat him as the child's natural parent, and he likely would have no obligation to support the child if he were alive. In such circumstances, no eligibility for benefits would exist unless the Commissioner made a determination that the claimant was the dependent child of the deceased wage earner for purposes of the Act by virtue of satisfying one of the requirements in §416(h).

[8] Because Juliet and Piers are Netting's legitimate children under Arizona state law, we need not consider whether they could be deemed dependent for another reason, such as their ability to inherit property from their deceased father under Arizona intestacy laws. See generally [Woodward v. Commissioner of Social Security, 760 N.E.2d 257 (Mass. 2002)]. As a practical matter, in most cases legitimate children would be able to inherit under state intestacy laws, but they need not *demonstrate* their ability to do so in order to be entitled to child's insurance benefits.

States also protect against unintentional disinheritance by means of "pretermitted heir" legislation, which provides a share for an omitted child born to (or adopted by) a testator *after* the testator executes a will. The rationale underlying such legislation is presumed intent (i.e., the idea that the testator would have wanted to provide a share for an accidentally omitted child).

(2) Do Parents Have the Legal Power to Disinherit Minor Children?   Every state except Louisiana empowers a parent to disinherit a child by will. As pointed out by Blackstone, the parent had this power at common law. Louisiana, whose law is influenced by the civil law tradition, has a system of "forced heirship." This requires, in effect, that children receive a minimum portion of a parent's estate unless certain conditions exist. Specifically, a parent in Louisiana has just cause to disinherit a child if:

> (1) The child has raised his hand to strike a parent, or has actually struck a parent, but a mere threat is not sufficient.
>
> (2) The child has been guilty, towards a parent, of cruel treatment, crime, or grievous injury.
>
> (3) The child has attempted to take the life of a parent.
>
> (4) The child, without any reasonable basis, has accused a parent of committing a crime for which the law provides that punishment could be life imprisonment or death.
>
> (5) The child has used any act of violence or coercion to hinder a parent from making a testament.
>
> (6) The child, being a minor, has married without the consent of the parent.
>
> (7) The child has been convicted of a crime for which the law provides that the punishment could be life imprisonment or death.
>
> (8) The child, after attaining the age of majority and knowing how to contact the parent, has failed to communicate with the parent without just cause for a period of two years, unless the child was on active duty in any of the military forces of the United States at the time. [La. Civ. Code Ann. art. 1621 (West Supp. 2004).]

May a parent evade this system of "forced heirship"? A Louisiana statute restricts parental evasion in some circumstances: "Donations inter vivos and mortis causa cannot exceed three-fourths of the property of the donor, if he leaves, at his death, one forced heir; and one-half, if he leaves at his death two or more forced heirs. La. Civ. Code Ann. art. 1495 (West 2000 & Supp. 2004). The Louisiana legislature subsequently restricted its forced share to those children who were 23 years old or younger or who were incapacitated; however, the state supreme court declared these restrictions unconstitutional. Succession of Lauga, 624 So. 2d 1156 (La. 1993); Succession of Terry, 624 So. 2d 1201 (La. 1993). In 1995, the voters approved a state constitutional amendment that required the legislature to implement legislation reinstating the above restrictions on testamentary freedom in terms of children's ages (23 and younger) and competency. Katherine Shaw Spaht, The Remnant of Forced Heirship: The Interrelationship of Undue Influence, What's Become of Disinherison, and The Unfinished Business of the Stepparent Usufruct, 50 La. L. Rev. 637, 641-643 (2000) (explaining background).

(3) Should Legislation Limit the Power of Disinheritance? The United States is almost alone among nations in allowing disinheritance of children by their parents.[27] Countries employ two different methods to protect children from intentional disinheritance: forced heirship (followed by civil law countries, and Louisiana, discussed supra, based upon the Napoleanic Code) and the family maintenance system (followed by many common law countries), which permits the court to exercise its discretion to provide for the needs of the heirs. Should the United States adopt one of these two schemes? If so, which?

May a father disinherit a child to defeat his child support obligation? See L.W.K. v. E.R.C., 735 N.E.2d 359 (Mass. 2000) (holding that a testator charged with an obligation to support his child cannot nullify that obligation by disinheriting the child because child support obligations should take precedence over testamentary dispositions).

(4) Special Family Protection Statutes. The general power of disinheritance is alleviated by statutory provisions protecting the surviving spouse and minor children. For example, homestead exemptions and personal property exemptions allow the setting apart of property to be exempt from execution for the decedent's debts. See, e.g., Cal. Prob. Code §6510 (West 1991). Also, during the period of probate administration, a family support allowance can be granted from the probate estate to a surviving spouse and minor children (sometimes also to adult children who were dependent upon the decedent). See, e.g., Cal. Prob. Code §6540(a)(2) (West 1991). More important, although minor children can be disinherited, the spouse ordinarily cannot. Because a surviving spouse has a legal duty to support the child and because the survivor generally receives property from the estate based on minimum share legislation (or through the operation of community property laws), some protection is provided indirectly for the children.

(5) Posthumous Children. A posthumous child is a child who was conceived while the intestate was alive but born after the deceased parent's death. What are the inheritance rights of a posthumous child? At common law, and according to the Uniform Probate Code (§2-108), posthumous children inherit as if they had been born during the decedent's lifetime. State intestacy statutes generally include similar provisions.

(6) Assisted Conception. New reproductive technologies, combined with cryopreservation of genetic material, have made possible the birth of an increasing number of children who are *conceived* posthumously. Cases like *Gillett-Netting* explore the extent of a posthumously conceived child's inheritance rights in the context of government benefits. On what basis did the court hold that the Netting children qualified for survivors' benefits under the Social Security Act?

Some states grant rights to posthumously conceived children if the decedent left written consent to be a parent. See, e.g., In re Estate of Kolacy, 753 A.2d 1257 (N.J. Super. Ct. 2000) (holding that twins conceived by in-vitro fertilization and born nearly 18 months after their father's death qualified as father's legal heirs under state intestacy law); Woodward v. Commissioner of Social Security, 760 N.E.2d 257 (Mass. 2002) (holding that posthumous children could inherit Social Security benefits if wife established their genetic relationship with the decedent and

[27] Ronald Chester, Should American Children Be Protected Against Disinheritance?, 32 Real Prob. Prob. & Tr. J. 405, 406 (1997).

that decedent consented both to reproduce posthumously and support any resulting child). Should consent of the deceased be a requirement for the child to succeed to governmental benefits? If so, what should be the scope of that consent — an intention to be a parent? To support the child? Both? How should that consent be manifested?

Gillett-Netting involves the right to governmental benefits. Should a posthumously conceived child be permitted to inherit from a father via intestate succession? (i.e., state laws applicable to decedents who died without a will.) Several states recently have amended their intestacy laws to include such children. Some of these states (e.g., Colorado, Delaware, Texas, Virginia, and Washington) permit these children to inherit if the decedent left written consent to be a parent. Other states add a requirement that the birth occur within a stated time following death (e.g., three years in Louisiana). Lindsay Fortado, Children Born Into Legal Limbo, Natl. L.J., July 19, 2004, at 1. Are these requirements sound policy? Why require the birth to occur within a stated time after the father's death? What period of time is preferable?

Although the father in *Gillett-Netting* supplied the genetic material, is a biological relationship essential to the child's right to inherit? Would a posthumously conceived child qualify as a dependent if the husband, prior to his death, consented to the wife's artificial insemination by means of third-party sperm? What light does *Gillett-Netting* shed on this question?

(7) Problem.   Gaby and Bruce Vernoff are a married couple. When Bruce dies unexpectedly in an accident, Gaby asks his physician to extract Bruce's sperm. Four years later, Gaby gives birth to a daughter using Bruce's genetic material. Gaby then files a claim for Social Security survivor benefits for the daughter. What are the daughter's inheritance rights? See Robert Salladay, Advancing the Issue: Reproduction and the Law; Controversy Continues to Dog a Procedure That Allows Human Embryos to Be Frozen for Use at a Later Date: "Dead Dads" Create Legal Issues, Daily Press, June 16, 2004, at A3.

See generally Kristine S. Knaplund, Postmortem Conception and a Father's Last Will, 46 Ariz. L. Rev. 91 (2004): Kayla VanCannon, Note, Father a Child from the Grave: What Are the Inheritance Rights of Children Born Through New Technology After the Death of a Parent?, 52 Drake L. Rev. 331 (2004).

D.   MANAGEMENT AND CONTROL OF THE PROPERTY OF A MINOR[28]

INTRODUCTORY PROBLEM

Ann Douglas is the 16-year-old daughter of Mr. and Mrs. Thomas Douglas. The Douglases are extremely wealthy, and it is clear that some day Ann will inherit a

---

[28] For an introduction to this topic, see generally Jesse Dukeminier et al., Wills, Trusts, and Estates 116-120 (7th ed. 2005); William M. McGovern & Sheldon F. Kurtz, Wills, Trusts and Estates Including Taxation and Future Interests 315 (2d ed. 2001).

great fortune. Her parents wish to provide her now with the practical experience of managing her own investments and money. They therefore wish to give her $50,000 to invest, spend, or use in any way she wishes. Is there any way as a practical matter this can be accomplished? What would you advise?

DISCUSSION: ALTERNATIVE MEANS TO HOLD AND CONTROL THE PROPERTY OF A MINOR

One element of the child's economic relationship to his family that is often overlooked has to do with the child's own property. A child may inherit stocks or bonds or real estate from a relative, or may receive as a gift a property that requires management. What are the child's powers to deal with his or her own property? What are the parents' powers with respect to the child's property? What are the alternative ways a child may "own" property?

What follows is a brief discussion of the four basic alternatives.

(1) Property Held in the Minor's Own Name: Practical Problems.   Property is sometimes simply held in the child's name without any indication of minority status. For example, a child may be the grantee in a real estate deed. Also, corporate securities or bank accounts may simply be registered in a child's name with no indication of age. Although holding title directly in the name of a minor is sometimes said to be against public policy, there are no criminal or civil sanctions — only substantial practical problems.

These practical difficulties arise because neither the child nor his or her parents may be able to manage the property or effectuate a transfer or sale. Apart from questions of maturity and competence, the child himself or herself may have severe practical difficulties because the contracts of minors are voidable — i.e., a minor may disavow a contract because of minority. See pp. 659-661, infra, for discussion of the power of disavowal of contract. This makes it risky for someone to do business with a minor. For example, if a minor owns real estate and signs a five-year lease with a tenant, the tenant risks having the lease set aside if the minor chooses to disavow. When property is sold or transferred by a minor, a title insurance company or a stock agent may decline to insure title or to transfer stock if the transferor is a minor. Indeed, special legislation has been enacted to protect banks against claims that might arise when they deal directly with a minor in connection with a bank account. See, e.g., Cal. Fin. Code §850 and §6751 (West 2004).

Nor do a child's parents as such have the legal power to manage or transfer a child's property. Although parents are said to be the "natural guardians" of a child's person (and as a consequence have broad powers and responsibilities with regard to custody, education, discipline, etc.), parents have no legal power *as parents* over the property of their children. This long-standing common law tradition persists to this day and is now sometimes expressed in state statutes. California Family Code §7502 (West 2004) provides, for example, "The parent, as such, has no control over the property of the child." In all events, if property is held simply in the name of the child, the child's parents lack the legal power to convey the property, or the right to manage or control the property, or even take the income and spend it on the child.

(2) Guardian of the Estate of a Child.   At common law, if a child inherited property or was given property requiring management, a court could appoint a guardian of the child's estate. This feudal relic is still available and at times required today. Even where the court-appointed guardian is a parent, the guardian of a child's estate is empowered to manage the child's assets and spend the income for the benefit of the child only with court supervision and approval and subject to inflexible and restrictive rules. Consequently guardianships are inconvenient, inefficient, and expensive.

There are a number of basic problems with guardianship administration. First, a guardianship is expensive to administer. Court supervision and approval is required for almost every action that the guardian takes, and this imposes court costs, attorneys' fees, and delays. In addition, a guardian must typically post a bond, pay an annual bond premium out of the income of the property, and file "accountings" in court. These all add to the administration costs. Second, the investment powers of the guardian are very limited, even with court approval. As a consequence, particularly in inflationary times, it is often extremely difficult for a guardian to obtain a decent return on the child's property. Third, a guardianship automatically terminates when a child reaches the age of majority, which is now typically 18. Where substantial property is involved, this may be undesirable because the 18-year-old may lack the maturity to manage his or her own property. Indeed, the disadvantages of guardianship for a child's estate are so substantial that a primary reason for parents of young children to write a will is to create alternative arrangements that avoid this necessity.[29]

(3) Trusts.[30]   The most flexible method of holding property on behalf of minors involves the use of a trust. With a trust, properties are held in the name of the trustee, who then has a fiduciary responsibility to manage, invest the property, and spend the proceeds in a manner consistent with the trust instrument. The trustee must be a competent adult or a responsible institution — like a bank. Management and control by the trustee is possible without going to court, and thus the inconvenience and expense of a guardianship can be avoided. Within very broad limits, the trust instrument itself may define the powers of the trustee, how the money is to be invested and expended, and the term of the trust. Thus, provision can be made for the distribution of the corpus or income of the trust in any manner that the trustor designates. There is no requirement that properties automatically be distributed to a young person when he or she reaches 18 or 21. Indeed, the trust instrument can permit the rights of several intended beneficiaries to be tailored to the precise wishes of the trustor, and can even provide for the interests of the beneficiaries to be limited or adjusted according to changed circumstances.

(4) Uniform Transfers to Minors Act.[31]   Every state now has some form of Uniform Transfers to Minors Act or its predecessor, the Uniform Gifts to Minors Act. These statutory provisions allow certain kinds of property (e.g., stocks, bonds,

---

[29] Dukeminier et al., supra note [28], at 118.

[30] See generally George G. Bogert, The Law of Trusts and Trustees (rev. 2d ed. 1993); Austin Wakeman Scott & William Fratcher, Trusts (4th ed. 1988).

[31] The Uniform Gifts to Minors Act (UGMA), 8A U.L.A. 297 (2003), was revised in 1983 as the Uniform Transfers to Minors Act (UTMA), 8C U.L.A. 1 (2001).

bank accounts) to be registered in the name of a qualified custodian, who then has broad powers to deal with the property, without court supervision. The act's provisions are triggered when property is put in the name of a custodian with an appropriate legend invoking the Uniform Act. Some states allow bequests to be subject to the act as well. In all events, the act provides a "canned trust" with standard provisions. The custodian, like a trustee, has fiduciary responsibilities to the minor and has broad statutory power to invest and reinvest the property and to spend the proceeds (whether income or principal) for the minor's support, maintenance, education, and benefit. The custodian has nearly complete discretion as to the time and amount of any such payments.

The age of distribution depends on the manner in which the property is transferred. If property is transferred by means of a gift, the exercise of a power of appointment, a will, or the terms of a trust, then the property may be distributed to a minor at age 21. The age of distribution for other transfers (e.g., employee benefit plans) is tied to the age of majority in the enacting state. Some states allow the transferor to vary the age of distribution within a fixed range (from 18 to 25 years). At the age designated for distribution, the custodianship terminates, and the custodian may distribute the property. While not as flexible as a custom-made trust, the act generally provides a convenient and inexpensive method of holding property for a minor.

E.   GOVERNMENTAL INCOME TRANSFER PROGRAMS THAT AFFECT CHILDREN

INTRODUCTORY NOTE

The initial topics in this chapter primarily concern how law provides a framework for private ordering as well as standards and a legal mechanism for the enforcement of certain rights. This section highlights the more active role of government in providing financial resources for child support. Specifically, many public programs provide money, goods, or services that help families fulfill their private support obligations.

In some programs, the benefits do not depend upon whether there is a child in the family. For example, unemployment insurance, first enacted in 1935 as part of the Social Security Act, provides income security for a limited period of time for employees who are out of work regardless of whether they have children. Similarly, workers' compensation provides income maintenance to workers injured in the course of employment without regard to the size of their families. Of course, children within these families may benefit substantially from the extra resources provided during hard times faced by their parents.

Other income maintenance programs base the amount of benefits on the presence or number of children. For example, the Old Age Survivors and Disability Insurance Program (OASDI), under Title II of the Social Security Act, is a federal program that provides benefits for (1) retired workers, (2) workers who are totally disabled, and (3) surviving dependents of workers. While the amount of family benefits is based in part on the worker's past earnings, benefits are increased by the presence of children under 18 (or under 22, if in school). The case of Jimenez v. Weinberger, 417 U.S. 628 (1974), established that nonmarital children born after the disability of a worker are eligible for benefits under this program. In 2003, approximately 3.1 million children received benefits as survivors of deceased workers or dependents of disabled or retired workers.[32]

In addition, in 1972 Congress enacted the Supplemental Security Income (SSI) program, 42 U.S.C. §§1381-1383d (2000), to assist needy aged, blind, and disabled persons.[33] In Sullivan v. Zebley, 493 U.S. 521 (1990), the Supreme Court invalidated, as contrary to congressional intent, Social Security Administration regulations that applied a different standard for determination of disability for children and adult claimants. *Sullivan* contributed to an increase in the number of children who were recipients of SSI.[34] In 1996, however, PRWORA §211 made the definition of "disability" more restrictive by establishing a new and separate disability definition for children under age 18 that requires a child to have a "medically determinable physical or mental impairment which results in marked or severe functional limitations, and which can be expected to result in death or which has lasted or can be expected to last for a continuous period not less than 12 months."[35] As a result, an estimated 135,000 children (13% of SSI child recipients) who were receiving aid no longer qualified. The number of children receiving SSI payments, and the percentage of the caseload they represent, has declined from 955,174 (14.4%) in December 1996 to 847,063 (12.9%) in December 1999.[36] To help remedy this problem, Congress mandated in the Balanced Budget Act of 1997, Pub. L. No. 105-33, §4913, 111 Stat. 251, 573 (1997), that states must continue Medicaid coverage for those children who were previously receiving SSI benefits but who failed to meet the more restrictive definition of "disability."

The food stamp program is another example of an income transfer program in which benefits are increased if there are children in the household. First enacted in 1964, the Food Stamp Act, 7 U.S.C. §§2011-2032, was amended in 1977 to permit low-income households to acquire stamps that may be used to purchase food. The coupon allotment of food stamps is based on the cost of a thrifty food plan, reduced by a fraction of the household's net income. For these purposes, the household includes all persons who are living as one economic unit and who customarily purchase food and prepare meals together (other than boarders, roomers, and certain unrelated live-in attendants). See United States Dept. of Agriculture v. Moreno, 413 U.S. 528 (1973) (invoking the equal protection component of the Fifth Amendment to strike the statutory exclusion of households containing a nonrelative). Eligibility depends on the household's monthly income, and the amount of allowable monthly income is influenced by the number of persons included in the household. Therefore,

---

[32] Social Security Administration, Fact Sheet on the Old-Age, Survivors, and Disability Insurance Program: 2003.

[33] House Comm. on Ways & Means, 106th Cong., 2d Sess., Background Material and Data on Programs Within the Jurisdiction of the Committee on Ways and Means ("2000 Green Book") 51 (Comm. Print. 2000).

[34] Id.

[35] 42 U.S.C. §1382c(a)(3)(C)(i) (2000).

[36] House Comm. on Ways & Means, 2000 Green Book, supra note [33], at 251.

the presence of children in the household can affect the maximum allowable monthly income and the coupon allotment of stamps.

Beginning in 1985 Congress enacted legislation significantly changing food stamp regulations. The Food Security Act, 7 U.S.C. §1281, required states to implement employment and training programs for recipients, provided automatic eligibility for recipients on Aid to Families with Dependent Children (AFDC) and SSI, prohibited collection of sales taxes on food stamp purchases, and increased benefits for those with high shelter costs and dependent care costs. Legislation in 1986 and 1987 increased benefits for the homeless and again for those with high shelter costs.[37] Subsequent legislation, the Hunger Prevention Act of 1988, Pub. L. No. 100-435, 102 Stat. 1645 (codified as amended in scattered sections of 7 U.S.C.), further expanded eligibility, increased benefits, and restructured the employment and training program. The 1990 Farm Bill, Pub. L. No. 101-624, 104 Stat. 3359 (codified in scattered sections of 7 U.S.C.) permitted states to authorize restaurants to accept food stamps from homeless households; authorized grants to organizations to conduct food stamps outreach targeted to rural, elderly, homeless, non-English-speaking and low-income working families with children; and provided that all persons applying for SSI at social security offices be given food stamp applications.[38]

The 1990 Farm Bill also gave authority to USDA to establish electronic benefits transfer systems, by which recipients could receive electronic cards (similar to automatic bank teller cards) rather than food stamps. 7 U.S.C. §2016(I)(1)(A) (2000). Purchases would be made with these cards and the amount deducted automatically from an account balance. The expansion of the use of electronic banking technology to deliver welfare benefits was intended to reduce welfare fraud and abuse.[39]

The Mickey Leland Childhood Hunger Relief Act, 7 U.S.C. §§2011 et seq. (2000), enacted August 10, 1993, as part of the Omnibus Budget Reconciliation Act (OBRA), provided for increased food stamp benefits to especially vulnerable recipients, such as those facing high shelter costs. In addition, the Act increased the penalties for fraud.

In 2002, the food stamp program served approximately 4.4 million households, including 10 million children, each month.[40] The characteristics of married-couple households with children varied considerably from those of single-adult households with children.[41] The average monthly food stamp benefit for single-adult households was lower than that of married-couple households ($248 versus $303), due to the smaller size of single-adult households.[42] The per capita benefit was higher

---

[37] House Comm. on Ways & Means, 103d Cong., 1st Sess., Overview of Entitlement Programs ("1993 Green Book") 1630 (Comm. Print 1993).

[38] Carrie Lewis, Recent Developments Affecting the Food Stamp Program, 26 Clearinghouse Rev. 1069, 1070 (Jan. 1993).

[39] See Electronic Food Stamps Prove Vulnerable to Fraud, S.F. Chron., July 13, 1994, at A3 (discussing use of the electronic technology by retailers in Maryland, the first state to implement the system).

[40] Office of Analysis, Nutrition & Evaluation, FSP-03-CHAR02, Characteristics of Food Stamp Households: Fiscal Year 2002, 15, 22.

[41] Id. at 15.

[42] Id. at 18.

for people in single-adult households than for people in married-couple households ($80 versus $65) in part because single-adult households were poorer. Among all households with children, 15 percent received child support, and 8 percent had no income.[43]

PRWORA, the federal welfare reform legislation enacted in 1996 (discussed infra), instituted major reductions in the food stamp program, cutting approximately $20 billion from the program over six years. As a result, between September 1996 and September 1997, the number of persons receiving food stamps decreased dramatically by 3.9 million.[44] Two-thirds of these reductions affected families with children. The Center on Budget and Policy Priorities estimated that in 1998 more than 5 million families with children lost an average of $36 per month in food stamp benefits.[45] The spending cuts led to a significant increase in requests for emergency food assistance.[46]

In May 2002, Congress enacted the Farm Security and Rural Investment Act, 7 U.S.C. §§7901 et seq., including reauthorization of the food stamp program. Program alterations restored food stamp eligibility for immigrant children under age 18, regardless of how long the children have been living in this country, and adjusted the standard deduction to varying household sizes.

Several other programs provide nutritional assistance to children. The National School Lunch Act, 42 U.S.C. §§1751 et seq. (2000), provides federal matching funds for public and private schools that serve meals to children. The program provides a reimbursement system for meals served to children based on household income; and children in the Temporary Assistance for Needy Families Program (TANF) and those in the food stamp program automatically receive free meals.[47] In 2001, more than 25.4 million children each day receive their lunch through the National School Lunch Program at a cost of 6.4 billion dollars.[48] In addition, the Special Supplemental Nutrition Program for Women, Infants, and Children (WIC) serves to safeguard the health of low-income women, infants, and children up to age five who are at nutritional risk by providing nutritious foods to supplement diets, information on healthy eating, and referrals to health care.[49] As of April 2002, approximately 8 million women, infants, and children were enrolled in the WIC program. Among these enrollees, approximately half are children; infants and women account for one-fourth respectively.[50] Additional child nutrition programs receiving federal funds include a surplus commodity program, a special milk program, the nonschool food program, and the school breakfast program.[51]

---

[43] Id.

[44] Children's Defense Fund, The State of America's Children, 1998 Yearbook 54-55 (1998).

[45] Id. at 545.

[46] Id.

[47] House Comm. on Ways & Means, 2000 Green Book, supra note [33], at 957.

[48] Office of Analysis, Nutrition, and Evaluation, Statistics on the National School Lunch Program (Aug. 2003).

[49] 42 U.S.C. §§1771 et seq. (2000). The Child Nutrition Act of 1966 was amended through Pub. L. No. 107-249 (Oct. 23, 2002).

[50] Office of Analysis, Nutrition, and Evaluation, WIC Participant and Program Characteristics 2002 (Sept. 2003).

[51] Id.

Medicaid is another federal program that provides in-kind benefits to children from low-income families. Medicaid Act, 42 U.S.C. §§1396 et seq. (2000). More than 42.8 million people received health care services through the Medicaid program in FY 2000 (the last year for which beneficiary data are available).[52] The total federal and state expenditures for Medicaid reached $258.2 billion in 2002, including direct payment to providers of $185.8 billion, payments for various premiums (for health maintenance organizations, Medicare, etc.) of $45.1 billion, payments to disproportionate-share hospitals of $15.4 billion, and administrative costs of $11.9 billion.[53] Begun in 1965, the program is jointly funded by the federal and state governments to assist states in providing medical long-term care assistance to eligible individuals. Medicaid enables states, inter alia, to furnish (1) medical assistance on behalf of needy families with dependent children and needy individuals, as well as those who are aged, blind, or permanently and totally disabled; and (2) rehabilitation and other services to help such families. For an eligible family, Medicaid can provide for full or partial payment for a child's medical care services. Traditionally, Medicaid eligibility depended on eligibility under the Aid to Families with Dependent Children (AFDC) or Supplemental Security Income (SSI) programs. This changed as eligibility was extended in 1986 to groups of low-income pregnant women and children without ties to the welfare system. Further, states were required, as of July 1, 1991, to cover all children under age 19 and whose family income was below 100 percent of the federal poverty level.[54]

Welfare reform legislation (PRWORA), enacted in 1996, established the conditional work program TANF (discussed infra) to replace AFDC. Unlike AFDC, TANF does not confer automatic Medicaid eligibility. However, PRWORA maintains Medicaid eligibility for those individuals who met AFDC standards but who do not qualify for assistance under TANF.[55] Further, to remedy some of the hardships caused by PRWORA, the Balanced Budget Act of 1997, Pub. L. No. 205-33, 111 Stat. 251, 573 (1997), created a new health insurance program under Title XXI of the Social Security Act called the State Children's Health Insurance Program (SCHIP). This program enabled states to initiate and expand health insurance coverage for uninsured children through an option of providing 12 months of Medicaid coverage regardless of whether the children met income eligibility tests and by allowing states to presume eligibility until it has been determined.[56]

For over 60 years, the primary means by which the federal government assisted needy children was the AFDC program. First enacted in 1935 as part of the Social Security Act, 42 U.S.C. §§601-617 (2000 & Supp. 2004), this program

---

[52] Centers for Medicare & Medicaid Services, An Overview of Medicaid: 2004, Mid-Session Review of the President's Fiscal Year 2004 Budget (2004).

[53] Id.

[54] House Comm. on Ways & Means, Overview of Entitlement Programs, supra note [37], at 1633-1635 (coverage mandatory for pregnant women, for services related to the pregnancy, and full coverage to children under age six with family incomes below 133 percent of the federal poverty income guidelines).

[55] House Comm. on Ways & Means, 105th Cong., 2d Sess., Background Material and Data on Programs Within the Jurisdiction of the Committee on Ways & Means (1998 Green Book) 952 (Comm. Print 1998).

[56] Id. at 953.

involved a partnership between the federal, state, and local governments. The program provided welfare payments for those needy children (and others in the child's household) who were deprived of support because a parent was absent, incapacitated, deceased, or unemployed. Under this program, federal statutes determined eligibility. States, however, decided the amount of benefits and administered the program.

In 1996, over 12.5 million individuals received AFDC benefits, of whom 8.5 million were children.[57] The number of children on AFDC rose steadily in the early 1990s. For example, in the years 1988 to 1992, which marked the largest increases in the AFDC population, the child recipient rate increased by over 50 percent in seven states alone. The rates were fueled in part by recession and rising unemployment.[58] Federal expenditures for the AFDC program in 1996 totaled almost $12.7 billion.[59] AFDC was replaced by PRWORA (discussed infra).

NOTE: THE PERSONAL RESPONSIBILITY AND WORK OPPORTUNITY RECONCILIATION ACT (PRWORA)

In 1996, Congress enacted the Personal Responsibility and Work Opportunity Reconciliation Act of 1996 (PRWORA), Pub. L. No. 104-193, 110 Stat. 2105 (codified primarily in scattered sections of 7 U.S.C. and 42 U.S.C.). As the first major reform of the welfare system since the New Deal, PRWORA aimed to: (1) aid needy families so that children may be cared for in their homes or those of relatives; (2) end dependency of needy parents upon government benefits by promoting job preparation, work, and marriage; (3) prevent and reduce out-of-wedlock pregnancies and establish goals for preventing and reducing their incidence; and (4) encourage formation and maintenance of two-parent families.[60]

PRWORA abolished several federally funded programs, including AFDC (the primary cash assistance program for families), Emergency Assistance for Needy Families (EA; emergency help to families with children for a maximum of one month per year), and the Job Opportunities and Basic Skills (JOBS) Training Program (the work and training program). In their place, PRWORA substitutes the Temporary Assistance for Needy Families Program (TANF). Unlike former law that *entitled* individuals and families to receive welfare assistance, TANF provides a block grant to the states for programs that are time-limited and conditioned on work.[61] TANF combined the funding for the repealed programs (AFDC, EA, and JOBS) into a single annual grant of $16.5 billion through the year 2002. Instead of receiving unlimited federal funds like under AFDC, states receive a "capped" block grant under PRWORA that has limited potential to increase following inflation, growth, or economic recession.

[57] Id. at 413.
[58] Id. at 689.
[59] Id. at 411.
[60] Id. at 495.
[61] Id. at 494.

TANF significantly enlarged states' discretion in operating their welfare systems. No longer required to provide matching state grants in order to receive federal funding, states instead only need to meet a "maintenance of effort" provision (MOE) requiring them to maintain spending equal to at least 75 percent of their 1994 spending level for AFDC, EA, and JOBS. (Those states that do not meet mandatory work requirements must satisfy an 80 percent maintenance requirement.) States may also choose to offer vouchers or services to recipients rather than cash assistance. In addition, states may decide which categories of needy families to assist, may choose to adopt financial rewards or penalties to induce work, and can continue to set benefit levels.[62] States also have the ability to transfer up to 30 percent of welfare block grant funds into other social service programs.

TANF imposes conditions of the receipt of federal funds. States must achieve certain minimum participation rates in the work program. For example, 50 percent of all recipients have to be working (or participating in work-related activities) by the year 2002 or the state's block grant would decrease. However, the "caseload reduction credit" allows states to have fewer than 50 percent of recipients in these activities if their welfare caseloads decrease. States must also spend a certain amount of state funds on behalf of eligible families, must impose a time limit on benefits, and must limit funds to unwed teenage mothers (discussed infra).

Some of the major provisions of the 1996 welfare reform legislation include the following:

a. Work requirements (PRWORA §103).   PRWORA requires states to impose work requirements and time-limited TANF grants. The head of every family must find work within two years of receiving aid or the family loses benefits. States may choose to impose more strict work requirements and time limits than those required by the Act.

Recipients in single-parent families must participate in a "qualifying work activity" for a minimum number of hours per week. Work requirements are increased for two-parent families. Recipients may not be penalized for failure to meet work requirements if their failure is based on their inability to find child care. Thus, the work requirement may be waived, at the option of the state, for parents with children under 12 months. For parents with children under age six, hours may be limited to 20 per week.

Payments to families are limited to two years for any one period of time. Further, adults are subject to a five-year lifetime cap for the receipt of welfare. If families' benefits are terminated because the head of the family is unwilling or unable to find work within the two-year period, states are not required to provide other services to meet the family's or children's needs. PRWORA also amended the Food Stamp Act (§801 et seq.) to link food stamp eligibility to work requirements (§824).

b. Unwed Teenage Mothers (PRWORA §§103, 905).   PRWORA prohibits states from providing benefits to unwed teenage mothers (under age 18) unless the young women meet certain conditions. First, they must live at home or in another adult-supervised setting. Certain exceptions exist for teenage parents who have no parent, guardian, or other adult relative, or who are victims of abuse (§103). Second,

[62] Id. at 495.

as soon as her child is three months old, the mother must attend high school or an alternative educational or training program. PRWORA also instituted family caps, permitting states to deny aid to children who are born more than ten months after the family goes on welfare (§103(a)). States receive bonuses (supplemental federal funds) if they show a decrease in the numbers of illegitimate births and pregnancies to teenage mothers (§103(a)).

The Act also provides for monitoring states' progress toward the goal of preventing teenage pregnancy. The Secretary of Health and Human Services must establish a plan for assuring that at least 25 percent of communities impose a teenage pregnancy prevention program. The Secretary is required to report annually on the success of preventing out-of-wedlock teenage pregnancies (§905).

c. Paternity Establishment (PRWORA §§301, 331, 332). PRWORA amended the Social Security Act, Title IV, Part D (Child Support and Establishment of Paternity), to require states to expand services relating to paternity establishment with the goal of increasing collection of child support payments. States must continue these services for families no longer eligible for aid under TANF (§301). Also, states must have procedures to require a child and other parties to submit to genetic testing in contested cases, and must establish a threshold probability level beyond which the genetic results create a rebuttable or conclusive presumption of paternity.

PRWORA expands the focus on *voluntary* paternity acknowledgment, requiring states to have in-hospital programs that attempt to establish paternity immediately at birth. Voluntary establishment programs must also be available from the state agency responsible for maintaining birth records. Such programs must inform the mother and father of the rights, legal consequences, and responsibilities that arise from signing a paternity acknowledgment. A voluntary acknowledgment of paternity is considered a legal finding of paternity (§331). Finally, states are also required to publicize and encourage the use of procedures for voluntary establishment of paternity and child support (§332).

d. Sanctions (PRWORA orders §103). PRWORA provided that states may sanction families for failure to comply with requirements of the Act, including the failure to ensure that minor children attend school. Similarly, the federal government may also sanction states for failure to comply with requirements of the Act and for failure to meet minimum participation rates.

Pending reauthorization legislation (H.R. 4, 108th Cong. (2004)) would continue TANF block grant funding at the current level of $16.5 billion but dramatically increase work requirements for the states from 50 to 70 percent over five years. The bill also increases the number of hours per week that recipients must be engaged in work and other activities; in general, recipients must work 40 hours per week, whereas parents with children under six are required to meet only a 20-hour per week work requirement. In addition, the activities defined as "work" are narrowed, and states' failure to meet the work requirements results in enhanced financial penalties. For the past several years, Congress has made unsuccessful attempts to reauthorize TANF. PRWORA expired on October 1, 2002, and is presently operating by continuing resolution.

Since its passage, commentators have highlighted shortcomings of the Act. Some question the ability of PRWORA to decrease poverty levels, arguing that the lack of focus on education merely moves recipients to low-salaried jobs that leave them unable to support a family. Instead, commentators suggest shifting the focus to education, subsidized salaries, and improved child care.[63] Others highlight the problems that would develop in a recession, particularly in central cities that have a concentration of welfare recipients.[64]

The most prevalent criticisms, however, focus on the work requirements. Specifically, many former welfare recipients and low-income workers struggle to keep their jobs because of lack of education and poor job skills.[65] Critics argue as well that programs do not help welfare recipients handle possible family problems (e.g., financial stress, lack of child care, or caring for disabled family members) while trying to maintain employment.[66]

Commentators generally commend the increased emphasis on paternity establishment and enforcement of child support obligations. However, many caution that these provisions alone do not result in decreased poverty levels. Instead, PRWORA must advocate expanded education and training opportunities, tax credits, a higher minimum wage, and, ideally, adequate paying jobs in the private sector.[67] In addition, others worry that the tougher measures toward paternity establishment and child support enforcement may have a negative impact for victims of domestic violence by alerting fathers to the location of mothers and forcing women to remain in abusive relationships because of the federal emphasis on self-sufficiency with its limitations on benefits.[68]

What are the long-term effects of the welfare reforms? Statistics reveal that welfare caseloads have declined dramatically during the past several years. In 2001, the average monthly number of TANF recipients was 5.4 million persons, 57 percent lower than the average monthly AFDC caseload in 1996 and the smallest number of people on welfare since 1968.[69] This decrease has been attributed to the PRWORA provisions of work requirements and time limits.[70] Whereas studies confirm that

[63] Lindsay Mara Schoen, Note, Working Welfare Recipients: A Comparison of the Family Support Act and the Personal Responsibility and Work Opportunity Reconciliation Act, 24 Fordham Urb. L.J. 635, 658-661 (1997).

[64] John Accordino, The Consequences of Welfare Reform for Central City Economies, 64 J. Am. Plan. Assn. 11, 11-14 (1998). See also Margaret Weir, The Uncertain Future of Welfare Reform in the Cities, 15 Brookings Rev. 30 (1997).

[65] Nancye Campbell et al., Job Retention and Advancement in Welfare Reform (Brookings Institute, 2002). See also Joel Handler, "Ending Welfare as We Know It": The Win/Win Spin or the Stench of Victory, 5 J. Gender Race & Just. 131 (2001).

[66] Courtney Jarchow, Job Retention and Advancement Strategies (Natl. Conf. of State Legislatures, 2003).

[67] Paul K. Legler, The Coming Revolution in Child Support Policy: Implications of the 1996 Welfare Act, 30 Fam. L.Q. 519, 562-563 (1996). See also Stacy L. Brustin, The Intersection Between Welfare Reform and Child Support Enforcement: D.C.'s Weak Link, 52 Cath. U.L. Rev. 621 (2003); Sheila Rafferty Zedlewski, Family Economic Resources in the Post-Reform Era, 12 The Future of Children: Children and Welfare Reform 121 (Winter/Spring 2002).

[68] Shelley Kintzel et al., Comments, The Effects of Domestic Violence on Welfare Reform: An Assessment of the Personal Responsibility and Work Opportunity Reconciliation Act as Applied to Battered Women, 50 U. Kan. L. Rev. 591 (2002). See also Jessica Pearson et al., Child Support and Domestic Violence: The Victims Speak Out, 5 Violence Against Women 427 (1999).

[69] Dept. of Health & Hum. Servs., Indicators of Welfare Dependence: 2003, Annual Report to Congress (2003).

[70] House Comm. on Ways & Means, 2000 Green Book, supra note [33], at 251.

welfare reforms have increased employment and earnings, particularly for single mothers, they also indicate that the favorable economy of the late 1990s was partly responsible for these effects.[71]

For further analysis of welfare reform policy, see Rebecca M. Blank & Ron Haskins, The New World of Welfare (2002); Lawrence B. Joseph, Families, Poverty, and Welfare Reform: Confronting a New Policy Era (2000); Alvin L. Schorr, Welfare Reform: Failures and Remedies (2001); Sanford F. Schram & Samuel H. Beer, Welfare Reform: A Race to the Bottom (2000); Alan Weil & Kenneth Finegold, Welfare Reform: The Next Act (2002).

[71] See, e.g., Jeffrey Grogger et al., Consequences of Welfare Reform: A Research Synthesis 98 (Rand Corp. 2002).

CHAPTER 3

Protecting the Child from Abuse and Neglect

A. PROBLEMS AND INTRODUCTION

(1) Eleanor Papillon is a 20-year-old single parent. She is a devoted member of a fundamentalist religious sect, one of the tenets of which is to strongly disapprove nonmarital sex. Eleanor's son Danny is four years old. When Eleanor took Danny in for an annual medical check-up, the pediatrician — Dr. Thomas Stein — noticed that Danny had bruise marks on his arms, stomach, back, and buttocks. The doctor asked Eleanor what had happened. Eleanor said that during a visit to his aunt's house three days before, Danny had been discovered under a bed with his pants off with a little girl, also aged four, who had her pants off. Eleanor reported that she had beaten Danny that night at home, after she became enraged by his refusal to admit what he had done.

a. Does Danny have a tort action for assault and battery against his mother? Under the standards of the Restatement (Second) of Torts, reprinted infra p. 230, would the mother's spanking be privileged? Would the doctrine of parental tort immunity prevent a suit? See infra p. 234. Are tort remedies appropriate?

b. Could Eleanor be criminally liable for the spanking she inflicted on Danny under the standards of the ALI Model Penal Code? (Reprinted p. 229, infra.) Are penal remedies appropriate?

c. What legal advice would you give to Dr. Stein? Is he obligated to make a report of this case to the police under the California reporting statute? See Ham v. Hospital of Morristown, p. 248, infra. What purposes are served by requiring a report?

d. Based on Eleanor's behavior, could a juvenile court assume jurisdiction over Danny as a neglected child? The California jurisdictional provisions, Welf. & Inst. Code §300, are reprinted at pp. 310-311, infra. Would it be appropriate for a juvenile court to take jurisdiction over Danny and to remove Danny from maternal custody and put him in foster care? To take jurisdiction and to leave Danny at home with supervision by a social worker? These issues are considered further in section E of this chapter, which deals more generally with the neglect jurisdiction of the juvenile court and the foster care system.

(2) Mission School, a public junior high school in Little Rock, Arkansas, has regulations that permit a classroom teacher to paddle a student if the teacher determines that (a) the student has behaved in a disruptive way and (b) the paddling is likely to improve class decorum. Four days ago Toby Rockland, a 13-year-old eighth grader, was paddled by his English teacher, Mr. Klaus. Klaus told Toby that Toby had disrupted the class by failing to raise his hand before speaking out in class and by whispering to other students during a study period. The paddling caused Toby considerable pain and has resulted in a large black and blue mark on his buttocks. As a consequence Toby visited a doctor and had to stay home from school for two days to recover.

a. Does Toby have any claim against the teacher under the tort law of your jurisdiction? Would he have a claim if the standards of the Restatement (Second) of Torts applied? See pp. 235-236, infra. Could this paddling offend the prohibition against cruel and unusual punishment? See Ingraham v. Wright, p. 242, infra.

b. Suppose Toby's parents object on principle to corporal punishment. As parents, do they have the right to prohibit the use of corporal punishment in school? Under the standards of the Restatement, would it be different if Mission School were a private school? What do the *Pierce, Meyer,* and *Yoder* cases, found in Chapter 1, suggest about parental prerogatives? See Baker v. Owen, p. 236, infra.

c. Does the Constitution require that Toby be given a hearing of some sort before he is paddled? See the Note on Procedural Due Process in school, p. 242, supra, and the material on Ingraham v. Wright, pp. 242-243, infra.

This chapter explores the tension generated by (1) the privilege of parents and those standing in loco parentis to use corporal punishment to discipline children; (2) the important social interest in protecting children (who ordinarily are in no position to defend themselves) from physical abuse from adults; and (3) the value our society places on family privacy. In studying the materials in this chapter you should focus on the questions of what legal standards should be used to evaluate the use of parental force towards children, whether the remedies of tort law or criminal law provide adequate protection, and what methods are available to discover parental excesses.

B. THE PARENTAL PRIVILEGE TO DISCIPLINE CHILDREN

Newby v. United States
797 A.2d 1233 (D.C. 2002)

GLICKMAN, Associate Judge:

. . . On a warm Monday afternoon in September, appellant brought her children to a park in southwest Washington, D.C., for a family outing. Before long a commotion broke out, attracting the attention of witnesses who were picnicking nearby. These witnesses watched as appellant, screaming obscenities, pummeled and kicked her six-year-old daughter, who was crying and trying to run away. Dismayed and alarmed, the witnesses summoned the police. Appellant was arrested and charged with second degree cruelty to children, a ten-year felony. The government later dropped that charge, choosing instead to prosecute appellant on one count of simple assault, a 180-day misdemeanor. . . .

Three eyewitnesses called by the government testified that appellant struck her daughter some ten to fifteen times on her head, neck and shoulders, and kicked her with a shod foot in the middle of her back. The beating continued after appellant knocked her daughter to the ground. The witnesses particularly remembered seeing appellant smack her daughter's face with the back of her hand, on which appellant was wearing several prominent rings.

Testifying in her own defense, appellant explained that her daughter had been misbehaving all afternoon and was especially wild and overexcited at the picnic area. Appellant feared that the child, who was running around in a "rage," would fall in the Potomac River, burn herself on a hot barbecue grill, or run in the path of a car. After exhausting non-violent efforts to distract and quiet her daughter, appellant said, she grabbed and hit the child. Appellant also kicked her in the back of her leg, in order, she said, to stop her from running away toward the river. Appellant admitted that she was angry and had lost control of the situation. She insisted, however, that she never intended to hurt her daughter, but only to discipline her for her own good. Appellant testified, without contradiction, that the child suffered no physical injuries.

. . . Appellant makes two arguments for reversal of her conviction. First, she argues that the misdemeanor simple assault statute, D.C. Code §22-404(a) (2001), does not apply at all to assaults by parents on their own children. Appellant argues that parent-child assaults may be prosecuted only under the felony cruelty to children statute, D.C. Code §22-1101 (2001). . . . Second, and alternatively, appellant argues that even if D.C. Code §22-404(a) is applicable to parent-child assaults, the government must prove that a parent acted with malice in order to overcome the "parental discipline" defense. Appellant contends that the government failed to prove malice in this case, and that the evidence therefore was insufficient to support her conviction. . . .

Novel though it is, appellant's claim that parent-child assaults may not be prosecuted as violations of the simple assault statute, but only as violations of the cruelty to children statute, does not persuade us. The simple assault statute has been on the books for over a hundred years, from 1901, when Congress codified the common law of the District of Columbia, to the present day. The statute provides that "[w]hoever unlawfully assaults, or threatens another in a menacing manner, shall be fined not more than $1,000 or be imprisoned not more than 180 days, or both." D.C. Code §22-404(a) (2001). This language makes no exceptions; it applies to parent-child assaults as to any other assaults. It is true that the statute admits of common law defenses, including the "parental discipline" privilege discussed [herein]. But the very existence of that qualified privilege confirms that the (now-codified) common law offense of assault encompassed unjustified assaults by parents on their children. Like the plain words of the statute, nothing in the relevant common law or more than a century of case law remotely suggests that the simple assault statute does not apply to parent-child assaults. . . .

Appellant theorizes, however, that when Congress enacted the original cruelty to children law some fifteen years earlier, in 1885, it intended that all prosecutions of parents for the use of unlawful force against their children would be brought under that statutory provision. Appellant argues that the 1885 statute codified and hence replaced the common law crime of parent-child assaults. This thesis suffers from manifold defects. To begin with, it finds no support in the statutory language[:] "a person" commits the crime of cruelty to children in either the first or second degree if that person "intentionally, knowingly, or recklessly tortures, beats, or otherwise willfully maltreats a child . . . or engages in conduct which creates a grave risk of bodily injury to a child. . . . " D.C. Code §22-1101(a). Nothing in this language implies that the cruelty to children statute precludes the prosecution of parents for simple assault or any other criminal offense. Indeed, the cruelty to children statute does not even mention parents or others acting in a parental capacity. Although the cruelty to children statute and the simple assault statute may overlap in their application to some crimes against children, the statutes "are fully capable of coexisting,". . . .

Furthermore, the legislative history contradicts appellant's claim that Congress intended to codify the common law when it enacted the new statutory offense of cruelty to children in 1885. . . . Nor does the legislative history disclose any intention to supplant the relevant common law. . . . Rather, according to the Senate Report [of 1884], the new statutory provision making it a crime to "torture, cruelly beat, abuse, or otherwise willfully maltreat" any child had a more limited object:

> The provision in question merely forbids and punishes torture and cruelty; and the police records of recent years show some cases of cruelties inflicted upon children in this District so revolting that "torture" is no more than an appropriate descriptive term for the offense. *It is this class of cases which the provision is specially designed to meet,* and it has been the law in regard to dumb animals since 1871.[8] [S. Rep. No. 94, 48th Cong., 1st Sess., at 2 (1884). (emphasis added).]

Thus, while it is true that Congress aimed at evils inflicted on children most commonly by parents or guardians, Congress did not intend to occupy the field or preclude prosecutions of parents for assault.

We turn to appellant's argument that her assault conviction must be reversed because the government did not prove that she acted out of malice when she punished her daughter. By the term "malice" in this context, appellant means the state of mind that this court described when it construed the offense of cruelty to children in Carson v. United States, 556 A.2d 1076, 1079 (D.C. 1989): "a parent acts with malice when a parent acts out of a *desire to inflict pain* rather than out of genuine effort to correct the child, or when the parent, in a genuine effort to correct the child, acts with a *conscious disregard* that serious harm will

---

[8] The criminal cruelty to children provisions enacted in 1885 were part of a larger bill that also extended to children the benefits of existing statutes for the prevention of cruelty to animals. Among other things, Congress renamed the Association for the Prevention of Cruelty to Animals the "Washington Humane Society," and authorized it to "prefer complaints, before any court in the District of Columbia having jurisdiction, for the violation of any law relating to or affecting the protection of children in said District." 23 Stat. 303, ch. 58, §1 (1885).

result." (Emphasis supplied.) . . . Appellant argues, however, that the government was obliged to prove malice to overcome her affirmative defense, the so-called parental discipline defense.

A parent's privilege to use reasonable force to discipline her minor child without being subjected to criminal liability for battery or assault is rooted in the common law, where it has a long pedigree. Blackstone, for example, deemed it settled that "battery is, in some cases, justifiable or lawful; as where one who hath authority, a parent or a master, gives moderate correction to his child, his scholar, or his apprentice." 2 William Blackstone, Commentaries *120. The privilege is recognized throughout the United States. Although some jurisdictions have embodied the parental discipline defense in statutes, often with refinements, it remains a common law defense in the District of Columbia. . . .

The precise contours of the parental discipline defense have not been articulated fully in the case law of this jurisdiction. [Our prior cases], summary though they are, emphasize not the non-malicious state of mind of the parent, but rather the purpose and the reasonableness of the force used. The widely accepted Criminal Jury Instructions [(No. 4.06 (4th ed., 1966 Supp.)] likewise states that "[t]o be justified, the force must have been used for the purpose of exercising parental discipline and must be reasonable."

This basic conception of the parental discipline defense is reinforced by decisions construing the common law of Maryland, to which we look for guidance when our own precedent is not dispositive. . . . The first limitation "is that the force truly be used in the exercise of domestic authority by way of punishing or disciplining the child — for the betterment of the child or promotion of the child's welfare — and not be a gratuitous attack." [Anderson v. State, 487 A.2d 294, 298 (Md. Ct. Spec. App. 1985).] The second limitation "is that the amount of force used be moderate and reasonable." Id. "The use of immoderate force is the thing that defeats the parental privilege, even where otherwise applicable." Id. at 299.

The District of Columbia and Maryland cases do not support appellant's contention that under the common law, "the government [is required] to prove malice before a parent, in a parental discipline case, could be found guilty of assault and battery." Much less do the cases support appellant's extravagant assertion that "what constitutes 'reasonable' parental discipline in our jurisdiction is therefore defined solely with reference to the parent's state of mind." Rather, the government could "defeat" the parental discipline defense by proving either that the parent did not have a genuine disciplinary purpose or that the force used was immoderate or unreasonable. This "reasonable force" standard for genuine parental discipline appears to be the common law rule in the majority of jurisdictions.

We recognize that not all jurisdictions employ the reasonable force standard. In the common law of some jurisdictions, the parental discipline privilege is based on a malice standard along the lines that appellant proposes. [W]e would not choose to follow the minority of courts that "hold that in the absence of malice, parents [have] almost unfettered discretion to physically dominate their children." [Kandice K. Johnson, Crime or Punishment: The Parental Corporal Punishment Defense — Reasonable and Necessary, or Excused Abuse?, 1998 U. Ill. L. Rev. 413, 435.] As Johnson reports, replacing the reasonable force standard with a malice standard would reduce the level of protection that the criminal law affords children:

In jurisdictions using the malice standard or variations thereof, great deference is given to the authority of parents to raise children as they see fit. Parental authority dominates the concern for the physical well-being of the child. As such, in all but the worst cases of abuse, when the child is subjected to conduct that could or does result in death, serious injury, or disfigurement, a parent's right to discipline is given priority over the consequences to the child. . . . [Johnson, supra, at 436 (footnotes omitted).]

A malice standard for the parental discipline defense also would run counter to the public policy reflected in the child neglect and abuse law of the District. That law states that a child whose parent inflicts, or fails to make reasonable efforts to prevent the infliction of, "excessive corporal punishment" is an "abused" child entitled to legal protection. D.C. Code §16-2301(23) (2001). Under this provision, we have stated, "a parent's right to manage a child has its limits," and corporal punishment "must be reasonable under the facts and circumstances of the case." In re L.D.H., 776 A.2d 570, 575 (D.C. 2001) (citations omitted). The test is an "objective" one that does not turn on the existence of parental malice. Parental good intentions do not excuse physical abuse.

Appellant nonetheless urges adoption of a malice standard in criminal prosecutions on the ground that "a general intent mens rea in parental discipline cases would not adequately safeguard a parent's constitutional right to decide how best to raise her child without undue interference from the government." This argument is flawed in that it ignores the availability of the parental discipline defense based on a reasonableness standard and assumes that nothing less than a malice standard will do to protect the due process "right of parents to make decisions concerning the care, custody and control of their children." Troxel v. Granville, 530 U.S. 57, 66 (2000) (citations omitted). But as the opinion in *Troxel* is careful to point out, the constitutional presumption against state intervention exists only "so long as a parent adequately cares for his or her children." Id. at 68. The "state has a wide range of power for limiting parental freedom and authority in things affecting the child's welfare." Prince v. Massachusetts, 321 U.S. 158, 167 (1944). Constitutionally protected parental prerogatives are sufficiently respected in a criminal assault prosecution by requiring the government to overcome the parental discipline defense beyond a reasonable doubt — by proving either that the punishment was unreasonable or that it was not genuinely disciplinary — without also requiring the government to prove that the parent acted with malice toward her child.

To say that much is not to say that the common law reasonableness standard is necessarily beyond criticism. One arguable shortcoming is that "[w]ith 'reasonableness' as their only guide, parents have little guidance as to the limits of a lawful physical interaction with their children, and fact finders are left to define the privilege on a case-by-case basis." Johnson, supra, at 467. . . . Perhaps the criminal sanction should be reserved for the most egregious cases, [as Professor Monrad Paulsen opines below[15]], or should entail a heightened *mens rea* requirement — if

_____

[15] In Paulsen's view, "[t]he harsh remedies of the criminal law are appropriate only in severe cases, cases which indicate that further harm may be done to others, cases which call for vengeance (if that call should ever be heeded), or cases which so disturb the community's sense of security that

not malice, then perhaps a lesser degree of recklessness. Refinements to the common law reasonableness standard implicate policy issues that are mainly for the legislative branch rather than the courts, however. . . .

We hold that the government was not required to prove malice in order to rebut appellant's assertion of the parental discipline defense. We therefore reject appellant's argument that her conviction must be overturned because there was insufficient evidence of malice. For the foregoing reasons, appellant's conviction of simple assault is affirmed.

ALI Model Penal Code §3.08

§3.08 Use of Force by Persons with Special Responsibility for Care, Discipline or Safety of Others

The use of force upon or toward the person of another is justifiable if:

(1) the actor is the parent or guardian or other person similarly responsible for the general care and supervision of a minor or a person acting at the request of such parent, guardian or other responsible person and:

(a) the force is used for the purpose of safeguarding or promoting the welfare of the minor, including the prevention or punishment of his misconduct; and   └ can be preemptive

(b) the force used is not designed to cause or known to create a substantial risk of causing death, serious bodily harm, disfigurement, extreme pain or mental distress or gross degradation; or

(2) the actor is a teacher or a person otherwise entrusted with the care or supervision for a special purpose of a minor and:

(a) the actor believes that the force used is necessary to further such special purpose, including the maintenance of reasonable discipline in a school, class or other group, and that the use of such force is consistent with the welfare of the minor; and   'in schools

(b) the degree of force, if it had been used by the parent or guardian of the minor, would not be unjustifiable under paragraph (1)(b) of this Section; or

(3) the actor is the guardian or other person similarly responsible for the general care and supervision of an incompetent person; and:

(a) the force is used for the purpose of safeguarding or promoting the welfare of the incompetent person, including the prevention of his misconduct, or, when such incompetent person is in a hospital or other institution for his care and custody, for the maintenance of reasonable discipline in such institution; and

(b) the force used is not designed to cause or known to create a substantial risk of causing death, serious bodily harm, disfigurement, extreme or unnecessary pain, mental distress, or humiliation. . . .

---

the events cannot go unremarked." [Monrad G. Paulsen, The Legal Framework for Child Protection, 66 Colum. L. Rev. 679, 692 (1966).]

Restatement (Second) of Torts §§147, 150, 151

§147 General Principle

(1) A parent is privileged to apply such reasonable force or to impose such reasonable confinement upon his child as he reasonably believes to be necessary for its proper control, training, or education.

(2) One other than a parent who has been given by law or has voluntarily assumed in whole or in part the function of controlling, training, or educating a child, is privileged to apply such reasonable force or to impose such reasonable confinement as he reasonably believes to be necessary for its proper control, training, or education, except in so far as the parent has restricted the privilege of one to whom he has entrusted the child.

§150 Factors Involved in Determining Reasonableness of Punishment

In determining whether force or confinement is reasonable for the control, training, or education of a child, the following factors are to be considered:

      (a) whether the actor is a parent;

      (b) the age, sex, and physical and mental condition of the child;

      (c) the nature of his offense and his apparent motive;

      (d) the influence of his example upon other children of the same family or group;

      (e) whether the force or confinement is <u>reasonably necessary and appropriate to compel obedience to a proper command;</u>

      (f) whether it is disproportionate to the offense, unnecessarily degrading, or likely to cause serious or permanent harm.

§151 Purpose of Punishment

Force applied or confinement imposed primarily for any purpose other than the proper training or education of the child or for the preservation of discipline is not privileged although applied or imposed in an amount and upon an occasion which would be privileged had it been applied for such purpose.

Dennis Alan Olson, Comment, The Swedish Ban of Corporal Punishment

1984 B.Y.U. L. Rev. 447-456

On July 1, 1979, Sweden became the first nation to prohibit corporal punishment of children by their parents. The Swedish Parenthood and Guardianship Code was amended to provide: "A child may not be subjected to corporal punishment or other injurious or humiliating treatment." The new Swedish law is distinctive because it allows greater intrusion into family life than the laws of other countries that have considered the relationship between corporal punishment and child abuse specifically and children's rights generally. The law also represents the final step in an attempt by lawmakers to change societal views without coercion. . . .

The 1979 law prohibiting corporal punishment reflects the major transformation of Swedish attitudes against the punishment of children that has occurred over the past thirty years. Traditionally, the right of parents to use corporal punishment in raising their children was wholly accepted in Sweden. Both religious and legal codes reiterated the proverbial dictum that sparing the rod spoils the child.

When Swedish family law was codified in 1920, it expressly gave parents the right to punish their children. This language of the statute was extensively criticized because it resulted in the widespread use of severe corporal punishment. In an effort to discourage the use of harsh punishments, the Parenthood and Guardianship Code was amended in 1949 to replace the word "punish" with reprimand. However, this change in the code was not accompanied by comparable changes in the criminal law. The Penal Code preserved the parental right to punish children and protected parents from criminal prosecution for actions against those under their supervision, as long as the injuries inflicted were not long-term. This exception from criminal liability for parents and guardians made child abuse cases difficult to prosecute until the exception was eliminated from the Penal Code in 1957.

In 1965, the rising number of child abuse cases led the justice minister to call for stronger statutory condemnation of corporal punishment. . . .

[I]n response to the Ministry's proposal to amend the code, the Riksdag adopted [a] proposal in 1966 [which] neither called for an acknowledgement of the right to punish nor expressly banned physical punishment. Despite the passive nature of simply removing all references to corporal punishment from the Code, the Riksdag considered this action a ban on corporal punishment. Even later, when the Riksdag expressly banned corporal punishment in 1979, it insisted that its action was merely a codification of the existing law.

The ban of corporal punishment was contrary to the prevailing public opinion in Sweden concerning corporal punishment. A public opinion poll in 1965 showed that 54% of all adult Swedes considered physical punishment occasionally necessary in child rearing. However, by 1968 the percentage of persons supporting physical punishment had fallen from 53% to 42% while opposition to corporal punishment had increased from 35% to 54%. This shift of opinion continued through 1971 when a survey indicated that support for corporal punishment had decreased to 35%. The 1971 survey also asked whether people thought the law prohibited corporal punishment. Sixty-one percent of the respondents felt that it was prohibited, while the remaining 39% either felt physical punishment was permitted by law or had no opinion on the issue. . . .

In preparation for the International Year of the Child, the Riksdag established the Commission on Children's Rights on February 24, 1977. The Commission was charged with investigating ways of strengthening the legal position of children. In 1978 the Commission issued its first report, entitled *Children's Rights: A Ban Against Corporal Punishment.* The report proposed the enactment of an explicit ban of physical punishment. Corporal punishment was viewed as "a form of degrading treatment" which results in a "lack of self-esteem and a personality change" that could affect the child for life. The report found that "[c]hild psychiatrists and psychologists have long been in agreement that physical punishment of children is inappropriate."

Influenced by such opinions and the need for society to "work against all forms of violence," the Commission found an express ban of corporal punishment necessary in order for children to grow up realizing that violence is not socially acceptable behavior. The Commission noted that, while most Swedes felt corporal punishment was prohibited, many people continued to violate the law. The Commission felt greater public knowledge of the law would result in increased compliance. However, the Commission recognized the difficulty of publicizing the mere absence of permission to reprimand or punish. Unless the ban were explicitly expressed, it would be difficult to increase public knowledge concerning the illegality of corporal punishment beyond the 1971 level. . . . The Commission's proposal was introduced in the Riksdag. In a report of its own, the government emphasized the role of the law in changing the attitudes of parents and guardians. The Riksdag's Law Committee proposed slight changes in some sections of the law but did not substantively alter the ban. A nearly unanimous vote of the Riksdag adopted the government proposal.

The law prohibiting corporal punishment of children was not intended to include criminal sanctions requiring changes in the Penal Code. The legislation was consciously designed as a prohibition "without teeth." The Commission on Children's Rights noted in its first report that no changes in the Penal Code were proposed. The remittance comments also made reference to the noncriminal nature of the ban and suggested use of a strong advertising campaign to increase public awareness and obedience to the law. The government adopted this suggestion as part of its own report. . . .

NOTES AND QUESTIONS

(1) Physical Abuse or Discipline?   Virtually all American states, either by statute or case law, permit "reasonable" corporal punishment by parents or guardians. Susan H. Bitensky, Spare the Rod, Embrace Our Humanity: Toward a New Legal Regime Prohibiting Corporal Punishment of Children, 31 Mich. J.L. Ref. 353, 356 & 356 n. 5 (1998). What distinguishes abuse from discipline?

(2) Reasonableness.   What factors determine whether the parent's degree of force was "reasonable"? According to the American Law Institute Model Penal Code? The Restatement (Second) of Torts? Should the law take into account a "cultural defense" in the determination of reasonableness (i.e., cultural practices among immigrant populations that permit various forms of corporal punishment)? See generally Michael Futterman, Comment, Seeking a Standard: Reconciling Child Abuse and Condoned Child Rearing Practices Among Different Cultures, 34 U. Miami Inter-Am. L. Rev. 491 (2003).

(3) Swedish Reform Movement.   How likely is Congress to enact a ban similar to the Swedish legislation? How would parents in the United States react to a ban similar to the Swedish legislation? Are American parents likely to respond to a prohibition without criminal penalties? If not, what penalties would be necessary to enforce the ban? Are criminal penalties, such as those for child abuse or assault, appropriate as redress for spanking or slapping?[1] See Calif. Welf. & Inst. Code

---

[1] In June 2004, the town of Brookline, Massachusetts, rejected a no-spanking resolution. Introduced by a town resident, the proposal carried no legal sanctions but would have banned the use

§300, reprinted infra, pp. 310-312. Could an American ban on corporal punishment be reconciled with the Supreme Court's decisions in *Meyer*, *Pierce*, and *Prince*? Note that in 1995 Congress unsuccessfully attempted to enact legislation that would have authorized a federal parental right to use "reasonable" corporal discipline. See Bitensky, supra, at 357, 357 n. 6 (citing the Parental Rights and Responsibilities Act of 1995, S. 984, 104th Cong. §3 (1995)).

As the above excerpt explains, the Swedish ban of 1979 was actually the third stage of legislative reform. The first reform occurred in 1957, when the Swedish Parliament eliminated the parental privilege from the Penal Code — i.e., removing parental physical punishment as a defense to criminal assault. In the second stage, in 1966, the Swedish Parliament removed references to even mild forms of corporal punishment from the Parents' Code.

(4) Effects of the Swedish Ban.

a. Attitudinal Change. The Swedish ban significantly changed attitudes toward corporal punishment. According to the above excerpt, before the ban, 54 percent of all adult Swedes considered such punishment necessary occasionally. Attitudes began to change following an aggressive public awareness campaign by the government. By 1995-1996, only 11 percent of respondents indicated that they were positively inclined to even mild forms of punishment. Joan E. Durrant, Legal Reform and Attitudes Toward Physical Punishment in Sweden, 11 Intl. J. Children's Rts. (No. 2) 147, 152 (2003). Durrant elaborates:

> The majority of youths born in 1980 reported never having been physically punished. Of those who were, the vast majority experienced it no more than once or twice in their lifetime. Virtually none were hit with implements. These findings suggest that the prevalence, frequency and harshness of physical punishment have indeed declined in Sweden since the 1950s. Id. at 159.

b. International Law. The Swedish ban initiated a worldwide trend. Ten other nations followed Sweden's example (Finland, Norway, Austria, Cyprus, Denmark, Latvia, Croatia, Israel, Germany, and Iceland) by enacting similar civil laws that assert the child's rights. Durrant, supra, at 168. Romania and the Ukraine banned corporal punishment in 2004. Alexandra Freanin London, How Laws on Child Punishment Differ Around World, Irish Independent, July 6, 2004. But cf. Canadian Foundation for Children, Youth & Law v. Canada, 234 D.L.R. (4th) 257 (2004) (upholding Canadian Criminal Code §43, which allows parents to physically discipline children if the force is "reasonable"). See generally Tamar Ezer, Children's Rights in Israel: An End to Corporal Punishment?, 5 Or. Rev. Intl. L. 139 (2003); Deanna Pollard, Banning Child Corporal Punishment, 77 Tul. L. Rev. 575 (2003).

c. Convention on the Rights of the Child. The Swedish ban also influenced international human rights law. Article 19 of the 1989 United Nations Convention on the Rights of the Child (which imposes human rights obligations on signatory nations) requires governments to protect children from all forms of maltreatment.

---

of corporal punishment of any kind by parents. Members of the town council viewed the measure as beyond the scope of their authority and left the matter for the state legislature. Jessica Bennett, Brookline Rejects Measure on Spanking Respect, Less Force Sought in Proposal, Boston Globe, June 4, 2004, at B1.

Moreover, Article 37 provides that no child shall be subjected to cruel, inhuman, or degrading punishment. Although the Convention does not contain an explicit prohibition of "physical punishment," the international committee that interprets the Convention has emphasized that "corporal punishment of children is incompatible with the Convention" and recommended that "the physical punishment of children in families be prohibited." Cited in Linda Rose-Krasnor et al., Physical Punishment and the U.N. Convention on the Rights of the Child, Intl. Soc. Study of Behav. Dev. Newsletter, No. 2, Serial No. 38 (2001), at 9. The United States has not yet ratified the U.N. Convention on the Rights of the Child.

(5) Challenges to the Ban. Several Swedish parents subsequently challenged the ban as a violation of the European Convention for the Protection of Human Rights and Fundamental Freedoms respecting private family life and freedom of religion (e.g., because some church tenets support corporal punishment). The European Court of Human Rights rejected their challenge in X, Y, and Z v. Sweden, 5 Eur. Ct. H.R. 147 (1983). Also, in 1998, the European Court of Human Rights held in A. v. United Kingdom, 27 Eur. Ct. H.R. 611 (1999), that a stepfather's beating of a nine-year-old boy with a bamboo garden stake violated the boy's human rights, even though a British court earlier deemed the punishment "reasonable chastisement." Sarah Lyall, European Court Rebukes Britain in Case of Stepfather Beating Son, Plain Dealer (Clev.), Sept. 24, 1998, at A6. In response, the British government promised to amend the law. In 2002, when no legislation was yet forthcoming, a United Nations committee criticized the British law of "reasonable chastisement" as incompatible with the nation's obligations under the Convention on the Rights of the Child. In 2004, Parliament considered but rejected a total ban on corporal punishment and decided instead to limit the scope of reasonable chastisement. Alan Cowell, The House of Lords Restrains the Hand That Hits the Child, N.Y. Times, July 6, 2004, at A4.

(6) Parental Tort Immunity. The parental tort immunity doctrine, prohibiting an unemancipated child from suing a parent for negligent injuries, was first recognized in Hewellette v. George, 9 So. 885 (1891). By the 1950s almost all states had adopted the doctrine. California started a trend toward abrogation in Gibson v. Gibson, 479 P.2d 648 (Cal. 1971), replacing the doctrine with the "reasonable parent standard" (permitting recovery if a parent fails to meet the standard of care required by a "reasonable and prudent parent"). Today, virtually all jurisdictions have abolished the doctrine. Joseph J. Basgier, III, Comment, Children's Rights: A Renewed Call for the End of Parental Immunity in Alabama and Arguments for the Further Expansion of a Child's Right to Sue, 26 Law & Psychol. Rev. 123 (2002). Is tort law an effective means of protecting children from physical abuse?

(7) Problem. T.A. is a 12-year-old special needs' child with Tourrette's syndrome (a motor disorder characterized by involuntary movements and vocal outbursts) and attention deficit hyperactivity disorder (ADHD) (a genetic dysfunction characterized by inattention, hyperactivity, and impulsivity). On the day that his family moves to a new home, T.A. is disobedient and defiant, and refuses to be helpful. When his mother asks him to retrieve a trash can, he empties the contents onto the kitchen floor. He later denies the act and begins crying and screaming. Determining that T.A. is "out of control," his stepfather spanks him eight to ten

times with a belt, leaving bruises that remain for several days. T.A.'s sister tells their biological father, who reports the incident to the authorities. The state statute provides:

step-parent is not
a parent

> [t]o use or attempt or offer to use force upon or toward the person of another is not unlawful if committed by a parent . . . in the exercise of a lawful authority to restrain or correct his child or ward and if restraint or correction has been rendered necessary by the misconduct of such child or ward, or by his refusal to obey the lawful command of such parent . . . and the force used is reasonable in manner and moderate in degree.

Should T.A. be adjudicated an abused/neglected child, or did the stepfather's spanking constitute "reasonable force"? See In re T.A., 663 N.W.2d 225 (S.D. 2003).

Corporal Punishment in Schools

Anglo-American law has permitted the use of physical force for disciplining children in schools as well as the home. In England, the basis of the teacher's right to administer corporal punishment was found in the doctrine of in loco parentis. That is, the school's authority derived from a partial delegation of the parental right to discipline. Blackstone wrote:

> [The father] may also delegate part of his parental authority, during his life, to the tutor or schoolmaster of his child; who is then in loco parentis, and has such a portion of the power of the parent committed to his charge, viz. that of restraint and correction, as may be necessary to answer the purposes for which he is employed. [2 Commentaries on the Laws of England *453 (Thomas M. Cooley ed. 1884).]

With the advent of compulsory education, it became difficult to find either a delegation or consent in the relation between parent and teacher, especially where the parent expressly objected to the use of corporal punishment. American courts have therefore emphasized maintenance of public order and control of the classroom in analyzing the teacher's right to administer corporal punishment. This analysis requires the court to weigh the parent's right to choose between means of discipline against the school's need to restrain or correct pupils. Note, in this regard, the balance struck by the Restatement (Second) of Torts §153, infra.

Restatement (Second) of Torts §§152-155

§152 Partial Control of Child

One who is charged only with the education or some other part of the training of a child has the privilege of using force or confinement to discipline the child only in so far as the privilege is necessary for the education or other part of the training which is committed or delegated to the actor.

§153 Power of Parent to Restrict Privilege

(1) One who is in charge of the control, training, or education of a child solely as the delegate of its parent is not privileged to inflict a punishment which the parent has forbidden or to punish the child for doing or refusing to do that which the parent has directed the child to do or not to do.

(2) One who is in charge of the education or training of a child as a public officer is privileged to inflict such reasonable punishments as are necessary for the child's proper education or training, notwithstanding the parent's prohibitions or wishes.

§154 Privilege of One in Charge of Group

One who is in charge of the training or education of a group of children is privileged to apply such force or impose such confinement upon one or more of them as is reasonably necessary to secure observance of the discipline necessary for the education and training of the children as a group.

§155 Effect of Excessive Force

If the actor applies a force or imposes a confinement upon a child which is in excess of that which is privileged, (a) the actor is liable for so much of the force or confinement as is excessive; (b) the child has the privilege stated in §§63-75 to defend himself against the actor's use or attempted use of the excessive force or confinement.

Baker v. Owen

395 F. Supp. 294 (M.D.N.C. 1975), *aff'd without opinion,* **423 U.S. 907 (1975)**

CRAVEN, Circuit Judge.

This three-judge court was convened to consider the claims of Russell Carl Baker and his mother that their constitutional rights were violated when Russell Carl was corporally punished by his teacher over his mother's objections and without procedural due process. Russell Carl, a sixth-grader, was paddled on December 6, 1973, for allegedly violating his teacher's announced rule against throwing kickballs except during designated play periods. Mrs. Baker had previously requested of Russell Carl's principal and certain teachers, that Russell Carl not be corporally punished, because she opposed it on principle. Nevertheless, shortly after his alleged misconduct her son received two licks in the presence of a second teacher and in view of other students.

Mrs. Baker alleges that the administration of corporal punishment after her objections violated her parental right to determine disciplinary methods for her child. Russell Carl charges that the circumstances in which the punishment was administered violated his right to procedural due process, and that the punishment itself in this instance amounted to cruel and unusual punishment. This special court was convened because both Mrs. Baker in her claim and Russell Carl in his procedural due process claim have challenged the constitutionality of

North Carolina General Statutes §115-146. They claim that this statute, which empowers school officials to "use reasonable force in the exercise of lawful authority to restrain or correct pupils and to maintain order,"[1] is unconstitutional insofar as it allows corporal punishment over parental objection and absent adequate procedural safeguards.

We hold that fourteenth amendment liberty embraces the right of parents generally to control means of discipline of their children, but that the state has a countervailing interest in the maintenance of order in the schools, in this case sufficient to sustain the right of teachers and school officials to administer reasonable corporal punishment for disciplinary purposes. We also hold that teachers and school officials must accord to students minimal procedural due process in the course of inflicting such punishment. We further hold that the spanking of Russell Carl in this case did not amount to cruel and unusual punishment. . . .

The Supreme Court first acknowledged the constitutional stature of parental rights over half a century ago in Meyer v. Nebraska, 262 U.S. 390 (1923). . . . Two years later the Court in Pierce v. Society of Sisters, 268 U.S. 510 (1925), struck down another state statute requiring public school attendance because it "unreasonably interfere[d] with the liberty of parents and guardians to direct the upbringing and education of children under their control," id. at 534-535.

The *Meyer* and *Pierce* decisions have since been interpreted by the Court as recognizing that, under our constitutional scheme, "the custody, care and nurture of the child reside first in the parents." Mrs. Baker urges that the right to determine disciplinary methods for Russell Carl is part of her primary right to and responsibility for his "custody, care and nurture"; that as such it is a fundamental right; and that the state therefore must show a compelling interest in order to punish Russell Carl corporally against her wishes.

. . . We agree with Mrs. Baker that the fourteenth amendment concept of liberty embraces the right of a parent to determine and choose between means of discipline of children, but few constitutional rights are absolute. Our inquiry does not end with the conclusion that Mrs. Baker has such a right but we must go on to consider the nature and extent of the state's interest in school discipline. . . .

We reject Mrs. Baker's suggestion that this right is fundamental and that the state can punish her child corporally only if it shows a compelling interest that outweighs her parental right. We do not read *Meyer* and *Pierce* to enshrine parental rights so high in the hierarchy of constitutional values. In each case the parental right prevailed not because the Court termed it fundamental and the state's interest

---

[1] N.C. Gen. Stat. §115-146 reads as follows:

> *Duties of teachers generally: principals and teachers may use reasonable force in exercising lawful authority.* — It shall be the duty of all teachers, including student teachers, substitute teachers, voluntary teachers, teachers' aides and assistants when given authority over some part of the school program by the principal or supervising teacher, to maintain good order and discipline in their respective schools. . . .
>
> Principals, teachers, substitute teachers, voluntary teachers, teachers' aides and assistants and student teachers in the public schools of this State may use reasonable force in the exercise of lawful authority to restrain or correct pupils and maintain order. No county or city board of education or district committee shall promulgate or continue in effect a rule, regulation or bylaw which prohibits the use of such force as is specified in this section.

uncompelling, but because the Court considered the state's action to be arbitrary, without reasonable relation to an end legitimately within its power . . .

A finding that Mrs. Baker's power of decision regarding corporal punishment is fundamental would require the state to show both a compelling interest and the unavailability of alternative means of fulfilling that interest before it could contravene her decision. A sensitive consideration of the nature of Mrs. Baker's right to preclude corporal punishment, and the context in which she seeks to assert it, simply forecloses the imposition of such a burden upon the state.

Insight into the nature of Mrs. Baker's right, for the purpose of deciding whether it should receive ultimate protection, can best be gained by comparing it to the parental rights at stake in *Meyer, Pierce*, and *Prince*. The Court in *Meyer* spoke of "the natural duty of the parent to give his children education," . . . 262 U.S. at 400; . . . In *Pierce* the Court was faced with a claim invoking "the right of parents to choose schools where their children will receive appropriate mental and religious training," 268 U.S. at 532, . . . And in *Prince* the parental right was the inculcation of one's religious beliefs in one's children. . . .

The common characteristic of the parental interests in all three cases is their venerability. In each instance the Court started with a premise that could provoke no quarrel — that the specific parental concern implicated was worthy of great deference due to its unquestioned acceptance throughout our history. Mrs. Baker's opposition to corporal punishment, on the other hand, enjoys no such universal approbation in our society even today, and certainly not historically. Quite the contrary, it bucks a settled tradition of countenancing such punishment when reasonable. See generally F. Harper & F. James, The Law of Torts §3.20 (1956); 68 Am. Jur. 2d, Schools §258 (1973). And though we accept Mrs. Baker's assertion that corporal punishment of children is today discouraged by the weight of professional opinion, we are also cognizant that the issue is unsettled and probably incapable of categorical resolution. We simply cannot foresee a parent's absolute disapproval of reasonable corporal punishment soon achieving the kind of societal respect that is clearly accorded the desire to expose one's child to certain fields of knowledge, to send him to a private or parochial school, or to pass on one's religious heritage to him. Thus, regardless whether the specific parental interests involved in *Meyer, Pierce*, and *Prince* should be considered fundamental, and without disparaging one whit Mrs. Baker's right to decide the methods of punishment to be employed with Russell Carl by herself or other private parties, we cannot say that her right of total opposition to his corporal punishment is fundamental in a constitutional sense.

We believe, therefore, that defendants can justify their corporal punishment of Russell Carl by showing that it furthered a legitimate state end. . . .

There can be no doubt about the state's legitimate and substantial interest in maintaining order and discipline in the public schools. Education may not be a fundamental interest, see [San Antonio School Dist. v. Rodriguez], 411 U.S. at 29-40, but the people of our states have long recognized its vital importance and provided it to their young people at public expense. It should be clear beyond peradventure, indeed self-evident, that to fulfill its assumed duty of providing an education to all who want it a state must maintain order within its schools. . . .

There are many, of course, including Mrs. Baker and the experts upon whose testimony and writings she relies, who believe that school officials can and should maintain [order] without using corporal punishment. We are aware that their view is shared by many professional educators, parents and others. But as we noted above, opinion on the merits of the rod is far from unanimous. On such a controversial issue, where we would be acting more from personal preference than from constitutional command, we cannot allow the wishes of a parent to restrict school officials' discretion in deciding the methods to be used in accomplishing the not just legitimate, but essential purpose of maintaining discipline. So long as the force used is reasonable — and that is all that the statute here allows — school officials are free to employ corporal punishment for disciplinary purposes until in the exercise of their own professional judgment, or in response to concerted pressure from opposing parents, they decide that its harm outweighs its utility. . . .

[The court then discussed whether corporal punishment was consistent with the child's rights under the Fourteenth Amendment.]

We believe that Russell Carl does have an interest, protected by the concept of liberty in the fourteenth amendment, in avoiding corporal punishment. . . . We believe that the concept must include, in appropriate instances, personal security in the seemingly small things of life as well as in the obviously momentous. . . . Secondly, the legal system, once quite tolerant of physical punishment in many contexts, has become less so. See generally Jackson v. Bishop, 404 F. 2d 571 (8th Cir. 1968) (prohibiting use of the strap on prisoners); 18 U.S.C. §2191 (1970) (outlawing flogging of sailors on United States ships); 1 F. Harper & P. James, The Law of Torts §3.20, at 289 (1956) (discussing husband's loss of the privilege of corporally disciplining his wife, and employer's similar loss of the privilege as to domestic employees). Indeed, it is questionable at best whether the law would now privilege any degree of corporal punishment of an adult. While the state historically has been granted broader powers over children than over adults, see, e.g., *Prince*, supra, 321 U.S. at 167-170, the Supreme Court has explicitly recognized that children have rights, too. Goss v. Lopez, supra, 419 U.S. at 570-576; *Tinker*, supra, 393 U.S. at 506, 511. Thus, although the weight of legal authority still permits corporal punishment of public school children, see Restatement (Second) of Torts §153(2) (1965), it seems uncontrovertible that the child has a legitimate interest in avoiding unnecessary or arbitrary infliction of a punishment that probably would be completely disallowed as to an adult. Moreover, North Carolina has itself given school children reasonable expectation of freedom from excessive or pointless corporal punishment by writing into section 115-146 the requirements that such punishment be reasonable and used for specific purposes only. Yet it has failed to provide any procedural protection to insure that those acting under the statutory authority will adhere to its dictates and neither punish arbitrarily nor use unreasonable force.

Having concluded . . . that North Carolina school children have a liberty interest, we must decide what procedural safeguards should protect it. . . . Our task is to fashion procedures that accommodate as best as possible the child's interest with the state's unquestioned interest in effective discipline. There is no dispute about the state's assertion that elaborate, time-consuming procedures antecedent to infliction of corporal punishment would destroy its value, as the essence of corporal punishment is swift and tangible wages for one's transgression. Plaintiffs concede, as we believe they must, that this basic consideration precludes our requiring the full panoply of procedural due process rights, i.e., such things as formal notice, right to counsel, right of confrontation and cross-examination.

Instead, plaintiffs request only those minimal procedures necessary to protect the student's interest without undercutting the disciplinary value of the punishment. We believe such procedures are few in number, but that is not to downplay their importance. First, except for those acts of misconduct which are so anti-social or disruptive in nature as to shock the conscience, corporal punishment may never be used unless the student was informed beforehand that specific misbehavior could occasion its use, and, subject to this exception, it should never be employed as a first line of punishment for misbehavior. The requirements of an announced possibility of corporal punishment and an attempt to modify behavior by some other means — keeping after school, assigning extra work, or some other punishment — will insure that the child has clear notice that certain behavior subjects him to physical punishment. Second, a teacher or principal must punish corporally in the presence of a second school official (teacher or principal), who must be informed beforehand and in the student's presence of the reason for the punishment. The student need not be afforded a formal opportunity to present his side to the second official; the requirement is intended only to allow a student to protest, spontaneously, an egregiously arbitrary or contrived application of punishment. And finally, an official who has administered such punishment must provide the child's parent, upon request, a written explanation of his reasons and the name of the second official who was present.

QUESTIONS ON CORPORAL PUNISHMENT IN SCHOOLS

(1) Who Decides on School Discipline?   Are you convinced by the way the *Baker* court squares *Meyer*, *Pierce*, and *Prince*? The court seems to knock down a straw man in rejecting Mrs. Baker's total opposition to corporal punishment. Isn't the real issue whether the parent or the state gets to decide on the means of discipline? Note that Mrs. Baker would apparently not strip the school of all disciplinary power, such as holding Russell Clark after school. Should this have made any difference to the court? What sources does the court draw upon in fixing the content of students' due process rights?

(2) Effectiveness of Corporal Punishment in Schools.   Approximately half of the states permit the use of corporal punishment in public schools as a means of discipline.[2] Are such disciplinary measures effective? Many commentators and social scientists are doubtful, arguing

> that corporal punishment is an ineffective disciplinary tool, causing more behavioral problems than it cures. Second, corporal punishment may produce many harmful side-effects — physical, sexual, emotional, and racial — that result even from its judicious application.[3]

[2] Lynn Roy, Corporal Punishment in American Public Schools and the Rights of the Child, 30 J.L. & Educ. 554, 557 & n. 22 (2001) (listing states).
[3] John M. Bylsma, Comment, Hands Off! New North Carolina General Statutes Section 115C-390 Allows Local School Boards to Ban Corporal Punishment, 70 N.C. L. Rev. 2058, 2069 (1992).

Critics contend that teachers and administrators are more likely to punish the economically disadvantaged, minorities, and males.[4] Some suggest that corporal punishment in the schools perpetuates notions of the acceptability of physical punishment.[5]

(3) Permission vs. Preclusion. Unlike the North Carolina statute at issue in Baker v. Owen that permitted school officials to inflict corporal punishment notwithstanding a parent's request, a few states specifically allow parents to forbid corporal punishment of their child. See, e.g., Utah Code Ann. §53A-11-802 (2000). See also Rinehart v. Board of Educ., 621 N.E.2d 1365 (Ohio Ct. App. 1993) (holding that *Baker* imposes a procedural requirement on a teacher before inflicting corporal punishment to verify the absence of a note from a parent forbidding it).

*(4) North Carolina Post-**Baker**.* North Carolina still permits corporal punishment in the schools. However, in 1991 the legislature replaced N.C. Gen. Stat. §115-146 with a statutory delegation of authority to local school boards. Whereas the former law permitted the use of reasonable force "to restrain or correct pupils and maintain order" and expressly precluded local regulations "which prohibit[ ] the use of such force," the most recent provision (N.C. Gen. Stat. §115C-390 (2001)) increases local autonomy by permitting school boards to restrict or prohibit the use of reasonable force. Seven months after passage of the law, one-third of North Carolina's school districts had banned the use of corporal punishment.[6] *local autonomy*

(5) Nationwide Trend. The change in North Carolina law is illustrative of a trend toward decreasing acceptance of corporal punishment in the public schools. Data reveal that 342,038 students were subjected to corporal punishment in 2000, compared to 1,521,896 students in 1976 (after *Baker*).[7] Following a legal setback in Ingraham v. Wright (discussed infra), opponents of corporal punishment directed their attention to legislative efforts to prohibit the practice in schools. Teachers, pediatricians, child abuse experts, and members of national organizations, such as the PTA and the AMA, lobbied legislators to enact protective legislation.[8]

Of the states that prohibit corporal punishment in schools, some dilute the prohibition by drawing a technical distinction between "corporal punishment" and

---

See also Susan H. Bitensky, The Constitutionality of School Corporal Punishment of Children as a Betrayal of Brown v. Board of Education, 37 Loy. U. Chi. L.J. 201, 210-211 (2004) (citing research of psychologist Elizabeth Gershoff, who identifies adverse outcomes of corporal punishment such as: increased aggression, criminal and antisocial conduct, and risk upon adulthood of abusing one's own child or spouse; and who theorizes that such effects may result from either parental or school discipline).

[4] John Dayton, Corporal Punishment in Public Schools: The Legal and Political Battle Continues, 89 Educ. L. Rep. 727, 735 (May 19, 1994). Data from the U.S. Department of Education, Office of Civil Rights, support the disproportionate racial nature of corporal punishment in the schools. For example, in 2000, African-American students received 39 percent of the paddlings, although they comprised 17 percent of students in the public schools. Center for Effective Discipline, "Discipline at School: Facts About Corporal Punishment," (compiled from U.S. Dept. of Education statistics) (available at *www.stophitting.com/disatschool/facts* (last visited Oct. 4, 2004)).

[5] Katherine Hunt Federle, Violence Is the Word, 37 Hous. L. Rev. 97, 106 (2000).

[6] Bylsma, supra note [3], at 2066.

[7] Center for Effective Discipline, Fact Sheet, supra note [4]. States with the highest percentage of students who are struck by educators are Mississippi, Arkansas, and Alabama. Id.

[8] Dayton, supra note [4], at 729.

"reasonable force" (permitting the latter in specified circumstances). See, e.g., Iowa Code Ann §280.21 (West Supp. 2004) (permitting use of reasonable force not designed to cause pain but for the protection of the employee, the student, or other students); Mass. Gen. Laws Ann. ch. 71 §37G(b) (West Supp. 2004) (permitting reasonable force to protect pupils, teachers, and others from assault); Mich. Comp. Laws Ann. §380.1312 (West Supp. 2004) (prohibition of corporal punishment was amended to allow use of reasonable force and to limit the definition of "corporal punishment" to "deliberate infliction of physical pain").

NOTE: INGRAHAM v. WRIGHT

In Ingraham v. Wright, 430 U.S. 651 (1977), the United States Supreme Court upheld the constitutionality of corporal punishment of school children. Two junior high students who alleged that their paddling by school officials limited their physical capacity for a week brought an individual action for damages and sought declaratory and injunctive relief on behalf of all public school students. The students claimed that (1) paddling constitutes cruel and unusual punishment in violation of the Eighth Amendment, and (2) if paddling were allowed, the Due Process Clause would require prior notice and an opportunity to be heard before the imposition of punishment. The Court, dividing 5 to 4, rejected both claims.

(1) Eighth Amendment Claim. The Court held that the Eighth Amendment did not apply to the public school setting based on the history of the Eighth Amendment, precedent, and a comparison with other institutions. The Court reasoned that students have little need for such protection because a school, unlike a prison, is an open institution in which other adults or pupils may witness and protest any mistreatment.

(2) Procedural Due Process Claim. Conceding that the child had a liberty interest under the Fourteenth Amendment (at least where the school punishment inflicts "appreciable physical pain" id. at 674), the majority held, however, that procedural due process was satisfied by the existence of civil remedies and criminal sanctions. A hearing prior to the imposition of corporal punishment was unnecessary and burdensome and would "entail a significant intrusion into an area of primary educational responsibility." Id. at 682.

Justice White, in a dissenting opinion joined by Justices Brennan, Marshall, and Stevens, argued that the remedy of a tort action was "utterly inadequate to protect against erroneous infliction of punishment"(id. at 693) and in all events could not undo the "infliction of physical pain." Id. at 695. Justice White (who wrote the Court's majority opinion in *Goss*, described at p. 129, supra) added:

> The majority emphasizes, as did the dissenters in *Goss*, that even the "rudimentary precautions" required by that decision would impose some burden on the school disciplinary process. But those costs are no greater if the student is paddled rather than suspended; the risk of error in the punishment is no smaller; and the fear of "a significant intrusion" into the disciplinary process . . . is just as exaggerated. Id. at 700.

(3) Substantive Due Process.   The Supreme Court declined to review the question of whether the infliction of severe corporal punishment upon public school students violates students' *substantive* due process rights under the Fourteenth Amendment. However, virtually every federal circuit court that has addressed this issue has allowed such claims. See Diane Heckman, Constitutional Due Process and Corporal Punishment Involving Athletics, 158 West Educ. L. Rep. 513 (2002) (analyzing substantive due process claims by circuit). But cf. Moore v. Willis Indep. Sch. Dist., 233 F.3d 871 (5th Cir. 2000) (denying a substantive due process claim based on the existence of an "adequate" state remedy against teacher). For a modern critique of *Ingraham,* see Lynn Roy, Chalk Talk: Corporal Punishment in American Schools and the Rights of the Child, 30 J.L. & Educ. 554, 557-563 (2001) (arguing that the Court "trivialized" students' need for protection from excessive or disproportionate physical discipline).

C.   CHILD ABUSE

1.   Scope of the Problem

Child Maltreatment: 2002[9]

U.S. Dept. of Health & Human Services, Administration for Children & Families

. . . An estimated 896,000 children were determined to be victims of child abuse or neglect for 2002. The rate of victimization per 1,000 children in the national population has dropped from 13.4 children in 1990 to 12.3 children in 2002.

More than 60 percent of child victims were neglected by their parents or other caregivers. Almost 20 percent were physically abused, 10 percent were sexually abused, and 7 percent were emotionally maltreated. In addition, almost 20 percent were associated with "other" types of maltreatment based on specific State laws and policies. A child could be a victim of more than one type of maltreatment.

Children ages birth to 3 years had the highest rates of victimization at 16.0 per 1,000 children. Girls were slightly more likely to be victims than boys.

American Indian or Alaska Native and African-American children had the highest rates of victimization when compared to their national population. While the rate of White victims of child abuse or neglect was 10.7 per 1,000 children of the same race, the rate for American Indian or Alaska Natives was 21.7 per 1,000 children and for African-Americans 20.2 per 1,000 children. . . .

More than one-half of all reports that alleged child abuse or neglect were made by such professionals as educators, law enforcement and legal personnel, social services personnel, medical personnel, mental health personnel, child day-care providers, and foster care providers. Educators made 16.1 percent of all reports, while law enforcement made 15.7 percent, and social services personnel made

[9] The above report is available at *http://www.acf.hhs.gov/programs/cb/publications/cm02/summary.htm.*

12.6 percent. Such <u>nonprofessionals</u> as friends, neighbors, and relatives submitted approximately 43.6 percent of reports.

After conducting interviews with family members, the alleged child victim, and sometimes other people familiar with the family, the CPS agency makes a determination concerning whether the child is a victim of abuse or neglect, or is at risk of abuse or neglect. This determination is often called a disposition.

Approximately 30 percent of the reports included at least one child who was found to be a victim of abuse or neglect. Sixty-one percent of the reports were found to be unsubstantiated (including intentionally false); the remaining reports were closed for additional reasons.

<u>Child fatalities a</u>re the most tragic consequence of maltreatment. For 2002, an estimated 1,400 children died due to child abuse or neglect. Three-quarters of children who were killed were younger than 4 years old, 12 percent were 4-7 years old, 6 percent were 8-11 years old, and 6 percent were 12-17 years old.

Infant boys (younger than 1 year old) had the highest rate of fatalities, nearly 19 deaths per 100,000 boys of the same age in the national population. Infant girls had a rate of 12 deaths per 100,000 girls of the same age. The overall rate of child fatalities was 2 deaths per 100,000 children. One-third of child fatalities were attributed to neglect. Physical abuse and sexual abuse also were major contributors to fatalities.

<u>More than 80 percent of perpetrators were</u> parents. Other relatives accounted for 7 percent and unmarried partners of parents accounted for 3 percent of perpetrators. The remaining perpetrators include persons with other (camp counselor, school employee, etc.) or unknown relationships to the child victims.

<u>Female perpetrators, mostly mothers, were typically younger than male perpe-</u><u>trators, mostly fathers.</u> Women also comprised a larger percentage of all perpetrators than men, 58 percent compared to 42 percent.

Nearly 29 percent of all perpetrators of sexual abuse were other relatives, and nearly one-quarter were in nonrelative or nonchildcaring roles. In addition, less than 3 percent of all parent perpetrators were associated with sexual abuse.

CPS agencies provide services to some families and their children during, and as a result of, an investigation or assessment. Approximately 59 percent of victims and 31 percent of nonvictims received services as a result of an investigation or assessment. Additional analyses indicated that children who were prior victims of maltreatment were more than 80 percent more likely to receive services than first time victims. Additionally, children with multiple types of maltreatment were more than 80 percent more likely to receive services than children with only one type of recorded maltreatment.

Services included both in-home and foster care services. Almost one-fifth of child victims were placed in foster care. About 4 percent of nonvictims also experienced a removal — usually a short-term placement during the course of the investigation. . . .

NOTE ON CAPTA

The above report is based on an annual data collection effort that was mandated by the first comprehensive federal legislation on the subject of child abuse and neglect. In 1974 Congress enacted the <u>Child Abuse Prevention and Treatment Act</u> of 1974 (CAPTA), 42 U.S.C. §§5101-5106 (2000), to provide funding for state child protective services. In order to qualify for federal funds, CAPTA requires states to adopt procedures for reporting and investigating reports of abuse, provide immunity from prosecution to persons who make good-faith reports, provide for confidentiality of records, and provide for the appointment of a guardian ad litem (who is not required to be an attorney) to represent children in judicial proceedings.

Congress recently amended and reauthorized CAPTA by the Keeping Children and Families Safe Act of 2003 (Pub. L. No. 108-36, 117 Stat. 800 (2003)). Recent amendments mandate that states require health care providers to report infants who are prenatally exposed to drug abuse to child protective services; disclose confidential information to governmental agencies if necessary for the purpose of child protection; promptly inform perpetrators of allegations of maltreatment; develop background checks of adults in prospective adoptive and foster care homes; and adopt procedures to improve the training and supervision of caseworkers.

2.   Definitions, Causes, and Consequences of Child Abuse

Diana J. English, The Extent and Consequences of Child Maltreatment
The Future of Children, vol. 8, no. 1 (Spring 1998), 40-42, 45-48

Defining Child Maltreatment

The concept of child maltreatment is relatively new in Western society, although there is historical evidence that children have long been murdered, abandoned, incarcerated, mutilated, sexually exploited, beaten, and forced into labor by their parents and caregivers. For instance, in colonial America, children were flogged to instill discipline, and in the early twentieth century, children routinely worked 14-hour days in mills and mines. Such actions were not formally defined as maltreatment, however, and public authorities seldom interceded on the children's behalf.

The emergence of official definitions of unacceptable treatment of children has helped to trigger and sustain efforts by authorities to protect children. Because they have important policy implications, however, definitions of maltreatment have been hotly debated. Despite efforts to create uniform approaches, the definitions used by state legislatures, agency officials, and researchers remain ambiguous and inconsistent. Some of the key differences are discussed below.

By the mid-twentieth century, legislation defining child maltreatment was introduced into many state statutes, and some states required physicians to report abuse or neglect. In 1974, the U.S. Congress passed the Child Abuse Prevention and Treatment Act (CAPTA), Public Law 93-247, to give a national definition of child maltreatment and prescribe actions states should take to protect children. That law established a broad definition of maltreatment as: "The physical and mental injury, sexual abuse, neglected treatment or maltreatment of a child under age 18 by a person who is responsible for the child's welfare under circumstances which indicate the child's health and welfare is harmed and threatened thereby, as determined in accordance with regulations prescribed by the Secretary of Health, Education, and Welfare."

This definition of child maltreatment specifies that only parents or caregivers can be perpetrators of child abuse and neglect. Abusive behavior by other individuals, whether known to the child or strangers, is considered assault. Of particular note, this national definition includes both mental injury and neglect. . . .

The federal CAPTA legislation sets <u>minimum definitional standards for</u> the states receiving federal funds, but the details of defining maltreatment fall to the states, and specific definitions vary considerably. For example, some states include educational neglect (when a child consistently fails to attend school) in their definition of child maltreatment, while others do not. States also vary in the criteria and procedures they use to first screen and later validate reports of alleged maltreatment. . . .

Debates over how broadly to define maltreatment began with the drafting of the CAPTA legislation, and they have continued. Underlying the debate is the difficulty of identifying an appropriate government role in the lives of children and families. Advocates for a narrow definition of child abuse and neglect argue that before the government has a right to intervene in the privacy of the family, the parental action should have resulted in observable harm or pose an imminent risk of such harm. Others stress the damage that persistent neglect or psychological abuse can do to children, even if that damage appears only later. Thus, arguments center on whether to include mental injury and neglect, whether cumulative harm should be considered, and whether threatened as well as actual harm should count as maltreatment. [S]upporters of a broad definition prevailed when the federal definition [in CAPTA] was established. . . .

Factors Associated with Abuse and Neglect

[U]nderstanding the factors that contribute to maltreatment and that shape its consequences for children is crucial to the development of prevention and treatment approaches. For instance, the likelihood that an individual child will experience abuse or neglect may be influenced by the characteristics of the parent or caregiver. . . .

Caregiver Characteristics

A wide variety of characteristics of the child's parents or caregivers have been linked to an increased likelihood of child abuse or neglect. For instance, individual attributes such as low self-esteem, poor impulse control, aggressiveness, anxiety, and depression often characterize maltreating parents of caregivers. Inaccurate knowledge of child development, inappropriate expectations of the child, and negative attitudes toward parenting contribute to child-rearing problems, as well. . . .

Domestic violence involving the child's caregiver is a problem that is more likely to contribute to physical abuse than neglect. [B]etween 1.5 and 3.3 million children in the United States witness domestic violence each year. Not only is the experience of witnessing violence likely to be psychologically harmful, but several studies have found that male batterers are more likely than other men to physically abuse their children. Women who are victims of domestic violence are also more likely to be reported for maltreating their children.

<u>Substance</u> abuse by the parent or caregiver is strongly associated with child maltreatment. Current estimates indicate that between 50 and 80% of families involved with child protective services are dealing with a substance-abuse problem. . . .

Socioeconomic Characteristics

[R]esearchers have focused on the relationship between child maltreatment and [poverty]. Although child abuse and neglect occur in families of all income brackets, cases of child maltreatment are drawn disproportionately from lower-income families. . . .

No one fully understands the links between poverty and maltreatment. The stress and frustrations of living in poverty may combine with attitudes toward the use of corporal punishment to increase the risk of physical violence. For instance, researchers have found that unemployment can lead to family stress and to child abuse. When a family lacks the basic resources needed to provide for a child, neglect is likely, although researchers suggest that dynamics over and above poverty (such as disorganization and social isolation) differentiate neglecting families from others. Indeed, most poor people do not mistreat their children. The effects of poverty appear to interact with other risk factors such as unrealistic expectations, depression, isolation, substance abuse, and domestic violence to increase the likelihood of maltreatment.

Child Characteristics

Studies suggest that young children, girls, premature infants, and children with more irritable temperaments are more vulnerable to abuse and neglect. Girls are more likely to suffer from sexual abuse than boys, but other types of maltreatment affect both sexes about equally. Maltreated infants and young children are significantly more likely to be reported to CPS agencies than are older children. About 16 per 1,000 children under age one were involved in substantiated reports in 1994, compared to only 9 per 1,000 adolescents ages 16 to 18. The youngest children, whose bodies are fragile, more often die from maltreatment: 45% of the maltreatment-related fatalities from 1993 to 1995 involved infants, and 85% involved children under age five.

Consequences of Child Maltreatment

. . . The psychological, emotional, or physical damage that a child suffers as a result of maltreatment depends on aspects of the abuse itself and on the child's stage of development. It should be noted that most research on maltreated children comes through clinical studies of young children who have been referred for treatment, who are typically those exhibiting the most serious behavioral problems. Moreover, most of the children studied are involved with public child welfare agencies and come from families of lower socioeconomic status and minority populations. For both reasons, the findings summarized below may not reflect the consequences of child maltreatment for the entire population of abused and neglected children.

In some cases, children do not appear to exhibit significant effects from maltreatment. These children may have been buffered by personal characteristics such as optimism, high self-esteem, high cognitive ability, or a sense of hopefulness despite their circumstances. Damaging effects may be limited if the abuse occurs only once, or if a supportive adult is available who lets the child feel he or she is believed and will be protected. In some cases, however, effects of abuse may surface long after the experience. For example, some preadolescent sexual-abuse victims do not exhibit the effects of the abusive relationship until adolescence or adulthood, when they become involved in intimate relationships.

Other children who suffer maltreatment evidence signs of serious emotional or physical harm. . . . Lasting growth retardation may result when the caregiver's feeding of an infant becomes disturbed; this response to neglect is called nonorganic failure to thrive. Other physical sequelae can affect victims of sexual abuse, who may become infected with sexually transmitted diseases.

Psychological problems are prevalent among victims of maltreatment. Physically abused children tend to be aggressive toward peers and adults, to have difficulty with peer relations, and to show a diminished capacity for empathy toward others. Studies of neglected toddlers show that their ability to trust others is often impaired. This may lead to feelings of being unloved and unwanted, and may inhibit the development of the social skills needed to form healthy relationships with peers and adults. When a child cannot master developmental tasks (like learning to trust) at the appropriate age, the accomplishment of later tasks becomes more difficult throughout the life span.

As they get older, children who have been abused and neglected are more likely to perform poorly in school and to commit crimes against persons. They more often experience emotional problems, depression, suicidal thoughts, sexual problems, and alcohol/substance abuse. Some children internalize reactions to maltreatment by becoming depressed or experiencing eating disorders, sleep disruption, and alcohol/drug abuse. Others externalize their reactions by engaging in physical aggression, shoplifting or committing other crimes, or attempting suicide. Retrospective studies of adults who were mistreated as children reveal a similar array of short- and long-term impairments.

As can be seen from this brief description, the effects of maltreatment on children are often severe and long-lasting, although for any given child, the consequences of abuse or neglect will be shaped by the intensity, duration, and type of abuse; the presence of supportive adults; and the age of the child at the time. The fact that each child and maltreatment experience is unique means that each child requires individual assessment and tailored supports. . . .

3. Discovery of Abuse: Reporting Laws

Ham v. Hospital of Morristown
917 F. Supp. 531 (E.D. Tenn. 1995)

JARVIS, Chief Judge.

. . . Plaintiffs allege that on March 21, 1993, the minor plaintiff, Desiree Levon Ham, who was then 16 months old, was brought to the emergency room of defendant Lakeway Regional Hospital in Morristown, Tennessee, by her mother Claudine D. Griffin. Ms. Griffin informed the hospital personnel that Desiree had been experiencing nausea and vomiting over the two to three preceding days. Desiree was then admitted to the hospital under the primary care of defendant Dan E. Hale, O.D.

On March 22, Desiree was seen in consultation by defendant <u>David V. Willbanks, M.D.</u>, a pediatrician, and by defendant <u>Everett G. Lynch, M.D.</u>, a family practice physician. Plaintiffs further allege that, during the course of Desiree's hospitalization, the defendants or their representatives all observed the child and noted that she had blisters on the palms and fingers of both hands. She also had an abrasion on her forehead. Desiree's mother was at a loss to explain these injuries, except to say that there was a mouse in the house and to speculate that Desiree might have been bitten by that mouse. At any rate, Desiree was treated for acute gastroenteritis for the next few days, improved, and was discharged on March 26 to her mother.

Two days later, on March 28, Ms. Griffin brought Desiree to the emergency room of the Morristown-Hamblen Hospital in an "unresponsive state and suffering seizures." Desiree was subsequently transferred to the East Tennessee Children's Hospital in Knoxville, Tennessee, where she was evaluated and placed in intensive care, apparently the victim of extreme child abuse. Desiree is presently afflicted with severe, irreversible brain damage as a result of this abuse. The complaint alleges that these injuries were sustained by Desiree after she was released from Lakeway Regional Hospital into the custody of her mother on March 26.

Ms. Griffin was subsequently charged with child abuse, although those charges have now been dismissed. The Hamblen County grand jury has since returned an indictment against Charles Ryan Dixon [the mother's boyfriend] for aggravated child abuse involving Desiree. Desiree has now been placed in the physical and legal custody of her paternal grandmother, Daisy Nadine Ham, who has brought this action on Desiree's behalf. [Physicians and hospital personnel moved to dismiss or for summary judgment.]

Before addressing whether Tenn. Code Ann. §37-1-403 creates a private cause of action, the court will turn briefly to defendants' contention that there is no common law duty to report suspected child abuse to anyone. The law is well settled in Tennessee that, in a cause of action for negligence, there must first be a duty of care owed by the defendant to the plaintiff. Thus, where there is no duty, then there can be no negligence. [T]he common law of Tennessee does not impose a duty on a treating physician to either report suspected child abuse or to prevent any such child abuse. This void in the common law was filled by the Tennessee legislature when it enacted Part 4 of the chapter in the [Tenn. Code Ann. §§37-1-101 through 616, which summarizes] the duty owed by the defendants in this case . . . : "*Mandatory* Child Abuse Reports." T.C.A. §37-1-401 (emphasis added). The specific subsection relied upon by plaintiffs is set forth in T.C.A. §37-1-403 ("Reporting of brutality, abuse, neglect or child sexual abuse"). This statute provides in pertinent part as follows:

(a) Any person, including, but not limited to, any:
　　(1) Physician, osteopath, medical examiner, chiropractor, nurse or hospital personnel engaged in the admission, examination, care or treatment of persons;
　　. . . having knowledge of or called upon to render aid to any child who is suffering from or has sustained any wound, injury, disability, or physical or mental condition which is of such a nature as to reasonably indicate that it has been caused by brutality, abuse or neglect or which on the basis of available

information reasonably appears to have been caused by brutality, abuse or neglect, shall report such harm immediately, by telephone or otherwise, to the judge having juvenile jurisdiction or to the county office of the department or to the office of the sheriff or the chief law enforcement official of the municipality where the child resides. . . .

There is no question, therefore, that this statute creates a duty on the part of these defendants; however, the issue to be determined by this court with respect to the pending motions is whether this statute creates a private cause of action.

In support of their position, defendants rely on a number of cases from other jurisdictions which clearly hold that similar reporting statutes do not create a private cause of action. See, e.g., Thelma D. v. Board of Education of City of St. Louis, 669 F. Supp. 947, 950 (E.D. Mo. 1987) (following Doe "A" v. Special School District of St. Louis County, 637 F. Supp. 1138 (E.D. Mo. 1986)). In fact, only one jurisdiction has held that a mandatory child abuse reporting statute creates a private cause of action under common law. See Landeros v. Flood, 551 P.2d 389 (Cal. 1976). There is also *dicta* in Doran v. Priddy, 534 F. Supp. 30, 33 (D. Kan. 1981), which indicates that court's willingness to follow *Landeros* had the issue been raised. Otherwise, there are no other courts outside of Tennessee which have held that a private cause of action is created for a child by a statute requiring a professional to report physical injuries to children which appear to have been inflicted other than by an accident.[*] Thus, if this court were to be persuaded simply by the weight of the authority on one side or the other of this issue from other jurisdictions, then defendants would readily prevail on their motion to dismiss.

However, as previously noted, the law of this case is controlled by Tennessee case law which interprets this reporting statute. [I]n Doe v. Coffee County Board of Education, 852 S.W.2d 899 (Tenn. Ct. App. 1992), the Court of Appeals for the Middle Section appears to have answered [affirmatively] the question presently confronting this court. In *Coffee County*, four students and their parents filed suit against the boys' basketball coach of the Manchester Central High School ("MCHS"), because of the coach's improper sexual activities with the students. Suit was also filed against the school board and four school employees [for failure to report the sexual misconduct and take appropriate action].

Finally, defendants contend that no private right of action can be created by the reporting statute because it is not designed to protect any particular class of people — rather, it is designed to protect the general public. The court disagrees. T.C.A. §37-1-402(a) sets forth the purpose and the focus of the reporting statute:

> The purpose of this part is to protect children whose physical or mental health and welfare are adversely affected by brutality, abuse or neglect by requiring reporting of suspected cases by any person having cause to believe that such case exists. It is intended that, as a result of such reports, the protective services of the state shall be brought to bear on the situation to prevent further abuses, to safeguard and enhance the welfare of children, and to preserve family life. This part shall be administered

[*] Cases which interpret Michigan's child protection law, Mich. Comp. Laws §§722.621, et seq., are easily distinguishable because that statute specifically provides that the failure to report may result in civil liability.

and interpreted to provide the greatest possible protection as promptly as possible for children.

The reporting statute, therefore, is not intended for the protection of the general public. It is intended to protect children only and, more specifically, those children who are the victims of brutality, neglect, and physical and sexual abuse. . . . In sum, while the court acknowledges that the defendants have raised many forceful arguments in support of their position that the reporting statute does not create a private cause of action, the court concludes that these arguments do not circumvent the clear import of the *Coffee County* case: the reporting statute creates a legal obligation to report suspected brutality, neglect, or physical or sexual abuse of children and the failure to report "can give rise to liability. . . ." *Coffee County*, 852 S.W.2d at 909. Defendants' motions to dismiss on this basis must therefore be denied.

[T]he inquiry now becomes whether, as with any other negligence claim, plaintiffs can establish that the failure to report the child abuse has proximately caused the injury to Desiree. If there is no proximate causation, then there can be no civil damage liability. . . . In support of their motion for summary judgment, the defendant doctors have filed their affidavits. The doctors admit that they saw blisters on Desiree's hands; however, they further opined that there was nothing about those blisters which indicated that they were caused by trauma. Rather, in the doctors' opinions, they were caused by Desiree's documented internal problems, i.e., viral gastroenteritis. The doctors also admit that Desiree had a bruise or abrasion on the left side of her forehead.

In response, plaintiffs have filed the affidavits of Carol M. White, a registered nurse, and Dr. Larry E. Wolfe, a family practitioner who has emergency room experience. In the court's opinion, these affidavits easily raise a genuine issue of material fact as to whether the defendant doctors should have been put on notice that Desiree was the victim of abuse. For example, Dr. Wolfe testifies that, within a reasonable degree of medical certainty, Desiree's "diarrhea could have been caused due to the stress from trauma." Dr. Wolfe further testifies as follows:

> No lab work was ordered in the Emergency Room, thus there was no monitoring of electrolytes. After admission, the lab work showed an elevated white blood cell count with lymphocytes being significantly elevated, indicative of an inflammatory process. Desiree Ham's hepatic enzymes were elevated which led Dr. Lynch to document "suspect hepatitis." The hepatitis survey showed no antibiotics or viruses detected. Possible liver trauma was not noted. In my professional opinion, within a reasonable degree of medical certainty, liver function studies are not this high in viremia. An elevation in liver function studies, which is as significant as this, is indicative of soft tissue injury.

Thus, Dr. Wolfe concludes that Desiree's injuries could have been caused by external trauma. This conclusion therefore creates a genuine issue of material fact as to the reasonableness of the doctors' conclusions that there was no child abuse and, consequently, no duty to report these injuries to one of the authorities enumerated by statute. Thus, defendants' motion for summary judgment must be denied.

QUESTIONS ON REPORTING REQUIREMENTS

(1) Mandatory Reporting Laws. Currently, all 50 states have mandatory reporting statutes that require designated individuals to report child abuse to specified authorities (e.g., law enforcement and/or social service agencies). When reporting laws were first enacted in the 1960s, the legislation mandated reporting of *physical* abuse by *physicians.* Since that time, states have broadened the definition of "abuse" and the mandated reporters (to include a variety of professionals). Some states include "any" individual as a designated reporter. See, e.g., Conn. Gen. Stat. Ann. §17a-101(b) (West 2003 & Supp. 2004).

How broadly should legislatures define "abuse"? Should statutory definitions include prenatal abuse? See, e.g., State v. McKnight, 576 S.E.2d 168 (S.C. 2003) (holding that homicide-by-child-abuse statute applied to stillbirth caused by ingestion of cocaine). See generally Deanna Ray Reitman, Note, The Collision Between the Rights of Women, The Rights of the Fetus and the Rights of the State: A Critical Analysis of the Criminal Prosecution of Drug Addicted Pregnant Women, 16 St. John's J. Legal Comment. 267 (2002).

Should statutory definitions include witnessing abuse? States are beginning to incorporate "child exposure to domestic violence" into their statutory definitions of abuse and neglect. See generally Lois A. Weithorn, Protecting Children from Exposure to Domestic Violence: The Use and Abuse of Child Maltreatment Statutes, 53 Hastings L.J. 1 (2001).

Should statutory definitions include prospective abuse of other siblings? See M.W. v. Department of Children & Family Services, p. 266 infra.

Are such broad definitions and the standard that evokes a report ("reasonable cause to suspect" or "reasonable cause to believe") void for vagueness? See State v. Brown, 140 S.W.3d 51 (Mo. 2004). See generally Jessica Ann Toth, Mandated Voices for the Vulnerable: An Examination of the Constitutionality of Missouri's Mandatory Child Abuse Reporting Statute, 72 UMKC L. Rev. 1083 (2004).

What is the purpose of reporting statutes? Given the preceding purpose(s), what are the advantages and disadvantages of enumerating each of the following report recipients (e.g., law enforcement, courts, and social service agencies)? Should the state mandate or merely encourage reporting of child abuse? See Marc A. Franklin & Matthew Ploeger, Of Rescue and Report: Should Tort Law Impose a Duty to Help Endangered Persons or Abused Children?, 40 Santa Clara L. Rev. 991 (2000) (questioning whether a mandate is appropriate).

(2) Liability for Failure to Report. All reporting statutes impose criminal penalties for failure to report child abuse. Only a few jurisdictions, by statute or case law, provide for additional civil liability. Curt Richardson, Comment, Physician/Hospital Liability for Negligently Reporting Child Abuse, 23 J. Legal Med. 131, 135 (2002). The judicial trend rejects a private cause of action. See, e.g., Cuyler v. United States, 362 F.3d 949 (7th Cir. 2004); Welker v. Southern Baptist Hosp. of Fla., Inc., 864 So. 2d 1178 (Fla. Dist. Ct. App. 2004); Meyer v. Lindala, 675 N.W.2d 635 (Minn. Ct. App. 2004).

Is civil and/or criminal liability the appropriate legal response for a designated professional's failure to report child abuse? What purpose of tort law is served by the imposition of liability on reporters? What purposes of the criminal law (e.g., deterrence, rehabilitation) are served by the imposition of penal sanctions against reporters? What are the advantages and disadvantages of invoking civil liability and/or criminal sanctions?

(3) Protection for Failure to Report.   What professionals should be subject to civil and/or criminal sanctions for nonreporting? Should liability extend as far as psychotherapists, clergy, and attorneys? That is, should the reporting obligation take precedence over the evidentiary privilege that attaches to confidential communications made during the relationship of physician-patient, attorney-client, and clergy-parishioner? Does the importance of the traditional evidentiary privileges outweigh the potential benefits to be gained in child protection? How far should liability extend — to babysitters? To "any person"?

(4) Clergy Privilege and Sex Abuse Scandal.   States adopt different approaches to the role of clergy in child abuse reporting. Most states exempt clergy from reporting requirements, whereas some states abrogate the clergy privilege for reporting purposes. In 2002, a large number of claims surfaced that involved sexual molestation of parishioners (mostly adolescent boys) by Catholic priests; claims included allegations of a cover-up by church authorities. See Fox Butterfield, 789 Children Abused by Priests Since 1940, Massachusetts Says, N.Y. Times, July 23, 2003, at A1. In response, many states revised their child abuse laws to strengthen criminal and civil penalties and extended criminal statutes of limitations to facilitate litigation of "stale" claims by victims. At the same time, many states amended their reporting laws to include clergy among mandatory reporters. See generally Susan Mangold, Reforming Child Protection in Response to the Catholic Church Child Abuse Scandal, 14 U. Fla. J.L. & Pub. Pol'y 155 (2003). How can the tension between a child's right to be protected from abuse and the constitutional right of free exercise be reconciled? See Norman Abrams, The Impact of Clergy Sexual Misconduct Litigation on Religious Liberty: Addressing the Tension Between the Clergy Communicant Privilege and the Duty to Report Child Abuse in State Statutes, 44 B.C. L. Rev. 1127 (2003).

(5) Immunity for Erroneous Reports.   Persons who file reports that are subsequently determined to be erroneous often are granted immunity from civil liability. Whereas a few states grant absolute immunity, most provide for immunity only where the report was made either from "reasonable cause" or in "good faith." Compare Cal. Penal Code §11164 (West 2000 & Supp. 2004) (absolute immunity) with Rine v. Chase, 765 N.Y.S.2d 648 (App. Div. 2003) ("good faith"). What are the advantages and disadvantages of granting absolute immunity from liability?

(6) Sanctions for a Parent's Failure to Protect.   In the *Ham* case, note that Ms. Griffin and her boyfriend originally were both charged with the crime of child abuse (although the charges against her were later dropped). Considerable controversy exists about the extent of liability for a mother who fails to protect her child from an abuser. If the mother fails to act, should she be liable for neglect or "passive" abuse? If so, should it matter if she is a victim of abuse herself? What should be the disposition in such cases? Should the child be removed from the mother's custody? See Nicholson v. Williams, 203 F. Supp. 2d 153 (E.D.N.Y. 2002) (finding that state agency's procedure of removal of children from battered mothers' custody solely on the ground of neglect violates substantive and procedural due process). Should the mother's parental rights be terminated? If the child dies as a result of the

abuse, should the passive mother be charged with murder? See Maureen K. Collins, Comment, Nicholson v. Williams: Who Is Failing to Protect Whom? Collaborating the Agendas of Child Welfare Agencies and Domestic Violence Services to Better Protect and Support Battered Mothers and Their Children, 38 New Eng. L. Rev. 725 (2004); Jeanne A. Fugate, Note, Who's Failing Whom? A Critical Look at Failure-to-Protect Laws, 76 N.Y.U. L. Rev. 272 (2001).

(7)   Keep in mind that a juvenile court may assume jurisdiction over an abused or neglected child and may remove such a child from parental custody. Indeed, child abuse can lead to the termination of parental rights. These issues are explored, infra.

4.   The Central Registry

Many states have incorporated into their reporting law a requirement that some state agency maintain a register of all reported cases of suspected child abuse.[10] The central registry originally was designed to act both as a central warehouse for statistical data to help ascertain the incidence and nature of child abuse, and as a practical tool for assisting professionals, allowing them to determine whether a particular child has been previously abused or neglected and to keep track of parents previously suspected of child abuse. More recently, social service agencies also rely on child abuse registries to identify and preclude individuals with abusive propensities from working in the field of child care. Central registries are not without their problems, as the following case reveals.

Valmonte v. Bane
18 F.3d 992 (2d Cir. 1994)

ALTIMARI, Circuit Judge.

[Plaintiff Anna Valmonte appeals the dismissal of her claim against the Commissioner of the New York Department of Social Services alleging that the inclusion of her name in the state central registry violated her due process rights.] The major issue presented in this appeal is whether the state's maintenance of a Central Register that identifies individuals accused of child abuse or neglect, and its communication of the names of those on the list to potential employers in the child care field, implicates a protectible liberty interest under the Fourteenth Amendment. If so, we must also determine whether the state's statutory procedures established to protect the liberty interest are constitutionally adequate. . . .

The Central Register procedures are triggered by reports to the Central Register of suspected child abuse. The state DSS maintains a telephone hotline with a toll-free telephone number that is staffed full-time in order to receive complaints. State law places an affirmative duty on designated individuals such as health care workers,

---

[10] Forty-three states and the District of Columbia have statutes establishing a central registry. U.S. Dept. of Health & Human Services, National Clearinghouse on Child Abuse and Neglect (NCCAN) Information, Statutes at a Glance, Disclosure of Confidential Records (June 2002) (available at *http://www.calib.com/nccanch/pubs/sag/confide.pdf* (last visited Oct. 13, 2004).

social workers, law enforcement agents, judicial officers, and education employees to report to the Central Register whenever they have reasonable cause to suspect that a child is maltreated. Calls to the hotline can be made, however, by any individuals, not only those with affirmative duties of reporting.

Upon receiving a complaint of suspected child abuse, hotline operators must determine whether the allegations, if true, would be legally sufficient to constitute child abuse. If so, the operator records the complaint on paper and relays it to the appropriate county or local DSS. The local DSS is responsible for investigating all complaints of suspected child maltreatment, and must investigate the truth of the charges and complete an investigation within 60 days.

At the conclusion of the investigation, the local department must determine whether the complaint is "unfounded" or "indicated." Unfounded reports are expunged from the Central Register and all records destroyed. If the local DSS finds that there is "some credible evidence" to support the complaint, the complaint is marked "indicated" and the individual who is the subject of the report is listed on the Central Register.

[T]he information in the Central Register is generally confidential. The names of individuals on the Central Register are not publicly available, although there are numerous exceptions for, among others, public agencies, law enforcement personnel, and judicial officers.

More significant, for purposes of this case, are the statutory provisions requiring certain employers in the child care field to make inquiries to the Central Register to determine whether potential employees are among those listed. The purpose of these provisions is to ensure that individuals on the Central Register do not become or stay employed or licensed in positions that allow substantial contact with children. . . .

When such employers make an inquiry, the state DSS will inform the potential employer if the individual is the subject of an indicated report on the Central Register. The state DSS will not inform the employer of the nature of the indicated report, but only that the report exists. If the potential employee is on the list, the employer can only hire the individual if the employer "maintain[s] a written record, as part of the application file or employment record, of the specific reasons why such person was determined to be appropriate" for working in the child or health care field. . . . SSL §424-a(2)(a). . . .

Valmonte became entangled in this system on November 30, 1989, when she slapped her eleven-year-old daughter Vanessa on the side of her face with an open hand. Valmonte states in her complaint that she slapped Vanessa because Vanessa had been caught stealing and other forms of discipline had not been successful. An unidentified employee at Vanessa's school made a complaint to the child abuse hotline that Valmonte had mistreated her daughter. Subsequently, child abuse investigators . . . concluded that Valmonte had engaged in "excessive corporal punishment," marked the complaint against her as "indicated," and commenced child protective proceedings against her.

The New York state family court subsequently dismissed the child protective proceedings against Valmonte on the condition that the Valmonte family receive counselling. This dismissal, however, had no impact on Valmonte's inclusion on the Central Register.

During this time, Valmonte requested expungement of her indicated report from the state DSS. This request was denied. Valmonte then exercised her right to an administrative hearing before an agent of the state DSS. The state DSS again denied expungement, finding some credible evidence to support the allegations. . . .

I. Does Disclosure Violate a Liberty Interest? . . .

A. Ripeness

The appellees [first] contend that Valmonte's claim is not ripe because Valmonte has not actually been deprived of employment or suffered any other injury. They argue that Valmonte has not made a showing that she has even looked for a job in the field of child care, and that she has only alleged that she had been a "paraprofessional in the school system" in the past.

As Valmonte responds, however, it is not necessary that she wait until she is actually injured to file this suit. . . .

In this case, Valmonte has sufficiently alleged facts that give rise to an existing controversy. We must accept as true Valmonte's assertions that she would look for a position in the child care field but for her presence on the Central Register. Should she apply for a position within the child care field, her chosen field, her potential employer will by operation of law automatically find out that she is named on the Central Register. If that happens, she will suffer at the very least the injury caused by the stigma of being placed on the list, and it is also likely that the employer will choose not to hire her due to her status.

Her presence on the Central Register, therefore, is a direct threat not only to her reputation but to her employment prospects. . . .

B. Whether Valmonte Has a Liberty Interest

The central issue in this case is whether Valmonte has sufficiently alleged the deprivation of a protected liberty interest. Valmonte's strongest argument on this issue is that the state's dissemination of information from the list to potential employers in the child care field not only stigmatizes those on the list but also denies them employment in their chosen field.

The question of whether one's good name and standing, and the interest in protecting that reputation, constitutes a protectible liberty interest has been considered in a string of Supreme Court and Second Circuit cases [which have held] loss of reputation must be coupled with some other tangible element in order to rise to the level of a protectible liberty interest. We have previously interpreted this holding to mean that "stigma plus" is required to establish a constitutional deprivation. See Neu v. Corcoran, 869 F.2d 662, 667 (2d Cir.), *cert. denied*, 493 U.S. 816 (1989). Consequently, we will examine Valmonte's claim first to determine whether inclusion on the Central Register constitutes "stigma," and then to determine whether the "plus" requirement has been satisfied. . . .

There is no dispute that Valmonte's inclusion on the list potentially damages her reputation by branding her as a child abuser, which certainly calls into question her "good name, reputation, honor, or integrity." Board of Regents v. Roth, 408 U.S.

564, 573 (1972) (quoting Wisconsin v. Constantineau, 400 U.S. 433, 437 (1971)). The state contends, however, that there is no "stigma" attached to her inclusion because there is no disclosure of information on the Central Register except to authorized state agencies or potential employers in the child care field.

Dissemination to potential employers, however, is the precise conduct that gives rise to stigmatization. . . . In the instant situation, although Valmonte's presence on the Central Register will not be disclosed to the public, it will be disclosed to any employer statutorily required to consult the Central Register. Since Valmonte states that she will be applying for child care positions, her status will automatically be disclosed to her potential employers. [T]hat dissemination satisfies the "stigma" requirement.

Because Valmonte has sufficiently alleged the defamation prong of the "stigma plus" test, we must now determine whether the second part of that test is met. [O]ur prior decisions indicate . . . that defamation is simply not enough to support a cognizable liberty interest.

. . . The Central Register does not simply defame Valmonte, it places a tangible burden on her employment prospects. Valmonte has alleged that because of her inclusion on the Central Register, and because all child care providers must consult that list, she will not be able to get a job in the child care field. In other words, by operation of law, her potential employers will be informed specifically about her inclusion on the Central Register and will therefore choose not to hire her. Moreover, if they do wish to hire her, those employers are required by law to explain the reasons why in writing.

This is not just the intangible deleterious effect that flows from a bad reputation. Rather, it is a specific deprivation of her opportunity to seek employment caused by a statutory impediment established by the state. . . .

This statutory scheme is unique . . . in that there will be no question in most cases whether the individual's inclusion on the Central Register was a causal factor in the individual's failure to secure employment, because SSL §424-a(2)(b)(i) requires that employers notify potential employees if they have been denied employment because of their presence on the list. Therefore, individuals on the Central Register who lose employment opportunities would have received offers but for their inclusion on the list. . . .

We hold that Valmonte has adequately stated a cause of action for deprivation of a liberty interest. . . .

II. Procedural Due Process

Even though the Central Register implicates Valmonte's liberty interest, Valmonte still must show that the procedural safeguards of her interest established by the state are insufficient to protect her rights. Valmonte argues that the existing procedures violate due process by prohibiting expungement of a subject's indicated record if there is "any credible evidence" to support the allegation and only holding the county DSS to a higher "preponderance of the evidence" standard after a subject loses an opportunity for employment.

[T]he statutory framework for the Central Register sets out the following procedural steps for the placement of an individual's name on the list:

1. Hotline Phone call to Central Register hotline, which requires the operator to make a determination on the complaint about whether to pass it on to the appropriate county DSS.

2. Investigation County DSS investigation, which must be completed in 60 days, and must determine whether a complaint is "unfounded" or "indicated" based on "some credible evidence."

3. State DSS Review Upon Request. If "indicated," the subject of the report has 90 days to request that the report be expunged. If a request is made, the state DSS has to conduct a review, determining whether there is "some credible evidence" for the allegations.

4. Administrative Hearing. If the expungement request is denied, an administrative hearing is held where the local DSS must prove the allegations by "some credible evidence."

5. Article 78 Proceeding. If the expungement request is again denied, the subject can commence an Article 78 proceeding, under the "arbitrary and capricious" standard.

6. Second Administrative Hearing. This is only for those who are denied employment based on their placement on the list. The hearing is to determine whether the person's record will be sealed in the future, although the name would still be on the list. The standard of proof in this hearing is "fair preponderance of the evidence."

The standards for evaluating the constitutionality of these procedures are clear. In Mathews v. Eldridge, 424 U.S. 319, 335 (1976), the Supreme Court articulated a three-factor test for evaluating administrative procedures, requiring examination of: (1) the nature of the private interest affected by the official action; (2) the risk of error and the effect of additional procedural safeguards; and (3) the governmental interest. We must balance these factors. . . .

The deciding factor in this case, the one that clearly shows the inadequacy of the procedural protections established by the state, is the enormous risk of error that has been alleged by Valmonte and acknowledged by the appellees. As noted earlier, the state only requires that the local DSS meet the "some credible evidence" standard in order to initially include a subject on the Central Register or to keep the subject on the list at the non-deprivation administrative hearing. It is only later, at the post-deprivation hearing, when the subject has already been denied employment due to his or her inclusion on the Central Register, that the local DSS is required to prove the allegations against the subject by a "fair preponderance of the evidence."

The distinction between the two standards is significant. Valmonte points out that, according to her figures, nearly 75% of those who seek expungement of their names from the list are ultimately successful. Half of that number obtain expungement only after they have lost employment or prospective employment because of their inclusion on the Central Register. This means that roughly one-third of those initially placed on the Central Register are eventually removed once the local DSS is required to prove the charges against the subject by a fair preponderance of the evidence. The fact that only 25% of those on the list remain after all administrative proceedings have been concluded indicates that the initial determination made by the local DSS is at best imperfect. . . .

Considering the minimal standard of proof, and the subjective nature of the inquiry, it is not altogether surprising that there is such a high risk of error. Another fact adduced at oral argument and noted in the record is that there are roughly 2,000,000 individuals on the rolls of the Central Register. This staggering figure has been cited to us by Valmonte, but it was not contested at oral argument. We find it difficult to fathom how such a huge percentage of New Yorkers could be included on a list of those suspected of child abuse and neglect, unless there has been a high rate of error in determinations. In any event, we rely more on the 75% than on the two million figure, the authenticity of which we are inclined to doubt.

The appellees, remarkably, do not challenge these figures, but argue that there is no real deprivation in cases where individuals contest the initial inclusion on the Central Register. According to the appellees, the subjects are not deprived of anything if their names are taken off the list. Moreover, they assert that the fact that reports are eventually expunged demonstrates that the state's procedures are working to correct mistakes in the original determination.

This is an inherently contradictory argument by the state. To argue that the extraordinarily high percentage of reversals supports the fairness of the system, as a desirable feature of that system, is a curious defense of administrative procedures. One does not normally purchase a car from a dealer who stresses that his repair staff routinely services and repairs the model after frequent and habitual breakdowns. If 75% of those challenging their inclusion on the list are successful, we cannot help but be skeptical of the fairness of the original determination. . . .

analogy

We hold that the high risk of error produced by the procedural protections established by New York is unacceptable. While the two interests at stake are fairly evenly balanced, the risk of error tilts the balancing test heavily in Valmonte's favor. . . .

For these reasons, we reverse the judgment of the district court and remand for further proceedings not inconsistent with this opinion. Although we recognize the grave seriousness of the problems of child abuse and neglect, and the need for the state to maintain a Central Register for ensuring that those with abusive backgrounds not be inadvertently given access to children, we find the current system unacceptable.

NOTES AND QUESTIONS ON CENTRAL REGISTRIES

(1) Early Problems. Soon after the enactment of central registries, commentators recognized their shortcomings, including: (a) the lack of an opportunity to challenge inclusion, (b) the broad criteria for inclusion, (c) the limited right of access to included information, and, (d) the inadequacy of expungement procedures. Gail Garringer & James N. Hyde, Child Abuse and the Central Registry, in Child Abuse: Intervention and Treatment 171-175 (Nancy B. Ebeling & Deborah A. Hill eds., 1975).

(2) Existing Shortcomings. Some of these early defects were corrected by statutory amendments. However, substantial problems persist, including: (a) significant delays in the expungement process, (b) the lack of predeprivation hearings in some states, (c) the low standard of proof for inclusion (as in *Valmonte*),

(d) inadequate notice of inclusion, and (e) the existence of a conflict of interest if the same official functions as investigator and adjudicator. Kate Hollenbeck, Between a Rock and a Hard Place: Child Abuse Registries at the Intersection of Child Protection, Due Process, and Equal Protection, 11 Tex. J. Women & L. 1, 16 (2001).

(3) Constitutionality of Central Registries.

a. Substantive Due Process.   *Valmonte* is one of several substantive and procedural due process challenges to registry statutes. See also Covell v. Department of Soc. Servs., 791 N.E.2d 877 (Mass. 2003); Benitez v. Rasmussen, 626 N.W.2d 209 (Neb. 2001). Most courts agree with *Valmonte* that inclusion in a registry that is accessible to employers does implicate the individual's due process rights to both employment and reputation. Hollenbeck, supra, at 23.

b. Procedural Due Process: Standard of Proof.   Following *Valmonte*, New York changed its standard of proof. The "some credible evidence" standard still applies to the filing of information at the early stages of an investigation. However, the "fair preponderance of the evidence" standard applies to determine whether an individual's name may be used for employment screening. What should be the standard of proof to determine whether there is sufficient evidence to include an individual in the registry? Should the standard be a "preponderance," as *Valmonte* suggests? Given the high number of unsubstantiated reports, should the standard be raised to "clear and convincing evidence"?

c. Procedural Due Process: Expungement.   CAPTA provides for expungement of records of child maltreatment in cases that are unsubstantiated or false. See 42 U.S.C. §5106(b)(2)(A)(xii) (2000) (requiring "prompt expungement of any records that are accessible to the general public or are used for purposes of employment or other background checks in cases determined to be unsubstantiated or false, except that nothing in this section shall prevent State child protective services agencies from keeping information on unsubstantiated reports in their casework files to assist in future risk and safety assessment"). How long should states maintain records of unsubstantiated cases before expungement? See Hollenbeck, supra, at 17 (practices range from 30 days to ten years).

(4) Equal Protection Challenges.   Some courts and commentators criticize child abuse procedures as a violation of equal protection, claiming that the procedures discriminate on the basis of gender, race, and class. See, e.g., People United for Children, Inc. v. City of New York, 108 F. Supp. 2d 275 (2000), Yuan v. Rivera, 48 F. Supp. 2d 335 (1999). Do you agree that strenthening procedural protections, such as central registries, "may reduce the incidence of racial, gender, and socioeconomic bias in child abuse investigations"? Hollenbeck, supra, at 34. If you were advising a state legislator, how would you suggest the registry statute be improved?

NOTE: SANCTIONS FOR FAILURE OF STATE TO ACT AFTER REPORT: DESHANEY v. WINNEBAGO COUNTY

Once a case of child abuse has been reported, does the child have a constitutional right to protection from the State? The Supreme Court addressed this issue in DeShaney v. Winnebago County Department of Social Services, 489 U.S. 189 (1989). A report of paternal abuse of two-year-old Joshua was made to the

Wisconsin Department of Social Services (DSS) in January 1982. After the father denied the charges, DSS dropped the case. However, after more reports of abuse, a caseworker was assigned to make monthly visits. During those visits, she noted numerous injuries to the child, although she never took any action to remove the child from the home. Two years later the child was beaten so severely by his father that the resulting brain damage left him retarded. Joshua and his mother filed an action under 42 U.S.C. §1983 claiming that the child had been deprived of his liberty without due process because of DSS's failure to protect him.

In an opinion by Chief Justice Rehnquist, the Court held that a State does not have a duty to protect an individual unless the State has taken him into custody against his will. Some active interference by the State is required because "[t]he affirmative duty to protect arises not from the State's knowledge of the individual's predicament or from its expressions of intent to help him, but from the limitation which it has imposed on his freedom to act on his own behalf." 489 U.S. at 200. No such limitation was found in this case because "[t]he most that can be said of the state functionaries . . . is that they stood by and did nothing when suspicious circumstances dictated a more active role." Id. at 203.

In the dissent, Justice Brennan (joined by Justices Marshall and Blackmun) found that DSS *had* limited Joshua's ability to act on his own behalf because, under Wisconsin law, only DSS handles child abuse cases. Once DSS receives a report, citizens and other governmental agencies feel their job is done. "If DSS ignores or dismisses . . . suspicions, no one will step in to fill the gap." Id. at 210. As the dissent stated, "[u]nfortunately for Joshua DeShaney, the buck effectively stopped with the Department." Id. at 209.

DeShaney left unresolved the question of which custodial relationships, short of incarceration, might trigger an affirmative obligation on the part of the state to protect children from abuse. For example, does the state have an affirmative duty to protect children placed in foster care? See, e.g., Burton v. Richmond, 276 F.3d 973 (8th Cir. 2002); Howard v. Malac, 270 F. Supp. 2d 132 (D. Mass. 2003) (both recognizing foster child's due process right). See generally Christine Dine, Protecting Those Who Cannot Protect Themselves: State Liability for Violation of Foster Children's Right to Safety, 38 Cal. W. L. Rev. 507 (2002). For further discussion of issues regarding foster care, see section E infra.

5. An Agenda for Reform

Douglas J. Besharov, Child Abuse Realities: Over-Reporting and Poverty

8 Va. J. Soc. Pol'y & L. 165, 188-192, 196-203 (2000)

For thirty years, advocates, program administrators, and politicians have joined the cause to encourage even more reports of suspected child abuse and neglect. [T]heir efforts have been spectacularly successful, with about three million children now reported each year. . . . All states now have specialized child protective agencies to receive and investigate reports, and treatment services for maltreated children and their parents have been expanded substantially. [However, at the present time] concerns other than non-reporting should come to the fore.

A. The Costs of Inappropriate Reports

The determination that a report is unfounded can only be made after an unavoidably traumatic investigation that is, inherently, a breach of parental and family privacy. To determine whether a particular child is in danger, caseworkers must inquire into the most intimate personal and family matters. Often, it is necessary to question friends, relatives, and neighbors, as well as school teachers, day care personnel, doctors, clergy, and others who know the family.

Laws against child abuse are an implicit recognition that family privacy must give way to the need to protect helpless children. But in seeking to protect children, it is all too easy to ignore the legitimate rights of parents. Each year, about 700,000 families are put through investigations of unfounded reports. This is a massive and unjustified violation of parental rights. . . .

The current flood of unfounded reports is overwhelming the limited resources of child protective agencies. For fear of missing even one abused child, workers perform extensive investigations of vague and apparently unsupported reports. Even when a home visit based on an anonymous report turns up no evidence of maltreatment, workers usually interview neighbors, schoolteachers, and day-care personnel to make sure that the child is not abused. And even repeated anonymous and unfounded reports do not prevent a further investigation. But all of this takes time.

As a result, children in real danger are getting lost in the press of inappropriate cases. Forced to allocate a substantial portion of their limited resources to unfounded reports, child protective agencies are less able to respond promptly and effectively when children are in serious danger. Some reports are left uninvestigated for a week and even two weeks after they are received. Investigations often miss key facts because workers rush to clear cases. Dangerous home situations receive inadequate supervision, as workers must ignore pending cases as they investigate the new reports that arrive daily on their desks. Decision-making also suffers. With so many cases of insubstantial or unproven risk to children, caseworkers are desensitized to the obvious warning signals of immediate and serious danger. . . .

Thirty years ago, even fifteen years ago, . . . this approach may have been needed. Now, all it does is ensure that child abuse hotlines will be flooded with inappropriate and unfounded reports. [A] relatively clear agenda for reform emerges. . . .

1. Clarify child abuse reporting laws

Existing laws are often vague and overbroad. They should be rewritten to provide real guidance about what conditions should, and should not, be reported. This can be accomplished without making a radical departure from present laws or practices. The key is to describe reportable conditions in terms of specific parental behaviors or conditions that are tied to severe and demonstrable harms (or potential harms) to children.

It would help, for example, to make a distinction between (1) direct evidence, meaning firsthand accounts or observations of seriously harmful parental behavior, and (2) circumstantial evidence, meaning concrete facts, such as the child's physical condition, which suggest that the child has been abused or neglected. (Behavioral indicators, however, should not, by themselves, be considered a sufficient basis for a report.) . . .

2. Provide continuing public education and professional training

Few people fail to report because they want children to suffer abuse and neglect. Likewise, few people make deliberately false reports. Most involve an honest desire to protect children coupled with confusion about what conditions are reportable. Thus, educational efforts should emphasize the conditions that do not justify a report, as well as those that do.

3. Screen reports

No matter how well professionals are trained and no matter how extensive public education efforts are, there will always be a tendency for persons to report cases that should not be investigated. Until recently, most states did not have formal policies and procedures for determining whether to accept a call for investigation. Such policies should be adopted by all states and they should provide explicit guidance about the kinds of cases that should not be assigned for investigation.

Reports should be rejected when the allegations fall outside the agency's definitions of "child abuse" and "child neglect," as established by state law. Often, the family has a coping problem for which they would be more appropriately referred to another social service agency. Prime examples include children beyond the specified age, alleged perpetrators falling outside the legal definition, and family problems not amounting to child maltreatment. Reports should also be rejected when the caller can give no credible reason for suspecting that the child has been abused or neglected. (Although actual proof of the maltreatment is not required, some evidence is.) Reports whose unfounded or malicious nature is established by specific evidence, of course, should also be rejected. Anonymous reports, reports from estranged spouses, and even previous unfounded reports from the same source should not be automatically rejected, but they need to be carefully evaluated. And, finally, reports in which insufficient information is given to identify or locate the child should likewise be screened (although the information may be kept for later use if a subsequent report about the same child is made). . . . When appropriate, rejected reports should be referred to other agencies that can provide services needed by the family.

4. Modify liability laws

Current laws provide immunity for anyone who makes a report in good faith, but give no protection to those who, in a good faith exercise of professional judgment, decide that a child has not been abused or neglected and, hence, should not be reported. This combination of immunities and penalties encourages the over-reporting of questionable situations.

5. Give feedback to persons who report — *Privacy concerns?*

If persons who report are not told what happened, they may conclude that the agency's response was ineffective or even harmful to the child, and the next time they suspect that a child is maltreated, they may decide not to report. In addition, finding out whether their suspicions were valid also refines their diagnostic skills and thus improves the quality and accuracy of their future reports. Reporters also need such information to interpret subsequent events and to monitor the child's condition.

6. Adopt an agency policy

Appropriate reporting of suspected child maltreatment requires a sophisticated knowledge of many legal, administrative, and diagnostic matters. To help ensure that staffs respond properly, an increasing number of public and private agencies are adopting formal agency policies about reporting. Some state laws mandate them. The primary purpose of these policies, or agency protocols, is to inform staff members of their obligation to report and of the procedures to be followed. . . .

B. Address Poverty-Related Neglect

In the wake of welfare reform, the ways in which child protective agencies respond to the condition of poverty takes on added importance. [Social agencies] overreact to cases of social deprivation in poor families. In fact, poor, socially deprived children are more likely to be placed in foster care than are abused children. These disadvantaged children, in no real danger of physical injury, languish for years in foster care. Living in emotionally traumatic conditions, hundreds of thousands of poor children suffer more harm than if they were simply left at home.

To say that poor children are inappropriately included in programs for abused and neglected children is not the same as saying that they do not have pressing needs, nor that they should not be the concern of public and private programs. But the nature of the intervention should be different — and it should be voluntary. Child protective agencies have not been established as society's response to poverty, and for them to assume this role misdirects their resources from their proper mission. Dr. Barton Schmitt explains:

> Including [poverty-related cases] in child abuse and neglect investigations will dilute the efforts of child protection units in responding to more serious cases and also lose them the respect of certain constituents of their community. We live in an imperfect world. Neglect is easily confused with poverty, ignorance, or parents who are overwhelmed by other problems. Some ethnic groups have defined neglect as "a failure to live up to the white middle classes' standards." For this reason neglect should not be reported automatically to the child protective service unit. Instead the

family should be offered help, especially financial assistance. Only if the family refuses services for their children, should the child neglect laws be implemented.[120]

Helping these families, usually involving single mothers, does not require mandatory reporting laws, involuntary investigations, central registers of reports, or psychologically oriented "treatment" interventions. In too many instances, such efforts are ineffectual, and even harmful.

Society should acknowledge the overlap between child maltreatment and poverty and adopt intervention strategies that address the families' broader problems. Such strategies might include compensatory child development programs housed in integrated service centers for teen mothers. But, even in the absence of such specialized services, society would do better if it did nothing in poverty-related cases, rather than the wrong — and often harmful — something. When it comes to the plight of these children, we should remember the ancient medical maxim: *Primum, non nocere* — first, do no harm. . . .

Writing almost twenty years ago, Schmitt [supra] concluded that the following factors were prone to over-reporting:

- Clothing neglect: Examples are wearing torn pants, wearing cast-off clothing, or not having a raincoat or gloves.
- Nutritional neglect: Examples are eating unbalanced meals, eating too many "junk foods," or cultural food preferences. Even skipping breakfast can be normal if it's the child's choice. We must remember that approximately one third of adults prefer not to eat breakfast.
- Hygiene neglect: Examples are coming to school with a dirty face, dirty hair, or dirty clothing. If the child is not malodorous and the problem is periodic, it is probably of minimal importance.
- Home environment neglect: Mildly unsanitary homes are quite common. We should not be over critical of housekeeping below standards, such as poorly washed dishes or a house that is covered with dog hair and needs vacuuming.
- Cultural deprivation or intellectual stimulation neglect: This term is often directed at families whose children allegedly are not talked to enough or presented with sufficient creative toys. All too often this term is applied to children with developmental delays due to normal variation or pre-maturity.
- Safety neglect: Many normal accidents are called safety neglect to the detriment of the parents, for example, blaming the parents for burns that occur on space heaters despite numerous precautions the parents have taken. On a practical level, some unsafe environments cannot be changed.
- Minor acute illness neglect: Insect bites, lice, scabies, and impetigo occur in children from all socioeconomic groups. Often parents are blamed for diaper rashes and cradle cap. Parents may be criticized because they have not given their child antipyretics before bringing them to the physician for

[120] Barton D. Schmitt, Child Neglect, in Child Abuse and Neglect: A Medical Reference 297, 305 (Norman S. Ellerstein ed., 1981).

a fever. Parents may be blamed for not coming to the clinic soon enough for an ear infection that they did not know existed. . . .

[I]n assessing such cases, a two-pronged inquiry is appropriate:

(1) Does the care of the child fall below commonly accepted community standards? To justify a report, the deviation must be clear and unambiguous, and should not be the product of responsible differences in culture or lifestyle. . . .

(2) Has the child's physical or mental condition been impaired or is it in danger of being impaired? [U]sing nutrition as an example, if the child seems hungry and emaciated, a report should be made.

Conclusion

This paper has proposed a broad agenda for reform. [M]uch more needs to be done if the nation's child protective system is to meet the high responsibilities assigned to it, without harming some of the children and families entrusted to its care.

6. The Problem of Sexual Abuse

M.W. v. Department of Children & Family Services
881 So. 2d 734 (Fla. Ct. App. 2004)

COPE, J.

M.W. appeals an order adjudicating his three natural daughters dependent. [O]n July 1, 2001, M.W. was arrested for sexual battery on his stepdaughter, J.G. The petition alleges that M.W. had sexual intercourse with his stepdaughter over a three-year period, beginning when the child was ten years old. As to the criminal charges, M.W. was released on bail and the criminal charges remain pending.

The Department filed a petition for dependency as to the stepdaughter J.G. (also referred to as "the stepdaughter") and M.W.'s natural daughters, J.W. 1, J.W. 2, and J.W. 3 (also referred to as "the natural daughters"). With regard to the stepdaughter, M.W. entered a consent plea to the dependency petition. Pursuant to this consent, the stepdaughter was adjudicated dependent as to M.W.

Four days later, the trial court conducted an adjudicatory hearing on the petition for dependency as to M.W.'s natural daughters. They were eight, seven, and three years old at the time of the dependency hearing. M.W. was present at the hearing and represented by counsel, but did not testify.

The trial court received testimony from a psychologist who had evaluated M.W., and took judicial notice of the consent order relating to the stepdaughter. The court entered an order adjudicating the natural daughters dependent as to M.W. The order states, in part:

> . . . 4b. Dr. Schzechowicz testified that there would be a high risk of sexual abuse re-occurring if [M.W.] had access to the Child [J.G.]. As such, no contact with

[J.G.] was recommended. Dr. Schzechowicz further recommended that [M.W.] be ordered to attend and successfully complete the Mentally Disordered Sex Offender (MDSO) Program.

4c. Dr. Schzechowicz testified that even though according to the testing [M.W.] had exhibited a low risk of recidivism [as to the natural daughters], there were concerns regarding his psychological functioning and he presented as a psychological[ly] maladjusted individual. [M.W.] showed no remorse and blamed the victim-child for any alleged misconduct. Hence, the risk to the Children [the natural daughters] according to Dr. Schzechowicz, was increased by [M.W.'s] commission of a similar act on another Child, to-wit: [J.G.], the Children's half-sister.

. . . 6. The Court finds, that based on the totality of the circumstances, and after reviewing the documents admitted into evidence as well as hearing expert testimony on the matter, the risk of imminent sexual abuse to the above captioned Children [the natural daughters] is increased by the Father's commission of a similar act on another Child, to-wit, the Children's half-sibling, [J.G.], his lack of remorse and his psychological functioning.

It is hereby ORDERED and ADJUDGED that the above captioned Children be adjudicated dependent within the meaning and intent of Florida Statutes Chapter 39.

[On appeal] M.W. argues that the evidence was legally insufficient to support the dependency order. He argues that his sexual abuse of his stepdaughter is insufficient to support a dependency adjudication as to his natural daughters. He contends that the psychologist's testimony defeats the Department's petition. We disagree.

The Florida Supreme Court has said, "The purpose of a dependency proceeding is not to punish the offending parent but to protect and care for a child who has been neglected, abandoned, or abused." M.F. v. Florida Department of Children and Families, 770 So. 2d 1189, 1193 (Fla. 2000).

In administering the child protection system, "The health and safety of the children served shall be of paramount concern." Fla. Stat. §39.001(1)(b)1. (2002).

Under the statute, a dependent child includes one who is "at substantial risk of imminent abuse, abandonment, or neglect by the parent or parents or legal custodians." Id. §39.01(14)(f). In making that determination, the trial court is to look at the totality of the circumstances.

M.W. relies on the *M.F.* decision, but that reliance is misplaced. In *M.F.*, the father had sexually abused one of his children, K.F. The father was convicted of sexual battery and imprisoned for fifteen years. K.F. was adjudicated dependent as to the father.

In further proceedings, the trial court found M.F.'s other children dependent, on the theory that the other children were at risk of prospective abuse. Rejecting that rationale for the dependency order, the Florida Supreme Court reasoned that since the father was imprisoned for fifteen years and presumably would have no contact with the children, it would follow that there was no risk of prospective abuse.

The present case differs from *M.F.* In the present case the father is at liberty on bail and there is thus no physical impediment to his having contact with the children. The remaining children are all younger daughters, who are plainly not old enough to protect themselves.

The *M.F.* court ruled that an adjudication of dependency based on the fact that a parent has sexually abused one child is a factor which can be considered in deciding whether the remaining children are at prospective risk. Id. The father has admitted to having repeated sexual intercourse with his stepdaughter and an adjudication of dependency as to that child has been entered.

M.W. argues, however, that the following testimony of the psychologist supports his position that the instant order should be reversed:

Q: Do you have an opinion regarding whether M.W. is at high risk to re-engage in sexually illegal behavior in the future?
A: If you're talking about M.W., and I'm going to make an assumption here that he did engage in the behavior he's charged with, if he actually did this, then if you were to give him unfettered access to the alleged victim in this case, then my opinion is there would be a very high risk to his stepdaughter. If we're talking about the other children, the signs would indicate that he is not a high risk and if these are his natural children. Based on both the Static Actuarial and Dynamic Risk Factors.
Q: Just so that we can be clear. Supposing, let's assume that M.W. is found guilty of this offense that he was arrested and charged with. Is there an increased risk for his natural children?
A: Of course, ma'am. Any time someone engages in sexually inappropriate behavior, the likelihood of future behavior increases. The results of the testing would indicate that the likelihood in terms of his sexually abusing his natural children *is below base rates, but it's not zero, by any means.* [Transcript, Mar. 27, 2003, at 19-20 (emphasis added).]

M.W. argues that since the psychologist said M.W. is not a high risk to his natural children, it follows that the legal standard for a dependency order has not been satisfied. We disagree.

In deciding whether there is a substantial risk of imminent abuse, the trial court is to examine all of the circumstances. This includes the severity of potential harm as well as the likelihood it will occur.

In this case the risk to be protected against is sexual abuse of minor children. It is among the greatest of harms that can be inflicted on children. It is physical harm which is serious criminal conduct.

Because the nature of the harm is so great, it is intolerable to allow even a low probability that M.W. will sexually abuse the other children. The psychologist here testified that while the danger to the natural children was below base rates, *"it's not zero, by any means."* (Emphasis added).

As we interpret M.W.'s position, he wants us to rule that the trial court cannot order protective services unless there is reason to believe that, more probably than not, he will sexually abuse his other children. The contention apparently is that if the likelihood is below fifty percent, then the young children must be left to fend for themselves. That analysis is incorrect under the statute and under the *M.F.* decision.

Quite apart from the psychological evaluation results, in M.W.'s own statements to the psychologist he denied responsibility and blamed the victim. Further, at the time of the proceeding below, treatment in the MDSO program had been recommended, but it is not clear whether treatment had begun. In any event, M.W. had completed no such program. These factors, too, support the conclusion that M.W. cannot be left to his own devices.

The trial court applied the correct legal standard and the dependency order is fully supported by the evidence. Affirmed.

Child Sexual Abuse: Intervention and Treatment Issues (1993)
U.S. Department of Health and Human Services,
National Clearinghouse on Child Abuse and Neglect

Definitions, Scope, and Effects of Child Sexual Abuse . . .

There are two types of statutes in which definitions of sexual abuse can be found — child protection (civil) and criminal. The purposes of these laws differ. Child protection statutes are concerned with sexual abuse as a condition from which children need to be protected. Thus, these laws include child sexual abuse as one of the forms of maltreatment that must be reported by designated professionals and investigated by child protection agencies. Courts may remove children from their homes in order to protect them from sexual abuse. Generally, child protection statutes apply only to situations in which offenders are the children's caretakers.

Criminal statutes prohibit certain sexual acts and specify the penalties. Generally, these laws include child sexual abuse as one of several sex crimes. Criminal statutes prohibit sex with a child, regardless of the adult's relationship to the child, although incest may be dealt with in a separate statute.

Definitions in child protection statutes are quite brief and often refer to State criminal laws for more elaborate definitions. In contrast, criminal statutes are frequently quite lengthy.

Child Protection Definitions

The Federal definition of child maltreatment is included in the Child Abuse Prevention and Treatment Act. Sexual abuse and exploitation is a subcategory of child abuse and neglect. The statute does not apply the maximum age of 18 for other types of maltreatment, but rather indicates that the age limit in the State law shall apply. Sexual abuse is further defined to include:

"(A) the employment, use, persuasion, inducement, enticement, or coercion of any child to engage in, or assist any other person to engage in, any sexually explicit conduct or simulation of such conduct for the purpose of producing a visual depiction of such conduct; or

(B) the rape, molestation, prostitution, or other form of sexual exploitation of children, or incest with children; . . . "

In order for States to qualify for funds allocated by the Federal Government, they must have child protection systems that meet certain criteria, including a definition of child maltreatment specifying sexual abuse.

Criminal Definitions

With the exception of situations involving Native American children, crimes committed on Federal property, interstate transport of minors for sexual purposes, and the shipment or possession of child pornography, State criminal statutes regulate child sexual abuse. Generally, the definitions of sexual abuse found in criminal statutes are very detailed. The penalties vary depending on:

- the age of the child, crimes against younger children being regarded as worse;
- the level of force, force making the crime more severe;
- the relationship between victim and offender, an act against a relative or household member being considered more serious; and
- the type of sexual act, acts of penetration receiving longer sentences.

Often types of sexual abuse are classified in terms of their degree (of severity), first degree being the most serious and fourth degree the least, and class (of felony), a class A felony being more serious than a class B or C, etc. . . .

Prevalence of Child Sexual Abuse

. . . Rates of victimization for females range from 6 to 62 percent, with most professionals estimating that between one in three and one in four women are sexually abused in some way during their childhoods. The rates for men are somewhat lower, ranging from 3 to 24 percent, with most professionals believing that 1 in 10 men and perhaps as many as 1 in 6 are sexually abused as children. As noted earlier, many believe that male victimization is more underreported than female, in part because of societal failure to identify the behavior as abusive. However, the boy himself may not define the behavior as sexual victimization but as sexual experience, especially if it involves a woman offender. Moreover, he may be less likely to disclose than a female victim, because he has been socialized not to talk about his problems. This reticence may be increased if the offender is a male, for he must overcome two taboos, having been the object of a sexual encounter with an adult and a male. Finally, he may not be as readily believed as a female victim. . . .

The Impact of Sexual Abuse

Regardless of the underlying causes of the impact of sexual abuse, the problems are very real for victims and their families. A number of attempts have been made to conceptualize the effects of sexual abuse. In addition, recent efforts to understand the impact of sexual abuse have gone beyond clinical impressions and case studies. They are based upon research findings, specifically controlled research in which sexually abused children are compared to a normal or nonsexually abused clinical population. There are close to 40 such studies to date.

Finkelhor, whose conceptualization of the traumatogenic effects of sexual abuse is the most widely employed, divides sequelae into four general categories, each having varied psychological and behavioral effects.

- *Traumatic sexualization.* Included in the psychological outcomes of traumatic sexualization are aversive feelings about sex, overvaluing sex, and sexual identity problems. Behavioral manifestations of traumatic sexualization constitute a range of hypersexual behaviors as well as avoidance of or negative sexual encounters.
- *Stigmatization.* Common psychological manifestations of stigmatization are what Sgroi calls "damaged goods syndrome" and feelings of guilt and responsibility for the abuse or the consequences of disclosure. These feelings are likely to be reflected in self-destructive behaviors such as substance abuse, risk-taking acts, self-mutilation, suicidal gestures and acts, and provocative behavior designed to elicit punishment.
- *Betrayal.* Perhaps the most fundamental damage from sexual abuse is its undermining of trust in those people who are supposed to be protectors and nurturers. Other psychological impacts of betrayal include anger and borderline functioning. Behavior that reflects this trauma includes avoidance of investment in others, manipulating others, re-enacting the trauma through subsequent involvement in exploitive and damaging relationships, and engaging in angry and acting-out behaviors.
- *Powerlessness.* The psychological impact of the trauma of powerlessness includes both a perception of vulnerability and victimization and a desire to control or prevail, often by identification with the aggressor. As with the trauma of betrayal, behavioral manifestations may involve aggression and exploitation of others. On the other hand, the vulnerability effect of powerlessness may be avoidant responses, such as dissociation and running away; behavioral manifestations of anxiety, including phobias, sleep problems, elimination problems, and eating problems; and revictimization.

[A] variety of factors influence how sexual maltreatment impacts on an individual. These factors include the age of the victim (both at the time of the abuse and the time of assessment), the sex of the victim, the sex of the offender, the extent of the sexual abuse, the relationship between offender and victim, the reaction of others to knowledge of the sexual abuse, other life experiences, and the length of time between the abuse and information gathering. For example, the findings for child victims and adult survivors are somewhat different.

It is important for professionals to appreciate both the incomplete state of knowledge about the consequences of sexual abuse and the variability in effects. . . .

Lindsay C. Arthur, Child Sexual Abuse: Improving the System's Response
37 Juv. & Fam. Ct. J. (No. 2) 1, 11-14 (1986)

. . . When a child is sexually abused there are two immediate and strong reactions; the abuser must be punished, the child must be helped. If the abuser is a stranger, there is no problem. The child and her family can be worked with and the abuser can be sent to prison with no one else hurt. . . . But if the abuser is a parent of the child, a choice may have to be made. Either treat the child or punish the abuser, usually not both. If the abusing parent is put in jail, the abused child will feel guilty, a parent who may be otherwise a valuable member of the family is gone, the family loses a paycheck, its standard of living tumbles, the abused child may be blamed by the rest of the family. The best treatment requires the whole family, the abuser and the abused, the mother who may be an enabler, the other children who are necessarily involved. Without the abuser, the treatment circle is not complete, the problems cannot be fully resolved, the children may yet grow up to be abusers themselves. . . .

Severe Punishment or Effective Prevention

The decision to punish severely or to concentrate on treatment is not simple. It requires legal input as to the probabilities of getting a conviction and what evidence is needed for the family members. It involves social input as to the possibilities and effectiveness of treatment and the impact on the family of participation in the criminal processes. It requires political input as to the demands of the public for punishment, for revenge and the political impact of not prosecuting.

Children who are abused will probably abuse their own children or stand by while others abuse them, and their children in turn will abuse or enable the abuse of their own children, and on and on. Children who are abused are likely to become status offenders, delinquents, and criminals. Children who are abused are likely to have unstable marriages with the consequent trauma to themselves and their children. But children who are abused can usually be treated. The impact of the abuse can be reduced. The cycle of abuse can be broken.

The purpose of the intervention is to remove the guilt feelings. To remove the insecurity, to remove the anger. If the impact of abuse can be ended, if this cycle can be broken, intervention can be of major significance.

The impact of the abuse can be treated, a sufficient degree of normalcy can be restored. But the treatment of intra-family abuse will usually require that the abuser, be it parent or sibling, be a part of the treatment, freely discussing what happened and why and working out understanding and relationships that can prevent a recurrence. But an abuser facing trial and a long term in prison is surely going to be advised by his lawyer not to discuss any part of what happened. He may harbor too much fear and resentment to truly participate in any understandings. An abuser facing a short term in prison upon condition of cooperation in treatment may be more than willing to assist the rehabilitative process.

And so the problem. If the only options are either to use mild punishment in order to rehabilitate the family or to punish the abuser severely and lose his cooperation, which should it be? A decision must be made, and early, as to whether there will be treatment including [the] abuser with his participation insured by the continuing threat of punishment, or whether there will be immediate heavy punishment of the abuser and treatment without his participation. There must be a professional assessment of both the possibilities of conviction and the possibilities of rehabilitation. All of the various options must be canvassed and weighed and a plan devised encompassing as much of every option as is appropriate. There must be coordination towards a single plan.

Assessment

Very early in cases of intra-family sexual abuse an assessment must be made to determine:

— If the evidence is sufficient for a conviction,
— If convicted, what is the probable sentence,
— How well can the family be rehabilitated if the abuser is not punished,
— How well can the family be rehabilitated if the abuser is punished,
— Is it politically possible not to punish. . . .

There are, of course, numerous options. . . .

. . . Prosecution for a felony, prosecution for a misdemeanor, prosecution in a plea bargained support of a rehabilitation process, a protective order, an action for neglect, even a civil action by the victim for damages or injunctive relief.

There are various possible felonies: rape, incest, carnal knowledge, aggravated assault, and their more modern and more sterile names: criminal sexual conduct in the first degree, etc. The choice depends on the credibility of the victim as a witness, the chances for conviction, the possible sentences, the public outcry, and the goals set for final disposition of the abuser, the abused, and the family. An incidental consideration is the unwillingness of the child to testify against a parent if it may result in a prison sentence but her willingness to testify if only a short jail sentence is possible.

There are also possible misdemeanors. If a rehabilitation package is being considered, contributing [to the delinquency of a minor] may be indicated because, in many States, venue for contributing is in the juvenile courts rather than the criminal courts making it more feasible to work out a rehabilitation plan based on neglect and supported by the criminal sanctions of contributing.

An increasingly common remedy is the protective order. It is frequently based upon a statute and is prosecuted at no cost to the victim. It has the flexibility of an injunction and can usually be obtained, at least in preliminary form, in a matter of hours.

For maximum flexibility, an action for neglect probably allows the widest possible scope in developing and monitoring a rehabilitation plan. The procedure was statutorily designed precisely for rehabilitation. The caselaw requires a preliminary plan and progress reports. It can be backed up by contempt. And if the plan fails, it can be converted to an action to terminate parental rights.

If there is a sexual abuse, there is a possibility of a divorce or action with the consequent powers of the court to determine and monitor custody and visitation, though the divorce monitoring procedures are usually rather more clumsy than monitoring a neglect rehabilitation plan. Spouses, however, are not usually interested in divorce even though their children have been sexually molested.

Civil actions are a possibility. Unless, however, it can somehow involve the family's liability insurance, there seems little point to it. Similarly actions in equity for injunctive relief seem to offer little that a protective order cannot provide and would be at the family's expense.

Coordination of Intervention

In sexual abuse cases there are often several agencies involved, sometimes several courts. The family may have to talk about the same things to many investigators. The media may play off the differences of approach. Conflicting plans may evolve. Coordination is needed. . . .

When abuse is reported, it is usually to the police. It may be required to notify the welfare agency. Both may send out investigators, each looking at the facts from a different perspective: the police need to decide if a crime was committed and to preserve the evidence for a prosecution; the welfare agency needs to know if a child is in danger and the steps needed to protect it. . . . If the prosecutor becomes involved, additional investigators may be sent out to look at the facts from their focus. The family can be overwhelmed. The memories of the witnesses may be tinkered with beyond recall.

There may be actions started in juvenile court, in family court, in criminal court, and some judge may be asked for a protective order. There may even be different lawyers for different family members, each making different motions for different purposes. In smaller communities this may present less of a problem because there may be a single judge for the various courts. In larger communities, there may be three or four judges, each unaware of what the other is doing, each getting slightly differently focussed versions of the same facts, each issuing orders which may well conflict with each other. . . .

The prosecutor will usually be involved in any neglect or criminal procedures. The police and the welfare agency are usually responsive to the prosecutor. The prosecutor, being usually elected, is aware of public sentiment. And the prosecutor is usually able to communicate well with the judges. Coordination thus seems best to lie with the prosecutor. Supported by the rationale and decisions of an assessment team, a reasonable amount of coordination should be possible. . . .

D. Kelly Weisberg, The "Discovery" of Sexual Abuse: Experts' Role in Legal Policy Formulation
18 U.C. Davis L. Rev. 1-2, 5, 6-10, 18-19, 25, 27-43, 45-56 (1984)

Introduction

Despite evidence of sexual abuse of children throughout history,[1] the labeling of this phenomenon as a pervasive social problem is relatively recent. The phenomenon has received so much attention that it has been labeled several times in the past half century. . . .

Legal policy directed at sexual abuse of children has undergone several successive reformulations in the past half century. In each stage, a new definition of criminal behavior and proscribed sanctions were enacted into law. Different participants were involved in each successive stage of the labeling process. . . .

---

[1] Sexual abuse of children has been noted to occur as far back in history as ancient Greece and Rome. See L. DeMause, The History of Childhood 43-47 (1974). . . .

I. Era of the Sexual Psychopath: From "Badness to Sickness"[15]

The first comprehensive legal labeling of child molestation appeared in the 1930s, and psychiatrists were the first experts relied upon to define the problem. Their initial reaction was to label such sexual crimes as indicative of an "illness," one they were uniquely qualified to treat. The impetus for this labeling came from several sexually-motivated murders of children in the late 1930s. . . .

A. Influence of Psychiatrists in Defining Sexual Crimes

The incomprehensibility of sexual crimes involving children spurred the call for experts — qualified to understand and assess the situation, to study the problem, and to make recommendations for its solution. The experts selected to make sense of both the criminal act and the offender were psychiatrists. . . .

The psychiatrists diagnosed child molestation as a form of mental illness, terming the illness "sexual psychopathy." They suggested a treatment for the patient: the patient should be hospitalized until "well" or normal again. . . .

Statutes utilized medical terminology and labeled the offender with psychiatric nomenclature. The terminology was made applicable specifically to child molesters.

Proper identification of the mental illness of sexual psychopathy necessitated the use of trained experts. Psychiatrists were required to interview the alleged perpetrator to determine both the malady's existence and the proper treatment. These dual functions of the psychiatric expert were embodied in the sexual psychopath legislation. . . .

The psychiatrist's role in the enactment of sexual psychopath legislation in the 1930s to 1940s has been previously noted in the literature. However, two important questions remain unanswered. First, why did these specific experts, rather than other scientists or behaviorists, play such an important role in the formulation of this legislation? Second, why was the role of psychiatrists enacted at this time in history? . . .

In short, the call for these experts came at a time when the public was increasingly aware of the promise of psychiatry. Social conditions made the public receptive to psychiatrists' input. Specifically, Freud's writings in the early twentieth century stimulated interest in the use of psychiatry to explain the irrational. World War I increased public awareness of psychiatry's value in treating war casualties. The Leopold-Loeb[11] trial revealed that psychiatry could have specific application to criminal law. These factors contributed to the emergence of psychiatrists in legal policymaking. When the public voiced concern about sex crimes, [t]he stage had been set for these experts to enact their roles.

---

[15] The term was coined by two sociologists in their social historical analysis of the transformation from religious and criminal to medical designations of deviance. See generally P. Conrad & J. Schneider, Deviance and Medicalization: From Badness to Sickness (1980).

[11] This trial in 1924 of two middle class youths for murder was the first time psychiatrists testified as expert witnesses to explain criminal behavior. See Note, The Leopold-Loeb Case, 97 Cent. L.J. 327 (1924).

II. The First Relabeling: the 1950s

Legislation in the 1950s reflects the reconstruction and relabeling of child molestation by psychiatrists. Several states repealed or amended their sexual psychopath statutes and enacted different legislation dealing with sex offenses. The new legislation renamed the patient's "illness." . . .

The sexual psychopath became the "mentally disordered sex offender" in California, the "sexually dangerous person" in Illinois, and the "sexual deviate" in Wisconsin. Not all jurisdictions adopted an entirely new label. Some jurisdictions merely modified and shortened the former label to "psychopathic offenders." One trend was evident: [m]edical nomenclature was deemphasized, and criminal terminology became more prominent. . . .

Several factors explain the relabeling of this social problem in the 1950s. First, the 1950s reflected a resurgence of interest in the application of psychiatry to legal problems. [S]ocietal recognition of psychiatry's shortcomings may also explain the relabeling process. Psychiatry was in a more advanced stage of development than in the 1930s; the legislation of the 1950s reflected a more realistic appraisal of the answers psychiatry could and could not supply. The realization was dawning that psychiatry was not an exact science nor one able to furnish precise solutions upon demand. The act of diagnosing an offender was not as simple as the weighing of a chemical compound. Nor could psychiatry permanently and completely "cure" sex offenders. With inadequate facilities, psychiatrists could barely hope to treat even a small number of patients.

The acute shortage of psychiatric personnel in public institutions after World War II frustrated hopes of treatment for sex offenders. . . .

The second wave of legislation clearly recognized the problem of psychiatric supply and demand. . . .

Another explanation for the relabeling process may be found in sexual behavior research. An important influence on policymakers was Alfred Kinsey. . . .

The reconstruction of the child molestation problem in the 1950s was . . . aided by research debunking the "old" social problem of the 1930s. The accumulation of research, especially that conducted by Kinsey's Institute for Sex Research, helped dispel certain widespread beliefs about sex offenders. These myths included the following: sex criminals progressed from minor sex crimes (exhibitionism and voyeurism) to major sex crimes (forcible rape and child molestation), and sex crimes were increasing. Sexual psychopathy had not proved to be of the magnitude and seriousness as first thought; a different approach was in order. The efforts of psychiatrists could be devoted best to treating only the serious sexual offenders. . . .

III. The Third Label—Policymaking in the 1970s

In the early 1970s child molestation received yet another label: "sexual abuse," or "child sexual abuse." The new label appeared in both federal and state legislation. The federal Child Abuse Prevention and Treatment Act, enacted in 1974, required each state to adopt a uniform definition of abuse that included "physical or mental injury, sexual abuse or exploitation, negligent treatment, or maltreatment" in order to qualify for federal monies for the prevention and treatment of abuse. The new nomenclature appeared also in state legislation on abused children.

New experts played a role in the labeling process: psychologists and social workers became preeminent in this period. These experts focused on the familial offender — the father or stepfather molester. Instead of hospitalization or civil commitment for the patient, the recommended treatment was family counseling. The experts viewed the entire family, rather than merely the perpetrator, as the source of the problem. For the first time attention was also focused on the child victim, for whom counseling was also recommended.

A. The Role of Psychologists and Social Workers in Relabeling

The definitional process of sexual abuse . . . began simultaneously by psychologists and social workers. A West Coast psychologist, Henry Giarretto, played a prominent role in this development. . . .

This new label of child sexual abuse was effectively promoted from its West Coast origins. [Giarretto] published articles discussing the problem. The media highlighted [his treatment center], and staff members appeared on local and national television and radio programs. The staff disseminated child sexual abuse information [and] also conducted presentations and training seminars for professionals. . . .

The director-psychologist also wanted [his treatment program] to serve as a model for similar centers in other communities. Not surprisingly, with such national publicity, similar programs were soon established in Washington, Connecticut, Georgia, New York, and Pennsylvania to provide services to sexually abused children and their parents. . . .

Social workers as well as psychologists influenced the construction of this "new" social problem. One social worker in particular, Vincent DeFrancis, played a prominent role. DeFrancis, a lawyer with post-graduate training in social work and Director of the American Humane Association, a prominent child protection organization, broadened the focus of national attention from battered children to sexually abused children. Early federal legislation defined child abuse as intentional physical injury. DeFrancis' efforts helped expand this definition to include sexual abuse.

DeFrancis, long interested in child protective services, had a special interest in child sexual abuse. In 1965, he became Project Director of a research project to study sexual abuse funded by the Children's Bureau of the Department of Health, Education and Welfare. . . .

DeFrancis' influence soon extended into the federal level. When Congress considered enacting national child abuse legislation. DeFrancis testified before the Senate. [He] attempted to put the battered child problem in its proper perspective, pointing to the lesser incidence of intentionally inflicted injuries compared with other types of abuse: "Based upon an estimate . . . there must be somewhere between 30,000 and perhaps 40,000 at the outside of truly battered children but there must be at least 100,000 children each year who are sexually abused. . . . " Largely because of his influence, Congress broadened the federal definition of child abuse from physical injury to include sexual abuse. . . .

B. Reasons for Acceptance of Psychology and Social Work Theories

The work of the social worker-lawyer DeFrancis, as well as that of psychologist Giarretto, came during a time that was receptive to the influence of their disciplines. [W]hy were the helping professions, especially psychology and social work, the primary labelers of the "new" social problem in the 1960s and 1970s? The answer may be found in important developments taking place in these two disciplines that led to increasing interest in the contribution of social work and psychology to legal problems.

First, the occurrence of several social conditions increased political activism by social workers. These conditions included: 1) an American foreign policy that highlighted discrepancies between affluent and poorer nations; 2) President John F. Kennedy's approach to social problems; 3) a mass urban movement by ethnic and racial minorities that swelled the relief rolls in the cities; 4) the civil rights movement; and 5) race riots in American cities that were fueled by unemployment and housing conditions. . . .

Social workers began to recognize the importance of utilizing the law to affect social change. . . .

Social workers also increased social action directed at child welfare reform, especially child abuse. Renewed interest developed in child protective services. Although the child welfare movement originally swept through America in the mid-nineteenth century,[180] the movement abated in the twentieth century until medical and social science research uncovered the abused child. . . .

[S]ocial workers played a central role in legal policymaking directed at the abused child. Two child welfare organizations historically interested in child protective services, the Children's Division of the American Humane Society and the United States Children's Bureau, contributed model legislation. Social workers not only called attention to physical abuse by conducting research and writing articles, but they also lobbied for passage of reporting statutes. . . . Social workers had developed an expertise in child abuse legislation and consequently were regarded as experts when the problem of sexual abuse was addressed. The social welfare emphasis on protective services, specifically for the child, contributed to the shift in focus of legal policy to the young victim.

The liaison between social work, psychology, and law provided for the expanded role of psychologists and social workers in child abuse legislation. The federal Child Abuse Prevention and Treatment Act authorized funding to public agencies and nonprofit organizations with training programs for professional and paraprofessional personnel in the fields of "medicine, law, education, *social work,*

---

[180] Protective services and programs for child abuse victims existed in America since the mid-nineteenth century. Early child protective services developed after the cause célèbre case of Mary Ellen in New York in 1866. For a description of this case, see V. DeFrancis, The Fundamentals of Child Protection 19 (1955). Several social conditions combined to generate a widespread interest in child protection. These conditions included industrialization, urbanization, immigration, and a changing concept of childhood. The early child protection movement took several forms, including the removal of dependent, neglected, and delinquent children from almshouses and other institutions and their placement in private homes; the creation of juvenile courts and probation systems; the passage of compulsory school attendance laws; and crusades against child labor. See generally W. Trattner, Social Welfare in America, ch. 6 ("Child Welfare") (1974).

and other related fields." (Emphasis added.) State legislation mandated reports of child abuse by psychologists and social workers, among other professionals. State departments of social services absorbed an increasing number of tasks. . . .

Professional interest in abuse was reflected in the law by the insertion of the social welfare and psychological objectives of prevention and treatment. This dual emphasis is apparent both from the title of the new legislation and its language. Moreover, the legislation voiced a concern for . . . the entire family unit. Broad purpose clauses of state legislation were directed at strengthening the family. The aim was "to assist those children and their parents or those persons legally responsible for them, in their own home, to aid in overcoming the problems leading to abuse and neglect, thereby strengthening parental care and supervision and enhancing such children's welfare and preserving family life whenever feasible."[218]

A constant refrain of the federal and state legislation was the emphasis on treatment and counseling. This emphasis may be traced to the growth and acceptance of family therapy in legal circles. In the mid-1960s social work professionals first advocated treating the whole family with conjoint family therapy techniques. These techniques were rapidly adopted in legal settings. . . . Social workers began advocating its use not only for delinquent children, but also for abused children and their families.

Thus, the new legal label emerging in the 1970s depended on the influence of both psychologists and social workers. The social problem was constructed in the 1970s, after it had been labeled initially in the 1930s and again in the 1950s. Now the problem was termed "child sexual abuse." Attention was focused for the first time on the child victim. To help the child victim and prevent recurrent abuse, the entire family and not merely the criminal offender received treatment.

IV. Reform in the 1980s: From "Sickness to Badness"

In the 1980s the social problem has again been relabeled. Beginning in the late 1970s, a number of states repealed their sex offender legislation and replaced it with more punitive statutes. New experts advocated law-and-order interests as primary goals for the new legislation. Psychiatrists no longer occupy a central role in policymaking or in handling of sex offenders. The pendulum's swing has reversed; current legal policy signals a movement away from rehabilitation and treatment and a return to more severe punishment of the sex offender. . . . Law reform was fueled by public and legislative concern about these crimes, as well as concern that existing legislation allowed parole of still dangerous persons. . . .

B. The Punitive Approach of the New Legislation

The most recent legislation reflects a harsher approach to the sex offender. Punishment has become the focus with treatment and rehabilitation receding into the background. In California, the legislature replaced the mentally disordered sexual offender statutes with long mandatory imprisonment terms for

---

[218] Del. Code Ann. tit. 16, §901 (Supp. 1980).

convicted child molesters and allowed hospitalization only during these prison terms. Hospitalization is no longer an alternative to a prison sentence. . . .

With the new legislation, psychiatric treatment of sex offenders is significantly curtailed. Child molestation is now being redefined by the criminal label of "sexual assault."[253] Medical influence over child molesters has yielded to criminal jurisdiction. Child molestation, originally defined as "badness," and later as "sickness," has been labeled again as "badness."

trend

C. Factors Behind the Emerging Punitive Policy

The emergence of the new legal policy on sex offenses in the 1980s may be explained in part by the growing reform movement to curtail the influence of psychiatrists in the law. Although psychiatrists have played a considerable role in sex offender policy since the 1930s, a number of events have contributed to the waning of their influence. First, psychiatric testimony on evaluation of defendants' mental state, in general, has come under increasing attack. A burgeoning literature has assailed psychiatry and psychiatrists. . . .

Criticisms of psychiatry and psychiatrists have also come from another front. The insanity defense has been under increasing attack, and with it, greater attention has been focused on the proper role of psychiatry and psychiatrists in the criminal law. . . .

The current trend in sex offender legislation heralds a movement from treatment and rehabilitation and a return to more punitive dispositions. Protection of society rather than rehabilitation of the offender is the paramount concern. This trend also signals a waning in the influence of psychiatry and psychiatrists. . . . Psychiatrists are less prominent in both legal policy formulation and in the processing of sex offenders from diagnosis and sentencing through treatment.

However, the reversal of the pendulum from rehabilitation and treatment to punishment has not been without gains. The differentiation among sex offenders which was first urged by Kinsey has been recognized. Legal dispositions now reflect the impact of social workers and psychologists in terms of a different and more "humanistic" approach towards intrafamilial offenders compared to stranger perpetrators. Specifically, incest offenders are more likely than stranger molesters to benefit in many jurisdictions from the rehabilitation model: they are more likely to receive shorter sentences, probation, and counseling. In addition, legal personnel now question whether commitment under sexual psychopath statutes is appropriate for intrafamilial offenders, and urge out-patient family treatment instead.

distiction made for intrafamilial offenders

Advances have also been made in treatment of sex offenders. Pioneering programs, many headed by psychiatrists, have been established across the country to treat sex offenders. Institutional and community-based programs work to change the attitudes and behaviors of sex offenders. Such programs aim to reduce recidivism

---

[253] See, e.g., Colo. Rev. Stat. §18-3-405 (1978 & Supp. 1983) ("sexual assault on a child"); N.H. Rev. Stat. Ann. §632-A:2 (1983) ("aggravated felonious sexual assault" — if actor is member of the same household of victim, or with victim less than 13 years of age); id. §632-A:3 ("felonious sexual assault" — if victim is between 13 and 16 years of age).

rates of convicted offenders and to increase knowledge about sex offenders in general to prevent future attacks.

Further, the child victims of sex offenders receive more attention. Many jurisdictions have adopted reforms minimizing the trauma of child victims in the investigation and hearing stages of the criminal process. Such reforms include special training for police, child protective service workers, and prosecutors for interviewing child victims; a team approach to interviewing children (utilizing social welfare and legal personnel); fewer investigative interviews; and videotaped testimony of the child victim. This humane response is the legacy of the intervention by members of the helping professions.

7. The Child Victim as Witness

In addition to the fundamental issue of how society ought to intervene in cases of child sexual abuse, many interesting procedural issues emerge during the prosecution of sexual abuse cases. These issues arise from the desire to protect a child victim from the trauma of the judicial process while at the same time safeguarding the defendant's constitutional rights. The following materials explore these conflicting interests.

Maryland v. Craig
497 U.S. 836 (1990)

Justice O'CONNOR delivered the opinion of the Court.

This case requires us to decide whether the Confrontation Clause of the Sixth Amendment categorically prohibits a child witness in a child abuse case from testifying against a defendant at trial, outside the defendant's physical presence, by one-way closed circuit television.

In October 1986, a Howard County grand jury charged respondent, Sandra Ann Craig, with child abuse, first and second degree sexual offenses, perverted sexual practice, assault, and battery. The named victim in each count was a six-year-old girl who, from August 1984 to June 1986, had attended a kindergarten and prekindergarten center owned and operated by Craig.

In March 1987, before the case went to trial, the State sought to invoke a Maryland statutory procedure that permits a judge to receive, by one-way closed circuit television, the testimony of a child witness who is alleged to be a victim of child abuse. To invoke the procedure, the trial judge must first "determin[e] that testimony by the child victim in the courtroom will result in the child suffering serious emotional distress such that the child cannot reasonably communicate." Md. Cts. & Jud. Proc. Code Ann. §9-102(a)(l)(ii) (1989). Once the procedure is invoked, the child witness, prosecutor, and defense counsel withdraw to a separate room; the judge, jury, and defendant remain in the courtroom. The child witness is then examined and cross-examined in the separate room, while a video monitor records and displays the witness' testimony to those in the courtroom. During this time the witness cannot see the defendant. The defendant remains in electronic communication with defense counsel, and objections may be made and ruled on as if the witness were testifying in the courtroom.

In support of its motion invoking the one-way closed circuit television procedure, the State presented expert testimony that the named victim as well as a number of other children who were alleged to have been sexually abused by Craig, would suffer "serious emotional distress such that [they could not] reasonably communicate," §9-102(a)(l)(ii), if required to testify in the courtroom. App. 7-59. The Maryland Court of Appeals characterized the evidence as follows:

> The expert testimony in each case suggested that each child would have some or considerable difficulty in testifying in Craig's presence. For example, as to one child, the expert said that what "would cause him the most anxiety would be to testify in front of Mrs. Craig. . . . " The child "wouldn't be able to communicate effectively." As to another, an expert said she "would probably stop talking and she would withdraw and curl up." With respect to two others, the testimony was that one would "become highly agitated, that he may refuse to talk or if he did talk, that he would choose his subject regardless of the questions" while the other would "become extremely timid and unwilling to talk." 560 A.2d 1120, 1128-1129 (Md. Ct. App. 1989).

[The trial court determined that each child would suffer serious emotional distress such that he or she would not be able to reasonably communicate, if forced to testify in the defendant's presence. The trial court then found the named victim and three other children competent to testify and accordingly permitted them to testify against Craig via the one-way closed circuit television procedure. The jury convicted Craig on all counts, and the Maryland Court of Special Appeals affirmed the convictions. The Court of Appeals reversed.]

II

The Confrontation Clause of the Sixth Amendment [provides:] "In all criminal prosecutions, the accused shall enjoy the right . . . to be confronted with the witnesses against him."

We observed in Coy v. Iowa that "the Confrontation Clause guarantees the defendant a face-to-face meeting with witnesses appearing before the trier of fact." 487 U.S., at 1016 (citing Kentucky v. Stincer, 482 U.S. 730, 748, 749-750 (1987) (Marshall, J., dissenting)). This interpretation derives not only from the literal text of the Clause, but also from our understanding of its historical roots.

We have never held, however, that the Confrontation Clause guarantees criminal defendants the *absolute* right to a face-to-face meeting with witnesses against them at trial. Indeed, in Coy v. Iowa we expressly "le[ft] for another day . . . the question whether any exceptions exist" to the "irreducible literal meaning of the Clause: 'a right to meet face to face all those who appear and give evidence at trial.'" 487 U.S., at 1021. The procedure challenged in *Coy* involved the placement of a screen that prevented two child witnesses in a child abuse case from seeing the defendant as they testified against him at trial. In holding that the use of this procedure violated the defendant's right to confront witnesses against him, we suggested that any exception to the right "would surely be allowed only when necessary to further an important public policy" — i.e., only upon a showing of something more than the generalized, "legislatively imposed presumption of trauma" underlying the statute at issue in that case. We concluded that "[s]ince there ha[d] been no individualized findings that these particular witnesses needed special protection, the judgment [in the case before us] could not be sustained by any conceivable exception." Because the trial court in this case made individualized findings that each of the child witnesses needed special protection, this case requires us to decide the question reserved in *Coy.*

The central concern of the Confrontation Clause is to ensure the reliability of the evidence against a criminal defendant by subjecting it to rigorous testing in the context of an adversary proceeding before the trier of fact. [T]he right guaranteed by the Confrontation Clause includes not only a "personal examination," but also "(1) insures that the witness will give his statements under oath — thus impressing him with the seriousness of the matter and guarding against the lie by the possibility of a penalty for perjury; (2) forces the witness to submit to cross-examination, the 'greatest legal engine ever invented for the discovery of truth'; [and] (3) permits the jury that is to decide the defendant's fate to observe the demeanor of the witness in making his statement, thus aiding the jury in assessing his credibility." [California v. Green, 399 U.S. 149, 158 (1970).]

The combined effect of these elements of confrontation — physical presence, oath, cross-examination, and observation of demeanor by the trier of fact — serves the purposes of the Confrontation Clause by ensuring that evidence admitted against an accused is reliable and subject to the rigorous adversarial testing that is the norm of Anglo-American criminal proceedings. . . .

Although face-to-face confrontation forms "the core of the values furthered by the Confrontation Clause," *Green*, 399 U.S., at 157, we have nevertheless recognized that it is not the *sine qua non* of the confrontation right.

For this reason, we have never insisted on an actual face-to-face encounter at trial in every instance in which testimony is admitted against a defendant. . . .

That the face-to-face confrontation requirement is not absolute does not, of course, mean that it may easily be dispensed with. As we suggested in *Coy,* our precedents confirm that a defendant's right to confront accusatory witnesses may be satisfied absent a physical, face-to-face confrontation at trial only where denial of such confrontation is necessary to further an important public policy and only where the reliability of the testimony is otherwise assured.

III

Maryland's statutory procedure, when invoked, prevents a child witness from seeing the defendant as he or she testifies against the defendant at trial. We find it significant, however, that Maryland's procedure preserves all of the other elements of the confrontation right: The child witness must be competent to testify and must testify under oath; the defendant retains full opportunity for contemporaneous cross-examination; and the judge, jury, and defendant are able to view (albeit by video monitor) the demeanor (and body) of the witness as he or she testifies. Although we are mindful of the many subtle effects face-to-face confrontation may have on an adversary criminal proceeding, the presence of these other elements of confrontation — oath, cross-examination, and observation of the witness' demeanor — adequately ensures that the testimony is both reliable and subject to rigorous adversarial testing in a manner functionally equivalent to that accorded live, in-person testimony. These safeguards of reliability and adversariness render the use of such a procedure a far cry from the undisputed prohibition of the Confrontation Clause: trial by ex parte affidavit or inquisition. Rather, we think these elements of effective confrontation not only permit a defendant to "confound and undo the false accuser, or reveal the child coached by a malevolent adult," *Coy*, supra, 487 U.S., at 1020, but may well aid a defendant in eliciting favorable testimony from the child witness. Indeed, to the extent the child witness' testimony may be said to be technically given out of court (though we do not so hold), these assurances of reliability and adversariness are far greater than those required for admission of hearsay testimony under the Confrontation Clause. We are therefore confident that use of the one-way closed circuit television procedure, where necessary to further an important state interest, does not impinge upon the truth-seeking or symbolic purposes of the Confrontation Clause.

The critical inquiry in this case, therefore, is whether use of the procedure is necessary to further an important state interest. The State contends that it has a substantial interest in protecting children who are allegedly victims of child abuse from the trauma of testifying against the alleged perpetrator and that its statutory procedure for receiving testimony from such witnesses is necessary to further that interest. . . .

[We] conclude today that a State's interest in the physical and psychological well-being of child abuse victims may be sufficiently important to outweigh, at least in some cases, a defendant's right to face his or her accusers in court. That a significant majority of States have enacted statutes to protect child witnesses from the trauma of giving testimony in child abuse cases attests to the widespread belief in the importance of such a public policy. Thirty-seven States, for example, permit the use of videotaped testimony of sexually abused children; 24 States have authorized the use of one-way closed circuit television testimony in child abuse cases; and 8 States authorize the use of a two-way system in which the child-witness is permitted to see the courtroom and the defendant on a video monitor and in which the jury and judge are permitted to view the child during the testimony.

The statute at issue in this case, for example, was specifically intended "to safeguard the physical and psychological well-being of child victims by avoiding, or at least minimizing, the emotional trauma produced by testifying." Wildermuth v. State, 530 A.2d 275, 286 (Md. Ct. App. 1987). . . .

Given the State's traditional and "transcendent interest in protecting the welfare of children," *Ginsberg*, 390 U.S., at 640, and buttressed by the growing body of academic literature documenting the psychological trauma suffered by child abuse victims who must testify in court, . . . we will not second-guess the considered judgment of the Maryland Legislature regarding the importance of its interest in protecting child abuse victims from the emotional trauma of testifying. Accordingly, we hold that, if the State makes an adequate showing of necessity, the state interest in protecting child witnesses from the trauma of testifying in a child abuse case is sufficiently important to justify the use of a special procedure that permits a child witness in such cases to testify at trial against a defendant in the absence of face-to-face confrontation with the defendant.

The requisite finding of necessity must of course be a case-specific one: The trial court must hear evidence and determine whether use of the one-way closed circuit television procedure is necessary to protect the welfare of the particular child witness who seeks to testify. The trial court must also find that the child witness would be traumatized, not by the courtroom generally, but by the presence of the defendant. Denial of face-to-face confrontation is not needed to further the state interest in protecting the child witness from trauma unless it is the presence of the defendant that causes the trauma. In other words, if the state interest were merely the interest in protecting child witnesses from courtroom trauma generally, denial of face-to-face confrontation would be unnecessary because the child could be permitted to testify in less intimidating surroundings, albeit with the defendant present. Finally, the trial court must find that the emotional distress suffered by the child witness in the presence of the defendant is more than de minimis, i.e., more than "mere nervousness or excitement or some reluctance to testify," *Wildermuth*, supra, 530 A.2d, at 289. We need not decide the minimum showing of emotional trauma required for use of the special procedure, however, because the Maryland statute, which requires a determination that the child witness will suffer "serious emotional distress such that the child cannot reasonably communicate," §9-102(a)(l)(ii), clearly suffices to meet constitutional standards.

To be sure, face-to-face confrontation may be said to cause trauma for the very purpose of eliciting truth, cf. *Coy*, supra, 487 U.S., at 1019-1020, but we think that the use of Maryland's special procedure, where necessary to further the important state interest in preventing trauma to child witnesses in child abuse cases, adequately ensures the accuracy of the testimony and preserves the adversary nature of the trial. Indeed, where face-to-face confrontation causes significant emotional distress in a child witness, there is evidence that such confrontation would in fact disserve the Confrontation Clause's truth-seeking goal.

In sum, we conclude that where necessary to protect a child witness from trauma that would be caused by testifying in the physical presence of the defendant, at least where such trauma would impair the child's ability to communicate, the Confrontation Clause does not prohibit use of a procedure that, despite the absence of face-to-face confrontation, ensures the reliability of the evidence by subjecting it to rigorous adversarial testing and thereby preserves the essence of effective confrontation. Because there is no dispute that the child witnesses in this case testified under oath, were subject to full cross-examination, and were able to be observed by the judge, jury, and defendant as they testified, we conclude that, to the extent that a proper finding of necessity has been made, the admission of such testimony would be consonant with the Confrontation Clause. . . .

Justice SCALIA, with whom Justice BRENNAN, Justice MARSHALL, and Justice STEVENS join, dissenting.

Seldom has this Court failed so conspicuously to sustain a categorical guarantee of the Constitution against the tide of prevailing current opinion. The Sixth Amendment provides, with unmistakable clarity, that "[i]n all criminal prosecutions, the accused shall enjoy the right . . . to be confronted with the witnesses against him." The purpose of enshrining this protection in the Constitution was to assure that none of the many policy interests from time to time pursued by statutory law could overcome a defendant's right to face his or her accusers in court. . . .

Because of this [Court's] subordination of explicit constitutional text to currently favored public policy, the following scene can be played out in an American courtroom for the first time in two centuries: A father whose young daughter has been given over to the exclusive custody of his estranged wife, or a mother whose young son has been taken into custody by the State's child welfare department, is sentenced to prison for sexual abuse on the basis of testimony by a child the parent has not seen or spoken to for many months; and the guilty verdict is rendered without giving the parent so much as the opportunity to sit in the presence of the child, and to ask, personally or through counsel, "it is really not true, is it, that I — your father (or mother) whom you see before you — did these terrible things?" Perhaps that is a procedure today's society desires; perhaps (though I doubt it) it is even a fair procedure; but it is assuredly not a procedure permitted by the Constitution. . . .

According to the Court, "we cannot say that [face-to-face] confrontation [with witnesses appearing at trial] is an indispensable element of the Sixth Amendment's guarantee of the right to confront one's accusers." That is rather like saying "we cannot say that being tried before a jury is an indispensable element of the Sixth Amendment's guarantee of the right to jury trial." The Court makes the impossible plausible by recharacterizing the Confrontation Clause, so that confrontation (redesignated "face-to-face confrontation") becomes only one of many "elements of confrontation." [T]hat the defendant should be confronted by the witnesses who appear at trial is not a preference "reflected" by the Confrontation Clause; it is a constitutional right unqualifiedly guaranteed. . . .

The Court's test today requires unavailability only in the sense that the child is unable to testify in the presence of the defendant. That cannot possibly be the relevant sense. [California v. Green, 399 U.S. 149 (1970)] held that the Confrontation Clause does not bar admission of prior testimony when the declarant is sworn as a witness but refuses to answer. But in *Green*, as in most cases of refusal, we could not know why the declarant refused to testify. Here, by contrast, we know that it is precisely because the child is unwilling to testify in the presence of the defendant. That unwillingness cannot be a valid excuse under the Confrontation Clause, whose very object is to place the witness under the sometimes hostile glare of the defendant. "That face-to-face presence may, unfortunately, upset the truthful rape victim or abused child; but by the same token it may confound and undo the false accuser, or reveal the child coached by a malevolent adult." *Coy*, 487 U.S., at 1020. . . .

The Court characterizes the State's interest which "outweigh[s]" the explicit text of the Constitution as an "interest in the physical and psychological well-being of child abuse victims," an "interest in protecting" such victims "from the emotional trauma of testifying." That is not so. A child who meets the Maryland statute's requirement of suffering such "serious emotional distress" from confrontation that he "cannot reasonably communicate" would seem entirely safe. Why would a prosecutor want to call a witness who cannot reasonably communicate? And if he did, it would be the State's own fault. Protection of the child's interest — as far as the Confrontation Clause is concerned — is entirely within Maryland's control. The State's interest here is in fact no more and no less than what the State's interest always is when it seeks to get a class of evidence admitted in criminal proceedings: more

defines state's interests differently

convictions of guilty defendants. That is not an unworthy interest, but it should not be dressed up as a humanitarian one.

And the interest on the other side is also what it usually is when the State seeks to get a new class of evidence admitted: fewer convictions of innocent defendants — specifically, in the present context, innocent defendants accused of particularly heinous crimes. The "special" reasons that exist for suspending one of the usual guarantees of reliability in the case of children's testimony are perhaps matched by "special" reasons for being particularly insistent upon it in the case of children's testimony. Some studies show that children are substantially more vulnerable to suggestion than adults, and often unable to separate recollected fantasy (or suggestion) from reality. . . .

In the last analysis, however, this debate is not an appropriate one. I have no need to defend the value of confrontation, because the Court has no authority to question it. . . . For good or bad, the Sixth Amendment requires confrontation, and we are not at liberty to ignore it. . . .

The Court today has applied "interest-balancing" analysis where the text of the Constitution simply does not permit it. We are not free to conduct a cost-benefit analysis of clear and explicit constitutional guarantees, and then to adjust their meaning to comport with our findings. . . . I would affirm the judgment of the Maryland Court of Appeals reversing the judgment of conviction.

People v. Vigil

104 P.3d 258 (Colo. Ct. App. 2004)

. . . Defendant was convicted of having sexually assaulted the seven-year-old son of a co-worker in the co-worker's home. The child's father testified at trial that, when he went to check on his son, he pushed open the door to the child's room and saw defendant leaning over the child. Both were partially undressed. Defendant fled. The child, who appeared frightened and confused, told his father that defendant "stuck his winkie in his butt and his butt hurt." He also told his father's friend, who was visiting in the home, that his "butt hurt."

The father called the police. Shortly thereafter, a police officer observed defendant, who matched the description of the suspect, walking on a sidewalk near the scene of the incident. When the officer stopped and got out of his car, defendant put a knife to his throat and, when the officer asked what he was doing, said, "I done bad." He then stabbed himself in the throat and chest. Defendant was transported to a hospital, where he told emergency room personnel that he wanted to die and that he "did a bad thing."

A police officer interviewed the child about the incident, and portions of the videotaped interview were shown to the jury at trial. The child, who had been ruled incompetent, did not testify.

Defendant contends on appeal that admission of the videotaped interview with the child violated his constitutional right to confront witnesses and requires reversal of his conviction. We agree.

The United States and Colorado Constitutions guarantee that persons accused of crimes shall have the right to confront the witnesses against them. See U.S. Const.

amends. VI ("In all criminal prosecutions the accused shall enjoy the right . . . to be confronted with the witnesses against him. . . . "), XIV; Colo. Const. art. II, §16 ("In criminal prosecutions the accused shall have the right . . . to meet the witnesses against him face to face. . . . ").

In Crawford v. Washington, 541 U.S. 36 (2004), announced during the pendency of this appeal, the Supreme Court prescribed a framework for evaluating Confrontation Clause claims that differs significantly from the analysis that was applicable at the time of defendant's trial.

In *Crawford*, the Court held that the petitioner's federal confrontation rights had been violated when the trial court played for the jury a tape-recorded statement to police by a witness whom the petitioner had not had the opportunity to cross-examine and who did not testify at trial. In so ruling, the Court departed from its prior confrontation analysis, which had permitted the use of an unavailable witness's statement if the statement bore sufficient indicia of reliability. See Ohio v. Roberts, 448 U.S. 56 (1980). After reviewing the historical background of the Confrontation Clause and the Court's prior case law, the *Crawford* Court held that a nontestifying witness's out-of-court "testimonial" statement, regardless of its reliability, may be admitted against an accused only if the witness is unavailable and the accused had an opportunity to cross-examine the witness when the statement was made.

Although the Court "le[ft] for another day any effort to spell out a comprehensive definition of 'testimonial,' " *Crawford*, supra, 541 U.S. at 68, it gave some guidance on the issue by noting various formulations of the "core class" of testimonial statements at which the Confrontation Clause was directed. These include (1) "ex parte in-court testimony or its functional equivalent — that is, material such as affidavits, custodial examinations, prior testimony that the defendant was unable to cross-examine, or similar pretrial statements that declarants would reasonably expect to be used prosecutorially"; (2) "extrajudicial statements . . . contained in formalized testimonial materials, such as affidavits, depositions, prior testimony, or confessions"; and (3) "statements that were made under circumstances which would lead an objective witness reasonably to believe that the statement would be available for use at a later trial." *Crawford*, supra, 541 U.S. at 51-52.

use of precedent

Observing that the involvement of government officers in the production of testimonial evidence presents a particular risk, the Court noted that "[s]tatements taken by police officers in the course of interrogations are also testimonial under even a narrow standard." Conversely, other types of hearsay, such as an "off-hand, overheard remark" or a "casual remark to an acquaintance," are not the sort of statements at which the Confrontation Clause was directed. *Crawford*, supra, 541 U.S. at 51 see also People v. Compan, 100 P.3d 533, 537 (Colo. Ct. App. 2004) (summarizing *Crawford* testimonial statements as generally being (1) solemn or formal statements, (2) made for the purpose of proving or establishing facts in judicial proceedings, (3) made to a government actor or agent, not to someone unassociated with government activity).

We conclude that the videotaped statement given by the child to the police officer in this case was "testimonial" under the *Crawford* formulations of that concept. In so concluding, we reject the People's argument that the statement could not be considered testimonial because it was not made during the course of police interrogation and because a seven-year-old child would not reasonably expect his statements to be used prosecutorially.

"Interrogation," under the *Crawford* Court's analysis, is used in a colloquial rather than a technical or legal sense. Thus, the witness's recorded statement knowingly given in response to structured police questioning in *Crawford* "qualifie[d] under any conceivable definition" of testimonial. *Crawford*, supra, 541 U.S. at 53 n. 4. Further, at least in the case of police interrogations, a statement need not be made under oath to be testimonial. *Crawford*, supra.

Although the interview in this case was conducted in a relaxed atmosphere, with open-ended, nonleading questions, and although no oath was administered at the outset, it nevertheless amounted to interrogation under *Crawford.* The police officer who conducted the interview had had extensive training in the particular interrogation techniques required for interviewing children. At the outset of the interview, she told the child she was a police officer, and, after ascertaining that the child knew the difference between being truthful and lying, she told him he needed to tell the truth. Thus, the absence of an oath, which in any event is not a requirement under *Crawford* for police interrogations, did not preclude the child's statements from being testimonial.

Nor can the statements be characterized as nontestimonial on the basis that a seven-year-old child would not reasonably expect them to be used prosecutorially. During the interview, the police officer asked the child what should happen to defendant, and the child replied that defendant should go to jail. The officer then told the child that he would need to talk to "a friend" of hers who worked for the district attorney and who was going to try to put defendant "in jail for a long long time." This discussion, together with the interviewer's emphasis at the outset regarding the need to be truthful, would indicate to an objective person in the child's position that the statements were intended for use at a later proceeding that would lead to punishment of defendant. See *Crawford*, supra, 541 U.S. at 52 (including among examples of testimonial statements those that were "made under circumstances which would lead an objective witness reasonably to believe that the statement would be available for use at a later trial").

Finally, we note that at least two other courts have concluded that, under *Crawford*, similar statements by children who did not testify were inadmissible testimonial hearsay. See People v. Sisavath, 13 Cal. Rptr. 3d 753 (Ct. App. 2004); Snowden v. State, 846 A.2d 36 (Md. Spec. App. 2004); see also People in Interest of R.A.S., — P.3d —, 2004 WL 1351383 (Colo. Ct. App. No. 03CA1209, June 17, 2004) (child victim's statements to police investigator during forensic interview were testimonial hearsay, and their use at trial violated juvenile's confrontation rights). But see People v. Geno, 683 N.W.2d 687 (Mich. Ct. App. 2004) (child victim's response to interviewer's question was not testimonial where interviewer was not government employee). Defendant had no opportunity to cross-examine the child regarding the statements he made to the interviewing officer. Based on the trial court's ruling that the child was incompetent, the child did not testify at trial. Accordingly, introduction of his statements to the interviewer violated defendant's right to confront the witnesses against him.

Having concluded that the admission of the videotaped interview violated defendant's confrontation rights, we next consider whether its admission requires reversal of defendant's conviction. We conclude that it does. [W]e cannot conclude that the erroneous admission of the videotaped interview was harmless beyond a reasonable doubt.

The interview was a significant part of the prosecution's case. Although there was other corroborative evidence . . . the child's statements to the interviewer provided the most detailed account of the incident and afforded the jurors the opportunity to hear what had happened from the child himself. See People v. Newbrough, 803 P.2d 155, 161 (Colo. 1990) ("A videotaped interview of a child victim is undoubtedly more powerful, and thus potentially more prejudicial, than testimony of a witness about what the child said.").

The prosecutor relied extensively on the child's videotaped interview in closing argument, citing the child's statements as proof that sexual contact, a necessary element of the charged offense, had occurred. . . . In sum, although there was unquestionably other corroborating evidence presented, we cannot say that the erroneous admission of the single most persuasive evidence of defendant's guilt was harmless beyond a reasonable doubt. . . .

Defendant contends that his confrontation rights were also violated by the admission of the child's hearsay statements to his father, the father's friend, and the examining doctor. We conclude that the child's statements to his father and his father's friend were properly admitted and will be admissible on retrial regardless of whether the child testifies. However, the child's statements to the doctor were "testimonial" within the meaning of *Crawford* and therefore may not be admitted on retrial if the child does not testify.

The child's statements to his father and his father's friend were made immediately after the incident, when the child was crying and upset. They were not solemn or formal statements and were made to persons unassociated with government activity. They therefore do not fall within the *Crawford* definition of testimonial hearsay.

Although the statements were not testimonial, we must nevertheless consider whether they amounted to a violation of defendant's right of confrontation under our state constitution, using the analysis set forth in Ohio v. Roberts, supra, and People v. Dement, 661 P.2d 675 (Colo. 1983) (applying *Roberts* test to determine whether admission of hearsay violated Colorado Constitution).

The child's statements were admissible under that test. It was undisputed that the child was unavailable at trial, and the statements were properly admitted under the excited utterance exception to the hearsay rule. . . .

We reach a different conclusion as to the child's statements to the doctor who examined him after the incident. The doctor was a member of a child protection team that provides consultations at Denver area hospitals in cases of suspected child abuse. He had previously provided extensive expert testimony in child abuse cases. He was asked to perform a "forensic sexual abuse examination" on the child and spoke with the police officer who accompanied the child before performing the examination. At trial, the doctor not only testified regarding his physical findings but also recounted what the child had told him about the incident.

We conclude that, under the particular circumstances present here, the child's statements to the doctor were testimonial under *Crawford*. The statements were made under circumstances that would lead an objective witness reasonably to believe that they would be used prosecutorially. Although the doctor himself was not a government officer or employee, he was not a person "unassociated with government activity." People v. Compan, 100 P.3d at 537. The doctor elicited the statements after consultation with the police, and he necessarily understood that information he obtained would be used in a subsequent prosecution for child abuse.

Thus, on retrial, the doctor may not testify regarding the child's statements to him if the child does not testify at trial. We note, however, that this conclusion does not require the exclusion of testimony by the doctor regarding his observations and physical findings. . . . The judgment of conviction is reversed, and the case is remanded for a new trial in accordance with the views set forth here.

NOTES AND QUESTIONS ON *CRAIG* AND *VIGIL*

(1) Maryland v. Craig involves the constitutionality of *in-court procedures* regarding the child victim. People v. Vigil addresses the constitutionality of admitting the child victim's *out-of-court statements* about the abuse. Both cases implicate the defendant's right of confrontation under the Sixth Amendment.

(2) Background.   *Craig* was the second child sexual abuse case to reach the Supreme Court concerning the right of confrontation. The Court first faced the issue of whether a special testimonial procedure violated the Sixth Amendment in Coy v. Iowa, 487 U.S. 1012 (1988), in which the defendant was charged with sexually assaulting two 13-year-old girls. Iowa law permitted a complaining witness to testify either via one-way closed-circuit television or behind a screen. The trial judge approved the use of a screen blocking the defendant from the girls' sight but permitting him to see them dimly and hear them. The Court, emphasizing the importance of a defendant's face-to-face meeting with witnesses, held that this procedure violated the defendant's right of confrontation. However, in dicta, the Court stated that exceptions would be allowed when necessary to further an important public policy. Id. at 1021.

(3) Epilogue.   *Coy* ruled unconstitutional a statute incorporating a *legislatively imposed* presumption of trauma and suggested the need for *individualized hearings* to support testimonial protection. In contrast, the statutory procedure invoked in *Craig* incorporated individualized findings that were based on expert testimony. On remand in *Craig*, the court of appeals reversed the defendant's conviction, interpreting the statute to require the trial judge to personally interview the victim before ordering the closed-circuit procedure. Craig v. Maryland, 588 A.2d 328 (Md. 1991). The daycare provider (as well as her son, who was also on trial) were not retried because the children's parents wanted to avoid traumatizing them further. Stephen Buckley, Prosecutors Reject New Trial in Sandra Craig Abuse Case, Wash. Post, July 3, 1991, at C1.

(4) Determination of Necessity.   What guidance does *Craig* provide for the trial judge in the determination of "necessity"? Is the judge *required* to rely on expert testimony to find trauma to the child or can the judge make that determination? See United States v. Rouse, 111 F.3d 561 (8th Cir. 1997), *cert. denied*, 522 U.S. 905 (1997) (holding that judge may make finding based on personal observations and questioning). How is a judge to determine the likelihood of potential trauma to the

child? See State v. Wright, 690 So. 2d 850 (La. Ct. App. 1997) (holding that fear of defendant is a requisite case-specific finding of necessity; nervousness in courtroom is insufficient). What should be the standard of proof for necessity? See, e.g., Cal. Penal Code §1347(b)(2) (West 2004) (requiring clear and convincing evidence of trauma). What relevance, if any, should the following factors play in the determination: the child's age, gender, severity, and frequency of the abuse or threats?

Both *Craig* and *Vigil* involve molestation by an unrelated adult. Most sexual abuse is perpetrated by family members rather than strangers. In the determination of "necessity" for child victims to qualify for special protective procedures, would victims of familial abuse be likely to suffer more or less trauma from testifying than other victims? See Kimberly Crnich, Redressing the Undressing: A Primer on Representation of Adult Survivors of Childhood Sexual Abuse, 14 Women's Rts. L. Rep. 65 (1991) (incest victims experience more emotional trauma than child rape victims).

(5) Note the evidence on which the Court relies in *Craig*. In particular, the Court draws support for the public policy of child protection from the literature documenting the psychological trauma of child victim witnesses and the number of states that have enacted special protective procedures. To what extent is a court's reliance on predictive evidence by expert witnesses justified? Might the experience of testifying actually have beneficial effects for child victims? See Gail Goodman et al., Innovations for Child Witnesses: A National Survey, 5 Psychol. Pub. Pol'y & L. 255, 258 (1999) (summarizing data). See also Dorothy F. Marsil et al., Child Witness Policy: Law Interfacing with Social Science, 65 Law & Contemp. Probs. 209, 214-215 (2002).

(6) Extension of Protective Procedures. How far should courts extend the rationale for special protective procedures for child victim witnesses? To child *eye-witnesses*? See Marx v. State, 987 S.W.2d 577 (Tex. Crim. App. 1999), *cert. denied*, 528 U.S. 1034 (1999). To child victims of crimes of a *nonsexual* nature? See Ex parte Taylor, 957 S.W.2d 43 (Tex. Ct. App. 1997) (to victims of domestic violence). See also Barbara Gilleran-Johnson & Timothy R. Evans, The Criminal Courtroom: Is It Child Proof?, 26 Loy. U. Chi. L.J. 681, 697 (1995) (arguing that testifying in crimes such as aggravated battery, kidnapping, cruelty to children, and domestic battery, can be just as damaging to the child). Should other special protective procedures that are applicable to adult victims of sexual assault be extended to children — such as rape shield laws that preclude the admissibility of prior sexual conduct evidence? See Churchfield v. State, 769 A.2d 313 (Md. Ct. App. 2001) (holding rape shield law inapplicable to child victim).

(7) Impact of **Craig.**

a. Federal Law Reform. In response to *Craig*, Congress enacted the Child Victims' and Child Witnesses' Rights Act (CVCWR), 18 U.S.C. §3509 (2000). The Act provides for an alternative to children's courtroom testimony — i.e., child witnesses may testify by means of two-way closed-circuit television or by video-taped depositions provided that: (a) the child is unable to testify because of fear; (b) there is a substantial likelihood (established by expert testimony) that the child will suffer emotional trauma from testifying, (c) the child suffers a mental or other infirmity, and (d) conduct by the defendant or defense counsel causes the child to be unable to continue testifying.

CVCWR goes further than *Craig* by permitting testimony via two-way closed circuit television (in contrast to the one-way closed circuit procedure authorized by statute in *Craig*). CVCWR also provides other protections, such as requiring that competency exams be appropriate in light of the child's age and development; protecting confidentiality; requiring the use of multidisciplinary child abuse teams; permitting the appointment of a guardian ad litem and the use of an adult support person; and allowing the use of testimonial aids, such as anatomical dolls. Janet Leach Richards, Protecting the Child Victim in Abuse Cases, 34 Fam. L.Q. 393, 400-401 (2000). Several federal courts have upheld the constitutionality of CVCWR. See, e.g., United States v. Garcia, 7 F.3d 885 (9th Cir. 1993); United States v. Carrier, 9 F.3d 867 (10th Cir. 1993).

b. Uniform Law. The Uniform Law Commissioners approved the Uniform Child Witness Testimony by Alternative Methods Act (UCWTAMA) in 2002. The Act provides authority for a judge in a civil or criminal proceeding to order a hearing (upon a motion by a party, child witness, or other individual with standing) to determine whether to allow a child to testify by an alternative method. The child's presence is not required at this hearing. Upon a showing of good cause, the judge will permit the child to testify outside the courtroom and outside the defendant's presence. To date, the Act has been approved by four states. See Uniform Child Witness Testimony by Alternative Methods Act, Legislative Fact Sheet, available at *http://nccusl.org/Update/uniformact_factsheets/uniformacts-fs-ucwtbama.asp* (last visited Oct. 15, 2004). Some commentators criticize the Act, claiming (1) it violates the federal Confrontation Clause, as interpreted by *Craig*, by encompassing *any* shielding procedure, by failing to limit the considerations by which judges permit shielding, and by not limiting the types of cases in which shielding is permissible; (2) it violates many state constitutional provisions requiring face-to-face confrontation; and (3) it has negative consequences from a public policy perspective by diminishing the presumption of innocence. See Katherine Grearson, Note, Proposed Uniform Child Witness Testimony Act: An Impermissible Abridgement of Criminal Defendants' Rights, 45 B.C. L. Rev. 467, 491-496 (2004).

(8) Constitutionality of Other Protective Procedures. States legislatures have enacted a number of protective mechanisms for child victims of sexual abuse, such as the following:

a. Videotaping. Many states authorize preservation of a child's testimony on videotape for later presentation at trial as a substitute for the presence of the child. Videotaping testimony eliminates the need for repeated interviews of the child. Some videotaping statutes require that the defendant be present and cross-examination be allowed at the videotaping session. Other statutes permit the videotape to be used subject to an opportunity for subsequent cross-examination at the judicial hearing. Is either type of statute constitutional after the Supreme Court's recent decision in Crawford v. Washington? See generally Michael D. Roth, Laissez-Faire Videoconferencing: Remote Witness Testimony and Adversarial Truth, 48 UCLA L. Rev. 185, 192 (2000).

b. Courtroom Closure. Despite the Sixth Amendment guarantee of a "public trial" in criminal prosecutions, trial judges have the discretion to close the courtroom to spectators and the press to lessen trauma to witnesses. The Supreme Court

[handwritten: issue of courtroom closure]

examined the constitutionality of one closure statute in Globe Newspaper v. Superior Court, 457 U.S. 596 (1982). Although finding mandatory courtroom closure unconstitutional, the Court permitted closure subject to a particularized finding on a case-by-case basis (taking into account the victim's age, maturity, and understanding; the nature of the crime; desires of the victims; and the interests of parents and relatives).

Note that federal legislation (the Child Victims' and Child Witnesses' Rights Act, supra) permits judges to close their courtrooms, at the judge's discretion, when child victims testify. See 18 U.S.C. §3509(e) (2000) (court may exclude all persons who do not have an interest in the case if the court determines that requiring the child to testify in open court would cause "substantial psychological harm to the child or would result in the child's inability to effectively communicate").

c. Child Courtroom.   One early suggestion for protecting child victims called for a special "child's courtroom."[12] Trial judges have discretion to modify trial practices to accommodate child witnesses, such as by making the courtroom setting more informal. Richards, supra, at 411.

(9) Hearsay Exceptions.   Reports of child abuse primarily come from teachers, law enforcement, and social and services personnel, as well as family friends and relatives (see supra p. 252).When the out-of-court statement of a child ("a declarant") to another person is offered at trial in order to establish the fact of the abuse ("the proof of the matter asserted"), the statement is termed "hearsay." Hearsay evidence is particularly useful in child abuse prosecutions because the child victim may be unavailable (i.e., unable) to testify.

Vigil raises the issue of the constitutionality of the admission of hearsay evidence under the Confrontation Clause. *Vigil* explains and applies the rule announced by the Supreme Court in Crawford v. Washington, 541 U.S. 36 (2004), a case that has created a "paradigm shift in confrontation clause analysis." Rene L. Valladares & Franny Forsman, Crawford v. Washington: The Confrontation Clause Gets Teeth, 12 Nev. Law. 12 (2004). According to *Crawford*, the admissibility of hearsay evidence now depends on whether the evidence is "testimonial." That is, nontestimonial statements are admissible based on traditional rules of evidence (i.e., traditional hearsay exceptions), whereas testimonial statements must not be admitted unless the declarant is *available* for cross-examination at trial or, *if the declarant is unavailable, the statement was previously subject to cross-examination.* Before *Crawford*, hearsay statements of an unavailable witness were admissible provided they fell within a "firmly rooted hearsay exception" (explained infra) or, alternatively, if they possessed sufficient indicia of reliability (i.e., the rule announced in Ohio v. Roberts, 448 U.S. 56 (1980)).

Although *Crawford* failed to define the meaning of "testimonial" for those statements that would evoke the need for cross-examination, the Court offered some guidance — statements that are the "functional equivalent" of in-court testimony (affidavits, custodial examinations, prior testimony) or "similar pre-trial statements that declarants would reasonably expect to be used prosecutorial." Id. at 1374. Clearly, a child's statement to law enforcement or government officers

---

[12] David Libai, The Protection of the Child Victim of a Sexual Offense in the Criminal Justice System, 15 Wayne L. Rev. 977 (1969).

is testimonial, in contrast to that of "a person who makes a casual remark to an acquaintance." Id. However, after *Crawford*, many statements made to others by child victims will be deemed inadmissible unless the statements fall within traditional exceptions to the hearsay rule (e.g., excited utterances or statements for the purpose of medical diagnosis and treatment, discussed infra).

As explained above, the Supreme Court in *Crawford* asserted that the determination of a statement as "testimonial" depends in part on whether the statement was made under circumstances that would lead a witness to believe that the statement would be available for use at a later trial. Should the admissibility of the child's out-of-court statement depend on whether *the child* reasonably believed that the statement could be used later for trial? How does *Vigil* respond to this issue? Is such a rule appropriate to characterize children's expectations? Why did the court in *Vigil* determine that some of the defendant's statements were "testimonial" and therefore should have been be excluded?

Beginning in the 1980s, many states responded to the problem of child sexual abuse by codifying "tender years" hearsay exceptions, by expanding two "firmly rooted" hearsay exceptions (the excited utterance and the medical diagnosis/treatment exception), and by increasing the use of residual or catch-all hearsay exceptions (which are admissible if statements have sufficient indicia of trustworthiness). The Federal Rules of Evidence, enacted in 1975, codify many of the preceding hearsay exceptions. What is the likely impact of *Crawford* on the following statutes?

a. Tender Years Hearsay Statutes. Prior to *Crawford*, many states have created special "tender years" hearsay exceptions that permit the admission of a sexually abused child's previous out-of-court statements (e.g., to a parent, friend, therapist), that would not be admissible under other hearsay exceptions. Most such statutes require that if the child is unavailable, there must be corroborative evidence. Some such statutes require that if the child is unavailable, the child must have been cross-examined when the statement was made. A few such statutes admit hearsay provided that, if the child is unavailable, the court determines that the statements are trustworthy. Robert G. Marks, Should We Believe the People Who Believe the Children?: The Need for a New Sexual Abuse Tender Years Hearsay Exception Statute, 32 Harv. J. On Legis. 207, 238-240 (1995)). Colorado, the jurisdiction in which *Vigil* was decided, has a "tender years" hearsay exception. See Colo. Rev. Stat. §§13-25-129, 18-3-411(3) (2003). Approximately 40 states currently have tender years hearsay statutes. Snowden v. State, 846 A.2d 36, 39 n. 7 (Md. Ct. App. 2003).

b. Excited Utterances or Spontaneous Declarations. An out-of-court statement is admissible provided that it was spontaneous and made under circumstances of shock or excitement. See Fed. R. Evid. 803(2). The rationale for this exception is that statements made while the declarant is in the throes of excitement are less likely to be fabricated. Many courts have expanded this exception for child sexual abuse victims to permit admission of a child's statement even if considerable time has elapsed between the abuse and the statement. Marks, supra, at 229.

c. Medical Diagnosis and Treatment. A statement is admissible under the medical diagnosis or treatment exception if the statement describes a medical condition and is pertinent to diagnosis or treatment. See Fed. R. Evid. 803(4). The rationale for this exception is that patients are likely to provide truthful information to health care providers because they know that false statements will affect their treatment. (Note that general statements about the abuse are admissible under this exception but not those relating to the identity of the perpetrator.) Marks, supra, at 230-231. In response to the difficulties of prosecuting child sexual abuse, states have expanded the medical diagnosis and treatment exception by broadly interpreting the terms "reasonably pertinent" and "medical diagnosis or treatment." Id. at 232.

Finally, a residual hearsay exception is sometimes used in child sexual abuse cases to admit statements that are not covered by another rule, provided that such statements have equivalent guarantees of trustworthiness. See Fed. R. Evid. 803(24) (for a declarant regardless of availability), 804(b)(5) (for a declarant who is unavailable).

Both excited utterance and medical diagnosis exceptions are considered "firmly rooted" hearsay exceptions. The residual exception and tender years statutory exception are not so considered. Marks, supra at 219.

The Supreme Court has decided two cases concerning the admissibility of a child's pretrial out-of-court statement to a physician. In Idaho v. Wright, 497 U.S. 805 (1990), a defendant was convicted of molestation of his five-year-old and two-year-old daughters based on the younger child's statements to a pediatrician. The statements were admitted under the state's "residual exception." (Resort to this exception was necessitated, rather than the exception for medical diagnosis and treatment, because the child incriminated her father as her *sister's* abuser.) Under the residual exception, to satisfy the Confrontation Clause, the prosecution has to produce the victim or, if he or she is unavailable, the statement has to manifest sufficient guarantees of reliability. Reversing the defendant's conviction, the Supreme Court held inadmissible the child's statements to her pediatrician because they lacked the requisite guarantees of trustworthiness for the reasons that the interview lacked procedural safeguards, contained leading questions, and was based on the doctor's preconceived ideas.

A subsequent case, White v. Illinois, 502 U.S. 346 (1992), also challenged the admissibility of statements about sexual assault in a case involving statements about a perpetrator made by a four-year-old girl to her mother, baby-sitter, police officer, emegency room nurse, and physician. The Supreme Court held that these statements were admissible (and that the prosecution was not required to produce the young victim at trial) under the spontaneous declaration and medical examination exceptions to the hearsay rule. Note that in *Crawford*, the Supreme Court admits that "Although our analysis in this case [*Crawford*] casts doubt on that holding [*White*], we need not definitively resolve whether it survives our decision today. . . . " 541 U.S. at 61.

(10) Other Protective Mechanisms.   States have developed additional protective evidentiary rules.

a. Child Sexual Abuse Accommodation Syndrome.   States have developed rules regarding the admissibility of evidence of a child sexual abuse accommodation syndrome (CSAAS) — a description of the behavioral characteristics of a child subjected to sexual abuse that explains his or her delays in reporting, half-truths, and recantations. Although the majority of jurisdictions reject CSAAS as direct evidence of the occurrence of the sexual abuse, many jurisdictions permit such evidence as rebuttal — i.e., to rehabilitate a child victim-witness. Pamela J. Jensen, Note, *Frye* v. *Daubert*: Practically the Same?, 87 Minn. L. Rev. 1579, 1604 (2003).

b. Anatomically Correct Dolls.   Many jurisdictions permit the use of anatomically correct dolls during the investigation of sexual abuse. Moreover, the trial judge has discretion to allow a child witness to testify using an anatomically correct doll. See, e.g., Commonwealth v. Trowbridge, 647 N.E.2d 413, 419 (Mass. 1995).

c. Abrogation of Marital Privilege.   Some states have statutory provisions eliminating the marital disqualification privilege (disqualifying a spouse as a witness against the other spouse) in cases of child sexual abuse. See, e.g., Mass. Gen. Laws ch. 233, §20 (West 2000).

d. Extensions of the Statute of Limitations; Delayed Discovery Rules.   Many states have adopted delayed discovery rules that extend the statute of limitations for tort recovery in child sexual abuse cases because many victims repress memories of the abuse for years afterward. See generally Elizabeth A. Wilson, Suing for Lost Childhood: Child Sexual Abuse, the Delayed Discovery Rule, and the Problem of Finding Justice for Adult-Survivors of Child Abuse, 12 UCLA Women's L.J. 145 (2003). See also Stogner v. California, 539 U.S. 607 (2003) (holding unconstitutional, as a violation of the Ex Post Facto Clause, the application of a state law extending the statute of limitations in a case of sexual child abuse to revive a prosecution that was time-barred at the time of enactment of the amendment). On the controversy about the admissibility of evidence based on repressed memories, see generally Lynn Holdsworth, Is It Repressed Memory with Delayed Recall or Is It False Memory Syndrome? The Controversy and Its Potential Legal Implications, 22 L. & Psychol. Rev. 103 (1998); Camille L. Fletcher, Note, Repressed Memories: Do Triggering Methods Contribute to Witness Testimony Reliability?, 13 Wash. U. J.L. & Pol'y 335 (2003).

Following the clergy sexual abuse scandal, the Massachusetts legislature extended the statute of limitations so that it began running three years after a minor reaches majority, and even further for victims of repressed memories. See Peter E. Smith, The Massachusetts Discovery Rule and Its Application to Non-Perpetrators in "Repressed Memory" Child Sexual Abuse Cases, 30 New Eng. J. Crim. & Civ. Confinement 179 (2004) (citing Mass. Gen. Laws ch. 260, §4C).

Are these protections necessary for child victims of sexual abuse? Should child witnesses be treated differently from adults by being accorded special treatment? In all cases? Or only in sexual abuse cases?

(11) **Vigil** *Epilogue.*   The Colorado Supreme Court subsequently granted certiorari to determine: (1) whether the victim's statements to the physician during the physical examination constitute "testimonial" evidence pursuant to *Crawford*; (2) whether the court of appeals correctly determined that the admission of the video-taped police interview was not harmless beyond a reasonable doubt; (3) whether the court of appeals erred in holding that admission of the victim's hearsay statements to his father and his father's friend did not violate the defendant's constitutional right of confrontation where the child was unavailable to testify at trial. People v. Vigil, No. O4SC 532, 2004 WL 2926003 (Colo. Dec. 20, 2004).

(12) **Problem.**   Defendant is charged with molesting three girls ranging in age from eight to ten years while he was living with the mother of one of the girls. The trial court admits the incriminating statement of a social worker from the County Department of Health and Human Services who conducted an unrecorded interview, using nonleading questions, with the victims after the social worker received a police

report. Maryland's tender years exemption statute permits child victims under age 12 not to testify in certain sexual abuse cases and authorizes testimony of certain persons in lieu of the child. Defendant complains that admission of the social worker's testimony violates his right to confrontation. What result? Snowden v. State, 846 A.2d 36 (Md. App. 2004).

D. STANDARD FOR INTERVENTION AND DISPOSITIONAL ALTERNATIVES

This section focuses on when the state should assume primary responsibility for the care and custody of children by intervention in the parent-child relationship. It examines the standard for intervention, which includes broad statutory definitions of parental neglect, and explores that standard in the context of both short-term summary removal, as well as long-term state-sponsored foster care. It presents criticisms of the foster care system as well as foster care reform. Finally, it discusses the remedy of termination of parental rights.

1. When Should the State Remove?

Roe v. Conn
417 F. Supp. 769 (M.D. Ala. 1976)

Before RIVES, Circuit Judge, JOHNSON, Chief District Judge, and VARNER, District Judge.

[These class actions challenge the constitutionality of Alabama's child neglect law. Ala. Code Tit. 13, §350 et seq. (1958). Plaintiff Wambles represents the class of mothers and plaintiff Roe represents the class of children who have been or may be subject to the removal provisions without a prior hearing where there was no showing of immediate or threatened harm.]

Findings of Fact

Margaret Wambles is a 25-year-old white woman who has never married. On September 15, 1971, Plaintiff Wambles gave birth to a son, Richard Roe, who lived with her continuously until June 2, 1975, when he was seized by Officer L. T. Conn of the Montgomery Police Department and placed in the custody of the Montgomery County Department of Pensions and Security. This seizure was ordered by Judge Thetford of the Montgomery County Family Court without affording Plaintiff Wambles prior notice and a hearing. Such authority as exists for this action is provided by Alabama Code, Title 13, §350(2) and 352(4), which purports to permit a juvenile court judge to summarily remove a "neglected child" from its home if the judge believes the child's welfare so warrants.[1]

---

[1] Title 13, §350(2) reads in pertinent part:

   The words "neglected child" shall mean any child, who, while under sixteen years of age . . . has no proper parental care or guardianship or whose home by reason of neglect,

The investigation which led to termination of Plaintiff Wambles' parental rights was prompted by Defendant Coppage. Mr. Coppage, who is white, lived intermittently with Plaintiff Wambles from 1970 until March, 1975, and claims to have fathered Richard Roe. On June 1, 1975, Mr. Coppage contacted the Montgomery Police Department and reported that Plaintiff Wambles might be neglecting Richard Roe, that she had been evicted from her former residence because she was keeping company with black males, and that she had moved to Highland Village (a black neighborhood) where she was living with a black man. On the basis of this information, Police Officer Conn initiated an investigation of Plaintiff Wambles. The records of the Montgomery Police Department were checked but revealed no previous complaints of child neglect against Plaintiff Wambles and no adult file on her.

Officer Conn went to the Wambles' residence . . . at approximately 7:30 P.M. on June 2, 1975. Plaintiff Wambles permitted Officer Conn to enter and inspect her dwelling, which the officer found was a two-bedroom apartment, where Plaintiff Wambles and her son were living with a black man to whom she was not married. Richard Roe was clothed, clean, and in "fairly good" physical condition with no signs of physical abuse. The home was "relatively clean" and stocked with "adequate food." Upon completing his inspection, Defendant Conn left the home and called Defendant Ward [director of the county youth facility] and reported his findings. He was then instructed by Defendant Ward to go to the Youth Facility and get a pick-up order. The only facts about Margaret Wambles known to Judge Thetford before he issued the pick-up order were that she was unemployed and that she and her child are white and were living with a black man in a black neighborhood. Judge Thetford had no information as to how long Margaret Wambles had lived in Montgomery, where she had worked, or how long she had been unemployed. He had no evidence that Richard Roe was being physically abused and no information as to the condition of the Wambles' home. Judge Thetford knew nothing about the man with whom Margaret Wambles was living, other than his race and the fact that he was not married to her. Judge Thetford testified that the race of the man with whom Plaintiff Wambles was living was relevant to his decision to order

---

cruelty, or depravity, on the part of his parent or parents, guardian or other person in whose care he may be, is an unfit and improper place for such child . . . or is under such improper or insufficient guardianship or control as to endanger the morals, health or general welfare of such child . . . or who for any other cause is in need of the care and protection of the state.

Sec. 350(4) provides that any child described as neglected shall be subject to the guardianship of the state and entitled to its care and protection. Sec. 352 sets forth the procedure to be followed in a child neglect case. A verified complaint is first filed with the juvenile court of the county of the child's residence by any person having knowledge of, or information concerning, the child. It is sufficient for the petition, after briefly stating the relevant facts, to aver that the named child is neglected and in need of the care and protection of the state. Upon the filing of the petition, the judge, clerk, or chief probation officer of the court shall cause an examination to be made and shall issue a summons requiring the child to appear before the court. Sec. 352(4) provides that, "If it appears from the petition that . . . the child is in such condition that its welfare requires that custody be immediately assumed, the judge of the court may endorse upon the summons a direction that the officer serving said summons shall at once take said child into his custody." The statute further provides that the custody of any child who has been summarily seized is subject to the discretion of the judge pending hearing of the case.

[The Alabama neglect provisions have been amended, effective January 15, 1977.]

Richard Roe removed from his mother's custody, particularly because they were living in a black neighborhood. Judge Thetford concluded that this habitation in a black neighborhood could be dangerous for a child because it was his belief that "it was not a healthy thing for a white child to be the only [white] child in a black neighborhood."

At approximately 8:30 P.M. on June 2, 1975, after obtaining the pick-up order, Defendant Conn, accompanied by two other Montgomery police officers, returned to Plaintiff Wambles' home. When Defendant Conn announced that he had come to take Richard Roe, Plaintiff Wambles picked up her child and ran to the back of the apartment. After Defendant Conn showed Plaintiff Wambles the pick-up order, she still refused to surrender the child. Thereupon, with the child crying, "No, mama, don't let him take me," Defendant Conn grabbed Plaintiff Wambles by the arm and pulled her back into the living room, took Richard Roe from her arms, and left without leaving a copy of the pick-up order. After the seizure, Defendant Conn took Richard Roe to a DPS-licensed shelter home in Montgomery.

No hearing was scheduled or held following Richard Roe's removal until July 10, 1975. No attorney was requested or appointed to represent Richard Roe at the July 10 hearing. At the hearing in the Family Court of Montgomery County, both Defendant Coppage and Plaintiff Wambles were present and represented by counsel. Judge Thetford entered an order on July 11, 1975, wherein he awarded Defendant Coppage custody of Richard Roe after making a finding that he was the natural father of the child. . . .

Expert Testimony

Plaintiffs Wambles and Roe have submitted the testimony of witnesses Dr. Sally A. Provence and Dr. Albert J. Solnit as experts in the field of child care and development. Drs. Provence and Solnit summarized their views as follows:

1. Summary removal of a young child from a parent who has been his major caregiver is a severe threat to his development. It disrupts and grossly endangers what he most needs, that is, the continuity of affectionate care from those to whom he is attached through bonds of love.

2. Summary removal should be allowed only under conditions in which physical survival is at stake.

3. In situations in which some interference is indicated because parents are unable to take good care of their child, there are alternatives to summary removal which should be used either singly or in combination. Among these are the following: (a) the provision in the child's home of assistance to parents with child care and with managing a household; (b) the provision of counselling to parents about how to care for a child in ways that enhance his development and well-being; (c) the provision of a day care center or day care family in which assistance to child and parent can be provided which is addressed to their specific needs; (d) the provision of a residential facility or foster family in which both parent and child can receive the nurture and guidance they may need (in extended families, relatives often supply such benevolent help, and when they are unavailable, it is one of society's responsibilities to organize and make available such assistance); and (e) the

provision of 24-hour substitute care for a child, which does not cut him off from contact with his parents. . . .

Conclusions of Law

The Fundamental Right to Family Integrity

A district court in Iowa recently reviewed the long line of Supreme Court cases addressed to the constitutional interests at stake where various aspects of family life are threatened and concluded that there is a fundamental right to family integrity protected by the Fourteenth Amendment to the United States Constitution. Alsager v. District Court of Polk County, Iowa, 406 F. Supp. 10, 15 (S.D. Iowa 1975). . . .

This Court is in full agreement . . . that the Constitution recognizes as fundamental the right of family integrity. This means that in our present case the state's severance of Plaintiff Wambles' parent-child relationship and of Plaintiff Roe's child-parent relationship will receive strict judicial scrutiny. Recognizing that fundamental right, this Court will now apply the pertinent constitutional principles to the facts of the present case.

Summary Seizure

This Court holds that Alabama Code, Title 13, §352(4), which authorizes summary seizure of a child "if it appears that . . . the child is in such condition that its welfare requires," violates procedural due process under the Fourteenth Amendment of the United States Constitution.

To determine the nature of the procedural safeguards that the Constitution mandates, the administrative needs of the State must be carefully balanced against the interests of the affected citizens. There is no question that the family members will suffer a grievous loss if the State severs the parent-child relationship; an interest, we have held, that is part of the liberty concept of the Fourteenth Amendment. The State of Alabama, on the other hand, does have a legitimate interest in protecting children from harm as quickly as possible. Normally, before intrusion into the affairs of the family is allowed, the State should have reliable evidence that a child is in need of protective care. In the absence of exigent circumstances, this fact-finding process, as a matter of basic fairness, should provide notice to the parents and child of the evidence of abuse and provide them with an opportunity for rebuttal at a hearing before an impartial tribunal.

The facts of this case dispel any notion that the State was faced with an emergency situation. As we earlier found, Officer Conn's investigation revealed that Richard Roe was clothed, clean, and in "fairly good" physical condition with no signs of physical abuse. The Wambles' home was "relatively clean" and stocked with "adequate food." Without danger of immediate harm or threatened harm to the child, the State's interest in protecting the child is not sufficient to justify a removal of the child prior to notice and a hearing. Additionally, even in the event summary seizure had been justified, a hearing would have had to follow the seizure "as soon as practicable" and not six weeks later as it did in the present case. . . . For these reasons, this Court is of the opinion that Alabama Code Title 13, §352(4) violates the procedural due process clause of the Fourteenth Amendment. . . .

Removal Upon a Finding of "Neglect"

After the hearing on July 10, 1975, Judge Thetford ordered the termination of the parental rights of Plaintiff Wambles to Richard Roe on the basis that the child was "a dependent or neglected child as defined by the laws of Alabama." . . .

. . . It is not disputed that the State of Alabama has a legitimate interest in the welfare of children. Minor intrusions into the affairs of the family may be permitted when the State has reason to believe that a child's best interest is at stake. In such cases, various options and alternatives are available to the State to achieve its objective of child protection. One possibility might be a requirement that the parents attend seminars and weekly counselling sessions on child care and the responsibilities of parenthood. Another situation might warrant supervision of the parents by a welfare counselor or the placing of a neutral person — such as an aunt — in the home to serve as a bridge between the parents and the child. The State's interest, however, would become "compelling" enough to sever entirely the parent-child relationship only when the child is subjected to real physical or emotional harm and less drastic measures would be unavailing.

Here, the State offered no assistance to Plaintiff Wambles, who was faced with the troubling predicament of raising a young child without the aid of a husband, nor did it explore the possibility of accomplishing its objective of protecting Richard Roe's welfare by use of alternatives other than termination of custody.

The Alabama statute defining "neglected" children sweeps far past the constitutionally permissible range of interference into the sanctity of the family unit. The fact that a home is "improper" in the eyes of the state officials does not necessarily mean that a child in that home is subject to physical or emotional harm.

[T]he state's burden is not only to show that the child is being disadvantaged but also to show that the child is being harmed in a real and substantial way. Accordingly, this Court declares Alabama Code, Title 13, §§350 and 352 unconstitutional, because it violates the family integrity of Margaret Wambles and all other mothers in the class represented by her and the family integrity of Richard Roe and all other children in the class represented by him.

This Court holds, as an alternative ground, that the challenged statutory provisions are unconstitutionally vague. . . . In the present case, not only is the statutory definition of neglect circular (a neglected child is any child who has no proper parental care by reason of neglect), but it is couched in terms that have no common meaning. . . . When is a home an "unfit" or "improper" place for a child? Obviously, this is a question about which men and women of ordinary intelligence would greatly disagree. Their answers would vary in large measure in relation to their differing social, ethical, and religious views. Because these terms are too subjective to denote a sufficient warning to those individuals who might be affected by their proscription, the statute is unconstitutionally vague. . . .

Appointment of Counsel for the Child

The Plaintiffs maintain that the Alabama child custody procedure violates the due process clause of the Constitution because that procedure does not provide for the appointment of independent counsel to represent a child in a neglect proceeding, and none was appointed here. We agree. . . .

. . . The juvenile court judge should, however, independently appoint counsel for the child, requiring the parents, if they are financially able, to pay for this legal representation. If the parents are indigent, free counsel should be afforded the child.

Consideration of Race

Plaintiffs contend that there was a racial animus behind the decision to remove Richard Roe from his mother's custody. It is undisputed that Judge Thetford, at the time he signed the pick-up order, knew only that Margaret Wambles was unemployed, that she and her child are white, and that they were living in a black neighborhood with a black man to whom Plaintiff Wambles was not married.

While a white child who is part of an interracial family unit and lives in a black neighborhood may be disadvantaged socially or culturally, this fact alone does not rise to the level of harm to the child that is required before the State can terminate the parent's right to custody of the child.[16] Since race per se can never amount to sufficient harm to justify a constitutional termination, this Court finds it unnecessary to decide whether consideration of racial factors by a juvenile court judge represents prohibited racial discrimination. . . .

[I]t is Ordered, Adjudged and Decreed by this Court that:

1. Defendants are hereby enjoined from enforcing the summary removal provision of Alabama Code, Title 13, §352(4) (1958), insofar as it permits summary removal of the child in the absence of the danger of immediate or threatened harm to the child.

2. Defendants are hereby enjoined from enforcing the standards of "neglect" found in Alabama Code, Title 13, §350(2) insofar as the statute permits removal of a child from parental custody in the absence of a showing of physical or emotional harm to the child.

3. Defendants are enjoined from instituting change of custody proceedings without independent counsel appointed to represent the child.

Since the State proceedings that terminated Margaret Wambles' custody over Richard Roe and the award of custody to Cecil Coppage are tainted with unconstitutionality, the rights of the parties should be returned to the status quo ante. This Court, however, believes that, when the interest of a young child is at stake, we should proceed cautiously, not unmindful of the changed circumstances of the child even though these changes were unconstitutionally accomplished. Accordingly, it is further ordered, adjudged and decreed by the Court that:

4. The State Department of Pensions and Security immediately reassume custody of Richard Roe pending further action in regard to his custody. If the State has not initiated within 30 days neglect proceedings consistent with the dictates of the United States Constitution, Defendants are further enjoined to deliver Richard Roe back to the custody of Margaret Wambles. . . .

---

[16] Neither is the fact that the parent is living with someone to whom he or she is not married. "Immorality" of the parent, without a showing that the child is being physically or emotionally harmed in a real way, is not sufficient justification for the State to terminate a parent-child relationship.

NOTES AND QUESTIONS

(1) Stages of Intervention.   Roe v. Conn reveals the stages of juvenile court intervention in cases of child abuse and neglect. Initial intervention takes two forms: *summary seizure* or the assertion of *temporary custody.* If the court determines that an emergency exists, the court may order (in an ex parte hearing) that the child be immediately removed from the home. On the other hand, the adversarial proceeding regarding temporary custody (termed a "jurisdictional hearing") determines whether the child falls within the statutory definition of an abused or neglected child. The next stage occurs after this jurisdictional determination when the court conducts a "dispositional hearing." At that time, the court chooses among various dispositions (e.g., conditions on custody, foster care, termination of parental rights).

(2) Threshold for Removal.   According to Roe v. Conn, what is the standard for summary seizure of a child from the home? What is the standard for termination of parental rights? How do the standards differ?

Roe v. Conn enjoined removal from parental custody under a neglect statute in the absence of a showing of "physical or emotional harm." How does one show emotional abuse or neglect? Should emotional maltreatment be a basis for removing a child via summary seizure or via termination of parental rights? Is it possible to predict when a child is emotionally endangered? Or does such an inquiry invite predictions beyond the capacity of the behavioral sciences? Can an inquiry requiring predictions of future emotional harm to the child do more harm than good? If there is a showing of physical or emotional harm, should removal be permitted even if there are reasonable means of protecting the child at home?

For a criticism that the practice of emergency removal is used far more frequently than necessary to protect children from harm and causes emotional damage to children, see Paul Chill, Burden of Proof Begone: The Pernicious Effect of Emergency Removal in Child Protective Proceedings, 42 Fam. Ct. Rev. 540 (2004).

(3) Emotional Maltreatment.   Courts have been slow to recognize emotional maltreatment as child abuse, in part because emotional maltreatment (unlike physical abuse) leaves no *physical* marks. Early definitions of "abuse" emphasized serious physical injuries. CAPTA, in requiring a minimal definition by states as a condition of their receiving federal funds, defines "child abuse" and "neglect" as

> the physical or *mental injury*, sexual abuse or exploitation, negligent treatment, or maltreatment of a child under the age of eighteen, or the age specified by the child protection law of the State, by a person including any employee of a residential facility or any staff person providing out of home care who is responsible for the child's welfare under circumstances indicating harm or threatened harm to the child's health or welfare. The term encompasses both acts and omissions on the part of a responsible person. [45 C.F.S. §1340.2(d) (2003) (originally codified at 42 U.S.C. §5106(g)) (emphasis added).]

States subsequently refined their definitions, thereby permitting considerable variation.

(4) In an omitted footnote, the court suggests that in a divorce proceeding, the more open-ended "best interest" standard would be "entirely appropriate." How is

this case different from a divorce custody fight? Is this case not simply a private dispute between the child's mother and a man who claims to be the child's father? The case makes plain that "race per se" and "parental immorality in itself "can never amount to sufficient harm" to justify state removal from parental custody in a neglect proceeding. In a divorce custody dispute, is it appropriate to take race and sexual conduct into consideration? For discussion of this issue, see Chapter 5.

(4) Counsel for the Abused Child. Do you agree that independent counsel for the child is constitutionally compelled in a child abuse and neglect proceeding? If so, is counsel required because the child's interest may not coincide with that of either the state or the parents? See discussion of Lassiter v. Department of Social Services, p. 360, infra. How should the child's representative decide what the child's interests are? By asking the child what he or she wants? By deciding on behalf of the child what is best for the child? See Donald N. Duquette, Legal Representation for Children in Protection Proceedings: Two Distinct Lawyer Roles Are Required, 34 Fam. L.Q. 441 (2000).

a. CAPTA and the GAL. Federal legislation spurred the adoption of guardian ad litem (GAL) programs for abused and neglected children. The Child Abuse Prevention and Treatment Act (CAPTA) of 1974, 42 U.S.C. §§5101-5707 (2000), requires that for states to qualify for federal funds for the prevention and treatment of abuse

> in every case involving an abused or neglected child which results in a judicial proceeding, a guardian ad litem, who has received training appropriate to the role, and who may be an attorney or a court appointed special advocate who has received training appropriate to that role (or both), shall be appointed to represent the child."
> [42 U.S.C. §5106a(b)(2)(A)(xiii) (2000 & West Supp. 2004).]

The Act does not require that the GAL be an attorney. Only about half of the states so require. Randi Mandelbaum, Revisiting the Question of Whether Young Children in Child Protection Proceedings Should Be Represented by Lawyers, 32 Loy. U. Chi. L.J. 1, 23 (2000). Should the child's representative be an attorney? Why or why not?

b. ABA Standards of Practice. The ABA approved the Standards of Practice for Lawyers Who Represent Children in Abuse and Neglect Cases in 1996. See Standards of Practice for Lawyers Who Represent Children in Abuse and Neglect Cases (reprinted in 29 Fam. L.Q. 375 (1995)). The Standards provide that the child's attorney should represent the child's expressed preferences. If the attorney believes that the child's preference would be seriously injurious to the child, the lawyer may request appointment of a separate guardian ad litem — while continuing to represent the child's expressed preference "unless the child's position is prohibited by law or without any factual foundation." According to the ABA Standards, the attorney shall not reveal to the judge the basis of the attorney's request for appointment of a guardian ad litem that would compromise the child's position. See generally David R. Katner, Coming to Praise, Not to Bury, the New ABA Standards of Practice for Lawyers who Represent Children in Abuse and Neglect Cases, 14 Geo. J. Legal Ethics 103 (2000).

*(5) **Child Abandonment as Neglect.*** The rising incidence of abandonment of newborns prompted legislatures to enact "Baby Moses" statutes. These statutes permit mothers who have given birth to surrender their newborn within the first hours of life to a hospital employee, anonymously and without fear of criminal prosecution. Are these safe haven laws an appropriate response to the problem of child abandonment? Do these laws violate the father's due process rights? See Dayna R. Cooper, Note, Fathers Are Parents Too: Challenging Safe Haven Laws with Procedural Due Process, 31 Hofstra L. Rev. 877, 878 (2003) (so arguing, and pointing out that 42 states have enacted such statutes).

In re Deborah G., Georgia G., Bruce G., and Elizabeth G.

2d Civil No. 40391, Cal. Ct. App., June 29, 1973 (unpublished opinion)

WOOD, J. . . .

George and Patricia G. are the parents of five children: Michael, age 15;[1] Deborah, age 11; Georgia, age 7; Bruce, age 5; and Elizabeth, age 2. . . . Deborah and Georgia had been adjudged dependent children in Alameda County in 1969, approximately two years prior to the herein proceedings; however, they remained in the family home.

The petitions herein were filed in 1971. In each petition, it is alleged that the child is under 21 years of age, and comes within the provisions of "Section 600b of the Juvenile Court Law of California" (Welf. & Inst. Code, §600, subd. (b)) in that the home of said minor "is an unfit place for him in that his home has become and is an unkempt and unsanitary place of living."

Evidence at the hearing of the petitions included testimony by a probation officer, a school nurse, the director of the housing authority, the maintenance foreman of the housing authority, a neighbor of the Gibsons, and a deputy sheriff. Some of that testimony . . . follows:

Prior to 1970, two of respondents' children had been adjudged dependent children of the juvenile court in Alameda County. In early 1970 respondents moved into San Luis Obispo County, and resided there with five of the children. Commencing in early 1970 employees of various governmental agencies visited the family home. In substance, they noticed that the house was "very filthy" and a strong odor emanated therefrom; the floors were "sticky" with food particles and dog hairs; the children were dirty and had body odors; lice were removed from the head of one child; garbage and litter were in the backyard; trash was in the living room; the bathroom was "terribly dirty" and "full of flies"; the kitchen floor was encrusted with food and dirt; pans of grease were on the stove, and there was an odor of stale food; the bedding was dirty; and the children were frequently absent from school.

The nurse testified that on several occasions she requested that respondents clean the house and that in her opinion the family was not being handled well and it would take a "superhuman" effort for respondents to become adequate parents through counseling. The director of the housing authority continuously urged

---

[1] Michael is not a party in this appeal. Apparently Mrs. G. is also the mother of three other children who were previously placed in foster homes.

respondents to clean their house; and the maintenance foreman of the housing authority testified that the condition of the kitchen was so filthy that he hated to go in there before his noon meal.

Respondents (parents) testified and called five witnesses, including a social worker. Such testimony was in part as follows:

Each of the respondents was overweight and in poor health (diabetes and gout), and their disabilities made it difficult to keep the house clean. They loved their children, and the children were not dirtier than ordinary children; the house (according to the social worker) was not dirtier than the average house;[2] there was mutual affection between the parents and the children; conditions of the home improved after the first visit by the social worker; a homemaker employed by the county visited the home on 20 or more occasions since 1970 to give Mrs. Gibson training and help; the homemaker did not think that the home presented a health hazard; the children were in good health, except for minor ailments; the children were happy; and there was no evidence of unkindness or cruelty by the parents.

Some of the petitioner's evidence was presented at a hearing on November 29, 1971, to determine jurisdiction of the juvenile court over Bruce and Elizabeth, and to consider the issue of dependent status of Deborah and Georgia (who had previously been adjudged dependent children of the juvenile court in Alameda County). The juvenile court temporarily removed the four children from the family home; and continued the hearing to December 6, 1971. Further evidence was presented by the parties on that date, and the matter was continued to December 13, 1972, at which time the parties presented further evidence.

The court found that Bruce and Elizabeth were dependent children within the provisions of section 600, subdivision (b), of the Juvenile Court Law (Welf. & Inst. Code, §600, subd. (b)), and that they should be removed from custody of the parents pursuant to section 726, subdivisions (a) and (c) of said code; and ordered that each of them be placed in the home of foster parents under supervision of the county, with arrangements for the parents to visit them. As to Deborah and Georgia, the court found that an order continuing the status of each of them as a dependent child for one year was necessary; and the provisions of said section 726, subdivisions (a) and (c), required that their custody be taken from the parents. It was ordered that the previous commitment of said children to the home of foster parents remain in effect, with arrangements for visits by their parents.

As to appellants' contention that the petitioner did not sustain the burden of proving the allegations of the petition, they argue: The allegations of the petition did not give fair notice of the grounds for adjudicating that the children were dependent children under section 600, subdivision (b), of said code; and petitioner (probation officer) did not present sufficient evidence to establish the alleged grounds for such adjudication.

---

[2] The testimony of that witness regarding the condition of the house was contradicted by a report which that witness had written previously. Also, testimony of another social worker was presented by respondents (parents) in the form of a letter; and on cross-examination that witness testified that in a previous letter he had stated that "this is a long-term case of a multiproblem family. The physical home environment has been a long-term chronic problem and does not appear to be improved."

In wardship proceedings the welfare of the child is of paramount concern. [T]he findings of the juvenile court will not be disturbed on appeal where there is substantial evidence to support them. . . .

In the present case each petition alleged in part that the minor came within the provisions of section "600b" of the Juvenile Court Law of California in that the home of the minor "is an unfit place for him in that his home has become and is an unkempt and unsanitary place of living." [T]he court said that there was "clear, competent and credible testimony . . . that the home of the parents is not a suitable place of abode for any said minors and that the home provided by the parents is an unfit place by reason of neglect." Findings (as to each minor) were in part that "all of the allegations of the petition are true, and that said minor is a person described by and coming within the provisions of Section 600(b) of the Juvenile Court Law." In the circumstances, the allegations of each petition gave the respondents reasonable notice of the grounds upon which deprivation of custody of the child was sought, evidence was presented on those grounds, and there was no material variance between the allegations of the petition and the findings. Respondents were not denied due process of law.

Also, there was substantial evidence to support the findings that each child was a dependent child within the provisions of said section 600, subdivision (b). . . . There was sufficient evidence to the effect that the home was unkempt and unsanitary so as to be an unfit place, by reason of neglect, and not a suitable abode for the children; efforts were made by various officials to help respondents remedy such neglect; such efforts were of no avail; such neglect continued for a substantial period of time; each parent was ill and overweight to the extent that it was difficult for them to keep the house clean; and extraordinary efforts would be required in order to improve the situation by counseling the parents. Petitioner was not required, as appellants assert, to prove that the conditions of the abode cause "sickness and disease of mind or body" in order to establish "neglect" within the meaning of said section 600, subdivision (b). As above stated, the welfare of the child is of paramount concern, and a purpose of the juvenile court law is to secure for each minor such care and guidance as will serve the spiritual, emotional, mental, and physical welfare of the minor and the best interests of the state. . . .

[T]he unfitness of a home for a particular child (as provided in said section 600, subd. (b)) is a relative concept, and it cannot be determined except by judicial appraisal of all available evidence bearing on the child's best interests. In the present case the findings that each child was a dependent child, under said section 600, subdivision (b), were supported by substantial evidence. . . .

Appellant further contends that the court erred in ordering removal of the children from the family home (dispositional orders). As to each child, the court made a finding and order that the child be removed from the family home pursuant to section 726, subdivisions (a) and (c), of the Welfare and Institutions Code, which provides in part: "In all cases wherein a minor is adjudged a ward or dependent child of the court, the court may limit the control to be exercised over such . . . dependent child by any parent . . . but no ward or dependent child shall be taken from the physical custody of a parent . . . unless upon the hearing the court finds one of the following facts: (a) That the parent . . . is incapable of providing or has failed or neglected to provide proper maintenance, training and education of the minor. . . . (c) That the welfare of the minor requires that his custody be taken from his parent."

Appellants argue that the court, in making its findings under the above cited provisions, failed to consider uncontradicted evidence that the family, when furnished with homemaking and other services to which they were entitled by law, were capable of maintaining a sanitary home. Although there was testimony to the effect that improvements in condition of the home occurred after homemaking and other social services were provided, there was also testimony (by nurse) that the improvements did not last longer than a month, then there would be another complaint. Appellants also argue that the court in making its order was influenced "erroneously" by references in the probation report to services which the parents had received for many years. It is to be noted, however, that section 706 of the Welfare and Institutions Code provides that the juvenile court, with reference to the question of the proper disposition of the minor, "shall receive in evidence the social study of the minor made by the probation officer . . . and in any judgment and order of disposition, shall state the social study made by the probation officer has been read and considered by the court." As to the court's rejection of further proposed testimony as to availability of additional services, no offer of proof was made as to such testimony, and in view of the continuing inability of the parents to remedy conditions of the home when services had been provided, it appears that the court could properly reject further evidence of services which might be available. The evidence was sufficient to support the findings that the minors should be removed from the home and to support the orders removing them.

The orders are affirmed.

QUESTIONS

(1) Do you think there was evidence that the children's health was seriously endangered? Without such a showing, should the state be allowed to remove the children from parental custody? Even if the filth did not endanger the children's health? Is this constitutional?

(2) Do you believe it is a good thing for the evaluation of parental attitudes and behavior to depend upon a judge's (or social worker's) personal values?

Most foster children come from poor families. The foster care system has long been criticized as being class biased.[13] Even though there are other plausible explanations for the high proportion of foster children from poor families, present day juvenile court standards allow a judge to impart his personal values into the decision-making process and therefore leave considerable scope for imposition of middle-class biases.

(3) If the parents are prepared to cooperate, should removal ever be allowed where the children can be protected in the home with reasonable services? Why shouldn't the state be required to provide services to protect children within the home rather than removing the children? Foster care is extremely expensive.[14]

[13] See Daan Braveman & Sarah Ramsey, When Welfare Ends: Removing Children from the Home for Poverty Alone, 70 Temple L. Rev. 447 (1997); Candra Bullock, Comment, Low-Income Parents Victimized by Child Protective Services, 11 Am. U. J. Gender Soc. Pol'y & L. 1023 (2003); Andrea Charlow, Race, Poverty, and Neglect, 28 Wm. Mitchell L. Rev. 763 (2001).

[14] The average monthly cost of foster care is $387 for children age 2, $404 for children age 9, and $462 for those age 16. U.S. Dept. of Health and Human Services, Foster Care, Basic Monthly

Wouldn't it be much cheaper simply to send in a housecleaning service to clean up the house at regular intervals? Consider the excerpt below on the policy dilemmas of home versus foster care placement. See also In re A.H., 842 A.2d 674 (D.C. 2004) (affirming removal of five children from parental custody for an unsanitary home environment).

(4) In *Deborah G.* note how vague, open-ended, and subjective the statutory standard of Welfare and Institutions Code §600(b) is. When is a home an "unfit place"? How is a judge to decide what is proper? Would section 600 be unconstitutional under the standards of Roe v. Conn?

Section 600 has since been amended to provide more specific standards for removal. It is now Welfare and Institutions Code §300, infra. Would *Deborah G.* have been decided differently under this new statutory standard?

California Welfare & Institutions Code §§300, 361 (West Supp. 1999)

§300. Children Subject to Jurisdiction . . .

Any child who comes within any of the following descriptions is within the jurisdiction of the juvenile court which may adjudge that person to be a dependent child of the court:

> (a) The child has suffered, or there is a substantial risk that the child will suffer, serious physical harm inflicted nonaccidentally upon the child by the child's parent or guardian. For the purposes of this subdivision, a court may find there is a substantial risk of serious future injury based on the manner in which a less serious injury was inflicted, a history of repeated inflictions of injuries on the child or the child's siblings, or a combination of these and other actions by the parent or guardian which indicate the child is at risk of serious physical harm. For purposes of this subdivision, "serious physical harm" does not include reasonable and age-appropriate spanking to the buttocks where there is no evidence of serious physical injury.

> (b) The child has suffered, or there is a substantial risk that the child will suffer, serious physical harm or illness, as a result of the failure or inability of his or her parent or guardian to adequately supervise or protect the child, or the willful or negligent failure of the child's parent or guardian to adequately supervise or protect the child from the conduct of the custodian with whom the child has been left, or by the willful or negligent failure of the parent or guardian to provide the child with adequate, food, clothing, shelter, or medical treatment, or by the inability of the parent or guardian to provide regular care for the child due to the parent's or guardian's mental illness, developmental disability, or substance abuse. No child shall be found to be a person described by this subdivision solely due to lack of an emergency

---

Maintenance Rates for Children Ages 2, 9, and 16, Selected Years 1994-2000 (cited in Comm. on Ways & Means., 108th Cong., 2d Sess., Background Material and Data on Programs Within the Jurisdiction of the Committee on Ways and Means (2004 Green Book 11-29 (Comm. Print 2004))).

shelter for the family. Whenever it is alleged that a child comes within the jurisdiction of the court on the basis of the parent or guardian's willful failure to provide adequate medical treatment or specific decision to provide spiritual treatment through prayer, the court shall give deference to the parent's or guardian's medical treatment, nontreatment, or spiritual treatment through prayer alone in accordance with the tenets and practices of a recognized church or religious denomination, by an accredited practitioner thereof, and shall not assume jurisdiction unless necessary to protect the child from suffering serious physical harm or illness. . . .

(c) The child is suffering serious emotional damage, or is at substantial risk of suffering serious emotional damage, evidenced by severe anxiety, depression, withdrawal, or untoward aggressive behavior toward self or others, as a result of the conduct of the parent or guardian or who has no parent or guardian capable of providing appropriate care. No child shall be found to be a person described by this subdivision if the willful failure of the parent or guardian to provide adequate mental health treatment is based on a sincerely held religious belief and if a less intrusive judicial intervention is available.

(d) The child has been sexually abused, or there is a substantial risk that the child will be sexually abused, as defined in Section 11165.1 of the Penal Code, by his or her parent or guardian or a member of his or her household, or the parent or guardian has failed to adequately protect the child from sexual abuse when the parent or guardian knew or reasonably should have known that the child was in danger of sexual abuse.

(e) The child is under the age of five and has suffered severe physical abuse by a parent, or by any person known by the parent, if the parent knew or reasonably should have known that the person was physically abusing the child. . . .

(f) The child's parent or guardian has been convicted of causing the death of another child through abuse or neglect.

(g) The child has been left without any provision for support; physical custody of the child has been voluntarily surrendered pursuant to Section 1255.7 of the Health and Safety Code [newborn abandonment provision] and the child has not been reclaimed within the 14-day period specified in subdivision (e) of that section; the child's parent has been incarcerated or institutionalized and cannot arrange for the care of the child; or a relative or other adult custodian with whom the child resides or has been left is unwilling or unable to provide care or support for the child, the whereabouts of the parent are unknown, and reasonable efforts to locate the parent have been unsuccessful. . . .

(i) The child has been subjected to an act or acts of cruelty by the parent or guardian or a member of his or her household, or the parent or guardian has failed to adequately protect the child from an act or acts of cruelty when the parent or guardian knew or reasonably should have known that the child was in danger of being subjected to an act or acts of cruelty.

(j) The child's sibling has been abused or neglected . . . and there is a substantial risk that the child will be abused or neglected. . . . The court shall consider the circumstances surrounding the abuse or neglect of the sibling, the age and gender of each child, the nature of the abuse or neglect of the sibling, the mental condition of the parent or guardian, and any other factors the court considers probative in determining whether there is a substantial risk to the minor.

It is the intent of the Legislature that nothing in this section disrupt the family unnecessarily or intrude inappropriately into family life, prohibit the use of reasonable methods of parental discipline, or prescribe a particular method of parenting. . . . The Legislature further declares that a physical disability, such as blindness or deafness, is no bar to the raising of happy and well-adjusted children and that a court's determination pursuant to this section shall center upon whether a parent's disability prevents him or her from exercising care and control.

§361. Grounds for Removal of Child

. . . (c) No dependent child shall be taken from the physical custody of his or her parents or guardian or guardians with whom the child resides at the time the petition was initiated unless the juvenile court finds clear and convincing evidence of any of the following:

(1) There is a substantial danger to the physical health of the minor or would be if the minor were returned home, and there are no reasonable means by which the minor's physical health can be protected without removing the minor from the minor's parents' or guardians' physical custody. . . .

(2) The parent or guardian of the minor is unwilling to have physical custody of the minor. . . .

(3) The minor is suffering severe emotional damage, as indicated by extreme anxiety, depression, withdrawal, or untoward aggressive behavior toward self or others, and there are no reasonable means by which the minor's emotional health may be protected without removing the minor from the physical custody of his or her parent or guardian.

(4) The minor or a sibling of the minor has been sexually abused, or is deemed to be at substantial risk of being sexually abused, by a parent, guardian, or member of his or her household, or other person known to his or her parent. . . .

(5) The minor has been left without any provision for his or her support, or a parent who has been incarcerated or institutionalized cannot arrange for the care of the minor, or a relative or other adult custodian with whom the child has been left by the parent is unwilling or unable to provide care or support for the child and the whereabouts of the parent is unknown and reasonable efforts to locate him or her have been unsuccessful.

(d) The court shall make a determination as to whether reasonable efforts were made to prevent or to eliminate the need for removal of the minor from his or her home or, if the minor is removed for one of the reasons stated in paragraph (5) of subdivision (c), whether it was reasonable under the circumstances not to make any such efforts. . . .

Michael S. Wald et al., Protecting Abused and Neglected Children

9-12 (1988) (references omitted)

The Policy Dilemma

I. Introduction

Policy preferences for or against the use of foster care to protect abused or neglected children rest ultimately on value judgments. Leaving such a child at home, even if the best treatment program is available, always entails some risk. Against that risk a legislature drafting a statute, or a judge in an individual case, must weigh any costs associated with placement. Critics of foster placement tend to focus on three factors: a preference for preserving biological ties or minimizing government intrusion in the family; concern over the financial cost of placement; and concern that foster care may actually be worse for children than living at home would be, even taking into account the risk of reabuse or continued neglect for children at home. . . .

The hard problem is how to evaluate the third concern. What is meant when it is said that foster care may be *worse* for children? It certainly does not mean that children are more likely to be abused or physically neglected in foster care: it appears clear that removal lowers the chances of reabuse or neglect. Although some children are injured by foster parents, the rate of reported abuse by foster parents is lower than that of the general population and far lower than the rate of reabuse by those who have once abused a child. Foster parents also are less likely to neglect children's physical needs. For the most part, they do not leave children unattended; they virtually always provide adequate food or shelter; they send foster children to school; their households tend to be stable and their care of the child regular. The attraction of foster care as a means of protecting children from further abuse or neglect is heightened by the relatively poor results of programs attempting to prevent reabuse by providing special services to parents. Several studies report reabuse in as many as 50 percent of all cases, even where the services to parents were intensive. Changing the behavior of neglectful parents may be even more difficult. Thus, if the major goal is to protect children from further *physical* harm, this is most likely achieved through foster care.

If one is concerned with *emotional* harm, however, the calculus may change. A number of researchers have reported problems in the emotional development of foster children. If placement with foster parents does have a significant negative impact on the emotional or social development of children, a policy designed only to avoid the risk of further abuse or physical neglect may be unwise. It is of interest, therefore, to review the research on the impact of foster care in order to identify particular possible harms to children. . . .

II. Research on Foster Care

A. The Case Against Foster Care

Awareness of the psychological impact of placement had its roots in the theoretical work of child analysts, especially that of John Bowlby, who asserted that separation from parents might have a negative impact on children, even children from "bad" homes. Bowlby was instrumental in identifying the importance to every child of having an emotional bond with her parents (or other primary caretaker). He labelled this relationship "attachment." It now has been well demonstrated that separation from attachment figures is extremely painful to children and, more significantly, may have long-term negative consequences, at least if the child is not able to establish an adequate new relationship.

Attachment theory predicts several different ways in which removal from home may be harmful to a child. In addition to the pain of separation, which often is very profound, a lengthy separation from a primary caretaker may permanently impair the child's attachment to that person, even if the separation is not permanent. Perhaps the greatest threat, however, occurs when the child is separated permanently from an attachment figure and is either unable to develop a new relationship or is denied the opportunity to do so. Deprivation of a secure attachment relationship with a primary caretaker may impair a child's ability to form other adequate relationships, both as a child, and as an adult. Deprivation of any attachment relationship also has been associated with diminished school performance and increased delinquency, though "causal" connections are still undetermined. Moreover, the quality as well as the existence of an attachment relationship may be important to the child's development. Several studies have found that a child's intellectual curiosity, personality development, and ability to get along with peers (up to age five) are related to how *secure* an attachment she has to a primary caretaker.

It is well documented that foster care frequently neither lends itself to maintaining ties with the biological parent nor facilitates establishment of emotional bonds with new caretakers. Foster care *is supposed to be temporary* — a way station until the child's home can be made safe. Yet if foster parents are told their custody of the child is only temporary, it seems unlikely they will allow themselves to become emotionally involved with the child. Adults, like children, suffer pain upon separation. A foster mother who has cared for many children may protect herself against that pain by limiting emotional involvement. Foster fathers may be even less involved. Thus, the foster families may act in ways that impede the development of a secure attachment relationship between the child and foster parents. . . .

[margin handwritten note: issue of emotional involvement]

Foster care may put children at risk in other ways. Many commentators assert that children need continuity and stability of environment in order to have normal emotional development. There also is clinical evidence that some children view foster home placement as punishment for wrongdoing or as rejection by their parents. . . . As a result, children placed in foster homes may experience identity problems, conflicts of loyalty, and anxiety about their future.

There also are studies showing high rates of behavioral problems, school problems, and delinquency among foster children, though none of these studies compared rates of such behavior in non-foster children or presented evidence about the children's behavior prior to placement. In addition, several studies find that children in foster care retain strong emotional bonds to their biological parents, even after lengthy stays in care. Even if foster children do not show developmental or social deficits, their preferences require some consideration.

Despite methodological problems with the research, there is reason to be concerned with the social, emotional, and academic development of children after they are placed in foster care, given the theoretical literature and the consistency of the clinical findings. If foster placement leads to substantial deterioration in these areas, it may be better to forgo foster placement and run the risk of further physical abuse or neglect by the biological parents, at least in situations where abuse or neglect is not life-threatening or likely to lead to permanent impairment.

PROBLEMS

Barbara Cardell.   Barbara Cardell, who was four months pregnant when she entered prison, recently gave birth to a child while serving a prison term for armed robbery. She is unmarried, has no immediate family, says that she does not know who the father is, and that she wishes to keep the child with her in prison. Should a juvenile court assume jurisdiction over the infant and place the child in foster care? If her expected prison term is six years, should her parental rights be terminated and the infant placed for adoption?

Eleanor Papillon.   Eleanor Papillon first came to the attention of the County Department of Social Services in 2003, when the parole agent from the California Youth Authority called the department to refer Eleanor, then 16 years old, because she was pregnant and needed to apply for welfare benefits. Eleanor, a Youth Authority parolee, had been in and out of institutions. Her main problems had been as a runaway. She could not get along with her mother and stepfather (who were observant Catholics) and would not stay in any placement, such as the Catholic Convent at the Good Shepherd, where she had been placed most recently. She was not precisely estranged from her mother, but her mother considered her incorrigible and always inclined to choose the wrong boyfriends.

After Danny was born, in February, 2004, Eleanor and Danny were placed together in a foster home where the foster mother could take care of Danny while Eleanor was attending school. Eleanor did attend high school, did very well, and eventually went into a medical assistant training program for which she had won a scholarship. Meanwhile she continued to live in the foster home with Danny. Eleanor had an excellent record on parole, and the record contained many references from the social worker to the effect that she was very mature for her age. She obtained a job as a medical technician, and both mother and child were placed in foster care.

About a year after placement, the receptionist in Eleanor's place of employment called the social worker to say that when she, the receptionist, had returned from work she found Eleanor chanting to herself in the office of one of the doctors. Eleanor was on her knees, and the receptionist could not get her to stop chanting or to get up. When the doctor returned, he also tried to get through to her but with no success. Finally Eleanor was sent to San Francisco General Hospital, where she was sedated. Doctors there discovered Eleanor was in a religious trance. After sedating her, they sent her home.

Eleanor's religion evidently had become an important part of her life. It was a fundamentalist religion, and Eleanor felt its strict and specific code had shown her "the way." This religion eschewed short skirts, cosmetics, and other things, including sex. At the time of the chanting incident when the caseworker spoke to Eleanor about her seizure, psychiatric help was suggested. Eleanor rejected this idea completely because she felt her religion had given her the answers that others might seek through psychiatry. She believed so firmly in her religion that she felt certain she did not need psychiatric help.

In the early part of 2004 Eleanor moved out of the foster home and made an arrangement for her mother to care for Danny while she was working. In September of 2004 a telephone report from the maternal grandmother was received in the agency to the effect that the maternal grandmother had noted Danny to be covered with bruise marks on his arms, stomach, and back. The caseworker immediately made a home visit, but Eleanor was not at home. The landlord stated that Eleanor and Danny usually left in the early morning and did not return until early evening.

That evening the caseworker and an officer from the Community Relations Department of the Police Department went to the home, and an examination of the child was made. It showed Danny to be covered with bruise marks and discoloration from his waist to his ankles. The only area not bruised was the genital area, although the insides of his thighs were also heavily discolored. Eleanor and Danny were taken to the Mount Zion emergency room, where a doctor examined Danny, and took x-rays. Eleanor was also seen by the attending psychiatrist, who recommended that an immediate psychiatric appointment be made by her for ongoing therapy.

Eleanor gave the following account of her beating of Danny. She was in her sister's home when one of the other children told her that Danny was under the bed with his panties off with a little girl, also aged four, who also had her panties off. Embarrassed and ashamed, Eleanor took Danny home immediately, but because she was so enraged she did not punish him then. However, that evening, the next day, and the day following she continually questioned him as to who had taken down his panties. At first Danny admitted that he had taken down his own pants, but with the continual emotional harassment left the question unanswered. It was three days later that she beat Danny for this incident, the reason being that he must be trained now not to let anyone pull his pants down until he was married. She stated that she did not do this out of anger, but out of love for him. She also stated that she knew sex play among children her son's age was normal, but she would not allow it anyway. She told the caseworker that she would do so again if this incident or a like one was repeated, although again she knew this to be a normal learning experience for all children.

The next day the maternal grandmother explained to the caseworker that her daughter had joined the Pentecostal religion two years earlier, telling her mother that she was doing this to save Danny because he was born in sin, and she was a sinner.

What would you have recommended regarding Danny and Eleanor? Should a neglect petition be filed? Should Danny be removed from Eleanor's custody?

Ritchie Adams.   It is February 1, 2004. Four weeks ago Ritchie Adams, six years old, was brought to Juvenile Hall by a baby-sitter. The child's mother told the baby-sitter to take him there because she had no way of caring for him.

When contacted by the Probation Officer, Ritchie's mother said she was unable to care for Ritchie. She told of her own unhappy childhood with quarrelsome parents, a sharp sibling rivalry, with preference given to boys in the family, and an early and unhappy marriage following her pregnancy with Ritchie. She described Ritchie as subject to temper tantrums beyond her control, hateful like his father, and hyperactive.

Ritchie's mother is in her late twenties. She talked of her wish to marry again and was very much involved with a new male friend. She reported that she had had no recent contact with Mr. Adams and did not know where he was living. Mrs. Adams explained that Ritchie's sister, Sheryl Adams, birthdate January 18, 2000, lived with her. An older brother, Dickie, born June 30, 1998, was in a mental hygiene foster home, having been placed through the Community Service Division of the Department of Social Welfare with a family in Fresno County.

Ritchie is large for his age, with light brown, somewhat wavy hair, fair complexion, and a moderately prominent nose. He is rough and somewhat aggressive in manner. He responds quickly to the attention and interest shown by cottage staff. However, the staff at Juvenile Hall, where Ritchie has been kept since he was brought in by the baby-sitter, vary somewhat in the way they describe him. One staff member described him as having temper tantrums and a short attention span, and as being difficult at school, impulsive, and quite a handful. When first at the detention hall he threw food around and was generally difficult, although he was responsive to attention. Another staff member saw him as determined but not unusually different from other children.

The psychiatrist at the Probation Department was asked to see Ritchie. Ritchie was seen once and the following report was rendered by Ralph Weiner, M.D., dated nearly seven months after Ritchie had first arrived at the Hall. The report stated:

> He is certainly disturbed. He is belligerent, a sourpuss and does not evoke a great deal of affection from others; plays poorly with other children; is selfish, demanding and easily frustrated. The ideal setting for him would be one in which he would receive individual attention plus some kind of small group activity, supervised by someone trained in dealing with emotionally disturbed youngsters. The usual school and the usual foster home would not be workable. He requires a treatment setting. He does not appear retarded but an intelligence test score will be forthcoming.

Mrs. Adams has not initiated any contact with Ritchie during his past month at Juvenile Hall and has seen him only when she came in for an interview. Mrs. Adams is willing and indeed appears eager to have Ritchie placed in foster care. She says she wants what is best for Ritchie.

Should Ritchie be returned to his mother or accepted into care? Does it matter whether placement is by court order, under a neglect statute, or by voluntary placement? Which, if any, would you recommend? What alternatives are there to placement? If your recommendation is for placement, what type of placement would you recommend?

Robert Doe. On October 30, 2005, Jeff and Wanda Doe were arrested on a public street for being under the influence of crack cocaine. Their 17-month-old son, Robert, was with them. Wanda was detained at the Elmwood Rehabilitation Center, and Jeff was released on his own recognizance. Robert was taken into temporary protective custody.

Robert was born June 4, 2003 with a toxicology screen positive for cocaine. At that time his father (Jeff) was incarcerated in the Santa Clara County Jail. Robert was made a dependent of the court on the basis of a petition filed June 15, 2003, which stated that no parent or guardian was exercising proper care and control.

Consequently, he was ordered into relative/foster home placement with his maternal grandparents. Robert had been returned to his parents about six months before the present incident.

Both parents gave accounts of the circumstances leading up to their arrest. According to Wanda, she had asked Jeff to buy some "rock." She "took a hit," then said to herself, "What are you doing?" She said that they were walking through the parking lot with Robert when the police arrested them. She also said she had been depressed about their current financial situation, which had resulted in Jeff leaving home so she could regain her welfare benefits, and she wanted to "sneak a hit." Wanda appeared remorseful after her arrest and said she knew she had "blown it."

Prior to this arrest it had appeared that Wanda was making progress in dealing with her drug problem. According to a counselor in the Santa Clara County Outpatient Drug Free Program, Wanda had been admitted into their program on July 18, 2004, and had since attended nine sessions and missed only two. She was tested for drugs on 10 occasions between July 18 and October 2, 2004, and all test results were negative. She was attending NA/AA meetings. Wanda was very serious about regaining custody of Robert and stated that she had not been involved in drugs since July 2003. Although Wanda had made excellent progress, the Drug Free Program continued to provide services as a support system.

Jeff claimed that he had not used crack cocaine immediately prior to the arrest but admitted that Wanda had. He is currently employed full-time. Prior to this incident he completed an alcohol residential rehabilitation program and had undergone random drug testing on a monthly basis since February 2004. The results of all these tests were negative.

Robert was placed in the home of his maternal grandparents on November 4, 2004. He is an energetic, outgoing 17-month-old who appears to have adjusted well to the reunion with his grandparents.

Both parents have expressed interest in reuniting with Robert. How should a court deal with this situation?

Mona Stay.   The family consists of a transracial couple, Mona Stay, 23, and her common law husband Frank Brown, aged 26. There are three children: Frank, three and a half; Sylvia, eighteen months; and Wilma, seven months. The couple has been together over five years. Although they quarrel and separate periodically, they seem very mutually dependent and likely to remain a couple.

Their original referral was from a nurse who had become aware of the eldest child's, Frank's, condition. He was difficult to discipline, was eating dirt and paint chips, and seemed hyperactive. Although over three, he was not speaking. His father reacted to him with impatience. He was often slapped and hardly ever spoken to with fondness. The caseworker persuaded Mona to cooperate in taking young Frank in for a test for lead poisoning and for a full developmental evaluation. This child had had several bouts with impetigo, had been bitten through the eyelid by a stray dog, and had had a series of ear infections resulting in a slight hearing loss. Although physically normal, developmentally he appeared already nearly a year retarded.

Often this child was found outside the house alone when the caseworker came to see the family. On one occasion he was seen hanging from a broken fire escape on the second floor. The worker was unable to rouse his mother or to enter the house until she got help from the nearby landlord, after which she ran upstairs and rescued the child. Only then did the sleeping Mona awaken.

With much effort expended on his behalf, this child has been attending a therapeutic nursery. His speech has already developed after four or five months, and his hyperactivity has calmed. He comes through as a lovable little boy.

Sylvia is surprisingly pale for a transracial child and indeed suffers from severe anemia. This child has had recurrent eye infections and a bout with spinal meningitis at three months, which, fortunately, seems to have left no effects. Much effort has gone into working with Mona concerning Sylvia's need for proper diet and iron supplement. After a year of contact this is still a problem.

The baby was born after the family had become known to the agency. Despite the agency's urging, Mona refused to go for prenatal care until she was in her second trimester, but she did maintain a fairly good diet, helped by small "loans" from the agency when her money for food ran out. When Wilma was born, she was left to lie most of the time in her bassinet, receiving very little attention from either parent. At four months of age, Wilma weighed only five pounds and was tentatively diagnosed as exhibiting "failure to thrive" by the hospital. Thereafter the mother avoided going to the clinic, and the caseworker spent much effort concerning the feeding and sheer survival of Wilma. The baby is now slowly gaining weight but is still limp and inactive.

In addition to an active caseworker, a homemaker was assigned to this family for months. Much more was involved than trying to help Mona learn to organize her day: she had almost no motivation to get started. Rather than learning how to manage, she tried to manipulate the homemaker into doing her housework for her. However, with time and patience, Mona has been persuaded to go with the caseworker on shopping trips, is learning how to buy groceries to best advantage, and from time to time manages to get the laundry into and out of the laundromat. So far as her plans for herself. Mona has talked of seeking training as a beauty operator, but has never followed through on this or on other positive plans.

The family's sole support is public assistance. Frank Brown, the father, was on drugs earlier in their relationship, but managed to get off them. Now, however, he drinks heavily, and although he manages to work, he never contributes to the household.

Mona, apparently, was herself a neglected child and was removed from her parents in infancy. Placed with an adoptive family, there was constant friction during her growing up, and she ran away from home several times. During her teens, she was placed in an institution for incorrigible girls. Later she spent a period in a mental hospital, during which she was withdrawn from heroin addiction. It is a commentary on her life that she regards this period in the adolescent ward as one of her happiest ever. Her adoptive mother is now dead, and her father wants nothing more to do with her, so she was more or less living on the streets when she met with Frank and set up their present establishment.

Mona and Frank, despite his obvious exploitativeness, seem to love each other and their children, and to want to keep the family together. They are able to relate to those who try to help them, so at least one is not operating constantly against hostile resistance. Mona is an intelligent woman and now shows adequate ability to handle the children. She can be an excellent cook — when there is food. Yet this remains a disorganized household. Bills are never paid, clothes are thrown around, the children never sleep on clean sheets, and trash is piled around the house so that flies and maggots abound. Mona still leaves the youngsters alone for brief periods. There is no heat in the house, and the family will soon have to move, with neither any idea where to go nor funds for rent deposits and the like.

What new action, if any, should the agency take with regard to the family? Is removal of the children appropriate? What specific facts should be determinative when deciding whether or not to remove?

2. The State as Parent: The Foster Care System

a. Introduction

Robert H. Mnookin, Foster Care — In Whose Best Interest?
43 Harv. Educ. Rev. 599 (1973) (footnotes omitted)

Most American parents raise their children free of intrusive legal constraints or major governmental intervention. Although compulsory education and child labor laws indicate there are some conspicuous legal limitations on parents, it is the family, not the state, which has primary responsibility for child rearing. Despite this predominant pattern, there are about [555,000 children among the nation's 72 million][15] for whom the state has assumed primary responsibility. These children live in state sponsored foster care, a term [used here] to include foster family homes, group homes, and child welfare institutions. For a number of the children in foster care, the state has assumed responsibility because no one else is available. Some children are orphans; others have been voluntarily given up by a family no longer willing or able to care for them. A significant number of children, however, are placed in foster care because the state has intervened and coercively removed the child from parental custody.

. . . When parents oppose foster care placement, a court can nevertheless order removal after a judicial proceeding if the state can demonstrate parental abuse or neglect. But if parents consent to foster care placement, no judicial action is necessary. Many foster care placements, perhaps one-half or more, are arranged by state social welfare departments without any court involvement.

A substantial degree of state coercion may be involved in many so-called voluntary placements, making the distinction between voluntary and coercive placement illusory. Many social welfare departments routinely ask parents to agree to give up their children before initiating neglect proceedings in court. Some parents who would have been willing to keep their children may consent to placement to avoid a court proceeding against them. If one were to use the legal standards of voluntariness and informed consent applied in the criminal law to confessions and

---

[15] Data are current as of 2000. U.S. Dept. of Health and Human Services, Trends in the Well-Being of America's Children and Youth 2002, "Children Living in Foster Care," pp. 18, 50, available at *http://aspe.hhs.gov/hsp/02trends* (last visited Oct. 23, 2004).

to the waiver of important legal rights, many cases of relinquishment after state intervention might not be considered voluntary. On the other hand, not all court-ordered foster care placements involve coercion of the parents. Some take place with their full concurrence.

How the State Removes Children from their Parents

Source of the Power

The power of government to protect children by removing them from parental custody has roots deep in American history. And in colonial times just as today, the children of the poor were the most affected. Seventeenth century laws of Massachusetts, Connecticut, and Virginia, for example, specifically authorized magistrates to "bind out" or indenture children *of the poor* over parental objections. . . .

By the early nineteenth century, the parens patriae power of the state, i.e., the sovereign's ultimate responsibility to guard the interests of children and others who lacked legal capacity, was thought sufficient to empower courts to remove a child from parental custody. Significantly, the reinforcement of public morality, and not simply the protection of children from cruelty, was seen as sufficient justification for the exercise of this power. Joseph Story, the renowned Massachusetts legal scholar who sat on the Supreme Court from 1811 to 1845, stated in his treatise on equity courts:

> Although, in general, parents are intrusted with the custody of the persons, and the education of their children, yet this is done upon the natural presumption, that the children will be properly taken care of, and will be brought up with a due education in literature, and morals, and religion; and that they will be treated with kindness and affection. But, whenever this presumption is removed; whenever (for example,) it is found, that a father is guilty of gross ill-treatment or cruelty towards his infant children; or that he is in constant habits of drunkenness and blasphemy, or low and gross debauchery, or that he professes atheistical or irreligious principles; or that his domestic associations are such as tend to the corruption and contamination of his children; or that he otherwise acts in a manner injurious to the morals and interests of his children; in every such case, the Court of Chancery will interfere, and deprive him of the custody of his children, and appoint a suitable person to act as guardian, and to take care of them, and to superintend their education. [Story, 2 Equity Jurisprudence Sec. 1341 (1857)].

The Process of Removal

[Compared to practices of] 100 years ago, far more complex administrative processes are involved. [A century ago] social workers and probation departments did not exist. Today a case usually reaches court after weaving through a complicated welfare bureaucracy where numerous officials including social workers, probation officers, and court personnel, may have had contact with the family.

. . . The process is usually initiated by a report from a social worker or the police, or less frequently from a neighbor, medical professional, or school staff member. Although practices vary, a member of a special unit of the social welfare or probation department is usually responsible for an initial investigation of the report. Customarily this investigation [involves] a visit to the home and a telephone conversation with the person who turned in the report. The investigator, sometimes together with a supervisor, then must decide whether to close the case, to suggest that the welfare agency informally (and non-coercively) provide services or supervision, or to file a petition in court.

Filing a petition initiates a judicial inquiry that usually has two stages. First, the court must determine whether it has jurisdiction over the child. This involves deciding on the basis of exceedingly broad and ill-defined statutory provisions whether the parents have failed to live up to acceptable social standards for child rearing. If it is determined that they have, then such jurisdiction empowers the court to intervene into the family. . . . The second stage involves a dispositional hearing, where the judge decides the manner of intervention. Removal from the home is by no means mandatory. The court can instead require supervision within the child's own home, psychological counseling for the parents and/or the child, or periodic home visits by a social worker, probation officer, or homemaker. . . .

After a court decides to remove a child from home, a public agency, often the social welfare or probation department, is assigned responsibility for placing the child. [Some children live in foster care under the auspices of voluntary agencies, while others are under the supervision of state social service agencies. Of state-supervised children, some live in foster family homes, group homes, or child welfare institutions.]

Foster family homes are usually licensed by the state, with regulations regarding aspects such as the size of the home, number of children, and age of foster parents. Under a contract, foster parents are paid a monthly fee for each child in their care. . . . Although foster parents are responsible for the day-to-day care of the children, the contract between the agency and the foster parents usually requires the foster parents to acknowledge that "the legal responsibility for the foster child remains with the Agency," and to "accept and comply with any plans the Agency makes for the child," including "the right to determine when and how the child leaves" the foster home.

[The author identifies three principles that should govern the operation of the foster care system:

(1) Removal should be a last resort to be used only when the child cannot be protected within the home;
(2) The decision to require foster care placement should be based on legal standards that can be applied in a consistent and evenhanded way, and not be profoundly influenced by the values of the particular deciding judge; and
(3) If removal is necessary, the state should actively seek, when possible, to help the child's parents overcome the problems that led to removal so that the child can be returned home as soon as possible. If the child cannot be returned home in a reasonable time despite efforts by the state, the state should find a stable alternative arrangement, such as adoption, for the child. A child should not be left in foster care for an indefinite period of time.

The above article was influential in the passage of federal legislation (discussed infra) that addresses the problem of "foster care drift" by facilitating the movement of children more promptly from foster care to either adoptive placements or reunification with their families.]

Sandra Bass et al., Children, Families and Foster Care: Analysis and Recommendations

The Future of Children
vol. 14, no. 1 (Winter 2004), pp. 6-8

The Current State of Foster Care

Foster care is intended to serve as a temporary haven for abused and neglected children who cannot safely remain with their families. However for some children, the journey through foster care is characterized by further trauma and abuse; and even in the best situations, foster care is inherently fraught with uncertainty, instability, and impermanence. The number of children and families who require foster care services has grown substantially over the past two decades, and these families are typically contending with a multitude of complex and interrelated life challenges such as mental illness, unemployment, substance abuse, and domestic violence. . . .

Children enter foster care for a number of reasons. For some children, the journey begins at birth, when it is clear that a mother cannot care for her newborn infant. Other children come to the attention of child welfare when a teacher, a social worker, a police officer, or a neighbor reports suspected child maltreatment to child protective services. Some of these children may have experienced physical or sexual abuse at the hands of a loved and trusted adult. More often, parents battling poverty, substance addiction, or mental illness woefully neglect their children's needs.

In 2001, approximately 3 million referrals were made to child protective services, and more than 900,000 children were found to be victims of maltreatment. When child maltreatment is unsubstantiated, caseworkers and courts must decide whether the child can safely remain home if the family is provided with in-home services, or whether the child should be placed into state care. In 2001, 290,000 children entered the foster care system.

The term *foster care* commonly refers to all out-of-home placements for children who cannot remain with their birth parents. Children may be placed with non-relative foster families, with relatives, in a therapeutic or treatment foster care home, or in some form of congregate care, such as an institution or group home. Nearly half of all children in foster care live with non-relative foster families, and about one-quarter reside with relatives. More than 800,000 children spent some time in the foster care system in 2001, with approximately 540,000 children in foster care at any one time.

After children are removed from their homes and placed in foster care, caseworkers develop a permanency plan based on an assessment of the child's individual needs and family circumstances. The plan is then reviewed by the court. For most children, the primary permanency plan is reunification with their birth parents. According to federal law [discussed infra p. 357], states must make "reasonable efforts" to provide birth parents with the services and supports they need to regain custody of their children. However, there are exceptions to this requirement. States are not required to pursue reunification under certain circumstances. In these circumstances, alternative permanency options such as adoption or legal guardianship are the goal for these children.

Under current law, if children are in foster care for 15 out of the previous 22 months, states are to recommend that parental rights be terminated and the child be made available for adoption. In 2001, there were 126,000 children who were no longer legally connected to their parents awaiting adoption. However, the child welfare agency can waive the termination requirement if birth parents are making progress in their case plans and workers believe they can *reunify* with their children soon, or if workers believe that another placement that does not require termination of parental rights, such as legal guardianship, is in the child's best interests.

The average length of stay for children in foster care is approximately 33 months, but some children stay a much shorter time and some much longer. According to 2001 data from the Adoption and Foster Care Analysis and Reporting System (AFCARS), approximately 38% of children who exited foster care in 2001 had spent 11 months or less in the system. At the other end of the spectrum, however, approximately 32% of children had been in care for 3 years or longer. The longer a child remains in care, the greater the likelihood that he or she will experience multiple placements. On average, approximately 85% of children who are in foster care for less than 1 year experience 2 or fewer placements, but placement instability increases with each year a child spends in the system.

More than half (57%) of the children in foster care exit through reunification with their birth parents, although in recent years, reunification rates have declined. Children who entered the system in 1997 had a 13% slower rate to reunification than those who entered in 1990. During this same period, the number of children who were adopted from foster care increased substantially. [M]ost states have more than doubled the number of adoptions from foster care over the last seven years and some states reported tripling the number. Additionally, many states have increased the number of children achieving permanence by offering caregivers the option of becoming legal guardians.

The Child Welfare System

When entering foster care, or the "child welfare system," a child does not enter a single system, but rather multiple systems that intersect and interact to create a safety net for children who cannot remain with their birth parents. State and local child welfare agencies, courts, private service providers, and public agencies that administer other government programs (such as public assistance or welfare, mental health counseling, substance abuse treatment), and Medicaid all play critical roles in providing supports and services to children and families involved in foster care. Indeed, families often find themselves juggling the requirements and paperwork of multiple systems.

Child welfare agencies are central to the system, but their policies and practices vary significantly from state to state. For example, each state determines its own definition of maltreatment, its own laws based on federal regulations, and its own level of investment in child welfare services. The organization of child welfare agencies also varies significantly across states. In some states the child welfare system is administered at the state level, whereas in others it is administered at the county level.

In every state, the courts also play a significant role in child welfare cases, from the initial decision to remove a child to the development of a permanency plan to the decision to return a child home or terminate parental rights and make the child available for adoption. . . .

Many jurisdictions rely on volunteer court appointed special advocates (CASAs) to ensure that children in foster care have a voice in the legal decision-making process. CASAs are assigned to one child (or a sibling group) for an extended period of time and are trained to serve as mentors and advocates. . . . Currently, more than 900 CASA programs operate in 45 states, and more than 250,000 children have been assigned CASAs. . . .

The emergence and convergence of several significant social problems in the mid-1980s had a tumultuous effect on the child welfare system. The crack epidemic, homelessness, the rapidly growing incarceration rate, and HIV/AIDS proved devastating for poor families and communities. In turn, families contending with multiple problems were unable to appropriately care for their children, and the number of children entering foster care rose. In 1980 approximately 300,000 children were in foster care; by 1998 that number had climbed to an unprecedented 568,000.

Today, children and families who enter the foster care system continue to wrestle with these complex and interrelated problems. Additionally, the population of children in the system has shifted. Children of color compose the majority of children in foster care, with disproportionate representation of African-American and American-Indian children. The changes in the severity of the needs of children in the system and in the diversity of populations that are represented, tax the system to provide appropriate services, delivered by trained workers, and in foster care homes that are tailored to children's individual needs. . . .

b. Standards to Guide the Operation of a Foster Care System After Removal

This section concerns what happens and should happen to a child who is in foster care, and the respective rights and responsibilities of the natural parents, foster parents, and state officials. Two ways a minor can leave foster care are (1) to be returned to his natural parents; or (2) to be adopted, which requires either the consent of the natural parents or termination of parental rights. In reading the cases that follow, keep in mind the following questions:

(1) Once a juvenile court assumes responsibility for a neglected or dependent child, when should its jurisdiction over the child end and the child be returned home? (a) When the original circumstances that gave rise to the intervention in the first place no longer exist? (b) When there are no longer any statutory grounds, old or new, for establishing jurisdiction? or (c) When a court thinks it is in the best interest of the child for jurisdiction to terminate?

(2) Under what circumstances should parental rights be terminated to free a foster child for adoption? Statutes traditionally allowed termination for "abandonment" of children by their biological parents or for egregious acts of child maltreatment.

What additional circumstances should give rise to termination of parental rights?[16]

Smith v. Organization of Foster Families for Equality and Reform
431 U.S. 816 (1977)

Mr. Justice BRENNAN delivered the opinion of the Court.

Appellees, individual foster parents[1] and an organization of foster parents, brought this civil rights class action pursuant to 42 U.S.C. §1983 on their own behalf and on behalf of children for whom they have provided homes for a year or more. They sought declaratory and injunctive relief . . . alleging that the procedures governing the removal of foster children from foster homes provided in New York Social Services Law §§383(2) and 400, and in Title 18, New York Codes Rules and Regulations §450.14 violated the Due Process and Equal Protection Clauses of the Fourteenth Amendment. . . . A group of natural mothers of children in foster care[5] were granted leave to intervene on behalf of themselves and others similarly situated.

[The district court determined that the preremoval procedures unconstitutionally deprived the foster child of a hearing before being either transferred to another foster home or returned to the natural parents, 418 F. Supp. 277 (1976).]

I . . .

The expressed central policy of the New York system is that "it is generally desirable for the child to remain with or be returned to the natural parent because the

---

[16] See generally Jacqueline D. Stanley, Annot., Grounds for Termination of Parental Rights, 32 Am. Jur. Proof of Facts 3d 83 (updated August 2004).

[1] Appellee Madeleine Smith is the foster parent with whom Eric and Danielle Gandy have been placed since 1970. The Gandy children, who are now 12 and 9 years old respectively, were voluntarily placed in foster care by their natural mother in 1968, and have had no contact with her at least since being placed with Mrs. Smith. The foster care agency has sought to remove the children from Mrs. Smith's care because her arthritis, in the agency's judgment, makes it difficult for her to continue to provide adequate care. . . .

Appellees Ralph and Christiane Goldberg were the foster parents of Rafael Serrano, now 14. His parents placed him in foster care voluntarily in 1969 after an abuse complaint was filed against them. [The Goldbergs eventually separated, placing Rafael in residential care.]

Appellees Walter and Dorothy Lhotan were foster parents of the four Wallace sisters, who were voluntarily placed in foster care by their mother in 1970. The two older girls were placed with the Lhotans in that year, their two younger sisters in 1972. In June 1974, the Lhotans were informed that the agency had decided to return the two younger girls to their mother and transfer the two older girls to another foster home. The agency apparently felt that the Lhotans were too emotionally involved with the girls and were damaging the agency's efforts to prepare them to return them to their mother. The state courts have ordered that all the Wallace children be returned to their mother. [The children eventually were returned to their mother.]

[5] Intervenor Naomi Rodriguez, who is blind, placed her newborn son Edwin in foster care in 1973 because of marital difficulties. When Mrs. Rodriguez separated from her husband three months later, she sought return of her child. Her efforts over the next nine months to obtain return of the child were resisted by the agency, apparently because it felt her handicap prevented her from providing adequate care. [She] finally prevailed, three years after she first sought return of the child. . . .

child's need for a normal family life will usually best be met in the natural home and . . . parents are entitled to bring up their own children unless the best interests of the child would be thereby endangered," Soc. Serv. L. §384-b(1)(a)(ii). But the State has opted for foster care as one response to those situations where the natural parents are unable to provide the "positive, nurturing family relationships" and "normal family life in a permanent home" that "offer the best opportunity for children to develop and thrive." Id., §384-b(1)(b), (1)(a)(i).

Foster care has been defined as "[a] child welfare service which provides substitute family care for a planned period for a child when his own family cannot care for him for a temporary or extended period and when adoption is neither desirable nor possible." Child Welfare League of America, Standards for Foster Family Care, 5 (1959). Thus, the distinctive features of foster care are first, "that it is care in a *family*, it is noninstitutional substitute care," and second, "that it is for a *planned* period — either temporary or extended. This is unlike adoptive placement, which implies a *permanent* substitution of one home for another." [Alfred Kadushin, Child Welfare Services 355 (1967).]

Under the New York scheme children may be placed in foster care either by voluntary placement or by court order. Most foster care placements are voluntary. They occur when physical or mental illness, economic problems, or other family crises make it impossible for natural parents, particularly single parents, to provide a stable home life for their children for some limited period. Resort to such placements is almost compelled when it is not possible in such circumstance to place the child with a relative or friend, or to pay for the services of a homemaker or boarding school.

Voluntary placement requires the signing of a written agreement by the natural parent or guardian, transferring the care and custody of the child to an authorized child welfare agency. Although by statute the terms of such agreements are open to negotiation, it is contended that agencies require execution of standardized forms. . . .

The agency may maintain the child in an institutional setting, but more commonly acts under its authority to "place out and board out" children in foster homes. Foster parents, who are licensed by the State or an authorized foster care agency, provide care under a contractual arrangement with the agency, and are compensated for their services. The typical contract expressly reserves the right of the agency to remove the child on request. Conversely, the foster parent may cancel the agreement at will.

The New York system divides parental functions among agency, foster parents and natural parents, and the definitions of the respective roles are often complex and often unclear. The law transfers "care and custody" to the agency, Soc. Serv. L. §384-a, but day-to-day supervision of the child and his activities, and most of the functions ordinarily associated with legal custody, are the responsibility of the foster parent. Nevertheless, agency supervision of the performance of the foster parents takes forms indicating that the foster parent does not have the full authority of a legal custodian.[18] Moreover, the natural parent's placement of the child with

---

[18] "The agency sets limits and advances directives as to how the foster parents are to behave toward the child — a situation not normally encountered by natural parents. The shared control and responsibility for the child is clearly set forth in the instruction pamphlets issued to foster parents."

the agency does not surrender legal guardianship; the parent retains authority to act with respect to the child in certain circumstances.[20] The natural parent has not only the right but the obligation to visit the foster child and plan for his future; failure of a parent with capacity to fulfill the obligation for more than a year can result in a court order terminating the parent's rights on the ground of neglect.

Children may also enter foster care by court order. . . . The consequences of foster care placement by court order do not differ substantially from those for children voluntarily placed, except that the parent is not entitled to return of the child on demand . . . ; termination of foster care must then be consented to by the court.

The provisions of the scheme specifically at issue in this case come into play when the agency having legal custodianship determines to remove the foster child from the foster home, either because it has determined that it would be in the child's best interests to transfer him to some other foster home, or to return the child to his natural parents in accordance with the statute or placement agreement. Most children are removed in order to be transferred to another foster home.[23] The procedures by which foster parents may challenge a removal made for that purpose differ somewhat from those where the removal is made to return the child to his natural parent.

Soc. Serv. L. §383(2) provides that the "authorized agency placing out or boarding [a foster] child . . . may in its discretion remove such child from the home where placed or boarded." Administrative regulations implement this provision. The agency is required, except in emergencies, to notify the foster parents in writing 10 days in advance of any removal. The notice advises the foster parents that if they object to the child's removal they may request a "conference" with the social services department. The department schedules requested conferences within 10 days of the receipt of the request. The foster parent may appear with counsel at the conference, where he will "be advised of the reasons [for the removal of the child], and be afforded an opportunity to submit reasons why the child should not be removed." 18 N.Y.C.R.R. §450.10(a). The official must render a decision in writing within five days after the close of the conference, and send notice of his decision to the foster parents and the agency. The proposed removal is stayed pending the outcome of the conference.

Kadushin, supra, at 394. Agencies frequently prohibit corporal punishment; require that children over a certain age be given an allowance; forbid changes in the child's sleeping arrangements or vacations out-of-State without agency approval; require the foster parent to discuss the child's behavioral problems with the agency. Id., at 394-395. Furthermore, since the cost of supporting the child is borne by the agency, the responsibility, as well as the authority, of the foster parent is shared with the agency. Ibid.

[20] "[A]lthough the agency usually obtains legal custody in foster family care, the child still legally 'belongs' to the parent and the parent retains guardianship. This means that, for some crucial aspects of the child's life, the agency has no authority to act. Only the parent can consent to surgery for the child, or consent to his marriage, or permit his enlistment in the armed forces, or represent him at law." Kadushin, supra, at 355. But see Soc. Serv. L. §383-b.

[23] The record shows that in 1973-1974 approximately eighty percent of the children removed from foster homes in New York State after living in the foster home for one year or more were transferred to another foster placement. Thirteen percent were returned to the biological parents, and seven percent were adopted. Tr. of Oral Arg., at 34; Brief for Appellees, at 20.

If the child is removed after the conference, the foster parent may appeal to the department of social services for a "[full adversary administrative hearing which is subject to judicial review]; however, the removal is not automatically stayed pending the hearing and judicial review.

This statutory and regulatory scheme applies statewide.[28] In addition, regulations . . . provide even greater procedural safeguards [in the form of a *preremoval* trial, upon request of the foster parents, if a child is being transferred to another foster home]. One further preremoval procedural safeguard is available. [Soc. Serv. Law §392] provides a mechanism whereby a foster parent may obtain preremoval judicial review of any agency's decision to remove a child who has been in foster care for 18 months or more.

Foster care of children is a sensitive and emotion-laden subject. . . . The New York regulatory scheme is no exception. . . .

From the standpoint of natural parents, such as the appellant intervenors here, foster care has been condemned as a class-based intrusion into the family life of the poor. See, e.g., Jenkins, Child Welfare as a Class System, in Children and Decent People, 3 (Schorr ed. 1974). It is certainly true that the poor resort to foster care more often than other citizens. . . .

The extent to which supposedly "voluntary" placements are in fact voluntary has been questioned on other grounds as well. For example, it has been said that many "voluntary" placements are in fact coerced by threat of neglect proceedings and are not in fact voluntary in the sense of the product of an informed consent. Mnookin, Foster Care — In Whose Best Interest? 43 Harv. Educ. Rev. 599, 601 (1973). Studies also suggest that social workers of middle-class backgrounds, perhaps unconsciously, incline to favor continued placement in foster care with a generally higher-status family rather than return the child to his natural family, thus reflecting a bias that treats the natural parents' poverty and life-style as prejudicial to the best interests of the child. This accounts,[35] it has been said, for the hostility of agencies to the efforts of natural parents to obtain the return of their children.

Appellee foster parents as well as natural parents . . . note that children often stay in "temporary" foster care for much longer than contemplated by the theory of the system. . . . The District Court found as a fact that the median time spent

---

[28] There is some dispute whether the procedures set out in 18 N.Y.C.R.R. §450.10 and Soc. Serv. L. §400 apply in the case of a foster child being removed from his foster home to be returned to his natural parents. Application of these procedures to children who have been placed voluntarily, for example, arguably conflicts with the requirements of Soc. Serv. L. §384a(2)(a) that children in that situation be returned to the natural parent as provided in the placement agreement or within 20 days of demand. . . .

Nevertheless, nothing in either the statute or the regulations limits the availability of these procedures to transfers within the foster-care system. Each refers to the decision to *remove* a child from the foster family home, and thus on its face each would seem to cover removal for the purpose of returning the child to its parents. . . .

[35] Other factors alleged to bias agencies in favor of retention in foster care are the lack of sufficient staff to provide social work services needed by the natural parent to resolve their problems and prepare for return of the child; policies of many agencies to discourage involvement of the natural parent in the care of the child while in foster care; and systems of foster care funding that encourage agencies to keep the child in foster care. Wald, [State Intervention on Behalf of 'Neglected' Children], 28 Stan. L. Rev. 623, 677-679 (1976).

in foster care in New York was over four years. Indeed, many children apparently remain in this "limbo" indefinitely. Mnookin, Child-Custody Adjudication: Judicial Functions in the Face of Indeterminacy, 39(3) Law and Contemp. Probs. 226, 273 (1975). The District Court also found that the longer a child remains in foster care, the more likely it is that he will never leave. . . . It is not surprising then that many children, particularly those that enter foster care at a very early age and have little or no contact with their natural parents during extended stays in foster care, often develop deep emotional ties with their foster parents.[40]

Yet such ties do not seem to be regarded as obstacles to transfer of the child from one foster placement to another. The record in this case indicates that nearly 60% of the children in foster care in New York City have experienced more than one placement, and about 28% have experienced three or more. [E]ven when it is clear that a foster child will not be returned to his natural parents, it is rare that he achieves a stable home life through final termination of parental ties and adoption into a new permanent family.

[W]e present this summary in the view that some understanding of those criticisms is necessary for a full appreciation of the complex and controversial system with which this lawsuit is concerned. But [o]ur task is only to determine whether the District Court correctly held that the present procedures preceding the removal from a foster home of children resident there a year or more are constitutionally inadequate. . . .

II

Our first inquiry is whether appellees have asserted interests within the Fourteenth Amendment's protection of "liberty." [A]ppellees' basic contention is that when a child has lived in a foster home for a year or more, a psychological tie is created between the child and the foster parents which constitutes the foster family the true "psychological family" of the child. That family, they argue, has a "liberty interest" in its survival as a family protected by the Fourteenth Amendment. . . . Upon this premise they conclude that the foster child cannot be removed without a prior hearing satisfying due process. Appointed counsel for the children, . . . however, disagrees, and has consistently argued that the foster parents have no such liberty interest independent of the interests of the foster children, and that the best interest of the children would not be served by procedural protections beyond those already provided by New York law. The intervening natural parents of children in foster care . . . also oppose the foster parents, arguing that recognition of the procedural right claimed would undercut both the substantive family law of New York, which favors the return of children to their natural parents as expeditiously as

---

[40] The development of such ties points up an intrinsic ambiguity of foster care that is central to this case. The warmer and more home-like environment of foster care is intended to be its main advantage over institutional care, yet because in theory foster care is intended to be only temporary, foster parents are urged not to become too attached to the children in their care. Mnookin, supra, 43 Harv. Educ. Rev., at 613. Indeed, the New York courts have upheld removal from a foster home for the very reason that the foster parents had become too emotionally involved with the child. In re Jewish Child Care Assn. (Sanders), 5 N.Y.2d 222 (1959). See also the case of the Lhotans, named appellees in this case, supra, n.l. . . .

possible . . . and their constitutionally protected right of family privacy, by forcing them to submit to a hearing and defend their rights to their children before the children could be returned to them. . . .

We [now] turn to appellees' assertion that they have a constitutionally protected liberty interest . . . in the integrity of their family unit. This assertion clearly presents difficulties. . . . There does exist a "private realm of family life which the state cannot enter," Prince v. Massachusetts, 321 U.S. 158, 166 (1944), that has been afforded both substantive and procedural protection. But is the relation of foster parent to foster child sufficiently akin to the concept of "family" recognized in our precedents to merit similar protection?[48] Although considerable difficulty has attended the task of defining "family" for purposes of the Due Process Clause, we are not without guides to some of the elements that define the concept of "family" and contribute to its place in our society.

First, the usual understanding of "family" implies biological relationships, and most decisions treating the relation between parent and child have stressed this element. Stanley v. Illinois, 405 U.S. 645, 651 (1972), for example, spoke of "[t]he rights to conceive and raise one's children" as essential rights. . . . A biological relationship is not present in the case of the usual foster family. But biological relationships are not exclusive determination of the existence of a family. [T]he importance of the familial relationship, to the individuals involved and to the society, stems from the emotional attachments that derive from the intimacy of daily association, and from the role it plays in "promot[ing] a way of life" through the instruction of children, Wisconsin v. Yoder, 406 U.S. 205, 231-233 (1972), as well as from the fact of blood relationship. No one would seriously dispute that a deeply loving and interdependent relationship between an adult and a child in his or her care may exist even in the absence of blood relationship. At least where a child has been placed in foster care as an infant, has never known his natural parents, and has remained continuously for several years in the care of the same foster parents, it is natural that the foster family should hold the same place in the emotional life of the foster child, and fulfill the same socializing functions, as a natural family.[52] For this reason, we cannot dismiss the foster family as a mere collection of unrelated individuals.

But there are also important distinctions between the foster family and the natural family. First, unlike the earlier cases recognizing a right to family privacy, the State here seeks to interfere not with a relationship having its origins entirely apart from the power of the State, but rather with a foster family which has its source

---

[48] Of course, recognition of a liberty interest in foster families for purposes of the procedural protections of the Due Process Clause would not necessarily require that foster families be treated as fully equivalent to biological families for purposes of substantive due process review. Cf. Moore v. City of East Cleveland, supra, at 6 (White, J., dissenting).

[52] The briefs dispute at some length the validity of the "psychological parent" theory propounded in Goldstein, Freud and Solnit, Beyond the Best Interests of the Child (1973). The book, on which appellee foster parents relied to some extent in the District Court, is indeed controversial. See, e.g., Strauss and Strauss, Book Review, 74 Colum. L. Rev. 996 (1974); Kadushin, Beyond the Best Interests of the Child: An Essay Review, 48 Soc. Sci. Rev. 508, 512 (1974). But this case turns not on the disputed validity of any particular psychological theory, but on the legal consequences of the undisputed fact that the emotional ties between foster parent and foster child are in many cases quite close, and undoubtedly in some as close as those existing in biological families.

in state law and contractual arrangements. . . . Here, however, whatever emotional ties may develop between foster parent and foster child have their origins in an arrangement in which the State has been a partner from the outset. . . .

A second consideration related to this is that ordinarily procedural protection may be afforded to a liberty interest of one person without derogating from the substantive liberty of another. Here, however, such a tension is virtually unavoidable. Under New York law, the natural parent of a foster child in voluntary placement has an absolute right to the return of his child in the absence of a court order obtainable only upon compliance with rigorous substantive and procedural standards, which reflect the constitutional protection accorded the natural family. Moreover, the natural parent initially gave up his child to the State only on the express understanding that the child would be returned in those circumstances. These rights are difficult to reconcile with the liberty interest in the foster family relationship claimed by appellees. It is one thing to say that individuals may acquire a liberty interest against arbitrary governmental interference in the family-like associations into which they have freely entered, even in the absence of biological connection or state-law recognition of the relationship. It is quite another to say that one may acquire such an interest in the face of another's constitutionally recognized liberty interest that derives from blood relationship, state law sanction, and basic human right — an interest the foster parent has recognized by contract from the outset. Whatever liberty interest might otherwise exist in the foster family as an institution, that interest must be substantially attenuated where the proposed removal from the foster family is to return the child to his natural parents.

As this discussion suggests, appellees' claim to a constitutionally protected liberty interest raises complex and novel questions. It is unnecessary for us to resolve those questions definitively in this case, however, for, like the District Court, we conclude that "narrower grounds exist to support" our reversal. We are persuaded that, even on the assumption that appellees have a protected "liberty interest," the District Court erred in holding that the preremoval procedures presently employed by the State are constitutionally defective.

III

Where procedural due process must be afforded because a "liberty" or "property" interest is within the Fourteenth Amendment's protection, there must be determined "what process is due" in the particular context. . . .

Consideration of the procedures employed by the City and State of New York [in light of the factors set forth in Mathews v. Eldridge, 414 U.S. 319 (1976), i.e., the private interest affected, the risk of an erroneous deprivation of such interest by the procedures, and the government's interest, including fiscal or administrative burdens that additional or substitute procedural requirements would entail] requires the conclusion that those procedures satisfy constitutional standards.

Turning first to the procedure applicable in New York City, SSC Procedure No. 5 provides that before a child is removed from a foster home, the foster parents may request an "independent review." . . . Such a procedure would appear to give a more elaborate trial-type hearing to foster families than this Court has found required in other contexts of administrative determinations. The District Court found the procedure inadequate on four grounds, none of which we find sufficient to justify the holding that the procedure violates due process.

First, the court held that the "independent review" administrative proceeding was insufficient because it was only available on the request of the foster parents. In the view of the District Court, the proceeding should be provided as a matter of course, because the interests of the foster parents and those of the child would not necessarily be coextensive, and it could not be assumed that the foster parents would invoke the hearing procedure in every case in which it was in the child's interest to have a hearing. . . . We disagree. As previously noted, the constitutional liberty, if any, sought to be protected by the New York procedures is a right of *family* privacy or autonomy, and the basis for recognition of any such interest in the foster family must be that close emotional ties analogous to those between parent and child are established when a child resides for a lengthy period with a foster family. If this is so, necessarily we should expect that the foster parents will seek to continue the relationship to preserve the stability of the family; if they do not request a hearing, it is difficult to see what right or interest of the foster child is protected by holding a hearing. [C]onsideration of the interest to be protected and the likelihood of erroneous deprivations, . . . do not support the District Court's imposition of [automatic hearings]. Moreover, automatic provision of hearings [would impose] a substantial additional administrative burden on the state. . . .

Second, the District Court faulted the city procedure on the ground that participation is limited to the foster parents and the agency, and the natural parent and the child are not made parties to the hearing. This is not fatal in light of the nature of the alleged constitutional interests at stake. When the child's transfer from one foster home to another is pending, the interest arguably requiring protection is that of the foster family, not that of the natural parents. Moreover, the natural parent can generally add little to the accuracy of factfinding concerning the wisdom of such a transfer. . . . Much the same can be said in response to the District Court's statement that " . . . it may be advisable, under certain circumstances, for the agency to appoint an adult representative better to articulate the interests of the child. In making this determination, the agency should carefully consider the child's age, sophistication and ability effectively to communicate his own true feelings." But nothing in the New York City procedures prevents consultation of the child's wishes. . . . Such consultation, however, does not require that the child or an appointed representative must be a party with full adversary powers in all preremoval hearings.

The other two defects in the city procedure found by the District Court must also be rejected. One is that the procedure does not extend to the removal of a child from foster care to be returned to his natural parent. But as we have already held, whatever liberty interest may be argued to exist in the foster family is significantly weaker in the case of removals preceding return to the natural parent, and the balance of due process interests must accordingly be different. . . . Similarly, the District Court pointed out that the New York City procedure coincided with the informal "conference" and postremoval hearings provided as a matter of state law. This overlap in procedures may be unnecessary or even to some degree unwise, but a State does not violate the Due Process Clause by providing alternative or additional procedures beyond what the Constitution requires.

Outside New York City, where only the statewide procedures apply, foster parents are provided not only with the procedures of a preremoval conference and postremoval hearing provided by 18 N.Y.C.R.R. §450.10 and Soc. Serv. L. §400, but also with the preremoval *judicial* hearing available on request to foster parents who have in their care children who have been in foster care for 18 months or more, Soc. Serv. L. §392. [A] foster parent in such case may obtain an order that the child remain in his care.

The District Court found three defects in this full judicial process. First, a §392 proceeding is available only to those foster children who have been in foster care for 18 months or more. . . . We do not think that the 18-month limitation on §392 actions renders the New York scheme constitutionally inadequate. The assumed liberty interest to be protected in this case is one rooted in the emotional attachments that develop over time between a child and the adults who care for him. But there is no reason to assume that those attachments ripen at less than 18 months or indeed at any precise point. Indeed, testimony in the record, . . . as well as material in published psychological texts, suggests that the amount of time necessary for the development of the sort of tie appellees seek to protect varies considerably depending on the age and previous attachments of the child. . . .

The District Court's other two findings of infirmity in the §392 procedure have already been considered and held to be without merit. . . . Finally, the §392 hearing is available to foster parents, both in and outside New York City, even where the removal sought is for the purpose of returning the child to his natural parents. Since this remedy provides a sufficient constitutional preremoval hearing to protect whatever liberty interest might exist in the continued existence of the foster family when the State seeks to transfer the child to another foster home, a fortiori the procedure is adequate to protect the lesser interest of the foster family in remaining together at the expense of the disruption of the natural family.

. . . Since we hold that the procedures provided by New York State in §392 and by New York City's SSC Procedure No. 5 are adequate to protect whatever liberty interests appellees may have, the judgment of the District Court is reversed.

Mr. Justice STEWART, with whom The Chief Justice and Mr. Justice REHNQUIST join, concurring in the judgment.

The foster parent-foster child relationship involved in this litigation is, of course, wholly a creation of the State. New York law defines the circumstances under which a child may be placed in foster care, prescribes the obligations of the foster parents, and provides for the removal of the child from the foster home. . . . The agency compensates the foster parents, and reserves in its contracts the authority to decide as it sees fit whether and when a child shall be returned to his natural family or placed elsewhere. . . . Were it not for the system of foster care that the State maintains, the relationship for which constitutional protection is asserted would not even exist.

The New York Legislature and the New York courts have made it unmistakably clear that foster care is intended only as a temporary way station until a child can be returned to his natural parents or placed for adoption. . . .

In these circumstances, I cannot understand why the Court thinks itself obliged to decide these cases on the assumption that either foster parents or foster children in New York have some sort of "liberty" interest in the continuation of their relationship.[1] Rather than tiptoeing around this central issue, I would squarely hold that the interests asserted by the appellees are not of a kind that the Due Process Clause of the Fourteenth Amendment protects.

[T]he predicate for invoking the Due Process Clause — the existence of state-created liberty or property — [is] missing here. New York confers no right on foster families to remain intact, defensible only upon proof of specific acts or circumstances. . . . Similarly, New York law provides no basis for a justifiable expectation on the part of foster families that their relationship will continue indefinitely. . . .

What remains of the appellees' argument is the theory that the relation of the foster parent to the foster child may generate emotional attachments similar to those found in natural families. The Court surmises that foster families who share these attachments might enjoy the same constitutional interests in "family privacy" as natural families. . . .

But under New York's foster care laws, any case where the foster parents had assumed the emotional role of the child's natural parents would represent not a triumph of the system, to be constitutionally safeguarded from state intrusion, but a failure. The goal of foster care, at least in New York, is not to provide a permanent substitute for the natural or adoptive home, but to prepare the child for his return to his real parents or placement in a permanent adoptive home by giving him temporary shelter in a family setting. Thus, the New York Court of Appeals has recognized that the development of close emotional ties between foster parents and a child may hinder the child's ultimate adjustment in a permanent home, and provide a basis

---

[1] The Court's opinion seems to indicate that there is no reason to distinguish between the claims of the foster parents and the foster children, either because the parents have standing to assert the rights of the children or because the parents' interest is identical to that of the children. I cannot agree.

First, it is by no means obvious that foster parents and foster children have the same interest in a continuation of their relationship. When the child leaves the foster family, it is because the agency with custody of him has determined that his interests will be better served by a new home, either with his natural parents, adoptive parents, or a different foster family. Any assessment of the child's alleged deprivation must take into account not only what he has lost, but what he has received in return. Foster parents, on the other hand, do not automatically receive a new child with whom they will presumably have a more profitable relationship.

Second, . . . this is not a case where the failure to grant the parents their requested relief will inevitably tend to "dilut[e] or adversely affec[t]" the alleged constitutional rights of the children. Denying the parents a hearing simply has no effect whatever on the children's separate claim to a hearing, and does not impair their alleged constitutional rights. There is therefore no standing in the parents to assert the children's claims.

I would nevertheless consider both the parents' and the children's claims in these cases, but only because the suit was originally brought on behalf of both the parents and the children, all of whom were parties plaintiff. While it is true that their interests may conflict, there was no reason not to allow counsel for the parents to continue to represent the children to the extent that their interests may be compatible. The conflict was avoided by the District Court's appointment of independent counsel, who took a position opposite to that of the foster parents as to where the children's welfare lay. The appointment of independent counsel, however, should not have left the children without advocacy for the position, right or wrong, that they are entitled to due process hearings. That position should have been left to be asserted by the counsel who originally brought the suit for the children. My view, therefore, is that the parents and the children are properly before the Court and entitled to assert their own separate claims, but that neither group has standing to assert the claims of the other.

for the *termination* of the foster family relationship. In re Jewish Child Care Assn. (Sanders), supra.[2] Perhaps it is to be expected that children who spend unduly long stays in what should have been temporary foster care will develop strong emotional ties with their foster parents. But this does not mean, and I cannot believe, that such breakdowns of the New York system must be protected or forever frozen in their existence by the Due Process Clause of the Fourteenth Amendment.

One of the liberties protected by the Due Process Clause, the Court has held, is the freedom to "establish a home and bring up children." Meyer v. Nebraska, supra, at 399. . . . But this constitutional concept is simply not in point when we deal with foster families as New York law has defined them. The family life upon which the State "intrudes" is simply a temporary status which the State itself has created. It is a "family life" defined and controlled by the law of New York, for which New York pays, and the goals of which New York is entitled to and does set for itself.

NOTES AND QUESTIONS

(1) Constitutional Procedures. Are the procedures provided in New York constitutionally compelled? Suppose a state did not have any procedures to allow foster parents either a trial-type hearing before removal or a preremoval conference and a postremoval hearing procedure? Would the Constitution be satisfied? Does the Constitution require some sort of trial-type hearing for foster parents *before* removal when (a) the child is not returning to his natural parents; (b) the foster parents and child have a substantial psychological relationship; (c) the child has lived with the foster parents more than 18 months; or (d) the foster parents request a hearing?

(2) Contractual Relationship. What effect do the terms of a contract between the state and foster parents have upon the foster parents' constitutional rights? If the foster parents' "contractual relationship with the state" had said nothing about the state's removal rights, would the foster parents then have had a constitutionally protected liberty interest? Would the outcome be different?

(3) Suppose the foster parents were the child's aunt and uncle (or grandparents), who had signed a contract with the state and received foster care payments from the state. Would they be entitled to greater constitutional protection? Would there be a "relationship having its origins entirely apart from the power of the state"?

(4) Where a child has no biological parents (either because they have died or abandoned the child), would foster parents have a constitutional liberty interest in the relationship with the child after the child had lived with them for some period of time?

---

[2] "That the Sanders have given Laura a good home and have shown her great love does not stamp as an abuse of discretion the Trial Justice's determination to take her from them. Indeed, it is the extreme of love, affection, and possessiveness manifested by the Sanders, together with the conduct which their emotional involvement impelled, that supplies the foundation of reasonableness and correctness for his determination. The vital fact is that Mr. and Mrs. Sanders are not, and presumably will never be, Laura's parents by adoption. Their disregard of that fact and their seizure of full parental status in the eyes of the child might well be, or so the Trial Justice was entitled to find, a source of detriment to the child in the circumstances presented." 5 N.Y.2d., at 229, 156 N.E.2d, at 703.

(5) Sibling Relationships. Do foster children have a liberty interest in sibling relationships? Compare B.H. v. Johnson, 715 F. Supp. 1387 (N.D. Ill. 1989) (finding no due process right to sibling visitation) with Cal. Welf. & Inst. Code §366.26 (West 1998) (termination of parental rights will not occur if it would result in substantial interference with the child's sibling relationships). See also Adoption of Pierce, 790 N.E.2d 680 (Mass. App. Ct. 2003) (holding that the best interests standard prevails over foster child's right to maintain sibling relationship). See generally William W. Patton, The Status of Siblings' Rights: A View into the New Millennium, 51 DePaul L. Rev. 1 (2001).

(6) Are the constitutional rights of the foster parents any greater in a case where the children have been placed in foster care by a juvenile court because of parental neglect? Does anything turn on the fact that the natural parents in these cases "voluntarily" place their children in foster care?

(7) Psychological Parent. Does OFFER adequately protect the relationship of the child to a "psychological parent"? Where it can be shown that a foster child has substantial psychological ties to foster parents who wish to adopt the child, should it be possible to terminate the parental rights of a biological parent who is not a "psychological parent"? The concept of the "psychological parent" was developed by Joseph Goldstein, Anna Freud, and Alfred Solnit in Beyond the Best Interests of the Child (1973) to denote an individual, who may or may not be the child's biological parent, who has strong emotional bonds with the child. See In re Phillip B., pp. 377-380 infra. Also compare In re J. & J.W., 365 A.2d 521 (Vt. 1976) (mother's failure to meet a foster child's need for a "psychological parent" does not constitute a substantial change of circumstances sufficient to warrant termination of parental rights) with In re J.S.R., 374 A.2d 860 (D.C. 1977) (upholding use of best interest standard in termination proceeding to allow adoption without parental consent).

(8) Kinship Care. An increasing number of children (especially African-American children) live with relatives (kinship care) either by informal agreement or formal child welfare arrangement. Kinship care became especially popular in the late 1980s with the AIDS epidemic and maternal substance abuse. What are the advantages of kinship care for children? For biological parents? For the state?

Federal child welfare policy promotes kinship foster care. For example, PRWORA, 42 U.S.C. §671(a)(19) (2000), encourages states to give preference to relative caregivers. And, for children who are in kinship care, the Adoption and Safe Families Act (ASFA) (discussed infra pp. 343-344) allows states to waive the rule requiring termination if children have been in out-of-home placements for 15 of the last 24 months. 42 U.S.C. §675(5)(E)(i) (2000). For criticisms of kinship care, see Dorothy E. Roberts, Kinship Care and the Price of State Support for Children, 76 Chi.-Kent L. Rev. 1619 (2001) (contending that kinship care harms families because state intrusion disrupts, rather than preserves, ties among kin).

(9) Voluntary Foster Care Placement. OFFER reveals that parents, rather than the state, often initiate foster care placement. What does OFFER reveal about the problems posed by such voluntary surrenders? See also In re Sanjivini K., 391 N.E.2d 1316 (N.Y. Ct. App. 1979) (finding that best interests of child were not served by freeing her for adoption by foster parents where mother voluntarily

surrendered child to agency but made considerable effort to preserve parental ties throughout child's life).

(10) Foster Care Subsidies for Children with Special Needs. Some children in foster care may be hard to place because of a disability. ASFA §201(codified at 42 U.S.C. §673A) provides financial incentives for states to increase adoptions of children with special needs. Is subsidized adoption like baby selling (discussed in Chapter 5)? Why is it that the symbolic repugnance of paying people to adopt a child seems to be less substantial than baby selling, where a biological mother is paid to give up a newborn?

(11) Liberty Interest: Other Jurisdictions. The Supreme Court in Smith v. OFFER refused to reach the question of whether foster parents can have a constitutionally protected "liberty" interest in the continued placement of a foster child in their home, but merely held that even if such a liberty interest existed, the New York agency had given the foster parents adequate procedural protection. Several circuits have since squarely held that foster parents do not possess a constitutionally protected liberty interest in the maintenance of the foster family relationship, because of the distinguishing factors mentioned by the majority in Smith v. OFFER. See, e.g., Rodriguez v. McLoughlin, 214 F.3d 328 (2d Cir. 2000); Gibson v. Merced County Dept. of Human Resources, 799 F.2d 582, 586 (9th Cir. 1986); Procopio v. Johnson, 994 F.2d 325 (7th Cir. 1993); Drummond v. Fulton County Dep't of Family and Children's Servs., 563 F.2d 1200, 1206 (5th Cir. 1977) (en banc), *cert. denied*, 437 U.S. 910 (1978). See generally Cassandra S. Haury, Note: The Changing American Family: A Reevaluation of the Rights of Foster Parents When Biological Parental Rights Have Been Terminated, 35 Ga. L. Rev. 313 (2000).

The Aftermath and Effects of Smith v. OFFER

David L. Chambers & Michael S. Wald, "Smith v. OFFER"
In the Interest of Children 114-117 (Robert H. Mnookin ed., 1985)

Despite the reversal by the Supreme Court the case was not without some impact. Beginning with the smallest but clearest impact of all, the Gandy children [see n. 1 of the opinion] stayed with Mrs. Smith. By the time that the Supreme Court had decided that New York's procedures were constitutionally permissible and vacated the restraining order that had been in effect for over three years, the Catholic Guardian Society had long abandoned its plans to move the children. The children seem to have thrived with Mrs. Smith. On May 7, 1981, seven years after the restraining order was entered, a New York state court approved a petition by Mrs. Smith to adopt the children.

In addition, . . . the litigation did result in New York City adopting new regulations providing for formal hearings prior to intra-foster-care transfers. These hearings, which are not available if the child is being returned home, must be requested by the foster parents. The placing agencies are required to notify all foster parents of their rights. The hearings are conducted in a far more formal manner than those held under the prior regulations. The foster parents can bring counsel and witnesses are sworn and subject to cross-examination. There is often expert testimony and several people from the agency, as well as the biological parents and their representatives, attend. These hearings generally last less than one day although some go on for several days. Occasionally, it takes months to complete the process.

Thus, for intra-foster-care moves, Lowry [the attorney representing the foster parents in *Smith*] obtained her goal in *New York City*. [However, the] New York State Department of Social Services declined to adopt the new regulations, and the New York State legislature has rejected bills that would have mandated New York City's approach across the state. . . .

We cannot determine whether children are "better off" as a result of the hearings that are held. Retta Friedman, who hears all these cases, is a former caseworker. She believes that hearings, although time-consuming and frequently subject to delays, have resulted in better information being gathered, and as a result, in more protection for children.

She believes that the effectiveness of the hearings is due to the fact that the agency worker must be present and is subject to cross-examination by the foster parent, who may be represented by counsel. In the past all the hearing officer had was a written report from the agency. Now the agencies do a much better job of substantiating the reasons for their actions and in providing documentation to the hearing officer. Friedman also believes that the hearings facilitate understanding and acceptance among foster parents. . . .

In addition to the actual requests for hearings, it may be that the regulations act to deter some inappropriate agency actions. . . . Most of the people we interviewed thought that there had been little change in agency behavior as a result of the new regulations. However, at least some people, including Gans [the attorney representing the interests of the natural parents in *Smith*], felt that the litigation did contribute to opening up the process in New York City to public attention and that this had led to some improvement in the system.

It may also be that the case accomplished the NYCLU's goals in some other ways. [T]he majority did indicate that there might be constitutionally-protected interests in permanence and stability in some foster care relationships. They implied that procedures similar to those in New York might be constitutionally required. States that did not afford foster parents any preremoval conferences or hearings were put on notice that their process might be unconstitutional. The *OFFER* decision has been cited by a few courts as a basis for protecting a *very* long-term foster relationship, although most of the ten to fifteen published opinions that have cited the case, for more than a passing reference in a string citation, have used it to deny foster parents any rights. *how OFFER is used as precedent*

c. Exit from Foster Care: The Aging Out of Older Foster Children

Occean v. Kearney
123 F. Supp. 2d 618 (S.D. Fla. 2000)

DIMITROULEAS, District Judge.

. . . Plaintiff brings these claims for injunctive and declaratory relief under Title 42 U.S.C. Section 1983, alleging that his substantive due process and procedural due process rights were violated when Defendants, in their official capacities as executives in a state agency, the Florida Department of Children and Family Services (hereinafter "DCF"), ended Plaintiff's foster care benefits when Plaintiff reached the age of eighteen without previously affording Plaintiff notice and an opportunity to be heard. . . .

The Amended Complaint alleges that Plaintiff, now nineteen years old, was born in the Bahamas and arrived thereafter in the United States with his mother. In March 1992, DCF removed Plaintiff from his parents' custody and placed him in foster care because he and his siblings were being left in their home inappropriately. On August 20, 1994, DCF transferred Plaintiff to Mel Blount Youth Home of Georgia, a behavioral modification facility, contracted to the Florida DCF to provide 24 hour, seven day a week care and education to juveniles under DCF control. In March 1995, the juvenile court in Fort Lauderdale entered an order providing that if DCF was to change the Plaintiff's placement, it shall present to the court a written report outlining what treatment plan is proposed for the Plaintiff and DCF's basis for such a recommendation. In June, 1995, the juvenile court changed the case plan goal for Plaintiff to long term foster care, and Plaintiff was given an Independent Living Skills Assessment to complete. Plaintiff stated that he wished to get his GED, attend technical school, and secure employment. According to the Amended Complaint, on May 6, 1997, Plaintiff met the eligibility criteria for receipt of Special Immigrant Status from the INS.

The Amended Complaint further alleges that according to the reports and recommendations to the juvenile court and from the Mel Blount facility's files, Plaintiff seemed to be making significant progress in this program and was working towards his GED. One month before his benefits were terminated, DCF recommended that Plaintiff continue individual and group counseling and explore vocational options for positive transition from youth home into the community. Furthermore, Plaintiff expressed his desire to remain in the youth home until he obtained his GED. On December 26, 1998, Plaintiff's eighteenth birthday, without any notice or an opportunity to be heard, his case was closed by DCF. Plaintiff was told on March 16, 1999 to immediately pack and leave on the next bus to Fort Lauderdale with only a few of his belongings and fifty dollars. Upon arrival in Fort Lauderdale, Plaintiff was unable to work because he never received legal immigration status from INS while in custody of the DCF nor his GED. While in South Florida, Plaintiff was arrested and incarcerated. Before his release from state custody, INS placed a hold on Plaintiff and he was transferred to an INS contract facility where he awaits deportation. . . .

Defendant argues that Plaintiff has no substantive due process claim because the continuance of foster care benefits after the age of eighteen and the assistance in obtaining a green card are not the type of liberty or property interest traditionally afforded due process. Defendants allege that the liberty interests the Plaintiff asserts are not those that are "objectively, deeply rooted in this Nation's history and tradition." Washington v. Glucksberg, 521 U.S. 702, 720-21 (1997). The Due Process Clause does not obligate states to provide its citizens with substantive services, even if those services are necessary to secure citizens' life, liberty, or property interest. However, a State owes a duty under the Due Process Clause to take care of those who have already been deprived of their liberty.

. . . When a person is institutionalized and wholly dependent on the state, a special relationship is created that requires a certain minimal standard of care. Youngberg v. Romeo, 457 U.S. 307, 317 (1982). In *Youngberg*, the Supreme Court held that the state was under a duty to provide respondent, a mentally retarded individual involuntarily committed to a state institution, with such training as an appropriate professional would consider reasonable to ensure safety and to facilitate his ability to function free from bodily restraint. The United States Court of Appeals for the Second Circuit has extended the meaning of *Youngberg* to children who are the responsibility of the state.

Defendants argue that Plaintiff has no substantive due process right to continued foster care benefits or assistance in obtaining a green card because no special relationship was created between Plaintiff and Defendants, and Plaintiff's claim simply does not rise to the level of a fundamental right secured by the Constitution. In the case at bar, Plaintiff argues Defendants accepted the responsibility of providing Plaintiff a residential placement in which he would be prepared to enter the adult world, thereby creating a special relationship, but instead abandoned the Plaintiff without a GED and without the legal ability to work because the Defendants did not obtain legal immigration status for Plaintiff while in foster care. Plaintiff, therefore, argues that Defendants deprived Plaintiff of his federal liberty interest in a humane and decent existence as a foster child in the care of the state, by not providing him with continued benefits in the form of participation in a GED program and legal immigration status.[3] However, if such a special relationship existed, when Plaintiff turned 18, such special relationship terminated for purposes of a substantive due process analysis. Moreover, Plaintiff is in INS custody due to his committing a crime while he was 18 years old and no longer in DCF care. Plaintiff's own intervening cause leads this Court to conclude that no substantive due process violation occurred in this case.

Ultimately, the Court is left with a claim that simply does not rise to the level of a fundamental right protected by the Due Process Clause of the Constitution. Even if Defendants' conduct in summarily terminating Plaintiff's foster care benefits upon turning age 18 was arbitrary and capricious, this Court concludes that such post-age 18 foster care benefits are not a fundamental right that merits protection under the substantive due process clause. *[handwritten: can't protect against this]*

The Court reaches a different conclusion as to Plaintiff's procedural due process claim. Defendant alleges that Plaintiff has no property right in continued foster care benefits and therefore, has failed to state a state procedural due process claim. There are two questions in the analysis of a procedural due process claim: first, did the plaintiff have a property interest of which he was deprived by state action, and if so, did the plaintiff receive sufficient process regarding that deprivation. Plaintiff alleges that he has a property interest in securing legal immigration status through the assistance of DCF, and in continued foster care as provided by Section 409.165(4) of the Florida Statutes. Plaintiff further alleges that once he turned eighteen he was

---

[3] Florida Statutes Section 409.145(a) authorizes the DCF to continue to provide the services of the children's foster care program to individuals 18 to 21 years of age who are enrolled in a program to obtain a high school equivalency diploma. In 2000, the statute was apparently amended to allow for such benefits until the age of 23.

entitled to the benefits until the age of twenty-one, that Defendants provided Plaintiff a plan calling for him to remain in foster care through May 31, 1999, and that Defendants violated the juvenile court judge's prohibition on terminating Plaintiff's existing foster placement without a court order. Finally, Plaintiff argues that the Florida Administrative Codes provides a procedure to be followed for mandatory administrative review, including notice of the conference, for children reaching age 18 but eligible for continued foster care benefits. See Florida Administrative Code Sections 65C-13.019 and 65C-16.003.

Defendants argue that Plaintiff's attainment of age 18 automatically terminates any property rights held by Plaintiff to continued benefits. Once reaching this "magic age," Defendants argue that Plaintiff's property rights ended, since Florida law allows DCF the discretion to continue benefits. However, the Defendants conceded at oral argument that there is an issue as to whether they failed to provide Plaintiff, prior to his turning 18, the assistance mandated by the Florida Administrative Code regarding aid in obtaining legal immigration status. Plaintiff also alleges that he never received a hearing or any type of process informing him of his denial of the extended foster care benefits.

When limitations exist on agency discretion to terminate or extend benefits, procedural due process must be afforded. In this case, both Florida Administrative Code and the continuing order of the juvenile court arguably provided such limitations on the discretion of Defendants in terminating Plaintiff's benefits. Taking Plaintiff's allegations as true, Plaintiff has sufficiently stated for purposes of defeating a motion to dismiss that he has a property interest entitled to procedural due process in these foster care benefits and immigration status assistance. Therefore, Plaintiff's allegations meet both requirements for a procedural due process claim and state a claim upon which relief can be granted. . . .

NOTE ON AGING OUT OF FOSTER CARE

Occean v. Kearney, supra, highlights the plight of the older foster care child who exits from foster care. Many foster children, particularly those who are not adopted or reunified with their families, exit foster care at the age of 18. These children "age out," i.e., they are no longer eligible for foster care benefits regardless of whether they have sufficient skills or resources to live on their own.

Approximately 20,000 teens leave foster care each year because they have reached the age of majority. Susan Vivian Mangold, Extending Non-Exclusive Parenting and the Right to Protection for Older Foster Children: Creating Third Options in Permanency Planning, 48 Buff. L. Rev. 835, 863 (2000) (citing congressional findings, H.R. 3443, 106th Cong. 1999). According to empirical studies, many of these youths face unemployment, homelessness, incarceration, and nonmarital pregnancy. Id. at 863-866.

In the mid 1980s federal legislation first recognized the needs of older foster care children. As a result, Congress enacted the Independent Living Initiative (ILI) 42 U.S.C. §677, in 1986, requiring specific planning to help these youth before their exit from foster care. The ILI required states to provide services to foster care children to prepare them for independent living.

Then, in 1999, Congress passed the Foster Care Independence Act (FCIA), 42 U.S.C. §677 (2000), to provide additional funding for improved services to these older youths who leave the foster care system. Specifically, FCIA offers programs in education, training or post-secondary education, employment, and financial support that may continue until age 21 if necessary. FCIA also allows Medicaid coverage to youths between the ages of 18 and 21 who were in foster care on their 18th birthday. FCIA also authorizes additional funding to assist states to find permanent homes for foster care youths. See generally Jill K. Jensen, Notes & Comments, Fostering Interdependence: A Family-Centered Approach to Help Youth Aging Out of Foster Care, 3 Whittier J. Child & Fam. Advoc. 329 (2004).

3. Foster Care Reform

a. Statutory Reform: AACWA and ASFA

Foster care was envisaged as a temporary solution to family disfunction or disruption. However, in the 1970s, public attention began focusing on the problem of "foster care drift." The term signifies the experience of foster care children who suffer multiple foster care placements, moving endlessly from foster home to foster home without any hope of family reunification or adoption. Many commentators criticized the practice and highlighted its psychological harm to children.[17] The United States Supreme Court added fuel to the debate wth its criticism of foster care drift in Smith v. OFFER (supra, pp. 326-336).

Concern about the "limbo" of foster care motivated substantial legislative reform on the federal and state level. In 1980 Congress passed the Adoption Assistance and Child Welfare Act (AACWA), 42 U.S.C. §§620-28, 670-79(a). The primary objective of the AACWA was to facilitate finding permanent homes for children (by preventing the need for removal, returning children to their families, or placing them for adoption). AACWA emphasizes preventive and reunification services.

The Act provides federal matching funds to states for foster care and adoptive services if states adopt certain standards. Specifically, AACWA requires that: (1) states must formulate case plans ("permanency planning") that are designed to achieve placement in the least possible restrictive setting, (2) states must conduct periodic case reviews, and (3) states must make "reasonable efforts" to prevent removal of children from the home and to reunify the family following removal (42 U.S.C. §671(a)(15)). Through these provisions Congress attempted to shift resources from temporary out-of-home care and to focus on channeling resources either to a child's natural family or to other permanent care alternatives.

---

[17] See, e.g., Joseph Goldstein et al., Beyond the Best Interests of the Child (1973); Robert H. Mnookin, Child-Custody Adjudication: Judicial Functions in the Face of Indeterminacy, 39 Law & Contemp. Probs. 226 (1975); Robert H. Mnookin, Foster Care — In Whose Best Interest?, 43 Harv. Educ. Rev. 599 (1973); Michael S. Wald, State Intervention on Behalf of 'Neglected' Children, 28 Stan. L. Rev. 623 (1976).

Even before Congress passed the AACWA, individual states were acting independently to adopt legislation that pointed in the same direction. After 1980, states adopted legislation to conform to the minimum requirements for federal funding set out by the AACWA.

Following federal legislative reform, several problems remained. The AACWA failed to define the term "reasonable efforts." That reform would be addressed in subsequent legislation (the Adoption and Safe Families Act, discussed infra). And, compliance with the AACWA varied considerably from state to state. Under the regulatory scheme contemplated by the Department of Health and Human Services (HHS), if a state asserted compliance with the AACWA, the state was automatically granted federal funding, and its practices were subject to only minimal scrutiny by HHS. As a result, many states received funding without in fact complying with the minimum requirements of the AACWA.

Congress turned again to address foster care reform with the enactment of the Adoption and Safe Families Act of 1997 (ASFA), 42 U.S.C. §675(5) (2000). ASFA strengthens the requirements of AACWA. One of ASFA's most important reforms is to clarify the meaning of the AACWA's "reasonable efforts" standard. Under AACWA, states had to make reasonable efforts to prevent the need for foster care and to reunify families after placement. However, AACWA failed to specify the extent of the efforts that were required.

In contrast, ASFA recognizes that reunification is not possible or advisable in all cases. Thus, ASFA eliminates the reasonable efforts requirement in the AACWA for the most severe cases (torture, sexual abuse, a parent murders another child, or a parent loses parental rights to a sibling), 42 U.S.C. §675(a)(15)(D). In addition, ASFA aims to facilitate adoption by reducing the amount of time that children spend in foster care. Thus, ASFA shortens the period triggering permanency hearings to no later than 12 months after the child's entry into foster care and also requires states to seek termination of parental rights for children who have been in foster care for 15 of the last 22 months (42 U.S.C. §675(5)(E)).

b. The Role of Litigation

Following the enactment of AACWA, class action lawsuits were brought by foster children against state and local agencies to secure regulatory enforcement of the Act. This effort began with Lynch v. King, 550 F. Supp. 325 (D. Mass. 1982), *aff'd sub nom.* Lynch v. Dukakis, 719 F.2d 504 (1st Cir. 1983), where, on the basis of the AACWA, a federal court for the first time recognized a private right of action against a state agency for the failure to live up to federal foster care requirements. In *Lynch*, the First Circuit upheld an injunction issued by the district court against the Massachusetts Department of Social Services (DSS) ordering DSS to comply with the requirements of the AACWA, specifically: (1) to reduce caseloads to no more than 20 per worker, or fewer if necessary to enable workers to meet their responsibilities; (2) to provide a detailed case plan for each child; (3) to periodically (at least every six months) review each child's status in foster care; and (4) to assign each case, i.e., deliver the file, to a specific social worker within 24 hours of its receipt by DSS. The court further ordered that if DSS failed to comply with the injunction it must forfeit its federal funding for foster care and child welfare programs, as provided by the Act.

After *Lynch*, several federal courts handed down similar decisions recognizing a private right of enforcement of the statutory provisions of the AACWA. See, e.g., LaShawn v. Dixon, 762 F. Supp. 959 (D.D.C. 1991); Norman v. Johnson, 739 F. Supp. 1182 (N.D. Ill. 1990); L.J. v. Massinga, 699 F. Supp. 508 (D. Md. 1988), *cert. denied*, 488 U.S. 1018 (1989); Joseph A. v. New Mexico Dept. of Soc. Servs., 575 F. Supp. 346 (D.N.M. 1983).

The Supreme Court called an abrupt halt in 1992 to this movement. Suter v. Artist M., 503 U.S. 347 (1992), involved a class action against the Illinois Department of Children and Family Services for failure to use "reasonable efforts" to assign caseworkers to child clients. Finding no congressional intent to permit private enforcement of the AACWA, the Court reasoned that the Act constituted only a vague directive which failed to provide guidance as to measurement of "reasonable efforts." Following *Suter*, compliance with the AACWA remains dependent on monitoring by HHS. As one commentator criticizes:

> By refusing to recognize a right to private enforcement of the AACWA, the Court has restricted enforcement of the Act to the one entity that consistently has refused to exercise its authority in the face of substantial statutory violations and systemic state failures to provide for children in its care.[18]

Congress subsequently disapproved the Supreme Court's holding in *Suter.* By an amendment to the Social Security Act, 42 U.S.C. §1320a-2, -10 (2000), Congress limited the Supreme Court's holding (that precluded private causes of action) to the "reasonable efforts" provision of the AACWA (§671(a)(15)). Further, one commentator[19] has speculated that children whom the state places in foster care (as opposed to those who are merely retained in their homes under state supervision) may still be able to seek redress after *DeShaney* (see discussion supra p. 260) for substantive due process violations. Several federal courts have recognized such a cause of action[20]; however, the Supreme Court has yet to address the issue.

Litigation to reform state child protective services continues. To avoid dismissal under *Suter*, lawsuits have relied on other constitutional, state statutory, and federal statutory causes of action. See, e.g., Occean v. Kearney, supra (recognizing a private cause of action under a different AACWA provision §671(a)(16)); LaShawn v. Barry, 87 F.3d 1389 (D.C. Cir. 1996) (post-*Suter* case recognizing a remedy under local law). However, this avenue of redress also may be curtailed by virtue of subsequent Supreme Court decisions limiting the ability of private citizens to recover in state or federal courts for violations of federal statutes. See College Savings Bank v. Florida Prepaid Postsecondary Educ. Expense Bd., 527 U.S. 627 (1999) (holding that states are immune from suits under Trademark Act); Kimel

---

[18] Arlene E. Fried, The Foster Child's Avenue of Redress: Questions Left Unanswered, 26 Colum. J.L. & Soc. Probs. 465 (1993).

[19] Id. at 479.

[20] See, e.g., Meador v. Cabinet for Human Res., 902 F.2d 474 (6th Cir. 1990), *cert. denied*, 498 U.S. 867 (1990); Burton v. Richmond, 276 F.3d 973 (8th Cir. 2002); T.M. ex rel. Cox v. Carson, 93 F. Supp. 2d 1179 (D. Wyo. 2000).

v. Florida Bd. of Regents, 528 U.S. 62 (2000) (same under Age Discrimination in Employment Act); Federal Maritime Commnr. v. S.C. State Ports Authority et al., 535 U.S. 743 (2000) (same under Shipping Act). But cf. Nevada Dept. Human Res. v. Hibbs, 538 U.S. 731 (2003) (permitting private suit under Family and Medical Leave Act); Tennessee v. Lane, 124 U.S. 1978 (2004) (same under Americans with Disabilities Act regarding access to federal facilities).

Nonetheless, litigation has been a major vehicle for foster care reform. To date, courts have ordered 27 states to improve their child welfare systems. Jensen, supra, at 338.

For critical commentary on the AACWA and AFSA, see Will L. Crossley, Defining Reasonable Efforts: Demystifying the State's Burden Under Federal Child Protection Legislation, 12 B.U. Pub. Int. L.J. 259 (2003); Terry Lyons, When Reasonable Efforts Hurt Victims of Abuse: Five Years of the Adoption and Safe Families Act of 1997, 26 Seton Hall Legis. J. 391 (2002); Amy Willinson-Hagen, Note: The Adoption and Safe Families Act of 1997: A Collision of Parens Patriae and Parent's Constitutional Rights, 11 Geo. J. on Poverty L. & Pol'y 137 (2004).

c. Criticisms and Proposals for Reform

Dorothy E. Roberts, Is There Justice in Children's Rights?: The Critique of Federal Family Preservation Policy
2 U. Pa. J. Const. L. 112, 118-138 (1999)

In November 1997 President Clinton signed the Adoption and Safe Families Act. . . . ASFA represents a dramatic shift in federal child welfare philosophy from an emphasis on the reunification of children in foster care with their biological families toward support for the adoption of these children into new families. . . .

A. ASFA's New Focus Cannot Solve the Foster Care Problem

ASFA's promotion of adoption is unlikely to improve the situation of most children in foster care. There are insufficient adoptive homes for the increasing number of children removed from their biological families. Moreover, unnecessarily separating children from their biological parents does not advance children's interests, but rather destroys family bonds that usually benefit children. . . .

The policy of promoting adoption at the expense of terminating parental rights assumes that adoption will significantly reduce the large numbers of children in out-of-home placements. The key supporters of ASFA operated according to the premise that the foster care problem stems from barriers to adoption. They criticized family preservation policies that made it difficult to terminate parental rights. They implied that if states removed these barriers — if courts terminated parental rights sooner — the foster care problem would dissipate and even disappear.

This is a false hope. There are not enough people wishing to adopt to absorb the high volume of children already pouring into foster care. Data on the foster care system over the last twenty years show that the number of parental rights terminations far outpaces the number of adoptions. Martin Guggenheim's study of statistics gathered from Michigan and New York over the period from 1987 to 1993 showed a dramatic increase in the number of children who become "state wards" — children whose parents' rights have been terminated and who are waiting in foster care to be adopted. . . . ASFA's accelerated deadlines for termination of parental rights will probably increase the state ward population; its adoption incentives, on the other hand, even if they achieve congressional goals, will probably fail to provide enough new homes for these children. This shortfall is exacerbated by the fact that the children most likely affected by ASFA's expedited termination process are the very ones least likely to be adopted. Black parents' rights are already terminated sooner than those of white parents, yet black children are less likely than white children to be adopted.

race issue

It is difficult to see how these children's interests are furthered by the extinction of their legal connection to their parents. "State governments appear to be destroying family ties of a large, and continually increasing number of children," Guggenheim charges, "with no concomitant benefit to children." Termination weakens family stability for many foster children by disrupting their relationship with their parents, while failing to result in permanent placement. . . .

There are alternatives to adoption that could ensure family stability while preserving the parent-child relationship. For example, children can often be safely placed in the long-term care of relatives or neighbors with parental visitation, leaving open the possibility of parents regaining custody if circumstances improve. In a 1994 survey of children in Illinois state custody who had been living with a relative for more than one year, 85% of relatives reported that the best plan for the children was to remain with them until the children were grown. . . .

ASFA's focus on terminating parental rights reflects the judgment that the risk of wrongful reunifications outweighs that of wrongful disruptions of families. This judgment, too, is misguided. The priority ASFA placed on child safety was cast as a correction of the 1980 Act's reasonable efforts requirement, which encouraged the return of foster children to violent homes. The reasonable efforts requirement, however, was itself enacted in response to evidence that agency caseworkers offered families minimal assistance and even obstructed parents' attempts to reunite with their children.

Even under the Child Welfare Act's reasonable efforts requirement, state agencies continued to make anemic efforts to prevent out-of-home placements and reunify families. Family preservation programs often fail because they do not address the needs of families, are inadequately funded, and do not last long enough. Caseworkers caught in the dual role of supporting families while recruiting foster and adoptive parents sometimes sabotage parents' quest to reunite with their children. A 1997 report issued by the General Accounting Office stated that more than half of the family support programs it surveyed "were not able to serve all families who needed services primarily due to the lack of funds and staff."

Services for families in California, for example, are permitted to continue for a maximum of six months and, on average, end after only half this time. How can agencies expect to solve problems arising from any combination of deplorable conditions — chronic poverty, dangerous neighborhoods, shoddy housing, poor health, drug addiction, profound depression, lack of childcare — with a three month parenting course or ephemeral crisis intervention? . . .

B. ASFA Mischaracterizes the Foster Care Problem

The pragmatic problems with ASFA's emphasis on adoption are related to a more fundamental philosophical flaw. Congress has misidentified the foster care problem. The injustice of the American foster care system does not stem from the small number of children being adopted. It stems, rather, from the large number of children removed from their homes.

The class and race dimensions of foster care magnify this problem — virtually all of the parents who lose custody of their children are poor, and a startling percentage are black. More than 200,000 children are removed from their homes and placed in foster care annually. In 1998, black children made up 45% of the foster care population while comprising only 15% of the general population under age eighteen. In the nation's urban centers, the racial disparity is even greater. Chicago's foster care population, for example, is almost 90% black. Of 42,000 children in foster care in New York City in 1997, only 1300 were white. Moreover, once black children enter foster care, they remain there longer, are moved more often, and receive less desirable placements than white children. . . .

The focus on adoption as the solution to the foster care problem directs attention away from the wide scale removal of poor black children from their homes. When Congress stated that its aim was "to make sure that every child has the opportunity to live in a safe, stable, loving and permanent home," it had in mind terminating parents' rights, not reducing poverty or building stronger supports for families. . . .

By promoting adoption so myopically, we forget that our ultimate goal should be to reduce the need for adoptions. [W]e can support adoption while working to curtail its causes. By combating poverty and its dangers to children, an ideal society would radically decrease its need for adoption. . . .

C. ASFA Disparages Biological Bonds

Perhaps the most disturbing aspect of ASFA's focus on adoption and its rescue mentality is the message it sends about the poor and minority families whose children have been placed in foster care. Throughout congressional testimony regarding the Act, adoption was portrayed as safer than the reunification of children with their biological families. Virtually every mention of biological families was negative, while adoptive homes were referred to as loving and stable. . . .

Perhaps the major reason for preferring extinction of parental ties in foster care is society's centuries-old depreciation of the relationship between poor parents and their children, especially those who are black. Most Americans can grasp a white middle-class child's emotional attachment to her biological father even though she is being raised by a stepfather. No one doubts the immediate re-connection of a wealthy child with his family when he returns from a year at boarding school. The public has a harder time, however, imagining a strong emotional bond between black parents and their children. . . . Poor black mothers are stereotyped as deviant and uncaring; they are blamed for transferring a degenerate lifestyle of welfare dependency and crime to their children. Black fathers are simply thought to be absent. When parents of children in foster care are portrayed as deranged and violent monsters, it becomes even more difficult for the public to believe that their children would want to maintain a relationship with them. . . .

Race and class politics are critical to understanding ASFA's impact because ASFA's emphasis on adoption was influenced by concurrent trends in federal welfare reform. ASFA was passed on the heels of the overhaul of federal welfare policy. The Personal Responsibility and Work Opportunity Reconciliation Act of 1996 ended the federal guarantee of cash assistance to America's children and allowed states to implement extensive welfare reform programs. State welfare reform measures hinder the ability of many poor mothers to care for their children: they reduce cash assistance to families, eliminate payments to some families altogether, and require mothers, often without adequate child care, to work and participate in job training, counseling, and other programs. What will happen to the children of mothers who fail to meet new work rules because of child care or transportation problems, who are unable to find work within the two-year time limit, or who leave their children at home without adequate care while they participate in required work programs? . . . Welfare-to-work programs may not rescue enough families from poverty to offset the numbers forced into the child welfare system by time limits, sanctions, and working conditions. In short, welfare reform may cause a net increase in the number of children entering foster care. . . .

The shift in federal policy from family preservation toward adoption also corresponded with the change in the federal position on trans-racial adoption. For decades, the federal government permitted public adoption agencies to enforce race-matching policies that sought to place black children exclusively with black adoptive families. In 1994 and 1996, however, Congress prohibited agencies receiving federal funding from placing children according to race or even from taking race into account in placement decisions. Federal support of trans-racial adoption has been championed as a critical step in increasing the numbers of adoptions of black children, the population with the lowest rate of permanent placements. Race-matching policies, it is argued, damage black children by not only denying them placements with white adoptive parents, but also by causing them to languish in foster care. . . .

The emphasis on freeing children for adoption heightens the tension between foster parents and biological parents, a contest that increasingly takes on a racial cast. . . . These contests bring to the surface a theme that runs more subtly through some of the discourse supporting trans-racial adoption — the belief that black children fare better if raised by white adoptive families than if returned home. Advocates of trans-racial adoption frequently assert the benefits of racial assimilation that black children and white parents experience by living together. In *Family Bonds*, for example, Elizabeth Bartholet rejects the claim that black children belong with black parents not only because "there is no evidence that black parents do a better job than white parents of raising black children with a sense of pride in their racial background," but also because black children reap substantial advantages from a white environment. Unlike black children "living in a state of relative isolation or exclusion from the white world," Bartholet contends, "black children raised in white homes are comfortable with their blackness and also uniquely comfortable in dealing with whites." As in the rhetoric promoting ASFA, the rhetoric promoting trans-racial adoption promotes the disruption of poor minority families by depicting adoptive homes as superior to children's existing family relationships.

(but there's a reason the child was removed!)

In sum, ASFA's emphasis on adoption and its popularity stemmed largely from concurrent developments in government policy related to welfare and trans-racial adoption. Determining whether ASFA furthers children's rights must take into account this political context. . . .

Elizabeth Bartholet, The Challenge of Children's Rights Advocacy: Problems and Progress in the Area of Child Abuse and Neglect
3 Whittier J. Child & Fam. Advoc. 215, 218-221 (2004)

A. Early Intensive Home Visitation

Early home visitation programs have developed in recent years as a way of addressing the problems of fragile families, typically first-time mothers whose children are identified as being at risk of child abuse and neglect because of the mothers' low socio-economic status and other factors. Inspired by Europe, where home visitation for young mothers is often provided as part of universal health care, some of the American programs have developed a more intensive visitation model better suited to a high risk population, with mothers visited on a regular basis both during pregnancy and through the first couple of years of the child's infancy.

I see this intensive form of home visitation as enormously promising. David Olds has demonstrated, through his careful research methodology, that his model, which uses nurse practitioners as the home visitors, works to reduce child abuse and neglect and is cost effective, at least when targeted to relatively high risk populations. His cost effectiveness research shows that his home visitation program saves the government money over the short term by reducing repeat pregnancies and helping to move young mothers into employment and off welfare.

This is an extremely conservative measure of cost effectiveness, since it does not even take into account the long term savings anticipated from reducing child abuse and neglect, and the enormous social costs associated with it. A comprehensive recent report on home visitation program research by an independent group of experts assembled by the U.S. Department of Health and Human Services constitutes a powerful endorsement of home visitation's success in reducing child abuse and neglect. The report concludes: "On the basis of strong evidence of effectiveness, the Task Force recommends early childhood home visitation for the prevention of child abuse and neglect." The Task Force's highest standard of effectiveness was met. The Task Force recommended home visitation for all at risk populations, including all disadvantaged and low-birthweight infants. It found that home visitation reduced the incidence of child abuse and neglect by about 40%, as compared with control populations, and concluded, as has David Olds, that the impact on child abuse and neglect was likely even greater because of the "surveillance" effect — the fact that the very presence of home visitors increases the likelihood that child abuse and neglect will be observed. The Task Force also endorsed Olds' cost effectiveness research and his conclusion that programs using nurse practitioners appeared to work better than those using paraprofessionals.

The kind of intensive and expensive home visitation programs which have actually been shown to be effective are the kind of general family support that our country has traditionally been reluctant to finance. Our politicians are all too ready to focus on the immediate expense of family support and ignore the horrendous long-term costs of child abuse and neglect — the costs associated with foster care and with the lives of crime, substance abuse, domestic violence, and unemployment that all too many victims of child maltreatment will live.

Also, our current early home visitation model is not likely to reach the families that are most at risk for child abuse and neglect. The model is voluntary not mandatory, offering home visitation to parents but not forcing it upon them. This is no surprise since the model has been built within the political realities of our deference to parental autonomy. The problem is that the parents who are most likely to be maltreating their children are those least likely to be willing to open the door to the home visitor who might witness the substance abuse and the child abuse and neglect that will put the parents at risk for criminal prosecution and child protective service intervention. Even the most enthusiastic home visitation advocates admit that a high percentage of parents refuse to participate and that the hard core problem parents are likely to be in this group. Yet as best I know I am virtually alone in advocating for mandatory home visitation, which seems to me essential if we are to reach the hard core group. . . .

C. Family Preservation

. . . Our child welfare policies place a high priority on family preservation even after serious child abuse and neglect has been identified. The Adoption and Safe Families Act (ASFA) passed by Congress in 1997 constitutes a major attempt to rebalance our society's priorities, placing a higher value on children's interests in safety and in moving on to permanent adoptive homes if their birth parents can not demonstrate within a reasonable period of time that they are capable of providing a nurturing home. ASFA is paralleled by numerous state and local policy initiatives placing a higher priority on children's interests when they seem in conflict with family preservation, such as expedited termination of parental rights (TPR) programs, and concurrent planning.

I have been an enthusiastic advocate for ASFA, for expedited TPR in egregious cases of child abuse and neglect, and for concurrent planning. I think we need to place a higher priority on children's interests than we have traditionally, and be more skeptical than we have traditionally as to whether those interests are always served by keeping them in their birth families. We need to recognize that what children victimized by child abuse and neglect, like battered women, often need is liberation from their families, rather than family preservation.

Critics of ASFA and other adoption-friendly policies argue that they are an unfair attack upon poor families. They are right that we don't do enough to enable poor families to succeed. We need to do more up front to support these families through intensive home visitation and other supportive programs. But once serious child abuse and neglect has been identified, many of the families at issue have fallen into such serious dysfunction that family support services are not likely to help create families that will really work for children. Research, including the most recent research, demonstrates that even well-funded, model family preservation programs have not succeeded in transforming dangerous family environments into ones that are safe and nurturing.

The critics of ASFA and other adoption-friendly policies are, like the critics of transracial adoption, both numerous and powerful. And ASFA leaves much discretion to state and other decision-makers: it is designed to set a new policy direction, but unlike MEPA [Multiethnic Placement Act, discussed in Chapter 5 infra] it mandates relatively little, and it contains many loopholes providing opportunities for those resistant to ASFA's spirit. The evidence to date indicates that some important ASFA provisions are having little impact. States are making liberal use of the exceptions to ASFA's requirement that parental rights be terminated for children held in foster care for 15 of the prior 22 months. States are generally not taking advantage of the opportunity ASFA provides to move children in egregious child abuse and neglect cases onto a fast track to adoption, bypassing any family preservation efforts. And after ASFA, as before, roughly one-third of all foster care children reunited with their birth families will reenter foster care, a statistic that speaks volumes about the harm we are doing to children in our efforts to keep them with their birth families.

Nonetheless, careful observers of ASFA see in their research evidence that this law, together with adoption-friendly state and local initiatives, is making a difference. There has been a dramatic increase in the number of adoptions from foster care. And many child welfare experts testify that ASFA has helped create a new pressure to expedite cases to permanency and to focus more on child safety. . . .

[The author also advocates the elimination of racial barriers to adoption placements and enforcement of federal legislation to that effect (discussed in Chapter 5). Finally, she advocates the enforcement of deadlines (one year) for substance-abusing parents to demonstrate that they are free of drugs and are able to parent before their parental rights are terminated.]

What do you think of the above criticisms and proposals of Professors Roberts and Bartholet?

4. Termination of Parental Rights: Procedural Safeguards

a. Reasonable Efforts Requirements

In re Ty M.
655 N.W.2d 672 (Neb. 2003)

WRIGHT, J.

Shawn M. and Holly M. each appeal from a judgment of the county court for Dodge County, sitting as a juvenile court, which terminated their parental rights to Ty M., born March 23, 1997, and Devon M., born June 10, 1998. . . . Ty and Devon were placed in the care, custody, and control of the Nebraska Department of Health and Human Services (DHHS) on November 20, 1998, after police were sent to the home to investigate a report that the children were in danger based on neglect. At the time, Ty was approximately 1 1/2 years old and Devon was approximately 5 months old. . . .

A petition to terminate parental rights was filed on February 27, 2001. The petition alleged that grounds for termination existed under Neb. Rev. Stat. §43-292(6) (Reissue 1998) because (1) the children had been determined to be children under §43-247(3)(a) [authorizing jurisdiction of any juvenile who lacks proper parental care] and (2) following that determination, reasonable efforts had been made to preserve and reunify the family, and the efforts had failed to correct the conditions which led to that determination. The petition also alleged that [distinct] grounds for termination existed under §43-292(7) [providing that] termination would be in the best interests of the children [for the reason that they] had been in out-of-home placement for 15 or more of the most recent 22 months. . . .

Best Interests of Children

Holly argues that the juvenile court erred in finding that it is in the best interests of the children to terminate her parental rights. She asserts that none of the witnesses could identify anything other than minor negative events which occurred while the children were in the parents' care. . . .

The children were initially removed from the home based upon the uncleanliness of the home. The home was filthy, and the conditions were inappropriate for children. Bottles contained spoiled formula or milk. Feces stains were seen on the carpet. The children's room had a strong odor of urine and spoiled formula or milk. The breathing treatment apparatus used by Devon was filthy and unusable, and no medication for the machine was found in the home.

The case plans that were implemented were not adopted merely to teach the parents how to clean a house. If cleanliness was the sole issue to be addressed prior to reuniting the family, it would not have been necessary for DHHS to expend more than $111,000 in resources trying to reunite the parents with the children. The conditions observed in the house were only a symptom of the problems which led to the adjudication and the subsequent plans for reunification. They did not represent a situation which could be remedied by simply hiring a cleaning service. . . .

The juvenile court agreed to a modified case plan received on April 21, 1999, which included goals for each parent. . . . Additional case plans were filed and received by the juvenile court on April 20 and October 20, 1999, April 21 and August 31, 2000, and January 12, 2001. At a hearing on November 30, 2001, Mary Goodwin, a protection and safety worker for DHHS who had been the caseworker for the parents since April 2000, testified as to the goals outlined in the final case plan for reunification of the family.

The first goal was for Holly to acquire skills to provide a clean and safe environment for the children. While Shawn was incarcerated between October 1999 and October 2000, Holly lived in various places, but did not have a residence of her own. In September 2000, Holly had obtained her own residence, but she said she was not ready to have the children returned to her. Holly had requested that the children be removed from the home in February 1999 because she was afraid of Shawn, who had broken a car window and "thrown the other son, Nicki, around."

A second goal was for Holly to address her mental health issues and comply with all mental health recommendations. Holly dropped out of therapy between August and November 2000 and again in May 2001.

The third goal called for Holly to acquire the skills needed to protect her children from domestic violence by participating in a domestic violence support group and to demonstrate an ability to assert herself in a way that would protect her and the children. Holly attended three sessions on domestic violence in November and December 2000. She received a psychiatric evaluation on July 31, 2000, and was given medication for depression. Psychological evaluations were later scheduled, but neither Holly nor Shawn appeared, and they did not reschedule the appointments.

The fourth goal was for Holly to demonstrate the ability to manage her children's behavior at all times during visits. Goodwin said the children's behavior was chaotic during visits, and Holly admitted that she could not control the children, who would be aggressive toward each other and would not listen to Holly. At times, she would "zone out" and would not notice that the children were "tearing up" the visitation room. On one occasion, they pulled down the drapes. They jumped off tables and climbed up on a file cabinet and jumped off. On another occasion, one boy jumped onto a pile of blankets, injuring another boy who was underneath the blankets. Goodwin stated that these problems were ongoing.

The fifth goal was for Holly to address her marital situation and determine whether it is in the best interests of her children to continue her relationship with Shawn. In September 2000, Holly reported that Shawn had threatened to break her hips, and in October 2000, she reported that she was hiding from Shawn because he was getting out of jail and she was afraid of him. However, the couple reunited when Shawn was released from jail.

The sixth goal was for Holly to learn to manage her finances to demonstrate that she can provide for the basic needs of her children and herself. Holly obtained her own home in September 2000.

The seventh goal was for Shawn to acquire the skills needed to provide a clean environment for his children. Goodwin said he was not able to work on the goal because he was incarcerated for a year.

The eighth goal was for Shawn to address mental health issues and to comply with mental health recommendations. Shawn completed a psychological evaluation in July 1999, which resulted in a finding that Shawn had an issue with anger management. It was recommended that Shawn receive counseling for anger management, parenting issues, and marital issues. After the parents missed appointments for counseling, they were referred to Susan Rippke, an in-home therapist. Shawn had several sessions with Rippke before Shawn was incarcerated. Holly missed approximately five appointments between August and November 1999. She was then scheduled to travel to Omaha for counseling, but dropped out after one appointment. Shawn received some therapy while in jail and was in therapy at the time of the November 2001 hearing.

The ninth goal was for Shawn to gain control over his temper and learn to manage his anger in appropriate ways. When he was released from jail in October 2000, he was referred to a men's group to address domestic violence, but he did not take part.

The 10th goal was for Shawn to increase his parenting knowledge and skills, demonstrate an understanding of child development, learn and utilize nonphysical ways to discipline, and respond to his children in a nurturing manner. Goodwin said the parents had taken advantage of parenting assistance on only a few occasions. Problems with managing the children's behavior during visits continued, and Goodwin reported occasions when Shawn yelled at Ty. Shawn countermanded consequences given by Holly and told the children they did not have to follow her directions. The parents continued to neglect safety issues by allowing the children to ride on the bottom of carts at stores, which resulted in injury to one of the children. The parents allowed Ty to ride a toy motorcycle into the street when a car was approaching. . . .

The 11th goal was for Shawn to learn to manage his finances to demonstrate an ability to provide for his and the children's needs. Shawn worked at one job from December 2000 to June 2001. At the end of June, he began working at another job, where he reported earning about $1,500 every 2 weeks and working "a lot" of overtime. Holly worked part-time jobs between February 1999 and June 2000, when she began working a full-time job, where she worked until September. She was unemployed between September and November 2000. She worked at another job from November 2000 until September 2001, was unemployed for a while, and then began working again.

Goodwin's testimony indicates that the parents have continued to behave in ways which are not in the best interests of the children. They have received various forms of assistance from DHHS staff, yet they have not been able to meet the goals set for them over a 2-year period.

While it appears that the parents have addressed some of the issues in the case plans, we have held that

> " 'participation in certain elements of the court ordered plan does not necessarily prevent the court from entering an order of termination where the parent has made no progress toward rehabilitation. A parent is required not only to follow the plan of the court to rehabilitate herself but also to make reasonable efforts on her own to bring about rehabilitation.' " [In re Interest of L.H. et al., 487 N.W.2d 279, 289 (Neb. 1992), quoting In re Interest of M., 453 N.W.2d 589 (Neb. 1990).]

This court has also held that partial compliance with one provision of a rehabilitation plan does not prevent termination of parental rights.

In addition, this court has held that the juvenile court is not limited to reviewing the efforts of the parent under the plan last ordered by the court; rather, the court looks at the entire reunification program and the parent's compliance with the various plans involved in the program, as well as any effort not contained within the program which would bring the parent closer to reunification. . . .

[W]e conclude that the record shows by clear and convincing evidence that it is in the best interests of the children to terminate the parental rights of Shawn and Holly. The parents have been provided many reasonable opportunities to rehabilitate, and they have failed to do so. The condition of the home was merely a manifestation of the parents' inability to properly care for their children. The evidence clearly and convincingly shows that the parents willfully failed to comply in whole or in part with the material provisions of the rehabilitation plans. . . .

Reasonable Efforts

Shawn argues that the juvenile court erred in finding that reasonable efforts had been made to preserve and reunify the family in the juvenile action and in the termination proceedings. He asserts that the State did not meet its burden because it relied on certified copies of prior court orders and did not elicit testimony on the reasonable efforts which had been made. . . . Holly argues that the State did not meet its burden to show that reasonable efforts would not result in reunification of the family. She suggests that the parents' opportunity to work toward reunification was thwarted by the actions of DHHS to decrease visitation. . . .

Section 43-292 identifies the grounds for termination of parental rights. It provides that termination may be ordered when it is in the best interests of the children and another condition exists. Subsection (6) allows for termination after a determination that the juveniles fall under §43-247(3)(a) and reasonable efforts to preserve and reunify the family if required under Neb. Rev. Stat. §43-283.01 (Reissue 1998), under the direction of the court, have failed to correct the conditions leading to the determination. Subsection (7) allows for termination after the juveniles have been in an out-of-home placement for 15 or more months of the most recent 22 months.

The parties stipulated to the dates of the children's out-of-home placement, which clearly showed that they had been out of the parental home for all but 2 of the approximately 36 months before the termination hearing. They were in foster care with nonrelatives for more than 24 months immediately preceding the hearing. Thus, §43-292(7) applies to these children, and if it is in their best interests to be removed from the home on this basis, the juvenile court may so order.

The record shows that DHHS worked with the family for almost 3 years before parental rights were terminated. The case plans in evidence and the court hearings and orders in the record support a finding that reasonable efforts were made to reunify the family. As we have held on numerous occasions, children cannot, and should not, be suspended in foster care or be made to await uncertain parental maturity. The assignment of error concerning reasonable efforts has no merit.

Unconstitutionality of §43-292(7)

The parents assert that §43-292(7) is unconstitutional because it uses an arbitrary and vague standard to terminate parental rights based solely on the length of time a child has been placed outside the home. The parents' arguments concerning the constitutionality of §43-292(7) are stated in broad terms and suggest only that the statute violates due process because it provides an arbitrary standard.

We have frequently held that where a parent is unable or unwilling to rehabilitate himself or herself within a reasonable time, the best interests of the children require termination of the parental rights. [S]ubsection (7) merely provides a guideline for the "reasonable time" given to the parents to rehabilitate themselves. . . . Section 43-292(7) is not unconstitutional. Adequate safeguards are provided to ensure that parental rights are not terminated based solely upon the length of time children are in an out-of-home placement.

Conclusion

The children in this case were initially removed from the home because it was filthy and unlivable. Although these conditions were apparently corrected at a later date, they were not the only basis upon which parental rights were terminated. The uncleanliness of the home was a manifestation of a lack of parenting skills on the part of Shawn and Holly. During a period of more than 2 years, the parents were unable to correct these deficiencies.

We find no error on the part of the juvenile court in its judgment terminating the parental rights of Shawn and Holly to Ty and Devon. The judgment is affirmed.

NOTES AND QUESTIONS

(1) Federal Mandate. Every state has statutory provisions authorizing the permanent removal of an endangered child from the home. Before termination of parental rights, however, the state must provide rehabilitation services, including reunification efforts. Federal legislation mandates the provision of these services. The Adoption Assistance and Child Welfare Act of 1980 (AACWA), 42 U.S.C. §§620 et seq., 670 et seq. (2000), provides that, to qualify for federal funding, states have to make *"reasonable efforts"* (id. at §671(a)(15)) to prevent placement of a child in foster care and to reunify a foster child with his or her parents. Some state statutes contained "reasonable efforts requirements" prior to the enactment of AACWA, but the AACWA triggered widespread adoption of such requirements.

Some jurisdictions (like Nebraska in In re Ty) now specify that a ground for termination of parental rights is the failure of the state's "reasonable efforts" to remedy the condition leading to the determination of the child as abused or neglected. See Neb. Rev. Stat. §43-292 (2003) (requiring best interests test plus failure of reasonable efforts).

(2) "Reasonable Efforts" Defined. What constitutes "reasonable efforts"? Because neither the AACWA nor many state statutes define the term, courts must interpret whether the provision of certain services satisfies the requirement. What services did the state provide in In re Ty? How does the court determine whether the provision of these services constituted "reasonable efforts"?

Federal legislation currently defines the nature of reunification services. The Adoption and Safe Families Act (ASFA) defines such services to include: (i) Individual, group, and family counseling; (ii) Inpatient, residential, or outpatient substance abuse treatment services; (iii) Mental health services; (iv) Assistance to address domestic violence; (v) Services designed to provide temporary child care and therapeutic services for families, including crisis nurseries. 42 U.S.C. §629(b) (2000).

(3) Time-Limited Services. How much time must the state devote to providing reasonable efforts before terminating parental rights? ASFA currently emphasizes the time-limited nature of rehabilitation services, restricting services to those provided within a 15-month period following placement of a child into foster care. See 42 U.S.C. §629a(b) (2000). See also State ex rel. Children, Youth & Families Dept., 47 P.3d 859 (N.M. Ct. App. 2002), *cert. denied sub nom.* In re Elizabeth H., 49 P.3d

76 (N.M. 2002) (declaring that states are not required to make reunification efforts for an indefinite period of time, reasoning that ASFA's 15-month period provides a measure of the state's duty).

Is ASFA's 15-month period sufficient time for the state to provide meaningful services? See Will L. Crossley, Defining Reasonable Efforts: Demystifying the State's Burden Under Federal Child Protection Legislation, 12 B.U. Pub. Int. L.J. 259, 292 (2003) (arguing that it is not sufficient, especially for parents who are substance abusers or serving jail sentences).

(4) Exceptions to "Reasonable Efforts" Requirement. Are "reasonable efforts" required even when they are likely to be futile? ASFA removed the "reasonable efforts" requirement in cases in which (1) the child has been the victim of aggravated circumstances, such as torture, abandonment, or sexual abuse; (2) the parent has killed another child or attempted to do so; or (3) the state has terminated the parent's rights with respect to a sibling. 42 U.S.C. §§671 (a)(15)(D)(i), (ii), (iii) (2000).

(5) Duration in Foster Care as Ground for Termination. To what extent can states rely on the duration that a child has spent in foster care to trigger termination proceedings? Note that the duration that Ty and his brother spent in out-of-home placement was a separate statutory ground for termination of parental rights (provided that the best interests test was also satisfied). The Nebraska statutory provision for termination of parental rights adopts ASFA's requirement that states must seek termination of parental rights for any child who has been in foster care for 15 of the last 22 months. 42 U.S.C. §675(5)(c).

Is the child's stay in foster care an appropriate indicator of parental unfitness? How does In re Ty respond to the parents' argument that the durational requirement violates their due process rights? Cf. In re H.G., 757 N.E.2d 846 (Ill. 2001) (holding that the statutory presumption of parental unfitness based on child's duration in foster care is not narrowly tailored to serve the compelling state interest in child protection and thus violates due process).

(6) Incarceration as Ground for Termination. In In re Ty, the father had been incarcerated for approximately one year. Should incarceration of a parent be a sufficient ground for termination of a parent's rights? Many states have such provisions, although the details vary considerably. Compare Tex. Fam. Code Ann. §161.001(1)(Q)(ii) (Vernon 2002) (terminating parental rights in cases of confinement and inability to care for the child for at least two years) with Fla. Stat. Ann. §39.806(1)(d) (West 2003) (incarceration is grounds for termination, provided that prison term comprises a substantial portion of the child's minority; parent comes within statutory designation of "violent career criminal"; or the court determines by clear and convincing evidence that continuation of the parent-child relationship would be harmful to the child such that termination of parental rights would be in the best interest of the child). See also Moran v. Weldon, 57 P.3d 898 (Or. Ct. App. 2002) (requiring a showing of additional statutory ground, other than incarceration, for termination of parental rights). See generally Philip M. Genty, Damage to Family Relationships as a Collateral Consequence of Parental Incarceration, 30 Fordham Urb. L.J. 1671 (2003) (suggesting that ASFA has had a disproportionate impact upon incarcerated parents who have children in foster care by increasing the rates of termination of parental rights based on incarceration).

(7) Does inclusion of "reasonable efforts" requirements before termination contribute to harm to children by creating unnecessary obstacles to termination of parental rights, as some commentators argue? Compare Elizabeth Bartholet, Nobody's Children: Abuse and Neglect, Foster Care Drift, and the Adoption Alternative (1999) with Martin Guggenheim, Somebody's Children: Sustaining the Family's Place in Child Welfare Policy, 113 Harv. L. Rev. 1716 (1999) (rebutting Bartholet's assumptions and conclusions).

b. Standard of Proof

The United States Supreme Court resolved the standard of proof issue for termination of parental rights in *Santosky v. Kramer,* 455 U.S. 745 (1982). In *Santosky,* the Court held that the New York Family Court Act's "fair preponderance of the evidence" standard for determining "permanent neglect" denied due process to parents where termination of rights was at stake.

In writing for the majority, Justice Blackmun emphasized that the fundamental liberty interest of natural parents in the care, custody, and control of their child does not disappear simply because they have not been model parents or have temporarily lost custody of their child to the state. For this reason, the Court held that before a state may sever completely and irrevocably the rights of parents in their natural child, due process requires the state to support its allegations by at least "clear and convincing" evidence. The Court declined to require the even more stringent "beyond a reasonable doubt" standard, but noted that state legislatures and courts are free to adopt the higher standard.

Justice Rehnquist, joined by three other Justices, dissented and argued that the standard of proof chosen by New York reflected a constitutionally permissible balance of the competing interests of the parents, the child, and the state. He emphasized the state's earnest efforts to aid the parents in regaining custody of their children and the numerous procedural protections afforded by other provisions of New York law. According to Justice Rehnquist, the majority's "obsessive focus on the standard of proof" was not required by the Due Process Clause and constituted a worrisome intrusion into an area of law traditionally entrusted to the states.

States have adopted different approaches to the standard of proof required by *Santosky.* See Brian C. Hill, Comment, The State's Burden of Proof at the Best Interests Stage of a Termination of Parental Rights, 2004 U. Chi. Legal F. 557, 565-566 (surveying jurisdictions). Most states follow *Santosky* and require clear and convincing evidence. However, some states hold that *Santosky* applies only to the initial determination of parental unfitness in a termination-of-parental-rights hearing but not to the dispositional stage of the proceeding (sometimes called the "best interests" stage after the legal standard employed by courts to decide whether a child should be removed from parental custody). These states apply a preponderance-of-the-evidence standard in the latter stage. An occasional state requires the strictest standard of beyond a reasonable doubt. Is the dispositional stage sufficiently different from the evidentiary stage to require the use of a different standard of proof? See Hill, supra (arguing that courts should apply the *Santosky* standard to both stages).

c. Right to Counsel

The Supreme Court has determined that an indigent parent has no constitutional right to counsel in a termination of parental rights proceeding. In Lassiter v. Department of Social Services, 452 U.S. 18 (1981), the Court held that the Due Process Clause does not give biological parents a right to counsel in every parental termination proceeding. Rather, according to the Court, the decision to appoint counsel should be made by the trial court on a case-by-case balancing test in light of the parents' interests, the state interests, and the risk of error. The Court reasoned that the failure to appoint counsel to petitioner did not deprive her of due process in light of the circumstances — i.e., the termination petition contained no allegations upon which criminal charges could be based, the case presented no complicated points of law, and the presence of counsel would not have made a difference for the petitioner (who had been sentenced to 25 to 40 years' incarceration for second-degree murder).

Most state legislatures and courts reject *Lassiter.* Some jurisdictions depart from *Lassiter* on state constitutional grounds. See, e.g., In re K.L.J., 813 P.2d 276 (Alaska 1991) (failure to appoint counsel in termination of parental rights proceeding violates father's due process rights under the state constitution). However, most states, by statute, give indigent parents the right to counsel in termination proceedings. See Rosalie R. Young, The Right to Appointed Counsel in Termination of Parental Rights Proceedings: The States' Response to *Lassiter*, 14 Touro L. Rev. 247 (1997) (finding that of 17 states that had no right to counsel prior to *Lassiter*, six require counsel in all instances and six require counsel only if requested; further, almost all of the 33 states that had provisions for a right to counsel prior to *Lassiter* continue to do so). See also Michele R. Forte, Notes and Comments, Making the Case for Effective Assistance of Counsel in Involuntary Termination of Parental Rights Proceedings, 28 Nova L. Rev.193 (2003) (arguing that indigent parents have a right to effective assistance of counsel at termination proceedings).

The Supreme Court subsequently addressed the procedural rights of indigent parents in parental rights proceedings in M.L.B. v. S.L.J., 519 U.S. 102 (1996), in which the Court held that an indigent parent has the right to record preparation fees (transcripts, binding, mailing). The Court concluded that a prepayment fee violates the parent's right to equal protection and due process. Noting that both *Santosky* and *Lassiter* speak to the primacy of the parent-child relationship, the Court reasoned that the stakes for the mother are substantial (i.e., the destruction of the parent-child bond) whereas the countervailing governmental interest (i.e., financial) is small.

CHAPTER 4

Medical Treatment: Who Speaks for the Child?

A. *INTRODUCTION*

As a general rule, informed parental consent is both a necessary and sufficient condition for the medical treatment of minors. This chapter examines the reasons for this general rule and its exceptions. It explores in several different contexts how power and responsibility to decide about the medical care of minors is now allocated among the child, the family, various medical professionals, and state officials, and asks how power *should* be allocated. What voice should the child have? What is the appropriate role of parents, doctors, and the state?

This chapter begins with some background material on the general requirement of parental consent and its exceptions. Excerpts from several statutes are provided, and questions are posed concerning the relationship of the consent requirement to the issue of who is and should be financially responsible for paying for a child's medical care. Next, some standard common law and statutory limitations and exceptions to the general parental consent requirement are explored. These relate to mandatory immunizations and screening procedures (applicable to all children), the neglect limitation (where a court may override a parental decision for an individual child), the emergency treatment of children (where no parental consent is required if the parent is unavailable), and various exceptions that allow minors themselves to consent to treatment.

The chapter then examines the parental consent requirement in the context of the decision to withhold or discontinue life-sustaining procedures for a newborn with birth defects. Materials are provided to explore the legal, ethical, and policy issues relating to when the state should overrule parental decisions in an extreme context. Adults may, under some circumstances, decide to withhold treatment for themselves (such as by the use of advance directives). Is it ever acceptable to withhold essential treatment from a severely handicapped newborn who cannot decide for itself? If so, what should the standards be? Who should decide? What procedure should be followed?

The same issues are examined in the context of medical experimentation on children. Should an exception to the general rule that allows parents to consent to the medical treatment of their child be made when the treatment is experimental, or when the child is exposed to a procedure that is not even for his therapeutic benefit?

The chapter also explores some of the legal issues that are implicated in the context of adolescent health. In particular, the chapter explores how power and responsibility for adolescent health decision making should be allocated among the child, the family, medical professionals, and the state.

The focus of this chapter is how power and responsibility should be allocated. It does not include materials addressing the state of children's health in the United States or the broad range of health policy issues relating to how the American health delivery system might better serve children.

B.   THE LEGAL CONTEXT FOR THE MEDICAL TREATMENT OF CHILDREN

1.   Battery and the Requirement of Informed Consent

As a general proposition, the primary legal principles governing the relationship of doctors to their adult patients are found in the tort law of battery and negligence. The tort of negligence is committed when the patient is harmed because a doctor's conduct falls below the standard of care reasonably to be expected from persons possessing the doctor's professional qualifications. For the most part, the standard of care is unaffected by whether the patient is an adult or a minor.

For battery, on the other hand, the legal framework for children is quite different from that for adults. Battery, in the most general terms, is committed when there is the touching of another without express consent.[1] A successful suit for battery does not require that the plaintiff be physically injured, that the plaintiff suffer a financial loss, or that medical treatment be unsuccessful. Moreover, once a battery has been established, the defendant is responsible for any and all damages that are a consequence of the nonprivileged touching. For negligence, in contrast to battery, the plaintiff must establish substantial injuries, typically with financial implications, and the defendant is in no event responsible for injuries that are not reasonably foreseeable.

For battery, "the central concept is the offense to personal dignity which occurs when another impinges on one's bodily integrity without full and valid consent."[2] In the medical context, to avoid committing a battery, a physician may ordinarily treat an adult patient only after the patient has given informed voluntary consent.[3]

---

[1] Bryan J. Warren, Pennsylvania Medical Informed Consent Law: A Call to Protect Patient Autonomy Rights by Abandoning the Battery Approach, 38 Duq. L. Rev. 917, 928 (2000) (citing William L. Prosser, Law of Torts §10 (4th ed., 1971)).

[2] Charles Fried, Medical Experimentation: Personal Integrity and Social Policy 16 (1974).

[3] On the history of the legal doctrine of informed consent, see Warren, supra note [1], at 927-935.

As a general proposition this requires that the doctor must give the patient the information necessary to make an informed choice. Typically, the diagnosis and prognosis of an illness must be evaluated and the benefits and risks of alternative treatments must be disclosed. There are limitations to the consent requirement for adults. These relate to emergencies (where consent may not be necessary), and the so-called therapeutic privilege (which allows a doctor to withhold information if the doctor reasonably believes that disclosure would not be in the patient's interest and would interfere with the best treatment).

A primary justification for this requirement of informed consent is protection of an adult's right of self-determination.[4] It also may serve to protect patients against depersonalized, authoritarian medical treatment.[5] Are these justifications any less important for children?

Because it was thought that children lacked the capacity to provide consent for purposes of avoiding a battery,[6] courts at common law held that until children reached majority, only a parent or legal guardian could give effective consent to medical treatment.[7] What policies does this rule serve? It protects the child from the responsibility of deciding for himself or herself. For infants or children who lack the maturity to evaluate alternatives and to make an informed choice, someone must decide on the child's behalf. But why parents? The general rule of parental consent is in accordance with broad notions of family privacy, parental autonomy, and the importance of familial bonds. But at the root of the common law rule was the narrower notion that parents are legally responsible for the care and support of their children. Among other things, the parental consent requirement protects parents from having to pay for unwanted or unnecessary medical care and from the possible financial consequences of supporting the child if unwanted treatment is unsuccessful. Indeed, as an Ohio court declared:

> [The rule that parents must consent for minors] is not based upon the capacity of a minor to consent, so far as he is personally concerned . . . but is based upon the right of parents whose liability for support and maintenance of their child may be greatly increased by an unfavorable result from [a surgeon's operation]. [Lacey v. Laird, 139 N.E.2d 25, 30 (Ohio 1956).]

Is there an alternative to the general rule of parental consent? One commentator advocates another approach: a bright-line rule that permits all adolescents over age 16 to have the right to make their own decisions regarding routine medical

---

[4] Pratt v. Davis, 118 Ill. App. 161, 166 (1905), *aff'd*, 79 N.E. 562 (Ill. 1906): " . . . the free citizen's first and greatest right, which underlies all others — the right to the inviolability of his person. . . . "

[5] Robert A. Burt, Taking Care of Strangers: The Rule of Law in Doctor-Patient Relations (1979); Raymond S. Duff & August B. Hollingshead, Sickness and Society (1968); Jay Katz, The Silent World of Doctor and Patient (1984).

[6] Commonwealth v. Nickerson, 87 Mass. (5 Allen) 518 (1863); William L. Prosser & W. Page Keeton, Handbook of the Law of Torts 115 (5th ed. 1984).

[7] Moss v. Rishworth, 222 S.W. 225 (Tex. Civ. App. 1920) (holding that father could recover from surgeon for child's death during operation to remove badly diseased tonsils and adenoids); Zoski v. Gaines, 260 N.W. 99 (Mich. 1935) (holding surgeon liable for operation without parental consent when boy was sent to hospital with note from city physician requesting removal of tonsils).

and surgical treatment.[8] What do you think of this suggestion? How capable are minors of various ages to understand a diagnosis, nature and risks of treatment (and risks of nontreatment), and alternatives to treatment, and then to give their opinions?

2.   Statutory Materials: When May a Minor Consent to Medical Treatment?

Ark. Stat. Ann. §20-9-602 (2000)

§20-9-602 Consent Generally

It is recognized and established that, in addition to such other persons as may be so authorized and empowered, any one of the following persons is authorized and empowered to consent, either orally or otherwise, to any surgical or medical treatment or procedures not prohibited by law which may be suggested, recommended, prescribed or directed by a duly licensed physician:

> (1) Any adult, for himself.
>
> (2) Any parent, whether an adult or a minor, for his minor child or for his adult child of unsound mind whether the child is of the parent's blood, is an adopted child, is a stepchild, or is a foster child; provided however, the father of an illegitimate child cannot consent for said child solely on the basis of parenthood.
>
> (3) Any married person, whether an adult or a minor, for himself;
>
> (4) Any female, regardless of age or marital status, for herself when given in connection with pregnancy or childbirth, except the unnatural interruption of a pregnancy;
>
> (5) Any person standing in loco parentis, whether formally serving or not, and any guardian, conservator or custodian, for his ward or other charge under disability;
>
> (6) Any emancipated minor, for himself.
>
> (7) Any unemancipated minor of sufficient intelligence to understand and appreciate the consequences of the proposed surgical or medical treatment or procedures, for himself.
>
> (8) Any adult, for his minor sibling or his adult sibling of unsound mind;
>
> (9) During the absence of a parent so authorized and empowered, any [grandparent]. . . .

---

[8] Andrew Newman, Adolescent Consent to Routine Medical and Surgical Treatment, 22 J. Legal Med. 501 (2001). See also Andrew Popper, Averting Malpractice by Information: Informed Consent in the Pediatric Treatment Environment 819, 831 (1998) (advocating a middle ground, between a rule of parental consent and a rule allowing unconditional veto power by the minor, which enables a child who is capable of meaningful speech and discussion to hear information and express an opinion.)

Ala. Code tit. 22 §§22-8-3 to 22-8-7 (1997)

§22-8-3 When Physician May Proceed Without Consent
of Parent

Any legally authorized medical, dental, health or mental health services may be rendered to minors of any age without the consent of a parent or legal guardian when, in the physician's judgment, an attempt to secure consent would result in delay of treatment which would increase the risk to the minor's life, health or mental health.

§22-8-4 When Minor May Give Consent Generally

Any minor who is 14 years of age or older, or has graduated from high school, or is married, or having been married is divorced or is pregnant may give effective consent to any legally authorized medical, dental, health or mental health services for himself or herself, and the consent of no other person shall be necessary.

§22-8-5 Consent of Minor for Self and Child

Any minor who is married, or having been married is divorced or has borne a child may give effective consent to any legally authorized medical, dental, health or mental health services for himself or his child or for herself or her child.

§22-8-6 Consent of any Minor as to Pregnancy, Venereal
Disease, Drug Dependency, Alcohol Toxicity
and Reportable Diseases

Any minor may give effective consent for any legally authorized medical, health or mental health services to determine the presence of, or to treat, pregnancy, venereal disease, drug dependency, alcohol toxicity or any reportable disease, and the consent of no other person shall be deemed necessary.

§22-8-7 Effect of Minor's Consent; Liability of
Physicians, etc.; Waiver of Rights or Causes
of Action

(a) The consent of a minor who professes to be, but is not, a minor whose consent alone is effective to medical, dental, health or mental health services shall be deemed effective without the consent of the minor's parent or legal guardian if the physician or other person relied in good faith upon the representations of the minor.

(b) Any physician or other person who has relied in good faith upon the representations of any persons under any of the provisions of this chapter or who acts in good faith under any of the provisions of this chapter shall not be liable for not having consent. . . .

Minn. Stat. Ann. §§144.341 to 144.347 (1998 & Supp. 2005)

Consent of Minors for Health Services

144.341 Living Apart from Parents and Managing Financial Affairs, Consent for Self

Notwithstanding any other provision of law, any minor who is living separate and apart from parents or legal guardian, whether with or without the consent of a parent or guardian and regardless of the duration of such separate residence, and who is managing personal financial affairs, regardless of the source or extent of the minor's income, may give effective consent to medical, dental, mental and other health services, and the consent of no other person is required.

144.342 Marriage or Giving Birth, Consent for Health Service for Self or Child

Any minor who has been married or has borne a child may give effective consent to personal medical, mental, dental and other health services, or to services for the minor's child, and the consent of no other person is required.

144.343 Pregnancy, Venereal Disease, Alcohol or Drug Abuse, Abortion

Subd. 1. Minor's consent valid.

Any minor may give effective consent for medical, mental and other health services to determine the presence of or to treat pregnancy and conditions associated therewith, venereal disease, alcohol and other drug abuse, and the consent of no other person is required.

Subd. 2. Notification concerning abortion.

Notwithstanding the provisions of section 13.02, subdivision 8, no abortion operation shall be performed upon an unemancipated minor or upon a woman for whom a guardian or conservator has been appointed pursuant to sections 525.54 to 525.551 because of a finding of incapacity, until at least 48 hours after written notice of the pending operation has been delivered in the manner specified in subdivisions 2 to 4.

(a) The notice shall be addressed to the parent at the usual place of abode of the parent and delivered personally to the parent by the physician or an agent.

(b) In lieu of the delivery required by clause (a), notice shall be made by certified mail addressed to the parent at the usual place of abode of the parent with return receipt requested and restricted delivery to the addressee which means postal employee can only deliver the mail to the authorized addressee. . . .

Subd. 3. Parent, abortion; definitions.

For purposes of this section, "parent" means both parents of the pregnant woman if they are both living, one parent of the pregnant woman if only one is living or if the second one cannot be located through reasonably diligent effort, or the guardian or conservator if the pregnant woman has one. . . .

Subd. 4. Limitations.

No notice shall be required under this section if:

(a) The attending physician certifies in the pregnant woman's medical record that the abortion is necessary to prevent the woman's death and there is insufficient time to provide the required notice; or

(b) The abortion is authorized in writing by the person or persons who are entitled to notice; or

(c) The pregnant minor woman declares that she is a victim of sexual abuse, neglect, or physical abuse as defined in section 626.556. Notice of that declaration shall be made to the proper authorities as provided in section 626.556, subdivision 3.

Subd. 5. Penalty.

Performance of an abortion in violation of this section shall be a misdemeanor and shall be grounds for a civil action by a person wrongfully denied notification. A person shall not be held liable under this section if the person establishes by written evidence that the person relied upon evidence sufficient to convince a careful and prudent person that the representations of the pregnant woman regarding information necessary to comply with this section are bona fide and true, or if the person has attempted with reasonable diligence to deliver notice, but has been unable to do so.

Subd. 6 . . .

Substitute notification provisions . . .

(c)(i) If such a pregnant woman elects not to allow the notification of one or both of her parents or guardian or conservator, any judge of a court of competent jurisdiction shall, upon petition, or motion, and after an appropriate hearing, authorize a physician to perform the abortion if said judge determines that the pregnant woman is mature and capable of giving informed consent to the proposed abortion. If said judge determines that the pregnant woman is not mature, or if the pregnant woman does not claim to be mature, the judge shall determine whether the performance of an abortion upon her without notification of her parents, guardian, or conservator would be in her best interests and shall authorize a physician to perform the abortion without such notification if said judge concludes that the pregnant woman's best interests would be served thereby.

(ii) Such a pregnant woman may participate in proceedings in the court on her own behalf, and the court may appoint a guardian ad litem for her. The court shall, however, advise her that she has a right to court appointed counsel, and shall, upon her request, provide her with such counsel.

(iii) Proceedings in the court under this section shall be confidential and shall be given such precedence over other pending matters so that the court may reach a decision promptly and without delay so as to serve the best interests of the pregnant woman. . . .

144.344 Emergency Treatment

Medical, dental, mental and other health services may be rendered to minors of any age without the consent of a parent or legal guardian when, in the professional's judgment, the risk to the minor's life or health is of such a nature that treatment should be given without delay and the requirement of consent would result in delay or denial of treatment.

144.3441 Hepatitis B Vaccination

A minor may give effective consent for a hepatitis B vaccination. The consent of no other person is required.

144.345 Representations to Persons Rendering Service

The consent of a minor who claims to be able to give effective consent for the purpose of receiving medical, dental, mental or other health services but who may not in fact do so, shall be deemed effective without the consent of the minor's parent or legal guardian, if the person rendering the service relied in good faith upon the representations of the minor.

144.346 Information to Parents

The professional may inform the parent or legal guardian of the minor patient of any treatment given or needed where, in the judgment of the professional, failure to inform the parent or guardian would seriously jeopardize the health of the minor patient.

144.347 Financial Responsibility

A minor so consenting for such health services shall thereby assume financial responsibility for the cost of said services.

3.   Model Statute

Institute of Judicial Administration and the American Bar Association, Juvenile Justice Standards: Standards Relating to Rights of Minors 9-12 (1980)

4.1 Prior Parental Consent

A. No medical procedures, services, or treatment should be provided to a minor without prior parental consent, except as specified in Standards 4.4-4.9.

B. Circumstances where parents refuse to consent to treatment are governed by the Abuse and Neglect volume.

4.2 Notification of Treatment

A. Where prior parental consent is not required to provide medical services or treatment to a minor, the provider should promptly notify the parent or responsible custodian of such treatment and obtain his or her consent to further treatment, except as hereinafter specified.

B. Where the medical services provided are for the treatment of chemical dependency, Standard 4.7, or venereal disease, contraception, and pregnancy, Standard 4.8, the physician should first seek and obtain the minor's permission to notify the parent of such treatments.

> 1. If the minor-patient objects to notification of the parent, the physician should not notify the parent that treatment was or is being provided unless he or she concludes that failing to inform the parent could seriously jeopardize the health of the minor, taking into consideration
>> a. the impact that such notification could have on the course of treatment;
>> b. the medical considerations which require such notification;
>> c. the nature, basis, and strength of the minor's objections;
>> d. the extent to which parental involvement in the course of treatment is required or desirable.
>
> 2. A physician who concludes that notification of the parent is medically required should:
>> a. indicate the medical justifications in the minor-patient's file; and
>> b. inform the parent only after making all reasonable efforts to persuade the minor to consent to notification of the parent.

C. Where the medical services provided are for the treatment of a mental or emotional disorder pursuant to Standard 4.9, after three sessions the provider should notify the parent of such treatment and obtain his or her consent to further treatment.

4.3 Financial Liability

A. A parent should be financially liable to persons providing medical treatment to his or her minor child if the parent consents to such services, or if the services are provided under emergency circumstances pursuant to Standard 4.5.

B. A minor who consents to his or her own medical treatment under Standard 4.6-4.9 should be financially liable for payment for such services, and should not disaffirm the financial obligation on account of minority.

C. A public or private health insurance policy or plan under which a minor is a beneficiary should allow a minor who consents to medical services or treatment to file claims and receive benefits, regardless of whether the parent has consented to the treatment.

D. A public or private health insurer should not inform a parent or policy holder that a minor has filed a claim or received a benefit under a health insurance policy or plan of which the minor is a beneficiary, unless the physician has previously notified the parent of the treatment for which the claim is submitted.

4.4 Emancipated Minor

A. An emancipated minor who is living separate and apart from his or her parent and who is managing his or her own financial affairs may consent to medical treatment on the same terms and conditions as an adult. Accordingly, parental consent should not be required, nor should there be subsequent notification of the parent, or financial liability.

> 1. If a physician treats a minor who is not actually emancipated, it should be a defense to a suit basing liability on lack of parental consent, that he or she relied in good faith on the minor's representations of emancipation. . . .

4.5 Emergency Treatment

A. Under emergency circumstances, a minor may receive medical services or treatment without prior parental consent.

> 1. Emergency circumstances exist when delaying treatment to first secure parental consent would endanger the life or health of the minor.
>
> 2. It should be a defense to an action basing liability on lack of parental consent, that the medical services were provided under emergency circumstances.

B. Where medical services or treatment are provided under emergency circumstances, the parent should be notified as promptly as possible, and his or her consent should be obtained for further treatment.

C. A parent should be financially liable to persons providing emergency medical treatment.

D. Where the emergency medical services are for treatment of chemical dependency (Standard 4.7); venereal disease, contraception, or pregnancy (Standard 4.8); or mental or emotional disorder (Standard 4.9), questions of notification of the parent and financial liability are governed by those provisions and Standards 4.2 B., 4.2 C., and 4.3.

4.6 Mature Minor

A. A minor of [16] or older who has sufficient capacity to understand the nature and consequences of a proposed medical treatment for his or her benefit may consent to that treatment on the same terms and conditions as an adult.

B. The treating physician should notify the minor's parent of any medical treatment provided under this standard, subject to the provisions of Standard 4.2 B.

4.7 Chemical Dependency

A. A minor of any age may consent to medical services, treatment, or therapy for problems or conditions related to alcohol or drug abuse or addiction.

B. If the minor objects to notification of the parent, the person or agency providing treatment under this standard should notify the parent of such treatment only if he or she concludes that failing to inform the parent would seriously jeopardize the health of the minor, and complies with the provisions of Standard 4.2.

4.8 Venereal Disease, Contraception, and Pregnancy

A. A minor of any age may consent to medical services, therapy, or counseling for:
    1. treatment of venereal disease;
    2. family planning, contraception, or birth control other than a procedure which results in sterilization; or
    3. treatment related to pregnancy, including abortion.

B. If the minor objects to notification of the parent, the person or agency providing treatment under this standard should notify the parent of such treatment only if he or she concludes that failing to inform the parent would seriously jeopardize the health of the minor, and complies with the provision of Standard 4.2.

4.9 Mental or Emotional Disorder

A. A minor of fourteen or older who has or professes to suffer from a mental or emotional disorder may consent to three sessions with a psychotherapist or counselor for diagnosis and consultation.

B. Following three sessions for crisis intervention and/or diagnosis, the provider should notify the parent of such sessions and obtain his or her consent to further treatment.

4. Who Pays for Medical Treatment?

Parents generally have the primary responsibility for paying for a child's medical treatment. Child support statutes in many jurisdictions are very broadly written (see Chapter 2) and have readily been construed to require the payment of necessary medical expenses. The common law made little provision for civil enforcement by the child or a third party of the parents' obligation to pay medical expenses; the modern trend, however, has been to allow third parties to sue the neglectful parent in quasi-contract.

Government also plays an important role in paying for medical care when parents are too poor to provide necessary medical treatment. For example, the Medicaid program was created expressly to provide health care and services to people who cannot afford them. There were 44 million people enrolled in Medicaid in 2000. Over one-half of them were under age 10.[9]

Formerly, Medicaid entitlement was automatic for people receiving Aid to Families with Dependent Children (AFDC). When welfare reform legislation (PRWORA) replaced AFDC with the Temporary Assistance for Needy Families (TANF) program in 1996, Congress severed the automatic eligibility provision between welfare and Medicaid. Under PRWORA, states may deny Medicaid to heads of households who lose TANF benefits because of their refusal to work. However, states must continue to provide Medicaid benefits to pregnant women and children.[10] (PRWORA is discussed in Chapter 2, pp. 217-221.)

The Balanced Budget Act of 1997, 47 U.S.C. §309(j) (2000), established the State Children's Health Insurance Program (SCHIP) to provide health insurance coverage to states for uninsured children in eligible low-income families. Recent revisions to SCHIP, 67 Fed. Reg. 61,956 (Oct. 2, 2002) (codified at 42 C.F.R. pt. 457 (2003)), redefine "child" (formerly those under 19 years of age) to include the unborn. See generally Elisabeth H. Sperow, Redefining Child Abuse Under the State Children's Health Insurance Program: Capable of Repetition, Yet Evading Results, 12 Am. U. J. Gender Soc. Pol'y & L. 137, 139 (2004).

As you can see from the above materials, some states provide statutory authority for young people in some circumstances to consent to their own medical treatment. See, e.g., pp. 364-369. When the child, not the parent, is providing the only consent for treatment, who should pay? Is it fair to impose the financial responsibility on the parents, especially in circumstances where parents can plausibly claim they would not have approved of treatment? Would not requiring parents to pay jeopardize the possible confidentiality interests of the minor? If parents are required to pay, would this create substantial risks that the parents might obstruct the young person's access to care?

If parents are not to pay directly, would it nonetheless be possible for the minor to be able to make use of his parent's health insurance? Without parental knowledge? Should the minor be able to bind himself contractually to be obligated for payment, notwithstanding his minority? Would the "necessaries" doctrine so provide? See

---

[9] House Comm. on Ways & Means, 108th Cong., 2d Sess., Background Material and Data on Programs Within the Jurisdiction of the Committee on Ways & Means (2004 Green Book) 15-41 (Comm. Printing 2004). On the history of Medicaid, see id. at 15-26 to 15-45.

[10] Id. at 15-33.

p. 152, supra. Should the state guarantee payment by the minor? Note how Section 4.3 of the Juvenile Justice Standards Relating to the Rights of Minors resolves these issues. See p. 370, supra.

C.   EXCEPTIONS AND LIMITATIONS TO PARENTAL CONSENT REQUIREMENTS

1.   Introductory Issues

PROBLEMS

Consider these problems in light of the preceding statutory materials:

(1) Twelve-year-old Jacqueline Parker fell off her bike after school at 3:15 P.M. while playing with a friend. Because Jacqueline appeared to be in extreme pain, the friend's mother took Jacqueline to the hospital emergency room. The friend's mother attempted unsuccessfully to contact Jacqueline's mother, who was out shopping and was not expected to return home until after 6:00 P.M. Jacqueline's father was away on a business trip. Whose consent, if any, should be required before:

a. The hospital may take x-rays to determine if her arm is broken?

b. The doctor may set the fracture, assuming he knows her arm is broken?

c. The physician may administer some pain-killing drug to make the child more comfortable until her mother is located? May the friend's mother consent? Would it make any difference if the adult accompanying Jacqueline had been her aunt? A paid baby-sitter? A camp counselor? A teacher? Suppose her parents were on a safari and might not be reached for a week or more? Would Jacqueline's consent be sufficient? Suppose Jacqueline's parents are divorced and she is injured during visitation with her noncustodial father. May he give effective consent?

(2) Karen is a 13-year-old suffering from irreversible kidney malfunction. She has had a kidney transplant, but the transplant has failed. Karen now has hemodialysis three times a week. She is tolerating dialysis poorly, and typically has severe headaches, chills, nausea, and weakness. Apart from dialysis, she is also on medication and has an extremely restricted diet. She is unable to attend school, is socially isolated, and always feels tired and uncomfortable.

On May 10, Karen was hospitalized after having had a high fever for ten days. With her parents' consent, the doctors operated and removed the transplanted kidney, the pathology of which indicated that any subsequent transplant would in all probability also fail.

Two weeks later, the arteriovenous shunt that had been placed in Karen's arm for hemodialysis was found to be infected. Part of her vein wall was removed, and the placement of the shunt was revised. Three days later, however, the shunt clotted and closed. This meant that the shunt would have to be further revised if dialysis were to continue. This would require minor (but uncomfortable) surgery. Without dialysis, Karen will die. With dialysis, she can be kept alive, but her condition will never improve.

a. If Karen and her parents together refuse to permit shunt revision and any further dialysis, must the medical staff accept their decision? Would it constitute battery if they were to proceed with treatment anyway?

b. Suppose Karen's parents insist on continuing the life-supporting treatment, but Karen objects? What would you advise the medical staff to do?

c. Suppose Karen's parents refuse to consent to further treatment, but Karen insists on continuing the treatment? What would you advise?[11]

(3) Kevin is a 15-year-old who suffers from extensive neurofibromatosis, or Von Recklinghausen's disease. It has caused a massive deformity of the right side of his face and neck involving a large overgrowth of facial tissue that has created a fold or flap which in turn has distorted his cheek, mouth, and right ear. The disease has not affected Kevin's sight or hearing and does not endanger his life.

Kevin's teachers and doctors all believe that Kevin should have surgery to correct this condition. The surgery will not cure the disease, for there is no known cure. But a plastic surgeon has indicated that an operation will improve both the "function and appearance" of his face. The surgery does involve substantial risks, however. A surgeon who is in favor of the operation has stated, "I think it is a dangerous procedure. I think it involves considerable risk. It is a massive surgery of six to eight hours duration with great blood loss." A psychiatrist has examined Kevin and has reported that he is not psychotic, that there is no evidence of any thinking disorder, but that he is extremely dependent on his mother, has feelings of inferiority and a "low self-concept." The doctors believe this is in part because of his grotesque appearance. Delaying the operation until Kevin is older will, if anything, decrease surgical risks but may increase the psychological risks to Kevin. Kevin's mother is a Jehovah's Witness. The mother is not opposed to have the recommended surgery performed upon her son, but she steadfastly refuses to give her consent to the administration of any blood transfusions during the course of the surgery, without which the proposed surgery may not safely be performed.

The county health commissioner and doctors petitioned the juvenile court to declare Kevin a "neglected child" so that a guardian may consent to the operation with a transfusion. Assume the relevant state statute permits the juvenile court to take jurisdiction when a parent "neglects or refuses when able to do so to provide or allow medical, surgical, or other care necessary for a child's health." You are the judge. What would you decide?[12]

---

[11] See generally Joseph Goldstein et al., Before the Best Interests of the Child 91-110 (1979); Joseph Goldstein, Medical Care for the Child at Risk: On State Supervention of Parental Autonomy, 86 Yale L.J. 645, 658-661 (1977).

Two highly publicized cases address problems of minors' consent. In the first case, a 16-year-old cancer patient ran away from Massachusetts to Texas to avoid chemotherapy (to which her parents had consented). In the second case, a 15-year-old girl fled her home in California after police, paramedics, and social workers compelled her to undergo chemotherapy for ovarian cancer (despite the fact that the girl and her parents refused their consent). See Susan D. Hawkins, Note, Protecting the Rights and Interests of Competent Minors in Litigated Medical Treatment Disputes, 64 Fordham L. Rev. 2075, 2075 (1996).

[12] See In re Sampson, 317 N.Y.S.2d 641 (Fam. Ct. 1970), *aff'd*, 323 N.Y.S.2d 253 (App. Div. 1971), *aff'd*, 278 N.E.2d 918 (N.Y. 1972).

(4) Helena is eight years old and has a malignant brain tumor. She is unlikely to survive more than another year. Her parents, who are married and live together, disagree about her treatment. Her father wants her to have more chemotherapy. Her mother feels this would put Helena through needless pain and suffering. Each parent now seeks a judicial declaration which will give that parent unilateral authority to grant or refuse consent to the treatment.

Is it appropriate to grant either parent this authority? If so, how would you decide which parent should have the power? If not, should the parents continue to share authority? Should decision making be delegated to a third party? What role in the decision making should Helena's opinions play? If she were 14 years old, would that alter your opinion? What special problems are posed by securing consent to medical treatment in cases involving dying children?[13]

2. State-Imposed Health Requirements Applicable to All Children

Some medical procedures are required for all children and in this sense represent generally applicable limitations on parental prerogatives. For example, the Supreme Court has upheld a compulsory state smallpox vaccination law as a reasonable and proper exercise of the police power. Jacobson v. Massachusetts, 197 U.S. 11 (1905). Vaccination requirements act to protect society from public health hazards created by communicable diseases where a parental decision may endanger not only a particular child but society at large. Consider circumstances where there is no risk of contagion — for example, a child with poor hearing or eyesight. In light of *Prince*, *Yoder*, *Pierce*, and *Meyer*, do you think there are any constitutional limitations on the state's power to impose generally applicable medical screening procedures without parental consent because it is thought to be beneficial for individual children? As a matter of policy, apart from constitutional law, what limit should there be?

The range of compulsory public interventions for children encompasses immunizations, school and newborn screening, and fluoridation of public water supplies. All states require that school children be immunized against certain contagious diseases, such as diphtheria, whooping cough, tetanus, measles, mumps, polio, Haemophilus influenzae type b (hib), and hepatitis B. The first mandatory smallpox vaccination requirements date from the mid 1800s.[14] Schools also generally require tuberculosis tests. All states offer medical exemptions when vaccination would have an adverse effect on the child's life or health. Virtually all states offer religious exemptions where vaccination is contrary to the individual's religious

[13] See generally Ann Eileen Driggs, The Mature Minor Doctrine: Do Adolescents Have the Right to Die?, 11 Health Matrix 687 (2001); Martin T. Harvey, Adolescent Competency and the Refusal of Medical Treatment, 13 Health Matrix 297 (2003). On the related problem of securing consent for research involving dying children, see Michael A. Grodin & Leonard H. Glantz, Children as Research Subjects 217 (1994).

[14] Steve P. Calandrillo, Vanishing Vaccinations: Why Are So Many Americans Opting Out of Vaccinating Their Children?, 37 U. Mich. J.L. Reform 353, 365 (2004).

beliefs. Less than half the states provide for exemptions on philosophical or moral grounds.[15]

Congress addressed the issue of immunization beginning in the 1980s. In the 1970s and 1980s, parents whose children had been harmed allegedly by vaccines filed several lawsuits against vaccine manufacturers. In response, Congress enacted the National Childhood Vaccine Injury Act of 1986, 42 U.S.C. §§300aa-1 to -34 (2000), to compensate children who were injured by vaccines and also to protect vaccine manufacturers from the threat of bankruptcy. At the same time, declining immunization rates resulted in epidemics of certain childhood diseases. For example, a measles epidemic in 1990 affected 55,000 children and caused 132 deaths.[16] In order to improve vaccination rates, Congress enacted a vaccine entitlement program (as part of the Omnibus Budget Reconciliation Act of 1993, Pub. L. No. 103-166, 107 Stat. 312), to provide free immunizations to uninsured children, children covered by Medicaid, and insured children whose health insurance failed to cover immunizations.

States also require medical screening of school children, although screening procedures vary from state to state (e.g., hearing and vision tests, etc.). In addition, states mandate screening of newborns. States screen 4 million newborns annually for particular disorders.[17] No federal guidelines require the inclusion of particular disorders; however, federal recommendations exist to screen newborns for phenylketonuria (PKU), congenital hypothyroidism, and sickle cell anemia. Many states recently expanded the number of blood tests for newborns based on new mass spectrometry equipment as well as new computer software and more comprehensive training of technicians. For example, New York state officials recently quadrupled the number of tests for newborns from 11 to 44.[18]

Statutes generally do not require parental consent for newborn screening. Most states provide medical exemptions from screening; several states allow exemptions for any reason. Many states require that results remain confidential, subject to exemptions for the purposes of research, law enforcement, and paternity establishment.[19]

Some states require HIV testing of newborns. Pediatric AIDS cases among children younger than age 13 represent 1.1 percent of all reported cases.[20] The majority of cases result from perinatal transmission (before or during birth). Because of concerns about invasion of the mother's privacy (e.g., a positive result for a newborn signifies that the mother is HIV-positive), the HIV screening initially was only for data collection purposes to determine the nationwide prevalence of infection.

---

[15] Sean Coletti, Note, Taking Account of Partial Exemptors in Vaccination Law, Policy, and Practice, 36 Conn. L. Rev. 1341, 1343 (2004).

[16] Calandrillo, supra note [14], at 373.

[17] U.S. General Accounting Office Report, Newborn Screening: Characteristics of State Programs, GAO 03-449 (Mar. 2003), available at *http://www.gao.gov/new.items/d03449.pdf* (last visited Oct. 26, 2004).

[18] Al Baker, State Will Expand Blood Tests That Seek Out Defects in Newborn Babies, N.Y. Times, Oct. 28, 2004, at A25.

[19] GAO Report, Newborn Screening, supra note [17].

[20] NCCAN, Trends in the Well-Being of America's Children and Youth 2002, Health Conditions and Health Care, Children and Youth with HIV/AIDS, p. 148.

Unlike many other newborn screening programs, however, the HIV screening led to the release of newborns from the hospital without their parents being informed of abnormal results. The ethics of this approach led the New York legislature to pass the AIDS Baby Bill, N.Y. Pub. Health §2500-f (2002) (effective in 1996), to allow for screening of newborns for HIV status and to provide for disclosure of this status to the babies' mothers.[21] In the 1990s, the number of children with AIDS declined dramatically due to implementation of guidelines for counseling, voluntary HIV testing of pregnant women, the use of medication for pregnant women with AIDS, and the administering of medication to affected newborns.[22]

Yet another public intervention is the fluoridation of public waters to prevent and retard tooth decay. Most courts have upheld the public power to fluoridate the water supply. See, e.g., Ill. Pure Water Comm. v. Director of Pub. Health, 470 N.E.2d 988 (Ill. 1984) (upholding constitutionality of statute requiring mandatory fluoridation of drinking water).

3. The Neglect Limitation

In re Phillip B.
156 Cal. Rptr. 48 (Ct. App. 1979)

CALDECOTT, Presiding Justice.

A petition was filed by the juvenile probation department in the juvenile court, alleging that Phillip B., a minor, came within the provision of [California] Welfare and Institutions Code section 300, subdivision (b), because he was not provided with the "necessities of life."

The petition requested that Phillip be declared a dependent child of the court for the special purpose of ensuring that he receive cardiac surgery for a congenital heart defect. Phillip's parents had refused to consent to the surgery. The juvenile court dismissed the petition. The appeal is from the order.

Phillip is a 12-year-old boy suffering from Down's Syndrome. At birth his parents decided he should live in a residential care facility. Phillip suffers from a congenital heart defect — a ventricular septal defect that results in elevated pulmonary blood pressure. Due to the defect, Phillip's heart must work three times harder than normal to supply blood to his body. When he overexerts, unoxygenated blood travels the wrong way through the septal hole reaching his circulation, rather than the lungs.

If the congenital heart defect is not corrected, damage to the lungs will increase to the point where his lungs will be unable to carry and oxygenate any blood. As a result, death follows. During the deterioration of the lungs, Phillip will suffer from

---

[21] Michele M. Contreras, Note, New York's Mandatory HIV Testing of Newborns: A Positive Step Which Results in Negative Consequences for Women and their Children, 20 Women's Rts. L. Rep. 21 (1998). See also Gina A. Angelletta, New York Public Health Law §2500-F: The Hand That Robbed the Cradle of Privacy, 8 St. John's J. Legal Comment. 175 (2003).

[22] NCCAN, Trends in Well-Being of America's Children, supra note [20].

a progressive loss of energy and vitality until he is forced to lead a bed-to-chair existence.

Phillip's heart condition has been known since 1973. At that time Dr. Gathman, a pediatric cardiologist, examined Phillip and recommended cardiac catheterization to further define the anatomy and dynamics of Phillip's condition. Phillip's parents refused.

In 1977, Dr. Gathman again recommended catheterization and this time Phillip's parents consented. The catheterization revealed the extensive nature of Phillip's septal defect, thus it was Dr. Gathman's recommendation that surgery be performed.

Dr. Gathman referred Phillip to a second pediatric cardiologist, Dr. William French of Stanford Medical Center. Dr. French estimates the surgical mortality rate to be five to ten percent, and notes that Down's Syndrome children face a higher than average risk of postoperative complications. Dr. French found that Phillip's pulmonary vessels have already undergone some change from high pulmonary artery pressure. Without the operation, Phillip will begin to function less physically until he will be severely incapacitated. Dr. French agrees with Dr. Gathman that Phillip will enjoy a significant expansion of his life span if his defect is surgically corrected. Without the surgery, Phillip may live at the outside 20 more years. Dr. French's opinion on the advisability of surgery was not asked.

It is fundamental that parental autonomy is constitutionally protected. The United States Supreme Court has articulated the concept of personal liberty found in the Fourteenth Amendment as a right of privacy which extends to certain aspects of a family relationship [citing Roe v. Wade, Wisconsin v. Yoder, Eisenstadt v. Baird, Griswold v. Connecticut, Meyer v. Nebraska, and Pierce v. Society of Sisters]. "It is cardinal with us that the custody, care and nurture of the child reside first in the parents, whose primary function and freedom include preparation for obligations the state can neither supply nor hinder." (Prince v. Massachusetts (1944) 321 U.S. 158, 166.) . . .

Parental autonomy, however, is not absolute. The state is the guardian of society's basic values. Under the doctrine of *parens patriae*, the state has a right, indeed, a duty, to protect children. (See, e.g., Prince v. Massachusetts, supra, 321 U.S. 158 at p. 166). State officials may interfere in family matters to safeguard the child's health, educational development and emotional well-being.

One of the most basic values protected by the state is the sanctity of human life. (U.S. Const., 14th Amend., §1.) Where parents fail to provide their children with adequate medical care, the state is justified to intervene. However, since the state should usually defer to the wishes of the parents, it has a serious burden of justification before abridging parental autonomy by substituting its judgment for that of the parents.

Several relevant factors must be taken into consideration before a state insists upon medical treatment rejected by the parents. The state should examine the seriousness of the harm the child is suffering or the substantial likelihood that he will suffer serious harm; the evaluation for the treatment by the medical profession; the risks involved in medically treating the child; and the expressed preferences of the child. Of course, the underlying consideration is the child's welfare and whether his best interests will be served by the medical treatment.

Section 300, subdivision (b), permits a court to adjudge a child under the age of 18 years a dependent of the court if the child is not provided with the "necessities of life."

The trial judge dismissed the petition on the ground that there was "no clear and convincing evidence to sustain this petition."

The rule is clear that the power of the appellate court begins and ends with a determination as to whether there is any substantial evidence, contradicted or uncontradicted, which will support the conclusion reached by the trier of fact. . . . The "clear and convincing evidence" standard for proof applies only to the trial court, and is not the standard for appellate review. . . .

Turning to the facts of this case, one expert witness testified that Phillip's case was more risky than the average for two reasons. One, he has pulmonary vascular changes and statistically this would make the operation more risky in that he would be subject to more complications than if he did not have these changes. Two, children with Down's Syndrome have more problems in the postoperative period. This witness put the mortality rate at five to ten percent, and the morbidity would be somewhat higher. When asked if he knew of a case in which this type of operation had been performed on a Down's Syndrome child, the witness replied that he did, but could not remember a case involving a child who had the degree of pulmonary vascular change that Phillip had. Another expert witness testified that one of the risks of surgery to correct a ventricular septal defect was damage to the nerve that controls the heart beat as the nerve is in the same area as the defect. When this occurs a pacemaker would be required.

The trial judge, in announcing his decision, cited the inconclusiveness of the evidence to support the petition.

On reading the record we can see the trial court's attempt to balance the possible benefits to be gained from the operation against the risks involved. The court had before it a child suffering not only from a ventricular septal defect but also from Down's Syndrome, with its higher than average morbidity, and the presence of pulmonary vascular changes. In light of these facts, we cannot say as a matter of law that there was no substantial evidence to support the decision of the trial court.

In denying the petition the trial court ruled that there was no clear and convincing evidence to sustain the petition. The state contends the proper standard of proof is by a preponderance of the evidence and not by the clear and convincing test. The state asserts that only when a permanent severance of the parent-child relationship is ordered by the court must the clear and convincing standard of proof be applied. Since the petition did not seek permanent severance but only authorization for corrective heart surgery, the state contends the lower standard of proof should have been applied. . . . [However,] the "clear and convincing standard" was proper in this case.

Section 353 requires that at the beginning of the hearing on a petition, "[t]he judge shall ascertain whether the minor and his parent or guardian or adult relative, as the case may be, has been informed of the right of the minor to be represented by counsel, and if not, the judge shall advise the minor and such person, if present, of the right to have counsel present and where applicable, of the right to appointed counsel."

Amicus Curiae contends the judge erred in failing to notify Phillip of his right to counsel, thus Phillip was not properly represented. . . .

In the present case, the facts show that a deputy district attorney was representing Phillip at the hearing. He was introduced to the judge as Phillip's attorney. The deputy district attorney proceeded to make an opening statement and continued to represent Phillip throughout the entire hearing.

The judge was under no statutory duty to inform Phillip of his right to counsel when it was evident to the court that Phillip was, in fact, represented by counsel.

The order dismissing the petition is affirmed.

A petition for a rehearing was denied June 7, 1979, and the opinion was modified to read as printed above. Appellants' petition for a hearing by the Supreme Court was denied July 19, 1979. Mosk, J., was of the opinion that the petition should be granted.

[For the fascinating aftermath of this case, see infra p. 449.]

NOTE: MEDICAL NEGLECT AND THE JUVENILE COURT

A very important legal constraint on parental prerogatives relates to child neglect laws. While there are historical antecedents related to the parens patriae power of equity courts, every state now has a statute allowing a court (typically a juvenile court) to assume jurisdiction over a child in order to override individual parental judgments concerning the medical treatment of their child.[23] As you can see from the materials in Chapter 3 on child abuse and neglect, neglect statutes are typically extremely vague and give courts substantial discretion to intervene to protect a child's health.

When should courts intervene? Only when a child's life is threatened? Whenever a judge believes the parents are not acting in the child's best interest? Many cases (e.g., In re Sampson)[24] represent expansive notions of the appropriate judicial role. Problem number three, supra p. 374, is based on *Sampson*, in which a New York family court judge declared Kevin Sampson, age 15, "a neglected child" in order to override Kevin's mother's decision — based on her religious objections — not to permit blood transfusions for Kevin during surgery. In ordering the operation, the court in effect assumed the parental role:

> [To] postpone the surgery merely to allow the boy to become of age so that he may make the decision himself as suggested by the surgeon and urged by both counsel for the mother and the Law Guardian . . . totally ignores the developmental and psychological factors stemming from his deformity which the Court deems to be of the utmost importance in any consideration of the boy's future welfare and begs the whole question.[25]

---

[23] In many jurisdictions, parents are guilty of a criminal homicide if their failure to provide medical attention results in the child's death. Failure to provide medical attention can also result in felony or misdemeanor criminal neglect charges.

[24] 317 N.Y.S.2d 641 (Fam. Ct. 1970), aff'd, 323 N.Y.S.2d 253 (App. Div. 1971), aff'd, 278 N.E.2d 918 (N.Y. 1972).

[25] 317 N.Y.S.2d at 655. For additional cases in which a parent objects to a child's medical treatment on religious grounds, see James G. Dwyer, The Children We Abandon: Religious Exemptions to

Many have argued that the neglect standard should impose only minimum standards and should be very narrowly construed. Professor Goldstein, for example, argues that:[26]

> State supervention of parental judgment would be justified to provide any proven, nonexperimental, medical procedure when its denial would mean *death* for a child who would otherwise have an opportunity for either a *life worth living* or a *life of relatively normal healthy growth* toward adulthood[18] — to majority when a person is freed of parental control and presumed competent to decide for himself. The state would overcome the presumption of parental autonomy in health-care matters only if it could establish: (a) that the medical profession is in agreement about what non-experimental medical treatment is right for the child; (b) that the expected outcome of that treatment is what society agrees to be right for any child, a chance for normal healthy growth toward adulthood or a life worth living; *and* (c) that the expected outcome of denial of that treatment would mean death for the child. . . .
>
> There would be no justification, however, for coercive intrusion by the state in those life-or-death situations (a) in which there is no proven medical procedure, *or* (b) in which parents are confronted with conflicting medical advice about which, if any, treatment procedure to follow, *or* (c), in which, even if the medical experts agree about treatment, there is less than a high probability that the nonexperimental treatment will enable the child to pursue either a life worth living or a life of relatively normal healthy growth toward adulthood. . . .
>
> Outside of narrow central core of agreement, "a life worth living" and "a life of relatively normal healthy growth" are highly personal terms about which there is no societal consensus. There can thus be no societal consensus about the "rightness" of always deciding for "life," or of always preferring the predicted results of the recommended treatment over the predicted result of refusing such treatment. It is precisely in those cases in which reasonable and responsible persons can and do disagree about whether the "life" after treatment would be "worth living" or "normal," and thus about what is "right," that parents must remain free of coercive state intervention in deciding whether to consent to or reject the medical program proffered for their child. . . .

Phillip B., supra p. 377, represents one of few reported cases in which a trial court decision refusing to require life-sustaining care was affirmed on appeal. In *Phillip B.*, Phillip's father testified that he would have no reluctance to authorize surgery for either of his other sons if they had the same physical problem. Is the result justified because Phillip was a mentally retarded child? Would this be a sufficient justification under Professor Goldstein's standard? Does Phillip have a chance toward "normal healthy growth toward adulthood or a life worth living"?[27]

Child Welfare and Education Laws as Denials of Equal Protection to Children of Religious Objectors, 74 N.C. L. Rev. 1321 (1996).

[26] Goldstein, Medical Care, supra note [11], at 651-654.

[18] While a life of relatively normal healthy growth is assumed to be a life worth living, it is not assumed that all lives worth living from a societal-consensus point of view could be characterized as relatively normal or healthy. For example, a quadriplegic child, in need of a blood transfusion for reasons unrelated to that condition might, for society, be a "life worth living" though not a life of normal healthy growth.

[27] For a discussion of *Phillip B.*, see Wesley Sokolosky, The Sick Child and the Reluctant Parent — A Framework for Judicial Intervention, 20 J. Fam. L. 69 (1981-82); Yolanda V. Vorys, The Outer

There is now federal legislation that requires child protection agencies to have a broader notion of when they should protect children. See section D, infra, on disabled newborns.

Most neglect cases are not appealed. Some commentators believe that the vague statutory standards frequently permit intervention at the trial level under circumstances where the child's life is not threatened, and the judge simply substitutes his or her judgment (or confirms a doctor's judgment) concerning the child's best medical interests. The neglect limitation in effect poses the critical question of defining when the state should coercively intervene into the family to override parental judgment concerning the health care of a child. Are special procedural safeguards necessary when the parent and child may have "conflicting interests"? *Parham*, which follows, and the materials later in this chapter concerning disabled newborns and the medical experimentation on children provide further opportunities to explore these questions.

Parham v. J.R.
442 U.S. 584 (1979)

Mr. Chief Justice BURGER delivered the opinion of the Court.

The question presented in this appeal is what process is constitutionally due a minor child whose parents or guardian seek state administered institutional mental health care for the child and specifically whether an adversary proceeding is required prior to or after the commitment.

[Appellees J.R. and J.L., children being treated in a Georgia state mental hospital, were plaintiffs in this class action, based on 42 U.S.C. §1983, against the state mental health authorities. Appellees sought a declaratory judgment that Georgia's voluntary commitment procedures for children under the age of 18 violated the Due Process Clause and requested an injunction against their future enforcement.

J.R. was declared a neglected child by the county and removed from his natural parents when he was three months old. He was placed in seven different foster homes prior to his admission to the state mental hospital at the age of seven. J.L., now deceased, was admitted to the state mental hospital at the age of six years. Prior to his admission, he had received out-patient treatment at the hospital for over two months. His natural parents were divorced, and his mother had remarried. He had been expelled from school because he was aggressive and uncontrollable. He was returned to his mother and stepfather two years later but the parents, unable to control J.L. to their satisfaction, requested his readmission. J.L.'s parents relinquished their parental rights two years later.]

Georgia Code §88-503.1 (1975) provides for the voluntary admission to a state regional hospital of children such as J.L. and J.R. Under that provision, admission begins with an application for hospitalization signed by a "parent or guardian." Upon application, the superintendent of each hospital is given the power to admit temporarily any child for "observation and diagnosis." If, after observation, the superintendent finds "evidence of mental illness" and that the child is "suitable for

---

Limits of Parental Autonomy: Withholding Medical Treatment from Children, 42 Ohio St. L.J. 813 (1981).

treatment" in the hospital, then the child may be admitted "for such period and under such conditions as may be authorized by law."

Georgia's mental health statute also provides for the discharge of voluntary patients. Any child who has been hospitalized for more than five days may be discharged at the request of a parent or guardian. Even without a request for discharge, however, the superintendent of each regional hospital has an affirmative duty to release any child "who has recovered from his mental illness or who has sufficiently improved that the superintendent determines that hospitalization of the patient is no longer desirable." §88-503.2 (1975). . . .

II

In holding unconstitutional Georgia's statutory procedure for voluntary commitment of juveniles, the District Court first determined that commitment . . . constitutes a severe deprivation of a child's liberty . . . in terms of both freedom from bodily restraint and freedom from the "emotional and psychic harm" caused by the institutionalization. Having determined that a liberty interest is implicated by a child's admission to a mental hospital, the court considered what process is required to protect that interest. It held that the process due "includes at least the right after notice to be heard before an impartial tribunal." [412 F. Supp. 112, 139 (M.D. Ga. 1976).]

In requiring the prescribed hearing, the court rejected Georgia's argument that no adversary-type hearing was required since the State was merely assisting parents who could not afford private care by making available treatment similar to that offered in private hospitals and by private physicians. The court acknowledged that most parents who seek to have their children admitted to a state mental hospital do so in good faith. It, however, relied on one of appellees' witnesses who expressed an opinion that "some still look upon mental hospitals as a 'dumping ground.' " Id., at 138. No specific evidence of such "dumping," however, can be found in the record.

The District Court also rejected the argument that review by the superintendents of the hospitals and their staffs was sufficient to protect the child's liberty interest. . . .

III

In an earlier day, the problems inherent in coping with children afflicted with mental or emotional abnormalities were dealt with largely within the family. . . . While some parents no doubt were able to deal with their disturbed children without specialized assistance, others especially those of limited means and education, were not. Increasingly, they turned for assistance to local, public sources or private charities. Until recently, most of the states did little more than provide custodial institutions for the confinement of persons who were considered dangerous.

As medical knowledge about the mentally ill and public concern for their condition expanded, the states, aided substantially by federal grants, have sought to ameliorate the human tragedies of seriously disturbed children. Ironically, as most states have expanded their efforts to assist the mentally ill, their actions have been subjected to increasing litigation and heightened constitutional scrutiny. . . .

. . . Assuming the existence of a protectible property or liberty interest, the Court has required a balancing of a number of factors [including the private interest affected, the risk of an erroneous deprivation of such interest, the value of other procedural safeguards, and the government's interest that other procedural requirements might entail. Mathews v. Eldridge, 424 U.S. 319 (1976)]. In applying these criteria, we must consider first the child's interest in not being committed. Normally, however, since this interest is inextricably linked with the parents' interest in and obligation for the welfare and health of the child, the private interest at stake is a combination of the child's and parents' concerns. Next, we must examine the State's interest in the procedures it has adopted for commitment and treatment of children. Finally, we must consider how well Georgia's procedures protect against arbitrariness in the decision to commit a child to a state mental hospital.

(a)

It is not disputed that a child, in common with adults, has a substantial liberty interest in not being confined unnecessarily for medical treatment and that the state's involvement in the commitment decision constitutes state action under the Fourteenth Amendment. . . . We also recognize that commitment sometimes produces adverse social consequences for the child because of the reaction of some to the discovery that the child has received psychiatric care. . . . For purposes of this decision, we assume that a child has a protectible interest not only in being free of unnecessary bodily restraints but also in not being labeled erroneously by some persons because of an improper decision by the state hospital superintendent.

(b)

We next deal with the interests of the parents who have decided, on the basis of their observations and independent professional recommendations, that their child needs institutional care. Appellees argue that the constitutional rights of the child are of such magnitude and the likelihood of parental abuse is so great that the parents' traditional interests in and responsibility for the upbringing of their child must be subordinated at least to the extent of providing a formal adversary hearing prior to a voluntary commitment.

Our jurisprudence historically has reflected Western civilization concepts of the family as a unit with broad parental authority over minor children. Our cases have consistently followed that course [and] asserted that parents generally "have the right, coupled with the high duty, to recognize and prepare [their children] for additional obligations." Pierce v. Society of Sisters, 268 U.S. 510, 535 (1925). See also Wisconsin v. Yoder, 406 U.S. 205, 213 (1972); Prince v. Massachusetts, 321 U.S. 158, 166 (1944); Meyer v. Nebraska, 262 U.S. 390, 400 (1923). Surely, this includes a "high duty" to recognize symptoms of illness and to seek and follow medical advice. The law's concept of the family rests on a presumption that parents possess what a child lacks in maturity, experience, and capacity for judgment required for making life's difficult decision. More important, historically it has recognized that natural bonds of affection lead parents to act in the best interests of their children. 1 W. Blackstone, Commentaries *447; 2 J. Kent, Commentaries on American Law *190.

As with so many other legal presumptions, experience and reality may rebut what the law accepts as a starting point. . . . That some parents "may at times be acting against the interests of their children" as was stated in Bartley v. Kremens, 402 F. Supp. 1039, 1047-1048 (E.D. Pa. 1975), vacated and remanded, 431 U.S. 119 (1977), creates a basis for caution, but is hardly a reason to discard wholesale those pages of human experience that teach that parents generally do act in the child's best interests. . . .

Nonetheless, we have recognized that a state is not without constitutional control over parental discretion in dealing with children when their physical or mental health is jeopardized. See Wisconsin v. Yoder, supra, 406 U.S., at 230; Prince v. Massachusetts, supra, 321 U.S., at 166. . . . Appellees urge that these precedents limiting the traditional rights of parents, if viewed in the context of the liberty interest of the child and the likelihood of parental abuse, require us to hold that the parents' decision to have a child admitted to a mental hospital must be subjected to an exacting constitutional scrutiny, including a formal, adversary, preadmission hearing.

Appellees' argument, however, sweeps too broadly. Simply because the decision of a parent is not agreeable to a child or because it involves risks does not automatically transfer the power to make that decision from the parents to some agency or officer of the state. The same characterizations can be made for a tonsillectomy, appendectomy, or other medical procedure. Most children, even in adolescence, simply are not able to make sound judgments concerning many decisions, including their need for medical care or treatment. Parents can and must make those judgments. Here, there is no finding by the District Court of even a single instance of bad faith by any parent of any member of appellees' class. . . . The fact that a child may balk at hospitalization . . . does not diminish the parents' authority to decide what is best for the child . . . Neither state officials nor federal courts are equipped to review such parental decisions. . . .

In defining the respective rights and prerogatives of the child and parent in the voluntary commitment setting, we conclude that our precedents permit the parents to retain a substantial, if not the dominant, role in the decision, absent a finding of neglect or abuse, and that the traditional presumption that the parents act in the best interests of their child should apply. We also conclude, however, that the child's rights and the nature of the commitment decision are such that parents cannot always have absolute and unreviewable discretion to decide whether to have a child institutionalized. They, of course, retain plenary authority to seek such care for their children, subject to a physician's independent examination and medical judgment.

(c)

The State obviously has a significant interest in confining the use of its costly mental health facilities to cases of genuine need. . . . To accomplish this purpose, the State has charged the superintendents of each regional hospital with the responsibility for determining, before authorizing an admission, whether a prospective patient is mentally ill and whether the patient will likely benefit from hospital care. . . .

The State in performing its voluntarily assumed mission also has a significant interest in not imposing unnecessary procedural obstacles that may discourage the mentally ill or their families from seeking needed psychiatric assistance. [M]any parents who believe they are acting in good faith would forgo state-provided hospital care if such care is contingent on participation in an adversary proceeding designed to probe their motives and other private family matters in seeking the voluntary admission. . . .

(d)

[T]he risk of error inherent in the parental decision to have a child institution-alized for mental health care is sufficiently great that some kind of inquiry should be made by a "neutral factfinder" to determine whether the statutory requirements for admission are satisfied. . . . That inquiry must carefully probe the child's back-ground using all available sources, including, but not limited to, parents, schools, and other social agencies. Of course, the review must also include an interview with the child. It is necessary that the decisionmaker have the authority to refuse to admit any child who does not satisfy the medical standards for admission. Finally, it is necessary that the child's continuing need for commitment be reviewed periodically by a similarly independent procedure. . . .

Due process has never been thought to require that the neutral and detached trier of fact be law trained or a judicial or administrative officer. Surely, this is the case as to medical decisions, for "neither judges nor administrative hearing officers are better qualified than psychiatrists to render psychiatric judgments." In re Roger S., 19 Cal. 3d 921, 942, 569 P.2d 1286, 1299 (1977) (Clark, J., dissenting). Thus, a staff physician will suffice, so long as he or she is free to evaluate independently the child's mental and emotional condition and need for treatment.

It is not necessary that the deciding physician conduct a formal or quasi-formal, hearing. A state is free to require such a hearing, but due process is not violated by use of informal traditional medical investigative techniques. . . . Another problem with requiring a formalized, factfinding hearing lies in the danger it poses for significant intrusion into the parent-child relationship. Pitting the parents and child as adversaries often will be at odds with the presumption that parents act in the best interests of their child. It is one thing to require a neutral physician to make a careful review of the parents' decision in order to make sure it is proper from a medical standpoint; it is a wholly different matter to employ an adversary contest to ascertain whether the parents' motivation is consistent with the child's interests. [Moreover,] there is a risk that it would exacerbate whatever tensions already exist between the child and the parents. . . .

It has been suggested that a hearing conducted by someone other than the admitting physician is necessary in order to detect instances where parents are "guilty of railroading their children into asylums" or are using "voluntary commit-ment procedures in order to sanction behavior of which they disapprov[e]." Ellis, Volunteering Children: Parental Commitment of Minors to Mental Institutions, 62 Calif. L. Rev. 840, 850-851 (1974). Curiously, it seems to be taken for granted that parents who seek to "dump" their children on the state will inevitably be able to conceal their motives and thus deceive the admitting psychiatrists and the other mental health professionals. . . . It is unrealistic to believe that trained psychia-trists, skilled in eliciting responses, sorting medically relevant facts, and sensing motivational nuances will often be deceived about the family situation surrounding a child's emotional disturbance. . . .

Georgia's statute envisions a careful diagnostic medical inquiry to be conducted by the admitting physician at each regional hospital [as well as periodic reviews and a duty to discharge a child who is no longer mentally ill].

We are satisfied that the voluminous record as a whole supports the conclusion that the admissions staffs of the hospitals have acted in a neutral and detached fashion in making medical judgments in the best interests of the children. The State, through its mental health programs, provides the authority for trained professionals to assist parents in examining, diagnosing, and treating emotionally disturbed children. Through its hiring practices, it provides well-staffed and well-equipped hospitals and — as the District Court found — conscientious public employees to implement the State's beneficent purposes. . . .

IV

Our discussion [above] was directed at the situation where a child's natural parents request his admission to a state mental hospital. Some members of appellees' class, including J.R., were wards of the State of Georgia at the time of their admission. Obviously their situation differs from those members of the class who have natural parents. While the determination of what process is due varies somewhat when the state, rather than a natural parent, makes the request for commitment, we conclude that the differences in the two situations do not justify requiring different procedures at the time of the child's initial admission to the hospital. [The Court then suggests that, on remand, the district court consider the need for more rigorous review procedures for wards of the state so they will not get "lost in the shuffle."]

On this record, we are satisfied that Georgia's medical factfinding processes are reasonable and consistent with constitutional guarantees. . . . The judgment is therefore reversed, and the case is remanded to the District Court for further proceedings consistent with this opinion.

NOTES AND QUESTIONS

The Mental Hospitalization of Troublesome Youth

(1) Vision of Family. Commentators on child mental health policy point out that the majority opinion in *Parham* "represents a construction of the supposed reality of how hospitalization occurs, derived from idyllic notions of how the family and the mental health professions should be." Gary B. Melton et al., No Place to Go: The Civil Commitment of Minors 126 (1998). What are the Court's assumptions about the family, mental health institutions, and the effects of formal, adversarial commitment procedures? See id. at 127-141.

(2) Procedures. What procedures does the majority in *Parham* require before a juvenile can be committed to a mental hospital? What limits, if any, are placed on the discretion of parents and doctors to decide what is best for the child?

(3) Due Process. *Parham* focuses on the due process question of what procedures are required. Consider the substantive question of what standards should

define when a young person should be committed. When is it appropriate to institutionalize a juvenile in a psychiatric hospital? In most states, an adult can be committed in one of two ways: (1) by voluntarily consenting to his own commitment; or (2) through an involuntary process that typically requires a showing that the person is a danger to himself or others by reason of a mental disorder. Are you persuaded that the substantive standards for juveniles should be different?

(4) Involuntary Commitment. When a young person does not wish to be committed, how would you define the circumstances when commitment is appropriate? Would you require a demonstration that the young person is suffering from a classic mental disorder, such as a psychosis, a severe depression, or an organic disorder? Would you require a showing that outpatient treatment is likely to be less effective? That commitment is likely to improve the young person's condition? More broadly, what benefits and risks do you see associated with committing a young person? What did the Court require?

(5) Troublemakers? Do you agree with the Court that the questions presented in the case are "essentially medical in character" and therefore are best resolved by medical personnel rather than judicial or administrative officers? Evidence suggests that most youths who are committed to inpatient psychiatric treatment have typically been given one of a number of vague labels that identify either "conduct disorders," which involve chronic violations of rules at home or school; or "personality disorders," which may involve uncertainty about a variety of issues relating to identity or long-term goals, excessive shyness, or overreactions to stressful situations such as parental fighting or divorce. Lois A. Weithorn, Mental Hospitalization of Troublesome Youth: An Analysis of Skyrocketing Admission Rates, 40 Stan. L. Rev. 773, 789 (1988). Further, a large proportion of children hospitalized in psychiatric facilities are considered "troublemakers" who disobey their parents, run away, miss school, take drugs, and engage in sexual activity. Some may even present a threat to persons or property or a psychological threat to family stability. Id. at 792.

(6) Trans-Institutionalization. In the late 1970s and 1980s the rates of juvenile admissions to psychiatric hospitals — particularly private psychiatric hospitals — increased substantially. At the same time, the number of young persons institutionalized as status offenders declined substantially. Could it be that the strict procedures in the delinquency process (see Chapter 7) and the move towards deinstitutionalizing status offenders (see Chapter 6) have resulted, as some commentators argue, in a "trans-institutionalization"? The argument is essentially that the population of teenagers cared for by the welfare system, the juvenile justice system, and the mental health system are substantially interchangeable. Pressure to reduce the rate of institutionalization in one system will simply increase the rate of institutionalization in the other systems. See Weithorn, supra, at 805-807.

(7) Role of Insurance. Commentators have argued that the Court's failure to impose substantial procedural safeguards in *Parham* has contributed to the increase in psychiatric populations — particularly in private mental hospitals for which in many states there are no safeguards imposed at all. There are other important factors at work as well, such as insurance. Both public and private insurance funding favors inpatient over outpatient treatment. State resources available for the juvenile justice system are often quite limited; however, insurance funding can pay for institutionalization in the mental health system. Weithorn, supra, at 826.

(8) State Protections.   State laws vary considerably in the protections they offer minors for whom psychiatric hospitalization is sought. One commentator points out some of these protections:

> In California, for example, minors ages fourteen and older have the right to a hearing before confinement in a public mental hospital [In re Roger S., 569 P.2d 1286 (Cal. 1977)] or an independent clinical review after hospitalization in a private facility. Illinois gives committed minors age twelve or older the right to seek judicial review of their hospitalization. Upon petition by the legal rights services, private or otherwise appointed counsel, a relative, or one acting as next friend, Ohio provides a right to judicial determination whether "voluntary" hospitalization is in the best interests of the minor. Beyond such statutory due process protections, minors held in public facilities or pursuant to state commitment laws may also seek review of their confinement by petition for a writ of habeas corpus. [Jan C. Costello, "The Trouble Is They're Growing, The Trouble Is They're Grown": Therapeutic Jurisprudence and Adolescents' Participation in Mental Health Care Decisions, 29 Ohio N.U. L. Rev. 607 (2003).]

4. Emergencies

NOTES AND QUESTIONS

(1) At common law a doctor may treat a child without parental consent in the event of an emergency, at least where the parent is unavailable and where delay endangers the child's life. Many states have express statutory exceptions from the parental consent requirement for emergencies. If the child's parents are available but refuse to consent, may the doctors proceed with life-saving treatment anyway? Or must the hospital first have the child declared "neglected" and secure a court order? See Miller ex rel. Miller v. HCA, infra p. 399. Where it would be neglect to withhold consent, why should a hospital delay treatment while reasonable efforts are made to contact the child's parents? More generally, what purposes are served by a consent requirement under circumstances where it would be neglect to withhold consent altogether? Would the "consent" of a second doctor serve as well or better?

(2) In an emergency situation where the child's parents are unavailable and the child is conscious, should the child have the capacity to refuse treatment? Can a rational adult refuse treatment that is essential to preserve his life?

(3) If doctors can be trusted in emergencies to act without parental consent, why can't they be trusted to act without such consent in more routine medical circumstances?

(4) Is abortion an emergency? See North Florida Woman's Health & Counseling Servs. v. State, supra p. 132.

(5) In light of the fact that state law allows doctors to proceed without parental consent in emergencies, why do you think schools, summer camps, and youth organizations like the Boy Scouts regularly request parents to sign consent forms stating that their child may be treated in an emergency if the parent cannot be located?

5.   Who Decides if the Parents Disagree and Based on What Standard?

In re K.I.
735 A.2d 448 (D.C. 1999)

REID, Associate Judge:

This poignant matter involves a "do not resuscitate" order ("the DNR") entered by the Superior Court of the District of Columbia in the case of a neglected child, K.I., who, since birth approximately two years ago, has suffered continuously from several serious medical problems. Currently the child is in a comatose state and has been described as "neurologically devastated." . . .

The record before us shows the following facts. On June 15, 1997, K.I. was born prematurely at twenty-six weeks gestation. K.I.'s treating physician at the Hospital for Sick Children, Dr. Glenn Hornstein, who testified at the DNR hearing, stated that as a result of the premature birth, K.I. "developed BPD; or broncho pulmonary dysplasia," an abnormal condition of the lung cells which requires the child to use oxygen. In addition, K.I. suffered from "hemoglobin SC disease, which is similar [to] or it is sickle cell disease, just a mild variance"; "reactive airways disease," characterized by wheezing; and "gastro-esophageal refl[u]x."

K.I. was released from the neonatal intensive care unit of the hospital in November 1997 to the biological mother, B.I. Beginning on November 24, 1997, for a period of five weeks, B.I. and K.I. stayed in an apartment in the Northwest sector of the District of Columbia with D.M., K.I.'s putative father who claims to be K.I.'s biological father. K.I. was required to wear a heart monitor and an apnea monitor, take medication for the lungs, and use oxygen continuously. D.M. became concerned when B.I. would take K.I. off the oxygen and heart monitor and fail to give the child the lung medication. He also was troubled when he saw B.I. consume about three "40-ounce . . . very strong beer[s]" every day. He stated, at the August 26, 1998 neglect proceeding, that B.I. became intoxicated and would "start stumbling and falling and get very silent and have a nasty attitude." B.I. would "leave the house and leave [D.M.] there with the baby and come back a day later or two days later." On December 28, 1997, B.I. left D.M.'s home. She carried K.I. with her but failed to take the oxygen. D.M. alerted Howard University that K.I. was without her oxygen.

On December 29, 1997, in response to D.M.'s alert, Edmond Lahai, then an employee of the District of Columbia Department of Human Services, Children and Family Services Administration, searched for B.I. and K.I. When he located B.I., she initially denied that K.I. was with her. Mr. Lahai found two Metropolitan Police officers, and when he returned with the police to the abode where B.I. was staying, she admitted that K.I. was with her. K.I. had no oxygen and no monitors.

A neglect petition was filed against B.I. on December 31, 1997, under D.C. Code §16-2301(9)(B), (C), and (F). The petition alleged that B.I. failed to: (1) provide K.I. with the requisite medical care; (2) schedule appointments for K.I.; and (3) use K.I.'s monitoring devices or tube feeding procedure. [At the hearing, K.I. was found to be a neglected child.]

On December 29, 1997, Mr. Lahai took K.I. to Howard University Hospital. Later, K.I. was transferred to the Hospital for Sick Children. When K.I. began to experience respiratory distress at the Hospital for Sick Children and her condition worsened, Dr. Hornstein transferred the child to Children's Hospital on July 21, 1998. On that same day, K.I. went into cardiac arrest and suffered hypoxia, which involves "a deprivation of oxygen to the cells and to the brain." Resuscitation efforts lasted for approximately twenty-five minutes. After the resuscitation efforts ceased, K.I.'s heart began to function again. However, the following day she experienced a seven-hour seizure which terminated only after the administration of "phenobarbital medication which . . . put K.I. into a pentobarb-like coma . . . to control the seizure."

On August 22, 1998, K.I. was returned to the Hospital for Sick Children, where she continued to experience severe medical problems. At the DNR hearing, Dr. Hornstein described the child's current condition — no "purposeful movements," persistent "myochronic jerks" [involving] "shaking of [the] arms and legs." In addition, according to Dr. Hornstein, K.I. "withdraws to pain or . . . feels discomfort when people do interventions such as . . . when [he] attempted to place [an] IV in [K.I.'s] . . . hand, [K.I.] actually was grimacing and sort of writhing and moving around as if in discomfort."

Due to K.I.'s persistent medical problems, the trial court "held a hearing to determine the propriety of aggressive resuscitation efforts in the event that [K.I.] suffered pulmonary or respiratory arrest." Several persons testified, including experts in pediatric critical care, bioethics, and ethics as well as B.I. and D.M. . . . Dr. Gabriel Jacob Hauser, a professor of bioethics at Georgetown University, the Chief of Pediatric Critical Care Service at the Georgetown University Hospital, and the former chair of the hospital's ethics committee, testified that: "While [K.I.] is capable of feeling pain and discomfort, [the child] responds to no other stimuli; . . . is unable to react to [the] environment, cannot contemplate events taking place [in close proximity], and is incapable of giving or receiving love." Furthermore, "the possible resuscitation efforts that would be used on [K.I.] in the event of cardiac arrest or respiratory failure, assuming no DNR order is in place . . . [w]ould entail substantial amounts of pain and discomfort."

[The trial court concluded that it had jurisdiction and that the best interests, rather than the substituted judgment, standard applied. Based on an application of that standard, the trial court granted the medical guardian ad litem's request to issue the DNR. The mother appealed.]

B.I. argues that, as a parent, she has the right to determine whether, and in what manner, K.I. should be resuscitated, and thus, the court erred by applying the best interests of the child instead of the substituted judgment standard in deciding whether to issue the DNR. She also maintains that the court based its judgment upon the preponderance of the evidence, the standard governing neglect proceedings, rather than clear and convincing evidence. . . . D.M. asserts that the DNR should be upheld . . .

. . . Finally, the amici curiae, consisting of the Hospital for Sick Children where K.I. receives medical care, the Medical Society of the District of Columbia, the American Medical Association . . . , two professors of law from the Georgetown University Law Center, and the Metropolitan Washington Bioethics Network, also support the DNR because "the best interest of [K.I.] is served by the establishment of a reasonable plan of medical care which is premised on the very limited benefits available to [K.I.] from medical science."

. . . We turn first to the issue of the trial court's jurisdiction over this matter. . . . The Family Division of the Superior Court ("the Division") has jurisdiction over cases pertaining to neglected children. . . . There is substantial evidence in the record showing that while K.I. was under the care of B.I., B.I. frequently consumed alcohol, took away K.I.'s required oxygen and monitors for apnea and the heart, and failed to provide adequate care for the child; thus, K.I. was properly adjudicated a neglected child.

Given the lack of appropriate attention and care by B.I., the trial court assumed its role as parens patriae "to promote [K.I.'s] best interest," and to provide necessary relief. . . . The court's exercise of its discretion as parens patriae was essential since the District government took no position on the resuscitation issue and because B.I. and D.M. had a fundamental disagreement concerning resuscitation — D.M. supported the need for the DNR, while B.I. opposed the DNR and favored the use of a variety of medical techniques, "including intubation, defibrillation (shock with electric paddles), and interosseous efforts at introducing medication into [K.I.'s] system" in an effort to reverse any cardiac arrest or respiratory distress. B.I.'s goal is to keep K.I. "breathing." Moreover, in light of the fact that K.I. has been described as "neurologically devastated," feels and reacts to pain and discomfort but not to other stimuli, has no reaction to the surrounding environment, cannot give or receive love or express a view; and because some of the resuscitation techniques engender substantial pain and discomfort, we cannot fault the trial court's decision to issue the DNR based upon guidance from medical experts and consistent with the best interests of K.I., rather than abiding by B.I.'s wishes.

Although biological parents have a "fundamental liberty interest . . . in the care, custody, and management of their child [which] does not evaporate simply because they have not been model parents or have lost temporary custody of their child to the State[,]" Santosky v. Kramer, 455 U.S. 745, 753 (1982), that interest is not absolute since "[t]he paramount concern is the child's welfare and all other considerations, including the rights of a parent to a child, must yield to its best interests and well-being." Davis v. Jurney, 145 A.2d 846, 849 (D.C. 1958). Although B.I. clearly has a liberty interest "in the care, custody and management of [K.I.]," *Santosky*, supra, 455 U.S. at 753, K.I.'s well-being takes precedence over B.I.'s parental rights.

In short, the trial court did not err in exercising jurisdiction over the DNR issue rather than yielding to B.I.'s wishes as a parent.

B.I. insists that, after the trial court decided to exercise jurisdiction over the DNR matter, the court should have applied the substituted judgment rather than the best interests of the child standard in determining whether to issue the DNR. . . .

Historically, the substituted judgment standard arose in estate cases involving incompetent persons, and generally has been invoked in cases of adults who at one time were competent but later became incompetent. In applying the doctrine, "[t]he court, as surrogate for the incompetent, is to determine as best it can what choice

[the] individual, if competent, would make with respect to medical procedures." In re Boyd, 403 A.2d 744, 750 (D.C. 1979) (footnote omitted). "[T]he substituted judgment inquiry is primarily a subjective one," [In re A.C., 573 A.2d 1235, 1249 (D.C. 1990)], and in both In re A.C. and In re Boyd, *supra*, we set forth factors to be followed in ascertaining the decision that the incompetent person would make. These factors include giving "the greatest weight . . . to the previously expressed wishes of the patient." In re A.C., *supra*, 573 A.2d at 1249-50. As we said in In re A.C.,

> to determine the subjective desires of the patient, the court must consider the totality of the evidence, focusing particularly on written or oral directions concerning treatment to family, friends, and health-care professionals. The court should also take into account the patient's past decisions regarding medical treatment, and attempt to ascertain from what is known about the patient's value system, goals, and desires what the patient would decide if competent. [Id. at 1251 (citations omitted).]

In In re Barry, 445 So.2d 365, 371 (Fla. App. 2 Dist. 1984), the court noted that: "The [substituted judgment] doctrine has been helpful in the case of adults, but it is difficult to apply to children or young adults." Indeed, most of the substituted judgment cases cited by B.I., including those from this jurisdiction, concerned adults. Moreover, unlike K.I.'s situation, in one of the cases cited by B.I. which involved a minor, there was no neglect adjudication, and both parents agreed to petition the court for approval to remove life support systems. See In re Barry, supra, . . .

To attempt to apply the substituted judgment test in this case where B.I. and D.M. disagree; where K.I., a child born in June 1997, has never been healthy; has issued no oral or written directives as to medical matters or formed any opinions about anything, let alone a value system; not only would be impossible, but also would violate the spirit of the substituted judgment standard, the purpose of which is to implement the wishes of the incompetent individual. Consequently, we hold, consistent with the trial court's memorandum opinion, that "in cases involving minor respondents who have lacked, and will forever lack, the ability to express a preference regarding their course of medical treatment," and where the parents do not speak with the same voice but disagree as to the proper course of action, the best interests of the child standard shall be applied to determine whether to issue a DNR.

[Next, the appellate court held that the correct standard of proof required for issuance of a DNA in the best interests of the child is clear and convincing evidence. The appellate court then turned to whether the trial court appropriately applied that standard.]

Contrary to B.I.'s argument, we are satisfied that the trial court applied the clear and convincing evidence test rather than relying primarily upon factual findings from the neglect adjudication which were made in accordance with the preponderance of the evidence standard. . . .

In this case, the trial court specifically stated that "the issuance of [its] DNR order must be predicated upon a finding by clear and convincing evidence both that it is in [K.I.'s] best interests to forego aggressive revival measures, and that [B.I.'s] refusal to consent to the issuance of the DNR order is unreasonably contrary to [K.I.'s] well-being." Further, the court "[was] satisfied, by clear and convincing evidence, that upon balancing the burdens of continued life against the benefits and rewards of furthering life, [K.I.'s] best interests will be served by issuing a DNR order." Thus, the main focus of the court was on the medical condition of K.I., the impact that aggressive and invasive resuscitation procedures would have on K.I. such as the inducement of pain, discomfort and additional neurological damage. The court did reference the findings of neglect relating to B.I. — her drinking and failure to keep K.I. on oxygen and required monitors. In concluding that B.I.'s "refusal to consent to the entry of [the DNR] is both unreasonable and contrary to [K.I.'s] best interests," however, the court emphasized B.I.'s lack of cooperation with the hospital staff and her singular goal of keeping K.I. breathing, as evidenced by her statement, "any amount of pain is worth it as long as [K.I.] breathes."

In short, in exercising its role as parens patriae and guided by testimony of several medical, bioethics, and ethics experts in this case where there was a prior adjudication of neglect, the trial court, carefully and thoughtfully, determined by clear and convincing evidence that it was in K.I.'s best interests to avoid use of aggressive resuscitation efforts which cause pain and discomfort. . . . We see no abuse of discretion in this matter. . . .

QUESTIONS

(1) In re K.I. involves medical decisionmaking regarding a child who is subject to the neglect jurisdiction. Suppose B.I. had not been a neglectful parent and that a court had not previously determined K.I. to be neglected. Would the case have been decided the same way? Should courts be the decisionmaker in cases of parental disagreement about a child's medical treatment? Might there be some alternative manner to resolve the dispute?

(2) In *K.I.*, the medical professionals (expert witnesses and *amici*) concurred that the court should issue the DNR order. Suppose the experts, as well as the parents, disagreed. How should a court adjudicate such a dispute? What factors should a court take into account?

(3) On what basis does the appellate court apply the best interests of the child standard? When should a court apply the substituted judgment standard in cases of medical disputes regarding ill children?

(4) Suppose the parents disagree not about medical treatment but rather about *telling* the child about the nature or consequences of the treatment or illness (e.g., if the illness is terminal). How should such a dispute be resolved? Should a court resort to the "best interests" standard? If so, is the "best interests of the child" a compelling state interest to permit an infringement of one parent's First Amendment rights? For a parental dispute in a related context, see Stephanie L. v. Benjamin L., 602 N.Y.S.2d 80 (N.Y. Sup. Ct. 1993) (refusing to enjoin husband from telling ten-year-old daughter that wife had terminal cancer).

6. Exceptions Where the Minor Alone May Consent to Medical Treatment

PRELIMINARY QUESTIONS

(1) Special Circumstances. A number of states permit a minor, regardless of age, to give effective consent to the diagnosis or treatment of venereal disease, drug addiction, alcoholism, pregnancy, or for purposes of giving blood. What purposes or interests are served by each of these exceptions? Are young people more likely to make mature decisions about treatment for these conditions? Or do these exceptions reflect predominant public health interests of society at large? Is the primary purpose to provide for treatment in circumstances where many young people are too embarrassed or fearful to discuss the matter with their parents? If such legislation reflects the privacy interest of minors, why is the doctor often given discretion to inform the young patient's parents that treatment has taken place? For example, see Minn. Stat. Ann. §144.346 (1998 & Supp. 2005), at p. 368 supra.

(2) Emancipation Exception. At common law an "emancipated" minor could consent to medical treatment and a doctor would not be liable for treatment without parental consent. Marriage was considered an act of emancipation. State statutes, in a variety of ways, provide for exceptions for "emancipated" or "mature" minors. Some statutes appear simply to codify the common law. Others modify the common law definition. Minnesota, for example, requires that the minor live "separate and apart from parents or legal guardian" and manage "personal financial affairs," but, unlike common law emancipation, does not require parental assent or consent to living away from home. See p. 366 supra. Still other states allow treatment of a minor without parental consent when the minor is of sufficient intelligence to understand and appreciate the "consequences" of the treatment. See Ark. Stat. Ann. §20-9-602 (2000), supra p. 364. Finally, some states by statute have simply lowered the age of consent. Ala. Code §22-8-4 (1997), supra p. 365. For an argument in favor of expanding the minor's right to consent, see Andrew Newman, Adolescent Consent to Routine Medical and Surgical Treatment, 22 J. Legal Med. 501 (2001).

(3) Alternative Forms of Consent. Consider these alternative methods of giving young people some say in their medical treatment:

a. Some states use an age-based line and simply adopt a lower age requirement. What are the advantages and disadvantages of age-based lines? Is the normal line today, drawn at 18, too high?

b. What are the advantages of using emancipation as the criterion? When parents no longer are responsible for a young person's support, does it necessarily follow that the self-supporting young person is mature enough to make his or her own medical decisions? Does the emancipation exception simply reflect the idea that parental consent is inconvenient when a young person is no longer living at home? Are 17-year-old college students, living in a dormitory and supported by their parents, emancipated at common law? Is living away from one's parents a better rule of thumb than age for determining when one is mature enough to weigh medical questions properly? If so, why should a "responsible" 17-year-old living at home have fewer rights than a Minnesota runaway?

c. What are the advantages and disadvantages of a more discretionary standard allowing the young person to consent to his own treatment if in a doctor's judgment the young person is sufficiently mature to understand the treatment and its consequences?

(4) Limits of Exception.   Where there is an exception for an emancipated or mature minor, should this exception apply to *all* kinds of medical treatment? Suppose a 17-year-old runaway wishes to have a vasectomy. Should an emancipated 14-year-old in Alabama have the same rights to refuse essential medical treatment as an adult? Can an adult refuse essential life-saving treatment? See Chapter 1, p. 33.

(5) Bypass Proceedings.   If parents cannot "veto" a young woman's medical decision to have an abortion, why should parental consent be required for other medical treatment of postpubescent adolescents? Alternatively, if bypass procedures are provided to minors in the abortion context, should such procedures also be available in the mental health context? See Richard E. Redding, Children's Competence to Provide Informed Consent for Mental Health Treatment, 50 Wash. & Lee L. Rev. 695, 719 (1993) (so arguing).

(6) Cognitive Competence.   Do adolescents have the cognitive competence to consent to medical treatment? Do they think the same way adults do? Consider the relevance of the psychological research that follows on the issue of when minors should have the right to consent to their own medical treatment.

Lois A. Weithorn, Children's Capacities in Legal Contexts
Children, Mental Health, and the Law 35-39 (N. Dickon Reppucci et al. eds., 1984)

The doctrine of informed consent requires that three conditions be met in order for a treatment decision to be considered legally valid. The decision must be informed (i.e., the patient must be provided with adequate information about the proposed and alternative treatments), voluntary (i.e., the patient must make the treatment decision free from coercion or unfair inducements), and competent. The predominant legal standard for competency emphasizes that the patient must have an "appreciation" of the nature, extent, and probable consequences of the conduct consented to. Although the notion of appreciation is not clearly defined by the law, it has been viewed by some as a higher level of understanding, requiring the individual to think abstractly and to make inferences about the implications of the proposed treatments for oneself.[3] In practice, however, competency to consent to treatment is typically evaluated by examining the patient's understanding of the basic factual information presented by the attending professional. Consent forms stress such factual information. Roth et al.[4] and Meisel[5] reviewed several additional standards of competency, which may be applied in various contexts. The "rational reasons" or "reasonable

---

[3] P.S. Appelbaum & L.H. Roth, Clinical Issues in the Assessment of Competency, Am. J. of Psychiatry 138(11), 1462-1467 (1981); Weithorn, L.A., Developmental Factors and Competence to Make Informed Treatment Decisions, 5 Child and Youth Services 85-100 (1982).

[4] L.H. Roth, A. Meisel, & C.W. Lidz, Tests of Competency to Consent to Treatment, Am. J. of Psychiatry 134, 279-284 (1977).

[5] A. Meisel, The "Exceptions" to the Informed Consent Doctrine: Striking a Balance Between Competing Values in Medical Decision Making, Wisc. L.J. 413-488 (1979).

decision-making process" standard emphasizes the manner in which the patient arrives at a decision. Did the patient consider the information about the risks and benefits of the various treatments provided by attending professionals? The "evidence of choice" test requires that patients merely express a preference regarding treatment. Finally, the "reasonable outcome" test examines the choice the patient has made to determine whether it is reasonable. This judgment may be made by comparing the patient's choice to prevailing professional opinion as to what are the "best" choices, or to a standard of the choice a "hypothetical reasonable person" might select. . . .

Weithorn[7] and Grisso and Vierling[8] provide discussions of the psychological skills that appear to be required in order to make a competent treatment decision. Based on a Piagetian analysis,[9] these authors predict that most adolescents will have the necessary cognitive skills to demonstrate competency according to the highest standard: appreciation. Since the standard of appreciation requires that individuals understand at a relatively abstract level information about future possibilities resulting from each of several choices, it appears that formal operational thinking would be a prerequisite. Formal operational structures allow individuals to conceptualize multiple abstract possibilities and to hypothesize about the consequences of various courses of action. Since children begin to develop formal operational structures at about age 11, and the stage reaches a point of equilibrium at about age 14, it would appear that 14-year-olds and older adolescents would meet the highest standards of competency.

Weithorn and Campbell[10] investigated the law's presumptions regarding the competency of minors to consent to treatment. Children aged 9 and 14 were compared with adults aged 18 and 21. All subjects were presented with four hypothetical vignettes about individuals suffering from medical or psychological disorders who had to choose among several treatment options. The subjects were presented with detailed information about the nature, purpose, risks, and benefits of the alternative treatments, and were asked to choose among them. The subjects were then asked a series of standardized questions about their decisions, and about the vignettes. The responses were scored according to criteria on several scales, each scale having been designed to measure competency according to one of the legal standards reviewed above.

In general, the findings strongly supported hypothetical predictions. Fourteen-year-olds were found not to differ from adults in most instances according to all scales of competency: inferential understanding (i.e., appreciation), factual understanding, reasoning, reasonable outcome, and evidence of choice. By contrast, 9-year-olds were found to perform significantly less well on the understanding and reasoning scales. However, despite the 9-year-olds' poorer performance on these scales, they did not differ significantly from the adults with respect to the choices

---

[7] [Weithorn, *supra* note 3].

[8] T. Grisso & L. Vierling, Minors' Consent to Treatment: A Developmental Perspective, Professional Psychology, 9, 412-427 (1978).

[9] Inhelder, B., & Piaget, J., The Growth of Logical Thinking (1958); Piaget, J., Intellectual Evolution From Adolescence to Adulthood, 15 Human Development 1-12 (1972).

[10] L.A. Weithorn & S.B. Campbell, The Competency of Children and Adolescents to Make Informed Treatment Decisions, Child Development 53, 1589-1599 (1982).

they selected (i.e., reasonable outcome test), in three or four instances. This finding suggests that full understanding and the most sophisticated reasoning process may not be prerequisites for reaching a reasonable decision. . . .

D. DISABLED NEWBORNS

1. Introduction

PROBLEMS

(1) Baby *A*, a newborn with Down's syndrome, has an intestinal obstruction that makes food digestion impossible. The chances of a successful operation to correct the obstruction are very good. Without the operation, the baby will starve to death within two weeks. Down's syndrome is a chromosomal disorder that produces mental retardation and several physical characteristics, such as a distinctively shaped head, neck, and abdomen. There is no known treatment. Many such babies can experience physical and mental growth, receive and give love, and be trained to feed and clothe themselves, as well as to perform simple kinds of work. Many live into adulthood. After consulting with family members, attending physicians, minister, and the hospital geneticist, Baby *A*'s parents decide not to consent to surgery to correct the intestinal blockage. See In re Infant Doe, No. GU 8204-004A (Monroe County Cir. Ct., Ind., Apr. 12, 1982).

(2) Baby *B* is an infant who is born with a medical condition known as anencephaly, a condition characterized by an absence of most of the brain but the presence of a functioning brain stem. Most such babies die within a short time after birth. When Baby *B* is born, she suffers severe respiratory difficulties. The hospital physicians, baby's father and members of the hospital ethics committee all recommend withholding the use of a mechanical ventilator to help the infant breathe, reasoning that such care would prolong the baby's inevitable death. They want to provide only comfort measures to Baby *B* (not life-sustaining treatment). However, Baby *B*'s mother, who is a fundamentalist Christian, insists that the baby be placed on the ventilator. See generally Matter of Baby K., 16 F.3d 590 (4th Cir. 1994), *cert. denied*, 513 U.S. 825 (1994).

(3) Mr. and Mrs. Smith come to the hospital when Mrs. Smith goes into premature labor at 23 weeks of pregnancy. The Smith's physician tells the Smiths that he has never seen such a premature baby survive and that if their infant did survive, the baby would be likely to suffer from severe physical and mental impairment. The Smiths decide that they do not want the hospital staff to undertake "heroic measures" to save their infant's life. They ask that the hospital not provide any life-sustaining measures. They are concerned about the effect of caring for a severely impaired infant on their two older children, their marriage, and their careers. The hospital administrator is concerned about the extent of the hospital's liability and orders the neonatologist to resuscitate the baby after birth. Baby *C* suffers from severe mental and physical impairment, requires constant operations to be kept

alive, and has no prospect of being able to feed himself or of becoming aware of his own existence. Compare Miller ex rel. Miller v. HCA, Inc., 118 S.W.3d 758 (Tex. 2003) (discussed infra) with Preston v. Meriter Hosp., Inc., 678 N.W.2d 347 (Wis. Ct. App. 2004).

a. In the above examples, do the parents have the right to withhold consent or insist on treatment? May the doctor and hospital rely on the parents' decision? Must the doctor and hospital rely on the parents' decision? Should the hospital staff ask a juvenile court to take jurisdiction of the baby as a "neglected child"? As an attorney, what would you advise the parents, the attending doctor, and the hospital about potential civil and criminal liability? (See also the federal Child Abuse Amendments of 1984, discussed infra.)

b. Would your answers be different if, rather than permitting the baby to die from nontreatment, a physician gave the baby a lethal injection?

c. What are the moral and legal responsibilities to these children? What factors should make a difference when deciding what treatment to give to a disabled newborn? Survival rate? Life expectancy? Self-awareness? Quality of the baby's life? Burdens on the family? Cost of treatment? Who should decide? By what procedure?

Consider the materials in this chapter in thinking about these questions.

2. Relevant Materials

One of the "miracles" of modern medicine has been the remarkable advances in neonatal care in the past few decades. Beginning in 1970, the neonatal mortality rate decreased significantly. For example, the neonatal mortality rate dropped by half in the decade from 1970 to 1980 — the greatest proportional decrease in any decade since national birth statistics were first gathered in 1915.[28] Particularly dramatic gains have been made in the survival rate of infants weighing less than 1,000 grams (2.2 lbs). However, not all seriously ill newborns will survive or thrive. Of those who do survive, many will suffer severe physical and/or mental impairments — either from their conditions or as a result of medical intervention. The extent of the infants' eventual impairment is often unknown at birth.

The case of Miller ex rel. Miller v. HCA, infra, explores the issue of parents' refusal of treatment in the context of a severely premature newborn whose prognosis is uncertain. The excerpt by Steven Smith explains the origins of the controversy about the ethics of forgoing treatment for seriously disabled newborns and the ensuing federal legislation. Subsequent excerpts highlight the moral and ethical issues raised by the withholding of medical care to disabled newborns.

Miller ex rel. Miller v. HCA, Inc.
118 S.W.3d 758 (Tex. 2003)

Justice ENOCH delivered the opinion of the Court.

The narrow question we must decide is whether Texas law recognizes a claim by parents for either battery or negligence because their premature infant, born alive

---

[28] President's Commission for the Study of Ethical Problems in Medicine and Biomedical and Behavioral Research, Deciding to Forgo Life-Sustaining Treatment, Pub. L. No. 83-17978, at 197-198.

but in distress at only twenty-three weeks of gestation, was provided resuscitative medical treatment by physicians at a hospital without parental consent. . . .

The unfortunate circumstances of this case began in August 1990, when approximately four months before her due date, Karla Miller was admitted to Woman's Hospital of Texas in premature labor. An ultrasound revealed that Karla's fetus weighed about 629 grams or 1 1/4 pounds and had a gestational age of approximately twenty-three weeks. Because of the fetus's prematurity, Karla's physicians began administering a drug designed to stop labor.

Karla's physicians subsequently discovered that Karla had an infection that could endanger her life and require them to induce delivery. Dr. Mark Jacobs, Karla's obstetrician, and Dr. Donald Kelley, a neonatologist at the Hospital, informed Karla and her husband, Mark Miller, that if they had to induce delivery, the infant had little chance of being born alive. The physicians also informed the Millers that if the infant was born alive, it would most probably suffer severe impairments, including cerebral palsy, brain hemorrhaging, blindness, lung disease, pulmonary infections, and mental retardation. Mark testified at trial that the physicians told him they had never had such a premature infant live and that anything they did to sustain the infant's life would be guesswork.

After their discussion, Drs. Jacobs and Kelley asked the Millers to decide whether physicians should treat the infant upon birth if they were forced to induce delivery. At approximately noon that day, the Millers informed Drs. Jacob and Kelley that they wanted no heroic measures performed on the infant and they wanted nature to take its course. Mark testified that he understood heroic measures to mean performing resuscitation, chest massage, and using life support machines. Dr. Kelley recorded the Millers' request in Karla's medical notes, and Dr. Jacobs informed the medical staff at the Hospital that no neonatologist would be needed at delivery. Mark then left the Hospital to make funeral arrangements for the infant.

In the meantime, the nursing staff informed other Hospital personnel of Dr. Jacobs' instruction that no neonatologist would be present in the delivery room when the Millers' infant was born. An afternoon of meetings involving Hospital administrators and physicians followed. Between approximately 4:00 P.M. and 4:30 P.M. that day, Anna Summerfield, the director of the Hospital's neonatal intensive care unit, and several physicians, including Dr. Jacobs, met with Mark upon his return to the Hospital to further discuss the situation. Mark testified that Ms. Summerfield announced at the meeting that the Hospital had a policy requiring resuscitation of any baby who was born weighing over 500 grams. Although Ms. Summerfield agreed that she said that, the only written Hospital policy produced described the Natural Death Act and did not mention resuscitating infants over 500 grams.

Moreover, the physicians at the meeting testified that they and Hospital administrators agreed only that a neonatologist would be present to evaluate the Millers' infant at birth and decide whether to resuscitate based on the infant's condition at that time. As Dr. Jacobs testified:

> [W]hat we finally decided that everyone wanted to do was to not make the call prior to the time we actually saw the baby. Deliver the baby, because you see there was this [question] is the baby really 23 weeks, or is the baby further along, how

big is the baby, what are we dealing with. We decided to let the neonatologist make
the call by looking directly at the baby at birth.

Another physician who attended the meeting agreed, testifying that to deny
any attempts at resuscitation without seeing the infant's condition would be
inappropriate and below the standard of care. . . .

Mark testified that, after the meeting, Hospital administrators asked him to
sign a consent form allowing resuscitation according to the Hospital's plan, but he
refused. Mark further testified that when he asked how he could prevent resuscitation, Hospital administrators told him that he could do so by removing Karla from
the Hospital, which was not a viable option given her condition. Dr. Jacobs then
noted in Karla's medical charts that a plan for evaluating the infant upon her birth
was discussed at that afternoon meeting.

That evening, Karla's condition worsened and her amniotic sac broke.
Dr. Jacobs determined that he would have to augment labor so that the infant would
be delivered before further complications to Karla's health developed. Dr. Jacobs
accordingly stopped administering the drug to Karla that was designed to stop labor,
substituting instead a drug designed to augment labor. At 11:30 P.M. that night, Karla
delivered a premature female infant weighing 615 grams, which the Millers named
Sidney. Sidney's actual gestational age was twenty-three and one-seventh weeks.
And she was born alive.

[Dr. Eduardo Otero, the neonatologist present in the delivery room when Sidney
was born] noted that Sidney had a heart beat, albeit at a rate below that normally
found in full-term babies. He further noted that Sidney, although blue in color and
limp, gasped for air, spontaneously cried, and grimaced. Dr. Otero also noted that
Sidney displayed no dysmorphic features other than being premature. He immediately "bagged" and "intubated" Sidney to oxygenate her blood; he then placed her
on ventilation. He explained why:

> Because this baby is alive and this is a baby that has a reasonable chance of living.
> And again, this is a baby that is not necessarily going to have problems later on.
> There are babies that survive at this gestational age that — with this birth weight,
> that later on go on and do well.

Neither Karla nor Mark objected at the time to the treatment provided.

Sidney initially responded well to the treatment. . . . But at some point during
the first few days after birth, Sidney suffered a brain hemorrhage — a complication
not uncommon in infants born so prematurely. [A]s predicted by Karla's physicians,
the hemorrhage caused Sidney to suffer severe physical and mental impairments.
At the time of trial, Sidney was seven years old and could not walk, talk, feed
herself, or sit up on her own. The evidence demonstrated that Sidney was legally
blind, suffered from severe mental retardation, cerebral palsy, seizures, and spastic
quadriparesis in her limbs. She could not be toilet-trained and required a shunt in
her brain to drain fluids that accumulate there and needed care twenty-four hours a
day. The evidence further demonstrated that her circumstances will not change.

[The Millers asserted battery and negligence claims against HCA and the
Hospital.] The Millers' claims stemmed from their allegations that despite their

instructions to the contrary, the Hospital not only resuscitated Sidney but performed experimental procedures and administered experimental drugs, without which, in all reasonable medical probability, Sidney would not have survived. . . . The jury concluded that HCA and the Hospital were grossly negligent and that the Hospital acted with malice. . . . The trial court rendered judgment jointly and severally against the HCA defendants on the jury's verdict of $29,400,000 in actual damages for medical expenses, $17,503,066 in prejudgment interest, and $13,500,000 in exemplary damages. HCA appealed.

[The appellate court reversed, holding that parents have the right to withhold life-sustaining treatment (under the state Natural Death Act) only when their baby's condition is certified as terminal. Here, because Sidney's condition was not certified as terminal, the Millers did not have the statutory right to refuse treatment. The appellate court also found that no court order was required to override the parents' refusal because the need for life-sustaining treatment became urgent only when the nonterminally ill baby was under a health provider's care. The dissenting judge disagreed, contending: (1) a court order was required to override the parents' decision; (2) the state Natural Death Act was not mandatory in this context; (3) the parents' choice was protected by the U.S. Constitution; and (4) the court erroneously applied an "emergency exception" when there was no finding of the existence of a medical emergency giving the hospital the right to intervene.]

This case requires us to determine the respective roles that parents and health-care providers play in deciding whether to treat an infant who is born alive but in distress and is so premature that, despite advancements in neonatal intensive care, has a largely uncertain prognosis. [N]either the Texas Legislature nor our case law has addressed this specific situation. . . .

Generally speaking, the custody, care, and nurture of an infant resides in the first instance with the parents. As the United States Supreme Court has acknowledged, parents are presumed to be the appropriate decision-makers for their infants:

> Our jurisprudence historically has reflected Western civilization concepts of the family as a unit with broad parental authority over minor children. Our cases have consistently followed that course; our constitutional system long ago rejected any notion that a child is "the mere creature of the State" and, on the contrary, asserted that parents generally "have the right, coupled with the high duty, to recognize and prepare [their children] for additional obligations." . . . Surely, this includes a "high duty" to recognize symptoms of illness and to seek and follow medical advice. The law's concept of the family rests on a presumption that parents possess what a child lacks in maturity, experience, and capacity for judgment required for making life's difficult decisions. More important, historically it has recognized that natural bonds of affection lead parents to act in the best interests of their children [citing Parham v. J.R., 442 U.S. 584, 602 (1979)].

. . . Of course, this broad grant of parental decision-making authority is not without limits. The State's role as parens patriae permits it to intercede in parental decision-making under certain circumstances. As the United States Supreme Court has noted:

[A]s persons unable to protect themselves, infants fall under the parens patriae power of the state. In the exercise of this authority, the state not only punishes parents whose conduct has amounted to abuse or neglect of their children but may also supervene parental decisions before they become operative to ensure that the choices made are not so detrimental to a child's interests as to amount to neglect and abuse. [Bowen v. American Hosp. Assn., 476 U.S. 610, 627 n. 13 (1986).]

But the Supreme Court has also pointed out:

[A]s long as parents choose from professionally accepted treatment options the choice is rarely reviewed in court and even less frequently supervened . . . [Id.].

[W]e now determine whether the Millers can maintain their battery and negligence claims against HCA. [W]e only address whether the Hospital was required to seek court intervention to overturn the lack of parental consent — which it undisputedly did not do — before Dr. Otero could treat Sidney without committing a battery.

The Millers acknowledge that numerous physicians at trial agreed that, absent an emergency situation, the proper course of action is court intervention when health care providers disagree with parents' refusal to consent to a child's treatment. And the Millers contend that, as a matter of law, no emergency existed that would excuse the Hospital's treatment of Sidney without their consent or a court order overriding their refusal to consent. . . . But the Millers' reasoning fails to recognize that, in this case, the evidence established that Sidney could only be properly evaluated when she was born. Any decision the Millers made before Sidney's birth concerning her treatment at or after her birth would necessarily be based on speculation. Therefore, we reject the Millers' argument that a decision could adequately be made pre-birth that denying all post-birth resuscitative treatment would be in Sidney's best interest. Such a decision could not control whether the circumstances facing Dr. Otero were emergent because it would not have been a fully informed one according to the evidence in this case.

The Millers point out that physicians routinely ask parents to make pre-birth treatment choices for their infants including whether to accept or refuse in utero medical treatment and to continue or terminate a pregnancy. While that may be entirely true, the evidence here established that the time for evaluating Sidney was when she was born. The evidence further reflected that Sidney was born alive but in distress. At that time, Dr. Otero had to make a split-second decision on whether to provide life-sustaining treatment. While the Millers were both present in the delivery room, there was simply no time to obtain their consent to treatment or to institute legal proceedings to challenge their withholding of consent, had the Millers done so, without jeopardizing Sidney's life. . . . . We agree that, whenever possible, obtaining consent in writing to evaluate a premature infant at birth and to render any warranted medical treatment is the best course of action. And physicians and hospitals should always strive to do so. But if such consent is not forthcoming, or is affirmatively denied, we decline to impose liability on a physician solely for providing life-sustaining treatment under emergent circumstances to a new-born infant without that consent. . . .

NOTES AND QUESTIONS

(1) Who Should Decide?   *Miller* focuses on the issue: who should decide whether an extremely premature infant who faces an uncertain prognosis (regarding the likelihood of suffering severe, permanent physical and mental impairment) should receive life-sustaining treatment? The parents? Medical professionals? The courts? According to what standard(s)? What factors should be taken into account?

(2) Additional Action.   What action do you think the hospital should have taken? Should it have sought a court order to override the parents' wishes? One commentator suggests that the physicians should have engaged in a "collaborative medical decisionmaking model" with the Millers, rather than unilaterally deciding to provide life-sustaining treatment. Holly O'Neal Rumbaugh, Miller v. HCA, Inc.: Disempowering Parents from Making Medical Treatment Decisions for Severely Premature Babies, 41 Hous. L. Rev. 675, 704 (2004). Do you agree? What additional action might the parents have taken? Could the parents be criminally liable for their nontreatment decision — i.e., the failure to provide necessary medical care to their infant?

(3) Emergency.   Was this an emergency situation that would excuse the hospital for treating the infant absent parental consent or a court order? Did the hospital's indecision and delay (between the physicians' meeting and the birth) create the emergency that justified their failure to obtain the parents' consent? *Miller* held that the provision of medical treatment to an infant during "emergent circumstances" (even in the face of parental refusal of consent) is an exception to the general rule that a physician commits battery by providing treatment without parental consent. Does this imply that a parent can never refuse consent to medical treatment for a severely premature infant *prior* to birth?

(4) Applicable Law.   Because *Miller* raised an issue of first impression, the state supreme court looked to relevant statutory and case law. How helpful in the determination to permit the withholding of life-sustaining treatment is a given state's Natural Death Act (i.e., giving parents the right to withhold treatment when the infant's condition is certifiably "terminal")? According to Texas law, a terminal condition is one caused "by injury, disease, or illness." Tex. Health & Safety Code §166.002(13). The Texas Natural Death Act was amended in 1999 and recodified as the Advance Directives Act. See Tex. Health & Safety Code Ann. §§166.001-.166 (Vernon Supp. 2000). Was the Miller's infant in a "terminal" condition? Alternatively, how helpful in the determination is the judicially applied best-interests-of-the-child standard?

(5) Tort Liability.   A few states (but not the jurisdiction in *Miller*) recognize a wrongful life cause of action — a tort claim brought on behalf of a child with major disabilities that were caused by another's negligence and that caused the child's severely impaired life. See Deana A. Pollard, Wrongful Analysis in Wrongful Life Jurisprudence, 55 Ala. L. Rev. 327, 329 (2004) (pointing out that three states currently recognize wrongful life claims). See also Willis v. Wu, 607 S.E.2d 63 (S.C. 2004) (rejecting cause of action). The cause of action is premised on the idea that no life is better than a significantly impaired life. Should courts be more willing to recognize such claims? Does recognition of such claims adequately address the issues raised by *Miller*?

On the issue of nontreatment, see also Preston v. Meriter Hosp., Inc., 678 N.W.2d 347 (Wis. Ct. App. 2004) (affirming summary judgment for hospital in suit by mother of infant (born at 23 weeks of gestation) who died shortly after birth when hospital refused to resuscitate or treat the child).

NOTE: FEDERAL LEGISLATION

Steven R. Smith, Disabled Newborns and the Federal Child Abuse Amendments: Tenuous Protection
37 Hastings L.J. 765, 789-804 (1986)

Infant Doe Case

Seldom in American law has such a small case had such an immediate impact as did Indiana's *Infant Doe* case.[88] It lasted less than six days, but led to various lawsuits, several state statutes, a new federal statute, and new federal regulations. *Infant Doe* was the first case of its kind to attract significant national attention.

. . . Infant Doe apparently was born with two serious defects: no connection between the esophagus and the stomach, and a connection between the trachea and the esophagus. Corrective surgery was possible. Without treatment, death was certain either from lack of food and water, which could not be provided because there was no connection to the stomach, or from suffocation. Infant Doe also suffered from Down's syndrome. The child's parents refused to consent to surgery and decided to withhold food and water. The state court refused to order treatment, and the Indiana Supreme Court declined to overturn the lower court's ruling. Six days after birth the infant died, as certiorari was being sought from the United States Supreme Court. This case is notable because it got to court at all. Ordinarily such decisions are made in private. Only if the physician seriously disagrees with the decision to withhold treatment is any court activity likely.

Initial Federal Response

At the time the *Infant Doe* case arose, no federal law explicitly prohibited withholding of treatment from infants. The federal government endeavored to use section 504 of the Rehabilitation Act of 1973, which prohibits discrimination against the disabled by federally funded programs, to fill this void.[95] About a month after Infant Doe's death, the Department of Health and Human Services ("HHS") sent a "Notice to Health Care Providers" concerning "discriminating against the handicapped by withholding treatment or nourishment."[96] The notice warned hospitals that they risked the loss of federal funding by failing to treat infants because of their mental or physical handicap. HHS pointed out current regulations implementing

---

[88] In re Infant Doe, No. GU 8204-004A (Monroe County Cir. Ct., Ind. Apr. 12, 1982) (declaratory judgment), *cert. denied sub nom.*, Infant Doe v. Bloomington Hosp., 464 U.S. 961 (1983). . . .

[95] 29 U.S.C. §794 (1982); . . .

[96] Notice to Health Care Providers from Betty Lous Dotson, Director, Office for Civil Rights, Department of Health & Human Services (May 18, 1982).

section 504[98] and informed hospitals that they should counsel parents against refusing treatment and refuse to aid parents who decide to withhold treatment or nourishment.

This notice was followed in 1983 by a formal HHS "interim final" regulation.[100] The regulation provided that withholding food or customary medical treatment from disabled infants violated section 504 of the Rehabilitation Act. It further required that hospitals post a notice indicating that such discrimination is prohibited by federal law. This notice had to include a "hotline" number that anyone could use to report known or suspected withholding of treatment. The regulations also provided for federal investigation and intervention to protect the life of a disabled individual.

Hospitals and medical groups immediately challenged these regulations in federal court,[101] and the court invalidated the regulations essentially on procedural grounds. HHS had adopted the rule without the public notice or thirty-day delay required by the Administrative Procedure Act and also apparently had neglected to consider a number of important factors, including the disruptive effect of the regulations, the harm that could result from removing an infant from a hospital, the malpractice risks, and the allocation of scarce medical and economic resources.

Shortly after the invalidation of the initial procedure, HHS proposed new procedures that, with very modest changes, were the same as the earlier interim final regulations. After receiving nearly 17,000 comments on the proposed regulations, HHS modified and adopted them early in 1984.[105] The new regulations continued the hotline and posting of notice requirements, but they still suffered from considerable ambiguity about what factors could be considered in deciding to withhold treatment. The regulations permitted medical factors to be taken into account, but prohibited "nonmedical considerations from being injected into the decision-making process." The final regulations also encouraged hospitals to establish infant care review committees ("ICRCs"). These committees were only to be advisory and were not authorized to permit the withholding of treatment from infants.

While the process of adopting federal regulations was underway, another case arose in New York that put them to rest. This case was considerably different from the Indiana *Infant Doe* case. While the New York infant, "Baby Doe," did suffer from a variety of mental and physical abnormalities, her situation was not as clearly life-threatening as had been Infant Doe's situation in Indiana. This child ultimately left the hospital and went home with her parents.[108] Both private individuals and the federal government sought to intervene to require treatment on the child's behalf. These private efforts were unsuccessful, however. The New York court held that, given the record in this case, as a matter of procedure, only the appropriate state agency could bring the action; private individuals could not.[109] The federal government attempted to enter the case under the new federal discrimination

---

[98] 45 C.F.R. pt. 84 (1981).

[100] 48 Fed. Reg. 9630 (1983) (codified at 45 C.F.R. pt. 84 (1985)).

[101] American Academy of Pediatrics v. Heckler, 561 F. Supp. 395 (D.D.C. 1983), *aff' d sub nom.* Bowen v. American Hosp. Ass'n, 106 S. Ct. 2101 (1986).

[105] 49 Fed. Reg. 1622 (1984) (codified at 45 C.F.R. 84 (1985)).

[108] See Vitiello, The Baby Jane Doe Litigation and Section 504: An Exercise in Raw Executive Power, 17 Conn. L. Rev. 95, 106 (1984).

[109] Weber v. Stony Brook Hosp., 60 N.Y.2d 208, 456 N.E.2d 1186, 469 N.Y.S.2d 63, *cert. denied,* 464 U.S. 1026 (1983).

provisions contained in section 504.[110] After a careful review of the Rehabilitation Act's legislative history, the Second Circuit ultimately rejected this attempt, concluding that Congress had not intended to authorize HHS to become involved in decisions to refuse treatment for seriously ill infants. The Supreme Court has reviewed the issues raised in this case and has agreed with the Second Circuit's holding.[112]

A Change of Focus

With the decision of the Second Circuit in the Baby Jane Doe case, the government's focus has changed from regulatory approaches interpreting section 504 to the establishment of new statutory authority dealing directly with life-saving treatment for infants. Its focus also has changed from protecting newborns under legislation intended to prohibit discrimination against the disabled to legislation intended to reduce the abuse and neglect of children. . . .

The major provision of the legislation regarding withdrawal of life-saving treatment from infants was the addition of a new clause to the federal child abuse law. Existing federal law required states to meet certain criteria to qualify for federal child abuse and neglect prevention funds. The 1984 amendment [codified at 42 U.S.C. §5103(b)(K) (West Supp. 1985)] provided that . . . states must have procedures or programs within the state child protective services to respond to instances of withholding medical treatment from disabled infants. States must provide for the appointment of someone in hospitals with whom the state can deal when nontreatment questions arise, who also must provide for prompt notification of instances of suspected medical neglect. Finally, the new law requires that states allow the state child protective services system "to pursue any legal remedies, including the authority to initiate legal proceedings in a court of competent jurisdiction, as may be necessary to prevent the withholding of medically indicated treatment from disabled infants with life-threatening conditions."

Central to the new provision is the term "withholding of medically indicated treatment," defined as the failure to "respond to the infant's life-threatening condition" in a way that is "most likely to be effective in ameliorating or correcting" all life-threatening conditions. Appropriate or necessary treatment must be determined according to the treating physician's "reasonable medical judgment" and specifically includes food, water, and medication. Presumably, treatment also includes surgery and the broad range of all forms of medical intervention.

The statute recognizes several categories in which treatment "other than appropriate nutrition, hydration, or medication" need not be provided to infants. These exceptions to the requirement that lifesaving treatment be given are:

1. When the child is irreversibly comatose.
2. When treatment would "merely prolong dying."
3. When the treatment would not be effective in ameliorating or correcting all of the life-threatening conditions.

---

[110] United States v. University Hosp., 575 F. Supp. 607 (E.D.N.Y. 1983), *aff'd*, 729 F.2d 144 (2d Cir. 1984).

[112] Bowen v. American Hosp. Assn., [476 U.S. 610 (1986)].

4. When the treatment "would otherwise be futile" in terms of the survival of the infant.

5. When imposing the treatment would be "virtually futile" in terms of survival and the treatment itself "under such circumstances would be inhumane."

The statute apparently excludes the provision of "appropriate" food, water, and medication from the treatment permitted to be withdrawn under these exceptions; therefore, these basic necessities must be provided even if one of the above treatment exceptions is present. Of course, by including the qualifying word, "appropriate," the statute implies that there are undefined conditions in which food, water, or medication are "inappropriate."

The Act also does not authorize the government to "establish standards prescribing specific medical treatment for specific conditions" and does not affect any rights or protections under section 504 of the Rehabilitation Act. Neither of these provisions should have a major impact on the Act's implementation. They merely leave open the question of whether the government may continue to push for the treatment of disabled newborns through section 504 of the Rehabilitation Act. The new statute also requires HHS to establish model guidelines concerning infant care review committees. . . .

HHS Regulations

[HHS's final regulations do provide] regulatory definitions of the terms "infant" and "reasonable medical judgment." An "infant" is defined as someone less than one year of age. The regulations also imply that "infant" status extends beyond the first year if the child has been "continuously hospitalized since birth, and was born extremely prematurely or . . . has a long term disability." The definition of "reasonable medical judgment" essentially tracks the common-law tort definition and requires that such judgments "be made by a reasonably prudent physician, knowledgeable about the case and the treatment possibilities with respect to the medical conditions involved." Both of these definitions were taken directly from the congressional conference report.

The appendix to the regulations is four times the length of the interpretive guidelines, and its length suggests the difficulty that HHS had in trying to establish acceptable but clear regulations. In this appendix, HHS notes that it "does not seek to establish these interpretive guidelines as binding rules of law." Instead, the guidelines are "intended to assist in interpreting the statutory definition so that it may be rationally and thoughtfully applied in specific contexts in a manner fully consistent with the legislative intent." . . .

Among the noteworthy points made in the appendix are the following:

(1) Decisions to withhold medically indicated treatment may *not* be based on "subjective opinions about the future 'quality of life' of a retarded or disabled person."

(2) Even when the statute permits the withholding of medically indicated treatment, "the infant must nonetheless be provided with appropriate nutrition, hydration, and medication."

(3) "Life-threatening" conditions include conditions that "significantly increase the risk of the onset of complications that may threaten the life of the infant."

(4) "Treatment" includes adequate evaluation, the referral of the infant to other physicians when necessary, and multiple medical or surgical procedures over a period of time.

(5) "Merely prolong dying" and related provisions that refer to treatments that would extend life only a short time do not apply only when death is "imminent." Treatment must be provided, however, when "many years of life will result from the provision of treatment or where the prognosis is not death in the near future but rather in the more distant future." It is up to the physician's exercise of reasonable medical judgment "to determine whether the prognosis of death, because of its nearness in time, is such that the treatment would not be medically indicated."

(6) The term "virtually futile" treatment means treatment that is highly unlikely to prevent death in the near future.

The regulations also propose model guidelines for establishing infant care review committees. Although the regulations encourage hospitals to establish ICRCs, they are not required to do so. If hospitals do establish them, the committees are not bound to conform to the guidelines suggested by HHS. The purposes of the ICRCs are: to offer counseling in specific cases involving disabled infants; to recommend institutional policies concerning disabled infants; and to educate hospital personnel and families of disabled infants concerning counseling, rehabilitative services, and support organizations. The regulations urge that the ICRC be able to be convened within twenty-four hours or less when there is disagreement between the infant's family and physician concerning withholding treatment or when the decision is made to withhold life-sustaining treatment "in certain categories of cases" identified in ICRC policies. The ICRC may "meet" by telephone when it cannot convene quickly enough in person. . . .

3. Philosophy

Robert H. Mnookin, Two Puzzles
1984 Ariz. St. L.J. 667, 677-679

. . . At a very basic level, there is fundamental disagreement among ethicists concerning the approach and the principles that should inform the analysis of decisions to withhold or withdraw treatment from handicapped newborns.[32] . . .

At one end of the spectrum are those who suggest that all non-dying neonates must be treated, irrespective of handicap, because of the "sanctity of life."[33] Under such an approach, the interests of the infant's family and social burdens are to be

---

[32] For a useful survey of ethical thought with respect to nontreatment issues, see R. Weir, Selective Nontreatment of Handicapped Newborns: Moral Dilemmas in Neonatal Medicine, chs. 6 &7 (1984).

[33] See, e.g., P. Ramsey, Ethics at the Edges of Life: Medical & Legal Intersections (1978). See generally R. Weir, supra note 32, at 146-152.

ignored. Nor is the expected quality of the child's handicapped life relevant. Paul Ramsey has argued, for example, that the severity of an infant's handicaps has no bearing on the decision whether or not to provide treatment: "We have no moral right to choose that some live and others die, when the medical indications for treatment are the same."[34] In more extreme forms, the sanctity of life approach involves a claim that every handicapped infant has an absolute and unwavering right to require that *all* measures be taken to preserve the child's life regardless of the quality of that life, the burdens imposed, the child's suffering, or the cost. This approach permits no balancing: human life, in whatever condition, is the ultimate good.

At the other extreme, there are utilitarians, Peter Singer and Michael Tooley most prominent among them, who find infanticide morally permissible in a wide range of circumstances.[35] Their moral calculus necessarily requires balancing, and it is legitimate and appropriate to consider both the parents' suffering and the social costs involved in raising handicapped children. They argue that it is not membership in the human species that matters, but rather, whether you have certain characteristics of personhood, such as self-consciousness or the ability to feel pain and suffering. If you lack these essential characteristics then your interests need not count in the calculus. "[E]veryday observation strongly suggests that there is no more reason for holding that a newborn baby has these capacities or enjoys these states (of personhood) than there is for holding that this is true of a newborn chimpanzee. [Consequently, the infanticide of newborns] is morally permissible in most cases when it is otherwise desirable."[36] And it makes no moral difference whether euthanasia is active or passive — i.e., whether the death occurs because treatment has been withheld or because a lethal injection has been given to end the neonate's life.

Between these extremes are a number of other approaches. For me the most persuasive is that suggested by Philippa Foot. She distinguishes between active and passive euthanasia, and suggests that withholding treatment is appropriate if, and only if, treatment is not in the patient's best interests. The question to ask is, "Is this death for the sake of the child himself?" If it is, and the doctor and parents are choosing death for that reason alone, then passive euthanasia is morally permissible. She forcefully argues that to take social burdens or familial interests into account is wrong.[37]

While this exclusive focus on the best interests of the child has substantial intuitive appeal, it does not provide a great deal of policy guidance in formulating more precise substantive standards or in deciding what to do in many cases. Even if one believes that the decision to terminate care for a handicapped newborn should be based only upon consideration of the infant's interests, what decision is best for the child? Often the best interests of a child are indeterminate and speculative. To decide what is best for a particular child, a decisionmaker must first make a set of predictions about the outcomes for the child under alternative courses of action. Then the decisionmaker must evaluate these different outcomes in light of some set of values in order to choose the best possible course of action under the

---

[34] P. Ramsey, supra note 33, at 19. . . .

[35] M. Tooley, Abortion and Infanticide (1983); P. Singer, Practical Ethics 122-57 (1979).

[36] M. Tooley, supra note 35.

[37] Foot, Euthanasia, 6 Phil. & Pub. Affairs 85-87, 109-12 (1977).

circumstances. For reasons I have developed at length in other contexts, making accurate predictions and choosing appropriate values are often very problematic.[38] The same uncertainty appears to hold with respect to handicapped newborns. Doctors acknowledge how difficult it often is accurately to predict at birth the severity of a child's eventual handicaps. And even with better predictions, there does not appear to be much of a social consensus about quality of life issues. An intolerable handicap for one person may be a challenging and fulfilling opportunity for another. What values should inform the choice for a particular child?. . .

DISCUSSION AND QUERIES

(1) Criminal prosecution for failure to treat a disabled newborn is rare. What explains the lack of prosecution of parents, doctors, and hospitals that decide to withhold treatment of disabled newborns? Is it the low visibility of the practice? Or is it because there is no social consensus that letting disabled newborns die is wrong? Or that the sanctions for homicide are too severe?

(2) Does the absence of prosecutions suggest that the criminal homicide laws should be changed to legalize apparent practices? Or does it suggest that the problems, if any, created by the possibility of criminal prosecutions are obviated by nonenforcement? John Robertson has described the present situation "as one in which prosecuting authorities, through the exercise of their discretion, have informally delegated authority to parents and physicians to decide the fate of defective newborns."[29] What are the advantages and disadvantages of this "informal delegation"? Consider the contrasting views that follow.

Raymond S. Duff & August B. Campbell, Moral and Ethical Dilemmas in the Special-Care Nursery
289 New Eng. J. Med. 890, 893-894 (1973)

Can families in the shock resulting from the birth of a defective child understand what faces them? Can they give truly "informed consent" for treatment or withholding treatment? Some of our colleagues answer no to both questions. In our opinion, if families regardless of background are heard sympathetically and at length and are given information and answers to their questions in words they understand, the problems of their children as well as the expected benefits and limits of any proposed care can be understood clearly in practically all instances. Parents *are* able to understand the implications of such things as chronic dyspnea, oxygen dependency, incontinence, paralysis, contractures, sexual handicaps and mental retardation. . . .

We do not know how often families and their physicians will make just decisions for severely handicapped children. Clearly, this issue is central in evaluation of the process of decision making that we have described. But we also ask, if these parties cannot make such decisions justly, who can?

[38] See R. Mnookin, In the Interest of Children (1985).
[29] John A. Robertson, Involuntary Euthanasia of Defective Newborns: A Legal Analysis, 27 Stan. L. Rev. 213, 243 (1975).

We recognize great variability and often much uncertainty in prognoses and in family capacities to deal with defective newborn infants. We also acknowledge that there are limits of support that society can or will give to assist handicapped persons and their families. Severely deforming conditions that are associated with little or no hope of a functional existence pose painful dilemmas for the laymen and professionals who must decide how to cope with severe handicaps. We believe the burdens of decision making must be borne by families and their professional advisers because they are most familiar with the respective situations. Since families primarily must live with and are most affected by the decisions, it therefore appears that society and the health professions should provide only general guidelines for decision making. Moreover, since variations between situations are so great, and the situations themselves so complex, it follows that much latitude in decision making should be expected and tolerated. Otherwise, the rules of society or the policies most convenient for medical technologists may become cruel masters of human beings instead of their servants. [W]e readily acknowledge that the extreme excesses of Hegelian "rational utility" under dictatorships must be avoided. Perhaps it is less recognized that the uncontrolled application of medical technology may be detrimental to individuals and families. . . . Physicians may hold excessive power over decision making by limiting or controlling the information made available to patients or families. It seems appropriate that the profession be held accountable for presenting fully all management options and their expected consequences. Also the public should be aware that professionals often face conflicts of interest that may result in decisions against individual preferences.

John A. Robertson, Involuntary Euthanasia of Defective Newborns: A Legal Analysis
27 Stan. L. Rev. 213, 262-264 (1975)

Duff and Campbell [supra] present the argument for granting parents and physicians final discretion to decide whether a defective infant should be treated and hence live or die. . . .

The logic of this argument, however, is unpersuasive. It rests on the assumption that parents have but two options — to withhold care or to be burdened with the care of the child throughout their lives. But a third option exists — termination of parental rights and obligations. However, while parental discretion to terminate the parental relationship may be justified, it does not follow that parents should also have the right to decide whether the child lives or dies. Clearly, discretion to terminate a relationship of dependency does not mandate that one have the power to impose death on the terminated party. Furthermore, a central element of procedural justice is impartial decisionmaking after full consideration of relevant information. Yet, neither parents nor physicians are impartial or disinterested; both have a strong personal interest in the outcome of their decision. Parents face the decision with the guilt, grief, and damaged image that birth of a defective child brings. They have a strong interest in maintaining previous life plans, and adjustment patterns, and in avoiding the psychic and financial costs of adjusting to care of a defective infant. Moreover, the treatment decision arises in highly emotional circumstances, when their rational faculties are weakest and full information concerning the defect and prognosis is wanting. In addition, the physician's objectivity may be compromised. The obstetrician, for example, may feel guilt or responsibility for the defect, and prefer that the problem be eliminated as soon as possible. He may think that the least he can do for the parents is to relieve them of a potential lifelong burden. Similarly, though less involved, the advice of a pediatrician or consultant is likely to be influenced by his own values concerning care for defective infants. In short, since parents and physicians face the treatment decision with conflicting interests and the pressure of strong emotions, giving them final, unguided discretion to decide whether defective infants live will often lead to hasty, biased choices. . . .

[A]rguably we can depend on the ethical commitments of the medical profession to prevent parental abuses. Physicians perhaps are better equipped than parents to consider these judgments and can intervene when parents misjudge the interests of society and child, thus operating as a check on parental decisionmaking. If the physician challenges the parental choice, . . . , he can seek judicial protection for the child. There is some merit to this claim, but one cannot reliably base a rule on the contingency that physicians will intervene in particularly egregious cases. There is no guarantee that physicians can adequately strike the most socially desirable balance. While nearness to extreme situations often requires physicians to make such judgments, nothing in their training or background qualifies them to identify, assess, and balance all interests involved — in short, to "play judge." In addition, decisions by physicians are likely to reflect specific class, economic, ethical, and cultural biases or interests arising out of prior relationships with the parents. . . .

President's Commission for the Study of Ethical Problems in Medicine and Biomedical and Behavioral Research: Deciding to Forgo Life-Sustaining Treatment
Pub. No. 83-17978, at 217-223 (1983)

. . . The Commission believes that decisionmaking will be improved if an attempt is made to decide which of three situations applies in a particular case — (1) a treatment is available that would clearly benefit the infant, (2) all treatment is expected to be futile, or (3) the probable benefits to an infant from different choices are quite uncertain. . . . The three situations need to be considered separately, since they demand differing responses. . . . [The Commission believes that medical intervention for a baby born with the physical disabilities of Down's syndrome (such as heart obstructions not affecting retardation) should be considered "clearly beneficial therapy."] The Commission has concluded that a very restrictive standard is appropriate: such permanent handicaps justify a decision not to provide life-sustaining treatment only when they are so severe that continued existence would not be a net benefit to the infant. . . . As in all surrogate decisionmaking, the surrogate is obligated to try to evaluate benefits and burdens from the infant's own perspective. The Commission believes that the handicaps of Down syndrome, for example, are not in themselves of this magnitude and do not justify failing to provide medically proven treatment, such as surgical correction of a blocked intestinal tract.

This is a very strict standard in that it excludes consideration of the negative effects of an impaired child's life on other persons, including parents, siblings, and society. Although abiding by this standard may be difficult in specific cases, it is all too easy to undervalue the lives of handicapped infants; the Commission finds it imperative to counteract this by treating them no less vigorously than their healthy peers or than older children with similar handicaps would be treated.

When there is no therapy that can benefit an infant, as in anencephaly or certain severe cardiac deformities, a decision by surrogates and providers not to try predictably futile endeavors is ethically and legally justifiable. Such therapies do not help the child, are sometimes painful for the infant (and probably distressing to the parents), and offer no reasonable probability of saving life for a substantial period. . . .

Just as with older patients, even when cure or saving of life are out of reach, obligations to comfort and respect a dying person remain. Thus infants whose lives are destined to be brief are owed whatever relief from suffering and enhancement of life can be provided, including feeding, medication for pain, and sedation, as appropriate. . . .

Ambiguous Cases

Although for most seriously ill infants there will be either a clearly beneficial option or no beneficial therapeutic options at all, hard questions are raised by the smaller number for whom it is very difficult to assess whether the treatments available offer prospects of benefit — for example, a child with a debilitating and painful disease who might live with therapy, but only a year or so, or a respirator-dependent premature infant whose long-term prognosis becomes bleaker with each passing day.

Much of the difficulty in these cases arises from factual uncertainty. For the many infants born prematurely, and sometimes for those with serious congenital defects, the only certainty is that without intensive care they are unlikely to survive; very little is known about how each individual will fare with treatment. Neonatology is too new a field to allow accurate predictions of which babies will survive and of the complications, handicaps, and potentials that the survivors might have.

The longer some of these babies survive, the more reliable the prognosis for the infant becomes and the clearer parents and professionals can be on whether further treatment is warranted or futile. Frequently, however, the prospect of long-term survival and the quality of that survival remain unclear for days, weeks, and months, during which time the infants may have an unpredictable and fluctuating course of advances and setbacks.

One way to avoid confronting anew the difficulties involved in evaluating each case is to adopt objective criteria to distinguish newborns who will receive life-sustaining treatment from those who will not. Such criteria would be justified if there were evidence that their adoption would lead to decisions more often being made correctly.

Strict treatment criteria proposed in the 1970s by a British physician for deciding which newborns with spina bifida[84] should receive treatment rested upon the location of the lesion (which influences degree of paralysis), the presence of hydrocephalus (fluid in the brain, which influences degree of retardation), and the likelihood of an infection. Some critics of this proposal argued with it on scientific grounds, such as objecting that long-term effects of spina bifida cannot be predicted with sufficient accuracy at birth. Other critics, however, claimed this whole approach to ambiguous cases exhibited the "technical criteria fallacy." They contended that an infant's future life — and hence the treatment decisions based on it — involves value considerations that are ignored when physicians focus solely on medical prognosis.

> The decision (to treat or not) must also include evaluation of the meaning of existence with varying impairments. Great variation exists about these essentially evaluative elements among parents, physicians, and policy makers. It must be an open question whether these variations in evaluation are among the relevant factors to consider in making a treatment decision. When Lorber uses the phrase "contraindications to active therapy," he is medicalizing what are really value choices.[88]

The Commission agrees that such criteria necessarily include value considerations. Supposedly objective criteria such as birth weight limits or checklists for severity of spina bifida have not been shown to improve the quality of decision-making in ambiguous and complex cases. Instead, their use seems to remove the weight of responsibility too readily from those who should have to face the value question — parents and health care providers.

Furthermore, any set of standards, when honestly applied, leaves some difficult or uncertain cases. When a child's best interests are ambiguous, a decision based upon them will require prudent and discerning judgment. . . .

PROBLEMS

(1) If the laws relating to disabled newborns are to be changed, how should they be changed? Should state legislatures define a new type of homicide involving disabled newborns that has a lesser sanction? Or should withholding care from a disabled newborn be legalized?

    a.   How would you define the class of disabled newborns for whom it would be legal to withhold care?

    b.   How would you take account of advances in medicine over time?

    c.   Would you permit "active" euthanasia — such as giving a lethal injection — as well as passive euthanasia, which involves simply withholding care?

---

[84] John Lorber, Early Results of Selective Treatment of Spina Bifida Cystica, 4 Brit. Med. J. 201 (1973); John Lorber, Results of Treatment of Myelomeningocele, 13 Dev. Med. & Child Neurol. 279 (1971). . . .

[88] Robert M. Veatch, The Technical Criteria Fallacy, 7 Hastings Ctr. Rep. 15, 16 (Aug. 1977).

     d.   Who would decide which babies would be untreatable? The parents? The attending doctor? A hospital committee? A judge?

     e.   By what procedure should the decision to withhold treatment be made?

Draft a statute that would legalize withholding care from disabled newborns.

    (2) Two Dutch physicians, Drs. Eduard Verhagen and Pieter J.J. Sauer, have developed guidelines (known as the Groningen Protocol) regarding the use of euthanasia for disabled infants. The physicians divide newborns who are at risk for end-of-life decisions into three groups: (1) infants with no chance of survival; (2) infants whose prognosis is poor and who have a poor quality of life and are dependent on intensive care (such as those with severe brain damage), and (3) infants whose prognosis is hopeless and who experience unbearable suffering but who may not need intensive medical care. According to the Groningen Protocol, the following conditions must be met in order to end the life of an infant whose suffering cannot be relieved and for whom no improvement can be expected: (a) full and informed consent of the parents regarding whether death would be more humane than continued life; (b) the agreement of a team of physicians; and (c) a subsequent review of each case by an independent legal body to determine whether the decision was justified and all procedures have been followed. What do you think of this proposal? See John Schwartz, When Torment Is Baby's Destiny, Euthanasia Is Defended, N.Y. Times, Mar. 10, 2005, at A3; Peter Singer, Pulling Back the Curtain on the Mercy Killing of Newborns, L.A. Times, Mar. 11, 2005; Eduard Verhagen & Pieter J.J. Sauer, The Groningen Protocol — Euthanasia in Severely Ill Newborns, 352 New Eng. J. Med. 959 (Mar. 20, 2005).

E. ADOLESCENT HEALTH CARE

This section highlights some of the legal issues that are implicated in the context of adolescent health. In particular, it explores how power and responsibility for adolescent health should be allocated among the child, the family, medical professionals, and state officials. The section begins with background material on adolescent health and then examines particular health issues affecting adolescents.

1. Introduction

The Centers for Disease Control and Prevention conducts an annual survey of the leading causes of health-risk behaviors among youths. The Youth Risk Behavior Surveillance System (YRBSS) provides information on risk behavior among youths in order to target and improve health programs.

Centers for Disease Control and Prevention, Youth Risk Behavior Surveillance — United States, 2003

. . . The Youth Risk Behavior Surveillance System monitors six categories of priority health-risk behaviors among youth and young adults — behaviors that contribute to unintentional injuries and violence; tobacco use; alcohol and other drug use; sexual behaviors that contribute to unintended pregnancy and sexually transmitted diseases (STDs), including human immunodeficiency virus (HIV) infection; unhealthy dietary behaviors; and physical inactivity — plus overweight. The YRBSS includes a national school-based survey conducted by CDC as well as state, territorial, and local school-based surveys conducted by education and health agencies. . . .

In the United States, 70.8% of all deaths among persons aged 10–24 years result from only four causes: motor-vehicle crashes, other unintentional injuries, homicide, and suicide. Results from the 2003 national Youth Risk Behavior Survey demonstrated that, during the 30 days preceding the survey, numerous high school students engage in behaviors that increase their likelihood of death from these four causes: 30.2% had ridden with a driver who had been drinking alcohol; 17.1% had carried a weapon; 44.9% had drunk alcohol; 22.4% had used marijuana.

In addition, during the 12 months preceding the survey, 33.0% of high school students had been in a physical fight, and 8.5% had attempted suicide. Substantial morbidity and social problems among young persons also result from unintended pregnancies and STDs, including HIV infection. In 2003, 46.7% of high school students had ever had sexual intercourse; 37% of sexually active students had not used a condom at last sexual intercourse; and 3.2% had ever injected an illegal drug. . . . In 2003, a total of 21.9% of high school students had smoked cigarettes during the 30 days preceding the survey; 78% had not eaten [more than] 5 servings/day of fruits and vegetables during the 7 days preceding the survey; 33.4% had participated in an insufficient amount of physical activity; and 13.5% were overweight. . . .

2. Suicide

Suicide is one of the primary causes of death among adolescents. Who, if anyone, should bear responsibility for a juvenile's suicide?

State v. Scruggs
2004 WL 1245557 (Conn. Super. Ct. 2004)

Stephen F. FRAZZINI, Judge.

This is a troubling case. A twelve-year-old boy who was facing constant bullying at school committed suicide. His mother, the defendant in this case, was then arrested and put on trial for risk of injury because of living conditions in the home. The defendant did not physically abuse her child. She was a single parent raising two children and working two jobs, sixty hours a week, to support her family. The family had already experienced sorrow several weeks earlier when the defendant's daughter suffered a miscarriage. Many people knew that the defendant's twelve-year-old son, Daniel, was in great distress. School officials knew that Daniel missed a lot of school and was often tardy, knew that he had severe personal hygiene problems, and did nothing to protect him from constant bullying. The Department of Children and Families ("DCF") was aware of Daniel's truancy, knew that the defendant wanted him placed in a different school, had been in the house during the period that the state claims the home living conditions endangered the child's health, but closed its case on the family six days before the suicide. Yet whatever the fault of the school or DCF, the state prosecuted and the jury convicted the defendant of risk of injury to Daniel's health because of the living conditions in the home.

The pertinent portion of the risk of injury statute under which the defendant was convicted provides as follows: "Any person who . . . wilfully or unlawfully causes or permits any child under the age of sixteen years to be placed in such a situation that . . . the health of such child is likely to be injured . . . " shall be guilty of the crime of risk of injury to a minor. General Statutes §53-21(a)(1). The first count of the amended information on which the defendant was convicted specifically accused her of committing this offense between August 1, 2001, and January 2, 2002, "by providing a home environment that was unhealthy and unsafe for such child."

. . . The critical issue for resolving these motions is whether the defendant caused or permitted Daniel to be placed in a situation that was likely to injure his health by providing a home environment that was unhealthy and unsafe for him. There was no evidence here that anything in the home environment was likely to injure a child's *physical* health.[1] The portion of the risk of injury statute under which the defendant was convicted, however, also prohibits conduct that places a child in a situation that poses a risk of injury to a child's mental health. . . .[2] [I]n considering the defendant's challenges to her conviction, the court must examine the evidence "in the light most favorable to sustaining the verdict" and ask whether, from the facts so construed and inferences reasonably drawn therefrom, the jury could reasonably have found guilt beyond a reasonable doubt." . . .

The jury heard testimony from several officials who went to the defendant's home on January 2, 2002, after receiving reports of a suicide there. Police testified that they found the dead body of the defendant's twelve-year-old son, Daniel, lying

---

[1] The only evidence about the safety of the home environment was that Daniel slept near knives and a home-made spear. Although there was evidence that the weapons were found in the closet near Daniel's body, there was no further evidence as to where near his body. There was no evidence whatsoever, either by direct or circumstantial proof, however, that these items or Daniel's use of them was likely to — i.e, would probably — injure either his mental or physical health. There is a difference between sharp implements being potentially unsafe, as many household items may be, and evidence showing that they were kept or used in an unsafe manner that made them likely to injure a child's health. There was also no evidence that the cluttered living conditions or unsanitary bathroom fixtures were likely to injure a child's physical health.

[2] It is important to keep in mind what is, and is not, at issue in this case. The crime being prosecuted here was creating or maintaining a situation that endangered the child's emotional health. The defendant was not charged with causing the child's suicide. The fact that the child committed suicide was relevant evidence concerning the risk to the child (and the defendant did not object to introduction of the evidence about the child's death), but was not itself an element of the offense charged here. The same violation, creating and maintaining a situation that endangered the child's mental health, would have existed even had the child not committed suicide.

on the floor of a walk-in closet in his bedroom. The defendant and her seventeen-year-old daughter, Kara Morris, told the police that Daniel had hung himself. Somewhere in the closet near the body, police found three long kitchen-type knives and a sharp implement affixed to a pole in a spear-like device, but there was no evidence that any of these objects played a role in causing the death.

The evidence, viewed most favorably to sustaining the verdict, would have reasonably permitted the jury to find that Daniel lived in a home with a foul and offensive odor. [T]he state's witnesses who went there on January 2 described that odor in various terms, as follows. Officer Michael Boothroyd testified that "a definite" and "a bit of offensive" odor "permeated throughout the whole home." Detective Gary Brandl described the odor as "very noticeable," "as if . . . you . . . stuck your head in a dirty clothes hamper . . . plus an odor of garbage" and said that although he noticed the odor upon entering the apartment, it was even stronger in the back of the house. Although Ronald Chase, an investigator for the state's medical examiner's office, described the odor as only "slightly offensive" and said he became accustomed to it after being in the premises and various defense witnesses denied that the apartment smelled bad, the jury was not required to believe witnesses denying the existence of any odor or minimizing its pungency.

The state's witnesses also described the apartment as very messy and cluttered. Boothroyd said the apartment was "extremely messy and dirty, very cluttered" and had a "chaotic atmosphere." He said that "It wasn't an easy place to walk through. . . . [Y]ou had to watch your step everywhere you went and made sure that you stayed on your feet" because of clothing and other articles piled everywhere on the floors throughout the house. He further testified that he saw dust accumulated on the top of various items. . . . [Brandl] said he could not even see the floor surface in Daniel's bedroom because of debris on the floor, some piled as high as the bed. When Brandl walked into the bedroom, he had to step on clothing and heard items cracking and breaking underneath. The police had to clear a path in the bedroom for the medical examiner's investigator to walk to the closet where Daniel's dead body lay. . . .

. . . In addition, the jury saw photographs, introduced into evidence by both parties, that were taken of the interior of the apartment on the day of Daniel's death. The photographs showed that most floors in the apartment were covered with furniture, piles of clothing and other debris, plastic bins, plastic garbage bags, and other items. . . . Flat surfaces above floor level — such as table tops, chairs, and other furniture — were also covered with items, often with no room for any additional items. For example, atop an ironing board in the living room sat an iron, coffee cup, coffee can with Styrofoam cups atop it, pencil, cellophane tape, socks and other clothing, a book, a roll of paper, and other items. There was no clear surface in the kitchen to prepare or eat food. . . . The only horizontal surfaces above floor level that were free of debris in the photographs taken of the defendant's apartment on January 2, 2002, were the three beds belonging to the defendant and her two children.

. . . The defendant's son-in-law, William Durrin, testified in the state's rebuttal case that he had been in the apartment in September and on Halloween of 2001 and that on those prior occasions clothing had also been strewn around the apartment, that the living room area of the apartment as depicted in state's exhibit two was a little cleaner than when he had earlier been there, and that the bathroom as depicted in state's exhibit seventeen was similar to how it had been on those earlier occasions. . . . Although Durrin admitted to personal animus against the defendant, the jury was nonetheless entitled to believe him.

In addition, evidence was presented from which the jury could reasonably have found that the bathroom and plumbing fixtures were unclean and unsanitary. . . . Boothroyd described the toilet as dirty inside and out. Brandl said that the sink bowl and bathtub walls were filthy and that the toilet bowl had mineral or rust stains and appeared dirty. . . .

There was thus ample evidence for the jury to find that Daniel lived in a home that had a foul and offensive odor and was so crowded with furniture, trash, clothing, and other debris on the floors that there was barely a place to walk anywhere. There was sufficient evidence for the jury to conclude that the bathroom facilities were dirty and unsanitary, had no privacy, with little or no clear floor space. Finally, the evidence overwhelmingly established that Daniel himself was in great distress: In addition to his truancy problems, he had bad hygiene, refused to bathe often, went to school with bad body odor and bad breath, and was so upset about the constant bullying at school that he defecated in his pants there. He was so fearful at home that he kept knives near him when he slept to protect himself. Since the defendant was no longer making Daniel go to school, he was facing the prospect of soon being home alone during the days.

The defendant's memorandum in support of her motions for acquittal argues that expert evidence was necessary to establish that the home environment was likely to injure the child's health. The defendant cites two recent decisions in which the Appellate Court reversed convictions for risk of injury for lack of expert evidence. In State v. Padua, 73 Conn. App. 386, 808 A.2d 361 (2002), *cert. granted*, 262 Conn. 941, 815 A.2d 672 (2003), police found children in a kitchen where marijuana was being packaged on a table near some cereal boxes and on the floor under the table. The state claimed that the marijuana was likely to injure the children's health because "the children could have eaten the marijuana that was present in the apartment." Id., at 393. The Appellate Court reversed a conviction under the same subsection of the risk of injury statute involved here because it concluded that a lay jury could not determine, without expert assistance, that being near or having access to marijuana can be injurious to the physical health of a child. As the court later explained in State v. Smith, 73 Conn. App. 809, 814, 809 A.2d 1146 (2002), *cert. granted*, 262 Conn. 948, 817 A.2d 108 (2003):

> a jury cannot be expected, absent the assistance of expert testimony, to understand or to appreciate the possible detrimental effects of eating marijuana or solely being in its presence.

Similarly, in *Smith*, police found a small child sitting near a bed where the defendant lay semiconscious and an aluminum foil packet containing crack cocaine on top of the mattress and bedding. The court held that, in the absence of expert testimony, there was insufficient evidence to support a finding that the presence of crack cocaine, even if ingested by the child, was likely to be injurious to the physical child's health. These cases do not stand for the proposition, however, that a jury always needs expert evidence to assess likely effect on health. In State v. Mancinone, 15 Conn. App. 251, 277, 545 A.2d 1131, *cert. denied*, 209 Conn. 818,

551 A.2d 757 (1988), *cert. denied*, 489 U.S. 1017 (1989), for example, the court upheld a conviction for risk of injury for providing alcohol and marijuana to children as harmful to their physical health without expert evidence.

The portion of the risk of injury statute under which the defendant was convicted does not require proof of any specific injury to a child's health, but only of a situation likely to injure a child's health. ("[W]hile . . . the children in this case did not sustain any actual injury . . . , the statute covers the situation where there need only be a risk of injury for the defendant to be convicted"). A jury may use its common sense and knowledge as to matters within general human experience. Expert testimony is necessary only for matters that go "beyond the common knowledge and comprehension, i.e., 'beyond the ken,' of the average juror." Conn. Code, Evidence, §7-2, Commentary.

The evidence in this case showed a child in severe distress — so distraught over bullying at school that he was defecating in his pants and missing school frequently and fearful at home. The evidence showed that he did not bathe often, smelled bad, had bad breath, problems probably compounded by fouling his pants at school. The jury could reasonably conclude that such a child needed to bathe more often and clean himself better. Yet the conditions of his home discouraged him from doing so. When bathing or using the toilet at home, he had no privacy because the door leading to his seventeen-year-old sister's bedroom could not be closed. The jury could certainly infer that the condition of the bathroom — clothing covering the floor, dirty and unsanitary fixtures, and articles in the tub — was a hindrance to using the bathroom, or at least would not encourage this twelve-year-child with severe hygiene problems to clean himself there.

Though a hard case, this was not a close case. Jurors may lack the personal experience to judge the effect on physical health of ingesting illegal narcotics substances, as the Appellate Court held in *Padua* and *Smith*. Their own lives, their knowledge of human experience, and their common sense would, however, provide an ample basis for them to assess the likely effect of the chaotic and filthy home environment in the defendant's household on the mental state of twelve-year-old Daniel Scruggs. The jury could use its everyday knowledge and common sense to conclude that the clutter and squalor throughout the home and lack of privacy in the bath were likely to harm Daniel's mental health, in light of his undisputedly fragile emotional state. Such a determination was not "beyond the ken of the average juror."

While this is undoubtedly a case in which expert evidence would have been *admissible*; it is not a case in which expert evidence was *required*. The specific nature of the risk charged is crucial in ascertaining whether expert evidence is necessary. If the question were whether the squalor here had caused the child's *suicide*, expert testimony would have been required, for such a causal link is by no means obvious. Similarly, in LePage v. Horne, 262 Conn. 116, 809 A.2d 505 (2002), the court held that an ordinary lay juror person could not determine, without expert testimony, the risks of various sleeping positions on an infant's physical safety. Yet while expert evidence may, in certain cases, be necessary to establish risk to physical health, our courts have never held expert evidence to be essential in cases involving claims of risk to mental or emotional health.

Our courts have long recognized that where an issue can be determined by the application of ordinary knowledge and experience, expert testimony is not required. . . . The risk to emotional health is far more self-evident in this case than in *Payne*. Any layperson with common sense could conclude that the squalor and home living environment here created a risk to Daniel's emotional health.

The law requires a parent to provide a home that does not cause risk of harm to a child's mental health. . . . The evidence here was sufficient for the jury to find that the home that the defendant provided for her son did not comply with that standard. . . . The only refuge for this troubled child, beset by bullies at school and fearful at home, was a closet. Even there, he felt unsafe.

This is not a case about a messy house. No law of which this court is aware regulates the frequency of vacuuming or prescribes specific housekeeping practices. The law, however, does seek to protect children, and mandates that adults not place a child "in such a situation that . . . [its] health . . . [is] likely to be injured." General Statutes §53-21(a)(1). The evidence here went far beyond messy or disorderly living conditions. The evidence showed extreme clutter and pervasive odor throughout the home, unsanitary bathroom facilities, and a child whose obvious emotional distress manifested itself in severe hygiene problems. It did not take an expert for this jury to conclude that the home living environment was likely to injure the mental, psychological, and emotional health of this troubled and fragile child. The motions for acquittal are, therefore, denied.

NOTES AND QUESTIONS

(1) Epilogue. The court suspended Mrs. Scruggs's 18-month sentence, placed her on probation for five years and sentenced her to 100 hours of community service. Her arrest occurred two months after she filed suit against the city and the middle school's vice principal and guidance counselor, alleging that they violated her son's civil rights by not providing him the education he was entitled to by law and by not preventing bullying by his classmates. Avi Salzman, Woman Is Spared Prison in Case Tied to Son's Suicide, N.Y. Times, May 15, 2004, at A14; Marc Santora, After Son's Suicide, Mother Is Convicted over Unsafe Home, N.Y. Times, Oct. 7, 2003, at A27. Following her sentencing, Mrs. Scruggs was evicted and lost her two jobs. Scruggs Can't Afford Lawyer, 30 Conn. L. Trib. 11 (June 14, 2004).

(2) Adolescent Suicide. Suicide is the third leading cause of death among children, after accidents and homicides. In 2001, 2,319 youths ages 10 to 20 committed suicide in the United States. The vast majority of youths who commit suicide are males (83%). Shankar Vedantam, Suicide Alert on Giving Antidepressants to Kids, S.F. Chron., Oct. 16, 2004, at A3. The most frequent manner of committing suicide for youths ages 10 to 20 is the use of a firearm. Id. The youth suicide rate fell dramatically during the past decade, particularly for children ages 10-14. Researchers attribute the drop to the passage of firearm laws, as well as the greater acceptance of gays and lesbians. Youth Suicides in U.S. Down by About 25%, S.F. Chron., June 11, 2004, at A3.

(3) Who Should Bear Responsibility? Who should bear responsibility for Daniel's suicide? Daniel himself? His mother? The school? The students who bullied him? If you believe liability should be imposed, should it take the form of tort damages? Criminal sanctions? Administrative remedies? If Daniel's mother had a younger child still living at home, should her parental rights to that child be terminated? Mrs. Scruggs later claimed that she did not clean the house because,

according to her view of childrearing, she believed that adolescents should help with the housekeeping. Salzman, supra, at B4. Does Mrs. Scruggs have a defense to criminal liability based on *Meyer, Pierce*, and *Yoder*?

Would your view about the imposition of parental liability be altered if Daniel had killed himself with a loaded gun that his mother kept in the home? Both federal and state law restrict the sale and delivery of firearms and ammunition to minors. See generally Katherine Hunt Federle, The Second Amendment Rights of Children, 89 Iowa L. Rev. 609 (2004). In addition, a number of states have child access prevention (CAP) laws that impose criminal penalties for the negligent storage of a firearm if a child uses the weapon to kill or injure himself or another person. See generally Andrew J. McClurg, Child Access Prevention Laws: A Common Sense Approach to Gun Control, 18 St. Louis U. Pub. L. Rev. 47, 50 (1999).

Prior to 1991, no court recognized the legal claims of a suicide victim's family against a school district. However, in Eisel v. Board of Education of Montgomery County, 597 A.2d 447 (Md. 1991), the Maryland supreme court held that a school district can be liable for an adolescent's suicide if the district's employees had knowledge that the student was suicidal and failed to warn the parents or take reasonable preventive action. See also Armijo v. Wagon Mound Public Schools, 159 F.3d 1253 (10th Cir. 1998) (establishing the possibility of school district's liability under §1983 of the Civil Rights Act using a "danger creation" theory, which provides that the state may be liable for an individual's safety if it created the danger that harmed the individual). See generally Richard Fossey & Perry Zirkel, Liability for Student Suicide in the Wake of *Eisel*, 10 Tex. Wesleyan L. Rev. 403 (2004).

(4) Purposes of Criminal Law. What purposes of the criminal law (general and specific deterrence, incapacitation, rehabilitation, retribution) are served by the imposition of criminal liability in the *Scruggs* case? Are you convinced by the court's comment (footnote 2) that this case is not about charging the mother "with causing the child's suicide" but rather about "maintaining a situation that endangered the child's mental health"?

(5) Antibullying Legislation. Should states enact legislation to protect children against peer harassment in the schools? Courts historically have rejected imposing tort liability on school officials for acts of bullying, relying on doctrines of sovereign immunity and proximate cause (viewing the perpetrator's acts as an intervening cause that precludes liability for negligent supervision). Daniel B. Weddle, When Will Schools Take Bullying Seriously?, Trial Mag., Oct. 2003, at 18.

However, school violence at Columbine High School in 1999 triggered a movement for states to pass "antibullying laws," which require schools to institute special procedures to address bullying. Following Daniel Scruggs' death, the Connecticut legislature enacted a bill mandating school officials to place an antibullying policy in student codes of conduct, require teachers and school staff who witness acts of bullying or receive reports to notify school administrators, promise anonymity to reporters, require administrators to investigate such reports, require the school to notify parents of the victim and perpetrator, and require the school to make public a list of verified acts of bullying. "Bullying" is defined as "any overt acts by a student or a group of students directed against another student with the intent to ridicule, humiliate or intimidate the other student while on school grounds or at a school-sponsored activity which acts are repeated against the same student over time." Conn. Gen. Stat. Ann. §10-222d (West 2003). If the Connecticut antibullying law had been in effect, do you think it would have prevented Daniel's death? See generally Alison Bethel, Keeping Schools Safe: Why Schools Should Have an Affirmative Duty to Protect Students From Harm by Other Students, 2 Pierce L. Rev. 183 (2004).

(6) *Role of Sexual Orientation.*   Gay students face a greater risk of bullying in schools. Sharon E. Rush, Lessons From and for "Disabled" Students, 8 J. Gender Race & Just. 75, 82 (2004). In Davis v. Monroe County Board of Education, 526 U.S. 629 (1999), the Supreme Court held that a school may be liable for student sexual harassment under Title IX of the Education Amendments Act of 1972, 20 U.S.C. §§1681-1687 (2000) (prohibiting sexual discrimination in education). Liability attaches when, after receiving notice of the sexual harassment, the school acts with deliberate indifference and the harassment is so severe that it effectively bars the victim's access to an educational opportunity or benefit. See generally Katie Feiock, The State to the Rescue: Using State Statutes to Protect Children from Peer Harassment in School, 35 Colum. J.L. & Soc. Probs. 317 (2002).

(7) *Adolescent Depression and Antipsychotic Drugs.*   Should medical professionals or drug manufacturers bear any responsibility in cases of adolescent suicide? For the past decade, controversy has raged concerning the correlation between antidepressant medication and increased risk of suicidal thoughts and behavior in adolescents. Such drugs are commonly prescribed for youth with depression and other psychiatric disorders. Clinical data suggest that children who are taking antidepressants are at increased risk of suicidal thoughts and behavior compared to a comparative sample of youth taking a placebo. In response to such clinical findings, many professionals argue that patients' suicidal thoughts and behavior are attributable to their illness rather than their medications. In October 2004, a scientific advisory panel of the Food and Drug Administration (FDA) ordered several pharmaceutical companies to place "black box" warnings on their antidepressant products disclosing that use of such medication increases suicidal behavior in children. The advisory is the government's strongest warning for dangerous drugs short of an outright ban. Marilyn Elias, Teen Suicide Warnings Going on Drug Labels, Deseret Morning News, Mar. 2, 2005, at A02; Gardiner Harris, Antidepressant Study Seen to Back Expert, N.Y. Times, Aug. 20, 2004, at A18.

Also, parents have attempted to impose liability on drug manufacturers in cases of children's suicides or homicides. See, e.g., Miller v. Pfizer, Inc., 356 F.3d 1326 (10th Cir. 2004) (affirming grant of summary judgment for defendant in suit by parents alleging that medication caused their 13-year-old son to commit suicide). And in June 2004, the New York Attorney General sued GlaxoSmithKline, alleging that the company withheld negative results about the effect of the antidepressant Paxil on children and adolescents. In a settlement, the company agreed to post the findings of clinical studies and to pay $2.5 million to the state. Glaxo Settles Legal Dispute, Chemical & Engineering News, Sept. 6, 2004, at 1617.

NOTE ON OTHER ADOLESCENT HEALTH ISSUES

Obesity in children and adolescents is a growing national concern. Research reveals that the percentage of children who are overweight has nearly doubled in the past two decades, whereas the percentage of overweight adolescents has nearly tripled. Eric Bost, Obesity Crisis, Cong. Testimony, 2004 WL 84559038 (Sept. 15, 2004). Obesity increases the likelihood that a child will develop childhood hypertension, heart disease, cancer, and Type 2 diabetes.

Who, if anyone, should bear responsibility for a child's obesity? The child? The parents? The schools? The food and beverage and entertainment industries? Recently, plaintiffs have instituted suits against the fast-food industry (modeled after tobacco litigation) charging that the industry has caused consumer obesity. In Pelman v. McDonald's Corp., 237 F. Supp. 2d 512 (S.D.N.Y. 2003), parents of two overweight teenage girls brought a class action suit on behalf of children in New York, alleging violations of state consumer protection laws (misleading and deceptive advertising) and negligence in connection with children's overconsumption of fast-food products that led to their children's health problems. The federal district court granted defendants' motion to dismiss, holding that the parents failed to allege specific deceptive acts or omissions; the defendants owed no duty to warn consumers of products' well-known attributes; and the parents failed to allege facts demonstrating that products were addictive.

Congress responded initially by proposing legislation (dubbed the "Cheeseburger Bill") that would preclude "frivolous lawsuits" in federal or state courts against the manufacturers, distributors, and sellers of fast food. See Personal Responsibility in Food Consumption Act, H.R. 339, 108th Cong. (2003). Subsequently, Congress commissioned a study of the problem of childhood obesity.

In the report mandated by Congress, the Institute of Medicine (a private organization associated with the National Academy of Sciences) found that efforts to slow the rise in childhood obesity rates need to involve schools, the food and beverage industries, government, and parents. The Institute's recommendations included having schools ensure that lunches are consistent with federal nutrition guidelines and put recess and physical-education classes back into the school day; the food, beverage, and entertainment industries should consider a plan to limit advertising of unhealthy products to children; the federal government should convene a task force to explore restrictions on advertising of unhealthy products and improve food labeling to give consumers more information about caloric intake; state and local governments should design communities to provide more opportunities to exercise by providing sidewalks, playgrounds, and other recreational areas; and, finally, parents should provide healthy meals and opportunities to exercise and should limit children's leisure television and computer time to less than two hours a day. Health Advisers Call for Action to Battle Childhood Obesity, Wall St. J., Oct. 1, 2004, at B2. What do you think of these recommendations?

See generally Lee J. Munger, Comment, Is Ronald McDonald the Next Joe Camel?: Regulating Fast Food Advertisements Targeting Children in Light of the American Overweight and Obesity Epidemic, 3 Conn. Pub. Int. L.J. 456 (2004); Samuel J. Romero, Comment, Obesity Liability: A Super-Sized Problem or a Small Fry in the Inevitable Development of Product Liability?, 7 Chap. L. Rev. 239 (2004).

Other adolescent health issues (contraception, sexually transmissible disease, drinking) are discussed in Chapter 6.

F.   MEDICAL EXPERIMENTATION ON CHILDREN

As we have seen, informed consent of parents is usually both a necessary and sufficient condition of medical treatment of children. So far, our concern has been with consent to standard medical therapy for a child requiring treatment, as well as the possible consequences if parents fail to provide essential treatment. In this section we explore the limits, if any, of parental power to consent when the child is participating in a medical experiment. Should parental prerogatives be limited when it comes to medical experiments? If so, what is an experiment — that is, how does one define the class of situations where parents should not be able to consent? In addition to parental consent, what other institutional safeguards are essential? As you will see, the legal, ethical, and policy issues posed by medical experimentation on children are profoundly difficult.

Consider the materials that follow in light of the following problems.

1.   Introductory Problem

Eight-year-old Johnny Smith has had leukemia for four years. For the last three years it has been in remission, but his most recent checkup revealed that his white cell count is again above normal, meaning the disease has reappeared. Existing data suggest that the prognosis of Johnny's surviving more than two years with conventional modes of treatment is poor, but not hopeless. Johnny's pediatrician has recommended that Johnny be given a new form of chemotherapy. There have been only a few preliminary tests with it, but the results seem promising. The doctor believes that this new therapy *may* help Johnny more than conventional therapy, and that under the circumstances "it is worth a try." May Johnny's parents consent to the chemotherapy? Should Johnny have any say as well?

Suppose the doctor is a professor at the state university medical school who is running a randomized clinical trial to compare the effectiveness of the new chemotherapy treatment with that of the standard treatment. May Johnny's parents consent to his participation in the experiment, under which the choice of treatment for Johnny will be made by random selection?

May Johnny's parents consent to Johnny's participation in some tests that are not part of Johnny's treatment but for the purpose of increasing knowledge about leukemia? These tests require that blood be taken from Johnny at more frequent intervals and in somewhat greater amounts than would be necessary for treatment.

Suppose that after standard therapy has failed to help Johnny, his doctor recommends an experimental drug that the Food and Drug Administration permits to be used only on a special protocol basis. If the parents refuse permission for the child to enter the study, and most medical professionals would agree that it might well cause a remission, do you think the doctor's petition to a juvenile court to require the drug would succeed? What if Johnny was 16 years old instead of 8 and wanted to try the drug? (See Angela R. Holder, Legal Issues in Pediatrics and Adolescent Medicine 159 (2d ed. 1985)).

2. Historical Background

[I]n eighteenth century England . . . Caroline, Princess of Wales, "begged the lives" of six condemned criminals for experimental smallpox vaccination before submitting her own children to the procedure. (She also procured, for further trial, "half a dozen of the charity children belonging to St. James' parish.") [Louis Lasagna, Special Subjects in Human Experimentation, 98 Daedalus (No. 2) 449 (1969).]

Ross G. Mitchell, The Child and Experimental Medicine
1 Brit. Med. J. 721-722 (1964)

Human experimentation is as old as medicine itself, but the experimental method of modern science is comparatively new. . . .

If the notorious experiments ordered by Queen Caroline on "charity children" . . . be excepted, one of the first experiments performed by a physician on living children was the experimental inoculation of young children with measles by Dr. Francis Home, a member of the College of Physicians of Edinburgh, in 1759. Forty years later, as the eighteenth century drew to a close, Edward Jenner made medical and paediatric history by selecting a healthy 8-year-old boy, James Phipps, for the purpose of inoculation with cowpox.

Throughout the nineteenth century paediatrics advanced as a scientific subject, although the concept of the controlled experiment was not yet established. . . .

With the development of bacteriology and biochemistry at the end of the century, the way was clear for the great advances in scientific paediatrics of our own century.

The first attempts at biochemical research in paediatrics were confined to comparatively simple measurements of the constituents of body fluids such as blood and urine. Paediatric journals of the early years of this century contain many reports of studies utilizing blood drawn from the superior sagittal sinus — a vessel first used for this purpose by Marfan in 1898 — or from the jugular vein of infants. Very few articles refer to parental permission for these studies, and there is seldom any expression of doubt about the morality of the work. Children from orphanages and "foundlings" were commonly used as subjects for these investigations. It is perhaps not surprising that this type of research was accepted unquestioningly, for infant and child mortality was still very high and methods of therapy were often drastic. Moreover, medicine had but recently emerged from an era in which children were little regarded, a world where foundlings were bought and sold and child labour was the rule. It is salutary to recall that a hundred years ago the American Society for Prevention of Cruelty to Animals was empowered by the courts to act in a case of cruelty to a child on the grounds that a child is an animal. A society for the prevention of cruelty to children was not founded until 1875 — nearly ten years later. . . . Against such a background, the use of orphans and foundlings for experiments would hardly have seemed to require permission or indeed justification. . . .

Our modern concern with the ethics of human experimentation dates from the Nuremberg trials of war criminals during World War II. The Nuremberg Code was formulated in response to Nazi medical experimentation on concentration camp prisoners. The Nuremberg Code proposes standards for the conduct of nontherapeutic research. It rests on the requirements of: (1) voluntary consent of informed subjects; (2) research that is unprocurable by other means and holds the promise of yielding "fruitful results" to benefit society; and (3) research that is conducted by scientifically qualified persons in a manner that avoids unnecessary physical and mental suffering.

The subsequent Declarations of Helsinki also serve as an international guide for the protection of human subjects in research. The initial Helsinki Declaration was promulgated in 1964 by the World Medical Association to rectify the failure of the Nuremberg Code to address research on subjects who are incapable of providing informed consent, such as children and mentally impaired persons. The Helsinki Declaration required proxy consent for all subjects who are legally incompetent. Subsequent revisions in 1983 (Helsinki Declaration III) emphasize the importance of allowing children's participation in medical decision making, requiring that the researcher obtain not only the consent of a minor's legal guardian but also that of the minor if the minor is able to provide such consent.

The Council for International Organizations of Medical Science, together with the World Health Organization, also developed guidelines for research on children (CIOMS/WHO Guidelines) in 1983. These Guidelines address pediatric research in therapeutic and nontherapeutic contexts. In both cases, the parent must give proxy consent, the child must consent to the extent that he or she is able, and, in the case of nontherapeutic research, the child's refusal to participate must be respected. The level of risk must be low and in proportion to the knowledge that the research is likely to yield.

The first binding international instrument protecting human rights in biomedicine, the Council of Europe Convention of Human Rights and Biomedicine, was adopted by the European Ministers of Justice in 1996. The Biomedical Convention's point of departure, similar to other international protocols, is the requirement that all subjects give voluntary and informed consent. Additional provisions require that research on incompetent persons (such as children) may be performed if: (1) the subject receives direct medical benefit; (2) research cannot be conducted on adults; (3) the subject's legal representative consents; and (4) the subject does not object. (The researcher must consider the child's opinion on whether to participate, based on the child's age and maturity.) Nontherapeutic research that does not benefit the child can be conducted provided it contributes to a greater understanding of the child's condition, will benefit patients of a similar age, and involves minimal risk and minimal burden to the child.

Federal legislation also addresses the protection of children in federally funded research. Beginning in the 1970s the federal government became concerned with the protection of the rights of research subjects. In 1974, Congress enacted the National Research Act (codified at 45 C.F.R. §46 (2001)), establishing a Commission for the Protection of Human Subjects of Biomedical and Behavioral Research, to identify ethical principles to guide research on human subjects. The Commission issued recommendations regarding pediatric research in 1977.

Many of the Commission's recommendations subsequently became the basis of federal regulations (known as the Common Rule) that govern the protection of human subjects generally applicable to federal agencies (codified at 45 C.F.R. §46.101(a) (2001)). For example, the Commission required consent from both parents and the child to participate in research. (The Commission replaced the term "consent" with the term of parental "permission" and the child's "assent.")

The Common Rule departs from the Commission's recommendations in some regards. For example, the Commission Report suggests that the assent of children seven years or older should be required. In contrast, the Common Rule permits a research institution's institutional review board (IRB) to determine a child's capacity to assent (based on the child's age, maturity, and psychological state) and also specifies circumstances in which the child's assent may be overridden (e.g., if the intervention holds out the prospect of increased well-being for the child). Thus, although the Commission Report required the child's refusal to participate to be binding, the Common Rule does not adhere to this recommendation.

Both the Commission Report and the Common Rule distinguish between various risk and benefit categories. For example, both distinguish between research that "poses not greater than minimal risk" and that involving "greater than minimal risk." Also, both distinguish between research that presents a direct benefit to the research subject versus research presenting no such benefit but likely to yield generalized benefit regarding the medical condition. For example,

- research that confers no therapeutic benefit to the child and does not involve greater than minimal risk requires both the child's assent and the parent's permission to participate in research;
- research that may directly benefit the child and that involves greater than minimal risk is permissible, subject to both parental permission and the child's assent, if the potential benefit justifies the risk or if the trial may be as beneficial to the child as an alternative treatment;
- research that will not directly benefit the child but is likely to provide general knowledge about a medical condition and that involves greater than minimal risk is permissible, subject to both parental permission and the child's assent, if the research represents a minor increase over minimal risk or involves approximately the same level of risk as involved in a medical or dental checkup;
- research that would not normally be approved but that presents an opportunity to understand, prevent or alleviate children's health is subject to external review to ensure that it meets the requisite standards.

On the development of protections for human subjects in medical research, see generally George J. Annas & Michael A. Grodin, The Nazi Doctors and the Nuremberg Code: Human Rights in Human Experimentation (1992); Joanne Roman, Note, U.S. Medical Research in the Developing World: Ignoring Nuremberg, 11 Cornell J.L. & Pub. Pol'y 441, 448-453 (2002); Ann E. Ryan, Comment, Protecting the Rights of Pediatric Research Subjects in the International Conference on Harmonisation of Technical Requirements for Registration of Pharmaceuticals for Human Use, 23 Fordham Intl. L.J. 848, 862-881 (2000).

3. Is Medical Experimentation on Children Essential?

Apart from the benefits or risks to the individual child who is a participant, is medical experimentation, considered in its own right, a social good? Is experimentation on children essential to medical progress? Both experimentation with no therapeutic purpose as well as therapeutic experimentation? What would be the consequences of prohibiting medical experimentation on children?

Ann E. Ryan, Comment, Protecting the Rights of Pediatric Research Subjects in the International Conference of Harmonisation of Technical Requirements for Registration of Pharmaceuticals for Human Use
23 Fordham Intl. L.J. 848, 855-857 (2000)

Even though medical studies that are conducted on children may be controversial, the scientific need for such experimentation is apparent. A child's physiology is significantly different from that of an adult or a child of a different age group. These differences may have a significant impact on whether and how a drug can be used on a pediatric patient. Drug studies conducted on adults, moreover, may not adequately predict whether a drug will be toxic if prescribed to a child. Pharmaceutical companies' failure to test medicines in children may result in death or serious illness. Without adequate pediatric testing, doctors encounter a serious ethical dilemma: either prescribe medication or perform a procedure that potentially may benefit the child, or refrain from this treatment because it has not been adequately tested on children. This problem, commonly referred to as therapeutic orphaning, hampers the development and use of potentially life-saving therapies for pediatric patients.

  Pediatric patients are likely to become therapeutic orphans, as many pharmaceutical companies resist conducting research on children because of ethical and legal issues involved in performing pediatric trials, difficulty recruiting subjects, and strains in raising adequate funds to conduct extra protocols. This situation creates grave dangers and risks for pediatric patients, as a large number of medications commonly prescribed for children are not tested on pediatric subjects. The problem is particularly pronounced in medications used to treat serious illnesses, such as the human immunodeficiency virus ("HIV"). Certain age groups are also commonly left out of drug trials, resulting in incomplete and unreliable results concerning the safety and effectiveness of drugs for these patients. . . .

4. May Parents Under Existing Law Consent to Medical Procedures Not Undertaken for the Treatment of the Child in Question?

Grimes v. Kennedy Krieger Institute, Inc.
782 A.2d 807 (Md. App. 2001)

CATHELL, Judge.

  [A] prestigious research institute [Kennedy Krieger Institute or KKI] created a nontherapeutic research program whereby it required certain classes of homes to have only partial lead paint abatement modifications performed[2]. . . . The research institute then encouraged, and in at least one of the cases at bar, required, the landlords to rent the premises to families with young children. . . . Apparently, the children and their parents involved in the cases *sub judice* were from a lower economic stratum and were, at least in one case, minorities. . . .

The purpose of the research was to determine how effective varying degrees of lead paint abatement procedures were. Success was to be determined by periodically, over a two-year period of time, measuring the extent to which lead dust remained in, or returned to, the premises after the varying levels of abatement modifications, and, as most important to our decision, by measuring the extent to which the theretofore healthy children's blood became contaminated with lead, and comparing that contamination with levels of lead dust in the houses over the same periods of time. . . . [Families were compensated $5 initially and $15 subsequently each time they completed a periodic questionnaire.]

Apparently, it was anticipated that the children, who were the human subjects in the program, would, or at least might, accumulate lead in their blood from the dust, thus helping the researchers to determine the extent to which the various partial abatement methods worked. There was no complete and clear explanation in the consent agreements signed by the parents of the children that the research to be conducted was designed, at least in significant part, to measure the success of the abatement procedures by measuring the extent to which the children's blood was being contaminated. It can be argued that the researchers intended that the children be the canaries in the mines but never clearly told the parents. (It was a practice in earlier years, and perhaps even now, for subsurface miners to rely on canaries to determine whether dangerous levels of toxic gasses were accumulating in the mines. Canaries were particularly susceptible to such gasses. When the canaries began to die, the miners knew that dangerous levels of gasses were accumulating.)

The researchers and their Institutional Review Board apparently saw nothing wrong with the research protocols that anticipated the possible accumulation of lead in the blood of otherwise healthy children as a result of the experiment, or they believed that the consents of the parents of the children made the research appropriate. [The minor participants in the research program brought negligence actions against the institute. The trial court granted the research institute's motion for summary judgment. The appellate court held, inter alia, that fact issues as to the existence of a duty precluded summary judgment. The appellate court also addressed, infra, the issue of proxy consent for children's participation in nontherapeutic research.]

[2] At least to the extent that commercial profit motives are not implicated, therapeutic research's purpose is to directly help or aid a patient who is suffering from a health condition the objectives of the research are designed to address — hopefully by the alleviation, or potential alleviation, of the health condition.

Nontherapeutic research generally utilizes subjects who are not known to have the condition the objectives of the research are designed to address, and/or is not designed to directly benefit the subjects utilized in the research, but, rather, is designed to achieve beneficial results for the public at large (or, under some circumstances, for profit).

VI. Parental Consent for Children to Be Subjects of Potentially Hazardous Nontherapeutic Research

The issue of whether a parent can consent to the participation of her or his child in a nontherapeutic health-related study that is known to be potentially hazardous to the health of the child raises serious questions with profound moral and ethical implications. What right does a parent have to knowingly expose a child not in need of therapy to health risks or otherwise knowingly place a child in danger, even if it can be argued it is for the greater good? The issue in these specific contested cases does not relate primarily to the authority of the parent, but to the procedures of KKI and similar entities that may be involved in such health-related studies. The issue of the parents' right to consent on behalf of the children has not been fully presented in either of these cases, but should be of concern not only to lawyers and judges, but to moralists, ethicists, and others. The consenting parents in the contested cases at bar were not the subjects of the experiment; the children were. Additionally, this practice presents the potential problems of children initiating actions in their own names upon reaching majority, if indeed, they have been damaged as a result of being used as guinea pigs in nontherapeutic scientific research. Children, it should be noted, are not in our society the equivalent of rats, hamsters, monkeys, and the like. Because of the overriding importance of this matter and this Court's interest in the welfare of children — we shall address the issue.

Most of the relatively few cases in the area of the ethics of protocols of various research projects involving children have merely assumed that a parent can give informed consent for the participation of their children in nontherapeutic research. The single case in which the issue has been addressed, and resolved, a case with which we agree, will be discussed further, infra.

It is not in the best interest of a specific child, in a nontherapeutic research project, to be placed in a research environment, which might possibly be, or which proves to be, hazardous to the health of the child. We have long stressed that the "best interests of the child" is the overriding concern of this Court in matters relating to children. Whatever the interests of a parent, and whatever the interests of the general public in fostering research that might, according to a researcher's hypothesis, be for the good of all children, this Court's concern for the particular child and particular case over-arches all other interests. It is, simply, and we hope, succinctly put, not in the best interest of any healthy child to be intentionally put in a nontherapeutic situation where his or her health may be impaired, in order to test methods that may ultimately benefit all children.

To think otherwise, to turn over human and legal ethical concerns solely to the scientific community, is to risk embarking on slippery slopes, that all too often in the past, here and elsewhere, have resulted in practices we, or any community, should be ever unwilling to accept.

We have little doubt that the general motives of all concerned in these contested cases were, for the most part, proper, albeit in our view not well thought out. The protocols of the research, those of which we have been made aware, were, in any event, unacceptable in a legal context. One simply does not expose otherwise healthy children, incapable of personal assent (consent), to a nontherapeutic research environment that is known at the inception of the research, might cause the children to ingest lead dust. It is especially troublesome, when a measurement of the success of the research experiment is, in significant respect, to be determined by the extent to which the blood of the children absorbs, and is contaminated by, a substance that the researcher knows can, in sufficient amounts, whether solely from the research environment or cumulative from all sources, cause serious and long term adverse health effects. Such a practice is not legally acceptable.

In Hart v. Brown, 29 Conn. Supp. 368, 289 A.2d 386 (1972), that court was faced, prospectively, with whether to approve the transplant of a kidney from one seven-year-old identical twin to the other twin. The medical information presented to the court indicated that without the transplant the recipient twin would have to undergo an extensive period of dialysis treatment with the expectation of only a 50% chance that she could survive that treatment for more than five years; the donor twin was expected to live a normal and productive life with one kidney. There were severe rejection problems with the transplant of a kidney from the parents that would have subjected the recipient twin to the possible side effects of immuno-suppressive drugs.

The parents brought an action in behalf of the recipient twin against the doctor and the hospital that had refused to perform the operation absent a court order that the parents or a guardian had the right to consent to the operation. The action, therefore, sought a declaratory judgment concerning whether the parents or a guardian ad litem had the right to consent to the transplant on behalf of the donor twin.

The court first appointed as guardian ad litems an attorney to represent the donor twin, and another person to represent the recipient twin. [The] Connecticut court adopted the "doctrine of substituted judgment." It upheld the giving of the consent of the parents, but only after noting the extensive process that the parties and the court had undertaken. . . . The court then cited the cases of Strunk v. Strunk, [445 S.W.2d 145 (Ky. 1969)]; Bonner v. Moran, 75 U.S. App. D.C. 156, 126 F.2d 121 (1941) and the unreported Massachusetts cases.

Bonner was an unusual case that involved the grafting of skin from a minor donor cousin to a badly burned donee cousin. In that case, the court did not answer whether a parent, or other appropriate relative or guardian, could give consent for a nontherapeutic (as to the donor cousin) procedure. The issue was whether their consent was necessary under the circumstances, in that the donor cousin had apparently donated the skin without any express consent (and may have already done so when an aunt improperly consented as a surrogate). The trial court found that the minor cousin was sufficiently mature so as to be able to assent to the procedure, thus avoiding a determination as to whether a parent, or appropriate relative, could have given surrogated consent. The trial court gave a "mature minor" instruction to the jury.[40] The trial court's decision was ultimately overturned. The appellate court, reversing, stated:

> "We are constrained, therefore, to feel that the court below should, in the cir-
> cumstances we have outlined, have instructed that the consent of the parent was
> necessary. . . . But by his own testimony, it clearly appears that he [the physician]

---

[40] The doctrine of "mature minor" recognizes that some minors are sufficiently mature to consent.

failed to explain, even to the infant, the nature or extent of the proposed first operation." [*Bonner*, 75 U.S. App. D.C. at 156, 126 F.2d at 123.]

As is clear, that court did not say that parental consent would always be sufficient itself, only that it was a necessary ingredient in the equation.

In the *Strunk* case, the proposed donor was a mentally incompetent adult. Her parents sought permission of the court to consent to having one of the incompetent adult's kidneys transplanted to her twenty-six-year-old brother. The court granted permission to the parents, adopting the "doctrine of substituted judgment."

What is of primary importance to be gleaned in the *Hart* and *Strunk* cases is not that the parents or guardians consented to the procedures, but that they first sought permission of the courts, and received that permission, before consenting to a nontherapeutic procedure in respect to some of their minor children, but that was therapeutic to other of their children.

In the case *sub judice*, no impartial judicial review or oversight was sought by the researchers or by the parents. Additionally, in spite of the IRB's improper attempt to manufacture a therapeutic value, there was absolutely no such value of the research in respect to the minor subjects used to measure the effectiveness of the study. In the absence of a requirement for judicial review, in such a circumstance, the researchers, and their scientific based review boards would be, if permitted, the sole judges of whether it is appropriate to use children in nontherapeutic research of the nature here present, where the success of an experiment is to be measured, in substantial part, by the degree to which the research environments cause the absorption of poisons into the blood of children. Science cannot be permitted to be the sole judge of the appropriateness of such research methods on human subjects, especially in respect to children. We hold that in these contested cases, the research study protocols, those of which we are aware, were not appropriate.

When it comes to children involved in nontherapeutic research, with the potential for health risks to the subject children in Maryland, we will not defer to science to be the sole determinant of the ethicality or legality of such experiments. The reason, in our view, is apparent from the research protocols at issue in the case at bar. Moreover, in nontherapeutic research using children, we hold that the consent of a parent alone cannot make appropriate that which is innately inappropriate. . . .

[The court then discusses the case of T.D. v. New York State Office of Mental Health, 626 N.Y.S.2d 1015 (1995), in which a mental health patient in a state facility challenged regulations governing the use of experimental drugs.] In respect to the reasonableness of accepting parental consent for minors to participate in potentially harmful, nontherapeutic research, that court stated:

> "We also find unacceptable the provisions that allow for consent to be obtained on behalf of minors for participation in greater than minimal risk[41] nontherapeutic research from the minor's parent or legal guardian, or, where no parent or guardian is available, from an adult family member involved in making treatment decisions for the child. . . .

---

[41] Minimal risk has been defined as "meaning 'that the probability and magnitude of harm or discomfort anticipated in the research are not greater in and of themselves than those ordinarily encountered in daily life or during the routine physical or psychological examinations or tests.' " . . .

We are not dealing here with parental choice among reasonable treatment alternatives, but with a decision to subject the child to nontherapeutic treatments and procedures that may cause harmful permanent or fatal side effects. It follows therefore that a parent or guardian, . . . may not consent to have a child submit to painful and/or potentially life-threatening research procedures that hold no prospect of benefit for the child . . . . We do not limit a parent or legal guardian's right to consent to a child's participation in therapeutic research that represents a valid alternative and may be the functional equivalent of treatment." [T.D. v. New York State Office of Mental Health, 228 A.D.2d 95, 123-124, 650 N.Y.S.2d 173, 191-192 (1996).]

We concur with that assessment.

Additionally, there are conflicting views in respect to nontherapeutic research, as to whether consent, even of a person capable of consenting, can justify a research protocol that is otherwise unjustifiable.

"This 'justifying' side of consent raises some timeless and thorny questions. What if people consent to activities and results which are repugnant, or even evil? Even John Stuart Mill worried about consensual slavery. . . . Today, we wonder whether a woman's consent to appear in graphic, demeaning, or even violent pornography justifies or immunizes the pornographer. If she appears to consent to a relationship in which she is repeatedly brutalized, does her consent stymie our efforts to stop the brutality or punish the brute?

These problems make us squirm a little, just as they did Mill. We have three ways out: We can say, first, 'Yes, consent justifies whatever is consented to — you consented, so case closed;' second, 'This particular consent is deficient — you did not really consent and so the result or action is not justified;' or third, 'You consented, but your consent cannot justify this action or result.' . . .

Note the subtle yet crucial difference between these three options: In the first, consent is king, while the third option assumes a moral universe shaped and governed by extra-consensual considerations. The second option, however, reflects the tension between the other two. We might block the consented-to action, but we pay lip service to consent's justifying role by assuring ourselves that had the consent been untainted, had it been 'informed,' it would have had moral force. In fact, we pay lip service precisely because we often silently suspect that consent cannot and does not always justify. . . . Rather than admit that the consent does not and could not justify the act, we denigrate the consent and, necessarily, the consenter as well.

This is cheating; it is a subterfuge designed to hide our unease and to allow us to profess simultaneous commitment to values that often conflict." [Garnett, Why Informed Consent? Human Experimentation and the Ethics of Autonomy, 36 Catholic Lawyer 455, 458-460 (1996) (footnotes omitted).]

The article continues:

"We should worry about the behavior of the experimenter, about our own culpability, and not about the subject's choosing capacities. . . .

Such restrictions on consent, which aim at objective behaviors and results rather than at subjective decision-making processes, are common in the criminal law. For example, guilty pleas must usually be supported by a factual basis, and be knowing and voluntary. We recognize that defendants might quite rationally plead guilty to crimes they did not commit and that prosecutors might be willing to accept such pleas. However, because such pleas embroil the legal system in a monstrous falsehood, we refuse to accept them while admitting that they might indeed be in the defendant's correctly perceived best interests. . . .

   Similarly, in contract and consumer law, we often balance our general preference for unfettered respect for consensual arrangements against other concerns. . . . One purpose of these rules is undeniably to substitute the supposedly better judgment of the legislature and the judiciary about what is really in a person's best interest. . . .

   . . . The Nuremberg Code explicitly recognized the need to place non-paternalistic limits on the scope of experiments. The Code asks more of an experiment, a researcher, or society than mere consent." [Id. at 494-497.][42] . . .

Based on the record before us, no degree of parental consent, and no degree of furnished information to the parents could make the experiment at issue here, ethically or legally permissible. It was wrong in the first instance.

   We hold that in Maryland a parent, appropriate relative, or other applicable surrogate, cannot consent to the participation of a child or other person under legal disability in nontherapeutic research or studies in which there is any risk of injury or damage to the health of the subject.

   [The court then ruled that informed consent agreements in nontherapeutic research projects, under certain circumstances, can constitute contracts and can evoke "special relationships" that give rise to duties out of the breach of which negligence actions may arise, and also that governmental regulations can create duties on the part of researchers towards human subjects out of which "special relationships" can arise. The court determined there was ample evidence to support a determination of the existence of defendant's duties arising out of contract, or out of a special relationship, or out of regulations and codes.]

   We hold that on the present record, the Circuit Courts erred in their assessment of the law and of the facts as pled in granting KKI's motions for summary judgment. . . .

NOTES AND QUESTIONS

(1) How does *Grimes* respond to whether the legal system currently provides adequate protection for children in nontherapeutic experiments? Can parents rely on federal regulations governing institutional review boards to protect their children's interests? Or is medical research flawed by a conflict of interest because research

---

[42] "Categorical limitations on human research and experimentation, [would] unavoidably slow us down. . . . Many might die of AIDS who would otherwise be willing to take risks on the slight chance that the next miracle drug might really work. . . . But these losses might be — like the occasionally guilty defendant going free — a price worth paying. The question is not so much whether we can afford to honor our commitment to human dignity, free from subterfuges . . . , but whether we can afford not to, or whether we ought to. . . . The lure of perfectionism and of the all-consuming pursuit of knowledge, both the conceit and the curiosity of the scientist, all conspire to tempt us to play fast and loose with the dignity of our research subjects and ourselves." Id. at 502.

institutions establish IRBs to review their *own* experiments? One commentator elaborates on the magnitude of the problem:

> The failure to protect children in research appears to be more problematic than the few incidents reported in the mainstream press. A study published in 2002 found 65 percent of published research on children did not comply with federal requirements for consent or review. This lack of compliance occurs despite the existence for more than 20 years of federal regulations and voluntary professional guidelines stipulating compliance with the regulations as a requirement for publication. . . . [William J. Wenner, Does the Legal System Provide Adequate Protection for Children in Scientific Experiments? The Unanswered Question of Grimes v. Kennedy Krieger Institute, 8 U.C. Davis J. Juv. L. & Pol'y 243 (2004).]

(2) Do you agree with the limitations imposed on parental rights by *Grimes*? How is a court to make the determination? Should the court appoint a guardian ad litem? If so, should the guardian ad litem (a) echo the child's desires; (b) argue against participation, if only as a "devil's advocate"; or (c) make an independent judgment of what is best from the child's perspective and then advocate that result?

Should the doctrine of informed consent apply *more* strictly in the research setting? In a Canadian case involving nontherapeutic research on human subjects, the Saskatchewan Court of Appeal imposed a duty of disclosure on medical researchers "as great as, if not greater than, the duty owed by the ordinary physician or surgeon." Halushka v. Univ. of Sask., [1965] 53 D.L.R. 2d 436, 443-444. If so, how should the informed consent doctrine be changed?

(3) In the case of Hart v. Brown (discussed in *Grimes*), parents asked a court to approve a kidney transplant from one seven-year-old twin to the other. The court considered the transplant as both nonexperimental and nontherapeutic for the donor and then determined that it had the equity power to approve nontherapeutic medical procedures. The court ruled that the parents had the right to consent because the transplant would be of benefit to the healthy twin based on her warm relationship to her sister. Is *Hart* truly an adversarial proceeding? How should a court evaluate the benefits and risks to the donor twin? Is it sound to rest a conclusion on psychological benefits to the donor? Compare Strunk v. Strunk, 445 S.W.2d 149 (Ky. 1969) (reasoning that a transplant was for the benefit of a mental patient donor with the mental age of six) with In re Pescinski, 226 N.W.2d 180 (Wis. 1975) (reasoning that no benefit was established for a prospective donor who was a 39-year-old catatonic schizophrenic with a mental age of 12 who had been institutionalized for 16 years).

(4) The death of a teenager in a biomedical experiment renewed concerns about the dangers of human experimentation. In 1999, a 19-year-old youth suffered a fatal immune-system reaction during a gene therapy experiment at the University of Pennsylvania. See Alice Dembner, Lawsuits Target Medical Research Patient Safeguards, Oversight Key Issues, Boston Globe, Aug. 12, 2002, at A1.

(5) As a society can we ever condone the sacrifice of a child? Remember Prince v. Massachusetts. Why should parents be permitted to make martyrs of their children? With regard to medical experiments on healthy children involving any risks whatsoever, is it too obvious that we are sacrificing children either for the parents' own purposes or for society's purpose? Is this acceptable, even if there is a scheme for compensation funds for those injured by unsuccessful experiments?

Do you agree that because of our commitment to the dignity of the individual and to human life, our society cannot condone the obvious or blatant sacrifice of an individual against his or her will? Is this a reason parents should not be permitted to consent to a medical experiment where it is obvious that the child has not consented, and the child will in no immediate sense benefit? Is there a practical necessity to place some values (i.e., the health of future children) above the health, comfort, and perhaps lives of some living children?

For a classic debate about proxy consent in the experimentation situation, see Richard A. McCormick, Proxy Consent in the Experimental Situation, 18 Persp. in Biology & Med. 2 (Autumn 1974) (arguing that parental consent is morally legitimate because it is a reasonable presumption of what the child would wish because he ought to do so); Paul Ramsey, A Reply to Richard McCormick: The Enforcement of Morals: Nontherapeutic Research on Children, 6 Hastings Center Rep. (No. 4) 21 (Aug. 1976) (arguing that proxy consent, based on the presumptive or implied consent of child, is "a violent and a false presumption" because a child is not a bearer of moral obligations).

CHAPTER **5**

Child Custody

A. INTRODUCTION

This chapter is concerned with who should have primary responsibility for the care and custody of children. The introductory section suggests broad questions that cut across the various strands of custody law. A section on adoption follows. The third section, relating to divorce custody, explores a variety of issues relating to the settlement of disputes between biological parents concerning their children. Finally, the last section examines issues involving custody law and the new reproductive technology.

In re Baby M
537 A.2d 1227 (N.J. 1988)

WILENTZ, Chief Justice.

In this matter the Court is asked to determine the validity of a contract that purports to provide a new way of bringing children into a family. . . .

In February 1985, William Stern and Mary Beth Whitehead entered into a surrogacy contract. It recited that Stern's wife, Elizabeth, was infertile, that they wanted a child, and that Mrs. Whitehead was willing to provide that child as the mother with Mr. Stern as the father.

The contract provided that through artificial insemination using Mr. Stern's sperm, Mrs. Whitehead would become pregnant, carry the child to term, bear it, deliver it to the Sterns, and thereafter do whatever was necessary to terminate her maternal rights so that Mrs. Stern could thereafter adopt the child. Mrs. Whitehead's husband, Richard, was also a party to the contract; Mrs. Stern was not. Mr. Whitehead promised to do all acts necessary to rebut the presumption of paternity under the Parentage Act. N.J.S.A. 9:17-43a(1), -44a. Although Mrs. Stern was not a party to the surrogacy agreement, the contract gave her sole custody of the child in the event of Mr. Stern's death. Mrs. Stern's status as a nonparty to the surrogate parenting agreement presumably was to avoid the application of the baby-selling statute to this arrangement. N.J.S.A. 9:3-54.

Mr. Stern, on his part, agreed to attempt the artificial insemination and to pay Mrs. Whitehead $10,000 after the child's birth, on its delivery to him. In a separate contract, Mr. Stern agreed to pay $7,500 to the Infertility Center of New York ("ICNY"). The Center's advertising campaigns solicit surrogate mothers and encourage infertile couples to consider surrogacy. ICNY arranged for the surrogacy contract by bringing the parties together, explaining the process to them, furnishing the contractual form, and providing legal counsel.

The history of the parties' involvement in this arrangement suggests their good faith. William and Elizabeth Stern were married in July 1974, having met at the University of Michigan, where both were Ph.D. candidates. Due to financial considerations and Mrs. Stern's pursuit of a medical degree and residency, they decided to defer starting a family until 1981. Before then, however, Mrs. Stern learned that she might have multiple sclerosis and that the disease in some cases renders pregnancy a serious health risk. . . . Based on the perceived risk, the Sterns decided to forgo having their own children. The decision had a special significance for Mr. Stern. Most of his family had been destroyed in the Holocaust. As the family's only survivor, he very much wanted to continue his bloodline. Initially the Sterns considered adoption, but were discouraged by the substantial delay apparently involved and by the potential problem they saw arising from their age and their differing religious backgrounds. . . . The paths of Mrs. Whitehead and the Sterns to surrogacy were similar. Both responded to advertising by ICNY. The Sterns' response, following their inquiries into adoption, was the result of their long-standing decision to have a child. Mrs. Whitehead's response apparently resulted from her sympathy with family members and others who could have no children (she stated that she wanted to give another couple the "gift of life"); she also wanted the $10,000 to help her family. . . .

. . . On February 6, 1985, Mr. Stern and Mr. and Mrs. Whitehead executed the surrogate parenting agreement. . . . [O]n March 27, 1986, Baby M was born. . . .

Mrs. Whitehead realized, almost from the moment of birth, that she could not part with this child. . . . Nonetheless, Mrs. Whitehead was, for the moment, true to her word. Despite powerful inclinations to the contrary, she turned her child over to the Sterns on March 30 at the Whiteheads' home.

The Sterns were thrilled with their new child [and] looked forward to raising their daughter, whom they named Melissa. While aware by then that Mrs. Whitehead was undergoing an emotional crisis, they were as yet not cognizant of the depth of that crisis and its implications for their newly-enlarged family.

Later in the evening of March 30, Mrs. Whitehead became deeply disturbed, disconsolate, stricken with unbearable sadness. . . . The next day she went to the Sterns' home and told them how much she was suffering. . . . She told them that she could not live without her baby, that she must have her, even if only for one week, that thereafter she would surrender her child. The Sterns, concerned that Mrs. Whitehead might indeed commit suicide, not wanting under any circumstances to risk that, and in any event believing that Mrs. Whitehead would keep her word, turned the child over to her. . . .

The struggle over Baby M began when it became apparent that Mrs. Whitehead could not return the child to Mr. Stern. Due to Mrs. Whitehead's refusal to relinquish the baby, Mr. Stern filed a complaint seeking enforcement of the surrogacy contract. . . . After the order [in favor of Stern] was entered, ex parte, the process server, aided by the police, in the presence of the Sterns, entered Mrs. Whitehead's home to execute the order. Mr. Whitehead fled with the child, who had been handed to him through a window while those who came to enforce the order were thrown off balance by a dispute over the child's current name.

The Whiteheads immediately fled to Florida with Baby M. They stayed initially with Mrs. Whitehead's parents, . . . [later] at roughly twenty different hotels, motels, and homes in order to avoid apprehension. From time to time Mrs. Whitehead would call Mr. Stern to discuss the matter; the conversations, recorded by Mr. Stern on advice of counsel, show an escalating dispute about rights, morality, and power, accompanied by threats of Mrs. Whitehead to kill herself, to kill the child, and falsely to accuse Mr. Stern of sexually molesting Mrs. Whitehead's other daughter.

Eventually the Sterns discovered where the Whiteheads were staying, commenced supplementary proceedings in Florida, and obtained an order requiring the Whiteheads to turn over the child. . . . The prior order of the court, issued ex parte, awarding custody of the child to the Sterns pendente lite, was reaffirmed. . . . Pending final judgment, Mrs. Whitehead was awarded limited visitation with Baby M. . . .

The trial [to enforce the surrogacy contract] took thirty-two days over a period of more than two months [and included testimony by 23 witnesses and 15 expert witnesses. The trial court] held that the surrogacy contract was valid; ordered that Mrs. Whitehead's parental rights be terminated and that sole custody of the child be granted to Mr. Stern; and . . . entered an order allowing the adoption of Melissa by Mrs. Stern. . . . Pending the outcome of the appeal, we granted a continuation of visitation to Mrs. Whitehead, although slightly more limited than the visitation allowed during the trial. . . .

II. Invalidity and Unenforceability of Surrogacy Contract

We have concluded that this surrogacy contract is invalid. Our conclusion has two bases: direct conflict with existing statutes and conflict with the public policies of this State, as expressed in its statutory and decisional law. . . .

A. Conflict and Statutory Provisions

The surrogacy contract conflicts with: (1) laws prohibiting the use of money in connection with adoptions; (2) laws requiring proof of parental unfitness or abandonment before termination of parental rights is ordered or an adoption is granted; and (3) laws that make surrender of custody and consent to adoption revocable in private placement adoptions.

(1) Our law prohibits paying or accepting money in connection with any placement of a child for adoption. N.J.S.A. 9:3-54a. . . . Considerable care was taken in this case to structure the surrogacy arrangement so as not to violate this prohibition.

The arrangement was structured as follows: the adopting parent, Mrs. Stern, was not a party to the surrogacy contract; the money paid to Mrs. Whitehead was stated to be for her services — not for the adoption; the sole purpose of the contract was stated as being that "of giving a child to William Stern, its natural and biological father"; the money was purported to be "compensation for services and expenses and in no way . . . a fee for termination of parental rights or a payment in exchange for consent to surrender a child for adoption"; the fee to the Infertility Center ($7,500) was stated to be for legal representation, advice, administrative work, and other "services." Nevertheless, it seems clear that the money was paid and accepted in connection with an adoption. . . .

Mr. Stern knew he was paying for the adoption of a child; Mrs. Whitehead knew she was accepting money so that a child might be adopted; the Infertility Center knew that it was being paid for assisting in the adoption of a child. The actions of all three worked to frustrate the goals of the statute. It strains credulity to claim that these arrangements, touted by those in the surrogacy business as an attractive alternative to the usual route leading to an adoption, really amount to something other than a private placement adoption for money.

The prohibition of our statute is strong. Violation constitutes a high misdemeanor, N.J.S.A. 9:3-54c, a third-degree crime, N.J.S.A. 2C:43-1b, carrying a penalty of three to five years imprisonment. N.J.S.A. 2C:43-6a(3). The evils inherent in baby bartering are loathsome for a myriad of reasons. The child is sold without regard for whether the purchasers will be suitable parents. The natural mother does not receive the benefit of counseling and guidance to assist her in making a decision that may affect her for a lifetime. In fact, the monetary incentive to sell her child may, depending on her financial circumstances, make her decision less voluntary. . . . Baby-selling potentially results in the exploitation of all parties involved. . . .

(2) The termination of Mrs. Whitehead's parental rights, called for by the surrogacy contract . . . fails to comply with the stringent requirements of New Jersey law. . . . Our statutes, and the cases interpreting them, leave no doubt that where there has been no written surrender to an approved agency or to DYFS [Division of Youth and Family Services], termination of parental rights will not be granted in this state absent a very strong showing of abandonment or neglect. That showing is required in every context in which termination of parental rights is sought, be it an action by an approved agency, an action by DYFS, or a private placement adoption proceeding, even where the petitioning adoptive parent is, as here, a step-parent. . . .

In this case a termination of parental rights was obtained not by proving the statutory prerequisites but by claiming the benefit of contractual provisions. . . .

Since the termination was invalid, it follows, as noted above, that adoption of Melissa by Mrs. Stern could not properly be granted.

(3) The provision in the surrogacy contract stating that Mary Beth Whitehead agrees to "surrender custody . . . and terminate all parental rights" contains no clause giving her a right to rescind. It is intended to be an irrevocable consent to surrender the child for adoption. . . .

Such a provision, however, making irrevocable the natural mother's consent to surrender custody of her child in a private placement adoption, clearly conflicts with New Jersey law.

. . . The provision in the surrogacy contract, agreed to before conception, requiring the natural mother to surrender custody of the child without any right of revocation is one more indication of the essential nature of this transaction: the creation of a contractual system of termination and adoption designed to circumvent our statutes.

B. Public Policy Considerations

The surrogacy contract's invalidity, resulting from its direct conflict with the above statutory provisions, is further underlined when its goals and means are measured against New Jersey's public policy. . . .

The surrogacy contract violates the policy of this State that the rights of natural parents are equal concerning their child, the father's right no greater than the mother's. . . . The whole purpose and effect of the surrogacy contract was to give the father the exclusive right to the child by destroying the rights of the mother.

The policies expressed in our comprehensive laws governing consent to the surrender of a child . . . stand in stark contrast to the surrogacy contract and what it implies. Here there is no counseling, independent or otherwise, of the natural mother, no evaluation, no warning. . . .

Mrs. Whitehead was examined and psychologically evaluated, but if it was for her benefit, the record does not disclose that fact. The Sterns regarded the evaluation as important. . . . Yet they never asked to see it, and were content with the assumption that the Infertility Center had made an evaluation and had concluded that there was no danger that the surrogate mother would change her mind. . . . It is apparent that the profit motive got the better of the Infertility Center. Although the evaluation was made, it was not put to any use, and understandably so, for the psychologist warned that Mrs. Whitehead demonstrated certain traits that might make surrender of the child difficult and that there should be further inquiry into this issue in connection with her surrogacy. . . . *Psych eval ignored*

Under the contract, the natural mother is irrevocably committed before she knows the strength of her bond with her child. She never makes a totally voluntary, informed decision, for quite clearly any decision prior to the baby's birth is, in the most important sense, uninformed, and any decision after that, compelled by a pre-existing contractual commitment, the threat of a lawsuit, and the inducement of a $10,000 payment, is less than totally voluntary. Her interests are of little concern to those who controlled this transaction. . . .

Worst of all, however, is the contract's total disregard of the best interests of the child. There is not the slightest suggestion that any inquiry will be made at any time to determine the fitness of the Sterns as custodial parents, of Mrs. Stern as an adoptive parent, their superiority to Mrs. Whitehead, or the effect on the child of not living with her natural mother.

This is the sale of a child, or, at the very least, the sale of a mother's right to her child, the only mitigating factor being that one of the purchasers is the father. Almost every evil that prompted the prohibition of the payment of money in connection with adoptions exists here.

The differences between an adoption and a surrogacy contract should be noted, since it is asserted that the use of money in connection with surrogacy does not pose the risks found where money buys an adoption. First, and perhaps most important, all parties concede that it is unlikely that surrogacy will survive without money. . . . That conclusion contrasts with adoption; for obvious reasons, there remains a steady supply, albeit insufficient, despite the prohibitions against payment. The adoption itself, relieving the natural mother of the financial burden of supporting an infant, is the equivalent of payment.

Second, the use of money in adoptions does not produce the problem — conception occurs, and usually the birth itself, before illicit funds are offered. With surrogacy, the "problem," if one views it as such, consisting of the purchase of a woman's procreative capacity, at the risk of her life, is caused by and originates with the offer of money.

Third, with the law prohibiting the use of money in connection with adoptions, the built-in financial pressure of the unwanted pregnancy and the consequent support obligation do not lead the mother to the highest paying, ill-suited, adoptive parents. She is just as well off surrendering the child to an approved agency. In surrogacy, the highest bidders will presumably become the adoptive parents regardless of suitability, so long as payment of money is permitted.

Fourth, the mother's consent to surrender her child in adoptions is revocable, even after surrender of the child, unless it be to an approved agency, where by regulation there are protections against an ill-advised surrender. In surrogacy, consent occurs so early that no amount of advice would satisfy the potential mother's need, yet the consent is irrevocable.

The main difference, that the plight of the unwanted pregnancy is unintended while the situation of the surrogate mother is voluntary and intended, is really not significant. [T]he essential evil is the same, taking advantage of a woman's circumstances (the unwanted pregnancy or the need for money) in order to take away her child, the difference being one of degree. . . .

Intimated, but disputed, is the assertion that surrogacy will be used for the benefit of the rich at the expense of the poor. In response it is noted that the Sterns are not rich and the Whiteheads not poor. Nevertheless, it is clear to us that it is unlikely that surrogate mothers will be as proportionately numerous among those women in the top twenty percent income bracket as among those in the bottom twenty percent. . . .

The point is made that Mrs. Whitehead agreed to the surrogacy arrangement, supposedly fully understanding the consequences. Putting aside the issue of how compelling her need for money may have been, and how significant her understanding of the consequences, we suggest that her consent is irrelevant. There are, in a civilized society, some things that money cannot buy. . . .

The long-term effects of surrogacy contracts are not known, but feared — the impact on the child who learns her life was bought, that she is the offspring of someone who gave birth to her only to obtain money; the impact on the natural mother as the full weight of her isolation is felt along with the full reality of the sale of her body and her child; the impact on the natural father and adoptive mother once they realize the consequences of their conduct. . . .

In sum, the harmful consequences of this surrogacy arrangement appear to us all too palpable. In New Jersey the surrogate mother's agreement to sell her child is void. . . .

III. Termination

We have already noted that under our laws termination of parental rights cannot be based on contract, but may be granted only on proof of the statutory requirements. . . . Nothing in this record justifies a finding that would allow a court to terminate Mary Beth Whitehead's parental rights under the statutory standard. It is not simply that obviously there was no "intentional abandonment or very substantial neglect of parental duties without a reasonable expectation of reversal of that conduct in the future," N.J.S.A. 9:3-48c(1), quite the contrary, but furthermore that the trial court never found Mrs. Whitehead an unfit mother and indeed affirmatively stated that Mary Beth Whitehead had been a good mother to her other children.

Although the best interests of the child is dispositive of the custody issue in a dispute between natural parents, it does not govern the question of termination. It has long been decided that the mere fact that a child would be better off with one set of parents than with another is an insufficient basis for terminating the natural parent's rights. . . .

IV. Constitutional Issues

Both parties argue that the Constitutions — state and federal — mandate approval of their basic claims. . . . The right asserted by the Sterns is the right of procreation; that asserted by Mary Beth Whitehead is the right to the companionship of her child. . . .

The right to procreate, as protected by the Constitution, has been ruled on directly only once by the United States Supreme Court. See Skinner v. Oklahoma, 316 U.S. 535 (1942) (forced sterilization of habitual criminals violates equal protection clause of fourteenth amendment). . . . The right to procreate very simply is the right to have natural children, whether through sexual intercourse or artificial insemination. It is no more than that. Mr. Stern has not been deprived of that right. Through artificial insemination of Mrs. Whitehead, Baby M is his child. The custody, care, companionship, and nurturing that follow birth are not parts of the right to procreation; they are rights that may also be constitutionally protected, but that involve many considerations other than the right of procreation. To assert that Mr. Stern's right of procreation gives him the right to the custody of Baby M would be to assert that Mrs. Whitehead's right of procreation does not give her the right to the custody of Baby M; it would be to assert that the constitutional right of procreation includes within it a constitutionally protected contractual right to destroy someone else's right of procreation. . . .

Mr. Stern also contends that he has been denied equal protection of the laws by the State's statute granting full parental rights to a husband in relation to the child produced, with his consent, by the union of his wife with a sperm donor. N.J.S.A. 9:17-44. The claim really is that of Mrs. Stern. It is that she is in precisely the same position as the husband in the statute: she is presumably infertile, as is the husband in the statute; her spouse by agreement with a third party procreates with the understanding that the child will be the couple's child. . . .

It is quite obvious that the situations are not parallel. A sperm donor simply cannot be equated with a surrogate mother. The State has more than a sufficient basis to distinguish the two situations — even if the only difference is between the time it takes to provide sperm for artificial insemination and the time invested in a nine-month pregnancy — so as to justify automatically divesting the sperm donor of his parental rights without automatically divesting a surrogate mother. Some basis for an equal protection argument might exist if Mary Beth Whitehead had contributed her egg to be implanted, fertilized or otherwise, in Mrs. Stern, resulting in the latter's pregnancy. That is not the case here, however.

Mrs. Whitehead, on the other hand, . . . claims the right to the companionship of her child. This is a fundamental interest, constitutionally protected. Furthermore, it was taken away from her by the action of the court below. Whether that action under these circumstances would constitute a constitutional deprivation, however, we need not and do not decide. . . . We have decided that both the statutes and public policy of this state require that that termination be voided and that her parental rights be restored. . . .

V. Custody

Having decided that the surrogacy contract is illegal and unenforceable, we now must decide the custody question without regard to the provisions of the surrogacy contract. . . . Under the Parentage Act the claims of the natural father and the natural mother are entitled to equal weight. . . . The applicable rule given these circumstances is clear: the child's best interests determine custody. . . .

 . . . The Whiteheads claim that even if the child's best interests would be served by our awarding custody to the Sterns, we should not do so. . . . Their position is that in order that surrogacy contracts be deterred, custody should remain in the surrogate mother unless she is unfit, regardless of the best interests of the child. We disagree. Our declaration that this surrogacy contract is unenforceable and illegal is sufficient to deter similar agreements. We need not sacrifice the child's interests in order to make that point sharper. . . .

The Whiteheads also contend that the award of custody to the Sterns pendente lite was erroneous and that the error should not be allowed to affect the final custody decision. . . .

The argument has considerable force. [However,] [t]he child's interests come first: we will not punish it for judicial errors, assuming any were made. . . . The custody decision must be based on all circumstances, on everything that actually has occurred, on everything that is relevant to the child's best interests. . . .

There were eleven experts who testified concerning the child's best interests, either directly or in connection with matters related to that issue. Our reading of the record persuades us that the trial court's decision awarding custody to the Sterns (technically to Mr. Stern) should be affirmed. . . .

Our custody conclusion is based on strongly persuasive testimony contrasting both the family life of the Whiteheads and the Sterns and the personalities and characters of the individuals. The stability of the Whitehead family life was doubtful at the time of trial. Their finances were in serious trouble (foreclosure by Mrs. Whitehead's sister on a second mortgage was in process). Mr. Whitehead's employment, though relatively steady, was always at risk because of his alcoholism, a condition that he seems not to have been able to confront effectively. Mrs. Whitehead had not worked for quite some time, her last two employments having been part-time. One of the Whiteheads' positive attributes was their ability to bring up two children, and apparently well, even in so vulnerable a household. Yet substantial question was raised even about that aspect of their home life. The expert testimony contained criticism of Mrs. Whitehead's handling of her son's educational difficulties. Certain of the experts noted that Mrs. Whitehead perceived herself as omnipotent and omniscient concerning her children. She knew what *—Baby M?* they were thinking, what they wanted, and she spoke for them. As to Melissa, Mrs. Whitehead expressed the view that she alone knew what that child's cries and sounds meant. Her inconsistent stories about various things engendered grave doubts about her ability to explain honestly and sensitively to Baby M — and at the right time — the nature of her origin. Although faith in professional counseling is not a sine qua non of parenting, several experts believed that Mrs. Whitehead's contempt for professional help, especially professional psychological help, coincided with her feelings of omnipotence in a way that could be devastating to a child who most likely will need such help. In short, while love and affection there would be, Baby M's life with the Whiteheads promised to be too closely controlled by Mrs. Whitehead. The prospects for a wholesome independent psychological growth and development would be at serious risk.

The Sterns have no other children, but all indications are that their household and their personalities promise a much more likely foundation for Melissa to grow and thrive. There is a track record of sorts — during the one-and-a-half years of custody Baby M has done very well, and the relationship between both Mr. and Mrs. Stern and the baby has become very strong. The household is stable, and likely to remain so. Their finances are more than adequate, their circle of friends supportive, and their marriage happy. Most important, they are loving, giving, nurturing, and open-minded people. They have demonstrated the wish and ability to nurture and protect Melissa, yet at the same time to encourage her independence. Their lack of experience is more than made up for by a willingness to learn and to listen, a willingness that is enhanced by their professional training, especially Mrs. Stern's experience as a pediatrician. They are honest; they can recognize error, deal with it, and learn from it. They will try to determine rationally the best way to cope with problems in their relationship with Melissa. When the time comes to tell her about her origins, they will probably have found a means of doing so that accords with the best interests of Baby M. All in all, Melissa's future appears solid, happy, and promising with them. . . .

Some comment is required on the initial ex parte order awarding custody pendente lite to the Sterns. . . . Any application by the natural father in a surrogacy dispute for custody pending the outcome of the litigation will henceforth require proof of unfitness [of the biological mother], of danger to the child, or the like, of so high a quality and persuasiveness as to make it unlikely that such application will succeed. . . .

VI. Visitation

The trial court's decision to terminate Mrs. Whitehead's parental rights precluded it from making any determination on visitation. . . . We therefore remand the visitation issue to the trial court for an abbreviated hearing and determination as set forth below. . . .

We also note the following for the trial court's consideration: First, this is not a divorce case where visitation is almost invariably granted to the non-custodial spouse. To some extent the facts here resemble cases where the non-custodial spouse has had practically no relationship with the child; but it only "resembles" those cases. In the instant case, Mrs. Whitehead spent the first four months of this child's life as her mother and has regularly visited the child since then. Second, she is not only the natural mother, but also the legal mother, and is not to be penalized one iota because of the surrogacy contract. . . .

In all of this, the trial court should recall the touchstones of visitation: that it is desirable for the child to have contact with both parents; that besides the child's interests, the parents' interests also must be considered; but that when all is said and done, the best interests of the child are paramount.

We have decided that Mrs. Whitehead is entitled to visitation at some point, and that question is not open to the trial court on this remand. The trial court will determine what kind of visitation shall be granted to her, with or without conditions, and when and under what circumstances it should commence. It also should be noted that the guardian's recommendation of a five-year delay is most unusual — one might argue that it begins to border on termination. . . .

Conclusion

This case affords some insight into a new reproductive arrangement: the artificial insemination of a surrogate mother. The unfortunate events that have unfolded illustrate that its unregulated use can bring suffering to all involved. Potential victims include the surrogate mother and her family, the natural father and his wife, and most importantly, the child. Although surrogacy has apparently provided positive results for some infertile couples, it can also, as this case demonstrates, cause suffering to participants, here essentially innocent and well-intended.

We have found that our present laws do not permit the surrogacy contract used in this case. Nowhere, however, do we find any legal prohibition against surrogacy when the surrogate mother volunteers, without any payment, to act as a surrogate and is given the right to change her mind and to assert her parental rights. Moreover, the Legislature remains free to deal with this most sensitive issue as it sees fit, subject only to constitutional constraints. . . . The problem is how to enjoy the benefits of the technology — especially for infertile couples — while minimizing the risk of abuse. The problem can be addressed only when society decides what its values and objectives are in this troubling, yet promising, area. . . .

QUESTIONS ON *BABY M*

See p. 624 infra.

POSTSCRIPT ON *BABY M*

Subsequent to the trial court ruling and by the time of oral argument in the above case, the Whiteheads had separated. Thereafter, Mrs. Whitehead became pregnant by New York accountant Dean Gould, divorced her husband, and married Gould.

She has two children from her new marriage as well as the two Whitehead children. The New Jersey Superior Court on remand granted Mary Beth Whitehead liberal visitation rights (542 A.2d 52 (N.J. Super. Ct. Ch. Div. 1988)).

Melissa Stern, who resembles her biological mother, turned 18 on March 27, 2004. She excels in mathematics, music, and sports. She visits regularly with her biological mother's family. "By all accounts, she is a friendly, happy girl, unaffected by her early fame and the continuing tension between her birth mother and the natural father and adoptive mother she lives with." Allen Salkin, She's Come a Long Way, Baby M! Gifted Child Born Amid a Two-Family Uproar Thrives, N.Y. Post, Mar. 21, 1999, at 5.

Mary Beth Whitehead Gould, who moved to Long Island after her remarriage, refuses to call her daughter the name given to her by the Sterns. Instead, she calls her "Sassy" (the child's mispronunciation of her name when she was two years old). Melissa calls Whitehead Gould "Mom," Elizabeth Stern "Betsy," and Bill Stern "Dad." The Sterns, fiercely protective of their daughter's privacy, obtained a court order prohibiting Whitehead Gould from talking about Melissa or releasing photos of her. However, Whitehead Gould continues to voice strong opposition to surrogacy and to express the pain it caused in her life. See Elaine D'Aurizio, Whatever Happened to Baby M? Surrogate Mom Still Mourning Loss After 16 Years, Calgary Herald, May 4, 2002, at 05; Elizabeth McNeil, Mary Beth Whitehead Gould Nurtures "Baby M," People Mag., Mar. 15, 1999, at 276; Cori Anne Natoli, Baby M, Away From Spotlight, Turns 13, The Record (N. New Jersey), Mar. 28, 1999, at N07; Salkin, supra. See also Phyllis Chesler, Sacred Bonds: The Legacy of Baby M (1988); Mary Beth Whitehead, A Mother's Story (1989).

Guardianship of Phillip B., a Minor
188 Cal. Rptr. 781 (Ct. App. 1983)

RACANELLI, Presiding Justice.

Few human experiences evoke the poignancy of a filial relationship and the pathos attendant upon its disruption in society's effort to afford every child a meaningful chance to live life to its fullest promise. This appeal, posing a sensitive confrontation between the fundamental right of parental custody and the well being of a retarded child, reflects the deeply ingrained concern that the needs of the child remain paramount in the judicial monitoring of custody. In reaching our decision to affirm, we neither suggest nor imply that appellants' subjectively motivated custodial objectives affront conventional norms of parental fitness; rather, we determine only that on the unusual factual record before us, the challenged order of guardianship must be upheld in order to avert potential harm to the minor ward likely to result from appellants' continuing custody and to subserve his best interests.

On February 23, 1981, respondents Herbert and Patsy H. filed a petition for appointment as guardians of the person and estate of Phillip B., then 14 years of age. Phillip's parents, appellants Warren and Patricia B., appeared in opposition to the petition. . . .

Phillip B. was born on October 16, 1966, with Down's Syndrome, a chromosomal anomaly — usually the presence of an extra chromosome attached to the number 21 pair — resulting in varying degrees of mental retardation and a number of abnormal physical characteristics. Down's Syndrome reportedly occurs in approximately 1/10 of 1 percent of live births.

Appellants, deeply distraught over Phillip's disability, decided upon institutionalization, a course of action recommended by a state social worker and approved by appellants' pediatrician. A few days later, Phillip was transferred from the hospital to a licensed board and care facility for disabled youngsters. Although the facility was clean, it offered no structured educational or developmental programs and required that all the children (up to 8 years of age) sleep in cribs. Appellants initially visited Phillip frequently; but soon their visits became less frequent and they became more detached from him.

When Phillip was three years old a pediatrician informed appellants that Phillip had a congenital heart defect, a condition afflicting half of Down's Syndrome children. Open heart surgery was suggested when Phillip attained age six. However, appellants took no action to investigate or remedy the suspected medical problem.

After the board and care facility had been sold during the summer of 1971, appellants discovered that the condition of the facility had seriously deteriorated under the new management; it had become dirty and cluttered with soiled clothing, and smelled strongly of urine. Phillip was very thin and listless and was being fed watery oatmeal from a bottle. At appellants' request, a state social worker arranged for Phillip's transfer in January, 1972, to We Care, a licensed residential facility for developmentally disabled children located in San Jose, where he remained up to the time of trial. . . . In April 1972, We Care employed Jeanne Haight (later to become program director and assistant administrator of the facility) to organize a volunteer program. . . . Mrs. Haight, who undertook a recruitment program for volunteers, soon recruited respondent Patsy H., who had helped to found a school for children with learning disabilities where Mrs. Haight had once been vice-principal. Mrs. H. began working at We Care on a daily basis. Her husband, respondent Herbert H., and their children, soon joined in the volunteer activities.

Mrs. H., initially assigned to work with Phillip and another child, assisted Phillip in experimenting with basic sensory experiences, improving body coordination, and in overcoming his fear of steps. Mr. H. and one of the H. children helped fence the yard area, put in a lawn, a sandbox, and install some climbing equipment.

Mrs. Haight promptly initiated efforts to enroll Phillip in a preschool program for the fall of 1972, which required parental consent.[4] She contacted Mr. B. who agreed to permit Phillip to participate provided learning aptitude could be demonstrated. Mrs. H. used vocabulary cards to teach Phillip 25 to 50 new words and to comprehend word association. Although Mr. B. failed to appear at the appointed time in order to observe what Phillip had learned, he eventually gave his parental consent enabling Phillip to attend Hope Preschool in October, 1972.

Respondents continued working with Phillip coordinating their efforts with his classroom lessons. Among other things, they concentrated on development of

---

[4] Apparently, Phillip had received no formal preschool education for the retarded even though such training programs were available in the community. Expert testimony established that early introduction to preschool training is of vital importance in preparing a retarded child for entry level public education.

feeding skills and toilet training and Mr. H. and the two eldest children gradually became more involved in the volunteer program.

Phillip subsequently attended a school for the trainable mentally retarded (TMR) where the children are taught basic survival words. They are capable of learning to feed and dress themselves appropriately, doing basic community activities such as shopping, and engaging in recreational activities. There is no attempt to teach them academics, and they are expected to live in sheltered settings as adults. . . .

A pattern of physical and emotional detachment from their son was developed by appellants over the next several years. In contrast, during the same period, respondents established a close and caring relationship with Phillip. Beginning in December, 1972, Phillip became a frequent visitor at respondents' home; with appellants' consent, Phillip was permitted to spend weekends with respondents, a practice which continued regularly and often included weekday evenings. At the same time, respondents maintained frequent contact with Phillip at We Care as regular volunteer visitors. Meanwhile, appellants visited Phillip at the facility only a few times a year; however, no overnight home visits occurred until after the underlying litigation ensued.

Respondents played an active role in Phillip's behavioral development and educational training. They consistently supplemented basic skills training given Phillip at We Care.[5]

Phillip was openly accepted as a member of the H. family whom he came to love and trust. He eventually had his own bedroom; he was included in sharing household chores. Mr. H. set up a workbench for Phillip and helped him make simple wooden toys; they attended special Boy Scout meetings together. And Phillip regularly participated in family outings. Phillip referred to the H. residence as "my house." When Phillip began to refer to the Hs. as "Mom" and "Dad," they initially discouraged the familiar reference, eventually succeeding in persuading Phillip to use the discriminate references "Mama Pat" and "Dada Bert" and "Mama B." and "Daddy B."[6] Both Mrs. Haight and Phillip's teacher observed significant improvements in Phillip's development and behavior. Phillip had developed, in Mrs. Haight's opinion, "true love and strong [emotional] feelings" for respondents.

Meanwhile, appellants continued to remain physically and emotionally detached from Phillip. The natural parents intellectualized their decision to treat Phillip differently from their other children. Appellants testified that Phillip, whom they felt would always require institutionalization, should not be permitted to form close emotional attachments which — upon inevitable disruption — would traumatize the youngster.

In matters of Phillip's health care needs, appellants manifested a reluctant — if not neglectful — concern. When Dr. Gathman, a pediatric cardiologist, diagnosed

[5] In addition to their efforts to improve Phillip's communication and reading skills through basic sign language and word association exercises, respondents toilet-trained Phillip and taught him to use eating utensils and to sleep in a regular bed (the latter frequently monitored during the night).

[6] At respondents' suggestion, Mrs. Haight requested a photograph of appellants to show Phillip who his parents were; but appellants failed to provide one.

Mr Hips B refuse to give him proper med treatments

a ventricular septal defect[7] in Phillip's heart in early 1973 and recommended catheterization (a medically accepted pre-surgery procedure to measure pressure and to examine the interior of the heart), appellants refused their consent.

In the spring of 1977, Dr. Gathman again recommended heart catheterization in connection with the anticipated use of general anesthesia during Phillip's major dental surgery. Appellants consented to the pre-operative procedure which revealed that the heart defect was surgically correctable with a maximum risk factor of 5 percent. At a conference attended by appellants and Mrs. Haight in June, 1977, Dr. Gathman recommended corrective surgery in order to avoid a progressively deteriorating condition resulting in a "bed-to-chair existence" and the probability of death before the age of 30.[8] Although Dr. Gathman — as requested by Mrs. B. — supplied the name of a parent of Down's Syndrome children with similar heart disease, no contact was ever made. Later that summer, appellants decided — without obtaining an independent medical consultation — against surgery. Appellants' stated reason was that Dr. Gathman had "painted" an inaccurate picture of the situation. They felt that surgery would be merely life-prolonging rather than life-saving, presenting the possibility that they would be unable to care for Phillip during his later years. A few months later, in early 1978, appellants' decision was challenged in a juvenile dependency proceeding initiated by the district attorney on the ground that the withholding of surgery constituted neglect within the meaning of Welfare and Institutions Code section 300, subdivision (b); the juvenile court's dismissal of the action on the basis of inconclusive evidence was ultimately sustained on appeal (In re Phillip B. (1979) 92 Cal. App. 3d 796, 156 Cal. Rptr. 48, *cert. den. sub nom.* Bothman v. Warren B., 445 U.S. 949 (1980)).

In September, 1978, upon hearing from a staff member of We Care that Phillip had been regularly spending weekends at respondents' home, Mr. B. promptly forbade Phillip's removal from the facility (except for medical purposes and school attendance) and requested that respondents be denied personal visits with Phillip at We Care. Although respondents continued to visit Phillip daily at the facility, the abrupt cessation of home visits produced regressive changes in Phillip's behavior: he began acting out violently when respondents prepared to leave, begging to be taken "home"; he resorted to profanity; he became sullen and withdrawn when respondents were gone; bed-wetting regularly occurred, a recognized symptom of emotional disturbance in children. He began to blame himself for the apparent rejection by respondents; he began playing with matches and on one occasion he set his clothes afire; on another, he rode his tricycle to respondents' residence a few blocks away proclaiming on arrival that he was "home." He continuously pleaded to return home with respondents. Many of the behavioral changes continued to the time of trial.

Appellants unsuccessfully pressed to remove Phillip from We Care notwithstanding the excellent care he was receiving. . . . Meanwhile, Phillip continued

---

[7] The disease, found in a large number of Down's Syndrome children . . . consists of an opening or "hole" between the heart chambers resulting in elevated blood pressure and impairment of vascular functions. The disease can become a progressive, and ultimately fatal, disorder.

[8] Dr. Gathman's explicit description of the likely ravages of the disease created anger and distrust on the part of appellants and motivated them to seek other opinions and to independently assess the need for surgery.

living at We Care, periodically visiting at appellants' home. But throughout, the strong emotional attachment between Phillip and respondents remained intact. . . .

[T]he right of parents to retain custody of a child is fundamental and may be disturbed " 'only in extreme cases of persons acting in a fashion incompatible with parenthood.' " . . . Accordingly, the Legislature has imposed the stringent requirement that before a court may make an order awarding custody of a child to a nonparent without consent of the parents, "it shall make a finding that an award of custody to a parent would be detrimental to the child and the award to a nonparent is required to serve the best interests of the child." (Civ. Code, §4600, subd. (c)). That requirement is equally applicable to guardianship proceedings under Probate Code section 1514, subdivision (b). . . .

The trial court expressly found that an award of custody to appellants would be harmful to Phillip in light of the psychological or 'de facto' parental relationship established between him and respondents. Such relationships have long been recognized in the fields of law and psychology. As Justice Tobriner has cogently observed, "The fact of biological parenthood may incline an adult to feel a strong concern for the welfare of his child, but it is not an essential condition; a person who assumes the role of parent, raising the child in his own home, may in time acquire an interest in the 'companionship, care, custody and management' of that child. The interest of the 'de facto parent' is a substantial one . . . deserving of legal protection" [citing the seminal study of Goldstein, Freud & Solnit, Beyond the Best Interests of the Child (1973) pp. 17–20, hereafter Goldstein]. Persons who assume such responsibility have been characterized by some interested professional observers as "psychological parents": "Whether any adult becomes the psychological parent of a child is based . . . on day-to-day interaction, companionship, and shared experiences. The role can be fulfilled either by a biological parent or by an adoptive parent or by any other caring adult — but never by an absent, inactive adult, whatever his biological or legal relationship to the child may be." (Goldstein, supra, p. 19.)

Appellants vigorously challenge the evidence and finding that respondents have become Phillip's de facto or psychological parents since he did not reside with them full-time. . . . They argue that the subjective concept of psychological parenthood, relying on such nebulous factors as "love and affection" is susceptible to abuse and requires the countervailing element of objectivity provided by a showing of the child's longterm residency in the home of the claimed psychological parent.

We disagree. Adoption of the proposed standard would require this court to endorse a novel doctrine of child psychology unsupported either by a demonstrated general acceptance in the field of psychology or by the record before us. Although psychological parenthood is said to result from "day-to-day attention to [the child's] needs for physical care, nourishment, comfort, affection, and stimulation" (Goldstein, supra, p. 17), appellants fail to point to any authority or body of professional opinion that equates daily attention with full-time residency. To the contrary, the record contains uncontradicted expert testimony that while psychological parenthood usually will require residency on a "24-hour basis," it is not an absolute requirement; further, that the frequency and quality of Phillip's weekend visits with respondents, together with the regular weekday visits at We Care, provided an adequate foundation to establish the crucial parent-child relationship. . . .

Appellants also challenge the sufficiency of the evidence to support the finding that their retention of custody would have been detrimental to Phillip. In making the critical finding, the trial court correctly applied the "clear and convincing" standard of proof necessary to protect the fundamental rights of parents in all cases involving a nonparent's bid for custody. . . .

The record contains abundant evidence that appellants' retention of custody would cause Phillip profound emotional harm. . . . [T]estimony indicated that, as with all children, Phillip needs love and affection, and he would be profoundly hurt if he were deprived of the existing psychological parental relationship with respondents in favor of maintaining unity with his biological parents.

Phillip's conduct unmistakably demonstrated that he derived none of the emotional benefits attending a close parental relationship largely as a result of appellants' individualized decision to abandon that traditional supporting role. Dr. Becking testified that no "bonding or attachment" has occurred between Phillip and his biological parents, a result palpably consistent with appellants' view that Phillip had none of the emotional needs uniquely filled by natural parents. We conclude that such substantial evidence adequately supports the finding that parental custody would have resulted in harmful deprivation of these human needs contrary to Phillip's best interests.

Finally, there was also evidence that Phillip would experience educational and developmental injury if parental custody remains unchanged. At Phillip's functioning level of disability, he can normally be expected to live at least semi-independently as an adult in a supervised residential setting and be suitably trained to work in a sheltered workshop or even a competitive environment (e.g., performing assembly duties or custodial tasks in a fast-food restaurant). Active involvement of a parent figure during the formative stages of education and habilitation is of immeasurable aid in reaching his full potential. Unfortunately, appellants' deliberate abdication of that central role would effectively deny Phillip any meaningful opportunity to develop whatever skills he may be capable of achieving. . . .

Nor can we overlook evidence of potential physical harm to Phillip due to appellants' passive neglect in response to Phillip's medical condition. Although it appears probable that the congenital heart defect is no longer correctable by surgery, the trial court could have reasonably concluded that appellants' past conduct reflected a dangerously passive approach to Phillip's future medical needs.

It is a clearly stated legislative policy that persons with developmental disabilities shall enjoy — inter alia — the right to treatment and rehabilitation services, the right to publicly supported education, the right to social interaction, and the right to prompt medical care and treatment. Moreover, the legislative purpose underlying Civil Code section 4600 is to protect the needs of children generally " ' . . . to be raised with love, emotional security and physical safety.' " When a trial court is called upon to determine the custody of a developmentally disabled or handicapped child, as here, it must be guided by such overriding policies rather than by the personal beliefs or attitudes of the contesting parties, since it is the child's interest which remains paramount. Clearly, the trial court faithfully complied with such legislative mandate in exercising its sound discretion based upon the evidence presented. We find no abuse as contended by appellants.

We strongly emphasize, as the trial court correctly concluded, that the fact of detriment cannot be proved solely by evidence that the biological parent has elected to institutionalize a handicapped child, or that nonparents are able and willing to offer the child the advantages of their home in lieu of institutional placement. Sound reasons may exist justifying institutionalization of a handicapped child. But the totality of the evidence under review permits of no rational conclusion other than that the detriment caused Phillip, and its possible recurrence, was due not to appellants' choice to institutionalize but their calculated decision to remain emotionally and physically detached — abdicating the conventional role of competent decision-maker in times of demonstrated need — thus effectively depriving him of any of the substantial benefits of a true parental relationship. It is the emotional abandonment of Phillip, not his institutionalization, which inevitably has created the unusual circumstances which led to the award of limited custody to respondents. We do not question the sincerity of appellants' belief that their approach to Phillip's welfare was in their combined best interests. But the record is replete with substantial and credible evidence supporting the trial court's determination, tested by the standard of clear and convincing proof, that appellants' retention of custody has caused and will continue to cause serious detriment to Phillip and that his best interests will be served through the guardianship award of custody to respondents. . . .

Robert H. Mnookin, The Guardianship of Phillip B.: Jay Spears' Achievement
40 Stan. L. Rev. 841, 852-854 (1988)

[Phillip's heart] catheterization was finally performed in the summer of 1983. . . . [1] It showed that Phillip had miraculously developed a new blockage that had not damaged his heart and yet had protected his lungs from further damage. The doctors reported that surgery was clearly indicated. . . . In September, Phillip underwent open heart surgery at the University of California hospital in San Francisco. [He] came through the surgery beautifully. . . .

Soon after the decision of the appellate court, the Beckers and the Heaths entered into a settlement agreement. The Beckers agreed to dismiss with prejudice the state court actions against the Heaths and further agreed that "unless there is a substantial and material change in the facts and circumstances currently known to the Beckers, the Beckers agree to take no legal action to remove custody of Phillip from the Heaths or to contest, limit or terminate the Heaths' status as Phillip's guardians and/or conservators."[56] The Heaths agreed that they would "provide and assume full responsibility for the cost of Phillip's care, and shall relieve the Beckers of and indemnify them against any liability for said costs."[57] They further agreed to permit either the Beckers or Phillip's brothers (after they reached adulthood) to

---

[1] For an earlier neglect proceeding brought on behalf of Phillip B. in an unsuccessful effort to compel the Beckers to consent to a heart catheterization, see In re Phillip B., 156 Cal. Rptr. 48 (Ct. App. 1979), reprinted and discussed supra pp. 377-380.

[56] Agreement entered into by Warren and Patricia Becker and Herbert and Patsy Heath at 3 (Aug. 16, 1983). . . .

[57] Id. at 3.

visit Phillip at least two days a year and to provide Phillip with Catholic last rites if he were near death. Each party agreed to assume their own costs on appeal.

The Heaths very much wanted to adopt Phillip; and in early 1984, they filed a petition requesting adoption. The Beckers would neither refuse nor grant consent, so that things remained at a standstill until Phillip turned 18, an event that created new legal options. At 18, the guardianship would, of course, end. Because of Phillip's disabilities, a conservatorship would be necessary. The Heaths promptly petitioned to become Phillip's limited conservators. We also petitioned for a decree of adoption.

Since Phillip was now an adult, it was necessary to proceed under the adult adoption statute, which provides that a court may issue a decree of adoption based on an agreement of adoption executed by the adopting parties. Because it was not clear that Phillip had the capacity to enter into such an agreement himself, we petitioned the court for an order authorizing the conservators to enter into a contract of adult adoption on behalf of their conservatee.

The court ordered an investigation; and the report plainly stated that although Phillip did not understand "the legalities" of the proceedings, he understood "perfectly the question, do you want Mr. and Mrs. Heath to continue to take care of you? His answer, given repeatedly, was that he does. He was most insistent that he wants to live with the Heaths and do things with them. Either as Phillip Heath-Becker or Phillip Becker-Heath." In February 1985, after full notice to the Beckers, who indicated that they did not object, the Heaths adopted Phillip.

Phillip Becker-Heath, a young man with Down syndrome, is now 21 years old. For six years he has lived with his adoptive parents, Pat and Herb Heath, in a comfortable home in San Jose. The Heaths are devoted to Phillip, who is now, more than ever, the center of their lives; their older sons are married, and their daughter is living on her own.

Phillip's life has settled into a comfortable routine. In the morning he gets himself up around 7:00, puts on his glasses and hearing aid, dresses himself, and helps "Mama Pat" with breakfast. The Heaths take him to the bus stop where he catches the county transit bus. The bus drops Phillip a few blocks from the Joseph McKinnon School in San Jose, and he walks the rest of the way on his own.

As part of his school program, Phillip works at the Santa Clara Valley Medical Center where he busses tables in the cafeteria. Earlier this year he worked in the Hewlett Packard cafeteria as part of a special county program for the disabled. He is learning to read, albeit not without a struggle. A tutor works with Phillip at home to supplement the program at McKinnon. Pat expects his reading skills to improve rapidly because Phillip recently began to use a reading program that he runs himself on the Apple computer he received from the Heaths for Christmas.

Phillip loves sports. Because the congenital heart defect that had threatened to cut his life short was corrected by surgery in 1983, Phillip now actively participates in the Special Olympics. He enjoys bowling, basketball, softball, and soccer. Joe Montana's picture hangs in his bedroom, and Phillip and the Heaths look forward to watching the Forty-Niners' games on television. Phillip roots for "number sixteen."

Phillip is a warm, affectionate, and optimistic young man who, according to Pat, is "a little bit cocky, and at times a smart aleck." He is helpful around the house. His chores include taking out the trash and raking the leaves in the yard. The Heaths are committed to seeing that Phillip develops the skills, discipline, and confidence necessary to hold down a job and lead a productive and largely independent life, notwithstanding his handicap. Pat and Herb feel certain that he will do so. "Two aspects of his character," according to Pat, "serve him very well. He wants to be a 'good boy' and he loves to work."

———————

Phillip Becker-Heath recently turned 38 years old. He is doing well. After two years of residence in a group home, he recently returned to the Heaths' home following the death of his girlfriend of 20 years. "They adored each other," says Pat Heath. Phillip's biggest problem now, according to Pat Heath, "is finding decent work — because of all the governmental cutbacks." He still participates in the Special Olympics in bowling, basketball, and golf. He had to give up his favorite hobby, computer art design, when his graphic arts teacher retired. Phillip loves music. "His tastes are very eclectic," describes Pat Heath, "from Pavorotti to rock and roll!"

"He's turned out to be the same sweet loving guy as when he was little," she adds. "He's bright and willing to learn new things. His vocabulary is still growing." Pat Heath says,"All my grandkids are wonderful with Phillip. He's got a lot of loving people in his life."

No one from Phillip's biological family contacted him since one week after his heart surgery in 1983. Mr. Becker passed away from cancer in 1995. "They don't know what they missed," says Pat Heath. "He's absolutely been the joy of my life." (Personal communication with Pat Heath, Jan. 4, 2005.)

1. The Problem of Delay

Note the delays involved in *Phillip B.* and *Baby M.* What do you think the effect of this delay is on the lives of the children?

In The Best Interests of the Child: The Least Detrimental Alternative,[2] Goldstein, Freud, and Solnit emphasize that "children have their own built-in time sense, based on the urgency of their instinctual and emotional needs and on the limits of their cognitive capacities. This results in their intolerance for postponement of gratification and their sensitivity to the length of separations."

What steps do you think might be taken to reduce the time social agencies and courts take in resolving custody disputes? Goldstein, Freud, and Solnit suggest that child placement decisions should be treated as "emergencies." Should appeals be eliminated? What effect would this have had in *Baby M* and *Phillip B.?*

2. Varieties of Custody Law

In many states, custody law reflects a complicated and chaotic multiplicity of such factors as the doctrinal thread invoked, the identity of the disputants, their prior

---

[2] Joseph Goldstein et al., The Best Interests of the Child: The Least Detrimental Alternative 9 (1996).

relationship to the child, and the setting from which the dispute arose. Most states have four separate strands of law that can be used to resolve a custody dispute: (a) divorce law, (b) guardianship law, (c) juvenile court child neglect laws, and (d) laws relating to termination of parental rights to free a child for adoption.[3] Typically, no single court has jurisdiction over all four strands. Each strand is invoked most often between particular kinds of parties, but the strands often have overlapping application. Moreover, the term "custody" is itself ambiguous because each of the four strands normally carries different legal implications for the parent-child relationship.

Phillip B. and *Baby M* illustrate the possibility of overlapping application of the various strands of custody law and the complexity of the custody determination. The first action brought on behalf of Phillip was a neglect proceeding (see Chapter 4, p. 377). Later, the Heaths sought custody of Phillip through a guardianship proceeding. Finally, they initiated an action to adopt Phillip. How do the custodial rights of a guardian differ from those of an adoptive parent? *Baby M* was an adoption dispute, but was treated by the lower court much like a divorce custody dispute. Why? How did this affect the court's disposition of the case?

As background for consideration of these sorts of questions, a brief summary of the four dominant strands of custody law follows.

a. Juvenile Court Child Neglect Laws

The power of government to protect children by removing them from parental custody has roots deep in American history. By the early nineteenth century, the parens patriae power of the state was thought sufficient to empower courts of equity to remove a child from parental custody and appoint a suitable person to act as guardian.

Every state today has a statute allowing a court, typically a juvenile court, to assume jurisdiction over an abused or neglected child and to remove the child from parental custody under broad and vague standards reminiscent of those invoked by courts of equity in the nineteenth century. A complex social welfare bureaucracy, however, now is responsible for discovering children in need of protection and initiating appropriate judicial action. A case usually reaches juvenile court only after weaving its way through a process where numerous officials — including social workers, probation officers, and court personnel — may have had contact with the family. The judicial inquiry itself usually contains two stages: first, the court must determine whether it has jurisdiction over the child; if so, the second stage involves a dispositional hearing, where the judge decides the manner of intervention. The court may leave the child at home and require supervision of the home, psychological counseling for the family, or both. But often the court will remove the child from parental custody, subject to some court review of the family situation at a later date.

If the court removes the child from parental custody, it normally orders that the care and custody of the child be supervised by the welfare or probation department, which, in turn, will place the child with relatives, foster parents, or in an

---

[3] See Robert H. Mnookin, Child Custody Adjudication: Judicial Functions in the Face of Indeterminacy, 39 Law & Contemp. Probs. 226 (1975).

institution. Placement does not extinguish the natural parent's duty to support the child financially, although ordinarily the state and the federal governments bear the cost because most affected families are very poor. The state agency and ultimately the court — not the foster parents — are responsible for deciding where the child will live.

This process can generate a variety of custody disputes. The natural parent may object to the initial attempt to remove the child.[4] After removal, the natural parent may seek the return of the child, and the social welfare department[5] or foster parents[6] may object. The foster parents may also object to the transfer of the child to some other foster home.[7] For all of these sorts of disputes, the law of juvenile neglect provides the principal framework for resolution. Initially, most juvenile court neglect proceedings involve the child protection function, for usually an agency of the state is asking a juvenile court to deny custody to a child's parent or parents on the basis of abuse or neglect that is thought to require state intervention in order to protect the child. Some juvenile court proceedings, however, may involve the private dispute settlement function as well, for there may be competing private claimants.

b. Involuntary Termination of Parental Rights — Adoption

Adoption[8] in this country normally requires that the rights of the natural parent first be extinguished. In most cases, the natural parent or parents consent to the adoption. But if the natural parents withhold consent, state laws provide for adoption without such consent under specified circumstances. Some states have separate proceedings for the involuntary termination of parental rights, and some authorize such termination as a remedy in neglect cases. Apart from contested termination proceedings, a custody dispute may arise if a natural parent challenges the adoption or attempts to withdraw his consent.

Termination cases often involve the child protection function: the state may initiate termination proceedings to free for adoption a child already a dependent of the juvenile court on the basis of allegations that the child has been neglected or abandoned by his natural parents. But termination proceedings may also arise out of situations where a stepparent wishes to adopt a spouse's child and therefore seeks to terminate the parental rights of the noncustodial natural parent. Where contested, these cases involve the private dispute settlement as well.

The legal consequences of termination are substantial. Termination extinguishes the natural parent's duty to support the child and may affect the intestate inheritance relationship between the child and his natural parents. More

---

[4] In re Rubisela E., 101 Cal. Rptr. 2d 760 (Ct. App. 2000).

[5] State ex rel. V.F.R., 815 So. 2d 1035 (La. Ct. App. 2002).

[6] In re Terrance G., 731 N.Y.S.2d 832 (Fam. Ct. 2001); John B. v. Niagara Cty. Dept. Soc. Servs., 735 N.Y.S.2d 333 (App. Div. 2001).

[7] Ex parte Rayer, 560 S.E.2d 397 (S.C. Ct. App. 2000).

[8] Adoption is the legal process by which a child acquires parents other than his biological parents, and parents acquire a child other than a biological child. The resulting legal relationship is identical to that of a biological parent and child. See infra p. 474.

significantly for present purposes, however, the natural parent's custodial rights are completely abolished.

c. Divorce Custody Law

Most child custody disputes requiring judicial resolution arise out of the dissolution of marriage. When a child's parents live together, the issue of which parent has the right to custody does not arise. But when each parent has a separate household, they may disagree about who should have primary responsibility to care for the child. If a divorce is granted, a court at that time normally will determine who will have custody. Courts resolve disputes between parents before or after divorce as well. A substantial body of law (which is here styled "divorce custody law") provides standards for the resolution of such disputes. Although it normally applies to disputes simply between two parents, the occasion of divorce may also lead a relative or friend to ask for custody. In all events the application of divorce custody law nearly always involves the private dispute settlement function, for there are competing private parties — usually the child's parents — seeking custody on the basis of their relationship to the child; but when the court must evaluate a claim that one of the parties would endanger the child, the child-protection function may be involved as well.

When courts award "custody" incident to separation or divorce, the winner usually has less than all the rights included in custody within the on-going two-parent family. In some cases, the parents can have joint custody, with the child periodically living with each parent. In other cases, only one parent has custody, lives with the child, and makes decisions about care and education, including religious training. Such custody is usually subject to the other parent's rights of visitation. Moreover, the divorce decree can provide that the noncustodial parent must be consulted or must consent before certain important decisions are made about the child's education. Finally, the duty of support is often separated from the right to have the child live with the particular parent. In short, divorce custody law permits courts great flexibility in dividing the various legal elements of the parent-child relationship.

d. Guardianship Custody Law

The appointment of a guardian of a child's person (personal guardian) is normally made by a probate court. While there are different types of guardians and the term is used to describe very different sorts of relationships, a personal guardian basically has the exclusive right to decide where the child lives, can control and discipline the child, has the power to consent to the child's medical care, but has no duty to support a child.

Guardianship proceedings typically arise when neither of a child's parents is alive or available and a nonparent wishes to have custodial rights. Most guardianship appointments are probably uncontested, but when there are competing claimants, the dispute is governed by guardianship law. Sometimes a natural parent can be involved in such disputes. This may occur after the death of the parent who has had custody following a divorce. If the child's stepparent (i.e., the spouse of the deceased parent) or some other relative of the deceased parent wishes to become the child's legal guardian, the noncustodial natural parent may object. Sometimes guardianship proceedings are initiated by a noncustodial spouse who wishes appointment to defeat an earlier divorce custody decision. Occasionally, after a neglected child has been placed in foster care by a juvenile court, the foster parents will seek appointment as the guardian. A guardianship custody dispute nearly always involves the private dispute settlement function, for there are competing private litigants; but it may involve the child protection function as well if the court must evaluate a claim that one of the claimants will endanger the child.

3. Two Functions of Custody Law: Private Dispute Settlement and Child Protection

Arguably, courts perform two very different functions in the resolution of custody disputes: private dispute settlement and child protection. The *private dispute settlement* function is involved when the court must choose between two or more private individuals, each of whom claims an associational interest with the child. While such a dispute ordinarily arises between adults, it also affects the child. The characterization of this function as "private" does not imply that a court should treat a child as an "object" and consider only the interests of the adults. By providing a judicial forum, the state protects the substantial public interest in resolving such disputes without resort to private force or violence and also protects the expectations and interests of the individuals directly affected, including the child. The second function, *child protection*, involves the judicial enforcement of standards of parental behavior believed necessary to protect the child. This function is consistent with the well-established principle that the *parens patriae* power of the state empowers courts to remove children from parental custody if such a step is necessary for their protection.

In *Baby M*, what role was the court playing? Was it settling a private dispute between the natural father and the natural mother? Or was it exercising *parens patriae* authority on behalf of a child who was one of its wards? What about in *Phillip B.?* What other interests were at stake in these two cases? What are other purposes and functions of custody law? What are the appropriate roles for the court to play?

As you proceed through this chapter, consider the following questions: in private disputes, what standard should be used in resolving the competing claims of adults who wish to care for the child? What mechanisms, other than adjudication, may be appropriate?

4. What Role Should Psychological Evidence Play in Deciding Custody Disputes? Should the Insights of Psychology and Psychiatry Be Used for Reformulation of Custody Standards?

Some time ago, a seminal note in the Yale Law Journal argued:

> Optimum custody goals [meeting the standard of the best interests of the child] may be further defined by concentration on the psychological well-being of the

child, where "psychological well-being" is used to denote the mental and emotional health of the child — specifically, a process of personality development within the framework of patterns of normal growth as posited by the behavior sciences. [Note, Alternatives to "Parental Right" in Child Custody Disputes Involving Third Parties, 73 Yale L.J. 151, 157 (1963).]

While suggesting that concern for the psychological welfare of the child, as opposed to the child's physical and material welfare, was implicit in the criteria sometimes referred to in cases applying the best interests of the child test, this note argued that courts should adopt a "psychological best interests test," id. at 162; and that "further inquiry should be made into the fundamental relationship between 'psychological' parent and child." Id. at 160. Under a psychological best interests test, it explained:

> [The] primary aim would be to identify and describe the existing affection-relationship(s), chiefly from the perspective of the particular child who is the subject of the custody dispute. Such relationships might be inferred from evidence shedding light on three questions: the continuity of the relationship between child and adult in terms of proximity and duration; the love of the adult toward the child; and the affection and trust of the child toward the adult. . . . [Id. at 162.]

A few years later, Professor Joseph Goldstein, himself trained in both law and psychiatry, wrote:

> If the law student (who is also hopefully the future judge) were to study the primary sources of psychoanalysis, he would see that at most and at best a psychoanalytically-informed definition of the child's *best interest* would assist court or adoption agency in deciding which disposition among available alternatives is likely to provide the child, whatever his endowments, with the best available opportunity to fulfill his potential in society as a civilized human being. [Joseph Goldstein, Psychoanalysis and Jurisprudence, 77 Yale L.J. 1053, 1076 (1968).]

And Professor Andrew S. Watson has suggested the appropriate roles for expert witnesses, lawyers, and judges in custody disputes and described various factors that would be relevant to the application of a psychological best interests of the child test.

There has been some movement to reformulate juvenile neglect and dependency standards on the basis of psychology as well. Some states have amended their child neglect statutes expressly to include "emotional" neglect. The Minnesota statute, for example, defines a neglected child in part as one whose parents fail to provide the child with "necessary food, clothing, shelter, education, and other care and control necessary for the child's physical, mental or *emotional* health and development, if the parent is physically and financially able." Minn. Stat. Ann. §260C. 301 (2003 & Supp. 2004) (emphasis added). In addition, state legislatures have enacted a broad range of civil and criminal statutes that take into account the negative impact of exposure to domestic violence upon children's psychological development.[9]

---

[9] Lois A. Weithorn, Protecting Children from Exposure to Domestic Violence: The Use and Abuse of Child Maltreatment, 53 Hastings L.J. 1, 12-26 (2001).

The best known proposal to use psychology and psychiatry to establish guidelines for the reformulation of custody standards is found in Joseph Goldstein et al., Beyond the Best Interests of the Child (2d ed. 1979). Suggesting that legal standards give too little weight to the psychological well-being of the child, Goldstein, Freud, and Solnit propose "generally applicable guidelines" to govern all "child placement" disputes.[10] And they would require a court to choose for a particular child the "least detrimental available alternative," which the authors define as:

> [T]hat child placement and procedure for child placement which maximizes, in accord with the child's sense of time . . . the child's opportunity for being wanted . . . and for maintaining on a continuous, unconditional, and permanent basis a relationship with at least one adult who is or will become the child's psychological parent.[11]

Any "intervenor" — whether the state, natural parents, or others — who wishes to alter a child's placement would have the burden of establishing that the child is unwanted and if so, that his current placement is not "the least detrimental alternative." The focus would be exclusively on the interests of the child, and no preference would be given to the natural parent as such.[12]

In recent years, a new controversial psychological theory has emerged in high-conflict custody disputes. Several courts have considered psychological evidence in custody battles of the "parental alienation syndrome" (PAS). See, e.g., In re Marriage of Bates, 289 Ill. Dec. 218 (Ill. 2004) (holding that trial court did not abuse its discretion by allowing expert's testimony on parental alienation syndrome). PAS, a theory developed by psychiatrist Richard A. Gardner, identifies a set of conscious and unconscious behaviors by one parent to undermine the child's affection toward the other parent by means of a campaign of vilification and denigration. Dr. Gardner recommends that custody should be transferred to the other parent in severe cases of PAS. PAS has been criticized by many legal and psychological commentators who argue that it lacks any scientific basis and fails to take into account the many possible explanations for parental behavior, such as domestic violence or child abuse, the child's developmental stage, and the parent's caregiving abilities.

See generally Richard A. Gardner, The Parental Alienation Syndrome (2d ed. 1998); Carol S. Bruch, Parental Alienation Syndrome: Getting It Wrong in Child Custody Cases, 35 Fam. L.Q. 527 (2001); Joan B. Kelly & Janet R. Johnston, The Alienated Child: A Reformulation of Parental Alienation Syndrome, 39 Fam. Ct. Rev. 249 (2001); Janet R. Johnston & Joan B. Kelly, Rejoinder to Gardner's "Commentary on Kelly and Johnston's 'The Alienated Child: A Reformulation of

[10] According to Goldstein, Freud, and Solnit, these procedures include "birth certification, neglect, abandonment, battered child, foster care, adoption, delinquency, youth offenses, as well as custody in annulment, separation, and divorce. These labels, in many ways reminiscent of the stultifying common law forms of action, have tended to obscure for scholar, draftsman, and practitioner, a problem common to all such procedures." Goldstein et al., Beyond the Best Interests of the Child 5 (1973).

[11] Id. at 99.

[12] See id. at 100. For a critical review of Goldstein, Freud, and Solnit's proposals, see Michael S. Wald, Thinking About Public Policy Toward Abuse and Neglect of Children: A Review of *Beyond the Best Interests of the Child*, 78 Mich. L. Rev. 645 (1980).

Parental Alienation Syndrome,' " 42 Fam. Ct. Rev. 622 (2004); Richard A. Gardner, Commentary on Kelly and Johnston's "The Alienated Child: A Reformulation of Parental Alienation Syndrome," 42 Fam. Ct. Rev. 611 (2004).

Having custody disputes determined by embracing more and more of the niceties of psychological and psychiatric theories requires careful analysis of the limits of these theories, their empirical bases, and the capacity of our legal system to absorb this new doctrine. Can psychologists and psychiatrists consistently differentiate between a situation where an adult and a child have a substantial relationship of the sort we characterize as parent-child and that where there is no such relationship at all? Do existing psychological theories provide a general basis for choosing between two adults when the child has some relationship and psychological attachment to each? In cases where, from the child's perspective, each claimant has a psychological relationship with the child, do you think there would often be widespread consensus among experts about which parent would prove psychologically better (or less detrimental) to the child? In many cases each parent will have a different sort of relationship with the child, with the child attached to each. One may be warm, easygoing, but incapable of discipline. The other may be fair, able to set limits, but unable to express affection. By what criteria is an expert to decide which situation is less detrimental? Moreover, even the proponents of psychological standards have acknowledged how problematic it is to evaluate relationships from a psychological perspective unless a highly trained person spends a considerable amount of time talking to the child or observing the parent and child interact. Superficial examinations by those without substantial training may be worse than nothing. And yet, such problems are surely high risks.

Even with the best trained experts, would the choice often be based on predictions that are beyond the demonstrated capacity of any existing theory?[13]

Note in *Baby M* the role played by experts in the original trial. Are you surprised by the lack of consensus?

5. How Much Weight Should Be Given to the Interests of the Biological Parents in Custody Disputes Involving Third Parties?

Goldstein, Freud, and Solnit in their book, Beyond the Best Interests of the Child (2d ed. 1979), define a "psychological parent" as "one who, on a continuing day-to-day basis, through interaction, companionship, interplay, and mutuality, fulfills the child's psychological needs for a parent, as well as the child's physical needs." Id. at 98.

(1) Should a "psychological parent" who is biologically unrelated to a child prevail in a custody dispute over a natural parent who is a stranger to the child? Third parties who have become "psychological parents" and who seek custody face

---

[13] Numerous authors have criticized the value of psychological testimony for deciding child custody cases. For recent critiques, see Dana Royce Baerger et al., A Methodology for Reviewing the Reliability and Relevance of Child Custody Evaluations, 18 J. Am. Acad. Matrim. Law. 35 (2002); James N. Bow & Francella A. Quinnell, A Critical Review of Child Custody Evaluations Reports, 40 Fam. Ct. Rev. 164 (2002); Daniel A. Krauss & Bruce D. Sales, Legal Standards, Expertise, and Experts in the Resolution of Contested Child Custody Cases, 6 Psychol., Pub. Pol'y & L. 843 (2000).

an obstacle: according to the "natural parent presumption," biological parents are deemed to be the best persons to raise their children absent a showing of unfitness. This was the situation in *Phillip B.* Does it make a difference if the parent is not unfit and is a stranger to the child through no fault of the parent's? For the child, do the risks of removing the child from a "psychological parent" for placement with a psychological stranger outweigh the psychological benefits the child might receive by maintaining a better sense of lineage by living with the natural parent? The court found this to be true in *Phillip B.* Is this always the case? Are courts qualified to make that determination? What evidence is most valuable in helping them decide?

(2) When state officials in the course of child protection treat a child's parents unfairly and violate their rights, what effect (if any) should this have on subsequent judicial proceedings relating to the child? Recall the discussion in *Baby M* about the lower court's error in awarding temporary custody to the father instead of the mother. Did the court adequately address the effect of this error? Should it affect the outcome of the case?

6. What Role Should the Child Have in the Resolution of a Custody Dispute?

Normally, the parties most obviously affected by a dispute have a right to participate in the adjudicatory process. The essential issue in a child custody dispute is what will become of the child, but ordinarily the child is not a true participant in the process. While the best interests principle requires that the primary focus be on the interests of the child, the child ordinarily does not define those interests, nor does the child have representation in the ordinary sense. Even in states that allow for independent representation for the child in the dispute, the role of the child's advocate is different from that in normal adjudication. A lawyer usually looks to the client for instructions about the goals to be pursued. Except in the case of older children, a child's representative in a custody dispute must himself normally define the child's interests.

Many states now require a judge to consider a child's expressed preference in applying the best interests standard in a divorce custody dispute between two parents, and sometimes, when those young persons are 12 to 14 years of age or older, statutes make their choice dispositive.[14] Under California law, once children are 12, they have the right to nominate their own guardian and petition the court for the appointment. The court is to appoint the nominated guardian unless it determines that the nominee is unsuitable. Cal. Prob. Code §§1510, 1514 (West 2002 & Supp. 2004).

California law provides no mechanism for considering the custody preferences of a child who is mentally disabled. However, the trial judge in *Phillip B.* used a hypothetical platonic dialogue between the court and Phillip as a way of considering Phillip's preference. Following is an account of the judge's presentation of this dialogue.

[14] On the child's preference, see infra pp. 611-612.

Robert H. Mnookin, The Guardianship of Phillip B.: Jay Spears' Achievement
40 Stan. L. Rev. 841, 849-850 (1988)

During the 10-day trial, the tension in the courtroom was palpable. The case aroused extraordinary emotions, and both sides viewed the stakes as profound. The Heaths believed that they were fighting for Phillip's chance to have a life worth living. The Beckers believed they were defending their integrity as parents.

On August 7, 1981, Judge William Fernandez summoned the parties and their lawyers to the courtroom, which was filled with reporters and well-wishers. When the judge began reading his opinion, [those gathered] had no idea what the result would be because during the trial, the judge had done nothing to tip his hand. Judge Fernandez wrote:

> California does not provide a method by which a mentally retarded child may state a preference. Other states have used a substituted judgment procedure to allow the court to state such a preference for the incompetent. This doctrine requires the court to ascertain as nearly as possible the incompetent person's "actual interests and preferences." . . .
>
> In our case the use of the substituted judgment method to arrive at Phillip's preference may best be stated in the form of a platonic dialogue with the court posing the choices to Phillip and Phillip's preference being ascertained from the more logical choice. The dialogue begins:
>
> *THE COURT*: Phillip . . . your first choice will lead you to a room in an institution where you will live. You will be fed, housed, and clothed but you will not receive any life prolonging medical care. . . . You will not be given an opportunity to add to your basic skills or to your motor skills and . . . will be treated as if you are incapable of learning and not fit to enter into society. You will not be allowed to become attached to any person, in fact efforts will be made to prevent any such attachments. Your biological parents will visit you occasionally, but their love and caring for you will at best be ambivalent. . . .
>
> Your second choice, Phillip, will lead you to a private home where you will be bathed in the love and affection of your psychological parents. . . . You will be given private tutoring and one on one training. . . . Your psychological parents believe that you are educable and will do all in their power to help you receive the education you may need to care for yourself and to secure work when you are an adult. You will have a chance for life prolonging surgery as well as receiving all the medical care that you need. Even if life prolonging surgery cannot be performed, your psychological parents will always be there to comfort you and care for you in the dark times of your final illness. Best of all, your psychological parents will do all in their power to involve your biological parents in your habilitation and to unite both families together in ensuring for you a life that is worth living.
>
> In my view, the dialogue would end with Phillip choosing to live with the Heaths.

Sad to say the foregoing legal analysis has no precedent in California law.

The judge went on to find that if detriment is defined as harm, then Phillip had suffered harm by the parenting of the Beckers: "severe emotional harm," "physical harm," "medical harm," and "the lasting harm by their stigmatization . . . as permanently mentally ill and disordered." He concluded by reading:

> [T]his is not a hearing to determine surgery for Phillip. That must wait another time and a sound parenting decision. This is a hearing for the purpose of giving Phillip Becker another parenting choice. It is a hearing responsive to Phillip's need for habilitation, and responsive to his desire for a chance to secure a life worth living. *I will give him that chance.*

When Judge Fernandez finished, the court personnel, the reporters in the courtroom, the Heaths, and their attorneys were in tears, not only because of the joyous result, but also because of this extraordinary demonstration of humanity by a courageous judge.

That day the judge signed the guardianship papers, appointing the Heaths guardians. He also authorized a heart catheterization to be done to determine if surgery was still possible. A court order also authorized the Heaths to take Phillip home for reasonable visitation, and later for custody. . . .

7. To What Degree Should the Legal Standards for the Resolution of Custody Disputes Be Discretionary?

Some time ago, Professors Foster and Freed wrote that nowhere has the task of achieving "a workable compromise between the values of flexibility and certainty . . . proved more challenging than in the area of child custody."[15] While some commentators have attacked the breadth of discretion granted judges in resolving custody disputes, the limited role of appellate review, and the inadequate protection of normal procedural safeguards,[16] courts, legislators, and other commentators have shown enormous hostility toward the development of rules that provided tight substantive standards for custody disputes. The differences among families generate great pressure to treat each case on its own facts. American custody law has come to require a highly individualized determination of what is in the best interests of a particular child.

Note the sort of evidence the court ultimately relied on in deciding the "best interests" test in *Baby M.* To what degree do the criteria mentioned by the court reflect subjective judgments on the part of the judges about what is in Baby M's best interests?

If the legal standards for resolving a custody dispute are vague and imprecise, will this necessarily mean that a judge will rely on his personal values (and biases)

[15] Henry H. Foster, Jr. & Doris Jonas Freed, Child Custody (Part I), 39 N.Y.U. L. Rev. 423 (1964).

[16] See, e.g., Robert J. Levy, Uniform Marriage and Divorce Legislation: A Preliminary Analysis 222-246 (1968); David L. Chambers, Rethinking the Substantive Rules for Custody Disputes in Divorce, 83 Mich. L. Rev. 477, 480-486 (1984); Michael Wald, State Intervention on Behalf of "Neglected" Children: A Search for Realistic Standards, 27 Stan. L. Rev. 985 (1975).

to inform his choice? Is this a bad thing? More generally, what are the benefits and costs of having discretionary legal standards?

8. One Set of Standards?

In order to simplify custody law, should there be a single set of legal standards for all custody disputes? As a matter of policy should the legal standards governing a custody dispute depend on the fortuity of which strand of custody law is invoked? Or since the legal consequences of a determination differ under the alternative strands (see pp. 457-461 supra), is there justification for different legal standards?

The distinction offered earlier between the child protection and the private dispute settlement functions helps explain why critics may be impatient with the remaining differences among the standards for the four strands of custody law. Either function can be involved in a judicial proceeding involving the application of any of the four strands of custody law, and a single case may involve both functions. Divorce custody law and guardianship law, for example, nearly always involve the private dispute settlement function, but either can involve the child protection function as well, if a court is required to evaluate a contention that one of the claimants would endanger a child. Cases involving the application of juvenile court child neglect laws or laws relating to termination of parental rights normally involve the child protection function — usually an agency of the state is asking the court to deny custody to a child's parent or parents on the basis of allegations that abuse or neglect endangers the child. The private dispute settlement function may be involved as well, however, if there are competing private parties, each prepared to make a long-term commitment to the child. And both functions are involved where, for example, a noncustodial father initiates a juvenile court child neglect proceeding in order to remove a child from his former wife's custody and have the child placed with him.[17] Similarly, a proceeding to terminate parental rights may also involve the judicial resolution of a private dispute, when it is initiated by a stepparent who wishes to adopt a child over the objection of a noncustodial natural parent.[18]

Significantly, both *Phillip B.* (see Chapter 4) and the *Rothman* case[19] used by Goldstein, Freud, and Solnit to illustrate their proposed standard, involved a custody fight between a biological parent who had no recent contact with the child and foster parents who had a substantial relationship with the child and did not wish to give up custody. Thus, both cases encompassed a juvenile court proceeding that was a private dispute involving claimants prepared to make a long-term commitment to the child. In such circumstances, to use a standard different from that employed in private disputes in the divorce or the guardianship context seems anomalous, particularly if one believes that the child's needs should be the primary focus and that biological parenthood should not be dispositive. After all, if one's chief concern is with the child rather than with the impact on the parents or the legal consequences of the proceeding, then the fortuity of the strand of law invoked

[17] See, e.g., James M.M. v. June O.O., 740 N.Y.S.2d 730 (App. Div. 2002).
[18] See, e.g., In re Adoption of B.M.W., 2 P.3d 159 (Kan. 2000).
[19] Rothman v. Jewish Child Care Assn., 167 N.Y.L.J. 17 (1972).

becomes an unacceptable basis for applying a different legal standard. But does the adoption of a single set of standards confuse the two different judicial functions and risk adverse policy consequences? To illustrate these consequences, the following article analyzes how the highly individualized determinations of what is either detrimental or in the best interests of a particular child contrast with the kinds of determinations usually required of courts in adjudication.

9. The Indeterminacy of Present-Day Standards

Robert H. Mnookin, Child-Custody Adjudication: Judicial Functions in the Face of Indeterminacy
39 Law & Contemp. Probs. 226, 255-268 (Summer 1975)

When a judge must resolve a custody dispute, he is committed to making a choice among alternatives. The very words of the best-interests-of-the-child principle suggest that the judge should decide by choosing the alternative that "maximizes" what is best for a particular child. Conceived this way, the judge's decision can be framed in a manner consistent with an intellectual tradition that views the decision process as a problem of rational choice. In analyzing the custody decision from this perspective, my purpose is not to describe how judges in fact decide custody disputes nor to propose a method of how they should. Instead, it is to expose the inherent indeterminacy of the best-interests standard.

1. Rational Choice

Decision theorists have laid out the logic of rational choice with clarity and mathematical rigor for prototype decision problems. The decision-maker specifies alternative outcomes associated with different courses of action and then chooses that alternative that "maximizes" his values, subject to whatever constraints the decision-maker faces. This involves two critical assumptions: first, that the decision-maker can specify alternative outcomes for each course of action; the second, that the decision-maker can assign to each outcome a "utility" measure that integrates his values and allows comparisons among alternative outcomes. . . .

2. A Custody Determination Under the Best-Interests-of-the-Child Principle

Assume that a judge must decide whether a child should live with his mother or his father when the parents are in the process of obtaining a divorce. From the perspective of rational choice, the judge would wish to compare the expected utility for the child of living with his mother with that of living with his father. The judge would need considerable information and predictive ability to do this. The judge would also need some source for the values to measure utility for the child. All three are problematic.

a. The Need for Information: Specifying Possible Outcomes
In the example chosen, the judge would require information about how each parent had behaved in the past, how this behavior had affected the child, and the child's present condition. Then the judge would need to predict the future behavior

and circumstances of each parent if the child were to remain with that parent and to gauge the effects of this behavior and these circumstances on the child. He would also have to consider the behavior of each parent if the child were to live with the other parent and how this might affect the child. If a custody award to one parent would require removing the child from his present circumstances, school, friends, and familiar surrounding, the judge would necessarily wish to predict the effects these changes would have on the child. These predictions would necessarily involve estimates of not only the child's mutual relationships with the custodial parent, but also his future contacts with the other parent and siblings, the probable number of visits by the noncustodial spouse, the probable financial circumstances of each of the spouses, and a myriad of other factors.

One can question how often, if ever, any judge will have the necessary information. In many instances, a judge lacks adequate information about even the most rudimentary aspects of a child's life with his parents and has still less information available about what either parent plans in the future. . . .

b. Predictions: Assessing the Probability of Alternative Outcomes

Obviously, more than one outcome is possible for each course of judicial action, so the judge must assess the probability of various outcomes and evaluate the seriousness of possible benefits and harms associated with each. But even where a judge has substantial information about the child's past home life and the present alternatives, present-day knowledge about human behavior provides no basis for the kind of individualized predictions required by the best-interests standard. There are numerous competing theories of human behavior, based on radically different conceptions of the nature of man, and no consensus exists that any one is correct.[161] No theory at all is considered widely capable of generating reliable predictions

---

[161] [A] comparison of five sample theories with competing implications [includes:]

1. Physiologically-oriented theories suggest that a child's personality is primarily determined by his physical structure or body type. See e.g., W. Sheldon, The Varieties of Human Physique: An Introduction to Constitutional Psychology (1940).
2. Behaviorist theories view the child as broadly malleable and suggest that his personality development is shaped by environment through a system of reward and punishment. See, e.g., J. Watson, Behaviorism (1920); B. Skinner, Walden II (1948) (affording an extreme perspective on the implications possible in child rearing).
3. Psychoanalytic theories suggest that the interaction between parent and child sets into motion various developmental and unconscious forces that are the wellsprings of behavior. Freud stresses the importance of the first few years of life, when the child goes through distinct developmental stages. The parents' response to these stages will be the major determinant of the child's later personality. See generally S. Freud, Beyond the Pleasure Principle, in 18 Collected Works 7, 20-21 (J. Strachey ed. & transl. 1955).
4. Child-development and learning theories present the child as an active participant in the world around him, basically self-generating and activated by innate tendencies towards involving himself with his environment. See, e.g., J. Piaget, The Origins of Intelligence in Children (1952).
5. Interpersonal theories suggest that a child's developing personality is largely determined by the roles and expectations assigned to him by his family. See, e.g., H. Sullivan, The Interpersonal Theory of Psychiatry (1953).

about the psychological and behavioral consequences of alternative dispositions for a particular child.

While psychiatrists and psychoanalysts have at times been enthusiastic in claiming for themselves the largest possible role in custody proceedings, many have conceded that their theories provide no reliable guide for predictions about what is likely to happen to a particular child. Anna Freud, who has devoted her life to the study of the child and who plainly believes that theory can be a useful guide to treatment, has warned: "In spite of . . . advances there remain factors which make clinical foresight, i.e., prediction, difficult and hazardous," not the least of which is that "environmental happenings in a child's life will always remain unpredictable since they are not governed by any known laws . . . ."[163]

c. Values to Inform Choice: Assigning Utilities to Various Outcomes

Even if the various outcomes could be specified and their probability estimated, a fundamental problem would remain unsolved. What set of values should a judge use to determine what is in a child's best interests? If a decision-maker must assign some measure of utility to each possible outcome, how is utility to be determined?

For many decisions in an individualistic society, one asks the person affected what he wants. Applying this notion to custody cases, the child could be asked to specify those values or even to choose. In some cases, especially those involving divorce, the child's preference is sought and given weight. But to make the child responsible for the choice may jeopardize his future relationship with the other parent. And we often lack confidence that the child has the capacity and the maturity appropriately to determine his own utility.

Moreover, whether or not the judge looks to the child for some guidance, there remains the question whether best interests should be viewed from a long-term or a short-term perspective. The conditions that make a person happy at age seven to ten may have adverse consequences at age thirty. . . .

Deciding what is best for a child poses a question no less ultimate than the purposes and values of life itself. Should the judge be primarily concerned with the child's happiness? Or with the child's spiritual and religious training? Should the judge be concerned with the economic "productivity" of the child when he grows up? Are the primary values of life in warm, interpersonal relationships, or in discipline and self-sacrifice? Is stability and security for a child more desirable than intellectual stimulation? These questions could be elaborated endlessly. And yet, where is the judge to look for the set of values that should inform the choice of what is best for the child? Normally, the custody statutes do not themselves give content or relative weights to the pertinent values. And if the judge looks to society at large, he finds neither a clear consensus as to the best child rearing strategies nor an appropriate hierarchy of ultimate values. . . .

3. Why Some Custody Cases Are Easy to Decide

An inquiry about what is best for a child often yields indeterminate results because of the problems of having adequate information, making the necessary

---

[163] A. Freud, Child Observation and Prediction of Development — A Memorial Lecture in Honor of Ernst Kris, in 13 The Psychoanalytic Study of the Child 92, 97-98 (1958). . . .

predictions, and finding an integrated set of values by which to choose. But some custody cases may still be comparatively easy to decide. While there is no consensus about what is best for a child, there is much consensus about what is very bad (e.g., physical abuse); some short-term predictions about human behavior can be reliably made (e.g., chronic alcoholism or psychosis is difficult quickly to modify). . . . Where one alternative plainly risks irreversible effects on the child that are bad and the other does not, there is no need to make longer-term predictions or more complicated psychological evaluations of what is likely to happen to the child's personality.

But to be easy, a case must involve only one claimant who is well known to the child and whose conduct does not endanger the child. If there are two such claimants or none, difficult choices remain. Most custody disputes pose difficult choices. . . . In many private disputes, the court must often choose between parties who each offer advantages and disadvantages, knowing that to deprive the child completely of either relationship will be disruptive. In a divorce custody fight, for example, where the mother is overprotective, possessive, and insecure and the father is demanding, aggressive, and hard-driving, how is the judge to decide where to place a seven-year-old child?

III. Implications of Indeterminacy

A. Would Rules Be Better?

Custody disputes are now decided on the basis of broad, person-oriented principles that ask for highly individualized determinations. The trial judge has broad discretion, but the question asked often has no meaningful answer. What are some of the implications of the use of indeterminate standards in custody disputes? Would more precise standards that ask an answerable question be better? . . .

More rule-like standards would avoid or mitigate some obvious disadvantages of adjudication by an indeterminate principle. For one thing, the use of an indeterminate standard makes the outcome of litigation difficult to predict. This may encourage more litigation than would a standard that made the outcome of more cases predictable. . . .

Indeterminate standards also pose an obviously greater risk of violating the fundamental precept that like cases should be decided alike. Because people differ and no two custody cases are exactly alike, the claim can be made that no process is more fair than one requiring resolution by a highly individualized, person-oriented standard. But with an indeterminate standard, the same case presented to different judges may easily result in different decisions. The use of an indeterminate standard means that state officials may decide on the basis of unarticulated (perhaps even unconscious) predictions and preferences that could be questioned if expressed. Because of the scope of discretion under such a standard, there is a substantial risk that decisions will be made on the basis of values not widely shared in our society, even among judges. . . .

. . . Today, custody disputes are ultimately assigned to courts for resolution, suggesting that a trial judge has the primary authority to decide, although it is not clear how decision-making responsibility is in fact shared by the trial judge with various other professionals (social workers, psychologists, psychiatrists) who also participate in the process. Implicit in some suggested reforms is the notion that the power to decide should be shifted from the judge to some other state official with different professional training. While judges may be ill-equipped to develop and evaluate information about the child, having some other state official decide or making various procedural adjustments (such as giving counsel to the child, providing better staff to courts, or making the proceedings more or less formal) will not cure the root problem. The indeterminacy flows from our inability to predict accurately human behavior and from a lack of social consensus about the values that should inform the decision. Procedural adjustments may make the system fairer and more efficient and may avoid some conspicuously erroneous determinations — goals worth pursuing. But neither greater use of existing expertise nor better procedures will make an indeterminate question answerable for an individual case.

Unlike procedural changes, adjudication by a more determinate rule would confront the fundamental problems posed by an indeterminate principle. But the choice between indeterminate standards and more precise rules poses a profound dilemma. The absence of rules removes the special burdens of justification and formulation of standards characteristic of adjudication. Unfairness and adverse consequences can result. And yet, rules that relate past events or conduct to legal consequences may themselves create substantial difficulties in the custody area. Our inadequate knowledge about human behavior and our inability to generalize confidently about the relationship between past events or conduct and future behavior make the formulation of rules especially problematic. Moreover, the very lack of consensus about values that makes the best-interests standard indeterminate may also make the formulation of rules inappropriate: a legal rule must, after all, reflect some social value or values. An overly ambitious and indeterminate principle may result in fewer decisions that reflect what is known to be desirable. But rules may result in some conspicuously bad decisions that could be avoided by a more discretionary standard. What balance should be struck? . . .

Like the choice in the judicial system of which party is to bear the burden of proof (or the risk of nonpersuasion), one's starting point as to the proper distribution of power can profoundly affect policy conclusions, particularly in the face of factual uncertainties and value clashes. Broadly speaking, there are three basic "starting points" for analyzing policies concerning children: (1) state paternalism, which assumes that the state has primary responsibility for children and ought to exercise full control over their lives, except where delegation to the family is justified; (2) family autonomy, which assumes that power and responsibility for children generally ought to be vested in private hands — essentially the family — except for cases where government rule can be justified; and (3) agnosticism, which rests on no preference and instead approaches individual policy issues on their own merits. . . .

. . . Even if one assumes that the sole criterion for evaluating the three alternative starting points is the interest of the child, there are affirmative justifications for making the family the presumptive locus of decision-making authority, particularly if there is no social consensus about what is best for children. Within the family, the child is more likely to have a voice in the decision, even if his wishes may not be determinative. Family members are more likely to have direct knowledge about a particular child. Affection for the child and mutual self-interest of family members are more likely to inform decisions. In all events, the evaluation of judicial functions in child custody that follows does not require a choice between family autonomy and agnosticism. Some of the policy recommendations do reflect, however, my rejection of state paternalism as a starting point, and it is useful here briefly to summarize the reasons.

First, state paternalism seems inconsistent with our historical and constitutional traditions. Indeed, family autonomy — the notion that those wishing a broader role for coercive governmental intrusion into the family carry a heavy burden of proof — has been the traditional American assumption. . . . The high value placed upon family autonomy . . . suggests a consensus that government may act coercively only when good cause is shown. Such a position would be consistent with our national ideological preference for decentralized decision-making, as generally evidenced by our economic and political system.

Second, state paternalism seems inconsistent with the present distribution of authority and responsibility for children. Most American families today enjoy substantial autonomy with regard to child rearing, and this has important implications for defining the limits of the child-protection function in custody disputes. The responsibility and opportunity of custody is assigned to a child's natural parents, and for the overwhelming majority of children, this simple rule suffices. For only a comparatively small proportion of children must a court resolve a custody dispute and perform either the private dispute-settlement or child-protection function.

Even if one were to accept paternalism as the starting point, broad definition of the child-protection function should be rejected because of its unfortunate consequences. What is best for children is often indeterminate; broad and discretionary standards for child-protection invite decisions based on the values of the particular judges and state officials responsible for a particular case. And apart from the internal integrity of the law, what has happened to children involved in the foster-care system — where the state has primary responsibility for the care of some children — should give pause to those seeking broader state authority. Indeed, even if one assumes that the family is simply a convenient instrument for the exercise of state power, an understanding of limitations with regard to resources, official talent, and what is known about human behavior is essential to the analysis of judicial role.

B.   ADOPTION

INTRODUCTORY PROBLEMS

(1) Eloise and Dan Bernheimer divorce when their two children are two and four years old. Eloise is awarded custody of the children, but the father visits regularly every other weekend, and the children stay with him for six weeks in the summer. The children look forward especially to summer visits when their father takes them on camping trips, picnics, and spends a considerable amount of time with them. The children are attached to their father and to their paternal grandparents.

Eloise remarries when the children are four and six years old. Over the next two years, the stepfather, Ben Taylor, develops a close relationship with the children and petitions for adoption. The children say they love both of their fathers, but want to have the same last name as their mother.

a. Where the children's mother favors adoption by the stepparent, should the biological father's consent be an absolute requirement to the adoption? Should termination of the father's rights be permitted if he abandons the children? If he fails to support them? If a judge thinks it is in the children's best interest? Should the children's expressed preference be considered? Should it be dispositive?

b. Is it more to the advantage of the children to have a "complete" and integrated new two-parent family even if that risks the loss of an ongoing relationship of the child to the excluded biological parent?

c. Under the existing laws of most states, if the former husband and natural father does not consent, there must be statutory grounds for termination of his parental rights before the child can be adopted by the stepfather. How would termination of the biological father's rights be possible in such a case?

d. If stepparent adoption is not possible and the mother later dies, what standard should govern a custody dispute between the noncustodial biological father and the stepfather?

e. At the present time, adoption terminates the biological father's duty to support, creates a duty of support in the adopting father, and would extinguish the visitation rights of the biological father. Can you imagine a system of adoption that would make the consequences of adoption less drastic?

(2) Eighteen-year-old Mary Ann Jones wants to relinquish her newborn to the Good Shepherd Adoption Agency but she refuses to tell the agency who the father is. What efforts must the agency make to determine the identity of the father before it can proceed with an adoption? What would be required under the Uniform Parentage Act, infra p. 488?

(3) Barbara and Carol have been in a committed relationship for ten years. One year ago, after being artificially inseminated with sperm from an anonymous donor, Barbara gives birth to a son, Jack. Carol petitions the trial court to adopt Jack in a "second parent" adoption. How should the court decide? If a judge thinks it is in the child's best interests? Should Barbara's approval and consent be required? Should Barbara retain her parental rights, or should the court terminate her parental rights so that Jack will have only one legal mother?

Suppose Barbara and Carol's relationship subsequently breaks up. Barbara moves for court approval to withdraw her own consent to the adoption. Should Barbara's prior consent to the adoption be irrevocable? In the decision-making process, what difference (if any) would it make if Carol was the egg donor of the embryo that was implanted in Barbara's uterus?

(4) An 11-year-old adopted child wants to know who her biological parents are. Should she have the right to learn? In all circumstances? Never? Only if it is persuasively shown that lack of knowledge of her roots is contributing to severe emotional problems? Should it matter whether the child's adoptive parents are willing to have her learn? Whether the natural mother is willing to be identified? Who should decide? By what process? According to what standard?

1.   Adoption: The Prerequisite of Consent or Involuntary Termination of Parental Rights

There are two primary methods for freeing a minor for adoption during the lives of the parents: (1) parental consent or (2) involuntary termination of parental rights. While state statutes vary considerably, "abandonment" of the child by the biological parent is the most common basis for allowing adoption without the parent's consent. Traditionally, such provisions have been rather inflexibly interpreted to require parental *intent to abandon* — that is, courts were reluctant to terminate parental rights merely because of the parent's demonstrated lack of interest.

However, the Uniform Adoption Act (UAA) facilitates termination in cases of abandonment. UAA was promulgated by the National Conference of Commissioners on Uniform State Laws in 1994 as a major reform of adoption law. Unif. Adoption Act §§1-8, 9 U.L.A. 11 (1994). UAA §3-504(c), 9 U.L.A. 52, provides for termination of parental rights if a parent fails to make reasonable and consistent support payments, or to communicate or visit regularly with a child for a consecutive six-month period. In addition, according to the modern trend, jurisdictions are more supportive of terminating a biological parent's rights in the case of stepparent adoption.

Furthermore, all states allow involuntary termination of parental rights for child maltreatment. Usually the "neglect" standard for termination purposes is somewhat more stringent than for the assertion of juvenile court jurisdiction. Some case law and statutes go so far as to allow adoption without a biological parent's consent if it is in the child's best interests.

Unless parental rights are terminated, adoption requires that both parents consent, and that consent be given without fraud, duress, or undue influence. In addition, consent must be obtained in accordance with prescribed statutory procedures. Some states also require the consent of the child being adopted if he or she is over a stated age, usually age 12 to 14.

This section and the next examine whether the general requirement of parental consent or termination of parental rights should be applied (1) in the case of a stepparent adoption; or (2) for unwed fathers when the mother is willing to relinquish the child for adoption.

In re Adoption of Williams
766 N.E.2d 637 (Ohio Prob. Ct. 2002)

Wayne F. WILKE, Judge.

This matter came before the court on November 29, 2001, pursuant to Civ.R. 53(E)(4)(b), regarding objections to the decision of the magistrate [which recommended] that the consent of Shawn Williams, the child's biological father, was not necessary for this proposed stepparent adoption petition to proceed. . . .

Facts and Procedural Posture

The child was born on May 22, 1993 in Cincinnati, Ohio. His mother is Ingrid Sandidge and his biological father is Shawn Williams. Ingrid Sandidge and Jeffrey

Sandidge were married on September 19, 1998, and Jeffrey Sandidge filed a petition to adopt the child on September 1, 2000.

The magistrate found that Shawn Williams made at least three telephone calls to the child in the year immediately prior to the filing of the adoption petition, although the respondent contends that he made even more calls than that. The magistrate also found that Shawn Williams sent birthday presents, consisting of toys and clothes, in the year immediately preceding the filing of the adoption and that Shawn Williams paid $125 for karate lessons on the child's behalf during that same one-year period. There is presently no court-mandated duty imposed upon Shawn Williams to pay any support. The question is whether Shawn Williams communicated with or supported his son in the year immediately preceding the filing of the adoption petition. If he did communicate with and support his son, then Shawn Williams's consent to the adoption is required. However, if he failed to communicate or to provide support for the child, then Shawn Williams's consent to the proposed adoption is not required.

Conclusions of Law

R.C. 3107.06 provides inter alia that a petition to adopt a minor may be granted only if the minor's biological mother and father consent to the adoption, unless a court finds that their consents are not required. A court may conclude that a biological parent's consent is not required if it finds that the parent has failed without justifiable cause to communicate with the minor or to provide for the maintenance and support of the minor as required by law or judicial decree for a period of at least one year immediately prior to the filing of the adoption petition. Failing to communicate with the minor and failing to provide for the minor are two reasons why a court might find a parent's consent to an adoption is not necessary. One of the problems in this area of law is that of defining what constitutes "failing to communicate" and "failing to support" (R.C. 3107.07[A]), so that a parent's consent is not required.

The seminal case in Ohio on what constitutes a lack of communication is In re Adoption of Holcomb, 481 N.E.2d 613 (Ohio 1985). In *Holcomb*, the court concluded that the legislature, in enacting R.C. 3107.07, opted for certainty. The court determined that a parent's consent is not required if there is a complete absence of communication for the one-year period and if there was no justifiable cause for the failure of communication.

Within a short time, members of the Supreme Court began to disagree about its holding in *Holcomb*. In In re Adoption of Bovett, 33 Ohio St. 3d 102, 515 N.E.2d 919 (Ohio 1987), the court shifted the burden to the parent opposing the adoption to show that any absence of communication or support was justifiable. The court in *Bovett* reaffirmed that it was obliged to strictly construe the statute's language but that it would not adopt a construction "so strict as to turn the statute into a sham." Id. at 106, 515 N.E.2d 919. Justice Douglas applauded the court's decision as a step in the right direction and wrote that trial courts need further guidance as to whether the making of one payment of support during the year or the sending of a Christmas card is enough to frustrate the operation of the statute. Id. at 107, 515 N.E.2d 919 (Douglas, J., concurring). Justice Douglas wrote that a probate court should not be bound "to negate the effect of the statute simply because a natural parent has made a payment or two during the year or has communicated once or twice during the year." Id. Indeed, R.C. 1.47(C) presumes that the intention behind every statute is a just and reasonable result. Several appellate decisions have subsequently followed Justice Douglas's position and have found de minimis efforts at communication and support insufficient to require that parent's consent. No statewide precedent has been established, however.

Recently, the First District Court of Appeals had the opportunity to interpret R.C. 3107.07 with respect to a man who, completely by chance, talked with his son for whom an adoption petition had been filed. The appellate court reversed this court's determination that one encounter was not sufficient "communication" within the meaning of R.C. 3107.07. In re Adoption of Tscheiner, 752 N.E.2d 292 (Ohio Ct. App. 2000). The court in *Tscheiner* stressed that there is an objective test for analyzing the failure of communication required by R.C. 3107.07(A) and that even one event of communication made that parent's consent to an adoption a requirement. In this case, there were at least three instances where the respondent communicated with his son and there was evidence that the respondent paid for some birthday gifts and for karate lessons. Accordingly, Shawn Williams's consent to this adoption is necessary and the objections to the decision of the magistrate are sustained.

Shawn Williams represents one of those parents written of by the Ohio Supreme Court in In re Adoption of Holcomb, supra. He is uncaring, unworthy, and unscrupulous. In this situation, three telephone calls and a petty amount of cash legally define and establish the respondent's relationship with his son and are sufficient to thwart an adoption by a well-meaning stepparent. That is sad and pathetic and reflects the development of case law that is inconsistent with social policy and values.

The underlying premise of adoption law is that a parent's consent to an adoption is required unless a court finds that it is not required. The next step after the consent phase is for a court to determine whether the adoption is in the child's best interest. Adoption proceedings should not, however, become "beauty contests" where a court is forced to make a subjective choice of who would make a better parent, in other words, to make a quasi-determination of the child's best interest at the beginning of the proceedings. On the other hand, a biological parent in many cases is voluntarily so far removed from a child's life that such a choice would be obvious. A chance encounter or single birthday card have been found to be sufficient communication to give standing to a biological parent to oppose an adoption, effectively preventing a child's best interest from ever being considered. Despite this harsh result for the child, this court is bound by the prior decisions of the Ohio Supreme Court and First District Court of Appeals.

There may very well come a time when a court, reviewing the facts in cases such as this, will be able to conclude that a parent's consent to an adoption is not necessary because the parent made only de minimis efforts at either communication or support. Unfortunately, this court is unable to make that determination today. The case law favors a black-letter rule that currently protects a nonconsenting parent's right to thwart an adoption at the expense of a child's best interest. In many cases, a nonconsenting parent is shielded by R.C. 3107.07, although his or her actions are in direct contravention of the common-law obligation of a parent to support a child and, of greater significance, the moral obligation to actually play a role in the child's life. The law should reflect that one's status as a parent requires more than being a name on a birth certificate. It should reflect that parenting is a full-time, on-going endeavor and not something to consider or address only when it is convenient. There seems to be growing recognition that the case law interpreting R.C. 3107.07 is not always beneficial to a child and can cause hardship. In many cases, a child who, through adoption, could have two loving and caring parents is shortchanged and left with one loving and caring parent, and one who gives his or her parental obligations as much thought as a "couch potato" would give in changing a television channel. This court is encouraged that eventually a fairer statute can be crafted (or a body of case law developed) that will more equitably determine whether a parent's consent to an adoption is required. . . .

QUESTIONS AND NOTES

(1) Background. In 2003, there were approximately four divorces per eight marriages.[20] The high rate of divorce results in an increasing number of steprelationships when custodial parents remarry. Although stepparent and stepchild relationships resemble biological parent-child relationships in many regards, the legal ramifications of the steprelationship are not identical unless the stepparent formally adopts the child.

Stepparent adoption may be completed with the consent of a noncustodial biological parent who voluntarily agrees to a termination of parental rights. The noncustodial parent may be required to file a petition with the court and attend a judicial hearing. The court then makes a finding that the parent's decision is informed and voluntary, and that termination would be in the best interests of the child. However, if the biological parent objects to the adoption and the forfeiture of all rights vis-à-vis the child (including visitation rights), then the stepparent desiring to effectuate a legal parent-child relationship may have to institute a proceeding for involuntary termination of the noncustodial parent's rights.

In this contested termination proceeding, the noncustodial parent is entitled to constitutional protection. A line of Supreme Court cases, starting with Stanley v. Illinois, infra, pp. 483-486 and including Santosky v. Kramer, supra p. 359, guarantees certain substantive and procedural rights to parents in the face of involuntary termination proceedings. Generally, termination of parental rights requires proof of parental misconduct by clear and convincing evidence (see discussion of Santosky v. Kramer).

Are these substantive and procedural protections, which were developed to protect parental rights in the face of attacks by the state, appropriate in the private dispute context of the steprelationship situation?

(2) Suppose the biological parent refuses to consent to the stepparent adoption, as in *Williams*. The child continues to live in the mother's household with the new stepfather. Several years later the mother dies. What are the rights of the surviving custodial stepparent as against the noncustodial biological parent?

Traditionally, courts would have difficulty awarding custody of children to the surviving stepparent. However, courts have become more willing to assign custody

[20] U.S. Bureau of the Census, Statistical Abstract of the United States: 2003 (123d ed. 2003) 72.

of children to a stepparent involved in a custody dispute with a biological parent after the death of the other biological parent. See, e.g., Doncer v. Dickerson, 81 S.W.3d 349 (Tex. App. 2002) (holding that stepmother had standing to file suit to gain custody of six-year-old boy following the death of the child's father). See also Stephen Hellman, Stepparent Custody Upon the Death of the Custodial Parent, 14 J. Suffolk Acad. L. 23 (2000); Danielle N. Rodier, Stepfather Prevails in Parental Fight with Biological Dad, Pa. L. Weekly, Nov. 28, 2000.

Another variation on this theme occurs if the stepparent and the custodial parent divorce. That is, suppose the Williams child lives with his mother and stepfather for several years. Then, the mother's second marriage is dissolved. The stepfather subsequently seeks either custody or postdivorce visitation regarding his former stepchild. How should this dispute be resolved?

Courts occasionally have granted custody in such situations to stepparents. However, stepparents must overcome a statutory presumption favoring biological preferences as against third parties. Many states now also have statutes that provide explicitly or implicitly for visitation by stepparents. Some states add the additional requirement for visitation that the stepparent must have contributed to the child's support or stood in loco parentis.[21] (Issues of visitation are discussed infra this chapter at pp. 583-603.) See generally John C. Mayoue, Stepping in to Parent: The Legal Rights of Stepparents, 25 Fam. Advoc. 36 (2002).

(3) Grandparents' Rights. The adoption of the child by a stepparent also raises the issue of grandparents' rights. Suppose Shawn Williams' mother has remarried and after adoption her new husband refuses to let child's paternal grandparents (the first father's parents) visit. What rights, if any, do the grandparents have? The problem is especially poignant if the noncustodial parent has died and the grandparents' sole connection with that deceased parent is the grandchild.

In response to lobbying by grandparents' rights organizations, all 50 states enacted legislation granting grandparent visitation in limited circumstances.[22] Some statutes permit visitation only in cases of the death or divorce of a parent. Other statutes permit grandparent visitation even when the children remain in an intact family.[23] Do grandparent visitation statutes unconstitutionally infringe on parental rights? See Troxel v. Granville, infra, p. 595.

(4) Support and Inheritance Rights. What are the consequences for the stepparent-child relationship if the biological parent refuses to give consent to adoption? A stepparent who has not adopted a stepchild generally has no legal obligation of support. Further, stepchildren who are not adopted by a stepparent have no right to inherit the stepparent's property through intestate succession laws — a rule that "undoubtedly is at odds with the wishes of many stepparents who die intestate." Ralph C. Brashier, Inheritance Law and the Evolving Family 157 (2004). In light of the increasing numbers of stepfamilies, should the above rules be changed? If

---

[21] John Dewitt Gregory, Blood Ties: A Rationale for Child Visitation by Legal Strangers, 55 Wash. & Lee L. Rev. 351, 362, 364 (1998).

[22] Stephen Elmo Averett, Grandparent Visitation Right Statutes, 13 BYU J. Pub. L. 355, 371 (1999).

[23] Id. at 371.

so, how? Should there be an automatic rule of inclusion for stepchildren in intestacy schemes? See generally Kim A. Feigenbaum, Note, The Changing Family Structure: Challenging Stepchildren's Lack of Inheritance Rights, 66 Brook. L. Rev. 167 (2000); Andrew L. Noble, Note, Intestate Succession for Stepchildren in Pennsylvania: A Proposal for Reform, 64 U. Pitt. L. Rev. 835 (2003).

(5) Problem. A legislator in the jurisdiction of Whiteacre proposes that the state legislature adopt the following progressive statute:

> A stepchild may inherit from a stepparent if (1) the parent-child relationship began during the stepchild's minority and continued throughout the parties' joint lifetimes and (2) clear and convincing evidence indicates that the stepparent would have adopted the child but for a legal barrier. [Cal. Prob. Code §6454 (West 2003).]

You are the legislator's intern. Advise the legislator on the merits and shortcomings of the proposed legislation.

(6) Parental Visitation Following Stepparent Adoption. How can we accommodate the desires and interests of both the biological noncustodial parent and the stepparent? Must it be an "all or none" situation — either severing the biological parent-child bond or giving the stepparent no real legal status vis-à-vis the child? In a classic law review article, Brigette M. Bodenheimer proposed a form of "weak" adoption — an intermediate form of adoption that permits the continuation of some contact between the biological parent and the child.[24] Courts were slow to adopt this proposal. However, "open adoption," which bears many similarities to Bodenheimer's proposal, has now become the trend. Indeed, adoption agencies that perform only closed adoptions have become the minority because agencies need to offer open adoption to stay competitive in the adoption market.[25]

In an open adoption, the birth mother and adoptive parents know each other's identities prior to the adoption, and the birth mother may exercise significant control over the choice of adoptive parents. The birth mother and adoptive parents then reach an agreement concerning the birth mother's postadoption relationship (often including visitation) with the child. Increasingly, courts are being asked to enforce such agreements and will generally uphold them if in the best interests of the child. Open adoption is discussed infra pp. 513-515.

(7) Uniform Adoption Act. The UAA includes several innovative provisions regarding stepparent adoptions. The UAA makes a distinction between stepparent adoptions and adoption of a child who is a stranger to the adopted family. Under the UAA, a stepparent adoption does not cut off all rights of the biological parent or the family of the biological parent whose parent-child relationship ends at adoption (as in the stranger adoption). Thus, for example, the child does not lose his or her inheritance rights.

Moreover, UAA does not terminate the visitation rights of the former biological parent (or grandparents). That is, UAA authorizes open adoption in cases of

---

[24] Brigette M. Bodenheimer, New Trends and Requirements in Adoption Law and Proposals for Legislative Change, 49 S. Cal. L. Rev. 10, 45-51 (1975).

[25] Amy L. Doherty, A Look at Open Adoption, 13 J. Contemp. Legal Issues 591, 592-593 (2000).

stepparent adoption. Specifically, UAA permits a court to enter a postadoption visitation order in favor of the former noncustodial parent — either by approving the parties' prior written agreement to that effect or, in the absence of such an agreement, by permitting visitation by a former parent (as well as by a grandparent or sibling of the adoptee) based on a determination of the child's best interests. UAA §4-113, 9 U.L.A. 1.75-76 (1999 & Supp. 2004).

What are the advantages and disadvantages of this statutory reform? See generally Margaret M. Mahoney, Open Adoption in Context: The Wisdom and Enforceability of Visitation Orders for Former Parents Under Uniform Adoption Act §4-113, 51 Fla. L. Rev. 89 (1999). To date, UAA has only been adopted in Vermont. Uniform Law Commissioners Web site, *http://nccusl.org/Update/ uniformact_ factsheets/uniformacts-fs-aa94.asp* (last visited Jan. 13, 2005).

(8) ALI Principles.   The American Law Institute, which conducted a decade-long project clarifying underlying principles of family law and making policy recommendations, also addresses the rights of stepparents. See ALI Principles of the Law of Family Dissolution: Analyis and Recommendations (2002). The Principles recognize several types of parents: legal parents (as defined by state law), "parents by estoppel," and "de facto parents." A "parent by estoppel" is a person who acts as a parent in circumstances that would estop the child's legal parent from denying the claimant's parental status. Parent-by-estoppel status may be created when an individual (1) is obligated for child support, or (2) has lived with the child for at least two years and has a reasonable belief that he is the father, or (3) has had an agreement with the child's legal parent since birth (or for at least two years) to serve as a co-parent provided that recognition of parental status would serve the child's best interests. ALI Principles §2.03(1)(b).

In contrast, a de facto parent is a person, other than a legal parent or a parent by estoppel, who has regularly performed an equal or greater share of caretaking as the parent with whom the child primarily lived, lived with the child for a significant period (not less than two years), and acted as a parent for nonfinancial reasons (and with the agreement of a legal parent) or as a result of a complete failure or inability of any legal parent to perform caretaking functions. Id at §2.03(1)(c).

If a stepparent qualifies as a parent by estoppel or a de facto parent, an application of the ALI Principles would result in the recognition of that stepparent's right to custody or visitation following the death of a custodial parent or the dissolution of the custodial parent's relationship with the stepparent. For a discussion and critique of these doctrines, see Mary Ann Mason & Nicole Zayac, Rethinking Stepparent Rights: Has the ALI Found a Better Definition?, 36 Fam. L.Q. 227 (2002); Sarah H. Ramsey, Constructing Parenthood for Stepparents: Parents by Estoppel, and De Facto Parents Under the American Law Institute's Principles of the Law of Family Dissolution, 8 Duke J. Gender L. & Pol'y 285 (2001).

2.   Adoption and the Unwed Father

A substantial portion of nonrelative adoptions involve nonmarital children. Before 1972 the fathers of such children had no substantial parental rights. Adoption required only the mother's consent, and the statutory adoption scheme did not require notice to the father that the child was being placed for adoption. In terms of the consent requirement many states distinguished between unwed fathers who had legitimated their offspring (whose consent was required) and those who had not legitimated their offspring (whose consent was not required). A father may legitimate a child by compliance with statutory requirements (e.g., by marrying the mother after the birth, or acknowledging the child publicly and/or receiving the child into his home).

The picture changed in 1972 with the case of Stanley v. Illinois and the subsequent promulgation of the Uniform Parentage Act in 1973. *Stanley* was proclaimed as a vindication of the rights of unwed fathers. Note that *Stanley* was not an adoption case, but rather a neglect case. Yet, its impressive shadow was cast on adoption as well.

Stanley v. Illinois
405 U.S. 645 (1972)

Mr. Justice WHITE delivered the opinion of the Court.

Joan Stanley lived with Peter Stanley intermittently for 18 years, during which time they had three children. When Joan Stanley died, Peter Stanley lost not only her but also his children. Under Illinois law, the children of unwed fathers become wards of the State upon the death of the mother. Accordingly, upon Joan Stanley's death, in a dependency proceeding instituted by the State of Illinois, Stanley's children were declared wards of the State and placed with court-appointed guardians. Stanley appealed, claiming that he had never been shown to be an unfit parent and that since married fathers and unwed mothers could not be deprived of their children without such a showing, he had been deprived of the equal protection of the laws guaranteed him by the Fourteenth Amendment. . . .

Stanley presses his equal protection claim here. . . . We granted certiorari to determine whether this method of procedure by presumption could be allowed to stand in light of the fact that Illinois allows married fathers — whether divorced, widowed, or separated — and mothers — even if unwed — the benefit of the presumption that they are fit to raise their children.

We must . . . examine [this] question. . . . Is a presumption that distinguishes and burdens all unwed fathers constitutionally repugnant? We conclude that, as a matter of due process of law, Stanley was entitled to a hearing on his fitness as a parent before his children were taken from him and that, by denying him a hearing and extending it to all other parents whose custody of their children is challenged, the State denied Stanley the equal protection of the laws guaranteed by the Fourteenth Amendment.

Illinois has two principal methods of removing nondelinquent children from the homes of their parents. In a dependency proceeding it may demonstrate that the children are wards of the State because they have no surviving parent or guardian. Ill. Rev. Stat., c. 37, §§702-1, 702-5. In a neglect proceeding it may show that children should be wards of the State because the present parent(s) or guardian does not provide suitable care. Ill. Rev. Stat., c. 37, §§702-1, 702-4.

The State's right — indeed, duty — to protect minor children through a judicial determination of their interests in a neglect proceeding is not challenged here. Rather, we are faced with a dependency statute that empowers state officials to circumvent neglect proceedings on the theory that an unwed father is not a "parent" whose existing relationship with his children must be considered. "Parents," say the State, "means the father and mother of a legitimate child, or the survivor of them, or the natural mother of an illegitimate child, and includes any adoptive parent," Ill. Rev. Stat., c. 37, §701-14, but the term does not include unwed fathers.

Under Illinois law, therefore, while the children of all parents can be taken from them in neglect proceedings, that is only after notice, hearing, and proof of such unfitness as a parent as amounts to neglect, an unwed father is uniquely subject to the more simplistic dependency proceeding. By use of this proceeding, the State, on showing that the father was not married to the mother, need not prove unfitness in fact, because it is presumed at law. Thus, the unwed father's claim of parental qualification is avoided as "irrelevant."

In considering this procedure under the Due Process Clause, we recognize, as we have in other cases, that due process of law does not require a hearing "in every conceivable case of government impairment of private interest." Cafeteria Workers v. McElroy, 367 U.S. 886, 894 (1961). That case explained that "[t]he very nature of due process negates any concept of inflexible procedures universally applicable to every imaginable situation" and firmly established that "what procedures due process may require under any given set of circumstances must begin with a determination of the precise nature of the government function involved as well as of the private interest that has been affected by governmental action." . . .

The private interest here, that of a man in the children he has sired and raised, undeniably warrants deference and, absent a powerful countervailing interest, protection. . . . The Court has frequently emphasized the importance of the family. The rights to conceive and to raise one's children have been deemed "essential," Meyer v. Nebraska, 262 U.S. 390, 399 (1923). . . . "It is cardinal with us that the custody, care and nurture of the child reside first in the parents, whose primary function and freedom include preparation for obligations the state can neither supply nor hinder." Prince v. Massachusetts, 321 U.S. 158, 166 (1944). . . .

Nor has the law refused to recognize those family relationships unlegitimized by a marriage ceremony. The Court has declared unconstitutional a state statute denying natural, but illegitimate, children a wrongful-death action for the death of their mother, emphasizing that such children cannot be denied the right of other children because familial bounds in such cases were often as warm, enduring, and important as those arising within a more formally organized family unit. Levy v. Louisiana, 391 U.S. 68, 71-72 (1968). "To say that the test of equal protection should be the 'legal' rather than the biological relationship is to avoid the issue. For the Equal Protection Clause necessarily limits the authority of a State to draw such 'legal' lines as it chooses." Glona v. American Guarantee Co., 391 U.S. 73, 75-76 (1968). These authorities make it clear that, at the least, Stanley's interest in retaining custody of his children is cognizable and substantial.

For its part, the State has made its interest quite plain: Illinois has declared that the aim of the Juvenile Court Act is to protect "the moral, emotional, mental, and physical welfare of the minor and the best interests of the community" and to "strengthen the minor's family ties whenever possible, removing him from the custody of his parents only when his welfare or safety or the protection of the public cannot be adequately safeguarded without removal. . . ." Ill. Rev. Stat., c. 37, §§701-2. These are legitimate interests, well within the power of the State to implement. We do not question the assertion that neglectful parents may be separated from their children.

But we are not asked to evaluate the legitimacy of the state ends, rather, to determine whether the means used to achieve these ends are constitutionally defensible. What is the state interest in separating children from fathers without a hearing designed to determine whether the father is unfit in a particular disputed case? We observe that the State registers no gain towards its declared goals when it separates children from the custody of fit parents. Indeed, if Stanley is a fit father, the State spites its own articulated goals when it needlessly separates him from his family. . . .

It may be, as the State insists, that most unmarried fathers are unsuitable and neglectful parents. It may also be that Stanley is such a parent and that his children should be placed in other hands. But all unmarried fathers are not in this category; some are wholly suited to have custody of their children. This much the State readily concedes, and nothing in this record indicates that Stanley is or has been a neglectful father who has not cared for his children. Given the opportunity to make his case, Stanley may have been seen to be deserving of custody of his offspring. Had this been so, the State's statutory policy would have been furthered by leaving custody in him. . . .

It may be argued that unmarried fathers are so seldom fit that Illinois need not undergo the administrative inconvenience of inquiry in any case, including Stanley's. The establishment of prompt efficacious procedures to achieve legitimate state ends is a proper state interest worthy of cognizance in constitutional adjudication. But the Constitution recognizes higher values than speed and efficiency. . . .

Procedure by presumption is always cheaper and easier than individualized determination. But when, as here, the procedure forecloses the determinative issues of competence and care, when it explicitly disdains present realities in deference to past formalities, it needlessly risks running roughshod over the important interests of both parent and child. It therefore cannot stand.[9]

. . . The State's interest in caring for Stanley's children is de minimis if Stanley is shown to be a fit father. It insists on presuming rather than proving Stanley's unfitness solely because it is more convenient to presume than to prove. Under the Due Process Clause that advantage is insufficient to justify refusing a father a hearing when the issue at stake is the dismemberment of his family.

The State of Illinois assumes custody of the children of married parents, divorced parents, and unmarried mothers only after a hearing and proof of neglect. The children of unmarried fathers, however, are declared dependent children

---

[9] We note in passing that the incremental cost of offering unwed fathers an opportunity for individualized hearings on fitness appears to be minimal. If unwed fathers, in the main, do not care about the disposition of their children, they will not appear to demand hearings. If they do care, under the scheme here held invalid, Illinois would admittedly at some later time have to afford them a properly focused hearing in a custody or adoption proceeding. . . .

without a hearing on parental fitness and without proof of neglect. Stanley's claim in the state courts and here is that failure to afford him a hearing on his parental qualifications while extending it to other parents denied him equal protection of the laws. We have concluded that all Illinois parents are constitutionally entitled to a hearing on their fitness before their children are removed from their custody. It follows that denying such a hearing to Stanley and those like him while granting it to other Illinois parents is inescapably contrary to the Equal Protection Clause.

NOTES AND QUESTIONS

(1) Whose rights are being vindicated in *Stanley*? The father's? The children's? Both?

(2) Unnamed Father's Due Process Rights.   Is *Stanley* a procedural case, dealing with the hearing rights of parents? A substantive case, limiting the circumstances when the state may remove children from parental circumstances? Or both? Does *Stanley* mean that a parent has a constitutional right to custody of his children vis-à-vis the state unless unfit? Or only that a parent is entitled to an opportunity to be heard before being deprived of custody? Suppose state law provides that the parental rights of the father of a nonmarital child could be terminated after notice to the father and a full hearing, if a court determines that termination is in the child's best interest. Would *Stanley* speak to this question? See pp. 500-505 infra.

(3) Stanley's Effect on Adoption Law.   Broadly speaking, there are several questions concerning *Stanley*'s effect on adoption law:

a.   In what circumstances is the consent to adoption by an unmarried father required? Does *Stanley* apply to all fathers of illegitimate children or only to those with some substantial contact with their children?

b.   When consent is required, should the adoption necessarily be frustrated by the birth father's refusal?

c.   If the unmarried father's consent is not required, does he nevertheless have a right to notice of a pending adoption and a right to participate in the proceedings?

d.   What affirmative obligation is there to determine who the father is? Suppose the mother will not say or cannot say who the father is? Should adoption be possible? If a man later shows up claiming that he is the father, what remedies should he have if inadequate steps were taken before the adoption?

(4) Uniform Parentage Act: Paternity Provisions.   In the aftermath of *Stanley*, these questions generated conflicting answers, both legislative and judicial. Some answers were provided by the Uniform Parentage Act (UPA) in 1973, which reformed the law regarding parentage, paternity actions, and child support. The UPA was adopted in its entirety by 19 states, but many additional states enacted significant portions of it. Unif. Parentage Act, Prefatory Note, 9B U.L.A. 296-298 (2000). According to the original UPA, judicial notice was required to a "presumed father" (as well as to one whose paternity was judicially established) before the

father's rights could be terminated. Under the UPA, a man was presumed to be the biological father of a child (1) if he married the mother (before or after the birth) or attempted to do so but the marriage was invalid (§4(a)(1), (2), and (3)); or (2) if he held out the child as his and received the child into his home (id. at (4)); or (3) if he acknowledged paternity in a writing that was filed with the appropriate authorities (id. at (5)). The presumption of paternity could be rebutted by clear and convincing evidence (id. at (b)). If conflicting presumptions arose, the presumption that was founded on "weightier considerations of policy and logic control[led]" (id.).

(5) Revised Uniform Parentage Act: Paternity Provisions. Technological advances in paternity establishment made the original UPA obsolete, and it was revised in 2000 and amended in 2002. The revised UPA replaces two other uniform acts that address parentage: the Uniform Status of Children of Assisted Conception Act (USCACA), created to establish legal parentage for children born via non-traditional means; and the Uniform Putative and Unknown Fathers Act (UPUFA), which allows the identification of putative and unknown fathers and the termination of their parental rights.

The revised UPA makes several improvements to the original Act. The new Act provides for four definitions of "father": (1) an "acknowledged father," who acknowledges paternity in accordance with the requirements established in Article 3 (with the concurrence of the mother and that is treated as an adjudication of paternity); (2) a judicially "adjudicated father"; (3) an "alleged father," who is asserted to be, or asserts himself to be or possibly to be, the father of a child (replacing the former term "putative" father); and (4) a "presumed father," who satisfies the circumstances establishing a presumption of paternity in §204.

For presumed fathers, the revised UPA clarifies the "holding out" requirement. The 1973 UPA neglected to specify a duration for the "holding out" requirement to establish a presumption of paternity (providing merely that any "holding out" was sufficient during a child's minority) (§4(a)(4)). This omission created uncertainty about whether the presumption arose either if the "holding out" occurred for a short time or if it commenced long after birth. The revised UPA requires that the man must reside with the child for the first two years of the child's life to establish the presumption of paternity.

In addition, the original UPA created a presumption of paternity for a man who acknowledged paternity in a writing filed with the appropriate agency (and if the mother failed to dispute that acknowledgment within a reasonable time). The revised UPA omits this presumption because it conflicts with a different provision of the revised Act that allows a valid acknowledgment actually to *establish* paternity rather than to establish a *presumption* of paternity. Because of the advent and accuracy of genetic testing, the revised UPA also omits the clear-and-convincing standard required to rebut the presumption as well as the provision regarding conflicting presumptions of paternity. Moreover, under the revised UPA, a court may use estoppel principles in appropriate circumstances to deny requests for genetic testing in the interest of preserving a child's ties to a presumed or acknowledged father who openly holds himself out as the child's father, regardless of whether he is in fact the genetic father.

The revised UPA also addresses the father's right to notice of a proceeding for adoption or termination of parental rights. Under the new UPA, if the man registers, he may protect his right to notice (assuming that the state of registration is the same state as the birth). The protection of his right to notice in other situations depends on the age of the child. For children aged one year and older at the time of the proceeding for adoption of termination of parental rights, notice must be given to every alleged father whether or not he has registered (§405). To facilitate infant adoptions, the revised UPA places a burden on the father to register if he wants to be notified of an adoption proceeding. The man's failure to register in cases of a child less than one year of age will result in waiver of his rights (§404), unless (1) a father-child relationship has been established under the Act or other law or (2) he has commenced a proceeding to adjudicate his paternity before the court terminates his parental rights.

The revised UPA also takes into account federal legislation regarding the acknowledgment procedure mandated by the Personal Responsibility and Work Opportunity Reconciliation Act (PRWORA) of 1996. Because PRWORA does not preclude the possibility that a child may have both a presumed and acknowledged parent, the new UPA provides that a presumed father must file a denial of paternity in order for another man's acknowledgment of paternity to be valid.

For critiques on the revised UPA, see generally Paula Roberts, Truth and Consequences: Part II. Questioning the Paternity of Marital Children, 37 Fam. L.Q. 55 (2003); Paula Roberts, Biology and Beyond: The Case for Passage of the New Uniform Parentage Act, 35 Fam. L.Q. 41 (2001). For a discussion of the requirements regarding efforts to identify unknown fathers, see infra pp. 500-503.

Uniform Parentage Act (2000, as amended in 2002)
9B U.L.A. 309-311, 313-314 (2001 & Supp. 2004)

§201. *Establishment of Parent-Child Relationship*

(a) The mother-child relationship is established between a woman and a child by:

(1) the woman's having given birth to the child[, except as otherwise provided in [Article] 8];

(2) an adjudication of the woman's maternity; [or]

(3) adoption of the child by the woman[; or

(4) an adjudication confirming the woman as a parent of a child born to a gestational mother if the agreement was validated under Article 8 or is enforceable under other law].

(b) The father-child relationship is established between a man and a child by:

(1) an unrebutted presumption of the man's paternity of the child under Section 204;

(2) an effective acknowledgment of paternity by the man under [Article] 3, unless the acknowledgment has been rescinded or successfully challenged;

(3) an adjudication of the man's paternity;

(4) adoption of the child by the man; [or]

(5) the man's having consented to assisted reproduction by a woman under [Article] 7 which resulted in the birth of the child[; or

(6) an adjudication confirming the man as a parent of a child born to a gestational mother if the agreement was validated under [Article] 8 or is enforceable under other law].

§204. Presumption of Paternity

(a) A man is presumed to be the father of a child if:

(1) he and the mother of the child are married to each other and the child is born during the marriage;

(2) he and the mother of the child were married to each other and the child is born within 300 days after the marriage is terminated by death, annulment, declaration of invalidity, or divorce[, or after a decree of separation];

(3) before the birth of the child, he and the mother of the child married each other in apparent compliance with law, even if the attempted marriage is or could be declared invalid, and the child is born during the invalid marriage or within 300 days after its termination by death, annulment, declaration of invalidity, or divorce[, or after a decree of separation];

(4) after the birth of the child, he and the mother of the child married each other in apparent compliance with law, whether or not the marriage is or could be declared invalid, and he voluntarily asserted his paternity of the child, and:

(A) the assertion is in a record filed with [state agency maintaining birth records];

(B) he agreed to be and is named as the child's father on the child's birth certificate; or

(C) he promised in a record to support the child as his own.

(b) A presumption of paternity established under this section may be rebutted only by an adjudication under [Article] 6.

§301. Acknowledgment of Paternity

The mother of a child and a man claiming to be the father of the child may sign an acknowledgment of paternity with intent to establish the man's paternity.

§302. Execution of Acknowledgment of Paternity

(a) An acknowledgment of paternity must:

(1) be in a record;

(2) be signed, or otherwise authenticated, under penalty of perjury by the mother and by the man seeking to establish his paternity;

(3) state that the child whose paternity is being acknowledged:

(A) does not have a presumed father, or has a presumed father whose full name is stated; and

(B) does not have another acknowledged or adjudicated father;

(4) state whether there has been genetic testing and, if so, that the acknowledging man's claim of paternity is consistent with the results of the testing; and

(5) state that the signatories understand that the acknowledgment is the equivalent of a judicial adjudication of paternity of the child and that a challenge to the acknowledgment is permitted only under limited circumstances and is barred after two years.

(b) An acknowledgment of paternity is void if it:

(1) states that another man is a presumed father, unless a denial of paternity signed or otherwise authenticated by the presumed father is filed with the [agency maintaining birth records];

(2) states that another man is an acknowledged or adjudicated father; or

(3) falsely denies the existence of a presumed, acknowledged, or adjudicated father of the child.

(c) A presumed father may sign or otherwise authenticate an acknowledgment of paternity.

§402. Registration for Notification

(a) Except as otherwise provided in subsection (b) or Section 405, a man who desires to be notified of a proceeding for adoption of, or termination of parental rights regarding, a child that he may have fathered must register in the registry of paternity before the birth of the child or within 30 days after the birth.

(b) A man is not required to register if[:

(1)]a father-child relationship between the man and the child has been established under this [Act] or other law[; or

(2) the man commences a proceeding to adjudicate his paternity before the court has terminated his parental rights].

(c) A registrant shall promptly notify the registry in a record of any change in the information registered. The [agency maintaining the registry] shall incorporate all new information received into its records but need not affirmatively seek to obtain current information for incorporation in the registry.

§403. Notice of Proceeding

Notice of a proceeding for the adoption of, or termination of parental rights regarding, a child must be given to a registrant who has timely registered. Notice must be given in a manner prescribed for service of process in a civil action.

§404. Termination of Parental Rights: Child Under One Year of Age

The parental rights of a man who may be the father of a child may be terminated without notice if:

(1) the child has not attained one year of age at the time of the termination of parental rights;

(2) the man did not register timely with the [agency maintaining the registry]; and

(3) the man is not exempt from registration under Section 402.

§405. Termination of Parental Rights: Child at Least One Year of Age

(a) If a child has attained one year of age, notice of a proceeding for adoption of, or termination of parental rights regarding, the child must be given to every alleged father of the child, whether or not he has registered with the [agency maintaining the registry].

(b) Notice must be given in a manner prescribed for service of process in a civil action.

Subsequent Supreme Court opinions generated additional answers to the many questions left unresolved in the wake of *Stanley*.

Quilloin v. Walcott, 434 U.S. 246 (1978), involved a Georgia statute providing that only the mother of nonmarital child need consent to the adoption of that child unless the father had legitimated the child by marriage and acknowledgment, or by court order. The biological father in *Quilloin* had never lived with the mother and the child, and had never legitimated the child. Shortly after the mother gave birth to the child, she married another man. Adoption was sought by the mother's new husband with whom the child had been living for approximately nine years. The child's biological father, although he had never sought custody before, had made some support payments and had visited the child on numerous occasions. At the time of the dispute, the child himself, then about 11 years old, expressed a desire to be adopted.

The child's biological father was given notice of the adoption petition and participated in a hearing at which he petitioned to be declared the child's legitimate father and to be granted visitation. He also petitioned that the adoption be denied. The Supreme Court affirmed the trial court's opinion granting the adoption on the ground that it was in the child's best interests. The Court rejected both Quilloin's due process and equal protection claims: (1) that due process prohibited termination of his parental rights without a finding of unfitness; and, (2) that the distinction between unmarried and married fathers violated the Equal Protection Clause. The Court held that the father's due process rights were not violated, although it conceded that due process probably would require a showing of unfitness before involuntarily separating a "natural family." Since Quilloin had never had or sought custody, the Court said this requirement was inapplicable to him. The Court also rejected his equal protection argument on the ground that his interests were distinguishable from those of a married father since the latter had borne legal responsibility for the rearing of his children.

Quilloin implied that the extent of an unwed father's rights depended on the nature of his relationship with his child(ren). A year after *Quilloin*, the Court further clarified its views on the rights of unwed fathers in Caban v. Mohammed, 441 U.S. 380 (1979). The New York statute challenged in *Caban* provided that a nonmarital child could be adopted with the consent of the mother alone, without the necessity for the biological father's consent. Although the unwed mother could block the adoption of her child by withholding her consent, the unwed father had no such right — even if his parental relationship was substantial. Such was the case in *Caban*. Abdiel Caban lived with Maria Mohammed for five years, during which time they had two children. When the couple separated, Mohammed went to live with another man whom she thereafter married. Caban continued to see the children frequently and at one point had custody of them. When the Mohammeds petitioned to adopt the children, the natural father and his new wife cross-petitioned for adoption. At the time of the hearing, the children were four and six years old. The trial judge approved the adoption on behalf of the Mohammeds.

In *Caban* the Supreme Court held that the statutory distinction between the rights of mothers and fathers of nonmarital children violated the Equal Protection Clause. The Court stated:

> We find that the distinction in [the statute] between unmarried mothers and unmarried fathers, as illustrated by this case, does not bear a substantial relation to the State's interest in providing adoptive homes for its illegitimate children . . . The New York Court of Appeals in In re Malpica-Orsini [331 N.E.2d 486 (N.Y. 1975)] suggested that the requiring of unmarried fathers' consent for adoption would pose a strong impediment for adoption because often it is impossible to locate unwed fathers when adoption proceedings are brought, whereas mothers are more likely to remain with their children. Even if the special difficulties attendant upon locating and identifying unwed fathers at birth would justify a legislative distinction between mothers and fathers of newborns,[11] these difficulties need not persist past infancy. When the adoption of an older child is sought, the State's interest in proceeding with adoption cases can be protected by means that do not draw such an inflexible gender-based distinction as that made in [the statute]. In those cases where the father never has come forward to participate in the rearing of his child, nothing in the Equal Protection Clause precludes the State from withholding from him the privilege of vetoing the adoption of that child. . . . But in cases such as this, where the father has established a substantial relationship with the child and has admitted his paternity, a State should have no difficulty in identifying the father even of children born out of wedlock. Thus, no showing has been made that the different treatment afforded unmarried fathers and unmarried mothers under [the statute] bears a substantial relationship to the proclaimed interest of the State in promoting the adoption of illegitimate children. [441 U.S. at 391-393.]

Thus, the Court in *Caban* again focused on the nature of the parent-child relationship and required certain indicia of parenthood in order to extend constitutional protection to the unwed father. Caban, unlike Mr. Quilloin, was a father who had provided support, had lived with his children for a substantial period of time, and visited them frequently after the relationship with their mother disintegrated.

Unanswered by *Quilloin* and *Caban* was the more troublesome question: what was the extent of constitutional protection required for the unwed father who has little more than a biological relationship with his child? Did he have a right to notice and an opportunity to be heard before his child could be adopted? This was the issue framed by the next case to be determined by the Supreme Court.

[11] Because the question is not before us, we express no view whether such difficulties would justify a statute addressed particularly to newborn adoptions, setting forth more stringent requirements concerning the acknowledgement of paternity or a stricter definition of abandonment.

Lehr v. Robertson
463 U.S. 248 (1983)

Justice STEVENS delivered the opinion of the Court.

The question presented is whether New York has sufficiently protected an unmarried father's inchoate relationship with a child whom he has never supported and rarely seen in the two years since her birth. The appellant, Jonathan Lehr, claims that the Due Process and Equal Protection Clauses of the Fourteenth Amendment, as interpreted in Stanley v. Illinois, give him an absolute right to notice and an opportunity to be heard before the child may be adopted. We disagree.

Jessica M. was born out of wedlock on November 9, 1976. Her mother, Lorraine Robertson, married Richard Robertson eight months after Jessica's birth. On December 21, 1978, when Jessica was over two years old, the Robertsons filed an adoption petition in the Family Court of Ulster County, New York. The court heard their testimony and received a favorable report from the Ulster County Department of Social Services. On March 7, 1979, the court entered an order of adoption. In this proceeding, appellant contends that the adoption order is invalid because he, Jessica's putative father, was not given advance notice of the adoption proceeding.

The State of New York maintains a "putative father registry." A man who files with that registry demonstrates his intent to claim paternity of a child born out of wedlock and is therefore entitled to receive notice of any proceeding to adopt that child. Before entering Jessica's adoption order, the Ulster County Family Court had the putative father registry examined. Although appellant claims to be Jessica's natural father, he has not entered his name in the registry.

In addition to the persons whose names are listed on the putative father registry, New York law requires that notice of an adoption proceeding be given to several other classes of possible fathers of children born out of wedlock — those who have been adjudicated to be the father, those who have been identified as the father on the child's birth certificate, those who live openly with the child and the child's mother and who hold themselves out to be the father, those who have been identified as the father by the mother in a sworn written statement, and those who were married to the child's mother before the child was six months old. Appellant admittedly was not a member of any of those classes. He had lived with appellee prior to Jessica's birth and visited her in the hospital when Jessica was born, but his name does not appear on Jessica's birth certificate. He did not live with appellee or Jessica after Jessica's birth, he has never provided them with any financial support, and he has never offered to marry appellee. Nevertheless, he contends that the following special circumstances gave him a constitutional right to notice and a hearing before Jessica was adopted.

On January 30, 1979, one month after the adoption proceeding was commenced in Ulster County, appellant filed a "visitation and paternity petition" in the Westchester County Family Court. In that petition, he asked for a determination of paternity, an order of support, and reasonable visitation privileges with Jessica. Notice of that proceeding was served on appellee on February 22, 1979. Four days later appellee's attorney informed the Ulster County Court that appellant had commenced a paternity proceeding in Westchester County; the Ulster County judge then entered an order staying appellant's paternity proceeding until he could rule on a motion to change the venue of that proceeding to Ulster County. On March 3, 1979, appellant received notice of the change of venue motion and, for the first time, learned that an adoption proceeding was pending in Ulster County.

On March 7, 1979, appellant's attorney telephoned the Ulster County judge to inform him that he planned to seek a stay of the adoption proceeding pending the determination of the paternity petition. In that telephone conversation, the judge advised the lawyer that he had already signed the adoption order earlier that day. According to appellant's attorney, the judge stated that he was aware of the pending paternity petition but did not believe he was required to give notice to appellant prior to the entry of the order of adoption.

Thereafter, the Family Court in Westchester County granted appellee's motion to dismiss the paternity petition, holding that the putative father's right to seek paternity " . . . must be deemed severed so long as an order of adoption exists." Appellant did not appeal from that dismissal. On June 22, 1979, appellant filed a petition to vacate the order of adoption on the ground that it was obtained by fraud and in violation of his constitutional rights. The Ulster County Family Court received written and oral argument on the question whether it had "dropped the ball" by approving the adoption without giving appellant advance notice. After deliberating for several months, it denied the petition, explaining its decision in a thorough written opinion. [The Appellate Division of the Supreme Court and the New York Court of Appeals both affirmed.]

Appellant . . . offers two alternative grounds for holding the New York statutory scheme unconstitutional. First, he contends that a putative father's actual or potential relationship with a child born out of wedlock is an interest in liberty which may not be destroyed without due process of law; he argues therefore that he had a constitutional right to prior notice and an opportunity to be heard before he was deprived of that interest. Second, he contends that the gender-based classification in the statute, which both denied him the right to consent to Jessica's adoption and accorded him fewer procedural rights than her mother, violated the Equal Protection Clause.

The Due Process Claim

. . . We therefore first consider the nature of the interest in liberty for which appellant claims constitutional protection and then turn to a discussion of the adequacy of the procedure that New York has provided for its protection. . . .

This Court has examined the extent to which a natural father's biological relationship with his illegitimate child receives protection under the Due Process Clause in precisely three cases: Stanley vs. Illinois, Quilloin v. Walcott, and Caban v. Mohammed. . . .

The difference between the developed parent-child relationship that was implicated in *Stanley* and *Caban*, and the potential relationship involved in *Quilloin* and this case, is both clear and significant. When an unwed father demonstrates a full commitment to the responsibilities of parenthood by "com[ing] forward to participate in the rearing of his child," *Caban*, 441 U.S., at 392, his interest in personal contact with his child acquires substantial protection under the due process clause.

At that point it may be said that he "act[s] as a father toward his children." Id., at 389, n.7. But the mere existence of a biological link does not merit equivalent constitutional protection. . . .

The significance of the biological connection is that it offers the natural father an opportunity that no other male possesses to develop a relationship with his offspring. If he grasps that opportunity and accepts some measure of responsibility for the child's future, he may enjoy the blessings of the parent-child relationship and make uniquely valuable contributions to the child's development.[18] If he fails to do so, the Federal Constitution will not automatically compel a state to listen to his opinion of where the child's best interests lie.

In this case, we are not assessing the constitutional adequacy of New York's procedures for terminating a developed relationship. Appellant has never had any significant custodial, personal, or financial relationship with Jessica, and he did not seek to establish a legal tie until after she was two years old.[19] We are concerned only with whether New York has adequately protected his opportunity to form such a relationship.

The most effective protection of the putative father's opportunity to develop a relationship with his child is provided by the laws that authorize formal marriage and govern its consequences. But the availability of that protection is, of course, dependent on the will of both parents of the child. Thus, New York has adopted a special statutory scheme to protect the unmarried father's interest in assuming a responsible role in the future of his child.

After this Court's decision in *Stanley*, the New York legislature [enacted] a statutory adoption scheme that automatically provides notice to seven categories of putative fathers who are likely to have assumed some responsibility for the care of their natural children. If this scheme were likely to omit many responsible fathers, and if qualification for notice were beyond the control of an interested putative father, it might be thought procedurally inadequate. Yet, . . . the right to receive notice was completely within appellant's control. By mailing a postcard to the putative father registry, he could have guaranteed that he would receive notice of any proceedings to adopt Jessica. The possibility that he may have failed to do so

---

[18] Of course, we need not take sides in the ongoing debate among family psychologists over the relative weight to be accorded biological ties and psychological ties, in order to recognize that a natural father who has played a substantial role in rearing his child has a greater claim to constitutional protection than a mere biological parent. New York's statutory scheme reflects these differences, guaranteeing notice to any putative father who is living openly with the child, and providing putative fathers who have never developed a relationship with the child the opportunity to receive notice simply by mailing a postcard to the putative father registry.

[19] This case happens to involve an adoption by the husband of the natural mother, but we do not believe the natural father has any greater right to object to such an adoption than to an adoption by two total strangers. If anything, the balance of equities tips the opposite way in a case such as this. In denying the putative father relief in *Quilloin*, we made an observation equally applicable here:

> Nor is this a case in which the proposed adoption would place the child with a new set of parents with whom the child has never before lived. Rather, the result of the adoption in this case is to give full recognition to a family unit already in existence, a result desired by all concerned, except appellant. Whatever might be required in other situations, we cannot say that the State was required in this situation to find anything more than that the adoption, and denial of legitimation, were in the "best interests of the child." 434 U.S., at 255.

because of his ignorance of the law cannot be a sufficient reason for criticizing the law itself. The New York legislature concluded that a more open-ended notice requirement would merely complicate the adoption process, threaten the privacy interests of unwed mothers, create the risk of unnecessary controversy, and impair the desired finality of adoption decrees. Regardless of whether we would have done likewise if we were legislators instead of judges, we surely cannot characterize the state's conclusion as arbitrary.

Appellant argues, however, that even if the putative father's opportunity to establish a relationship with an illegitimate child is adequately protected by the New York statutory scheme in the normal case, he was nevertheless entitled to special notice because the court and the mother knew that he had filed an affiliation proceeding in another court. This argument amounts to nothing more than an indirect attack on the notice provisions of the New York statute. The legitimate state interests in facilitating the adoption of young children and having the adoption proceeding completed expeditiously that underlie the entire statutory scheme also justify a trial judge's determination to require all interested parties to adhere precisely to the procedural requirements of the statute. The Constitution does not require either a trial judge or a litigant to have special notice to nonparties who are presumptively capable of asserting and protecting their own rights. Since the New York statutes adequately protected appellant's inchoate interest in establishing a relationship with Jessica, we find no merit in the claim that his constitutional rights were offended because the family court strictly complied with the notice provisions of the statute.

The Equal Protection Claim

. . . The legislation at issue in this case, sections 111 and 111a of the New York Domestic Relations Law, is intended to establish procedures for adoptions [that] promote the best interests of the child, protect the rights of interested third parties, and ensure promptness and finality. To serve those ends, the legislation guarantees to certain people the right to veto an adoption and the right to prior notice of any adoption proceeding. The mother of an illegitimate child is always within that favored class, but only certain putative fathers are included. Appellant contends that the gender-based distinction is invidious. . . .

We have held that these statutes may not constitutionally be applied in that class of cases where the mother and father are in fact similarly situated with regard to their relationship with the child. In Caban v. Mohammed, 441 U.S. 380 (1979), the Court held that it violated the Equal Protection Clause to grant the mother a veto over the adoption of a four-year-old girl and a six-year-old boy, but not to grant a veto to their father, who had admitted paternity and had participated in the rearing of the children. The Court made it clear, however, that if the father had not "come forward to participate in the rearing of his child, nothing in the Equal Protection Clause [would] preclude [ ] the State from withholding from him the privilege of vetoing the adoption of that child."

Jessica's parents are not like the parents involved in *Caban*. Whereas appellee had a continuous custodial responsibility for Jessica, appellant never established any custodial, personal, or financial relationship with her. If one parent has an established custodial relationship with the child and the other parent has either abandoned or never established a relationship, the Equal Protection Clause does not prevent a state from according the two parents different legal rights.

The judgment of the New York Court of Appeals is affirmed.

Justice WHITE, with whom Justice MARSHALL and Justice BLACKMUN join, dissenting.

The question in this case is whether the State may, consistent with the Due Process Clause, deny notice and an opportunity to be heard in an adoption proceeding to a putative father when the State has actual notice of his existence, whereabouts, and interest in the child.

I

It is axiomatic that "[t]he fundamental requirement of due process is the opportunity to be heard 'at a meaningful time and in a meaningful manner.'" As Jessica's biological father, Lehr either had an interest protected by the Constitution or he did not. If the entry of the adoption order in this case deprived Lehr of a constitutionally protected interest, he is entitled to notice and an opportunity to be heard before the order can be accorded finality.

According to Lehr, he and Jessica's mother met in 1971 and began living together in 1974. The couple cohabited for approximately 2 years, until Jessica's birth in 1976. Throughout the pregnancy and after the birth, Lorraine acknowledged to friends and relatives that Lehr was Jessica's father; Lorraine told Lehr that she had reported to the New York State Department of Social Services that he was the father [as required for her to receive benefits under Aid to Families with Dependent Children]. Lehr visited Lorraine and Jessica in the hospital every day during Lorraine's confinement. According to Lehr, from the time Lorraine was discharged from the hospital until August, 1978, she concealed her whereabouts from him. During this time Lehr never ceased his efforts to locate Lorraine and Jessica and achieved sporadic success until August, 1977, after which time he was unable to locate them at all. On those occasions when he did determine Lorraine's location, he visited with her and her children to the extent she was willing to permit it. When Lehr, with the aid of a detective agency, located Lorraine and Jessica in August, 1978, Lorraine was already married to Mr. Robertson. Lehr asserts that at this time he offered to provide financial assistance and to set up a trust fund for Jessica, but that Lorraine refused. Lorraine threatened Lehr with arrest unless he stayed away and refused to permit him to see Jessica. Thereafter Lehr retained counsel who wrote to Lorraine in early December, 1978, requesting that she permit Lehr to visit Jessica and threatening legal action on Lehr's behalf. On December 21, 1978, perhaps as a response to Lehr's threatened legal action, appellees commenced the adoption action at issue here. . . .

Lehr's version of the "facts" paints a far different picture than that portrayed by the majority. The majority's recitation, that "[a]ppellant has never had any significant custodial, personal, or financial relationship with Jessica, and he did not seek to establish a legal tie until after she was two years old," obviously does not tell the whole story. Appellant has never been afforded an opportunity to present his case.

The legitimation proceeding he instituted was first stayed, and then dismissed, on appellees' motions. Nor could appellant establish his interest during the adoption proceedings, for it is the failure to provide Lehr notice and an opportunity to be heard there that is at issue here. We cannot fairly make a judgment based on the quality or substance of a relationship without a complete and developed factual record. This case requires us to assume that Lehr's allegations are true — that but for the actions of the child's mother there would have been the kind of significant relationship that the majority concedes is entitled to the full panoply of procedural due process protections.[3]

I reject the peculiar notion that the only significance of the biological connection between father and child is that "it offers the natural father an opportunity that no other male possesses to develop a relationship with his offspring." A "mere biological relationship" is not as unimportant in determining the nature of liberty interests as the majority suggests.

The "biological connection" is itself a relationship that creates a protected interest. Thus the "nature" of the interest is the parent-child relationship; how well-developed that relationship has become goes to its "weight," not its "nature."[4] Whether Lehr's interest is entitled to constitutional protection does not entail a searching inquiry into the quality of the relationship but a simple determination of the fact that the relationship exists — a fact that even the majority agrees must be assumed to be established.

Beyond that, however, because there is no established factual basis on which to proceed, it is quite untenable to conclude that a putative father's interest in his child is lacking in substance, that the father in effect has abandoned the child, or ultimately that the father's interest is not entitled to the same minimum procedural protections as the interests of other putative fathers. Any analysis of the adequacy of the notice in this case must be conducted on the assumption that the interest involved here is as strong as that of any putative father. That is not to say that due process requires actual notice to every putative father or that adoptive parents or the State must conduct an exhaustive search of records or an intensive investigation before a final adoption order may be entered. The procedures adopted by the State, however, must at least represent a reasonable effort to determine the identity of the putative father and to give him adequate notice.

---

[3] In response to our decision in Caban v. Mohammed, 441 U.S. 380 (1979), the statute governing the persons whose consent is necessary to an adoption has been amended to include certain unwed fathers. The State has recognized that an unwed father's failure to maintain an actual relationship or to communicate with a child will not deprive him of his right to consent if he was "prevented from doing so by the person or authorized agency having lawful custody of the child." N.Y. Dom. Rel. Law §111(1)(d) (as amended by Chap. 575, L. 1980). Thus, even the State recognizes that before a lesser standard can be applied consistent with due process requirements, there must be a determination that there was no significant relationship and that the father was not prevented from forming such a relationship.

[4] The majority's citation of *Quilloin* and *Caban* as examples that the Constitution does not require the same procedural protections for the interests of all unwed fathers is disingenuous. Neither case involved notice and opportunity to be heard. In both, the unwed fathers were notified and participated as parties in the adoption proceedings.

II

In this case, of course, there was no question about either the identity or the location of the putative father. The mother knew exactly who he was and both she and the court entering the order of adoption knew precisely where he was and how to give him actual notice that his parental rights were about to be terminated by an adoption order. Lehr was entitled to due process, and the right to be heard is one of the fundamentals of that right, which "has little reality or worth unless one is informed that the matter is pending and can choose for himself whether to appear or default, acquiesce or contest."

The State concedes this much but insists that Lehr has had all the process that is due to him. It relies on §111-a, which designates seven categories of unwed fathers to whom notice of adoption proceedings must be given, including any unwed father who has filed with the State a notice of his intent to claim paternity. The State submits that it need not give notice to anyone who has not filed his name, as he is permitted to do, and who is not otherwise within the designated categories, even if his identity and interest are known or are reasonably ascertainable by the State.

I am unpersuaded by the State's position. In the first place, §111-a defines six categories of unwed fathers to whom notice must be given even though they have not placed their names on file pursuant to the section. Those six categories, however, do not include fathers such as Lehr who have initiated filiation proceedings, even though their identity and interest are as clearly and easily ascertainable as those fathers in the six categories. Initiating such proceedings necessarily involves a formal acknowledgement of paternity, and requiring the State to take note of such a case in connection with pending adoption proceedings would be a trifling burden, no more than the State undertakes when there is a final adjudication in a paternity action. Indeed, there would appear to be more reason to give notice to those such as Lehr who acknowledge paternity than to those who have been adjudged to be a father in a contested paternity action.

The State asserts that any problem in this respect is overcome by the seventh category of putative fathers to whom notice must be given, namely those fathers who have identified themselves in the putative father register maintained by the State. Since Lehr did not take advantage of this device to make his interest known, the State contends, he was not entitled to notice and a hearing even though his identity, location and interest were known to the adoption court prior to entry of the adoption order. I have difficulty with this position. First, it represents a grudging and crabbed approach to due process. The State is quite willing to give notice and a hearing to putative fathers who have made themselves known by resorting to the putative fathers' register. It makes little sense to me to deny notice and hearing to a father who has not placed his name in the register but who has unmistakably identified himself by filing suit to establish his paternity and has notified the adoption court of his action and his interest. [H]e effectively made himself known by other means, and it is the sheerest formalism to deny him a hearing because he informed the State in the wrong manner.

No state interest is substantially served by denying Lehr adequate notice and a hearing. The State no doubt has an interest in expediting adoption proceedings to prevent a child from remaining unduly long in the custody of the State or foster parents. But this is not an adoption involving a child in the custody of an authorized state agency. . . . The State's undoubted interest in the finality of adoption orders likewise is not well served by a procedure that will deny notice and a hearing to a father whose identity and location are known. As this case well illustrates, denying notice and a hearing to such a father may result in years of additional litigation and threaten the reopening of adoption proceedings and the vacation of the adoption. . . .

Because in my view the failure to provide Lehr with notice and an opportunity to be heard violated rights guaranteed him by the Due Process Clause, I need not address the question whether §111-a violates the Equal Protection Clause by discriminating between categories of unwed fathers or by discriminating on the basis of gender.

Respectfully, I dissent.

QUESTIONS AND NOTES

Lehr and prior case law reveal that the unwed father is entitled to constitutional protection of his parental rights so long as he is willing to accept the responsibilities of parenthood. The extent of this constitutional protection varies according to the degree to which the unwed father manifests a willingness to assume a custodial, personal, or financial relationship with his child. Although an unwed father has the right to establish a constitutionally protected relationship with his child, he may lose this right by his failure to act promptly.

(1) Notice. Currently, more than half the states authorize, by statute, the creation of putative father registries.[26] Registries place the burden of protecting the parent-child relationship on the unwed father who has to take the initiative to register with the statutorily designated state agency in order to receive subsequent notice of an adoption proceeding. In *Lehr*, the Court held that New York's scheme for providing notice to an unwed father (through the requirement that he enter his name in a putative father's registry entitling him to receive subsequent notice of an adoption proceeding) did not violate the Due Process Clause. According to *Lehr*, if a biological father fails to seize the opportunity to establish a relationship with his child, he may lose his parental rights, including the right to notice of, and to participate in, adoption proceedings.

Lehr, similar to preceding Supreme Court cases *(Quilloin, Caban)* dealt with adoptions of older children. The dilemma left unanswered by *Lehr* and other post-*Stanley* cases concerns their implications for infants. If an unmarried mother is relinquishing a newborn for adoption, what does due process demand if the father is never given an opportunity to comply with the registration requirement for any number of reasons?

Does due process require that the father in the following situations be permitted to show that he never had an opportunity to comply with the requirement of filing a notice in the putative father registry?

---

[26] Mary Beck, Toward a National Putative Father Registry, 25 Harv. J.L. & Pub. Pol'y 1031, 1036-1037 (2002) ("over thirty states currently have putative father registries" based on state survey).

a. Unknown Whereabouts of Mother. A man and woman conceive a child out of wedlock. Because of her family's disapproval of her pregnancy, the woman leaves the state and refuses to disclose her whereabouts to the father. He is unable to locate her, although the couple continues to communicate by e-mail. When the mother gives birth in Minnesota, she leaves blank the name of the father on the birth certificate and relinquishes the child for adoption. After the baby is placed with adoptive parents, the father discovers the infant's whereabouts. He then sends the required forms to the Minnesota paternity registry to seek abrogation of the adoption. See Heidibreder v. Carton, 636 N.W.2d 383 (Minn. Ct. App. 2001) (holding that father's parental rights were not violated when he failed to timely register, and registry procedure did not violate his rights to due process and equal protection).

b. False Information that Baby Died. Daniella Janikova and Otakar Kirchner, both Czechoslovakian immigrants, are living together when Daniella becomes pregnant. The man leaves for a short visit with a dying relative in Czechoslovakia. Upon being told, falsely, by a meddlesome aunt that Otakar is having an affair with a former girlfriend, Daniella moves out and tells him that their child died at birth. Two months later, he learns that the child was placed for adoption. They subsequently marry and seek the return of the child from the adoptive parents. See In re Petition of John Doe, 638 N.E.2d 181 (Ill. 1994), *cert. denied*, 513 U.S. 994 (1994) (setting aside adoption because father had shown sufficient interest to preclude termination of parental rights). The father successfully sought a writ of habeas corpus, requiring the transfer of the four-year-old boy (known as Baby Richard) to the father's custody. In re Petition of Kirchner, 649 N.E.2d 324 (Ill. 1995), *stay denied sub nom.* O'Connell v. Kirchner, 513 U.S. 1138 (1995).

Baby Richard's birth parents subsequently separated, then reconciled and had two daughters. The boy, 12 years old in 2003, is reportedly doing well. He told his psychologist, "I got stolen when I was a baby. There was a big argument about who I should stay with and about the truth. The other people — I don't know their names — wanted to keep me." Abdon M. Pallash, "Baby Richard", Doing Fine — 7th-Grader Has Straight A's; Psychologist's Book Says Boy Not Scarred by Adoption Ordeal, Chicago Sun-Times, Nov. 18, 2003, at 4. See also Karen Moriarty, Baby Richard: A Four-Year-Old Comes Home (2004).

c. Misrepresentation of Biological Father. Cara Claussen, an unmarried woman, gives birth to a girl in Iowa, misrepresenting Scott Seefeldt as the father. When Michigan residents Roberta and Jan DeBoer file a petition to adopt Baby Jessica, an Iowa court terminates the parental rights of Clausen and Seefeldt and grants custody during the pendency of the proceeding to the DeBoers, who return to Michigan. Nine days later, Clausen admits that she falsely identified the father and seeks to revoke her consent. Clausen subsequently marries the baby's father, Daniel Schmidt, and they seek the return of the child.

In In re B.G.C., 496 N.W.2d 239 (Iowa 1992), the Iowa Supreme Court held that the biological father's parental rights could not be terminated because his abandonment was not established by clear and convincing evidence. In Michigan, Baby Jessica's prospective adoptive parents unsuccessfully petitioned for modification of the Iowa court order denying their adoption petition and granting custody to the child's biological parents. In re Baby Girl Clausen, 502 N.W.2d 649 (Mich. 1993).

The United States Supreme Court refused to stay the order entered pursuant to the Michigan Supreme Court's opinion. 509 U.S. 1301 (1993).

Baby Jessica was returned to the Schmidts and was renamed Anna. Daniel Schmidt was injured in a construction accident in 1998. His subsequent unemployment contributed to the parents' divorce in 2000. Anna and her younger sister reside with their father, although the parents share legal custody. According to her parents, 12-year-old Anna is well adjusted and happy. See "Baby Jessica" Celebrates 10 Years with Birth Family; Her Adoptive Parents in Ann Arbor and Her Birth Parents Fought their Case All the Way to the Supreme Court, Grand Rapids Press, Aug. 3, 2003, at A19, available at 2003 WL 58547327; Profile: Effect of Highly Publicized Custody Battles on Children, NBC News: Today, June 3, 2004, available at 2004 WL 81873945. The cases of Baby Richard and Baby Jessica spurred many states to enact putative father registries to facilitate newborn adoptions.[27]

   d. Ignorance of Pregnancy.   On the other hand, suppose that the birth father is not aware of the mother's pregnancy. What due process protection, if any, does the father have?

In Robert O. v. Russell K., 604 N.E.2d 99 (N.Y. 1992), a man and woman live together for a year. When they break up, the woman chooses not to inform the man of her pregnancy and her relinquishment of the child for adoption. Several months later, they reconcile and marry. After the woman informs the father about the child, he registers in the putative father registry and commences proceedings to vacate the adoption (18 months after the child's birth and 20 months after the adoption is finalized). The New York Court of Appeals concludes that the father failed to manifest a willingness to assume full custody within the time provided by statute. The court explains that prompt action was necessary because of the state's legitimate interest in the child's need for stability. "Promptness is measured in terms of the baby's life not by the onset of the father's awareness." Id. at 103. The court limited the time in which a father must act to the six-month period immediately preceding the child's placement for adoption. See also In re Baby Girl U., 638 N.Y.S.2d 253 (App. Div. 1996) (finding that unwed father was not entitled to veto adoption where he failed to seek declaration of paternity until six months after learning of birth and never sought to be financially responsible for the child). Is it realistic to characterize a father as exhibiting no interest in his child if he does not know of its existence?

What does due process require if the identity and/or whereabouts of a father are unknown? The original UPA required that efforts be made to identify the biological father through appropriate inquiries (§25(b)). If such inquiries were unsuccessful, the unknown father's rights could be terminated, subject to a six-month period during which the matter could be reopened if the man came forward and demonstrated that he was the father. However, after the six-month period, the termination was final (§25(d)).

The revised Uniform Adoption Act, 9 U.L.A. 11 (1994), also addresses efforts to identify the father. The revised UAA requires inquiry of the mother. If such inquiry fails to identify the father and there is no reasonable likelihood that publication or posting will lead to actual notice, the Act rules out that method of notice. If the mother refuses to identify the father or his whereabouts, UAA §3-404(e) requires

[27] Id. at 1036.

the court to explain to her the importance of disclosure (for finality of adoption and medical history) and to advise her that she may be subject to civil liability for misidentification of the father.

(2) Opportunity to Develop a Relationship.   In *Lehr*, the Court noted:

> The significance of the biological connection is that it offers the natural father an opportunity that no other male possesses to develop a relationship with his offspring. If he grasps that opportunity and accepts some measure of responsibility for the child's future, he may enjoy the blessings of the parent-child relationship and make uniquely valuable contributions to the child's development. If he fails to do so, the Federal Constitution will not automatically compel a State to listen to his opinion of where the child's best interests lie. [463 U.S. at 261-262.]

Thus, according to *Lehr*, unwed fathers gain from their biological connection an opportunity interest to develop a relationship that is constitutionally protected. The opportunity interest can be lost by a parent who fails to develop a relationship, in the case of a father, for example, who shows little interest in his child, fails to visit, or support the child.

It is one case if the father voluntarily abandons his "opportunity interest." But what if he involuntarily does so because of the mother's actions, as in the cases discussed supra, pp. 501-502. May the state deny such a father an opportunity to establish this relationship with the child? In the case of the newborn, how does an unwed father develop a parental relationship with a fetus? How relevant in the evaluation of the father's seizing the "opportunity to develop a relationship" is his prebirth conduct toward the *mother*?

In Bowers v. Pearson, 609 S.E.2d 174 (Ga. Ct. App. 2005), when Margaret Pearson learned that she was pregnant after the termination of a brief affair with David Bowers, she informed David by phone. He made several subsequent attempts to speak with her and her parents, but they all refused to talk with him. Before the child's birth, he had filed with the putative father's registry and petitioned to legitimate the child. At the child's birth, Margaret placed the child for adoption. In the legitimation proceeding, the trial court found that David abandoned his opportunity to develop a relationship with the child by failing to provide financial or other support to Margaret during her pregnancy. The Georgia Court of Appeals reversed, concluding that the finding of abandonment was not supported by the evidence because, by the father's registering and instituting the legitimation proceeding, he agreed to assume parental responsibilities and to submit himself to a claim by the mother for expenses. See also In re Adoption of Vest, No. 00AP-1150, 2001 WL 242594 (Ohio Ct. App. Mar. 13, 2001) (refusing to dispense with consent to adoption of a biological father, finding that he did not willfully abandon the birth mother, in the face of the maternal grandmother's prohibiting him from contacting the birth mother, because he registered with the putative father registry prior to the birth and offered support to both the mother during her pregnancy and to a child support enforcement agency).

Note that in Bowers v. Peterson, supra, the biological father petitioned to legitimate the child prior to the child's birth. Recall that in Lehr v. Robertson, supra, the biological father did not register in New York's putative fathers registry but did file a paternity petition. In the ensuing adoption proceeding, although the trial judge therefore knew Lehr's identity, the court nonetheless granted the adoption and terminated his parental rights without notice. The new UPA §402(b)(2) would accord considerable weight to a father's filing of a paternity action, by exempting an alleged father from the requirement of registration if he "commences a proceeding to adjudicate his paternity before the court has terminated his parental rights."

How promptly does the father have to seize his "opportunity interest"? Does he have to act promptly after the *birth* or upon *learning* of the pregnancy? If the father comes forward long after the adoption, how should a court balance the father's constitutional rights against the child's need for stability in its adoptive placement? See Smith v. Soligon, 561 S.E.2d 850 (Ga. Ct. App. 2002) (concluding, in a stepparent adoption proceeding, that the biological father, who filed a petition to legitimate a child six years after the child's birth, had abandoned his opportunity interest to develop a relationship with the child by his failure to provide significant emotional or financial support).

A student note writer argues that putative father registries do not adequately protect the rights of many unwed fathers. She suggests that states should ensure that the putative fathers (whose rights were terminated) actually knew of the registration requirement and should provide exceptions for genuinely thwarted fathers. See Rebeca Aizpuru, Note, Protecting the Unwed Father's Opportunity to Parent: A Survey of Paternity Registry Statutes, 18 Rev. Litig. 703, 707 (1999). Do you agree with these criticisms?

Another criticism of state putative father registries is that they fail to protect fathers' rights in interstate adoptions because a father's registration in the state of birth will not ensure his notice of an adoption proceeding that takes place in another state. Mary Beck, Toward a National Putative Father Registry Database, 25 Harv. J.L. & Pub. Pol'y 1031, 1033 (2002). In response to this problem, should federal legislation create a national putative father registry? See id; Donna L. Moore, Implementing a National Putative Father Registry by Utilizing Existing Federal/State Collaborative Databases, 36 J. Marshall L. Rev. 1033 (2003).

Is tort law (for the intentional interference with parental rights) an appropriate method of protecting the rights of unwed fathers in such cases of thwarting the father's opportunity to develop a relationship with a newborn? See, e.g., Kessel v. Leavitt, 511 S.E.2d 720 (W. Va. 1998) (holding that father could maintain action for fraud against mother's relatives and attorney for concealment of information regarding location and adoption of child).

(3) Standard to Be Applied.   What standard should be applied to proceedings terminating the rights of the unwed father for adoption purposes? Suppose the father petitions to establish paternity and requests custody. Should the court apply a best interests standard, or require a finding that a grant of custody would be detrimental to the child, or require a finding of unfitness?

Adoption of Kelsey S., 823 P.2d 1216 (Cal. 1992), examined the constitutionality of the standard to be applied in terminating a father's rights. At the time of Kelsey's birth, the biological father had instituted a paternity action and request for custody, which was consolidated with the prospective adoptive parents' petition for adoption. The prospective adoptive parents alleged that only the mother's consent was required for an adoption because there was no "presumed father" under California law. The California version of the Uniform Parentage Act (Cal. Civ. Code

§7004(a), now Cal. Fam. Code §7611 (West 1994 & Supp. 2004)), adopted a different standard in terminating parental rights of "presumed" versus other fathers: "presumed fathers" were permitted, similar to mothers, to withhold consent to adoption. However, the parental rights of other fathers could be terminated more easily based only upon a best interests standard. Kelsey's biological father was unable to establish that he was a "presumed father" because, although he openly held out the child as his own, he was unable to meet the statutory requirement of receiving the child into his home because he was prevented from doing so by the mother.

The trial court ruled, and the appellate court affirmed, that he was not a "presumed father" and that the child's best interest required termination of his parental rights. On appeal, the California Supreme Court held: (1) the statute creating a category of "presumed father" whose consent was required prior to adoption violates federal constitutional guarantees of equal protection and due process for unwed fathers to the extent that the statutes allow a mother's unilateral action to preclude the biological father from becoming a presumed father; and (2) if an unwed father promptly comes forward and demonstrates a full commitment to his parental responsibilities (e.g., emotional, financial), his federal constitutional right to due process prohibits termination of his parental relationship absent a showing of unfitness as a parent. The court remanded the case for a determination of whether the father had demonstrated sufficient commitment to his parental responsibilities. See also In re Raquel Marie, 559 N.E.2d 418 (N.Y. 1990) (holding a similar statute unconstitutional on equal protection grounds). But cf. Adoption of Daniele G., 105 Cal. Rptr. 2d 341 (Ct. App. 2001) (standard for *approval of guardianship petition* is a finding that granting custody to the biological parent would be detrimental and that granting custody to the prospective guardians would be in child's best interest).

(4) Empirical Data. What are the characteristics of unwed fathers? A national study profiled a large sample of unwed fathers (n=12,686). Robert I. Lerman & Theodora J. Ooms, Young Unwed Fathers: Changing Roles and Emerging Policies (1993). That study reveals: (1) unwed fatherhood is not limited to teens but also occurs among men aged 20-26 who constitute almost 8 percent of unwed fathers (id. at 31); (2) young unwed fatherhood is more prevalent among African Americans (id. at 47); (3) unwed fathers tend to come from families of lower socioeconomic status, be less well educated, have lower academic abilities, and have sexual intercourse at early ages (id.); (4) few unwed fathers have more than one child (id. at 46); and (5) most unwed fathers (80%) remain absent fathers (id. at 32, 46).

Empirical research also suggests that a desire to search for the relinquished child is a common experience of parents who surrender their children for adoption. However, the motivating factor in searching is different for fathers and for mothers. Birth mothers generally search for their children out of a need to alleviate guilt and restore self-esteem through the assurance that the child is well. On the other hand, birth fathers often search for their children with thoughts of taking them back. See Eva Y. Deykin et al., Fathers of Adopted Children: A Study of the Impact of Child Surrender on Birth Fathers, 58 Am. J. Orthopsychiatry 240, 244 (April 1988). What do you think are the implications of such findings for adoption professionals and prospective adoptive parents?

3.   Independent Adoption Versus Agency Adoption

Broadly speaking, if one puts aside cases where children are adopted by a known relative (such as a stepparent), there are two procedures for adoptions: "agency adoptions" and "independent" (or "private") adoptions. Both require that the biological parents' rights be extinguished, either by consent or by termination.

In an agency adoption, a social agency acts as an intermediary between the biological mother and the adoptive family. Often after substantial counseling, the mother typically consensually relinquishes her parental rights and consents to having the agency place the child for adoption. The agency chooses an adoptive family from applicants, after investigating and evaluating alternatives. After placing the child in its new home, the agency provides counseling services, may evaluate the family's adjustment during a trial period, and will then assist the family in completing the legal adoption. Should the adoption for some reason fail, the agency will take the child back. Some adoption agencies are actually state agencies. Most are private, often sectarian organizations, licensed by the state.

An independent or private adoption is one where the child is not placed with its new family by an adoption agency. Instead, the biological parent(s) may place the child directly with the adoptive family, or some nonagency intermediary — a friend, a relative, doctor, lawyer, or spiritual advisor — may act as a go-between and place the child. Private adoptions account for a significant amount of domestic adoptions annually.[28] Independent adoptions rose in the 1970s when several factors (i.e., the increased use of contraception, liberalization of abortion, and society's acceptance of women raising nonmarital children) contributed to a shortage of adoptable white infants.[29] In response, many states enacted standards to protect children in independent adoptions.

In a private adoption, if the biological mother receives payment for more than her medical expenses, or if a third-party intermediary who arranges the adoption receives more than an appropriate fee, a crime may be committed. Many states have criminal statutes making baby selling illegal. Concern resulted in congressional hearings over the so-called black market adoptions. There are reports of situations in which adoptive families have paid up to $40,000 for a baby.[30] Despite newspaper articles and congressional hearings decrying the black market for babies, prosecutions for baby selling are infrequent. Complaints rarely arise from the adoptive family, the biological mother, or the go-betweens. Moreover, it is difficult to distinguish cases in which the money that has changed hands is for legitimate expenses and professional fees, from those where a mother is selling her baby. In all events, some proponents of agency adoptions argue that the existence of a black market (and a "gray market," as the intermediary mechanism is called) suggests the need to abolish independent or private adoptions, and allow only agency adoptions.

---

[28] Kathy S. Stolley, Statistics on Adoption in the United States, in The Future of Children 31 (Packard Foundation, 1993).

[29] Bobbi W.Y. Lum, Privacy v. Secrecy: The Open Adoption Records Movement and Its Impact on Hawaii, 15 U. Haw. L. Rev. 483, 486 (1993).

[30] Melinda Lucas, Adoption: Distinguishing Between Gray Market and Black Market Activities, 34 Fam. L.Q. 553, 557 (2000).

Proponents of agency adoptions argue that without the safeguards provided by agency adoptions, all parties risk inadequate protection because of lack of concern for (1) the biological mother, (2) the qualifications of the would-be parents, and (3) the safety and welfare of the child. By employing the skills of professionals, agencies investigate the maternal and paternal history of the child; give the child a physical, mental, and psychological examination; and evaluate the health, financial situation, and motivation for adoption of the adoptive parents. In addition, they provide follow-up services, especially during a probationary period when the integration of the child into the adoptive family can be evaluated. The agency also provides for the permanent retention of adoption records and confidentiality.

Opponents of independent adoption not only fear that private adoption fosters a "black market,"[31] but also that several serious risks are augmented by failure to take the safeguards provided by agency adoption. These risks are said to include several dangers: (1) biological parents may be pressured into a hasty and ill-considered decision, particularly because the mother is often unwed and therefore faces social stigma and financial difficulties; (2) adoptive parents may enter the arrangement blindly; (3) adoptive parents may be harassed by biological parents, especially those who change their minds and later regret having consented to the adoption; (4) the adoptive home may not "match" the needs of the particular child; (5) the child is an unprotected pawn if the adoptive parents change their minds about the adoption or are motivated to adopt a child solely to bolster their unsatisfactory marriage; (6) unbeknownst to the adoptive family the child may have some mental or physical disability; (7) there will be no funds or personnel to care for the child if the adoption should fail.

Banning independent adoptions may have its faults as well. Some commentators point to the decrease in adoptions in states that have abolished independent adoption.[32] For example, in Connecticut before a law was passed prohibiting all but agency adoptions, there were 1092 adoptions in a given year, of which 58 percent were independent. After the law was passed, only 573 adoptions were made, and of these almost half had been made the year before.[33] Moreover, other commentators point to the overall success of independent adoptions.[34] It appears that adoptive parents who have had a private adoption are as happy with their decision years afterwards as those with an agency adoption. Agency practices have also been criticized. Some believe that agency adoptions give too much discretion to professionals to use their personal values to choose among the competing applicants, thus disadvantaging many potential adoptive families. This concern becomes especially acute if adoption agencies are given a monopoly, through the elimination of private adoptions.[35]

---

[31] See L. Jean Emery, Agency Versus Independent Adoption: The Case for Agency Adoption, in The Future of Children 139 (Packard Foundation, 1993).

[32] Pearl S. Buck, Children for Adoption 205-206 (1964).

[33] Id.

[34] William Meezan et al., Adoptions Without Agencies: A Study of Independent Adoptions 42 (1978).

[35] HEW Funds Study of Independent Adoptions (quoting Anne Shyne, Director of the Child Welfare League), 2 Fam. L. Rep. 2149 (1976).

4. Adoption Failure

Under the present law of most states, an adoption can be abrogated even after a child is placed with the adoptive family. In some circumstances, it is possible for the biological mother to reclaim the child if she demonstrates that her relinquishment of parental rights was induced by force or duress.[36] In addition, it is possible for adoption to be upset upon a demonstration that the required consent of a biological parent was not obtained or that there was a failure to give notice to a parent. These attacks can be made after an adoption has become final, although many states have statutes of limitation that bar attacks on adoption decrees after a certain period of time, typically ranging from six months to three years.[37]

During the probation period, before the adoption decree is entered, the agency placing the child for adoption may also reclaim the child typically upon the discovery of alcoholism, drug abuse, or threatened child abuse in the adoptive family.[38]

Finally, in some states, under certain circumstances, an adoption can be abrogated by the adoptive parents. Adoptive parents may seek abrogation of adoptions on the basis of fraud, misrepresentation, and undue influence, as well as on procedural grounds, including lack of compliance with statutory requirements.[39] The majority of cases involving abrogation by adoptive parents include two common situations: (1) both adoptive parents seek abrogation due to some abnormality or defect in the

---

[36] A noted example of a mother changing her mind took place in the famous "Baby Lenore" case. See Scarpetta v. Spence-Chapin Adoption Serv., 269 N.E.2d 787 (N.Y. 1971). For criticisms of the decision, see Henry H. Foster, Revocation of Consent to Adoption: A Covenant Running with the Child?, N.Y.L.J., Aug. 6, 1971, at 1; Sanford N. Katz, The Adoption of Baby Lenore: Problems of Consent and the Role of Lawyers, 5 Fam. L.Q. (No. 4) 405 (1971); Monroe L. Inker, Expanding the Rights of Children in Custody and Adoption Cases, id. at 417.

Jurisdictions have assumed a variety of positions regarding withdrawal of parental consent to adoption. Some states focus on the timing of the parents' revocation of consent after the child's birth. See, e.g., Uniform Adoption Act (UAA), 9 U.L.A. pt. I, at 36-38 (Supp. 1999), §§2-408 & 2-409 (permitting a parent to revoke consent within eight days after the birth); In re Adoption of Anderson, 248 N.W. 657 (Minn. 1993) (consent is revocable until final decree of adoption is issued). Other states invalidate consent that is procured by fraud or duress or based on a parent's immaturity. See, e.g., Ill. Ann. Stat. ch. 750 ¶50/11 (West 1993 & Supp. 1999) (consent is irrevocable absent fraud or duress); Adoption of Thomas, 559 N.E.2d 1230 (Mass. 1990) (immaturity). Still other states differentiate between surrender to an approved agency or to a private adoption, making revocation of consent more difficult for relinquishments to approved agencies. See Sees v. Baber, 377 A.2d 628 (N.J. 1977).

[37] See Homer H. Clark, Law of Domestic Relations 934-935 (2d ed. 1988). For further discussion of adoption consent laws, see Karen D. Laverdiere, Context over Form: The Shifting of Adoption Consent Laws, 25 Whittier L. Rev. 599 (2004).

[38] Agencies supervise the child in the applicant's home for a probationary period, which varies from state to state — usually six months or a year. Because there are no definite criteria for either placement or its revocation, an agency worker may terminate a placement on the basis of nothing more than a hunch of parental unfitness or even of an anonymous telephone call. See C.V.C. v. Superior Court, 106 Cal. Rptr. 123, 126 (Ct. App. 1973) (test changed from whether the agency had any acceptable reason for its decision to whether the agency's decision to terminate the placement was justified by the best interest of the child).

[39] See Clark, supra note [37], at 937.

child; and (2) adoptive fathers seek abrogation, usually after divorcing the child's biological mother. The outcomes of abrogation in each case are quite different: if an adoptive father successfully abrogates an adoption, the child is left in the care of the child's biological mother; however, if the adoptive parents successfully abrogate an adoption, the child effectively is abandoned.

In a famous Rhode Island case, In re Lisa Diane G., 537 A.2d 131 (R.I. 1988), the adoptive parents petitioned to have the adoption of their adoptive daughter set aside on the basis of misrepresentation.

> The gist of the parents' complaint is that the adoption decree was procured by the fraudulent conduct or misrepresentations of certain representatives of the Department of Children and Their Families (DCF). The parents contend that DCF never informed them that the staff at Bradley Hospital, an institution noted for its treatment of the emotionally disturbed, had informed DCF that the child, because of her emotional problems, should not be placed for adoption. In the Family Court the parents sought nullification of the adoption decree and compensation for the expenses they incurred in caring for the child. . . . [Id. at 132.]

Do you think relief should be granted? Does it alter your opinion that the child was eight years old when adopted and now is a teenager? Most states do not permit adoptive parents to rescind an adoption, and most commentators would agree that "adoptors, who voluntarily assumed the responsibility of natural parents, must not expect to be able to give them back again at will any more than they could relieve themselves of the responsibility if the child had been born to them."[40]

However, in response to the problems of misrepresentation by adoption agencies and judicial reluctance to nullify adoption decrees, some states are recognizing a remedy of wrongful adoption. The cause of action does not seek annulment of the adoption but rather damages from the agency for the extraordinary expenses and emotional distress associated with caring for the child. Ross v. Louise Wise Servs., Inc., 777 N.Y.S.2d 618 (N.Y. App. Div. 2004) (awarding compensatory damages to adoptive parents by adoption agency that had promised to give them a healthy baby but instead gave them an infant with a double family history of paranoid schizophrenia). See generally Amanda Trefethen, The Emerging Tort of Wrongful Adoption, 11 J. Contemp. Legal Issues 620 (2000); Erica Shultz, Note, Ignoring Distress Signals: Why Courts Should Recognize Emotional Distress Damages in Wrongful Adoption Claims, 52 Fla. L. Rev. 1073 (2000).

5. Baby Selling

At the present time there is a severe shortage of adoptable Caucasian babies, for the demand has remained high while the supply of children available for adoption has substantially diminished. Improvements in contraception techniques, the

---

[40] See In re Adoption of a Minor, 214 N.E.2d 281, 282 (Mass. 1966) ("Adoption is said to create 'a for better, for worse situation' ").

legalization of abortion, and the decrease in social stigma attached to an unmarried mother raising a child all have contributed to the shrinking supply.

Consider whether a market for baby selling, with appropriate safeguards, might not substantially increase the sum total of human happiness and correct this shortage of adoptable babies. For example, imagine a system where it was legal for a mother (or father?) to be paid any agreed-upon amount for placement of a newborn child in an adoptive home, as long as the adoptive parents met appropriate minimum objective standards that ensured the child would not be cruelly or neglectfully treated.

Who would be harmed by such a system? Would not the adoptive parents (who might otherwise be childless), the child (who might not otherwise be born), and the biological parents (who had received compensation) all be better off? What, then, are the objections to baby selling? Would low-income families who wished to adopt be worse off than today? Would a market for babies lead to overreaching middlemen who would take advantage of "vulnerable" biological and adoptive parents? Should we be fearful of the implications for the eugenic alteration of the human race since baby selling might lead to baby breeding? Or are the primary objections symbolic? By creating a property right of sorts in the biological parents, does baby selling seem too much like slavery? Does baby selling undermine the "best interests of the child" premise of modern child custody law?

At the forefront of the debate over the desirability of a market approach to adoption is Judge Richard A. Posner. In a classic article[41] he considers a "free market theory" of adoption and explores how changes in the law might make the existing market in babies for adoption operate more efficiently and equitably. He further refines his theory in the following article.

Richard A. Posner, The Regulation of the Market in Adoptions
67 B.U. L. Rev. 59, 64-72 (1987)

[In] this article I shall describe briefly how such a market might operate, under what regulatory constraints, and with what likely consequences, and in doing so will try to respond to the most frequently expressed objections to allowing the market to function in this area.

II. Characteristics of and Desirable Constraints on the Baby Market

A. The Question of Price

For heuristic purposes (only!), it is useful to analogize the sale of babies to the sale of an ordinary good, such as an automobile or a television set. We observe, for example, that although the supply of automobiles and of television sets is rationed by price, not all the automobiles and television sets are owned by wealthy people. On the contrary, the free market in these goods has lowered prices, through competition

---

[41] Posner began the debate with an article by Richard A. Posner & Elizabeth Landes, The Economics of the Baby Shortage, 7 J. Legal Stud. 323 (1978).

and innovation, to the point where the goods are available to a lot more people than in highly controlled economies such as that of the Soviet Union. There is even less reason for thinking that if babies could be sold to adoptive parents the wealthy would come to monopolize babies. Wealthy people (other than those few who owe their wealth to savings or inheritance rather than to a high income) have high costs of time. It therefore costs them more to raise a child — child rearing still being a time-intensive activity — than it costs the nonwealthy. As a result, wealthy couples tend to have few rather than many children. [Citations omitted.] This pattern would not change if babies could be bought. Moreover, since most people have a strong preference for natural, as distinct from adopted, children, wealthy couples able to have natural children are unlikely (to say the least) to substitute adopted ones.

It is also unlikely that allowing people to bid for babies with dollars would drive up the price of babies, thereby allocating the supply to wealthy demanders. Today we observe a high black market price conjoined with an artificially low price for babies obtained from adoption agencies and through lawful independent adoptions. . . . The low price in the lawful market is deceptive. . . . Quality-adjusted prices in free markets normally are lower than black market prices, and there is no reason to doubt that this would be true in a free market for adoptions. Thus, while it is possible that "[i]nherent in the baby black market is the unfairness that results from the fact that only the affluent can afford to pay the enormous fees necessary to procure a baby," the words "black market" ought to be italicized. It is not the free market, but unwarranted restrictions on the operation of that market, that has raised the black market price of babies beyond the reach of ordinary people. . . .

B. The Question of Quality

As soon as one mentions quality, people's hackles rise and they remind you that one is talking about a traffic in human beings, not in inanimate objects. The observation is pertinent, and at least five limitations might have to be placed on the operation of the market in babies for adoption. The first, already mentioned and already in place, is that the buyers can have no "right to abuse the thing bought." . . . [The second limitation concerns screening for fitness.] Today, all adoptive parents are, in theory anyway, screened for fitness. Adoption agencies are charged with this responsibility, and if we moved toward a freer market in babies the agencies could be given the additional function of investigating and certifying prospective purchasers, who would pay the price of the service. . . .

The third limitation on a baby market concerns remedies for breach of contract. In an ordinary market a buyer can both reject defective goods and, if the seller refuses to deliver and damages would be an inadequate remedy for the refusal, get specific performance of the contract. Natural parents are not permitted to reject their baby, either when it is born or afterward, because it turns out to be handicapped or otherwise not in conformity with their expectations; no more should adoptive parents who buy their babies. . . . For the welfare of the baby must be considered along with that of the contracting parties. . . . The child is an interested third party whose welfare would be disserved by a mechanical application of the remedies available to buyers in the market for inanimate goods.

For the same reason (the child's welfare) neither natural nor adopting parents should be allowed to sell their children after infancy, that is, after the child has established a bond with its parents. . . .

The last limitation on the baby market that I shall discuss relates to eugenic breeding. Although prospects still seem remote, one can imagine an entrepreneur in the baby market trying to breed a race of *Ubermenschen* who would command premium prices. The external effects of such an endeavor could be very harmful, and would provide an appropriate basis for governmental regulation. . . .

One reason people fear the operation of a free market in babies for adoption is that they extrapolate from experience with the illegal market. Critics who suggest that baby selling offers the promise of huge profits to middlemen — the dreaded "baby brokers" — fail to distinguish between an illegal market, in which sellers demand a heavy premium (an apparent, though not real, profit) in order to defray the expected costs of punishment, and a legal market, in which the premium is eliminated. Seemingly exorbitant profits, low quality, poor information, involvement of criminal elements — these widely asserted characteristics of the black market in babies are no more indicative of the behavior of a lawful market than the tactics of the bootleggers and rum-runners during Prohibition were indicative of the behavior of the liquor industry after Prohibition was repealed.

III. The Objection from Symbolism and the Issue of Semantics

Even if partial deregulation of the baby market might make practical utilitarian sense along the lines just suggested, some will resist on symbolic grounds. If we acknowledge that babies can be sold, the argument goes, we open the door to all sorts of monstrous institutions — including slavery. . . . Allowing parents to sell their children into slavery would be a monstrous idea. Allowing the prospective mother of an illegitimate child to receive money in exchange for giving the child up for adoption, when described in shorthand as "baby selling," seems to many people uncomfortably close to the type of real baby selling that is found in slave societies — that was found in the slave societies of the South before the Civil War. No doubt it requires more thought than most people are willing to give to the problem to hold these quite different concepts separate in their minds. But if they are not held separate we find ourselves condemned to perpetuate the painful spectacle of mass abortion and illegitimacy in a society in which, to a significant extent, children are not available for adoption by persons unwilling to violate the law.

One should always be suspicious of arguments against the market when they are made by people who have no desire to participate in it themselves, people who want to restrict the availability of goods to other people. Most people who invoke vague symbols in opposition to "baby selling" have no interest in or expectation of either adopting a child or conceiving one out of wedlock. They have little empathy with the needs of people who find themselves involuntarily childless or involuntarily pregnant.

The opponents of "baby selling" are unwilling to acknowledge that what we have today, even apart from the black market, is closer to a free market in babies than a free market in babies would be to slavery. . . . As I said at the outset, adoption agencies do lawfully "sell" babies, and many charge thousands of dollars. Moreover, in independent adoptions, the mother herself may "sell" her baby, for it is not considered unlawful to use a part of the fee paid by the adoptive parents to defray the medical and other maintenance costs of the mother during pregnancy. . . .

Two other important examples of legal baby selling should be mentioned. One is the "family compact" doctrine, which allows a woman to enter into an enforceable contract to give up her baby for adoption by a close relative. The other is surrogate motherhood. . . .

So we have legal baby selling today; the question of public policy is not whether baby selling should be forbidden or allowed but how extensively it should be regulated. I simply think it should be regulated less stringently than is done today.

Posner's proposal regarding baby selling has been widely criticized. See, e.g., Tamar Frankel & Francis H. Miller, The Inapplicability of Market Theory to Adoptions, 67 B.U. L. Rev. 99 (1987); Mark Kelman, Consumption Theory, Production Theory and the Ideology of the Coase Theorem, 52 S. Cal. L. Rev. 669 (1979); J. Robert Pritchard, A Market for Babies?, 34 U. Toronto L.J. 341 (1984); Margaret Jane Radin, What, if Anything, Is Wrong with Baby Selling? 26 Pac. L.J. 135 (1995).

6. Adopted Children's Right to Learn Their Origins

There is a tradition in adoptions, particularly agency adoptions, of strict confidentiality. Agencies typically have elaborate safeguards to insure that (1) the biological parents can never determine the identity of a child relinquished for adoption, and (2) the adopted child, even as an adult, cannot find out the identity of the biological parents. Court adoption records are typically sealed, and allow disclosure only by court order based on some urgent necessity. In independent adoptions, on the other hand, although the court records may be sealed, the adoptive parents often know the identity of the biological mother and sometimes that of both parents. In such circumstances, the adoptive parents decide whether the child will be informed.

An adoption reform movement began in the 1970s to open adoption records and thereby allow the exchange of information between the adopted child and the biological parents. States take different approaches to the provision of identifying information: (1) most states still require that the original birth certificate and adoption records be sealed but permit access upon a judicial finding of "good cause"; (2) a few states grant adult adoptees, upon request and without restriction, access to their adoption records or original birth certificates;[42] (3) some states have "search and consent" statutes under which an adoptee may request a public or private adoption agency to investigate the location of the biological parent and to request consent to release identifying information; and (4) some states have "mutual consent"

---

[42] Recently, New Hampshire became the fifth state (in addition to Alabama, Alaska, Kansas, and Oregon) to allow adult adoptees unrestricted access to birth records. New Hampshire: Adoption Veil Lifted, N.Y. Times, Jan. 4, 2005, at A16. Scotland has permitted unrestricted access to adopted children (after age 17) since 1930. The Adoption of Children (Scotland), 1930, 20 & 21 Geo. 5, ch. 37 §11(9).

registries that allow for the release of identifying information if both parties have registered their consent to the release of information.[43]

What interests of the adopted child, the adoptive parents, and the biological parents are affected by confidentiality? Should a biological parent's constitutional right to privacy trump a child's right to know? In a case where both the biological parents and an adult adoptee want to find each other (and the adoptive parents have no objection), are there still any arguments for confidentiality? As a practical matter, which of the above approaches should be established?

What motivates adoptees to search for their birth parents? Empirical data reveal that adoptees' searches are not "a vindictive venture, but an attempt to understand themselves and their situations better." John P. Triseliotis, In Search of Origins: The Experiences of Adopted People 166 (1973). Even when the information they learned was upsetting, a large percentage of adoptees felt they benefited from their searches. Id. at 139-140. See also Arthur D. Sorosky et al., The Adoption Triangle 121-142 (1978) (finding that the search for biological parents does not indicate a rejection of the adoptive parents and also that the reunions with biological parents do not appear to harm the relationships of the adoptees).

On the sealed record debate, see Katarina Wegar, Adoption, Identity, and Kinship: The Debate over Sealed Birth Records (1997). See also E. Wayne Carp, Adoption, Blood Kinship, Stigma, and the Adoption Reform Movement: A Historical Perspective, 36 Law & Soc'y Rev. 433 (2002) (book review of Wegar's book).

Another aspect of the adoption reform movement is the trend toward open adoption. Whereas the sealed record debate involves the rights of adult adoptees, the open adoption movement generally involves infants. Open adoption signifies the sharing of information and contact between the adoptive and biological parents before and after placement of the child. Open adoption differs from closed adoption because, in an open adoption, the biological mother and adoptive parents know each other's identity; the birth mother may exercise significant control over the choice of adoptive parents; and the parties have an agreement concerning the birth mother's postadoption relationship to the child.[44] Whereas most states still hold that open adoption is violative of public policy, a few states recognize such agreements. Some of these states, however, refuse to enforce agreements in the case of disputes, but other states enforce such agreements provided they are part of the adoption decree.[45]

 Because the majority of adoptions are by relatives and stepparents, most adoptions today are not anonymous.[46] The Uniform Adoption Act provides for judicial enforcement of postadoption visitation agreements only for stepparent adoptions. UAA §4-113, 9 U.L.A. (pt. IA) 110-112 (1999). In other cases, the UAA permits "mutually agreed-upon communication between birth and adoptive families," but does not make such agreements enforceable. Id. at 15 (Prefatory Note). Advocates of

[43] Jennifer R. Racine, A Fundamental Rights Debate: Should Wisconsin Allow Adult Adoptees Unconditional Access to Adoption Records and Original Birth Certificates?, 2002 Wis. L. Rev. 1435, 1458-1459.

[44] Amy L. Doherty, Foster Care and Adoption: A Look at Open Adoption, 11 J. Contemp. Legal Issues 591, 592 (2000).

[45] Id. at 594 (finding eight states permit such agreements but refuse to enforce them, and another eight states enforce them if they are included in the adoption decree).

[46] Annette Ruth Appell, The Move Toward Legally Sanctioned Cooperative Adoption: Can It Survive the Uniform Adoption Act?, 30 Fam. L.Q. 483, 488-489 (1996).

open adoption emphasize that the practice increases the number of children available for adoption because it comports with many birth parents' desires, eliminates the need for adoptees subsequently to search for their origins, and permits children to avoid the trauma of a complete rupture from their biological parents. In contrast, opponents contend that the practice deters adoption because it creates a fear of disruption of the adoptive family, breaches the traditional principle of confidentiality, and interferes with the establishment of new parent-child relationships. Which approach do you favor and why?

7. The Relevance of Sexual Orientation to Adoption

What relevance, if any, should be given to the role of sexual orientation in adoption decisionmaking?

Lofton v. Secretary of the Department of Children and Family Services
358 F.3d 804 (11th Cir. 2004)

BIRCH, Circuit Judge:

[W]e decide the states' rights issue of whether Florida Statute §63.042(3), which prevents adoption by practicing homosexuals, is constitutional. . . . Since 1977, Florida's adoption law has contained a codified prohibition on adoption by any "homosexual" person. 1977 Fla. Laws, ch. 77-140, §1, Fla. Stat. §63.042(3) (2002). For purposes of this statute, Florida courts have defined the term "homosexual" as being "limited to applicants who are known to engage in current, voluntary homosexual activity," thus drawing "a distinction between homosexual orientation and homosexual activity." Fla. Dept. of Health & Rehab. Servs. v. Cox, 627 So. 2d 1210, 1215 (Fla. Dist. Ct. App. 1993), aff'd in relevant part, 656 So. 2d 902, 903 (Fla. 1995). . . .

Six plaintiffs-appellants bring this case. The first, Steven Lofton, is a registered pediatric nurse who has raised from infancy three Florida foster children, each of whom tested positive for HIV at birth. By all accounts, Lofton's efforts in caring for these children have been exemplary, and his story has been chronicled in dozens of news stories and editorials as well as on national television. . . . John Doe, also named as a plaintiff-appellant in this litigation, was born on 29 April 1991. Testing positive at birth for HIV and cocaine, Doe immediately entered the Florida foster care system. Shortly thereafter, Children's Home Society, a private agency, placed Doe in foster care with Lofton. . . . Lofton filed an application to adopt Doe but refused to answer the application's inquiry about his sexual preference and also failed to disclose Roger Croteau, his cohabitating partner, as a member of his household. After Lofton refused requests from the Department of Children and Families ("DCF") to supply the missing information, his application was rejected. . . .

Appellants assert three constitutional arguments on appeal. First, appellants argue that the statute violates . . . rights to familial privacy, intimate association, and family integrity under the Due Process Clause of the Fourteenth Amendment. Second, appellants argue that the Supreme Court's recent decision in Lawrence v. Texas, 539 U.S. 558 (2003), recognized a fundamental right to private sexual intimacy and that the Florida statute, by disallowing adoption by individuals who engage in homosexual activity, impermissibly burdens the exercise of this right. Third, appellants allege that, by categorically prohibiting only homosexual persons from adopting children, the statute violates the Equal Protection Clause of the Fourteenth Amendment. . . .

. . . Under Florida law, "adoption is not a right; it is a statutory privilege." *Cox*, 627 So. 2d at 1216. Unlike biological parentage, which precedes and transcends formal recognition by the state, adoption is wholly a creature of the state.

In formulating its adoption policies and procedures, the State of Florida acts in the protective and provisional role of *in loco parentis* for those children who, because of various circumstances, have become wards of the state. Thus, adoption law is unlike criminal law, for example, where the paramount substantive concern is not intruding on individuals' liberty interests, see, e.g., *Lawrence*, 539 U.S. 558; Roe v. Wade, 410 U.S. 113 (1973), and the paramount procedural imperative is ensuring due process and fairness. Adoption is also distinct from such contexts as government-benefit eligibility schemes or access to a public forum, where equality of treatment is the primary concern. By contrast, in the adoption context, the state's overriding interest is the best interests of the children whom it is seeking to place with adoptive families. . . .

Because of the primacy of the welfare of the child, the state can make classifications for adoption purposes that would be constitutionally suspect in many other arenas. For example, [in] screening adoption applicants, Florida considers such factors as physical and mental health, income and financial status, duration of marriage, housing, and neighborhood, among others. . . .

The decision to adopt a child is not a private one, but a public act. [A] person who seeks to adopt is asking the state to conduct an examination into his or her background and to make a determination as to the best interests of a child in need of adoption. In doing so, the state's overriding interest is not providing individuals the opportunity to become parents, but rather identifying those individuals whom it deems most capable of parenting adoptive children and providing them with a secure family environment. . . .

Appellants' Due Process Challenges

1. Fundamental Right to "Family Integrity"

[A]ppellants argue that, by prohibiting homosexual adoption, the state is refusing to recognize and protect constitutionally protected parent-child relationships between Lofton and Doe. . . . Noting that the Supreme Court has identified "the interest of parents in the care, custody, and control of their children" as "perhaps the oldest of the fundamental liberty interests recognized by this Court," Troxel [v. Granville, 530 U.S. 57, 65 (2000)], appellants argue that they are entitled to a similar constitutional liberty interest because they share deeply loving emotional bonds that are as close as those between a natural parent and child. . . . Only by being given the opportunity to adopt, appellants assert, will they be able to protect their alleged right to "family integrity."

Although the text of the Constitution contains no reference to familial or parental rights, Supreme Court precedent has long recognized that "the Due Process

Clause of the Fourteenth Amendment protects the fundamental right of parents to make decisions concerning the care, custody, and control of their children." Id. at 66. A corollary to this right is the "private realm of family life which the state cannot enter that has been afforded both substantive and procedural protection." Smith v. Org. of Foster Families for Equal. & Reform, 431 U.S. 816, 842 (1977). Historically, the Court's family- and parental-rights holdings have involved biological families. . . . Appellants, however, seize on a few lines of dicta from *Smith*, in which the Court acknowledged that "biological relationships are not [the] exclusive determination of the existence of a family," id., and noted that "adoption, for instance, is recognized as the legal equivalent of biological parenthood," id. at 844 n. 51. Extrapolating from *Smith*, appellants argue that parental and familial rights should be extended to individuals such as foster parents and legal guardians and that the touchstone of this liberty interest is not biological ties or official legal recognition, but the emotional bond that develops between and among individuals as a result of shared daily life.

We do not read *Smith* so broadly. [Lofton entered into a relationship to be a foster parent with an implicit understanding that this relationship] would not be immune from state oversight and would be permitted to continue only upon state approval. The emotional connections between Lofton and his foster child . . . originate in arrangements that have been subject to state oversight from the outset. We conclude that Lofton [and the other appellants] could have no justifiable expectation of permanency in their relationships. Nor could [they] have developed expectations that they would be allowed to adopt, in light of the adoption provision itself.

Even if Florida law did create an expectation of permanency, appellants misconstrue the nature of the liberty interest that it would confer upon them. The resulting liberty interest at most would provide *procedural* due process protection in the event the state were to attempt to remove Doe. . . . See *Smith*, 431 U.S. at 845. Such a procedural right does not translate, however, into a substantive right to be free from state inference. Nor does it create an affirmative right to be accorded official recognition as "parent" and "child." . . .

[W]e decline appellants' invitation to recognize a new fundamental right to family integrity for groups of individuals who have formed deeply loving and interdependent relationships. Under appellants' theory, any collection of individuals living together and enjoying strong emotional bonds could claim a right to legal recognition of their family unit, and every removal of a child from a long-term foster care placement — or simply the state's failure to give long-term foster parents the opportunity to adopt — would give rise to a constitutional claim. Such an expansion of the venerable right of parental control would well exceed our judicial mandate as a lower federal court.

2. Fundamental Right to "Private Sexual Intimacy"

. . . Appellants argue that the Supreme Court's recent decision in Lawrence v. Texas, 539 U.S. 558 (2003), which struck down Texas's sodomy statute, identified a hitherto unarticulated fundamental right to private sexual intimacy. They contend that the Florida statute, by disallowing adoption to any individual who chooses to engage in homosexual conduct, impermissibly burdens the exercise of this right.

We begin with the threshold question of whether *Lawrence* identified a new fundamental right to private sexual intimacy. *Lawrence*'s holding was that substantive due process does not permit a state to impose a criminal prohibition on private consensual homosexual conduct. The effect of this holding was to establish a greater respect than previously existed in the law for the right of consenting adults to engage in private sexual conduct. Nowhere, however, did the Court characterize this right as "fundamental." . . .

We are particularly hesitant to infer a new fundamental liberty interest from an opinion whose language and reasoning are inconsistent with standard fundamental-rights analysis. . . . First, the *Lawrence* opinion contains virtually no inquiry into the question of whether the petitioners' asserted right is one of "those fundamental rights and liberties which are, objectively, deeply rooted in this Nation's history and tradition and implicit in the concept of ordered liberty, such that neither liberty nor justice would exist if they were sacrificed." [Washington v. Glucksberg, 521 U.S. 703, 720-721 (1997)]. Second, the opinion notably never provides the " 'careful description' of the asserted fundamental liberty interest" that is to accompany fundamental-rights analysis. Id. at 721. Rather, the constitutional liberty interests on which the Court relied were invoked, not with "careful description," but with sweeping generality. . . . Most significant, however, is the fact that the *Lawrence* Court never applied strict scrutiny, the proper standard when fundamental rights are implicated, but instead invalidated the Texas statute on rational-basis grounds. . . .

We conclude that it is a strained and ultimately incorrect reading of *Lawrence* to interpret it to announce a new fundamental right. . . . Moreover, the holding of *Lawrence* does not control the present case. Apart from the shared homosexuality component, there are marked differences in the facts of the two cases. . . . Here, the involved actors are not only consenting adults, but minors as well. The relevant state action is not criminal prohibition, but grant of a statutory privilege. And the asserted liberty interest is not the negative right to engage in private conduct without facing criminal sanctions, but the affirmative right to receive official and public recognition. Hence, we conclude that the *Lawrence* decision cannot be extrapolated to create a right to adopt for homosexual persons.

Appellants' Equal Protection Challenge

. . . Florida contends that the statute is only one aspect of its broader adoption policy, which is designed to create adoptive homes that resemble the nuclear family as closely as possible. Florida argues that the statute is rationally related to Florida's interest in furthering the best interests of adopted children by placing them in families with married mothers and fathers. Such homes, Florida asserts, provide the stability that marriage affords and the presence of both male and female authority figures, which it considers critical to optimal childhood development and socialization. In particular, Florida emphasizes a vital role that dual-gender parenting plays in shaping sexual and gender identity and in providing heterosexual role modeling. Florida argues that disallowing adoption into homosexual households, which are necessarily motherless or fatherless and lack the stability that comes with marriage, is a rational means of furthering Florida's interest in promoting adoption by marital families.

Florida clearly has a legitimate interest in encouraging a stable and nurturing environment for the education and socialization of its adopted children. It is chiefly from parental figures that children learn about the world and their place in it, and the formative influence of parents extends well beyond the years spent under their roof, shaping their children's psychology, character, and personality for years to come. In time, children grow up to become full members of society, which they in turn influence, whether for good or ill. The adage that "the hand that rocks the cradle rules the world" hardly overstates the ripple effect that parents have on the public good by virtue of their role in raising their children. . . .

. . . Florida argues that its preference for adoptive marital families is based on the premise that the marital family structure is more stable than other household arrangements and that children benefit from the presence of both a father and mother in the home. Given that appellants have offered no competent evidence to the contrary, we find this premise to be one of those "unprovable assumptions" that nevertheless can provide a legitimate basis for legislative action. Although social theorists from Plato to Simone de Beauvoir have proposed alternative child-rearing arrangements, none has proven as enduring as the marital family structure, nor has the accumulated wisdom of several millennia of human experience discovered a superior model. Against this "sum of experience," it is rational for Florida to conclude that it is in the best interests of adoptive children, many of whom come from troubled and unstable backgrounds, to be placed in a home anchored by both a father and a mother.

Appellants offer little to dispute whether Florida's preference for marital adoptive families is a legitimate state interest. Instead, they maintain that the statute is not rationally related to this interest. Arguing that the statute is both overinclusive and underinclusive, appellants contend that the real motivation behind the statute cannot be the best interest of adoptive children. . . .

a. Adoption by Unmarried Heterosexual Persons

Appellants note that Florida law permits adoption by unmarried individuals and that, among children coming out [of] the Florida foster care system, 25% of adoptions are to parents who are currently single. Their argument is that homosexual persons are similarly situated to unmarried persons with regard to Florida's asserted interest in promoting married-couple adoption. According to appellants, this disparate treatment lacks a rational basis and, therefore, disproves any rational connection between the statute and Florida's asserted interest in promoting adoption into married homes. . . .

. . . The Florida legislature could rationally conclude that homosexuals and heterosexual singles are not "similarly situated in relevant respects." It is not irrational to think that heterosexual singles have a markedly greater probability of eventually establishing a married household and, thus, providing their adopted children with a stable, dual-gender parenting environment. Moreover, as the state noted, the legislature could rationally act on the theory that heterosexual singles, even if they never marry, are better positioned than homosexual individuals to provide adopted children with education and guidance relative to their sexual development throughout pubescence and adolescence. In a previous challenge to Florida's statute, a Florida appellate court observed:

> Whatever causes a person to become a homosexual, it is clear that the state cannot know the sexual preferences that a child will exhibit as an adult. Statistically, the state does know that a very high percentage of children available for adoption will develop heterosexual preferences. As a result, those children will need education and guidance after puberty concerning relationships with the opposite sex. . . . It is in the best interests of a child if his or her parents can personally relate to the child's problems and assist the child in the difficult transition to heterosexual adulthood. Given that adopted children tend to have some developmental problems arising from adoption or from their experiences prior to adoption, it is perhaps more important for adopted children than other children to have a stable heterosexual household during puberty and the teenage years. [*Cox*, 627 So. 2d at 1220.]

"It could be that the assumptions underlying these rationales are erroneous, but the very fact that they are arguable is sufficient, on rational-basis review, to immunize the legislative choice from constitutional challenge." . . . [Heller v. Doe, 509 U.S. 312, 333 (1993)]

. . . We conclude that there are plausible rational reasons for the disparate treatment of homosexuals and heterosexual singles under Florida adoption law and that, to the extent that the classification may be imperfect, that imperfection does not rise to the level of a constitutional infraction.

b. Current Foster Care Population

Appellants make much of the fact that Florida has over three thousand children who are currently in foster care and, consequently, have not been placed with permanent adoptive families. According to appellants, because excluding homosexuals from the pool of prospective adoptive parents will not create more eligible married couples to reduce the backlog, it is impossible for the legislature to believe that the statute advances the state's interest in placing children with married couples.

We do not agree that the statute does not further the state's interest in promoting nuclear-family adoption because it may delay the adoption of some children. Appellants misconstrue Florida's interest, which is not simply to place children in a permanent home as quickly as possible, but, when placing them, to do so in an optimal home, i.e., one in which there is a heterosexual couple or the potential for one. According to appellants' logic, every restriction on adoptive-parent candidates, such as income, in-state residency, and criminal record — none of which creates more available married couples — are likewise constitutionally suspect as long as Florida has a backlog of unadopted foster children. The best interests of children, however, are not automatically served by adoption into *any* available home merely because it is permanent. Moreover, the legislature could rationally act on the theory that not placing adoptees in homosexual households increases the probability that these children eventually will be placed with married couple families, thus furthering the state's goal of optimal placement. Therefore, we conclude that Florida's current foster care backlog does not render the statute irrational. . . .

Noting that Florida law permits homosexuals to become foster parents and permanent guardians, appellants contend that this fact demonstrates that Florida must not truly believe that placement in a homosexual household is not in a child's best interests. We do not find that the fact that Florida has permitted homosexual foster homes and guardianships defeats the rational relationship between the statute and the state's asserted interest. . . . Foster care and legal guardianship are designed to address a different situation than permanent adoption. . . .

Appellants cite recent social science research and the opinion of mental health professionals and child welfare organizations as evidence that there is no child welfare basis for excluding homosexuals from adopting. They argue that the cited studies show that the parenting skills of homosexual parents are at least equivalent to those of heterosexual parents and that children raised by homosexual parents suffer no adverse outcomes. Appellants also point to the policies and practices of numerous adoption agencies that permit homosexual persons to adopt.

In considering appellants' argument, we must ask not whether the latest in social science research and professional opinion *support* the decision of the Florida legislature, but whether that evidence is so well established and so far beyond dispute that it would be irrational for the Florida legislature to believe that the interests of its children are best served by not permitting homosexual adoption. Also, we must credit any conceivable rational reason that the legislature might have for choosing not to alter its statutory scheme in response to this recent social science research. We must assume, for example, that the legislature might be aware of the critiques of the studies cited by appellants — critiques that have highlighted significant flaws in the studies' methodologies and conclusions, such as the use of small, self-selected samples; reliance on self-report instruments; politically driven hypotheses; and the use of unrepresentative study populations consisting of disproportionately affluent, educated parents. Alternatively, the legislature might consider and credit other studies that have found that children raised in homosexual households fare differently on a number of measures, doing worse on some of them, than children raised in similarly situated heterosexual households. Or the legislature might consider, and even credit, the research cited by appellants, but find it premature to rely on a very recent and still developing body of research, particularly in light of the absence of longitudinal studies following child subjects into adulthood and of studies of adopted, rather than natural, children of homosexual parents.

We do not find any of these possible legislative responses to be irrational. Openly homosexual households represent a very recent phenomenon, and sufficient time has not yet passed to permit any scientific study of how children raised in those households fare as adults. . . . Given this state of affairs, it is not irrational for the Florida legislature to credit one side of the debate over the other. . . . Accordingly, we conclude that appellants' proffered social science evidence does not disprove the rational basis of the Florida statute.

Finally, we disagree with appellants' contention that *Romer* [v. Evans, 517 U.S. 620 (1996)] requires us to strike down the Florida statute. In *Romer*, the Supreme Court invalidated Amendment 2 to the Colorado state constitution, which prohibited all legislative, executive, or judicial action designed to protect homosexual persons from discrimination. . . . Unlike Colorado's Amendment 2, Florida's statute is not so "sweeping and comprehensive" as to render Florida's rationales for the statute "inexplicable by anything but animus" toward its homosexual residents. [T]he Florida classification is limited to the narrow and discrete context of access to the statutory privilege of adoption and, more importantly, has a plausible connection with the state's asserted interest. . . .

. . . The State of Florida has made the determination that it is not in the best interests of its displaced children to be adopted by individuals who "engage in current, voluntary homosexual activity," *Cox*, 627 So. 2d at 1215, and we have found nothing in the Constitution that forbids this policy judgment. . . .

NOTES AND QUESTIONS

(1) Epilogue.   On appeal, the United States Supreme Court denied certiorari. Lofton v. Secretary, Florida Dept. of Children and Families (125 S. Ct. 869 (2005)). In the midst of the litigation, plaintiff and his partner moved to Oregon with their foster children. Several of these children, however, remain under the jurisdiction of the Florida adoption agency. Plaintiffs also challenged the Florida ban on *state* constitutional grounds. See Cox v. Florida Dept. of Health & Rehabilitative Servs., 656 So. 2d 902 (Fla. 1995) (holding that Florida ban did not violate state constitutional protection against privacy or due process and was not unconstitutionally vague, but failing to reach equal protection issue because of insufficient record).

(2) State Restrictions.   A few jurisdictions expressly consider sexual orientation in adoption decision making. Florida was the first state to enact a ban in 1977. Some state proscriptions address the *individual's* sexual orientation, whereas other statutes restrict gay and lesbian *couples* from adopting children. Some states contain both prohibitions. See, e.g., Conn. Gen. Stat. Ann. §45a-726a (West Supp. 2001) (prohibiting placement "with a prospective adoptive or foster parent or parents who are homosexual or bisexual"); Miss. Code Ann. §93-17-3(2) (Supp. 2002) ("Adoption by couples of the same gender is prohibited"). See also Utah Code §78-30-1(3)(b) (2003) (barring unmarried couples, whether same-sex or heterosexual, from adopting). Do such statutes manifest an animus toward gays and lesbians that is constitutionally suspect? Are you convinced by *Lofton's* attempt to distinguish *Romer*?

(3) Foster Parenting Bans Distinguished.   As *Lofton* explains, Florida permits gays and lesbians to serve as foster parents but not as adoptive parents. In contrast, some states attempted to ban gays as foster parents. See Howard v. Child Welfare Agency Review Bd., No. CV199-9881, 2004 WL 3154530 (Ark. Cir. Ct. Dec. 29, 2004) (invalidating state regulation prohibiting gays from becoming foster parents and foster children from being placed in a household with gay members). See also Clay Robison, Legislature, House OKs Proposal to Ban Gay Marriage, Houston Chron., Apr. 26, 2005, at A1 (describing measure that recently passed the Texas House of Representatives to prohibit gays from becoming foster parents).

Does it make sense to permit gays and lesbians to serve as foster parents but to deny them the right to adopt? How does *Lofton* respond? Do the differences between foster parenting and adoption justify different treatment of the role of sexual orientation?

(4) Validity of Second-Parent Adoptions.   Some jurisdictions recognize "second-parent adoptions" by members of gay and lesbian couples. Generally,

in such adoptions, the biological parent's same-sex partner petitions a court for permission to adopt the child (although such adoptions can occur in situations in which neither prospective adoptive parent has a biological relationship to the child). New York was one of the first jurisdictions to recognize second-parent adoptions among gay and lesbian couples in 1992. See Jane S. Schacter, Counted Among the Blessed: One Court and the Constitution of Family, 74 Tex. L. Rev. 1267, 1267 (1996).

In second-parent adoptions, some courts wrestle with the issue of whether granting the adoption requires the court to terminate the parental rights of the biological parent in order to permit the assumption of parental rights by the second parent. Compare Sharon S. v. Superior Court, 2 Cal. Rptr. 3d 699 (Cal. 2003) (holding that termination of a birth parent's rights is not a mandatory prerequisite to every adoption and that second-parent adoptions are valid under California's independent adoption law), with In re Adoption of Luke, 640 N.W.2d 374 (Neb. 2002) (holding that a child was not eligible for adoption by the biological mother's companion because the biological mother had not relinquished her parental rights). The underlying rationale is that children should have only one parent of a given gender. Does this rationale make sense in contemporary society, with its high rate of divorce and myriad family forms?

Traditionally, the stepparent adoption procedure (which permits a stepparent to adopt a child without terminating the parental rights of the birth parent) has not been available to gay and lesbian couples because they have not been allowed to marry. While *Sharon S.*, supra, was pending, California's domestic partnership law went into effect permitting registered same-sex partners to use the expedited stepparent adoption procedure of Cal. Fam. Code §9000. California is one of eight states that allow adoption by a nonbiological same-sex parent without terminating the biological parent's rights. Stephanie Francis Ward, "Alternative Families" Gaining Acceptance, 31 A.B.A. J. E-Report 2 (2003).

For other recent cases permitting second-parent adoption, see In re Adoption of K.S.P., 804 N.E.2d 1253 (Ind. Ct. App. 2004); In re Adoption of Carolyn B., 774 N.Y.S.2d 227 (App. Div. 2004). For a recent empirical study of couples involved in second-parent adoptions, see Catherine Connolly, The Voice of the Petitioner: The Experiences of Gay and Lesbian Parents in Successful Second-Parent Adoption Proceedings, 36 Law & Soc'y Rev. 325 (2002).

(5) Uniform Parentage Act. Should the Uniform Parentage Act, a model statute that was promulgated originally to adjudicate the paternity of unwed fathers, be applied to same-sex custody and adoption cases? See Melanie B. Jacobs, Micah Has One Mommy and One Legal Stranger: Adjudicating Maternity for Nonbiological Lesbian Coparents, 50 Buff. L. Rev. 341 (2002) (proposing the use of the Uniform Parentage Act to adjudicate maternity for lesbian co-parents and thereby confer all the rights and privileges of legal parenthood).

(6) Relevance of Social Science Data on the Impact of Gay Parenting. Some courts have concluded that social science data do not support the ban on adoption by gay parents and also have pointed out that various child welfare organizations (e.g., the American Psychological Association and the American Academy of Pediatricians) concur with those findings. See, e.g., Howard v. Child Welfare Agency Review Board, supra; In re Evan, 583 N.Y.S.2d 997, 1002 n. 1. (Sur. Ct.

N.Y. Cty. 1992). How does *Lofton*, supra, respond to the issue of the relevance of the social science data to adoption by gays and lesbians?

For additional empirical research on the impact of gay parenting on children, see Suzanne M. Johnson & Elizabeth O'Connor, The Gay Baby Boom: A Psychological Perspective (2002); Charlotte J. Patterson & Anthony R. D'Augelli, Lesbian, Gay, and Bisexual Identities in Families: Psychological Perspectives (1998); Ellen C. Perrin et al., Technical Report: Coparent or Second-Parent Adoption by Same-Sex Parents, 109 Pediatrics 341 (2002); Fiona L. Tasker & Susan Golombok, Growing Up in a Lesbian Family: Effects on Child Development (1998); Judith Stacey & Timothy J. Biblarz, (How) Does the Sexual Orientation of Parents Matter?, 66 Am. Soc. Rev. 199 (2001).

8.   The Relevance of Race to Adoption

What relevance, if any, should be given to the role of race in adoption decision making?

Adoption of Vito
728 N.E.3d 292 (Mass. 2000)

MARSHALL, C.J.

This appeal arises from the denial of a petition to dispense with parental consent to adoption. The case concerns a child [who] has lived with his foster parents (also his preadoptive parents) since he was discharged from the hospital one month after his birth. Vito has never lived with his biological mother.[3] He is now eight and one-half years old. [Vito's foster family is from the Dominican Republic; his foster parents speak only Spanish. Vito speaks both Spanish and English. His biological family is African-American.]

We summarize in some detail the findings of fact and conclusions of law made by the judge. In 1990 Vito's biological mother began using crack cocaine, which she continued to do until 1995, with occasional periods of nonuse. Prior to May, 1991, when a judge in the Boston Juvenile Court awarded temporary custody of her three oldest children to the department, she had been trading food stamps and using public welfare benefits to purchase crack cocaine. Her children were often left at home alone. When Vito tested positive for cocaine at birth [in 1992], an abuse and neglect report concerning him was filed. . . .

Vito was discharged from the hospital one month after his birth and was placed in the home of his foster parents; his siblings had been placed in other homes. In March, 1992, the Boston Juvenile Court ordered the department to assume permanent custody of Vito and his three older siblings; the mother's whereabouts were unknown to the department at that time.

From the time of his removal from his mother's care in January, 1992, while in the hospital, until January, 1995, his biological mother visited Vito only once. During that ninety-minute visit, Vito responded minimally to his biological mother, withdrew from her and attached himself to his foster mother. At the end of that visit,

---

[3] Vito's biological father did not object to the department's petition, nor did he appeal.

the mother agreed to visit Vito again at the end of the month, on his first birthday, but although the foster mother and Vito arrived for the birthday visit, the mother failed to attend; she did not telephone to cancel the visit. Following the failed January, 1993, birthday visit, the biological mother made no request for a visit with her son for the remainder of 1993. During 1994 there were no visits with Vito, and little contact between the biological mother and the department; she told the department she had relocated to Florida.

In 1995, while back in Massachusetts in prison on shoplifting charges, Vito's mother signed a department service plan, entered a drug rehabilitation program and began visits with Vito and his siblings.[10] Vito's mother was released from prison in October, 1995. The judge found that the mother's visits with Vito have been generally consistent since March, 1995, and that she has attended monthly supervised visits since her release. The judge found that Vito and his biological mother have "no emotional sharing" between them and remain dissociated, despite pleasant play and conversation. The judge found that Vito did not show any genuine interest in his biological siblings and did not appear to have formed any emotional attachment to his biological mother; he did not appear to be excited to see her and separated from her with no difficulties or emotional overtones. The judge nevertheless made an ultimate finding that Vito had formed "a positive relationship" with his biological mother that has developed since visitation began when she was incarcerated.[11] The judge found that Vito's mother, however, had not fully complied with the department's service plan tasks, and concluded that Vito's biological mother cannot now resume care and custody of Vito because "she has not secured adequate stable housing, has not adequately addressed her issues of lengthy substance abuse history and has not acquired any meaningful parenting skills training." She also concluded that Vito's mother's drug abuse and resultant neglect "was severe and of a lengthy duration," although she had improved in the last two years.

In contrast, the judge found that Vito is "fully integrated into his foster family both emotionally and ethnically." The judge found that it was "important" to Vito to belong to his foster family "because that was the only family he had known," and that "[t]he foster parents are invested in adopting [Vito]; they perceive him as their own son." She found that Vito "has a significant attachment to his foster family," and that separating Vito from his foster family could result in a range of negative responses, from severe depression to less severe trauma.

The judge concluded that, by clear and convincing evidence, Vito's mother is currently unfit to parent him. . . . Despite the fact that the biological mother

---

[10] Because the department now knew where Vito's biological mother was located, it initiated the effort to begin visits between Vito and her. The first such visit took place in March, 1995, at the Massachusetts Correctional Institution at Framingham. Department regulations provide that the department shall make reasonable efforts to work with incarcerated parents to promote a healthy relationship with their children, such efforts to include regular visitation at the correctional facility.

[11] During a May, 1995, visit Vito's mother was seen attempting to interact with Vito, talking to him and exchanging toys. During subsequent visits Vito began to direct more conversation to his mother, although he did not refer to her by name or by any version of "mother." One social worker testified that as Vito began to understand English better, between May and September of 1995, he began to relate better to his mother. Another social worker observed that in 1996 Vito referred to his biological mother as his "other mother." The guardian ad litem reported that Vito told her he liked the visits with his mother and that she brings him toys when they visit.

"cares deeply for and has good intentions toward the child," however, "[g]ood intentions . . . are insufficient to establish fitness to parent a child."

The judge further determined that "racial issues *may* at sometime in the future" become a problem for Vito (emphasis added). She found that Vito's relationship with his biological mother is "crucial" for his "racial and cultural development and adjustment," that his best interests will be served by continued "significant" contact with her after any adoption, and that under the department's adoption plan Vito would have limited or no connection to his African-American family or culture.[13] She found that the department's plan is not in Vito's "best interest so long as it does not provide for significant ongoing contact with [his][m]other and [biological] siblings."

[The probate judge therefore denied the petition to dispense with parental consent to adoption but stated that she might enter a new judgment should the department submit an adoption plan that provided for postadoption contact, including eight yearly visits with his biological mother, as long as the mother is not abusing drugs and the contact continues to be in Vito's best interests. The department appealed. Vacating the probate decree, the Appeals Court directed that the department's petition be granted to dispense with the mother's consent. The Appeals Court further found the judge's proposal for postadoption visitation was permissible but ordered that, given the passage of time, the probate court should rehear any petition for postadoption visitation filed within 30 days. The department petitioned for further appellate review, challenging the judge's requirement of postadoption visitation in the adoption plan and departmental involvement after the adoption.]

Despite numerous appellate decisions to the contrary, the department argues that there is no authority for the judge to enter an order requiring postadoption visitation in a termination proceeding, pursuant to G.L. c. 210, §3, or at least, that such an order cannot be made where there is an identified, pre-adoptive family and the child has no bond with the biological parent. . . . We concluded in [Petition of the Dept. of Social Servs. to Dispense with Consent to Adoption, 467 N.E.2d 861 (Mass. 1984)] that the equitable powers of courts in this area permit a judge, in her discretion, to evaluate an adoption plan proposed by the department [and] decide whether [postadoption] visitation is in the child's best interests. Since our 1984 decision, numerous Appeals Court decisions have expressed an understanding that judges may effect or require postadoption visitation as an outcome of termination proceedings. That was a correct understanding of our law.

A judge's equitable power to order postadoption contact, however, is not without limit. . . . Constitutional considerations also guide the exercise of this equitable power. Adoptive parents have the same legal rights toward their children that biological parents do. Parental rights to raise one's children are essential, basic rights that are constitutionally protected [citing Wisconsin v. Yoder, Stanley v. Illinois, Meyer v. Nebraska, and Prince v. Massachusetts]. State intrusion in the rearing of children by their parents may be justified only in limited circumstances.

At a pragmatic level, unnecessary involvement of the courts in long-term, wide-ranging monitoring and enforcement of the numerous postadoption contact

[13] The judge found that there was no evidence that the adoptive family had any significant contacts with the African-American community at this time.

arrangements could result from too ready an application of the court's equitable power to issue contact orders. The postadoption contact arrangements contemplated by the judge in this case were both long term and wide ranging, and necessarily would have involved the court in ongoing arrangements between the biological mother and the adopting family for many years to come. But courts are not often the best place to monitor children's changing needs. . . . We also recognize the concern raised by the department and the amici that untrammeled equitable power used to impose postadoption contact might reduce the number of prospective parents willing to adopt. . . . Where, as here, the child has formed strong, nurturing bonds with his preadoptive family, and there is little or no evidence of a significant, existing bond with the biological parent, judicial exercise of equitable power to require postadoption contact would usually be unwarranted. . . .

Transitional provision for posttermination or postadoption contact in the best interests of the child, however, is a far different thing from judicial meddling in the child's and adoptive family's life, based not on evidence of the emotional ties and current dynamics between the child and the biological parent, but on speculation concerning some hypothetical dynamic between parent and child several years hence, later in adolescence, for example. Parental and familial autonomy cannot be so lightly cast aside. . . .

Looking at the evidence of the actual circumstances of Vito's life and relationships, testimony of the guardian ad litem made clear that Vito's monthly visits with the biological mother had little or no impact on Vito's sense of identity. Rather, the judge's findings reveal that Vito strongly identified with his preadoptive family, emotionally and ethnically. . . .

There was also little in the record before us to suggest that Vito's relationship with his biological mother was likely to become important to Vito's adolescent identity. There was evidence of some possible future significance of the relationship in the guardian ad litem's acknowledgment that, generally, adolescence *may* be a time when a transracial adoptee *may* experience adjustment problems, and that Vito would have little connection to an African-American family or culture living with his adoptive family. Generalities about what may be in the best interests of some children, without more, cannot be the basis of judicial orders concerning postadoption contact of a particular child; the best interests of the child standard is one grounded in the particular needs and circumstances of the individual child in question.

Assuming that it was proper to use racial grounds for determining Vito's best interest, there was no evidence in the record that showed Vito would be deprived of all African-American contacts in his adolescence if regular visits with his biological mother were not mandated. While Vito's foster family "currently" has no significant contacts with the African-American community, that fact says little, if anything, about contacts that his adoptive family might develop in the future, if this becomes important for their son. We discern no support for a determination that Vito's relationship with his biological mother is "crucial" for his "racial and cultural development and adjustment." . . .

We conclude, therefore, that, although the probate judge had a statutory mandate to review the department's adoption plan to determine whether the best interests of the child would be served by a termination decree with that plan, and although the judge had equitable authority to order postadoption contact, including visitation, the judge's determination that such postadoption contact was required was clearly erroneous in this case. . . .

NOTES AND QUESTIONS

(1) Background of Race-Matching Policies.   Should African-American children be adopted by white parents? The issue of transracial adoption has evoked controversy for decades. During the 1960s and early 1970s, the Civil Rights Movement led to a supportive climate for transracial adoption. However, the climate changed in 1972 when the National Association of Black Social Workers (NABSW) denounced transracial adoption in an influential statement at their national conference. NABSW contended that white parents could not teach their African-American children to deal with the prejudice endemic to society. Moreover, NABSW argued that transracial adoption constituted a form of genocide and an attack on the African-American family.

In response, the Child Welfare League of America (the nation's oldest and largest child welfare organization) promptly amended their adoption standards to support race matching. This action resulted in a significant decline in transracial adoptions. See Hawley Fogg-Davis, The Ethics of Transracial Adoption 3 (2002) (pointing out that transracial adoption steadily increased following the first documented placement in 1948 until it peaked in 1971, before the NABSW statement); Randall Kennedy, Interracial Intimacies: Sex, Marriage, Identity, and Adoption 450-453 (2003) (similarly explaining the influence of the NABSW position paper).

What are the arguments supporting and opposing transracial adoption? Consider the excerpt (reprinted infra) by Cynthia Hawkins-Leon and Carla Bradley, Race and Transracial Adoption: The Answer Is Neither Simply Black or White Nor Right or Wrong, 51 Cath. U. L. Rev. 1227 (2002). For different views of transracial adoption, compare Elizabeth Bartholet, Nobody's Children: Abuse and Neglect, Foster Drift, and the Adoption Alternative (1999); Randall Kennedy, Interracial Intimacies: Sex, Marriage, Identity, and Adoption (2003) (both supporting transracial adoption) with Ruth-Arlene W. Howe, Transracial Adoption (TRA): Old Prejudices and Discrimination Float Under a New Halo, 6 B.U. Pub. Int. L.J. 409 (1997); Twila L. Perry, The Transracial Adoption Controversy: An Analysis of Discourse and Subordination, 21 N.Y.U. Rev. L. & Soc. Change 33 (1993) (both supporting race-matching policies when feasible).

(2) The trial judge in Adoption of Vito proposed postadoption visitation with the child's African-American mother and siblings as a method of promoting the child's racial identity. Why did the state supreme court hold that this ruling was erroneous? What is the best way to maintain a transracial adoptee's appreciation of his or her racial heritage? In what circumstances is postadoption visitation appropriate for transracial adoptees? When is it inappropriate?

(3) Empirical Research.   Most research on the effects of transracial adoption has found that transracially adopted children adjust well in their adoptive homes. The most comprehensive longitudinal research concludes that these adoptions serve the children's best interests. That empirical study (spanning three decades and studying 366 children) found no differences in the children's self-esteem or racial self-perception and determined that the children were at ease in

both African-American and white worlds. See Rita J. Simon & Howard Altstein, Adoption, Race & Identity: From Infancy to Young Adulthood (2d ed. 2002). An earlier study (of 153 families) reported that the age of the child at the time of adoption, as well as opposition to the adoption by friends and relatives, had a more significant impact on the child's development than the transracial adoption. Arnold R. Silverman & William Feigelman, The Adjustment of Black Children Adopted by White Families, 62 Social Casework 529 (1981). See also Arnold R. Silverman, Outcomes of Transracial Adoption, in The Future of Children: Adoption 115 (David & Lucille Packard Foundation ed., 1993). For recent first-person accounts of transracial adoption, see Sharon E. Rush, Loving Across the Color Line: A White Adoptive Mother Learns About Race (2000); Rita J. Simon & Rhonda M. Roorda, In Their Own Voices: Transracial Adoptees Tell Their Stories (2000).

(4) Federal Legislation. In 1994 Congress enacted the Multiethnic Placement Act (MEPA), 42 U.S.C. §5115a (1994), prohibiting the delay or denial of child placements (in adoption and foster care) by any federally funded agency *solely* on the basis of race, color, or national origin. However, MEPA contained a loophole: agencies could consider the race, color, or national origin when relevant and in conjunction with other factors. As a result, agencies continued race matching despite the legislation. In response, Congress repealed portions of MEPA in 1996 and substituted new legislation, Inter-Ethnic Adoption Act (IEAA) (enacted as part of the Small Business Job Protection Act, 42 U.S.C. §§671[a], 674). IEAA strengthened the federal policy against race matching by penalizing federally funded programs that violate the prohibition against race matching by reduction of their federal funds. Following the enactment of IEAA, many commentators contend that race may no longer be considered in placements. See, e.g., Kennedy, supra, at 400; Cynthia Hawkins-León & Carla Bradley, supra, at 1248. That view, however, is not unanimous. Compare Fogg-Davis, supra, at 49; Joan Heifetz Hollinger, ABA Center on Children and the Law, A Guide to the Multiethnic Placement Act of 1994 as amended by the Inter-Ethnic Adoption Provisions of 1996, 9-10 (1998) (both arguing that IEAA did not completely eliminate consideration of race).

In the principal case, did the probate judge's denial of the agency's petition to dispense with the mother's consent — based on the importance of maintaining Vito's racial identity — delay Vito's adoption, in violation of the IEAA? See Adoption of Vito, 728 N.E.3d at 305 (vacating the denial of the petition to dispense with the mother's consent on other grounds, thereby obviating the need to address this question). Might Vito's prospective adoptive parents have a federal cause of action for a potential violation of IEAA? See 42 U.S.C. §674 (d)(3)(A) (S2000) (conferring such a private right or action).

(5) Influence of **Palmore v. Sidoti.** The United States Supreme Court has not addressed the role of race in adoption decision making. However, in Palmore v. Sidoti (infra, p. 566), the Supreme Court held that consideration of race as the sole basis for the denial of *custody* to a Caucasian mother married to an African-American man violates equal protection. According to some commentators, *Palmore*'s application to the context of adoption is unclear. See, e.g., Twila L. Perry, Power, Possibility and Choice: The Racial Identity of Transracially Adopted Children, 9 Mich. J. Race & L. 215, 218 (2003) (book review of Hawley Fogg-Davis, The

Ethics of Transracial Adoption (2002)). Following *Palmore*, several state and federal courts have upheld consideration of race as one of several factors in adoption. Id.

(6) What are the similarities and differences between legal and societal responses toward adoption by gay and lesbian parents and transracial adoption? See, e.g., Kenneth L. Karst, Law, Cultural Conflict, and the Socialization of Children, 91 Cal. L. Rev. 967 (2003) (pointing out both contexts are dominated by public concerns about the socialization of children).

(7) The Relevance of Religion. Religious-matching laws, which match the religion of the adoptive child (or the biological parents) to that of the adoptive parents, have long been upheld as constitutional. See, e.g., Dickens v. Ernesto, 281 N.E.2d 153 (N.Y. 1972), *appeal dismissed*, 407 U.S. 917 (1972). Although the modern trend reflects a diminution in the importance of such matching, many states still require religious matching. Amanda C. Pustilnik, Note, Private Ordering, Legal Ordering, and the Getting of Children: A Counterhistory of Adoption Law, 20 Yale L. & Pol'y Rev. 263, 289 nn. 130 & 131 (2002) (pointing out that from 1954 to 1989, the number of states with such provisions diminished from 43 to 17). What constitutional issues do such statutory provisions raise? From the child's perspective, does such a policy make sense?

(8) The Relevance of Ethnicity: the Indian Child Welfare Act. The Indian Child Welfare Act of 1978 (ICWA), 25 U.S.C. §1915(a) (2000), makes ethnic background decisive in the placement of Native American children. The ICWA provides that the Indian tribe has exclusive jurisdiction as against the state concerning any "child custody proceeding" (including adoptive and foster care placements) involving an Indian child. 25 U.S.C. §§1903[1], 1911[a]. Thus, upon the petition of either parent, a Native American custodian, or the child's tribe, a state court must transfer the proceeding to the jurisdiction of the tribe.

Congress enacted the legislation in an attempt to reduce the incidence of adoption of Native American children by white families, with the resulting loss of the children's heritage. The purpose of the Act is to "promote the best interests of Indian children and the stability and security of Indian tribes and families by the establishment of minimum federal standards for the removal of Indian children from their families and the placement of such children in foster or adoptive homes which reflect the unique values of the Indian culture." 25 U.S.C.§1902. Absent good cause, preference is given to placement with: (1) a member of the child's extended family; (2) other members of the child's tribe; or (3) other Native American families.

In Mississippi Band of Choctaw Indians v. Holyfield, 490 U.S. 30 (1989) (overturning adoption of Choctaw twins), the Supreme Court held that state courts lack authority to permit adoption of Native Americans by non-Native Americans, even when the biological parents leave the reservation to give up the children.

Several state courts have adopted an "existing Indian family doctrine," refusing to apply the Act if a child is not being removed from an existing Indian family because the purpose of the Act (to keep Indian children with Indian families) is not served. See, e.g., In re Santos Y., 112 Cal. Rptr. 2d 692, 716 (Ct. App. 2001) (pointing out that nine states have adopted this exception). See also Carole E. Goldberg, Individual Rights and Tribal Revitalization, 35 Ariz. St. L.J. 889, 903-904 (2003) (criticizing the "existing Indian family doctrine" as harming tribal revitalization efforts). For recent critiques of the ICWA, see Randall Kennedy, Interracial

Intimacies: Sex, Marriage, Identity, and Adoption 480-518 (2003); Richard P. Barth et al., Adoption of American Indian Children: Implications for Implementing the Indian Child Welfare and Adoption and Safe Families Acts, 24 Child. & Youth Servs. Rev. 139 (2002).

(9) Problem. Sixteen-year-old Tiffany becomes pregnant during an affair with a schoolmate, Christopher, who is a member of the Muscogee Nation tribe. (Tiffany is not a member of any Native American tribe.) Christopher, although technically a tribal member, does not participate in any tribal activities or live within tribal boundaries. For a short time during the pregnancy, Tiffany moves into Christopher's household. His grandmother provides support, and Christopher begins working at a restaurant to help with expenses. Christopher and Tiffany subsequently break up, and she moves out. Tiffany then tells Christopher that she has miscarried. However, upon deciding to relinquish the baby for adoption, she is advised to notify the father of her plans and that she is still pregnant. After she does, Christopher protests the adoption. Later, he attempts to visit the mother and child at the birth, but the mother and the hospital staff refuse.

Tiffany seeks an order that the child is eligible for adoption without the father's consent and for termination of his parental rights. The father objects to the adoption. The Muscogee Nation files a motion to intervene, contending that the ICWA applies. What result under the ICWA? Irrespective of the ICWA, does dispensing with the father's consent to adoption violate his constitutional rights? See In re Baby Boy L., 103 P.3d 1099 (Okla. 2004).

Consider the following arguments favoring and opposing transracial adoption. Which do you find most persuasive?

Cynthia G. Hawkins-León & Carla Bradley, Race and Transracial Adoption: The Answer Is Neither Simply Black or White Nor Right or Wrong
51 Cath. U. L. Rev. 1227, 1255-1267 (2002)

In Opposition to Transracial Adoption

1. One-Way Nature

One of the primary reasons that African Americans and organizations purporting to represent the interests of African Americans are opposed to transracial adoption is that the phenomenon of transracial adoption occurs unilaterally; the overwhelming trend in transracial adoption is for White adults to adopt African American children. . . .

2. Racial Identity

The earliest adoptions attempted to mimic the biological family. Transracial adoptions make this attempt impossible and are not in the best interests of African American children. It is in the best interests of a child to preserve a child's racial, ethnic, and cultural heritage in adoption placement decisions. . . . It is virtually impossible for White parents to raise African American children in a White environment and have the children retain their African American identity. . . . When an African American child is adopted by White parents who do not have a significant number of African American friends or contacts and who are uninterested in teaching the child about African American culture, the child is left with little or no African American identity. These children struggle unsuccessfully to acquire a positive racial identity; their parents simply cannot provide a same-race role model. This lack of nurturing makes it virtually impossible for the child to develop pride, acceptance, and understanding of his or her heritage. . . .

3. Cultural Genocide

According to some perspective, transracial adoptions actually harm African American children. Taking African American children away from the African American community, it is argued, is a form of "[cultural] genocide." . . . The concern is that African American children are both literally and figuratively stolen from the African American community. . . .

The notion that a parent's love is enough to overcome external racism is naïve. . . . Even in this new millennium, African Americans are victims of racism and are subject to verbal attacks, physical altercations, employment discrimination, higher arrest rates, and discriminatory sentencing guidelines. Without experiencing such discriminatory behavior themselves, White parents do not have and cannot share adequate survival skills to cope with racism. . . .

4. African American Adoptive Parents

To claim that there are many more African American children in foster care awaiting adoption than the number of prospective African American adoptive parents is inaccurate and insults the strength of the African American family. African American adoptive homes can be found for African American children. . . . African American adoptive parents are in short supply because they encounter roadblocks in the adoption process, not because they are disinterested in adopting. [Problems include institutional racism because guidelines are derived from white middle-class perspectives; adoption agencies lack persons of color as staff decision makers; high adoption fees serve as a barrier; prospective adoptive parents of color may possess negative perceptions of adoption agencies; persons of color tend to favor informal adoption; agencies have inflexible standards that favor young, two-parent, wealthier families and disadvantage prospective parents of color; agencies fail to set aside sufficient resources for recruitment of minority parents; and communities of color remain unaware of the need for their services.]

Furthermore, transracial adoption will not relieve the number of African American children in foster care. [W]hile the median age of children in foster care is nine years, the majority of White adoptive parents are not interested in adopting older children (of any race) or children with handicaps. . . . Therefore, even with the phenomenon of transracial adoptions, some hard-to-place children will remain hard-to-place and will continue to linger in the foster care system. Aggressive recruitment of prospective African American adoptive parents will tend to make transracial adoptions unnecessary. . . .

In Support of Transracial Adoption

1. Statistics

Significant support for transracial adoption stems from the existence and effect of race-related statistics for foster care and domestic adoption. [A]pproximately forty-six percent of children who are available for adoption are African American. Meanwhile, sixty-seven percent of American families waiting to adopt are White. . . . [Additionally], African American children remained in foster care thirty-three percent longer than the national median; on average, Black children remain in foster care for two years. Although African Americans adopt at the same rate as Whites, African Americans would have to adopt at a rate many times that of Whites to provide homes for all of the African American children available for adoption. . . .

Evidence demonstrates that children suffer irreparable harm from growing up without permanent parents. Almost thirty percent of children who grow up in unstable circumstances, including foster care, have reported instances of crime, alcoholism, or both. This startling figure is even more disturbing considering that the number of children in foster care is now double what it was during the 1970s. . . .

2. Race Matching Harms Children

In passing the [MEPA/IEPA], Congress determined that racial matching and same-race placements were responsible, at least in part, for the length of time children spent in foster care. Furthermore, children are less likely to find permanent placements as they age. Thus, race matching decreases the probability that children, particularly African American children, will be placed into permanent homes for adoption. Rather than same-race placement, it is more important that children receive love, attention, and permanency and that they do not languish in foster care.

3. Success Rate

Adoptions are not all successful; however, the failure rate is unrelated to adoptions across racial lines. There is no evidence that transracial adoptions harm children; in fact, transracial adoptions have proven to be successful. Pointedly, research data indicates that transracial adoptees fare well. Over seventy-five percent of transracial adoptions are considered successful — a number comparable to same-race adoptions. Sixty-eight percent of children who were adopted transracially do not feel any discomfort with their appearance compared to their adoptive parents or the community in which they were raised. It can be concluded from these statistics that transracially adopted children are proud of their heritage. Finally, "there is no evidence that adoptive parents form weaker bonds to dissimilar looking children than to similar ones."

4. Self Identity and White Privilege

While identity is admittedly a complex topic, social and cultural attitudes are learned, not inherited. Individuals are not born with a sense of self, but develop self-awareness through social interaction. . . . Most White parents meet the identity needs of their adopted African American children. Many adoptive parents create a multi-racial environment for their children to offset potential identity problems and to provide same-race mentors. Furthermore, White adoptive parents are in a unique position to teach their Black children how to "maneuver in the White world of power and privilege." . . .

C.   PARENTAL CUSTODY AFTER DIVORCE

1.   Introduction

Divorce affects large numbers of children. Approximately 1 million children experience the divorce of their parents annually.[47] How should the opportunities and responsibilities for various aspects of child rearing be allocated in the event of divorce? In Chapter 2 we considered the economic claims a child should have against each of his parents in the context of divorce. Here we shall consider issues relating to custody and visitation.

INTRODUCTORY PROBLEM

John and Mary Anderson are legally separated and are in the process of getting divorced. Their only child, Jimmy, is seven years old. Because Mary has been attending law school for the previous three years, Jimmy has spent a great deal of time with John. John, a college teacher who writes fiction, hates doing laundry, housekeeping, and grocery shopping. Despite his strong affection for his son, John agrees that Mary should have custody of Jimmy.

(1) Upon being informed of his parent's decision, Jimmy expresses his strong wish to live with his father. Should the parental agreement nevertheless be dispositive? Before the divorce is made final, should Jimmy have a lawyer? Should the judge consider Jimmy's views? Should Jimmy's views be dispositive? Or should the judge make an independent evaluation? By what standard? Should the judge be able to force Jimmy to live with Mary?

(2) Suppose that upon hearing Jimmy's objection to living with Mary, John and Mary enter into a new agreement providing that Jimmy will spend six months a year with each parent. Suppose that Jimmy objects to this arrangement because he wants to be with his father all the time, because "Mommy has too much work to do and does not like to build model airplanes," and because the arrangement will require that he "move around too much."

(3) Suppose that John changes his mind and decides to seek full custody of Jimmy. Mary then vows to fight such an arrangement. What factors should be taken into consideration for choosing which parent should prevail? Is it relevant that Mary discovered that she is a lesbian and plans to live with her new partner?

(4) Before the divorce Jimmy used to visit Mary's parents for three weeks during the summer. Jimmy is especially fond of his grandfather, who takes him on fishing trips and to baseball games. Mary's parents have never liked John and

---

[47] Bureau of the Census, Statistical Abstract of the United States 2003 72 (table 83) (23rd ed. 2003).

encouraged Mary to divorce him. Now that he has custody of Jimmy, they are afraid that John will seek revenge by not permitting them to see Jimmy. Suppose Jimmy enjoys spending time with his grandparents. Who should decide whether and how often these visits should take place? Should grandparents have a right to see their grandchildren?

(5) Two years after the decree John is offered and accepts the opportunity to teach English literature in France. John plans to take Jimmy with him. Mary is now a well-paid lawyer but considers having to travel to Europe to visit her son outrageous. She seeks modification of the custody decree.

(6) Suppose Jimmy is the child of Mary and Julie, who have been partners for ten years. Mary is Jimmy's biological mother via artificial insemination by an anonymous donor, and Julie has been a parent to Jimmy since his birth. When Jimmy is seven, Mary and Julie's relationship dissolves, and Mary refuses to let Julie have further contact with Jimmy. Does Julie have standing to sue for custody of Jimmy? If a court refuses to grant Julie custody rights, should she be allowed visitation rights even though she has no biological tie to Jimmy? If a court fails to find a legal relationship between Jimmy and Julie, should Julie still be required to pay child support?

For each of the above described circumstances consider the following questions: Should Jimmy have an attorney? Should Jimmy's views be considered? Should they be dispositive? Should the parents' agreement be dispositive? Should the judge make an independent evaluation? By what standard?

NOTES AND QUESTIONS ON CONTESTED CHILD CUSTODY

It appears that in approximately 10 to 20 percent of divorces involving children, the parents cannot agree concerning custody.[48] In these cases, the critical question is how should these disputes be resolved? Through what process? With what standards? Who should decide?

(1) For disputes between parents, what would be the advantage of more precise legal standards? Would it lead to less controversy?

(2) Evaluate critically the advantages and disadvantages of the following standards and compare them to the best interests standard:

a. A standard that awards custody on the basis of the sex of the parents — e.g., a maternal preference.[49]

b. A standard that awards custody to the parent of the same sex as that of the child.

c. A standard that awards custody to the richer parent.

d. A standard that awards custody to the parent who would be expected to spend more time with the child.

e. A standard that awards custody to the parent chosen by the child.

f. A standard that awards custody to the parent whose psychological relationship to the child would be "less detrimental."

[48] Eleanor E. Maccoby & Robert H. Mnookin, Dividing the Child: Social and Legal Dilemmas of Custody 103, 134 (1992).

[49] For data showing that mothers obtain custody more often, see id. at 112-113 (mothers receive sole physical custody in two out of three cases).

(3) Consider modes of dispute resolution other than traditional adjudication. What problems do you foresee with each suggestion?

    a.   A system that involved mediators or family counselors who could not impose a resolution upon the parents, but who pressed a private resolution of the custody dispute.

    b.   A form of adjudication or arbitration that required the disputing parents to choose a "judge," who is given the power to resolve the dispute. If the judge knows the family, the custody decision might better reflect an intuitive appreciation of the parties' values, psychology, and goals. The decision might also be more acceptable to the parents. What problems could you foresee with such a mechanism?

    c.   The flip of a coin would avoid the pain associated with an adversarial proceeding that requires an open exploration of the intimate aspects of family life and an ultimate judgment that one parent is preferable to another.

(4) While a substantial argument can be made that the primary responsibility of courts in contesting divorce custody cases is to decide the issue and to decide it once and for all, the legal system at present allows parents to relitigate these questions over a considerable period of time. For a discussion of the legal standards relating to modification of custody, see infra, pp. 615-617. Additional complexities arise when the divorcing parents live in different states; see infra, pp. 617-622.

2. Effects of Parental Divorce

Both popular and expert opinion agree that divorce affects children in many ways. As stated above, divorce is an increasingly common experience of childhood. What are the consequences of divorce for children? What are the psychological effects of divorce on children? Also, what impact does divorce have on children's day-to-day reality? Finally, what are the implications of these questions for custody decision making?

    The past several decades have witnessed considerable social science research that has increased our understanding of the responses of children to the divorce process. The excerpts below summarize the findings of some of this research.

Judith S. Wallerstein, Child of Divorce: An Overview
4 Behav. Sci. & L. 105, 112-116 (1986) (citations omitted)

To the child, divorce signifies the collapse of the structure that provides support and protection. The child reacts as to the anticipated cutting of his or her lifeline. . . .

    Boys are reported to be more vulnerable than girls to the acute stress of the marital rupture, as well as to the more chronic stresses of the transitional phase in the preschool and latency ages. Major differences between preschool boys and girls in a wide range of cognitive, social, and developmental measures have been reported. Boys from divorced families perform less well on a range of learning measures than boys in intact families. . . . While boys and girls did not differ in the overall psychological adjustment at the time of the marital breakup, at 18 months

boys have
harder
time

later the boys' psychological adjustment had deteriorated markedly, whereas that of the girls had greatly improved, making for a growing gap between the two groups. Other evidence shows that marital turmoil has a greater impact on boys than on girls, both in divorced families and in intact, discordant families. . . .

Developmental factors are critical in the responses of children and adolescents at the time of the marital rupture. Despite significant individual differences in the child, in the family, and in parent-child relations, the child's age and developmental stage appear to be the most important factors governing the initial response. . . .

A major finding in divorce research has been the common patterns of response within different age groups. The age groups which share significant commonalities in perceptions, responses, underlying fantasies, and behaviors are the preschool ages 3-5, early school age or early latency ages 5 1/2-8, later school age or latency ages 8-11, and finally, adolescent ages 12-18. . . .

Preschool children are likely to show regression following one parent's departure from the household. The regression usually occurs in the most recent developmental achievement of the child. Intensified fears are frequent and are evoked by routine separations from the custodial parent during the day and at bedtime. Sleep disturbances are also frequent. The preoccupying fantasy of many of the little children is fear of abandonment by both parents. Yearning for the departed parent is intense. Young children are likely to become irritable and demanding and to behave aggressively with parents, with younger siblings, and with peers.

Children in the 5- to 8-year-old group are likely to show open grieving. They are preoccupied with feelings of concern and longing for the departed parent. Many share the terrifying fantasy of replacement. "Will my daddy get a new dog, a new mommy, a new little boy?" were the comments of several boys in this age group. Little girls wove elaborate Madame Butterfly fantasies, asserting that the departed father would some day return to them, that he loved them "the best." Many of the children in this age group could not believe that the divorce would endure. About half suffered a precipitous decline in their school work.

In the 8 1/2- to 12-year-old group, the central response often seems to be intense anger at one or both parents for causing the divorce. In addition, these children suffer from grief over the loss of the intact family, from anxiety, loneliness, and the humiliating sense of their own powerlessness. Youngsters in this age group often see one parent as the "good" parent and the other as "bad," and they appear especially vulnerable to the blandishments of one or the other parent to engage in marital battles. Children in later latency also have a high potential for assuming a helpful and empathic role in the care of a needy parent. School performance and peer relationships suffer a decline in approximately one-half of these children.

Contrary to community expectations, adolescents are very vulnerable to their parents' divorce. The precipitation of acute depression, accompanied by suicidal preoccupation and acting out, is frequent enough to be alarming. Anger can be intense. . . . Preoccupied with issues of morality, adolescents may judge the parents' conduct during the marriage and the divorce, and they may identify with one parent and do battle against the other. A good number become anxious about their own future entry into adulthood, concerned that they may experience marital failure like their own parents. Researchers have also called attention to the adolescents' impressive capacity to grow to maturity and independence as they respond to the family crisis and the parents' need for help. . . .

. . . No single theme appeared among those children who enhanced or continued their good developmental progress after the divorce crisis had finally ended. . . . Instead, a set of complex configurations was found, in which the relevant components appear to include (1) the extent to which the parent has been able to resolve and put aside conflict and angers and to make use of the relief from conflict provided by the divorce; (2) the course of the custodial parent's handling of the child and the resumption or improvement of parenting within the home; (3) the extent to which the child does not feel rejected by the noncustodial or visiting parent and the extent to which this relationship has continued regularly and kept pace with the child's growth; (4) the extent to which the divorce has helped to attenuate or dilute a psychopathological parent-child relationship; (5) the range of assets and deficits which the child brought to the divorce, including both the child's history in the predivorce family and his or her capacities in the present, particularly intelligence, the capacity for fantasy, social maturity, and the ability to turn to peers and adults; (6) the availability to the child of a supportive human network; (7) the absence in the child of continued anger and depression; and (8) the sex and age of the child at the marital rupture and the remarriage. . . .

The problems that marital rupture poses to children are grave and potentially enduring. The initial responses of children and parents at the height of the crisis during the separation are serious. . . . In the long term, however, the central hazards to the psychological health of children are not the result of the divorce, per se, but rather in the diminished or disputed parenting that so often follows in the wake of marital breakdown. . . .

E. Mavis Hetherington & John Kelly, For Better or For Worse: Divorce Reconsidered
228-229 (2002)

The big headline in my data is that 80 percent of children from divorced homes eventually are able to adapt to their new life and become reasonably well adjusted. A subgroup of girls even become exceptionally competent as a result of dealing with the challenges of divorce, enjoy a normal development, and grow into truly outstanding young adults. The 20 percent who continue to bear the scars of divorce fall into a troubled group, who display impulsive, irresponsible, antisocial behavior or are depressed. At the end of the [study], troubled youths were having difficulty at work, in romantic relationships, and in gaining a toehold in adult life. They had the highest academic dropout rate and the highest divorce rate in the study, and were more likely to be faring poorly economically. In addition, being troubled and a girl made a young woman more likely to have left home early and to have experienced at least one out-of-wedlock pregnancy, birth, or abortion.

However, coming from a non-divorced family did not always protect against growing into a troubled young adult. Ten percent of youths in non-divorced families, compared to 20 percent in divorced and remarried families, were troubled. Most of our troubled young men and women came from families where conflict was frequent and authoritative parenting rare. In adulthood as was found in childhood and adolescence, those who had moved from a highly contentious intact home situation to a more harmonious divorced family situation, with a caring, competent parent, benefited from the divorce and had fewer problems. But the legacy of the stresses and inept parenting associated with divorce and remarriage, and especially with living in a complex stepfamily, are still seen in the psychological, emotional, and social problems in 20 percent of young people from these families. . . .

What about the other 80 percent of young people from divorced and remarried families? While most were not exactly the New Man or New Woman that the divorce revolution's supporters had predicted, they were behaving the way young adults were supposed to behave. They were choosing careers, developing permanent relationships, ably going about the central tasks of young adulthood, and establishing a grown-up life. They ranged from those who were remarkably well adjusted to Good Enoughs and competent-at-a-cost, who were having a few problems but coping reasonably well to very well.

Finally, it should be a reassuring finding for divorced and remarried parents, and their children, that for every young man or woman who emerged from postnuclear family life with problems, four others were functioning reasonably or exceptionally well . . .

The Wallerstein excerpt above is based on her original study, Surviving the Breakup: How Children and Parents Cope with Divorce (1980) (co-authored with Joan Kelly), which pointed out that the effects of divorce on children vary according to gender, age, and developmental stage at the time of divorce. Wallerstein's study of 60 divorced families with 131 children highlighted many negative consequences of divorce in terms of children's psychological well-being. Her follow-up research, Second Chances: Men, Women, and Children a Decade After Divorce (1989) (co-authored with Sandra Blakeslee), and The Unexpected Legacy of Divorce: A 25-Year Landmark Study) (2000) (co-authored with Julia M. Lewis and Sandra Blakeslee), illuminated the continuing long-term effects of parental divorce, especially in terms of children's relationships with their mothers and fathers, as well as their difficulty in forming and maintaining intimate, adult interpersonal relationships. In contrast, Hetherington's more optimistic findings emphasize the resiliency of the children of divorce. Her longitudinal study of 1,400 families (including divorced and intact families) concludes that the vast majority of the children of divorce become well-adjusted adults.

Social psychologist Paul Amato has attempted to reconcile the two psychologists' seemingly disparate findings. Amato confirms that several of Wallerstein's claims are consistent with the research literature, in particular: (1) children with divorced parents are more likely to experience psychological problems in adulthood than are children with continuously married parents; (2) children of divorced parents, compared with children with continuously married parents, have more problems in forming and maintaining stable intimate relationships; and (3) children of divorce reach adulthood with weaker ties to parents than do children with continuously married parents. Paul R. Amato, Reconciling Divergent Perspectives: Judith Wallerstein, Quantitative Family Research, and Children of Divorce, 52 Fam. Relations 332, 334 (2003).

Nonetheless, based on his longitudinal research of 671 children of divorce (including a control group of intact families), Amato concludes that the long-term effects of divorce are "not as pervasive or as strong as Wallerstein claims." Id. at 336. That is, whereas Wallerstein finds that over one-third of children with divorced parents become psychologically troubled adults, Amato indicates that only 10 percent of such children manifest serious psychological problems in adulthood. Id. at 337. In this regard, Amato's findings more closely approximate those of Hetherington, supra, who found that 20 percent of the children of divorced parents had psychological difficulties as adults. (Wallerstein's more negative findings may be partly attributable to the fact that her sample consisted of families referred to a counseling center by family law attorneys.)

In addition, Amato, like Wallerstein and Hetherington, recognizes that pre-divorce as well as postdivorce factors play an important role in the children's psychological well being. "Moderating factors may be present in the family prior to marital disruption, or they may exist in postdivorce family arrangements." Id. For example, one important postdivorce factor is a parent's remarriage. Amato notes that the evidence regarding parental remarriage is mixed in terms of its beneficial or harmful effects for children. However, he points out that multiple family transitions (involving multiple divorces and remarriages) are more problematic for children than the experience of a single divorce. Id. at 338.[50]

What is the day-to-day reality for children in the aftermath of divorce? How do legal labels, whether sole custody or joint legal custody, or joint physical custody, translate into contemporary reality for children of divorce? The following study in one jurisdiction of the custodial arrangements of 1,129 families with 1,884 children sheds some light on these questions.

Eleanor E. Maccoby et al., Custody of Children Following Divorce

Impact of Divorce, Single-Parenting and Step-Parenting on Children 91, 96-113 (E. Mavis Hetherington & Josephine D. Arasteh eds., 1988)

Although it is possible to document some rapid changes in the nature of the legal labels for the custodial arrangements, little is known concerning the realities that

---

[50] For additional recent discussion of the effects of divorce on children, see Robert E. Emery, The Truth About Children and Divorce: Groundbreaking Research and Advice for Dealing with the Emotions So You and Your Children Can Thrive (2004); Robert E. Emery, Marriage, Divorce, and Children's Adjustment (2d ed. 1999); Robert E. Emery, Postdivorce Family Life for Children: An Overview of Research and Some Implications for Policy, in The Postdivorce Family: Children, Parenting, and Society (Ross A. Thompson & Paul R. Amato eds., 1999); Paul R. Amato, Children of Divorce in the 1990's: An Update of the Amato & Keith Meta-Analysis, 15 J. of Fam. Psychol. 355 (2001); Paul R. Amato, The Consequences of Divorce for Adults and Children, 62 J. Marriage & Fam. 1269 (2000); Joan B. Kelly, Children's Adjustment in Conflicted Marriage and Divorce: A Decade of Research, 39 J. of Am. Acad. of Child & Adolescent Psychiatry (2000); Kim Leon, Risk and Protective Factors in Young Children's Adjustment to Parental Divorce: A Review of the Research, 52 Fam. Relations 258 (2003); Heidi R. Riggio, Parental Marital Conflict and Divorce, Parent-Child Relationships, Social Support, and Relationship Anxiety in Young Adulthood, 11 Personal Relationships 99 (2004); Ronald L. Simons et al., Explaining the Higher Incidence of Adjustment Problems Among Children of Divorce Compared with Those in Two-Parent Families, 61 J. Marriage & Fam. 1020 (1999).

underlie these legal labels. It is possible that some of the changes are more apparent than real. For example, a decree of joint legal custody with maternal physical custody may not mean that families live their lives differently than they did under the traditional pattern of maternal custody with father visitation. On the other hand, having a legitimized role — even a pro forma one — in decisions concerning the child may sustain a father's interests and prevent the "father dropout" that so commonly occurs [citations omitted].

Further questions concern interspousal conflict. In some number of cases, joint custody — physical or legal — is being settled upon by the couple despite the fact that one of the parents might have preferred an alternative arrangement. It is reasonable to suppose that there may be more conflict, at least initially, in these cases than for the couples who fully agreed on the form of custody they preferred. Some writers assume that joint custody implies more than increased father-child interaction. They present a picture of shared parenting. Furstenberg and Nord (1985) [citation omitted] challenged the assumption of co-parenting, reporting that they found evidence for "parallel parenting" at best. . . . What kind and degree of shared parenting is possible between parents who separate under conditions of high conflict (over custody or other issues)? We need to know more about the conditions under which co-parenting can actually occur, and what role is played in this by the degree of initial agreement or conflict between the divorcing couple. Do hostility and conflict drop away over time? Do they grow faster, or more slowly, if the parents remain in contact because of their mutual involvement with the child? Our study is designed to obtain information relevant to these questions. . . . The purpose of the present chapter is to provide a description of the existing de facto arrangements for physical custody, and to examine how these arrangements vary according to the age and sex of the children and the number of children in the family. The existing studies of divorce give some intriguing indications that the impact of family disruption may be different for children of different ages . . . and has highlighted the possibility that the children's welfare may in part depend on whether they are in the custody of the same-sex versus opposite-sex parent. . . .

Where the Children Were Living at Time 1

. . . We find that over a third of the children in our sample were spending no overnights with father at the time of our Time 1 interview, and 6 percent were spending no overnights with mother. We hasten to point out, however, that the absence of overnights does not imply a total lack of contact with the secondary parent. . . .

Why do most parents continue to choose maternal residence? The reasons are various. . . . Parents make assumptions concerning which of them would be the better parent, and these may be implicitly agreed upon even if never discussed. Beyond the individual skills of the parents involved, many parents of both sexes assume that mothers have a natural talent for child-rearing, especially for children of "tender years," and that fathers do not understand young children as well. Also, there are many parents who seem to assume that it is natural for fathers to give higher priority to their work than mothers will do. . . .

The practicalities of the father's situation often led to maternal custody, at least in the short run. More often than not, it was the fathers who had moved out, leaving the mothers and children in the family dwelling. The father might initially have moved in with relatives or stayed in some other temporary residence where there was no room for the children. . . .

With children of school age, both parents usually saw advantages to keeping them in their familiar school, and the father's residence was seldom close enough to make this convenient. Parents frequently spoke of the importance of maintaining as much stability as possible for the children. As long as the mother stays in the family home, this implies maternal custody. . . .

Custody of Boys and Girls

[T]here is a tilt in the direction of children residing with the same-sex parent. . . . The trend toward living with the same-sex parent is characteristic of all ages, although it is strongest for children age 11 or older. At this age, there are over twice as many boys as girls residing primarily with their fathers. Between the ages of 2 and 11, the numbers of boys and girls residing with father are very similar. . . .

Research conducted when mother custody was the norm showed an overwhelming trend toward father disengagement from the family. This was true uniformly for fathers of sons and daughters. New child-custody options offer fathers the opportunity for greater involvement without assuming sole custody. Our data show that fathers, particularly those with boys, seem to be taking advantage of this option. . . . In our research, we hear respondents expressing related themes of identification with the same-sex parent and the father's superior ability to exercise control over older boys. . . .

Residence of Children of Different Ages

Not surprisingly, [our research] shows that children under the age of 2 are more likely than any other age group to be living with their mothers. . . . Divided residence, where the child regularly spends a substantial number of overnights with each parent, is highest for the children aged 2 through 7, and drops off after that age to a very low level among teenagers. Residence with father is most common among teenagers, although as noted previously this applies to boys only. . . .

We may speculate as to what lies behind these age trends. The low incidence of overnight visits and divided residence for children under 2 reflects a number of logistical problems, such as the need for special equipment for a very young child — crib, stroller, potty chair — all of which would need to be transferred or replicated in a second household. . . .

Why are overnight stays and divided residence most frequent at age 2 through 7, and why do they decline thereafter? The logistics of having children spend time in two households appear to become more complex as children develop their own activity agendas and grow old enough to go back and forth to friends' houses without being accompanied by a parent. We suspect that with increasing age, children have more and more voice in where they will reside, and that when they do have a choice, many prefer to have a single residence for sleeping and to use as a base of operations. . . .

Residential Custody and Family Size

Whether or not children live with their mothers following divorce does not appear to depend on the number of children in the family. The kind and amount of residence with father, however, does vary according to family size. . . .

It appears that maintaining divided residential arrangements for children, where they spend a substantial number of nights in each household, is more difficult for larger families than it is with only one child. Nearly 20 percent of the "only" children have a shared residential pattern, whereas this pattern is found in only 4 percent of the children who have two or more siblings. . . .

About 25 percent of the children in the study have a great deal of contact with their father. Family size is a key determinant of the way in which that contact is affected. In smaller families, divided residence is more common. In larger ones, it is more likely that at least some children in the family will reside with their father. . . .

Summary and Conclusions

. . . Our findings reflect interesting compromises between opposing viewpoints in the joint custody debate. Parents appear to be embracing the norm that fathers should remain involved with their children after divorce. Still, they are not rejecting the idea that children, particularly very young ones, should have their major residence with their mothers. The level of father physical custody is not increasing; but joint physical custody is. Most parents elect an arrangement that assigns physical custody to the mother and legal custody to both parents.

Another key debate about joint custody centers on whether the stability of a single-home environment should be compromised in order to permit frequent contact with each parent. The families in our study seem to weigh stability versus contact differently depending on the age and gender of the child. Very young children are less often alternated between parental households. Divided residence is also less frequent among older children, who have established ties to school and friends. Considerations of parental contact versus a stable environment also seem to be weighted somewhat differently for boys and girls. Boys are more likely than girls to divide their time between two parental households. As boys grow older, however, the need for stability of a single home environment seems to be added to the need for father contact. Consequently, more adolescent boys live with their fathers.

It is important to remember that these findings are drawn from interviews taken shortly after filing for divorce. We do not know whether arrangements that involve the participation of both parents can be sustained over time. . . .

In the following excerpt, Professors Maccoby and Mnookin describe their subsequent findings regarding the participation of parents in custody over a three-year period after divorce (i.e., comparing the period shortly after the divorce petition was filed, one year later, and two years later).

Eleanor E. Maccoby & Robert H. Mnookin, Dividing the Child: Social and Legal Dilemmas of Custody
274-275 (1992)

... For a substantial majority of the families in our study, fathers as well as mothers have remained in regular contact with the children. For those families with dual residence, obviously both parents are deeply involved. For the small minority with father residence, mothers have maintained contact very well indeed. Our most significant finding is that in a majority of families where the children lived with their mother, visitation with the non-residential father was maintained over the period of our study, and the visits most commonly involved overnight stays. At Time 3, only 14% of the children living with their mothers had not seen their fathers within the past year.

The proportion of mother-resident families in which the children had overnight visits with their father remained remarkably constant over three and a half years. On the other hand, when the father had only daytime visits at Time 1, with no overnights, this arrangement proved quite unstable: it often evolved either to no regular visitation at all, or (less commonly) to overnight visitation. Because of this decline in visitation by fathers with only daytime visits, the proportion of mother-resident families having no visits with the father increased from 23 percent at Time 1 to 39 percent at Time 3. On the other hand, almost a quarter of the families who initially had no visitation had established some by Time 3. Thus, within the overall picture of declining visitation with fathers — particularly for those who only had daytime visits — there was a substantial minority of mother-resident families in which visitation was increasing over time.

What factors affect whether children living with their mother maintain contact with the father? A mother's conviction that it is good for the children to sustain their relationship with their father is strongly associated with sustaining contact. Remarriage of the mother has a slight effect; it tends to diminish the amount of time children spend with their father. A residential move of one or both parents has a more powerful effect: when the distance between the two households increases, the children, not surprisingly, see their fathers less.

It is possible, of course, that the amount of contact between children and their fathers will continue to erode, and perhaps at a faster rate, as more time passes. However, we should note that in the follow-up of adolescent children conducted a year after the present study, the large majority of the children in the sample were still seeing their fathers on a fairly regular basis, and very few had not seen him during the past year. In short, during the more than four years following the initial separation, a high proportion of the children in our study maintained "frequent and continuing contact" with both parents.

3. Limits on Private Ordering

A preliminary question is the degree to which the parents themselves should be able to decide who should have custody and to what extent. At the time of separation or dissolution, it is usually possible for parents to agree on these matters and spell out their respective rights and obligations in a separation agreement. Evidence suggests that approximately 80-90 percent of divorced parents agree,[51] although often after difficult bargaining. The traditional doctrine is, however, that when the divorce is granted the court is responsible for independently determining whether a parental agreement serves the child's best interests, and even today parental agreement is not considered binding on the court.[52] Moreover, even if the court at the time of the divorce accepts the parental agreement, the court is free at any time during the child's minority to reopen and modify its decree in light of any change in circumstances. The parties cannot bind themselves by agreement and thus deprive the court of the power to evaluate or reopen custody issues.

What justifications are there for these substantial limitations on parental power? Do they derive from the fact that the child is not normally a meaningful participant in the bargaining process? Can you imagine situations in which a parental agreement concerning custody or visitation reflects the parents' interests rather than the child's?

Do judicial scrutiny of parental agreements and the possibility of subsequent judicial reexamination really safeguard the child's interest? Available empirical evidence suggests that courts typically rubber-stamp parental agreements concerning custody or support. This is less surprising when one considers the general lack of judicial resources for a thorough or independent investigation of the family's circumstances, the vagueness of the applicable legal standards, and the limitations on a court's practical power to control parental behavior once they leave the courtroom. Most courts behave as if their function in the divorce process were private dispute settlement. By the time most divorcing parents reach the courtroom, they no longer have disputes concerning custody, visitation, and child support. Busy judges are typically quite willing to rubber-stamp any private agreement, thus conserving judicial resources for disputed cases.

Provided custody does not go to a parent who endangers the child according to appropriate neglect standards, what interest does the state have, and what function is a court serving by requiring judicial approval of a parental agreement? Is not the function in these cases simply "private dispute settlement"? If so, when there is no dispute, what need is there for judicial intervention or supervision?

4. Parental Disputes Concerning Child Custody

a. Standards for Selecting the Custodial Parent: What Should the Standard Be?

Over the years, courts have applied a variety of presumptions to determine child custody disputes. What are the advantages and disadvantages of presumptions?

---

[51] Maccoby & Mnookin, supra note [48], at 134.

[52] The Uniform Marriage and Divorce Act, 9A U.L.A. (pt. I) 159 (1998 & Supp. 2004), for example, expressly provides that the terms of a separation agreement not having to do with the children "are binding upon the court unless it finds . . . the agreement is unconscionable." There is an express exception, however, for terms "providing for the support, custody, and visitation of children." See UMDA §306(f).

(The most important standard, the best interests of the child, is explored infra, pp. 548-549.)

Traditionally, courts applied the maternal preference, also known as the "tender years" presumption. Under this doctrine, courts gave custody of children of "tender years" (generally preschoolers, but sometimes older children as well) to the mother. Although the United States Supreme Court has never addressed the constitutionality of the doctrine, several state courts in the 1970s and 1980s found that a maternal preference violates equal protection. See, e.g., Ex Parte Devine, 398 So. 2d 686 (Ala. 1981); Watts v. Watts, 350 N.Y.S.2d 285 (Fam. Ct. 1973); Pusey v. Pusey, 728 P.2d 117 (Utah 1986). However, some courts continue to consider it as a relevant factor in custody decision making. See, e.g., Daniel v. Daniel, 770 So. 2d 562 (Miss. App. 2000); Rosero v. Blake, 581 S.E.2d 41 (N.C. 2003); Donnelly v. Donnelly, 92 P.3d 298 (Wyo. 2004). See also Jeff Atkinson, The Current State of Best Interests, 26 Family Advocate 18, 18 (2004) (explaining that a few states apply a weak version of the "tender years" presumption). Note that the American Law Institute (ALI) Principles of the Law of Family Dissolution prohibits a court from considering the gender of either the parent or the child in determining custody arrangements. ALI Principles §2.12(1)(b) (2002).

The "primary caretaker" presumption, which replaced the maternal preference, favors granting custody to the parent who is able to establish that she or he is the child's primary caretaker. West Virginia was the first state to adopt the presumption in Garska v. McCoy, 278 S.E.2d 357, 363 (W. Va. 1981). Primary caretaker status was determined by the performance of such duties as preparation and planning of meals; bathing, grooming, and dressing the children; purchasing, cleaning, and caring for the clothes; medical care; arranging for children's social interactions with peers; arranging alternative care; putting the child to bed at night; discipline; religious, cultural, or social education; and teaching elementary skills. Id. at 363. Minnesota soon followed by adopting the presumption in Pikula v. Pikula, 374 N.W.2d 705 (Minn. 1985), but abrogated it subsequently.

The primary caretaker doctrine generated considerable criticism. Advocates argued that the doctrine was preferable to the maternal preference because it was gender-neutral, encouraged less litigation, and was predictable. Opponents argued that the preference was simply a "tender years" presumption in disguise because the mother is the parent who usually performs caretaking duties and also because it put too much weight on traditional gender roles in society. For discussion of these criticisms, see David L. Chambers, Rethinking the Substantive Rules for Custody Disputes in Divorce, 83 Mich. L. Rev. 477, 527-528 (1984); Martha L. Fineman & Anne Opie, The Uses of Social Science Data in Legal Policy Making: Custody Determinations and Divorce, 1987 Wis. L. Rev. 107; Paul L. Smith, Notes, The Primary Caretaker Presumption: Have We Been Presuming Too Much?, 75 Ind. L.J. 731, 732-733 (2000).

Although only West Virginia and Minnesota adhered to the presumption, many states considered primary caretaker status as a relevant factor in custody decision making. However, criticisms of the doctrine led to abrogation of primary caretaker status as a presumption (although some states continue to consider it as a relevant factor). Minnesota abolished the presumption in 1989 as the sole determinant of custody, replacing it with a hybrid standard in which the status of the child's primary caretaker is one of numerous factors. Minn. Stat. Ann. §518.17 (West 1990 & Supp. 1999). West Virginia also abrogated the presumption and replaced it with the ALI "approximation" standard (explained infra). W. Va. Code Ann. §48-9-206(a) (Michie 2002).

The ALI standard creates a presumption that "custodial responsibility" after divorce should be allocated to approximate the parents' caretaking roles in the intact family. ALI Principles §2.08(1). The standard recognizes the variations in parental roles — i.e., that parents' roles and responsibilities often diverge from the primary caretaker model. The ALI standard replaces the traditional physical custody terms of "custody" and "visitation" with the term "custodial responsibility" (to differentiate it from the term "decision making responsibility" for legal custody), in part to abolish the stigma often associated with the noncustodial "visitor" parent. The approximation standard, also known as the "past caretaking standard," may be rebutted by specific factors, such as a prior parental agreement, the child's preference, the need to keep siblings together, harm to the child's welfare (based on emotional attachment to a parent and the parent's ability/availability to meet the child's needs), avoidance of custodial arrangements that would be impractical or interfere with the child's need for stability, and the need to deal with parental relocation (§2.08(1)(a) to (g)). See generally Katharine T. Bartlett, U.S. Custody Laws and Trends in the Context of ALI Principles of the Law of Family Dissolution, 10 Va. J. Soc. Pol'y & L. 16 (2002) (discussion of standard); Elizabeth Scott, Pluralism, Parental Preference, and Child Custody, 80 Cal. L. Rev. 615 (1992) (first proposing approximation standard).

The ALI Principles favor private ordering in custody decision making. According to the Principles, courts should base custody awards on the arrangements to which the parties once agreed (i.e., the approximation standard) in cases in which divorcing parents are unable to agree on a custodial allocation. Moreover, the ALI requires those parents who are able to reach agreement about custody to submit a "parenting plan." This ALI provision mirrors statutory developments in a number of jurisdictions that require parents who seek custody to file a written agreement in which they specify caretaking and decision making authority for their children as well as the manner in which future disputes are to be resolved. According to the Principles, the court should enforce such agreements unless an agreement is not voluntary or would be harmful to the child (§§2.06(1)(a) 2.06(1)(b)).

Finally, some states provide that evidence of domestic violence creates a rebuttable presumption against awards of custody (often including joint custody) to the abusive parent. Other states include such evidence as a factor in the best interests standard. Amy B. Levin, Comment, Child Witnesses of Domestic Violence: How Should Judges Apply the Best Interests of the Child Standard in Custody and Visitation Cases Involving Domestic Violence? 47 UCLA L. Rev. 813, 827 & nn. 31-37 (2000) (state survey). The ALI also addresses the role of domestic violence in custody, providing that batterers may not receive custodial responsibility unless the court orders appropriate measures to ensure protection of the child and the other parent (e.g., by mandating counseling) (§2.11(2)(I)). For further discussion of this presumption, see infra p. 566.

NOTE ON SEPARATING SIBLINGS

Gender issues may also arise in terms of separation of siblings. When more than one child is involved in a custody dispute, some courts separate the siblings — awarding custody of girls to mothers and boys to fathers. Courts may justify such "split" or "divided" custody awards on the rationale that such arrangements allow the child to develop feelings of sexuality. However, the majority of states have a presumption against separating siblings in the event of divorce absent exceptional or compelling circumstances. To meet this standard, courts consider the siblings' proximity in age, relationships between the siblings, and their involvement in similar activities or experiences. See generally Ellen Marrus, "Where Have You Been, Fran?" The Right of Siblings to Seek Court Access to Override Parental Denial of Visitation, 66 Tenn. L. Rev. 977 (1999); Dana E. Prescott, Biological Altruism, Splitting Siblings and the Judicial Process: A Child's Right to Constitutional Protection in Family Dislocation, 71 UMKC L. Rev. 623 (2003).

(1) Best Interests of the Child

The primary consideration in determinations of child custody is the best interests of the child. Judges typically have broad discretion in custody decision making. The best interest standard has been uniformly adopted either by state statutes, which include expanded lists of relevant factors, or by statutes giving courts a general directive. Although state laws vary, certain factors are commonly considered to be relevant in determining the best interests of the child. The following materials first present the historical background on the development of this standard, and next explore several relevant factors.

Robert H. Mnookin, Child-Custody Adjudication: Judicial Functions in the Face of Indeterminacy
39 Law & Contemp. Probs. 226, 235-237 (1975)

The history of the legal standards governing custody disputes between a child's parents reveals a dramatic movement from rules to a highly discretionary principle gradually shorn of narrowing procedural devices. In the early nineteenth century, adjudication of a custody dispute between a husband and wife was controlled by a simple rule: the father, in Lord Ellenborough's words, was "the person entitled by law to the custody of his child."[32] Deciding any custody dispute under these standards required a single factual determination: whether one of the claimants was the biological father of the child who was born while that claimant was married to the child's mother.[33]

---

[32] King v. DeManneville, 102 Eng. Rep. 1054, 1055 (K.B. 1804).

[33] The force of these rules is illustrated by an early habeas corpus case where a mother's custody claims against an estranged husband were denied even though the child was young, the separation had been forced by the father's ill-treatment of the mother, and there were uncontested allegations of continuing misconduct by the father. King v. DeManneville, 102 Eng. Rep. 1054 (K.B. 1804). Similarly, neither a husband's "cruelty" and "brutality" to his wife nor his cohabitation with another woman after desertion would justify a court of law giving custody to his wife even though he was at

An absolute rule of paternal preference does not appear to have been generally applied in nineteenth-century America, and in many jurisdictions courts were authorized to award custody to either parent as part of a divorce proceeding.[34] While some statutes expressed a preference for the father, it appears a rule based on fault emerged: "The children will be best taken care of and instructed by the innocent party."[35] This standard was not as open-ended as first appears because divorce in the nineteenth century required a showing of fault on the part of a spouse. Particularly given the social convention that the wife filed for divorce, courts no doubt awarded custody to the mother more frequently than to the father.

Gradually, in the twentieth century, courts came to acknowledge formally what had perhaps long been the reality. The statutory language, by now putting the wife on an equal footing with the husband, came to be interpreted as giving a substantial preference to the mother, particularly if the children were young. In the words of a New York appellate court, "the child at tender age is entitled to have such care, love, and discipline as only a good and devoted mother can usually give."[39] This maternal-preference rule was achieved in various ways: sometimes by statute, often by a judicially constructed rule that it was in the best interests of the child "of tender years" for the mother — unless shown to be unfit — to have custody.

At the present time, maternal-preference standards are being displaced by a formal insistence on a neutral application of the best-interests standard. . . .

Divorce custody standards now show the overwhelming dominance of the best-interests principle. A majority of the states provide by statute for a best-interests-of-the-child standard. Other states have no statutory standard but have relied on their courts to develop a best-interests standard. Most of the remaining states have broad and vague statutory standards — calling for determination by such principles as "right and proper," "expedient," or "just and reasonable" — that have been judicially construed as involving the best-interests inquiry. . . .

---

the time apparently in jail, where the child was brought to him every day. Ex parte Skinner, 27 Rev. R. 710, 713 (C.P. 1824). See also King v. Greenhill, 111 Eng. Rep. 922 (K.B. 1836).

Early English custody cases suggest that the settlement of such private disputes over custody was kept separate from the child-protection function. The courts of equity and the Chancellor — but not the law courts — were seen as having the power to control an abusive father's legal right to custody or, in an appropriate case, appoint someone else as guardian, if that were necessary to protect the child. See Shelley v. Westbrooke, 37 Eng. Rep. 850 (Ch. 1817). The Chancellor could also enjoin the husband's removal of the child from the Kingdom. See DeManneville v. DeManneville, 32 Eng. Rep. 762 (Ch. 1804). But no discretionary power appears to have existed in courts of law to adjudicate a custody dispute in favor of a wife as against her husband.

[34] . . . Many early cases demonstrate that the mother as well as the father could claim custody [citations omitted]. In 1839, the English Parliament modified the absolute rule of paternal preference for legitimate children by passing the so-called Talfourd's Act, which gave a mother the right to custody of infants under the age of seven years. An Act to Amend the Law Relating to the Custody of Infants, 2 & 3 Vict., c. 54 (1839); and later for infants of any age. An Act to Amend the Law as to the Custody of Infants, 36 & 37 Vict., c. 12 (1873).

[35] [J. Bishop, Commentaries on the Law of Marriage and Divorce 520 (1852).]

[39] Ullman v. Ullman, 151 App. Div. 419, 424-425, 135 N.Y.S. 1080, 1083 (1912).

(a) Fitness

Hollon v. Hollon
784 So. 2d 943 (Miss. 2001)

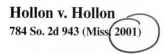

DIAZ, Justice, for the Court:

This matter arises from a divorce action decided by the Chancery Court of Jackson County, wherein Timothy Paul Hollon (Tim) and Dorothy Elisabeth Hollon (Beth) were granted a divorce on the grounds of irreconcilable differences. . . . Beth appeals the chancellor's decision to award custody of their son to Tim. . . .

Tim and Beth were married on April 9, 1994, in Jackson County, Mississippi. During the course of the marriage, Zachary Thomas Hollon was born on July, 16, 1996. . . . The family resided in Bonaparte Square Apartment complex in Pascagoula, where Beth served as the on-site manager. The apartment complex owners provided Beth and Tim with a rent-free apartment as part of her compensation package. Tim served the City of Moss Point as a police officer.

Soon after Zach's birth, Tim and Beth's marriage began to deteriorate. They separated in January of 1997, for approximately eight weeks. After reconciling, their marriage again drifted into troubled waters leading to a second separation on January 11, 1998. Tim moved out of the marital apartment and into his parents' home, leaving Zach and Tyler [a son from Beth's previous marriage] in Beth's care. In an effort to alleviate the financial strain placed upon her during her separation, Beth took in a roommate, Beth Dukes (Dukes). Prior to this arrangement, Bonaparte Square Apartment complex also provided Dukes, an officer with the Pascagoula Police department, with a rent-free apartment in exchange for her service as a "courtesy officer." . . .

As roommates, Beth and Dukes split expenses, such as utilities and groceries. In addition, they each served as a baby sitter for the children when one was otherwise occupied. At the time, five people inhabited Beth's three-bedroom apartment; Beth and her two children, Tyler and Zach, as well as Dukes and her son Seth. Tyler, a teenager, was given his own bedroom, while Seth and Zach shared a bedroom as they were both under the age of five. Beth and Dukes shared the third bedroom.

At trial, Beth freely admitted that she and Dukes slept in the same bed. However, she vehemently denied any sexual relationship existed between her and Dukes, continually characterizing their relationship as platonic. Donna Mauldin, a friend of Beth's, testified that Beth told her that she and Dukes were engaged in a sexual relationship. Mauldin further testified that Beth wanted her to deny, if asked, that she ever admitted having a sexual relationship with Dukes. . . .

Tim heard the surfacing allegations surrounding Beth and Dukes' relationship. In order to investigate, Tim borrowed a key to the apartment, his former marital residence, from Donna Mauldin. While Beth and Dukes were away, Tim and Calvin Hutchins entered the apartment without permission and made a photographic record of things Tim felt were "inappropriate." These photographs and rumors led him to become concerned with "the environment that [Zach] would be raised in." Among other things, Tim took photographs of Dukes' clothing and police equipment in the shared bedroom, beer bottles in the refrigerator and wastebasket, liquor bottles on the counter, and one red light bulb in a ceiling fixture. These photographs were admitted into evidence over Beth's objection. . . .

Tim lives with his parents in their four-bedroom house and pays them fifty dollars a month in rent. During the trial, Beth moved out of the apartment complex with her two children and into her parents' five-bedroom house. She initiated this move during the break in the trial because she felt the judge disapproved of her living situation. Beth's plan to reside with her parents is temporary. She and Tyler will move into a newly remodeled three-bedroom house provided, in part, by her new job as the rental property manager for R.J. Homes. Beth no longer lives with Dukes and her son, although they remain friends. . . .

The polestar consideration in child custody cases is the best interest and welfare of the child. [F]actors used to determine what is, in fact, in the "best interests" of a child in regard to custody are as follows: 1) age, health and sex of the child; 2) determination of the parent that had the continuity of care prior to the separation; 3) which has the best parenting skills and which has the willingness and capacity to provide primary child care; 4) the employment of the parent and responsibilities of that employment; 5) physical and mental health and age of the parents; 6) emotional ties of parent and child; 7) moral fitness of parents; 8) the home, school and community record of the child; 9) the preference of the child at the age sufficient to express a preference by law; 10) stability of home environment and employment of each parent; and 11) other factors relevant to the parent-child relationship. [Albright v. Albright, 437 So. 2d 1003, 1005 (Miss. 1983).] It should further be noted that marital fault should not be used as a sanction in custody awards, nor should differences in religion, personal values and lifestyles be the sole basis for custody decisions. Id. at 1005.

[W]e review the evidence and testimony presented at trial under each factor [to determine if the] ruling was supported by the record.

1) The age, health and sex of the child

Although this Court has weakened the "tender years" doctrine in recent years, there is still a presumption that a mother is generally better suited to raise a young child [citations omitted]. [T]he child was barely three years old at the time the trial ended. . . . The chancellor did not explicitly say that this factor favored one party over another. This factor favors Beth because the legal presumption, although weakened, still favors the mother to raise a very small child.

2) The determination of which parent had continuous care of the child prior to the separation

Chancellor Watts was mindful of the fact that since the parties separated, the mother retained primary care of the child, with the father retaining visitation privileges. The chancellor failed to note that Tim did not have custody of Zach during the previous separation, nor express any interest in becoming the custodial parent until the allegations of homosexuality arose. The chancellor did not point out that Tim rarely exercised his visitation rights, nor did he make a specific finding that this favored one parent over the other. Clearly, this factor weighs in favor of Beth.

3) The determination of which parent has the best parenting skills as well as the willingness and capacity to provide primary child care

. . . Prior to the separation, Beth testified that she had the primary responsibility of caring for her two children. She estimated that she provided approximately ninety percent of the direct care for Zach, such as changing, feeding, and supervising him, as well as doing laundry and other housework. Beth shared cooking duties with Tim. Tim testified that he helped change and feed Zach, but qualified his testimony adding that he provided said care in the evenings or on his days off. Tim's work schedule prohibits consistent, in depth care of the child.

The chancellor found that neither parent held an advantage over the other here. From the entirety of the record, it is clear that Beth provided primary child care and if from familiarity or practice alone, holds an advantage over Tim in this area.

4) The employment of the parent and responsibilities of that employment

In his analysis of this factor, the chancellor gave a detailed recitation of the employment circumstances of both Beth and Tim. Although he did not cite a preference for either parent in the record, it is obvious that Beth's working situation is far more conducive to caring for a young child. Tim serves the public as a police officer and thus logs eighty-four hours on duty during his two-week shift. The schedule follows a two days on, two days off, three days on, two days off, two days on, three days off pattern with Tim on duty twelve hours each working day, rotating from a day shift to a night shift every twenty-eight days.

Beth works approximately thirty-five hours a week as a rental property manager in an office environment. Her position requires her to work only during the day, never on weekends and never during the holidays. This is in stark contrast to the regimented schedule that Tim must adhere to, regardless of weekends, holidays, or the hour of the day. . . . Beth also has the option of taking Zach to work with her if she chooses. Without question, this factor weighs heavily in Beth's favor.

5) The physical and mental health and age of the parents

Chancellor Watts noted that, at the time of trial, Beth was 36, Tim was 38, and both were in good physical and mental health. Although not specifically stated by the trial judge, this factor balances equally between Beth and Tim.

6) The emotional ties of parent and child

[T]he trial court held that no testimony was presented that showed Zach exhibited a stronger attachment to one parent over the other. Despite this finding, the trial court noted that Zach has been in Beth's continual care throughout both separations and subsequent divorce proceedings. The trial court implied that this factor also balanced equally between Tim and Beth, again never specifying for the record who, if anyone, benefitted from this factor.

7) The moral fitness of the parents

The seventh factor, moral fitness, took the lion's share of the chancellor's attention and is essentially what Beth argues dealt the fatal blow to her attempt to retain custody of Zach. Chancellor Watts noted that neither parent attended church regularly, which was "disturbing to the Court to some degree." The chancellor further stated Beth having a red light bulb in a fixture is "somewhat unusual, but not determinative of the issues herein." It is impossible to understand why the color of a light bulb is mentioned under this heading.

The chancellor then dove into the allegations of the homosexual affair. Chancellor Watts found Beth's testimony regarding this issue to be untrustworthy. In fact, because Beth's testimony denying her relationship with Dukes directly contradicted Donna Mauldin's testimony confirming it, he asked the District Attorney's office to consider conducting an investigation into whether or not Beth committed perjury by denying she had a homosexual relationship with Dukes. The chancellor further noted that he ought to have confidence that the custodial parent is a truthful, forthright person, and he stated that he lacked that confidence in Beth. Accordingly, he found that this factor weighed heavily in Tim's favor.

Chancellor Watts also noted that evidence of a homosexual relationship is not, per se, a basis to determine that child custody should be denied. He then went on to rehash, in detail, all of the testimony regarding Beth's alleged sexual relationship with Dukes. This Court has held that:

> In divorce actions, as distinguished from proceedings for modification of custody, sexual misconduct on the part of the wife is not per se grounds for denial of custody. A husband may upon proof of his wife's adultery be granted an absolute divorce on that grounds and yet in the same case custody of the children may be awarded to the mother. Our cases well recognize that it may be in the best interest of a child to remain with its mother even though she may have been guilty of adultery. Cheek v. Ricker, 431 So. 2d 1139, 1144-45 n. 3 (Miss. 1983). . . .

This view of custody arrangements is comparable to that employed in other states in similar fact situations.

The trial court never found the mother unfit to care for Zach, and no evidence was presented regarding any detrimental effects the child may have suffered as a result of living with his mother. The chancellor failed to mention that Tim admitted drinking a couple of beers every other day, that he drank to the point of being under the influence in the past, and formerly gambled every other week, but had not gambled recently because he did not have the money to do so. Beth also admitting to drinking to the point of intoxication in the past, but admitted that she gambled only once every six months.

While this factor is as important as any other and should be given its due consideration, it appears that the allegations offered under this heading were far and away the most scrutinized among the evidence reviewed at trial.

[The chancellor noted that no evidence had been presented with regard to the two factors of "the home, school and community record of the child" and "the preference of the child at an age sufficient to express a preference by law," and therefore did not weigh against either parent.]

10) The stability of home environment and employment of each parent

The chancellor found, after considering the stability of the home environment and employment of each parent, that this factor favored Tim. This reasoning is inexplicable. Beth's current employment situation, discussed above, is clearly more favorable to child-rearing than Tim's schedule.

By the time the second day of the trial arrived, both Tim and Beth lived with their parents, although Beth stated her intention to move into a house of her own. The trial court seemed to hold this relocation and change in employment against her, although a less than subtle warning offered by the chancellor was the sole reason that Beth initiated the change in living situations.

. . . . After considering all of the evidence and weighing the enumerated factors, the trial judge found that it would be in the best interest of the child to be relocated to Tim's care. A cursory glance at the above analysis reveals that the evidence supports a finding that more factors weigh in favor of Beth than Tim. . . .

Tim testified that his only concern with leaving Zach in Beth's permanent custody was the "homosexual environment" in which Zach would be raised. Tim felt that she was qualified in every other way to raise the child. Tim specifically testified that "[i]t's wrong, it's — and I don't care what society says. It's morally wrong. It totally goes against the laws of God. It is wrong, period. I want my son to grow up a healthy, happy, young man." Despite this admonition, he testified that Beth was a good mother. It is clear from the record that the chancellor's defining consideration in determining custody of Zach centered on the allegations of Beth's homosexual affair. In doing so, the chancellor committed reversible error. . . .

Within his analysis of the [best interest] factors, the chancellor abused his discretion by placing too much weight upon the "moral fitness" factor and ignoring the voluminous evidence presented under the remaining factors supporting Beth as the preferred custodial parent. Therefore, we reverse the decision of the Chancery Court of Jackson County and award Beth custody of Zach and remand the case for a determination of Tim's visitation rights. . . .

NOTES AND QUESTIONS

(1) Different Views.   Prior to the 1970s few gay and lesbian parents were successful in custody cases.[53] Currently, courts treat the issue of sexual orientation in custody decision making in several different ways: (a) some courts view homosexuality as evidence of parental unfitness per se; (b) other courts employ a "nexus test," which requires proof that the parent's sexual orientation has an adverse impact on the child; and (c) some courts presume adverse impact and require that the gay or lesbian parent has the burden of proof of the absence of adverse impact. The second view, followed by most courts, is also the view supported by most commentators.[54]

[53] Rhonda R. Rivera, Queer Law: Sexual Orientation Law in the Mid-Eighties, 11 U. Dayton L. Rev. 275, 335 (1986). Exact data on the number of gay and lesbian parents are unknown; however, the 2000 Census found that more than 150,000 same-sex couples have at least one child under age 18 in the home. Dirk Johnson & Adam Piore, Home in Two Worlds, Newsweek, Oct. 10, 2004, at 53. The Census data undoubtedly are low because of under-reporting.

[54] See 2 Child Custody and Visitation: Law and Practice §10.12[2], at 10-216 (Sandra Morgan Little ed., 1999) [hereinafter Little]. This is also the view of the Uniform Marriage and Divorce Act §402.

(2) Showing of Adverse Impact.   Under the majority view, sexual orientation is an issue only insofar as the parent's sexual orientation can be proven to have harmed the child. However, courts differ as to the amount and type of harm required for a showing of adverse impact. For example, is teasing by peers sufficient harm? Compare Jacoby v. Jacoby, 763 So. 2d 410 (Fla. Dist. Ct. App. 2000) (negative thoughts by peers of children not enough to deny or change custody) with Bottoms v. Bottoms, 457 S.E.2d 102 (Va. 1995) (determining that social condemnation is a factor when making a custody determination). Is actual harm required, or is potential future harm sufficient? See, e.g., Boswell v. Boswell, 721 A.2d 662 (Md. 1998). What role do judges' values play in custody disputes involving a gay or lesbian parent?

(3) Negative Effects?   What are the possible negative effects on a child from having a gay or lesbian parent? Common beliefs include (a) the concern that children raised in homes with gay or lesbian parents are more likely to become homosexual; (b) the fear that a gay or lesbian parent is more likely than a heterosexual parent to molest the children; and (c) children of gay and lesbian parents suffer stigma from peers and the community.[55]

Do the foregoing assumptions have any empirical basis? Studies of children of gay and lesbian parents conclude that sexual orientation of the parent is not an important factor in sex role development.[56] The other two issues have not been researched as extensively. However, evidence suggests that child molestation is generally heterosexual in nature.[57] Furthermore, peer pressure may not be as significant a problem as many courts believe.[58] For a controversial debate on the effect of parenting by gays and lesbians, see Lynn D. Wardle, The Potential Impact of Homosexual Parenting on Children, 1997 U. Ill. L. Rev. 833 (1997) (encouraging legislatures to enact statutes with a rebuttable presumption that homosexual parenting is not in children's best interests); Carlos A. Ball & Janice Farrell Pea, Warring with Wardle: Morality, Social Science, and Gay and Lesbian Parents, 1998 U. Ill. L. Rev. 253 (1998) (rebuttal challenging the constitutionality of such a presumption).

(4) Effect of Openness.   In custody decisions involving gay parents, what other factors should be relevant in the determination of the best interests of the child? Should it matter whether the parent is discreet about his or her sexual

---

[55] David Cramer, Gay Parents and Their Children: A Review of Research and Practical Implications, 64 J. Counseling & Dev. 504, 504-505 (1986).

[56] Charlotte J. Patterson & Anthony R. D'Augelli, Lesbian, Gay, and Bisexual Identities and Youth: Psychological Perspectives (2001); Jennifer L. Wainright et al., Psychosocial Adjustment, School Outcomes, and Romantic Relationships of Adolescents with Same-Sex Parents, 75 Child Development 1886 (Dec. 2004); Fiona L. Tasker & Susan Golombok, Growing Up in a Lesbian Family: Effects on Child Development (1998). See also Eileen P. Huff, The Children of Homosexual Parents: The Voices the Courts Have Yet to Hear, 9 Am. U. J. Gender Soc. Pol'y & Law 695 (2001).

[57] Marny Hall, Lesbian Families: Cultural and Clinical Issues, 23 Soc. Work 380 (1978); Carole Jenny et al., Are Children at Risk for Sexual Abuse by Homosexuals?, 94 Pediatrics 41, 44 (1994).

[58] See, e.g., Richard Green, Sexual Identity of 37 Children Raised by Homosexual or Transsexual Parents, 135 Am. J. Psychiatry 692, 695 (1978) (only 3 out of 21 children recalled being teased by peers because of their mother's homosexuality).

relationship(s)? See, e.g., Ex parte J.M.F., 730 So. 2d 1190 (Ala. 1998) (granting change of custody to father when lesbian mother ceased to maintain discreet relationship). Is it clear that a parent's admission of homosexuality to a child is more harmful than secrecy?[59] Whether the parent places the sexual relationship above the children's interests? See, e.g., Charpentier v. Charpentier, 536 A.2d 948 (Conn. 1988) (father awarded custody because lesbian mother neglected children because of partner). How the partner treats the children? See, e.g., Sims v. Sims, 253 S.E.2d 763 (Ga. 1979) (cohabiting partner of lesbian mother physically abused children). Should it matter whether the dispute is between parents or whether the state or a third party is seeking custody? See White v. Thompson, 569 So. 2d 1181 (Miss. 1990) (awarding custody of children of lesbian mother to paternal grandparents based on mother's sexual orientation). Should it matter whether the parent exposes the child to the gay lifestyle? See Marlow v. Marlow, 702 N.E.2d 733 (Ind. Ct. App. 1998) (finding award of paternal custody was not in child's best interests because of father's exposure of child to gay lifestyle).

   (5) Risk of Loss of Custody or Visitation.   Gay and lesbian parents face the possibility of losing custody not only in initial awards but also in child custody modifications and juvenile court neglect determinations. See, e.g., In re E.C. and S.C. Children, 2004 WL 2903808 (Ga. Ct. App. 2004) (reversing a juvenile court finding of neglect that resulted in transfer of custody of children of lesbian mother); L.A.M. v. B.M., — So.2d —, 2004 WL 2829052 (Ala. Civ. App. 2004) (holding that evidence was sufficient to warrant change of custody to father when mother was engaged in homosexual affair).

   Further, gay and lesbian parents face restrictions on, or loss of, their visitation rights. Such restrictions frequently take the form of prohibitions on gay and lesbian parents from associating with a same-sex partner in the presence of the child. See, e.g., Davis v. Davis, 2004 WL 2806433 (Ohio Ct. App. 2004) (affirming trial court order prohibiting lesbian mother from having her "female paramour" present during her parenting time). Do such judicial decisions implicate the "child protection" and/or "private dispute resolution" strand of custody law? For additional discussion of conditions on visitation, see infra, pp. 590-595. For additional discussion of second-parent custody and visitation rights, see infra, pp. 601-603.

   (6) Influence of Lawrence v. Texas.   The United States Supreme Court held in Lawrence v. Texas, 539 U.S. 558 (2003), that state sodomy laws (which banned homosexual, but not heterosexual, sodomy) violated the individual's constitutional rights to due process and privacy. In holding that the individual had a constitutionally protected right of intimate association, the Court concluded that moral disapproval

----

[59] Courts often emphasize the harm to a child stemming from a parent's openness about his or her homosexuality. Paradoxically, researchers conclude that a parent's openness may have a positive influence on parent-child relationships. See Frederick W. Bozett, Gay Fathers: How and Why They Disclose Their Homosexuality to Their Children, 29 Fam. Relations 173, 175-176 (1980) (such gay fathers serve as role models for tolerance of others); Dorothy I. Riddle, Relating to Children: Gays as Role Models, 34 J. Soc. Issues 38, 52-53 (No. 3) (1978) (such parents help set framework for more honest, open, and intimate relationship with their children).

is not a sufficiently legitimate state interest to justify such differential treatment under the Equal Protection Clause.

What is the likely impact of *Lawrence* on custody determinations? See Erisa Gesing, Note, The Fight to Be a Parent: How Courts Have Restricted the Constitutionally-Based Challenges Available to Homosexuals, 38 New Eng. L. Rev. 841 (2004); Matt Larsen, Note, Lawrence v. Texas and Family Law: Gay Parent's Constitutional Rights in Child Custody Proceedings, 60 N.Y.U. Annual Survey Am. L. 53 (2004); Jennifer Naeger, Note, And Then There Were None, The Repeal of Sodomy Laws After Lawrence v. Texas and Its Effect on the Custody and Visitation Rights of Gay and Lesbian Parents, 78 St. John's L. Rev. 397 (2004).

ALI Principles. The ALI Principles of the Law of Family Dissolution prohibit a court from considering either the sexual orientation or the extramarital sexual conduct of a parent except upon a showing that such conduct causes harm to the child. ALI Principles §2.12(1)(d) (sexual orientation); §2.12(1)(e) (extramarital sexual conduct) (2002).

(7) Recent Developments. The advent of same-sex marriage in Massachusetts (following Goodridge v. Department of Pub. Health, 798 N.E.2d 941 (Mass. 2003)), and statutorily created domestic partnerships in some jurisdictions (e.g., California, New Jersey, Hawaii, and Vermont) focuses renewed attention on the role of sexual orientation in custody decision making. These states provide varying degrees of benefits for nonbiological parents. Should domestic partners have the same rights in child custody decisions as marital parties? The California Supreme Court recently granted review in three cases to determine the extent of the custody and visitation rights of the members of same-sex couples. See K.M. v. E.G., 13 Cal. Rptr. 3d 136 (Ct. App.), *review granted*, 97 P.3d 72 (Cal. 2004); Kristine H. v. Lisa R., 16 Cal. Rptr. 3d 123 (Ct. App.), *review granted*, 97 P.3d 72 (Cal. 2004). Elisa B. v. Emily B., 13 Cal. Rptr. 3d 494 (Ct. App.), *review granted*, 97 P.3d 72 (Cal. 2004). See generally William S. Friedlander, Do Mom and Mom and Baby Make a Family?, 40 Trial 36 (Dec. 2004); Margaret S. Osborne, Note, Legalizing Families: Solutions to Adjudicate Parentage for Lesbian Co-Parents, 49 Vill. L. Rev. 363 (2004). See also the discussion of visitation disputes involving same-sex couples, infra pp. 601-603.

(b) Wealth

In re Custody of Tara Marie Pearce
456 A.2d 597 (Pa. Super. Ct. 1983)

Rowley, Judge:

This is an appeal from an order granting custody of the parties' minor child, Tara Marie, to appellee Ernest Pearce.

The parties were married February 29, 1973 and Tara was born August 6, 1977. . . . Tara's parents were divorced on October 25, 1977. . . . Tara resided with her mother, the appellant, from the date of her birth until January of 1981.

On January 15, 1981, appellant entered a hospital for an operation. She arranged for her three children, Michael Knecht, age 11, Shane Wolford, age 8, and Tara to be cared for by her (appellant's) mother and sister. Complications slowed appellant's recovery following the operation and she was unable to care for her children for approximately four weeks. During this period Tara's father, the appellee, offered to care for Tara until appellant's health was improved. Appellant agreed. However, appellee refused to return Tara to appellant when requested to do so.

On February 23, 1981, appellant filed a Petition for a Writ of Habeas Corpus. That same day, the trial court entered an order directing that Tara be returned to appellant. On March 9, 1981, the court entered an order confirming primary custody of Tara in appellant, Judith Pearce, pending a full hearing on her petition for custody. Several hearings were held. . . . A final order, dated June 14, 1982, was entered granting custody of Tara to appellee Ernest Pearce. This appeal followed.

The primary consideration in a custody dispute is the best interest of the child. Therefore, the issue before us is whether the court erred in concluding that placing Tara in appellee's custody would be in Tara's best interest. . . .

In this case, the trial court based its decision granting custody to appellee on three factors: 1) the court concluded that appellee is able to provide better housing facilities for Tara than is appellant; 2) the court found that appellant exhibited unstable behavior characterized by religious delusions; and 3) the court decided that appellant failed to provide adequate supervision for Tara.

We have concluded that these conclusions of the hearing judge are not supported by the record.

The record reveals the following uncontradicted facts. Appellant is thirty-two years old. While pregnant with Tara, she was laid off from her job at Woolrich Woolen Mills and has not worked since. Appellant and her three children live in a three bedroom apartment in Lock Haven Gardens. Tara has her own bedroom and sleeps in a single twin bed. Appellant's income consists of $369.00 a month from Public Assistance. In addition, she has a medical card for the family and receives $157.00 a month in food stamps. Appellant is able to adequately feed, clothe and house her family, including Tara, on her present income.

Appellee is twenty-seven years old and was remarried in June of 1980. Both he and his twenty year old wife are employed at Woolrich Woolen Mills. Appellee has a net income of approximately $135.00 per week. His wife's net income is $115.00 per week. They live in a newly built home on approximately one acre of land. Tara has her own bedroom and a double bed when in appellee's custody. When at appellee's, Tara is cared for at the home of a baby-sitter during the day while appellee and his wife are at work.

The relative wealth of the parties is not a decisive factor in determining custody unless it appears that one parent is unable to provide adequately for the child. In this case, it is undisputed that appellant has been adequately providing for Tara's needs. The home evaluations performed by Clinton County Children and Youth Services concluded that both homes were suitable for a child to grow up in. Therefore, the fact that appellee could provide "somewhat better" living facilities should have been given very little, if any, weight.

The court's finding of mental instability[2] and religious delusions on the part of appellant is unsupported by the record. It is true that appellant's family and friends were concerned about her behavior in late January and early February of 1981 and urged her to seek mental health counseling. The trial court placed great emphasis on one particular incident that occurred in late January of that year. Appellant and a girlfriend entered a bar during the afternoon and ordered cokes. According to witnesses, they were "talking about God" and reportedly left a $15.00 tip.

All of the claimed incidents of "unstable" behavior occurred during the time that appellant admittedly was having difficulty recovering from surgery and was taking medication. She was weak and depressed during that period. There is no evidence, however, that appellant has not fully recovered from her health problems. A psychological evaluation of appellant found no psychosis, no major depressive disorder and no paranoid delusions. While finding some "vague paranoid trends," the report stated that any such feelings had a partial basis in reality in view of recent events. Although appellant was tense and somewhat evasive, this reaction was explained as "normal distress" over the difficulties of obtaining custody of Tara.

Unless it can be shown that a parent's conduct has had harmful effects on a child, it should have little weight in making a custody decision. In this case, there is no evidence that appellant's health problems had any harmful effect on Tara. On the contrary, appellant realized that she could not adequately care for her children following her operation and made satisfactory arrangements for alternate care during that period.

As to appellant's religious beliefs, she is a "born again" Christian who reads the Bible often and admits that religion is an important part of her life. The fact that appellant's family and friends have problems understanding her new beliefs does not establish that she is unfit to raise Tara. There is no evidence that appellant suffers from any delusions or that she has removed herself from reality. Nor is there any evidence that her "intense interest in religion" has had any harmful effect on her children.

Finally, the court also concluded that appellant did not provide adequate supervision for Tara. The court emphasized that Tara "liberally uses" the playground across the street from her apartment with no apparent adult supervision. The record shows that the playground in question can be seen from appellant's apartment and is surrounded by other apartment buildings. When playing there and in other areas near her home, Tara is in the company of other neighborhood children and often is accompanied by one or both of her older brothers. These facts do not indicate any negligence on the part of appellant. There is no evidence that the playground in the apartment complex poses any special danger. It is not necessary for a normal,

---

[2] The trial court did not seem to be overly concerned with appellee's history of past instability. It notes that he was convicted of statutory rape at age eighteen, has a history of alcohol and drug abuse, and is "somewhat prone to violence." However, the court accepted the conclusion in appellee's phyciatric [sic] evaluation that "his most recent marriage and its concomitant stability has tended to ameliorate these faults."

healthy four year old to have an adult constantly at her side when she is playing outdoors.

The court seemed especially concerned with an incident which occurred in the summer of 1980 when Tara ran into the street and was almost hit by a car. Appellant acknowledged that the incident occurred and her testimony as to the circumstances was uncontradicted. She had sent Tara downstairs to get a broom, unaware that it was across the street. She did not know that the child had left the house until she looked out the window and saw her returning. The record indicates that appellant was very upset by the incident and responded appropriately. Appellant testified that Tara knows she is not to cross the street alone and that on the few occasions when the child has done so, she had been disciplined.

The final evidence of appellant's "lack of supervision" occurred in September of 1980. Appellant worked for four evenings that month at the Oak Inn, leaving her son Michael in charge of the younger children for three to four hours on each of the four evenings. Michael had instructions to call appellant or Donna, a close neighbor, if there were any problems. This was an isolated incident. The record indicates that at all other times when appellant went out Tara would either have a babysitter or be left with relatives. It is our opinion that none of the above-mentioned evidence supports a finding of lack of adequate supervision on the part of appellant.

Although it is briefly mentioned in the trial court's opinion, we believe that the court failed to give adequate consideration to the effect a change of custody would have on Tara. Continued residence of the child with one parent is a factor which may, in certain cases, be controlling. Tara has resided with appellant since birth. All of the evidence indicates that there is a very close and loving relationship between appellant and her daughter. Tara also has a close relationship with her two half brothers. The psychological evaluation of Tara indicates that she has flourished under appellant's care. She was found to be a typical happy four year old of high average intelligence, with no indication of any emotional problems.

Furthermore, Tara expressed a strong preference for remaining with her mother. While the wishes of the child are not controlling, they do constitute an important factor which must be carefully considered in determining the child's best interest. When asked why she preferred to live with appellant, Tara responded that appellee and his wife always fight when she is there, which upsets her. When Tara was returned to appellant after briefly living with appellee, she was upset, withdrawn and reluctant to leave her mother's side. She initially refused to go on visitations with appellee, and had to be forced to go, kicking and crying. While the situation had improved during the proceedings in the trial court, Tara continued to be reluctant to go on visitations with appellee. On several occasions, Tara asked to be taken back to her mother's home early. While there was inconsistent testimony from Tara herself as to whether she actually enjoyed her visits with appellee once she got there, she made it very clear that she did not desire to live with appellee.

In conclusion, the hearing court's finding that it would be in Tara's best interest to reside with appellee is not supported by the record and therefore constitutes an abuse of discretion. . . . We will remand this case, therefore, for the entry of an appropriate order. . . .

NOTES AND QUESTION

Pearce examines the relevance of various factors in the determination of what constitutes the best interests of the child. Consider the role the following factors should have in custody decision making:

(1) Wealth.   What weight, if any, should be given to the superior financial position of one of the parents? The general rule, as *Pearce* reveals, is that the relative wealth of the parties is not a decisive factor unless one parent is unable to provide adequately for the child. See also Kovacs v. Kovacs, No. 205692, 1998 WL 1989809 (Mich. Ct. App., Sept. 29, 1998). Although not a decisive factor, should wealth be a relevant factor? Several cases hold that it is. See In re Haley, No. 1998CA0297, 1999 WL 1071962 (Ohio. Ct. App., Nov. 8, 1999) (finding that parent's ability to provide a stable environment and to satisfy child's educational needs are relevant factors); Hammers v. Hammers, 890 So. 2d 944 (Miss. Ct. App. 2004) (finding that stability of employment is relevant factor). Does such a policy raise equal protection issues?

ALI Principles.   The ALI Principles prohibit a court from considering parents' relative earning capacities or financial circumstances unless the parents' combined financial resources "set practical limits on the custodial arrangements." ALI Principles §2.12(1)(f).

The following excerpt explores the advantages and disadvantages of reliance on wealth as a factor in custody decision making.

David L. Chambers, Rethinking the Substantive Rules for Custody Disputes in Divorce
83 Mich. L. Rev. 477, 538–540 (1984)

A large income disparity typically exists between divorcing parents. . . . If, in general, secondary caretakers have substantial resources, are there advantages to children from access to such resources that neutralize the advantages of placing children with primary caretakers? Similarly, should the systematic higher earnings of men be considered as yet another reason for rejecting the arguments considered earlier for preferring women as caretakers for very young children?

. . . The disparity in income is, nonetheless, likely to make important differences in the quality of life available to the child in the two [custodial] settings. Studies have shown that in successive income groups of the general population from low to high, the proportion of people who report themselves to be happy rises steadily. For the divorcing family, access to resources can determine whether or not the custodial parent can afford to remain in the home the couple lived in during the marriage and, as it does for all Americans, it can mean access to opportunity for the child — to a more expensive education, summer camp, or music lessons. Moreover, even when most basic needs can be met, a parent accustomed to living at a higher standard is likely to worry a great deal about money, which in turn may produce stress for the child.

At least in the abstract, it would thus appear wholly defensible for courts to give weight in custody decisions to the comparative financial positions of the parties. . . .

The problem with giving substantial weight to resources or income potential is that, in this country today, the effect of doing so is to disadvantage mothers in two ways that many people would consider unfair. First, women in general earn much less than men in general. This disparity in income is widely perceived to be the result of systematic discrimination against women in the labor market. Second, even in families in which the particular parent, usually a woman, could have earned as much as her spouse, a parent who has, with her spouse's concurrence, stayed at home or worked less than full time because of children is at a disadvantage as to resources for reasons that we should applaud, not count against her. For these reasons, it might well be argued that because of the effect it has on mothers, courts should ignore systematic income differences in forming rules. . . .

For a more recent discussion of the role of wealth as a factor in custody decision making, see Carolyn J. Frantz, Note, Eliminating Consideration of Parental Wealth in Post-Divorce Child Custody Disputes, 99 Mich. L. Rev. 216 (2000).

(2) Mental Disability.   *Pearce* also raises the issue of the relevance of a parent's mental disability in custody decision making. In *Pearce* the mother's erratic behavior led family and friends to urge her to seek mental health counseling. Psychological evaluation of the mother revealed some "vague paranoid trends." Why did the court decide not to give much weight to such evidence?

Cases generally hold that the fact of a parent's mental illness per se does not establish unfitness. Rather, as *Pearce* reveals, the focus is the nexus between the mental illness and parenting abilities, specifically whether the parent's mental illness is likely to affect the child adversely. See generally Martha A. Field & Valerie A. Sanchez, Equal Treatment for People with Mental Retardation: Having and Raising Children (2000); Linda A. Francis, Annotation, Mental Health of Contesting Parent as Factor in Award of Child Custody, 53 A.L.R. 5th 375 (2001). Certain factors often influence courts to minimize the importance of mental problems — the effect of medication and treatment, the willingness to look at one's own weaknesses, and the presence of normal stress that anyone might manifest in a similar situation. Are any of these factors present in *Pearce*?

Physical illness or disability is another factor that enters into the determination of the best interests of the child. How should physical disabilities be treated, similarly to mental disability? Should the type of physical disability be relevant? For example, should deafness or blindness be treated differently than motor disabilities? See, e.g., Bednarski v. Bednarski, 366 N.W.2d 69 (Mich. Ct. App. 1985) (inappropriate weight given to mother's deafness).

What relevance, if any, should attach to a parent's terminal illness? For example, should a parent with AIDS, or one infected with HIV (the AIDS virus) be granted custody? See AIDS Patient Gets Custody of Son, S.F. Chron., Oct. 20, 1988, at A-2. See also Pierce J. Reed & Laura Davis Smith, HIV, Judicial Logic and Medical Science: Toward a Presumption of Noninfection in Child-Custody and Visitation Cases, 31 New Eng. L. Rev. 471 (1997).

Until recently, it was often assumed that the severely physically disabled parent could not adequately care for a child. Increasingly, however, appellate courts are rejecting such assumptions and focusing instead on whether the parent's disability will have an adverse effect on the child. See, e.g., Matta v. Matta, 693 N.E.2d 1063 (Mass. App. Ct. 1998); Clark v. Madden, 725 N.E.2d 100 (Ind. Ct. App. 2000).

In Carney v. Carney, 598 P. 2d 36 (Cal. 1979), custody was awarded to the father. Five years later the father became a quadriplegic as a result of a Jeep accident while serving in the military reserve, and the mother requested a modification in her behalf. The California Supreme Court reversed the modification award to the mother because the lower court relied solely on the evidence of physical disability. The California Supreme Court noted:

> the essence of parenting is not to be found in the harried rounds of daily carpooling endemic to modern suburban life, or even in the doggedly dutiful acts of "togetherness" committed every weekend by well-meaning fathers and mothers across America. Rather, its essence lies in the ethical, emotional, and intellectual guidance the parent gives to the child throughout his formative years, and often beyond. The source of this guidance is the adult's own experience of life; its motive power is parental love and concern for the child's well-being; and its teachings deal with such fundamental matters as the child's feelings about himself, his relationships with others, his system of values, his standards of conduct, and his goals and priorities in life. Even if it were true, as the court herein asserted that William [the father] cannot do "anything" for his sons except "talk to them and teach them, be a tutor," that would not only be "enough" — contrary to the court's conclusion — it would be the most valuable service a parent can render. Yet his capacity to do so is entirely unrelated to his physical prowess: however limited his bodily strength may be, a handicapped person is a whole person to the child who needs his affection, sympathy, and wisdom to deal with the problems of growing up. Indeed, in such matters, his handicap may well be an asset: few can pass through the crucible of a severe physical disability without learning enduring lessons in patience and tolerance [598 P.2d at 44.]

How much difference did it make, do you think, that this was a modification hearing rather than an initial award of custody? See generally Megan Kirshbaum et al., Issues Facing Family Court, Parents with Disabilities, Problems in Family Court Practice, 4 J. Center for Families, Child & Cts. 27 (2003).

(3) Religion. The mother in *Pearce* was a "born again" Christian who had an "intense interest in religion." What role should religion play in custody decision making? Although few states have statutes specifically including religion as a factor to consider in awards of custody,[60] many judges do consider religion in their determination of the child's best interest. The question is complicated by constitutional overlays. When may judges consider religious practices without violating the Constitution? In conformity with the First Amendment, courts may not interfere with religious freedom or prefer one religion to another. Each parent has a constitutionally protected right to practice his or her religion, or to practice none at all. Frequently, disputes involve parents of different religions who allege that the child should be raised in their respective religious faith. The Establishment Clause,

---

[60] See Hawaii Rev. Stat. §571-46 (1993 & Supp. 2003); Minn. Stat. Ann. §518.17 (West 1990 & Supp. 2004); S.C. Code Ann. §20-3-160 (1985 & Supp. 2002); Wis. Stat. Ann. §764.24(5) (West 1998).

however, prevents courts from favoring one religion over another. Consequently, courts must refrain from weighing the comparative merits of various religions. See, e.g., Garrett v. Garrett, 527 N.W.2d 213 (Neb. 1985); Hoedebeck v. Hoedebeck, 948 P.2d 1240 (Okla. Ct. App. 1997). Although courts may not judge the merits of a particular religion, they may properly examine the effect that the particular religion has on the development of the child. See Ficker v. Ficker, 62 S.W.2d 496 (Mo. 2001).

Suppose the dispute involves two parents, one religious and the other nonreligious? May a court prefer a parent who has religious beliefs over one who does not? In an action by a father to have custody transferred to him, the Idaho Supreme Court ruled that the trial court had abused its discretion by basing its decisions on a belief that the father was able to provide superior moral training. Osteraas v. Osteraas, 859 P.2d 948 (Idaho 1993). But cf. Hamilton v. Hamilton, 42 P.3d 1107 (Alaska 2002); Wilson v. Wilson, 716 N.E.2d 486 (Ind. 1999).

Suppose there is an allegation that one custodian's religion exposes the child to actual or potential physical harm? In this instance, what weight should be given to a parent's religion or religious beliefs? Should it matter whether the religion exposes the child to the risk of dying as a result of the parent's opposition to a blood transfusion or whether it merely occasions social harm due to deprivation of radio, television, or toys? Compare Kendall v. Kendall, 687 N.E.2d 1228 (Mass. 1997) (evidence of parent's religious practices admissible if there is clear evidence that the religious practices caused substantial harm to the child's physical or mental health) with Gago v. Acevedo, 625 N.Y.S.2d 250 (App. Div. 1995) (law does not require proof of actual harm to the child, nor need the court disregard the issue of the parent's suitability to have custody even though the parent claims a religious basis for the practices at issue). If courts require some element of harm, do they require actual harm, a substantial threat of harm, or merely some risk of harm? See Jennifer Ann Drobac, Note, For the Sake of the Children: Court Consideration of Religion in Child Custody Cases, 50 Stan. L. Rev. 1609, 1631 (1998) (concluding that courts use all three tests but most courts use actual harm). See generally Carl E. Schneider, Religion and Child Custody, 25 U. Mich. J.L. Ref. 879 (1992).

ALI Principles. The ALI Principles of the Law of Family Dissolution prohibit a court from considering the "religious practices" of either the parent or the child in custody decision making except in the following situations: (a) if the religious practices present "severe and almost certain harm" to the child (and then a court may limit the religious practices only to the minimum degree necessary to protect the child), or (b) if necessary to protect the child's ability to practice a religion "that has been a significant part of the child's life." ALI Principles §2.12(1)(c). Joann Ross Wilder, Special Concerns of Children, Religion and Best Interests in Custody Cases, 18 J. Am. Acad. Matrim. Law 211 (2002).

(4) Other Factors: Time, Daycare, and Breastfeeding. What other factors should be relevant in determining the best interests of the child? For example, should time be a relevant factor — that is, the amount of time a parent has available to spend with the children? A few cases have held that professionals (specifically, in law and medicine) may be at a disadvantage in custody battles. See, e.g., Prost v. Green, 652 A.2d 621 (D.C. 1995); In re Rebecca B., 611 N.Y.S.2d 831 (N.Y. App. Div. 1994); Richmond v. Tecklenberg, 396 S.E.2d 111 (S.C. Ct. App. 1990). See

also Young v. Hector, 740 So.2d 1153 (Fla. Dist. Ct. App. 1999) (reversing custody denial to lawyer-mother). See generally Amy D. Ronner, Women Who Dance on the Professional Track: Custody and the Red Shoes, 23 Harv. Women's L.J. 173 (2003). D. Kelly Weisberg, Professional Women and the Professionalization of Motherhood: Marcia Clark's Double Bind, 6 Hastings Women's L.J. 295 (1995).

What might be problematic about utilizing time as a relevant factor in the best interests determination? Consider the following:

> A standard that awards custody to the parent able to spend more time with the child would ignore qualitative differences in time spent with the child and thus might not be justifiable from the perspective of what is good for the child. In all events, because the test would require a prediction of the amount of time each parent would spend with the child, it would be very difficult to apply and would invite exaggeration and dishonesty in litigation. Monitoring the time a parent would actually spend with a child after the custody dispute was resolved would be intrusive and impractical. Moreover, what remedy would there be if a parent later spent less time than expected? . . . [61]

Should a parent's reliance on day care be relevant? In a famous case, a university student was denied custody of her nonmarital child because the mother placed the child in day care while she attended class. The trial court accepted the father's contention that his mother (the child's grandmother) would provide better care for the child while he worked. The Michigan Supreme Court overturned the trial court award of paternal custody. Smith v. Ireland, 547 N.W.2d 686 (Mich. 1996). See also In re Marriage of Loyd, 131 Cal. Rptr. 2d 80 (Ct. App. 2003) (holding that custody modification to mother based on father's reliance on day care was abuse of discretion); Lynda Gorov, California Woman Gets Custody, Harvard; Ruling Allows Single Mother to Return to Studies in Fall, Boston Globe, May 7, 1997, at 3 (awarding custody to single mother who was student at Harvard despite her reliance on day care compared to father whose parents could care for child while he worked in the family restaurant). See generally Cynthia A. McNeely, Comment, Lagging Behind the Times: Parenthood, Custody, and Gender Bias in the Family Courts, 25 Fla. St. U. L. Rev. 891, 955 (1998); Debra L. Swank, Comment, Day Care and Parental Employment: What Weight Should They Be Given in Child Custody Disputes?, 41 Vill. L. Rev. 909 (1996).

ALI Principles. The ALI Principles of the Law of Family Dissolution provide that placement of a child in day care does not constitute sufficiently changed circumstances to warrant custody modification. ALI Principles §2.15(3)(c).

Should breastfeeding play a role in child custody decisions? Or, does taking this factor into account merely resurrect the tender years presumption? See Kristin D. Hofheimer, Breastfeeding as a Factor in Child Custody and Visitation Decisions, 5 Va. J. Soc. Pol'y & L. 433 (1998). Should cigarette smoking be a factor? See In re Julie Anne, 780 N.E.2d 635 (Ohio Ct. App. 2002). See also Jeannette Igbenebor, Comment, Smoking as a Factor in Child Custody Cases, 18 J. Am. Acad. Matrim. Law. 235 (2002).

---

[61] Mnookin, Child-Custody Adjudication, supra note [1], at 284-288.

(5) Other Factors: Substance Abuse and Domestic Violence.   *Pearce* mentions several additional factors that might play a role in custody decision making. For example, if a father has a history of alcohol and drug abuse, what weight, if any, should be given to evidence of substance abuse? See generally Sandra Morgan Little ed., Child Custody and Visitation: Law and Practice §10.11[2][e] at 10-201 (2004).

Furthermore, *Pearce* contains allegations of maternal neglect. How relevant should the factors of abuse and neglect be in custody decision making? What about sexual abuse? Most states address abuse as a factor in custody.[62] The majority of these states provide that courts should consider domestic violence in the determination of the best interests of the child. A few states provide that courts may take domestic violence into account in decisions regarding joint custody (e.g., joint custody would not be in the child's best interests in such a case), and some states establish rebuttable presumptions against awards of custody (sole or joint) to perpetrators of domestic violence.[63] Some states now consider exposure to domestic abuse in custody decision making.[64] Other statutes address the role of abuse in custody decision making indirectly by providing that if a parent leaves the home to escape spousal abuse, this absence shall not be held against the parent in determining the best interests of the child. See, e.g., Colo. Rev. Stat. §14-10-124(l) (West 1997 & Supp. 2003); Ky. Rev. Stat. §403-270(2) (1999 & Supp. 2003).

Recall (from Chapter 3) that neglect runs the gamut from inadequate supervision to withholding necessary food, clothing, or medical care. Similarly, abuse ranges from isolated acts of physical discipline to more serious acts of beating, burning, and mutilation. Abuse also includes sexual abuse. Where did the alleged acts of the mother in *Pearce* fall on this continuum? How did the court treat this issue?

(6) *Pearce* found both parents to be "fit." Yet, given the record (a mother who allegedly is mentally unstable with religious delusions versus a father who has a history of alcohol and drug abuse), *Pearce* may also be characterized as a case involving two equally "unfit" parents. Cases of equal fitness or unfitness present especially difficult problems for judges. How should such tiebreaker cases be resolved? And by what process — by the courts using rules, preferences, presumptions? By the parties through mediation? Or coin-flipping? See pp. 603-611, infra.

(c) Race

Palmore v. Sidoti
466 U.S. 429 (1984)

Chief Justice BURGER delivered the opinion of the Court.

We granted certiorari to review a judgment of a state court divesting a natural mother of the custody of her infant child because of her remarriage to a person of a different race.

---

[62] See Family Violence Project, Family Violence in Child Custody Statutes: An Analysis of State Codes and Legal Practice, 29 Fam. L.Q. 197, 197 (1995).

[63] Lois A. Weithorn, Protecting Children from Exposure to Domestic Violence: The Use and Abuse of Child Maltreatment, 53 Hastings L.J. 1, 13-14 (2001).

[64] Id. at 15-21 (discussing different types of statutes).

I

When petitioner Linda Sidoti Palmore and respondent Anthony J. Sidoti, both Caucasians, were divorced in May 1980 in Florida, the mother was awarded custody of their 3-year-old daughter.

In September 1981 the father sought custody of the child by filing a petition to modify the prior judgment because of changed conditions. The change was that the child's mother was then cohabiting with a Negro, Clarence Palmore, Jr., whom she married two months later. Additionally, the father made several allegations of instances in which the mother had not properly cared for the child.

After hearing testimony from both parties and considering a court counselor's investigative report, the court noted that the father had made allegations about the child's care, but the court made no findings with respect to these allegations. On the contrary, the court made a finding that "there is no issue as to either party's devotion to the child, adequacy of housing facilities, or respectability of the new spouse of either parent."

The court then addressed the recommendations of the court counselor, who had made an earlier report "in [another] case coming out of this circuit also involving the social consequences of an interracial marriage." From this vague reference to that earlier case, the court turned to the present case and noted the counselor's recommendation for a change in custody because "[t]he wife [petitioner] has chosen for herself and for her child, a life-style unacceptable to the father *and to society*. . . . The child . . . is, or at school age will be, subject to environmental pressures not of choice." (emphasis added).

The court then concluded that the best interests of the child would be served by awarding custody to the father. The court's rationale is contained in the following:

> The father's evident resentment of the mother's choice of a black partner is not sufficient to wrest custody from the mother. It is of some significance, however, that the mother did see fit to bring a man into her home and carry on a sexual relationship with him without being married to him. Such action tended to place gratification of her own desires ahead of her concern for the child's future welfare. *This Court feels that despite the strides that have been made in bettering relations between the races in the country, it is inevitable that Melanie will, if allowed to remain in her present situation and attains school age and thus more vulnerable to peer pressures, suffer from the social stigmatization that is sure to come.* (emphasis added).

The Second District Court of Appeal affirmed without opinion, thus denying the Florida Supreme Court jurisdiction to review the case. We granted certiorari, and we reverse.

II

The judgment of a state court determining or reviewing a child custody decision is not ordinarily a likely candidate for review by this Court. However, the court's opinion, after stating that the "father's evident resentment of the mother's choice of a black partner is not sufficient" to deprive her of custody, then turns to what it regarded as the damaging impact on the child from remaining in a racially mixed household. This raises important federal concerns arising from the Constitution's commitment to eradicating discrimination based on race.

The Florida court did not focus directly on the parental qualifications of the natural mother or her present husband, or indeed on the father's qualifications to have custody of the child. The court found that "there is no issue as to either party's devotion to the child, adequacy of housing facilities, or respectability of the new spouse of either parent." This, taken with the absence of any negative finding as to the quality of the care provided by the mother, constitutes a rejection of any claim of petitioner's unfitness to continue the custody of her child.

The court correctly stated that the child's welfare was the controlling factor. But that court was entirely candid and made no effort to place its holding on any ground other than race. Taking the court's findings and rationale at face value, it is clear that the outcome would have been different had petitioner married a Caucasian male of similar respectability.

A core purpose of the Fourteenth Amendment was to do away with all governmentally imposed discrimination based on race. Classifying persons according to their race is more likely to reflect racial prejudice than legitimate public concerns; the race, not the person, dictates the category. Such classifications are subject to the most exacting scrutiny; to pass constitutional muster, they must be justified by a compelling governmental interest and must be "necessary . . . to the accomplishment" of their legitimate purpose.

The State, of course, has a duty of the highest order to protect the interests of minor children, particularly those of tender years. In common with most states, Florida law mandates that custody determinations be made in the best interests of the children involved. Fla. Stat. §61.13(2)(b)(1) (1983). The goal of granting custody based on the best interests of the child is indisputably a substantial governmental interest for purposes of the Equal Protection Clause.

It would ignore reality to suggest that racial and ethnic prejudices do not exist or that all manifestations of those prejudices have been eliminated. There is a risk that a child living with a stepparent of a different race may be subject to a variety of pressures and stresses not present if the child were living with parents of the same racial or ethnic origin.

The question, however, is whether the reality of private biases and the possible injury they might inflict are permissible considerations for removal of an infant child from the custody of its natural mother. We have little difficulty concluding that they are not.[2] The Constitution cannot control such prejudices, but neither can it tolerate them. Private biases may be outside the reach of the law, but the law cannot, directly or indirectly, give them effect. . . .

The effects of racial prejudice, however real, cannot justify a racial classification removing an infant child from the custody of its natural mother found to be an appropriate person to have such custody.

The judgment of the District Court of Appeal is reversed.

[2] In light of our holding based on the Equal Protection Clause, we need not reach or resolve petitioner's claim based on the Fourteenth Amendment's Due Process Clause.

NOTES AND QUESTIONS

(1) Relevance of Race: Different Views.   Prior to *Palmore*, several courts considered the weight to be given to race. Three views appeared to predominate: (1) racial differences are not relevant to custody; (2) racial differences may be considered as one of the factors that would be in the child's best interests; and (3) race may not be used as the determinative factor in awarding custody. See cases cited in Lee R. Ross, Annotation, Race as Factor in Custody Award or Proceedings, 10 A.L.R.4th 796 (1981). Which view does *Palmore* follow?

(2) Epilogue.   The day the Supreme Court announced its decision, the father, who had moved to Texas with his new wife, filed an application for a temporary restraining order with a Texas court. The mother subsequently filed (1) in Texas, a petition for a writ of habeas corpus to recover possession of the child, and (2) in Florida, a motion to compel return of the child to her custody. The father, in turn, filed a motion to dismiss the mother's motion in the Florida court. Ultimately, the Texas court found that it had jurisdiction for purposes of further interim orders, and the Florida court declined jurisdiction in favor of the Texas court. The mother appealed, arguing that the Florida trial court erred in declining to exercise jurisdiction under the Uniform Child Custody Jurisdiction Act, 9 U.L.A. pt. 1A 104 (1999 & Supp. 2004) (see Post-Decree Problems, pp. 615-616, infra). The mother also argued that as a result of the Supreme Court's opinion, custody should revert to the situation prior to the order and that she should again have custody.

The court of appeals of Florida replied: "We cannot agree under the particular facts of this child custody case. . . . The Supreme Court's decision was that the modification of custody could not be predicated upon the mother's association with a black man. Its opinion did not direct a reinstatement of the original custody decree and the immediate return of the child. The Supreme Court did not say that a Florida court could not defer to a Texas court. . . ." Palmore v. Sidoti, 472 So. 2d 843, 846 (Fla. Dist. Ct. App. 1985). The court of appeals concluded: "Under all the circumstances we cannot say that at this time it has been established to be in Melanie's best interest that she be ordered returned to her mother and that the trial court erred in not so ordering. The eight-year-old child appears to have had substantial upheavals of her life, and we find no compelling reason at this point to add a further upheaval. . . ." Id. at 846-847. Do you agree?

(3) Inappropriate Consideration?   How difficult is it to determine whether the court gave inappropriate weight to the role of race? For example, in one of the few post-*Palmore* cases to consider the role of race, Parker v. Parker, 986 S.W.2d 557 (Tenn. Sup. Ct. 1999), a woman who was dating an African-American man (also her employer) sought custody of her child. The trial court awarded custody to the child's father, stating that its decision was not based on race but rather on disapproval of the extramarital relationship and the fact that the relationship was causing the mother to neglect the child. The appellate and state supreme courts upheld the award of paternal custody, accepting the trial court's judgment on the fitness of the parents. See also Parker v. Parker, 986 S.W.2d 557 (Tenn. 1999); Dansby v. Dansby, No. CA 03-741, 2004 WL 1465757 (Ark. Ct. App. June 30, 2004).

See generally Katherine T. Bartlett, Essay, Comparing Race and Sex Discrimination in Custody Cases, 28 Hofstra L. Rev. 877 (2000); Randall Kennedy,

Interracial Intimacies: Sex, Marriage, Identity, and Adoption (2003); Rachel F. Moran, Interracial Intimacy: The Regulation of Race and Romance (2001).

(4) ALI Principles.   The ALI Principles of the Law of Family Dissolution, §2.12(1)(a), prohibit a court from considering the race or ethnicity of the child, parent, or other member of the household in determining custody arrangements.

(5) Custody vs. Adoption.   Compare the treatment of race in the custody and adoption contexts (see The Relevance of Race to Adoption, supra, pp. 524-533). Is the state's interest in adoption proceedings greater than in custody proceedings? If so, should this interest justify differential treatment of the relevance of race?

(6) Extension of **Palmore.**   The Supreme Court based its holding in *Palmore* on the ground that private biases and possible injury therefrom are not permissible considerations for removal from the custody of a biological parent. May this reasoning justify an extension of *Palmore* to other situations? For cases that have extended *Palmore* beyond questions of race, see Jacoby v. Jacoby, 763 So. 2d 410, 413 (Fla. Ct. App. 2000) (holding that perceived community bias against homosexuals is improper basis for a residential custody determination); Inscoe v. Inscoe, 700 N.E.2d 70, 82 (Ohio Ct. App. 1997) (reversing custody award to wife on ground of husband's homosexuality because courts may not consider adverse impact on a child that flows from the unpopularity of gays and lesbians in our society). Consider also the impact of Lawrence v. Texas, discussed supra pp. 556-557.

(2) Joint Custody

PROBLEMS

(1) Sandra and Rick have been married for ten years. They have two children: Andrew, age six, and Kristin, age four. The past year has been particularly stressful for the family as Sandra and Rick have realized the extent of their marital differences. Finally, the couple decides to obtain a divorce. Both parents have been extremely involved with the children throughout their relationship. Neither is happy at the prospect of losing custody of Andrew and Kristin. The parents consult you, their attorney, to inquire as to the advisability of a "joint custody-type" arrangement.

Sandra and Rick pose several questions to you. What does joint custody mean in terms of future shared responsibilities for child rearing? Is an award of joint custody appropriate if both Sandra and Rick desire this custodial arrangement? What might be the advantages of joint custody for the respective family members — mother, father, and children? What are the disadvantages? What problems might joint custody involve, even in the best possible situation, when both parents agree to it? Is there any "scientific evidence" investigating how joint custody actually works for most families? What else might Sandra and Rick want to know to assist them in making their decision to secure joint custody?

(2) After many discussions with each other and with legal counsel, Sandra and Rick come to a decision. Rick is firm in his desire for joint custody; Sandra, however, would prefer an award of sole custody to her. Each petitions the court. Suppose you are the judge deciding such a case. Is an award of joint custody

appropriate in circumstances when one parent does not desire it? What problems might arise if one parent is coerced into accepting a joint custodial arrangement? Are these problems different from the situation in which one parent initially wants sole custody but later agrees to joint custody through negotiation? What are the prospects for such couples to reach consensus in subsequent decisions about child custody?

(3) Alternatively, suppose that after much discussion, Rick and Sandra decide that joint custody is not appropriate for them. Each decides to petition the court for sole custody. Is an award of joint custody ever appropriate in circumstances when neither parent wants it? That is, should a judge ever award joint custody over both parents' objections? If so, in what circumstances?

Consider these questions in light of the materials that follow.

Taylor v. Taylor
508 A.2d 964 (Md. 1986)

McAULIFFE, Judge.

. . . The parties to this appeal are Judith Ann Taylor (Appellant) and Neil Randall Taylor, III (Appellee). The Taylors were married on November 26, 1977, and are the parents of Christina Lee Taylor, born April 9, 1979, and Neil Randall Taylor, IV, born August 5, 1980.

During the summer of 1982, the Taylors began experiencing marital difficulties and on September 10, 1982, they separated. . . . Appellee filed a Bill of Complaint in the Circuit Court for Cecil County seeking an absolute divorce and temporary and permanent custody of the children. Appellant filed an answer in which she requested custody of the children pendente lite and permanently.

On November 24 a "visitation schedule," signed only by counsel, was filed, detailing an apparent agreement between the parties, and specifying the days and times that each party would have the children. On December 7, Judge Donaldson Cole entered a pendente lite order granting the parties "joint custody" of the children "in consideration of the agreement of the parties." The order further provided that the children were to reside with Appellee in the family home, and incorporated by reference the visitation schedule previously filed.

On April 7, 1983, Appellant changed attorneys. Five days later she filed an amended and supplemental answer in which she requested that the order of December 7, 1982, be stricken, and that she be awarded care and custody of the children. Appellant alleged that the order providing joint custody pendente lite was the result of "a meeting with the court without her knowledge," and of action taken by her attorney without her authority. Trial on the merits occurred shortly thereafter, and following a five day trial Judge H. Kenneth Mackey granted Appellee's request for an absolute divorce, and ordered continuation of the arrangement spelled out in the "visitation agreement," which he characterized as "a sort of joint custody." . . . Appellant's Motion for Reconsideration was denied, and she noted an appeal to the Court of Special Appeals. That court affirmed. Taylor v. Taylor, 60 Md. App. 268, 482 A.2d 164 (1984). We granted certiorari to consider the following two questions:

1) Whether a trial judge in Maryland has the authority to grant joint custody; and

2) Whether, if the trial judge did have the authority to grant such an award, he abused his discretion under the facts of this case.

I. Definition of Joint Custody

This dynamic and emotionally charged field of law is unfortunately afflicted with significant semantical problems, described by one writer as a "frightful lack of linguistic uniformity."[3] The inability of courts and commentators to agree on what is meant by the term "joint custody" makes difficult the task of distilling principles and guidelines from a rapidly growing body of literature and case law. What one writer sees as an amorphous concept another sees as a structured legal arrangement. While it is clear that both parents in a joint custody arrangement function as "custodians" in the sense that they are actually involved in the overall welfare of their child, a distinction must be made between sharing parental responsibility in major decision-making matters and sharing responsibility for providing a home for the child.

Embraced within the meaning of "custody" are the concepts of "legal" and "physical" custody. Legal custody carries with it the right and obligation to make long range decisions involving education, religious training, discipline, medical care, and other matters of major significance concerning the child's life and welfare.[4] Joint legal custody means that both parents have an equal voice in making those decisions, and neither parent's rights are superior to the other.

Physical custody, on the other hand, means the right and obligation to provide a home for the child and to make the day-to-day decisions required during the time the child is actually with the parent having such custody. Joint physical custody is in reality "shared" or "divided" custody.[5] Shared physical custody may, but need not, be on a 50/50 basis, and in fact most commonly will involve custody by one parent during the school year and by the other during summer vacation months, or division between weekdays and weekends, or between days and nights.

With respect to physical custody, there is no difference between the rights and obligations of a parent having temporary custody of a child pursuant to an order of shared physical custody, and one having temporary custody pursuant to an award of visitation. Thus, a determination to grant legal custody to one parent and to allocate

---

[3] D. Miller, Joint Custody, 13 Fam. L.Q. 345, 376 (1979).

[4] The parent not granted legal custody will, under ordinary circumstances, retain authority to make necessary day-to-day decisions concerning the child's welfare during the time the child is in that parent's physical custody. Thus, a parent exercising physical custody over a child, whether pursuant to an order of visitation or to an order of shared physical custody, necessarily possesses the authority to control and discipline the child during the period of physical custody. Similarly, that parent has the authority to consent to emergency surgery or emergency major medical care when there is insufficient time to contact the parent having legal custody. We need not here consider the issues that may arise when the parent having legal custody cannot agree with the parent exercising physical custody concerning emergency medical care. . . .

[5] The term "split custody" is generally used to describe the situation in which one parent is given sole custody of some of the children of the parties, with sole custody of the remaining children going to the other parent, and cross rights of visitation. Again, however, the use of terms is not uniform and some courts speak of "divided custody" to describe a situation involving split custody.

physical custody between the parents may be accomplished either by granting sole custody to one parent and specified rights of visitation to the other, or by granting legal custody to one parent and specified periods of physical custody to each parent. In either instance the effect will be the same.

Proper practice in any case involving joint custody dictates that the parties and the trial judge separately consider the issues involved in both joint legal custody and joint physical custody, and that the trial judge state specifically the decision made as to each.

II. Authority to Award Joint Custody

Appellant argues that "[t]here is no express statutory authority for an award of joint custody in Maryland" and that in the absence of such authority a court of equity lacks jurisdiction to grant joint custody. A strong argument can be made that authority to award joint custody is implicit in the language of the several statutes relating to child custody. We need not decide that issue, for we hold the authority to grant joint custody is an integral part of the broad and inherent authority of a court exercising its equitable powers to determine child custody. . . .

III. Joint Custody Considerations

This Court last considered the issue of joint custody in McCann v. McCann, 167 Md. 167, 172, 173 A. 7 (1934), in which our predecessors denounced joint control of a child as an arrangement "to be avoided, whenever possible, as an evil fruitful in the destruction of discipline, in the creation of distrust, and in the production of mental distress in the child." Significant societal changes that have occurred over the ensuing half century mandate our reexamination of those views.

Proponents of joint custody point out that it offers an opportunity for a child to enjoy a meaningful relationship with both parents, and may diminish the traumatic effects upon the child that can result from a dissolution of the marriage. While sole custody may reduce the noncustodial parent to the second class status of a visitor, joint custody allows both parties to function as, and be perceived as, parents. The sharing of the burdens as well as the joys of child-rearing may be particularly helpful in the many instances where both parents are employed. Where joint custody has been appropriate, benefits have accrued not only to the child, but to parents as well.

The principal criticism leveled at joint custody is that it creates confusion and instability for children at the very time they need a sense of certainty and finality in their lives. Additionally, it is said to present too great an opportunity for manipulation of the parents by the child. Critics also contend that the option of joint custody creates too great a temptation to the trial judge to avoid choosing one parent and disappointing the other by simply awarding custody to both. Certainly, joint custody is not appropriate in every case. Indeed, it has been suggested that it is appropriate only in a small minority of cases. But when appropriate, joint custody can result in substantial advantages to children and parents alike, and the feasibility of such an arrangement is certainly worthy of careful consideration.

Formula or computer solutions in child custody matters are impossible because of the unique character of each case, and the subjective nature of the evaluations and decisions that must be made. At best we can discuss the major factors that should be considered in determining whether joint custody is appropriate, but in doing so we recognize that none has talismanic qualities, and that no single list of criteria will satisfy the demands of every case.

We emphasize that in any child custody case, the paramount concern is the best interest of the child. . . . The best interest of the child is therefore not considered as one of many factors, but as the objective to which virtually all other factors speak. . . .

Capacity of the Parents to Communicate and to Reach Shared Decisions Affecting the Child's Welfare

This is clearly the most important factor in the determination of whether an award of joint legal custody is appropriate, and is relevant as well to a consideration of shared physical custody. Rarely, if ever, should joint legal custody be awarded in the absence of a record of mature conduct on the part of the parents evidencing an ability to effectively communicate with each other concerning the best interest of the child, and then only when it is possible to make a finding of a strong potential for such conduct in the future. . . .

When the evidence discloses severely embittered parents and a relationship marked by dispute, acrimony, and a failure of rational communication, there is nothing to be gained and much to be lost by conditioning the making of decisions affecting the child's welfare upon the mutual agreement of the parties. Even in the absence of bitterness or inability to communicate, if the evidence discloses the parents do not share parenting values, and each insists on adhering to irreconcilable theories of child-rearing, joint legal custody is not appropriate. The parents need not agree on every aspect of parenting, but their views should not be so widely divergent or so inflexibly maintained as to forecast the probability of continuing disagreement on important matters. In S. Steinman, Joint Custody: What We Know, What We Have Yet to Learn, and the Judicial and Legislative Implications, 16 U.C.D. L. Rev. 739, 745-46, the author listed the characteristics of coparental relationships found to be important in a study of successful joint custody arrangements:

> Foremost was the sense of respect for one another as parents, despite the disappointment in each other as marriage partners. Each appreciated the value of the other to the child, and was sensitive to the possible loss of a parent-child relationship. The parents' relationships were characterized by a similarity in basic child-rearing values. There was the capacity to tolerate the minor differences that existed and to distinguish the important from the unimportant ones. These parents were able to relinquish control and not interfere in the other parent's relationship with the child. They were personally flexible and able to accommodate to the needs of the arrangement, the child, and even to the other parent. These were not people who were rigid in their thinking or behavior. There was a capacity to contain their anger and hostility and to divert it away from the children. There was an ability to take responsibility for their part in the break-up and their current life rather than project blame onto their ex-mate. Finally, there was a sense of parity in these coparental relationships. They accepted the premise that they were equally significant to and capable of caring for the children. This meant not only the genuine

valuing of the other as a parent in raising the child but, equally as important, it enhanced the parents' own self-confidence. It was important that each parent had a sense of self-esteem as a parent in his or her own right in order to maintain the balance in the co-parental relationship.

These parents were able to separate out their roles and feelings as parents from the marital- and divorce-engendered conflicts. They had rarely argued about the children during the marriage, and were able to maintain a "conflict free" sphere around the children, which they protected through the divorcing process. This capacity was central to a smooth running co-parental arrangement.

Ordinarily the best evidence of compatibility with this criterion will be the past conduct or "track record" of the parties. We recognize, however, that the tensions of separation and litigation will sometimes produce bitterness and lack of ability to cooperate or agree. The trial judge will have to evaluate whether this is a temporary condition, very likely to abate upon resolution of the issues, or whether it is more permanent in nature. Only where the evidence is strong in support of a finding of the existence of a significant potential for compliance with this criterion should joint legal custody be granted. Blind hope that a joint custody agreement will succeed, or that forcing the responsibility of joint decision-making upon the warring parents will bring peace, is not acceptable. In the unusual case where the trial judge concludes that joint legal custody is appropriate notwithstanding the absence of a "track record" of willingness and ability on the part of the parents to cooperate in making decisions dealing with the child's welfare, the trial judge must articulate fully the reasons that support that conclusion.

Willingness of Parents to Share Custody

Generally, the parents should be willing to undertake joint custody or it should not be ordered. We are asked by Appellant, and by the Women's Legal Defense Fund as amicus curiae, to hold that a trial judge may never order joint legal custody over the objection of one parent. They argue, with some force, that unwillingness on the part of one parent to share custody inevitably presages intransigence or inability to cooperate in making decisions affecting the welfare of the child. While we agree that the absence of an express willingness on the part of the parents to accept a joint custody arrangement is a strong indicator that joint legal custody is contraindicated, we are unwilling to fashion a hard and fast rule that would have the effect of granting to either parent veto power over the possibility of a joint custody award. A caring parent, believing that sole custody is in the best interest of the child, may forcefully advance that position throughout the litigation but be willing and able to fully participate in a joint custody arrangement if that is the considered decision of the court.

Fitness of Parents

The psychological and physical capabilities of both parents must be considered, although the determination may vary depending upon whether a parent is being evaluated for fitness for legal custody or for physical custody. A parent may be fit for one type of custody but not the other, or neither, or both.

Relationship Established Between the Child and Each Parent

When both parents are seen by the child as a source of security and love, there is a favorable climate for joint custody. . . .

Preference of the Child

The reasonable preference of a child of suitable age and discretion should be considered. In addition to being sensitive to the possible presence of the "lollipop" or "rescue" syndromes,[12] the trial judge must also recognize that children often experience a strong desire to see separated parents reunited, and this motivation may produce an unrealistic preference for joint custody.

Potential Disruption of Child's Social and School Life

Joint physical custody may seriously disrupt the social and school life of a child when each parent has the child for half the year, and the homes are not in close proximity to one another. In such cases the amount of time each parent has physical custody may be adjusted without interfering with the concept of continued joint custody.

Geographic Proximity of Parental Homes

Parental homes within the same school district offer certain advantages in a joint custody situation. The child may enjoy joint physical custody without changing schools or being required to constantly change a circle of friends, and the parents may find proximity a benefit in discussing the decisions to be made concerning the child. However, distance is not a bar, and when the distance between homes is great, a joint custody arrangement may offer the only practical way to preserve to the child a meaningful relationship with each parent. . . .

Demands of Parental Employment

In some situations, joint physical custody will be appropriate only if the work hours of the parents are different, or there is flexibility in the demands of the employment of each.

Age and Number of Children

The factor of age obviously interrelates with other factors already discussed. The number of children involved may pose practical difficulties to a joint custody arrangement, but on the other hand may be helpful to both parents in bringing about

[12] The so-called "lollipop syndrome" relates to the situation where one parent in a custody battle may shower the child with gifts and pleasant times, and impose no discipline in order to win the child's preference. The "rescue syndrome" relates to the expression of preference by a child for the parent perceived by the child to be the "weaker" of the two, in the belief that the stronger parent will survive in any event, but the weaker parent needs the child.

a sharing of the pressures of single family parenting of a number of children. In rare cases, split custody may be preferred over sole or joint custody.

Sincerity of Parents' Request

A number of interested observers have opposed the concept of joint custody absent mutual agreement on the ground that one spouse may interpose a demand for joint custody solely to gain bargaining leverage over the other in extracting favorable alimony, child support or property concessions. Drawing upon the reasoning of King Solomon writers have suggested that a parent truly interested in the welfare of a child will give up almost anything to protect the child, and thus the threat of enforced joint custody can be used to extract unwarranted concessions. While the remedy they suggest — denial of joint custody in the absence of parental agreement — is unnecessarily restrictive, we acknowledge the legitimacy of these concerns and highlight the necessity to carefully examine the motives and sincerity of each parent.

Financial Status of the Parents

Joint physical custody imposes financial burdens upon the parents because of the necessity of maintaining two homes for the child, with separate furnishings and often separate toys, equipment, and clothing. . . .

Benefit to Parents

Although the primary focus is properly upon the best interest of the child, it is also appropriate to consider the salutary effect that joint custody may have on the parents, not only because their feelings and interests are worthy of consideration, but also because their improved self-image as parents is likely to redound to the ultimate benefit of the child.

Other Factors

The enumeration of factors appropriate for consideration in a joint custody case is not intended to be all-inclusive, and a trial judge should consider all other circumstances that reasonably relate to the issue.

IV

In our review of the record to determine whether the trial judge abused his discretion, we are initially confronted with the problem of understanding the exact nature of the custody arrangement he intended. It is clear he intended to perpetuate the arrangement found to exist at the time of trial, which he characterized as "a sort of joint custody." This was basically the arrangement stipulated by the "visitation schedule". . . . The trial judge described the arrangement as follows:

> Both parents teach school. The father's work day is from about 8:30 A.M. to 4:15 P.M. and the mother's 12:30 P.M. to 4:15 P.M. . . . In November 1982 the parties agreed upon a sort of joint custody of the children. Their base is in the

father's home but the mother probably sees them more of their waking hours. The mother is in the home with the children Monday to Friday from 7:30 A.M. to 12:30 P.M. The mother has the children in her home from 4:15 P.M. to 8:00 P.M. Tuesday and on alternate [weekends] from 10:00 A.M. Saturday until 8:00 P.M. Sunday. The paternal grandmother babysits Monday to Friday from 12:30 P.M. to 4:15 P.M., i.e. from the time the mother leaves the children until the father gets home. The father pays his mother $29.00 weekly. The mother contributes no money for child support.

It is difficult to determine from an examination of the "visitation schedule" filed by the parties whether they were using "visitation" to mean custody, or whether the agreement assumed custody by Appellee with specific visitation rights reserved to Appellant. The temporary custody order provided for "joint custody," but also established a "visitation" schedule for Appellant. The final order, while perpetuating the existing arrangement with respect to physical care of the children, is silent on the question of legal custody.

We think it likely the trial judge intended to grant joint physical custody, but we would have to speculate concerning his intent as to legal custody. Any uncertainty should be resolved by the trial court, and we shall remand for that purpose. Additionally, we conclude that under the particular facts of this case our remand should mandate full reconsideration of the issue of child custody. This disposition will enable the parties and the trial court to address specifically the issues of physical and legal custody, and to measure the facts of this case against the criteria for joint custody that we have discussed above. Particular attention must be given to the ability and inclination of these parties to effectively communicate with each other, and to agree on those important matters affecting the welfare of the children. Although the record supports the finding of the trial judge that the parties, with the aid of counsel, were able to successfully establish a schedule for the physical care of the children, the record also strongly suggests the presence of considerable hostility between these parents and an inability to effectively communicate directly with each other. We recognize that significant changes may have taken place in the three years that have elapsed since the trial of this matter, and that additional evidence should be received. . . .

Judgment of the Court of Special Appeals vacated. Case remanded. . . .

NOTES ON JOINT CUSTODY

(1) Definition.   As Taylor v. Taylor reveals, the concept of joint custody is beset with "significant semantical problems." An award of custody, in general, encompasses two concepts: legal custody and physical custody. Legal custody involves responsibility for significant and long-range decisions regarding care, upbringing, health, welfare, and education of the child. Physical custody involves decision making regarding the child's daily activities. In an award of joint custody (more accurately termed joint legal custody), each parent shares responsibility for major child-rearing decision making irrespective of which parent has physical custody. Courts fashion joint custody awards in varying manners. *Taylor* illustrates

that an award of joint physical custody does not always encompass an award of joint legal custody and vice versa.

In *Taylor*, review how joint custody differs from other traditional custodial arrangements. An award of "sole custody" vests one parent with legal control and permanent physical custody; the noncustodial parent has only temporary physical custody during specified visitation periods. "Divided custody," sometimes called "alternating custody," involves a custody order that divides or alternates the legal and physical custody of a child between parents. "Split custody" refers to a situation in which one parent is given sole custody of one or more of the children, while the other parent has sole custody of other children.

(2) Benefits and Criticisms of Joint Custody. What are the benefits of joint custody — for parents and for children? What are the disadvantages of joint custody for the participants? Are short-range advantages and disadvantages different from long-range ones? The author of one empirical study (involving 24 families who voluntarily selected joint custody) points to the overriding parental benefit of sharing the pleasures and burdens of childrearing compared to the disadvantage of experiencing a sense of discontinuity of being a part-time parent. Children had a sense of being loved by both parents, recognition that both their parents were making considerable efforts to care for them, and physical access to both parents that mitigated loyalty conflicts. See Susan Steinman, Joint Custody: What We Know, What We Have to Learn, and the Judicial and Legislative Implications, 16 U.C. Davis L. Rev. 739, 743-749 (1983).

On the other hand, the concept of joint custody has many critics. One criticism concerns the unequal bargaining position involved in the joint custody choice that disfavors women.

> Critics argue that joint custody statutes increase men's rights at divorce and their bargaining strength with respect to women, making women more vulnerable to claims and threats made by men. [Citations omitted.] Underlying this critique are the assumptions that women take more responsibility for their children than do men, love their children more than men do, and are more willing than men to sacrifice in order to retain custody of their children. As a result, women will sacrifice their own financial rights, and even those of their children, in negotiations at divorce in order to preserve maximum custody of their children. This distortion in bargaining at divorce occurs, it is claimed, even if men do not really want joint custody of their children or do not intend to exercise their joint custody rights.
>
> Particular forms of joint custody provisions may disfavor women still further. For example, a "friendly parent" provision operates in sole custody disputes to favor the parent who demonstrates the greater willingness to allow the other parent access to the children. This rule may make it too risky for a woman to oppose a father's request for joint custody, even in justifiable circumstances, for to do so might imply that the mother is unwilling to permit the child the greatest access to both parents and thus is less suitable as a custodian. To avoid this implication, the woman may accept joint custody even when she feels it is in neither her nor her child's best interests . . . . [65]

[65] Katharine T. Bartlett & Carol B. Stack, Joint Custody, Feminism and the Dependency Dilemma, 2 Berkeley Women's L.J. 9, 19-20 (1986).

(3) Presumption, Preference, or Option.   In *Taylor*, the appellate court held that trial courts may make awards of joint custody even without express statutory authority. Today, however, almost all states provide for awards of joint custody either by statute or case law.[66] States follow different approaches: some statutes create a presumption for joint custody, others a preference, and others merely list joint custody as an option. Presumption and preference statutes each accord different weight to joint custody. Preference statutes give joint custody preference over other custodial forms; presumption statutes contain an assumption that joint custody is assumed to be in the child's best interests and will be ordered unless rebutted.

In recent years, states have retreated from joint custody, with some states removing joint custody presumptions, or precluding joint custody absent an agreement, or simply decreasing the number of joint custody awards. This retreat derives from the belief that joint custody (physical or legal) may not be in the child's best interests, especially when judicially imposed or when there is considerable parental discord. James G. Dwyer, A Taxonomy of Children's Existing Rights in State Decision Making About Their Relationships, 11 Wm. & Mary Bill Rts. J. 845, 911 (2003).

(4) Effect of Parental Agreement.   In many states, joint custody will not be awarded unless both parents agree to the arrangement. However, in other states, courts may decree an award of joint custody over the objection of one, or both, of the parents. See, e.g., Kay v. Ludwig, 686 N.W.2d 619 (Neb. Ct. App. 2004) (if parties do not agree, court may award joint custody upon finding of best interests).

There is considerable debate by commentators about whether an award of joint custody is appropriate over the objection of one, or both, of the parents. Consider the following two views:

> Most authorities agree that joint custody is only appropriate and in a child's best interests when both parents agree to such a plan and are capable of joint decision-making regarding the child's welfare. [Citations omitted.] This type of joint custody legislation [joint custody upon request of one party] is antithetical to the above criteria since the court can force joint custody on those parents who are not in agreement or who have not shown themselves capable of co-parenting. Legal edicts cannot force parents to agree on childrearing questions. Nor can the fate of children rest on the *possibility* of success.[67]
>
> A further resistance to joint custody is expressed in the widely held belief that joint custody should never be awarded unless both parents agree. Proponents of this view state that it is not in the "best interest" of the child to be involved in such a shared parenting arrangement because the hostile environment between parents will be perpetuated. . . . First, this position seems to ignore the finding that parents with sole custody orders also experience a period of intense conflict to

---

Inherent in the first criticism is the suggestion that some men request joint custody in order to reduce their child support liability. Some states address this issue specifically by providing either that an award of joint custody does not preclude support (see, e.g., Fla. Stat. Ann. §61.13(1)(a) (West 1997 & Supp. 1999); Mo. Rev. Stat. §452.375 (1997 & Supp. 1999)), or justify modification of a support order.

[66] See Margaret F. Brinig & F.H. Buckley, Joint Custody: Bonding and Monitoring Theories, 73 Ind. L.J. 393, 397 (1998) (surveying law).

[67] Joanne Schulman & Valerie Pitt, Second Thoughts on Joint Custody: Analysis of Legislation and Its Impact for Women and Children, 12 Golden Gate L. Rev. 539, 550 (1982).

which the children are witnesses. There is not yet evidence available that, on a daily basis, children in unilaterally desired joint custody arrangements experience *more* hostility, or that the hostility they initially experience would not be balanced by the opportunity to continue their relationship in a meaningful way with both parents. And, in denying joint custody *solely* on the basis of one parent's opposition, the child's wishes and developmental needs are not even being considered as a relevant factor in decision making . . . . [68]

(5) Factors Considered by Courts. *Taylor* mentions several factors that are relevant in determining whether joint custody is appropriate.

a. Parent-Related Factors. Case law emphasizes the necessity for parental cooperation for a successful joint custody arrangement. Although the court in *Taylor* found that the capacity of the parents to communicate and reach shared decisions affecting the child's welfare is the "most important factor" in determining the appropriateness of joint custody, many courts do not consider communication difficulties to present an insurmountable obstacle.[69]

Among the parent-related factors, the issue of parental cooperation elicits considerable controversy. Critics of joint custody argue that if parents could not agree during marriage, how can they be forced to agree after divorce? Consider the following rebuttal to this argument:

Another concept contributing to resistance among lawyers, judges, and mental health professionals to joint custody has been the belief that parents who divorce are unable to cooperate about anything, including their parenting after the divorce. This concept actually draws upon two somewhat erroneous and simplistic notions about divorce. The first is that a marriage that fails has done so in every regard, and that the conflict that led to the termination of the marriage permeated child-rearing issues and parental decision making as well. While this is clearly true in some marriages, there is evidence that substantial conflict regarding child-rearing practices is not present in a majority of marriages. Lawyers, in particular, seem to share the belief that if parents could cooperate regarding their children, they would not be divorcing in the first place. Adults divorce for many reasons related to adult needs and dissatisfactions, but dissatisfaction or conflict stemming from the spouse's parental behavior is not among the more prevalent reasons expressed for obtaining a divorce. The second notion is that the anger which attorneys and mental health professionals observe during the divorcing period will remain undiminished during the years following divorce. However, there is evidence that the intense anger between parents diminishes within the first year post-divorce. . . . After two years post-separation, only a small percentage of parents (close to 15%) remain intensely or pathologically enraged. . . . [70]

Another parent-related factor, geographic proximity between parental residences, also has an impact on the appropriateness of joint custody. This is especially

[68] Joan B. Kelly, Examining Resistance to Joint Custody in Joint Custody and Shared Parenting, in Joint Custody and Shared Parenting, (43 Jay Folberg, ed. 1984).

[69] See, e.g., McCarty v. McCarty, 807 A.2d 1211 (Md. App. 2002); Murphy v. Miller, 932 P.2d 722 (Wash. Ct. App. 1997).

[70] Schulman & Pitt, supra note [67].

true in cases in which parents share joint physical, as well as joint legal, custody. In some cases, courts assume that geographically distant residences lead to too much disruption to make joint custody feasible.[71] Other courts hold that distance is no bar to an award of joint custody.[72] Still another parent-related factor is financial resources. Maintenance of two parental residences appropriate for child rearing may place a burden on both parents. Should the inferior financial ability of one party preclude an award of joint custody? Review the discussion of wealth as a factor in custody decision making, pp. 557-562, supra.

b. Child-Related Factors.   Among the child-related factors, research has been conducted on the possible disruptive effect of joint custody. One commentator, reporting on her research, concludes that potential disruption may vary as a function of age:

> A major concern about joint custody is whether switching homes generates confusion and anxiety in the child about where he belongs. Most of the children [in our study] were impressively able to keep their complex schedules in mind and demonstrated a sense of mastery over switching between homes. Twenty-five percent of the children, however, were anxious and insecure about switching homes. They worried about themselves, their parents, possessions, and exhibited an overall sense of instability. . . .
>
> The continuity of school life and friendships was found to be very important to all the children in the study, but particularly to the latency age and adolescent children. They valued the stability of remaining in one school and used school as an anchoring place. The adolescents' age-appropriate involvement in school-based social activities, as well as the loosening of psychological ties to the parents, made the long established dual-home arrangement antithetical to their needs when they became teen-agers . . . . [73]

Another study concurs that the appropriateness of joint custody may depend on the age of the child. It suggests, however, that the preschool child (age three to five) has an even more difficult adjustment than the adolescent. See Rosemary McKinnon & Judith S. Wallerstein, Joint Custody and the Preschool Child, 4 Behav. Sci. & Law 169 (1986). What implication does this finding have for awards of joint custody? Should awards of joint custody be modified automatically when a child reaches adolescence?

c. Contraindicated Factors.   In some contexts, joint custody may be particularly inappropriate. What might those contexts be? Some commentators suggest that joint custody should never be awarded if there is evidence of spousal abuse, since

---

[71] See, e.g., West v. Lawson, 951 P.2d 1200 (Alaska 1998) (vacating joint custody arrangement when co-custodian moved from Anchorage to Las Vegas); Doyle v. Doyle, 955 S.W.2d 478 (Tex. Ct. App. 1997) (affirming award of sole custody to mother where father's military training obligations might require child to be left in care of non-parent for extended periods and might prevent father from making daily decisions about child).

[72] See, e.g., Rusin v. Rusin, 426 N.Y.S.2d 701 (Sup. Ct. 1980) (modification refused when co-custodian moved from New York to Denver). In this situation, some courts think joint custody is especially appropriate in order to facilitate continued parental participation in childrearing. Little, supra note [54], §13.07[5] at 13-56.

[73] Susan Steinman, Joint Custody: What We Know, What We Have Yet to Learn, and the Judicial and Legislative Implications, 16 U.C. Davis L. Rev. 739 (1983).

joint custody ensures continued contact with the abuser.[74] Most states now take this factor into account, either specifically in statutes providing for awards of joint custody, or more generally, in terms of determining any custodial arrangement. Can you think of similar situations that would militate against awards of joint custody?

(6) ALI Principles.   The ALI Principles favors joint custody when parents have adhered to it in the past. ALI Principles §2.08(1). The ALI Principles defers to private ordering by requiring all parents who seek to allocate custodial responsibility to file a parenting plan. Id. at §2.05(1). (Recall that the ALI substitutes the term "custodial responsibility" for the former terms "custody" and "visitation" and also uses the term "decision making responsibility" rather than the term "legal custody.") If the parents are unable to agree how to allocate custodial responsibility, the court follows the approximation standard — i.e., the division of parental responsibilities adopted by the parents prior to the divorce. See generally Katharine T. Bartlett, U.S. Custody Law and Trends in the Context of the ALI Principles of the Law of Family Dissolution, 10 Va. J. Soc. Pol'y & L. 5 (2002).

(7) Do parents have a constitutionally protected liberty interest in the joint legal custody of their children upon dissolution? If so, should states protect that right by providing for a rebuttable presumption of joint decision making? See James W. Bozzomo, Note, Joint Legal Custody: A Parent's Constitutional Right in a Reorganized Family, 31 Hofstra L. Rev. 547 (2002) (so arguing).

b. Standards Regarding the Noncustodial Parent: Visitation

Traditionally, an award of custody to one parent (typically the mother) is accompanied by a grant of visitation rights to the noncustodial parent. A trial judge has considerable discretion to determine the scope and frequency of visitation. Visitation can later be the occasion of disputes and tension because (1) it ordinarily requires the divorced parents to have at least *some contact* with one another; and (2) it may create conflicts of *loyalty* for the child. To avoid judicial intervention in family relationships after a divorce, and to protect the relationship between the child and the custodial parent, Goldstein, Freud and Solnit[75] suggested that "the noncustodial parent should have no legally enforceable right to visit the child," thus giving the custodial parent the full power and responsibility of deciding whether there should be visitation, and if so, when and for how long.

Commentators have been especially critical of this suggestion. For example, the Benedeks have written that

> experience has shown that custodial parents may be motivated to deny visitation by a number of reasons or emotions to which the child's best interests are entirely irrelevant. Ironically, it is the most meaningful relationships between children and noncustodial parents that are frequently the most threatening to custodial parents and, consequently, such relationships would often be in the greatest jeopardy.[76]

[74] See, e. g., Tonia E. Hinger, Domestic Violence and Joint Custody: New York Is Not Measuring Up, 11 Buff. Women's L.J. 89 (2002-2003).

[75] Joseph Goldstein et al., The Best Interests of the Child, supra note [2], at 23.

[76] Elissa P. Benedek & David M. Benedek, Postdivorce Visitation: A Child's Right, 16 J. Am. Acad. of Clinical Psychiatry 256, 263 (Spring 1977).

Does the Goldstein, Freud, and Solnit proposal raise constitutional problems?

The following section focuses on visitation. First, it explores the issue of the denial of visitation rights. Is it ever appropriate to deny visitation to a parent? If so, in what circumstances? Next, it examines conditions on visitation. Is it ever appropriate to restrict a parent's conduct during visitation periods? If so, in what circumstances? What restrictions are justifiable? Are there any limitations on a court's authority to condition visitation rights? Finally, it examines the rights of third parties to petition for visitation. Do persons such as grandparents, stepparents, and same-sex partners have visitation rights? Should a court be able to undermine a parent's decision to deny visitation to a person who has no legally cognizable relationship with the child? In what instances is such judicial interference in the family appropriate? In what circumstances does it violate the parent's right to raise a child as the parent sees fit?

(1) No Visitation?

Peterson v. Jason
513 So. 2d 1351 (Fla. Ct. App. 1987)

MILLS, Judge.

William E. Peterson appeals from a non-final order terminating visitation for non-payment of child support. . . . We reverse.

The parties herein were married in 1980 and produced one child in 1981. The final judgement of dissolution was entered in November 1985, granting primary custody of the child to the wife and visitation rights to Peterson. Based upon his then monthly income of $800.00, Peterson was ordered to pay $150.00 per month in child support, plus $50.00 per month against support arrearages which had accumulated during the period before final judgement was entered.

The ensuing months brought numerous motions for contempt from both parties, the wife alleging failure to pay child support, Peterson alleging wrongful denial of visitation. In November and December 1986, Peterson filed *pro se* motions for modification of his child support obligations based on allegations of illness and inability to pay. These motions were heard in April 1987 after which, despite evidence of Peterson's illness and a reduction in his income from $800.00 per month to $200.00 per month in welfare benefits, the trial court denied Peterson's motions for modification and further held him in "willful contempt" for failure to pay child support.

Despite the stated denial of modification of child support, the order went on to provide that "due to the financial status of petitioner (Peterson), the court will reduce the monthly support obligation from $150.00 to $75.00 per month"; the wife does not challenge this reduction. The order concluded that "visitation would be reinstated" if Peterson paid his May child support payment by 2 May and continued to keep it current. It is not clear if visitation had been terminated orally at the April hearing or by some other written order which does not appear in the record.

On 5 May 1987, the court entered another order noting that Peterson had not paid his child support as required by the first order and stating that "the court hereby stays petitioner's visitation with the minor child until he complies [with the 1 May order]." [R]einstatement of visitation to [occur] at such time as Peterson should appear and show that his child support was current. This appeal followed, on the sole issue of whether the trial court erred in conditioning Peterson's visitation rights on the payment of child support.

It is the general rule that visitation may not be changed or denied based merely on nonpayment of child support. However, there are some cases holding that, while the right to visitation does not terminate upon an *excusable failure* to pay support, in the face of a *willful and intentional refusal* to pay child support which is detrimental to the welfare of the child, the right to visitation may be terminated. [Citations omitted.] Therefore, it appears that a trial court can terminate a parent's right to visitation with a minor child for nonpayment of support only when the nonpayment has been willful and intentional *and* detrimental to the welfare of the child so that termination would be in the child's best interest.

Implicit in a finding of "willful and intentional refusal" to pay support is the ability to pay. . . . In the instant case, although the trial court found Peterson in "willful" contempt for nonpayment of support, withholding visitation until the payments were brought current, at the same time it halved his support obligation from $150.00 to $75.00 per month, specifically based on "the financial status of the petitioner." We cannot hold these equivocal findings sufficient to support the drastic measure of terminating visitation. As has been noted, a court has at its disposal a wide variety of other methods to coerce compliance with a final judgement of divorce.

Reversed.

NOTES AND QUESTIONS

(1) General Rule. The general rule is that the right to visitation and the duty of support are not interdependent variables. That is, visitation may not be conditioned on timely payment of child support. On the other hand, child support may not be withheld because an ex-spouse denies or interferes with visitation rights. See Hastings v. Rigsfee, 875 So. 2d 772 (Fla. Ct. App. 2004) (order conditioning mother's visitation upon payment of support was abuse of discretion). (For a discussion of the Parental Support Obligation, see Chapter 2, section B.)

(2) Exceptions. As *Peterson* reveals, courts are reluctant to impose total denial of visitation. Nonetheless, some situations may result in this "drastic measure." What might be such situations? For example, should a noncustodial parent's lack of interest constitute grounds for denying visitation? Compare J.L.M. v. R.L.C., 132 S.W.3d 279 (Mo. Ct. App. 2004) (denying visitation rights to father who failed to make contact for ten years, despite being financially able to do so) with Jackson v. Jackson, No. 2003-CA-000929-MR, 2004 WL 1299988 (Ky. Ct. App., June 11, 2004) (reversing denial of visitation by mother who had not seen child for two years).

What if the noncustodial parent physically abuses the children? Is this a basis to deny visitation? In Painter v. Painter, 688 A.2d 479 (Md. Ct. App. 1997), a father was denied visitation with his son and awarded only limited visitation with his daughter because of the father's severe physical and emotional physical abuse. Similarly, in Stitzel v. Brown, 767 N.Y.S.2d 510 (App. Div. 2003), the father was denied visitation because he committed domestic violence against the mother in the children's presence and injured the youngest child.

Proof of sexual abuse of the child is another ground for denying visitation. See, e.g., Appolon v. Faught, 796 N.E.2d 297 (Ind. Ct. App. 2003) (affirming denial of visitation by father where he molested one of the children); Lewis v. Butler, 794 So. 2d 1015 (Miss. 2001) (holding that father's improper sexual advances to his 14-year-old daughter warranted denial of visitation as to that daughter and another daughter); In re Marriage of M.A., 149 S.W.3d 562 (Mo. Ct. App. 2004) (affirming denial of visitation based on father's sexual abuse).

Suppose a parent is incarcerated. Is that sufficient reason to deny visitation? See Wright v. Wooden, No. 2001-CA-002295-MR, 2003 WL 22744370 (Ky. Ct. App., Nov. 21, 2003) (holding that visitation should be denied based upon a finding of serious endangerment caused by visiting incarcerated father rather than upon "best interests" standard). Should the underlying reason for the parent's incarceration be relevant in the determination of that parent's visitation rights? See, e.g., Cal. Fam. Code §3030(b) (West 2003) (providing a conclusive presumption that an award of custody or visitation to a convicted rapist, when the child was born as a result of the rape, is not in the child's best interests); Cal. Fam. Code §3030(c) (West 2003) (providing a rebuttable presumption against custody or unsupervised visitation with a person who has been convicted of first-degree murder of the child's other parent unless the court finds that there is no risk to the child's health, safety, and welfare).

See generally Deborah Ahrens, Not in Front of the Children: Prohibition on Child Custody as Civil Branding for Criminal Activity, 75 N.Y.U. L. Rev. 737 (2000); Dana Lowy & Mary Redfield, Criminal Histories and Parental Custody and Visitation Rights, 26 L.A. Law. 25 (Oct. 2003); Benjamin Guthrie Stewart, Comment, When Should a Court Order Visitation Between a Child and an Incarcerated Parent?, 9 U. Chi. L. Sch. Roundtable 165 (2002).

(3) Purpose of Visitation Denial.   What purpose does denial of visitation serve in these cases? If the purpose is punishment of the noncustodial parent, is this an appropriate use of punishment? If denial of visitation is based on the best interests of the child, is it ever in the child's best interests to be deprived of all contact with a parent? *abuse*

(4) Empirical Evidence.   *Peterson* raises the question of the appropriateness of a denial of visitation for failure to pay child support. The relationship of visitation to child support is much debated. Numerous questions arise. What is the incidence of visitation denial by custodial mothers? How often does visitation denial lead to nonpayment of child support? And conversely, how often does nonpayment of support contribute to problems with the exercise of visitation rights? The following article explores the complex relationship between visitation denial and child support, and suggests some areas for reform.

Jessica Pearson & Nancy Thoennes, The Denial of Visitation Rights: A Preliminary Look at Its Incidence, Correlates, Antecedents and Consequences
10 Law & Pol'y 363, 375-379 (1988)

This paper explores the nature and incidence of the denial of visitation rights and the nonpayment of child support. It relies on a secondary analysis of three different longitudinal data sets. . . .

The analysis reveals that visitation denial is a problem with approximately 22 percent of sample mothers reputedly failing to comply with the visitation terms of their divorce decree. This is consistent with reports of [other studies], however, it should be noted that these levels fall far below the reported levels of non-compliance with child support. Only about half of all custodial parents owed child support receive the full amount of support owed to them in any given year. Even fewer custodians receive all the payments on time. [Citations omitted]

Estimated levels of visitation denial also fall below levels of non-contact by absent parents noted in previous research. For example, in their longitudinal study of 1,747 households, Furstenburg and North (1983:10) discovered that in cases involving children living in one-parent families where the non-custodian is believed to be alive, "over a third of the children . . . lost contact altogether with the biological parent living outside the home." Hetherington, et al. (1978) report that two years following the divorce, 30 percent of the children saw their fathers about once a month or less. Luepnitz (1982) reports that in 24 percent of the 34 maternal custody families she studied, all of whom had separated at least two years, the non-custodian parent "never" saw the children. Fulton's (1979) study also notes that after two years, 30 percent of the fathers no longer visit their children. And at the five year follow-up study with their volunteer sample of 60 families, Wallerstein and Kelly (1980) report that only nine percent of the children had no contact with the non-custodian, although another 17 percent were visited only sporadically.

Clearly, it is inaccurate to assume that all of these are cases in which custodians encourage sporadic visitation or deny the non-custodian regular access to the children. Indeed in her study, Luepnitz notes that:

> In half of the cases when the non-custodial father visits rarely or never, it is because the children dislike him and have decided not to see him. But in many other cases, custodial mothers report that their ex had split the scene "in order to evade child support payments" (Luepnitz, 1982:34).

Further investigation of visitation non-compliance reveals that it rarely stands alone as a post-divorce problem and that such allegations are accompanied by a host of other visitation-related complaints. Moreover, for most parents visitation difficulties appear to become established fairly early on and fail to deviate over time.

Couples with visitation problems are decidedly more embittered than their compliant counterparts and their lack of cooperation, conflict and anger are apparent at the earliest interview, well before the promulgation of a divorce decree and are corroborated by independent interviewer ratings. Although non-payment of child support cases do not always involve a visitation problem, the two phenomena are related and cases with visitation problems are substantially more likely to involve child support nonpayment or disputes over support. Both phenomena appear to stem from conflict patterns between the parents, although we were unable to assess causal order in cases that involved both types of non-compliance. In half the cases, visitation preceded child support; in the other half of the cases, the opposite was true. In most instances, both problems were apparent at the time of the first interview and it was impossible to trace problem sequence. . . .

Policy Considerations

These findings inspire several policy recommendations. Minimally, there is a need for reliable record keeping of both child support and visitation arrears. Without reliable record keeping, violations are difficult to prove, make-up policies are impossible to establish or supervise. To date, several states require child support payments to be made through the Clerk of the Court rather than directly to the custodial parent. . . . Objective accounts of visitation denial, however, are harder to come by. One model approach is found in a Michigan law which requires the child support enforcement agency, the Friend of the Court, to keep track of alleged visitation denials (with the custodial parent having an opportunity to contest the allegation) and to supervise make-up visitation orders (Mich. Comp. Laws F25.164 (42) (4)-(5)).

Secondly these findings underscore the importance of interventions with divorcing couples aimed at enhancing their communication skills and reducing levels of anger and hostility. [A] preliminary assessment of relationships between the noncustodial parent and his children reveals that conflict between divorced parents is a good prediction of both child support payment, visitation and other types of involvement (Braver et al., 1985). [I]t appears that neglect of therapeutic elements of the process may vastly diminish its potential effectiveness in reducing post-divorce conflict over visitation and support.

A third conclusion of this research is the need to consider child support and visitation issues concurrently. While there is no evidence to suggest that the two issues should be made contingent upon one another, so that the denial of one should be a remedy for the withholding of the other, policy should reflect the fact that they co-occur and that grievances in both areas should be jointly aired. This conclusion runs counter to current practice. To date most court-based mediation services deal with the issues of contested child custody and/or visitation only. Child support and the other financial issues of divorce are considered to be beyond the purview of the mediation intervention. In the few settings where child support issues are mediated in court settings, they tend to be handled by a separate staff. . . .

For recent discussion of the relationship between custody and support, see Ira Mark Ellman, Should Visitation Denial Affect the Obligation to Pay Support?, 36 Ariz. St. L.J. 661 (2004) (contending that the rule of independence of support and visitation should be applied in more narrow range of cases); W. Fabricius & S. Braver, Non-Child Support Expenditures on Children by Nonresidential Divorced Fathers, 42 Fam. Ct. Rev. 321 (2003) (arguing that nonresidential fathers incur considerable visitation expenses and that should lead to a reduction in their child support obligations); Irwin Garfinkel et al., Visitation and Child Support Guidelines: A Comment on Fabricius and Braver, 42 Fam. Ct. Rev. 342 (2004) (rebuttal to Fabricius and Braver study).

(5) As aforementioned, Goldstein, Freud, and Solnit in *Beyond the Best Interests of the Child* suggest that the custodial parent be given the power to determine the visitation rights of the noncustodial parent. Putting aside for the moment the

constitutional implications of such a proposal, does it constitute sound policy? Consider the following:

Eleanor E. Maccoby & Robert H. Mnookin, Dividing the Child: Social and Legal Dilemmas of Custody
285-287 (1992)

Some children would no doubt benefit from a rule that gave the custodial parent control over the other parent's access. What concerns us, however, is the risk that many other children might well be harmed by such a rule. Our research suggests that a significant if declining portion of parents do remain enmeshed in conflict. For some of these conflicted families, ending visitation might benefit the children. But among the families in our study, the conflicted pattern of co-parenting was not the most common pattern several years after parental separation. Rather, spousal disengagement became the norm as time passed. . . . Our concern is that because of difficulties related to the spousal divorce, a significant number of custodial mothers might put an end to paternal visitation in circumstances where the children would not in fact suffer long-run harm by reason of parental conflict, and where they would receive important long-run benefits from a continuing relationship with their father.

We suggested earlier that children who are primarily residing with their mother can nevertheless receive a variety of benefits — psychological, social, and economic — from a continuing relationship with their father. [T]he evidence in both our study and others makes it clear that there is better compliance with support obligations by fathers who maintain contact with their children. In many states, a father's legal obligation to support his children ends when the child reaches age 18. We think it quite plausible that fathers who remain in contact are more likely to help a child with college expenses after this age. Moreover, in addition to possible economic benefits, we think children can benefit in other ways from a continuing relationship. We have seen that a significant minority of children who start out living with one parent go to live with the other at a later time, at least temporarily. . . . And in cases where the children continue to live with the mother, the relationship with the father — although not nearly so important to a child's development as the relationship with the custodial mother — can nevertheless provide emotional support in times of crisis and possible guidance for the child over the years. . . .

In recent years, there has been considerable debate concerning the wisdom of children's having continuing contact with a non-custodial parent in families where there is a history of domestic violence (Cahn, 1991; Ellis, 1990). We do not doubt that when the *child* has been abused by the non-custodial parent, the court is justified in denying visitation or limiting it to supervised situations. However, in cases of violence between the spouses, the issue is more complex. Incidents of violence (for example, hitting, throwing objects) are quite common at the time a marriage breaks up, and husbands and wives are almost equally likely to engage in violent acts, though women are much more likely to get hurt (Johnston, in press; Straus, Gelles, and Steinmetz, 1981). Further, allegations of physical abuse are common during divorce negotiations (Depner, Cannata, and Simon, in press), and verifying their frequency or severity is difficult indeed. We believe that allegations of violent acts should not be automatic grounds for denying visitation. A history of chronic physical abuse must be taken very seriously, however. While it may not be possible to devise a blanket statutory rule that would be applicable to all cases, we certainly believe that courts should retain the power to eliminate visitation in order to protect mother and children from a physically abusive father.

In families where no abuse has occurred, there are nevertheless some potential risks of maintaining visitation in families in which the parents have disengaged. The child may become the carrier of necessary messages, and may get caught up in parental conflict in the process. Beyond this, children — particularly teenagers — may well be able to weaken the authority of the custodial parent by playing off the two parents against each other. . . .

Despite these potential disadvantages, we are not persuaded that on balance the potential benefits of a general policy giving the custodial parent the legal right to terminate visitation would outweigh the potential costs. Of course, we are constrained by the existing research, which does not allow precise quantification and comparison of the benefits and costs of a legal rule that would give a custodial parent the legal power to end visitation. It is certainly conceivable that research in the future might suggest that on balance the benefits of such a rule would outweigh the costs. But on the basis of existing evidence, and in the absence of a showing of abuse, we are not persuaded this would be so. . . .

(2) Conditions on Visitation

Khalsa v. Khalsa
751 P.2d 715 (N.M. Ct. App. 1988)

GARCIA, Judge.

The parties were married in 1973. At the time, they were Sikhs and believed in and practiced the Sikh religion. In June 1976, the parties' oldest child, Mari Jap Singh Khalsa, was born, and in January 1981, the parties had a second child, Kartar Singh Khalsa. Both children's Sikh names appear on their birth certificates and, while the parties were married, both children were raised as Sikhs. The family observed the requirements of their religion, including the wearing of distinct apparel and turbans, reading from the Guru Granath, the Sikh scriptures, and the assumption of Sikh names. Their adherence to principles and tenets of their faith continued throughout their marriage.

Marital discord ultimately led to the breakdown of their marriage and in December 1982, mother filed an uncontested petition for divorce. Mother was granted the divorce and awarded sole custody of the two children.

In December 1983, mother remarried. Shortly thereafter, mother abandoned the Sikh religion and began discouraging the children from practicing Sikhism. Mother also began calling the children by other than the Sikh names. Father objected to the children not being raised as Sikhs, and the parties' disagreements over religious differences escalated. In May 1984, father filed a motion requesting sole custody of the children or, in the alternative, joint custody.

In violation of father's discovery request, mother failed to timely disclose the names of any expert witnesses whom she planned to call at trial on her behalf. . . . Over father's objections, both witnesses testified.

In December 1986, following a hearing on the merits, the trial court entered its order regarding custody, [and] visitation. . . .

[T]he court ordered that sole custody of the children remain with mother; that father have visitation with the children at his residence for one month each summer; and that the children not participate voluntarily or involuntarily in any Sikh religious activities with father. Father appeals. . . .

Father raised the following . . . on appeal: . . . whether the trial court erred in enjoining father from encouraging his children to practice and participate in the Sikh religion during their visits with father. . . .

This issue presents a matter of first impression. [W]e deem it necessary to give guidance as to the scope of a court's intervention in religious beliefs and practices in child custody disputes.

Without any finding that participation in religious activities was harmful to the children here, the trial court enjoined the parties from freely discussing their religious beliefs with their children. Specifically, the trial court ordered that when the children were with the father, they could not voluntarily or involuntarily participate in any Sikh activity, including any church activity, Sikh camp or Sikh day care center.

It is well established that in child custody matters the best interests and welfare of the children are the primary and controlling considerations. Similarly, where there is a conflict between the parents regarding the religious faith and training of the children, the paramount concern is the welfare of the children.

Courts should proceed cautiously and with circumspection when dealing with religious issues. . . . In Munoz v. Munoz, [489 P.2d 1133 (Wash. 1971)] the court noted:

> The courts are reluctant . . . to interfere with the religious faith and training of children where the conflicting religious preferences of the parents are in no way detrimental to the welfare of the child. The obvious reason for such a policy of impartiality regarding religious beliefs is that, constitutionally, American courts are forbidden from interfering with religious freedoms or to take steps preferring one religion over another.

Thus, the rule appears to be well established that the courts should maintain an attitude of strict impartiality between religions and should not disqualify any applicant for custody or restrain any person having custody or visitation rights from taking the children to a particular church, except where there is a clear and affirmative showing that the conflicting religious beliefs affect the general welfare of the child.

In justifying a prohibition of religious restrictions on visitation rights, physical or emotional harm to the child cannot be assumed, but must be demonstrated in detail. Factual evidence of harm rather than "mere conclusions and speculation" is required.

Thus, a custodial parent's general testimony that the child is upset or confused because of the non-custodial parent's religious practice is insufficient to demonstrate harm. Further, general testimony that the child is upset because the parents practice conflicting religious beliefs is likewise insufficient. Hanson v. Hanson [404 N.W.2d 460 (N.D. 1987)] (mother's testimony that father, a member of the Pentecostal Apostolic church, had told the children, among other things, that the

Catholic church believes in cannibalism, which upset the children, was insufficient to prohibit father from taking the children to his church); Munoz v. Munoz [supra] (parent's speculation that six-year-old son, who attended both Mormon services with his mother and Catholic services with his father, was emotionally harmed thereby, was insufficient. The court concluded that duality of religious beliefs, do not, per se, create a conflict upon young minds.)

Although most disputes involve conflicting religious practices between the divorced parents, the same principles apply equally where one parent practices no religion. . . .

A court's reluctance to interfere with the religious upbringing of children, however, is not absolute. Religious restrictions placed upon visitation rights have been upheld where evidence of physical or emotional harm to the child has been substantial. See Funk v. Ossman, 150 Ariz. 578, 724 P.2d 1247 (App. 1986) (court upheld order enjoining noncustodial parent from taking his eight-year-old son to formal Jewish religious training. Evidence presented at trial included the testimony of three psychologists, one of whom testified that child had anxiety problems caused by the religious differences of his parents, which manifested itself in encopresis); Bentley v. Bentley, 86 A.D.2d 926, 448 N.Y.S.2d 559 (1982) (court affirmed order prohibiting non-custodial father from instructing his children in the teachings of the Jehovah's Witnesses. The custodial mother was Catholic and the court found that the children were "emotionally strained and torn" as a result of the parties' conflicting religious beliefs).

Thus, although the courts are reluctant to enjoin a non-custodial parent from practicing his religion with his children, the courts can and will enjoin such practice where the testimony concerning physical or emotional harm to the child is detailed and the best interests of the child will be served through the prohibition. Here, the evidence concerning the impact on the children consisted of testimony by Father Burtner and mother's general testimony that the children appeared upset and disturbed after visitations with father. Because we have held that the trial court abused its discretion in permitting Father Burtner to testify, however, the trial court could not restrict father from practicing his religion with his children based on such testimony. Mother's general testimony alone, however, was insufficient to support the restriction.

In sum, we adopt the view [that] [c]ourts should adhere to a policy of impartiality between religions, and should intervene in this sensitive and constitutionally protected area only where there is a clear and affirmative showing of harm to the children. Restrictions in this area present the danger that court-imposed limitations will unconstitutionally infringe upon a parent's freedom of worship or be perceived as having that effect.

Thus, we hold that, in determining whether a parent involved in a child custody dispute should be restricted from practicing or encouraging the child in a religious belief or practice, the trial court must consider the following:

1. Whether there exists detailed factual evidence demonstrating that the conflicting beliefs or practices of the parents pose substantial physical or emotional harm to the child;

2. Whether restricting the religious interaction between the parent and child will necessarily alleviate this harm; and

3. Whether such restrictions are narrowly tailored so as to minimize interference with the parents' religious freedom.

Here, there was no evidence that either child was harmed by exposure to father's religion. Accordingly, we further hold the trial court's judgment enjoining both parents from freely discussing their religious beliefs with the children, and specifically prohibiting father from encouraging his children to participate in any Sikh activity, to be error. . . .

NOTES AND QUESTIONS

(1) General Rule. In general, the custodial parent has the right to determine the child's upbringing. In some instances the custodial parent can place conditions, which courts will enforce, on visitation between the noncustodial parent and the child. In what situations are courts likely to enforce such restrictions? In what situations will courts refuse? *Khalsa* reveals that one frequent source of contention involves religious differences between parents. Mr. Khalsa wants the children to participate in Sikh religious activities during periods of visitation with him; the mother objects. In this conflict, what are the various interests of the noncustodial father, the custodial mother, and the children? How should the court balance these interests? *Khalsa* reveals that, as a general rule, courts are reluctant to infringe on visitation rights of the noncustodial parent. Visitation will not be restricted because of a noncustodial parent's religious beliefs absent a showing that the child will be harmed thereby.

(2) Constitutional Issues. What constitutional problems are inherent in a court's resolution of visitation disputes between divorced parents? Is visitation a constitutionally protected right of the noncustodial parent? Marsha B. Freedman, Reconnecting the Family: A Need for Sensible Visitation Schedules for Children of Divorce, 22 Whittier L. Rev. 779 (2001).

First Amendment concerns make courts reluctant to become involved in religious disputes. The First Amendment provides that "Congress shall make no law respecting an establishment of religion, or prohibiting the free exercise thereof." U.S. Const. amend. I.[77] The two clauses of the amendment, the Establishment Clause and the Free Exercise Clause, present separate requirements. State action in the form of a judicial opinion that prefers one religion to another may violate both clauses. By favoring one parent over another for religious reasons, judicial action violates the disfavored parent's right to the free exercise of religion. Similarly, favoring a parent for religious reasons also may violate the prohibition against a state's establishing a religion by violating the goals of ensuring separation of church and state and of promoting governmental neutrality towards religion.

(3) Requisite Harm. Although courts will condition or refuse visitation rights to a noncustodial parent (or even deny custody to a parent) whose religious practices will harm a child, courts differ on the certainty and amount of harm that must be shown. What harm might result from a child's exposure to different religious beliefs

---

[77] The amendment applies to the states through the Fourteenth Amendment. In addition, it applies to judicial as well as legislative actions.

of its parents? Courts sometimes look to the amount and intensity of confusion, frustration, guilt, or anxiety, especially in conjunction with physical manifestations. See, e.g. In re Marriage of Dorworth, 33 P.3d 1260 (Colo. Ct. App. 2001) (impairment of emotional development); Meyer v. Meyer, 789 A.2d 921 (Utah 2001) (tension and severe anxiety). Is a child's confusion about the doctrinal differences between the parents' different religions sufficient harm? See In re Marriage of Minix, 801 N.E. 2d 1201 (Ill. App. Ct. 2003).

What evidence is necessary to meet the requisite showing of harm? Is the custodial parent's testimony sufficient? Court conjecture? Or is expert testimony required? *Khalsa* is indicative of cases that require a higher standard of harm: harm must not be assumed or surmised but rather demonstrated in detail. See also Sagar v. Sagar, 781 N.E.2d 54 (Mass. App. Ct. 2003). What were the allegations of harm in *Khalsa*, and how did the mother attempt to substantiate them? Further, for the necessary showing of harm, must there be actual harm or is the probability of future harm sufficient?[78] Compare Shepp v. Shepp, 821 A.2d 635 (Pa. Super. Ct. 2003) (actual harm), with Osherow v. Osherow, 757 So. 2d 519 (Fla. Ct. App. 2003) (likelihood of harm).

(4) Other Religious Issues.   Suppose that the religious differences between the parents pertain to other issues. For example, should courts reduce or change visitation to accommodate the custodial parent's desires (such as the wish to take the child to Sunday church services or instructional classes)? On the other hand, may a court require the *noncustodial* parent to take the child to church and Sunday school during visitation periods? Compare Johns v. Johns, 918 S.W.2d 728 (Ark. Ct. App. 1996) (father required to take children to church during visitation) with Johnson v. Nation, 615 N.E.2d 141 (Ind. App. Ct. 1993) (contra). May a court require the noncustodial parent to conform to the custodial parent's religious practices during visitation? See Brown v. Szakal, 514 A.2d 81 (N.J. Super. Ct. 1986) (court cannot compel noncustodial parent to enforce custodial parent's Sabbath and dietary laws during visitation). See generally Carl E. Schneider, Religion and Child Custody, 25 U. Mich. J.L. Ref. 879 (1992); Joann Ross Wilder, Religion and Best Interests in Custody Cases, 18 J. Am. Acad. Matrim. Law 211 (2002).

(5) Conditions on Sexual Conduct and Sexual Orientation.   The issue of judicial enforcement of conditions on visitation also arises in several other contexts, frequently in the area of sexual behavior. For example, a noncustodial parent's sexual orientation may give rise to conditions on visitation. In many cases involving a gay or lesbian noncustodial parent, courts either award nonovernight visitation or condition visitation on the requirement that the child never be in the presence of the parent's partner. Compare In re Marriage of Dorworth, supra (upholding restriction), with Donovan v. Muffley, 767 N.E.2d 1014 (Ind. Ct. App. 2002), and Eldridge v. Eldridge, 42 S.W.3d 82 (Tenn. 2001) (invalidating restriction). See also Robin Cheryl Miller, Annotation, Restrictions on Parent's Child Visitation Rights Based on Parent's Sexual Conduct, 99 A.L.R.5th 475 (2002).

---

[78] See Jennifer Ann Drobac, Note, For the Sake of the Children: Court Consideration of Religion in Child Custody Cases, 50 Stan. L. Rev. 1609, 1631 (1998) (concluding that different courts require actual harm, a substantial threat of harm or merely some risk of harm although some courts require no showing of harm).

Suppose the noncustodial parent violates the judicially ordered condition. What result? See, e.g., Arms v. Arms, 803 N.E.2d 1201 (Ind. Ct. App. 2004) (affirming transfer of custody).

Do these conditions violate any constitutional rights of the noncustodial parent? Does Lawrence v. Texas, supra pp. 556-557, have any impact on the imposition of such conditions on visitation?

In contrast to cases involving a gay or lesbian parent, many courts are reluctant to condition visitation regarding a parent's involvement in a nonmarital heterosexual relationship. Harper v. Harper, 777 So. 2d 1275 (La. Ct. App. 2001). But cf. Ford v. Ford, 65 S.W.3d 432 (Ark. 2002) (parties prohibited from having nonrelatives of opposite sex staying overnight while children were present).

(6) Supervised Visitation. What additional factors might lead to conditions on visitation? Courts have allowed visitation between the noncustodial parent and child in cases of physical or sexual abuse or substance abuse. Usually, however, visitation is strictly supervised. See In re Anna H.M., No. WD-03-033, 2003 WL 22946179 (Ohio App. Ct. Dec. 12, 2003) (sexual abuse); Street v. May, 803 So. 2d 312 (La. Ct. App. 2001) (substance abuse); Madison v. Madison, 27 S.W.3d 853 (Mo. App. Ct. 2000) (physical abuse).

Supervised visitation often leads to difficulties in framing the order. For example, should supervised visitation begin only after a parent seeks treatment? See Keith Allen A. v. Jennifer J.A., 500 S.E.2d 552 (W. Va. 1997). Completes treatment? Who should supervise visitation — a social worker, mental health professional, relative, friend? Should the child's feelings about the supervisor be taken into account? See Monette v. Hoff, 958 P.2d 434 (Ark. 1998); In re Santoro, 594 N.W.2d 174 (Minn. 1999). When should supervised visitation give way to unsupervised visitation? See generally Nat Stern & Karen Oehme, The Troubling Admission of Supervised Visitation Records in Custody Proceedings, 75 Temp. L. Rev. 271 (2002).

(7) Other Conditions: Smoking. Given the danger posed by "secondhand smoke," should visitation be conditioned on a parent's not smoking? See Johnita M.D. v. David D.D., 740 N.Y.S.2d 811 (N.Y. 2002) (holding that trial court would take judicial notice that it was in best interest of child that mother and father be ordered not to smoke); Judge William F. Chinnock, No Smoking Around Children: The Family Courts' Mandatory Duty to Restrain Parents and Other Persons from Smoking Around Children, 45 Ariz. L. Rev. 801 (2003); Jeanette Igbenebor, Comment, Smoking as a Factor in Child Custody Cases, 18 J. Am. Acad. Matrim. Law. 235 (2002).

(3) Third-Party Visitation Rights

What are the rights of third parties (such as grandparents, stepparents, and gay and lesbian partners) to visit with children in the face of parental objection?

Troxel v. Granville SupCt
530 U.S. 57 (2000)

Justice O'CONNOR announced the judgment of the Court and delivered an opinion, in which the Chief Justice, Justice GINSBURG, and Justice BREYER join. . . .

ts   Tommie Granville and Brad Troxel shared a relationship that ended in June
1991. The two never married, but they had two daughters, Isabelle and Natalie.
Jenifer and Gary Troxel are Brad's parents, and thus the paternal grandparents of
Isabelle and Natalie. After Tommie and Brad separated in 1991, Brad lived with
his parents and regularly brought his daughters to his parents' home for weekend visitation. Brad committed suicide in May 1993. Although the Troxels at first
continued to see Isabelle and Natalie on a regular basis after their son's death,
Tommie Granville informed the Troxels in October 1993 that she wished to limit
their visitation with her daughters to one short visit per month.

[Two months later, the Troxels filed this petition for visitation.] At trial, the
Troxels requested two weekends of overnight visitation per month and two weeks of
visitation each summer. Granville did not oppose visitation altogether, but instead
asked the court to order one day of visitation per month with no overnight stay.
[T]he Superior Court [ordered] visitation one weekend per month, one week during
the summer, and four hours on both of the petitioning grandparents' birthdays.
Granville appealed, during which time she married Kelly Wynn. [Before addressing
Granville's appeal, the Washington Court of Appeals remanded the case to the
Superior Court, which found that visitation was in the children's best interests.
Nine months later, Granville's husband adopted the girls. The Court of Appeals
reversed the visitation order based on their statutory interpretation that nonparents
lack standing unless a custody action is pending.] Having resolved the case on
the statutory ground, however, the Court of Appeals did not expressly pass on
Granville's constitutional challenge to the visitation statute.

II

The demographic changes of the past century make it difficult to speak of an average American family. The composition of families varies greatly from household to
household. While many children may have two married parents and grandparents
who visit regularly, many other children are raised in single-parent households. In
1996, children living with only one parent accounted for 28 percent of all children
under age 18 in the United States. U.S. Dept. of Commerce, Bureau of Census, Current Population Reports, 1997 Population Profile of the United States 27 (1998).
Understandably, in these single-parent households, persons outside the nuclear family are called upon with increasing frequency to assist in the everyday tasks of child
rearing. In many cases, grandparents play an important role. For example, in 1998,
approximately 4 million children — or 5.6 percent of all children under age 18 —
lived in the household of their grandparents. U.S. Dept. of Commerce, Bureau
of Census, Current Population Reports, Marital Status and Living Arrangements:
March 1998, p. I (1998).

The nationwide enactment of nonparental visitation statutes is assuredly due,
in some part, to the States' recognition of these changing realities of the American family. Because grandparents and other relatives undertake duties of a parental
nature in many households, States have sought to ensure the welfare of the children
therein by protecting the relationships those children form with such third parties.
The States' nonparental visitation statutes are further supported by a recognition,
which varies from State to State, that children should have the opportunity to benefit

from relationships with statutorily specified persons — for example, their grand-parents. The extension of statutory rights in this area to persons other than a child's parents, however, comes with an obvious cost. For example, the State's recognition of an independent third-party interest in a child can place a substantial burden on the traditional parent-child relationship. . . .

The liberty interest at issue in this case — the interest of parents in the care, custody, and control of their children — is perhaps the oldest of the fundamental liberty interests recognized by this Court. More than 75 years ago, in Meyer v. Nebraska, 262 U.S. 390, 399, 401 (1923), we held that the "liberty" protected by the Due Process Clause includes the right of parents to "establish a home and bring up children" and "to control the education of their own." Two years later, in Pierce v. Society of Sisters, 268 U.S. 510, 534-535 (1925), we again held that the "liberty of parents and guardians" includes the right "to direct the upbringing and education of children under their control." We explained in *Pierce* that "[t]he child is not the mere creature of the State; those who nurture him and direct his destiny have the right, coupled with the high duty, to recognize and prepare him for additional obligations." Id., at 535. We returned to the subject in Prince v. Massachusetts, 321 U.S. 158 (1944), and again confirmed that there is a constitutional dimension to the right of parents to direct the upbringing of their children. "It is cardinal with us that the custody, care and nurture of the child reside first in the parents, whose primary function and freedom include preparation for obligations the state can neither supply nor hinder." Id., at 166.

In subsequent cases also, we have recognized the fundamental right of parents to make decisions concerning the care, custody, and control of their children [citing Stanley v. Illinois, Wisconsin v. Yoder, Quilloin v. Walcott, etc.]. In light of this extensive precedent, it cannot now be doubted that the Due Process Clause of the Fourteenth Amendment protects the fundamental right of parents to make decisions concerning the care, custody, and control of their children.

Section 26.10.160(3), as applied to Granville and her family in this case, unconstitutionally infringes on that fundamental parental right. The Washington nonparental visitation statute is breathtakingly broad. According to the statute's text, "*[a]ny person* may petition the court for visitation rights at any time," and the court may grant such visitation rights whenever "visitation may serve *the best interest of the child.*" §26.10.160(3) (emphases added). That language effectively permits any third party seeking visitation to subject any decision by a parent con-cerning visitation of the parent's children to state-court review. Once the visitation petition has been filed in court and the matter is placed before a judge, a parent's decision that visitation would not be in the child's best interest is accorded no deference. Section 26.10.160(3) contains no requirement that a court accord the parent's decision any presumption of validity or any weight whatsoever. Instead, the Washington statute places the best-interest determination solely in the hands of the judge. Should the judge disagree with the parent's estimation of the child's best interests, the judge's view necessarily prevails. Thus, in practical effect, in the State of Washington a court can disregard and overturn any decision by a fit custodial parent concerning visitation whenever a third party affected by the decision files a visitation petition, based solely on the judge's determination of the child's best interests. . . .

Turning to the facts of this case, the record reveals that the Superior Court's order was based on precisely the type of mere disagreement we have just described and nothing more. The Superior Court's order was not founded on any special factors that might justify the State's interference with Granville's fundamental right to make decisions concerning the rearing of her two daughters. To be sure, this case involves a visitation petition filed by grandparents soon after the death of their son — the father of Isabelle and Natalie — but the combination of several factors here compels our conclusion that §26.10.160(3), as applied, exceeded the bounds of the Due Process Clause.

First, the Troxels did not allege, and no court has found, that Granville was an unfit parent. That aspect of the case is important, for there is a presumption that fit parents act in the best interests of their children. [S]o long as a parent adequately cares for his or her children (i.e., is fit), there will normally be no reason for the State to inject itself into the private realm of the family to further question the ability of that parent to make the best decisions concerning the rearing of that parent's children.

The problem here is not that the Washington Superior Court intervened, but that when it did so, it gave no special weight at all to Granville's determination of her daughters' best interests. More importantly, it appears that the Superior Court [adopted a "commonsensical approach [that] it is normally in the best interest of the children to spend quality time with the grandparent," and placing] on Granville, the fit custodial parent, the burden of *disproving* that visitation would be in the best interest of her daughters. . . .

The decisional framework employed by the Superior Court directly contravened the traditional presumption that a fit parent will act in the best interest of his or her child. In that respect, the court's presumption failed to provide any protection for Granville's fundamental constitutional right to make decisions concerning the rearing of her own daughters. In an ideal world, parents might always seek to cultivate the bonds between grandparents and their grandchildren. Needless to say, however, our world is far from perfect, and in it the decision whether such an intergenerational relationship would be beneficial in any specific case is for the parent to make in the first instance. And, if a fit parent's decision of the kind at issue here becomes subject to judicial review, the court must accord at least some special weight to the parent's own determination.

Finally, we note that there is no allegation that Granville ever sought to cut off visitation entirely. Rather, the present dispute originated when Granville informed the Troxels that she would prefer to restrict their visitation with Isabelle and Natalie to one short visit per month and special holidays. . . . The Superior Court gave no weight to Granville's having assented to visitation even before the filing of any visitation petition or subsequent court intervention. . . . Significantly, many other states expressly provide by statute that courts may not award visitation unless a parent has denied (or unreasonably denied) visitation to the concerned third party.

Considered together with the Superior Court's reasons for awarding visitation to the Troxels, the combination of these factors demonstrates that the visitation order in this case was an unconstitutional infringement on Granville's fundamental right to make decisions concerning the care, custody, and control of her two daughters. The Washington Superior Court failed to accord the determination of Granville, a fit custodial parent, any material weight. In fact, the Superior Court made only two formal findings in support of its visitation order. First, the Troxels "are part of a large, central, loving family, all located in this area, and the [Troxels] can provide opportunities for the children in the areas of cousins and music." App. 70a. Second, "[t]he children would be benefitted from spending quality time with the [Troxels], provided that that time is balanced with time with the childrens' [sic] nuclear family." Ibid. These slender findings, in combination with the court's announced presumption in favor of grandparent visitation and its failure to accord significant weight to Granville's already having offered meaningful visitation to the Troxels, show that this case involves nothing more than a simple disagreement between the Washington Superior Court and Granville concerning her children's best interests. The Superior Court's announced reason for ordering one week of visitation in the summer demonstrates our conclusion well: "I look back on some personal experiences. . . . We always spen[t] as kids a week with one set of grandparents and another set of grandparents, [and] it happened to work out in our family that [it] turned out to be an enjoyable experience. Maybe that can, in this family, if that is how it works out." Verbatim Report 220-221. As we have explained, the Due Process Clause does not permit a State to infringe on the fundamental right of parents to make child rearing decisions simply because a state judge believes a "better" decision could be made. Neither the Washington nonparental visitation statute generally — which places no limits on either the persons who may petition for visitation or the circumstances in which such a petition may be granted — nor the Superior Court in this specific case required anything more. Accordingly, we hold that §26.10.160(3), as applied in this case, is unconstitutional. . . .

Because we rest our decision on the sweeping breadth of §26.10.160(3) and the application of that broad, unlimited power in this case, we do not consider the primary constitutional question passed on by the Washington Supreme Court — whether the Due Process Clause requires all nonparental visitation statutes to include a showing of harm or potential harm to the child as a condition precedent to granting visitation. We do not, and need not, define today the precise scope of the parental due process right in the visitation context. [T]he constitutionality of any standard for awarding visitation turns on the specific manner in which that standard is applied. . . . Because much state-court adjudication in this context occurs on a case-by-case basis, we would be hesitant to hold that specific nonparental visitation statutes violate the Due Process Clause as a *per se* matter. . . .

[In separate omitted concurring opinions, Justice Souter upheld the state court's determination of the statute's facial unconstitutionality, and Justice Thomas noted that strict scrutiny ought to apply. In separate omitted dissenting opinions, Justice Scalia declined to recognize unenumerated constitutional rights, and Justice Kennedy reasoned that the best interest doctrine is not always an unconstitutional standard in visitation cases. Justice Stevens' dissent is excerpted supra, pp. 79-80.]

NOTES AND QUESTIONS

(1) Background: Common Law. At common law, grandparents had no right to visitation with grandchildren in the face of parental objection. All states now

have third-party visitation statutes that permit grandparents (and sometimes other persons, as *Troxel* reveals) to petition for visitation in certain circumstances.

(2) Background: Biological-Parent Presumption.   A presumption favors biological parents in custody, as opposed to visitation, disputes involving parents versus nonparents. That is, courts apply a rebuttable presumption that custody should be awarded to a biological parent absent evidence of parental unfitness. In a landmark grandparents' rights case, a state supreme court refused to follow that presumption. In Painter v. Bannister, 140 N.W.2d 152 (Iowa 1966), *cert. denied*, 385 U.S. 949 (1966), a father left his young son with the maternal grandparents when the boy's sister and mother died in an automobile accident. When the father remarried and requested the return of his son, the grandparents refused. The father brought a habeas corpus action. Refusing to apply the parental presumption, the court held that the child's best interests would be served by remaining with the stable, churchgoing Midwestern grandparents rather than with the bohemian writer-father. How does a custody dispute between parents and nonparents, such as *Painter*, differ from a visitation dispute such as *Troxel*?

(3) Unconstitutional as Applied.   In *Troxel*, the plurality held that the Washington statute, as applied to Tommie Granville, violated the Due Process Clause. In what way(s) was the application defective? Why did the Court determine that the Washington visitation statute unconstitutionally infringed on the mother's rights? How influential are Meyer v. Nebraska and Pierce v. Society of Sisters in the Court's analysis?

(4) Why is it significant that the Court held the statute unconstitutional as applied rather than facially unconstitutional? How should the Washington state legislature redraft the statute after *Troxel*?

(5) Standard of Review.   In *Troxel*, the Court avoided identifying the appropriate standard of review for evaluating infringements on parental rights. After *Troxel*, should courts apply the strict scrutiny test (out of deference to parental rights) or the rational basis test? See Stephen A. Newman, Five Critical Issues in New York's Grandparent Visitation Law after Troxel v. Granville, 48 N.Y.L. Sch. L. Rev. 489, 516 (2003-2004) (pointing out that several state supreme courts post-*Troxel* have adopted strict scrutiny).

(6) Degree of Deference to Fit Parent's Decision.   *Troxel* established that courts must give deference to a fit parent's decision to restrict or deny third-party visitation. However, the Court failed to define the requisite degree of deference. In response, a majority of courts have agreed that the parent's decision regarding visitation is entitled to a rebuttable presumption that the parent is acting in the child's best interests. Solangel Maldonade, When Father (or Mother) Doesn't Know Best: Quasi-Parents and Parental Deference After Troxel v. Granville, 88 Iowa L. Rev. 865, 884-888 (2003). What factors should rebut the presumption?

(7) Showing of Harm?   The various Justices in *Troxel* disagreed about the need for a showing of harm as a condition precedent to granting third-party visitation. In the wake of *Troxel*, "[s]tate courts have differed on whether the constitutionality of [state] statutes should be weighed against the harm standard for state intervention or merely against the 'best interest of the child' standard." Laurence C. Nolan, Beyond *Troxel*: The Pragmatic Challenges of Grandparent Visitation Continue, 50 Drake L. Rev. 267 (2002). What should the test be — potential harm to the

child if visitation is not granted? Or the best interests test? What factors are relevant in the determination of potential harm or best interests? What are the advantages and disadvantages of each test? Should the same standard be applicable in cases involving *modification* or *termination* of grandparent visitation orders? See Denardo v. Bergamo, 863 A.2d 686 (Conn. 2005) (applying same standard in request to modify and terminate grandparents' visitation). Because of the Court's failure to resolve these issues, response to *Troxel* has been mixed: courts in some jurisdictions find their statutes to be unconstitutional as applied, whereas others uphold the constitutionality of their statutes by distinguishing them from the Washington statute in *Troxel*. John DeWitt Gregory, Defining the Family in the Millennium: The *Troxel* Follies, 32 U. Mem. L. Rev. 687, 719 (2002).

(8) Role of Law. What should be the role of the law in the resolution of such private disputes as those between parents and third parties? Do you agree that "[m]any courts, especially trial courts, have little or no concern for the challenges inherent in court-ordered visitation when deciding the appropriateness of granting visitation or in fashioning the order"? Nolan, supra, at 270. What are the stereotypes of grandparents that influence these visitation disputes? To counter these criticisms, should courts always appoint guardians ad litem for the child? See Newman, supra (so arguing).

(9) Stepparent Visitation. Third-party visitation rights also arise in cases involving stepparents, especially in cases of the divorce of a stepparent and the child's biological parent or the death of a child's biological custodial parent who had remarried. In each case, a stepparent who has been actively involved in childrearing wishes to continue the relationship with the child. See, e.g., Riepe v. Riepe, 91 P.3d 312 (Ariz. Ct. App. 2004) (holding that court has authority to award visitation to widowed stepmother pursuant to statutory criteria). In what ways are stepparent visitation disputes similar to, and different from, grandparent visitation disputes? Should stepparent visitation disputes be treated the same as, or different from, grandparent visitation disputes? About one-third of the states have statutes that either explicitly provide for stepparent visitation or contain language regarding third-party visitation that is broad enough to apply to stepparents. Gregory, supra, at 690.

Application of the concept of "psychological parent" (as influenced by the views of Goldstein, Freud, and Solnit, supra p. 453) has sometimes led courts to recognize the rights of third parties such as stepparents. Recall too that, under the ALI Principles, if a stepparent qualifies as a "parent by estoppel" or a "de facto parent," a court would have to recognize that stepparent's right to custody or visitation following the death of a custodial parent or the dissolution of the custodial parent's relationship with the stepparent. ALI Principles §2.03(1)(b) (parenthood by estoppel); §2.03(1)(c) (de facto parent).

After *Troxel*, are stepparent visitation statutes constitutional that allow courts to grant reasonable visitation to a stepparent if the court determines that it is in the child's best interests? See In re Marriage of Engelkens, 821 N.E.2d 799 (Ill. App. Ct. 2004). On stepparent disputes in the adoption context, see supra, pp. 481-482. On stepparents' support obligation, see supra, pp. 183-185.

(10) Second-Parent Visitation Rights. Traditionally, courts have not been receptive to recognition of co-parent's rights to custody and/or visitation after dissolution of a same-sex relationship. In such disputes, courts have tended to recognize

the biological mother as the sole legal parent and thereby to exclude the same-sex partner as a legal stranger. In two famous cases, courts refused to permit custody or visitation rights for the same-sex partner of a biological parent when the relationship terminated. In Nancy S. v. Michele G., 279 Cal. Rptr. 212 (Ct. App. 1991), two children were conceived via artificial insemination during the couple's relationship. The nonbiological mother was listed as "father" on the birth certificates. When the couple separated, they agreed that the daughter would live with the partner but the son with the birth mother, with each adult having liberal visitation with the other child. When a subsequent disagreement arose, the California Court of Appeal denied custody and visitation rights to the nonbiological mother based on a strict interpretation of the Uniform Parentage Act's definition of a legal parent. Because of this ruling, after the biological mother died in an automobile accident, the nonbiological mother faced difficulties obtaining guardianship of the son. Elaine Herscher, Family Circle, S.F. Chron., Aug. 29, 1999, at 1, 4.

Similarly, in Alison D. v. Virginia M., 572 N.E.2d 27 (N.Y. 1991), soon after the same-sex relationship dissolved, the biological mother decided to terminate all contact between the child and the former partner. The partner brought a habeas corpus petition to obtain visitation rights. The New York Court of Appeals refused to read the state domestic relations law broadly (which conferred custody rights on a "parent") to include nonparents who have developed a relationship with the child.

However, recent cases' reliance on a variety of theories signals a greater willingness of some courts to recognize lesbian parents' rights. See Kristine H. v. Lisa R., 16 Cal. Rptr. 3d 123 (Ct. App. 2004) (holding that the presumed-father provision of California's version of UPA could be applied to establish legal parentage of the former same-sex partner), *review granted*, 97 P.3d 72 (Cal. 2004); V.C. v. M.J.B., 748 A.2d 539 (N.J. 2000) (holding that former partner, as "psychological parent," was entitled to visitation rights although not entitled to joint legal custody); E.N.O. v. L.M.M., 711 N.E.2d 886 (Mass. 1999) (recognizing nonbiological parent as child's de facto parent with a right to visitation). But cf. K.M. v. E.G., 13 Cal. Rptr. 3d 136 (Ct. App. 2004) (holding that donor of eggs to lesbian partner who bore twins had standing to bring action to determine parentage under UPA, but that evidence supported finding that her signature on the donor consent form constituted a waiver of her parental rights), *review granted*, 97 P.3d 72 (Cal. 2004). On the application of the Uniform Parentage Act to second-parent adoption and custody disputes, see Melanie B. Jacobs, Micah Has One Mommy and One Legal Stranger: Adjudicating Maternity for Nonbiological Lesbian Coparents, 50 Buff. L. Rev. 341 (2002) (proposing the use of the UPA to adjudicate maternity for lesbian co-parents and thereby confer all rights and privileges of legal parenthood).

After dissolution of the same-sex relationship, should the nonbiological parent-partner be obliged to pay child support to the biological parent for a child who was conceived with both partners' consent? Should it matter whether the former partner would be entitled to custody and/or visitation under state law? See Maria B. v. Superior Court, 13 Cal. Rptr.3d 494 (Ct. App. 2004) (holding that former partner was not a parent within meaning of UPA and thus was not obligated to pay child support), *review granted sub nom.* Elisa B. v. Emily B., 97 P.3d 72 (Cal. 2004). In January 2005, new statewide domestic partnership legislation (California Domestic Partner Rights and Responsibilities Act, A.B. 205) became effective in

California that equated domestic partners' rights to that of spouses in terms of community property, child custody, child support, and spousal support. As a result, the California Supreme Court granted review of three previously decided cases involving same-sex custody/visitation support rights. See Elisa B. v. Emily B., supra; K.M. v. E.G., supra; Kristine H. v. Lisa R., supra.

What is the likely impact of Troxel v. Granville on visitation disputes involving gay and lesbian parents? See generally Laura S. Brown, "Relationships More Enduring," Implications of the *Troxel* Decision on Gay and Lesbian Families, 41 Fam. Ct. Rev. 60 (2003); Brooke N. Silverthorn, Notes and Comments, When Parental Rights and Children's Best Interests Collide: An Examination of Troxel v. Granville as It Relates to Gay and Lesbian Families, 19 Ga. St. U. L. Rev. 893 (2003).

(11) Child's Interests. Do cases addressing second-parent custody and visitation disputes give adequate respect to the child's wishes and interests? See Jacobs, supra (arguing that courts fail to take into account the child's perspective). On the context of adoption by second parents, see supra p. 515.

(12) Problem. Karen and Charles separate after a brief marriage, shortly before the birth of their daughter Emily. Karen moves in with Charles' parents for a week and then moves into a shelter for battered women. She files for dissolution, claiming that Charles was abusive. Karen is granted sole legal and physical custody. Charles is granted supervised visitation. One month later, the paternal grandparents petition for visitation, alleging that Karen has refused them access to Emily. The grandparents want Emily to spend ten days at their home every other month. Karen protests because Emily is still nursing and also because of her concern that Charles was abused as a child by the paternal grandfather. Over Karen's objections, but with Charles' approval, the trial court grants liberal visitation to the grandparents. Several week-long visits occur with the grandparents. Six months later Karen petitions to terminate the grandparents' visitation, alleging that the visits give Emily nightmares and distress her. The state statute provides that a court may grant reasonable visitation to a grandparent if the court determines that visitation would be in the child's best interests or if there is a preexisting relationship between the grandparent and grandchild that has engendered a bond such that visitation would be in the child's best interests. Karen challenges the statute as unconstitutional on its face and as applied. What result? See In re Marriage of Harris, 96 P.3d 141 (Cal. 2004).

5. Process: What Process Should Be Used to Resolve Disputes?

This section explores the issue of which process should be utilized to settle child custody disputes. Three approaches are presented: (1) the traditional adversarial process; (2) the alternative dispute resolution processes of mediation and collaborative law; and (3) a random process of "coin-flipping." Advantages and disadvantages of each alternative are examined. Finally, this section explores the role of the child in custody decision making: specifically, should the child's wishes be considered in the process?

a. Adversarial Process

Most divorced parents reach private agreements regarding responsibility for child rearing in the postdivorce period. Only a small minority of custody decisions are actually settled by the judicial process. This small percentage of cases, however, involves particularly acrimonious disputes with far-reaching consequences for the participants. Consider the following criticism of the adversarial process:

Donald T. Saposnek, Mediating Child Custody Disputes
7-16 (rev. ed. 1998) (citations omitted)

"The Adversarial Approach"

Traditionally, contested cases had been dealt with exclusively by an adversarial process. For the most part, the adversarial process has proved itself a just and effective approach for discovering the facts and critical issues in criminal and other matters, so that decisions could be made to attribute blame and responsibility or to resolve disputes. However, this same adversarial process, when applied to domestic conflicts, tends to do more harm than good. As Coogler (1978, p. 8) noted, "Whatever may be said in support of the adversarial process for resolving other kinds of controversies, in marital disputes this competitive struggle is frequently more damaging for the marriage partners and their children than anything else that preceded it."

Because divorces and custody decisions were, in the recent past, made on the basis of finding one person at fault, and/or unfit, the adversarial process seemed fully appropriate as the most efficient method for arriving at such decisions. Each contest had a winner and a loser, and the courts assumed that, once the decisions were made, the matter was settled. While the matters of property and the legal dissolution of the marriage were indeed settled, the matters of custody and visitation were very often far from settled. Frequently, in reaction to the humiliation of defeat, the losing spouse would try to get back at the winning spouse by gathering damaging evidence regarding the spouse's unfitness, the quality of care given the children, or the spouse's immorality, and by filing an order to show cause (OSC) petition to reverse the custody decision. Relitigation frequently continued for years beyond the initial decision. . . .

The recent trends toward no-fault divorces and custody decisions based on the best interests of the child rather than on the fitness of the parent have been attempts to reduce the acrimonious nature of such domestic conflicts. Yet the adversarial process by which these new standards are applied inherently breeds acrimony. Moreover, when children are involved in the process, they typically become repeat victims. This victimization can be obvious and publicly painful, as when a child must betray one parent by testifying in court on behalf of the other. Or, it can be more subtle and insidious, as when a parent or lawyer solicits an "evaluation" of, or "treatment" for, the youngster by a child psychologist or psychiatrist as a tactic to help achieve the goal of obtaining custody.

. . . Typically, in such cases, the parent who is about to launch a bid for custody of a child seeks a therapist to help the child deal with the emotional upset manifested in the aftermath of the divorce. However, what that parent often does not tell the therapist until later is that the parent was sent there by the attorney in hopes of documenting some harm that has occurred or will occur to the child as a result of being in the custody of the other parent. If there is no chance of finding harm, the attorney may hope that the therapist, by seeing the one parent and child together, can be enticed into writing a report and perhaps even testifying to the effect that a "strong bond of attachment clearly exists between this parent and the child." . . .

Regardless of whether the request to evaluate the child or child-parent relationship is presented in a straightforward or in an indirect manner, the experience of the child will be nearly the same. The child will be led to consider and/or express a preference for a custodial parent and will be coerced in various ways to participate in discussions that will likely result in the betrayal of one parent. Moreover, when evidence of harm to the child is sought or suspected, the child will feel the intensity of focused probing for pathology. This can cause considerable discomfort in the child. . . .

It is also noteworthy that children who participate in such evaluations occasionally feel betrayed when they find out that a judge made the custody decision based upon what they told the therapist. For in spite of what they may be told to the contrary, they often believe that their conversations will be confidential. . . .

While the adjustment problems that children have following a divorce are commonly attributed by each parent to the quality of caregiving by the other parent, it is much more often the case that they are due to the many stressful changes that children must endure in a parental separation and to the interparental conflict that either begins at separation or continues from the marriage to play out after separation. It has also been found that the adversarial approach exacerbates the effects of these factors. . . .

The adversarial process trains parents, through discussions and modeling, to fight even more effectively, using slander, accusation, defamation, and any other weapons available. Yet such contests are construed as a proper means of achieving the best interests of the child. By any standard of common sense, as well as the accumulated research data showing that children need co-parenting and a cessation of interparental conflict, the adversarial process must rank very low as a method of making satisfactory and lasting postdivorce parenting arrangements. . . .

b. Mediation

Mediation, as an alternative to the formal adversarial process, has a long and varied history. Its roots are found in ancient Chinese, Japanese, African, and even Biblical law.[79] Mediation is a process by which parties to a disagreement, with the aid of a neutral third party, isolate disputed issues in order to develop options, consider alternatives, and reach a consensual settlement.[80] Many statutes currently

---

[79] Jay Folberg & Alison Taylor, Mediation: A Comprehensive Guide to Resolving Conflicts Without Litigation 1-3 (1984); Forest S. Mosten, Institutionalization of Mediation, 42 Fam. Ct. Rev. 292 (2004).

[80] Folberg & Taylor, supra note [79], at 7.

provide for mediation in custody disputes: some by mandatory mediation requiring mediation in all disputed custody cases; others by authorizing a court to order mediation in some circumstances;[81] and still others by authorizing mediation only at the request of the parties.

Mediation represents a shift from third-party, external decision making in child custody disputes toward private ordering.[82] In the adversarial process, the law restricts private ordering. That is, the state asserts broad authority not only over the financial aspects of the dissolution, but also over the parties' relationships with their children. With the increasing acceptance of mediation, states confer broad latitude on the divorcing couple to decide for themselves, outside the courtroom, many aspects relevant to the dissolution of their relationship.

Mediation includes many different professionals. Lawyers and mental health professionals comprise a significant percentage of the profession. As a result, mediation is heavily influenced by the diverse orientations of these professions. Given that different professionals are involved, certain issues arise. This section explores several of these issues. First, what is the role of the mediator in a child custody dispute? How do the values and concerns of each profession help define the role of the mediator? Second, how much deference do these different professionals give to the principle of private ordering? That is, what circumstances cause mediators, who are generally neutral, to limit private ordering by questioning custody agreements which the parties accept? Do different professional orientations result in different proclivities for intervention? Finally, should the child have a role in the mediation process? If so, what should that role involve?

(1) Roles of the Mediator

Divorce mediation has many forms. "Each form reflects the setting in which the service is being offered, the framework from which the mediator shapes his or her process, and the prior profession of the mediator."[83] Despite these variables, it is possible to identify several models which provide the major frameworks for most mediators.

Commentators have suggested various theoretical models and modes of mediation. For example, Becker-Haven suggests four conceptual frameworks for child custody mediation and the corresponding roles of the mediator derived from each framework.[84] These include:

(a)   the therapeutic framework, with the mediator as healer;
(b)   the educational framework, with the mediator as teacher;
(c)   the rational/analytic framework, with the mediator as strategist;
(d)   the normative/evaluative framework, with the mediator as judge.

---

[81] Joan B. Kelly, Psychological and Legal Interventions for Parents and Children in Custody and Access Disputes: Current Research and Practice, 10 Va. J. Soc. Pol'y & L. 129, 138 (2002) (pointing out that 13 states have mandatory mediation and 24 states have statutes conferring discretion on judges to order mediation).

[82] Robert H. Mnookin & Lewis Kornhauser, Bargaining in the Shadow of the Law: The Case of Divorce, 88 Yale L.J. 950 (1979).

[83] Susan M. Brown, Models of Mediation, in Divorce and Family Mediation 49 (James C. Hansen ed., 1985).

[84] See Jane Becker-Haven, Modes of Mediating Child Custody Disputes, Ph.D. Dissertation, Stanford University (1988).

In the therapeutic framework, the mediator views an essential part of divorce mediation as addressing the emotional upheaval associated with the divorce (i.e., encouraging the expression of feelings, interpreting behaviors, etc.) in order to facilitate the resolution of parenting problems. In contrast, the educational mode of mediation places the mediator in the role of a teacher who provides information and builds problem-solving skills to enable the parents to resolve current and future disputes for themselves.

The rational/analytic framework puts the mediator in the role of rational decision manager by helping the parents evaluate options to maximize their values and preferences (i.e., delineating the parameters of decisions, eliciting preferences, generating alternatives, weighing trade-offs, and pointing out flaws in reasoning). The normative/evaluative mode places the mediator in the role of judge by promoting normative prescriptions, sometimes quite forcefully, for decision and inaction into the mediation process. Mediators in this role emphasize giving opinions, directing the parents' attention to the child's interests, acting as advocate for the child, and revealing a potential recommendation if the case were to go to trial.

Mediators may adopt aspects of one or more of the above role(s), depending on their philosophy, value orientation, and the characteristics of the couple and conflict being mediated.[85] In addition, professional background appears to play a role in determining the mode of mediation. Lawyers tend to subscribe to the rational/analytic mode; mental health professionals to the therapeutic mode; counseling psychologists and educators to the educational mode; and juvenile probation workers to the normative/evaluative mode.[86] For a discussion of other models of divorce mediation, see Connie J.A. Beck & Bruce D. Sales, Family Mediation: Facts, Myths, and Future Prospects 9 (2001) (including legal model, labor management model, therapeutic model, and communication/information model).

(2) Degrees of Intervention

Mediators adopt different degrees of intervention. Some mediators are nondirective, relying instead on the participants' sense of fairness. Other mediators may be quite directive, challenging decisions or agreements reached by the divorcing parties and even refusing to write an agreement that they believe is unfair. An empirical study of mediation concluded that most mediators mix these approaches to balance the values of autonomy and protection. The researchers found no strong association between background characteristics and interventionist approaches, hypothesizing that those practitioners who enter divorce mediation are less committed to either traditional adversarial practice or traditional therapy.[87]

(3) Children's Role in Mediation

Should children have a role in mediation? What might be the advantages to the child for inclusion? The disadvantages? If children should have a role, what should that role be?

---

[85] Brown, supra note [83].
[86] Becker-Haven, supra note [84].
[87] Joseph P. Folger & Sydney E. Bernard, Divorce Mediation: When Mediators Challenge the Divorcing Parties, 10 Mediation Q. 5, 11 (1985).

First, what might be the benefits to children of their inclusion? One commentator argues that

> [T]here are benefits to be gained by allowing them to observe and participate in negotiation sessions. For many children, this may be the first time in months or years that they actually observe these dynamics between their parents. When the children understand that one of the primary motivations for the parents' mediating is their love and concern for them, it can be very supportive for the children.
>
> Another advantage of having children present during mediation is the potential for positive reinforcement for the existing parenting and caring relationships . . . . This provide[s] the mediator with an opportunity to observe and indicate to the parents how comfortable this child was with both and to commend them for their nurturance of the child's attachment to both parents.
>
> Finally, children's concerns tend to be somewhat more concrete and immediate than those of their parents. They want to know which toys will be in which house, which furniture will be moved, and the exact day and hour that the moves will be made. Their presence in mediation allows them to express these questions and concerns and receive direct responses from parents.[88]

On the other hand, there may be severe disadvantages to children from participating in mediation.

> Including children in sessions also has potentially negative consequences. Parents sometimes express reluctance to expose children to their disagreements and hostility. [T]hese feelings can make for highly volatile mediation sessions. It is undesirable to expose children to continued accusations, diatribes, and discord if the parents are not progressing toward settlement of the custody issues.
>
> Children tend to display their feelings of sadness, anger, fear and confusion openly. This can become a problem in mediation sessions if the mediator is unwilling or unable to respond to these feelings or if parents blame each other and/or the mediator for the children's emotions. . . .[89]

Just as mediators differ about intervention in the face of an unfair agreement, they also disagree about the role of children in the mediation process. Some mediators believe children should be actively included in the decision-making process. On the other hand, in their respect for parental autonomy, other mediators believe that parents alone should make decisions regarding custody, especially when children are young.

For a debate on children's appropriate role in mediation, compare Joan B. Kelly, Psychological and Legal Interventions for Parents and Children in Custody and Access Disputes: Current Research and Practice, 10 Va. J. Soc. Pol'y & L. 129 (2002) (urging greater participation of children) with Robert E. Emery, Easing the Pain of Divorce for Children: Children's Voices, Causes of Conflict, and Mediation, Comments on Kelly's "Resolving Child Custody Disputes," 10 Va. J. Soc. Pol'y & L. 164 (2002) (voicing the fear that inclusion of children inappropriately gives them responsibility for adult decisions).

---

[88] Karen K. Irvin, Including Children in Mediation: Considerations for the Mediator, in Divorce and Family Mediation at 94, 98.

[89] Id. at 98.

The most recent efforts by the American Bar Association establishing standards of practice for family mediators also address the role of children in mediation. Standard VIII of the Model Standards of Practice for Family and Divorce Mediation (adopted by the House of Delegates in 2001) provides that children should not participate without the consent of both parents and the children's court-appointed representative except in extraordinary circumstances (VIII.D). In addition, before including children, the mediator should consult with parents and a children's court-appointed representative not only about whether children should participate but the form of their participation (VIII.E) and should discuss the various options (e.g., personal participation, an interview with a mental health professional, the mediator reporting to the parents, a videotape statement) (VIII.F). On the Standards, see generally Andrew Schepard, An Introduction to the Model Standards of Practice for Family and Divorce Mediation, 35 Fam. L.Q. 1 (2001).

Assuming that children's inclusion might be beneficial, what form do you think their participation should take? Should certain circumstances dictate special consideration of children's roles — e.g., if a parent alleges abuse or neglect of the other parent? If so, should children be excluded or included in such cases? Many states provide special protections for the parties in mediation proceedings in cases of domestic violence. See, e.g., Cal. Fam. Code §§3181 (separate sessions), 6303(c) (victim may have support person attend mediation) (West 2003). See also Andrew I. Schepard, Children, Courts, and Custody: Interdisciplinary Models for Divorcing Families 102-104 (2004) (contrasting the different views on mandatory mediation in the domestic violence context of the ALI Principles, which reject mandatory mediation, and the ABA Model Standards of Practice for Family and Divorce Mediation, which rejects mediation in inappropriate cases); Nancy Ver Steegh, Yes, No, and Maybe: Informed Decision Making About Divorce Mediation in the Presence of Domestic Violence, 9 Wm. & Mary J. Women & Law 145 (2003).

c. Collaborative Law

Another form of alternative dispute resolution is collaborative law. The collaborative law movement was launched in 1990 by Minneapolis family law attorney Stuart Webb.[90] In such procedures, the parties and their attorneys sign a binding agreement in which they agree to use cooperative techniques without resort to judicial intervention except for court approval of the parties' agreement. Attorneys are prohibited from participating in contested court proceedings for their clients. That is, if the parties are unable to reach agreement through collaborative law procedures, their attorneys must withdraw from representation.

The attorney's role in collaborative law procedures differs from that of the attorney as mediator. The traditional mediation model involves two parties and the neutral mediator; legal services (if any) are provided outside the mediation process (e.g., review of documents). In contrast, collaborative lawyers are advocates for their clients (rather than neutral facilitators). In addition, collaborative lawyers are more directive than traditional mediators in helping their clients realize their

---

[90] Pauline H. Tesler, Collaborative Family Law, 4 Pepp. Disp. Resol. L.J. 317 (2004).

goals.[911] Texas became the first state in 2001 to provide, by statute, for resolution of family matters by collaborative law procedures. See Tex. Fam. Code §153.0072 (West 2003).

d. Coin-Flipping

Robert H. Mnookin, Child-Custody Adjudication: Judicial Functions in the Face of Indeterminacy
39 Law & Contemp. Probs. 226, 289-291 (1975)

Random Selection

Assuming that an "intimate" acceptable to both parents cannot be found to make an individualized decision, would not a random process of decision be fairer and more efficient than adjudication under a best-interests principle? Individualized adjudication means that the result will often turn on a largely intuitive evaluation based on unspoken values and unproven predictions. We would more frankly acknowledge both our ignorance and the presumed equality of the natural parents were we to flip a coin. Whether one had a separate flip for each child or one flip for all the children, the process would certainly be cheaper and quicker. It would avoid the pain associated with an adversary proceeding that requires an open exploration of the intimate aspects of family life and an ultimate judgment that one parent is preferable to the other. And it might have beneficial effects on private negotiations.[254]

Resolving a custody dispute by state-administered coin-flip would probably be viewed as unacceptable by most in our society. Perhaps this reaction reflects an abiding faith, despite the absence of an empirical basis for it, that letting a judge choose produces better results for the child. Alternatively, flipping a coin might be unacceptable for some because it represents an abdication of the search for wisdom. While judgments about what is best for the child may be currently beyond our capacity in many cases, this need not be true in fifty years. Movement toward better judgments implies, however, that judges and decision-makers as a group learn from the process of decision. In the absence of systematic feedback, this is

---

[911] Id. at 329-330. See also Andrew I. Schepard, Children, Courts, and Custody: Interdisciplinary Models for Divorcing Families (2004) (especially Chapter 10, discussing the differences between mediation and collaborative law).

[254] The effect on negotiation would depend on each parent's risk preferences and on how much each wanted the child. Because each parent would face a 50 per cent chance of losing, this might encourage private compromise if both wanted the child and were very risk-averse. But because a coin-flip would be less painful than an adversary proceeding, the threat of holding out for such a resolution might be more frequently and credibly used than the threat of litigation is today by a party who did not much want the child but who was bargaining for advantage with regard to other elements of the marriage dissolution. To avoid these bargaining problems, the state might insist that the coin-flip occur at the time of the marriage. Through state-supervised random process, one of the parents could then be designated as the parent who would have custody (absent a showing of neglect) if the parents should later separate and be unable themselves to decide who should have custody. . . . It is interesting to speculate whether such a rule would affect the loser's emotional commitment to the child or willingness to stay married to avoid losing custody of the child.

not likely. Indeed, adopting a coin-flip now means neither that at a time when more were known and a consensus existed an adjudicatory system might not be adopted, nor that efforts to discover an adjudicatory standard would cease.

Deciding a child's future by flipping a coin might be viewed as callous. Is it more callous, however, than drafting for the military by lottery? In the same way that a lottery is a social affirmation of equality among those upon whom the government might impose the risks of war, a coin-flip would be a government affirmation of the equality of the parents. In a custody case, however, a coin-flip also symbolically abdicates government responsibility for the child and symbolically denies the importance of human differences and distinctiveness. Moreover, flipping a coin would deprive the parents of a process and a forum where their anger and aspirations might be expressed. In all, these symbolic and participatory values of adjudication would be lost by a random process.

While forceful arguments can be made in favor of the abandonment of adjudication and the adoption of an openly random process, the repulsion many would probably feel towards this suggestion may reflect an intuitive appreciation of the importance of the educational, participatory, and symbolic values of adjudication as a mode of dispute settlement. Adjudication under the indeterminate best-interests principle may yield something close to a random pattern of outcomes, while at the same time serving these values, affirming parental equality, and expressing a social concern for the child. Insofar as judges as a group may have value preferences that systematically bias the process and make the pattern less than random, these value preferences may reflect widespread values that have not been acknowledged openly in the form of legal rules. . . .

e. What Role for the Child in Custody Decision Making?

(1) Consideration of the Child's Preference

Most states have statutes that call for consideration of the child's wishes. In recent years, an increasing number of states have adopted legislation requiring consideration of children's preferences.[92] States assign different weight to such preferences: (1) some mandate consideration of children's wishes and grant controlling weight to these preferences (sometimes dependent on the age of the child); (2) some mandate consideration of children's preferences based on the judge's discretion; and (3) still others give courts complete discretion to consider a child's preference.[93]

Generally, trial courts treat the wishes of 14- to 18-year-olds as deserving of greater weight or even as dispositive. See, e.g., Reinke v. Reinke, 670 N.W.2d 841 (N.D. 2003); Wheeler v. Mazur, 793 A.2d 929 (Pa. Super. Ct. 2001) (both reversing

---

[92] Randi L. Dulaney, Note, Children Should Be Seen and Heard in Florida Custody Determinations, 25 Nova L. Rev. 815, 819 (2001) (pointing out that since 1977, the number of states mandating consideration of children's preferences has more than doubled from 16 to 34).

[93] Id. at 823-824. Many states' statutes reflect the influence of UMDA §402, 9A U.L.A. 282, providing that a court shall consider the child's wishes, but the appropriate weight to be accorded to preference is left to the trial judge's discretion.

trial court decisions that failed to give sufficient weight to the preferences of 13- or 14-year olds). On the other hand, trial judges sometimes examine the underlying reasons for a child's preference and refuse to recognize the preference in certain circumstances (e.g., coercion by a parent, sympathy for a parent, or a desire for a more permissive environment).[94] See also Kirkendall v. Kirkendall, 844 A.2d 1261 (Pa. Super. Ct. 2004) (affirming award of paternal custody, and rejecting five-year old's preference for maternal custody as immature). The ALI Principles §2.08 specifies that if the court adopts the approximation presumption (for those parents unable to formulate a parenting plan), one of the factors that shall rebut that presumption is the "firm and reasonable preference" of children of statutorily designated ages (and proposing 11 to 14 years as the range of ages for a uniform rule).

Should courts assign less weight to children's preferences in specific contexts? For example, in cases of domestic violence, children may be pressured to choose the perpetrator as the custodial parent. Or in custody disputes involving gay and lesbian parents, children may be unduly influenced by their initial negative response to the parent's disclosure of his or her sexual orientation. See Kirsten Lea Doolittle, Note, Don't Ask, You May Not Want to Know: Custody Preferences of Children of Gay and Lesbian Parents, 73 S. Cal. L. Rev. 677, 679 (2000).

(2) Procedures for Ascertaining a Child's Preference

Once it is agreed that the child's preference should be taken into account, the question remains of the proper procedure for learning that preference. Consider the advantages and disadvantages of the following alternatives:

a. having the child testify,
b. having other persons testify regarding the child's preference,
c. having the child's preference recorded in a videotape that is introduced at trial,
d. having the trial judge elicit the child's preference in a private interview in chambers (i) with opposing counsel present or (ii) without counsel present.

A recent empirical study found that most judges prefer to ascertain children's wishes through court-ordered custody evaluations or party testimony rather than through in-court testimony or an in-camera interview. Barbara A. Atwood, The Child's Voice in Custody Litigation: An Empirical Survey and Suggestions for Reform, 45 Ariz. L. Rev. 629, 642 (2003). What do you think explains judges' preferences?

Although in-camera testimony may protect the child from the pain of openly choosing sides, it may present constitutional concerns. Atwood, supra, at 641. How? Does the Supreme Court's decision in Troxel v. Granville strengthen or weaken parents' claim that procedural due process entitles them to access their children's in-camera statements? See Cynthia Starnes, Swords in the Hands of Babes: Rethinking Custody Interviews After *Troxel*, 2003 Wis. L. Rev. 115. Does a child have a due

---

[94] Barbara A. Atwood, The Child's Voice in Custody Litigation: An Empirical Survey and Suggestions for Reform, 45 Ariz. L. Rev. 629, 640 (2003).

process right to have a voice in custody decision making? In response to constitutional concerns, many states now require that in-camera interviews be recorded, the record be made available to the parties, and attorneys be present. Atwood, supra, at 643. Although the ALI Principles recommend that judges have discretion to interview children and that parents' counsel should have the right to propose questions that may be asked of the child, the Principles are silent regarding the presence of counsel at the interview and the recording of the interview. See, e.g., ALI Principles §2.14.

(3) Counsel for the Child?

The debate about mandatory representation for children in custody and visitation disputes began in the 1960s and 1970s, prompted by the rising rate of divorce (especially, concerns about the effects of divorce on children) and the Supreme Court's decision in In re Gault, 387 U.S. 1 (1967) (granting a right to counsel for the child in delinquency proceedings) (supra Chapter 1). Commentators have manifested long-standing support for the appointment of legal representation for the child in custody proceedings.[95] However, virtually all states provide for discretionary appointment.[96]

Should representation for the child in contested custody disputes be mandatory? Or will the court's independent investigative powers and duties ensure protection of the child's interests? One critic of mandatory representation urges judges to be more cautious in appointing counsel for children. Professor Martin Guggenheim argues that the appointment of counsel may actually undermine the nature of the proceedings. Guggenheim believes that children's representatives should be mere fact-finders, ensuring that the process is fair and that judges have sufficient information to make informed decisions about children's best interests. He bases his view on concerns about children's lack of capacity, the undue weight a judge may attach to children's legal advocates, and the invasion of family privacy that may stem from the adversarial nature of the proceedings.[97] Which position do you find persuasive?

[95] See, e.g., Linda Elrod, Counsel for the Child in Custody Disputes: The Time Is Now, 26 Fam. L.Q. 53 (1992); Monroe L. Inker & Charlotte Anne Perretta, A Child's Right to Counsel in Custody Cases, 5 Fam. L.Q. 108 (1971).

[96] Raven C. Lidman & Betsy R. Hollingsworth, The Guardian Ad Litem in Child Custody Cases: The Contours of Our Judicial System Stretched Beyond Recognition, 6 Geo. Mason L. Rev. 255, 262 (1998). Cf. Wis. Stat. Ann. §767.045(1) (West 1997) (mandatory representation in child custody disputes).

[97] See Martin Guggenheim, The Right to Be Represented but Not Heard: Reflections on Legal Representation for Children, 59 N.Y.U. L. Rev. 76 (1984); Martin Guggenheim, A Paradigm for Determining the Role of Counsel for Children, 64 Fordham L. Rev. 1399 (1996); Martin Guggenheim, Reconsidering the Need for Counsel for Children in Custody, Visitation and Child Protection Proceedings, 29 Loy. U. Chi. L.J. 299 (1998).

In contrast to the widespread discretionary policy on representation in custody proceedings, many jurisdictions now provide for mandatory appointment of counsel in those contested custody cases that involve allegations of abuse or neglect. Why might representation in these proceedings be advisable? Under the Child Abuse Prevention and Treatment Act (CAPTA), 42 U.S.C. §5106a(b)(6) (2000), states are required, in order to qualify for federal funding, to provide guardians ad litem to all children involved in child protective proceedings. Despite the CAPTA requirement, however, states are not required to appoint attorneys as guardians ad litem. (Guardians ad litem may come from many professions, such as law, social work, psychology, etc.) See Chapter 3, supra p. 305. Should the child's representative be an attorney? Is there a greater need, lesser need, or the same need for legal representation for children in abuse/neglect proceedings compared to contested custody proceedings?

If the appointment of a separate representative for the child is preferable in custody proceedings, what role should the representative play? Courts and legislatures often fail to give guidance as to the appropriate role and/or responsibilities of children's representatives. Should the child's representative be an advocate for the child's wishes or advocate the best interests of the child (even if that might differ from the child's wishes)?

In recent years, considerable attention has focused on the issue of legal representation for children. The American Academy of Matrimonial Lawyers (AAML) promulgated Standards for Attorneys and Guardians Ad Litem in Custody or Visitation Proceedings, which address when representation should be appointed as well as what the lawyers' and guardians' responsibilities are.[98] The ABA promulgated two sets of standards: for abuse, neglect and termination of parental rights cases and also for custody and visitation cases.[99]

The ABA Standards of Practice for Lawyers Representing Children in Custody Cases (Custody Standards), approved by the ABA Family Law Section in 2003, clarify the roles of lawyers in representing children in all types of custody proceedings. Such proceedings include legal or physical custody, parenting plans, and visitation; and cover the contexts of divorce, parentage, domestic violence, contested adoptions, and contested private guardianship cases but not child abuse and neglect (for which the ABA Standards of Practice for Representing a Child in Abuse and Neglect Cases are applicable).

The Custody Standards provide that a lawyer should fulfill the role of either (1) a "child's attorney" who provides independent legal counsel to the child in the same manner as to any other client; or (2) a "best interests attorney," who advocates the child's best interests without being bound by the child's directives. (The Custody Standards abandon the term "guardian ad litem" because of its inherent ambiguity.) These Standards define the duties associated with each role. The court determines which type of lawyer to appoint and makes the participants aware of the duties and

---

[98] See Representing Children: Standards for Attorneys and Guardians Ad Litem in Custody or Visitation Proceedings, 13 J. Am. Acad. Matrim. Law. 1 (1995).

[99] See ABA Standards of Practice for Lawyers Who Represent Children in Abuse and Neglect Cases, 29 Fam. L.Q. 375 (1995) (discussed supra, p. 305); ABA Section of Family Law Standards of Practice for Lawyers Representing Children in Custody Cases, 37 Fam. L.Q. 131 (2003).

limitations of each role. The child's representative always functions as a lawyer, not as a witness.

6. Postdecree Problems

a. Modification

(1) Traditional Rules and Variations. For modification of an initial custody decree, a court must determine that a substantial change of circumstances has occurred that warrants an alteration in custody to promote the best interests of the child. Some states follow a stricter rule that further limits modification.[100] Other states adopt a more liberal test that permits modifications based on the "best interests of the child." The rationale behind the traditional rule is that the child's need for stability militates against relitigation of custody issues.

The usual meaning of the term "changed circumstances" dictates that courts consider only facts that have occurred since entry of the initial decree, as do the general rules of res judicata. However, some states, in the view that the child's welfare outweighs the policy of finality of judgments, hold that custody may be modified for facts existing at the time of that decree if those facts were not presented to or known by the court.

(2) Modification of Agreements. As discussed previously, the majority of custody cases are disposed of by agreement rather than by judicial order. Some courts hold that custody *agreements* may be modified more easily than judicial awards of custody. See, e.g., Elmer v. Elmer, 776 P.2d 599 (Utah 1999). What are the policy reasons behind this relaxation of the traditional modification standard?

(3) Remarriage and Relocation. Special circumstances, such as a parent's remarriage or relocation, frequently give rise to requests for modification of custody or visitation. Remarriage generally is not sufficient basis for modification unless the remarriage per se, or in conjunction with other factors, has a substantial impact upon the child's welfare. See Davis v. Flickinger, 674 N.E.2d 1159 (Ohio 1997).

A custodial spouse also might desire to move because of better employment or educational opportunities. Some states, by statute or case, regard a move as a sufficient change of circumstances, whereas other states do not. Linda D. Elrod, When Should Custody Orders Be Modified, 26 Fam. Advoc. 40, 41 (2004).

When faced with an impending move by the custodial spouse, a noncustodial parent may request a custody modification or even a transfer of custody. Until recently, the trend in "move-away" cases has been toward decreasing the restrictions on relocation.[101] See, e.g., Burgess v. Burgess, 51 Cal. Rptr.2d 44 (Cal. 1996); Tropea v. Tropea, 642 N.Y.S.2d 575 (N.Y. 1996). But cf. In re Marriage of La Musga, 88 P.3d 81 (Cal. 2004) (holding that noncustodial father did not have

---

[100] Some states follow the Uniform Marriage and Divorce Act §9A U.L.A. (pt. II) 439 (1998 & Supp. 1999) (requiring serious endangerment or a two-year period). See, e.g., Ill. Rev. Stat. 1979, ch. 750, ¶5/610 (1999).

[101] Janet M. Bowermaster, Sympathizing with Solomon: Choosing Between Parents in a Mobile Society, 31 J. Fam. L. 791, 795-831 (1992-1993).

to show detriment). Do restrictions on relocation raise constitutional concerns? See, e.g., In re Marriage of Ciesluk, 100 P.3d 527 (Colo. Ct. App. 2004), *review granted*, 2004 WL 2504503 (Colo. 2004); Watt v. Watt, 971 P.2d 608 (Wyo. 1999). See also Tabitha Sample & Teresa Reiger, Comment, Relocation Standards and Constitutional Considerations, 10 J. Am. Acad. Matrim. Law. 229 (1998).

(4) ALI Principles: Relocation.   The ALI Principles permit a parent with primary custody to relocate if he or she acts in good faith and for a "valid purpose." ALI Principles §2.17. According to the Principles, the following reasons constitute valid purposes: proximity to family, employment or educational opportunity, and a desire to be with a spouse or domestic partner or to improve significantly the family's quality of life.

(5) Modification of Joint Custody.   Modification of joint custody decrees poses special problems. In many states, the policy favoring joint custody has eased modifications to joint custody by relaxing the traditional rule to require only that the change to joint custody be in the best interests of the child.[102] Requests for modification from joint to *sole* custody arise for a number of reasons, including a breakdown in cooperation, violation of religious or education provisions of the original joint custody order, relocation, and remarriage. Some courts view parental tension and lack of cooperation as sufficient changes of circumstances to necessitate modification to sole custody.[103] Because joint custody is intended to assure continuing contact with parents, should courts be less willing to permit modification from joint to sole custody on these grounds than modification transferring sole custody from one parent to the other?

(6) Child's Preference. What role should the child's preference play in modification of custody? The use of the child's preference in modification proceedings raises many of the same problems as in initial custody determinations. See supra, pp. 611-613.

(7) ALI Principles: Modification.   The ALI recommends modification of a parenting plan upon a showing of a substantial change in circumstances (of the child or one or both parents), based on facts that were unknown or that arose since the entry of the prior order and were unanticipated, that makes modification "necessary to the child's welfare." ALI Principles §2.15(1) & (2). Modification based on a more liberal standard is available for consensual changes, minor modifications to the parenting plan, or the attainment of a statutorily designated age for a child who expresses a preference for a custodial change. §2.15, cmt. a. None of the following circumstances justify modification absent a showing of harm: a parent's loss of income or employment, remarriage or cohabitation, or use of day care. §2.15(3).

b. Jurisdiction Over and Enforcement of Custody Decrees

Modification of another state's custody decree raises questions of jurisdiction and sometimes enforcement as well. Modification is permitted subject to the

---

[102] See, e.g., Alaska Stat. §25.20.110 (2002); Mont. Code Ann. §40-4-219 (2003).
[103] See, e.g., White v. Moore, 58 S.W.3d 73 (Mo. Ct. App. 2001); Stanton v. Stanton, 484 S.E.2d 875 (S.C. Ct. App. 1997).

Uniform Child Custody Jurisdiction Act (UCCJA), 9 U.L.A. 115 (1999), Uniform Child Custody Jurisdiction and Enforcement Act, (UCCJEA), 9 U.L.A. 257 (1999), and the Parental Kidnapping Prevention Act (PKPA), 28 U.S.C. 1738A (2000) (discussed below).

PROBLEM

Heidi and Michael Leyda were divorced in Iowa in 1982. The parties were awarded joint legal custody of their daughter Kim, with physical care entrusted to Heidi. In September 1984, the Iowa court modified the decree, as a result of what it believed to be a substantial change of circumstances. Sole custody and care of Kim was awarded to Michael. During these proceedings, from September 1983 to September 1984, Kim lived with Heidi in Florida.

In October 1984, Heidi filed an action in a Florida trial court requesting that the Iowa judgment granting custody to Michael be declared void or, in the alternative, that the Florida court modify the Iowa judgment to grant custody of Kim to Heidi. An ex parte temporary order was issued by the Florida court to restrain Michael from removing Kim from Florida.

Michael appeared at a hearing before the Florida trial court on July 12, 1985. He submitted to in personal jurisdiction but challenged the subject matter jurisdiction of the court. Following the hearing, another temporary order was issued that stipulated Michael's challenge and further recited that Florida was the home state jurisdiction under the UCCJA. This order provided that Heidi would have primary physical custody with reasonable visitation rights awarded to Michael. Kim could visit Michael outside of Florida for six weeks during the summer. Furthermore, the order stipulated that the parties both acknowledge that Michael's failure to return Kim to Heidi's custody would be a third-degree felony.

Between the July 12th temporary order and August 26, 1985, Michael returned to Iowa with Kim. On August 26, Heidi filed a petition for a writ of habeas corpus. Does the Iowa court have continuing jurisdiction to resolve this dispute? Or did the Florida trial court act properly in granting the temporary custody order? See In re Marriage of Leyda, 398 N.W.2d 815 (Iowa 1987). The answer lies in an understanding of the UCCJA, UCCJEA, and the PKPA.

NOTES AND QUESTIONS ON JURISDICTION AND ENFORCEMENT

(1) UCCJA. The UCCJA was enacted to avoid jurisdiction competition and confusion and to deter removals of children in order to obtain custody. The Act provides for jurisdiction if

> (1) th[e] State
> > (i) is the home state of the child at the time of commencement of the proceeding, or
> > (ii) had been the child's home state within six months before commencement of the proceeding and the child is absent from th[e] State because of his removal or retention by a person claiming his custody or for other reasons, and a parent or person acting as parent continues to live in this State; or

(2) it is in the best interest of the child that a court of th[e] State assume jurisdiction because

(i) the child and his parents, or the child and at least one contestant, have a significant connection with th[e] State, and

(ii) there is available in this State substantial evidence concerning the child's present or future care, protection, training, and personal relationships; or

(3) the child is physically present in th[e] State and

(i) the child has been abandoned or

(ii) it is necessary in an emergency to protect the child because he has been subjected to or threatened with mistreatment or abuse or is otherwise neglected [or dependent]; or

(4)(i) it appears no other state would have jurisdiction under prerequisites substantially in accordance with paragraphs (1), (2), or (3), or another state has declined to exercise jurisdiction on the ground that th[e] State is the more appropriate forum to determine the custody of the child and

(ii) it is in the best interest of the child that this court assume jurisdiction.

The UCCJA applies to both original and modification decrees. Consider whether the Iowa court above had jurisdiction to modify its original decree or whether the Florida court had authority to grant the temporary order. Section 14 of the Act provides that a court cannot modify a foreign custody decree unless (1) the state which rendered the decree does not now have jurisdiction or has declined to assume jurisdiction and (2) the court seeking to modify has jurisdiction.

Under the UCCJA, a court may decline to exercise jurisdiction if the petitioner for an initial decree has wrongfully taken the child from another state or has engaged in similar reprehensible conduct. Consider Michael's knowing violation Florida's temporary order. Does this preclude further jurisdiction in Iowa? Does it matter that Florida may not have been the home state? Knowing of the action in Iowa, should the Florida court have declined to take action?

(2) PKPA. The Parental Kidnapping Prevention Act (PKPA) is also relevant in cases involving jurisdiction over child custody determinations. One of its chief purposes is to avoid jurisdictional competition and conflict between state courts. The Act sets forth jurisdictional criteria for determining which custody decree shall be afforded full faith and credit by a sister court. In addition, the Act assists victimized parents in locating the abductor by making the Federal Parent Locator Service available to state agencies and applying the Fugitive Felon Act, 18 U.S.C. §1073 (2000), to all state felony parental kidnapping cases. Jurisdiction to modify a decree under the PKPA is established if

(1) such court has jurisdiction under the law of such State; and

(2) one of the following conditions is met:

(A) such State

(i) is the home State of the child on the date of the commencement of the proceeding, or

(ii) had been the child's home State within six months before the date of the commencement of the proceeding and the child is absent from such State because of his removal or retention by a contestant or for other reasons, and a contestant continues to live in such State;

(B)(i) it appears that no other State would have jurisdiction under sub-paragraph (A), and

(ii) it is in the best interest of the child that a court of such State assume jurisdiction because

(I) the child and his parents, or the child and at least one contestant, have a significant connection with such State other than mere physical presence in such State and

(II) there is available in such State substantial evidence concerning the child's present or future care, protection, training, and personal relationships;

(C) the child is physically present in such State and

(i) the child has been abandoned, or

(ii) it is necessary in an emergency to protect the child because he has been subjected to or threatened with mistreatment or abuse;

(D)(i) it appears that no other State would have jurisdiction under sub-paragraph (A), (B), (C), or (E), or another State has declined to exercise jurisdiction on the ground that the State whose jurisdiction is in issue is the more appropriate forum to determine the custody of the child, and

(ii) it is in the best interest of the child that such court assume jurisdiction; or

(E) the court has continuing jurisdiction pursuant to subsection (d) of this section.

Consider the distinctions in the jurisdictional requirements under the UCCJA and PKPA. Would the Iowa court in *Leyda*, supra, retain jurisdiction to modify its original order under the PKPA? Section 1738A(d) says that if a state has made a child custody determination consistently with the provisions of this section, its jurisdiction continues as long as the requirement of subsection (c)(1) of this section continues to be met and such state remains the residence of the child or of any contestant. Does analysis under the PKPA change the result in the *Leyda* case? Would the result be different had Florida been the jurisdiction where the "best interests of the child" could have best been served?

One author criticizes the PKPA as follows:

Intrinsically the UCCJA and PKPA involve philosophical differences. The UCCJA deliberately provided for jurisdictional flexibility to insure procurement of its dominant concern, the best interests of children. Some stability and certainty as to child custody jurisdiction was sacrificed where the best interests of the child presumably call[ ] for an assumption of jurisdiction by a state other than the home state. . . . The PKPA, on the other hand, attacks the vice of uncertainty and instability head on. By practically eliminating the "significant connection" alternative for child custody jurisdiction, it vests continuing jurisdiction in the home state alone, except in emergency or vacuum situations.

See Henry H. Foster, Child Custody Jurisdiction: UCCJA and PKPA, 27 N.Y.L. Sch. L. Rev. 297, 302 (1981).

(3) Federal Court Jurisdiction? Suppose different states assert jurisdiction over the same custody matter. May a federal court assert jurisdiction to settle the dispute? Before 1988 a series of decisions interpreted the PKPA to imply federal court jurisdiction when courts of two different states asserted jurisdiction over a custody determination. See, e.g., Flood v. Braaten, 727 F.2d 303 (3d Cir. 1984); Meade v. Meade, 812 F.2d 1473 (4th Cir. 1987). The Supreme Court finally resolved the issue of federal court jurisdiction in Thompson v. Thompson, 484 U.S. 174 (1988), holding:

> The PKPA does not provide an implied cause of action in federal court to determine which of two conflicting state custody decisions is valid. The context in which the PKPA was enacted — the existence of jurisdictional deadlocks among the States in custody cases and a nationwide problem of interstate parental kidnapping — suggests that Congress principal aim was to extend the requirements of the Full Faith and Credit Clause to custody determinations and not to create an entirely new cause of action. The language and placement of the Act reinforce this conclusion, in that the Act is an addendum to, and is therefore clearly intended to have the same operative effect as, the federal full faith and credit statute, the Act's heading is "Full faith and credit given to child custody determinations," and, unlike statutes that explicitly confer a right on a specified class of persons, the Act is addressed to States and to state courts. [T]he PKPA's legislative history provides an unusually clear indication that Congress did not intend the federal courts to play the enforcement role. [Id. at 175.]

The Court rejected the argument that failure to infer a cause of action would render the PKPA nugatory, reasoning that the argument, based on the presumption that the states are either unable or unwilling to enforce provisions of the Act, was one in which the Court was not willing to indulge. What effect will this decision have on a party with two conflicting state decrees?

(4) UCCJEA. In 1997, the National Conference of Commissioners on Uniform State Laws promulgated the Uniform Child Custody Jurisdiction and Enforcement Act (UCCJEA), 9 U.L.A. 257 (1999), to remedy inconsistent application of state laws under the UCCJA and PKPA. The UCCJEA, which is intended eventually to replace the UCCJA, makes several improvements in the UCCJA: "It provides clearer standards for which states can exercise original jurisdiction over a child-custody determination. It also, for the first time, enunciates a standard of continuing jurisdiction and clarifies modification and emergency jurisdiction. Other aspects of the jurisdiction provisions harmonize the law on simultaneous proceedings, clean hands, and forum non conveniens." Linda D. Elrod & Robert G. Spector, A Review of the Year in Family Law: A Search for Definitions and Policy, 31 Fam. L.Q. 613, 619 (1998).

Specifically, the UCCJEA:

(a)   includes a new definition of the term "custody determination" in order to clarify the custody proceedings that are covered by the Act (all custody and visitation cases with the exception of adoption and issues of tribal custody that remain subject to state determination applicability);

    (b)   incorporates the stricter jurisidictional standards of the PKPA by explicitly prioritizing home-state jurisdiction (instead of merely listing the four bases of jurisdiction as did the UCCJA);

    (c)   clarifies the meaning and application of "emergency" jurisdiction by providing that emergency jurisdiction may be used to protect the child on a temporary basis until the court issues a permanent order and defines the term to specify the inclusion of domestic violence; and,

    (d)   clarifies the meaning of "exclusive continuing jurisdiction" by providing for exclusive continuing jurisdiction in specific situations and facilitates the determination of when a state has relinquished continuing jurisdiction.

In addition, the UCCJEA eliminates a perennial source of confusion in the UCCJA by deleting the term "best interest" from the jurisdictional standards. The UCCJEA explicitly specifies that the Act is not intended to be used to address the underlying merits of a custody dispute or to provide a basis for jurisdiction based on the substantive custody best interests standard. To date, the UCCJEA has been enacted by 41 states. See Child Custody Jurisdiction and Enforcement Act, Legislative Fact Sheet, *http://nccusl.org/Update/uniformact_ factsheets/ uniformacts-fs-uccjea.asp* (last visited Jan. 30, 2005).

In 1998 Congress amended the Parental Kidnapping Prevention Act with the Visitation Rights Enforcement Act, 28 U.S.C. §1738A (2000). The PKPA now encompasses visitation as well as custody disputes (§1738A(a)), specifies that a court cannot modify the visitation or custody determination of another state unless the other state no longer has jurisdiction (or has declined to exercise it) (§1738A(h)), and revises the definition of "contestant" to include grandparents who claim a right to custody or visitation (§1738A(b)(2)).

(5) Extradition.   Suppose that in the *Leyda* case, Heidi instituted criminal charges against Michael, in the Florida courts, for kidnapping their daughter. Could the Florida court execute an extradition warrant to compel Michael's presence in Florida? Could Michael's home state grant a writ of habeas corpus to block the extradition warrant? See California v. Superior Court of California ex rel. Smolin, 482 U.S. 400 (1987), holding that, under the Extradition Act, "surrender is not to be interfered with by the summary process of habeas corpus upon speculations as to what ought to be the result of a trial in the place where the Constitution provides for its taking place." These issues raise problems of enforcement of custody decrees.

(6) Enforcement Remedies.   The traditional method of enforcing custody decrees is a civil contempt proceeding. A defendant is found in contempt if the parent could have complied with the decree yet willfully failed to do so. Since the purpose of civil contempt is to coerce compliance, a conditional punishment (such as a fine, imprisonment, or a temporary custody change) is imposed until the parent complies. See, e.g., In re Marriage of Fair & Martin, 940 P.2d 679 (Wash. Ct. App. 1997). If a parent ultimately fails to comply, problems arise in punishing the noncomplying parent. Imprisonment or a permanent custody change, for instance, may be deemed inappropriate as adverse to the best interests of the child.

Some jurisdictions authorize a parent to withhold child support in the face of the other parent's noncompliance with the custody decree. Case law and commentators, however, criticize this remedy because it may impose undue hardship on the child if the custodial parent needs the added support to care adequately for the child. See Carter v. Carter, 479 S.E.2d 681 (W. Va. 1996) for a discussion of diverging case law. See also Homer H. Clark, Law of Domestic Relations 848 (2d ed. 1988).

A writ of habeas corpus is another traditional enforcement mechanism. Originally used by prisoners claiming illegal arrest or unlawful detention, the writ is also utilized in child custody cases. Courts are reluctant to use this remedy, however, unless no other means of relief exists. See Hudson v. Purifoy, 986 S.W.2d 870 (Ark. 1999); Amenson v. Iowa, 59 F.3d 92 (8th Cir. 1995).

Complications in enforcement arise when the noncustodial parent leaves the forum state with the child. Because a custody determination is modifiable, it is not a final judgment and therefore not subject to the Full Faith and Credit Clause of Article IV, §1 of the Constitution. This possibility of modification encourages forum-shopping for a favorable decree. The UCCJA, UCCJEA, and the PKPA attempt to limit a state from modifying another state's custody decree. However problems still arise in enforcing that decree. For example, a significant problem may be locating the fleeing parent. Under the PKPA, states have access to the Federal Parental Locator Service to facilitate discovery of the address and employer of the abducting parent. The Act permits such access only to certain parties (e.g., court, state attorney, state or federal law enforcement agency) and not to a custodial parent. See generally Anne B. Goldstein, The Tragedy of the Interstate Child: A Critical Examination of the Uniform Child Custody Jurisdiction Act and the Parental Kidnapping Prevention Act, 25 U.C. Davis L. Rev. 845, 918 M. 335 (1992).

Some states also recognize, by case law or statute, the tort of custodial interference. See, e.g., Matsumoto v. Matsumoto, 762 A.2d 224 (N.J. Super. Ct. App. Div. 2000). However, a minority of jurisdictions refuse to recognize the tort, contending that the action merely increases hostilities for families already suffering from the consequences of divorce. See Zaharias v. Gammill, 844 P.2d 137 (Okla. 1992); Kessel v. Leavitt, 511 S.E.2d 710 (W. Va. 1998). Criminal liability also exists for custodial interference. See, e.g., State v. Wood, 8 P.3d 1189 (Ariz. Ct. App. 2000); Ex parte Jones, 36 S.W.3d 139 (Tex. Ct. App. 2000).

D.   *CUSTODY AND THE NEW REPRODUCTIVE TECHNIQUES*

INTRODUCTORY PROBLEMS

(1) Mary and John Jones have been married for several years but have been unable to have a child because John is sterile. Mary and John wish to have a biologically related child. They consult Mary's gynecologist, Dr. Pendleton, who suggests artificial insemination with semen from a third-party donor. After discussion, both Mary and John agree to the procedure. The insemination is performed by Dr. Pendleton with semen from Dan Duncan, a first-year medical student at a nearby university, where Dr. Pendleton is on the faculty. Dr. Pendleton keeps all parties' identities secret. After two insemination attempts, Mary becomes pregnant. Following an uneventful pregnancy, a daughter, Samantha, is born. What are the respective rights and responsibilities of Mary, John, and Dan? Who is Samantha's

"father" for purposes of custody and support? If Dan wishes, may his name be placed on Samantha's birth certificate? May he assert rights to visitation?

(2) Margaret and Joe Smith have been married for several years but have been unable to have a child because Margaret has damaged fallopian tubes. They would like to have a child biologically related to Joe. After advertising in the local newspaper, they meet Diane Cady, a 23-year-old graduate student. They wish to enter into a contract with Diane, who would agree to become artificially inseminated using Joe's sperm, with appropriate medical supervision. The agreement would provide that Diane give up the child to the Smiths immediately at birth and furnish any necessary consent for the Smiths to adopt the child. The Smiths would pay her $25,000 plus medical expenses: $12,500 when she becomes pregnant and $12,500 when the adoption becomes final. Advise the Smiths concerning the applicable law in the following circumstances: *Connect to Baby M*

a. All goes according to plan and Diane delivers a healthy male child whom the Smiths name Sam. Diane relinquishes Sam to the Smiths who have agreed to raise him. In the absence of any dispute, what is the legality of this arrangement? Are the parties subject to any criminal liability?

b. After Sam's birth, Diane changes her mind and decides to keep the child. Can the Smiths adopt the child without Diane's consent? If not, would the Smiths prevail over Diane in a custody fight? Would the contract be specifically enforceable? Does Joe Smith have any support obligation if his efforts at adoption and custody are unsuccessful?

c. Diane gives birth to a mentally retarded child. The Smiths decide they do not want the disabled infant. Neither does Diane. Are the Smiths liable for damages for breach of contract? What are the custody and support obligations of the respective parties?

Should the law's response to the Smith's situation(s) differ from the case in which Mary Jones is impregnated by artificial insemination when her husband is sterile? If so, why?

(3) Joe Smith learns he has a serious illness requiring chemotherapy. His physician informs him that the treatment may render him sterile. He decides to freeze semen samples so that he and Margaret may have a child in the future. Following Joe's recovery from his illness, the Smiths decide to have a child. Margaret's gynecologist surgically removes an ovum from Margaret and fertilizes it in a petri dish with Joe's semen. Since Margaret previously underwent a hysterectomy (involving removal of her uterus but not ovaries), she is unable to bear the child. They enter into a contract with Diane Cady to receive the fertilized embryo and to give birth to the resulting child.

What should be the custodial and support rights and responsibilities of the respective parties? Who is the child's "mother" — the ovum donor or the surrogate? What should be the law's response if Diane should refuse to relinquish the child? By the Smiths if they refuse to accept the child?

(4) Shortly after Dr. Pendleton fertilizes Margaret Smith's ovum in a petri dish with Joe's semen, Margaret and Joe are killed in an automobile accident. Numerous infertile couples apply to Dr. Pendleton for the fertilized embryos. He chooses a couple, Susan and Charles White. After a female child is born, the Smiths' relatives

bring a custody action against the Whites. What are the custodial rights and support obligations of the respective parties?

(5) Sally and Daniel White have been married for seven years. Shortly after their marriage, Sally suffers a tubal pregnancy that results in the surgical removal of one of her fallopian tubes. After several other tubal pregnancies, her other fallopian tube is removed, leaving Sally unable to conceive a child by sexual intercourse. The Whites decide to undergo in vitro fertilization whereby Sally's egg is surgically removed and then fertilized in a laboratory medium with Daniel's sperm. After the procedure, eight embryos result. Before some of these embryos can be implanted in Sally's womb, the Whites' marriage breaks up. At the divorce proceeding, Sally requests that the embryos be distributed to her for implantation. Daniel protests, arguing that he no longer wants to father a child with Sally. He wants the embryos destroyed.

How should the dispute be resolved? Are the embryos akin to "property" that should be distributed in the course of dissolution proceedings? Or are they "persons" whose "custody" should be determined according to the best interests of the child?

In re Baby M
See pp. 439-448, supra.

NOTES AND QUESTIONS ON *BABY M*

(1) Artificial Insemination. In the case of artificial insemination (termed "AID") a woman is impregnated with sperm from a third-party donor. AID raises a number of legal issues. Who, for instance, is regarded as the child's father for custody and support purposes? Cases typically arise following a divorce, when the wife refuses the husband visitation rights on the ground that the children conceived by AID are therefore not his children.[104] Or upon separation or divorce, the father of a child conceived by AID alleges he is not liable for child support because there is no issue of the marriage.[105]

Case law generally holds that the husband's consent is often decisive in such disputes. That is, by giving consent to the insemination, the husband is entitled to visitation rights and also is estopped from denying liability for support. This result is also dictated by states that follow the original version of the Uniform Parentage Act §5, 9B U.L.A. 287 (1987).

What are the rights and responsibilities of the sperm donor? In several states, including those following the Original Uniform Parentage Act §5, the sperm donor "is treated in law as if he were not the natural father." Hence, the biological father has no duty of support and no custodial rights. In the absence of legislation, the common law presumption of legitimacy (discussed below) also suggests that the child is the legitimate issue of the woman's husband, rather than of the sperm donor. The UPA was revised in 2000 (and amended in 2002). What are the similarities and differences between the versions?

---

[104] See, e.g., People ex rel. Abajian v. Dennett, 184 N.Y.S.2d 178 (Super. Ct. 1958).
[105] See, e.g., Levin v. Levin, 645 N.E.2d 601 (Ind. Ct. App. 1994).

Uniform Parentage Act (2000, as amended 2002)
9B U.L.A. 355-356 (2001 & Supp. 2004)

[The following provisions are not applicable to children conceived by sexual intercourse or those subject to gestational agreements.]

§702. Parental Status of Donor

A donor is not a parent of a child conceived by means of assisted reproduction.

§703. Paternity of Child of Assisted Reproduction

A man who provides sperm for, or consents to, assisted reproduction by a woman as provided in Section 704 with the intent to be the parent of her child, is a parent of the resulting child.

§704. Consent to Assisted Reproduction

(a) Consent by a woman, and a man who intends to be a parent of a child born to the woman by assisted reproduction must be in a record signed by the woman and the man. This requirement does not apply to a donor.

(b) Failure of a man to sign a consent required by subsection (a), before or after birth of the child, does not preclude a finding of paternity if the woman and the man, during the first two years of the child's life resided together in the same household with the child and openly held out the child as their own.

(2) Surrogacy: Background. Surrogate motherhood is the female counterpart of artificial insemination. Whereas artificial insemination addresses problems regarding a man's infertility, surrogate motherhood presents a solution to a woman's fertility problems (and sometimes also for gay parents, as discussed below). A surrogate mother agrees to be inseminated with the sperm of a man whose wife is unable to conceive or bear a child. The surrogate agrees to bear the child and to relinquish all parental rights to the child after birth. Then the husband and his wife petition to adopt the child.

Estimates suggest that as many as 10,000 babies have been born as a result of these agreements.[106] The majority of cases, apparently, involve no disputes. May the parties, nonetheless, be subject to criminal liability?

In Doe v. Kelly, 307 N.W.2d 438 (Mich. Ct. App. 1981), a couple and a surrogate agreed to the arrangement. Stemming from concerns about criminal prosecution, the parties brought suit via a declaratory judgment to declare the Michigan baby-selling statute void for vagueness and violative of their constitutional right to privacy. The trial court upheld the statute, and the appellate court affirmed. Although holding that the baby-selling statute did not prohibit the couple from proceeding with the surrogacy arrangement, the court did not rule on the validity of such contracts. Subsequent Michigan legislation, however, prohibited surrogacy as contrary to public

---

[106] Aaron Derfel, More Americans "Renting" Canadian Wombs, Nat. Post, Oct. 24, 2003, at A2.

policy. See Michigan Comp. Law. Ann. §722.855 (West 2002). See also Surrogate Parenting Assocs., Inc. v. Commonwealth, 704 S.W.2d 209 (Ky. 1986) (holding that surrogate motherhood contracts are not violative of Kentucky law against baby selling). The Kentucky legislature overruled the decision by enacting a statute that prohibited compensation for surrogacy and made such contracts void. Ky. Rev. Stat. Ann. 199.590 (Baldwin 1999).

(3) Baby Selling. Baby-selling statutes, which forbid compensation to a surrogate in connection with an adoption or termination of parental rights, raise a number of constitutional problems. For example, do these statutes constitute a denial of equal protection, since the surrogate mother is being treated differently from the "surrogate father" in artificial insemination? The Fourteenth Amendment forbids certain forms of governmental interference: in general persons who are similarly situated may not be treated differently. The court in *Baby M* stated, "A sperm donor simply cannot be equated with a surrogate mother." Do you agree? How is the sperm donor analogous to the surrogate mother who donates her egg? How is he different?

Further, is the surrogate being paid for a "product" or a "service"? If a product, then why not permit payment, since sperm donors and blood donors are compensated? If a service, then why not allow compensation, since wet nurses, nannies, and other child caretakers have historically been compensated for child-rearing services?

(4) Baby-selling statutes in the surrogate context were also challenged in *Baby M* as violating the constitutional right to privacy. Roe v. Wade (supra Chapter 1), as well as other Supreme Court cases, have held that the constitutional right of privacy, relative to procreation, guarantees the right to be free from state interference in the decision to bear or beget a child. Is the right to hire or to be a surrogate mother guaranteed by the constitutional right of privacy?[107] If the practice of surrogate motherhood is within the protected right of privacy, can the state still interfere on the basis of any compelling interests?

(5) The policy behind baby-selling statutes is to relieve the economic incentive for a mother to give up her child under adverse circumstances. Is the same rationale underlying the antipathy to baby selling present in the surrogacy situation? Consider the following:

> We conclude that . . . there are fundamental differences between the surrogate parenting procedure . . . and the buying and selling of children as prohibited by [the baby-selling statute]. . . .
>
> There is no doubt but that [the baby-selling statute] is intended to keep baby brokers from overwhelming an expectant mother or the parents of a child with financial inducements to part with the child. But the central fact in the surrogate parenting procedure is that the agreement to bear the child is entered into *before* conception. The essential considerations for the surrogate mother when she agrees to the surrogate parenting procedure are *not* avoiding the consequences of an unwanted pregnancy or fear of the financial burden of child rearing. On the contrary,

---

[107] A prominent proponent of the view that the right to use assisted technologies is part of constitutionally protected procreative liberty is Professor John A. Robertson. See John A. Robertson, Children of Choice: Freedom and the New Reproductive Technologies (1994).

the essential consideration is to assist a person or couple who desperately want a child but are unable to conceive one in the customary manner to achieve a biologically related offspring. Surrogate Parenting Assocs., Inc. v. Commonwealth, 704 S.W.2d 209, 211 (Ky. 1986).

(6) Feminist Concerns. *Baby* M, with its suggestion that surrogate motherhood is "potentially degrading to women," raises a concern about the possible exploitative aspects of surrogate motherhood. Is surrogate parenting exploitative of women?[108] If women desire to enter into such arrangements, is it paternalistic for the law to forbid this conduct?

Baby M suggests that women may still serve as surrogates if they do so voluntarily and without remuneration. Is this a realistic solution to the problems of surrogate motherhood?

(7) Breach of Contract. As we have seen, the law interposes limits on private ordering in the surrogacy context (in the form of criminal sanctions in some jurisdictions) even when all parties agree to the arrangement. What occurs when disputes arise — either on the part of the surrogate, or less frequently perhaps, on the part of the prospective adoptive parents?

In *Baby M*, the mother breaches by refusing to relinquish the child for adoption by the Sterns as promised. Following Mrs. Whitehead's breach, Mr. Stern attempts to establish his parental rights by enforcement of the surrogacy contract. Is the contract enforceable according to *Baby M*? If the Sterns are without a contract remedy, one legal recourse they have is to attempt to proceed with the adoption. Could such an attempt ever be successful without the consent of the biological mother? If, as in *Baby M*, the mother refuses to consent, what must be shown to overcome this obstacle? If adoption is unsuccessful, the couple's next recourse is a custody proceeding. Given the indeterminacy of the best interests standard, is there ever a likely result? Consider too the *Baby M* court's view on temporary custody orders. Existing law, thus, appears to be characterized by considerable uncertainty for the infertile couple, as well as for the child. See also Johnson v. Calvert, 851 P.2d 776 (Cal. 1993) (recognizing the parental rights of the genetic parents according to an intent-based rationale).

(8) Other possibilities also exist for breach on the part of the surrogate. For example, suppose the surrogate delivers a premature infant, who subsequently dies. Or the surrogate wants an abortion? May the biological father prevent her from exercising her right? Or suppose she neglects normal precautions of pregnancy and abuses alcohol or other harmful substances? If the surrogate contract were to be held valid, what should be the remedy in each case? What problems might these remedies pose? For example, are money damages adequate for loss of the couple's "expectation interest"? Could a court order a surrogate mother's specific performance?

---

[108] Radical feminists are the most outspoken proponents of this point of view. See, e.g., Gena Corea, The Mother Machine: Reproductive Technologies from Artificial Insemination to Artificial Wombs (1985); Robyn Rowland, Living Laboratories: Women and Reproductive Technologies (1992). See also Margaret Jane Radin, Contested Commodities (2001) (claiming that commodification of women's reproductive capacity is harmful to women's self-concept).

(9) Breach by Sperm Donor. Custody disputes also arise when the sperm donor and his wife breach the agreement. For example, suppose that the child is born with a disability, and the prospective adoptive parents refuse to accept the child. How should this breach of contract be treated? In Malahoff v. Stiver, 848 F.2d 192 (6th Cir. 1988), the surrogate mother, Judy Stiver, gave birth to a mentally retarded child. The sperm donor, Alexander Malahoff, decided he did not want the child; neither did the Stivers. Blood tests revealed that the child had actually been fathered by the surrogate's husband. Malahoff sued the surrogate for not producing the child he ordered. In Stiver v. Parker, 975 F.2d 261 (6th Cir. 1992), the Stivers sued the doctor, lawyer, and psychiatrist of the surrogate program for not advising them about the timing of intercourse. They also sued Malahoff for violating their privacy by making the matter public and for transmitting a virus to the child through his semen that contributed to the child's illness. What result?

Or suppose that twins are born as a result of the insemination of the surrogate. The intended parents agree to accept only the girl but not the boy. What remedy, if any, is available to the surrogate in this breach of contract situation? Would you advise a suit for specific performance? Cited in Nick Craven, Dilemma Over the Surrogate Twins with No Parents, Daily Mail, May 8, 2000, at 8.

(10) Presumption of Legitimacy. In the biological father's bid for custody, several obstacles stand in his path regarding acknowledgment of his paternity. The first obstacle is a common law doctrine specifying that a child born of a married woman is presumed conclusively to be fathered by the woman's husband. Thus, in the case of a married surrogate, the sperm donor will not be recognized as the biological father.

This presumption is frequently an issue in surrogacy cases. In In re Baby Girl, 9 Fam. L. Rep. 2348 (Ky. Cir. Ct., Mar. 8, 1983), a surrogate and her husband attempted to terminate their parental rights to enable the sperm donor to take permanent custody. The Kentucky court denied the petition. The court, in dicta, stated that the doctor's affidavit regarding the artificial insemination was not sufficient evidence to rebut the presumption of paternity. The same presumption arose in Syrkowski v. Appleyard, 362 N.W.2d 211 (Mich. 1985). In order to seek legal custody of a child carried by a surrogate mother, the sperm donor sought an order of filiation before the child was born. The jurisdiction had a rebuttable presumption of legitimacy in favor of the surrogate's husband. The lower court ruled that it lacked jurisdiction, since Michigan paternity law applied only to actions involving non-marital children. The Michigan Supreme Court reversed, finding that the court did have jurisdiction to rule on plaintiff's paternity claim.

A second presumption, statutory rather than common law, presents an additional obstacle to biological fathers seeking to establish paternity of children conceived through surrogacy arrangements: Statutes regulating artificial insemination in many states, modeled after the original Uniform Parentage Act, specify that if a husband consents to artificial insemination of his wife by a third-party semen donor, the woman's husband is presumed to be the father of the resulting child. Such statutes imply that the biological father in a surrogacy contract would not be the child's legitimate father. How is this issue handled by the surrogacy contract in *Baby* M?

The purpose of the common law presumption is to protect the rights of the nonmarital child and to preserve family integrity; the purpose of the statutory presumption is to ensure support for the AID child. Are these purposes relevant to surrogacy? Do these difficulties suggest that couples desiring to enter surrogacy agreements should always select single surrogates?[109] What problems might then arise?

(11) Adoption Consent Statutes. Another obstacle is adoption consent statutes that prohibit pre-birth consent. As part of the surrogacy agreement, Mrs. Whitehead agreed to surrender the child to the Sterns, giving them permanent and sole custody, and to terminate her parental rights. When she breached, she was protected by state laws governing revocation of consent to adoption (see supra pp. 508-509). All 50 states have legislation prohibiting a mother from granting irrevocable consent to adoption before the child's birth or for some period after birth. The purpose of such laws is to ensure that the biological mother's consent be knowing, voluntary, and without duress. Should such laws be applicable to the surrogacy situation in which the surrogate has considerable time, even before conception, to reflect? Is it relevant that her decision is not the product of impaired judgment resulting from an unplanned pregnancy?

One solution to the obstacle of such pre-birth consent statutes is a determination of parentage prior to the birth. Will a court issue a pre-birth determination of parentage? Compare Culliton v. Beth Israel Deaconess Med. Ctr., 756 N.E.2d 1133 (Mass. 2001) (approving the issuance of a pre-birth parentage order) with A.H.W. v. G.H.B., 772 A.2d 948 (N.J. Super. Ct. Ch. Div. 2000) (contra). See generally Vanessa S. Browne-Barbour, Bartering for Babies: Are Preconception Agreements in the Best Interests of Children?, 26 Whittier L. Rev. 429 (2004) (arguing that preconception agreements constitute baby selling violative of federal and state law, exploit women and children, and devalue humans).

(12) Is it possible for a child conceived by surrogacy to have no legal parent(s)? In In re Marriage of Buzzanca, 72 Cal. Rptr. 2d 280 (Ct. App. 1998), a married couple contracted with a surrogate mother to implant an embryo and bear a child for them. The embryo was produced by donated genetic material (not their egg or sperm). Thus, none of the parties was biologically related to the child. Although the surrogate carries the child to term, the contracting couple divorces. The contracting husband disclaims all responsibility for the child. The contracting wife seeks to be declared the child's mother. The trial court, determining that the child has no lawful parents, terminates the husband's obligations. The appellate court reverses, analogizing the situation to that of artificial insemination whereby parenthood can be established by conduct and by consent without the necessity for biological ties.

(13) Gay and Lesbian Parents. Application of assisted reproductive techniques to gay and lesbian couples raises many of the foregoing issues and some additional ones. For example, such couples must face the prohibition on baby-selling and (in the case of gay male couples hiring a married surrogate) overcome

---

[109] Some professionals who are involved in surrogate parenting advocate use of single surrogates. David Gelman & Daniel Shapiro, Infertility: Babies by Contract, Newsweek, Nov. 4, 1985, at 74-75; Noel P. Keane & Dennis L. Breo, The Surrogate Mother 49 (1981). Others prefer that the surrogate be married, preferably with children of her own. See M. Louise Graham, Surrogate Gestation and the Protection of Choice, 22 Santa Clara L. Rev. 291, 293 n. 7 (1982).

the presumption that the surrogate's husband is the father. On the other hand, lesbian couples who resort to artificial insemination with a known sperm donor occasionally must face the prospect of a sperm donor who demands visitation rights. How should such disputes be resolved? See, e.g., Thomas v. Robin, 618 N.Y.S.2d 356 (N.Y. App. Div. 1994). See also In re Parentage of L.B., 89 P.3d 271 (Wash. Ct. App. 2004) (holding that lesbian nonbiological mother could petition for parenting rights despite biological mother's and sperm donor's attempts to thwart her claims by their marriage and his signing an acknowledgment of paternity), *petition for review granted*, 101 P.3d 107 (Wash. 2004). See generally Fred A. Bernstein, This Child Does Have Two Mothers . . . And a Sperm Donor with Visitation, 22 N.Y.U. Rev. L. & Soc. Change 1 (1996).

(14) Different State Approaches.   States adopt a variety of approaches to surrogacy. Some jurisdictions deny enforcement, declaring all surrogacy agreements void. Others prohibit compensation (but permit payment of expenses). Still other states regulate isolated aspects of surrogacy agreements (e.g., by providing exemptions from criminal sanctions for baby selling). Finally, other states permit surrogacy but with significant procedural regulation. Adam P. Plant, With a Little Help from My Friends: The Intersection of the Gestational Carrier Surrogacy Agreement, Legislative Inaction, and Medical Advancement, 54 Ala. L. Rev. 639, 650-655 (2003) (surveying jurisdictions).

(15) Forum Shopping.   The lack of uniformity in different jurisdictions' treatment of surrogate contracts may lead to forum shopping, precipitating issues of federalism and conflicts of law. In this event, which law should prevail — that of the jurisdiction where the contract was entered into, where the insemination was performed, or where the child was born? Or should it be the law of the domicile of the surrogate? Of the infertile couple? See Susan Frelich Appleton, Surrogacy Arrangements and the Conflict of Laws, 1990 Wis. L. Rev. 399.

(16) Model Legislation.   Model legislation also addresses surrogate parenting agreements. In 1988, the National Conference of Commissioners on Uniform State Laws (NCCUSL) approved the Uniform Status of Children of Assisted Conception Act (USCACA), 9B U.L.A. 184 (Supp. 1999), with alternative proposals: Alternative A regulates surrogacy through a preconception adoption proceeding (i.e., providing that contracts are valid if they are judicially pre-approved), and Alternative B makes surrogacy agreements void. Only two states adopted USCACA (Virginia adopted Alternative A and North Dakota adopted Alternative B). Plant, supra, at 650.

In 2000, a revised Uniform Parentage Act (UPA) replaced USCACA. Because reproductive technology was in its infancy when the UPA was enacted in 1973, the original version addressed the issue of legal fatherhood only in the context of artificial insemination (i.e., the rights of the husband versus the sperm donor) (UPA §5(a)). The UPA was revised substantially in 2000 (and subsequently amended in 2002) in light of scientific advances in paternity testing and the new reproductive technologies.

The revised UPA Act (excerpted below) provides limited regulation of surrogacy. It authorizes "gestational agreements" if they are validated by a court. The Act permits payment to a surrogate mother. Also, it provides that the intended parents may be married or unmarried. Once it is satisfied that certain requirements are met, the court may issue an order validating the agreement and declaring that the intended parents are the parents of the child. The new UPA provides a mechanism for determining parentage of children in the event that the agreement is not enforceable and also provides for liability for child support in such cases.

The new UPA departs from USCACA in several ways: (1) it provides that only validated gestational agreements are enforceable, thereby providing an incentive for the participants to seek judicial approval; (2) the new UPA has abandoned the requirement that at least one of the intended parents be genetically related to the child; and (3) individuals who enter into nonvalidated gestational agreements and later refuse to adopt the resulting child now may be liable for support. To date, only four states have enacted this new legislation (Delaware, Texas, Washington, and Wyoming). See Uniform Parentage Act, Legislative Fact Sheet, *http://nccusl.org/Update/uniformact_factsheets/uniformacts-fs-upa.asp* (last visited Jan. 31, 2005).

(17) International Perspective. The international response to surrogacy also varies considerably. Some countries ban surrogacy (e.g., France, China, Italy, Vietnam). However, many countries now permit private surrogacy arrangements. England, for example, recognizes private agreements (permitting payment for expenses but not services), although it bans commercial surrogacy. Surrogacy Arrangements Act of 1985, ch. 49. See also Human Fertilization and Embryology Act of 1990, ch. 37 (regulating fertility programs and authorizing courts to declare the infertile couple as the legal parents of a child born via surrogacy). See generally Amy Garrity, Comment, A Comparative Analysis of Surrogacy Law in the United States and Great Britain — A Proposed Model Statute for Louisiana, 60 La. L. Rev. 809 (2000). Similarly, noncommercial surrogacy (with payment permitted for expenses) is also allowed in parts of Australia, including the Australian Capital Territory and New South Wales. Gareth Malpeli, Baby Traders, West Australian, June 15, 2002 (available at 2002 WL 20275905).

Israel has adopted the most progressive approach with its government-sponsored program. The Surrogate Motherhood Agreements Act, 1996, S.H. 1577, establishes a governmental committee to approve all requests for surrogacy. The legislation permits payment to the surrogate mother for her services and also specifies eligibility criteria, the status of the child (including custody, guardianship, and the manner of delivery to the intended parents), and the limited conditions under which the surrogate mother may revoke consent. See generally D. Kelly Weisberg, The Birth of Surrogacy in Israel (2005).

(18) Problem. You are the legislative assistant to a state legislator who has asked you to draft a statute on surrogate parenting. What do you think the law's response to surrogate parenting should be? At one extreme, should it be a crime to enter into such contracts? At the other extreme, should such contracts be enforceable and the parties held to their promises, subject to traditional breach of contract remedies? Or should the law adopt an intermediate stance? If so, what should this intermediate stance be: should such contracts be enforceable only if there is a prior judicial hearing, approving the contract and requiring a showing that the surrogate has made a voluntary, informed, and knowing waiver of parental rights? Should the law require all surrogates to be married and already to have children? Should the law require that the infertile couple be married? Should there be medical

certification that the wife is physically unable to conceive or carry a child, rather than merely unwilling? Should the law screen the prospective adoptive parents for fitness, as in all agency adoptions? What provision should be made for subsequent disclosure to the child of his or her origins? Finally, should the legislature adopt the new Uniform Parentage Act provisions on gestational agreements (excerpted below)?

Uniform Parentage Act (2000, as amended 2002)
9B U.L.A. 362, 367-369 (2001 & Supp. 2004)

§801. *Gestational Agreement Authorized*

(a) A prospective gestational mother, her husband if she is married, a donor or the donors, and the intended parents may enter into a written agreement providing that:

(1) the prospective gestational mother agrees to pregnancy by means of assisted reproduction;

(2) the prospective gestational mother, her husband if she is married, and the donors relinquish all rights and duties as the parents of a child conceived through assisted reproduction; and

(3) the intended parents become the parents of the child.

(b) The man and the woman who are the intended parents must both be parties to the gestational agreement.

(c) A gestational agreement is enforceable only if validated as provided in Section 803.

(d) A gestational agreement does not apply to the birth of a child conceived by means of sexual intercourse.

(e) A gestational agreement may provide for payment of consideration.

(f) A gestational agreement may not limit the right of the gestational mother to make decisions to safeguard her health or that of the embryos or fetus.

§806. *Termination of Gestational Agreement*

(a) After issuance of an order under this [article], but before the prospective gestational mother becomes pregnant by means of assisted reproduction, the prospective gestational mother, her husband, or either of the intended parents may terminate the gestational agreement by giving written notice of termination to all other parties.

(b) The court for good cause shown may terminate the gestational agreement.

(c) An individual who terminates a gestational agreement shall file notice of the termination with the court. On receipt of the notice, the court shall vacate the order issued under this [article]. An individual who does not notify the court of the termination of the agreement is subject to appropriate sanctions.

(d) Neither a prospective gestational mother nor her husband, if any, is liable to the intended parents for terminating a gestational agreement pursuant to this section.

§807. *Parentage Under Validated Gestational Agreement*

(a) Upon birth of a child to a gestational mother, the intended parents shall file notice with the court that a child has been born to the gestational mother within 300 days after assisted reproduction. Thereupon, the court shall issue an order:
(1) confirming that the intended parents are the parents of the child;
(2) if necessary, ordering that the child be surrendered to the intended parents; and
(3) directing the [agency maintaining birth records] to issue a birth certificate naming the intended parents as parents of the child.

(b) If the parentage of a child born to a gestational mother is alleged not to be the result of assisted reproduction, the court shall order genetic testing to determine the parentage of the child.

(c) If the intended parents fail to file notice required under subsection (a), the gestational mother or the appropriate State agency may file notice with the court that a child has been born to the gestational mother within 300 days after assisted reproduction. Upon proof of a court order issued pursuant to Section 803 validating the gestational agreement, the court shall order the intended parents are the parents of the child and are financially responsible for the child.

§809. *Effect of Nonvalidated Gestational Agreement*

(a) A gestational agreement, whether in a record or not, that is not judicially validated is not enforceable.

(b) If a birth results under a gestational agreement that is not judicially validated as provided in this [article], the parent-child relationship is determined as provided in [Article] 2.

(c) Individuals who are parties to a nonvalidated gestational agreement as intended parents may be held liable for support of the resulting child, even if the agreement is otherwise unenforceable. . . .

NOTE ON IN VITRO FERTILIZATION

In vitro fertilization[110] raises additional provocative legal issues. Early controversy centered around the medical ethics of "experimenting" with human sperm and ova. In Del Zio v. Presbyterian Hospital, 74 Civ. 3588 (S.D.N.Y. 1978), a couple began the in vitro procedure by surgical removal of the woman's egg and its introduction into the medium with the husband's sperm. Before fertilization had occurred, the hospital's chief of obstetrics and gynecology destroyed the embryo, contending that it constituted experimentation unapproved by the hospital ethics committee. A jury returned a verdict for $50,000 to the couple for pain and suffering.

[110] In in vitro fertilization, ova are surgically removed and placed in a laboratory medium together with sperm. After fertilization, the embryo is implanted in the uterus of either the ovum donor or another woman. The procedure enables women with blocked or damaged fallopian tubes to conceive or bear children.

To date, little federal legislation deals with in vitro fertilization. The Fertility Clinic Success Rate and Certification Act of 1992, 42 U.S.C. §§263a-1 to 263a-7 (2000), requires that IVF clinics report the number of procedures performed and the resulting number of live births. The Act was enacted to counter claims of inflated success rates by some clinics. It specifies that "age, diagnosis, and other significant factors" be taken in account in reporting. 42 U.S.C. §263a-1(2) (2000).

Another controversial issue concerns the use of in vitro fertilization by post menopausal women. More older women have been using reproductive technology to become pregnant. In January 2005, a 66-year-old Romanian woman gave birth to a girl conceived by in vitro fertilization with donor sperm and eggs.[111] The number of such births to older women has been steadily increasing[112] and presents many ethical and policy concerns. In the use of such technology by older women, how does one balance the respective interests of the child, the woman, the family, and the state?[113]

Legal issues also arise in conjunction with disposition of embryos. For example, to whom do the embryos belong? Are they "property" of the ovum donor, and/or the sperm donor? What should happen to the frozen embryos if the parents divorce or die? In March 1981, a wealthy couple, Mr. and Mrs. Rios, flew to Australia in order to impregnate the wife through in vitro fertilization. Three eggs were removed and fertilized from an anonymous donor. Of the three, one was implanted but did not result in a pregnancy, and the other two were frozen. Before another attempt, the Rios died in an airplane crash in South America, leaving no indication as to what should be done with the frozen embryos.[114] Should the embryos be donated to other infertile couples? If a child is born from the embryo transfer, does it have any rights to the property of its deceased "mother" and "father"?

What should happen if the couple subsequently divorces, for example, after the woman's eggs have been fertilized by the husband's sperm but before implantation? If the couple attempts to address this eventuality in a prior agreement, will such an agreement be enforceable?

In Kass v. Kass, 696 N.E.2d 174 (N.Y. 1998), Maureen and Steven Kass had five frozen embryos, the result of their attempts at in vitro fertilization. They had executed an informed consent agreement with the clinic that provided that any remaining prezygotes would be donated to science in the event of subsequent disagreements about disposition. However, Maureen Kass petitioned for distribution

---

[111] Alison Muther, Mom, 66, Is "More than Happy," Charlotte Observer, Jan. 18, 2005, at 6A.

[112] In 2002, the National Center for Health Statistics reported 263 births to women 50 and older. Cited in Michael Stroh, Growing Trend: New Mothers in Their 50s, 60s, Baltimore Sun, Dec. 30, 2004, at A1.

[113] Italy recently enacted legislation restricting fertility treatments to "stable heterosexual" couples who live together and are of childbearing age and who use their own eggs and sperm. An Italian court subsequently cleared the way for a referendum on the controversial legislation. See Church Tells Italians to Abstain or Vote "No" in Fertility Referendum, Agence France Presse, Jan. 17, 2005.

[114] Subsequently, an ethics commission (the Waller Committee) recommended destruction of the embryos; however, the legislature reversed the recommendation. Ultimately, the embryos were implanted unsuccessfully in the wombs of two women. For an account of the case, see Nicole L. Cucci, Note, The Constitutional Implications of In Vitro Fertilization Procedures, 72 St. John's L. Rev. 417, 432 (1998).

of the embryos to her (alleging that implantation would provide her with her only chance of biological motherhood). Stephen Kass protested the imposition of coerced fatherhood and counterclaimed to enforce the couple's consent agreement.

The New York Court of Appeals held that a woman has no privacy right to control embryos before implantation. Finding no reason to release the parties from their agreement based either on public policy or changed circumstances, the court reasoned that it was especially important to honor parties' choices made before disputes arise. "To the extent possible, it should be the progenitors — not the State and not the courts — who by their prior directive make this deeply personal life choice." Id at 180. Do you agree?

Similarly, in A.Z. v. B.Z., 725 N.E.2d 1051 (Mass. 2000), and J.B. v. M.B., 783 A.2d 707 (N.J. 2001), two couples executed respective agreements providing that, in the event of divorce, their embryos would be implanted in the infertile wife. Subsequently, courts in both jurisdictions held that the agreements violated public policy. See also Litowitz v. Litowitz, 48 P.3d 261 (Wash. 2002) (awarding embryos to husband postdivorce, with instructions to donate them to an infertile couple, reasoning that the "best interests" test did not dictate that ensuing children should be raised by the single, divorced older wife). For a discussion of these cases, see Ellen Waldman, The Parent Trap: Uncovering the Myth of "Coerced Parenthood" in Frozen Embryo Disputes, 53 Am. U. L. Rev. 1021 (2004).

CHAPTER 6

State-Enforced Limitations on the Liberty of Minors

A. INTRODUCTION

In a variety of areas, law constrains the liberty of adolescents more than that of adults. This chapter explores circumstances where, because of age, the freedom of juveniles is limited. The materials in this chapter relate to important aspects of a teenager's life: limitations on their rights to work, drive automobiles, and consume liquor; and the requirements that they attend school and generally be subject to parental controls.

Whether a young person should have the same freedom as an adult is a critical question considered earlier in the book. For example, the *Ginsberg* case, Chapter 1, posed the question of whether a state could prohibit the sale of sexually explicit materials to juveniles in situations in which adult access would be constitutionally protected. The degree of a juvenile's autonomy with regard to medical treatment was a principal concern of Chapter 4. The case of North Florida Women's Health and Counseling Services v. State, Chapter 1, like Carey v. Population Services International, infra, p. 674, involves the privacy rights of sexually active young persons. There are also parallels between the *Yoder* case, Chapter 1, and the status offender material, infra, p. 698, in that each concerns aspects of the requirement that young people attend school.

Certain common questions should frame your inquiry into the topics that follow:

1. What interests are being served by treating teenagers by different standards from those applying to adults? Is the primary purpose protection of the young person? The enforcement of parental prerogatives? The protection of society?

2. How substantial is the evidence offered to justify limiting the young person's freedom?

3. Are age-based lines appropriate? Are there alternatives? What opportunities are there for standards based on "competence" or "maturity" that would apply

irrespective of age? Are the existing age-based lines drawn at the appropriate age?

4. What method is being used to limit the young person's liberty? What are the consequences of a violation? Are sanctions imposed on minors? Their parents? Persons dealing with minors in the marketplace?

5. What role does the young person's family have in enforcement of the constraints on the minor's liberty? To what extent may parents "liberate" their own children?

6. According to Virginia Coigney, "The relationship between the child, his parents, and society is fundamentally a property relationship. . . . Most of the laws relating to children reflect the prevailing attitude that they are the possessions of their parents and/or the state and not very valuable possessions at that."[1] To correct this, she proposes the adoption of "A Child's Bill of Rights," the first right being:

> *The Right to Self-Determination.* Children should have the right to decide the matters which affect them most directly. This is the basic right upon which all others depend. Children are now treated as the private property of their parents on the assumption that it is the parents' right and responsibility to control the life of the child. The achievement of children's rights, however, would reduce the need for this control and bring about an end to the double standard of morals and behavior for adults and children.[2]

Using the topics considered in this chapter,

a. Evaluate critically the extent to which children are treated as the "private property of their parents" or "possessions of their parents and/or the state";

b. Describe and compare the degree to which under present law a minor has "the right to decide";

c. Consider alternative ways in which the law might be changed to broaden the minor's "right to decide" in the relevant areas and then analyze critically the implications of such changes for related areas of the law, for the family, and for society.

B. CHILD LABOR[3]

Federal and state laws restrict the ability of young people to work for pay. These laws were the culmination of reform efforts to prevent the exploitation of children, to ensure their education, and to protect them from the hazards of the workplace. But have such laws outlived their appropriateness? The regulation of child labor presents a fascinating context to explore how reform legislation, enacted in an earlier time to

---

[1] Virginia Coigney, Children Are People Too: How We Fail Our Children and How We Can Love Them 137 (1975).

[2] Id. at 197; Richard E. Farson, Birthrights (1974).

[3] This section on child labor draws on historical source materials reprinted in Children and Youth in America: A Documentary History, Vol. 2, pp. 601-749 (Robert H. Bremner ed., 1971) and vol. 3, pp. 299-518 (Robert H. Bremner ed., 1974) [hereinafter Children and Youth in America].

protect young people, may now act as a substantial and unwise constraint on their liberty. Should the state "protect" children from employment or instead encourage young people to gain work experience outside the home? What role should parents have in deciding whether their children should work?

Supporters of child labor laws maintain that the laws protect children from being forced to work at too early an age, for too many hours a day, or in occupations where chances of accident and injury are high. On the other hand, in an era of heightened sensitivity to human rights, both children and their adult spokespersons have objected to child labor laws that pose undesirable restrictions on children's rights to work and deprive them of experience and opportunities beneficial to social development.[4] The following materials explore these issues.

1. Historical Perspective

Laws restricting the employment of children spring largely from social reform movements of the late nineteenth century. Although work had traditionally been seen as essential to a child's upbringing, the growth of industrialism in America gradually changed the nature of the work and attitudes toward it. Critics suggested that children sent to meet the increasing demand for workers in factories suffered in economic terms: they were no longer being trained in a vocation but typically learned only how to do a small task that was part of a larger process. Children who were taught manufacturing skills at an early age tended to remain in the same jobs at the same factory, and were thus deprived of upward social mobility.[5] More noticeably, work in the factories was physically harmful to children. Often the unhealthiest work was given to the child workers, as concerned reformers pointed out with increasing vividness:

> It is a sorry but indisputable fact that where children are employed, the most unhealthful work is generally given them. In the spinning and carding rooms of cotton and woollen mills, where large numbers of children are employed, clouds of lint-dust fill the lungs and menace the health. The children have often a distressing cough, caused by the irritation of the throat, and many are hoarse from the same cause. In bottle factories and other branches of glass manufacture, the atmosphere is constantly charged with microscopic particles of glass. In the woodworking industries, such as the manufacture of cheap furniture and wooden boxes, and packing cases, the air is laden with fine sawdust. Children employed in soap and soap-powder factories work, many of them, in clouds of alkaline dust which inflames the eyelids and nostrils. Boys employed in filling boxes of soap-powder work all day long with handkerchiefs tied over their mouths. In the coal-mines the breaker boys breathe air that is heavy and thick with particles of coal, and their lungs become black in consequence. In the manufacture of felt hats, little girls are often employed at the machines which tear the fur from the skins of rabbits and other animals. Recently, I stood and watched a young girl working

---

[4] 3 Children and Youth in America 299.

[5] Owen R. Lovejoy, Cutting Child Labor Out of the Vicious Circle, 3 Child Lab. Bull. 59 (1914-1915).

at such a machine; she wore a newspaper pinned over her head and a handkerchief tied over her mouth. She was white with dust from head to feet, and when she stooped to pick anything from the floor the dust would fall from her paper headcovering in little heaps. About seven feet from the mouth of the machine was a window through which poured thick volumes of dust as it was belched out from the machine. I placed a sheet of paper on the inner sill of the window and in twenty minutes it was covered with a layer of fine dust, half an inch deep. Yet that girl works midway between the window and the machine, in the very center of the volume of dust, sixty hours a week. These are a few of the occupations in which the dangers arise from the forced inhalation of dust.[6]

Increasing awareness of the abuse and exploitation accompanying child labor produced demands for reform. At the beginning of the nineteenth century, industrial working conditions for both children and adults had been largely unregulated, and there were few legal limitations on child labor. In reaction to this situation, three primary groups pressed for reform. First, from as early as the 1830s, educators began insisting that work not interfere with a child's formal education. Pressure for compulsory education began to grow at the same time as pressure for child labor laws, and the two movements developed alongside in the years from 1830 to 1930. Second, in the late nineteenth century and early twentieth century, increasing numbers of middle-class "progressive" reformers came to oppose child labor as physically dangerous to the child, destructive of family values, and inconsistent with the child's and society's own long-run interests. Third, in the same period, many in the labor movement, and some economists as well, pressed for child labor laws on the grounds that unregulated child labor depressed wages for adult workers and hindered efforts to organize a strong labor movement through which improvements for adult workers might be won. Labor groups also stressed the humanitarian concerns of the progressive reformers.

State Reform

Efforts for legislative reform began at the state level. The first reform campaigns concentrated on ensuring children an education by requiring the factories to set up their own schools or to send the children to school for a specified number of hours each day or for a certain number of months a year. As early as 1813, Connecticut passed a law providing for the education of working children by the proprietors of manufacturing establishments in which children were employed. By 1860, at least five states had laws requiring children under 15 employed in manufacturing establishments to attend school for three months each year, and by 1930 38 states restricted child labor by requiring some kind of educational qualification for children entering employment. Direct regulation of the conditions of employment of children followed a similar pattern, becoming more widespread as knowledge increased of the harmful effects of working conditions on children. By 1860 eight states had laws restricting the number of hours a day that children could work. By 1930 most states had established minimum age requirements for

---

[6] John Spargo, The Bitter Cry of the Children 175-180 (1906), reprinted in 2 Children and Youth in America 641-642.

the employment of children and had reduced the allowable working hours to eight a day.[7]

Federal Reform

Shortly after the turn of the century, the child labor reform movements shifted their attention from local to national solutions. Although many states had adopted child labor laws, some of the laws were felt to be inadequate, and many states still lacked any regulations. This disparity at the state level was seen as creating an unhealthy economic competition: states with strict child labor laws saw themselves as being at a disadvantage, since they were forced to compete with other states where child labor produced goods of the same quality at a lower cost. States that contemplated adopting child labor laws were vulnerable to threats by manufacturers to move their plants to unregulated states. This unsatisfactory situation prompted reformers to seek national standards.

The first federal legislation passed to regulate child labor, the Keating-Owen bill of 1916, sought to prevent interstate commerce in the products of child labor.[8] In 1918, however, the Supreme Court declared the law unconstitutional on the grounds that (1) by aiming to regulate the production of goods rather than their transportation, the act exceeded the permissible scope of congressional authority over commerce, and (2) in aiming to prevent unfair competition, the act exerted a power as to a purely local matter, over which federal authority has no jurisdiction. Hammer v. Dagenhart, 247 U.S. 251 (1918). Shortly after this ruling, Congress again attempted to regulate child labor, this time by exercising its taxation power and imposing a 10 percent tax on all products of child labor.[9] This act, too, met with constitutional challenges and was repealed.[10] By this time the Supreme Court had also declared it to be unconstitutional on the grounds that because the tax represented a penalty aimed at regulating conduct which constitutionally it was for the states to regulate, the act exceeded the federal taxing power. The Child Labor Tax Case, 259 U.S. 20 (1922).

Frustrated by the Supreme Court's actions, reformers pressed for an amendment to the Constitution to empower Congress to regulate child labor directly. In 1924 Congress approved and submitted to the states for ratification the Child Labor Amendment, authorizing Congress to regulate the labor of persons under age 18.[11] The proposed amendment met with substantial opposition, and by 1931 it had been rejected by 38 states and ratified by only six. In 1933, however, interest in the amendment was rekindled (no doubt by the effects of the Depression and the coming of the "New Deal"), and 14 more states ratified the amendment. Since 12 of these had previously rejected it, their action raised new constitutional challenges and delays.

The questions concerning the proposed constitutional amendment became moot when in 1938 Congress enacted the Fair Labor Standards Act, with its provision relating to "oppressive child labor." In United States v. Darby, 312 U.S. 100 (1940),

---

[7] United States Children's Bureau, Child Labor Facts and Figures, Pub. L. No. 197, pp. 4-8 (Washington D.C. 1930), reprinted in 2 Children and Youth in America 666-667.

[8] Child Labor Act of 1916, 39 Stat. 675 (1916).

[9] Child Labor Tax Act, 40 Stat. 1148 (1918).

[10] See 42 Stat. 321 (1921).

[11] 43 Stat. 670 (1924).

the Supreme Court upheld the constitutionality of this act, expressly overruling Hammer v. Dagenhart.

Though the Fair Labor Standards Act is a landmark in the regulation of child labor, in its original form it represented only a modest achievement. Because of its broad exemptions (including a total exemption for agricultural employment outside school hours) and the indirectness of its prohibition of the products of child labor, "[i]t is estimated that of the approximately 850,000 children under 16 gainfully employed in 1938, only about 50,000 were subject to the act. Children in industrial agriculture, intrastate industries, the street trades, messenger and delivery service, stores, hotels, restaurants, beauty parlors, bowling alleys, filling stations, garages, etc., were outside the law."[12]

The limitations of the law were further revealed in one of the earliest cases brought under it, Western Union Telegraph v. Lenroot, 323 U.S. 490 (1945). This case involved the question of whether the Western Union Telegraph Company should be restrained from submitting its messages in interstate commerce because it (1) employed some messengers under 16 years of age and (2) permitted messengers between the ages of 16 and 18 to drive motor vehicles. The Court ruled that the legislative history was inconclusive as to the congressional purpose but that the language of the statute providing that "no producer . . . shall ship or deliver for shipment in commerce any goods produced in any establishment" did not apply to the transmission of telegraph messages. As far as its child labor provisions were concerned, the act seems rather to have confirmed a social reality than to have initiated significant reform.

For a historical analysis of the effectiveness of early child labor restrictions, see Adriana Lleras-Muney, Were Compulsory Attendance and Child Labor Laws Effective?, An Analysis From 1915 to 1939, 45 J.L. & Econ. 401 (2002).

2.   Contemporary Regulation of Child Labor

Every state now has laws regulating child labor, though they vary considerably in their details. The basic feature of these laws is the minimum age at which a minor can be employed: typically, the minimum age is 14 for safe work outside of school hours, 16 for work in industrial plants or for work during school hours. Many state laws prohibit or restrict the employment of minors in specified occupations considered hazardous, in specified establishments, or with specified machinery. Most states limit the number of hours and designate the hours between which minors of various ages can work. Many states require minors to have a working permit or educational certificate from either the local school system or from government official in order to be employed.[13] Further, many state child labor laws are connected to compulsory

---

[12] Youth: Transition to Adulthood, Report of the Panel on Youth of the President's Science Advisory Committee (Chicago and London: University of Chicago Press, 1972), p. 36.

[13] See Sy Moskowitz, American Youth in the Workplace: Legal Aberration, Failed Social Policy, 67 Alb. L. Rev. 1071, 1077-1078 (2004) (reporting that 18 states limit employment of children under age 16; 27 states require parental consent for employment of children of designated ages; 36 states allow children aged 16 and 17 to work 40 hours or more while school is in session). See generally U.S. General Accounting Office, Child Labor: Labor Can Strengthen Its Efforts to Protect Children

school attendance laws that proscribe minimum ages for withdrawal from school.[14]

Fair Labor Standards Act
29 U.S.C. §§203, 212 & 213 (2000 & Supp. 2004)

§203(1): Definitions

"Oppressive child labor" means a condition of employment under which
        (1) any employee under the age of sixteen years is employed by an employer (other than a parent or a person standing in place of a parent employing his own child or a child in his custody under the age of sixteen years in an occupation other than manufacturing or mining or an occupation found by the Secretary of Labor to be particularly hazardous for the employment of children between the ages of sixteen and eighteen years or detrimental to their health or well-being) in any occupation, or
        (2) any employee between the ages of sixteen and eighteen years is employed by an employer in any occupation which the Secretary of Labor shall find and by order declare to be particularly hazardous for the employment of children between such ages or detrimental to their health or well-being. . . . The Secretary of Labor shall provide by regulation or by order that the employment of employees between the ages of fourteen and sixteen years in occupations other than manufacturing and mining shall not be deemed to constitute oppressive child labor if and to the extent that the Secretary determines that such employment is confined to periods which will not interfere with their schooling and to conditions which will not interfere with their health and well-being.

§212: Child Labor Provisions

        (a) No producer, manufacturer, or dealer shall ship or deliver for shipment in commerce any goods produced in an establishment situated in the United States in or about which within 30 days prior to the removal of such goods therefrom any oppressive child labor has been employed: *Provided*, That any such shipment or delivery for shipment of such goods by a purchaser who acquired them in good faith in reliance on written assurance from the producer, manufacturer, or dealer that the goods were produced in compliance with the requirements of this section, and who acquired such goods for value without notice of any such violation, shall not be deemed prohibited by this subsection. . . .
        (b) The Secretary of Labor, or any of his authorized representatives, shall make all investigations and inspections under section 211 (a) of this title with respect to the employment of minors, and, subject to the direction and control of the Attorney General, shall bring all actions under section 217 of this title to enjoin any act or

---

Who Work (Sept. 2002), available at *http://www.gao.gov/new.items/d02880.pdf* (last visited Jan. 3, 2005).
    [14] Most states give parents the right to notice and to consent for children to drop out of school; however, a large number of states allow 16-year-olds to make this decision. Moskowitz, supra note [13], at 1078.

practice which is unlawful by reason of the existence of oppressive child labor, and shall administer all other provisions of this chapter relating to oppressive child labor.

(c) No employer shall employ any oppressive child labor in commerce or in the production of goods for commerce or in any enterprise engaged in commerce or in the production of goods for commerce.

(d) In order to carry out the objectives of this section, the Secretary may by regulation require employers to obtain from any employee proof of age.

§213: Exemptions From the Child Labor Provision

... (c)(1) Except as provided in paragraph (2) or (4), the provisions of section 212 of this title relating to child labor shall not apply to any employee employed in agriculture outside of school hours for the school district where such employee is living while he is so employed, if such employee —

(A) is less than twelve years of age and

(i) is employed by his parent, or by a person standing in the place of his parent, on a farm owned or operated by such parent or person, or

(ii) is employed, with the consent of his parent or person standing in the place of his parent, on a farm, none of the employees of which are (because of subsection (a)(6)(A) of this section) required to be paid at the wage rate prescribed by section 206(a)(5) of this title,

(B) is twelve years or thirteen years of age and

(i) such employment is with the consent of his parent or person standing in the place of his parent, or

(ii) his parent or such person is employed on the same farm as such employee, or

(C) is fourteen years of age or older.

(2) The provisions of section 212 of this title relating to child labor shall apply to an employee below the age of sixteen employed in agriculture in an occupation that the Secretary of Labor finds and declares to be particularly hazardous for the employment of children below the age of sixteen, except where such employee is employed by his parent or by a person standing in the place of his parent on a farm owned or operated by such parent or person.

(3) The provisions of section 212 of this title relating to child labor shall not apply to any child employed as an actor or performer in motion pictures or theatrical productions, or in radio or television productions.

(4)(A) An employer or group of employers may apply to the Secretary for a waiver of the application of section 212 of this title to the employment for not more than eight weeks in any calendar year of individuals who are less than twelve years of age, but not less than ten years of age, as hand harvest laborers in an agricultural operation which has been, and is customarily and generally recognized as being, paid on a piece rate basis in the region in which such individuals would be employed. The Secretary may not grant such a waiver unless he finds, based on objective data submitted by the applicant, that —

(i) the crop to be harvested is one with a particularly short harvesting season and the application of section 212 of this title would cause severe economic disruption in the industry of the employer or group of employers applying for the waiver;

(ii) the employment of the individuals to whom the waiver would apply would not be deleterious to their health or well-being;

(iii) the level and type of pesticides and other chemicals used would not have an adverse effect on the health or well-being of the individuals to whom the waiver would apply;

(iv) individuals age twelve and above are not available for such employment; and

(v) the industry of such employer or group of employers has traditionally and substantially employed individuals under twelve years of age without displacing substantial job opportunities for individuals over sixteen years of age.

(B) Any waiver granted by the Secretary under subparagraph (A) shall require that —

(i) the individuals employed under such waiver be employed outside of school hours for the school district where they are living while so employed;

(ii) such individuals while so employed commute daily from their permanent residence to the farm on which they are so employed; and

(iii) such individuals be employed under such waiver (I) for not more than eight weeks between June 1 and October 15 of any calendar year, and (II) in accordance with such other terms and conditions as the Secretary shall prescribe for such individuals' protection.

(d) The provisions of sections . . . 212 of this title shall not apply with respect to any employee engaged in the delivery of newspapers to the consumer or to any homeworker engaged in the making of wreaths composed principally of natural holly, pine, cedar, or other evergreens (including the harvesting of the evergreens or other forest products used in making such wreaths). . . .

NOTES AND QUESTIONS CONCERNING THE CONSEQUENCES OF CHILD LABOR VIOLATIONS

(1) Sanctions. If a young person works illegally, what sanctions should be imposed? A variety of penalties and remedies is often available. The most commonly employed remedy for a violation of the federal statute is injunctive relief against the employer enjoining future employment of minors. Federal and state child labor laws also provide for criminal sanctions; see 29 U.S.C. §216(a) (2000 & Supp. 2004) (allowing fines of up to $10,000 for a willful violation or imprisonment for not more than one month, or both); civil fines may also be imposed. See 29 U.S.C. §216(e) (2000 & Supp. 2004) and Cal. Lab. Code §§1287-1288 (West 2003).

In 1990 Congress amended the child labor provisions of the Fair Labor Standards Act. The amendments provided for an expansion of civil penalties, that is, increasing the maximum civil penalty for a nonwillful violation from $1,000 to $10,000. 29 U.S.C. §216(e) (2000 & Supp. 2004). Also in 1990, then Secretary of Labor Elizabeth Dole initiated increased federal efforts (termed "Operation Child Watch") to identify violations of the child labor regulations.

Recent years have witnessed additional attempts to amend the Fair Labor Standards Act regarding child labor. In 1998, Congress passed the Drive for Teen Employment Act to amend the Fair Labor Standards Act for the protection of teenage employee-drivers. The legislation prohibits employees under 17 years of age from driving automobiles or trucks on public roadways except in daylight hours, provided that the automobile or truck does not exceed 6,000 pounds of gross vehicle weight and that the driving is not beyond a 30-mile radius from the employee's place of employment and is occasional and incidental to the employee's employment. Drive for Teen Employment Act, 29 U.S.C. §213(c)(6) (2000 & Supp. 2004).

In addition, Representative Tom Lantos (D.-Cal.) and 57 cosponsors unsuccessfully proposed The Young American Workers' Bill of Rights Act, H.R. 2119, 106th Cong., 1st Sess. (1999). The bill proposed to amend the Fair Labor Standards Act by requiring a minor to obtain certification from the state verifying age, school enrollment, and parental consent; limiting the number of hours per day that a minor can work; and prohibiting minors from working before 6 A.M. and after 10 P.M. while school is in session.

In December 2003, Lantos dedicated another bill (the Youth Worker Protection Act, H.R. 3139) to the memory of Adam Carey, a 16-year-old boy who died as the result of an accident on a golf course where he was illegally driving a golf cart. Lantos cited statistics from the National Institute for Occupational Safety and Health stating than an average of 67 teenagers die annually from employment-related injuries and 230,000 teens are injured each year. 149 Cong. Rec. E. 2501-02, 108th Cong., 1st Sess. (2003). The bill is currently pending before the House Committee on Education and the Workforce.

Finally, Congress has repeatedly considered the Child Labor Deterrence Act (CLDA), first proposed in 1989 (S. 1551, 106th Cong., 1st Sess. (1999)). The CLDA would prohibit the entry into the United States of goods produced abroad by child labor. The Act provides that any importer of such goods be fined or jailed. It also provides that the Secretary of Labor shall compile an annual report that identifies countries that condone the use of children under the age of 15 in manufacturing or mining, in order to boycott all manufactured articles by that country. Although several commentators support the objective of the legislation to enforce international minimum-age standards, the legislation has little chance of passage because of concerns about its effect on international relations. See generally William E. Myers, The Right Rights? Child Labor in a Globalizing World, 575 Annals 38 (2001).

(2) Liability. Who should be held responsible for violations of the child labor law? The employer? The child? Parents?

a. Employer. Sanctions are most commonly directed at employers. Should an employer be held responsible for violating the child labor provisions when the employer lacks knowledge that the young person is underage? Must the employer inquire? Compare American Belt Co. v. W.C.A.B., 755 A.2d 77 (Pa. 2000) (employer liable for 50% penalty under state law if it knew or should have known that employee was a minor), with Beard v. Lee Enterprises, Inc., 591 N.W.2d 156 (Wis. Sup. Ct. 1999) (refusing to impose tort liability on employer for minor's negligence unless employer had actual or constructive knowledge of employment relationship with minor).

b. Parents. In some jurisdictions parents may be subject to criminal sanctions if they permit their child to be employed in violation of the child labor laws. See, e.g., Cal. Lab. Code §1303 (West 2003). Is this consistent with provisions in some child labor laws that allow minors to work under parental supervision in otherwise prohibited or restricted occupations? Should parental consent preempt application of the child labor laws?

c. The Child. Federal and state laws appear not to contain express provisions subjecting a minor to criminal sanctions for a violation of child labor provisions.

Why shouldn't the minor be held responsible, especially in cases where the minor obtains work through misrepresenting age? If a minor accepted a job knowing that the child labor laws were being violated, would this justify a determination by a juvenile court that the minor was a delinquent? See Chapter 7 for a discussion of delinquency. Could a juvenile court take jurisdiction over the young person on the ground that he was "in need of supervision" or "beyond parental control?" See infra p. 718.

(3) Compensation for Injury. If an illegally employed young person is injured on the job, what recovery is available? Should the child labor violation be sufficient proof of employer negligence to allow tort recovery for the youth's personal injury? Should the employer be able to assert as defenses that the young person "assumed the risk" or was "contributorily negligent," or that the child's parents had consented to the employment? See Fire Ins. Exch. v. Cincinnati Ins. Co., 610 N.W.2d 98 (Wis. Ct. App. 2000) (holding employer strictly liable for violation of child labor law regardless of fault of child employee).

The worker's compensation laws of approximately one-third of the states require employers to pay extra compensation (often double) for a minor who is injured while illegally employed. (See, e.g., Mich. Comp. Laws Ann. §418.161(1)(b) (West 1999 & Supp. 2004)). Some states provide that this additional compensation cannot be covered by insurance, and that the employer must be liable. See e.g., N.J. Stat. Ann. §34:15-10 (2000 & Supp. 2004). See also Dugan v. General Servs. Co., 799 So. 2d 760 (3d Cir. 2004) (workers' compensation is exclusive remedy even though minor was employed illegally). See generally Ronald B. Grayzel, Department Off the Beaten Track: A Primer on Child Labor Torts, 216 N.J. Law. 38 (2002); Annotation, Workers' Compensation Statute as Barring Illegally Employed Minor's Tort Action, 77 A.L.R. 4th 844, 848-849 (1990 & Supp. 2004).

(4) Reexamining Child Labor Laws.   Legal challenges to the Fair Labor Standards Act have been infrequent. Likewise, state child labor laws have gone largely unchallenged or revised. In light of the changing social, economic, and legal status of youth, do these laws represent an undue restraint on children's rights?[15] Should children be treated differently from adults in the area of employment? Can we still justify the restrictions embodied in the child labor laws? Whose rights and what rights are at stake? Examine the following arguments in favor of child labor restrictions:

- children need to be protected from physical harm;
- sending children to work at an early age prevents them from securing an education essential for their development;
- child labor produces harmful effects on society as a whole.

A reexamination of the bases of existing child labor laws suggests several alternatives to the present system. Consider each of the following possibilities and the problems it raises:

---

[15] In 2001, approximately 3.7 million youths aged 15-17 were employed in the United States. Further, the United States has the highest percentage of employed youth of any developed nation. Cited in id., at 1071.

- eliminate all age-based restrictions and give children the same freedom to work as adults, relying on regulations of general applicability to protect both children and adults;
- maintain the current age-based provisions, but allow a broad exemption whenever parents consent to the employment of their minor children;
- maintain the current age-based regulations, but allow a broad exemption whenever it can be shown that the minor needs to work to support his or her family.

C. DRIVING PRIVILEGES

1. Introduction

Minors are allowed to drive in every state, although age-based limits are universally imposed. The laws relating to driving by minors reflect various social concerns: the need for protection of the public from unsafe drivers; the need for easily administered rules; the need to hold someone financially responsible for the costs of accidents; and the economic and social importance of transportation to minors, their families, and employers.

In reading through the material that follows, consider these questions. How are power and responsibility for a minor's driving allocated? How are minors treated differently from adults, and why are they so treated? What power and responsibility do minors themselves have? To what extent does the law give the parent responsibility? What special limitations on the minor's liberty does the state impose? What social interests are reflected in the allocation of power?

Age Limits

Every state imposes age restrictions on driving, which vary according to the type of activity involved. The usual practice is to give regular licenses to minors between ages 15 and 17 (usually 16); however, these licenses do not extend to driving for hire, driving oversized vehicles (usually an 18-year-old minimum), or driving a school bus (often a 21-year-old minimum). Special permits are also available for learning to drive. These are sometimes available to persons as young as 14 years old, provided that a parent or certified teacher accompanies the learner.

Many states will give restricted licenses to minors as young as 14 years old if they can show a special need (to go to school or to provide for a needy family) or are employed on a family farm. Such licenses cannot be used for any purpose other than that specified in the restrictions. See, e.g., Cal. Veh. Code §12513 (West 2000).

What should be the minimum driving age, given the existence of competence testing?

Special Rules for Minors Old Enough to Be Eligible for Licenses

While the states recognize the desirability of giving minors driving privileges, state laws do *not* simply treat minors above the cutoff age exactly like adults. The following are a few examples. What social interests do these rules reflect? Should similar rules apply to adults?

(1) Many states require any driver under 18 to complete driver education (in a classroom) or driver training (behind the wheel). See e.g., Cal. Veh. Code §12509 (West 2000 & Supp. 2004).

(2) Most states make it easier to suspend or revoke the license of minor drivers. In New York, for example, a minor who becomes a ward of the family court as a "youthful offender" may have the license suspended for up to one year (N.Y. Veh. & Traf. Law (Consol.) §510(3)(j) (McKinney 1996 & Supp. 2004)). Colorado uses a point system for all drivers in determining suspensions or revocations. A minor in that jurisdiction loses his license after collecting far fewer points than older drivers would have to accumulate (Colo. Rev. Stat. §42-2-127 (West 2004)). Many states impose a suspension of license or even impound the car if a minor possesses alcoholic beverages while driving, whether or not the bottle is open. See e.g., Cal. Veh. Code §23224 (West 2000 & Supp. 2004).

(3) Some states have curfew laws affecting young drivers. In Illinois, no one under 17 may be on the streets or highways between 11:00 P.M. and 6:00 A.M. on Sunday to Friday, and 12:01 A.M. and 6:00 A.M. on Saturday and Sunday. However, the statute has two exceptions: minors may be on the streets during curfew hours if they are (1) accompanied by a parent, legal guardian, or other responsible companion at least 18 years of age who has been approved by the minor's parent or guardian or (2) engaged in some business activity that the law allows them to perform during those hours. (Ill. Stat. Ann. ch. 720 ¶555/1(a) (West 2003).) In Massachusetts, a minor under age 18 cannot drive between 12:00 A.M. and 5:00 A.M. unless accompanied by a parent or legal guardian (Mass. Gen. Laws Ann. ch. 90, §8 (West 2001 & Supp. 2004)).

(4) Almost 40 states have three-tier *graduated licensing* statutes for minors. Typical statutes specify: (1) minors of a minimum specified age are able to obtain a *learner's permit* provided that they pass vision and knowledge tests, drive at all times with a licensed adult who is at least age 21, never drive while intoxicated, and remain crash- and conviction-free for six months; (2) minors of a minimum specified age are able to obtain a *provisional license* provided that they pass a road test, never drive while intoxicated, drive during night hours only with a licensed adult, and remain crash- and conviction-free for 12 months; and (3) minors are able to obtain a *full license* by completing the previous stage and reaching the specified age. Research reveals that graduated licensing programs reduce automobile accidents significantly, although minors continue to have the highest rate of fatal crashes. Limits on Teenage Drivers Lower Accidents, Data Show, N.Y. Times, Feb. 19, 2003 (data from the National Safety Council reveals a 33% decrease in accident rate in states with such programs). See generally Christine Branche et al., Graduating Licensing for Teens: Why Everybody's Doing It, 30 J.L. Med. & Ethics 146 (2002); Carol Jones, Note: The Unintended Consumer: Protecting Teen Drivers Through Graduated Licensing Laws, 15 Loy. Consumer L. Rev. 163 (2003).

By enacting these statutes, is the state venturing into an area of supervision that is best left to parents? Alternatively, do such statutes violate minors' constitutional rights? See Robert Diaz de Leon, California's Teen Driving Law: Violation of Constitutional Rights?, 21 J. Juv. L. 86 (2000).

2.   The Necessity of Parental Consent and Implied Parental Liability

Jackson v. Houchin
144 S.W.3d 764 (Ark. Ct. App. 2004)

Robert J. GLADWIN, Judge.

On March 15, 1996, appellant Freddie Jackson signed a driver's license application for his cousin, Charles Jackson, who was a minor at that time. Under the provisions of Ark. Code Ann. §27-16-702 (Supp. 1995), appellant was not authorized to sign the application for Charles because the boy's mother was living and appellant did not have custody or guardianship of him. On August 5, 1996, Charles was involved in an automobile accident with appellee David Houchin. Appellee filed a negligence suit, naming appellant as a co-defendant. A jury found for appellee on his complaint against Charles Jackson and appellant Freddie Jackson, and assessed damages in the amount of $11,088.55, plus costs. Appellant contends on appeal that because he was not authorized to sign the application of the minor, he cannot be held liable for the minor's negligent conduct. We affirm.

Arkansas Code Annotated section 27-16-702 (Supp. 1995) provides in relevant part:

> (a)(1)(A) The original application of any person under the age of eighteen (18) years for an instruction permit, driver's license, motor-driven cycle or motorcycle license shall be signed and verified before a person authorized to administer oaths by either the father or mother of the applicant, if either is living and has custody.
>
> (B) In the event neither parent is living or has custody, then the application shall be signed by the person or guardian having custody or by an employer of the minor.
>
> (C) In the event there is no guardian or employer, then the application shall be signed by any other responsible person who is willing to assume the obligations imposed under this subchapter upon a person signing the application of a minor. . . .
>
> (b) Any negligence or willful misconduct of a minor under the age of eighteen (18) years when driving a motor vehicle upon a highway shall be imputed to the person who signed the application of the minor for a permit or license, *regardless of whether the person who signed was authorized to sign under subsection (a) of this section*, which person shall be jointly and severally liable with the minor for any damages caused by negligence or willful misconduct. (Emphasis added.)

In arguing that he cannot be held liable under the above statutory provisions because, under these same provisions, he was not authorized to sign the application, appellant is seeking to benefit from his wrongdoing. The language of the statute makes it clear that even though appellant was not authorized to sign for the minor, once he did sign, he became jointly and severally liable for any damages suffered as a result of the minor's negligence.

Appellant cites two cases to support his contention that he cannot be held liable for the minor's negligence, neither of which is applicable here. The first is

Richardson v. Donaldson, 220 Ark. 173, 246 S.W.2d 551 (1952), wherein the father of the minor did not sign an application, but did allow his daughter, who had no driver's license, to drive his vehicle. The court said that negligence could not be imputed to the father under a statutory provision similar to the one in the case now before us because the father had never signed an application. Letting his daughter drive without a license was a misdemeanor, and while violation of the traffic laws was evidence of negligence, it did not establish negligence as a matter of law. The statutory provisions imputing negligence did not apply because Richardson, unlike appellant, had never signed an application at all.

Appellant also cites Jones v. Davis, 300 Ark. 130, 777 S.W.2d 582 (1989). In *Jones*, a vehicle driven by seventeen-year-old Charles Volpert struck a motorcycle driven by Mark Jones. Volpert's mother, Barbara Davis, had signed Volpert's application for a driver's license. Jones contended that Charles Davis, Volpert's stepfather, stood in loco parentis to Volpert; was required to sign Volpert's application; and was liable for his stepson's negligence. The language of the statute in effect at that time required that either parent, if living, sign a minor's application for a driver's license. Only if neither parent was living would anyone else be authorized to sign. Volpert's mother and father were both living, and his mother signed the application. Davis was neither required nor authorized under the statute to sign the application, and had not done so. The court found that Davis could not be held liable under the statute for his stepson's negligence.

The distinction between *Jones* and the case before us is obvious: Davis did not sign an application, while appellant herein did sign the application for his minor cousin. The act of signing the application brought appellant within the purview of the statute, and appellant cannot now say he should be excused from the liability incurred under the statutory provisions because he acted in a manner not authorized by that statute. Affirmed. Decide in Houchin's favor

NOTES AND QUESTIONS

(1) Parental Consent — Imputed Liability. Most states insist upon parental consent before a minor may obtain a driver's license and require parental signatures on the minor's application. This requirement gives the parents control over their children's activities and in many jurisdictions serves as a basis for imputing the child's negligence to the consenting adult(s). The statutes sometimes allow someone other than the parent to consent. In some states, a parent's, guardian's, or employer's signature is sufficient, no matter who has custody. A few states allow a "responsible person" to sign the application if there is no parent, guardian, or employer.

As *Jackson* illustrates, in many states imputed liability for a minor's negligence or willful misconduct while driving is imposed on whoever signs a minor's application for a license. This measure is viewed as a further protection of the public and as an inducement to provide closer supervision of a minor's driving. Is it realistic to expect such supervision? Yes, to a degree

Suppose the minor's driver's license has been revoked by the state but the minor nevertheless continues to drive. Should this discharge the liability of a parent who signed the license application for the minor's negligence while driving? See

Keating v. Hollstein, 557 N.E.2d 1253 (Ohio 1990) (holding that mother's permission automatically terminated upon revocation of her son's driving privileges).

(2) Emancipation.   Some statutes allow a parent to withdraw the driving privileges of a minor even if emancipated, despite his or her increased need for independent transportation. Some jurisdictions provide exceptions to imputed liability for married or emancipated minors. Compare Lay v. Suggs, 559 So. 2d 740 (Fla. Dist. Ct. App. 1990) (emancipation terminates signatory's vicarious liability) with State Auto. Ins. Co. v. Reynolds, 32 S.W.3d 508 (Ky. Ct. App. 2000) (holding father liable for negligent acts of emancipated daughter). In California emancipated minors may verify their own applications if they can provide proof of financial responsibility (Cal. Veh. Code §17705 (West 2000 & Supp. 2004)). If a minor, whether or not emancipated, can provide proof of sufficient financial responsibility, why should parental consent be required as a condition for a license?

3.   Parental Negligence and Other Special Liability Provisions

Dortman v. Lester
155 N.W.2d 846 (Mich. 1968)

Souris, Justice:

This appeal involves two cases brought in behalf of the Dortmans to recover damages from the defendants for injuries suffered by Mrs. Dortman when the car in which she was riding was struck from the rear by a car driven by defendant Barre Lester, the 18-year-old [minor] son of the other defendants. Title to the car Barre Lester was driving was in his name and his mother's. Plaintiffs planted their claim against defendant father on the theory that he was casually negligent in permitting his son to drive a car knowing that the son was an incompetent driver and that the father's negligence and the son's negligence were concurrent proximate causes of Mrs. Dortman's injuries. . . .

. . . The circuit judge granted summary judgments dismissing the actions against defendant father for failure to state causes of action against him. The Court of Appeals affirmed. 3 Mich. App. 600, 143 N.W.2d 130.

Following the Court of Appeals decision in this case, this Court decided Muma v. Brown (1967), 378 Mich. 637, 148 N.W.2d 760. We divided equally on the sufficiency of proofs to support the jury's verdict in favor of plaintiff. The dissenters who voted for reversal considered the crucial legal issue on the appeal to be the applicability of the rule of negligent entrustment to the facts of the case. The Justices who joined in the controlling opinion, on the other hand, like the circuit judge and the Court of Appeals, considered the legal issue to be whether parents are liable for the negligent acts of their children resulting from the parents' negligent failure to exercise parental supervision. See their opinion at [378 Mich. at 644] where it is said that the question was one of first impression. If the question addressed by the Justices who joined in the controlling opinion was a negligent entrustment question, then clearly it was not one of first impression. They were, instead, addressing the issue of parental liability, in a case in which the rules of negligent entrustment would have been adequate to support plaintiffs' claim.

In discussing the issue of parental liability, those Justices who joined in the controlling opinion quite properly did so in the factual context of the *Muma* case, in which the parents happened to own the vehicle with which their child negligently committed a tortious injury. The fact of the parents' ownership and control of the vehicle was legally irrelevant to the legal issue of their parental liability, although it would have been legally relevant to their liability under the rules of negligent entrustment. Unfortunately, the controlling opinion's language seems to limit its otherwise valid conclusions regarding parental liability for a child's negligent operation of a motor vehicle only to those situations in which the parents not only can exercise control over the child, but, also can control the availability of the motor vehicle to the child. While I do not believe such limitation is legally justifiable, I concede the case of Muma v. Brown, supra, does not contribute much to our decision herein. We must, instead, look elsewhere for our authority.

Earlier, in May v. Goulding (1961), 365 Mich. 143, 111 N.W.2d 862, this Court cited and applied, among others, the following authorities pertinent to the issue framed by the pleadings in this case of *Dortman:*

1 Harper and James, Law of Torts, §8.13, p. 662:

Aside from the relationship of master and servant, the parent may be liable for harm inflicted by a child under circumstances that constitute negligence on the part of the parent. This, of course, is not a case of responsibility of a parent for the child's tort, but liability for his own wrong. . . .

2. Restatement of Torts, §316:

§316. Duty of Parent to Control Conduct of Child

A parent is under a duty to exercise reasonable care so to control his minor child as to prevent it from intentionally harming others or from so conducting itself as to create an unreasonable risk of bodily harm to them, if the parent (a) knows or has reason to know that he has the ability to control his child, and (b) knows or should know of the necessity and opportunity for exercising such control.

4. Restatement of Torts, §877:

§877. A Person Directing or Permitting Conduct of Another

For harm resulting to a third person from the tortious conduct of another, a person is liable if he . . . (c) controls, or has a duty to use care to control, the conduct of another who is likely to do harm if not controlled, and fails to exercise care in such control. . . .

The theory upon which plaintiffs relied in these cases as against the defendant father is squarely within the above quoted rules of the common law. The motions for summary judgment, therefore, should not have been granted for failure to state causes of action. We reverse and remand to the circuit court for further proceedings. . . .

Kavanagh, Adams and Brennan, JJ., concurred with Souris, J.

O'HARA, Justice.

I disagree with Mr. Justice Souris. First, I am not in accord with his application of Muma v. Brown, 378 Mich. 637, 148 N.W.2d 760 (1967). I regard the case as inapposite.

In *Muma*, we were concerned with an unlicensed and inexperienced minor of the age of 14 driving the family automobile titled in the mother and father jointly. The theory of the plaintiff was that the parents were negligent in leaving the 14-year-old boy at home alone unsupervised for a week end, with a set of keys to the family car in the house.

In the case at bar the minor was 18 years of age. He was a licensed driver. The title to the automobile involved was in his name and the name of his mother. His license to drive was granted him by the State. He was legally entitled to be an owner and he was by the certificate of title a co-owner. His father was a stranger to the title and could not under any statute we have cited have prohibited his son from obtaining title thereto legally, nor legally could he compel his son as co-owner to divest himself of his co-ownership. This is a far factual cry from the situation presented in *Muma*.

With the general principles quoted by Justice Souris I have no basic disagreement. In the pleaded factual context of this case I do not think they control. Plaintiff alleged as to the father only that Barre E. Lester was under 21, and "was subject to the orders, direction and control of his parents." Literally, such a legal conclusion can hardly be challenged. It is little more than a restatement of the parent-child relationship. Such relationship does not per se render a parent liable for the tort of a child. . . .

I would affirm the Court of Appeals. . . .

NOTE: OTHER SPECIAL LIABILITY PROVISIONS

Under the common law parents were not held liable for the consequences of the torts of their minor children solely because of the existence of the parent-child relationship. See 59 Am. Jur. 2d. Parent and Child §116 (1987). Exceptions to this traditional rule were developed when a parent (1) participated in the minor's tort, (2) permitted the tort to occur as the result of the parent's negligent supervision of the minor, or (3) maintained some additional relationship with the child (such as principal and agent) that allowed imputation of the child's negligence.

Apart from imputed liability and parental negligence in controlling their child, most states apply other doctrines (explained below) in certain circumstances to impose responsibility for a minor's negligence on parents or others.

(1) Family Car Doctrine.   If a head of household makes his or her auto available to other members of the family, his or her consent is assumed and vicarious liability may be imposed. This does not extend to a car owned by a minor or one provided for the minor and under his or her exclusive control. See, e.g., Aurbach v. Giallina, 753 So. 2d 60 (Fla. 2000); McPhee v. Tuffy, 623 N.W.2d 390 (N.D. 2001).

(2) Expressed or Implied Permission.   Most states impose liability on the parents or persons with custody of minors if they give expressed or implied permission to their children to drive in violation of state law. California extends this

doctrine to include all parental permission regardless of any violations (Cal. Veh. Code §17708 (West 2000)).

(3) Negligent Entrustment. Any person who negligently and knowingly supplies, entrusts, permits, or lends a vehicle to an incompetent or habitually careless driver may be held liable for negligent entrustment. Such liability arises out of the combined negligence of the owner and the driver — negligence of the owner entrusting the vehicle to the incompetent driver and negligence of the driver in its operation. See Joseph v. Dickerson, 754 So. 2d 912 (La. 2000).

(4) Providing an Unlicensed Minor with a Motor Vehicle. Any person (whether or not a parent) supplying a minor with a vehicle to drive when the minor is not licensed to do so usually faces liability. See State v. King, 620 N.E.2d 30 (Ohio Mun. Ct. 1993).

4. The Minor's Liability: Standard of Care for Adult Activities

Dellwo v. Pearson
107 N.W.2d 859 (Minn. 1961)

LOEVINGER, Justice.

This case arises out of a personal injury to Jeanette E. Dellwo, one of the plaintiffs. She and her husband, the other plaintiff, were fishing on one of Minnesota's numerous and beautiful lakes by trolling at a low speed with about 40 to 50 feet of line trailing behind the boat. Defendant, a 12-year-old boy, operating a boat with an outboard motor, crossed behind plaintiffs' boat. Just at this time Mrs. Dellwo felt a jerk on her line which suddenly was pulled out very rapidly. The line was knotted to the spool of the reel so that when it had run out the fishing rod was pulled downward, the reel hit the side of the boat, the reel came apart, and part of it flew through the lens of Mrs. Dellwo's glasses and injured her eye. Both parties then proceeded to a dock where inspection of defendant's motor disclosed 2 to 3 feet of fishing line wound about the propeller.

The case was . . . submitted to the jury upon instructions which, in so far as relevant here, instructed . . . : (1) In considering the matter of negligence the duty to which defendant is held is modified because he is a child, a child not being held to the same standard of conduct as an adult and being required to exercise only that degree of care which ordinarily is exercised by children of like age, mental capacity, and experience under the same or similar circumstances; (2) "A person guilty of negligence is liable for all consequences which might reasonably have been foreseen as likely to result from one's negligent act or omissions under the circumstances. . . . A wrongdoer is not responsible for a consequence which is merely possible according to occasional experience, but only for a consequence which is probable according to ordinary and usual experience." . . . Several hours after the jury retired it returned and asked for additional instructions with respect to "foreseeable responsibility" and "the responsibility of a youngster compared to a more mature person." The court thereupon repeated the instructions relating to negligence, the standard of care, and proximate cause, including the language quoted above.

The jury returned a general verdict for defendant, and plaintiffs appeal. Plaintiffs contend that the trial court erred in its instruction that a defendant is not responsible for unforeseen consequences of negligence. . . .

The instruction of the trial court limiting liability for negligence to foreseeable consequences was a part of the instruction on proximate cause and, in effect, made foreseeability of a test of proximate cause. . . .

[The court reversed the trial court's judgment because the trial court erred in making foreseeability the test of proximate cause.]

Since the case must be retried, it is appropriate for us to indicate the principles which should govern the submission upon a second trial. . . .

[An] important point involves the instruction that defendant was to be judged by the standard of care of a child of similar age rather than of a reasonable man. There is no doubt that the instruction given substantially reflects the language of numerous decisions in this and other courts. However, the great majority of these cases involve the issue of contributory negligence and the standard of care that may properly be required of a child in protecting himself against some hazard. The standard of care stated is proper and appropriate for such situations.

However, this court has previously recognized that there may be a difference between the standard of care that is required of a child in protecting himself against hazards and the standard that may be applicable when his activities expose others to hazards. Certainly in the circumstances of modern life, where vehicles moved by powerful motors are readily available and frequently operated by immature individuals, we should be skeptical of a rule that would allow motor vehicles to be operated to the hazard of the public with less than the normal minimum degree of care and competence.

To give legal sanction to the operation of automobiles by teen-agers with less than ordinary care for safety of others is impractical today, to say the least. We may take judicial notice of the hazards of automobile traffic, the frequency of accidents, the often catastrophic results of accidents, and the fact that immature individuals are no less prone to accidents than adults. While minors are entitled to be judged by standards commensurate with age, experience, and wisdom when engaged in activities appropriate to their age, experience, and wisdom, it would be unfair to the public to permit a minor in the operation of a motor vehicle to observe any other standards of care and conduct than those expected of all others. A person observing children at play with toys, throwing balls, operating tricycles cycles or velocipedes, or engaged in other childhood activities may anticipate conduct that does not reach an adult standard of care of prudence. However, one cannot know whether the operator of an approaching automobile, airplane, or powerboat is a minor or an adult, and usually cannot protect himself against youthful imprudence even if warned. Accordingly, we hold that in the operation of an automobile, airplane, or powerboat, a minor is to be held to the same standard of care as an adult.

Undoubtedly there are problems attendant upon such a view. However, there are problems in any rule that may be adopted applicable to this matter. They will have to be solved as they may present themselves in the setting of future cases. The latest tentative revision of the Restatement of Torts proposes an even broader rule that would hold a child to adult standards whenever he engages "in an activity which is normally undertaken only by adults, and for which adult qualifications are required." [§238A, comment *c*] However, it is unnecessary to this case to adopt a rule in such broad form, and, therefore, we expressly leave open the question whether or not that rule should be adopted in this state. For the present it is sufficient to say that no reasonable grounds for differentiating between automobiles, airplanes, and powerboats appears, and that a rule requiring a single standard of care in the operation of such vehicles, regardless of the age of the operator, appears to us to be required by the circumstances of contemporary life.

Reversed and remanded for new trial.

5.   The Standard of Care for the Negligence of Minors

The Restatement (Third) of Torts §10 (Proposed Final Draft No. 1, Apr. 6, 2005) reads as follows:

> (a) A child's conduct is negligent if it does not conform to that of a reasonably careful person of the same age, intelligence, and experience, except as provided in Subsection (b) or (c).
> (b) A child less than five years of age is incapable of negligence; and
> (c) The special rule in Subsection (a) does not apply when the child is engaging in a dangerous activity that is characteristically undertaken by adults.

The justification for §10(a) is that children, because of their inexperience, have less ability to perceive the probable consequences of their acts or omissions than do adults. Although some courts still generally apply this conventional standard (which allows age and experience to be taken into account), the majority follows that expressed by §10(c) and the court in Dellwo v. Pearson, supra, p. 655, which found that the societal interest in protecting potential victims of negligence requires that there not be an age-based standard of care where a minor is performing an adult activity. See also Summerill v. Shipley, 890 P.2d 1042 (Utah Ct. App. 1995). Do you think the availability of liability insurance to cover people injured by minors should influence the standard of care applied to their behavior?

Traditionally, contributory negligence has been a bar to recovery by plaintiffs even though the defendant was negligent. When children are injured by negligent acts, a question arises concerning the standard to be applied when a minor is contributorily negligent. The so-called Massachusetts standard, which is the majority view, rejects the idea that age is the major factor in determining a child's capacity. The Massachusetts rule on contributory negligence, like the Restatement Rule on negligence, determines the capacity of the child to be contributorily negligent by comparing his intelligence, experience, and discretion with those of other children of the same age, intelligence, and experience, acting under the same or similar circumstances. Other courts, however, have adopted presumptions based on age and have held, for example, that a child below the age of seven cannot be held contributorily negligent.[16] Is it realistic to say that a child seven years old has absolutely

---

[16] See generally Lori Rinella, Children and the Law: Children of Tender Years and Contributory Negligence, 63 UMKC L. Rev. 475 (1995). For a critical analysis of the current Restatement rule, see John Goldberg & Benjamin Zipursky, Symposium: The Restatement (Third) and the Place of Duty in Negligence Law, 54 Vand. L. Rev. 657 (2001).

no capacity to take care of himself? A majority of jurisdictions apply the "reasonable person of like age" standard to both negligence and contributory negligence. However, a few jurisdictions apply the adult standard of care for a child's negligence but the lesser standard for his contributory negligence. Does this rule make any sense?

Also consider whether it is not somehow inconsistent to apply an adult standard of care to minors who drive, see *Dellwo*, supra, p. 655, and at the same time impose imputed liability on parents who are formally empowered to withdraw a minor's license, see *Dortman*, supra, p. 652.

PROBLEM

On his 16th birthday, Larry Mosk passed his driver's test and received a license to drive. On the same day he purchased a 2000 Toyota from Allen Blum. Larry found the car from a want ad that Blum had placed in the newspaper. The two of them agreed on a price of $4,200. Larry paid Blum $300 cash and signed a note for the remaining $3,900, secured by a security interest in the car itself.

The day after he purchased the car, Larry was involved in an accident in which the car was seriously damaged and seven-year-old Jessica Finn was injured. It was raining at the time, and Larry was driving 30 miles per hour in a 35 miles per hour zone. After turning a corner, the rear end of the car skidded and "spun out." Because of his inexperience as a driver, Larry turned the steering wheel the "wrong" way — that is, instead of turning into the skid, he turned away from the skid. As a consequence, the car went out of control, smashed into a tree, and then went back into the street, where it hit Jessica who was playing near the curb making mud pies and splashing in puddles. As a result of the accident, Jessica broke her leg and the car was very nearly "totaled." The car's value now is about $550.

Larry obviously needs a lawyer. He reports that he has liability insurance, but no collision coverage for the damage to the car. He asks for your advice concerning the following questions:

1. How likely is it that a court would find Larry's driving to be negligent? Assume that he could show that most beginning drivers do not know which way to turn when there is a skid.
2. What are the chances that Larry could successfully assert that Jessica was contributorily negligent and thus escape liability to her?
3. Larry no longer wants to own a car. Is there any way he can avoid paying the $3,900 to Blum? Can he get his $300 back?

Consider the conceptions of childhood and responsibility underlying (1) the ordinary negligence standard for children, which imposes a standard of care "common to children of like age, intelligence, and experience"; (2) the adult activities exception; (3) the treatment of contributory negligence for children; and (4) the doctrine that contracts entered into by a minor are "voidable" (discussed below). Are these standards consistent?

6. The Power of Minors to Make Contracts and the Defense of Infancy

According to Professor Corbin,

> [a]t common law the contracts of an infant are said to be voidable, but not void. That they are not void is made clear by the fact that the infant can almost always enforce them against the other party. In most cases it is equally true however that the contract cannot be enforced against the infant if he cares to take advantage of his infancy as a defense.[17]

Except where changed by statute or case law, this is still the majority rule. Consequently, a minor who purchases goods or services by contract is allowed to disaffirm at any time during minority or even within a reasonable time after reaching majority.[18] Disaffirmance may be accomplished by any act indicating that the minor does not wish to be bound by the contract made during minority.[19]

Three states have changed the common law rule by case law: New Hampshire, Minnesota, and Arizona. Hall v. Butterfield, 59 N.H. 354 (1879); Bergland v. American Multigraph Sales Co., 160 N.W. 191 (Minn. 1916), Worman Motor Co. v. Hill, 94 P.2d 865 (Ariz. 1939). Under the minority view, a minor must make restitution for benefits received. According to the New Hampshire Supreme Court in *Hall*, the infancy defense "is to be used as a shield, not as a sword; not to do injustice, but to prevent it." 59 N.H. at 355.

In states following the majority rule, disaffirmance requires the minor to give back to the seller those purchased goods that remain in his possession.[20] Some courts have allowed a minor to disaffirm when what he gives back has depreciated or is worthless,[21] or even when the goods have been lost or squandered.[22] Moreover, the minor would have no obligation to put the other party back into a position similar to the one existing before the agreement was made.[23] Some courts, however, avoid this extreme result by holding the minor responsible for quasi-contractual damages, requiring the minor to return not only the goods, but also whatever value the minor got from them.[24] Indeed this is always the rule for "necessaries," a term that usually encompasses an actual requirement of food, clothing, shelter, medical aid, or minimal education while considering the particular minor's station in life. (See Chapter 2 p. 152 for a discussion of necessaries.)

[17] Arthur L. Corbin, Contracts §227, at 318 (1952). On the history of the infancy doctrine, see Larry A. DiMatteo, Deconstructing the Myth of the "Infancy Law Doctrine": From Incapacity to Accountability, 21 Ohio N.U.L. Rev. 481 (1994).

[18] Corbin, supra note [17], at §239. What constitutes a "reasonable time" is a question of fact. See, e.g., Hoblyn v. Johnson, 55 P.3d 1219 (Wyo. 2002).

[19] Corbin, supra note [17], at §234.

[20] See, e.g., Mitchell v. Mitchell, 963 S.W.2d 222 (Ky. Ct. App. 1998).

[21] See, e.g., Dodson v. Shrader, 824 S.W.2d 545 (Tenn. 1992).

[22] See, e.g., Freiburghaus v. Herman Body Co., 102 S.W.2d 743 (Mo. Ct. App. 1937) (depreciation); Bowling v. Sperry, 184 N.E.2d 901 (Ind. Ct. App. 1962) (damage).

[23] See, e.g., Halbman v. Lemke, 298 N.W.2d 562 (Wis. 1980).

[24] Annotation, Infant's Liability for Use or Depreciation of Subject Matter in Action to Recover Purchase Price upon his Disaffirmance of Contract to Purchase Goods, 12 A.L.R.3d 1174 (1967 & Supp. 2004).

The policy behind permitting minors to disaffirm contracts is to protect them from overreaching by unscrupulous adults[25] and from their own inexperience. But the defense of infancy also acts as a constraint on the freedom of minors to contract because the person dealing with the minor will not be certain that he can enforce the contract. While this may not substantially affect the minor's ability to buy for cash, merchants may be very reluctant to sell to them on credit. For instance, unless a parent co-signs a note, a merchant may refuse to sell to a minor on credit. If the practical operation of the rule is to allow young people to buy for cash but require parental cooperation if they are to buy on credit, is this a bad thing? In all events, disaffirmance frequently operates inequitably as to the other contracting party, who, having acted innocently, may be compelled to bear the burden of his contract without being assured of any of its benefits.

Some courts, however, have recognized that times have changed.[26] Teenagers spend billions of dollars annually on clothing, video games, CD players, stereos, and cars.[27] Does it make sense for Macy's to bear the loss when a stereo purchased by a student is stolen or smashed at a weekend party? Some courts have allowed a minor to recover the consideration he has paid, even though the minor misrepresented his age.[28] This harsh result is usually justified by the argument that to permit the other contracting party to obtain a benefit under the contract would undermine the protective policy. On the other hand, an increasing number of courts have held that a fraudulent misrepresentation of age by an infant may estop him from disaffirming the contract. Even when a minor is a defendant, estoppel is frequently applied against him.

Several highly publicized cases involve famous adults attempting to disaffirm contracts entered into when they were minors. In Shields v. Gross, 448 N.E.2d 108 (N.Y. 1983), actress Brooke Shields sought damages and injunctive relief to prevent a photographer from using nude photographs taken when she was 10 years old. The New York Court of Appeals held that the plaintiff could not disaffirm the contract because the model's mother effectively had consented on her behalf. The majority reasoned that there was an important need "to bring certainty to an important industry that necessarily uses minors" (id. at 111). On the other hand, the dissent countered that "children must be placed above any concern for trade or commercialism" (id. at 112).

In another famous disaffirmance case, Stephen Barry left royal service after 12 years as Prince Charles' valet. Barry published a book about his experiences with the royal family notwithstanding his pledge of confidentiality when he began service. Barry was able to disaffirm the earlier contract as he was only 17 when he

---

[25] See, e.g., McGuckian v. Carpenter, 110 A. 402 (R.I. 1920) (the reason the law allows the infant the privilege of disaffirming is for protection against the immaturity and improvidence that led to making unwise contracts).

[26] See, e.g., Kiefer v. Fred Howe Motors, Inc., 158 N.W.2d 288 (Wis. 1968).

[27] According to a study by the Rand Youth Poll (a New York City market research firm), 36.7 million teens spent a total of $105.1 billion in 1998. Rand Youth Poll, Teen-Age Personal Spending Continues to Climb, While Youths' Overall Impact on Economy Intensifies (press release available from Rand Youth Poll), undated, at 1-2.

[28] See Annotation, Infant's Misrepresentation as to His Age as Estopping Him from Disaffirming His Voidable Transaction, 29 A.L.R. 3d 1270 (1970 & Supp. 2004).

had entered royal service. See Royal Fink? Stephen Barry, Prince Charles' Ex-Valet Slips Through a Loophole and Talks, People Weekly, Apr. 11, 1983, at 124.

There has been a legislative response to the inequities caused by disaffirmance. A student commentator[29] noted six common statutory ways of holding a minor bound to his contract: (1) estoppel by misrepresentation of age, (2) lowering the age of majority on petition to a court, (3) reaching majority status by marriage, (4) holding a minor to his reasonable contracts made while he is engaged in business, or at least putting him under an affirmative duty to warn those with whom he deals about his minority, (5) forcing a restoration of the consideration (or its equivalent) if the contract was made when the minor was 18 or older, and (6) removing disability of a minor veteran so that he can get education loans.

Another commentator[30] would add to this list statutes allowing the infant to make nonvoidable contracts for insurance, for education loans, and for other agreements made pursuant to statute. In addition, in both California and New York special legislation was made applicable to the entertainment industry. Initially, the legislation was prompted by a need to uphold the validity of contracts with minors. Subsequently, state legislatures enacted laws to protect child performers. See generally Jessica Krieg, Comment, There's No Business Like Show Business: Child Entertainers and the Law, 6 U. Pa. J. Lab. & Emp. L. 429 (2004). Do you think this piecemeal approach is an effective means of reforming the infancy rule?

D. DRINKING

INTRODUCTORY PROBLEM

Puerto Rico maintains its minimum legal drinking age of 18 despite the federal government's law that will reduce the amount of federal funding for surface transportation unless the United States territory raises its drinking age to 21. You are the staff director of a federal commission charged with preparing a report that addresses the question of whether the laws should be revised. The commission's charge is to make recommendations on the following issues: (1) Should age-based limitations relating to drinking be continued? (2) If so, should the legal drinking age be raised from 18 to 21? (3) What are the most appropriate means of enforcing age-based limitations on drinking? (4) What exceptions, if any, should be in the new law? (5) What role should parents have?

Your first task is to prepare a research agenda for the commission. Those who are in favor of raising the drinking age rely basically on four arguments: (1) Drinking by minors can lead to increases in juvenile crime and other antisocial behavior; (2) Raising the drinking age to 21 prevents children younger than 18 from experimenting

---

[29] H.H.W., Note, The Status of Infancy as a Defense to Contracts, 34 Va. L. Rev. 829, 831-833 (1948).

[30] Robert C. Edge, Voidability of Minor's Contracts: A Feudal Doctrine in a Modern Economy, 1 Ga. L. Rev. 205, 226-227 (1967).

with alcohol and may reduce the incidence of adult alcoholism; (3) Raising the drinking age will reduce the problems of teenage driving under the influence of alcohol; and (4) Drinking is an immoral or socially undesirable activity for adults, and raising the drinking age will emphasize the undesirability of this activity for young people. You should suggest, as part of the commission's agenda, what empirical research might bear on these arguments. You should also spell out what arguments (other than financial) might be made in favor of changing the law and suggest how those arguments might best be evaluated.

1.   State Controls on Consumption of Alcoholic Beverages by Minors[31]

a. Legal Drinking Age: Background

Prohibitions on the sale of alcohol to youths date from the beginning of the twentieth century.[32] States enacted strict minimum age drinking laws after the repeal of Prohibition. Most state laws set the age of drinking at 21 and made it illegal for any person (including parents) to provide youths with alcoholic beverages. In 1970, in response to the enactment of the Twenty-Sixth Amendment lowering the federal voting age to 18, most states lowered their drinking age from 21 to 18. A few years later, the Supreme Court reviewed the first challenge to minimum age drinking laws when it held that Oklahoma's different minimum age for males and females to drink low-alcohol-content beer was unconstitutional. Craig v. Boren, 429 U.S. 190, 199 (1976).

In 1984, President Reagan's Commission on Drunk Driving recommended age 21 as the uniform minimum legal drinking age, in reliance on statistics showing that a higher drinking age would reduce the number of fatal traffic accidents. In response, Congress enacted the National Minimum Drinking Age Act of 1984 (23 U.S.C. §158(a)(1) & (2)), which requires states to raise their minimum age for the purchase and public possession of alcohol to age 21 or face a reduction in federal highway funds. By 1988, all states had enacted legislation to raise the drinking age.

The United States Supreme Court reviewed another state minimum age law in South Dakota v. Dole, 483 U.S. 203 (1987), upholding the state statute against a challenge that the statute was unconstitutional as an unauthorized use of Congress' spending power. Yet another minimum age law was challenged on the state level in Manuel v. State, 692 So. 2d 320 (La. 1996). In *Manuel*, the Louisiana Supreme Court initially held that the statute constituted age discrimination under the state constitution. However, on rehearing, the state supreme court upheld the constitutionality of the law, reasoning that it substantially furthered the appropriate governmental purpose of improving highway safety.

---

[31] This section draws on James Mosher, The Prohibition of Youthful Drinking: A Need for Reform (Unpublished), Social Research Group Working Paper No. 29, University of California-Berkeley (1973).

[32] On the history of minimum age drinking laws, see Alexander C. Wagenaar, Alcohol, Young Drivers and Traffic Accidents 1-4 (1983).

Critics of the federal minimum age law point to several problems. One major criticism is that society has conferred so many responsibilities of adulthood upon 18-year-olds. The frequent argument has been that if 18-year-olds are old enough to drive, vote, marry, and fight in a war, then they are certainly old enough to drink alcohol. What weight should be given to this argument? Do the statistics on fatal traffic accidents involving young drivers under age 21 who have been drinking justify limiting the rights of 18- to 20-year-olds?

b. The Variety of Sanctions

(1) Criminal Sanctions Against the Minor

State laws vary concerning what acts by a minor relating to alcoholic drinks constitute a crime. All states prohibit purchase or possession in public of alcoholic beverage by minors, but many do not extend this to possession in a private home. The potential penalties vary considerably. In Arkansas, for example, a judge may impose a fine between $100 and $500 or may require a minor to write an essay on intoxicating liquor, wine, or beer. Ark. Stat. Ann. §3-3-203 (1987 & Supp. 2001). In some states, a minor will face only small discretionary fines. In contrast, other states impose a minimum fine of $100, while several others allow for one-year jail sentences and fines up to $1,000. Special provisions with even stiffer penalties are imposed in most states for use of false identification. In addition, many states have "loitering" statutes (a minor is prohibited from entering and remaining on premises in which liquor is on sale). See, e.g., Conn. Gen. Stat. §30-90a (West Supp. 2003).

Minors who violate a drinking statute also subject themselves to juvenile court jurisdiction as delinquents. In California, for example, Cal. Welf. & Inst. Code §602 (West 1998 & Supp. 2004) expressly states that a violation by a person under 18 of any state law defining a crime satisfies the jurisdictional requirement of the juvenile court and gives the court power to make the minor a ward of the court. In states with a 21-year-old drinking age, however, 18- to 21-year-olds are exempt from juvenile court jurisdiction.

(2) Criminal Sanctions Against the Adult Supplier

The adult who supplies a minor with liquor is generally subject to harsher sanctions than the minor, reflecting perhaps a notion that a child is the "victim." Most states distinguish between a "seller" and other suppliers, the former being subject to more severe sanctions. A few states, in fact, have provisions covering only the "sale" of alcoholic beverages. The range of penalties among states varies greatly. Oklahoma, for example, has a felony provision for the first offense with a maximum sentence of five years and/or a $5,000 fine. Okla. Stat. Ann. tit. 37 §538 (West 1999 & Supp. 2004). Arkansas, for a first offense, provides for a fine not to exceed $100. Ark. Stat. Ann. §3-3-204 (Michie 1987 & Supp. 2001). Most states have misdemeanor statutes with light, discretionary sentences and fines.

Other provisions usually prohibit furnishing a minor with false identification or allowing a minor to remain on premises serving alcohol. There are also sanctions for contributing to the delinquency of a minor. A supplier, after all, is encouraging minors to break state laws and encouraging "immoral" behavior.

(3) Exemptions for Parents Who Supply Liquor to Their Children

Many states have express exemptions in their statutes or case law for supplying liquor to minors under specific circumstances. A number of states have general provisions allowing parents to procure, supply, or give alcoholic beverages to their children. For example, Wisconsin and Texas allow drinking in the presence of a parent. Wis. Stat. Ann. §125.07 (West 1999 & Supp. 2003); Tex. [alcoholic beverages] Code Ann. §106.06 (West 1995 & Supp. 2004). A few states provide for drinking in the parent's home. Several others exempt married minors.

These exemptions and their constriction over time reflect an interesting historical trend toward increasing skepticism concerning family social control. Criminal statutes concerning child drinking first appeared in the second half of the nineteenth century and gave considerable discretionary authority to parents and other adults. For example, at least three states, Georgia, Texas, and Arkansas, allowed a parent to give written permission for their children to drink.[33] Three other states, Michigan, Connecticut, and Pennsylvania, had exemptions similar to the present New York provisions, N.Y. Penal Law §260.20 (McKinney 2000 & Supp. 2004).[34] But in this century the move has been toward greater regulation. Why do you think this has occurred?

(4) Regulatory and Civil Provisions

Civil controls against commercial suppliers are widespread and are more likely to be enforced than criminal sanctions. Usually, fines can be assessed and liquor licenses revoked if a bar or liquor store sells to minors. The owners are subject to strict liability in many states; an honest mistake is not a defense.

At common law, a supplier of liquor could not be held liable for injury or death to either a consumer of alcoholic beverages or to a third party who was harmed by the acts of the intoxicated consumer. A majority of jurisdictions have rejected this rule of nonliability by the enactment of "dram shop acts" — legislation that imposes civil liability on vendors under certain circumstances.[35]

In addition, a few state courts have found a cause of action against any adult supplier, not simply commercial sellers. See, e.g., Camp v. Lummino, 800 A.2d 234 (N.J. Super. Ct. 2002); Barnes v. Cohen Dry Wall, Inc., 592 S.E.2d 311 (S.C. Ct. App. 2003). Should courts impose liability on an adolescent host who collects

---

[33] See, e.g., Gill v. State, 13 S.E. 86 (Ga. 1891); State v. Jarvis, 427 S.W.2d 531 (Ark. 1968).

[34] People v. Bird, 100 N. W. 1003 (Minn. 1904); State v. Hughes, 209 A.2d 872 (Conn. Cir. Ct. 1965).

[35] Angela M. Easley, Note, Vendor Liability for the Sale of Alcohol to an Underage Person: The Untoward Consequences of Estate of Mullis v. Monroe Oil Co., 21 Campbell L. Rev. 277, 285 (1999) (as of 1988, 37 states had such legislation). See also Implementation of the National Minimum Drinking Age Act, Hearing before the Subcomm. on Surface Transportation of the Comm. on Public Works and Transportation, 102d Cong., 2d Sess. 56 (1992) (testimony of Surgeon General Antonia G. Novello) (the ABA recommended in 1985 that all states should enact such statutes).

a "cover charge" from other minors at a party and then supplies them with alcohol?
See Koehnen v. Dufuor, 590 N.W.2d 107 (Minn. 1999).

See generally Richard Smith, Note: A Comparative Analysis of Dramshop
Liability and a Proposal for Uniform Legislation, 25 J. Corp. L. 553 (2003).

(5) Enforcement

While the laws on the books seem formidable, enforcement policies by state
and local agencies reflect greater acceptance of youthful drinking. In California,
for example, informal interviews suggest that the criminal laws are rarely, if ever,
invoked against sellers. Instead, the California Alcoholic Beverage Control Board
may bring civil disciplinary action against a store or bar that serves anyone under 21.
The initial fines are usually lenient — $500 or less, depending on income. Only
if there are repeated, blatant violations will the liquor license be revoked. No
"contributing to delinquency" prosecution has been reported in recent years for
selling or giving liquor to a minor. The local police do not recall taking any action
against a minor unless the youth's drinking is combined with driving or some other
crime.

> Police also point out that parents do not like their children arrested for "doing
> what everyone else does." One official described enforcement of alcohol laws
> as "a no-win" situation. And another commented, "Local police have another
> priority — [illicit] drugs. They ignore alcohol."
>
> Frequently, there are only nominal penalties against vendors and minors when
> they violate these laws. While vendors may have fines or their licenses suspended,
> license revocations are rare. The penalties against the youth who violate the laws
> are often not deterrents. Even when strict penalties exist, courts are lenient and do
> not apply them.[36]

Furthermore, additional constraints on enforcement exist. As James Mosher notes:

> While the ABC [Alcoholic Beverage Control Board] has exclusive authority to
> revoke or suspend liquor licenses, its ability to effectively carry out its responsi-
> bilities is limited by the law of enforcement personnel. The department currently
> has 198 enforcement agents assigned to approximately 68,000 licensees, a ratio of
> one enforcement agent for every 343 outlets. As department enforcement capac-
> ity has eroded, enforcement responsibilities have increasingly been left to local
> officials. Yet, the role of local government is severely restricted because the ABC
> Department retains exclusive authority to conduct disciplinary actions against a
> business' state liquor license.
>
> To date, the state has failed to expand local control of sales-to-minors laws
> despite these problems in enforcement and despite overwhelming public support
> for the action. Yet, it is important for policy-makers to recognize that local control
> is a linchpin of the environmental approach to prevention because of its emphasis
> on community norms and practices.[37]

[36] Hearing, Implementation of the National Minimum Drinking Age Act, supra note [35], at 55
(testimony of Surgeon General Antonia C. Novello).

[37] James F. Mosher, Preventing Alcohol Problems Among Young People: Californians Support
Key Public Policies, Growing Up Well: Focus on Prevention 5 (1998).

Do these enforcement patterns suggest the laws should be changed to reflect actual practices? Or that there is no need for change because of an informal accommodation of present social mores?

2. Teenagers and Alcohol: Research Findings

In 2003, the U.S. Department of Health and Human Services published The National Survey on Drug Use and Health, a study of drug use that included an extensive exploration of alcohol use among minors. The study examined the pattern and frequency of the consumption of alcoholic beverages, including beer, wine, whiskey, brandy, and mixed drinks. The results revealed that 10.9 million people aged 12 to 20 reported drinking alcohol in the past month. Of those who drink, nearly 7.2 million (19.2 percent) were binge drinkers and 2.3 million (6.1 percent) were heavy drinkers. The prevalence of current alcohol use increases with age, from 2.0 percent at 12 to 6.5 percent at age 13, 13.4 percent at age 14, 19.9 percent at age 15, 29.0 percent at age 16, and 36.2 percent at age 17. The rate reaches a peak of 70.9 percent for persons 21 years old.[38]

A decade earlier, a study conducted by the Office of the Inspector General (OIG), titled Youth and Alcohol: A National Survey, investigated youths' motivations for drinking, the amount of alcohol consumed, and attitudes about drinking and driving. Of those students who drink, their reasons include: 25 percent drink to get high, 25 percent drink when they are bored, 41 percent drink when they are upset, and 31 percent drink alone. When queried about their attitudes about drinking and driving, 92 percent of the youths responded that a person who has been drinking should not drive; however, one-third of the students had driven with a friend who had been drinking. These findings, according to the OIG, indicate a need for increased education and peer approval of designated drivers.[39]

In other research, Patrick M. O'Malley and Alexander C. Wagenaar examined the effects of different minimum drinking ages on the alcohol-related behavior of high school seniors. Their purpose was to explore differences in drinking behavior in states with high versus low minimum drinking ages. Specifically, they compared alcohol consumption of youths in states that changed their minimum drinking age law from 18 to 21 during 1976 to 1987 with that of youth in states that maintained a minimum age of 21 throughout the same period. The authors found that the minimum age of 21 does indeed lead to lower consumption of alcohol by high school seniors and that, surprisingly, the lower rate of drinking appears to continue into early adulthood.[40]

[38] U.S. Dept. of Health & Human Servs., Substance Abuse and Mental Health Servs. Admin., Results from the 2003 National Study on Drug Use and Health: National Findings, Pub. No. SMA 04-3964 (2004).

[39] Office of Inspector General, "Youth and Alcohol: A National Survey," reprinted in Hearing, Implementation of the National Minimum Drinking Age Act, supra note [35] at 19-51. See also Catalina Arata et al., High School Drinking and Its Consequences, 38 Adolescence (No. 151) 567 (2003).

[40] Patrick M. O'Malley & Alexander C. Wagenaar, Effects of Minimum Drinking Age Laws on Alcohol Use, Related Behaviors and Traffic Crash Involvement among American Youth, 1976-1987, 52 J. Stud. Alcohol (No. 5) 478, 482, 489 (1991).

They also noted that increases in the minimum drinking age did not lead to significantly more alcohol consumption by underage persons in private settings such as cars. Nor did increases in the minimum drinking age lead to increased abuse of other illicit substances.

The following excerpt (although written before the 1984 federal legislation) presents a provocative analysis of the public policy implications of raising the minimum drinking age.

James Mosher, The History of Youthful-Drinking Laws: Implications for Public Policy
Minimum-Drinking-Age Laws: An Evaluation 26-31 (Henry Wechsler ed., 1980)

Youthful-Drinking Laws and the Prevention of Alcohol-Related Problems

The Symbolic Nature of Youthful-Drinking Laws

Perhaps the most striking characteristic of current youthful-drinking regulations is the gulf that they create between adults and children in the legal availability of alcohol. Until either ages 18 or 21, depending on the jurisdiction, children are legally expected neither to possess alcohol nor to be present in premises where alcohol is the primary product being served. Any attempts by a child to do so may, in theory, lead to serious legal consequences. Adults, including in most cases parents, who aid a child in drinking or permit them in forbidden premises face even stiffer penalties. After the magic age is reached, however, the "new adult" is expected to be a moderate drinker, using alcohol as a pleasant social lubricant in an increasing number of social settings. The new adult is also expected to avoid the serious dangers that alcohol poses to long-term personal health, traffic accidents and fatalities, and other forms of accidents and injuries.

The legal structuring of alcohol availability is obviously not designed as a real guide for actual behavior, as current youthful-drinking patterns strongly suggest. "Learning to drink" involves experimentation that our society actually encourages in many ways. That the law does not provide a guideline for behavior, however, does not necessarily lead to a conclusion that the law needs to be reformed. As Bonnie points out, there are numerous methods for utilizing the law to shape individual behavior. Youthful-drinking laws, in Bonnie's terms, are "symbolic" and "moralistic" prescripts, used to denote the official posture toward youthful drinking — that is, they articulate what is held to be desirable or undesirable behavior. The vast majority of adolescents are not punished for their drinking; the law functions more as a flashing red light, a warning that social norms discourage this form of behavior.

Youthful-drinking laws might also be viewed as vestiges of moral or symbolic prescripts against drinking generally, a flashback to earlier attitudes about alcohol as an evil or undesirable force in our society. In pre-Prohibition times, in fact, youthful-drinking laws served just such a purpose. Drinking was considered dangerous for everyone, but particularly for youth. Laws directed at youths served as a subset for an overall legal strategy of discouragement. The difference today is that while the law provides that drinking is undesirable behavior for youth, it provides a different message to the society generally.

"Moral" or "symbolic" laws aimed at youth that are in conflict with societal norms are not limited to alcohol availability. We tend to act out our moral ambiguities by "protecting" our children. Obscenity law provides the most obvious parallel — as the society has become increasingly permissive about public displays of sexuality, laws concerning youthful exposure to sexually-oriented materials have become stricter. . . .

The problem with subjecting youths to special symbolic laws that are not relevant to adult behavior is the confusion that they create. Youths, after all, do become adults, and to prescribe radically different behavior norms breeds contempt rather than respect for the laws. Perhaps the success that the Temperance movement had in enlisting children to their cause was that the adults themselves passionately believed in the norms the children were expected to follow. By contrast, adolescents today view drinking-age laws with either indifference or contempt. Further, the law not only loses its moral suasion, it also loses its potential for guiding youths toward healthy personal choices through other strategies.

Closing the Gap Between Childhood and Adult Drinking Norms

The destruction of the symbolic value of drinking-age laws points to two possible policy initiatives. The first involves reform in youthful-drinking laws themselves. Stringent, symbolic controls without a real expectation of compliance preclude the use of law as a guidepost for desired behavior. Adolescents are going to experiment with alcohol; the law could serve to regulate the circumstances of this experimentation to deter undesired behavior and consequences.

As the historical analysis shows, there are numerous variables that may be considered. Most obviously, parents could be given explicit permission to regulate their children's drinking behavior. Complete adult availability could be staggered in various ways. Commercial sale could remain prohibited, but non-commercial furnishing could be decriminalized. Civil controls making adult suppliers civilly responsible for harms caused by minors they serve could be expanded. [D]rinking-age laws may be structured in various ways to discourage specific undesired behavior.

For instance, driving laws in this country do use such a strategy. Typically, young drivers are placed under stricter controls than adults. Parental permission to drive is usually required prior to the child's eighteenth birthday. Successful completion of driver education and/or training may be required before licensing, and a young person's license is typically subject to prompter revocation than adults. The law's message is not merely that "driving is dangerous," which would be the case if driving laws were mainly treated symbolically. Rather, it attempts to provide youths with special guidelines for learning to drive and for avoiding harmful consequences. Similar but less stringent deterrents are placed on adults. Thus, the youthful regulations are but a consistent subset of overall driving laws. It is obviously not a perfect system. However, it can be forcefully argued that it provides more guidance than a system that, on the one hand, prohibits young persons under 18 or 21 from driving and, on the other, grants unlimited driving privileges to those over that age.

Driving, unlike drinking, is not a morally ambiguous activity, which accounts at least in part for the difference in legal approvals. There is no innate reason for the differing treatment, however. Permitting increased adolescent responsibility is consistent with recent trends in children's law. Beginning in the 1960s, the U.S. Supreme Court has expanded recognition of the rights of families and children to resist state intrusion in private decisions concerning religion, schooling, and social protest. . . . Thus, the trend toward increased state power over adolescents, which began in the nineteenth century concurrently with the adoption of strict youthful-drinking laws, is being partially reversed. Adolescence, in the eyes of the law, has become an age of only partial incompetence.

Although these constitutional protections probably do not include a child's right to purchase or consume alcohol, they do provide insights into issues raised by drinking-age laws. Encouraging adolescents to take on increased responsibility for their lives may have a beneficial long-term effect on their ability to learn and manage adult roles. This is particularly important in drinking behavior, which focuses attention on individual restraints and responsibility as the primary mode for discouraging harmful drinking practices.

Promoting increased responsibility among adolescents is limited, however, as shown by the recent reduction in the drinking age. In the present social climate, loosening the symbolic restrictions on youthful drinking may well be interpreted as measures to encourage drinking. Thus, increased youthful experimentation with alcohol should not be permitted without legal attention being given to the second area of legal policy initiatives — the availability of alcohol to adults.

The failure of symbolic youthful-drinking laws can be explained in part by the societal acceptance of alcohol generally and the relative disinterest in controlling its legal use. Today, the law more often serves to encourage rather than discourage drinking. As discussed earlier, federal and state governments and an increasing number of businesses outside the alcohol industry are profiting from alcohol use. The relaxing of availability regulations has been accomplished to increase this profitability. Alcohol advertising is widespread, and, despite recent media campaigns to the contrary, the dominant message remains alcohol's ability to increase life's pleasures and enhance one's social success and sexual appeal. This combination of increased availability and massive advertising appeals has contributed to the integration of alcohol use into an ever-expanding matrix of daily experience. These are particularly potent messages to adolescents, who are expected to experiment with adult behaviors. An adolescent's desire to experiment freely with this seemingly safe and exciting adult product can hardly be taken as surprising.

Those concerned with promoting the public health among drinking minors must examine seriously the laws which promote this positive alcohol environment. The government's economic role in alcohol policy must be balanced more evenly against public health responsibilities. This does not mean that legal prohibition should be reinstituted but rather that the alcohol messages in the mass media, the laws concerning availability of alcohol, and the economic structure of the alcohol market must be examined from a public health perspective. In short, the legal treatment of alcohol as merely another commercial commodity, the chief characteristic of which is its profitability both for the state and for an expanding range of businesses and industries, must be challenged.

Such a reorientation does, inevitably, raise wider, conflicting social policies. As Bonnie points out, using regulation to discourage unhealthy personal choices must be balanced against an individual's right of free choice. However, freedom of choice hardly necessitates a societal encouragement of alcohol use. Clearly, there is much that can be done in this area.

By providing a public health perspective to overall availability, youthful-drinking laws will become more effective. Minors will be given a more consistent message concerning alcohol use and the public health issues involved. The law's symbolic import will be less ambiguous. Most importantly, regulations that limit availability to minors can be more effectively molded to deter harmful drinking and to promote safer experimentation without the appearance of encouraging overall use.

Conclusion

The controversy concerning drinking-age laws has been notable for its limited scope. It has, for the most part, ignored the complexity of legal issues that form a drinking-age law and has failed to examine them in terms of overall social attitudes toward alcohol consumption and availability. When the trend was to reduce the drinking age to 18 during the 1970s, the primary issue was the abstract, legal rights of 18- to 20-year-olds. No concern was given to the fact that the age reduction placed the contradictions of adult-child drinking norms at a younger, even less mature age. In fact, as Richard Douglass' excellent study shows, alcohol availability in Michigan — particularly Sunday sales, when adolescents would be expected to be drinking — was actually expanded during the same period that the drinking age was lowered. The relationship of the two was not even considered. These policy reforms together provided a clear message of approval to young drinkers.

Today, the move is in the opposite direction. Permitting adult availability to 18- to 20-year-olds has apparently increased consumption and the risk of alcohol problems, particularly driving problems. However, the debate has centered on the age of legal drinking, treating it as an either/or choice and as a problem divorced from the overall alcohol environment.

History suggests that the drinking age in fact includes a number of availability issues and that various forms of youthful experimentation can be encouraged or discouraged through careful use of the variables. It also suggests that youthful drinking must be regulated in such a way as to be consistent with a general alcohol policy.

Drinking/driving problems among adolescents, the most forceful rationale for returning to a drinking age of 21, illustrates these points. Drunk driving is a societal problem, not merely an adolescent problem. That adolescents have particular problems with learning to drink and drive reflects the conflicts of adult roles — adults are expected to drink in a wide range of social settings and to drive to and from those settings. Serious consideration must be given to limiting alcohol availability in situations where driving is likely to occur and to providing safer transportation. Regulation of young drinkers and drivers, which will undoubtedly necessitate stricter controls, can then be set within the overall strategy.

As Douglass suggests, raising the drinking age to deter drunk driving is at best an indirect strategy. It avoids the basic conflict and raises serious policy questions of possible constitutional proportions. No doubt raising the drinking age to 25, 30, or even 50, as one house of the Mississippi legislature recently passed, would also tend to reduce drunk driving. The youngest age group is being chosen as a symbolic gesture because of its political impotence and because, unlike other possible reforms, there are no major economic consequences involved for the state or for the national alcohol industry. It serves to demonstrate our inability to face the hard issues at hand.

The political shuffling of the legal drinking age has also raised serious practical problems for college administrators — problems that legislatures have widely ignored. When drinking ages are raised, college programs to supervise drinking and to integrate younger students into college social settings are disrupted, and colleges' legal responsibilities became clouded. Instead of attempting to regulate college drinking, administrators are forced officially to prohibit most college drinking, which in practical terms leads to ignoring actual student practices. A more careful attempt to regulate youthful drinking could avoid these unintended results.

In sum, a coherent youthful-drinking policy requires careful attention to wider issues. The needs of children and adolescents for learning and experimenting with adult roles in limited ways and the need for a consistent alcohol policy must be carefully examined. . . . Hopefully, a wider debate of youthful-drinking laws will result in effective legal reform.

3. Drinking and Driving Among Teenagers

Perhaps the most serious problem connected with drinking is drunk driving, particularly among teenagers. Teenagers are involved in a disproportionately high percentage of fatal car accidents, and a substantial portion of these involve drinking. Consider that youth between the ages of 15 and 20 years old account for 6.6 percent of the total number of drivers in the United States. Yet 14 percent of all drivers involved in fatal crashes are drivers in this age group. Moreover, of these victims, 24 percent were intoxicated at the time of the crash.[41] As a group, teenagers have the least amount of experience with either drinking or driving and thus are more likely to misjudge their abilities and reactions. They are affected by small amounts of alcohol to a greater degree than more experienced drinkers.

There is considerable debate concerning the relationship of increases in the minimum drinking age to the accident rate. Research reveals that the number of teenage deaths decreased after states returned to 21 as the drinking age. One study, conducted in selected states three years before and three years after changes in minimum drinking age laws (based on self-report and crash data) reported a significant decline in single-vehicle night-time (SVN) fatal automobile crashes among drivers of under 21 years of age following increases in the minimum drinking age. "The largest rate change occurred among states whose change in minimum drinking age was 3 years (i.e., from 18 to 21); in these states, there was a decline of 26.3% in

[41] National Highway Traffic Safety Admin. (NHTSA), U.S. Dept. of Transportation, Traffic Safety Facts 2002. Motor vehicle crashes are the leading cause of death for 15- to 20-year-olds. Id.

the rate per licensed driver of alcohol-involved SVN fatal crashes involving drivers under 21. . . . "[42]

Do these findings signify that the decrease in alcohol-related deaths is attributed solely to changes in the minimum drinking age laws? This is a difficult question to answer because the number of alcohol-related injuries decreased in all age categories during the same time period. Thus, while the 15- to 20-year-old group witnessed the greatest decline in involvement in alcohol-related fatal crashes, other factors may account for this phenomenon.

For example, independent researcher Mike Males suggests that research overestimates the lifesaving potential of the 21-year-old drinking age because data reveal that increases in minimum drinking age laws merely shift the number of fatal crashes from a lower to a higher age group.[43] In addition, he concludes that "[t]he facile assumption that an increase in age alone correlates with more mature practices toward alcohol — and the exclusion of more important factors such as quality of family supervision, experience and individual learning abilities — may be the deadliest myth of the drinking age debate."[44]

Other critics raise similar questions. Some experts say that the 21- to 24-year-old age group is just as dangerous on the road as the 18- to 20-year-old group. So if "adulthood" is not a factor, then why not raise the drinking age to 25 if the only aim is to reduce the number of traffic accidents caused by drunken driving? Why, too, prohibit home consumption of alcohol for 18- to 20-year-olds?

Another question is: is it fair to limit drinking by women between 18 and 20? Data reveal that, for young drivers, alcohol involvement is higher among males than females. For example, in 2002, 27 percent of the young male drivers involved in fatal crashes had been drinking, compared with 22 percent of young female drivers.[45] However, to limit access to alcohol by males probably would be unconstitutional. In Craig v. Boren, 429 U.S. 190 (1976), the United States Supreme Court held that an Oklahoma law prohibiting sale of low-alcohol content beer to males under the age of 21 and to females under the age of 18 was a gender-based difference that violated the equal protection rights of males aged 18 to 20.

If it is impermissible to use gender-based restrictions in order to reduce the number of fatal drunk driving accidents, perhaps a better solution would be to find ways to reduce drunk driving for all age groups, such as enforcing stiffer penalties for drunk driving, adopting stronger controls on sale and distribution of alcohol, adopting stronger controls on driver licensing, or providing special mass transit service to give drivers another option after consuming alcohol.

Another criticism of raising the drinking age to 21 is that to do so is unduly restrictive and/or intrusive and thus unconstitutional. This criticism was voiced not only by commentators but also by courts, when the states began raising the minimum legal drinking age on their own initiative. For example, in Felix v. Milliken, 463 F. Supp. 1360 (E.D. Mich. 1978), the federal district court ruled that a state constitutional amendment passed by voters that raised the minimum drinking age

[42] O'Malley & Wagenaar, supra note [40], at 478, 487.

[43] Mike A. Males, The Minimum Purchase Age for Alcohol and Young-Driver Fatal Crashes: A Long-Term View, 15 J. Leg. Stud. 181, 183 (1986).

[44] Id. at 211.

[45] NHTSA Traffic Safety Facts, supra note [41].

from 19 to 21 did not violate parental rights of parents or the right to privacy, based on rational basis review applicable to age-based discrimination (according to Massachusetts Board of Retirement v. Murgia, 427 U.S. 307 (1976)). The district court reasoned that the data showing a strong correlation between lowering the drinking age and the increase in teenage involvement in fatal crashes demonstrated a rational relationship between raising the drinking age and the constitutionally permissible purpose of increasing traffic safety. For similar reasoning, see Manuel v. State, 677 So. 2d 116 (La. 1996) (upholding state minimum drinking age law).

Increases in the minimum drinking age have been followed by a resort to additional methods of enforcement. For example, many states enacted legislation (referred to as "abuse and lose" statutes) providing for revocation or suspension of juveniles' driving privileges upon conviction of drunk driving or substance abuse. Other states preclude juveniles from driving while intoxicated by means of their graduated licensing programs (discussed supra, p. 649). Do "abuse and lose" statutes violate equal protection? See R.T.M. v. State, 677 So. 2d 801 (Ala. Ct. App. 1995) (upholding statute as a legitimate state purpose in protecting the public from juvenile substance abusers). See also Freed v. Ryan, 704 N.E.2d 746 (Ill. Ct. App. 1998) (holding that state "abuse and lose" statutes did not violate due process).

In addition, enforcement of laws restricting the sale of liquor to minors coupled with the growing incidence of traffic accidents involving young drivers prompted the National Traffic Safety Board (NTSB) to recommend that states establish lower blood-alcohol content (BAC) levels for youth.[46] In response, Congress enacted the National Highway Safety Designation Act (NHSDA) of 1995, Pub. L. No. 104-59, 109 Stat. 568 (codified as amended in scattered sections of 23 U.S.C.), a coercive measure that withholds federal highway funds to states that do not consider a 0.02 BAC to be "driving while intoxicated" for drivers under the age of 21. Conversely, states that consider a 0.02 BAC (or less) to be "driving while intoxicated" for drivers under age 21 may qualify for drunk-driving-incentive-grant funds under §410 of the Highway Safety Act.[47]

SOME FINAL QUESTIONS ON TEENAGE DRINKING

(1) The sale of liquor to minors is illegal in every state, but most teenagers drink before reaching 18. Does this suggest the need for stricter laws? Repeal? Neither?

(2) Alcoholism and drunken driving are both serious social problems: do they suggest the need for stricter laws directed at young and old alike? Or better methods of teaching young people good drinking habits?

(3) In a world where some adults consider drinking by adults to be immoral and inappropriate, while other adults consider drinking an acceptable social activity, what role should parents have in the regulation or development of their children's drinking? Is it possible to satisfy parents who want to make it more difficult for their children to drink as well as those who are prepared to allow their children to experiment?

---

[46] National Transportation Safety Board, Safety Recommendation 15 (Mar. 11, 1993).

[47] National Highway Traffic Safety Admin., U.S. Dept. of Transportation, State Legislative Fact Sheet: Zero-Tolerance Laws to Reduce Alcohol Impaired Driving by Youth (1996).

REVIEW PROBLEM: DRINKING, DRIVING, AND OBSCENITY

You will recall that in Prince v. Massachusetts (Chapter 1), the Supreme Court suggested that "streets afford dangers" for children "not affecting adults." The Court further suggested that "this is so not only when children are unaccompanied but certainly to some extent when they are with their parents. What may be wholly permissible for adults therefore may not be so for children, either with or without their parents' presence."

Compare the age-based restrictions relating to driving, drinking, and viewing sexually explicit materials (that would not be pornographic for adults). See pp. 648-674, supra. (1) Analyze whether there are dangers for young people that are different in kind or degree from the dangers for adults in each of these areas. Is it appropriate in each area to give young people less freedom than adults? (2) What power should parents have to teach their children how to drive, to let them drink in their parents' presence, and to permit them to view sexually explicit materials? (3) Are there similarities in the problems of enforcement in the three areas? (4) Compare for each area the possibilities for "licensing" based on "competence" rather than age. Could the licensing procedures used in driving be applied to drinking? Sexual activities? (5) In each area, do the legal prohibitions facilitate a young person's transition into adulthood? Or make it more problematic? Does the law strengthen the role of parents and the family? Or contribute to intra-family conflict?

E. CONTRACEPTION

Carey v. Population Services International
431 U.S. 678 (1977)

Mr. Justice BRENNAN delivered the opinion of the Court (Parts I, II, III, and V), together with an opinion (Part IV) in which Mr. Justice STEWART, Mr. Justice MARSHALL, and Mr. Justice BLACKMUN joined.

Under New York Education Law §6811(8) it is a crime (1) for any person to sell or distribute any contraceptive of any kind to a minor under the age of 16 years; (2) for anyone other than a licensed pharmacist to distribute contraceptives to persons over 16; and (3) for anyone, including licensed pharmacists, to advertise or display contraceptives.

[A distributor of mail-order contraceptives challenged the constitutionality of the statute, asserting that it violated the constitutionally protected right to privacy of potential purchasers. The federal district court declared the statute unconstitutional. In omitted portions of the case below, the Supreme Court held that the limitation on distribution only by *licensed pharmacists* served no compelling state interest and also that the prohibition on *advertisement or display* could not be justified as offensive to consumers or as legitimate of sexual activity. Below, the Court examines the prohibition on the *sale or distribution of contraceptives to minors under age 16.*]

Although "[t]he Constitution does not explicitly mention any right of privacy," the Court has recognized that one aspect of the "liberty" protected by the Due Process Clause of the Fourteenth Amendment is "a right of personal privacy, or a guarantee of certain areas or zones of privacy." Roe v. Wade, 410 U.S. 113, 152 (1973). . . . While the outer limits of this aspect of privacy have not been marked by the Court, it is clear that among the decisions that an individual may make without unjustified government interference are personal decisions "relating to marriage, procreation, contraception, family relationships, and child rearing and education [citing Loving v. Virginia, Eisenstadt v. Baird, Meyer v. Nebraska, Pierce v. Society of Sisters, and Roe v. Wade].

The decision whether or not to beget or bear a child is at the very heart of this cluster of constitutionally protected choices. That decision holds a particularly important place in the history of the right of privacy, a right first explicitly recognized in an opinion holding unconstitutional a statute prohibiting the use of contraceptives, Griswold v. Connecticut, 381 U.S. 479 (1965), and most prominently vindicated in recent years in the contexts of contraception and abortion. This is understandable, for in a field that by definition concerns the most intimate of human activities and relationships, decisions whether to accomplish or to prevent conception are among the most private and sensitive. "If the right of privacy means anything, it is the right of the individual, married or single, to be free of unwarranted governmental intrusion into matters so fundamentally affecting a person as the decision whether to bear or beget a child." Eisenstadt v. Baird, supra, 405 U.S., at 453. (Emphasis omitted.)

That the constitutionally protected right of privacy extends to an individual's liberty to make choices regarding contraception does not, however, automatically invalidate every state regulation in this area. [E]ven a burdensome regulation may be validated by a sufficiently compelling state interest. . . .

With these principles in mind, we turn to the question whether the District Court was correct in holding invalid the provisions of §6811(8) as applied to the distribution of nonprescription contraceptives. . . .

IV

A

Appellants contend that [the prohibition on the sale or distribution of contraceptives to minors] is constitutionally permissible as a regulation of the morality of minors in furtherance of the State's policy against promiscuous sexual intercourse among the young.

The question of the extent of state power to regulate conduct of minors not constitutionally regulable when committed by adults is a vexing one, perhaps not susceptible to precise answer. . . . Certain principles, however, have been recognized. "Minors, as well as adults, are protected by the Constitution and possess constitutional rights." Planned Parenthood of Central Missouri v. Danforth, [428 U.S. 52, 74 (1976)]. "[W]hatever may be their precise impact, neither the Fourteenth Amendment nor the Bill of Rights is for adults alone." In re Gault, [387 U.S. 1, 13 (1967)]. On the other hand, we have held in a variety of contexts that "the power of the state to control the conduct of children reaches beyond the scope of its authority over adults." Prince v. Massachusetts, [321 U.S. 158, 170 (1994)]; Ginsberg v. New York, 390 U.S. 629 (1968).

Of particular significance to the decision of this case, the right to privacy in connection with decision affecting procreation extends to minors as well as to adults. Planned Parenthood of Central Missouri v. Danforth, supra, held that a State "may not impose a blanket provision . . . requiring the consent of a parent or person in loco parentis as a condition for abortion of an unmarried mother during the first 12 weeks of her pregnancy." 428 U.S., at 74. As in the case of the spousal consent requirement struck down in the same case, "the State does not have the constitutional authority to give a third party an absolute, and possibly arbitrary, veto," id., at 74, "which the state itself is absolutely and totally prohibited from exercising." Id., at 69. State restrictions inhibiting privacy rights of minors are valid only if they serve "any significant state interest . . . that is not present in the case of an adult." Id., at 75. *Planned Parenthood* found that no such interest justified a state requirement of parental consent.

Since the State may not impose a blanket prohibition, or even a blanket requirement of parental consent, on the choice of a minor to terminate her pregnancy, the constitutionality of a blanket prohibition of the distribution of contraceptives to minors is *a fortiori* foreclosed. The State's interests in protection of the mental and physical health of the pregnant minor, and in protection of potential life are clearly more implicated by the abortion decision than by the decision to use a nonhazardous contraceptive.

Appellants argue, however, that significant state interests are served by restricting minors' access to contraceptives, because free availability to minors of contraceptives would lead to increased sexual activity among the young, in violation of the policy of New York to discourage such behavior.[17] The argument is that minors' sexual activity may be deterred by increasing the hazards attendant on it. The same argument, however, would support a ban on abortions for minors, or indeed support a prohibition on abortions, or access to contraceptives, for the unmarried, whose sexual activity is also against the public policy of many States. Yet, in each of these areas, the Court has rejected the argument, noting in Roe v. Wade, that "no court or commentator has taken the argument seriously." 410 U.S., at 148. The reason for this unanimous rejection was stated in Eisenstadt v. Baird, supra: "It would be plainly unreasonable to assume that [the state] has prescribed pregnancy and the birth of an unwanted child [or the physical and psychological dangers of an abortion] as punishment for fornication." 405 U.S., at 448. We remain reluctant to attribute any such "scheme of values" to the State.

---

[17] Appellees argue that the State's policy to discourage sexual activity of minors is itself unconstitutional, for the reason that the right to privacy comprehends a right of minors as well as adults to engage in private consensual sexual behavior. We observe that the Court has not definitively answered the difficult question whether and to what extent the Constitution prohibits state statutes regulating such behavior among adults. But whatever the answer to that question, Ginsberg v. New York, 390 U.S. 629 (1968), indicates that in the area of sexual mores, as in other areas, the scope of permissible state regulation is broader as to minors than as to adults. In any event, it is unnecessary to pass upon this contention of appellees, and our decision proceeds on the assumption that the Constitution does not bar state regulation of the sexual behavior of minors.

Moreover, there is substantial reason for doubt whether limiting access to contraceptives will in fact substantially discourage early sexual behavior. Appellants themselves conceded in the District Court that "there is no evidence that teenage extramarital sexual activity increases in proportion to the availability of contraceptives," 398 F. Supp., at 332, and n.10 and accordingly offered none. . . . Appellees, on the other hand, cite a considerable body of evidence and opinion indicating that there is no such deterrent effect. Although we take judicial notice . . . that with or without access to contraceptives, the incidence of sexual activity among minors is high, and the consequences of such activity are frequently devastating, the studies cited by appellees play no part in our decision. It is enough that we again confirm the principle that when a State, as here, burdens the exercise of a fundamental right, its attempt to justify that burden as a rational means for the accomplishment of some significant State policy requires more than a bare assertion, based on a conceded complete absence of supporting evidence, that the burden is connected to such a policy.

B

Appellants argue that New York does not totally prohibit distribution of contraceptives to minors under 16, and that accordingly §6811(8) cannot be held unconstitutional. Although §6811 (8) on its face is a flat unqualified prohibition, Education Law §6807(b), . . . provides that nothing in Education Law §§6800-6826 shall be construed to prevent "[a]ny physician . . . from supplying his patients with such drugs as [he] . . . deems proper in connection with his practice." This narrow exception, however, does not save the statute. As we have held above as to limitations upon distribution to adults, less than total restrictions on access to contraceptives that significantly burden the right to decide whether to bear children must also pass constitutional scrutiny. Appellants assert no medical necessity for imposing a medical limitation on the distribution of nonprescription contraceptives to minors. Rather, they argue that such a restriction serves to emphasize to young people the seriousness with which the State views the decision to engage in sexual intercourse at an early age. But this is only another form of the argument that juvenile sexual conduct will be deterred by making contraceptives more difficult to obtain. Moreover, that argument is particularly poorly suited to the restriction appellants are attempting to justify, which on appellants' construction delegates the State's authority to disapprove of minors' sexual behavior to physicians, who may exercise it arbitrarily, either to deny contraceptives to young people, or to undermine the State's policy of discouraging illicit early sexual behavior. This the State may not do. . . .

Affirmed.

Mr. Justice WHITE, concurring in part and concurring in the result in part. . . .

I concur in the result in Part IV primarily because the State has not demonstrated that the prohibition against distribution of contraceptives to minors measurably contributes to the deterrent purposes which the State advances as justification for the restriction. . . .

Mr. Justice POWELL, concurring in part and concurring in the judgment. . . .

New York has made it a crime for anyone other than a physician to sell or distribute contraceptives to minors under the age of 16 years. This element of

New York's program of regulation for the protection of its minor citizens is said to evidence the State's judgment that the health and well-being of minors would be better assured if they are not encouraged to engage in sexual intercourse without guidance. Although I have no doubt that properly framed legislation serving this purpose would meet constitutional standards, the New York provision is defective in two respects. First, it infringes the privacy interests of married females between the ages of 14 and 16, . . . in that it prohibits the distribution of contraceptives to such females except by a physician. In authorizing marriage at that age, the State also sanctions sexual intercourse between the partners and expressly recognizes that once the marriage relationship exists the husband and wife are presumed to possess the requisite understanding and maturity to make decisions concerning sex and procreation. Consequently, the State interest that justifies a requirement of prior counseling with respect to minors in general simply is inapplicable with respect to minors for whom the State has affirmatively approved marriage.

Second, this provision prohibits parents from distributing contraceptives to their children, a restriction that unjustifiably interferes with parental interests in rearing their children [citing Meyer v. Nebraska, Pierce v. Society of Sisters, Wisconsin v. Yoder]. Moreover, this statute would allow the State "to enquire into, prove, and punish," Poe v. Ullman, 367 U.S. 497, 548 (1961) (Harlan, J., dissenting), the exercise of this parental responsibility. The State points to no interest of sufficient magnitude to justify this direct interference with the parental guidance that is especially appropriate in this sensitive area of child development.

But in my view there is considerably more room for state regulation in this area than would be permissible under the Court's opinion. It seems clear to me, for example, that the State would further a constitutionally permissible end if it encouraged adolescents to seek the advice and guidance of their parents before deciding whether to engage in sexual intercourse. The State justifiably may take note of the psychological pressures that might influence children at a time in their lives when they generally do not possess the maturity necessary to understand and control their responses. Participation in sexual intercourse at an early age may have both physical and psychological consequences. These include the risks of venereal disease and pregnancy, and the less obvious mental and emotional problems that may result from sexual activity by children. Moreover, society has long adhered to the view that sexual intercourse should not be engaged in promiscuously, a judgment that an adolescent may be less likely to heed than an adult.

Requiring minors to seek parental guidance would be consistent with our prior cases. In Planned Parenthood of Central Missouri v. Danforth, 428 U.S. 52 (1976), we considered whether there was "any significant state interest in conditioning [a minor's] abortion [decision] on the consent of a parent or person in loco parentis that is not present in the case of an adult." Id., at 75. Observing that the minor necessarily would be consulting with a physician on all aspects of the abortion decision, we concluded that the Missouri requirement was invalid because it imposed "a special-consent provision, exercisable by a person other than the woman and her physician, as a prerequisite to a minor's termination of her pregnancy and [did] so without a sufficient justification for the restriction." Ibid. But we explicitly suggested that a materially different constitutional issue would be presented with respect to a statute assuring in most instances consultation between the parent and child. Ibid., citing

Bellotti v. Baird, 428 U.S. 132 (1976). See Planned Parenthood, 428 U.S., at 90-91 (Stewart, J., concurring).

A requirement of prior parental consultation is merely one illustration of permissible regulation in this area. As long as parental distribution is permitted, a State should have substantial latitude in regulating the distribution of contraceptives to minors. . . .

Mr. Justice STEVENS, concurring in part and concurring in the judgment.

. . . I also agree with the conclusion that New York's prohibition against the distribution of contraceptives to persons under 16 years of age is unconstitutional, . . . but my reasons differ from those set forth in Part IV of Mr. Justice Brennan's opinion. . . .

There are two reasons why I do not join Part IV. First, the holding in Planned Parenthood of Missouri v. Danforth, 428 U.S. 52, 72-75, [1976] that a minor's decision to abort her pregnancy may not be conditioned on parental consent, is not dispositive here. The options available to the already pregnant minor are fundamentally different from those available to nonpregnant minors. The former must bear a child unless she aborts; but persons in the latter category can and generally will avoid childbearing by abstention. Consequently, even if I had joined that part of *Planned Parenthood*, I could not agree that the Constitution provides the same measure of protection to the minor's right to use contraceptives as to the pregnant female's right to abort.

Second, I would not leave open the question whether there is a significant state interest in discouraging sexual activity among unmarried persons under 16 years of age. Indeed, I would describe as "frivolous" appellee's argument that a minor has the constitutional right to put contraceptives to their intended use, notwithstanding the combined objection of both parents and the State.

For the reasons explained by Mr. Justice Powell, I agree that the statute may not be applied to married females between the ages of 14 and 16, or to distribution by parents. I am not persuaded, however, that these glaring defects alone justify an injunction against other applications of the statute. Only one of the three plaintiffs in this case is a parent who wishes to give contraceptives to his children. The others are an Episcopal minister who sponsors a program against venereal disease, and a mail order firm, which presumably has no way to determine the age of its customers. I am satisfied, for the reasons that follow, that the statute is also invalid as applied to them.

The State's important interest in the welfare of its young citizens justifies a number of protective measures. Such special legislation is premised on the fact that young persons frequently make unwise choices with harmful consequences; the State may properly ameliorate those consequences by providing, for example, that a minor may not be required to honor his bargain. It is almost unprecedented, however, for a State to require that an ill-advised act by a minor give rise to greater risk of irreparable harm than a similar act by an adult.

Common sense indicates that many young people will engage in sexual activity regardless of what the New York Legislature does; and further, that the incidence of venereal disease and premarital pregnancy is affected by the availability or unavailability of contraceptives. Although young persons theoretically may avoid those harms by practicing total abstention, inevitably many will not. The statutory prohibition denies them and their parents a choice which, if available, would reduce their exposure to disease or unwanted pregnancy.

The State's asserted justification is a desire to inhibit sexual conduct by minors under 16. It does not seriously contend that if contraceptives are available, significant numbers of minors who now abstain from sex will cease abstaining because they will no longer fear pregnancy or disease. Rather its central argument is that the statute has the important symbolic effect of communicating disapproval of sexual activity by minors. In essence, therefore, the statute is defended as a form of propaganda, rather than a regulation of behavior.[4]

Although the State may properly perform a teaching function, it seems to me that an attempt to persuade by inflicting harm on the listener is an unacceptable means of conveying a message that is otherwise legitimate. The propaganda technique used in this case significantly increases the risk of unwanted pregnancy and venereal disease. It is as though a State decided to dramatize its disapproval of motorcycles by forbidding the use of safety helmets. One need not posit a constitutional right to ride a motorcycle to characterize such a restriction as irrational and perverse.

Even as a regulation of behavior, such a statute would be defective. Assuming that the State could impose a uniform sanction upon young persons who risk self-inflicted harm by operating motorcycles, or by engaging in sexual activity, surely that sanction could not take the form of deliberately injuring the cyclist or infecting the promiscuous child. If such punishment may not be administered deliberately, after trial and a finding of guilt, it manifestly cannot be imposed by a legislature, indiscriminately and at random. This kind of government-mandated harm, is, in my judgment, appropriately characterized as a deprivation of liberty without due process of law.

Mr. Justice REHNQUIST, dissenting.

Those who valiantly but vainly defended the heights of Bunker Hill in 1775 made it possible that men such as James Madison might later sit in the first Congress and draft the Bill of Rights to the Constitution. The post-Civil War Congresses, which drafted the Civil War Amendments to the Constitution, could not have accomplished their task without the blood of brave men on both sides which was shed at Shiloh, Gettysburg, and Cold Harbor. If those responsible for these Amendments, by feats of valor or efforts of draftsmanship, could have lived to know that their efforts had enshrined in the Constitution the right of commercial vendors of contraceptives to peddle them to unmarried minors through such means as window displays and vending machines located in the men's room of truck stops, notwithstanding the considered judgment of the New York Legislature to the contrary, it is not difficult to imagine their reaction. . . .

No questions of religious belief, compelled allegiance to a secular creed, or decisions on the part of married couples as to procreation are involved here. New York has simply decided that it wishes to discourage unmarried minors in the 14- to 16-years-age bracket from having promiscuous sexual intercourse with one another.

---

[4] The State presents no empirical evidence to support the conclusion that its "propaganda" is effective. Simply as a matter of common sense, it seems unlikely that many minors under 16 are influenced by the mere existence of a law indirectly disapproving their conduct.

Even the Court would scarcely go so far as to say that this is not a subject with which the New York Legislature may properly concern itself.

That legislature has not chosen to deny to a pregnant woman, after the *fait accompli* of pregnancy, the one remedy which would enable her to terminate an unwanted pregnancy. It has instead sought to deter the conduct which will produce such *faits accomplis*. The majority of New York's citizens are in effect told that however deeply they may be concerned about the problem of promiscuous sex and intercourse among unmarried teenagers, they may not adopt this means of dealing with it. The Court holds that New York may not use its police power to legislate in the interests of its concept of the public morality as it pertains to minors. The Court's denial of a power so fundamental to self-government must, in the long run, prove to be but a temporary departure from a wise and heretofore settled course of adjudication to the contrary. I would reverse the judgment of the District Court.

[handwritten: deterrent argument]

NOTES AND QUESTIONS

(1) State's Interest. What did the various *Carey* opinions assume about the legitimacy of a state's attempt to deter sexual activity? Note that there are two reasons a state could wish to inhibit teenage sexual activity. One is based on moral justifications: sexual intercourse outside marriage or by the immature members of our society is wrong. The second relates to the problem of unwanted teenage pregnancies.

(2) Data on Teen Contraceptive Use. Research reveals that 78 percent of teenage girls use contraceptives at first intercourse.[48] The two most popular forms of contraception by young men and women are condoms and birth control pills. Slightly more than half of sexually active youth in grades 9 through 12 reported using a condom during their last sexual intercourse, while approximately one-fifth reported use of birth control pills.[49] However, although more youths are using contraceptives, these youths are likely to practice contraception sporadically.[50] Not surprisingly, the percentage of sexually active youths rises with each subsequent grade. However, condom use among 12th graders is lower than among youths in earlier grades.[51]

(3) Constitutionality of Condom Distribution Programs. Should parental consent be required for the distribution of condoms in schools? If parents are opposed on religious grounds, does the distribution of condoms violate parents' freedom of religion? Does condom distribution interfere with the parents' right to raise a child free from state interference as established in *Meyer*, *Pierce*, and *Yoder*? These issues were raised in Curtis v. School Committee of Falmouth, 652 N.E.2d 580 (1st Cir. 1995), *cert. denied*, 516 U.S. 1067 (1996), which held that a condom distribution program that contained no "opt-out" provision did not violate plaintiffs' liberty to raise their children as they saw fit or their right to privacy or

[48] Alan Guttmacher Institute, Teen Sex and Pregnancy (1999).
[49] U.S. Dept. of Health & Human Servs., Trends in the Well-Being of America's Children and Youth 2002, Contraceptive Use, 284.
[50] Id.
[51] Id. at 282, 284.

to free exercise. See also Parents United for Better Public Schools v. School Dist. of Phila., 148 F.3d 260 (3d Cir. 1998) (holding that condom distribution program did not violate parents' fundamental right to bring up their children without unnecessary governmental interference when participation is voluntary and the program reserves to parents the right to opt out). See generally Stephen Lease et al., Condom Distribution Programs, 68 Am. Jur. 2d Schools §312 (2004).

(4) Data on Teens and Sexually Transmissible Disease (STD).   Data reveal that about one in four sexually experienced teens acquire an STD each year. Chlamydia is more common among teens than among older men and women. Teens have higher rates of gonorrhea than sexually active men and women aged 20-44. Further, teenage girls are more likely to be hospitalized than older women for acute pelvic inflammatory disease (PID) (which is often caused by untreated gonorrhea or chlamydia and can lead to infertility and ectopic pregnancy).[52]

(5) Teen Pregnancy. Studies reveal the high rates of teenage sexual activity and pregnancy as well as the serious implications that pregnancy has for the teenage mother, teenage father, child, and society. The Alan Guttmacher Institute notes the following statistics: only about one in five young people do *not* have intercourse while teenagers, and over half of 17-year-olds have had intercourse. Each year, almost one million teenage women — 10 percent of all women aged 15-19 and 19 percent of those who have had sexual intercourse — become pregnant; nearly 4 in 10 of these pregnancies end in abortion. More than three-quarters of teen pregnancies are unplanned and occur outside of marriage.[53]

A national study by the U.S. Department of Health and Human Services elaborates on the societal consequences of teen pregnancies:

> Research indicates that giving birth as a youth can have negative consequences on both mothers and their children. Giving birth at an early age can limit a young female's options regarding education and employment opportunities, increase the likelihood that she will need public assistance, and can have negative effects on the development of her children. Young mothers are less likely to complete high school (only one third receive a high school diploma) and are more likely to end up on welfare (nearly 80 percent of unmarried young mothers end up on welfare). The sons of young mothers are 13 percent more likely to serve time in prison, while their daughters are 22 percent more likely to become young mothers themselves.[54]

Despite these statistics, it is important to note that the rate of teenage pregnancy decreased dramatically during the 1990s (for teens aged 15 to 17 as well as for older teens aged 18-19).[55] Researchers attribute the decline to a decrease in sexual activity, more effective use of contraceptives, and, to a lesser degree, increased abstinence among teenagers.[56]

[52] Guttmacher Report, supra note [48].

[53] Id.

[54] Trends in Well-Being, supra note [49].

[55] Center for Disease Control (CDC), Births: Final Data for 2002, 51 Natl. Vital Statistics Reports (No. 10), at 5 (2003) (the pregnancy rate for teens aged 15-17 fell from 38.6 per 1,000 in 1991 to 23.2 per 1,000 in 2002. The rate for teens aged 18-19 decreased from 94 per 1,000 in 1991 to 72.8 per 1,000 in 2002).

[56] Jacqueline Darroch & Susheela Singh, Why Is Teenage Pregnancy Declining? The Roles of Abstinence, Sexual Activity, and Contraceptive Use 9 (Guttmacher Institute, 1999).

See generally Helen Cothran, Teen Pregnancy and Parenting: Current Controversies (2000); Melissa Ludtke, On Our Own: Unmarried Motherhood in America 34-101 (1999) (focus on unmarried teen mothers); Rebecca A. Maynard, Kids Having Kids: Economic Costs and Social Consequences of Teen Pregnancy (1997).

(6) Minors' Sexual Privacy. Could a state pass a law making it a crime for minors to engage in sexual intercourse? Does the Constitution ensure the right to private consensual sexual activity for adults, let alone for minors? You would think after cases like *Griswold, Roe,* and the Supreme Court's recent pronouncement in Lawrence v. Texas, 539 U.S. 558 (2003), the answer for adults, at least, would be yes. In *Lawrence,* the Supreme Court held that a Texas statute criminalizing homosexual sodomy violated petitioners' due process right to engage in private consensual sexual conduct. A broad reading of *Lawrence* would suggest that adults possess a constitutionally protected right of sexual privacy. However, subsequent federal and state case law is not in agreement as to how broadly to interpret *Lawrence.* Compare Williams v. Attorney General, 378 F.3d 1232, 1236 (11th Cir. 2004) (refusing to invalidate prohibition on commercial distribution of sex toys on the basis that there is no fundamental substantive due process right of consenting adults to engage in private intimate sexual conduct as would trigger a strict scrutiny review); and Lofton v. Department of Children and Family Servs., 358 F.3d 804, 815-817 (11th Cir. 2004) (upholding statutory prohibition on adoption by gays and lesbians, reasoning that *Lawrence* did not announce a new fundamental right that protects gay and lesbian intimate relationships) with Goodridge v. Department of Pub. Health, 798 N.E.2d 941, 948 (Mass. 2003) (citing *Lawrence* with approval in support of right of same-sex couples to marry).

Note that in *Carey,* Justice Brennan observed that "our decision proceeds on the assumption that the Constitution does not bar state regulation of the sexual behavior of minors" (p. 676 n. 17, supra). Moreover, the Supreme Court in *Lawrence* differentiated the right of adults to engage in consensual private sexual conduct from that of minors ("[t]his case does not involve minors") (539 U.S. at 578), thereby indicating a reluctance to extend the right to engage in consensual sexual activity to minors. And the Eleventh Circuit relied on this protective rationale in *Lofton,* supra, to uphold Florida's ban on gay and lesbian adoptions of children. See also Michael M. v. Superior Court, 450 U.S. 464 (1981) (upholding gender-discriminatory statutory rape statute against a claim that it violated equal protection by reasoning that the statute was sufficiently related to the state's objective to prevent teenage pregnancy); In re G.T., 758 A.2d 301 (Vt. 2000) (holding that the statutory rape statute does not apply to consensual sexual activity between minors, thereby avoiding the underlying constitutional issues).

See generally Charles A. Phipps, Misdirected Reform: On Regulating Consensual Sexual Activity Between Teenagers, 12 Cornell J.L. & Pub. Pol'y 373 (2003); Kate Sutherland, From Jailbird to Jailbait: Age of Consent Laws and the Construction of Teenage Sexualities, 9 Wm. & Mary J. Women & L. 313 (2003).

(7) Effectiveness of Regulation. What is the relationship between the state's attempt to regulate access to contraceptives and its attempt to regulate teenage sexual activity? Some people believe access to contraceptives will have *no* effect on the level of teenage sexual activity but will reduce unwanted pregnancies. Others fear that access to contraceptives will encourage more sexual activity and may

ironically lead to more unwanted pregnancies, because despite the availability, teenagers are not very good contraceptive users. In *Carey*, the state argued that "significant state interests are served by restricting minor's access to contraceptives, because free availability to minors of contraceptives would lead to increased sexual activity among the young, in violation of the policy of New York to discourage such behavior." (p. 676, supra.) The state apparently felt that preventing access to contraceptives would deter teenage sexual activity by "increasing the hazards attendant on it." (p. 676, supra.) The state also argued that their restrictions served to "emphasize to young people the seriousness with which the state views the decision to engage in sexual intercourse at an early age." (p. 677, supra.) How does the Court treat this argument? Consider Justice Steven's response (p. 679, supra). Do you agree that prohibiting contraceptives will increase the risk of unwanted pregnancies and venereal disease? Is it really "as though a State decided to dramatize its disapproval of motorcycles by forbidding the use of safety helmets"? (p. 680, supra.)

The evidence regarding the deterrent effect of limited contraceptive availability on sexual activity is not conclusive. Critics of family planning services point out that the significant increase in teenage sexual activity in the 1970s was accompanied by a significant growth in the availability of contraceptive services for both adult women and adolescents. Yet some researchers point out that the existence of a causal connection between these trends is not clear; they criticize that prior research does not always control for other factors that might affect levels of sexual activity among different subgroups or different points in time.[57] One recent study on the effects of condom availability programs in schools on teenage sexual activity found that: "Adolescents in schools where condoms were available were more likely to receive condom use instruction and less likely to report lifetime or recent sexual intercourse."[58]

Furthermore, the Children's Defense Fund finds:

> Teaching teens about sex has been found to increase their knowledge without increasing their sexual activity, despite assumptions to the contrary. In *No Easy Answers: Research Findings on Programs to Reduce Teen Pregnancy*, the National Campaign to Prevent Teen Pregnancy reported in 1997 that making condoms and school-based health clinics available as part of pregnancy prevention efforts does not increase teens' sexual activity. However, simply providing access to contraception is not enough to prevent pregnancy. The weight of the research evidence indicates that making contraceptives available in school-based clinics — without adding other important program components that address teens' motivations — does not affect teen pregnancy or birth rates. *No Easy Answers* notes that even though abstinence-only programs may be appropriate for many young people, especially junior high and middle school youths, no published scientific research of adequate quality measures whether or not such initiatives actually delay sexual activity. The report's author, Douglas Kirby, cautions that because some young

---

[57] National Research Council, Risking the Future: Adolescent Sexuality, Pregnancy and Childbearing, vol. I, 165-166 (1986).

[58] Susan Blake et al., Condom Availability in Massachusetts High Schools: Relationships with Condom Use and Sexual Behavior, 93 Am. J. Pub. Health 955, 957 (2003).

people have sexual relations and others refrain, "programs need to address both abstaining from or postponing sex and using contraceptives."[59]

Abstinence-based sex education programs are discussed infra.

(8) Parental Involvement Laws. What role should parents have when their teenagers seek access to contraceptives? Parental notification or consent rules are extremely controversial. Some states and health care providers require parental notification or consent before providing minors with contraceptives. See Ruth Padawer, Sex Study Fuels Debate on Parental Notification, The Record (New Jersey), Jan. 19, 2005, at A1 (pointing out that Utah, Texas, and an Illinois county prohibit state funding for clinics that do not require written parental consent before giving minors contraception).

Federal legislation currently provides confidentiality to teenage clients of federally funded health providers, although reformers are attempting to change that rule. In 1970, Congress adopted Title X of the Public Health Service Act, Family Planning Services & Population Research Act of 1970, 42 U.S.C. §§300 to 300a-41 (2000), to provide family planning and preventive health screening services (e.g., contraceptives, infertility management, prenatal information and counseling, and treatment of STDs, but not abortion) to low-income women by means of grants to private and public health care providers. In 1978 Congress amended Title X to place special emphasis on "preventing unwanted pregnancies among sexually active adolescents."[60] The federal program mandates confidentiality in the physician-patient relationship. Subsequent interpretive notes and decisions about Title X prohibit parental notification or consent requirements, even when required by state law, on the basis that state parental involvement laws interfere with the federal policy of providing health care to sexually active minors. Jessica Bertuglia, Note, Preserving the Right to Choose: A Minor's Right to Confidential Reproductive Health Care, 23 Women's Rts. L. Rep. 63, 75 (2001).

Various attempts have been made to change the confidentiality rule. In 1983 the Department of Health and Human Services, acting under authority granted by Title X, amended its regulations governing the family planning services program. The regulation, known as the "squeal rule," provided that (a) federally funded clinics would have to notify parents of unemancipated minors' receiving prescription contraceptives within ten days of receipt (42 C.F.R. §59.5(a)(12)(I)(A) (1983), and (b) federally funded clinics would have to comply with state notification or consent laws (42 C.F.R §59.5(a)(12)(ii) (1983). Two federal courts of appeal invalidated the regulations as inconsistent with congressional intent under Title X to make family planning services available to adolescents. New York v. Heckler, 719 F.2d 1191 (2d Cir. 1983); Planned Parenthood Federation of America v. Heckler, 712 F.2d 650 (D.C. Cir. 1983).

Efforts continue to abrogate the confidentiality provision of Title X. In June 2003, Representative Todd Akin (R-Mo.) introduced the Parents' Right to Know

[59] Children's Defense Fund, The Status of America's Children: Yearbook 1998: 87 (1998).
[60] Center for Reproductive Rights Publication, Forced Parental Involvement Defeats the Goals of the Title X, available at *http://crlp.org/pub_fac_adolesdom.html* (Jan. 2004) (last visited Feb. 5, 2005).

Act of 2003 (108th Cong., 1st Sess., H.R. 2444) to require federally funded health care providers to notify a custodial parent or legal guardian of the intent to provide contraceptive drugs or devices at least five business days beforehand and also to secure the written consent of that parent or guardian. Exceptions are provided for emancipated minors and minors who have obtained a judicial waiver of parental consent and notification.

What do you think would be the effect of federal legislation mandating parental involvement before teenagers are permitted to obtain contraceptives? Recent research reveals that many adolescents would refuse to seek reproductive health care if health care providers insist on parental notification or consent. The first national study of teenagers' attitudes on parental notification (including more than 1,500 female minors in 33 states) found that parental notification requirements would result in only 30 percent of the teenagers continuing to patronize health care providers for contraceptives and that nearly one in five females would stop using contraceptives. Diane M. Reddy et al., Effect of Mandatory Parental Notification on Adolescent Girls' Use of Sexual Health Care Services, 288 JAMA (No. 6) 710 (Aug. 14, 2002).

See generally Jessica Arons, Misconceived Laws: The Irrationality of Parental Involvement Requirements for Contraception, 41 Wm. & Mary L. Rev. 1093 (2000); Stephanie Bornstein, The Undue Burden: Parental Notification Requirements for Publicly Funded Contraception, 15 Berkeley Women's L.J. 40 (2000).

(9) AIDS Prevention Programs.   Teenagers are one of the fastest growing groups contracting acquired immunodeficiency syndrome (AIDS).[61] Indeed, the prevalence of infected youths may be higher than reported because many adolescents fail to get tested for the disease. A key problem in AIDS testing is that most statutes that permit adolescents themselves to consent to medical care for specific conditions (such as substance abuse or sexually transmitted diseases) omit any reference to HIV or AIDS testing. Rhonda Gay Hartman, AIDS and Adolescents, 7 J. Health Care L. & Pol'y 280, 284 (2004).

Currently, 35 states mandate HIV, STD, and/or AIDS education; 18 states and the District of Columbia merely mandate sexuality education.[62] See also Roger J.R. Levesque, Sexuality Education: What Adolescents' Educational Rights Require, 6 Psychol. Pub. Pol'y & L. 953, 966-967 (2000) (discussing statutes). Is preventing the spread of AIDS a sufficiently compelling state interest to justify the burden of imposing such educational programs on teenagers' sexual decision making?

(10) Abstinence-based Sex Education.   As explained above, many states require that sex education programs be offered in the schools. Such programs are known by different labels (e.g., "family life education," "health," "sexual health,"

---

[61] Eugene S. Bjorklun, Condom Distribution in the Public Schools: Is Parental Consent Required?, 91 Educ. L. Rep. 11 (July 28, 1994) (citing United States House of Representatives Select Committee on Children, Youth, and Families, The Risky Business of Adolescence: How to Help Teens Stay Safe — Part II (Washington, D.C.: U.S. Government Printing Office, 1992), p. 30)).

[62] Naomi K. Seiler, Abstinence-Only Education and Privacy, 24 Women's Rts. L. Rep. 27, 31 (2002).

etc.) and cover a variety of topics. Most statutes on sex education provide "opt out" provisions for parents who do not want their children taught certain subjects. Moreover, as a result of federal legislation (discussed below), most such statutes emphasize abstinence-only education. Levesque, supra, at 967. Abstinence-based programs generally prohibit discussion of contraceptives and convey the message that premarital sexual activity leads to psychological and physical harm.

Abstinence-based sex education received a boost from federal legislation. The Adolescent Family Life Act of 1981 (AFLA), 42 U.S.C. §§300z(a)(1)-300z(a)(10) (2000), provided funding for abstinence-only education through federal matching grants to the states. In Bowen v. Kendrick, 487 U.S. 589 (1988), the United States Supreme Court upheld the constitutionality of AFLA against a challenge that it violated the Establishment Clause. The Court reasoned that the Act would not lead to excessive government entanglement with religion and did not have a primary effect of advancing religion.

Subsequently, in 1996, federal welfare reform legislation (PRWORA), Pub. L. No. 104-193, §912, 110 Stat. 2105 (1996) (codified in scattered sections of 42 U.S.C.), reaffirmed the federal commitment to an abstinence-only approach. In an effort to reduce teen pregnancy, PRWORA allocates money ($50 million annually from 1998 to 2002) to states that adopt abstinence education programs. 42 U.S.C. §912 (2000). Congress doubled the funding for such programs to $100 million in 2003; the proposed budget for these programs for fiscal year 2005 is $270 million. James McGrath, Abstinence-Only Adolescent Education: Ineffective, Unpopular, and Unconstitutional, 38 U.S.F. L. Rev. 665, 666 (2004). Another governmental program that funds abstinence-only education is Special Projects of Regional and National Significance — Community-Based Abstinence Education, administered by the Department of Health and Human Services Maternal and Child Health Bureau, which began in 2001. Under the program, a recipient organization must agree not to provide a participating adolescent with any form of education regarding sexual conduct except abstinence. For an argument that the program violates the "unconstitutional conditions" doctrine (placing an unconstitutional condition on the receipt of federal funds), see McGrath, supra, at 667-668.

Is an "abstinence-only" form of sex education an effective deterrent to sexual activity? Recent research on the effectiveness of abstinence programs suggests that such programs are ineffective in delaying teens' sexual activity and reducing unintended pregnancies. A study of 4,877 sexually active females ages 15 to 19 (conducted by the Guttmacher Institute and published in Perspectives on Sexual and Reproductive Health) reveals that the youth are much less likely to become pregnant if they have a positive attitude toward contraception. Further, the vast majority (88%) of those adolescents who take virginity pledges break them. Researchers concluded that comprehensive sex education (i.e., an "abstinence-plus" instead of "abstinence-only" approach) produces the best results. Cited in Marina Pisano, Studies Challenge Abstinence-Only; Researchers Share Their Results on Teen Sex at News Briefing, San Antonio Express-News, Jan. 21, 2005, at B5. Do abstinence-based sex education programs violate minors' right to privacy? Parents' right to family privacy?

F. JUVENILE CURFEWS

Hodgkins v. Peterson (*Hodgkins II*)
355 F.3d 1048 (7th Cir. 2004)

ROVNER, Circuit Judge. . . .

Shortly after 11:00 P.M. on August 26, 1999, Colin Hodgkins and his three friends left a Steak'n Shake restaurant in Marion County, Indiana where they had stopped to eat after attending a school soccer game. As they left the restaurant, police arrested and handcuffed them for violating Indiana's curfew regulation. The police took Colin and his friends to a curfew sweep processing site where he was given a breathalyser test and escorted to a bathroom where he was required to submit a urine sample to be tested for drugs. Later, both tests were determined to be negative. After the tests, a community volunteer interviewed Colin, asking him various personal questions about his friends and family including whether his family attended church. Two and a half hours later, at 1:30 A.M., a member of the Marion County Sheriff's Department went to the Hodgkins residence to inform Nancy Hodgkins that her son had been arrested and had to be picked up at the local high school. When she arrived to pick up her son, a community volunteer interviewed her and asked her personal questions about the Hodgkins family.

Colin's arrest spurred a series of legal challenges to the constitutionality of the statute. [At the time of Colin's arrest, the Indiana statute (Ind. Code 31-37-3-2) set a curfew of 11 P.M. on weekday nights and 1 A.M. on weekend nights for youth aged 15-17 with additional restrictions for those under age 15. Exemptions applied for any child who was accompanied by a parent or guardian or by an adult designated by the parent or guardian; or participating in employment, a school activity, or a religious event.] Pursuant to a challenge by Colin, his mother, and a certified class of minors similarly situated, the district court determined that the statutes were constitutionally flawed as they lacked any exceptions for First Amendment activity. Hodgkins v. Goldsmith, No. IP99-1528-C-T/G, 2000 WL 892964, at *18 (S.D. Ind. July 3, 2000) (*Hodgkins I*). Following this decision, the defendants appealed. While the appeal was pending, the Indiana General Assembly passed the current version of the curfew law, effective May 1, 2001 [which incorporated the prior exceptions to the curfew rule and added a new provision] which, rather than creating an exception for First Amendment activity, created an affirmative defense for those engaged in protected expressive activity. [Plaintiffs again sought to preliminarily enjoin the enforcement of the law in the belief that the statutory revisions did not cure the constitutional defects. The district court denied the plaintiffs' motion.]

Named plaintiff Nancy Hodgkins is a resident of Indianapolis, Indiana, and is the mother of named plaintiffs Colin and Caroline Hodgkins. Ms. Hodgkins would like to allow her children to participate in the activities protected by the curfew law's First Amendment exception, however, she is concerned that if they do so, they will be subject to arrest. Ms. Hodgkins recognizes that if one of her children is arrested while participating in a First Amendment activity she and the child could later use that activity as a defense to the charges. She is nevertheless concerned about the potential expense and time involved in launching such a defense, and, we surmise, she is wary of again placing herself in a position where she will be summoned by the police in the middle of the night to come to a curfew processing center or detention center and of placing her children in a position where they will be subject to arrest, a breathalyser test, urine test, and an intrusive interview. Ms. Hodgkins states that she will certainly consider the risk of arrest when deciding whether to allow her children to participate in First Amendment activities after curfew. Consequently, she asserts that the current statute chills her children's ability to engage in these types of activities.

Furthermore, Ms. Hodgkins wishes to assert her rights as a parent to measure out more privileges and responsibilities to her children as they mature and grow more capable of acting responsibly with additional freedom. She believes that it is part of a parent's job to prepare a child for adulthood by doling out greater freedoms, including the freedom to remain out past curfew without being accompanied by an adult. [Defendants (i.e., the Indianapolis mayor, county sheriff, and county prosecutor)] claim that the curfew law is constitutional and serves the compelling governmental interest in lowering the incidence of drug and alcohol use by youth, decreasing crime committed by and against minors, fostering parental involvement in children's conduct, and empowering parents who wish to set limits on their children's nightime activities. . . .

[J]uvenile curfew laws have existed throughout our nation's history, and state and local governmental attempts at enacting constitutional curfew statutes have met with varying degrees of success. See Ramos v. Town of Vernon, 353 F.3d 171, 172 (2d Cir. 2003) (amended Dec. 19, 2003) (Equal Protection challenge to curfew law). In this case, the plaintiffs are concerned with two burdens that the Indianapolis curfew law imposes: the burden on the First Amendment rights of the youths themselves and the burden on the due process rights of the parents and legal guardians to direct their children's upbringing. . . .

We must begin by exploring the baseline question: Do minors have a fundamental right to freedom of expression worthy of constitutional protection? The Supreme Court answered this question affirmatively in Tinker v. Des Moines Indep. Cmty. Sch. Dist., 393 U.S. 503, 511 (1969). It is oft said that those rights are not coextensive with the rights of adults, at least in the context of the rights of students in public schools. Bethel Sch. Dist. No. 403 v. Fraser, 478 U.S. 675, 682 (1986); Hazelwood Sch. Dist. v. Kuhlmeier, 484 U.S. 260, 266 (1988). The question as to whether a minor's First Amendment rights are diluted outside of the school context is not as clear. *Hazelwood*, 484 U.S. at 266 (noting that student speech which disrupts the educational environment need not be tolerated "even though the government could not censor similar speech outside the school").

The strength of our democracy depends on a citizenry that knows and understands its freedoms, exercises them responsibly, and guards them vigilantly. Young adults, as Judge Tinder [in *Hodgkins I*] pointed out, are not suddenly granted the full panoply of constitutional rights on the day they attain the age of majority. We not only permit but expect youths to exercise those liberties — to learn to think for themselves, to give voice to their opinions, to hear and evaluate competing points of view — so that they might attain the right to vote at age eighteen with the tools to exercise that right. A juvenile's ability to worship, associate, and speak freely is therefore not simply a privilege that benefits her as an individual, but a necessary means of allowing her to become a fully enfranchised member of democratic society. "People are unlikely to become well-functioning, independent-minded adults and responsible citizens if they are raised in an intellectual bubble." [American Amusement Mach. Assoc. v. Kendrick, 244 F.3d 572, 577 (7th Cir. 2001).] In short, minors have First Amendment rights worthy of protection. How we balance those rights against other legitimate governmental interests is, of course, the key question in this case and will be discussed at length below.

The Hodgkins maintain that the revisions to the curfew law have not cured the constitutional defect found in the previous version of the law which was struck down by the district court in *Hodgkins I*. The affirmative defenses added to the revised curfew law, they argue, do not adequately protect minors' First Amendment rights, as the curfew law requires them to subject themselves to arrest — including the possibility of breathalyser tests, urine tests and intrusive questioning about their family life — and then prove at a later time that the activity they were engaging in fell within the affirmative defense for First Amendment activity. They assert that the consequences of violating the curfew law are so burdensome and intrusive that, rather than risk arrest, they will be discouraged from participating in expressive activity during curfew hours. In other words, the plaintiffs claim that the curfew regulation creates a "chill" that imposes on their First Amendment rights. . . .

[Our first task] is to decide through which of the many First Amendment lenses we will analyze the constitutionality of the curfew law. [The court adopts an intermediate level of scrutiny applicable to content-neutral government regulations affecting speech.][5]

These intermediate scrutiny tests can be applied only to governmental regulation of conduct that has an expressive element or to regulations directed at activity with no expressive component but which nevertheless impose a disproportionate burden on those engaged in protected First Amendment activity. The government claims that plaintiffs cannot mount a facial challenge to the curfew law . . . because they have not demonstrated either that the curfew law imposes a disproportionate burden on those engaged in First Amendment activities or that it regulates conduct with an expressive element.

We agree that the Indiana curfew ordinance does not disproportionately impact First Amendment rights. As Colin Hodgkins can attest, it burdens minors who want to attend soccer games as much as it burdens those who wish to speak at a political rally. On the other hand, the curfew ordinance regulates minors' abilities to engage

---

[5] Other courts that have reviewed curfew laws challenged on Equal Protection grounds and the right to travel or to free movement have struggled to decide whether minors' constitutional rights should be subject to strict scrutiny, intermediate scrutiny, or an amalgam of both. See Ramos, 353 F.3d 171, 2003 WL 22989226, at *5-6 (including discussion of the various methodologies courts have chosen to incorporate the status of minors into the Equal Protection framework). We find it unnecessary to reach any conclusion regarding the level of scrutiny minors should receive in Equal Protection cases, as the minor plaintiffs in this case challenge the statute on First Amendment grounds only. As we will discuss further, under this type of First Amendment challenge to a content neutral statute, a level of intermediate scrutiny . . . applies.

in some of the purest and most protected forms of speech and expression. As Judge Tinder [in *Hodgkins I*] recognized, a wide range of First Amendment activities occur during curfew hours, including political events, death penalty protests, late night sessions of the Indiana General Assembly, and neighborhood association meetings or nighttime events. *Hodgkins I*, 2000 WL 892964, at *10. A number of religions mark particular days or events with late-night services, prayers, or other activities: many Christians, for example, commemorate the birth of Christ with a midnight service on Christmas Eve and the Last Supper with an all-night vigil on Holy Thursday; Jews observe the first night of Shavuot by studying Torah all through the night; and throughout the month of Ramadan, Muslims engage in late-evening prayer. Late-night or all-night marches, rallies, and sleep-ins are often held to protest government action or inaction. And it is not unusual for political campaigns, particularly in the whirlwind final hours before an election, to hold rallies in the middle of the night. Thus, during the last weeks of the 1960 presidential campaign, then-Senator John F. Kennedy addressed a group of University of Michigan students at 2:00 A.M. on the steps of the Michigan Union. In unprepared remarks, he asked the students whether they would be willing to devote a few years of their lives working in underdeveloped countries in order to foster better relations between the people of those nations and the United States. The students responded with a petition calling for the creation of the Peace Corps, which came into being the following year. These are but a few examples. The curfew ordinance regulates access to almost every form of public expression during the late night hours. The effect on the speech of the plaintiffs is significant.

Despite this extensive regulation, the State of Indiana argues that the curfew law is a general regulation of conduct and not a regulation of expressive conduct. . . . In this case, however, the government regulation of nonspeech (the nocturnal activity of minors) is intimately related to the expressive conduct at issue. Being out in public is a necessary precursor to almost all public forums for speech, expression, and political activity. Its relationship to expressive conduct is intimate and profound.

. . . The lynchpin questions in this case then are first, whether the curfew law furthers an important or substantial governmental interest and, second, whether the restrictions imposed by the curfew regulation are no greater than are essential to further that interest [— that is] whether the statute is narrowly tailored to serve a significant governmental interest — [and] whether the curfew law allows for ample alternative channels for expression.

The district court found that the curfew law advanced the important governmental interest in providing for the safety and well-being of children and combating juvenile crime. *Hodgkins II*, 175 F. Supp. 2d at 1150. Even the plaintiffs agree that the interests asserted by the government are legitimate (though they stop short of calling the interests substantial or important). And we agree that they are indeed important and substantial.

The question remains, however, whether the nexus between the curfew law and those significant governmental interests is close enough to pass constitutional muster. . . . We look to see whether the curfew law is no more restrictive than necessary to further the governmental interest. . . . The district court in *Hodgkins I* concluded that without the affirmative defense, the curfew ordinance indeed did

[handwritten margin note: law does have purpose]

burden speech more than was necessary to serve the state's legitimate interests. *Hodgkins I*, 2000 WL 892964, at *10-11. After the affirmative defense for First Amendment activity was added, however, the district court concluded that the defense sufficiently protected children's abilities to engage in protected communication during curfew hours. *Hodgkins II*, 175 F. Supp. 2d at 1150-51. After all, the court noted,

> an officer would not have probable cause to arrest children who appear to be under the age of 18 and who also appear to be participating in an early morning protest at the Governor's residence. Similarly, an officer would not have probable cause to arrest children apparently under the age of 18 attending Midnight Mass at the Cathedral. In those cases, the officer would have knowledge of facts and circumstances which would conclusively establish the First Amendment activity affirmative defense; the officer would not have to conduct any investigation into the defense as it would be readily apparent that the children were engaging in protected activity. [*Hodgkins II*, 175 F. Supp. 2d at 1149.]

But there is no reason to think that the minors whom the affirmative defense will shield from arrest represent most or even many of those who are at risk of being stopped by the police. A police officer has probable cause to arrest when "the facts and circumstances *within the officer's knowledge* . . . are sufficient to warrant a prudent person, or one of reasonable caution, in believing, in the circumstances shown, that the suspect has committed, is committing, or is about to commit an offense." Michigan v. DeFillippo, 443 U.S. 31, 37 (1979) (emphasis ours). Under Indiana law, "[r]easonable suspicion exists where the facts *known to the officer*, together with the reasonable inferences arising from such facts, would cause an ordinarily prudent person to believe that criminal activity has or is about to occur." Baldwin v. Reagan, 715 N.E.2d 332, 337 (Ind. 1999) (emphasis ours). Once a police officer discovers sufficient facts to establish probable cause, she has no constitutional obligation to conduct any further investigation in the hope of discovering exculpatory evidence. A police officer may not ignore conclusively established evidence of the existence of an affirmative defense, but the officer has no duty to investigate the validity of any defense. In fact, both the defendants in this case and the court below, ruling in their favor, conceded that a police officer need not investigate an individual's claim of an affirmative defense to determine facts unknown to the officer. See *Hodgkins II*, 175 F. Supp. 2d at 1147. A legislature can draft a curfew law which specifies that a law enforcement official must look into whether an affirmative defense applies before making an arrest. See Hutchins v. District of Columbia, 188 F.3d 531, 535 (D.C. Cir. 1999) (en banc) (noting that before police officer may detain juvenile for violation of District of Columbia's curfew ordinance, officer must "reasonably believe . . . that an offense has occurred under the curfew law *and* that no defense exists") (emphasis ours); [Qutb v. Strauss, 11 F.3d 488, 490-491] (noting that Dallas curfew ordinance requires police officer to inquire into minor's reasons for being in public place during curfew hours and permits officer to issue citation or make arrest "only if the officer reasonably believes that the person has violated the ordinance *and* that no defenses apply") (emphasis ours). The Indiana Legislature did not impose that requirement.

Thus, a police officer who actually sees a sixteen-year-old leaving a late-night religious service or political rally could not properly arrest the youth for staying out past curfew. But, as Judge Tinder held, the statute's affirmative defenses do not compel the officer to look beyond what he already knows in order to decide whether one of the affirmative defenses applies. *Hodgkins II*, 175 F. Supp. 2d at 1148. Thus, if a police officer stops a seventeen-year-old on the road at 1:00 A.M., and the teen informs the officer that she is returning home from a midnight political rally, the officer need not take the teen at her word nor attempt to ascertain whether she is telling the truth. Lacking first-hand knowledge that the juvenile indeed has been participating in First Amendment activity, the officer is free to arrest her and leave assessment of the First Amendment or any other affirmative defense for a judicial officer. . . . Any juvenile who chooses to participate in a late-night religious or political activity thus runs the risk that he will be arrested if a police officer stops him en route to or from that activity and he cannot prove to the officer's satisfaction that he is out after hours in order to exercise his First Amendment rights.

Consequently, because the defense imposes no duty of investigation on the arresting officer, as a practical matter it protects only those minors whom the officer has actually seen participating in protected activity. This strikes us as a small subset of minors participating in late-night First Amendment activities, and therefore we conclude that the statute reaches a substantial amount of protected conduct. . . .

Furthermore, we think the district court took too narrow a view when determining that the curfew law left open adequate alternative channels of communication. Judge Tinder noted that minors could engage in protected activity during the ample non-curfew hours, during curfew hours under the shield of the affirmative defense, when accompanied by an authorized adult, or within the confines of their home by telephone or through the internet. No doubt many if not most of the participants would find it more convenient to exercise their First Amendment rights other than in the dead of night. It is by no means a coincidence, however, that so many of the expressive activities we illustrated above occur late in the evening. In some instances, the late hour of the activity may be dictated by necessity — as, for example, when citizens wish to observe or influence a legislative session that extends into the late hours, or a down-to-the-wire election postpones a celebration for the winning candidate until the wee hours of the morning. More often, however, the late hour is closely linked with the purpose and message of the activity. Take Back the Night marches and rallies frequently extend to and after midnight in order to protest the crimes that jeopardize the security of women at night. Executions of prisoners on death row often are carried out shortly after midnight or in the early hours of the day, and so are routinely attended by all-night vigils held by those for and against the death penalty. Kristallnacht (Night of Glass) is commemorated with late-night prayers and vigils because it was after midnight one evening sixty-five years ago when Nazi hooligans looted and destroyed Jewish businesses, homes, and synagogues in Germany. In the final days of Ramadan, mosques remain open all night so that Muslims may mark Lailat al-Qadr (Night of Power), the night when the prophet Mohammed first received revelations from the angel Jibra'el (Gabriel), by holding vigil in prayer, Qur'anic reading, and contemplation. And it was after midnight one evening in October 1998 when young Matthew Shepard was beaten, burned, and lashed to a fence, and left for dead outside of Laramie, Wyoming;

and so it is that candlelight vigils were and are held in the middle of the night to protest the homophobia that motivated his killers. Thus, to the extent that the curfew prevents a minor from being outside of the home during curfew hours, it does not mean simply that she must shift the exercise of her First Amendment rights to noncurfew hours or to the telephone or internet; it means that she must surrender her right to participate in late-night activities whose context and message are tied to the late hour and the public forum. There is no internet connection, no telephone call, no television coverage that can compare to attending a political rally in person, praying in the sanctuary of one's choice side-by-side with other worshipers, feeling the energy of the crowd as a victorious political candidate announces his plans for the new administration, holding hands with other mourners at a candlelight vigil, or standing in front of the seat of state government as a legislative session winds its way into the night. . . .

Granted, Indiana's curfew does not forbid minors from exercising their First Amendment rights during curfew hours, but it does forcefully discourage the exercise of those rights. The First Amendment defense will shield a minor from conviction, assuming that she can prove to the satisfaction of a judge that she was exercising her First Amendment rights, but, as discussed, it will not shield her from arrest if the officer who stops her has not actually seen her participating in a religious service, political rally, or other First Amendment event. The prospect of an arrest is intimidating in and of itself; but one should also have in mind what else might follow from the arrest [as did occur in this case]. We have no doubt that the authorities are well meaning in administering the drug and alcohol testing and in questioning the minor and his parents about his friends and family life. But these are also rather serious intrusions upon one's personal and familial privacy, and they represent a substantial price for a minor to have to pay in order to take part in a late-night political or religious event. The chill that the prospect of arrest imposes on a minor's exercise of his or her First Amendment rights is patent.

The only way that a minor can avoid this risk is to find a parent or another adult designated by his parent to accompany him. See Ind. Code §31-37-3-3.5(b)(1), (2). But that alternative itself burdens a minor's expressive rights: adults may be reluctant or unable to accompany the minor to a late-night activity; a seventeen-year-old attending college away from home may be unable to recruit a parent or designated adult; and the minor himself may decide that participation is not worth the bother if he must bring a parent or other adult along with him. To condition the exercise of First Amendment rights on the willingness of an adult to chaperone is to curtail them. . . .

In sum, we hold that the curfew law, even with the new affirmative defenses for First Amendment activity, is not narrowly tailored to serve a significant governmental interest and fails to allow for ample alternative channels for expression. . . .

NOTES AND QUESTIONS ON CURFEWS

(1) Background.   The central issue in the litigation regarding curfew ordinances concerns their constitutionality. The United States Supreme Court was first presented with the constitutionality of a curfew ordinance in Bykofsky v.

Middletown, 401 F. Supp. 1242 (M.D. Pa. 1975), *aff'd*, 535 F.2d 1245, *cert. denied*, 429 U.S. 964 (1976), challenged on grounds of vagueness, minors' due process rights, minors' First Amendment rights, the right to travel, parents' rights to direct the upbringing of their children, and minors' right to equal protection. The district court upheld the ordinance with the exception of a few vague words and phrases, which it deleted. The Third Circuit Court of Appeals affirmed. The Supreme Court denied certiorari, but three Justices (White, Marshall, and Brennan) indicated that they would have granted certiorari and set the case for oral argument. Justice Marshall, joined by Justice Brennan, dissented from the denial of certiorari as follows:

> The freedom to leave one's house and move about at will is "of the very essence of a scheme of ordered liberty," Palko v. Connecticut, 302 U.S. 319, 325 (1937), and hence is protected against state intrusions by the Due Process of the Fourteenth Amendment. To justify a law that significantly intrudes on this freedom, therefore, a State must demonstrate that the law is "narrowly drawn" to further a "compelling state interest." . . . I have little doubt but that, absent a genuine emergency, a curfew aimed at all citizens could not survive constitutional scrutiny. . . .
>
> The question squarely presented by this case, then, is whether the due process rights of juveniles are entitled to lesser protection than those of adults. The prior decisions of this Court provide no clear answer. We have recognized that, "Constitutional rights do not mature and come into being magically only when one attains the state defined age of majority. Minors, as well as adults, are protected by the Constitution and possess constitutional rights." Planned Parenthood v. Danforth, 428 U.S. 52 (1976); see also Tinker v. Des Moines Independent Community School Dist., 393 U.S. 503, 511 (1969). But we also have acknowledged that "the State has somewhat broader authority to regulate the activities of children than of adults." Planned Parenthood v. Danforth, supra; see also Ginsberg v. New York, 390 U.S. 629 (1968); Prince v. Massachusetts, 321 U.S. 158 (1944). Not surprisingly, therefore, the lower courts have reached conflicting conclusions in addressing the issue raised here.
>
> Because I believe this case poses a substantial constitutional question — one which is of great importance to thousands of towns with similar ordinances — I would grant a writ of certiorari. [429 U.S. 964 (1976).]

Federal courts continue to reach "conflicting conclusions" regarding the constitutionality of curfew ordinances. Compare Hutchins v. District of Columbia, 188 F.3d 531 (D.C. Cir. 1999) (en banc); Schliefer v. City of Charlottesville, 159 F.3d 843 (4th Cir. 1998); Qutb v. Strauss, 11 F.3d 488, 492 (5th Cir. 1993) (upholding curfew laws), with Ramos v. Town of Vernon, 353 F.3d 171 (2d Cir. 2003); Nunez v. City of San Diego, 114 F.3d 935 (9th Cir. 1997) (contra). For recent state court decisions, see State v. J.P., — So.2d. —, 2004 WL 2609242 (Fla. 2004); City of Sumner v. Walsh, 61 P.3d 1111 (Wash. 2003) (both invalidating juvenile curfew ordinances).

(2) Applicable Level of Scrutiny.   The success of challenges to juvenile curfew laws often depends on the level of scrutiny applied by particular courts to evaluate juveniles' constitutional rights. Courts differ on the level of scrutiny applicable to juvenile curfew laws. (The level of scrutiny dictates the level of protection given to a constitutional right. Ordinances that infringe upon fundamental rights are given strict scrutiny.) What level of scrutiny did the *Hodgkins II* court apply to invalidate the Indiana curfew ordinance? Note that other courts have applied a higher level

of scrutiny based on their perception of the federal or state constitutional right at issue. See Nunez v. City of San Diego, 114 F.3d 935, 944-946 (9th Cir. 1997) (finding juveniles' fundamental rights implicated and applying strict scrutiny); State v. J.P., supra (applying strict scrutiny to infringement on juveniles' rights to privacy and travel). What level of constitutional scrutiny do you think is appropriate? See generally Calvin Massey, Juvenile Curfews and Fundamental Rights Methodology, 27 Hastings Const. L.Q. 775 (2000) (comparing the different approaches of federal courts of appeal).

(3) Equal Protection. Some courts (e.g., *Bykofsky*, supra; *Hutchins*, supra) have held that curfew laws do not violate minors' right to equal protection, reasoning that minors are subject to greater governmental regulation of their conduct. Other courts have disagreed that the constitutional rights of minors are less deserving of protection that those of adults. See, e.g., Waters v. Barry, 711 F. Supp. 1125 (D.D.C. 1989). The Supreme Court has recognized three reasons to allow courts to treat the rights of minors differently from those of adults: the peculiar vulnerability of youth, their inability to make critical decisions in an informed mature manner, and the importance of the parental role in childrearing. Bellotti v. Baird, 443 U.S. 622, 634 (1979). How applicable is the *Bellotti* rationale, developed for juvenile abortion decision making, to the curfew context? Compare People ex rel. J.M., 768 P.2d 219 (Colo. 1989); Village of Deerfield v. Greenberg, 550 N.E.2d 12 (Ill. App. Ct. 1990) (relying on *Bellotti* rationale to uphold juvenile curfew ordinances) with Johnson v. City of Opelousas, 658 F.2d 1065 (5th Cir. 1981); Waters v. Barry, supra (relying on *Bellotti* rationale to invalidate juvenile curfew ordinances).

(4) Exemptions. Many juvenile curfew laws, like those of Indiana in *Hodgkins*, contain exceptions for various juvenile activities. Second-generation curfew laws are more narrowly drawn than the curfew laws of the 1960s and 1970s (i.e., they contain more exceptions) in an effort to pass constitutional muster. Common exceptions include parental consent or travel for work- or school-related purposes.

Some recent decisions, such as *Hodgkins II*, invalidate curfew laws for failure to include an exception that allows the expression of minors' First Amendment rights. After the district court initially enjoined the statute, the state legislature amended the statute to include a First Amendment exception. Why does the court in the principal case find that the curfew law with its First Amendment exception is still unconstitutional? See also City of Maquoketa v. Russell, 484 N.W.2d 179 (Iowa 1992) (similarly invalidating ordinance on First Amendment grounds). How should the state legislature amend the Indiana statute to shift the burden *from* youth to prove their activity exempts them from the curfew — *to* police to determine that a youth is not engaged in protected First Amendment activities?

(5) Parental rights. Many courts have considered whether juvenile curfew laws interfere with parental rights by injecting government in the role of childrearing. Do juvenile curfews promote the role of parents in childrearing or infringe on parental rights? How do *Meyer*, *Pierce*, and *Prince* affect the analysis? Although the holding in *Hodgkins II* rendered it unnecessary to rule on the parents' due process claims, the court did make the following observations on the issue:

> In this case, the exceptions covering a broad variety of circumstances do give parents greater flexibility to allow their children to stay out after hours and in

that way minimize the interference with parental autonomy. But the affirmative defenses in the Indiana curfew statute present a risk that a minor will be arrested whenever the arresting officer lacks direct knowledge that the minor is on an emergency errand, coming from a school sanctioned activity, or engaging in some other activity encompassed by the specified defenses. For that reason, we are not convinced that the affirmative defenses actually do minimize the state's restraint on parental authority in a manner sufficient to overcome a constitutional attack. 355 F.3d at 1065.

In contrast, many courts have held that the curfew laws do not violate parents' constitutional rights. See, e.g., Hutchins v. District of Columbia, supra; Schleifer v. City of Charlottesville, supra; Treacy v. Municipality of Anchorage, 91 P.3d 252 (Alaska 2004); Panora v. Simmons, 445 N.W.2d 363 (Iowa 1989).

(6) Social Interests. What social interests are served by juvenile curfews, according to the defendants in *Hodgkins II*? Historically, curfews have functioned as a vehicle of social control. Prior to the Civil War, Southern towns enacted curfew ordinances to prohibit the presence of slaves and free blacks on public streets during certain hours. Peter L. Scherr, Note, The Juvenile Curfew Ordinance: In Search of a New Standard of Review, 41 J. Urb. & Contemp. L. 163, 164-165 (1992). Curfew ordinances were enacted in the 1890s to decrease crime among immigrant youth. Later, they were perceived as an effective method of control for parents who were busy helping with the war effort during World War II. Current ordinances have been enacted in response to problems of drugs and/or crime. To the extent that the purpose of juvenile curfew laws is to control juvenile crime, particularly gang activity, why not limit the application of curfew laws to prohibit groups of people on the street late at night? For further issues relating to gangs and juvenile delinquency, see Chapter 7.

Some commentators suggest that juvenile curfews disproportionately target minority youth. See Carol M. Bast & K. Michael Reynolds, A New Look at Juvenile Curfews: Are They Effective?, 39 Crim. L. Bull. 5 (May 2003); Ronald Smothers, Atlanta Sets a Curfew for Youths, Prompting Concern on Race Bias, N.Y. Times, Nov. 20, 1990, at A1. Data also suggest that enforcement of curfew restrictions disproportionately targets females. Howard N. Snyder, Juvenile Arrests 2002, Juvenile Justice Bulletin (Office of Juvenile Justice & Delinquency Prevention, Sept. 2004) at 8 (juvenile arrest rate for female curfew violators is significantly higher than for males).

(7) Deterrent Effect of Curfew Laws. Do curfew laws prevent crime and victimization? Most studies observe no change in crime rates upon implementation of a new or revised curfew law. While some studies note a decrease in certain types of crimes (e.g., criminal mischief), other studies actually report a slight increase in violent crimes and felonies. See Kenneth Adams, The Effectiveness of Juvenile Curfews at Crime Prevention, 587 Annals of Am. Acad. of Pol. & Soc. Sci. 136 (May 1, 2003); Center on Juvenile and Criminal Justice, Impact of Juvenile Curfew Laws in California 1, 3, available at *www.cjcj.org/pubs/curfew* (last visited Jan. 6, 2005) (finding that "[c]urfew enforcement generally had no discernible effect on youth crime").

For further commentary on juvenile curfews, see Deirdre Norton, Why Criminalize Children? Looking Beyond the Express Policies Driving Juvenile Curfew

Legislation, 4 N.Y.U. J. Legis. & Pub. Pol'y 175 (2000); Todd Kaminsky, Rethinking Judicial Attitudes Toward Freedom of Association Challenges to Teen Curfews: The First Amendment Exception Explored, 78 N.Y.U. L. Rev. 2278 (2003); Cheri L. Lichtensteiger Baden, Note, When the Open Road Is Closed to Juveniles: The Constitutionality of Juvenile Curfew Laws and the Inconsistencies Among the Courts, 37 Val. U. L. Rev. 831 (2003); Adam W. Poff, Comment: A Tale of Two Curfews (And One City): What Do Two Washington, D.C. Juvenile Curfews Say About the Constitutional Interpretations of District of Columbia Courts and the Confusion Over Juvenile Curfews Everywhere?, 46 Vill. L. Rev. 277 (2001).

G.   *"STATUS" OFFENSES*

> If a man has a stubborn and rebellious son, who will not obey his father or his mother who will not listen to them even when they chastise him, then his father and mother shall lay hands upon him and bring him before the sheikhs of his town at the local gateway, telling the sheikhs of his town, "This son of ours is a stubborn and rebellious fellow who will not obey our orders: he is a spendthrift and is a drunkard." Whereupon all his fellow-citizens shall stone him to death. So shall you eradicate evil from you, and all Israel shall hear and fear. [Deuteronomy 21:18-21.]

1.   Status Offense Jurisdiction of the Juvenile Court

In re Walker
191 S.E.2d 702 (N.C. 1972)

On 2 August 1971 Mrs. Katherine Walker, mother of Valerie Lenise Walker, filed a petition in the district court alleging [that Valerie was an "undisciplined child as defined by G.S. §7A-278"]. . . .

The matter came on for hearing before Judge Gentry on 17 August 1971. Valerie was present with her mother and the court counselor, Mrs. Ann M. Jones. Valerie was not represented by an attorney at this hearing. Judge Gentry heard evidence and found (a) that Valerie Lenise Walker . . . is a child under sixteen years of age in the custody and under the supervision and control of her parents . . . ; (b) that Valerie has been regularly disobedient to her parents in that she goes and comes without permission, keeps late hours, associates with persons that her parents object to, and goes to places where her parents tell her not to go; and (c) that Valerie is an undisciplined child and in need of the discipline and supervision of the State. This order was signed on 19 August 1971.

Based on the foregoing findings, it was ordered, adjudged and decreed that Valerie was an undisciplined child within the meaning of the law. She was placed on probation subject to the following conditions:

1. That she be of good behavior and conduct herself in a law-abiding manner;
2. That she mind and obey her parents and not leave home without permission and

then to go only to places that she has permission to go and return as directed; 3. That she attend school regularly during the school year and obey the school rules and regulations; 4. That she report to the court counselor as directed, truthfully answer questions put to her concerning her conduct, behavior, associates and activities and carry out requests given her concerning such; 5. That this matter be reopened for further orders on March 22, 1972. . . .

Thereafter on 21 September 1971 Ann M. Jones, Court Counselor, filed a verified petition and motion in the cause for further consideration and review of the case, alleging:

> That the said child is a delinquent child as defined by G.S. §7A-278(2) in that the said child has violated Conditions No. 1, 2, and 3 of the probation order dated August 19, 1971, in that the said child continuously disobeys her parents in that she goes and comes as she pleases; keeps late hours; and frequents places not approved by her parents; further, the said child refuses to obey school rules and regulations in that she misbehaves in the classroom and is disrespectful to school officials; further, the said child is beyond the control of her parents.

A juvenile summons was thereupon issued and served upon Valerie and her parents, notifying them to appear in juvenile court for a further hearing. . . .

Prior to the hearing the public defender . . . was appointed to represent Valerie, and the matter came on for hearing before Judge Gentry on 15 October 1971. . . .

Prior to the introduction of evidence, Valerie's counsel moved to vacate the order dated 19 August 1971 finding that Valerie was an undisciplined child and placing her on probation for that she was not represented by counsel at that time and was unable to defend herself on the charge that she was an undisciplined child, resulting in a denial of due process. Her counsel further moved to dismiss the petition and motion in the cause filed 21 September 1971 [because] G.S. §7A-278 violates the Equal Protection Clause of the Fourteenth Amendment in that the statute provides for an adjudication of delinquency when the respondent has violated none of the laws of the State of North Carolina. Both motions were denied and respondent duly excepted.

Katherine Walker, mother of Valerie, testified that she lives with her husband and seven small children, including Valerie; that she and her husband both work and that Valerie is usually not at home when she returns from work; that Valerie fails to do the chores which have been assigned to her, such as cleaning her room, the bathroom, and taking her turn washing dishes; that when Valerie comes home she usually says she has been at Mrs. Cunningham's house with Vanessa Cunningham; that Valerie has been told not to leave home without telling her mother where she is going but she continues to disobey in that respect; that Valerie keeps late hours and sometimes comes in at eleven, twelve, one and two o'clock at night; that Valerie has been to Paradise Inn in violation of parental instructions; that Paradise Inn sells beer and has a bad reputation and is no place for a fourteen-year-old girl; that during Valerie's nocturnal absences her parents do not know where she is.

Mrs. Walker further testified that she is the mother of ten children; that Valerie is lazy and disobedient; that Valerie signed for a registered letter from school officials, addressed to her mother, and then destroyed the letter. Mrs. Walker said: "All I want her to do is to behave like a fourteen year old should."

Howard King, Assistant Principal at Mendenhall Junior High School, testified that Valerie came to his school on September 8, 1971, and was placed in special education with a group of students who had similar defects in adjusting; that . . . he saw Valerie in his office many times on referral from all of her teachers except one for disrupting the class; that he had numerous conferences with Valerie and specifically recalls one problem which arose due to Valerie's refusal . . . to dress for physical education practically every day . . . ; that he could not communicate very well with Valerie because she sucked her thumb, did not talk for a while, "and when she does start talking it's almost impossible to keep her from talking and it doesn't have any meaning to what we're talking about when she comes to the office. . . . It was not something that was relevant."

Mr. King further testified that Valerie was large for her age and as compared to the other children in the class; that Valerie was sent by her teachers to the office practically every day, does not fit into the classroom and disrupts whatever the teachers try to do; that he would have suspended her each day but had no way to get her home; that he simply required her to sit in the office and occasionally she would leave the office without permission; that Valerie does not respond to any methods of discipline available at the school.

The probation officer testified that Valerie had problems at her previous school similar to those described by Mr. King; that her attitude was bad toward her probation officer as well as others and that her behavior has not shown improvement; that Valerie does not have a receptive attitude toward her probation officer or the school or her mother in regard to discipline.

The respondent elected to offer no evidence and moved to dismiss the proceeding at the close of all the evidence. The motion was denied, and under date of 27 October 1971 Judge Gentry signed an order providing in pertinent part as follows:

> The court finds, upon hearing evidence, that the child was before the court on August 17, 1971 and that she was adjudged to be an undisciplined child and placed on probation, one of the conditions of probation being that she be of good behavior and conduct herself in a law-abiding manner; another condition being that she mind and obey her mother and not be away from home without permission. Another condition was that she attend school regularly and obey the school rules and regulations. The court finds that the said child did not obey her parents in that she left home without permission and did keep late hours at night. That she went to places that she was told not to go to by her parents and that she failed to do chores assigned to her by her mother. The court further finds that the child was sent out of the classroom in school a number of times for disobeying the teachers and disturbing the class. That she also refused to dress for her Physical Education classes without giving any reasons for doing so. The court finds that these acts of the child constitute a violation of the conditions of probation and that she is a delinquent child for having violated the conditions of probation and that she is in need of the discipline and supervision of the state. The court further finds that since September 21, 1971, the said child has been a constant behavior problem in school and has not responded to disciplinary actions taken and that she continues

to disobey her mother. The court finds that she is in need of more discipline and supervision than can be provided for her within Guilford County.

It is now therefore ordered, adjudged and decreed that Valerie Walker, having been found to be a delinquent child, that the said child is hereby committed to the North Carolina Board of Juvenile Correction and is to be in the custody and under the control and supervision of the officials thereof until discharged. [S]he is to remain in the temporary custody of the court until she can be delivered to the designated correction school. . . .

> *B. Gordon Gentry*
> *Judge presiding*

From the foregoing order respondent appealed to the Court of Appeals which found no error. Respondent thereupon appealed to the Supreme Court . . . asserting involvement of substantial constitutional questions. . . .

HUSKINS, Justice.

Appellant Valerie Walker contends that she had a constitutional right to counsel at the hearing on the initial petition alleging her to be an *undisciplined* child. We first consider whether the Constitution affords her such right.

In In re Gault, 387 U.S. 1 (1967), the United States Supreme Court held, inter alia, that

> the Due Process Clause of the Fourteenth Amendment requires that in respect of proceedings to determine delinquency which may result in commitment to an institution in which the juvenile's freedom is curtailed, the child and his parents must be notified of the child's right to be represented by counsel retained by them, or if they are unable to afford counsel, that counsel will be appointed to represent the child.

A similar statutory right to counsel for indigent juveniles at a hearing which could result in commitment to an institution is afforded by G.S. §7A-451(a)(8).

The initial petition alleging that Valerie was an *undisciplined* child was heard on August 17, 1971. At that time the 1969 version of Article 23, Chapter 7A of the North Carolina General Statutes (Jurisdiction and Procedure Applicable to Children) was in effect. . . .

> (1) "Child" is any person who has not reached his sixteenth birthday.
>
> (2) "Delinquent child" includes any child who has committed any criminal offense under State law or under an ordinance of local government . . . or a child who has violated the conditions of his probation under this article. . . .
>
> (5) "Undisciplined child" includes any child who is unlawfully absent from school, or who is regularly disobedient to his parents or guardian or custodian and beyond their disciplinary control, or who is regularly found in places where it is unlawful for a child to be, or who has run away from home.

G.S. §7A-286(1969) . . . makes the following alternatives available to any judge exercising juvenile jurisdiction: "(4) In the case of any child who is delinquent or undisciplined, the court may: a. Place the child on probation . . . ; or b. Continue the case . . . ; or, *if the child is delinquent*, the court may: c. Commit the child to the care of the North Carolina Board of Juvenile Correction . . . . " (Emphasis added.)

Despite the somewhat awkward structure of G.S. §7A-286 (1969), it is clear that under its terms, no judge exercising juvenile jurisdiction had any authority upon finding the child to be *undisciplined* to commit such child to the Board of Juvenile Correction for assignment to a State facility in which the juvenile's freedom is curtailed. The statute permitted incarceration of *delinquent* children only.

Therefore, we hold that neither *Gault*, supra, nor G.S. §7A-451(a)(8) afforded Valerie Walker the right to counsel at the hearing on the initial petition alleging her to be an undisciplined child, for under the wording of G.S. §7A-286(4) (1969) that hearing could not result in her commitment to an institution in which her freedom would be curtailed. Nor would there be such a right under the statute as presently written. See G.S. §7A-286(5) (1971).

Appellant would have this Court go further than *Gault* requires. She argues for the right to counsel at the hearing of an *undisciplined child* petition on the theory that such a hearing is a critical stage in the juvenile process since it subjects the child to the risk of probation and since a violation of probation means that the child is *delinquent* and subject to commitment. In such fashion appellant seeks to engraft upon the juvenile process the "critical stage" test used by the United States Supreme Court in determining the scope of the Sixth Amendment right to counsel in *criminal prosecutions*. We find no authority for such engraftment. Whatever may be the proper classification for a juvenile proceeding in which the child is alleged to be undisciplined, it certainly is not a criminal prosecution within the meaning of the Sixth Amendment which guarantees the assistance of counsel. . . .

The right to counsel delineated in *Gault* has not been extended to other procedural steps in juvenile proceedings. Neither this Court nor the United States Supreme Court has ever applied the "critical stage" test to the juvenile process. Accordingly, we hold that counsel is not constitutionally required at the hearing on an *undisciplined child* petition. See In re Gault, supra (n.48) in which it is stated: "[W]hat we hold in this opinion with regard to the procedural requirements at the adjudicatory stage has no necessary applicability to other steps of the juvenile process."

The fact that a child initially has been found to be undisciplined and placed on probation is merely incidental to a later petition and motion alleging delinquency based on violation of the terms of probation. The initial finding can never legally result in commitment to an institution in which the juvenile's freedom is curtailed. It is only the latter petition and motion, and the finding that the child is a *delinquent* child by reason of its conduct since the initial hearing, that may result in the child's commitment. . . .

Appellant's second contention is that G.S. §7A-286 violates the Equal Protection Clause of the Fourteenth Amendment in that it subjects an undisciplined child to probation and the concomitant risk of incarceration when the child has committed no criminal offense, while adults are subjected to probation and incarceration only for actual criminal offenses. . . .

The purpose of the Juvenile Court Act "is not for the punishment of offenders but for the salvation of children." Commonwealth v. Fisher, 213 Pa. 48, 62 A. 198 (1905). The Act treats "delinquent children not as criminals, but as wards, and undertakes . . . to give them the control and environment that may lead to their reformation, and enable them to become law-abiding and useful citizens. . . ." State v. Burnett, 179 N.C. 735, 102 S.E. 711 (1920). The State must exercise its power as "parens patriae to protect and provide for the comfort and well-being of such of its citizens as by reason of infancy . . . are unable to take care of themselves." County of McLean v. Humphreys, 104 Ill. 378 (1882). Thus, juveniles are in need of supervision and control due to their inability to protect themselves. In contrast, adults are regarded as self sufficient.

Therefore, the classification here challenged is based on differences between adults and children; and there are so many valid distinctions that the basis for challenge seems shallow. These differences are "reasonably related to the purposes of the Act." . . . Consequently, the classification does not offend the Equal Protection Clause. [I]t is our view that the desire of the State to exercise its authority as parens patriae and provide for the care and protection of its children supplies a "compellingly rational" justification for the classification.

The conclusion we reach — that G.S. §7A-278 and related statutes do not violate the Equal Protection Clause by classifying and treating children differently from adults — has also been reached in numerous cases upholding juvenile Acts in other states. [Citations omitted]. . . .

Appellant makes the further contention that North Carolina's statutory scheme, G.S. §§7A-278(5), 7A-285 and 7A-286(2) and (4), allowing a child to be adjudged *undisciplined* and placed on probation *without benefit of counsel*, while at the same time requiring counsel before a child may be adjudged *delinquent*, denies equal protection of the laws to the undisciplined child.

This argument has no merit and cannot be sustained. The Equal Protection Clause is offended only if the classifications of "undisciplined" and "delinquent" rest on grounds wholly irrelevant to the achievement of the State's objective. . . . In seeking solutions which provide in each case for the protection, treatment, rehabilitation and correction of the child, it is impellingly relevant to the achievement of the State's objective that distinctions be made between undisciplined children on the one hand and delinquent children on the other. The one may need protection while the other needs correction. . . .

Finally, appellant urges that the trial judge's failure to state in his order that he found "beyond a reasonable doubt" that appellant had violated the conditions of her probation was constitutional error under In re Winship, 397 U.S. 358 (1970).

In *Winship*, the juvenile was accused of stealing $112 from a woman's pocketbook. . . . The juvenile was adjudged delinquent and placed in a training school, subject to confinement for as long as six years. The juvenile judge acknowledged that pursuant to a New York statute his determination of the delinquency issue was based on a preponderance of the evidence. The juvenile, contending that due process required proof beyond a reasonable doubt, carried the case by successive appeals to the Supreme Court of the United States. The Court held that the Due Process Clause requires proof beyond a reasonable doubt in delinquency proceedings wherein the child is charged with an act that would constitute a crime if committed by an adult. Here, Valerie Walker was charged with delinquency by reason of probation violations, none of which violations amounted to a crime. See G.S. §7A-278(2). Therefore, *Winship* does not apply to these findings. . . .

For the reasons stated, the result reached by the Court of Appeals upholding the order entered by Judge Gentry is

Affirmed.

BOBBITT, Chief Justice (dissenting). . . .

G.S. §7A-285 includes the following: "In cases where the petition alleges that a child is delinquent *or* undisciplined *and* where the child *may* be committed to a State institution, the child shall have a right to assigned counsel as provided by law in cases of indigency." (Our italics.)

Valerie was found delinquent and committed solely on the ground she had violated certain of the probation conditions imposed when she was adjudicated an "undisciplined child" on August 19th. The adjudication that she was an "undisciplined child" was absolutely essential to a valid commitment for violation of probation conditions. The Court holds that she was entitled to assigned counsel *only at the final hearing* to determine whether the probation conditions had been violated. In my opinion, she was equally entitled to assigned counsel at the earlier hearing to determine whether she should be adjudged an "undisciplined child."

Here a fourteen-year-old girl was brought before the juvenile court upon the complaint of her mother. Absent counsel, she stood alone before the court. In addition to the statutory requirement, it is my opinion that due process required that counsel be assigned to represent her at any hearing which might result in an adjudication prejudicial to her.

For the reasons indicated, I would reverse the decision of the Court of Appeals, vacate Judge Gentry's order of October 27, 1971, and remand the case with direction that a plenary hearing be conducted when Valerie is represented by counsel for de novo consideration and determination of the charge in the original petition that she is an "undisciplined child."

District of Columbia v. B.J.R.

332 A.2d 58 (D.C.), *cert. denied*, 421 U.S. 1016 (1975)

YEAGLEY, Associate Judge.

This is an appeal from an order of the Family Division dismissing a petition, as amended, filed under D.C. Code 1973, §16-2301(8)(A)(iii) and 16-2301(8)(B), on the ground that the definition of "children in need of supervision" in that statute (hereinafter CINS) is "unconstitutionally vague" and cannot be saved by reasonable construction. The amended petition alleged that the appellee was a "child in need of supervision in that she is habitually disobedient of the reasonable and lawful commands of her parent and is ungovernable." Appellee was specifically charged with absconding from home in April and October 1969, in June and August of 1972, and on February 26, 1973. The last three abscondances were within the nine months preceding the March 6, 1973, filing of the CINS petition in the trial court.

The pertinent portion of §16-2301 reads as follows: . . . "(8) The term 'child in need of supervision' means a child who — . . . (iii) is habitually disobedient of the reasonable and lawful commands of his parent, guardian, or other custodian and is ungovernable; and (B) is in need of care or rehabilitation." The sole issue on appeal is whether or not this language under attack for vagueness passes constitutional muster. We find that it does.

The Supreme Court in Parker v. Levy, 417 U.S. 733, 752 (1974), recently summarized the due process elements of the "void-for-vagueness" doctrine:

> The doctrine incorporates notions of fair notice or warning. Moreover, it requires legislatures to set reasonably clear guidelines for law enforcement officials and triers of fact in order to prevent "arbitrary and discriminatory enforcement." Where a statute's literal scope, unaided by narrowing state court interpretation, is capable of reaching expression sheltered by the First Amendment, the doctrine demands a greater degree of specificity than in other contexts. Smith v. Goguen, 415 U.S. 566, 572-573 (1974).

It is difficult to perceive how our CINS statute could violate these requirements when considered in regard to the conduct of the appellee.

Children of ordinary understanding know that to repeatedly abscond from home in defiance of the lawful commands of one's parent is a rather drastic form of disobedience that may well precipitate some disciplinary or punitive action. The statute here gave the appellee adequate warning that to abscond from home five times in four years, three of those times within the nine months preceding the instant petition, would subject her to the sanctions provided for a child who "is habitually disobedient of the reasonable and lawful commands of [her] parent. . . . " Such conduct establishes the "frequent practice or habit acquired over a period of time" required to satisfy the "habitually" element as that term was authoritatively construed under an earlier version of our juvenile statute in In re Elmore, D.C. App., 222 A.2d 255, 258-259 (1966), *rev'd on other grounds*, 127 U.S. App. D.C. 176, 382 F.2d 125 (1967).

When a child's conduct clearly falls within the common understanding of the statutory language, the officials charged with enforcing the CINS statute are not compelled to make arbitrary decisions in applying it to juveniles such as the appellee. If a parent makes reasonable efforts to control a child from running away, it seems clear that the child is "ungovernable" in his present home situation and may be in need of closer supervision than is available at home. Section 16-2301 (8) was explicitly designed to provide such supervision.

While it may be said that the wording of the CINS statute is somewhat broad and general, we must recognize, as did the Supreme Court . . . that " . . . there are limitations in the English language with respect to being both specific and manageably brief, and it seems to us that although the prohibitions may not satisfy those intent on finding fault at any cost, they are set out in terms that the ordinary person exercising ordinary common sense can sufficiently understand and comply with, without sacrifice to the public interest." [United States Civil Service Commn. v. National Assn. of Letter Carriers, 413 U.S. 548, 578-579 (1973).]

Our juvenile code, particularly the CINS section, is not a criminal statute in the ordinary sense. Further, language limitations are particularly acute for the draftsmen of juvenile laws designed to implement the broad social policy of reinforcing parents in carrying out their responsibility to support and promote the welfare of their children. To enable parents to carry out this legal obligation, the law gives them the authority to control their children through the giving of reasonable and lawful commands. The CINS statute reinforces this authority and may be invoked when children repeatedly refuse to recognize their obligation to obey such commands.

The court is also mindful that our present CINS statute, adopted in 1970, is the product of highly competent, contemporaneous legal expertise in the drafting of juvenile court statutes. The definition of "children in need of supervision" is substantially identical to those proposed in the Uniform Juvenile Court Act (U.L.A.) §2(4)(1973) and the Legislative Guide for Drafting Family and Juvenile Court Acts §2(p) (Dept. of H.E.W., Children's Bureau Pub. No. 472-1969). The 1970 statute eliminated, inter alia, troublesome language from D.C. Code 1967, §§111551(a)(1)(H) and (1), which gave the juvenile court jurisdiction over children who engaged in "immoral" activities.[3] Neither the lower court nor the appellee has provided us with convincing suggestions for further improvement in our present act....

Our conclusion that the CINS statute is not unconstitutionally vague is supported by the overwhelming weight of authority from other jurisdictions which have considered the validity of juvenile statutes with similar language. [Citations omitted].... Interpretations by sister jurisdictions of statutory language so strikingly parallel to our own cannot be dismissed, as the trial court attempted to do, merely because the language is not "identical" or is a "less-than-perfect fit."

The trial court, in finding the CINS statute unconstitutionally vague, limited itself to an examination of the statute's facial validity without consideration of whether its language gave one such as the appellee fair warning that to repeatedly abscond from home would subject her to CINS sanctions. Appellee attempts to continue this line of reasoning on appeal by anticipating potentially abusive applications of the statute in a variety of hypothetical situations, particularly emphasizing possible infringements upon First Amendment rights of children. But the Supreme Court in Parker v. Levy, supra, 417 U.S., at 759, rejected that approach when it said: ... "[e]mbedded in the traditional rules governing constitutional adjudication is the principle that a person to whom a statute may constitutionally be applied will not be heard to challenge that statute on the ground that it may conceivably be applied unconstitutionally to others, in other situations not before the Court." [Broadrick v. Oklahoma, 413 U.S. 601, 610 (1973).] ... "[T]he Court has recognized some limited exceptions to these principles, but only because of the most 'weighty countervailing policies.'" Id., at 611. One of those exceptions "has been carved out in the area of the First Amendment." Ibid....

We find no "weighty countervailing policies" in this case to justify an attack on the facial validity of the CINS statute by one whose conduct clearly falls within its parameters....

Neither the plainly legitimate sweep of the language of the CINS statute nor the facts of this case suggest a substantial infringement upon the constitutionally

---

[3] Similar language in other statutes had been struck down on "vagueness" grounds in several jurisdictions. See, e.g., Gesicki v. Oswald, 336 P. Supp. 371 (S.D.N.Y. 1971) (holding unconstitutional N.Y. Code Crim. Proc. §913-a(5) and (6) which allowed incarceration of children "morally depraved or in danger of becoming morally depraved"). But see A. v. City of New York, 31 N.Y.2d 83, 286 N.E.2d 432 (1972) (upholding the "persons in need of supervision" portion of the same New York juvenile court act which consists of language remarkably similar to our own).

protected conduct of children so as to merit facial invalidation. The statute reinforces parents as they attempt to discipline their children in the broad ambit of family life. We conclude that the sort of activity that would establish a child as "habitually disobedient of the reasonable and lawful commands of his parent" would seldom directly and principally involve First Amendment activity such as expressive conduct or pure speech. . . .

To the extent that First Amendment activities may be infringed when the CINS statute is applied, we suggest that in balancing such infringement against the right and duty of a parent to teach, control, and discipline a child, we are obliged, if we are to accord some recognition to reality, to grant the parent greater latitude in the First Amendment area than is permitted the state. However, such parental authority would be seriously undermined if not given some official support. It strikes us that in applying the First Amendment, the strict enforcement of those rights must be tempered when we consider disciplinary problems involving a parent-child relationship. . . .

Reversed and remanded for further proceedings not inconsistent with this opinion.

NOTE: RUNAWAYS — WHERE DO THEY GO?

Both *Walker* and *B.J.R.* involve young people who ran away from home. Consider what life is like for a runaway. Evidence indicates that most runaways, although they may travel within their own state, stay close to home.[63] According to the National Incidence Studies (NIS) of Runaway and Thrownaway Children, almost 1.7 million youths had a runaway or thrownaway episode in 1999.[64]

(1) Runaway Shelters. One option for runaways is to seek the shelter and services of a runaway shelter. This is a viable alternative only for those fortunate enough to arrive in a community with one of the relatively small number of runaway houses in the United States. Of the estimated 500,000 to 1.5 million runaways annually, at most 70,000 find shelter in a runaway shelter.[65]

The federal government provides funding for runaway shelters through the Runaway Youth Act.[66] In passing the act in 1974, Congress acknowledged the effectiveness of community-based runaway youth centers to provide shelter and emergency assistance to runaway youth. Federal funds provide support to existing runaway youth centers and help establish new programs in unserved communities.

---

[63] Only 23 percent of runaways travel more than 50 miles from home. Office of Juvenile Justice and Delinquency Prevention, National Incidence Studies (NIS) of Missing, Abducted, Runaway and Throwaway Children, "Runaway/Thrownaway Children: National Estimates and Characteristics," Table 3, at 7 (Oct. 2002).

[64] Id. at 5.

[65] Patricia Montoya (Commissioner, Administration on Children, Youth and Families, Dept. of Health & Human Servs.), Prepared Statement Before the House Education and the Workforce Subcomm. On Early Childhood, Youth and Families, The Reauthorization of the Runaway and Homeless Youth Act, 1999 WL 8086486, Mar. 25, 1999.

[66] Title III of the Juvenile Justice and Delinquency Prevention Act of 1974, 42 U.S.C. §§5700-5702, 5711-5713, 5715-5716, 5731-5732, 5751 (2000).

To qualify for federal funding a runaway house must (1) be located in an area accessible to runaway youth; (2) have a maximum capacity of no more than 20 children with an adequate staff-child ratio; (3) develop plans for contacting the child's parents or relatives and assuring the safe return of the child, and for providing other appropriate alternative living arrangements; (4) develop an adequate plan for assuring proper relations with law enforcement personnel, social service personnel, and welfare personnel and for the return of runaway youths from correctional institutions; (5) develop an adequate plan for aftercare counseling of youth and their parents; (6) develop an adequate plan for establishing or coordinating with outreach programs; (7) keep statistical records profiling the children and their parents while assuring the confidentiality of records; and (8) submit annual reports and budget estimates to the Secretary of Health and Human Services.[67]

In addition to federal funding, some states provide funding to runaway shelters. Runaway shelters offer a variety of services to the youth. All centers provide the basic services required by law, including outreach, temporary shelter, and individual and family counseling services. In addition, the centers furnish aftercare assistance in such areas as health, education, legal, and employment services, either directly or through referrals to other social service agencies.

(2) Profile of Runaway Youth.   According to the NIS Study of Runaway and Thrownaway Children, most runaway youths (68 percent) are older teens, aged 15 to 17. However, a surprisingly large percentage (28 percent) are aged 12 to 14. A considerable number of runaway episodes occur during the summer months, when young people are less constrained by weather and school activities. While most runaways are gone from home for less than one week (77 percent), 7 percent are away for more than one month. Of the possible reasons for youths to leave home, 21 percent leave due to physical or sexual abuse and 19 percent due to addiction. In addition, 18 percent were in the company of someone known to be abusing drugs; 17 percent were using hard drugs; 11 percent engaged in criminal activity; and 4 percent had previously attempted suicide. Police are contacted to locate less than one-third of runaway/thrownaway youths. The two most common reasons for not contacting police are that the child's caretakers know the child's location or do not believe that police are needed.[68]

Researchers have explored in depth the relationship between running away and adolescent prostitution. The NIS Study reveals that many runaway/thrownaway youths engage in sexual activity in exchange for money, drugs, food, or shelter during the episode.[69] See generally D. Kelly Weisberg, Children of the Night: A Study of Adolescent Prostitution (1985).

In recognition of the large numbers of youth who are homeless because they were throwaways, rather than runaways, Congress reenacted the Runaway Youth Act in 1980 and broadened its scope, renaming it the Runaway and Homeless Youth Act, Pub. L. No. 96-509, 94 Stat. 2750 (codified as amended in scattered sections of 42 U.S.C.). In April 1999, the Senate passed legislation (S. 249, 106th Cong., 1st Sess. (1999)), titled the "Missing, Exploited and Runaway Children Protection

---

[67] 42 U.S.C. §5712(b)(3)-5712(b)(7) (2000).

[68] NIS Studies of Missing Children, supra note [63], Table 3, at 6-7.

[69] Id. at 6.

Act," which provided funding for the National Center for Missing and Exploited Children and also re-authorized funding for the Runaway and Homeless Youth Act for the years 2000-2004. In October 2003, Congress reauthorized programs under the Runaway and Homeless Youth Act and also the Missing Children's Assistance Act (S. 1451, 108th Cong., 1st Sess. (2003)).

2. Should Status Offenses Be Abolished?

Randy Frances Kandel & Anne Griffiths, Reconfiguring Personhood: From Ungovernability to Parent Adolescent Autonomy Conflict Actions
53 Syracuse L. Rev. 995, 1002-1003, 1032-1042, 1059-1063 (2003)

. . . Reconfiguration of the rights basis of ungovernability is essential because it remains a resilient populist resource, in the face of more than thirty years of governmental and professional efforts to abolish or curtail it. Ungovernability or PINS ["persons in need of supervision"] jurisdiction is easy to condemn, but it is very hard to kill. Disparaged by such entities as the Department of Justice, the American Bar Association and the Institute of Judicial Administration, ungovernability actions are increasingly seen as a resource by the largely poor and working class families who become caught in the web, often generation after generation.

In 1967, the President's Commission on Law Enforcement and Administration of Justice opined that "serious consideration . . . should be given to complete elimination of the court's power over children for noncriminal conduct." In 1974, during consideration of the major federal juvenile justice overhaul statute, the Juvenile Justice and Delinquency Prevention Act of 1974 (JJDPA), numerous august advisory and standard-setting groups recommended the reduction or elimination of juvenile court status offense jurisdiction and increased reliance on voluntary community-based services. The National Council on Crime and Delinquency issued a policy statement stating that:

> Subjecting a child to judicial sanction for a status offense . . . helps neither the child nor society; instead, it often does considerable harm to both. [It] serves no humanitarian or rehabilitative purpose. It is, instead, unwarranted punishment, unjust because it is disproportionate to the harm done by the child's noncriminal behavior. It cannot be justified under either a treatment or a punishment rationale.

[Nonetheless,] the 1974 version of the JJDPA stopped short of eliminating status offense jurisdiction. . . . The 1992 reauthorization of the JJDPA included a State Challenge Program amendment authorizing grants to states for innovative programming consistent with the Act's goals, including "[d]eveloping and adopting policies and programs to remove, where appropriate, status offenders from the jurisdiction of the juvenile court." Yet, since 1993, ungovernability cases have increased significantly. . . .

An ungovernability finding places the court in the position of enforcer of cultural stasis. . . . First, it places a particular onus on teens whose own personal development may be out of step with the mainstream chronological cultural norm. For example, girls whose physical and sexual maturity comes early may find themselves in foster homes or even institutions, branded as promiscuous merely because in the United States the length of required schooling is relatively long in a global sense, although many of the world's cultures may consider such girls ready for marriage and adult roles.

Second, teens who are considered rebellious in their local communities for violation of their cultural norms may find themselves branded ungovernable, even though, on a global scale, innovation in everything from music to politics often begins with teens, especially because it is a time of risk taking and experimentation. Constraining teens who "act-out" to follow traditional community norms may limit cultural diversity and may change society as a whole in a way which curtails creativity and diversity. As the norms of the legal culture approximate those of the middle class, the dampening of diversity results in an unconscious bias against the mores of lower class communities and ethnic and racial minorities. . . .

[A]dolescence and its constraints are especially prolonged in modern Western society, which requires a long, generally expensive, period of post-childhood formal training before entry into the work world as an adult and a relatively high average age for childbirth. Many youths are PINSed because they are or seem to be ready to leave their period of formal school and to begin bearing children at an age that only postmodern technological twenty-first century Western society would find too young. However, this amounts to a class bias because many working class youths who are PINSed come from the kinds of backgrounds where "coming of age" has been relatively early. . . .

I. Summing Up: The Wrongs of Rights

Ungovernability jurisdiction is difficult to rationalize from either a parental rights or children's rights perspective. First, although seemingly buttressed by a conservative policy of enlisting the power and authority of the court in support of parental efforts to control a difficult or disobedient child and to maintain their fundamental liberty to raise their children as "they see fit," PINS jurisdiction . . . often accomplishes the reverse.

In seeking judicial intervention in the raising of their children, parents weaken the presumption that parental custody is in the child's best interests, in practice and effect if not in black letter law. The sad irony is that the court, in its parens patriae role, substitutes for, rather than strengthens, parental control. The initiation of a petition itself suggests an inability to personally and independently perform what the petitioner believes to be his or her parental responsibilities and duties. [T]he probation officer is empowered to prepare an influential report to the judge that details what the probation officer has learned from parents, child, and others and sets forth the probation officer's views about inadequacies or difficulties with the parents as well as the child. The confrontation of working-class and middle class views of rights, protection, and discipline . . . may now become part of the case. . . .

As an ungovernability finding is based only upon the child's behavior (ungovernable, habitually disobedient, beyond the control of custodian or lawful authority) and a disposition after such finding is based only upon the child's best interest, the custodial parent may (however initially willingly) lose custody of the child to a non-parent (the Department of Social Services) without any finding that parental custody is detrimental to the child, the stricter standard most often applied in custody disputes between parent and non-parent. . . .

Second, even if ungovernability jurisdiction did support parents' rights in the strong sense, the justification and rationale for enlisting judicial support in the process of child rearing weakens dramatically in the adolescent and teen years. In conflicts between parents and young children, children's autonomy rights are generally trumped by the custodial parents' fundamental constitutional liberty to control their children and the presumption that fit parents act in their children's best interests. With young children, parental rights, children's interests, and protective rights are tied together through the Gordian Knot of the child's relative immaturity. But the knot unravels in adolescence when people begin to think, choose, and act for themselves along lines that differ from those of their parents. . . .

Third, in ungovernability jurisdiction, the emphasis is almost totally on protective rights, at a developmental stage when the balance should be tipping towards autonomous choice. . . . The rights that [an adolescent] may constitutionally enjoy independently or with parental consent and the privileges that may be extended to her in her own family give way to institutional rules when a PINS is "placed" in a group home or institutional setting. The protective custody given to PINS youths resembles other non-criminal semi-incarcerations, such as detention of undocumented alien children or hospitalization of mentally ill teenagers, at least as much as the protective warmth of a loving parent.

Fourth, the protective emphasis is legitimated in "ungovernability" jurisprudence by the idea that there is something especially wrong, troubled, or at risk about the ungovernable adolescent. The exercise of "protective rights" as used in the PINS action is rationalized by a fuzzy pastiche of quasi-criminal and quasi-psychological-medical discourses that cloak the child and the parents in the context of social and psychological pathology and make it possible to avoid the hard issue of whether or not the PINS child may have good reasons for disobedience. Running away, cutting class, staying out late, "trashing" one's room, "stealing" a sibling's or stepparents' clothes, and defying household rules are often the instrumentalities of rational youths who, as subordinated actors, have no other means to resist unfairness, exercise independence, or influence family dynamics. . . .

Fifth, by definition, "ungovernable" adolescents and teens are neither criminal nor insane, so that it is only by a collaboration and conflation of discipline and therapy . . . that the action can be sustained as a way to provide protective custody and help to "soft" deviants. An entire "behavioral disorder" universe of symptoms and syndromes, such as oppositional/defiant disorder (ODD), has been developed largely for forensic purposes. The diagnostic features of these syndromes parallel the noncriminal behaviors that typify "ungovernable" youths either before or after they are so legally labeled. Diagnosis of syndromes that track legal charges becomes one reason to "place" adolescents and teens "for their own good," just at the age when the mix of rights begins to tip towards the autonomy pole. As the term of an ungovernability placement is renewable and ultimately indeterminate and follows the old juvenile justice rule of "best interests," mere naughtiness, renamed as "ungovernability" and/or "psychopathology" may lead to a longer institution-alization than criminality, and would come close to unconstitutionality in any non parens patriae context.

Sixth, in many situations, the forensic syndromes overtake and swamp the developmental stage of adolescence itself. The terms "ungovernability" and "habit-ual disobedience" virtually define adolescence as it is culturally understood and celebrated in the United States, and as it is defined in core Western psychological theory as a time of rebellion, turmoil and increasing conflict with parents. The heart of the problem is that adolescence and the teenage years are a time when it is both normal and normative to be deviant and therefore the syndromes, applied broadly, may apply to any adolescent. "[O]ppositional-defiant disorder" is a forensic syn-drome with which almost any teenager may be loosely labeled. The jurisdiction is, indeed, an offense of being in a developmental "status."

Seventh, in ungovernability actions, adolescents and teens are at a procedu-ral disadvantage as they are necessarily placed in the role of the quasi-criminal defendant. Substantively, the ungovernability allegation (Is the child ungovern-able, habitually disobedient, or out of control?) and the presumption that parental decision-making is in the child's best interests, effectively deny the respondent youth any positive agency, choice, or intelligent wisdom. Either he is following what his parents prescribe, and he is not ungovernable, or he is not following what his parents prescribe, and he is ungovernable, either because he is naughty and will-ful or because he is diagnosable (e.g. with oppositional-defiant disorder). There is no defense of justification, better judgment, or personal choice and no counterclaim or action, if his parents are not neglectful or abusive but merely arbitrary, authoritar-ian, or insensitive. Not surprisingly, even respondents with excellent committed law guardians, rarely put on a case. The respondent has no real choice. She may receive protective rights under parental custody or the custody of the state but, unless the youth meets the standards for emancipation, there will not be a considered decision as to whether the respondent is in need of protective rights or entitled to rights of autonomy regarding any issue. . . .

The key question that brings families to the ungovernability court is who should make the decisions about the youth's day-to-day life. Parents PINS their sons and daughters because they believe that they must control and constrain the acts and autonomy of their youths to keep them on the path to productive adulthood, while the youths themselves feel the need to disagree, make defiant choices, do nothing, rebel, or experiment with possibly wild and risky decisions in order to be autonomous and independent adults. These are core questions of liberty, autonomy, and choice that are essentially legal ones, not psychological ones (although like divorce actions, they are intertwined with emotional matters). . . .

We suggest revamping the ungovernability action as a new Parent-Adolescent Autonomy Conflict action [PAAC]. . . . First, rather than a quasi-criminal action that requires a status offense determination to make a specific disposition, the PAAC would be a purely civil action between the parents (or other custodial caregiver) and the adolescent or teen. Both the parents and their son or daughter would have affirmative rights of standing to bring an initial action, assert claims and counter-claims, and to terminate a placement or modify a decision or order. To make the right a reality, adolescents and teens who lacked their own funds would be assigned attorneys.

Without any "status" finding the court would be empowered to determine the rights, responsibilities, obligations, directives, and breaches between the parties regarding specific issues, as in a contract dispute. Alternatively, the allegations might be more general, like a no fault divorce, speaking to the overall tension between a parent who wants to control and an offspring who wants to rebel. In emulation of some Australian juvenile statutes, they might allege "substantial and presently irretrievable breakdown" or "substantial and presently irreconcilable difference" between parent and child. . . .

Second, there would be a change of emphasis from disobedience and psychological dysfunction to disagreement between the parties. Third, there would be a change in emphasis from an exclusively welfare or protective rights rationale to a predominantly autonomy rights rationale. And fourth, at the same time, the essence and gravamen of the action would be to forthrightly address on an individualized case-by-case basis the nuances and tensions that exist in the gray area where parental control gradually slips away as children attain autonomy. In making decisions that cannot be determined by bright line rules, the court would be guided by the principles of legal personhood for adolescents and teens . . . (1) maturing decisional capacity; (2) the affirmative value and normality of experiment, risk, and rebellion; and (3) the standard of the "reasonable teen" as it incorporates context, culture, and class, and subordination as well as psychological and biological development.

[J]ust as adolescents and teens may sometimes be ordered to follow the dictates of their parents, so should parents, who are presumed to be capable of sufficient understanding of diverse personal views and their measurement against social and cultural norms, be charged with the obligation to recognize the independent ideas and decisions of their adolescents, even if they are in disagreement with them, and may be court ordered to respect their adolescent's ideas, behaviors, and decisions at the risk of losing custody of their teens.

Inevitably, the court would have authority to make a broad range of findings and dispositions and be able to open access to a wide range of resources. At one extreme, a court might make a finding of emancipation, enabling the youth to entirely live independently and self-responsibly if the youth meets the requisite criteria of maturity and potential self-sufficiency. At the other extreme, and as a last resort, the court might find, as it now often does, that the youth is truly out of parental control, yet too immature, wild, or unstable to make his or her daily decisions and should be adjudicated ungovernable, taken into the custody of social services, and "placed" in a foster family, group home, or institution.

But more often, the court would use its jurisdiction for intermediate decisions. For example, the court might order the parents to respect certain decisions of their son, not because he is a "mature minor" but because he is "mature enough" to make the decisions at issue, and enforce their custodial obligation to guide him in the expression of autonomy rights.

Adolescents and teens would have the right to assert, by petition or counter-claim, that specific parental demands or controls are unreasonable, and have an affirmative substantive right to petition the court to be removed from their parents because of unreasonable parental constraints or parental inadequacies (even those that do not constitute neglect or abuse). The court would be able to find that the child is a mature minor who is able to make an informed autonomous decision about a change of custody — in other words a rearrangement of residence and custody could be accomplished without a finding that the child is a wrongdoer. Alternatively, if the court found that the child was not a mature minor, the court would be able to arrange a placement on the grounds of irreconcilable parent-child conflict — a no fault decision, analogous to a divorce determination.

Parents or youths should be able to contract for a placement for a specified time through an expansion of respite, emergency, and short-term placements. In situations where an adolescent or teen is removed from the parental home, he or she should have a meaningful right to petition to go home that is not conditioned upon the preferences of the Department of Social Services. By the same token, parents should be able to petition to have their son or daughter temporarily, voluntarily "placed," and then returned without the present elaborate investigations and procedures. . . .

This reconceptualization of the PINS would also . . . require a greater use of mediation and other alternative dispute resolution options, either as mandated by the court or initiated by the parties. [M]ediation or other negotiated solutions might include contracts between parents and children regarding the reciprocal behavior of each, which would be legally enforceable.

Educational and residential alternatives would be needed. . . . Instead of providing only schools and homes that are based on disciplinary and behavior modification techniques, alternative environments that are facilitative of teens' evolving capacities and maturing decisional, emotional, and managerial capacities, and respectful of teens' choices, emotional connections, and developing ethics should be created. Upon a youth's petition, the court would have authority to issue an order permitting a youth, on the basis of the youth's decisional autonomy and against the parents' wishes, to live in an educational, vocational, or cooperative living situation that is facilitative to the youth's interests, and development, and that is "maturity enhancing," and not primarily intended to be correctional, rehabilitative, or therapeutic. . . . [A]lternatives should [facilitate] alternative ways to acquire a basic education, apprenticeships, mentorships and "vacations" from education, which would allow adolescents and teens to take a semester or a year off from school and then return without being labeled as truants or drop outs. Earlier opportunities to obtain the GED should be available so that people who do not want to study further could enter the job market sooner. . . .

In this way the legal system would promote a new approach to dealing with cases of conflict between parent and child, one that is based on a positive view of adolescents' and teens' agency, and an empowering vision of their rights. . . .

3. Status Offenders

NOTES AND QUESTIONS

(1) Justification for Status Offense Statutes.   Note that in *Walker* the court suggests that an "undisciplined child" proceeding was "not a criminal prosecution"

and that in *B.J.R.* the court says that the "CINS section is not a criminal statute in the ordinary sense." What are these courts saying? That the state's purpose is rehabilitative, not retributive? Was the young person's liberty constrained substantially as a result of juvenile court jurisdiction in each case? Consider what Professor Francis A. Allen has written:

> Measures which subject individuals to the substantial and involuntary deprivation of their liberty contain an inescapable punitive element, and this reality is not altered by the facts that the motivations that prompt incarceration are to provide therapy or otherwise contribute to the person's well-being or reform. As such, these measures must be closely scrutinized to insure that power is being applied consistently with those values of the community that justify interference with liberty for only the most clear and compelling reasons.[70]

Do you agree?

What are the "clear and compelling" reasons consistent with community values to interfere with the liberty of the young people in *B.J.R.* and *Walker*? Was there any showing that the young person was in danger? Or was endangering others? Is the enforcement of parental controls over children a clear and compelling justification? Why?

Are status offenders substantially similar enough to juvenile delinquents that they should be handled by the same system? Or is the behavior of most status offenders a normal part of growing up and thus unlike the more hardened, deviant behavior of delinquents? Will early court intervention at the point of status offense prevent an escalation into more serious forms of delinquency? Or does juvenile court intervention itself cause escalation by encouraging youth to think of themselves as delinquent and to associate with others who have been similarly identified? For a recent discussion of the research, see Alex R. Piquero et al., The Criminal Career Paradigm, 30 Crime & Just. 359 (2003).

(2) The Procedural Rights of Youth "In Need of Supervision."   Are young people allegedly "in need of supervision" entitled to the same procedural rights, such as the privilege against self-incrimination as young people accused of a crime? The juvenile justice system differentiates status offenders from delinquents in many ways. For example, the Supreme Court has required proof beyond a reasonable doubt in delinquency cases. In re Winship, 397 U.S. 358 (1970). However, the proof standard is not uniform for status offenses. Many states require only a preponderance of the evidence or clear and convincing evidence. See, e.g., Ark. Stat. Ann. §9-27-325 (Michie 2002 & Supp. 2003); N.C. Gen. Stat. §7B-805 (2002). Some states, however, do require proof beyond a reasonable doubt. See, e.g., N.Y. Fam. Ct. Act §744(b) (McKinney 1999 & Supp. 2004); S.D. Codified Laws Ann. §26-7A-96/87 (1999).

Moreover, it is likely that evidence may be admissible at a PINS hearing that would not be admissible in the trial of a delinquency petition, and some statutes expressly authorize this. See, e.g., Cal. Welf. & Inst. Code §701 (West 1998 & Supp. 2004), providing that admissibility of evidence in a beyond-control case is governed by rules of evidence applicable to trial of a civil case, rather than by rules

---

[70] Francis A. Allen, The Borderland of Criminal Justice: Essays in Law and Criminology 37 (1964).

of evidence applicable to trial of a criminal case that govern in case of delinquency. This, together with the lower standard of proof commonly required, may explain in part why criminal offenses sometimes are dealt with under the PINS or other unruly child rubric.

Should a juvenile be entitled to counsel in status offense proceedings? Recall that *Walker*, supra p. 698, said no (like many jurisdictions). But cf. Mass. Gen. Laws ch. 119 §39E (1998) (conferring right to counsel on status offenders). After *Walker*, the North Carolina legislature expressly provided for a right to representation in all juvenile court proceedings. N.C. Gen. Stat. §7B-2000 (2002). Some courts maintain there is no right to counsel if institutionalization is not authorized. See, e.g., M.J.M. v. Department of Health & Rehabilitation Servs., 397 So. 2d 755 (Fla. Dist. Ct. App. 1981).

(3) Vagueness and Overbreadth.   Many commentators have suggested that the statutes conferring status offense jurisdiction are unconstitutionally vague and overbroad.[71] But as *B.J.R.* suggests, appellate courts have generally upheld the constitutional validity of PINS statutes against such attacks. The Supreme Court has not explicitly dealt with these issues, although it summarily affirmed Oswald v. Gesicki, 406 U.S. 913 (1972) without opinion. In Gesicki v. Oswald, 336 F. Supp. 371 (S.D.N.Y. 1971), a three-judge federal district court invalidated a New York youthful offender statute that allowed jurisdiction over a wayward minor, defined as one who was "morally depraved or . . . in danger of becoming morally depraved."

(4) Sex Discrimination.   Note that both *Walker* and *B.J.R.* involved teenage girls. Research reveals that status offense jurisdiction is invoked more frequently for girls than for boys. Parents refer girls to the juvenile justice system at a much higher rate than they refer boys, and girls are more likely to be arrested for these offenses. Thus, for example, in 1995, 27.5 percent of all girls' arrests were for status offenses, whereas only 10.5 percent of boys arrested were for status offenses.[72]

A number of states have set different age levels for the assertion of ungovernability (and sometimes delinquency and neglect) jurisdiction as between girls and boys. Courts, however, have invalidated such different age levels as violative of equal protection. See, e.g., People v. Ellis, 311 N.E.2d 98 (Ill. 1974); In re Patricia A., 286 N.E.2d 431 (N.Y. 1972). Courts that have struck down these laws have rejected the state's reliance on concerns about female pregnancy. Note, however, that in Michael M. v. Superior Court, 450 U.S. 464 (1981), in an equal protection challenge to California's statutory rape law, the United States Supreme Court found that the state's asserted concern about teenage pregnancy was a legitimate interest to justify the gender-discriminatory statute.

See generally Meda Chesney-Lind, The Female Offender (1997); Meda Chesney-Lind & Randall G. Shelden, Girls, Delinquency, and Juvenile Justice (2d ed., 1997); Cheryl Dalby, Gender Bias Toward Status Offenders: A Paternalistic

---

[71] See, e.g., Al Katz & Lee E. Teitelbaum, PINS Jurisdiction, the Vagueness Doctrine and the Rule of Law, 53 Ind. L.J. 1 (1978); Irene Merker Rosenberg, Juvenile Status Offender Statutes — New Perspectives on an Old Problem, 16 U.C. Davis L. Rev. 283, 294-300 (1983); Patricia M. Wald, The Rights of Youth, 4 Hum. Rts. 13, 21 (1974).

[72] Alecia Humphrey, The Criminalization of Survival Attempts: Locking Up Female Runaways and Other Status Offenders, 15 Hastings Women's L.J. 165, 173 (2004) (citing research).

Approach Carried Out Through the JJDPA, 12 Law & Ineq. J. 429 (1994); Laura A. Barnickol, Note, The Disparate Treatment of Males and Females Within the Juvenile Justice System, 2 Wash. U. J.L. & Pol'y, 429, 434 (2000).

(5) Proposed ABA Juvenile Justice Standards. The American Bar Association Juvenile Justice Standards Project has proposed the elimination of the general juvenile court jurisdiction over status offenses in noncriminal juvenile misbehavior. Instead, the standards place primary reliance on "a system of voluntary referral to service provided outside the juvenile justice system."[73]

> It is the position of these standards that the dejudicialization of status offenses and reliance on voluntarily based services will make those services more appropriate to the needs of the youth and his or her family; it is both true and a truism that help that a person elects to receive and in which he or she willingly participates has a better likelihood of success than services imposed at the end of a writ. Removal of the status offense jurisdiction will, it is submitted, encourage more people to get more effective help; stimulate the creation and extension of a wider range of voluntary services than is presently available; end the corrosive effects of treating noncriminal youth as though they had committed crimes; and free up a substantial part of the resources of the juvenile justice system to deal with the cases of delinquency and of abused and neglected children that belong in it.[74]

The proposed standards do not eliminate coercive instruction completely, however. One commentator notes:

> [B]ecause of the particular problems presented by certain kinds of cases — youths who run away, who are in circumstances of immediate jeopardy, who are in need of alternative living arrangements when they and their parents cannot agree, and who evidence a need for emergency medical services — some carefully limited official intervention is preserved, though in all cases wardship as a result of the child's noncriminal behavior or circumstances is precluded.[75]

The standards permit a law enforcement officer to take a juvenile into limited custody for no more than six hours if the juvenile (a) is "absent from home without [parental] consent";[76] or (b) "is in circumstances which constitute a substantial and immediate danger to the juvenile's physical safety."[77] The officer must then notify the child's parent or guardian "as soon as practicable" unless there are "compelling circumstances why the parent or guardian should not" be notified.[78] If a parent or other responsible person is unavailable, or if the child refuses to go home with the parents, the officer is authorized to take the juvenile to a state licensed "temporary nonsecure residential facility."[79] The juvenile may stay there for no more than 21 days, unless the parent consents or a neglect petition is filed.[80]

---

[73] American Bar Association, Juvenile Justice Standards for Noncriminal Misbehavior 2 (1982).
[74] Id. at 15.
[75] Id. at 2.
[76] Id. at 25.
[77] Id. at 23.
[78] Id. at 24.
[79] Id.
[80] Id. at 25.

If the juvenile chooses not to return home, the juvenile may file a motion to have the juvenile court approve some alternative residential placement.[81] The court is required to approve the placement requested by the juvenile unless the court finds upon a preponderance of the evidence that that placement imperils or would imperil the juvenile — that is, that it "fails to provide physical protection, adequate shelter, or adequate nutrition; or seriously and unconscionably obstructs the juvenile's medical care, education, or physical and emotional development, as determined according to the needs of the juvenile in the particular case; or exposes the juvenile to unconscionable exploitation."[82] In such circumstances the court may direct some alternative "non-secure" placement.

The standards also allow for a juvenile to be taken into "emergency custody" for a period not to exceed 72 hours in limited circumstances that show an "immediate need for emergency psychiatric or medical evaluation and possible care." Beyond that period, however, the standards envision that the juvenile may be held only pursuant to the state's adult procedures for mental health commitments.[83]

4. Dispositions in PINS Cases

State v. Damian R.
591 S.E.2d 168 (W. Va. 2003)

STARCHER, C.J.

. . . The appellant, D.R., was born on September 4, 1987, and was fourteen years old at the time of the proceedings below. During the 2001-2002 school year the juvenile resided with his mother [a single parent] in Berkeley County, and was enrolled in the seventh grade. The juvenile had truancy and anger management problems at school; in the Fall of 2001 he was expelled from school and the school system offered him alternative educational services on two nights a week after school. A truancy diversion social worker was assigned to work with the juvenile and his family. The juvenile attended some of the alternative education sessions, but missed most of them.

In late 2001, the juvenile's mother, seeking further assistance in dealing with her problems with her son,[2] consulted with the Berkeley County Prosecuting Attorney's Office. As a result of this consultation and with the mother's consent, on December 12, 2001, the Berkeley County Prosecuting Attorney filed a petition pursuant to W.Va. Code, 49-5-7 [1998], requesting that the juvenile be adjudged to be a status offender.

A probable cause hearing was held by the circuit court on January 29, 2002, where a truancy diversion social worker and the juvenile's mother testified briefly to the juvenile's misconduct. The social worker testified that the juvenile would

---

[81] Id. at 29.

[82] Id. at 29-30.

[83] Id. at 31-34.

[2] These problems included emotional outbursts, not following household rules, throwing things, not saying where he was going when he left the house, smoking marijuana; and, as previously noted, refusing to go to school.

benefit from counseling; the mother testified that while the juvenile's behavior had already improved noticeably since the petition was filed, the mother still felt she needed help from the court. The circuit court ruled that probable cause had been established and set a date about one month later for an adjudicatory hearing.

On February 27, 2002, the circuit court held the adjudicatory hearing. There was no evidence presented of any further misconduct by the juvenile since the probable cause hearing. The juvenile's counsel advised the court that the juvenile would admit to the factual allegations in the petition and that the juvenile wished to remain with his mother. The circuit court questioned the juvenile to be sure that he understood his rights and then accepted the juvenile's acknowledgment of the truth of the allegations in the petition.

The circuit court entered an order adjudicating the juvenile as a status offender, based on incorrigibility and truancy. The court referred the juvenile to the West Virginia Department of Health and Human Resources ("DHHR") "for treatment according to statute." The court also ordered a psychological examination of the juvenile. The court cautioned the juvenile that his truancy was unacceptable; that he needed above all to attend school regularly; and that he would face more serious consequences if he did not attend school as required.

After this hearing the juvenile began to attend school again. Then, on March 1, 4 and 7, the juvenile reportedly "acted out" in school, by yelling at a teacher and not following directions. The school contacted the DHHR, and on March 15, 2002 the DHHR filed a petition with the circuit court, briefly describing the reported "acting out" incidents and further alleging that "[t]he Juvenile is not amenable to services in the community because he will not remain in a safe residence long enough for services to be offered nor is there a community service available that can supervise the Juvenile to prevent him from skipping school, being incorrigible, and running away, so therefore it is in the best interest of this fourteen-year-old Juvenile if he is placed in the custody of the Department and placed in a staff secure facility." The DHHR sought an order awarding custody of the juvenile to the DHHR for out-of-home placement.

A hearing on this petition was held on March 25, 2002, following which the circuit court entered an order — without making any specific written findings — granting custody of the juvenile to the DHHR for the purpose of making placement at a place to be determined, and pending such placement ordering that the juvenile be held at the Romney Child Care Center. . . .

[On appeal, appellant argues] that awarding custody to the DHHR was improper because the DHHR had not even attempted to provide the services that would be a less restrictive alternative than removal from his mother's custody. . . .

The proceedings at issue in the instant case alleged that the juvenile was a "status offender" — i.e., a child whose complained-of conduct would not be a crime if the conduct was engaged in by an adult. . . . [W.Va. Code 49-5-11.] The referral from the circuit court pursuant to W.Va. Code, 49-5-11(d) [1998] triggers a duty by the DHHR to provide services to the juvenile, under the mandate of W.Va. Code, 49-5-11a [1998], which states in part:

(a) Services provided by the department for juveniles adjudicated as status offenders shall be consistent with the provisions of article five-b of this chapter

[49-5B-1] and shall be designed to develop skills and supports *within families* and to resolve problems related to the juveniles or conflicts *within their families.* Services may include, but are not limited to, referral of juveniles and parents, guardians or custodians and other family members to services for psychiatric or other medical care, or psychological, welfare, legal, educational or other social services, as appropriate to the needs of the juvenile and his or her family. (Emphasis added.) . . .

The DHHR's petition for custody in the instant case is grounded in the language in the foregoing-quoted statute authorizing the DHHR to "[i]f necessary . . . petition the circuit court [to] . . . place a [referred status offender] out of home in a nonsecure or staff-secure setting, and/or to place a juvenile in custody of the department." Id.

The appellant suggests that as a matter of law and in all cases, in order for the DHHR to seek under W.Va. Code, 49-5-11a(b)(2) [1998] to have custody of an adjudicated status offender transferred from the child's parent to the DHHR — as a quasi-jurisdictional and necessary precursor for such a request, the DHHR must first have provided services to the juvenile and his or her family while the juvenile is in the parent's home and custody, and the DHHR must show that these in-home services have been ineffective, thus rendering a further court order "necessary."

However, such a reading of W.Va. Code, 49-5-11a [1998] is not compelled by the language of the statute, nor would such a reading comport with common sense. Certainly there could be a severe case in which the provision of services to a status offender necessarily requires, in the first instance, an order placing a juvenile out of his or her parents' custody or home in the first instance — such as when a juvenile's parent is gravely ill, for example. Having said this, however, we must emphasize that the entire statutory scheme for status offenders contemplates that removal from the home and/or transfer of custody from a parent be undertaken only when necessary and upon clear and convincing proof that no less restrictive alternative is feasible.

The removal of a juvenile status offender or delinquent from his parent's custody is authorized "only when the child's welfare or the safety and protection of the public cannot be adequately safeguarded without removal . . . . " W.Va. Code, 49-1-1(a)(12)(b) [1999].[5] While the 1997 revisions to the child welfare statutes "grant courts broader discretion in determining the precise placement for status offenders that will meet the best interests of the juvenile and the community [,]" the requirement of selecting the least restrictive appropriate alternative remains.

In the law concerning custody of minor children, no rule is more firmly established than that the right of a natural parent to the custody of his or her infant child is paramount to that of any other person; it is a fundamental personal liberty protected and guaranteed by the Due Process Clauses of the West Virginia and United States Constitutions. . . .

---

[5] Additionally, W.Va. Code, 49-5-13(b)(4) [1999], which applies to delinquents and not status offenders, requires the court to determine whether the Department made reasonable efforts to prevent an out-of-home placement before such a placement may be ordered. Certainly there is no less of a requirement for status offenders.

Based on the foregoing, we hold that the prior actual provision of services by the State Department of Health and Human Resources to a status offender is not in all cases a jurisdictional prerequisite for the filing of a petition seeking an order transferring custody of the status offender to the Department and/or out-of-home placement under W.Va. Code, 49-5-11a(b)(2) [1998]; however, such a petition may only be granted upon a showing by clear and convincing evidence that such a custody or placement order is actually necessary; that the effective provision of services cannot occur absent such an order; and that all reasonable efforts have been made to provide appropriate services without an out-of-home placement and/or custody transfer; additionally, orders granting such placement or transfer must be based on specific findings and conclusions by the court with respect to the grounds for and necessity of the order.

Applying the foregoing principles to the facts of the instant case, we first note that the DHHR was required upon receipt of the initial referral from the court to establish an individualized plan of rehabilitation for the juvenile. W.Va. Code, 49-5B-4(b) [1999]. No evidence was adduced regarding the establishment of such a plan in the instant case. Moreover, while the DHHR alleged in its post-adjudication petition for custody and transfer that "services were provided to the Juvenile by the Children's Home Society of West Virginia[,]" and that "[t]he juvenile will not remain in a safe residence long enough for services to be provided nor is there a community service available that can supervise the Juvenile to prevent him from skipping school, being incorrigible, and running away . . . [,]" in fact none of these allegations were addressed, much less proven, at the March 25, 2002 hearing.[7] [T]he evidence at the March 25, 2002 hearing did not legally establish the necessity — for the protection of the juvenile or the public — of transferring legal custody of the juvenile to the DHHR and removing him from his home.

For this reason, the circuit court's order removing the juvenile from his parent's custody and transferring it to the DHHR and placing him out of his home must be reversed. . . .

NOTES AND QUESTIONS

(1) Deinstitutionalization Movement.   No state has adopted the ABA Juvenile Justice Standards that eliminate general juvenile court jurisdiction over noncriminal juvenile behavior.[84] However, there has been an important movement to

---

[7] Additionally, no evidence showed that the DHHR had, prior to filing its post-adjudication petition for custody and placement, attempted to implement any less restrictive alternative. A lecture from a trial judge and "fear of consequences" is not the provision of rehabilitative services that the DHHR is required to deliver to status offenders. In the instant case, the DHHR had a responsibility after adjudication to promptly meet with the juvenile and his parent and to discuss how to implement a home-based services plan. Certainly, after the first reported incident at school of March 1, 2002, the DHHR was on notice of a pressing need to immediately begin to work with the juvenile to try to avoid further incidents in school — or to return to an effective alternative education plan. Nothing in the record demonstrates any such attempt.

[84] See John Murray, Status Offenders: A Sourcebook 28 (table 8) (1983).

deinstitutionalize status offenders.[85] The deinstitutionalization movement began in the 1970s as concerns were raised about incarcerating juveniles for noncriminal behavior. The federal government facilitated the movement by enacting in 1974 the Juvenile Justice and Delinquency Prevention Act (JJDPA), 42 U.S.C. §§5601-5751 (2000 & Supp. 2003). Prior to the JJDPA, most states provided for secure detention for status offenders. However, the JJDPA discouraged the practice of commingling status offenders and delinquents, encouraged the diversion of status offenders from the juvenile justice system whenever possible, and encouraged alternatives to the traditional juvenile detention and correctional facilities. The JJDPA required states to remove all status offenders from secure institutions in order to be eligible for federal funds.

Juvenile Justice and Delinquency Prevention Act
42 U.S.C. §5633 (2000 & Supp. 2003)

State Plans

(a) Requirements

In order to receive formula grants under this part, a State shall submit a plan for carrying out its purposes. [S]uch plan . . .

(11) shall, in accordance with rules issued by the Administrator, provide that —

(A) juveniles who are charged with or who have committed an offense that would not be criminal if committed by an adult [with some exceptions, such as youths who knowingly possess a handgun or ammunition, who have committed a violation of a valid court order, etc.] shall not be placed in secure detention facilities or secure correctional facilities; and

(B) juveniles —

(i) who are not charged with any offense; and

(ii) who are [aliens or alleged to be dependent, neglected, or abused];

shall not be placed in secure detention facilities or secure correctional facilities;

(12) provide that —

(A) juveniles alleged to be or found to be delinquent or juveniles within the purview of paragraph (11) will not be detained or confined in any institution in which they have contact with adult inmates; . . .

(13) provide that no juvenile will be detained or confined in any jail or lockup for adults except —

(A) juveniles who are accused of nonstatus offenses and who are detained in such jail or lockup for a period not to exceed 6 hours —

---

[85] "Deinstitutionalization" refers to the removal of status offenders from secure detention or correctional facilities or preventing their placement in such facilities. (In contrast to secure facilities, nonsecure facilities permit greater freedom of movement by the juvenile, offer minimal supervision by staff, and generally have no locked areas.)

(i) for processing or release;

(ii) while awaiting transfer to a juvenile facility; or

(iii) in which period such juveniles make a court appearance;
and only if such juveniles do not have contact with adult inmates. . . .

(B) juveniles who are accused of nonstatus offenses, who are awaiting an initial court appearance that will occur within 48 hours after being taken into custody (excluding Saturdays, Sundays, and legal holidays), and who are detained in a jail or lockup —

(i) in which —

(I) such juveniles do not have contact with adult inmates; and

(II) that [is located outside a metropolitan area and has no existing acceptable alternative placement available; or is located where travel conditions do not allow for court appearances within 48 hours]; or

(III) [is located where adverse conditions of safety exist (such as adverse weather conditions)]

(14) provide for an adequate system of monitoring jails, detention facilities, correctional facilities, and non-secure facilities to insure that the requirements of paragraphs (11), (12), and (13) are met, and for annual reporting of the results of such monitoring to the Administrator, except that such reporting requirements shall not apply in the case of a State which is in compliance with the other requirements of this paragraph, which is in compliance with the requirements in paragraphs (11) and (12), and which has enacted legislation which conforms to such requirements and which contains, in the opinion of the Administrator, sufficient enforcement mechanisms to ensure that such legislation will be administered effectively. . . .

Subsequent amendments changed the deinstitutionalization (DSO) requirements. The Juvenile Justice Amendments of 1977, Pub. L. No. 95-115, 91 Stat. 1054 (1977), revised the timetable by adding two years to the three-year limit within which states must comply. In addition, the amendments defined what was required for substantial compliance with the JJDPA — "achievement of deinstitutionalization of not less than 75 per centum of such juveniles." The Juvenile Justice Amendments of 1980, 42 U.S.C. §5633(a)(12) (2000), contained additional revisions that authorized the confinement of status offenders who had violated a valid court order. Further, states are still eligible for grants if their failure to comply is "de minimus," according to a legal opinion of the Law Enforcement Assistance Administration Office of General Counsel.[86]

---

[86] Cited in Robert W. Sweet, Jr., Deinstitutionalization of Status Offenders: In Perspective, 18 Pepperdine L. Rev. 389, 408 (1991).

(2) Compliance Data. The Office of Juvenile Justice and Delinquency Prevention (OJJDP) is the agency responsibility for administering JJDPA funds. In regard to states' compliance with deinstitutionalization requirements, OJJDP notes:

> During 2002, 7 States with no violations were in compliance with the deinstitutionalization of status offenders provision of the JJDP Act, which stipulates that status offenders and nonoffenders cannot be detained or confined in secure detention or correctional facilities. Forty-four States were in full compliance with de minimis exceptions, with fewer than 29.4 violations per 100,000 persons under age 18 in the State.
>
> Forty-three States with no violations were in compliance with the separation provision of the JJDP Act, which requires that accused and adjudicated delinquent, status offender, and nonoffender juveniles not have contact with incarcerated adults. Ten States were in compliance with separation based on regulatory exceptions.
>
> The jail and lockup removal provision of the JJDP Act stipulates that juveniles cannot be detained in any adult jail or lockup. Twelve States with zero violations were in full compliance with this provision. Forty States were in compliance with de minimis exceptions, while two states were out of compliance with this provision.[87]

The above statistics, however, do not reveal the full picture. In order to meet governmental requirements to comply with the JJDPA, many states did prohibit the secure detention of status offenders. However, states then were torn between satisfying governmental funding requirements and popular demands to respond to the many problems of status offenders. In response to this dilemma, as commentators explain, states developed certain tactics to circumvent the JJDPA's requirements: "(a) referring or committing a status offender to a secure mental health facility (public or private), (b) alleging juvenile delinquency instead of status offense in petition to permit detention in juvenile hall, (c) developing "semi-secure" facilities which would technically comply with the JJDPA definition but which operated as secure in fact, and (d) using the court's contempt power to "bootstrap" a status offender into a delinquent."[88]

(3) The "Re-Institutionalization" Movement. Subsequent to the JJDPA, the wisdom of the deinstitutionalization movement was called into question, particularly in regard to runaway children. The U.S. Attorney General Advisory Board on Missing and Exploited Children issued a report recommending that both federal and state legislatures amend their laws to allow the institutionalization of runaways. OJJDP America's Missing and Exploited Children: Their Safety and Their Future 19-20 (March 1986). Some authorities who worked with runaway prostitutes believed that police officers should be able to place the youth in secure facilities at least for short periods. This would keep the youth safe from pimps, as well as facilitate both rehabilitation services and criminal investigation.

---

[87] Office of Juvenile Justice and Delinquency Prevention, U.S. Dept. of Justice, Annual Report 42 (2002).

[88] Bruce J. Winick et al., "Wayward and Noncompliant" People with Mental Disabilities, 9 Psychol. Pub. Pol'y & L. 233, 240 (2003).

In response to calls for reform, in 1995 the Washington state legislature passed the "Becca's Bill," Wash Rev. Code §13.32 (West 2004), to provide for the detention of status offenders in secure facilities for at least 24 hours and up to five consecutive days. (A more stringent provision, to hold habitual runaways in secure facilities for up to six months, was vetoed by the governor.) The bill was passed in response to the murder of a 13-year-old runaway prostitute. Following her death, her adoptive parents sought legislation to address the frustration caused by the fact that police could detain runaways only for a short time and only in unsecured facilities.[89] Does Becca's Bill detention provisions, which place runaways in secure facilities, violate juveniles' due process rights? See Carrie A. Tracy, Note, A Proposal to Bring the Becca's Bill Runaway-Detention Provisions into Compliance with Juvenile's Procedural Due Process Rights, 75 Wash. L. Rev. 1399 (2000) (so arguing).

(4) Policy Arguments. What are the arguments in support of, and in opposition to, the institutionalization of status offenders? Is it fair to lock up children who have done nothing criminal? Will exposure to delinquents be harmful to status offenders? Is it wasteful to spend juvenile court resources on non-criminal youth? What light does *Damian R.* shed on this issue?

(5) Some commentators argue that deinstitutionalization results in the practice of relabelling or in the phenomenon of a "hardening of the record." Often minors commit two offenses — a status offense and a delinquent offense. Before the dein-stitutionalization movement, the system would have labeled the juvenile a status offender to avoid the stigma of delinquency. However, after the deinstitutionaliza-tion requirements, the child would have to be relabeled a delinquent or mentally ill to become eligible for services or to provide for detention. See Status Offender Incarceration Decreases Partly Offset by Relabelling, Net Widening, 12 Crim. Just. Newsletter 1 (April 27, 1981). Is this a result of the prohibition against placing children in secure facilities or of a systems failure elsewhere?

(6) Bootstrapping. May a status offender be institutionalized as a delin-quent for violating a court order (for instance, to attend school regularly or not run away)? "Bootstrapping" refers to the practice of using the court's contempt power to change a "status offender" into a "delinquent." Initially, the Juvenile Jus-tice and Delinquency Prevention Act, 42 U.S.C. §§5601-5751 (2000), prohibited incarcerating status offenders after elevating them to delinquency status for failure to comply with a court order. However, as explained above, §5633(a)(12)(A) of the Act was amended in 1980 to permit the incarceration in secure facilities of status offenders, who violated valid court orders. Courts have split over the question of whether they can use their contempt power to place children in secure facilities. Note the ease with which the West Virginia Department of Health and Human Services in the principal case requested that Damian be placed in a secure facil-ity for violating the court order that he attend school regularly. Most states have affirmed their courts' use of the contempt power to order the secure detention of contemptuous status offenders, despite an expression of legislative intent gener-ally banning such detention. Bruce J. Winick et al., "Wayward and Noncompliant

---

[89] On the history of the legislation, see Tiffany Zwicker Eggers, The "Becca Bill" Would Not Have Saved Becca: Washington State's Treatment of Young Female Offenders, 16 Law & Ineq. 219, 219-225, 230-235 (1998).

People" with Mental Disabilities, 9 Psychol. Pub. Pol'y & L. 233, 242 (2003). But cf. Commonwealth v. Florence F., 709 N.E.2d 418 (Mass. 1999) (disapproving the practice).

(7) Juvenile Diversion Programs. Many states offer juvenile diversion programs by which status offenders (and sometimes, first-offender delinquents) are diverted out of the juvenile court and channeled to community-based treatment-oriented programs. As Professor Franklin Zimring explains, diversion "has been an important motive in juvenile justice from the beginning, and became the dominant purpose of a separate juvenile court after In re Gault in 1967."[90] As mentioned above (supra, p. 722), the federal government gave such programs a boost when the JJDPA emphasized the need to establish programs "to divert juveniles from the traditional juvenile justice system and to provide critically needed alternatives to institutionalization." Juvenile diversion programs have several benefits:

> By maintaining the youth's ties with his family and the community, diversion avoids the potential effect of a formal delinquent label which could adversely affect his self-image and contribute to subsequent delinquent behavior. Studies show that diversion programs are reducing the number of repeat offenders. In addition, in the long run, diversion programs are cheaper than expanding juvenile police, courts, and corrective functions. Diversion offers the possibility of reallocating funds and resources to community programs that may satisfy a more rational public policy than traditional static juvenile corrections programs.[91]

Professor Zimring concludes that "The past thirty years have been the juvenile court's finest hour as a diversion project; the rate of juvenile incarceration has been stable, while incarceration of young adults has soared."[92]

(8) Anti-Truancy Reforms. The juvenile in *Damian R.* came to the attention of the juvenile justice system because of truancy. School districts increasingly are enacting tough new measures to curb truancy. Many states now punish *parents* with fines and imprisonment if their children are habitually truant. The definition of "habitually truant" varies considerably (e.g., 15 unexcused absences within 90 days in Florida; 6 unexcused absences in Oakland, California). See Julian Guthrie, Parents Face Jail Time if Kids Miss Class, S.F. Examiner, Sept. 19, 1999, at A1. Punishments also vary. For example, parents in Florida face fines of $500 and 60 days in jail compared to fines of $2,500 and a year in jail for parents in Kern County, California. Id. at A13. Moreover, in some jurisdictions, parents of truant children can be made to attend parenting class and are subject to prosecution for contributing to the delinquency of a minor. Jennifer Radcliffe, Warning Issued on Truancy, Consequences Spelled Out for Offenders, L.A. Daily News, Dec. 2, 2004, at N4. Is this approach likely to be effective? Is it sound policy?

[90] Franklin E. Zimring, The Common Thread: Diversion in Juvenile Justice, 88 Cal. L. Rev. 2477, 2479 (2000).
[91] S'Lee Arthur Hinshaw II, Juvenile Diversion: An Alternative to Juvenile Court, 1993 J. Disp. Resol. 305, 312-313 (1993).
[92] Zimring, supra note [90], at 2479.

5. Should Children Be Able to Divorce Their Parents?

In re Snyder
532 P.2d 278 (Wash. 1975)

EN BANC.

HUNTER, Associate Justice.

Paul Snyder and Nell Snyder, petitioners, seek review of the King County Juvenile Court's finding that their daughter, Cynthia Nell Snyder, respondent, was an incorrigible child as defined under RCW 13.04.010(7). . . .

Cynthia Nell Snyder is 16 years old, attends high school, and has consistently received above average grades. Prior to the occurrences which led to this action, she resided with her parents in their North Seattle home. The record shows that as Cynthia entered her teen years, a hostility began to develop between herself and her parents. This environment within the family home worsened due to a total breakdown in the lines of communication between Cynthia and her parents. Cynthia's parents, being strict disciplinarians, placed numerous limitations on their daughter's activities such as restricting her choice of friends, and refusing to let her smoke, date, or participate in certain extracurricular activities within the school, all of which caused Cynthia to rebel against their authority. These hostilities culminated in a total collapse of the parent-child relationship. This atmosphere resulted in extreme mental abuse to all parties concerned.

On June 18, 1973, Mr. Snyder, having concluded that the juvenile court might be able to assist him in controlling his daughter, removed Cynthia from the family home and delivered her to the Youth Service Center. As a result, Cynthia was placed in a receiving home. On July 19, 1973, in an attempt to avoid returning home, Cynthia filed a petition in the Juvenile Department of the Superior Court for King County, alleging that she was a dependent child as defined by RCW 13.04.010(2) and (3), which provide:

> This chapter shall be shown as the "Juvenile Court Law" and shall apply to all minor children under the age of eighteen years who are delinquent or dependent, and to any person or persons who are responsible for or contribute to, the delinquency or dependency of such children.
>
> For the purpose of this chapter the words "dependent child" shall mean any child under the age of eighteen years: . . .
>
> (2) Who has no parent, guardian or other responsible person; or who has no parent or guardian willing to exercise, or capable of exercising, proper parental control; or
>
> (3) Whose home by reason of neglect, cruelty or depravity of his parents or either of them, or on the part of his guardian, or on the part of the person in whose custody or care he may be, or for any other reason, is an unfit place for such child; . . .

On July 23, 1973, Cynthia was placed in the temporary custody of the Department of Social and Health Services and an attorney was appointed to be her guardian ad litem. On October 12, 1973, the juvenile court held that the allegations attacking the fitness of Cynthia's parents were incorrect, at least to the extent that they alleged dependency, and that Cynthia should be returned to the custody of her parents. Cynthia did return to the family residence, where she remained until November 16, 1973. At that time, following additional confrontations in her home, Cynthia went to Youth Advocates, a group which assists troubled juveniles, who in turn directed her to the Youth Service Center. On November 21, 1973, Margaret Rozmyn, who was in charge of the intake program at the center, filed a petition alleging that Cynthia was incorrigible as defined under RCW 13.04.010(7), which provides:

> For the purpose of this chapter the words "dependent child" mean any child under the age of eighteen years: . . .
>   (7) Who is incorrigible; that is, who is beyond the control and power of his parents, guardian, or custodian by reason of the conduct or nature of said child; . . .

A hearing was held on December 3, 1973, to determine temporary custody. The court limited the proceedings to arguments of opposing counsel and ultimately decided that Cynthia should be placed in a foster home pending the outcome of the fact-finding hearing. This hearing was held on December 10 and 11, 1973. At that time, Commissioner Quinn found that Cynthia was incorrigible and continued the matter for one week in order for the entire family to meet with a counselor. Originally, the commissioner indicated that he was inclined to have Cynthia return home, while at the same time being placed under supervised probation. However, on December 18, 1973, Commissioner Quinn upon hearing the comments and conclusions of the counseling psychiatrists chosen by the parents, decided that Cynthia was to be placed in a foster home, under the supervision of the probation department of the juvenile court, and that she and her parents were to continue counseling, subject to subsequent review by the court. The parents immediately filed a motion for revision of the commissioner's decision, which was denied by the Superior Court for King County in August of 1974.

This court assumed jurisdiction of the case upon our issuance of the requested writ of certiorari.

The sole issue presented by these facts is whether there is substantial evidence in the record, taken as a whole, to support the juvenile court's determination that Cynthia Nell Snyder is incorrigible. Her parents contend that Cynthia is not incorrigible, as a matter of law, since the only evidence to support such a finding is their daughter's own statements. We disagree.

A child is incorrigible when she is beyond the power and control of her parents by reason of her own conduct. RCW 13.04.010(7). In reviewing the record in search of substantial evidence, we must find "evidence in sufficient quantum to persuade a fair-minded, rational person of the truth of a declared premise." Helman v. Sacred Heart Hospital, 62 Wash. 2d 136, 147, 381 P.2d 605, 612 (1963). In applying this criteria for review, we are mindful that our paramount consideration, irrespective of the natural emotions in cases of this nature, must be the welfare of the child . . . . When the questions of dependency and incorrigibility arise, "we have often noted what we think is a realistic and rational appellate policy of placing very strong reliance on trial court determinations of what course of action will be in the best interests of the child." In re Todd, 68 Wash. 2d [587] at 591, 414 P.2d [605] at 608. In reviewing the record, we find no evidence which would indicate that Commissioner Quinn acted unfairly, irrationally, or in a prejudicial manner in reaching his conclusion. Therefore, we must give "very strong" credence to his determinations. We feel it is imperative to recognize that the issue of who is actually responsible for the breakdown in the parent-child relationship is irrelevant to our disposition of this case. The issue is whether there is substantial evidence to support a finding that the parent-child relationship has dissipated to the point where parental control is lost and, therefore, Cynthia is incorrigible. It is for this reason that Cynthia's conduct, her state of mind, and the opinion of Doctor Gallagher, the psychiatrist chosen by Mr. and Mrs. Snyder, are of such paramount importance. This child has established a pattern of refusing to obey her parents and, on two occasions, has, in effect, fled her home by filing petitions in the juvenile court in order that she might be made a ward of the court. Cynthia's adamant state of mind can be best understood by considering her *clear* and *unambiguous* testimony in response to her attorney's direct examination.

> Q. Your petition alleges that you absolutely refuse to go home and obey your parents, is that correct?
>
> A. Yes.
>
> Q. You are under oath today, of course, and is that the statement you would make to the Court today?
>
> A. Yes.
>
> Q. Cindy, do you understand the consequences of filing a petition of this nature?
>
> A. Yes.
>
> Q. Did we discuss this matter?
>
> A. Yes.
>
> Q. Have we discussed this on several occasions?
>
> A. Yes.
>
> Q. What is your understanding of what might be the consequences of this type of petition?
>
> A. I could be put in the Youth Center or I could be put in another institution of some kind or I could go into the custody of the Department of Social and Health Services.
>
> Q. So you understand it is conceivable that you might not be able to go back home, is that correct?
>
> A. Yes.
>
> Q. In spite of all that, is it still your statement today that at the time of the petition anyway you refused to go back home?
>
> A. Yes.
>
> Q. Is that your position right now?
>
> A. Yes.
>
> Q. The position then, why don't you state that for the Court?
>
> A. I refuse to go back there. I just won't do it.

MR. SANDERS [Attorney for parents]. I object to the whole line of testimony. I think it is irrelevant whether she refuses to go back home. That is not an issue in the case.

THE COURT. Overruled.

> A. *I just absolutely refuse to go back there. I can't live with them.* (Italics ours.)

In addition, the parents and the older sister, by their testimony, admitted that a difficult situation existed in the home. The court also considered the testimony of the intake officer from the Youth Service Center as to the attitude of Cynthia. Finally, the court considered the opinion of Dr. Gallagher, who met with Cynthia and her parents, and reported that counseling would not be beneficial until all of the individuals concerned backed away from the hard and fast positions they now held in regard to this matter, which, in his opinion, was the cause of the tension which resulted in overt hostility. In other words, the finding of incorrigibility is not supported solely by Cynthia's testimony and her refusal to return home. But in addition thereto, the commissioner's opinion finds support in the testimony of other individuals who are familiar with the situation, either from a personal or a professional standpoint. . . .

Having found the juvenile court's finding of incorrigibility, as defined in RCW 13.04.010(7), to be supported by substantial evidence within the entire record, we are constitutionally bound to affirm the juvenile court's decision.

The parents also contend that RCW 13.04.010(7), is unconstitutionally vague. Our recent upholding of this statute in Blondheim v. State, 84 Wash. 2d 874, 529 P.2d 1096 (1974), is dispositive of this issue, and no further discussion is warranted.

It is implicit in the record that the petitioner parents believe the juvenile court has given sympathy and support to Cynthia's problems in disregard of their rights as parents, and that the juvenile court has failed to assume its responsibility to assist in the resolution of the parent's problems with their minor child. We find this presumption of the petitioners to be unsupported by the evidence.

The record clearly shows that numerous attempts were made by the juvenile court commissioner to reconcile the family differences, as evidenced by its unsuccessful attempt at sending Cynthia home subsequent to the disposition of the first petition, the attempt to gain assistance through professional counseling, and the numerous and extensive exchanges between Commissioner Quinn and the Snyder family during the proceeding. The avenues for counseling were to remain open and counseling of both parties was to continue, which was interrupted by the interposition of the application by the parents for our review. In view of our disposition of this case, we are satisfied that the juvenile court, in exercising its continuing jurisdiction, will continue to review the progress of the parties to the end of a hoped for reconciliation.

The decision of the juvenile court for King County is affirmed.

NOTES AND QUESTIONS

(1) As applied to the facts in the case, does the incorrigibility statute violate parental prerogatives that *Prince, Meyer,* and *Yoder* (Chapter 1) suggest may have constitutional dimensions?

(2) Epilogue.   In 1979, a jury awarded Mr. and Mrs. Snyder $140,000 against the State of Washington and King County for alienation of the affections of their child. The award was affirmed on appeal by a Washington state appellate court without opinion. Cynthia Snyder never returned home. (Richard Sanders, attorney for the parents, telephone conversation, May 13th, 1987.)

Snyder is analyzed and discussed in Comment, Status Offenses and the Status of Children's Rights: Do Children Have the Legal Right to Be Incorrigible? 1976 B.Y.U. L. Rev. (No. 3) 659.

(3) Emancipation. Emancipation is the process by which a minor becomes free from parental authority. An emancipated minor is considered an adult for legal purposes. At common law, a minor could be emancipated by marriage or service in the armed forces. Today, most states have statutes regulating emancipation. For example, according to California law, the petitioner must be at least 14 years old, willingly live separate and apart from his parents or legal guardian with their consent, have a legal source of income and manage his or her own financial affairs; and emancipation must not be contrary to the minor's best interest. Cal. Fam. Code §7120 (West 2003).

Minors seek emancipation for several reasons. Some are unmarried parents who want custody of their children, to qualify for government assistance, or to engage in such activities as obtaining a lease and consenting to medical care. Other youths seek to leave abusive homes. Kristine Alton, Rights of Children: Emancipation in San Diego County, 11 J. Contemp. Legal Issues 662, 662 (2000). One empirical study of 90 cases reported, surprisingly, that in many cases, parents initiate the idea of emancipation in order to abdicate their caretaking responsibilities (e.g., child support duty). Carol Sanger & Eleanor Willemsen, Minor Changes: Emancipating Children in Modern Times, 25 U. Mich. J.L. Ref. 239 (1992).

(4) Another interesting case, like *Snyder*, in which a PINS statute was used in an attempt to gain a minor's freedom from his parents was In re Polovchak, 454 N.E.2d 258 (Ill. 1983). Two children (12-year-old Walter and his 17-year-old sister Natalie) ran away from home when their parents, who had recently immigrated to the United States, decided to return to the Soviet Union. After the police found the children, the juvenile court determined that both Natalie and Walter were minors in need of supervision. The parents appealed, and the appellate court reversed. When Walter appealed, the state supreme court affirmed, concluding that "Walter should have been released to the custody of his parents, who were in the courtroom requesting permission to take their son home." Id. at 263. The court determined that Walter was not "beyond control." By the time the litigation concluded, however, Walter had turned 18 and was free to remain in the United States on his own. For a discussion of the case, see Irene Merker Rosenberg, Juvenile Status Offender Statutes — New Perspectives on an Old Problem, 16 U.C. Davis L. Rev. 283, 300-310 (1983).

(5) Several additional cases also involve a child's right to "divorce" his or her parents. Kimberly Mays was mistakenly switched at birth and sent home with a couple who were not her biological parents. The biological parents (the Twiggs) learned of the mistake ten years later when blood tests were taken while their daughter was dying of a congenital heart condition. Although the Twiggs agreed not to seek custody of Kimberly, they did seek visitation rights. The court denied the request for visitation, finding that such contact would be detrimental to the child. Twiggs v. Mays, 543 So. 2d 241 (Fla. Dist. Ct. App.), *aff'd*, No. 88-4489CA01, 1993 WL 330624 (Fla. Cir. Ct. Aug. 18, 1993). Kimberly (then 14) told the judge at first that she wanted nothing to do with her biological parents but subsequently changed her mind and moved in with the Twiggs. William Booth, Tangled Family

Ties and Children's Rights, Teen's Change of Mind Revives Debate, Wash. Post, Mar. 11, 1994, at A3.

In another highly publicized case, Gregory K. was placed in foster care after his mother abandoned him. At age 11, he filed a petition in the juvenile division of the circuit court for termination of his mother's parental rights (his father died during the proceedings). The trial court ruled that Gregory had standing to initiate the action even though he was an unemancipated minor. The appellate court, however, ruled that a minor did not have the capacity to bring a termination of parental rights proceeding in his own right but that the error was rendered harmless by the fact that separate petitions for termination were filed on his behalf by other parties (i.e., his foster parents, who filed for adoption). Kingsley v. Kingsley, 623 So. 2d 780 (Fla. Ct. App. 1993).

More recently, a 14-year-old Massachusetts boy, Daniel Holland, petitioned to terminate his father's parental rights. The father had murdered the boy's mother and left the boy, then eight years old, to find her body. After the mother's death, Daniel went to live with his mother's best friend and her husband, who wanted to adopt him. Before the matter came to trial, the father (who is serving life in prison without parole for first-degree murder) agreed to relinquish his parental rights. James Compton, Couple Wanting to Adopt Son of Killer Dad Are Called into Court, Patriot Ledger, Nov. 29, 2004, at 1.

The case inspired proposed legislation in Massachusetts (called "Patrick's Law") that would provide for termination of parental rights in cases when a person is convicted of first- or second-degree murder of the other parent unless the child refuses or if the surviving parent (i.e., the perpetrator) was the victim of domestic violence. State News in Brief, Providence J., Dec. 7, 2004, at C3.

(6) Does *Snyder* suggest that young people may now themselves initiate governmental intervention into the family in order to diminish parental prerogatives? Do you think a likely legacy of *Snyder*, and the cases of *Gregory K.*, and Kimberly Mays, will be "kids . . . suing their parents for being told to do their homework or take out the trash?" Mark Hansen, Boy Wins "Divorce" from Mom: Critics Claim Ruling Will Encourage Frivolous Suits by Dissatisfied Kids, 78 A.B.A. J. 16 (1992).

Bruce C. Hafen, Children's Liberation and the New Egalitarianism: Some Reservations About Abandoning Youth to Their "Rights"
1976 B.Y.U. L. Rev. (No. 3) 605, 656-658

The individual tradition is at the heart of American culture. Yet the fulfillment of individualism's promise of personal liberty depends, paradoxically, upon the maintenance of a set of corollary traditions that require what may seem to be the opposite of personal liberty: submission to authority, acceptance of responsibility, and the discharge of duty. The family tradition is among the most essential corollaries to the individual tradition, because it is in families that both children and parents experience the need for and the value of authority, responsibility, and duty in their most pristine forms. When individualism breaks loose from its corollaries, however, its tendency to destroy personal fulfillment and human relationships is exposed. This result was anticipated in the infancy of the American democratic experiment by Alexis de Tocqueville:

> As social conditions become more equal, the number of persons increases who, although they are neither rich nor powerful enough to exercise any great influence over their fellows, have nevertheless acquired or retained sufficient education and fortune to satisfy their own wants. They owe nothing to any man, they expect nothing from any man; they acquire the habit of always considering themselves as standing alone, and they are apt to imagine that their whole destiny is in their own hands.
>
> Thus, not only does democracy make every man forget his ancestors, but it hides his descendants and separates his contemporaries from him; it throws him back forever upon himself alone, and threatens in the end to confine him entirely within the solitude of his own heart.[159]

Perhaps it is no coincidence that the recent period of expansive egalitarianism is also the period of the most widespread loneliness and alienation Western culture has known. It may also be that the tendency of democracy to make men forget both their ancestors and their descendants is causing some adults to seek the liberation of children as a way of liberating themselves from the duties, the ambiguities, and the self-denial that are necessarily required of parents and communities committed to the pattern of family life.

But individualism must remain embedded in the context of its corollary obligations to family and community if the individual tradition itself is to survive in a meaningful form. Family life, rather than subjecting the young to the permanent disadvantages caused by certain unfair discriminations against other classes, has served to nurture children's readiness for responsible participation in the individual tradition. The natural need to prepare children for entry into the fray of individualism, with its risks and obligations as well as its opportunities, has, until the last decade, kept children within the walls of the family tradition. We may now be on the verge of seeing a rejuvenated egalitarian movement break down those walls. To date, however, there is no serious evidence that society has outgrown the need for the preparatory role of the family tradition, nor has industrial society discovered substitute institutions or relationships adequate to fulfill the functions historically performed by the family.

Because of its preparatory role, maintenance of the family tradition is in fact a prerequisite to the existence of a rational and productive individual tradition. John Locke concluded his discussion of the role of children in the individual tradition with this statement: "And thus we see how natural freedom and subjection to parents may consist together and are both founded on the same principle."[161] The principle upon which both freedom and subjection to parents is founded has to do with the most fundamental human processes of learning. Locke believed that parents were obliged by "Nature" to "nourish and educate" children in developing the minimal capacities one must possess before the liberty to make binding choices can be meaningful. The related obligation of children is to submit to some degree of parental authority;

---

[159] A. de Tocqueville, Democracy in America 194 (R. Heffner ed., 1956).
[161] J. Locke, The Second Treatise of Government §55 (1952).

otherwise, little significant learning can take place. In his important work on the development of individual knowledge, philosopher Michael Polanyi has pointed out that neither basic nor sophisticated skills can be learned without the kind of personal master-apprentice relationship Locke saw as existing between parents and children:

> An art which cannot be specified in detail cannot be transmitted by prescription, since no prescription for its exists. It can be passed only by example from master to apprentice.... To learn by example is to submit to authority. You follow your master because you trust his manner of doing things even when you cannot account in detail for its effectiveness. By watching the master and emulating his efforts in the presence of his example, the apprentice unconsciously picks up the rules of the art, including those which are not explicitly known to the master himself. These hidden rules can be assimilated only by a person who surrenders himself to that extent uncritically to the imitation of another. A society which wants to preserve a fund of personal knowledge must submit to tradition.[162]

It is more than coincidental that for the ancient Greeks and Romans, as well as for Western society in the post-1500 period, a strong commitment to the idea of childhood and lasting family relationships grew parallel with a strong commitment to the idea of education. Childhood, as a time of life and as a frame of mind, is intimately related to educational development.

Ardent advocates of children's rights may believe that "in this society . . . we are not likely to err in the direction of too much freedom,"[164] but too much freedom can undermine and finally destroy the most fundamental processes and the human relationships that sustain them. To the extent that these relationships and processes are undetermined, it is ultimately the tradition of individual liberty that will be damaged.

WRITTEN REVIEW PROBLEMS

(1) Legislative Proposal to Give Teenagers the Vote.   A state senator introduces a bill, titled "Training Wheels for Citizenship," to amend the Blackacre state constitution to give youths a partial vote in state-wide elections. According to the bill, youths aged 16 and 17 would receive a fractional vote equal to one-half of an adult; and youths aged 14 and 15 would have a fractional vote equal to one-quarter of an adult. The senator who sponsored the legislation claims that the proposal would boost voter participation, which has hit historic lows. He argues that the modern teenager is much better informed than youths in the past because of the technological innovations such as the Internet, cell phones, and multichannel television. Ken McNeill, Proposed Amendment Would Reduce Minimum Age from 18 to 14, Daily Review (Hayward, CA), Mar. 9, 2004 (describing similar legislative efforts by California state senator John Vasconcellos). The senator adds that lowering the voting age would develop youths' sense of responsibility while at the same time

---

[162] M. Polanyi, Personal Knowledge: Towards a Post-Critical Philosophy 53 (1964).
[164] R. Farson, Birthrights 2 (1974).

their fractional representation would recognize that they are not yet fully mature. John M. Hubbell, Partial Vote for Teenagers Proposed, S.F. Chron., May 6, 2004, at A10.

Supporters of the bill explain that some countries allow youths younger than age 18 to vote (e.g., Austria and Germany allow 16-year-olds to vote; Israel allows 17-year-olds to vote). McNeill, supra. A delegation of local high school youths lobby the state legislature to adopt the bill by arguing that teenagers contribute to the state economy (by means of their employment, income taxes, and sales tax) and therefore should have the right to decide how their taxes are spent. Hubbell, supra. On the other hand, one lobbyist contends that teens do not have the life experience to be voters and that teenage voters would be "susceptible to peer pressure, even a rock or a rap song." Id. Additional opponents point out that the proposal would create a "logistical nightmare" in tallying an election. Id. In addition, an African American legislator opposes the proposal, by "allud[ing] to a time in history when blacks were viewed as three-fifths of a man in determining representation." Id.

You are the legislative intern to the state senator in Blackacre who is sponsoring the legislation. Please write a memorandum explaining your opinion of the proposal. In your memorandum, consider the following: the various age-based limitations on the liberty of minors, the issue whether young persons should have the same rights as adults, the interests that are served by treating youths by different standards, and the appropriateness of age-based lines generally and as applied to the voting context.

(2) Parent-Child Divorce. A husband and wife have some legal power to change their marital status. They may go to court and secure a judicial determination of whether and how the marriage should be dissolved or modified. Write an essay on the legal ability and desirability of allowing young people aged 14 to 18 to divorce themselves from their parents. You may use the law of your own state.

a. First consider the case in which the parents and young person agree that they wish to change their legal relationship and have the young person assume more adult responsibilities. Under existing law, what legal impediments lie in the way of such emancipation? Put another way, are there limits under existing law to the power of young people and their parents to change consensually their legal relationship? What would you advise them? Consider this question, in light of parental support obligations, parental rights and duties to discipline, parental duties with regard to the child's torts and contracts, and the young person's ability to secure medical treatment, a job, a driver's license, a car, and the control of his or her own property; and to make decisions about his or her education. Does the state have an independent interest if the young person and the parents agree? Would you change their power to modify their relationship in any of these areas? Why? How? If young people "run away," and the parents do ask for them back, is this a different situation?

b. Now consider the situation if the parents and the young person do not agree — the young person wants to emancipate himself or herself and the parents will not consent. Briefly describe those areas (if any) where the young person can assert autonomy under existing law before reaching 18. Should the law be changed to allow a young person to invoke the judicial process to change the legal relationship with his or her parents? Should there be a proceeding (analogous to a contested divorce?) in which young people can "free" themselves or modify the legal relationship with their parents? What difficulties do you see with such an approach? If there were such a judicial inquiry, what factors would be relevant to the decision — what legal standards and process would you suggest? Describe those areas, if any, where you think such an approach would be appropriate.

c. Finally, consider whether there is a need for a uniform statutory emancipation of minors act. If so, how should the act take into account the following issues: (1) the minimum age for emancipation, (2) the proper court of jurisdiction, (3) the specific standards by which the court may judge the petition, (4) whether the minor needs parental consent before the court may grant the petition, (5) the purposes for which the minor may be considered emancipated? See generally H. Jeffrey Gottesfeld, Comment, The Uncertain Status of the Emancipated Minor: Why We Need a Uniform Statutory Emancipation of Minors Act (USEMA), 15 U.S.F.L. Rev. 473 (1981) (explaining how modern statutes generally address these issues).

CHAPTER **7**

Juvenile Delinquency

A. *INTRODUCTION*

How are juvenile offenders treated differently from adult offenders? To what extent should they be? These questions, closely related to the general issues in this book, provide the focus for this examination of delinquency.[1]

As background for these questions, the various purposes of criminal punishment (rehabilitation, deterrence, incapacitation, and retribution) are examined in order to analyze whether delinquents and adult offenders should be treated differently. Introductory materials are provided next concerning juvenile crime and the juvenile court: its history, philosophy, and bureaucratic context. Then, the jurisdictional and dispositional authority of the juvenile court are examined.

Next, various procedures governing the juvenile delinquency process and the adult criminal process are compared in light of the questions presented earlier: whether delinquents and adult offenders are and should be treated differently. The final section of the chapter concerns the role of the lawyer in the juvenile court process. Again, the core question examined is whether a lawyer's professional responsibility is different with a juvenile, rather than an adult client, who is accused of a criminal act.

Throughout the chapter, consider how the difference between the juvenile delinquency process and the adult criminal process is affected by or should be affected by:

1. the parent-child relationship,
2. the young person's possible lack of maturity and competence, and
3. the rehabilitative goals of the juvenile court.

[1] For additional materials on the procedural and substantive law concerning the juvenile court's delinquency jurisdiction, see generally Robert Agnew, Juvenile Delinquency: Causes and Control (2001); Dean John Champion, The Juvenile Justice System: Delinquency, Processing, and the Law (4th ed. 2003); Joseph G. Weis et al., Juvenile Delinquency: Readings (2001).

INTRODUCTORY PROBLEM

Thirteen-year-old Tony is a member of the Jets, a loose gang of boys who are mostly 15 to 17 years old. As his initiation into the Jets, Tony was told he must mug an old lady. Two days later Tony knocked down a 73-year-old woman as she was leaving a grocery store and snatched her purse. The woman was hospitalized with a broken hip. A bystander recognized Tony, and reported the incident to the police.

(1) Should Tony be held responsible for his act? How? Should he be adjudicated a delinquent? If so, should he be sent to a training school? Put in foster care? Put on probation? What information would be relevant to these decisions? What criteria should be used to decide?

(2) Suppose the day after the mugging, the police went to Tony's home where his parents allowed the police to search his room. The police find the victim's purse under Tony's bed. Is the search valid?

(3) Suppose the police ask Tony's parents to be allowed to question Tony. Tony's parents agree. The police then question Tony in the family's living room for 30 minutes with his parents present. Is Tony entitled to his *Miranda* rights? Is he entitled to counsel? Does it matter if the interrogation takes place at the police station instead? If the questioning lasts three hours? May the police exclude Tony's parents from the interrogation despite their request to be present?

(4) Suppose Tony at first denies involvement but then confesses to the police after his father threatens to beat him if he doesn't tell the truth. Should Tony's confession be admissible as evidence?

(5) A delinquency petition is filed against Tony, and you are appointed to represent him. Tony tells you he wants to "beat the rap" and not be adjudicated a delinquent. Most of all, he doesn't want to be sent to training school. Suppose the probation officer offers to put Tony on informal supervision without his being adjudicated a delinquent, provided Tony agrees to cooperate with the police in their investigation of the Jets? Tony says that he doesn't want to "rat" on his friends, but that he is afraid of his parents' reaction if he refuses to cooperate. How would you advise him?

(6) Would it be appropriate to hold Tony's parents financially responsible for his actions? To what extent? Suppose $500 of the victim's medical bills was not paid for by her health insurance. Should Tony's parents be made to pay?[2] Would your opinion change if the victim does not have medical insurance and her bills total $25,000?

(7) If Tony were 18 instead of 13, would any of your answers be different? From a policy perspective, is there a single age that defines an appropriate cutoff point for distinguishing youth crime from adult crime?

---

[2] For a discussion of parents' civil liability for acts committed by their minor children, see Linda A. Chapin, Out of Control? Uses and Abuses of Parental Liability Laws to Control Juvenile Delinquency in the United States, 37 Santa Clara L. Rev. 621 (1997); Pamela K. Graham, Parental Responsibility Laws: Let the Punishment Fit the Crime, 33 Loy. L.A. L. Rev. 1719 (2000); Daniel W. Rinaldelli, Parent's Right to Contest Amount of Restitution, 21 J. Juv. L. 196 (2000).

B.   BACKGROUND

1.   The Purposes of Punishment and Juvenile Justice

Various justifications have been offered for punishing adult criminal conduct: (a) rehabilitation; (b) deterrence, special and general; (c) incapacitation; and (d) retribution. Is each a legitimate purpose with regard to delinquents?

a. Rehabilitation

Treatment and rehabilitation traditionally have served as *the* justification for the juvenile justice system. As Professor Herbert Packer has written: "The most immediately appealing justification for punishment is the claim that it may be used to prevent crime by so changing the personality of the offender that he will conform to the dictates of the law; in a word, by reforming him."[3] In theory, delinquency proceedings allowed a benevolent judge to provide the necessary help and guidance to a young person who might otherwise travel further down the road of crime. This rehabilitative ideal had several important consequences for the juvenile court process: since the underlying justification was prevention, not punishment, proof that a youth in fact committed a particular crime was traditionally thought less relevant than the youth's need for rehabilitation; judges were given broad discretion with regard to dispositions; and the length of sentences was typically indeterminate, so that "treatment" could continue as long as it was thought appropriate.

In re Gault (discussed infra p. 782) and its progeny imposed procedural safeguards intended to ensure an adequate factual determination concerning a past criminal act. Nevertheless, the rehabilitative premises of the juvenile court still have important consequences that remain open to question: judges and corrections personnel still have broad discretionary power with regard to disposition. Once jurisdiction is established, the disposition does not typically depend on the seriousness of the crime proven. "The murderer was as eligible for the indeterminate commitment as was the beggar."[4] Indeed, notwithstanding the criticisms of the rehabilitative ideal that have become increasingly vociferous since *Gault*, the juvenile justice system remains largely wedded to this purpose; McKeiver v. Pennsylvania, infra p. 798, suggests as much.

With regard to rehabilitation, should children be treated differently than adults? Are children easier to rehabilitate than adults? Or more difficult to treat? Two behavioral assumptions underlie claims that rehabilitation is more relevant for youthful offenders than for adult criminals: (1) juvenile offenders will become adult offenders unless they are treated, (2) youthful offenders are particularly amenable to rehabilitative treatment. Available social science evidence fails to establish either assumption.[5]

[3] Herbert L. Packer, The Limits of the Criminal Sanction 53 (1968).

[4] Sanford J. Fox, Philosophy and the Principle of Punishment in the Juvenile Court, 8 Fam. L.Q. (No. 4) 373, 377 (1974).

[5] See generally Anna Louise Simpson, Comment, Rehabilitation as the Justification of a Separate Juvenile Justice System, 64 Cal. L. Rev. 984 (1976).

In terms of the first assumption, it appears that most adolescents at one time or another engage in unlawful conduct. But most do not go on to pursue a life of crime. This necessarily implies that many young people who have committed a criminal act "do not graduate to criminal careers."

There have been several studies that followed, over an extended period of time, the careers of juvenile offenders. The most important of these traced the arrest histories of males born in Philadelphia in 1945. See Marvin E. Wolfgang et al., Delinquency in a Birth Cohort (1972). Of the 9,945 cohort subjects, about 35 percent were involved with the police at least once to the extent that an official recording of the act resulted. Of these offenders, 54 percent were recidivists and 46 percent were one-timers. About 18 percent of the offenders were categorized as "chronic offenders" — they each committed more than four violations. As a group, the chronic offenders committed over one-half of all the juvenile offenses recorded. Id. at 244-248.

Subsequently, the Wolfgang study was replicated with surprisingly similar results. See Paul E. Tracy et al., Delinquency in Two Birth Cohorts, Executive Summary, U.S. Dept. Justice, Office of Juvenile Justice and Delinquency Prevention (Sept. 1985). In the later study, of 13,160 male cohort subjects, about 33 percent were involved with the police at least once, to the extent that an official record ensued. Of these offenders, 58 percent were recidivists, and 42 percent were one-timers. About 23 percent of the recidivists were termed "chronic offenders" (with more than four violations). A comparison of the two birth cohorts revealed an enduring effect regarding the chronic offenders' share of offenses. That is, compared to the earlier study in which 18 percent of the chronic delinquent subset committed 52 percent of the delinquent acts, in the later group 23 percent of the chronic delinquents committed 61 percent of the delinquent offenses. Id. at 5, 9, 10. It must be remembered, of course, that this study, like most of the empirical research bearing on rehabilitation, is based on subsequent arrest records — such records are obviously an imperfect measure of subsequent criminal behavior.

Analysis is complicated by the fact that youthful offenders tend to commit somewhat different sorts of crimes than older offenders. The more serious offenses are more likely to be committed by older delinquents.[6] To the extent that the young tend to commit different sorts of crimes, does this in itself justify greater reliance on rehabilitation? Does it imply that a 16-year-old who steals a car is more likely to be rehabilitated than a 16-year-old who commits aggravated assault? The earlier Wolfgang study (referred to above) suggested that "the choice of the type of the next offense is only very slightly related to the type of the prior offense or offenses." Wolfgang et al., Delinquency in a Birth Cohort, supra, at 254.

As imperfect as our knowledge today is, it nevertheless appears that ". . . the clearest finding from the statistics on the age distribution of offenders and the studies following the later lives of juvenile offenders is that the probability of offenses decreases with age. There is no generally accepted explanation of this decrease."[7]

---

[6] Paul E. Tracy et al., Delinquency in Two Birth Cohorts, Executive Summary, U.S. Dept. Justice, Office of Juvenile Justice and Delinquency Prevention 15 (Sept. 1985).

[7] Simpson, supra note [5], at 984-985.

The second assumption, that juvenile offenders are more amenable to rehabilitative treatment than adult offenders, also finds little support in the evidence:

> Despite the evidence that juvenile and adult offenders share important characteristics [with regard to moral reasoning, decision making, and control of impulses] the supposition that juvenile offenders, because less fixed in their ways, are more amenable to rehabilitative treatment than adults, might make the special treatment of juveniles appropriate. But there is little evidence to support this simple and popular view. Maturational reform is not evidence of greater amenability to rehabilitative programs; the reform associated with age appears to occur whether or not the offender is apprehended. Apparently, variables that account for maturational reform are not influenced by treatment programs. The evidence does not lead to the conclusion that all rehabilitative programs should be eliminated; rather, it suggests that an emphasis on rehabilitative treatment for juveniles is not justified by the assumption that juveniles are especially amenable to rehabilitative treatment.[8]

In a thoughtful essay on delinquency prevention, Professor Frank Zimring cautions against primary reliance on rehabilitation and "people programs" that treat young offenders:

> A treatment emphasis is particularly risky given the track record of the great number of such programs that have been evaluated. Most programs have had no measurable impact on the criminality of their clientele. In a few cases, programs have apparently produced some improvement in some subjects. Overall, there is no present treatment technology that appears capable of substantially reducing recidivism, and there is no reason to suppose that we are approaching a breakthrough.[9]

Some critics go beyond simply doubting the efficacy of rehabilitation within the juvenile justice system. They suggest that, particularly for youthful offenders, intervention may increase the probability of future criminal conduct. If intervention were more likely to affect adversely recidivism for the young, then should not youthful offenders become "priority targets for non-intervention"?[10] See generally Edwin M. Schur, Radical Non-Intervention (1973).

Even if existing evidence does not demonstrate that juveniles are especially amenable to rehabilitation, does this necessarily imply that rehabilitation should be abandoned as the primary goal of the juvenile justice process? After all, in the last century rehabilitation has become an increasingly important goal for adult offenders.

Consider the institutional consequences of the rehabilitative ideal for the juvenile justice system. Some commentators have suggested that the rehabilitation rationale provides extraordinarily broad discretion to correctional personnel and "is to some extent a smokescreen to satisfy an ambivalent public, which sometimes feels guilty at merely punishing; and is primarily a managerial device to make it

---

[8] Id. at 1012-1013.

[9] Franklin E. Zimring, Dealing with Youth Crime: National Needs and Federal Priorities 8 (Sept. 1975) (unpublished policy paper prepared for the Federal Coordinating Council for Juvenile Justice and Delinquency Prevention).

[10] Id. at 23.

easier to manipulate prisoners in ways that minimize administrative problems."[11] On the other hand, might the abandonment of rehabilitation as the primary goal of the delinquency process make the juvenile justice system less humane? For example, at the present time, social workers and probation officers assume primary responsibility for delinquents. Are their attitudes different from those of prison guards? Is it not possible that juvenile institutions, because of the rehabilitation ideal, are, on average, better facilities than adult prisons? Put another way, even if we do not know how to rehabilitate, is it not possible that the goal nevertheless makes the custodial arrangements for young people better than they would be if rehabilitation were abandoned?

b. Deterrence

The classical utilitarian justification for punishment is that it has an inhibiting effect on the future conduct of those who might otherwise commit crimes. Punishing a youthful offender may thus serve as a threat that deters others from committing crimes ("general deterrence"). It may also deter the youth being punished from future criminal conduct because of increased sensitivity to threatened punishment in the future ("intimidation" or "special deterrence").[12]

From the victim's perspective, and probably from society's as well, the fact that a criminal act has been committed by a young person rather than by an adult hardly makes it of *less* social concern. To the victim of a mugging the age of the attacker is not of primary concern. If the short-run undesirable consequences of a criminal act do not depend upon the age of the offender, is not deterrence (both general and special) as valid a purpose with regard to youthful offenders as for adult offenders?

Deterrence has been criticized by psychologists on the ground that the behavioral model underlying deterrence "assumes a perfectly hedonistic, perfectly rational actor, whose object it is to maximize pleasure and minimize pain." To such an actor contemplating the possibility of a criminal act, the decision is based on a calculus: "How much do I stand to gain by doing it? How much do I stand to lose if I am caught doing it? What are the chances of my getting away with it? What is the balance of gain and loss as discounted by the chance of apprehension?"[13] Some psychological critics suggest that a person's behavior is largely determined by unconscious drives that impel actions, which are therefore not rationally based. Such critics reject the notion that punishment will deter future behavior.

The high recidivism rate for juvenile offenders who are punished is often cited as evidence that special deterrence or intimidation does not in fact work. Indeed, it might be argued that

---

[11] Caleb Foote, quoted in Leigh, Corrections and the Courts: A Plea for Understanding and Implementation, Resolution (1974) at 23.

[12] It should be noted that special deterrence is not unrelated to rehabilitation. Both aim to curb future criminal misconduct of the person being "punished" or "treated." Special deterrence is based on a model that punishment will reduce the commission of future crimes by the individual being punished, specifically by causing that individual to realize that the consequences outweigh the benefits of future criminal acts. See generally Packer, supra note [3].

[13] Packer, supra note [3], at 40-41.

the corrupting influence of criminal associations in prison with the feelings of bitterness, hatred, and desire for revenge that are engendered by inhumane treatment in a backward prison may well produce a net loss in crime prevention. Whatever feelings of intimidation are produced on the prisoner by the severity of his punishment may be outweighed by the deterioration of his character in prison. His punishment may contribute to the effect of deterrence on others, but in the process he is lost to society.[14]

It should be pointed out, however, that "we do not know how much higher the recidivism rate would be if there had been no criminal punishment in the first place."[15] Moreover, threats of punishment may be more effective in curbing some types of crimes than others. For example, intuition suggests that it might be easier to deter economic crime (such as income tax evasion) than certain assaultive crimes (e.g., rape or murder).[16] It appears that much juvenile delinquency occurs as a result of group activities. There has been a considerable amount of sociological research relating to the juvenile gang. Unfortunately, no empirical research has been specifically directed at examining the degree to which group pressures within juvenile gangs may affect deterrence. To the extent that more juvenile crime is a result of group pressures than adult crime, it is certainly possible that deterrence has a differential effectiveness. In all events, empirical studies to date do not establish the differential effects on compliance with criminal law resulting from changes in particular sanctions. Still less do they disclose the differential effect of deterrence on young people as opposed to adults. See generally Franklin E. Zimring, American Youth Violence (1998); Franklin E. Zimring & Gordon J. Hawkins, Deterrence: The Legal Threat in Crime Control (1973).

Consider the implications of accepting deterrence as a valid purpose for imposing sanctions on juvenile offenders. If deterrence is adopted as a goal, this necessarily implies that we are prepared to punish a young person not because we necessarily believe it will help that particular youth but because we believe it may help society by altering the behavior of others. In other words, the state is *using* this young person to achieve state objectives. This, of course, is an accepted feature of the adult criminal process. But is it consistent with the claim that intervention is occurring in order to serve the child's "best interests"? If the juvenile justice system is premised in part on deterrence, is there any justification for denying juveniles the full range of due process protections afforded adults, including a jury trial? See *McKeiver* and the materials that follow, infra.

Acceptance of deterrence as a goal has other implications as well. For deterrence to be effective, potential offenders must be made aware of the probable consequences of their conduct. A threat must be communicated, and sanctions must be imposed. If in fact the sentences meted out by the juvenile process today are typically less severe than those imposed on adults, even insubstantial, then deterrence will suffer, at least if one assumes that juveniles are susceptible to threats and have learned that the sanctions are light. There does exist anecdotal evidence that the

---

[14] Id. at 47.

[15] Id. at 46.

[16] Id. at 46-47.

insubstantiality of the sanctions imposed by the juvenile justice process may affect behavior. For example, a New York Times article suggested that "thousands of Harlem drug runners, [aged] 9 to 16, find the rewards are high, the risks low." The article goes on to suggest:

> Arrests are commonly viewed as minor inconveniences. The youths are treated as juvenile delinquents and released to the custody of a parent or guardian. Sometimes they are back on the street dealing before the sun rises and sets. Under the present law, the maximum sentence a juvenile can receive is 18 months.[17]

c. Incapacitation

Past misconduct may lead to the belief that in the future if permitted to remain at large in society, the offender will in all likelihood commit further crimes. By putting the offenders somewhere where they can no longer endanger members of society at large, the streets have thereby been made safer by being rid of troublemakers.

Is incapacitation as valid a purpose for youthful offenders as it is for adult criminals? As suggested earlier, "statistics on the age distribution of offenders and the studies following the later lives of juvenile offenders" demonstrate that "the probability of offenses decreases with age" and that by 25 or 30 most criminal careers will end.[18] Consider the implications of this social science finding. If most youthful offenders "grow out" of their delinquency, why not incapacitate a delinquent found guilty of several offenses during the years when it is likely he will commit further crimes and release him only when he reaches an age that makes further criminal behavior unlikely — say, 25 or 30?

Various criticisms of incapacitation have been made. For one thing, keeping someone locked up is quite expensive. In California in 2004-2005, for example, the Youth Authority indicated that it cost $71,700 annually to keep a delinquent in a secure facility.[19] Second, long-term incarceration may make successful reintegration of the offender into the community more difficult when he or she finally is released. In addition, incapacitation may often offend notions of proportionality. Note that it would imply that a young offender (whose potential criminal career had more years remaining) would be given a more severe sentence than an older offender, even though their past conduct was largely identical. Finally, how confident are we about the implicit prediction that a youthful offender who has been convicted for several offenses will in all probability have a long criminal career? In this sense, incapacitation poses the same problems as *preventive detention.*

[17] Lena Williams, Thousands of Harlem Drug Runners, 9 to 16, Find the Rewards Are High, the Risks Low, N.Y. Times, Apr. 21, 1977, at B1.

[18] Simpson, supra note [5], at 1005, 1010-1013.

[19] Telephone interview with Nancy Lungren, Chief Information Officer, California Youth Authority, Sacramento, California (Feb. 10, 2004).

d. Retribution

By imposing a sanction on persons who engage in serious misconduct, society can express a sense of injury and moral outrage at the conduct and give the criminals their commensurate deserts. Punishment is "the deserved infliction of suffering on evildoers."[20]

It has been suggested that two different theories explain retribution. One is "revenge theory." A society pays a criminal back for his bad conduct, and punishment is a desirable community expression of hatred and fear aroused by the criminal's act. The second theory, "expiation theory," rests on the idea that through suffering the criminal expiates sin. This theory focuses on the demands that the offender should make on himself. Punishment represents an external expression of condemnation that usefully reinforces or creates an adequate sense of guilt on the part of the offender.

In recent years, the legal response to crime, in general, and juvenile crime, in particular, has shifted from rehabilitation to an increased emphasis on retribution (as the excerpt below illustrates). Justifications for this shift to punishment include: (1) punishment will deter juveniles from committing future offenses, (2) punishment will incapacitate juvenile offenders and thereby prevent the commission of future offenses, and (3) punishment satisfies the societal desire for accountability. Consider whether retribution is a valid goal of punishment with regard to juvenile offenders. Implicit in notions of retribution is the idea that people are responsible for their actions. Are juveniles as "responsible" for their own conduct as adult offenders? Is it fair to hold young people accountable for their actions? Consider again the notions of responsibility underlying the legal treatment of young people in other contexts, such as the decision to have an abortion (Chapter 1), to secure medical treatment (Chapter 4), as well as the various topics considered in Chapter 6.

Recent scientific research reveals that the adolescent brain processes information differently from that of an adult. Studies that used modern scientific techniques (e.g., magnetic resonance imaging) and that focused on the causes of attention deficit hyperactivity disorder (ADHD) and autism, in fact, led to discoveries about adolescents' cognitive development that have relevance to juvenile justice. Research has demonstrated that certain characteristics of adolescents (e.g., their impulsivity, disregard of consequences, irresponsibility, vulnerability to peer pressure, and tendency to take risks) are products of their neurological immaturity rather than symptoms of deviance. Based on such evidence, are you convinced that juvenile offenders are less culpable than they are often thought to be?

For a review of this research and a discussion of its implications, see Barry Feld, Competence, Culpability, and Punishment: Implications of *Atkins* for Executing and Sentencing Adolescents, 32 Hofstra L. Rev. 463 (2003) (arguing that the psychological characteristics that were recognized by the Supreme Court in Atkins v. Virginia, 536 U.S. 304 (2002), as rendering mentally retarded offenders less blameworthy, also characterize adolescents and should therefore lead to a prohibition on their execution); Elizabeth Scott & Laurence Steinberg, Blaming Youth,

---

[20] Packer, supra note [3], at 36.

81 Tex. L. Rev. 799 (2003) (analyzing the culpability of juvenile offenders within the framework of criminal law doctrine and theory in order to enlighten lawmakers about how to assign criminal responsibility); Robert E. Shepherd, The Relevance of Brain Research to Juvenile Defense, 19 Crim. Just. 51 (2005) (arguing that an understanding of the neurological basis of adolescent functioning is essential for lawyers who represent youths).

Andrew R. Strauss, Note, Losing Sight of the Utilitarian Forest for the Retributivist Trees: An Analysis of the Role of Public Opinion in a Utilitarian Model of Punishment
23 Cardozo L. Rev. 1549, 1571-1581 (2002)

Public Opinion at Work in the Criminal Law: Rehabilitation and the Evolution of the Juvenile Justice System

Since the early 19th century, a system of juvenile justice has existed largely independently of the system of adult justice. The original premise behind the separateness of the juvenile justice system was that the juvenile is "unable to comprehend the wrongness of his acts and needs to be treated as though he were ill, instead of being punished like a criminal." Juvenile courts were to be guided by the best interests of the child rather than by the protection of society. In the past thirty years, however, the juvenile justice system has seen a shift in philosophy away from rehabilitation and towards retribution. . . .

C. The Fall of the Rehabilitative Ideal

[The author points out that the juvenile justice system "began its convergence towards the adult system" during the "due process revolution" of the 1960s and 1970s, consisting of cases such as Kent v. United States, In re Winship, and In re Gault (all discussed infra), which recognized procedural safeguards in delinquency proceedings.]

[Subsequent] events occurred that caused the rehabilitative ideal to lose favor with the public. First, the arrest rates for juveniles increased dramatically: between 1962 and 1972, the number of arrests of juveniles increased almost one hundred percent. This led the public to believe that juvenile delinquency was a major problem. Secondly, several studies were published that suggested that rehabilitation did not work. The most influential of these studies was the work conducted by Robert Martinson and his colleagues in the mid-1970s. This work consisted of a review of over two hundred studies of rehabilitation programs conducted from 1945 to 1967. Although some of these programs proved to be effective, the overall conclusion drawn by Martinson and his colleagues was that rehabilitation in general was an ineffective strategy for controlling juvenile crime. Soon after, the National Academy of Sciences commissioned a further study of the issue and came to similar conclusions. Both of these studies were used to support the "nothing works" philosophy, which claimed that the rehabilitative ideal was ineffective and should be scrapped.

Around the same time as the due process cases and the publication of Martinson's work, the book *Struggle for Justice* was published. This document, prepared for the American Friends Service Committee, presented an extremely harsh and compelling attack on rehabilitation. The authors argued that the rehabilitative model was a product of a class society, and that it resulted in a two-tiered system of criminal justice that gave preferential treatment to upper- and middle-class criminals. *Struggle for Justice* was extremely influential because it combined a political critique of rehabilitation based on inequality with empirical studies demonstrating the failure of rehabilitation. This document was subsequently cited by other, less radical, commentators who also advocated reform of the criminal justice system.

Also around the same period, the Joint Commission on Juvenile Justice Standards, a collaboration between the Institute of Judicial Administration and the American Bar Association, initiated a study of the juvenile justice system called the Juvenile Justice Standards Project. The fundamental working principle of the study was to create standards "to establish the best possible juvenile justice system for our society, not to fluctuate in response to transitory headlines or controversies." This ten-year study culminated in the publication of a twenty-three-volume report, which included a set of ten principles that a juvenile justice system should follow and which would impose more of an adult criminal law-like structure and emphasis on the juvenile system.

Although the Joint Commission founded these principles on the "idealized design of the family court as the centerpiece of [an] idealized juvenile justice system," it rejected the need for treatment as the basis for the court's jurisdiction. Instead, influenced by the In re Gault decision [discussed infra], it adopted "a due process model governed by equity and fairness."

D. The Political and Legislative Response

The shift in public opinion away from rehabilitation and towards greater punitive policies has had a significant effect on politics and state legislatures over the last thirty years. The politicization of crime and juvenile justice policies began in the 1960s, when conservative Republicans began to use crime control as an issue to distinguish themselves from Democrats. Political candidates such as Richard Nixon, Gerald Ford, and George Wallace ran "law and order" and "get tough" campaigns. Public statements about the "crime issue" by these politicians "who 'ought to know' contributed to the collective public perceptions that there was a 'crime problem,' and, in turn, contributed to the election of those who were making the statements." Since then, politicians have avoided running on platforms that can be characterized "soft on crime."

More importantly, public opinion has also prompted significant state legislative activity that has greatly altered the way in which juvenile crime is handled. Much of this activity has consisted in the increased use of waiver, which allows prosecutors, under certain circumstances, to try juveniles as adults in criminal court, and in the increased use of mandatory minimum sentences that depend on the seriousness of the offense. These changes reflect the shift in philosophy from rehabilitation to retribution, from individualized justice to just deserts, from offender to offense. This shift is also seen in state juvenile codes, which have increasingly used the language of accountability, responsibility, punishment, and public safety rather than the best interests of the child. . . .

2.   The Problem of Juvenile Crime

Howard N. Snyder, Juvenile Arrests 2001, Juvenile Justice Bulletin
Office of Juvenile Justice and Delinquency Prevention (Dec. 2003), pp. 1, 4, 6-10

In 2001, law enforcement agencies in the United States made an estimated 2.3 million arrests of persons under age 18. This number was 4% below the 2000 level and 20% below the 1997 level. According to the Federal Bureau of Investigations (FBI), juveniles accounted for 17% of all arrests and 15% of all violent crime arrests in 2001. The substantial growth in juvenile crime arrests that began in the late 1980's peaked in 1994. In 2001, for the seventh consecutive year, the rate of juvenile arrests for Violent Crime Index offenses — murder, forcible rape, robbery, and aggravated assault — declined. Specifically, between 1994 and 2001, the juvenile arrest rate for Violent Crime Index offenses fell 44%. As a result, the Juvenile Violent Crime Index arrest rate in 2001 was the lowest since 1983. From its peak in 1993 to 2001, the juvenile arrest rate for murder fell 70%.

These findings are derived from data reported annually by local law enforcement agencies across the country to the FBI's Uniform Crime Reporting (UCR) Program.

Female arrest rates continued to increase.

In 2001, 28% of juvenile arrests were arrests of females. Law enforcement agencies made 645,000 arrests of females under age 18 in 2001. Between 1992 and 2001, arrests of juvenile females generally increased more (or decreased less) than male arrests in most offense categories. The change in the female juvenile arrest rate between 1980 and 2001 was greater than the change in the male rate for aggravated assault (113% vs. 22%), simple assault (275% vs. 109%), and weapons law violations (140% vs. 16%).

Juvenile arrests disproportionately involved minorities.

The racial composition of the juvenile population in 2001 was 78% white, 17% black, 4% Asian/Pacific Islander, and 1% American Indian. Most Hispanics (an ethnic designation, not a race) were classified as white. In contrast to their representation in the population, black youth were overrepresented in juvenile arrests for violent crimes, and, to a lesser extent, property crimes. Of all juvenile arrests for violent crimes, 55% involved white youth, 43% involved black youth, 1% involved Asian youth, and 1% involved American Indian youth.

Despite the fact that there is still a notable disparity in proportional arrest rates between black and white juvenile offenders, over the period from 1980 through 2001, the black-to-white disparity in juvenile arrest rates for violent crimes declined. In 1980, the black juvenile Violent Crime Index arrest rate was 6.3 times the white rate; in 2001, the rate disparity had declined to 3.6. In 2001, the robbery arrest rates for both white youth and black youth were at a 20-year low. Unlike the white rate, the black rate in 2001 was substantially below its levels of the

1980s. Murder arrest rates in 2001 were near their lowest levels since at least 1980 for both white youth and black youth. Between 1993 and 2001, murder arrest rates for white juveniles declined 62%, while the rate for black juveniles declined 79%.

Murder

- The juvenile arrest rate for murder more than doubled between the mid-1980s and 1993.
- Between 1993 and 2001, the juvenile arrest rate for murder fell 70%, resting at a level lower than any experienced in the 1980s and 1990s.

Forcible Rape

- The juvenile arrest rate for forcible rape did not vary as much as the rates for the other violent crimes over the period of 1980 to 2001, although it did follow the general pattern of growth and decline over the period.
- The juvenile arrest rate for forcible rape increased 44% between 1980 and 1991 and then fell; by 2001, it was 13% below the 1980 rate, at its lowest level in at least two decades.

Robbery

- Juvenile arrests for robbery declined 30% between 1980 and 1988.
- Between 1988 and the peak years of 1994 and 1995, the juvenile arrest rate increased 70%, to a level 19% above the 1980 rate.
- Between the peak years and 2001, the juvenile arrest rate for robbery declined 59%, falling to its lowest level in two decades.

Aggravated Assault

- The juvenile arrest rate for aggravated assault doubled between 1980 and 1994. Its increase between the mid-1980s and the mid-1990s generally paralleled the increases for murder and robbery.
- Unlike the juvenile arrest rate trends for murder and robbery, the decline in juvenile arrest rates for aggravated assault between 1994 and 2001 did not erase the increase that began in the mid-1980s.
- Although the juvenile arrest rate for aggravated assault fell 33% between 1994 and 2001, the 2001 rate was still 37% above the 1980 level.

Burglary

- The juvenile arrest rate for burglary declined consistently and substantially between 1980 and 2001. Over this period, the burglary arrest rate was cut by 66%.
- In 1980, there were an estimated 230,500 juvenile arrests for burglary; by 2001, this figure had fallen to 90,300.

Juvenile arrest rates for weapons law violations mirrored the arrest rates for murder between 1980 and 2001.

- The juvenile arrest rates for weapons law violations and for murder more than doubled between 1987 and the peak year of 1993.
- After 1993, both rates fell substantially. The juvenile arrest rate for weapons law violations was cut in half, falling 49% and returning to the 1987 level.

Drug abuse violation arrests for juveniles soared in the mid-1990s.

- Between 1980 and 1993, the juvenile arrest rate for drug abuse violations remained within a limited range. Between 1993 and 1997, however, the rate grew 77%. By 2001, the rate had fallen only 16% from its 1997 high.
- During the period from 1992 to 2001, juvenile arrests for drug abuse violations increased 121%, while adult arrests grew 33%.

Two economists have proposed a novel and controversial theory to explain the decrease in crime rates over the past two decades. Professors John J. Donohue III and Steven D. Levitt posit a relationship between the legalization of abortion and the reduction in the crime rate. The authors theorize, "Crime began to fall roughly eighteen years after abortion legalization. The five states that allowed abortion in 1970 experienced declines earlier than the rest of the nation, which legalized abortion in 1973 with Roe v. Wade. States with high abortion rates in the 1970s and 1980s experienced greater crime reductions in the 1990s. . . . Legalized abortion appears to account for as much as 50 percent of recent drop in crime." John J. Donohue III & Steven D. Levitt, The Impact of Legalized Abortion on Crime, 116 Q. J. Econ. 379 (2001). Donohue and Levitt speculate that, as a result of legalization of abortion, fewer unwanted children were born to mothers in straitened circumstances — children who would have been more likely to grow up to be criminals.

NOTE: YOUTH GANGS AND ANTI-GANG LEGISLATION

Despite evidence of a decline in violent youth crime, gang crimes have become an increasing social problem. In the past decade, national concern with youth gangs has escalated. Nearly 21,500 gangs having 731,500 members were active in the United States in 2002, according to the Department of Justice. The highest concentration of gangs is found in Los Angeles (city and county) and Chicago, Illinois.[21] Moreover, modern street gangs are manifesting heightened levels of violence and, increasingly, are injuring innocent bystanders by their criminal activities.[22]

---

[21] U.S. Department of Justice, Office of Juvenile Justice and Delinquency Prevention, 2002 National Youth Gang Survey (2004).

[22] Id. See also Fox Butterfield, Guns and Jeers Used by Gangs to Buy Silence, N.Y. Times, Jan. 16, 2005, at 11 (juvenile gang homicides have increased by 25 percent since 2000).

Stemming from these concerns, many states have enacted anti-gang measures. In 1988 California became the first state to pass anti-gang legislation. The Street Terrorism Enforcement and Prevention Act (STEP) (Cal. Penal Code §§186.20-186.28 (West 2004)) was modeled after the federal Racketeer Influenced and Corrupt Organizations Act (RICO), 18 U.S.C. §1962(c) (2000). STEP creates a new crime of participation in criminal street gang activity by specifying that "any person who actively participates in any criminal street gang with knowledge that its members engage in or have engaged in a pattern of criminal gang activity, and who willfully promotes, furthers, or assists in any felonious criminal conduct by members of that gang" is guilty of a criminal offense (§186.22(a)). STEP also provides for sentence enhancements of one to three years for felonies committed in conjunction with gang activity (§186.22(b)), enhancements of two to four years for felonies committed on or near occupied schools (id.), forfeiture of weapons that are in the possession of gang members (§186.22(e)(1)), and criminalizes gang recruitment of a minor by means of violence or threats of violence ((§186.22(a)). STEP has withstood constitutional challenges on the basis of overbreadth, vagueness, and violations of due process and freedom of association. See People v. Gardeley, 59 Cal. Rptr. 2d 356 (Cal. 1996); People v. Green, 278 Cal. Rptr. 140 (Ct. App. 1991).

The California statute served as an important influence on other states' responses to street gang criminal activity. Some states, however, adopted provisions that went beyond STEP by penalizing gang intimidation, gang recruitment not only by force but also by mere encouragement, and gang drive-by shootings; and providing for broad forfeiture of gang assets as well as broad definitions of gang membership.[23]

Legislators and law enforcement have turned to other anti-gang remedies as well. Federal prosecutors began using RICO to prosecute urban street gangs in the 1980s. Congress enacted RICO in 1970 to eradicate the infiltration of organized crime, especially the Mafia. RICO statutes give prosecutors several advantages: use of more severe penalties, prosecution of *groups* of criminals and gang leaders, use of evidence of related crimes, and encouragement of witnesses' testimony because witnesses are likely to feel less threatened when groups of members are prosecuted.[24]

Some states target gangs by means of such civil remedies as injunctions that apply general nuisance statutes to gang members' conduct. Civil injunctions prohibit gang members from engaging in *legal* as well as illegal activities. "In addition to barring gang members from gathering in public, some injunctions prohibit them from wearing gang colors or symbols and possessing everyday items like cellular phones, pagers, tools, and spray paint cans — objects they typically use to conduct drug sales or vandalize property."[25]

---

[23] See Beth Bjerregard, The Constitutionality of Anti-Gang Legislation, 12 Campbell L. Rev. 31, 32-33 (1998); Carol J. Martinez, Note, The Street Terrorism Enforcement and Prevention Act: Gang Members and Guilt by Association, 28 Pac. L.J. 711, 714 (1997) (discussing statutes).

[24] Janice A. Petrella, Note, Equal Protection — What Is in a Name? Sign? Symbol? Gang Members and RICO Considered: State v. Frazier, 649 N.W.2d 828 (Minn. 2002), 34 Rutgers L.J. 1237, 1257 (2003).

[25] Julie Gannon Shoop, Gang Warfare: Legal Battle Pits Personal Liberty Against Public Safety, Trial, Mar. 1998, at 12.

California courts have granted preliminary injunctions against gangs on behalf of other citizens living in the neighborhood. The California Supreme Court upheld the constitutionality of such anti-gang injunctions in People ex rel. Gallo v. Acuna, 929 P.2d 596 (Cal. 1997), *cert. denied sub nom.* Gonzalez v. Gallo, 521 U.S. 1121 (1997) (holding that anti-gang injunctions do not violate freedom of association and are not vague or overbroad).

Some jurisdictions have also passed anti-loitering measures that are directed at gangs. For example, in 1992 Chicago passed a "gang loitering ordinance" that allowed Chicago police officers who reasonably believed they saw a gang member loitering in any public place with one or more persons to order the group to disperse. Failure to comply with the officer's order to leave the area gave the police power to arrest. In City of Chicago v. Morales, 697 N.E.2d 11 (Ill. 1995), the Illinois Supreme Court invalidated the ordinance as unconstitutional. Affirming, the United States Supreme Court held that the ordinance was unconstitutionally vague (reasoning that the statutory definition of "loiter" would not enable the ordinary citizen to confirm his or her conduct to the law). 527 U.S. 41, 60 (1999).

Some states address gang-related violence by expanding the circumstances that evoke the death penalty to include gang-related murders. See H. Mitchell Caldwell, Stalking the Jets and the Sharks: Exploring the Constitutionality of the Gang Death Penalty Enhancer, 12 Geo. Mason L. Rev. 601, 603 (2004) (identifying four states with these provisions).

Congressional concerns with juvenile gang violence led, in part, to enactment of the Violent Crime Control and Law Enforcement Act of 1994 (VCCLEA), Pub. L. No. 103-322, 108 Stat. 1796 (codified in scattered sections of U.S.C.), which imposes federal criminal liability for participation in street gangs. 18 U.S.C. §521(d) (2000). In addition, a juvenile's role in gang activity may serve as a factor in the judicial decision to transfer a youth to adult criminal court. 18 U.S.C. §5032 (2000).

Congress is presently considering the Criminal Gang Abatement Act (CGAA) (S. 1236, 107th Cong.), first introduced in 2001 by Senators Dianne Feinstein (D-Cal.) and Orrin Hatch (R-Utah). The CGAA encourages creation of regional task forces composed of local, state, and federal agencies to fight gangs, criminalizes gang recruitment of minors, increases funding to law enforcement for fighting gangs, enhances sentences for gang-related crimes, and creates a new federal crime of interstate witness intimidation.[26]

Commentators voice concerns about the constitutional shortcomings of the various anti-gang measures.[27] Nonetheless, most courts that have reviewed anti-gang legislation have rejected challenges on grounds of overbreadth or vagueness.[28] Aside from constitutional concerns, some commentators criticize

[26] For an explanation and criticism of CGAA, see Andrew E. Goldsmith, Criminal Gang Abatement Act, 39 Harv. J. on Legis. 503 (2002).

[27] See, e.g., Peter W. Poulos, Comment, Chicago's Ban on Gang Loitering: Making Sense of Vagueness and Overbreadth in Loitering Laws, 83 Calif. L. Rev. 379 (1995); Christopher S. Yoo, Comment, The Constitutionality of Enjoining Criminal Street Gangs as Public Nuisances, 89 Nw. U.L. Rev. 212 (1994); Matthew Mickle Werdegar, Note, Enjoining the Constitution: The Use of Public Nuisance Abatement Injunctions Against Urban Street Gangs, 51 Stan. L. Rev. 409 (1999) (suggesting anti-gang injunctions are unconstitutional).

[28] Bjerregaard, supra note [23], at 41-42.

anti-gang civil injunctions for their negative social connotations for minority youth.[29]

3. The Early Juvenile Court: Historical Origins and Philosophy

a. Historical Origins of the Juvenile Court[30]

The Invention of the Juvenile Court
Juvenile Justice Philosophy: Readings, Cases and Comments 550-557 (Frederic L. Faust & Paul J. Brantingham eds. 1974)

Historical analysis of the origin of the juvenile court is in flux. Two separate interpretations of juvenile court history — agreeing only on the year 1899 as the formal date of founding — have currency. . . .

The orthodox interpretation of the founding of the juvenile court is a tale of humane impulse merging with social science through a legal catalyst to replace the barbarous and vengeful cruelties of the criminal law with something better. At common law, and in the American criminal laws formed under the influence of classical criminology during the course of the 19th century, all persons capable of mature reasoning were held criminally accountable for their actions. Built into that general rule was the ancient common law exception of *doli incapax* which held children under the age of seven years legally incapable of criminal intent and hence crime. Children aged seven to fourteen years were presumed incapable of mature reasoning and so not criminally punishable. But the state could rebut the presumption. Where the presumption was successfully rebutted, children were held to answer in criminal court. Children above the age of 14 were treated as adults by the criminal law. The result was that children were arrested and jailed with adults, were tried under the same grueling procedures used for adults, and could be sentenced to the same punishments as adults. The orthodox histories of the juvenile court cite examples of children being hung, tortured, transported and imprisoned to make their point. In the orthodox interpretation, the founders of juvenile courts were first and foremost searching for a way to save children from the scourges of criminal law and prison discipline. The founders sought a humane and beneficial method for controlling offensive conduct and alleviating juvenile misery.

During the latter part of the 19th century nascent social science made its first impact on penology. The American version of positive criminology suggested that the causes of delinquency could be found in the heredity, and social and physical

---

[29] See, e.g., Gary Stewart, Note, Black Codes and Broken Windows: The Legacy of Racial Hegemony in Anti-Gang Civil Injunctions, 107 Yale L.J. 2249, 2250 (1998); Toni Massaro, The Gang's Not Here, 2 Green Bag 2d 25, 32 (1998).

[30] A great deal has been written on the origins of the juvenile court. Two examples of the traditional, orthodox view are Herbert H. Lou, Juvenile Courts in the United States (1927) and Julian W. Mack, The Juvenile Court, 23 Harv. L. Rev. 104 (1909). See also Sanford Fox, The Early History of the Court, in the Future of Children: The Juvenile Court 29 (Packard Foundation, 1996); Anthony M. Platt, The Child Savers: The Invention of Delinquency (2d ed. 1977); Margaret K. Rosenheim, A Century of Juvenile Justice (2002).

environments of the individual offenders. Where the causes could be identified, the medical analogy suggested that cures could be found and administered. Beyond that, the religious-humanistic child-saving movement, which dated from 1825, offered support and guidance for the positive school conclusions: children were infinitely malleable, the best possible subjects for the new social sciences to work wonders upon; and the source of most troubled children's problems could be identified in the social environment in the home created by irresponsibly indulgent or incompetent parents.

But to work its wonders, social science had to have early access to children, before they were molded into a life of depravity. . . . What was needed was a legal bridge between the troubled child and the agencies of amelioration. That legal bridge was found in the informal procedures of equity jurisdictions; in the doctrine of parens patriae. American ingenuity extended the parens patriae concept — the idea that the state was the ultimate parent — from its traditional role as guardian of the persons and property of wealthy orphans to a new and nobler role as guardian of all children. Suddenly the state took up the burden of parenthood and stood between all children and the manifest dangers of parental laxness and urban temptation. At the same time, equity procedure protected children from the stigma of criminality and the horrors of prison discipline. Parens patriae doctrine became the legal catalyst necessary to the formal foundation of the juvenile court. . . .

The revisionist interpretation of the founding of the juvenile court rejects ortho-dox history as both self-serving and ingenuous. The juvenile court was not a major departure in legal process, but rather an evolutionary culmination of at least a half-century's developments in penology and legal practice. The juvenile court was a steel fist of social control — fired in a blast furnace of class conflict and women's liberation and tempered in the fluid doctrines of positive criminology.

In the revisionist retelling of the creation of the juvenile court, it is no more than the last in a series of institutions created by 19th century Americans to deal with troubled and troublesome urban children. . . .

By the 1890s there was general agreement on reformatory theory. Anthony M. Platt has identified and articulated a nine-point statement of the ideal reformatory scheme: (1) segregation of young deviants from adult deviants; (2) removal of deviant children from unsound environments to reformatories for their own good; (3) denial of need for trial or due process legal trappings in the removal process because reformatories helped rather than hurt; (4) indeterminate commitments; (5) denial of sentimentality and resort to punishment where it became a necessary means to reform; (6) military drill, physical exercise, labor, and constant supervision to protect reformatory inmates from idleness and indulgence; (7) cottage plan physical plants in rural locations; (8) tripartite school program based on elementary education, industrial and agricultural training, and religious education; and (9) constant training in the value of sobriety, thrift, industry, prudence, realistic ambition, and life adjustment.

[T]he civil poor laws — marked by informal legal procedures and biased against the social environment implicit in pauper homes — were expanded and used to break up pauper families and direct pauper children into reformatory institutions. Penal theory made little distinction between delinquent and dependent children. As the 19th century progressed, courts came to blur the distinctions between delinquents and dependents in the same way penal theory did and to move toward use of the informal procedures of the poor laws as the most efficient method for delivering troubled and troublesome children to the child savers. On the eve of its founding, the revisionist interpretation concludes, all of the elements of the juvenile court existed in well-developed form. The Illinois juvenile court act merely codified extant practice.

The revisionist interpretation also rejects the orthodox history's analysis of the motives of the founders of the juvenile court. Far from seeing the founders as humanitarians, the revisionist interpretation sees them as members of social and political interest groups: a socio-economic elite manipulating the juvenile laws to hold the impoverished and immigrant lower classes in their places; professional child savers seeking protection and expansion of their careers; and middle-class feminists seeking both political power and socially acceptable careers outside the home. . . . The juvenile court gave a patina of respectability to and a rationale for the destruction of lower-class families. Deviance was a product of biology and environment. The juvenile court allowed the child savers to identify and save children by painlessly substituting healthy environments for sickly environments. It was all so scientific.

b. Philosophy of the Early Juvenile Court

Rehabilitative Ideal

The early juvenile court acts promised a new brand of justice for the child. Although this justice was to be dispensed in a court proceeding, the goals of the proceeding were investigation, diagnosis, and prescription of treatment, rather than adversary determination of facts and impositions of punitive sanctions. Rehabilitation, rather than deterrence and retribution, was to be emphasized. These objectives were set out by the court in Commonwealth v. Fisher, 62 A. 198 (Pa. 1905):

> The act is not for the trial of a child charged with a crime, but is mercifully to save it from such an ordeal, with the prison or penitentiary in its wake, if the child's own good and the best interests of the state justify such salvation. . . . The act is but an exercise by the state of its supreme power over the welfare of its children. . . .
>
> The design is not punishment, nor the restraint imprisonment, any more than is the wholesome restraint which a parent exercises over his child. . . . There is no probability, in the proper administration of the law, of the child's liberty being unduly invaded. Every statute which is designed to give protection, care, and training to children, as a needed substitute for parental authority and performance of parental duty, is but a recognition of the duty of the state, as the legitimate guardian and protector of children where other guardianship fails. No constitutional right is violated.

Procedural Informality

Judge Julian Mack, writing of the early twentieth century juvenile court, depicted a benevolent and paternalistic institution in which legalistic formalities would be not only inappropriate, but counterproductive:

The child who must be brought into court should, of course, be made to know that he is face to face with the power of the state, but he should at the same time, and more emphatically, be made to feel that he is the object of its care and solicitude. The ordinary trappings of the courtroom are out of place in such hearings. The judge on a bench, looking down upon the boy standing at the bar, can never evoke a proper sympathetic spirit. Seated at a desk, with the child at his side, where he can on occasion put his arm around his shoulder and draw the lad to him, the judge, while losing none of his judicial dignity, will gain immensely in the effectiveness of his work.[31]

Individualization

Justice for children was to be personalized, individualized. Mack describes the court's obligation as one of determining the child's need for treatment and writing out the correct prescription, rather than adjudicating criminal conduct:

> The problem for determination by the judge is not, Has this boy or girl committed a specific wrong, but what is he, how has he become what he is, and what had best be done in his interest and in the interest of the state to save him from a downward career. It is apparent at once that the ordinary legal evidence in a criminal court is not the sort of evidence to be heard in such a proceeding. A thorough investigation, usually made by the probation officer, will give the court much information bearing on the heredity and environment of the child.[32]

Separation of Juvenile and Adult Offenders

The juvenile court movement sought to ensure that children were not incarcerated with adults in order to protect children from being physically brutalized or taught criminal habits by hardened adult offenders. Indeed this goal of establishing separate and specialized juvenile detention facilities had been pressed by reformers with occasional success much earlier in the nineteenth century — New York City founded a House of Refuge for children only in 1825. Building on this tradition, juvenile court acts typically prohibited a court from committing a delinquent child to a correctional facility that also housed adult convicts.

4.   The Juvenile Justice System Today: The Bureaucratic Process

The juvenile court is one part of a larger juvenile justice system that includes police and correctional agencies. The number of children who actually go through the court's adjudicatory process and are placed in institutions represent a small fraction of those children who come in contact with some part of the total system. Most juveniles who appear in juvenile court are sent there by the police. However, some youths may also be sent to juvenile court by social agencies or parents.

[31] Mack, supra note [30], at 120.
[32] Id. at 119-120.

Howard N. Snyder, The Juvenile Court and Delinquency Cases
The Future of Children: The Juvenile Court 53, 55-58 (1996)

The Juvenile Court's Response to Delinquency Cases

In general, the juvenile court process can be conceptualized as a series of decision points. . . . All juvenile justice systems contain the same series of decision points; however, who performs these tasks (for example, police, prosecutor, court clerk, judge, or probation officer) may differ from jurisdiction to jurisdiction.

Diversion

Once a juvenile is arrested and the case is referred to court intake, an intake official (for example, a juvenile probation officer with intake responsibility or a prosecutor) decides if the referral should be processed by the court. The intake official's first consideration is the case's legal sufficiency — whether there is enough evidence to prosecute the matter successfully. If not, the case is dismissed. If the intake official decides that the case has legal sufficiency, the case may either go to the court or be diverted for handling outside the formal court process. Cases are likely to be diverted if the youth admits to the act, if it is the youth's first referral, if the charge is not serious, and if the victim is satisfied with the agreed-upon outcome such as the level of restitution. [A]pproximately one quarter of all delinquency cases [are] either dismissed or diverted to community agencies at the intake level.

Preadjudicatory Detention

At the time of referral to court intake, it is often the intake official who determines if the juvenile should be placed in a secure detention facility prior to the court's first hearing on the case. The intake official typically is employed by the detention center or by the intake department of the court. Detention may be ordered if the juvenile is a threat to the community, to ensure the juvenile's appearance at court hearings, or for the juvenile's own safety. State statutes require that, if detention is ordered, a judge must review the detention decision within a short period of time (generally 24 to 71 hours). Juveniles may also be detained later in the processing of the case if the court believes it is necessary. [I]n about one in five delinquency cases, the juveniles [are] securely detained for some period between the date of intake and the date of court disposition. . . .

Informal versus Formal Processing

If there is sufficient reason to believe the youth committed the delinquent act and it is determined that the matter requires some form of court intervention, the intake officer must then decide if the case should be handled informally or formally. In many jurisdictions, the youth must admit that he or she committed the act before informal processing is permitted. If the case is handled informally, the juvenile *voluntarily agrees* to serve a period of informal probation, to pay victim restitution, to pay a fine, to perform community service, or to submit to some other sanction. If the youth successfully adheres to this informal agreement, the case is then dismissed. If the youth fails to abide by the agreement, the case can then be reassessed and in most instances, handled formally. . . .

Transfers to Juvenile Court

There are three basic pathways for a juvenile to be tried in a criminal court: statutory exclusion, prosecutorial discretion, and judicial waiver or transfer. Statutes in many states exclude from juvenile court jurisdiction certain cases involving a person who by age alone would be classified as a juvenile and require that they be processed in a criminal court. Along with statutory exclusions, some states give prosecutors the discretion to file certain types of cases in either the juvenile or criminal court. The criteria for statutory exclusion and prosecutorial discretion normally involve factors of age, seriousness of the offense, and prior record. The third pathway enables juvenile court judges to waive the juvenile court's jurisdiction over a case and send the matter to criminal court. In addition to the factors mentioned above, the judge's decision is influenced by the juvenile's amenability to treatment in the juvenile justice system. . . .

Adjudication

Instead of a transfer petition, a petition may be filed asking the court to find (adjudicate) the youth to be delinquent. [Juveniles are] adjudicated delinquent in nearly three of every five, or more than 2 million, of these cases. In nearly two-thirds of those cases in which the youth was not found delinquent, the case was dismissed. In the other nonadjudicated cases, the youth *voluntarily agreed* to some form of probation, restitution, or other sanction(s).

Court-Ordered Dispositions

Once a youth is found to be delinquent, the judge can place the youth on formal probation, order the youth to a residential facility, invoke other sanctions such as restitution, fines, or community service, or dismiss the case in consideration of actions already taken. . . . When juveniles are placed in residential facilities, a variety of options are available to the court ranging from large state training schools with hundreds of beds to small, 30-bed, community-based facilities, to residential group homes for fewer than six youths. It is not uncommon for juveniles to move through different levels of security within a single institution or through more than one type of facility before completing their court-ordered disposition. . . .

Although there is some variation, in most states the juvenile court may keep juveniles in a residential placement or on probation until their 21st birthdays. Courts in a few states lose jurisdiction at age 18. . . .

C.   JURISDICTION AND DISPOSITION IN THE JUVENILE COURT

1.   Who Is Subject to the Delinquency Jurisdiction of the Juvenile Court?

In re Michael B.
118 Cal. Rptr. 685 (Ct. App. 1975)

FLEMING, J.

Nine-year-old Michael B. appeals the order of the juvenile court declaring him a ward of the court under Welfare and Institutions Code section 602.[1] The court based its order on a finding that Michael committed a burglary in violation of Penal Code section 459.

Richard Lewis testified that on 16 April 1974 he parked and locked his 1967 Mercedes Benz automobile in the parking area of his apartment building on North Maltman Avenue in Los Angeles. On his return to the automobile he found the outside rearview mirror broken off, the antenna bent, and the windwing pried open. Lewis gave no one permission to enter his automobile.

Police Officer John Murphy testified that on 16 April 1974 he was searching for a missing juvenile, Michael B., in the area of Bellvue Park, where Michael had been seen riding a purple, girl's bicycle. Murphy saw Michael hiding behind a shed in the park and asked him for his name and the whereabouts of the bicycle he had been riding. The boy showed the officer the bicycle in the bushes. Murphy took Michael into custody and advised him of his constitutional rights to silence and to counsel. Michael said he had heard his rights before and understood them, he did not want counsel, and he wanted to talk. At the police station, Murphy asked Michael where he had been the night before. Michael said he had been with friends, and they had gone into three or four cars on Maltman Avenue near the park. He then took Murphy to Richard Lewis' Mercedes Benz, told him he had broken off the rearview mirror so he could get his hands in to pry open the windwing and that when he had done so, one of his friends reached inside and unlocked the door. They took a package of cigarettes, the only thing they could find of value.

Murphy asked Michael if he knew right from wrong, if he knew it was wrong to break into cars and steal. Michael said yes. Murphy asked Michael how he would feel if someone took something that meant a lot to him. Michael said he never had anything that meant a lot to him, so it really didn't matter.

Penal Code section 26, which applies to proceedings under Welfare and Institutions Code section 602 (In re Gladys R., 1 Cal. 3d 855, 862-867), provides in pertinent part: "All persons are capable of committing crimes except those belonging to the following classes: One — Children under the age of 14, in the absence of clear proof that at the time of committing the act charged against them, they

---

[1] Section 602 provides in pertinent part: "Any person who is under the age of 18 years when he violates any law of this state . . . defining crime . . . is within the jurisdiction of the juvenile court, which may adjudge such person to be a ward of the court."

knew its wrongfulness." The Supreme Court declared in In re Gladys R., at page 867: "Only if the age, experience, knowledge, and conduct of the child demonstrate by clear proof that he has violated a criminal law should he be declared a ward of the court under section 602." The evidence here falls far short of that necessary to establish "clear proof" that Michael knew the wrongfulness of his acts.

The only evidence on that issue was the brief statement of the police officer that Michael said yes when asked if he knew the difference between right and wrong. Penal Code section 26 requires more substantial evidence than that to clearly prove that a nine-year-old boy, no more than a third-grade pupil, harbored the necessary capacity to commit a serious criminal offense. No such substantial evidence was presented here, nor do the nature and circumstances of the crime itself furnish that clear proof of knowledge of the wrongfulness of the conduct that is required by the statute. We think nine-year-old Michael was improperly adjudicated a ward of the court under Welfare and Institutions Code section 602.

In re Gladys R., 1 Cal. 3d 855, suggests alternative procedures under Welfare and Institutions Code sections 600 or 601 for disposition of cases involving, as here, a child too young to appreciate the wrongfulness of his acts (at p. 867):

> Section 601 provides that a child who disobeys the lawful orders of his parents or school authorities, who is beyond the control of such persons, or who is in danger of leading an immoral life may be adjudged a ward of the court. Section 601 might clearly cover younger children who lack the age or experience to understand the wrongfulness of their conduct. If the juvenile court considers section 601 inappropriate for the particular child, he may be covered by the even broader provisions of section 600. . . . Section 602 should apply only to those who are over 14 and may be presumed to understand the wrongfulness of their acts and to those under the age of 14 who clearly appreciate the wrongfulness of their conduct.

While Michael may be receiving the same care and treatment as a ward under section 602 that he would be receiving if a ward under section 600 or 601, disposition under section 602 carries a stigma of criminal conduct which is not justified by the record in this case.

The judgment (order) is reversed, and the cause is remanded to the juvenile court for further proceedings consistent with this opinion.

NOTE: JURISDICTIONAL REQUIREMENTS

From the outset, delinquency jurisdiction of a juvenile court has included young persons whose conduct would constitute "a crime if committed by an adult" (Or. Rev. Stat. §419.C453 (2003)) or who violated "any law . . . defining crime" (Cal. Welf. & Inst. Code §602 (West 2004)). In other words, the jurisdiction is defined in terms of age and in terms of violation of a criminal law.[33]

---

[33] As indicated in Chapter 6, young people who violate curfews, are truants, or are ungovernable may also be subject to the delinquency jurisdiction in some states, although the tendency in modern juvenile statutes is to create a special category for them.

(1) Minimum Age.   Most jurisdictional statutes do not establish a minimum age for persons to be subject to the original jurisdiction of the juvenile court.[34] There are exceptions, however. For example, 11 states set the minimum age at ten years old; 1 state sets the minimum age at eight; and 3 states set it at seven; North Carolina has the lowest statutory minimum age: six years.[35] In In re Michael B., note that California Welfare & Institutions Code §602 does not itself establish a jurisdictional lower limit. Instead, the court's ruling that nine-year-old Michael was not a delinquent turned on the statutory provision that excludes from the category of persons "capable of committing crimes" those children under 14, at least "in the absence of clear proof that at the time of committing the act charged against them, they knew its wrongfulness." That case suggests, however, how an infancy defense or the mens rea requirement may, as a practical matter, exclude younger children from being adjudicated delinquents. See also infra, In re S.H.

(2) Maximum Age.   The majority of state statutes provide that persons 17 and younger are subject to the jurisdiction of the juvenile court. Ten states set the maximum age for juvenile court jurisdiction at 16. Only three states set it even younger, at 15.[36] In addition to the variations in the maximum ages, statutes differ in terms of whether that age limit applies to the time when the alleged *crime* took place, or the age when *proceedings* are brought. States are split on this issue, and even among those states that set the age limit at the time when proceedings are brought, numerous interpretations of the standard exist.[37]

Although very young children might not be adjudicated as delinquents, a juvenile court may nevertheless assume jurisdiction over children because they are "neglected" or are beyond parental control. As a practical matter, what difference does this make? Is it less stigmatizing? Are the consequences for the child less severe?

(3) Violation of a Criminal Statute.   Every state incorporates "in some form and with various exceptions the criminal law applicable to adults as the dominant source of substantive rules governing the behavior of juveniles."[38] Precise limits of this incorporation vary substantially from state to state. Many states specifically exclude traffic offenses as a basis for delinquency. See, e.g., Colo. Rev. Stat. Ann. §§19-2-104(1)(a)(I) & (1)(a)(II) (West 2004). Questions can arise as to

---

[34] Melanie Bozynski & Linda Szymanski, State Juvenile Justice Profiles: National Overviews (2003), available at *http://www.ncjj.org/stateprofiles/* (last visited Feb. 10, 2005).

[35] Id.

[36] Id.

[37] H.D. Warren & C.P. Jhong, Annotation, Age of Child at Time of Alleged Offense or Delinquency, or at Time of Legal Proceedings, as Criterion of Jurisdiction of Juvenile Court, 89 A.L.R.2d 506 (2004).

[38] American Bar Association, Juvenile Justice Standards, Standards Relating to Juvenile Delinquency and Sanctions 18 (1980). In 1971 the Institute of Judicial Administration, a private nonprofit research and educational organization at N.Y.U. School of Law, began a Juvenile Justice Standards Project to address juvenile justice issues. The ABA became cosponsor of the project in 1973. More than 30 scholars undertook the task of writing standards and accompanying commentary. Their efforts culminated in tentative drafts. An executive committee was formed to review individual volumes. Twenty of the 23 volumes subsequently were approved by the ABA House of Delegates. The result is a set of standards and commentary intended to serve as a compilation of current thought and guidelines for action at local, state, and federal levels.

whether municipal ordinances, regulations concerning fish and game laws, and various other regulatory laws that allow the imposition of a fine satisfy the jurisdictional requirement that the conduct would be criminal if committed by an adult.

The Juvenile Justice Standards advocate the following:

2.2 Offense

A. The delinquency jurisdiction of the juvenile court should include only those offenses which are:

     1. punishable by incarceration in a prison, jail, or other place of detention, and

     2. except as qualified by these standards, in violation of an applicable federal, state, or local criminal statute or ordinance, or

     3. in violation of an applicable state or local statute or ordinance defining a major traffic offense.[39]

(4) Mens Rea and the Infancy Defense.   Most crimes require that a mental element — mens rea — be proven for conviction. Mens rea focuses on whether an accused possesses the specific state of mind required to commit a blameworthy act. The required state of mind varies with the crime: often, but not always, fault (not simply an unhappy result) must be shown.[40] Responsibility for criminal acts also involves the issue of capacity — whether the accused has the capacity to understand wrongfulness. In a sense, capacity is a prerequisite to mens rea — an individual must have the capacity to be culpable, that is to know wrongfulness, in order to maintain a specific mens rea. The criminal law permits the accused to prove defects in capacity, in the form of defenses such as insanity, mistake, or justification, in order to show that the accused is not a proper object of criminal sanctions.

In cases in which the accused is a minor there are additional complexities. Several questions can be posed. *First*, should age sometimes be a complete defense to a crime? An infancy defense did exist at common law: it centered on the question whether a child had sufficient maturity or capacity to know right from wrong. Special rules existed concerning the capacity of children to commit crimes. Children under seven were conclusively presumed to lack capacity to commit a crime. Children between seven and 14 were presumed to be without capacity, but this presumption could be rebutted. Finally, children 14 and above were held to the same standards as adults.[41]

In only a few jurisdictions today is a defense based on infancy available. When a general defense based on infancy is unavailable, a *second* and separate question concerns whether the minor had the requisite mens rea for the particular crime alleged. For example, a 15-year-old accused of the theft of a book would not at common law have an infancy defense available, but might nevertheless avoid conviction if

---

[39] Id. at 4.

[40] Professors LaFave and Scott have written: "Crimes may be classified according to their mental aspects into (1) crimes requiring subjective fault, (2) crimes requiring objective fault, and (3) crimes imposing liability without fault. The principal types of mental culpability in crimes requiring fault are (1) intention, (2) knowledge, (3) recklessness, and (4) negligence." Wayne R. LaFave & Austin W. Scott, Jr., Criminal Law 191 (1972).

[41] Id. at 399-403.

there was insufficient proof that he had intentionally taken the book knowing it was not his book but belonged to some other student.

Francis McCarthy has suggested that

> The principles of criminal liability at common law applied equally to both adults and children. In both instances the criminal sanction was imposed only upon proof of the commission of an offense and all the requisite elements, including mens rea, of that offense. The only difference between the child and the adult was that the former was aided by a presumption which had the same force for those children between ages seven and 14 as that which would be occasioned by a prima facie showing of insanity by an adult. If this obstacle to prosecution were overcome, the principles of criminal responsibility for adults and children were identical.[42]

A *third* set of questions concerns whether and how the creation of a juvenile court (and its delinquency jurisdiction) changed, if at all, these common law notions of children's criminal responsibility. Does an infancy defense exist in juvenile court? Must there be proof of the mens rea element of the crime upon which delinquency is to be based?

A number of state courts have considered whether the infancy defense is applicable to juvenile court proceedings. The traditional view, based on the rehabilitative ideal upon which the juvenile court was founded, is that since the juvenile court is not penal, children do not need to be protected from its jurisdiction by presumptions of incapacity.[43] As one commentator has described:

> Because parens patriae theory depends on the notion that the child is being helped and thus is not being tried for a crime and punished as a criminal, there was no need to determine whether the child had the capacity to act in a culpable fashion. Indeed, assertion of the defense could be viewed as wrongfully precluding treatment for those very children most susceptible to the benefits of intervention. . . . [44]

Only a small number of jurisdictions hold that the infancy defense is applicable to juvenile proceedings.[45] One commentator suggests that the shift in focus of the juvenile justice to a punishment-based rationale calls forth a new consideration of the infancy defense:

> Since 1992 all but 10 of the states have greatly liberalized the ability of the state to try juveniles as adults, a number of them at earlier ages than previously. In addition, public and law enforcement access to juvenile court records has broadened considerably. In more than half the states juveniles may be transferred to criminal court by judicial waiver, prosecutorial waiver, or statute for certain serious offenses committed prior to their fourteenth birthday, with a significant number of these

[42] Francis B. McCarthy, The Role of the Concept of Responsibility in Juvenile Delinquency Proceedings, 10 U. Mich. J.L. Ref. 181, 187 (1977).

[43] Lara A. Bazelon, Exploding the Superpredator Myth: Why Infancy Is the Preadolescent's Best Defense in Juvenile Court, 75 N.Y.U. L. Rev. 159, 161 (2000).

[44] Andrew Walkover, The Infancy Defense in the New Juvenile Court, 31 UCLA L. Rev. 503, 516-517 (1984).

[45] Bazelon, supra note [43], at 161 n. 7 (pointing out that only four states apply the infancy defense in juvenile court proceedings).

jurisdictions permitting adult treatment for children of any age for at least some offenses.

Even those youths retained in the juvenile or family court for handling as delinquents are increasingly exposed to sanctions that focus more on accountability than treatment, and they may be deprived of their liberty for longer periods of time pursuant to serious offender statutes. Juvenile court adjudications may be utilized more freely to enhance subsequent adult sentences under three-strikes laws or pursuant to sentencing guidelines in both the federal and criminal justice systems. In other words, the once large gulf between juvenile or family court rehabilitation and treatment and adult criminal court handling has narrowed considerably, if it has not disappeared entirely. In light of these major developments, the defense of infancy deserves a new look and fresh consideration by those involved in the juvenile justice process.[46]

See also Steven A. Drizin & Allison McGowen Keegan, Abolishing the Use of the Felony-Murder Rule When the Defendant Is a Teenager, 28 Nova L. Rev. 507 (2004) (arguing that the infancy defense should supersede the felony-murder rule). For the classic proposal to resurrect the infancy defense, see Andrew Walkover, The Infancy Defense in the New Juvenile Court, 31 UCLA L. Rev. 503 (1984).

Few reported cases explicitly consider whether mens rea must be shown in delinquency proceedings. However, most commentators, as well as the ABA Standards, have suggested that the state should have to prove the same mental element of the underlying crime for delinquency as in adult proceedings.[47] The ABA Juvenile Justice Standards require the state to prove mens rea — or the appropriate culpable mental state — in all cases in which it would be required if an adult were accused of the underlying crime. In addition, the Standards provide for a "reasonableness defense" for risk-creating conduct (that the juvenile's conduct conformed to the standard of care that a reasonable person of the juvenile's age, maturity, and mental capacity would observe in the juvenile's situation) and an "insanity defense" (that as a result of mental disease or defect, the juvenile lacked substantial capacity to appreciate the criminality of conduct or to conform conduct to the requirements of the law).[48]

(5) Fitness Hearings, Waiver, and Transfer for Trial in Adult Criminal Court. There are circumstances in which a minor may be tried for a crime in adult criminal court rather than juvenile court. The possibility of transfer or waiver has been a feature of the juvenile court system since its inception, and nearly every state allows for it. The recent "get tough on crime" movement has resulted in an increasing number of youths being transferred to criminal court. Juveniles may be transferred from the juvenile court to the adult criminal court in three ways: judicial waiver, legislative waiver, or prosecutorial discretion.

First, juvenile court judges may transfer cases to adult criminal court following a hearing. Common judicial waiver provisions allow a juvenile court judge to transfer

---

[46] Robert E. Shepherd, Jr., Juvenile Justice, 12 Crim. Just. 45, 45 (1997). See also Bazelon, supra note [43] (advocating use of a reformulated infancy defense requiring proof of a juvenile's capacity *and* mens rea).

[47] See, e.g., McCarthy, supra note [43]; Sanford J. Fox, Responsibility in the Juvenile Court, 11 Wm. & Mary L. Rev. 650 (1970).

[48] American Bar Association, Juvenile Justice Standards, supra note [38], at 5-6.

a juvenile to criminal court if the judge determines that the youth is not a "fit and proper" subject for juvenile court processing or that the youth "cannot benefit" from the "guidance" or "treatment" available in the juvenile court system."[49]

In Kent v. United States, 383 U.S. 541 (1966), the United States Supreme Court mandated certain procedural safeguards for judicial waiver (a hearing, representation, access by counsel to social and probation records, and a statement of reasons justifying the transfer). In an attempt to provide guidelines for the exercise of judicial discretion, the Court enumerated certain factors that should be considered in the waiver determination — i.e., seriousness of the offense to the community, manner in which the offense was committed (violence or premeditation), person-based or property-based offense, sufficiency of the evidence, desirability of trying the offense in one court, maturity of juvenile, record and previous arrest history of juvenile, protection of public, and likelihood of rehabilitation of juvenile by use of juvenile court procedures. Id. at 566-567. *Kent* required that judges make explicit findings based on individualized determinations of amenability to treatment or dangerousness to the community.

The ABA Juvenile Justice Standards also attempted to limit judicial discretion by requiring the following findings for transfer:

2.2 Necessary Findings

A. The juvenile court should waive its jurisdiction only upon finding:
1. that probable cause exists to believe that the juvenile has committed the class one [punishable by more than 20 years or the death penalty] or class two [punishable by 5 to 20 years] juvenile offense alleged in the petition; and
2. that by clear and convincing evidence the juvenile is not a proper person to be handled by the juvenile court.

B. A finding of probable cause to believe that a juvenile has committed a class one or class two juvenile offense should be based solely on evidence admissible in an adjudicatory hearing of the juvenile court.

C. A finding that a juvenile is not a proper person to be handled by the juvenile court must include determinations, by clear and convincing evidence, of:
1. the seriousness of the alleged class one or class two juvenile offense;
2. a prior record of adjudicated delinquency involving the infliction or threat of significant bodily injury, if the juvenile is alleged to have committed a class two juvenile offense;
3. the likely inefficacy of the dispositions available to the juvenile court as demonstrated by previous dispositions of the juvenile; and
4. the appropriateness of the services and dispositional alternatives available in the criminal justice system for dealing with the juvenile's problems and whether they are, in fact, available.

---

[49] See, e.g., Cal. Welf. & Inst. Code §707(c) (West 2004), which creates a presumption that a juvenile who commits certain felonies defined under §707(b) is not a fit and proper subject to be dealt with under juvenile court jurisdiction unless the court finds that the minor "would be amenable to care, treatment and training programs available through facilities of the juvenile court."

Expert opinion should be considered in assessing the likely efficacy of the dispositions available to the juvenile court. A finding that a juvenile is not a proper person
to be handled by the juvenile court should be based solely on evidence admissible
in a disposition hearing of the juvenile court and should be in writing, as provided
in Standard 2.1E.

D. A finding of probable cause to believe that a juvenile has committed a
class one or class two juvenile offense may be substituted for a probable cause
determination relating to that offense (or a lesser included offense) required in
any subsequent juvenile court proceeding. Such a finding should not be substituted for any finding of probable cause required in any subsequent criminal
proceeding.[50]

Fitness hearings result in a considerable amount of litigation and introduce
substantial complexity into the juvenile justice process. For example, Breed v.
Jones, discussed infra p. 806, posed a double jeopardy issue because a juvenile
court transferred a case to adult court *after* the adjudicatory hearing in juvenile
court. After *Kent*, supra, recurring issues regarding waiver included the following:
(1) Does a minor have a right to counsel at the waiver hearing? (2) Does the minor
and/or minor's parents have a right to notice of the transfer hearing? (3) Are the
rules of evidence applicable at the hearing, especially the admissibility of hearsay?
(4) What is the standard of proof at the hearing? (5) Is the privilege against self-
incrimination applicable, especially the admissibility in subsequent proceedings of
incriminating statements? (6) Does a right of appeal exist?

Judicial waiver practice received considerable criticism in the years following *Kent.* Such criticisms triggered statutory reforms focusing on an offense-based
system. In this second form of waiver, "legislative" or "automatic waiver," many
state statutes exclude certain crimes or chronic offenders from juvenile court
jurisdiction. For example, juvenile court jurisdiction is automatically precluded
in some states when the child is charged with an act that would be a capital crime or an extremely serious felony (e.g., murder, kidnapping, rape, armed
robbery, crimes committed with a firearm). Some states include drug offenses
and felonies committed in furtherance of gang activities. In the past few years,
many states revised their transfer statutes to facilitate transfers to adult court —
by reducing the minimum age for transfer,[51] expanding the list of transferable
offenses, and eliminating some of the factors that must be considered (such
as no longer requiring that the juvenile must first be found "unamenable to
treatment").[52]

Finally, in the third form of waiver, prosecutors in some states may file certain
cases involving juveniles directly in either juvenile or adult criminal court. Unlike
judicial waiver, prosecutorial waiver of juveniles to criminal court is unreviewable

---

[50] American Bar Association, Juvenile Justice Standards, Standards Relating to Transfer
Between Courts, at 10-11 (1980).

[51] Richard E. Redding, Juveniles Transferred to Criminal Court: Legal Reform Proposals Based
on Social Science Research, 1997 Utah L. Rev. 709, 714. All states have lowered the minimum age
for transfer to age 14 or younger. The federal transfer statute, the Violent Crime Control and Law
Enforcement Act, 18 U.S.C. §5032 (2000), permits juveniles as young as age 13 to face federal
prosecution for some offenses.

[52] Redding, supra note [51], at 714.

and final.[53] In addition, the prosecutor's decision is made without the benefit of a hearing at which information about the juvenile can be presented.[54] Furthermore, prosecutorial discretion is subject to political pressure.[55]

Formerly, judicial waivers constituted the most popular form of transfer of juveniles to adult court. However, today, prosecutorial and legislative waivers are considerably more common. For example, in one multi-jurisdictional study of adult courts in 18 large urban counties in 1998, 45 percent of all transfer decisions were made by prosecutors and 40 percent were made by legislatures, rather than judges.[56] The increasing use of transfer raises questions regarding juvenile justice policy. For example, commentators disagree about the effectiveness of transfer. Some suggest that transfer is worthwhile for its symbolic value (as a statement that juvenile crime is taken seriously), its deterrent value (to deter juveniles from criminal behavior), or its protective function (to provide due process protections conferred on adults).[57] Other commentators claim that research findings do not substantiate the belief that transfer reduces the rate of reoffending by juvenile offenders.[58] Furthermore, questions arise about who should make the initial decision about waiver — the prosecutor, the judge, or the legislature — and how much discretion should be permitted.

Other commentators criticize the trend of expanding waiver that results in the transfer to adult court of juveniles at increasingly younger ages.[59] A highly publicized example of this trend is the Florida case of 12-year-old Lionel Tate, who killed a 6-year-old friend while he was practicing professional wrestling moves that he saw on television (Tate v. Florida, 864 So. 2d 44 (Fla. Dist. Ct. App. 2003)). Prosecutorial waiver resulted in Lionel being tried as an adult. After the boy was convicted of first-degree murder (carrying a mandatory sentence of life in prison without the possibility of parole), public outcry led to his being granted a retrial and, subsequently, his acceptance of a plea bargain with a reduced sentence. See generally Mike Clary, Teen's Life Sentence Sparks Juvenile Punishment Debate, Chicago Tribune, Mar. 21, 2001, at 11.

One commentator, who analyzed transfer decision making with reference to empirical research on offending and recidivism patterns, points out additional problems with transfer practice: (1) immature and incompetent juveniles are being transferred to be tried as adults, (2) older juveniles are being transferred to ensure their incarceration past the age of majority, (3) transfer laws often target first-time

[53] Janet Ainsworth, The Court's Effectiveness in Protecting the Rights of Juveniles in Delinquency Cases, in The Future of Children: The Juvenile Court 64, 68 (Packard Fdn. 1996).

[54] The Juvenile Court: Analysis and Recommendations, in The Future of Children: The Juvenile Court 4, 10 (Packard Fdn. 1996).

[55] Id. at 10.

[56] Cited in Stephen A. Drizin & Allison McGowen Keegan, Abolishing the Use of the Felony-Murder Rule When the Defendant Is a Teenager 507, 539 (2004).

[57] The Juvenile Court: Analysis and Recommendations, supra note [54], at 9.

[58] Id.

[59] See, e.g., David O. Brink, Immaturity, Normative Competence, and Juvenile Transfer: How (Not) to Punish Minors for Major Crimes, 82 Tex. L. Rev. 1555, 1557 (2004); Marcy R. Podkopacz & Barry Feld, The Back-Door to Prison: Waiver Reform, "Blended Sentencing," and the Law of Unintended Consequences, 91 J. Crim. L. & Criminology 997, 999 (2001).

violent offenders although repeat offenders are more likely to be recidivists, and (4) transfer decision making is highly variable and arbitrary. In response to these problems, the author suggests the following reforms: abolish mandatory transfer laws, provide explicit transfer decision making guidelines for judges, require a competency evaluation before the transfer hearing, and extend juvenile court jurisdiction to allow it to impose adult sentences.[60] What do you think of these proposed reforms?

For recent commentary on juvenile waiver, see John D. Burrow, Punishing Serious Juvenile Offenders: A Case Study of Michigan's Prosecutorial Waiver Statute, 9 U.C. Davis J. Juv. L. & Pol'y 1 (2005); Randall T. Salekin et al., Juvenile Waiver to Adult Criminal Courts: Prototypes for Dangerousness, Sophistication — Maturity, and Amenability to Treatment, 7 Psychol. Pub. Pol'y & L. 381 (2001); Joshua T. Rose, Note, Innocence Lost: The Detrimental Effect of Automatic Waiver Statutes on Juvenile Justice, 41 Brandeis L.J. 977 (2003).

2. Disposition and Treatment

Juvenile court delinquency proceedings have two aspects: (a) the adjudicatory or jurisdictional phase, in which the court must decide whether the young person's conduct warrants juvenile court jurisdiction; and (b) the dispositional phase, in which the judge is faced with the task of deciding what to do with a youth over whom jurisdiction has been established. Basically the dispositional choices (apart from a possible fine) are (1) allowing the young person to remain living at home, under the supervision of a probation officer or the court; (2) placement of the child in the home of a relative or foster parent; (3) placement of the child in a "group home," often under the supervision of a child care agency; or (4) placement in a state or local institution — typically a "training school" or a juvenile "ranch."

State juvenile court acts typically give the judge the same dispositional power over all delinquents: it makes no difference whether the judge is dealing with a first-time shoplifter or a fourth-time armed robber. Statutes *do not* set out punishments according to the offense. In this respect, the disposition power of a juvenile court differs from adult penal sanctions, which are often graduated in proportion to the specific violation. The statutes themselves typically give the judge extraordinarily broad discretion in making the dispositional decision, often subject to the best-interests-of-the-child standard.

Judge Ketcham commented on the problems flowing from giving such vast discretion to judges:

> The high degree of autonomy which the juvenile court judge typically enjoys has the corollary effect of focusing upon him virtually the total responsibility for a just adjudication and an astute disposition. In a great majority of jurisdictions, however, he is hampered not only by his own lack of training in the necessarily specialized

---

[60] Redding, supra note [51], at 716. For recent criticism of the policy of transferring juveniles to adult criminal court, see Brink, supra note [59]; Joshua T. Rose, Innocence Lost: The Detrimental Effect of Automatic Waiver Statutes on Juvenile Justice, 41 Brandeis L.J. 977 (2003); Marissa Slaten, Juvenile Transfers to Criminal Court: Whose Right Is It Anyway?, 55 Rutgers L. Rev. 821 (2003).

skills demanded by his job and by overloaded calendars, but also by administrative duties and essential extracurricular activities far beyond those demanded by judges in other courts. His task is further complicated in many jurisdictions by intake and probation staffs that are overworked, underpaid, and poorly trained.[61]

The judge typically receives information on which to base his or her decision from a *social study* prepared by the probation officer who has investigated the child's circumstances. The report often contains evidence that would not be legally admissible during the adjudicatory hearing. For this reason many statutes prohibit the judge from seeing any predisposition study before jurisdiction is established, e.g., N.Y. Fam. Ct. Act §750(1) (McKinney 2004), and courts have held it reversible error for a judge to consider the report prior to a jurisdictional finding. E.g., In re Gladys R., 464 P.2d 127 (Cal. 1970).

To aid in the court's effort to provide "individualized justice," the report may contain (1) facts concerning the family background, the child's past and present behavior in the home and community, and his or her medical and social history; (2) the views of interested third parties, such as teachers, social workers, and court-appointed clinicians; (3) the probation officer's estimate of the nature and seriousness of the child's "problem"; and (4) the probation officer's recommendation as to the appropriate treatment. While many juvenile court statutes are silent on the question of what access the juvenile and his attorney have to the report, "denial of access to these materials may constitute a denial of the right to the effective assistance of counsel and, therefore, be a mistake of constitutional dimensions."[62] Cf. Kent v. United States, 383 U.S. 541 (1966).

The judge is not bound by this social study. The report does, however, furnish the bulk of the information that influences the dispositional decision. In the majority of cases the probation officer's recommendation is followed. One of the problems with this system was pointed out by Judge Polier:

> The value of diagnostic studies and recommendations is too often reduced to a paper recommendation. In shopping for placement, probation officers are forced to lower their sights from what they know a child needs to what they can secure. Their sense of professional responsibility is steadily eroded. The judge, in turn, becomes a ceremonial officer who in many cases approves a disposition which he knows is only a dead end for the child.[63]

The Supreme Court has never considered what procedural requirements the Constitution imposes with regard to the dispositional phase of the juvenile court proceeding. Indeed, in In re Gault (discussed infra p. 782), the Court stated in a footnote:

> The problems of pre-adjudication treatment of juveniles, and of post-adjudication disposition, are unique to the juvenile process; hence, what we hold in this opinion

[61] Orman W. Ketcham, The Unfulfilled Promise of the Juvenile Court, 7 Crime & Delinq. 97, 104 (1961).

[62] Sanford J. Fox, The Law of Juvenile Courts in a Nutshell 224 (3d ed. 1984).

[63] Justine Wise Polier, A View from the Bench 30 (1964).

with regard to the procedural requirements at the adjudicatory stage has no necessary applicability to other steps of the juvenile process. [387 U.S. 1, 31 n.48 (1967).]

Nevertheless, it seems clear that because the disposition stage is "critical" and because many juvenile court statutes provide for a right to counsel for disposition, e.g., N.Y. Fam. Ct. Act §741 (McKinney 2004), the right to counsel is firmly established.

How long may a juvenile who is adjudicated a delinquent be supervised under probation or required to stay in an institution? As a general rule, juvenile court statutes allow commitment or probation until a juvenile reaches majority. Lowering the age of majority from 21 to 18 automatically reduced in some states the term of a possible commitment. Some states still provide by statute that probation or commitment can continue until the 21st birthday. See, e.g., Cal. Welf. & Inst. Code §607 (West 2004); Minn. Stat. Ann. §260B.153(5)(b) (2005). In many states, although commitment normally ends at 18, it is possible for an extension until the age of 21 to be authorized by the juvenile court upon an appropriate request from the institution. See, e.g., Me. Rev. Stat. Ann. tit. 15, §3316 (2004).

Since commitment may typically extend until the child reaches the age of majority, some children may possibly serve longer terms at institutions than an adult convicted for violating the same law. Several cases have challenged this on equal protection grounds, but no court has held that the possibility of a longer term violates equal protection. Courts have typically sustained the juvenile court's dispositional authority by refusing to equate delinquency adjudication with criminal proceedings. See, e.g., In re A.M.H., 447 N.W.2d 40 (Neb. 1989); In re J.K., 228 N.W.2d 713 (Wis. 1975).

However, departing from the traditional mode of analysis, the United States Supreme Court decided United States v. R.L.C., 503 U.S. 291 (1992). The case involved a juvenile offender who was originally sentenced for a longer period of time (three years) for involuntary manslaughter (i.e., an automobile accident on an Indian reservation) than a similarly situated adult would have received pursuant to the United States Sentencing Guidelines (21 months). The United States Supreme Court affirmed the court of appeals' opinion, thereby opting for the lesser sentence under the federal sentencing guidelines.

Justice O'Connor, joined by Justice Blackmun, dissented, arguing that

> [r]equiring a district court to calculate a Guideline maximum for each juvenile imports formal factfinding procedures foreign to the discretionary sentencing system Congress intended to retain. Juvenile proceedings, in contrast to adult proceedings, have traditionally aspired to be "intimate, informal [and] protective." McKeiver v. Pennsylvania, 403 U.S. 528, 545 (1971). One reason for the traditional informality of juvenile proceedings is that the focus of sentencing is on treatment, not punishment. The presumption is that juveniles are still teachable and not yet "hardened criminals." S. Rep. No. 1989, 75th Cong., 3d Sess., 1 (1938). . . . As a result, the sentencing considerations relevant to juveniles are far different from those relevant to adults. [503 U.S. at 314.]

(Note that the Court's decision in *R.L.C.* was based on statutory rather than constitutional grounds.)[64]

Some statutes have established a maximum term of juvenile commitment; see, e.g., N.C. Gen. Stat. §7B-2513 (2003) (definite term of commitment restricted to two years), or established a schedule of maximum detention terms based on the seriousness of the delinquent act. See, e.g., N.J. Stat. Ann. §2A:4A-44(d) (West 2004).

The ABA Juvenile Justice Standards recommended a rather radical restructuring of the dispositional authority of the juvenile courts. The Standards generally require a determinate sentence to be established at the time of the adjudication. The maximum confinement would be 36 months, and the maximum probation would be 36 months. These would apply only to "class one" offenses, which would for adults be punishable by sentences in excess of 20 years or the death penalty. For "class five" offenses, on the other hand, which for an adult could result in imprisonment of six months or less, a juvenile may be committed to a "nonsecure facility or residence for a period of two months" if the juvenile has a prior record, or "conditional freedom for a period of six months" if the juvenile does not have a prior record.[65]

3.   Segregation of Juvenile Offenders from Adult Offenders

Are there special dangers if young people are committed to the same correctional institutions as adults? Do these dangers justify treating youthful offenders differently from adult offenders?

As earlier noted, an important goal of the original movement to create juvenile courts was to ensure that juvenile offenders were kept separate and apart from adult offenders. Most juvenile court acts today do not permit a juvenile court at the time of the original disposition to commit a delinquent child to a correctional facility that also houses adult prisoners. Section 223(a)(14) of the Juvenile Justice and Delinquency Prevention Act (Pub. L. No. 93-415 (1974), codified at 42 U.S.C. §5600 et seq.) specifically provides that no juvenile will be detained or confined in any jail or lock-up for adults. Subsequent implementing regulations clarify this requirement by providing that brief and inadvertent contact in nonresidential areas is not a violation. Regulations also exempt those juveniles who are transferred from

---

[64] The impact on juvenile sentencing policy posed by recent United States Supreme Court decisions is presently unknown. See United States v. Booker, 125 S. Ct. 738 (2005) (holding that the federal criminal sentencing guidelines violate the Sixth Amendment right to a jury trial; the federal sentencing guidelines are now only advisory); Blakely v. Washington, 124 S. Ct. 2531 (2004) (ruling that state sentencing guidelines permitting enhancements above the statutory minimum sentence based on a judge's findings violate the Sixth Amendment right to jury trial); Apprendi v. New Jersey, 530 U.S. 466 (2000) (invalidating state statute that allowed judges to add enhancements; holding that any fact that increases penalty beyond prescribed statutory maximum must be submitted to a jury and be proved beyond a reasonable doubt).

[65] See American Bar Association, Juvenile Justice Standards, Standards Relating to Juvenile Delinquency and Sanctions, supra note [38], at 7-9.

a juvenile institution to an adult one, such as those juveniles who are being tried for felonies or who have been convicted as felons.[66]

According to the Bureau of Justice Statistics' Annual Survey of Jails, an estimated 7,600 youths younger than 18 were being held in adult jails on June 30, 2000. These inmates account for 1.2 percent of the total jail population.[67] Most jail inmates younger than 18 (80%) were convicted or awaiting trial as adult criminal offenders — some who were transferred to criminal court and others who resided in states where all 17-year-olds (or all 16- and 17-year-olds) are considered adults for purposes of criminal prosecution.[68]

Several commentators highlight an additional problem of intermingling juveniles and adult offenders that is caused by the Immigration and Naturalization Service's failure to segregate non-delinquent alien juveniles (those who enter the country unlawfully) in facilities with either serious juvenile offenders or adult offenders. See generally Devon A. Corneal, On the Way to Grandmother's House: Is U.S. Immigration Policy More Dangerous Than the Big Bad Wolf for Unaccompanied Juvenile Aliens?, 109 Penn St. L. Rev. 609 (2004); Areti Georgopoulos, Beyond the Reach of Juvenile Justice: The Crisis of Unaccompanied Immigrant Children Detained by the United States, 23 Law & Ineq. 117 (2005).

To what hazards are juveniles exposed if committed to the same facilities as adults? One commentator explains:

> Foremost is the increased exposure of these children to emotional and physical abuse from other prisoners and, sadly, sometimes from the jail employees themselves. . . . The hard facts are most dramatically illustrated in a simple statistic compiled by the Community Research Center. The suicide rate for juveniles placed in adult jails and lock-ups is nearly eight times greater than for juveniles placed in separate, secure juvenile detention centers.
>
> But there is a more generalized, less dramatic harm. Adult jails are simply not designed, intended, equipped, or staffed to supervise juveniles, nor are they required to provide the counseling, educational, recreational, and other ancillary services to the same extent as are secure juvenile detention facilities. . . . [69]

4. Capital Punishment for Persons Who Commit Crimes as Juveniles

Roper v. Simmons
125 S. Ct. 1183 (2005)

Justice KENNEDY delivered the opinion of the Court.

. . . At the age of 17, when he was still a junior in high school, Christopher Simmons, the respondent here, committed murder. . . . There is little doubt that

---

[66] Melissa Sickmund, Juveniles in Corrections, Office of Juvenile Justice and Delinquency Prevention 18 (June 2004).

[67] Id.

[68] Id.

[69] Gordon Raley, Removing Children from Adult Jails: the Balance of Legislation, 3 Children's Legal Rts. J. 4, 6 (1982).

Simmons was the instigator of the crime. Before its commission Simmons said he wanted to murder someone. In chilling, callous terms he talked about his plan, discussing it for the most part with two friends, Charles Benjamin and John Tessmer, then aged 15 and 16 respectively. Simmons proposed to commit burglary and murder by breaking and entering, tying up a victim, and throwing the victim off a bridge. Simmons assured his friends they could "get away with it" because they were minors.

The three met at about 2 A.M. on the night of the murder, but Tessmer left before the other two set out. (The State later charged Tessmer with conspiracy, but dropped the charge in exchange for his testimony against Simmons.) Simmons and Benjamin entered the home of the victim, Shirley Crook, after reaching through an open window and unlocking the back door. Simmons turned on a hallway light. Awakened, Mrs. Crook called out, "Who's there?" In response Simmons entered Mrs. Crook's bedroom, where he recognized her from a previous car accident involving them both. Simmons later admitted this confirmed his resolve to murder her. Using duct tape to cover her eyes and mouth and bind her hands, the two perpetrators put Mrs. Crook in her minivan and drove to a state park. They reinforced the bindings, covered her head with a towel, and walked her to a railroad trestle spanning the Meramec River. There they tied her hands and feet together with electrical wire, wrapped her whole face in duct tape and threw her from the bridge, drowning her in the waters below. . . .

. . . The State sought the death penalty. As aggravating factors, the State submitted that the murder [involved] depravity of mind and was outrageously and wantonly vile, horrible, and inhuman. [As a mitigating factor, Simmons' attorneys argued that he had no prior criminal record.]

During closing arguments, both the prosecutor and defense counsel addressed Simmons' age, which the trial judge had instructed the jurors they could consider as a mitigating factor. Defense counsel reminded the jurors that juveniles of Simmons' age cannot drink, serve on juries, or even see certain movies, because "the legislatures have wisely decided that individuals of a certain age aren't responsible enough." Defense counsel argued that Simmons' age should make "a huge difference to [the jurors] in deciding just exactly what sort of punishment to make." In rebuttal, the prosecutor gave the following response: "Age, he says. Think about age. Seventeen years old. Isn't that scary? Doesn't that scare you? Mitigating? Quite the contrary I submit. Quite the contrary." . . .

Accepting the jury's recommendation, the trial judge imposed the death penalty. [The defendant unsuccessfully petitioned for postconviction relief, claiming ineffective counsel, i.e., during sentencing, counsel should have established Simmons' immaturity, impulsivity, susceptibility to being influenced, difficult home environment, and negative associations with other youths. After the United States Supreme Court decided Atkins v. Virginia, 536 U.S. 304 (2002), Simmons brought a new petition for postconviction relief.] We granted certiorari, and now affirm.

The Eighth Amendment provides: "Excessive bail shall not be required, nor excessive fines imposed, nor cruel and unusual punishments inflicted." . . . By protecting even those convicted of heinous crimes, the Eighth Amendment reaffirms the duty of the government to respect the dignity of all persons.

The prohibition against "cruel and unusual punishments," like other expansive language in the Constitution, must be interpreted according to its text, by considering history, tradition, and precedent, and with due regard for its purpose and function in the constitutional design. To implement this framework we have established the propriety and affirmed the necessity of referring to "the evolving standards of decency that mark the progress of a maturing society" to determine which punishments are so disproportionate as to be cruel and unusual. Trop v. Dulles, 356 U.S. 86, 100-101 (1958) (plurality opinion).

In Thompson v. Oklahoma, 487 U.S. 815 (1988), a plurality of the Court determined that our standards of decency do not permit the execution of any offender under the age of 16 at the time of the crime. The plurality opinion explained that no death penalty State that had given express consideration to a minimum age for the death penalty had set the age lower than 16. The plurality also observed that "[t]he conclusion that it would offend civilized standards of decency to execute a person who was less than 16 years old at the time of his or her offense is consistent with the views that have been expressed by respected professional organizations, by other nations that share our Anglo-American heritage, and by the leading members of the Western European community." Id., at 830. The opinion further noted that juries imposed the death penalty on offenders under 16 with exceeding rarity; the last execution of an offender for a crime committed under the age of 16 had been carried out in 1948, 40 years prior.

The next year, in Stanford v. Kentucky, 492 U.S. 361 (1989), the Court, over a dissenting opinion joined by four Justices, referred to contemporary standards of decency in this country and concluded the Eighth and Fourteenth Amendments did not proscribe the execution of juvenile offenders over 15 but under 18. The Court noted that 22 of the 37 death penalty States permitted the death penalty for 16-year-old offenders, and, among these 37 States, 25 permitted it for 17-year-old offenders. These numbers, in the Court's view, indicated there was no national consensus "sufficient to label a particular punishment cruel and unusual." Id., at 370-371. . . .

The same day the Court decided *Stanford*, it held that the Eighth Amendment did not mandate a categorical exemption from the death penalty for the mentally retarded [because there was not sufficient evidence of a national consensus to ban the practice]. Penry v. Lynaugh, 492 U.S. 302 (1989). . . . Three Terms ago the subject was reconsidered in *Atkins*. We held that standards of decency have evolved since *Penry* and [that] the execution of the mentally retarded is cruel and unusual punishment. . . .

The evidence of national consensus against the death penalty for juveniles is similar, and in some respects parallel, to the evidence *Atkins* held sufficient to demonstrate a national consensus against the death penalty for the mentally retarded. When *Atkins* was decided, 30 States prohibited the death penalty for the mentally retarded. . . . By a similar calculation in this case, 30 States prohibit the juvenile death penalty, comprising 12 that have rejected the death penalty altogether and 18 that maintain it but, by express provision or judicial interpretation, exclude juveniles from its reach. *Atkins* emphasized that even in the 20 States without formal prohibition, the practice of executing the mentally retarded was infrequent. . . . In the present case, too, even in the 20 States without a formal prohibition on executing juveniles, the practice is infrequent. Since *Stanford*, six States have executed prisoners for crimes committed as juveniles. In the past 10 years, only three have done so: Oklahoma, Texas, and Virginia. . . .

There is, to be sure, at least one difference between the evidence of consensus in *Atkins* and in this case. Impressive in *Atkins* was the rate of abolition of the death penalty for the mentally retarded. . . . By contrast, the rate of change in reducing the incidence of the juvenile death penalty, or in taking specific steps to abolish it, has been slower. [However, any difference] between this case and *Atkins* with respect to the pace of abolition is thus counterbalanced by the consistent direction of the change. . . .

As in *Atkins*, the objective indicia of consensus in this case — the rejection of the juvenile death penalty in the majority of States; the infrequency of its use even where it remains on the books; and the consistency in the trend toward abolition of the practice — provide sufficient evidence that today our society views juveniles, in the words *Atkins* used respecting the mentally retarded, as "categorically less culpable than the average criminal." 536 U.S., at 316.

. . . Because the death penalty is the most severe punishment, the Eighth Amendment applies to it with special force. Capital punishment must be limited to those offenders who commit "a narrow category of the most serious crimes" and whose extreme culpability makes them "the most deserving of execution." *Atkins*, supra, at 319. . . .

Three general differences between juveniles under 18 and adults demonstrate that juvenile offenders cannot with reliability be classified among the worst offenders. First, as any parent knows and as the scientific and sociological studies respondent and his amici cite tend to confirm, "[a] lack of maturity and an underdeveloped sense of responsibility are found in youth more often than in adults and are more understandable among the young. These qualities often result in impetuous and ill-considered actions and decisions." [Johnson v. Texas, 509 U.S. 350, 367 (1993).] It has been noted that "adolescents are overrepresented statistically in virtually every category of reckless behavior." Arnett, Reckless Behavior in Adolescence: A Developmental Perspective, 12 Developmental Review 339 (1992). In recognition of the comparative immaturity and irresponsibility of juveniles, almost every State prohibits those under 18 years of age from voting, serving on juries, or marrying without parental consent.

The second area of difference is that juveniles are more vulnerable or susceptible to negative influences and outside pressures, including peer pressure. This is explained in part by the prevailing circumstance that juveniles have less control, or less experience with control, over their own environment. See Steinberg & Scott, Less Guilty by Reason of Adolescence: Developmental Immaturity, Diminished Responsibility, and the Juvenile Death Penalty, 58 Am. Psychologist 1009, 1014 (2003) (hereinafter Steinberg & Scott) ("[A]s legal minors, [juveniles] lack the freedom that adults have to extricate themselves from a criminogenic setting").

The third broad difference is that the character of a juvenile is not as well formed as that of an adult. The personality traits of juveniles are more transitory, less fixed. See generally E. Erikson, Identity: Youth and Crisis (1968).

These differences render suspect any conclusion that a juvenile falls among the worst offenders. The susceptibility of juveniles to immature and irresponsible behavior means "their irresponsible conduct is not as morally reprehensible as that of an adult." *Thompson*, supra, at 835. Their own vulnerability and comparative lack of control over their immediate surroundings mean juveniles have a greater claim than adults to be forgiven for failing to escape negative influences in their whole environment. The reality that juveniles still struggle to define their identity means it is less supportable to conclude that even a heinous crime committed by a juvenile is evidence of irretrievably depraved character. From a moral standpoint it would be misguided to equate the failings of a minor with those of an adult, for a greater possibility exists that a minor's character deficiencies will be reformed. Indeed, "[t]he relevance of youth as a mitigating factor derives from the fact that the signature qualities of youth are transient; as individuals mature, the impetuousness and recklessness that may dominate in younger years can subside." *Johnson*, supra, at 368; see also Steinberg & Scott 1014 ("For most teens, [risky or antisocial] behaviors are fleeting; they cease with maturity as individual identity becomes settled. Only a relatively small proportion of adolescents who experiment in risky or illegal activities develop entrenched patterns of problem behavior that persist into adulthood"). In *Thompson*, a plurality of the Court recognized the import of these characteristics with respect to juveniles under 16, and relied on them to hold that the Eighth Amendment prohibited the imposition of the death penalty on juveniles below that age. We conclude the same reasoning applies to all juvenile offenders under 18.

Once the diminished culpability of juveniles is recognized, it is evident that the penological justifications for the death penalty apply to them with lesser force than to adults. We have held there are two distinct social purposes served by the death penalty: " 'retribution and deterrence of capital crimes by prospective offenders.' " *Atkins*, 536 U.S., at 319. As for retribution, we remarked in *Atkins* that "[i]f the culpability of the average murderer is insufficient to justify the most extreme sanction available to the State, the lesser culpability of the mentally retarded offender surely does not merit that form of retribution." 536 U.S., at 319. The same conclusions follow from the lesser culpability of the juvenile offender. Whether viewed as an attempt to express the community's moral outrage or as an attempt to right the balance for the wrong to the victim, the case for retribution is not as strong with a minor as with an adult. Retribution is not proportional if the law's most severe penalty is imposed on one whose culpability or blameworthiness is diminished, to a substantial degree, by reason of youth and immaturity.

As for deterrence, it is unclear whether the death penalty has a significant or even measurable deterrent effect on juveniles. [Here], the absence of evidence of deterrent effect is of special concern because the same characteristics that render juveniles less culpable than adults suggest as well that juveniles will be less susceptible to deterrence. In particular, as the plurality observed in *Thompson*, "[t]he likelihood that the teenage offender has made the kind of cost-benefit analysis that attaches any weight to the possibility of execution is so remote as to be virtually nonexistent." 487 U.S., at 837. To the extent the juvenile death penalty might have residual deterrent effect, it is worth noting that the punishment of life imprisonment without the possibility of parole is itself a severe sanction, in particular for a young person.

In concluding that neither retribution nor deterrence provides adequate justification for imposing the death penalty on juvenile offenders, we cannot deny or overlook the brutal crimes too many juvenile offenders have committed. Certainly it can be argued, although we by no means concede the point, that a rare case might arise in which a juvenile offender has sufficient psychological maturity, and at the same time demonstrates sufficient depravity, to merit a sentence of death. Indeed, this possibility is the linchpin of one contention pressed by petitioner and his amici. They assert that even assuming the truth of the observations we have made about juveniles' diminished culpability in general, jurors nonetheless should be allowed to consider mitigating arguments related to youth on a case-by-case basis, and in some cases to impose the death penalty if justified. A central feature of death penalty sentencing is a particular assessment of the circumstances of the crime and the characteristics of the offender. The system is designed to consider both aggravating and mitigating circumstances, including youth, in every case. Given this Court's own insistence on individualized consideration, petitioner maintains that it is both arbitrary and unnecessary to adopt a categorical rule barring imposition of the death penalty on any offender under 18 years of age.

We disagree. The differences between juvenile and adult offenders are too marked and well understood to risk allowing a youthful person to receive the death penalty despite insufficient culpability. An unacceptable likelihood exists that the brutality or cold-blooded nature of any particular crime would overpower mitigating arguments based on youth as a matter of course, even where the juvenile offender's objective immaturity, vulnerability, and lack of true depravity should require a sentence less severe than death. In some cases a defendant's youth may even be counted against him. In this very case, as we noted above, the prosecutor argued Simmons' youth was aggravating rather than mitigating. While this sort of overreaching could be corrected by a particular rule to ensure that the mitigating force of youth is not overlooked, that would not address our larger concerns.

It is difficult even for expert psychologists to differentiate between the juvenile offender whose crime reflects unfortunate yet transient immaturity, and the rare juvenile offender whose crime reflects irreparable corruption. As we understand it, this difficulty underlies the rule forbidding psychiatrists from diagnosing any patient under 18 as having antisocial personality disorder, a disorder also referred to as psychopathy or sociopathy, and which is characterized by callousness, cynicism, and contempt for the feelings, rights, and suffering of others. American Psychiatric Association, Diagnostic and Statistical Manual of Mental Disorders 701-706 (4th ed. text rev. 2000); see also Steinberg & Scott 1015. If trained psychiatrists with the advantage of clinical testing and observation refrain, despite diagnostic expertise, from assessing any juvenile under 18 as having antisocial personality disorder, we conclude that States should refrain from asking jurors to issue a far graver condemnation — that a juvenile offender merits the death penalty. When a juvenile offender commits a heinous crime, the State can exact forfeiture of some of the most basic liberties, but the State cannot extinguish his life and his potential to attain a mature understanding of his own humanity.

Drawing the line at 18 years of age is subject, of course, to the objections always raised against categorical rules. The qualities that distinguish juveniles from adults do not disappear when an individual turns 18. By the same token, some under 18 have already attained a level of maturity some adults will never reach. For the reasons we have discussed, however, a line must be drawn. The plurality opinion in *Thompson* drew the line at 16. In the intervening years the *Thompson* plurality's conclusion that offenders under 16 may not be executed has not been challenged. The logic of *Thompson* extends to those who are under 18. The age of 18 is the point where society draws the line for many purposes between childhood and adulthood. It is, we conclude, the age at which the line for death eligibility ought to rest. . . .

Justice O'CONNOR, dissenting.

[T]he rule decreed by the Court rests, ultimately, on its independent moral judgment that death is a disproportionately severe punishment for any 17-year-old offender. I do not subscribe to this judgment. . . .

Seventeen-year-old murderers must be categorically exempted from capital punishment, the Court says, because they "cannot with reliability be classified among the worst offenders." That conclusion is premised on three perceived differences between "adults," who have already reached their 18th birthdays, and "juveniles," who have not. First, juveniles lack maturity and responsibility and are more reckless than adults. Second, juveniles are more vulnerable to outside influences because they have less control over their surroundings. And third, a juvenile's character is not as fully formed as that of an adult. Based on these characteristics, the Court determines that 17-year-old capital murderers are not as blameworthy as adults guilty of similar crimes; that 17-year-olds are less likely than adults to be deterred by the prospect of a death sentence; and that it is difficult to conclude that a 17-year-old who commits even the most heinous of crimes is "irretrievably depraved." . . .

It is beyond cavil that juveniles as a class are generally less mature, less responsible, and less fully formed than adults, and that these differences bear on juveniles' comparative moral culpability. But even accepting this premise, the Court's proportionality argument fails to support its categorical rule.

First, the Court adduces no evidence whatsoever in support of its sweeping conclusion, that it is only in "rare" cases, if ever, that 17-year-old murderers are sufficiently mature and act with sufficient depravity to warrant the death penalty. The fact that juveniles are generally less culpable for their misconduct than adults does not necessarily mean that a 17-year-old murderer cannot be sufficiently culpable to merit the death penalty. At most, the Court's argument suggests that the average 17-year-old murderer is not as culpable as the average adult murderer. But an especially depraved juvenile offender may nevertheless be just as culpable as many adult offenders considered bad enough to deserve the death penalty. Similarly, the fact that the availability of the death penalty may be less likely to deter a juvenile from committing a capital crime does not imply that this threat cannot effectively deter some 17-year-olds from such an act. Surely there is an age below which no offender, no matter what his crime, can be deemed to have the cognitive or emotional maturity necessary to warrant the death penalty. But at least at the margins between adolescence and adulthood — and especially for 17-year-olds such as respondent — the relevant differences between "adults" and "juveniles" appear to be a matter of degree, rather than of kind. It follows that a legislature may reasonably conclude that at least some 17-year-olds can act with sufficient moral culpability, and can be sufficiently deterred by the threat of execution, that capital punishment may be warranted in an appropriate case. Indeed, this appears to be just such a case. . . .

The Court's proportionality argument suffers from a second and closely related defect: It fails to establish that the differences in maturity between 17-year-olds and young "adults" are both universal enough and significant enough to justify a bright-line prophylactic rule against capital punishment of the former. The Court's analysis is premised on differences *in the aggregate* between juveniles and adults, which frequently do not hold true when comparing individuals. Although it may be that many 17-year-old murderers lack sufficient maturity to deserve the death penalty, some juvenile murderers may be quite mature. Chronological age is not an unfailing measure of psychological development, and common experience suggests that many 17-year-olds are more mature than the average young "adult." In short, the class of offenders exempted from capital punishment by today's decision is too broad and too diverse to warrant a categorical prohibition. Indeed, the age-based line drawn by the Court is indefensibly arbitrary — it quite likely will protect a number of offenders who are mature enough to deserve the death penalty and may well leave vulnerable many who are not.

For purposes of proportionality analysis, 17-year-olds as a class are qualitatively and materially different from the mentally retarded. "Mentally retarded" offenders, as we understood that category in *Atkins*, are defined by precisely the characteristics which render death an excessive punishment. A mentally retarded person is, "by definition," one whose cognitive and behavioral capacities have been proven to fall below a certain minimum. Accordingly, for purposes of our decision in *Atkins*, the mentally retarded are not merely less blameworthy for their misconduct or less likely to be deterred by the death penalty than others. Rather, a mentally retarded offender is one whose demonstrated impairments make it so highly unlikely that he is culpable enough to deserve the death penalty or that he could have been deterred by the threat of death, that execution is not a defensible punishment. There is no such inherent or accurate fit between an offender's chronological age and the personal limitations which the Court believes make capital punishment excessive for 17-year-old murderers. Moreover, it defies common sense to suggest that 17-year-olds as a class are somehow equivalent to mentally retarded persons with regard to culpability or susceptibility to deterrence. Seventeen-year-olds may, on average, be less mature than adults, but that lesser maturity simply cannot be equated with the major, lifelong impairments suffered by the mentally retarded.

The proportionality issues raised by the Court clearly implicate Eighth Amendment concerns. But these concerns may properly be addressed not by means of an arbitrary, categorical age-based rule, but rather through individualized sentencing. ....

[The separate dissenting opinion of Justice Scalia, with whom Justices Rehnquist and Thomas join, is omitted.]

NOTES AND QUESTIONS

(1) Background.   The issue of the appropriateness of capital punishment for minors is raised initially upon waiver — i.e., the decision whether to transfer a juvenile from the juvenile justice system to the adult system. If tried as an adult, the

juvenile is subject to the same range of punishments, including capital punishment, imposed upon adults. (Waiver is discussed, supra p. 840.) As of June 2003, a total of 78 persons were on death row for crimes committed as juveniles. All of these offenders were either 16 or 17 at the time of their offenses. Victor L. Streib, The Juvenile Death Penalty Today: Death Sentences and Executions for Juvenile Crimes, Jan. 1, 1973-June 30, 2003, at 10, available at *http://www.law.onu.edu/faculty/streib* (last visited Feb. 13, 2005).

As the *Roper* case explains, the Supreme Court previously explored the constitutionality of capital punishment for juveniles in Thompson v. Oklahoma, 487 U.S. 815 (1988) (declaring the death penalty unconstitutional for defendants who were 15 years old at the time of the offense), and Stanford v. Kentucky, 492 U.S. 361 (1989) (upholding the imposition of the death sentence for offenders who were at least 16 years old at the time of the offense). Why did the Supreme Court decide these two cases differently?

(2) Sniper Case. A highly publicized series of murders focused renewed interest in the juvenile death penalty. In October 2002, Lee Boyd Malvo was arrested in connection with the Washington, D.C., area "sniper slayings," a series of 13 random shootings that terrorized residents in Virginia, Maryland, and Washington, D.C. Malvo was the triggerman in the murder spree that was masterminded by 41-year-old John Allan Muhammad. Malvo's attorneys argued that the impressionable teen was brainwashed by Muhammad, and that Malvo's susceptibility to Muhammad's influence resulted from Malvo's troubled background (an absent father and abusive mother). Malvo was tried initially in Virginia (a state that permits the imposition of the death penalty on juveniles) and received a sentence of life imprisonment. Muhammad received the death penalty. See generally Joseph W. Goodman, Overturning Stanford v. Kentucky: Lee Boyd Malvo and the Execution of Juvenile Offenders, 2003 Mich. St. DCL L. Rev. 389; Warren Richey, Sniper Case Revisits Juvenile Death Penalty, Christian Science Monitor, Nov. 21, 2003, at 2.

(3) Eighth Amendment. The debate over the juvenile death penalty centers around the application of the Eighth Amendment's prohibition on cruel and unusual punishment. Because the Supreme Court has interpreted the Eighth Amendment to require an evaluation of the punishment in terms of "the evolving standards of decency that mark the progress of a maturing society," an analysis is required of these standards and their evolution. According to *Roper*, what factors are relevant in that analysis?

(4) Purposes of Punishment. Does the death penalty serve valid penological purposes when applied to juveniles, according to *Roper*? Review the material supra pp. 739-746 on the purposes of punishment and juvenile justice. In terms of retribution, is it appropriate to punish juveniles with the same degree of severity as adults? In terms of deterrence, does capital sentencing send a message to other potential juvenile offenders? Are there inherent characteristics of youth that might prevent this message from being received? Do juveniles modify their actions rationally so as to avoid crime and punishment? Do age-based lines make sense in light of these penological purposes?

(5) Arguments Pro and Con. Professor Victor Streib, who has written extensively on the juvenile death penalty, summarizes the policy debate. Streib, supra, at 11-12. Assess the following arguments he identifies in favor of the imposition of the

death penalty on juveniles: (a) the incidence of violent juvenile crime, particularly homicide, is higher in America than in other countries; (b) juvenile homicide rates increased substantially until the mid- to late-1990s and, although they are on the decline, public fear of juvenile homicide remains very high; (c) juvenile murders seem to be particularly brutal and senseless; (d) political leaders advocate harsher punishments for violent juvenile crime; and (e) correcting the societal conditions that contribute to violent juvenile crime is an impossible task. Opposing arguments include: (a) almost all serious juvenile offenders have had troubled childhoods; (b) research indicates that the brain maturation does not occur until the late teens or early twenties, with impulse control developing last; (c) the threat of capital punishment does not deter teenagers, who tend to see themselves as immortal; (d) the retribution rationale is less weighty if the offender is a child; and (e) harsh punishment for violent juvenile offenders is an ineffective solution to the problem of juvenile crime because society should address the causes (environments, neighborhoods, schools, and societal structures).

(6) Who Should Decide?   The debate over the juvenile death penalty raises the issue of the state and legislature's traditional role in determining appropriate punishments. In an omitted dissent, Justice Scalia notes: "Today's opinion provides a perfect example of why judges are ill equipped to make the type of legislative judgments the Court insists on making here." 125 S. Ct. at 1222. Given the test of the evolving standards of decency, should the determination of the permissibility of the juvenile death penalty be made more appropriately by state legislatures rather than the federal judiciary?

(7) Are Juveniles Analogous to the Mentally Retarded?   In *Roper*, the United States Supreme Court analogizes the juvenile offender to the mentally retarded defendant. Do the reasons supporting the unconstitutionality of the death penalty for mentally retarded defendants apply with equal force to the execution of juvenile offenders? How does Justice O'Connor in her dissent distinguish juvenile offenders from the mentally retarded? Do you find her arguments persuasive? See also Robin M. A. Weeks, Comparing Children to the Mentally Retarded: How the Decision in Atkins v. Virginia Will Affect the Execution of Juvenile Offenders, 17 BYU J. Pub. L. 451 (2003).

(8) Equal Protection.   Consider that a substantial number of juveniles who are executed are African Americans and that a similar high percentage of offenders on death row who committed offenses as juveniles are African American. See General Accounting Office, Death Penalty Sentencing: Research Indicates Pattern of Racial Disparities 5 (Feb. 1990) (discussing data). Is the imposition of the death penalty on these offenders a violation of equal protection, a form of racial discrimination?

(9) Supreme Court's Treatment of Maturity in Different Contexts.   In his omitted dissent, Justice Scalia highlights the Court's inconsistent treatment of the issue of minors' maturity. He points out that several psychological studies reveal that many minors are mature enough to make the abortion decision without parental involvement. 125 S. Ct. at 1223. How does consideration of the issue of maturity differ in the contexts of abortion and capital punishment? That is, how can a minor be sufficiently mature to make the abortion decision but not mature enough to be subject to the death penalty? See generally Nicole A. Saharsky, Consistency as a

Constitutional Value: A Comparative Look at Age in Abortion and Death Penalty
Jurisprudence, 85 Minn. L. Rev. 1119 (2001).

(10) International Consensus.   In an omitted portion of *Roper*, the majority
asserts that various international human rights documents (U.N. Convention on
the Rights of the Child, the International Covenant on Civil and Political Rights)
and the law of other countries support the abolition of the juvenile death penalty.
In his omitted dissent, Justice Scalia contends that consideration of international
human rights law and foreign law should play no role in the determination of the
constitutionality of the death penalty. 125 S. Ct. at 1225-1229. Which view do
you find more persuasive and why? See generally Leo R. McIntyre III, Of Treaties
and Reservations: The International Covenant on Civil and Political Rights and the
Juvenile Death Penalty in the United States, 40 Hous. L. Rev. 147 (2003).

For additional perspectives on capital punishment for juveniles, see William J.
Bowers et al., Too Young for the Death Penalty: An Empirical Examination of Community Conscience and the Juvenile Death Penalty from the Perspective of Capital
Jurors, 84 B.U. L. Rev. 609 (2004); Mirah A. Horowitz, Kids Who Kill: A Critique
of How the American Legal System Deals with Juveniles Who Commit Homicide, 63 Law & Contemp. Probs. 133 (Summer 2000); Adam Caine Ortiz, Juvenile
Death Penalty: Is It "Cruel and Unusual" in Light of Contemporary Standards?,
17 Crim. Just. 21 (Winter 2003); Victor L. Streib, Adolescence, Mental Retardation, and the Death Penalty: The Siren Call of Atkins v. Virginia, 33 N.M. L. Rev.
183 (2003); Victor L. Streib, Executing Juvenile Offenders: The Ultimate Denial
of Juvenile Justice, 14 Stan. L. & Pol'y Rev. 121 (2003); David S. Tenenhaus &
Steven A. Drizin, "Owing to the Extreme Youth of the Accused": The Changing
Legal Response to Juvenile Homicide, 92 J. Crim. L. & Criminology 641 (2002).

D.   PROCEDURAL DIFFERENCES BETWEEN THE DELINQUENCY PROCESS AND THE ADULT CRIMINAL PROCESS

In re Gault
387 U.S. 1 (1967)

Mr. Justice FORTAS delivered the opinion of the Court.

This is an appeal . . . from a judgment of the Supreme Court of Arizona affirming the dismissal of a petition for a writ of habeas corpus. The petition sought the
release of Gerald Francis Gault, appellants' 15-year-old son, who had been committed as a juvenile delinquent to the State Industrial School by the Juvenile Court
of Gila County, Arizona. The Supreme Court of Arizona affirmed dismissal of the
writ. . . . We do not agree, and we reverse. . . .

I

On Monday, June 8, 1964, at about 10 A.M., Gerald Francis Gault and a friend,
Ronald Lewis, were taken into custody by the Sheriff of Gila County. Gerald

was then still subject to a six months' probation order which had been entered on February 25, 1964, as a result of his having been in the company of another boy who had stolen a wallet from a lady's purse. The police action on June 8 was taken as the result of a verbal complaint by a neighbor of the boys, Mrs. Cook, about a telephone call made to her in which the caller or callers made lewd or indecent remarks . . . of the irritatingly offensive, adolescent, sex variety.

At the time Gerald was picked up, his mother and father were both at work. No notice that Gerald was being taken into custody was left at the home. No other steps were taken to advise them that their son had, in effect, been arrested. Gerald was taken to the Children's Detention Home. When his mother arrived home at about 6 o'clock, Gerald was not there. Gerald's older brother was sent to look for him at the trailer home of the Lewis family. He apparently learned then that Gerald was in custody. He so informed his mother. The two of them went to the Detention Home. The deputy probation officer, Flagg, who was also superintendent of the Detention Home, told Mrs. Gault "why Jerry was there" and said that a hearing would be held in Juvenile Court at 3 o'clock the following day, June 9.

Officer Flagg filed a petition with the court on the hearing day, June 9, 1964. It was not served on the Gaults. Indeed, none of them saw this petition until the habeas corpus hearing on August 17, 1964. The petition . . . made no reference to any factual basis for the judicial action which it initiated. It recited only that "said minor is under the age of eighteen years, . . . [and that] said minor is a delinquent minor." It prayed for a hearing and an order regarding "the care and custody of said minor." . . .

On June 9, Gerald, his mother, his older brother, and Probation Officers Flagg and Henderson appeared before the juvenile judge in chambers. . . . Mrs. Cook, the complainant, was not there. No one was sworn at this hearing. No transcript or recording was made. . . . Our information about the proceedings of the subsequent hearing on June 15, derives entirely from the testimony of the Juvenile Court Judge, Mr. and Mrs. Gault and Officer Flagg at the habeas corpus proceeding conducted two months later. From this, it appears that at the June 9 hearing Gerald was questioned by the judge about the telephone call. There was conflict as to what he said. His mother recalled that Gerald said he only dialed Mrs. Cook's number and handed the telephone to his friend, Ronald. Officer Flagg recalled that Gerald had admitted making the lewd remarks. Judge McGhee testified that Gerald "admitted making one of these [lewd] statements." . . . Gerald was taken back to the Detention Home. . . . On June 11 or 12, after having been detained since June 8, Gerald was released. . . . There is no explanation in the record as to why he was kept in the Detention Home or why he was released. At 5 P.M. on the day of Gerald's release, Mrs. Gault received a note signed by Officer Flagg. It was on plain paper, not letterhead. Its entire text was as follows:

> Mrs. Gault:
>   Judge McGhee has set Monday, June 15, 1964 at 11:00 A.M. as the date and time for further Hearings on Gerald's delinquency.
>
> /s/ Flagg

At the appointed time on Monday, June 15, Gerald, his father and mother, Ronald Lewis and his father, and Officers Flagg and Henderson were present before Judge McGhee. Witnesses at the habeas corpus proceeding differed in their recollections of Gerald's testimony at the June 15 hearing Mr. and Mrs. Gault recalled that Gerald again testified that he had only dialed the number and that the other boy had made the remarks. Officer Flagg agreed that at this hearing Gerald did not admit making the lewd remarks. But Judge McGhee recalled that "there was some admission again of some of the lewd statements. He — he didn't admit any of the more serious lewd statements." Again, the complainant, Mrs. Cook, was not present. Mrs. Gault asked that Mrs. Cook be present. . . . The juvenile judge said "she didn't have to be present at that hearing." The judge did not speak to Mrs. Cook or communicate with her at any time. Probation Officer Flagg had talked to her once — over the telephone on June 9.

At this June 15 hearing a "referral report" made by the probation officers was filed with the court, although not disclosed to Gerald or his parents. This listed the charge as "Lewd Phone Calls." At the conclusion of the hearing, the judge committed Gerald as a juvenile delinquent to the State Industrial School "for the period of his minority [that is, until 21], unless sooner discharged by due process of law." . . .

No appeal is permitted by Arizona law in juvenile cases. [A] petition for a writ of habeas corpus was filed with the Supreme Court of Arizona and referred by it to the Superior Court for hearing.

At the habeas corpus hearing on August 17, Judge McGhee was vigorously cross-examined as to the basis for his actions. He testified that he had taken into account the fact that Gerald was on probation. He was asked "under what section of . . . the code you found the boy delinquent?"

His answer is set forth in the margin.[5] In substance, he concluded that Gerald came within ARS §8-201, subsec. 6(a), which specifies that a "delinquent child" includes one "who has violated a law of the state or an ordinance. . . ." The law which Gerald was found to have violated is ARS §13-377 [which] provides that a person who "in the presence or hearing of any woman or child . . . uses vulgar, abusive or obscene language, is guilty of a misdeameanor. . . ." The penalty specified in the Criminal Code, which would apply to an adult, is $5 to $50, or imprisonment for not more than two months. The judge also testified that he acted under ARS §8-201, subsec. 6(d) which includes in the definition of a "delinquent child" one who, as the judge phrased it, is "habitually involved in immoral matters."

Asked about the basis for his conclusion that Gerald was "habitually involved in immoral matters," the judge testified, somewhat vaguely, that two years earlier, on July 2, 1962, a "referral" was made concerning Gerald, "where the boy had stolen a baseball glove from another boy and lied to the Police Department about it." The judge said there was "no hearing, . . . because of lack of material foundation." But it seems to have remained in his mind as a relevant factor. The judge also testified

---

[5] Q. All right. Now, judge, would you tell me under what section of the law or tell me under what section of — of the code you found the boy delinquent?

A. Well, there is a — I think it amounts to disturbing the peace. I can't give you the section, but I can tell you the law, that when one person uses lewd language in the presence of another person, that it can amount to — and I consider that when a person makes it over the phone, that it is considered in the presence, I might be wrong, that is one section. The other section upon which I consider the boy delinquent is Section 8-201, Subsection (d), habitually involved in immoral matters.

that Gerald had admitted making other nuisance phone calls in the past which, as the judge recalled the boy's testimony, were "silly calls, or funny calls, or something like that."

[The Superior Court dismissed the writ of habeas corpus. The Arizona Supreme Court affirmed.]

II

The Supreme Court of Arizona held that due process of law is requisite to the constitutional validity of proceedings in which . . . a juvenile . . . has engaged in conduct prohibited by law, or has otherwise misbehaved with the consequence that he is committed to an institution in which his freedom is curtailed. This conclusion is in accord with the decisions of a number of courts under both federal and state constitutions.

This Court has not heretofore decided the precise question. In Kent v. United States, 383 U.S. 541 (1966), we considered the requirements for a valid waiver of the "exclusive" jurisdiction of the Juvenile Court of the District of Columbia so that a juvenile could be tried in the adult criminal court of the District. Although our decision turned upon the language of the statute, we emphasized the necessity that "the basic requirements of due process and fairness" be satisfied in such proceedings. [383 U.S. at 553.] [I]n Haley v. State of Ohio, 332 U.S. 596 (1948), [t]he Court held that the Fourteenth Amendment applied to prohibit the use of the coerced confession [of a 15-year-old boy]. [T]hese cases . . . unmistakably indicate that, whatever may be their precise impact, neither the Fourteenth Amendment nor the Bill of Rights is for adults alone.

We do not in this opinion . . . consider the entire process relating to juvenile "delinquents." For example, we are not here concerned with the procedures or constitutional rights applicable to the pre-judicial stages of the juvenile process, nor do we direct our attention to the post-adjudicative or dispositional process. We consider only . . . proceedings by which a determination is made as to whether a juvenile is a "delinquent" as a result of alleged misconduct on his part, with the consequence that he may be committed to a state institution. As to these proceedings, . . . the Due Process Clause has a role to play. The problem is to ascertain the precise impact of the due process requirement upon such proceedings.

From the inception of the juvenile court system, wide differences have been tolerated — indeed insisted upon — between the procedural rights accorded to adults and those of juveniles. In practically all jurisdictions, there are rights granted to adults which are withheld from juveniles. [F]or example, it has been held that the juvenile is not entitled to bail, to indictment by grand jury, to a public trial or to trial by jury. It is frequent practice that rules governing the arrest and interrogation of adults by the police are not observed in the case of juveniles.

The history and theory underlying this development are well known. . . . The Juvenile Court movement began in this country at the end of the last century. From the juvenile court statute adopted in Illinois in 1899, the system has spread to every State in the Union, the District of Columbia, and Puerto Rico. The constitutionality of juvenile court laws has been sustained in over 40 jurisdictions against a variety of attacks.

The early reformers were appalled by adult procedures and penalties, and by the fact that children could be given long prison sentences and mixed in jails with hardened criminals. . . . They believed that society's role was not to ascertain whether the child was "guilty" or "innocent," but "What is he, how has he become what he is, and what had best be done in his interest and in the interest of the state to save him from a downward career." The child — essentially good, as they saw it — was to be made "to feel that he is the object of [the state's] care and solicitude," not that he was under arrest or on trial. The rules of criminal procedure were therefore altogether inapplicable. The apparent rigidities, technicalities, and harshness which they observed in both substantive and procedural criminal law were therefore to be discarded. The idea of crime and punishment was to be abandoned. The child was to be "treated" and "rehabilitated" and the procedures, from apprehension through institutionalization, were to be "clinical" rather than punitive.

These results were to be achieved . . . by insisting that the proceedings were not adversary, but that the state was proceeding as parens patriae. The Latin phrase proved to be a great help to those who sought to rationalize the exclusion of juveniles from the constitutional scheme; but its meaning is murky. . . . The phrase was taken from chancery practice, where, however, it was used to describe the power of the state to act in loco parentis for the purpose of protecting the property interests and the person of the child. . . .

The right of the state, as parens patriae, to deny to the child procedural rights available to his elders was elaborated by the assertion that a child, unlike an adult, has a right "not to liberty but to custody." He can be made to attorn to his parents, to go to school, etc. If his parents default in effectively performing their custodial functions — that is, if the child is "delinquent" — the state may intervene. In doing so, it does not deprive the child of any rights, because he has none. It merely provides the "custody" to which the child is entitled. On this basis, proceedings involving juveniles were described as "civil" not "criminal" and therefore not subject to the requirements which restrict the state when it seeks to deprive a person of his liberty.

Accordingly, the highest motives and most enlightened impulses led to a peculiar system for juveniles, unknown to our law in any comparable context. The constitutional and theoretical basis for this peculiar system is — to say the least — debatable. And in practice, as we remarked in the *Kent* case, supra, the results have not been entirely satisfactory. Juvenile Court history has again demonstrated that unbridled discretion, however benevolently motivated, is frequently a poor substitute for principle and procedure. In 1937, Dean Pound wrote: "The powers of the Star Chamber were a trifle in comparison with those of our juvenile courts. . . ." The absence of substantive standards has not necessarily meant that children receive careful, compassionate, individualized treatment. The absence of procedural rules based upon constitutional principle has not always produced fair, efficient, and effective procedures. . . .

Failure to observe the fundamental requirements of due process has resulted in instances, which might have been avoided, of unfairness to individuals and inadequate or inaccurate findings of fact and unfortunate prescriptions of remedy. Due process of law is the primary and indispensable foundation of individual freedom.

It is the basic and essential term in the social compact which defines the rights of the individual and delimits the powers which the state may exercise. . . . But, in addition, the procedural rules which have been fashioned from the generality of due process . . . enhance the possibility that truth will emerge from the confrontation of opposing versions and conflicting data. . . .

It is claimed that juveniles obtain benefits from the special procedures applicable to them which more than offset the disadvantages of denial of the substance of normal due process. [I]t is important, we think, that the claimed benefits of the juvenile process should be candidly appraised. . . .

[T]he high crime rates among juveniles . . . could not lead us to conclude that the absence of constitutional protections reduces crime, or that the juvenile system, functioning free of constitutional inhibitions as it has largely done, is effective to reduce crime or rehabilitate offenders. We do not mean by this to denigrate the juvenile court process or to suggest that there are not aspects of the juvenile system relating to offenders which are valuable. But the features of the juvenile system which its proponents have asserted are of unique benefit will not be impaired by constitutional domestication. For example, the commendable principles relating to the processing and treatment of juveniles separately from adults are in no way involved or affected by the procedural issues under discussion. Further, we are told that one of the procedural benefits of the special juvenile court procedures is that they avoid classifying the juvenile as a "criminal." The juvenile offender is now classed as a "delinquent." There is, of course, no reason why this should not continue. . . .

Beyond this, it is frequently said that juveniles are protected by the process from disclosure of their deviational behavior. [T]he summary procedures of Juvenile Courts are sometimes defended by a statement that it is the law's policy "to hide youthful errors from the full gaze of the public and bury them in the graveyard of the forgotten past." This claim of secrecy, however, is more rhetoric than reality. Disclosure of court records is discretionary with the judge in most jurisdictions. [M]any courts routinely furnish information to the FBI and the military, and on request to government agencies and even to private employers. . . .

Further, it is urged that the juvenile benefits from informal proceedings in the court. The early conception of the Juvenile Court proceeding was one in which a fatherly judge touched the heart and conscience of the erring youth by talking over his problems, by paternal advice and admonition, and in which, in extreme situations, benevolent and wise institutions of the State provided guidance and help "to save him from a downward career." [R]ecent studies have, with surprising unanimity, entered sharp dissent as to the validity of this gentle conception. They suggest that the appearance as well as the actuality of fairness, impartiality and orderliness — in short, the essentials of due process — may be a more impressive and more therapeutic attitude so far as the juvenile is concerned. For example, in a recent study, the sociologists Wheeler and Cottrell observe that when the procedural laxness of the "parens patriae" attitude is followed by stern disciplining, the contrast may have an adverse effect upon the child, who feels that he has been deceived or enticed. They conclude as follows: "Unless appropriate due process of law is followed, even the juvenile who has violated the law may not feel that he is being fairly treated and may therefore resist the rehabilitative efforts of court personnel."[37] . . . While due process requirements will, in some instances, introduce a degree of order and regularity to Juvenile Court proceedings to determine delinquency, and in contested cases will introduce some elements of the adversary system, nothing will require that the conception of the kindly juvenile judge be replaced by its opposite. . . .

Ultimately, however, we confront the reality of that portion of the Juvenile Court process with which we deal in this case. A boy is charged with misconduct. The boy is committed to an institution where he may be restrained of liberty for years. It is of no constitutional consequence — and of limited practical meaning — that the institution to which he is committed is called an Industrial School. The fact of the matter is that, however euphemistic the title . . . an "industrial school" for juveniles is an institution of confinement. . . . His world becomes "a building with whitewashed walls, regimented routine and institutional hours. . . ." Instead of mother and father and sisters and brothers and friends and classmates, his world is peopled by guards, custodians, state employees, and "delinquents" confined with him for anything from waywardness to rape and homicide.

In view of this, it would be extraordinary if our Constitution did not require the procedural regularity and the exercise of care implied in the phrase "due process." Under our Constitution, the condition of being a boy does not justify a kangaroo court. The traditional ideas of Juvenile Court procedure, indeed, contemplated that time would be available and care would be used to establish precisely what the juvenile did and why he did it — was it a prank of adolescence or a brutal act threatening serious consequences to himself or society unless corrected? Under traditional notions, one would assume that in a case like that of Gerald Gault, where the juvenile appears to have a home, a working mother and father, and an older brother, the juvenile judge would have made a careful inquiry and judgment as to the possibility that the boy could be disciplined and dealt with at home, despite his previous transgressions.[41] Indeed, so far as appears in the record before us, except for some conversation with Gerald about his school work and his "wanting to go to . . . Grand Canyon with his father," the points to which the judge directed his attention were little different from those that would be involved in determining any charge of violation of a penal statute. The essential difference between Gerald's case and a normal criminal case is that safeguards available to adults were discarded in Gerald's case. The summary procedure as well as the long commitment was possible because Gerald was 15 years of age instead of over 18.

If Gerald had been over 18, he would not have been subject to Juvenile Court proceedings. For the particular offense immediately involved, the maximum punishment would have been a fine of $5 to $50, or imprisonment in jail for not more than two months. Instead, he was committed to custody for a maximum of

[37] Juvenile Delinquency — Its Prevention and Control (Russell Sage Foundation, 1966), p. 33. . . .

[41] The juvenile judge's testimony at the habeas corpus proceeding is devoid of any meaningful discussion of this. He appears to have centered his attention upon whether Gerald made the phone call and used lewd words. He was impressed by the fact that Gerald was on six months' probation because he was with another boy who allegedly stole a purse — a different sort of offense, sharing the feature that Gerald was "along," and he even referred to a report which he said was not investigated because "there was no accusation" "because of lack of material foundation." . . .

six years. If he had been over 18 and had committed an offense to which such a sentence might apply, he would have been entitled to substantial rights under the Constitution of the United States as well as under Arizona's laws and constitution. The United States Constitution would guarantee him rights and protections with respect to arrest, search, and seizure, and pretrial interrogation. It would assure him of specific notice of the charges and adequate time to decide his course of action and to prepare his defense. He would be entitled to clear advice that he could be represented by counsel, and, at least if a felony were involved, the State would be required to provide counsel if his parents were unable to afford it. If the court acted on the basis of his confession, careful procedures would be required to assure its voluntariness. If the case went to trial, confrontation and opportunity for cross-examination would be guaranteed. So wide a gulf between the State's treatment of the adult and of the child requires a bridge sturdier than mere verbiage, and reasons more persuasive than cliche can provide. . . .

We now turn to the specific issues which are presented to us in the present case.

III. Notice of Charges

Appellants allege that . . . the proceedings before the Juvenile Court were constitutionally defective because of failure to provide adequate notice of hearings. No notice was given to Gerald's parents when he was taken into custody on Monday, June 8. On that night, when Mrs. Gault went to the Detention Home, she was orally informed that there would be a hearing the next afternoon and was told the reason why Gerald was in custody. The only written notice Gerald's parents received at any time was a note on plain paper from Officer Flagg delivered on Thursday or Friday, June 11 or 12, to the effect that the judge had set Monday, June 15, "for further Hearings on Gerald's delinquency."

A "petition" was filed with the court on June 9 by Officer Flagg, reciting only that he was informed and believed that "said minor is a delinquent minor and that it is necessary that some order be made by the Honorable Court for said minor's welfare." The applicable Arizona statute provides for a petition to be filed in Juvenile Court, alleging in general terms that the child is "neglected, dependent or delinquent." The statute explicitly states that such a general allegation is sufficient, "without alleging the facts." There is no requirement that the petition be served and it was not served upon, given to, or shown to Gerald or his parents.

The Supreme Court of Arizona rejected appellants' claim that due process was denied because of inadequate notice. It stated that "Mrs. Gault knew the exact nature of the charge against Gerald from the day he was taken to the detention home." . . . It held that the appropriate rule is that "the infant and his parents or guardian will receive a petition only reciting a conclusion of delinquency.[51] But no later than the initial hearing by the judge, they must be advised of the facts involved in the case. . . ."

We cannot agree. . . . Notice, to comply with due process requirements, must be given sufficiently in advance of scheduled court proceedings so that reasonable opportunity to prepare will be afforded, and it must "set forth the alleged misconduct

---

[51] No such petition was served or supplied in the present case.

with particularity." . . . The "initial hearing" in the present case was a hearing on the merits. Notice at that time is not timely; and even if there were a conceivable purpose served by the deferral . . . it would have to yield to the requirements that the child and his parents or guardian be notified, in writing, of the specific charge or factual allegations . . . at the earliest practicable time, and in any event sufficiently in advance of the hearing to permit preparation. Due process of law requires notice of the sort we have described. . . . It does not allow a hearing to be held in which a youth's freedom and his parents' right to his custody are at stake without giving them timely notice, in advance of the hearing, of the specific issues that they must meet. Nor, in the circumstances of this case, can it reasonably be said that the requirements of notice was waived.[54]

IV. Right to Counsel

Appellants charge that the Juvenile Court proceedings were fatally defective because the court did not advise Gerald or his parents of their right to counsel, and proceeded with the hearing, the adjudication of delinquency and the order of commitment in the absence of counsel for the child and his parents or an express waiver of the right thereto. The Supreme Court of Arizona pointed out that "[t]here is disagreement [among the various jurisdictions] as to whether the court must advise the infant that he has a right to counsel." It noted its own decision . . . to the effect "that the *parents* of an infant in a juvenile proceeding cannot be denied representation by counsel of their choosing." (Emphasis added.) It referred to a provision of the Juvenile Code which it characterized as requiring "that the probation officer shall look after the interests of neglected, delinquent and dependent children," including representing their interests in court. The court argued that "The parent and the probation officer may be relied upon to protect the infant's interests." Accordingly it rejected the proposition that "due process requires that an infant have a right to counsel." It said that juvenile courts have the discretion, but not the duty, to allow such representation. . . . We do not agree. Probation officers, in the Arizona scheme, are also arresting officers. They initiate proceedings and file petitions which they verify, as here, alleging the delinquency of the child; and they testify, as here, against the child. . . . The probation officer cannot act as counsel for the child. . . . Nor can the judge represent the child. There is no material difference in this respect between adult and juvenile proceedings of the sort here involved. In adult proceedings, this contention has been foreclosed by decisions of this Court.[57]

---

[54] Mrs. Gault's "knowledge" of the charge against Gerald, and/or the asserted failure to object, does not excuse the lack of adequate notice. Indeed, one of the purposes of notice is to clarify the issues to be considered, and as our discussion of the facts, supra, shows, even the Juvenile Court Judge was uncertain as to the precise issues determined at the two "hearings." Since the Gaults had no counsel and were not told of their right to counsel, we cannot consider their failure to object to the lack of constitutionally adequate notice as a waiver of their rights. Because of our conclusion that notice given only at the first hearing is inadequate, we need not reach the question whether the Gaults ever received adequately specific notice even at the June 9 hearing, in light of the fact they were never apprised of the charge of being habitually involved in immoral matters.

[57] Powell v. State of Alabama, 287 U.S. 45, 61 (1932); Gideon v. Wainwright, 372 U.S. 335 (1963).

A proceeding where the issue is whether the child will be found to be "delinquent" and subjected to the loss of his liberty for years is comparable in seriousness to a felony prosecution. The juvenile needs the assistance of counsel to cope with problems of law, to make skilled inquiry into the facts, to insist upon regularity of the proceedings, and to ascertain whether he has a defense and to prepare and submit it. The child "requires the guiding hand of counsel at every step in the proceedings against him." [Powell v. Alabama, 287 U.S. 45, 69 (1932).]

We conclude that the Due Process Clause of the Fourteenth Amendment requires that in respect of proceedings to determine delinquency which may result in commitment to an institution in which the juvenile's freedom is curtailed, the child and his parents must be notified of the child's right to be represented by counsel retained by them, or if they are unable to afford counsel, the counsel will be appointed to represent the child. . . .

V. Confrontation, Self-Incrimination, Cross-Examination

Appellants urge that the writ of habeas corpus should have been granted because of the denial of the rights of confrontation and cross-examination in the Juvenile Court hearings, and because the privilege against self-incrimination was not observed. The Juvenile Court Judge testified at the habeas corpus hearing that he had proceeded on the basis of Gerald's admissions at the two hearings. Appellants attack this on the ground that the admissions were obtained in disregard of, the privilege against self-incrimination. . . .

Our first question, then, is whether Gerald's admission was improperly obtained. . . . For this purpose, it is necessary briefly to recall the relevant facts.

Mrs. Cook, the complainant, and the recipient of the alleged telephone call, was not called as a witness. Gerald's mother asked the Juvenile Court Judge why Mrs. Cook was not present and the judge replied that "she didn't have to be present." So far as appears, Mrs. Cook was spoken to only once, by Officer Flagg, and this was by telephone. The judge did not speak with her on any occasion. Gerald had been questioned by the probation officer after having been taken into custody. The exact circumstances of this questioning do not appear but any admissions Gerald may have made at this time do not appear in the record. Gerald was also questioned by the Juvenile Court Judge at each of the two hearings. . . . There was conflict and uncertainty among the witnesses at the habeas corpus proceeding — the Juvenile Court Judge, Mr. and Mrs. Gault, and the probation officer — as to what Gerald did or did not admit.

. . . Neither Gerald nor his parents were advised that he did not have to testify or make a statement, or that an incriminating statement might result in his commitment as a "delinquent."

The Arizona Supreme Court rejected appellants' contention that Gerald had a right to be advised that he need not incriminate himself. . . .

In reviewing this conclusion of Arizona's Supreme Court, we emphasize again that we are here concerned only with a proceeding to determine whether a minor is a "delinquent" and which may result in commitment to a state institution. Specifically, the question is whether, in such a proceeding, an admission by the juvenile may be used against him in the absence of clear and unequivocal evidence that the admission was made with knowledge that he was not obliged to speak and would not be penalized for remaining silent. In light of Miranda v. State of Arizona, 384 U.S. 436 (1966), we must also consider whether, if the privilege against self-incrimination is available, it can effectively be waived unless counsel is present or the right to counsel has been waived.

It has long been recognized that the eliciting and use of confessions or admissions require careful scrutiny. . . .

The privilege against self-incrimination is, of course, related to the question of the safeguards necessary to assure that admissions or confessions are reasonably trustworthy, that they are not the mere fruits of fear or coercion, but are reliable expressions of the truth. The roots of the privilege are, however, far deeper. They [insist] upon the equality of the individual and the state. In other words, the privilege has a broader and deeper thrust than the rule which prevents the use of confessions which are the product of coercion because coercion is thought to carry with it the danger of unreliability. One of its purposes is to prevent the state, whether by force or by psychological domination, from overcoming the mind and will of the person under investigation and depriving him of the freedom to decide whether to assist the state in securing his conviction.

It would indeed be surprising if the privilege against self-incrimination were available to hardened criminals but not to children. The language of the Fifth Amendment, applicable to the States by operation of the Fourteenth Amendment, is unequivocal and without exception. . . .

Against the application to juveniles of the right to silence, it is argued that juvenile proceedings are "civil" and not "criminal," and therefore the privilege should not apply. It is true that the statement of the privilege in the Fifth Amendment . . . is that no person "shall be compelled in any *criminal case* to be a witness against himself." However, it is also clear that the availability of the privilege does not turn upon the type of proceeding in which its protection is invoked, but upon the nature of the statement or admission and the exposure which it invites. . . .

It would be entirely unrealistic to carve out of the Fifth Amendment all statements by juveniles on the ground that these cannot lead to "criminal" involvement. In the first place, juvenile proceedings to determine "delinquency," which may lead to commitment to a state institution, must be regarded as "criminal" for purposes of the privilege against self-incrimination. To hold otherwise would be to disregard substance because of the feeble enticement of the "civil" label-of-convenience which has been attached to juvenile proceedings. [C]ommitment is a deprivation of liberty. It is incarceration against one's will, whether it is called "criminal" or "civil." And our Constitution guarantees that no person shall be "compelled" to be a witness against himself when he is threatened with deprivation of his liberty. . . .

In addition, . . . there is little or no assurance in Arizona, as in most if not all of the States, that a juvenile apprehended and interrogated by the police or even by the Juvenile Court itself will remain outside of the reach of adult courts as a consequence of the offense for which he has been taken into custody. In Arizona, as in other States, provision is made for Juvenile Courts to relinquish or waive jurisdiction to the ordinary criminal courts. In the present case, when Gerald Gault was interrogated concerning violation of a section of the Arizona Criminal Code, it could not be certain that the Juvenile Court Judge would decide to "suspend" criminal prosecution in court for adults by proceeding to an adjudication in Juvenile Court.

It is also urged, as the Supreme Court of Arizona here asserted, that the juvenile and presumably his parents should not be advised of the juvenile's right to silence because confession is good for the child as the commencement of the assumed therapy of the juvenile court process, and he should be encouraged to assume an attitude of trust and confidence toward the officials of the juvenile process. This proposition has been subjected to widespread challenge on the basis of current reappraisals of the rhetoric and realities of the handling of juvenile offenders.

In fact, evidence is accumulating that confessions by juveniles do not aid in "individualized treatment," as the court below put it, and that compelling the child to answer questions, without warning or advice as to his right to remain silent, does not serve this or any other good purpose. In light of the observations of Wheeler and Cottrell, and others, it seems probable that where children are induced to confess by "paternal" urgings on the part of officials and the confession is then followed by disciplinary action, the child's reaction is likely to be hostile and adverse — the child may well feel that he has been led or tricked into confession and that despite his confession, he is being punished.

Further, authoritative opinion has cast formidable doubt upon the reliability and trustworthiness of "confessions" by children. . . .

We conclude that the constitutional privilege against self-incrimination is applicable in the case of juveniles as it is with respect to adults. We appreciate that special problems may arise with respect to waiver of the privilege by or on behalf of children, and that there may well be some differences in technique — but not in principle — depending upon the age of the child and the presence and competence of parents. The participation of counsel will, of course, assist the police, Juvenile Courts and appellate tribunals in administering the privilege. If counsel was not present for some permissible reason when an admission was obtained, the greatest care must be taken to assure that the admission was voluntary, in the sense not only that it was not coerced or suggested, but also that it was not the product of ignorance of rights or of adolescent fantasy, fright or despair.

The "confession" of Gerald Gault was first obtained by Officer Flagg, out of the presence of Gerald's parents, without counsel and without advising him of his right to silence, as far as appears. The judgment of the Juvenile Court was stated by the judge to be based on Gerald's admissions in court. Neither "admission" was reduced to writing, and, to say the least, the process by which the "admissions" were obtained and received must be characterized as lacking the certainty and order which are required of proceedings of such formidable consequences. Apart from the "admission," there was nothing upon which a judgment or finding might be based. There was no sworn testimony. Mrs. Cook, the complainant, was not present. The Arizona Supreme Court held that "sworn testimony must be required of all witnesses including police officers, probation officers and others who are part of or officially related to the juvenile court structure." We hold that this is not enough. No reason is suggested or appears for a different rule in respect of sworn testimony in juvenile courts than in adult tribunals. Absent a valid confession adequate to support the determination of the Juvenile Court, confrontation and sworn testimony by witnesses available for cross-examination were essential for a finding of "delinquency" and an order committing Gerald to a state institution for a maximum of six years. . . .

VI. *Appellate Review and Transcript of Proceedings*

Appellants urge that the Arizona statute is unconstitutional under the Due Process Clause because, as construed by its Supreme Court, "there is no right of appeal from a juvenile court order. . . . " The court held that there is no right to a transcript because there is no right to appeal and because the proceedings are confidential and any record must be destroyed after a prescribed period of time. Whether a transcript or other recording is made, it held, is a matter for the discretion of the juvenile court.

This Court has not held that a State is required by the Federal Constitution "to provide appellate courts or a right to appellate review at all." In view of the fact that we must reverse the Supreme Court of Arizona's affirmance of the dismissal of the writ of habeas corpus for other reasons, we need not rule on this question in the present case or upon the failure to provide a transcript. [T]he consequences of failure to provide an appeal, to record the proceedings, or to make findings or state the grounds for the juvenile court's conclusion may be to throw a burden upon the machinery for habeas corpus, to saddle the reviewing process with the burden of attempting to reconstruct a record, and to impose upon the juvenile judge the unseemly duty of testifying under cross-examination as to the events that transpired in the hearings before him. . . .

Judgment reversed and cause remanded with directions.

[The separate concurring opinions of Justices Black, Harlan, and White are omitted.]

Mr. Justice STEWART, dissenting.

The Court today uses an obscure Arizona case as a vehicle to impose upon thousands of juvenile courts throughout the Nation restrictions that the Constitution made applicable to adversary criminal trials. I believe the Court's decision is wholly unsound as a matter of constitutional law, and sadly unwise as a matter of judicial policy. Juvenile proceedings are not criminal trials. . . .

The inflexible restrictions that the Constitution so wisely made applicable to adversary criminal trials have no inevitable place in the proceedings of those public social agencies known as juvenile or family courts. And to impose the Court's long catalog of requirements . . . is to invite a long step backwards into the nineteenth century. In that era . . . a child was tried in a conventional criminal court with all the trappings of a conventional criminal trial. So it was that a 12-year-old boy named James Guild was tried in New Jersey for killing Catharine Beakes. A jury found him guilty of murder, and he was sentenced to death by hanging. The sentence was executed. It was all very constitutional [State v. Guild, 5 Hals. 163, 10 N.J. L. 163, 18 Am. Dec. 404 (1828)].

[D]ue process may require that some of the same restrictions which the Constitution has placed upon criminal trials must be imposed upon juvenile proceedings. For example, I suppose that all would agree that a brutally coerced confession could not constitutionally be considered in a juvenile court hearing. But it surely does not follow that the testimonial privilege against self-incrimination is applicable in all justice proceedings. Similarly, due process clearly requires timely notice of the purpose and scope of any proceedings affecting the relationship of parent and child. But it certainly does not follow that notice of a juvenile hearing must be framed with all the technical niceties of a criminal indictment.

In any event, there is no reason to deal with issues such as these in the present case. The Supreme Court of Arizona found that the parents of Gerald Gault "knew of their right to counsel, to subpoena and cross examine witnesses, of the right to confront the witnesses against Gerald and the possible consequences of a finding of delinquency." 407 P.2d 760, 763. It further found that "Mrs. Gault knew the exact nature of the charge against Gerald from the day he was taken to the detention home." 407 P.2d, at 768. And, as Mr. Justice White correctly points out, no issue of compulsory self-incrimination is presented by this case.

I would dismiss the appeal.

NOTES AND QUESTIONS

(1) **Gault***: Wellspring for the Rights of Children.* *Gault* has served as a wellspring for the development of the constitutional rights of minors. Although the holdings were limited to the adjudicatory stage of juvenile court delinquency proceedings where a young person risked incarceration, the principles underlying the decision and the approach taken by the court have broader implications for delinquency proceedings, for other sorts of juvenile court proceedings, and for the rights of children generally. *Gault* represented the first unequivocal holding that young people, as individuals, have constitutional rights of their own: "[W]hatever may be their precise impact, neither the Fourteenth Amendment nor the Bill of Rights is for adults alone." Moreover, the Court displayed a willingness to base its decision on what it perceived as the realities of the juvenile justice system. Neither the high motives and "enlightened impulses" of state officials, nor the parens patriae power of the state were accepted as sufficient justifications for the denial of procedural rights to a young person.

The cases considered in Chapter 1, *Roe, Meyer, Pierce, Prince*, and *Yoder*, all reflect the tension between two principles: (a) The family has a broad range of authority over the child, and the parent-child relationship itself has a constitutional dimension; and (b) the state has legitimate interests in child rearing, and need not treat children like adults. *Gault* established a third principle: Young people may have rights of their own, some of which are of constitutional dimension. *Gault*'s principle thus represents a third point in the triangular relationship between the child, the family, and the state.

(2) **Gault***: Implications for Juvenile Delinquency.* Consider the following questions:

a. Due Process v. Equal Protection. Does *Gault* suggest that a juvenile accused of criminal conduct must be treated in all respects like an adult accused of criminal conduct? Are society's interests with regard to juvenile offenders any different from those with regard to adult offenders? What significance do you attach to the fact that *Gault* was decided on the basis of the Due Process Clause and not the Equal Protection Clause?

*b. Post-*Gault *Constitutional Developments.*   Does the Court's approach in *Gault* suggest that a juvenile accused of delinquency must have all the procedural rights constitutionally guaranteed for an adult accused of a crime? Since *Gault*, the Supreme Court has considered whether delinquents are entitled to the "beyond a reasonable doubt" standard of proof, In re Winship, 397 U.S. 358 (1970) (discussed infra p. 803); jury trials, McKeiver v. Pennsylvania, 403 U.S. 528 (1971) (discussed infra p. 798); protection against double jeopardy, Breed v. Jones, 421 U.S. 519 (1975) (discussed infra p. 806); certain interrogation-related rights, Fare v. Michael C., 442 U.S. 707 (1979) (discussed infra p. 834); the right not to be detained prior to trial, Schall v. Martin, 467 U.S. 253 (1984) (discussed infra p. 809); and unreasonable search and seizure, New Jersey v. T.L.O., 469 U.S. 325 (1985) (discussed infra p. 811).

c. Parental Role.   What does *Gault* suggest concerning the question of the role of a young person's parents in a delinquency proceeding? Why did the court say that "the child *and his parents* must be notified of the child's right to be represented by counsel retained by them, or if they are unable to afford counsel, that counsel will be appointed to represent the child"? (Supra p. 791.) Even if a young person is notified of the charges against him, and his right of counsel, would the Constitution be violated if his parents were not notified? Should a young person be able to insist that his parents *not* be notified? Who should be able to waive the youth's right to counsel, the young person or his parents? Neither alone? See generally pp. 849-850.

d. Procedural Safeguards.   Consider the implications of a youthful offender's possible immaturity. Because *Gault* implies that young persons are entitled to certain procedural safeguards that adults also have, does this imply that young people should be held responsible for their criminal misconduct like adults? Is it possible that certain procedural safeguards that may be adequate for an adult offender, may not sufficiently protect a young person who is immature? Can a 13-year-old give a "knowing and informed" waiver of his constitutional rights?

Do you think it is more important for a young person than for an adult to be encouraged to "tell the truth" and confess to a misdeed? What message is a 12-year-old receiving when he is told that he has a right to remain silent and not confess to a crime? In everyday child rearing, how do you think most parents would feel if they were required to tell their child that he or she had a right to remain silent when asked about involvement in possible misdeeds? How is the delinquency process different?

(3) **Gault:** *Implications for Procedural Due Process in Contexts Other than Delinquency Proceedings.*   *Gault* has had implications far broader than the delinquency process itself, and has provided the foundation for arguments in a variety of contexts that a young person is constitutionally entitled to various procedural safeguards because of the Due Process Clause. In applying the Due Process Clause, the Supreme Court has generally indicated that a two-stage analysis is necessary; first, the court must determine whether the individual's interests involved in a particular case are encompassed within the Fourteenth Amendment's protection of "life, liberty, or property." While these concepts are hardly self-defining, the court has made plain that only if protected interests are implicated does the Constitution require procedural safeguards. Second, assuming protected interests are implicated,

the court must then decide what procedures in a particular context constitute "due process of law."

In *Gault*, the young person obviously had a "liberty" interest at stake: he was charged with misconduct and risked commitment to an institution for a period of years. Because the possible consequences for a youth are so akin to those of an adult accused, *Gault* and its progeny have interpreted due process to require a highly adversary and formal process in a delinquency proceeding: these include the right to counsel, a right to confront witnesses, a high standard of proof, etc. See infra p. 854. In other contexts, however, the Court has determined that the Due Process Clause is satisfied with fewer procedural safeguards, or none at all. See infra pp. 128-129.

The following questions suggest the variety of contexts in which procedural due process claims might be made on behalf of a young person.

a. Juvenile Court Cases Involving Alleged Noncriminal Misconduct. A juvenile court may assume jurisdiction over a young person based on allegations that the youth is in need of supervision, has been a truant, is a runaway, or is engaged in other noncriminal misbehavior. As a consequence, the young person's liberty can be constrained. What does the Due Process Clause require in such cases? See Chapter 6.

b. Child Neglect Cases. What procedural safeguards should be required before the state may coercively remove a young person from parental custody on the grounds that the parent is neglecting or abusing the child? Must there be a hearing before an initial removal? Must there be counsel for the parents? Independent counsel for the child? See Chapter 3. Are more substantial safeguards necessary if the court is considering termination of parental rights in order to free the child for adoption?

c. Divorce Proceedings. Should the child have independent counsel in all cases where parents are divorcing? All disputed cases? Only in cases where custody is disputed? Divorce custody issues are considered in Chapter 5.

d. Commitment to State Mental Hospital. Must there be a hearing, and must the child be represented by independent counsel before his parents can commit him to a state mental hospital? See Parham v. J.R., supra p. 382.

e. Due Process Rights in Schools. Is a young person constitutionally entitled to a hearing before being expelled from school? Before being suspended from school for a short period? See supra pp. 128-129. Before being subjected to corporal punishment for disciplinary purposes? See supra p. 131. If a hearing is required, what sort of hearing?

(4) *Social Science Evidence.* Notice how the court in *Gault* relies on various types of social science evidence in reaching its conclusion. Do you think this is a firm basis for the result reached? Consider the following elements.[70]

a. Increase in Crime. The Court suggests that juvenile crime has increased since the juvenile court was established. Is this relevant? Does the Court mean to imply that this demonstrates the failure of the juvenile court? Does the Court address the question of how much crime there would be under an alternative scheme

---

[70] The questions that follow in the text are suggested by William V. Stapleton & Lee E. Teitelbaum, In Defense of Youth: A Study of Counsel in American Juvenile Courts (1972).

that was of a more adversary nature? Is it possible that crime rates may have been even greater without juvenile courts? Was there a "control" that would allow the Court to evaluate what difference having the juvenile court made?

   b. Stigma.   The Court suggests that the information that a juvenile has been adjudicated a delinquent could be stigmatizing if the information became available, and the Court suggested that in fact this information often did become available. Does guaranteeing counsel in the delinquency proceeding in any way limit access to the information that a juvenile has been adjudicated a delinquent? Does it keep that information more secret? Is not the problem raised by the Court the illegitimate use of juvenile records? If this is the problem, are there alternative procedures, quite apart from representation by counsel, that might attack this problem directly?

   c. The Juvenile's Perception of the System's Fairness.   The majority opinion sharply questions the value of informality as a molder of desirable views of justice. Citing Juvenile Delinquency: Its Prevention and Control, the Court suggested that "recent studies" indicated that the essentials of due process "may be a more impressive and more therapeutic attitude so far as the juvenile is concerned." But the primary study cited by the Court was described by its own authors as a "brief overview of major problems, issues, and developments in the field of juvenile delinquency," *not* a report of actual findings. Moreover, as Stapleton and Teitelbaum write,

> Recent studies on the attitudes of juvenile offenders suggest that, for many, there is little understanding of the system or perception of "unfairness." In addition, data from an as yet unreleased portion of this study indicate that relatively few juveniles processed through [juvenile] courts regard the system as "unjust." Generally, therefore, it may be said that the theories connecting juveniles' perceptions of justice with the court's processes are little more than current and provocative, but untested, ideas, and that the Supreme Court's evaluation rested on intelligent guesswork rather than empirical data. [William V. Stapleton & Lee E. Teitelbaum, In Defense of Youth: A Study of the Role of Counsel in American Juvenile Courts 171 (1972).]

   d. Punishment and Loss of Liberty.   The final empirical observation upon which the Court's decision rests seems to be the punitive nature of the sanctions. Indeed, this may be the critical aspect. The Court emphasized that a juvenile sent to a "home" or "school" was deprived of his liberty, and was, in effect, incarcerated. Does *Gault* require counsel when there is no possibility of incarceration? For example, could a state establish informal proceedings without the various procedural safeguards in circumstances in which the minor did not risk incarceration, and the only issue concerned the conditions of his probation? See In re K., 554 P.2d 180 (Or. Ct. App. 1976) (holding that due process required fewer guarantees when child is not subject to incarceration).

McKeiver v. Pennsylvania
403 U.S. 528 (1971)

Mr. Justice BLACKMUN announced the judgments of the Court and an opinion in which The Chief Justice, Mr. Justice STEWART, and Mr. Justice WHITE join.

These cases present the narrow but precise issue whether the Due Process Clause of the Fourteenth Amendment assures the right to trial by jury in the adjudicative phase of a state juvenile court delinquency proceeding. . . .

II

[W]e turn to the facts of the present cases:

No. 322. Joseph McKeiver, then age 16, in May 1968 was charged with robbery, larceny, and receiving stolen goods (felonies under Pennsylvania law) . . . as acts of juvenile delinquency. At the time of the adjudication hearing he was represented by counsel. His request for a jury trial was denied. . . . McKeiver was adjudged a delinquent upon findings that he had violated a law of the Commonwealth. Pa. Stat. Ann., Tit. 11, §243 (4) (a) (1965). He was placed on probation. . . .

It suffices to say that McKeiver's offense was his participating with 20 or 30 youths who pursued three young teenagers and took 25 cents from them; that McKeiver never before had been arrested and had a record of gainful employment; that the testimony of two of the victims was described by the court as somewhat inconsistent and as "weak" . . .

[Edward Terry, age 15, was charged with assault and battery on a police officer and conspiracy (misdemeanors under Pennsylvania law) for hitting a police officer who broke up a fight that Terry and others were watching. Barbara Burrus was one of the 45 African-American children, ages 11 to 15, whose charges arose from their participation in a series of demonstrations regarding school assignments and a school consolidation plan. The request for jury trial in each case was denied. The cases were consolidated. On appeal, the Supreme Court of North Carolina affirmed the appellate courts' delinquency adjudications and denials of the right to jury trial. In re Burrus, 169 S.E.2d 879 (N.C. 1969).]

IV

The right to an impartial jury "[i]n all criminal prosecutions" under federal law is guaranteed by the Sixth Amendment. Through the Fourteenth Amendment that requirement has now been imposed upon the States "in all criminal cases which — were they to be tried in a federal court — would come within the Sixth Amendment's guarantee." This is because the Court has said it believes "that trial by jury in criminal cases is fundamental to the American scheme of justice." . . .

This, of course, does not automatically provide the answer to the present jury trial issue, if for no other reason than that the juvenile court proceeding has not yet been held to be a "criminal prosecution," within the meaning and reach of the Sixth Amendment, and also has not yet been regarded as devoid of criminal aspects merely because it usually has been given the civil label.

Little, indeed, is to be gained by any attempt simplistically to call the juvenile court proceeding either "civil" or "criminal." The Court carefully has avoided this wooden approach. Before *Gault* was decided in 1967, the Fifth Amendment's guarantee against self-incrimination had been imposed upon the state criminal trial. . . . So, too, had the Sixth Amendment's rights of confrontation and cross-examination. . . . Yet the Court did not automatically and peremptorily apply those rights to the juvenile proceeding. A reading of *Gault* reveals the opposite. And the same separate approach to the standard-of-proof issue is evident from the carefully separated application of the standard, first to the criminal trial, and then to the juvenile proceeding, displayed in *Winship.* [397 U.S. 358, 361, 365.]

Thus, accepting "the proposition that the Due Process Clause has a role to play," *Gault,* 387 U.S., at 13, our task here with respect to trial by jury, as it was in *Gault* with respect to other claimed rights, "is to ascertain the precise impact of the due process requirement." Id., at 13-14.

V

The Pennsylvania juveniles' basic argument is that they were tried in proceedings "substantially similar to a criminal trial." They say that a delinquency proceeding in their State is initiated by a petition charging a penal code violation in the conclusory language of an indictment; that a juvenile detained prior to trial is held in a building substantially similar to an adult prison; . . . that counsel and the prosecution engage in plea bargaining; that motions to suppress are routinely heard and decided; that the usual rules of evidence are applied; that the customary common-law defenses are available; that the press is generally admitted in the Philadelphia juvenile courtrooms; that members of the public enter the room; that arrest and prior record may be reported by the press (from police sources, however, rather than from the juvenile court records); that, once adjudged delinquent, a juvenile may be confined until his majority in what amounts to a prison and that the stigma attached upon delinquency adjudication approximates that resulting from conviction in an adult criminal proceeding.

The North Carolina juveniles particularly urge that the requirement of a jury trial would not operate to deny the supposed benefits of the juvenile court system [flexible sentencing permitting emphasis on rehabilitation]; that realization of these benefits does not depend upon dispensing with the jury; that adjudication of factual issues on the one hand and disposition of the case on the other are very different matters with very different purposes; that the purpose of the former is indistinguishable from that of the criminal trial; that the jury trial provides an independent protective factor; that experience has shown that jury trials in juvenile courts are manageable; that no reason exists why protection traditionally accorded in criminal proceedings should be denied young people subject to involuntary incarceration for lengthy periods; and that the juvenile courts deserve healthy public scrutiny.

VI

All the litigants here agree that the applicable due process standard in juvenile proceedings, as developed by *Gault* and *Winship,* is fundamental fairness. As that standard was applied in those two cases, we have an emphasis on factfinding procedures. The requirements of notice, counsel, confrontation, cross-examination, and standard of proof naturally flowed from this emphasis. But one cannot say that in our legal system the jury is a necessary component of accurate factfinding. There is much to be said for it, to be sure, but we have been content to pursue other ways for determining facts. Juries are not required, and have not been, for example, in equity cases, in workmen's compensation, in probate, or in deportation cases. Neither have they been generally used in military trials. . . .

We must recognize, as the Court has recognized before, that the fond and idealistic hopes of the juvenile court proponents and early reformers of three generations ago have not been realized. The devastating commentary upon the system's failures as a whole, contained in the President's Commission on Law Enforcement and Administration of Justice, Task Force Report: Juvenile Delinquency and Youth Crime 7-9 (1967), reveals the depth of disappointment in what has been accomplished. Too often the juvenile court judge falls far short of that stalwart, protective, and communicating figure the system envisaged. The community's unwillingness to provide people and facilities and to be concerned, the insufficiency of time devoted, the scarcity of professional help, the inadequacy of dispositional alternatives, and our general lack of knowledge all contribute to dissatisfaction with the experiment. . . .

Despite all these disappointments, all these failures, and all these shortcomings, we conclude that trial by jury in the juvenile court's adjudicative stage is not a constitutional requirement. We so conclude for a number of reasons:

1. The Court has refrained, in the cases heretofore decided, from taking the easy way with a flat holding that all rights constitutionally assured for the adult accused are to be imposed upon the state juvenile proceeding. . . .

2. There is a possibility, at least, that the jury trial, if required as a matter of constitutional precept, will remake the juvenile proceeding into a fully adversary process and will put an effective end to what has been the idealistic prospect of an intimate, informal protective proceeding.

3. The Task Force Report, although concededly pre-*Gault*, is notable for its not making any recommendation that the jury trial be imposed upon the juvenile court system. This is so despite its vivid description of the system's deficiencies and disappointments. . . .

4. The Court specifically has recognized by dictum that a jury is not a necessary part even of every criminal process that is fair and equitable. . . .

5. The imposition of the jury trial on the juvenile court system would not strengthen greatly, if at all, the factfinding function, and would, contrarily, provide an attrition of the juvenile court's assumed ability to function in a unique manner. It would not remedy the defects of the system. . . .

6. The juvenile concept held high promise. We are reluctant to say that, despite disappointments of grave dimensions, it still does not hold promise, and we are particularly reluctant to say, as do the Pennsylvania appellants here, that the system cannot accomplish its rehabilitative goals. . . . We are reluctant to disallow the States to experiment further and to seek in new and different ways the elusive answers to the problems of the young, and we feel that we would be impeding that experimentation by imposing the jury trial. . . . If, in its wisdom, any State feels the jury trial is desirable in all cases, or in certain kinds, there appears to be no impediment to its installing a system embracing that feature. That, however, is the State's privilege and not its obligation. . . .

10. Since *Gault* . . . the great majority of States, in addition to Pennsylvania and North Carolina, that have faced the issue have concluded that the considerations

that led to the result in those two cases do not compel trial by jury in the juvenile court. . . .

12. If the jury trial were to be injected into the juvenile court system as a matter of right, it would bring with it into that system the traditional delay, the formality, and the clamor of the adversary system and, possibly, the public trial. . . .

13. Finally, the arguments advanced by the juveniles here are, of course, the identical arguments that underlie the demand for the jury trial for criminal proceedings. The arguments necessarily equate the juvenile proceeding — or at least the adjudicative phase of it — with the criminal trial. Whether they should be so equated is our issue. Concern about the inapplicability of exclusionary and other rules of evidence, about the juvenile court judge's possible awareness of the juvenile's prior record and of the contents of the social file; about repeated appearances of the same familiar witnesses in the persons of juvenile and probation officers and social workers — all to the effect that this will create the likelihood of prejudgment — chooses to ignore, it seems to us, every aspect of fairness, of concern, of sympathy, and of paternal attention that the juvenile court system contemplates.

If the formalities of the criminal adjudicative process are to be superimposed upon the juvenile court system, there is little need for its separate existence. Perhaps that ultimate disillusionment will come one day, but for the moment we are disinclined to give impetus to it.

Affirmed.

[The separate concurring opinions of Justice Harlan and Justice White have been omitted.]

Mr. Justice DOUGLAS, with whom Mr. Justice BLACK and Mr. Justice MARSHALL concur, dissenting.

These cases from Pennsylvania and North Carolina present the issue of the right to a jury trial for offenders charged in juvenile court and facing a possible incarceration until they reach their majority. I believe the guarantees of the Bill of Rights, made applicable to the States by the Fourteenth Amendment, require a jury trial. . . .

Conviction of each of these crimes would subject a person, whether juvenile or adult, to imprisonment in a state institution. In the case of these students the possible term was six to 10 years; it would be computed for the period until an individual reached the age of 21.

[W]here a State uses its juvenile court proceedings to prosecute a juvenile for a criminal act and to order "confinement" until the child reaches 21 years of age or where the child at the threshold of the proceedings faces that prospect, then he is entitled to the same procedural protection as an adult. . . .

Just as courts have sometimes confused delinquency with crime, so have law enforcement officials treated juveniles not as delinquents but as criminals. . . .

In the present cases imprisonment or confinement up to 10 years was possible for one child and each faced at least a possible five-year incarceration. No adult could be denied a jury trial in those circumstances. Duncan v. Louisiana, 391 U.S. 145, 162. The Fourteenth Amendment, which makes trial by jury provided in the Sixth Amendment applicable to the States, speaks of denial of rights to "any person," not denial of rights to "any adult person". . . .

NOTES AND QUESTIONS

(1) **McKeiver's** *Role in the Due Process Revolutions.* During the years following *Gault*, the Supreme Court decided a number of cases that raised questions concerning the constitutional requirements of delinquency proceedings. Among *Gault's* Supreme Court progeny, *McKeiver* stood alone in denying a constitutional safeguard to children accused of delinquency. Another of *Gault's* progeny, In re Winship, 397 U.S. 358 (1970), alluded *to* in *McKeiver*, supra p. 800, held that the standard of proof beyond a reasonable doubt was constitutionally required during the adjudicatory stage of a delinquency proceeding. Is *McKeiver* consistent with *Gault, Winship*, and *Breed* (holding that the Double Jeopardy Clause attached to juvenile waiver proceedings)? (See infra p. 806.)

(2) Premise: Reliability of Judicial Fact Finding. *McKeiver* is based in part on the premise of the reliability of judicial fact finding. Specifically, the plurality in *McKeiver* asserts that the use of a jury "would not strengthen greatly, if at all, the factfinding function [of the juvenile court]" (supra p. 801). Is the premise correct that judicial fact finding is as reliable as jury fact finding?

In response to this question, Professors Martin Guggenheim and Randy Hertz concluded (based on their empirical study of bench versus jury trials) that judges are more likely to convict alleged delinquents on insufficient evidence, to lean unduly in the prosecution's favor when appraising the evidence, to be less likely to subject police officers' testimony to critical evaluation even when their accounts seem dubious, and to be biased by highly incriminating evidence that would be inadmissible at trial and would be kept from a jury. Martin Guggenheim & Randy Hertz, Reflections on Judges, Juries, and Justice: Ensuring the Fairness of Juvenile Delinquency Trials, 33 Wake Forest L. Rev. 553 (1998). In contrast, the authors claim that the use of juries (by drawing on the experiences and perspectives of many persons from diverse backgrounds) "increases the likelihood that witnesses' credibility will be assessed accurately and facts correctly found" (id. at 576), and that "salient facts will not be overlooked or forgotten" (id. at 578). See also Recent Cases, Constitutional Law — Right to Jury Trial — Eighth Circuit Holds an Adjudication of Juvenile Delinquency to Be a "Prior Conviction" for the Purpose of Sentence Enhancement at a Subsequent Criminal Proceeding — United States v. Smalley, 294 F.3d 1030 (8th Cir. 2002), 116 Harv. L. Rev. 705, 709 (2002) (pointing out that the *McKeiver* plurality's assertion of the reliability of judicial fact finding is "belied by empirical evidence the Court itself has accepted").

Professors Guggenheim and Hertz suggest that certain procedures should be adopted by legislatures and judges in jurisdictions that deny juveniles the right to jury trial. First, they advocate guarding against the juvenile court judge's exposure to prejudicial information in all pretrial matters (e.g., detention hearings, transfers to adult court, and hearings to suppress evidence) by having a judge different from the one who will preside over the trial. Second, they suggest that juvenile court judges should make a routine practice of discussing cases with other judges before rendering a verdict to improve the quality of judicial decision making. Guggenheim & Hertz, supra, at 583-585. What do you think of the proposed reforms?

(3) Premise: Need for Special Characteristics of Juvenile Court. Another premise of *McKeiver* was that the introduction of jury trials would erode the unique

characteristics of the juvenile court system, in particular its paternal approach to the juvenile offender. Does the recent criminalization trend of the juvenile justice system undermine this assumption? Several commentators have argued that it does. For example, one student commentator writes:

> Even admitting that the juvenile justice system had fallen short of its ideal of reha-
> bilitating juveniles in a noncriminal context, the *McKeiver* plurality was "reluctant
> to say that, despite disappointments of grave dimensions, [the system] still does not
> hold promise." The plurality was therefore wary of any reform that would "place
> the juvenile squarely in the routine of the criminal process" — implicitly assuming
> that the juvenile process had not already done so. Whether or not there was a great
> practical distinction — beyond the procedural protections at issue — between the
> criminal and juvenile justice systems of 1971, the systems have since converged to
> the point that *McKeiver*'s idealistic conception of the juvenile justice system is hard
> to sustain. Whereas early juvenile courts emphasized flexibility in order to serve
> the best interests of individual offenders, today states increasingly use fixed or
> mandatory-minimum sentences in defining punishments for juvenile delinquents.
> Some states even allow juvenile courts to impose "blended" sentences that include
> incarceration in both juvenile and adult correctional facilities. . . . One juvenile
> justice scholar summarizes: "Within the past three decades, judicial decisions,
> legislative amendments, and administrative changes have transformed the juvenile
> court from a nominally rehabilitative social welfare agency into a scaled-down,
> second-class criminal court for young offenders that provides neither therapy nor
> justice." The increasing convergence of the juvenile and criminal courts under-
> mines one of *McKeiver*'s key reasons for denying juries to juveniles — preservation
> of the unique aspects of the juvenile system — as the system loses the unique
> aspects the Court wanted to preserve. . . . [Recent Cases, supra, at 711-712.]

Do you agree?

(4) Effects of Denial of Jury Trial.   How does denial of the right to jury trial hurt juveniles? Possible ways include the following:

> First, and foremost, juries acquit more readily than do judges, so juveniles are
> more likely to be convicted than if they could opt for jury trial. [The author spec-
> ulates that because juvenile court judges hear so many cases, they are less careful
> in weighing the evidence and more cynical in evaluating juveniles' credibility.] In
> addition, the parties in a jury trial have an opportunity to exclude jurors whose
> personal biases may prevent them from fairly trying the case. . . .
>   [Finally,] [d]enial of the right to jury trial disadvantages juveniles even after
> the fact-finding stage. In a jury trial, jurors must be explicitly instructed in the
> law to be applied in the case by the trial judge through written jury instructions.
> Any error of law can be later reviewed by an appellate court. However, when a
> judge sits without a jury, she need not expressly articulate her understanding of the
> law; therefore, the appellate court has no way of determining whether the juvenile
> court judge misunderstood or misapplied the law to the juvenile's detriment. Thus,
> depriving juveniles of jury trial puts them at a double disadvantage compared to
> adult defendants: they are more likely to be convicted at trial and are less likely to
> be able to demonstrate an error of law on appeal.[71]

[71] Ainsworth, supra note [53], at 67-68.

(5) Implication of the Right to Jury Trials for Juvenile Courts. One commentator elaborates on the reasons that the majority of states deny the right to a jury trial in juvenile court, including: juvenile court proceedings would become adversarial; jury trials would result in considerable delay in juvenile court proceedings and complicate the rehabilitative process.[72] If *McKeiver* required a jury trial in delinquency adjudications, would this have jeopardized the long-range survival of a separate system for juvenile offenders? Would pressure have increased for the abolition of the juvenile justice system, with young offenders simply treated the same as adult offenders?

(6) Effects of Denial of Jury Trial on Sentence Enhancements. Denial of the right to jury trial in juvenile proceedings has other ramifications in terms of the offender's subsequent processing by the criminal justice system. Several federal courts recently have wrestled with whether a juvenile adjudication may be considered a prior conviction for subsequent sentence enhancement purposes. Traditionally, juvenile delinquents' "adjudications" were not considered "convictions," from a semantic point of view, because of the differences between the juvenile and adult criminal courts. Nonetheless, in United States v. Smalley, 294 F.3d 1030 (8th Cir. 2002), a district court enhanced the sentence of a convicted felon based on his two adjudications of delinquency for violent crimes involving firearms. The Eighth Circuit affirmed, counting the juvenile adjudications toward sentence enhancements. But cf. United States v. Tighe, 266 F.3d 1187 (9th Cir. 2001) (holding that judge's use of defendant's prior, nonjury juvenile adjudication to increase the statutorily mandated maximum punishment to which he was exposed violated due process). Does the use of juvenile adjudications for sentence enhancement purposes strengthen or weaken the argument for the right to a jury trial in delinquency proceedings?

(7) State Provisions for Jury Trials for Delinquents. While holding that the federal Constitution did not require a jury trial in delinquency proceedings, *McKeiver* also indicated that a state could allow them in some or all cases. Roughly one-fifth of the states provide by statute for jury trial in delinquency cases,[73] and at least two by judicial decision based on interpretation of state constitutional guarantees that predated *McKeiver* (see R.L.R. v. State, 487 P.2d 27 (Alaska 1971); Peyton v. Nord, 437 P.2d 716 (N.M. 1968)).

(8) Public Trial. Typically, delinquency proceedings are not open to the public. Most closure statutes provide that the public and press will be excluded from juvenile proceedings unless the juvenile judge finds that such persons have a "direct" or "proper" interest in the matter. Stephan E. Oestreicher, Jr., Note, Toward Fundamental Fairness in the Kangaroo Courtroom: The Due Process Case Against Statutes Presumptively Closing Juvenile Proceedings, 54 Vand. L. Rev. 1751, 1755

---

[72] Korine L. Larsen, With Liberty and Juvenile Justice for All: Extending the Right to a Jury Trial to the Juvenile Courts, 20 Wm. Mitchell L. Rev. 835, 862-866 (1994). See also Kerrin C. Wolf, Note, Justice by Any Other Name: The Right to a Jury Trial and the Criminal Nature of Juvenile Justice in Louisiana, 12 Wm. & Mary Bill Rts. J. 275, 299 (2003) (discussing advantages and disadvantages of juries for the juvenile justice system).

[73] Martin Guggenheim & Randy Hertz, Reflections on Judges, Juries, and Justice: Ensuring the Fairness of Juvenile Delinquency Trials, 33 Wake Forest L. Rev. 553, 582 (1998).

n. 13 (2001). This policy is usually rationalized as a means of safeguarding the privacy of the youth.

Beginning in the 1990s, the "get tough on crime" attitude resulted in many states abrogating their closure statutes and mandating that delinquency proceedings be open to the public. See id. (pointing out that 12 states reverse the traditional presumption by providing that juvenile proceedings are presumptively open unless the juvenile judge finds good cause for closing them; 15 other states provide that juvenile proceedings shall be closed in the case of minor offenses but open if the offense would be a felony or other serious crime under the state criminal code). Does the closure policy still serve the rehabilitative ideal of the juvenile court? Or do presumptive closure statutes violate due process? See id. (so arguing). Does this trend signify yet another reason to grant juvenile delinquents the right to a jury trial?

(9) Note on Double Jeopardy.   In Breed v. Jones, 421 U.S. 519 (1975), the Supreme Court held that the protections of the Double Jeopardy Clause applied to juveniles. In that case, a 17-year-old, accused of armed robbery, was adjudicated a delinquent by a juvenile court at a jurisdictional (or "adjudicatory") hearing. Two weeks later, having not yet decided on the youth's sentence or disposition, the juvenile court determined at a "fitness" hearing that the youth was not "amenable" to juvenile court "care, treatment, and training" and ordered that the youth be prosecuted as an adult. At a subsequent trial in adult court, the youth was convicted of first-degree robbery. The Supreme Court held that the juvenile had been put in jeopardy at the original adjudicatory hearing in which jurisdiction was established and that the Double Jeopardy Clause had been offended by his subsequent criminal trial for the same offense.

The Court distinguished *McKeiver* in a single sentence: "We deal here, not with the 'formalities of the criminal adjudicative process' [citing *McKeiver*], but with analysis of an aspect of the juvenile court system in terms of the kind of risk to which jeopardy refers." Id. at 531. Chief Justice Burger, for a unanimous court, wrote:

> We believe it is simply too late in the day to conclude . . . that a juvenile is not put in jeopardy at a proceeding whose object is to determine whether he has committed acts that violate a criminal law and whose potential consequences include both the stigma inherent in such a determination and the deprivation of liberty for many years. [I]n terms of potential consequences, there is little to distinguish an adjudicatory hearing such as was held in this case from a traditional criminal prosecution. [Id. at 529-530.]

The Court rejected the state's argument that applying "the constitutional protection against multiple trials . . . will diminish flexibility and informality to the extent that those qualities relate uniquely to the goals of the juvenile court system." Id. at 535. The Court in *Breed* recognized that its decision "will require, in most cases, that the transfer decision be made prior to an adjudicatory hearing" and that "where transfer is considered and rejected there may be some added burden on juvenile courts by reason of duplicative proceedings." Id. at 536. Nevertheless, the Court concluded:

[T]he burdens that [the state] envisions appear to us neither qualitatively nor quantitatively sufficient to justify a departure in this context from the fundamental prohibition against double jeopardy.

A requirement that transfer hearings be held prior to adjudicatory hearings affects not at all the nature of the latter proceedings. More significantly, such a requirement need not affect the quality of decisionmaking at transfer hearings themselves. [Id. at 537.]

Gault and its immediate progeny narrowed the differences between the adult criminal process and the juvenile process. Nevertheless, *McKeiver* and subsequent Supreme Court decisions (e.g., Schall v. Martin, New Jersey v. T.L.O. Roper v. Simmons) are doctrinal reminders that the requirements imposed by the Constitution are not identical for delinquents and adult criminals.

This lack of identity is not surprising for several reasons. First, as *McKeiver* suggests, the traditions of the juvenile court and the values of informality and flexibility still may carry weight. Second, a youth accused of a crime will often have a parent or guardian who generally has certain legal powers and responsibilities with regard to the youth. Because minors are involved, various questions necessarily arise in the delinquency process about the appropriate parental role. Finally, the Court has not repudiated the notions, broadly reflected in a variety of other areas of the law, that young people are less able to make mature and responsible decisions and perhaps more susceptible to coercion or undue influence. Therefore, it is not surprising that in the delinquency context courts have considered age relevant as to a number of issues, such as determining the voluntariness of a confession or the validity of a waiver of constitutional rights.

The materials that follow suggest some of the ways the parent-child relationship and concept about the relationship between age, maturity, and competence create procedural differences between the juvenile process and the adult criminal process.

1. Arrest

Generally, the same substantive standards apply to juveniles and adults concerning the legality of an arrest. In some states, however, a youth may be arrested for delinquency even though the youth came to the attention of law enforcement for an act that would be a misdemeanor or noncriminal conduct for an adult. See D.L.C. v. State, 298 So. 2d 480 (Fla. Dist. Ct. App. 1974) (upholding a conviction for possession of marijuana based on a search incident to an arrest for curfew violation and drinking alcohol).

The United States Supreme Court subsequently let stand a similar California case upholding a search incident to an arrest of a youth for truancy. James D., a youthful looking 17-year-old, was spotted by police walking on a sidewalk at 10:30 A.M. on a school day carrying a book bag. The officers stopped and questioned the youth for allegedly violating a provision of the California Education Act mandating full-time school attendance for youths between ages 6 and 16. While conducting the truancy investigation, they proceeded to search the youth and discovered

LSD. James D. subsequently was charged in juvenile court with possession of a controlled substance. In the petition for certiorari, his attorneys argued, "California has chosen to afford greater Fourth Amendment protection to individuals suspected of crimes than to youthful appearing persons. . . ." James D. v. California, 741 P.2d 161 (1987), *cert. denied*, 485 U.S. 959 (1988).

At common law, law enforcement personnel could arrest an individual only after obtaining a warrant from a court having jurisdiction (except where the gravity of the offense justified an immediate arrest or the crime was committed in the officer's presence). Linda J. Collier & Deborah D. Rosenbloom, Warrant Requirement, 5 Am. Jur. 2d Arrest §11 (2004). However, some states allow arrest of juveniles without a warrant, even though a warrant would be required in the arrest of an adult in the same circumstances. See Garcia v. State, 661 S.W.2d 754 (Tex. Ct. App. 1983) (statute authorizing the taking of a juvenile into custody does not violate equal protection by not requiring arrest warrant). But see In re Martin S., 429 N.Y.S.2d 1009 (Fam. Ct. 1980) (standard of probable cause governing adult arrest is applicable to instances when children under the age of 16 are taken into custody without a warrant).

Further, while some states require police to offer an arrested juvenile the opportunity to telephone parents, other states do not explicitly grant this protection. Compare Cal. Welf. & Inst. Code §308(b) (West 2004) (minors ten years of age or older shall be advised within one hour of being taken into custody that they have a right to make at least two telephone calls, one to a parent or responsible relative and one to an attorney) with People v. Stachelek, 495 N.E.2d 984 (Ill. Ct. App. 1986) (no requirement that police officer spontaneously offer a suspect the opportunity to telephone parents). See also Federal Juvenile Delinquency Act, 18 U.S.C. §5033 (2000) (requiring parental notification whenever juvenile is taken into custody for act of delinquency that violates federal law).

Should juveniles receive protections in addition to those provided adults? Special provisions exist allowing for the arrest records of juveniles to be sealed or expunged in some circumstances. In what circumstances should courts allow expungement? Are there some circumstances when juvenile records should be sealed but not expunged? See Commonwealth v. Gavin G., 772 N.E.2d 1067 (Mass. 2002) (holding that juvenile court lacks authority to order expungement of probation records of juveniles wrongfully accused of criminal conduct given alternative statutory remedy for sealing records). See also Luz A. Carrion, Note, Rethinking Expungement of Juvenile Records in Massachusetts: The Case of Commonwealth v. Gavin G., 38 New Eng. L. Rev. 331 (2004). On the gradual erosion of the confidentiality standard for juvenile records, see Kristin Henning, Eroding Confidentiality in Delinquency Proceedings: Should Schools and Public Housing Authorities Be Notified?, 79 N.Y.U. L. Rev. 520 (2004).

2. Pretrial Detention

Two types of youth are generally eligible for pretrial detention: (1) those who might run away and (2) those who might commit another offense. Does the Due Process Clause require that adult standards should govern the pretrial detention of a youth accused of delinquency?

In Schall v. Martin, 467 U.S. 253 (1984), the United States Supreme Court upheld the constitutionality of pretrial detention for juveniles detained after arrest but prior to a determination of guilt. (The statutory provision at issue, New York Family Court Act §320.5(3)(b), permits pretrial detention based on a finding of a "serious risk" that an arrested juvenile may commit a crime before his return date.) The Supreme Court concluded that preventive detention of juveniles does not violate due process because it does not constitute punishment, but rather serves a legitimate governmental objective of protecting the community and the juvenile from the hazards of pre-hearing crime.

At the time of the case, no comparable authority existed for the pretrial detention of adults charged with crimes. Subsequent to *Schall*, a provision of the Bail Reform Act of 1984, 18 U.S.C. §3142 (2000), permitted federal judicial officers to consider dangerousness in pretrial release decisions; the provision was upheld in United States v. Salerno, 481 U.S. 739 (1987).

The majority in *Schall* bases its holding in part on tradition: prediction of future criminal conduct forms a basis for decisions involving capital sentencing, parole-release determinations, parole revocations, and sentencing of dangerous special offenders. In holding that pretrial detention for juveniles does not violate due process, the Court explains that it previously rejected the contention "that it is impossible to predict future behavior and that the question is so vague as to be meaningless" [*Schall*, supra, at 279]. How accurate are predictions of future criminal conduct in general? Are predictions of juveniles' future dangerousness more or less likely to be speculative than predictions of adults' behavior? Many studies reveal that a large number of offenders predicted to be dangerous are erroneously labeled. A few studies that examine the accuracy of such predictions for juveniles report a significantly higher rate of false positives for juveniles. See Ernst A. Wenk & Robert L. Emrich, Assaultive Experience and Assaultive Potential of California Youth Authority Wards, 9 J. Res. Crime & Delinq. 171 (1972); Stephen E. Schlesinger, The Prediction of Dangerousness in Juveniles: A Replication, 24 Crime & Delinq. 40 (1978).

The Court gives additional justifications for its conclusion that pretrial detention of juveniles comports with due process: (1) every state allows such detention, and some state courts have expressly upheld state statutes permitting it; (2) any risk of erroneous deprivation of a juvenile's liberty interest is small because "juveniles, unlike adults, are always in some form of custody" [467 U.S. at 265]; and (3) any risk of unnecessary deprivation of a juvenile's liberty interest is reduced by procedural safeguards (notice of charges, record of proceedings, the right of representation, subsequent probable cause hearings, right to habeas corpus review).

What do you think of these rationales? Is the existence of uniform state practice persuasive evidence to support the view that preventive detention conforms with due process? Can parental custody properly be compared to institutional custody? Do you agree that preventive detention does not constitute "punishment"? The Court reaches this last conclusion in part because confinement for juvenile detainees is either in nonsecure facilities or else in separate secure facilities for juveniles. Is a juvenile who is detained after arrest likely to view such detention other than as punishment? Do *postdetention* safeguards provide adequate protection against "erroneous and unnecessary deprivations of liberty"? [Id. at 254.]

What hazards are posed by pretrial detention of juveniles? See Jonathan Schuppe, Where Mentally Ill Youths Are Left to Despair — Child Advocate Says County Detention Centers Are Being Illegally Used, Star-Ledger (Newark, N.J.), Nov. 23, 2004, at 1 (reporting chronic overcrowding, intermingling of detainees with dangerous offenders, and high suicide rate); Mental Healthcare, Mentally Ill California Youths Unnecessarily Detained, Report Says, Obesity, Fitness & Wellness Wk., Feb. 19, 2005, at 1029 (pointing out that detention centers are not equipped to treat mental illness of detainees). See also National Juvenile Defender Center, The Use and Abuse of Juvenile Detention, Jan. 2004, at 1, available at *http://www.njdc.info/pdf/factsheet-detention.pdf* (last visited April 4, 2005) (citing research that reveals that juveniles who are detained prior to adjudication are more likely to be incarcerated at disposition, when compared with youths who have not been detained, regardless of the charges against them).

Additional questions arise in the context of what pretrial procedures are due a juvenile. First, do detained juveniles have a right to bail? Most states conclude that they do not because juveniles do not have contractual capacity to enter into bail agreements and because statutory criteria often favor release to parents. Ellen Marrus, Best Interests Equals Zealous Advocacy: A Not So Radical View of Holistic Representation for Children Accused of Crime, 62 Md. L. Rev. 288, 306 n. 95 (2003). But cf. Cal. Welf. & Inst. Code §207.1(c) (West 2004) (mandating right to bail for juveniles who have been transferred to adult court); Minn. Stat. Ann. §260B.176 (West 2005) (allowing reasonable bail).

Second, how long may minors be detained pending a hearing? While the length of time varies by jurisdiction, the remedy is the same. See In re McCall, 438 N.E.2d 1269 (Ill. Ct. App. 1982) (proper remedy for 36-hour rule is to release the juvenile from custody prior to the adjudicatory hearing).

Third, what is the appropriate evidentiary standard for pretrial detention decisions in juvenile court? See Julia Colton-Bell & Robert J. Levant, Clear and Convincing Evidence: The Standard Required to Support Pretrial Detention of Juveniles Pursuant to D.C. Code §16-2310, 3 D.C. L. Rev. 213 (1995) (arguing for a clear-and-convincing standard).

Fourth, what criteria should govern decision making regarding pretrial detention of juveniles? See Facilities Review Panel v. Coe, 420 S.E.2d 532 (W. Va. 1992) (adopting objective standards based on the type of offense, judicial findings of dangerousness, whether juvenile is an escapee from commitment or has a record of failure to appear in juvenile court, and whether less restrictive method has been tried).

Finally, where may the juvenile be detained? Section 10.2 of the Juvenile Justice Standards Relating to Interim Status (1977) states a prohibition against the detention of juveniles in any facility also used to detain adults. See also Segregation of Juvenile Offenders from Adult Offenders, supra, p. 771.

For discussion of pretrial detention, see generally Barry C. Feld, Juvenile Justice Administration (2000) (especially ch. 5); Marc Miller & Martin Guggenheim, Pretrial Detention and Punishment, 75 Minn. L. Rev. 335 (1990); David A. Geller, Note, Putting the "Parens" Back into Parens Patriae: Parental Custody of Juveniles as an Alternative to Pretrial Juvenile Detention, 21 New Eng. J. on Crim. & Civ.

Confinement 509 (1995); William J. Meade, Note, Pretrial Detention — Preventive Detention — Due Process, 82 Mass. L. Rev. 209 (1997).

3. Searches

Does the law compel public school students to submit to searches that would be unconstitutional as applied to adults?

New Jersey v. T.L.O.
469 U.S. 325 (1985)

Justice WHITE delivered the opinion of the Court. . . .

I

On March 7, 1980, a teacher at Piscataway High School in Middlesex County, N.J., discovered two girls smoking in a lavatory. One of the two girls was the respondent T.L.O., who at that time was a 14-year-old high school freshman. Because smoking in the lavatory was a violation of a school rule, the teacher took the two girls to the Principal's office, where they met with Assistant Vice Principal Theodore Choplick. In response to questioning by Mr. Choplick, T.L.O.'s companion admitted that she had violated the rule. T.L.O., however, denied that she had been smoking in the lavatory and claimed that she did not smoke at all.

Mr. Choplick asked T.L.O. to come into his private office and demanded to see her purse. Opening the purse, he found a pack of cigarettes, which he removed from the purse and held before T.L.O. as he accused her of having lied to him. As he reached into the purse for the cigarettes, Mr. Choplick also noticed a package of cigarette rolling papers. In his experience, possession of rolling papers by high school students was closely associated with the use of marijuana. Suspecting that a closer examination of the purse might yield further evidence of drug use, Mr. Choplick proceeded to search the purse thoroughly. The search revealed a small amount of marijuana, a pipe, a number of empty plastic bags, a substantial quantity of money in one-dollar bills, an index card that appeared to be a list of students who owed T.L.O. money, and two letters that implicated T.L.O. in marijuana dealing.

Mr. Choplick notified T.L.O.'s mother and police, and turned the evidence of drug dealing over to the police. At the request of the police, T.L.O.'s mother took her daughter to police headquarters, where T.L.O. confessed that she had been selling marijuana at the high school. On the basis of the confession and the evidence seized by Mr. Choplick, the State brought delinquency charges against T.L.O. in the Juvenile and Domestic Relations Court of Middlesex County. Contending that Mr. Choplick's search of her purse violated the Fourth Amendment, T.L.O. moved to suppress the evidence found in her purse as well as her confession, which, she argued, was tainted by the allegedly unlawful search. [The Juvenile Court denied the motion to suppress, found T.L.O. to be a delinquent, and sentenced her to a year's probation. The appellate court affirmed. The New Jersey Supreme Court reversed.]

Although we originally granted certiorari to decide the issue of the appropriate remedy in juvenile court proceedings for unlawful school searches [i.e., the appropriateness of the exclusionary rule as a remedy], our doubts regarding the wisdom of deciding that question in isolation from the broader question of what limits, if any, the Fourth Amendment places on the activities of school authorities prompted us to order reargument on that question.[2] Having heard argument on the legality of the search of T.L.O.'s purse, we are satisfied that the search did not violate the Fourth Amendment.[3]

II

In determining whether the search at issue in this case violated the Fourth Amendment, we are faced initially with the question whether that Amendment's prohibition on unreasonable searches and seizures applies to searches conducted by public school officials. We hold that it does.

[T]he State of New Jersey has argued that the history of the Fourth Amendment indicates that the Amendment was intended to regulate only searches and seizures carried out by law enforcement officers; accordingly, although public school officials are concededly state agents for purposes of the Fourteenth Amendment, the Fourth Amendment creates no rights enforceable against them.

[T]his Court has never limited the Amendment's prohibition on unreasonable searches and seizures to operations conducted by the police. Rather, the Court has long spoken of the Fourth Amendment's strictures as restraints imposed upon "governmental action" — that is, "upon the activities of sovereign authority." Accordingly, we have held the Fourth Amendment applicable to the activities of civil as well as criminal authorities. . . .

Notwithstanding the general applicability of the Fourth Amendment to the activities of civil authorities, a few courts have concluded that school officials are exempt from the dictates of the Fourth Amendment by virtue of the special nature of their authority over schoolchildren. Teachers and school administrators, it is said, act in loco parentis in their dealings with students: their authority is that of the parent, not the State, and is therefore not subject to the limits of the Fourth Amendment.

Such reasoning is in tension with contemporary reality and the teachings of this Court. We have held school officials subject to the commands of the First

---

[2] . . . [Courts have] split over whether the exclusionary rule is an appropriate remedy for Fourth Amendment violations committed by school authorities. The Georgia courts have held that although the Fourth Amendment applies to the schools, the exclusionary rule does not. Other jurisdictions have applied the rule to exclude the fruits of unlawful school searches from criminal trials and delinquency proceedings.

[3] In holding that the search of T.L.O.'s purse did not violate the Fourth Amendment, we do not implicitly determine that the exclusionary rule applies to the fruits of unlawful searches conducted by school authorities. The question whether evidence should be excluded from a criminal proceeding involves two discrete inquiries: whether the evidence was seized in violation of the Fourth Amendment, and whether the exclusionary rule is the appropriate remedy for the violation. Neither question is logically antecedent to the other, for a negative answer to either question is sufficient to dispose of the case. Thus, our determination that the search at issue in this case did not violate the Fourth Amendment implies no particular resolution of the question of the applicability of the exclusionary rule.

Amendment; see Tinker v. Des Moines Independent Community School District, 393 U.S. 503 (1969), and the Due Process Clause of the Fourteenth Amendment; see Goss v. Lopez, 419 U.S. 565 (1975). If school authorities are state actors for purposes of the constitutional guarantees of freedom of expression and due process, it is difficult to understand why they should be deemed to be exercising parental rather than public authority when conducting searches of their students. . . . Today's public school officials do not merely exercise authority voluntarily conferred on them by individual parents; rather, they act in furtherance of publicly mandated educational and disciplinary policies. . . . In carrying out searches and other disciplinary functions pursuant to such policies, school officials act as representatives of the State, not merely as surrogates for the parents, and they cannot claim the parents' immunity from the strictures of the Fourth Amendment.

III

To hold that the Fourth Amendment applies to searches conducted by school authorities is only to begin the inquiry into the standards governing such searches. Although the underlying command of the Fourth Amendment is always that searches and seizures be reasonable, what is reasonable depends on the context within which a search takes place. The determination of the standard of reasonableness governing any specific class of searches requires "balancing the need to search against the invasion which the search entails." On one side of the balance are arrayed the individual's legitimate expectations of privacy and personal security; on the other, the government's need for effective methods to deal with breaches of public order.

We have recognized that even a limited search of the person is a substantial invasion of privacy. . . . A search of a child's person or of a closed purse or other bag carried on her person,[5] no less than a similar search carried out on an adult, is undoubtedly a severe violation of subjective expectations of privacy. . . .

The State of New Jersey has argued that because of the pervasive supervision to which children in the schools are necessarily subject, a child has virtually no legitimate expectation of privacy in articles of personal property "unnecessarily" carried into a school. This argument has two factual premises: (1) the fundamental incompatibility of expectations of privacy with the maintenance of a sound educational environment; and (2) the minimal interest of the child in bringing any items of personal property into the school. Both premises are severely flawed.

Although this Court may take notice of the difficulty of maintaining discipline in the public schools today, the situation is not so dire that students in the schools may claim no legitimate expectations of privacy. We have recently recognized that the need to maintain order in a prison is such that prisoners retain no legitimate expectations of privacy in their cells, but it goes without saying that "[t]he prisoner and the schoolchild stand in wholly different circumstances, separated by the harsh facts of criminal conviction and incarceration." Ingraham v. Wright, supra, at 669.

---

[5] We do not address the question, not presented by this case, whether a schoolchild has a legitimate expectation of privacy in lockers, desks, or other school property provided for the storage of school supplies. Nor do we express any opinion on the standards (if any) governing searches of such areas by school officials or by other public authorities acting at the request of school officials.

We are not yet ready to hold that the schools and the prisons need be equated for purposes of the Fourth Amendment.

Nor does the State's suggestion that children have no legitimate need to bring personal property into the schools seem well anchored in reality. Students at a minimum must bring to school not only the supplies needed for their studies, but also keys, money, and the necessaries of personal hygiene and grooming. In addition, students may carry on their persons or in purses or wallets such nondisruptive yet highly personal items as photographs, letters, and diaries. Finally, students may have perfectly legitimate reasons to carry with them articles of property needed in connection with extracurricular or recreational activities. In short, schoolchildren may find it necessary to carry with them a variety of legitimate, noncontraband items, and there is no reason to conclude that they have necessarily waived all rights to privacy in such items merely by bringing them onto school grounds.

Against the child's interest in privacy must be set the substantial interest of teachers and administrators in maintaining discipline in the classroom and on school grounds. Maintaining order in the classroom has never been easy, but in recent years, school disorder has often taken particularly ugly forms: drug use and violent crime in the schools have become major social problems. . . .

How, then, should we strike the balance between the schoolchild's legitimate expectations of privacy and the school's equally legitimate need to maintain an environment in which learning can take place? It is evident that the school setting requires some easing of the restrictions to which searches by public authorities are ordinarily subject. The warrant requirement, in particular, is unsuited to the school environment: requiring a teacher to obtain a warrant before searching a child suspected of an infraction of school rules (or of the criminal law) would unduly interfere with the maintenance of the swift and informal disciplinary procedures needed in the schools. . . .

The school setting also requires some modification of the level of suspicion of illicit activity needed to justify a search. Ordinarily, a search — even one that may permissibly be carried out without a warrant — must be based upon "probable cause" to believe that a violation of the law has occurred. However, "probable cause" is not an irreducible requirement of a valid search. The fundamental command of the Fourth Amendment is that searches and seizures be reasonable, and although "both the concept of probable cause and the requirement of a warrant bear on the reasonableness of a search, . . . in certain limited circumstances neither is required." Thus, we have in a number of cases recognized the legality of searches and seizures based on suspicions that, although "reasonable," do not rise to the level of probable cause. . . .

We join the majority of courts that have examined this issue in concluding that the accommodation of the privacy interests of schoolchildren with the substantial need of teachers and administrators for freedom to maintain order in the schools does not require strict adherence to the requirement that searches be based on probable cause to believe that the subject of the search has violated or is violating the law. Rather, the legality of a search of a student should depend simply on the reasonableness, under all the circumstances, of the search. Determining the reasonableness of any search involves a twofold inquiry: first, one must consider "whether the . . . action was justified at its inception"; second, one must determine whether the search as actually conducted "was reasonably related in scope to the circumstances which justified the interference in the first place." Under ordinary circumstances, a search of a student by a teacher or other school official[7] will be "justified at its inception" when there are reasonable grounds for suspecting that the search will turn up evidence that the student has violated or is violating either the law or the rules of the school.[8] Such a search will be permissible in its scope when the measures adopted are reasonably related to the objectives of the search and not excessively intrusive in light of the age and sex of the student and the nature of the infraction.

This standard will, we trust, neither unduly burden the efforts of school authorities to maintain order in their schools nor authorize unrestrained intrusions upon the privacy of school children. By focusing attention on the question of reasonableness, the standard will spare teachers and school administrators the necessity of schooling themselves in the niceties of probable cause and permit them to regulate their conduct according to the dictates of reason and common sense. At the same time, the reasonableness standard should ensure that the interests of students will be invaded no more than is necessary to achieve the legitimate end of preserving order in the schools.

IV

There remains the question of the legality of the search in this case. We recognize that the "reasonable grounds" standard applied by the New Jersey Supreme Court in its consideration of this question is not substantially different from the standard that we have adopted today. Nonetheless, we believe that the New Jersey court's application of that standard to strike down the search of T.L.O.'s purse reflects a somewhat crabbed notion of reasonableness. Our review of the facts surrounding the search leads us to conclude that the search was in no sense unreasonable for Fourth Amendment purposes. . . .

Reversed.

[The separate concurring opinion of Justice Powell has been omitted.]

---

[7] We here consider only searches carried out by school authorities acting alone and on their own authority. This case does not present the question of the appropriate standard for assessing the legality of searches conducted by school officials in conjunction with or at the behest of law enforcement agencies, and we express no opinion on that question.

[8] We do not decide whether individualized suspicion is an essential element of the reasonableness standard we adopt for searches by school authorities. In other contexts, however, we have held that although "some quantum of individualized suspicion is usually a prerequisite to a constitutional search or seizure[,] . . . the Fourth Amendment imposes no irreducible requirement of such suspicion." United States v. Martinez-Fuerte, 428 U.S. 543, 560-561 (1976). Exceptions to the requirement of individualized suspicion are generally appropriate only where the privacy interests implicated by a search are minimal and where "other safeguards" are available "to assure that the individual's reasonable expectation of privacy is not 'subject to the discretion of the official in the field.'" Delaware v. Prouse, 440 U.S. 648, 654-655 (1979). Because the search of T.L.O.'s purse was based upon an individualized suspicion that she had violated school rules, . . . we need not consider the circumstances that might justify school authorities in conducting searches unsupported by individualized suspicion.

Justice BLACKMUN, concurring in the judgment.

I join the judgment of the Court and agree with much that is said in its opinion. I write separately, however, because I believe the Court omits a crucial step in its analysis of whether a school search must be based upon probable cause. The Court correctly states that we have recognized limited exceptions to the probable-cause requirement "[w]here a careful balancing of governmental and private interests suggests that the public interest is best served" by a lesser standard. I believe that we have used such a balancing test, rather than strictly applying the Fourth Amendment's Warrant and Probable-Cause Clause, only when we were confronted with "a special law enforcement need for greater flexibility." Florida v. Royer, 460 U.S. 491, 514 (1983) (Blackmun, J., dissenting). I pointed out in United States v. Place, 462 U.S. 696 (1983):

> While the Fourth Amendment speaks in terms of freedom from unreasonable [searches], the Amendment does not leave the reasonableness of most [searches] to the judgment of courts or government officers; the Framers of the Amendment balanced the interests involved and decided that a [search] is reasonable only if supported by a judicial warrant based on probable cause.

Only in those exceptional circumstances in which special needs, beyond the normal need for law enforcement, make the warrant and probable-cause requirement impracticable, is a court entitled to substitute its balancing of interests for that of the Framers.

[Blackmun gives examples of stops that are permitted based on less than probable cause in cases of "stop and frisks" when the police believe a crime has occurred or is about to occur, and for border stops.] The Court's implication that the balancing test is the rule rather than the exception is troubling for me because it is unnecessary in this case. The elementary and secondary school setting presents a special need for flexibility justifying a departure from the balance struck by the Framers. As Justice Powell notes, "[w]ithout first establishing discipline and maintaining order, teachers cannot begin to educate their students." Maintaining order in the classroom can be a difficult task. A single teacher often must watch over a large number of students, and, as any parent knows, children at certain ages are inclined to test the outer boundaries of acceptable conduct and to imitate the misbehavior of a peer if that misbehavior is not dealt with quickly. Every adult remembers from his own schooldays the havoc a water pistol or peashooter can wreak until it is taken away. Thus, the Court has recognized that "[e]vents calling for discipline are frequent occurrences and sometimes require immediate, effective action." Goss v. Lopez, 419 U.S. 565, 580 (1975). Indeed, because drug use and possession of weapons have become increasingly common among young people, an immediate response frequently is required not just to maintain an environment conducive to learning, but to protect the very safety of students and school personnel.

Such immediate action obviously would not be possible if a teacher were required to secure a warrant before searching a student. Nor would it be possible if a teacher could not conduct a necessary search until the teacher thought there was probable cause for the search. A teacher has neither the training nor the day-to-day experience in the complexities of probable cause that a law enforcement officer possesses, and is ill-equipped to make a quick judgment about the existence of probable cause. The time required for a teacher to ask the questions or make the observations that are necessary to turn reasonable grounds into probable cause is time during which the teacher, and other students, are diverted from the essential task of education. . . . The special need for an immediate response to behavior that threatens either the safety of schoolchildren and teachers or the educational process itself justifies the Court in excepting school searches from the warrant and probable-cause requirement, and in applying a standard determined by balancing the relevant interests. . . .

Justice STEVENS, with whom Justice MARSHALL joins, and with whom Justice BRENNAN joins as to Part I, concurring in part and dissenting in part.

. . . The Court embraces the standard applied by the New Jersey Supreme Court as equivalent to its own, and then deprecates the state court's application of the standard as reflecting "a somewhat crabbed notion of reasonableness." There is no mystery, however, in the state court's finding that the search in this case was unconstitutional; the decision below was not based on a manipulation of reasonable suspicion, but on the trivial character of the activity that promoted the official search. The New Jersey Supreme Court wrote:

> We are satisfied that when a school official has reasonable grounds to believe that a student possesses evidence of *illegal activity or activity that would interfere with school discipline and order*, the school official has the right to conduct a reasonable search for such evidence.
> In determining whether the school official has reasonable grounds, courts should consider "the child's age, history, and school record, *the prevalence and seriousness of the problem in the school to which the search was directed*, the exigency to make the search without delay, and the probative value and reliability of the information used as a justification for the search." [State in Interest of T.L.O., 463 A.2d 934, 941-942 (N.J. 1983).]

The emphasized language in the state court's opinion focuses on the character of the rule infraction that is to be the object of the search. In the view of the state court, there is a quite obvious and material difference between a search for evidence relating to violent or disruptive activity, and a search for evidence of a smoking rule violation. . . .

Like the New Jersey Supreme Court, I would view this case differently if the Assistant Vice Principal had reason to believe T.L.O.'s purse contained evidence of criminal activity, or of an activity that would seriously disrupt school discipline. There was, however, absolutely no basis for any such assumption — not even a "hunch."

In this case, Mr. Choplick overreacted to what appeared to be nothing more than a minor infraction — a rule prohibiting smoking in the bathroom of the freshmen's and sophomores' building. It is, of course, true that he actually found evidence of serious wrongdoing by T.L.O., but no one claims that the prior search may be justified by his unexpected discovery. As far as the smoking infraction is concerned, the search for cigarettes merely tended to corroborate a teacher's eyewitness account of T.L.O.'s violation of a minor regulation designed to channel student smoking behavior into designated locations. Because this conduct was neither unlawful nor significantly disruptive of school order or the educational process, the invasion of privacy associated with the forcible opening of T.L.O.'s purse was entirely unjustified at its inception.

A review of the sampling of school search cases relied on by the Court demonstrates how different this case is from those in which there was indeed a valid justification for intruding on a student's privacy. In most of them the student was suspected of a criminal violation; in the remainder either violence or substantial disruption of school order or the integrity of the academic process was at stake. Few involved matters as trivial as the no-smoking rule violated by T.L.O. The rule the Court adopts today is so open-ended that it may make the Fourth Amendment virtually meaningless in the school context. Although I agree that school administrators must have broad latitude to maintain order and discipline in our classrooms, that authority is not unlimited. . . .

Board of Education v. Earls
536 U.S. 822 (2002)

Justice THOMAS delivered the opinion of the Court.

. . . The city of Tecumseh, Oklahoma, is a rural community located approximately 40 miles southeast of Oklahoma City. The School District administers all Tecumseh public schools. In the fall of 1998, the School District adopted the Student Activities Drug Testing Policy (Policy), which requires all middle and high school students to consent to drug testing in order to participate in any extracurricular activity. In practice, the Policy has been applied only to competitive extracurricular activities sanctioned by the Oklahoma Secondary Schools Activities Association, such as the Academic Team, Future Farmers of America, Future Homemakers of America, band, choir, pom-pom, cheerleading, and athletics. Under the Policy, students are required to take a drug test before participating in an extracurricular activity, must submit to random drug testing while participating in that activity, and must agree to be tested at any time upon reasonable suspicion. The urinalysis tests are designed to detect only the use of illegal drugs, including amphetamines, marijuana, cocaine, opiates, and barbituates, not medical conditions or the presence of authorized prescription medications.

. . . Respondent Lindsay Earls was a member of the show choir, the marching band, the Academic Team, and the National Honor Society. Respondent Daniel James sought to participate in the Academic Team. Together with their parents, Earls and James brought a Rev. Stat. §1979, 42 U.S.C. §1983, action against the School District, challenging the Policy both on its face and as applied to their participation in extracurricular activities. They alleged that the Policy violates the Fourth Amendment [and] requested injunctive and declarative relief. . . . [The district court rejected respondents' claim that the school policy was unconstitutional and granted summary judgment to the School District. The Tenth Circuit Court of Appeals reversed, holding that the policy violated the Fourth Amendment.]

The Fourth Amendment to the United States Constitution protects "[t]he right of the people to be secure in their persons, houses, papers, and effects, against unreasonable searches and seizures." Searches by public school officials, such as the collection of urine samples, implicate Fourth Amendment interests. We must therefore review the School District's Policy for "reasonableness," which is the touchstone of the constitutionality of a governmental search.

In the criminal context, reasonableness usually requires a showing of probable cause. The probable-cause standard, however, "is peculiarly related to criminal investigations" and may be unsuited to determining the reasonableness of administrative searches where the "Government seeks to *prevent* the development of hazardous conditions." Treasury Employees v. Von Raab, 489 U.S. 656, 667-668 (1989). The Court has also held that a warrant and finding of probable cause are unnecessary in the public school context because such requirements " 'would unduly interfere with the maintenance of the swift and informal disciplinary procedures [that are] needed.' " [Vernonia School Dist. v. Acton, 515 U.S. 646, 653 (1995) (quoting New Jersey v. T.L.O., 469 U.S. 325, 340-341 (1985).]

Given that the School District's Policy is not in any way related to the conduct of criminal investigations, respondents do not contend that the School District requires probable cause before testing students for drug use. Respondents instead argue that drug testing must be based at least on some level of individualized suspicion. It is true that we generally determine the reasonableness of a search by balancing the nature of the intrusion on the individual's privacy against the promotion of legitimate governmental interests. But we have long held that "the Fourth Amendment imposes no irreducible requirement of [individualized] suspicion." United States v. Martinez-Fuerte, 428 U.S. 543, 561 (1976). "[I]n certain limited circumstances, the Government's need to discover such latent or hidden conditions, or to prevent their development, is sufficiently compelling to justify the intrusion on privacy entailed by conducting such searches without any measure of individualized suspicion." *Von Raab*, supra, at 668. Therefore, in the context of safety and administrative regulations, a search unsupported by probable cause may be reasonable "when 'special needs, beyond the normal need for law enforcement, make the warrant and probable-cause requirement impracticable.' " Griffin v. Wisconsin, 483 U.S. 868, 873 (1987) (quoting *T.L.O.*, supra, at 351 (Blackmun, J., concurring in judgment)).

Significantly, this Court has previously held that "special needs" inhere in the public school context. See *Vernonia*, supra, at 653; *T.L.O.*, supra, at 339-340. While schoolchildren do not shed their constitutional rights when they enter the schoolhouse, see Tinker v. Des Moines Independent Community School Dist., 393 U.S. 503 (1969), "Fourth Amendment rights . . . are different in public schools than elsewhere; the 'reasonableness' inquiry cannot disregard the schools' custodial and tutelary responsibility for children." *Vernonia*, 515 U.S., at 656. In particular, a finding of individualized suspicion may not be necessary when a school conducts drug testing.

In *Vernonia*, this Court held that the suspicionless drug testing of athletes was constitutional. The Court, however, did not simply authorize all school drug testing, but rather conducted a fact-specific balancing of the intrusion on the children's Fourth Amendment rights against the promotion of legitimate governmental interests. Applying the principles of *Vernonia* to the somewhat different facts of this case, we conclude that Tecumseh's Policy is also constitutional.

balancing

A

We first consider the nature of the privacy interest allegedly compromised by the drug testing. As in *Vernonia*, the context of the public school environment serves as the backdrop for the analysis of the privacy interest at stake and the reasonableness of the drug testing policy in general. [Citing *Vernonia*] ("Central . . . is the fact that the subjects of the Policy are (1) children, who (2) have been committed to the temporary custody of the State as schoolmaster"); see also id., at 665 ("The most significant element in this case is the first we discussed: that the Policy was undertaken in furtherance of the government's responsibilities, under a public school system, as guardian and tutor of children entrusted to its care"); ibid. ("[W]hen the government acts as guardian and tutor the relevant question is whether the search is one that a reasonable guardian and tutor might undertake").

A student's privacy interest is limited in a public school environment where the State is responsible for maintaining discipline, health, and safety. Schoolchildren are routinely required to submit to physical examinations and vaccinations against disease. Securing order in the school environment sometimes requires that students be subjected to greater controls than those appropriate for adults. See *T.L.O.*, 469 U.S., at 350 (Powell, J., concurring) ("Without first establishing discipline and maintaining order, teachers cannot begin to educate their students. And apart from education, the school has the obligation to protect pupils from mistreatment by other children, and also to protect teachers themselves from violence by the few students whose conduct in recent years has prompted national concern").

Respondents argue that because children participating in nonathletic extracurricular activities are not subject to regular physicals and communal undress, they have a stronger expectation of privacy than the athletes tested in *Vernonia*. This distinction, however, was not essential to our decision in *Vernonia*, which depended primarily upon the school's custodial responsibility and authority.

In any event, students who participate in competitive extracurricular activities voluntarily subject themselves to many of the same intrusions on their privacy as do athletes. Some of these clubs and activities require occasional off-campus travel and communal undress. All of them have their own rules and requirements for participating students that do not apply to the student body as a whole. For example, each of the competitive extracurricular activities governed by the Policy must abide by the rules of the Oklahoma Secondary Schools Activities Association, and a faculty sponsor monitors the students for compliance with the various rules dictated by the clubs and activities. This regulation of extracurricular activities further diminishes the expectation of privacy among schoolchildren. We therefore conclude that the students affected by this Policy have a limited expectation of privacy.

B

Next, we consider the character of the intrusion imposed by the Policy. Urination is "an excretory function traditionally shielded by great privacy." Skinner v. Railway Labor Executives' Assn., 489 U.S. 602, 626 (1989). But the "degree of intrusion" on one's privacy caused by collecting a urine sample "depends upon the manner in which production of the urine sample is monitored." *Vernonia*, supra, at 658.

Under the Policy, a faculty monitor waits outside the closed restroom stall for the student to produce a sample and must "listen for the normal sounds of urination in order to guard against tampered specimens and to insure an accurate chain of custody." The monitor then pours the sample into two bottles that are sealed and placed into a mailing pouch along with a consent form signed by the student. This procedure is virtually identical to that reviewed in *Vernonia*, except that it additionally protects privacy by allowing male students to produce their samples behind a closed stall. Given that we considered the method of collection in *Vernonia* a "negligible" intrusion, the method here is even less problematic.

In addition, the Policy clearly requires that the test results be kept in confidential files separate from a student's other educational records and released to school personnel only on a "need to know" basis. Respondents nonetheless contend that the intrusion on students' privacy is significant because the Policy fails to protect effectively against the disclosure of confidential information and, specifically, that the school "has been careless in protecting that information: for example, the Choir teacher looked at students' prescription drug lists and left them where other students could see them." Brief for Respondents 24. But the choir teacher is someone with a "need to know," because during off-campus trips she needs to know what medications are taken by her students. Even before the Policy was enacted the choir teacher had access to this information. In any event, there is no allegation that any other student did see such information. This one example of alleged carelessness hardly increases the character of the intrusion.

Moreover, the test results are not turned over to any law enforcement authority. Nor do the test results here lead to the imposition of discipline or have any academic consequences. Rather, the only consequence of a failed drug test is to limit the student's privilege of participating in extracurricular activities. . . .

Given the minimally intrusive nature of the sample collection and the limited uses to which the test results are put, we conclude that the invasion of students' privacy is not significant.

C

Finally, this Court must consider the nature and immediacy of the government's concerns and the efficacy of the Policy in meeting them. This Court has already articulated in detail the importance of the governmental concern in preventing drug use by schoolchildren. The drug abuse problem among our Nation's youth has hardly abated since *Vernonia* was decided in 1995. In fact, evidence suggests that it has only grown worse.[5] As in *Vernonia*, "the necessity for the State to act is magnified by the fact that this evil is being visited not just upon individuals at large, but upon children for whom it has undertaken a special responsibility of care and direction." Id., at 662. The health and safety risks identified in *Vernonia* apply with equal force to Tecumseh's children. Indeed, the nationwide drug epidemic makes the war against drugs a pressing concern in every school.

Additionally, the School District in this case has presented specific evidence of drug use at Tecumseh schools. Teachers testified that they had seen students who

---

[5] For instance, the number of 12th graders using any illicit drug increased from 48.4 percent in 1995 to 53.9 percent in 2001. The number of 12th graders reporting they had used marijuana jumped from 41.7 percent to 49.0 percent during that same period. See Department of Health and Human Services, Monitoring the Future: National Results on Adolescent Drug Use, Overview of Key Findings (2001) (Table 1).

appeared to be under the influence of drugs and that they had heard students speaking openly about using drugs. A drug dog found marijuana cigarettes near the school parking lot. Police officers once found drugs or drug paraphernalia in a car driven by a Future Farmers of America member. And the school board president reported that people in the community were calling the board to discuss the "drug situation." We decline to second-guess the finding of the District Court that "[v]iewing the evidence as a whole, it cannot be reasonably disputed that the [School District] was faced with a 'drug problem' when it adopted the Policy" [115 F. Supp.2d 1281, 1287 (W.D. Okla. 2000)].

Respondents consider the proffered evidence insufficient and argue that there is no "real and immediate interest" to justify a policy of drug testing nonathletes. We have recognized, however, that "[a] demonstrated problem of drug abuse . . . [is] not in all cases necessary to the validity of a testing regime," but that some showing does "shore up an assertion of special need for a suspicionless general search program." Chandler v. Miller, 520 U.S. 305, 319 (1997). The School District has provided sufficient evidence to shore up the need for its drug testing program.

Furthermore, this Court has not required a particularized or pervasive drug problem before allowing the government to conduct suspicionless drug testing. For instance, in *Von Raab* the Court upheld the drug testing of customs officials on a purely preventive basis, without any documented history of drug use by such officials. In response to the lack of evidence relating to drug use, the Court noted generally that "drug abuse is one of the most serious problems confronting our society today," and that programs to prevent and detect drug use among customs officials could not be deemed unreasonable. [489 U.S. at 674]; cf. *Skinner*, 489 U.S., at 607, and n. 1, 109 S. Ct. 1402 (noting nationwide studies that identified on-the-job alcohol and drug use by railroad employees). Likewise, the need to prevent and deter the substantial harm of childhood drug use provides the necessary immediacy for a school testing policy. Indeed, it would make little sense to require a school district to wait for a substantial portion of its students to begin using drugs before it was allowed to institute a drug testing program designed to deter drug use.

Given the nationwide epidemic of drug use, and the evidence of increased drug use in Tecumseh schools, it was entirely reasonable for the School District to enact this particular drug testing policy. . . .

Respondents also argue that the testing of nonathletes does not implicate any safety concerns, and that safety is a "crucial factor" in applying the special needs framework [to override the usual protections of the Fourth Amendment]. Respondents are correct that safety factors into the special needs analysis, but the safety interest furthered by drug testing is undoubtedly substantial for all children, athletes and nonathletes alike. We know all too well that drug use carries a variety of health risks for children, including death from overdose.

We also reject respondents' argument that drug testing must presumptively be based upon an individualized reasonable suspicion of wrongdoing because such a testing regime would be less intrusive. In this context, the Fourth Amendment does not require a finding of individualized suspicion, and we decline to impose such a requirement on schools attempting to prevent and detect drug use by students. Moreover, we question whether testing based on individualized suspicion in fact would be less intrusive. Such a regime would place an additional burden on public school teachers who are already tasked with the difficult job of maintaining order and discipline. A program of individualized suspicion might unfairly target members of unpopular groups. The fear of lawsuits resulting from such targeted searches may chill enforcement of the program, rendering it ineffective in combating drug use. In any case, this Court has repeatedly stated that reasonableness under the Fourth Amendment does not require employing the least intrusive means, because "[t]he logic of such elaborate less-restrictive-alternative arguments could raise insuperable barriers to the exercise of virtually all search-and-seizure powers." [United States v. Martinez-Fuerte, 428 U.S. 543, 556-557, n. 12 (1976).]

Finally, we find that testing students who participate in extracurricular activities is a reasonably effective means of addressing the School District's legitimate concerns in preventing, deterring, and detecting drug use. While in *Vernonia* there might have been a closer fit between the testing of athletes and the trial court's finding that the drug problem was "fueled by the 'role model' effect of athletes' drug use," such a finding was not essential to the holding. *Vernonia* did not require the school to test the group of students most likely to use drugs, but rather considered the constitutionality of the program in the context of the public school's custodial responsibilities. Evaluating the Policy in this context, we conclude that the drug testing of Tecumseh students who participate in extracurricular activities effectively serves the School District's interest in protecting the safety and health of its students. . . .

[Omitted are the concurring opinion of Justice Breyer as well as the separate dissenting opinion of Justice O'Conner in which Justice Souter joins.]

Justice GINSBURG, with whom Justice STEVENS, Justice O'CONNOR, and Justice SOUTER join, dissenting.

Seven years ago, in Vernonia School Dist. v. Acton, 515 U.S. 646 (1995), this Court determined that a school district's policy of randomly testing the urine of its student athletes for illicit drugs did not violate the Fourth Amendment. In so ruling, the Court emphasized that drug use "increase[d] the risk of sports-related injury" and that Vernonia's athletes were the "leaders" of an aggressive local "drug culture" that had reached " 'epidemic proportions.' " Id., at 649. Today, the Court relies upon *Vernonia* to permit a school district with a drug problem its superintendent repeatedly described as "not . . . major," to test the urine of an academic team member solely by reason of her participation in a nonathletic, competitive extracurricular activity — participation associated with neither special dangers from, nor particular predilections for, drug use.

"[T]he legality of a search of a student," this Court has instructed, "should depend simply on the reasonableness, under all the circumstances, of the search." New Jersey v. T.L.O., 469 U.S. 325, 341 (1985). Although " 'special needs' inhere in the public school context," see *ante*, at 2564 (quoting Vernonia, 515 U.S., at 653), those needs are not so expansive or malleable as to render reasonable any program of student drug testing a school district elects to install. The particular testing program upheld today is not reasonable; it is capricious, even perverse: Petitioners' policy targets for testing a student population least likely to be at risk from illicit drugs and their damaging effects. I therefore dissent. . . .

NOTES AND QUESTIONS ON *T.L.O.* AND *EARLS*

(1) Attenuation of the Fourth Amendment.   The trilogy of juvenile search cases (*T.L.O.*, Vernonia v. Acton, and *Earls*) reflects a gradual attenuation of Fourth Amendment protection as applied to schoolchildren. According to *T.L.O.*, school officials may conduct a warrantless search provided that they have reasonable suspicion (a lower standard than probable cause) that a student violated a school rule or a criminal law. The Court applied a balancing test (discussed below) to test the reasonableness of the search. However, *T.L.O.* left unresolved whether the "reasonableness" standard for school searches requires individualized suspicion (see footnote 8). Because Vice Principal Choplick had individualized suspicion that T.L.O. had violated school rules, the Supreme Court did not consider the validity of school searches in the absence of individualized suspicion. *Vernonia*, in sustaining random drug testing for student athletes, subsequently answers that question by rejecting the need for individualized suspicion. *Earls* carries *Vernonia* further by extending random warrantless searches beyond athletes to participants in extracurricular activities.

Should the Court in *T.L.O.* have lowered the standard as it did? In an age of drugs and crime, do public school officials function in a manner similar to law enforcement officers? As such, should they be subject to the same standard of probable cause, especially if the purpose of their search is to uncover evidence of a crime (e.g., drug use, possession of a dangerous weapon)? In refusing to adopt the probable cause standard, the Court was concerned with the desire to spare school officials the necessity of educating themselves about the requirements of probable cause. Is such solicitousness appropriate, given that school officials have to educate themselves about legal requirements for many other purposes, such as immunizations, child abuse, and neglect reporting?

(2) Nature of School Setting and Special Needs Doctrine.   *T.L.O.* holds that the Fourth Amendment applies in the public school context; as a result, a search in a school setting must be "reasonable." The Supreme Court then applies a balancing test to determine the reasonableness of the particular search. The test involves a two-pronged inquiry: (a) whether the action was justified at its inception (i.e., was likely to turn up evidence of a violation of the law or school rule) and (b) whether the actual search was reasonably related in scope to the circumstances (i.e., it was not overly intrusive in light of the age and sex of the student and the nature of the infraction).

Subsequently, *Vernonia* upheld the reasonableness of a school policy that required athletes to submit to random, warrantless drug tests based on the "special needs" of the school environment. The determination of reasonableness in *Vernonia* (and later *Earls*) was based on the "special needs" doctrine as derived from a statement in Justice Blackmun's concurring opinion in *T.L.O.* in which he asserts that the requirements of a warrant and probable cause may be dispensed with when exigent circumstances make these requirements impracticable (see supra p. 816). The *Vernonia* Court found the existence of such "special needs" in the need to secure order in the educational setting and to deter drug use in the schools.

In *Vernonia*, the Court balanced (a) the student athletes' legitimate expectations of privacy (finding that athletes have lowered expectations of privacy than other students); and (b) the character of the intrusion (finding that the invasion of privacy caused by a urinanalysis test was minimal); against (c) the nature of the governmental concern and the efficacy of the chosen method of meeting that concern (finding that the concern was the deterrence of drug use, and the means was efficacious because athletes serve as role models and also because drugs pose a particular danger to them and to others due to the risk of sport-related injuries). How does the Court in *Earls* apply this balancing test to a similar search of student participants in extracurricular activities? How do the majority and dissent in *Earls* differ on the issue of whether the drug testing of participants in extracurricular activities was justified?

As Earls explains, the Supreme Court previously applied the "special needs" doctrine to probationers and railroad employees. How is the public school context similar and/or different? What special characteristics of the school setting justify such a limitation, according to the Court? Do you agree with the Court's assessment? How is the school's mission, as characterized by the Court in *T.L.O.* and *Earls*, similar to or different from that previously characterized by the Court in *Tinker*, *Hazelwood*, and *Bethel*? See generally Bernard James & Joanne E.K. Larson, The Doctrine of Deference: Shifting Constitutional Presumptions and the Supreme Court's Restatement of Student Rights After Board of Education v. Earls, 56 S.C. L. Rev. 1, 35-37 (2004) (discussing changing views of schools' mission).

What criteria does the Court in *Earls* use to determine whether a given need is "special"? Do you think Justice Blackmun, whose concurring opinion in *T.L.O.* was the basis for the special needs doctrine, would agree with the application of the doctrine in *Earls*? That is, does *Earls* represent one of "those exceptional circumstances [like "stop and frisks" during the commission of crimes or border patrol stops] in which special needs, beyond the normal need for law enforcement, make the warrant and probable-cause requirement impracticable," (supra p. 816) such that a court is entitled to substitute its balancing for the view of the Framers [of the Constitution]?

The special needs doctrine has received its share of scholarly criticism. See Robert D. Dodson, Ten Years of Randomized Jurisprudence: Amending the Special Needs Doctrine, 51 S.C. L. Rev. 258, 274 (2000) ("More disturbing is the fact that the Court has never invalidated a law under the special needs balancing test"); Irene Merker Rosenberg, The Public Schools Have a "Special Need" for Their Students' Urine, 31 Hofstra L. Rev. 303, 307 (2002) (criticizing the "special needs" doctrine for its lack of fixed or objective criteria and also for its "double counting" of the governmental interest — once to determine if the need is special, and then again in the balancing of governmental vs. private interests).

(3) Striking the Balance: Weighing Minors' Privacy Rights. As explained above, *T.L.O.* set forth a two-prong test of reasonableness to evaluate the constitutionality of a particular search: whether the search was justified at its inception and whether it was reasonably related in scope to the circumstances (i.e., not overly intrusive in light of the age and sex of the student and the nature of the infraction). In *T.L.O.*, was the vice principal's search justified at its inception? Was it reasonably related to the objectives of the search? How intrusive was the search in light of the age and sex of the student and the nature of the infraction? In *Earls*, the Court similarly dismisses the privacy concerns of the participants in extracurricular

activities who must submit to urinanalysis tests. Consider the following comments regarding the privacy interest at issue in the urinanalysis testing of students:

> The unfortunate consequence of [the Court's] finding [of a negligible invasion of privacy] is that it completely minimizes the horrors of adolescence — the time when male junior high students begin growing pubic hair and become self-conscious of their genitalia and the new and, often, uncomfortable bodily responses that accompany puberty. Likewise, junior high is often the time when female students begin menstruating. Imagine the humiliation and embarrassment of a menstruating junior high student required to provide school officials with a urine sample that will possibly reveal that she is taking birth control pills, is HIV positive, is on medication for depression, or perhaps suffers from a sexually transmitted disease. To assert that providing a urine sample during these formative and agonizing years presents only a "negligible" privacy violation denies a very real fact of adolescence — every little act or action is generally amplified and overwhelming. It is disingenuous to suggest that taking a state-compelled urine sample from an adolescent does not invoke the most intimate of privacy interests. [Meg Penrose, Shedding Rights, Shredding Rights: A Critical Examination of Students' Privacy Rights and the "Special Needs" Doctrine After *Earls*, 3 Nev. L.J. 411, 435 (2002/2003).]

In *Earls*, the Court analogizes the level of intrusion of a urinanalysis to that of physical examinations and vaccinations. Do you agree?

Was the character of the intrusion mitigated, as the Court suggests, by the nature of the specimen collections and the limited uses to which the test results are put? Are you reassured by the Court's assertion that the results of the drug test would remain confidential? See Aaron Marcus, Comment, Beyond the Classroom: A Reality-Based Approach to Student Drug Testing, 3 Whittier J. Child & Fam. Advoc. 365, 390 (2004) (claiming that the Court undervalued the intrusiveness of the disclosure of students' private medical information and suggesting that schools will break confidentiality by informing parents); Dodson, supra, at 277 (pointing out that prosecutors frequently use evidence obtained in school searches in criminal prosecutions and delinquency proceedings).

(4) Limits of **Earls.**   Both *Vernonia* and *Earls* upheld limitations on the Fourth Amendment rights of *some* public school students. *Vernonia* applies to student athletes, who, according to the Court, have lowered expectations of privacy because of their practice of dressing and undressing in communal locker rooms. *Earls* applies to participants in competitive extracurricular activities. Do you agree with the Court's characterization that the latter students "voluntarily subject themselves to many of the same intrusions on their privacy as do athletes"?

Does the Court recognize *any* limits to the ability of a school to conduct random warrantless searches? That is, do *Vernonia* and *Earls* permit the random suspicion-less testing of all public school students? See Jacob Brooks, Note, Constitutional Law — Suspicionless Drug Testing of Students Participating in Non-Athletic Competitive School Activities: Are All Students Next? Board of Education v. Earls, 4 Wyo. L. Rev. 365 (2004); Penrose, supra, at 412 (*Earls* "seemingly limitless breadth . . . sounds the death knell of the assurance that students do not shed their Constitutional rights at the school house gate"); Brad Setterberg, Note, Privacy Changes, Precedent Doesn't: Why Board of Education v. Earls Was Judged by the Wrong Standard, 40 Hous. L. Rev. 1183, 1202 (2003) (so arguing). Does the governmental interest in deterring drug use justify such a significant expansion of schools' investigative authority? In its reliance on the policy justification of the drug epidemic, has the Supreme Court "supplemented a concern for safety with rhetoric of fear"? Marcus, supra, at 395.

For a post-*Earls* case rejecting *Earls'* reasoning, see Doe ex rel. Doe v. Little Rock Sch. Dist., 380 F.3d 349 (8th Cir. 2004) (holding that a school's policy of random, suspicionless searches of all students' persons and belongings was unconstitutional, based on a finding that the school's generalized concern about weapons or drugs was insufficient to overcome students' expectation of privacy, the all-encompassing nature of the search, and the fact that the fruits of the search were routinely submitted to law enforcement).

(5) Unanswered Questions. T.L.O., *Vernonia*, and *Earls* left several unanswered questions.

a. Should the exclusionary rule apply to exclude evidence illegally seized by public school officials? In *T.L.O.*, the state originally appealed to the United States Supreme Court on the issue of whether the exclusionary rule should bar consideration in delinquency proceedings of evidence that was illegally seized by school officials without the involvement of law enforcement officials. However, the Court decided to address only the threshold Fourth Amendment issue (see supra p. 812 and footnote 3). Since *T.L.O.*, a majority of states have held that the exclusionary rule applies to delinquency proceedings. See Irene Merker Rosenberg, A Door Left Open: Applicability of the Fourth Amendment Exclusionary Rule to Juvenile Court Delinquency Hearings, 24 Am. J. Crim. L. 29, 58-59 (1996).

If the exclusionary rule applies, should evidence be excluded from school disciplinary proceedings as well as delinquency proceedings? Compare Juan C. v. Cortines, 647 N.Y.S.2d 491 (App. Div. 1996) (holding that the exclusionary rule should apply in suspension hearing), *rev'd on other grounds*, 679 N.E.2d 1061 (N.Y. 1997), with Thompson v. Carthage Sch. Dist., 87 F.3d 979 (8th Cir. 1996) (rejecting application of exclusionary rule in disciplinary hearing). See also Dodson, supra, at 286 (advocating exclusion of illegally seized evidence from criminal prosecutions and delinquency proceedings); Mai Linh Spencer, Note, Suppress or Suspend: New York's Exclusionary Rule in School Disciplinary Proceedings, 72 N.Y.U. L. Rev. 1494 (1997).

b. What standard should apply if school officials conduct the search "in concert with" or "at the behest of" law enforcement? T.L.O. left this question unresolved (see footnote 7) because Vice Principal Choplick acted alone in searching T.L.O.'s belongings. In setting the standard, case law makes distinctions regarding whether (1) the law enforcement officer is responsible to a law enforcement agency (applying the probable cause standard) or the school (applying reasonable suspicion standard); (2) the law enforcement officer initiates the search in furtherance of the school's mission to maintain a proper educational environment (applying reasonable suspicion); (3) the purpose of the search is to uncover evidence that violates a school rule (applying reasonable suspicion) or to uncover evidence pertaining to a potential criminal violation (applying probable cause); and (4) the situation is potentially dangerous — for example, involving firearms (applying reasonable suspicion). See Michael Pinard, From the Classroom to the Courtroom: Reassessing Fourth Amendment Standards in Public School Searches Involving Law Enforcement Authorities, 45 Ariz. L. Rev. 1067, 1083-1088 (2003) (analyzing different standards and suggesting reforms).

(6) *Constitutionality of Other School Searches.* Another question unanswered by *T.L.O.*, *Vernonia*, and *Earls* is what standard should apply to searches of
students' personal belongings in lockers and automobiles parked on school grounds
and to canine searches (see footnote 3). The trilogy of cases seems to imply that
"searches in areas previously deemed murky, involving metal detectors, dogs, and
other devices, [henceforth will] be subject to fewer Fourth Amendment challenges."
James & Larson, supra, at 51.

paper?
topic

a. *Locker Searches.* Many courts have held that lockers are school property
and therefore students have no legitimate expectation of privacy therein. Rebecca
N. Cordero, No Expectation of Privacy: Should School Officials Be Able to Search
Students' Lockers Without Any Suspicion of Wrong Doing? A Study of In re
Patrick Y. and Its Effect on Maryland Public School Students, 31 U. Balt. L. Rev.
305, 316 (2002). In these jurisdictions, random locker searches are permissible
without the necessity of individualized suspicion. See, e.g., In re Patrick Y., 746
A.2d 405 (Md. 2000); Shoemaker v. State, 971 S.W.2d 178 (Tex. App. 1998); In
re Isiah B., 500 N.W.2d 637 (Wis. 1993). Other courts have held that students do
have legitimate expectations of privacy in their lockers. See, e.g., State v. Jones, 666
N.W.2d 142 (Iowa 2003) (holding that, despite student's legitimate expectation of
privacy, search was permissible because it was conducted as part of routine annual
cleanout of lockers). Some courts base their decisions on whether the schools have
an explicit policy and give notice of it. See, e.g., Commonwealth v. Snyder, 597
N.E.2d 1363 (Mass. 1992) (existence of school policy established legitimacy of
students' expectation of privacy).

Jurisdictions holding that students have no expectation of privacy in school
lockers adopt one of the following rationales: (1) students' expectation of privacy
is diminished because school officials have a master key; (2) lockers are school
property; and (3) the expectation of privacy is diminished because lockers are
located in public areas. Cordero, supra, at 317. On the other hand, those jurisdictions
that support students' expectation of privacy take the position that lockers are for
students' exclusive use and also that the lock indicates restricted entry. Id. at 318.

b. *Automobile Searches on School Grounds.* Analogizing car searches to
locker searches, many courts hold that students do not have a legitimate expectation
of privacy in cars that are parked on school premises. Christine Pedigo, Protecting
Students' Fourth Amendment Rights: Alternatives to School-Mandated Urinalysis, 4 U.C. Davis J. Juv. L. & Pol'y 175, 193 (2000). See also J. Bates McIntyre,
Note, Empowering Schools to Search: The Effect of Growing Drug and Violence
Concerns, 2000 U. Ill. L. Rev. 1025, 1046 (2000) (suggesting that students enjoy a
lowered expectation of privacy in their automobiles, especially if a school requires
them to sign a parking agreement in which students agree to abide by school rules
and policies). This view is in accordance with the general rule that permits warrantless searches of an automobile if police have probable cause to believe the car
contains contraband or evidence of criminal activity (based on the rationale of the
inherent mobility of an automobile). Annual Review of Criminal Procedure, Note,
Search Incident to Valid Arrest, 91 Geo. L. J. 54, 85 (2003).

c. *Metal Detectors.* In the wake of increasing incidents of school violence
in the 1990s (see supra p. 129), school officials became increasingly concerned
about the presence of weapons on school grounds. As a result, Congress enacted

the Safe School Act of 1994, 20 U.S.C. §§5961, 5962 (2000), which permits school districts with high crime rates to compete for federal grants for violence prevention. The Act provides that federal funds may be used for the purchase of metal detectors to prevent weapons from being brought to school (id. at §5965(a)(13)). In response, the use of metal detectors in schools increased significantly.

Most courts hold that the use of metal detectors in schools does not violate the Fourth Amendment. For example, in In re F.B., 726 A.2d 361 (Pa. 1999), the Pennsylvania Supreme Court upheld the constitutionality of a search that confiscated a Swiss army knife. Applying the reasonableness test of *Vernonia*, the court reasoned: (1) students have a limited privacy interest; (2) the particular student suffered a minimal invasion of privacy by the scanner passing over his clothing; and (3) the government had a strong interest in keeping weapons out of the schools. Do you agree that the standard by which to assess the constitutionality of metal detector searches should be "reasonable suspicion" because such searches do not constitute police action? See, e.g., People v. Pruitt, 662 N.E.2d 540 (Ill. App. Ct. 1996) (upholding the constitutionality of a metal detector search directed by a school official although carried out by police). Are metal detectors an effective means of reducing school violence? See Robert S. Johnson, Metal Detector Searches: An Effective Means to Help Keep Weapons Out of Schools, 29 J.L. & Educ. 197, 200-201 (2000) (so arguing).

The United States Supreme Court has also addressed the issue of weapons in schools. In United States v. Lopez, 514 U.S. 549 (1995), a high school student was arrested, on the basis of an anonymous tip, for bringing a 38-caliber handgun to school. The student (Lopez) was carrying the Unloaded gun and five bullets for another person who planned to use the weapon in a gang war. Lopez was prosecuted for violating the federal Gun-Free School Zones Act of 1990, 18 U.S.C. §922(q)(1)(A)-2(A) (1994), prohibiting possession of a firearm within 1,000 feet of a school zone. The Supreme Court, in affirming the decision of the Fifth Circuit Court of Appeals, held that Congress exceeded the scope of its authority under the Commerce Clause in enacting the Act. Reasoning that the federal commerce power extends to noncommercial interstate commerce, the Court invalidated the Act after concluding that bearing weapons near schools does not substantially affect interstate commerce.

d. Dog Sniffs. School searches are sometimes conducted by specially trained canine units. To what extent does "dog sniffing" violate a student's constitutional rights? Most courts hold that a dog sniff of a student's *property* is not a search within the meaning of the Fourth Amendment, in line with Supreme Court authority. See United States v. Place, 462 U.S. 696 (1983) (holding that dog sniffings of luggage are not subject to the Fourth Amendment). However, searches of a minor's *person* have engendered more disagreement. James & Larson, supra, at 51. How intrusive is dog sniffing according to the "reasonableness" factors set forth in *Vernonia* and *Earls*: (1) the privacy interest, (2) the nature of the intrusion, and (3) the nature and immediacy of the governmental concern and the efficacy of the means used? In Horton v. Goose Creek Independent School District, 690 F.2d 470 (5th Cir. 1982), *reh'g denied*, 693 F.2d 524 (5th Cir. 1982), the Fifth Circuit Court of Appeals held a canine search unconstitutional, based in part on the fact that the search was unjustified because of the student's strong interest in bodily integrity and the lack of individualized suspicion. Is *Horton* valid after *Vernonia* and *Earls*? See James & Larson, supra, at 51 (speculating that "dog sniffs as part of a random, suspicionless search policy enjoy a presumption of validity after *Earls*"). See also Reuters, Parents Sue Police, School Over Drug Raid, Natl. Post, Dec. 16, 2003, at A12 (discussing incident involving allegations of illegal search and seizure, excessive force, assault, battery, and false imprisonment during an early morning canine search of minority high school students in Goose Creek, South Carolina, by police with guns drawn and handcuffs which netted no drugs or weapons).

   e. Strip Searches.   Courts have upheld the constitutionality of strip searches of school children. Rosemary Spellman, Comment, Strip Searches of Juveniles and the Fourth Amendment: A Delicate Balance of Protection and Privacy, 22 J. Juv. L. 159, 161 (2001/2002). Some courts exempt school officials from liability based on the doctrine of qualified immunity. See, e.g., Thomas ex rel. Thomas v. Roberts, 323 F.3d 950, 951 (11th Cir. 2003); Doe v. Renfrow, 475 F. Supp. 1012 (N.D. Ind. 1979), *aff'd in part, remanded in part on other grounds*, 631 F.2d 91 (7th Cir. 1980), *reh'g denied*, 635 F.2d 582 (7th Cir. 1980). Only six states (California, Iowa, Oklahoma, South Carolina, Washington, and Wisconsin) expressly prohibit strip searches by school officials. Dana Ingrassia, Note, Thomas ex rel. Thomas v. Roberts: Another Photo Finish Where School Officials Win the Race for Qualified Immunity, 26 Whittier L. Rev. 621, 622 (2004).

   Some courts that uphold strip searches of students insist on individualized suspicion. See, e.g., Holmes v. Montgomery, No. 2001-CA 002550-MR, 2003 WL 1786518 (Ky. Ct. App. 2003) (reversing summary judgment against parents in school officials' strip search of middle school students and identifying prior case law that upholds such searches of students based on individualized suspicion). Other courts find reasonable those strip searches that are intended for the purpose of finding weapons or drugs. See, e.g., Cornfield v. Consolidated High Sch. Dist., 991 F.2d 1316 (7th Cir. 1993); Williams v. Ellington, 936 F.2d 881 (6th Cir. 1991).

   In addition, some juvenile detention facilities have routine policies that permit strip searches. See, e.g., Cuesta v. School Board of Miami-Dade County, 285 F.3d 962 (11th Cir. 2002) (holding that strip search of juvenile in pretrial detention facilities does not require probable cause because of security danger). But cf. Smook v. Minnehaha County, 353 F. Supp. 2d 1059 (D.S.D. 2005) (holding that detention center policy of strip searching juvenile non-felon detainees violates Fourth Amendment).

   The Supreme Court previously upheld the constitutionality of strip searches for prison inmates following contact visits with outside visitors in Bell v. Wolfish, 441 U.S. 520 (1979) (in which the Court initially applied the "special needs" doctrine but without the label). Is the school setting analogous?

   What is the harm suffered by juveniles as a result of strip searches? Is a strip search analogous to rape? Are strip searches more damaging to juveniles than to adults? One commentator points out that courts give little guidance to school officials regarding the conduct of strip searches. Spellman, supra, at 162. Research on strip searches of juveniles concludes that lower courts fail to take into account the nature and potential impact of the strip search or the significance of the child's age. The authors of one study suggest that research in developmental psychology could help courts determine how to apply Fourth Amendment protections to children of different ages. Steven F. Shatz et al., The Strip Search of Children and the Fourth Amendment, 26 U.S.F. L. Rev. 1 (1991). Do you agree? Or should strip searches of children be per se unconstitutional? See Scott A. Garnter, Note, Strip Searches of Juveniles: What Johnny Really Learned in School and How Local School Boards Can Help Solve the Problem, 70 S. Cal. L. Rev. 921 (1997) (so arguing).

The constitutionality of strip searches also arises in other contexts, such as the investigation of child maltreatment. See N. Dickon Reppucci & Carrie S. Fried, Child Abuse and the Law, 69 UMKC L. Rev. 107, 118-119 (2000). In addition, commentators criticize the policy of routine strip searches in juvenile detention centers or of alien juveniles who are detained by the Immigration and Naturalization Service. Compare Flores v. Meese, 681 F. Supp. 665 (C.D. Cal. 1988) (holding that routine strip searches of juvenile detainees were unconstitutional) with N.G. v. Connecticut, 382 F.3d 225 (2d Cir. 2004) (holding that strip searches of juvenile detainees at initial admission did not violate Fourth Amendment). See generally Areti Georgopoulos, Beyond the Reach of Juvenile Justice: The Crisis of Unaccompanied Immigrant Children Detained by the United States, 23 Law & Ineq. 117 (2005); Molly McDonough, Unusual Settlement Proposed in Strip-Search Case, 20 A.B.A. J. E-Report 7 (May 24, 2002) (describing settlement provision that gives juvenile detainees, who were routinely strip searched, vouchers for education, food, lodging, and health care).

(7) Other Search-Related Issues. The issue of minority is relevant with regard to other aspects of the law of search and seizure. For example, there are circumstances that permit the valid arrest of a child, thus allowing a search incident to an arrest, in circumstances in which an adult could not be arrested. See James D. v. California, 741 P.2d 161 (Cal. 1987), *cert. denied*, 485 U.S. 959 (1988) (discussed supra p. 807). In addition, if a youth has acquiesced in or consented to a search, presumably the determination of the "voluntariness" of the consent may take into account the factor of the youth's age. See In re Williams, 267 N.Y.S.2d 91 (Fam. Ct. 1966) (15-year-old's submission to authority does not constitute consent to search). Indeed, the American Law Institute's Model Code of Pre-Arraignment Procedure (§240.2(1)(a)148 (1975)) would go much further and require parental consent to search if a youth is under age 16.

The parent-child relationship is also relevant in other ways in the context of searches. May parents consent to a warrantless search directed against a child living at home? A number of courts have so held. See, e.g., United States v. Evans, 27 F.3d 1219 (7th Cir. 1994); State v. Rodriguez, 828 P.2d 636 (Wash. Ct. App. 1992). On the other hand, may children consent to a warrantless search directed against a parent in the home? Do children have the same access and control to the family's living space? Are children as cognizant of the implications of their consent and their ability to refuse consent? See generally Matt McCaughey, Note, And a Child Shall Lead Them: The Validity of Children's Consent to Warrantless Searches of the Family Home, 34 U. Louisville J. Fam. L. 747 (1995-1996).

(8) Problem. School officials from several Indiana high schools, concerned about drug and alcohol use, formulate a new policy, which is adopted by the school board. In addition to permitting testing for students on the basis of individualized suspicion, the policy requires a drug and alcohol test for any student who (1) possesses or uses tobacco products; (2) is suspended for three or more days for fighting;

(3) is habitually truant; or (4) violates any other school rule that results in at least a three-day suspension. Test results are disclosed only to parents. Although students are not punished, they may be expelled if they refuse to participate in a drug education program. Students who refuse to undergo a test are considered to have admitted unlawful substance use.

James Willis, a freshman, is suspended for fighting with a fellow student. Upon his return to school, James is informed that he will be tested for drug and alcohol use. He refuses and is suspended again. He is then advised that if he refuses again to submit to a urinanalysis test, he will be deemed to have admitted unlawful drug use and will be expelled. James files suit, claiming that the policy violates the Fourth and Fourteenth Amendments. Although no school official observed James using drugs or alcohol at any time, the school contends that the fight itself was enough to create a reasonable suspicion that James was using an illegal substance and also claims that students who use illegal substances are "more than twice as likely to get into physical fights." What result? See Willis by Willis v. Anderson Community Sch., 158 F.3d 415 (7th Cir. 1998).

4. Notice of Charges

You will recall that *Gault* required that "the child *and* his parents or guardian be notified, in writing, of the specific charge or factual allegations. . . ." 387 U.S. 1, 33 (1967) (emphasis added). Obviously, this notice requirement does not apply to adults who are accused of a crime and thus distinguishes delinquency proceedings. Consider the purposes served by giving notice to a youth's parents. Whose rights are violated by the failure to give the parents notice? The youth's? The parents'? Both? Does the omission amount to a constitutional violation? Compare McDonald v. Black, 820 F.2d 260 (8th Cir. 1987); United States v. Doe, 155 F.3d 1070 (9th Cir. 1998) (both holding that juvenile defendant was not deprived of due process by lack of parental notification) with In re J.P.J., 485 N.E.2d 848 (Ill. 1985) (adequate notice to minor and his parents is a requirement of due process).

May a parent waive various procedural rights, such as notice requirements, on behalf of his child? If the minor has notice, but his parents are not given adequate notice, does this necessarily vitiate the juvenile court's jurisdiction? See United States v. Watts, 513 F.2d 5 (10th Cir. 1975) (parental notice is a prophylactic safeguard but not a "separate and independent" constitutional requirement); State v. Whitter, 245 So. 2d 913 (Fla. Dist. Ct. App. 1971) (when parent has actual notice, failure to comply with statutory notice requirement does not render a judgment void).

Suppose the juvenile's parents are divorced. Must a state use due diligence in finding and serving the noncustodial parent? Compare In re J.P.J., supra, (service of process adequate although divorced father not served and father's whereabouts unknown) with In re T.M.F., 508 N.E.2d 1160 (Ill. App. Ct. 1987) (rule of In re J.P.J. not applicable when mother's whereabouts are known). Does failure to provide the required notice deprive a court of subject matter jurisdiction? See In re T.B., 382 N.E.2d 1292 (Ill. App. Ct. 1978) (juvenile court lacked jurisdiction when a state did not exercise due diligence in trying to find mother's address and failed to give mother proper notice).

Following *Gault*, Congress amended the Federal Juvenile Delinquency Act, 18 U.S.C. §5033 (2000), to provide for parental notification whenever a minor is taken into custody for a federal offense. The arresting officer must immediately notify the parents that the juvenile is in custody and explain to the parents both the juvenile's rights and the nature of the juvenile's offense. However, the Act does not clarify the meaning of "immediately" or specify which of the juvenile's rights must be explained to the parents (i.e., whether notification that the minor is in custody also requires notification of the minor's *Miranda* rights).

The Ninth Circuit Court of Appeals recently addressed many of these gaps. See, e.g., United States v. Juvenile (RRA-A), 229 F.3d 737 (9th Cir. 2000) (holding that a border agent did not "immediately" advise juvenile of her rights by waiting four hours to give *Miranda* warnings and also that he violated notification provision by failing to personally contact the Mexican consulate when unable to reach minor's parents by phone and by failing to wait a reasonable amount of time to begin interrogation); United States v. Doe (*Doe III*), 170 F.3d 1162 (9th Cir. 1999) (holding that parental notification of the juvenile's *Miranda* rights must be given contemporaneously with the parental notification of custody). For those juveniles whose parents live outside the United States, the government may notify the relevant foreign consulate in the United States if it is not feasible to provide parental notification (e.g., if the parents do not have a phone). United States v. Doe, 701 F.2d 819, 822 (9th Cir. 1983).

May juveniles waive their right to parental notification (e.g., if they do not want their parents to know of their arrest)? See United States v. L.M.K, 149 F.3d 1033 (9th Cir. 1998) (holding that parental notification requirement is nonwaivable by the minor).

5.   The Voluntariness of Juvenile Confessions

The admissibility of a juvenile's confession has been frequently litigated. In two cases decided before *Gault*, the Supreme Court held that the confession of a juvenile was not "voluntary" and that its admission as evidence therefore violated the juvenile's due process rights under the Fourteenth Amendment. In each case, the Court made plain that the age of the accused was a relevant factor in applying the voluntariness test.

The first of these cases, Haley v. Ohio, 332 U.S. 596 (1948), involved a 15-year-old who confessed after police questioning from midnight to 5 A.M. Writing for a plurality of the Court, Justice Douglas stated:

> What transpired would make us pause for careful inquiry if a mature man were involved. And when, as here, a mere child — an easy victim of the law — is before us, special care in scrutinizing the record must be used. Age 15 is a tender and difficult age for a boy of any race. He cannot be judged by the more exacting standards of maturity. That which would leave a man cold and unimpressed can overawe and overwhelm a lad in his early teens. This is the period of great instability which the crisis of adolescence produces. A 15-year-old lad, questioned through the dead of night by relays of police, is a ready victim of the inquisition. Mature men possibly might stand the ordeal from midnight to 5 A.M. But we cannot believe that a lad of tender years is a match for the police in such a contest. He needs counsel

and support if he is not to become the victim first of fear, then of panic. He needs someone on whom to lean lest the overpowering presence of the law, as he knows it, crush him. No friend stood at the side of this 15-year-old boy as the police, working in relays, questioned him hour after hour, from midnight until dawn. No lawyer stood guard to make sure that the police went so far and no farther, to see to it that they stopped short of the point where he became the victim of coercion. No counsel or friend was called during the critical hours of questioning. A photographer was admitted once this lad broke and confessed. But not even a gesture towards getting a lawyer for him was ever made. [332 U.S. at 599-600.]

The second case, Gallegos v. Colorado, 370 U.S. 49 (1962), involved a 14-year-old boy's formal confession. Writing the opinion for the Court, Justice Douglas stated:

The fact that petitioner was only 14 years old puts this case on the same footing as Haley v. Ohio, supra. There was here no evidence of prolonged questioning. But the five-day-detention — during which time the boy's mother unsuccessfully tried to see him and he was cut off from contact with any lawyer or adult advisory — gives the case an ominous cast. The prosecution says that the boy was advised of his right to counsel, but that he did not ask either for a lawyer or for his parents. But a 14-year-old boy, no matter how sophisticated, is unlikely to have any conception of what will confront him when he is made accessible only to the police. That is to say, we deal with a person who is not equal to the police in knowledge and understanding of the consequences of the questions and answers being recorded and who is unable to know how to protect his own interests or how to get the benefits of his constitutional rights.

The prosecution says that the youth and immaturity of the petitioner and the five-day detention are irrelevant, because the basic ingredients of the confession came tumbling out as soon as he was arrested. But if we took that position, it would, with all deference, be in callous disregard of this boy's constitutional rights. He cannot be compared with an adult in full possession of his senses and knowledge-able of the consequences of his admissions. He would have no way of knowing what the consequences of his confession were without advice as to his rights — from someone concerned with securing him those rights — and without the aid of more mature judgment as to the steps he should take in the predicament in which he found himself. A lawyer or an adult relative or friend could have given the petitioner the protection which his own immaturity could not. Adult advice would have put him on a less unequal footing with his interrogators. Without some adult protection against this inequality, a 14-year-old boy would not be able to know, let alone assert, such constitutional rights as he had. To allow this conviction to stand would, in effect, be to treat him as if he had no constitutional rights. [Id. at 53-55.]

The United States Supreme Court examined issues surrounding juvenile con-fessions in two subsequent cases (Fare v. Michael C., 442 U.S. 707 (1979), and Yarborough v. Alvarado, 541 U.S. 652 (2004)). In *Fare*, the Court adopted the totality-of-the-circumstances test to evaluate the voluntariness of a juvenile's con-fession. In prior case law, the Court had emphasized that "special care" must be taken when assessing the voluntariness of a juvenile's confession; however, in *Fare*, the Court applied the adult totality standard. This test considers factors such as age, intelligence, previous experience with police officers, and the circumstances sur-rounding the interrogation (e.g., length of the interrogation, etc.). Following *Fare*, a majority of states adopted this standard for juvenile offenders. (*Fare* is discussed in more detail infra p. 839.)

However, dissatisfaction with *Fare* led some states to adopt a per se rule that treats interrogations of juveniles with more care. Although there is some variation in states' per se tests, the most common test is the "interested adult" rule, which requires courts to consider whether the juvenile had an opportunity to consult (before or during the interrogation) with an interested adult before waiving the privilege against self-incrimination.

In recent years, several highly publicized cases have focused attention on the voluntariness of juvenile confessions. In Chicago in 1999, police arrested two boys, ages 7 and 8, on charges of murdering an 11-year-old girl for her bicycle. The boys confessed to the crime, but police dropped the charges when investigators discovered semen in the victim's underpants that matched that of a known sex offender. See Robyn E. Blumner, Children Confess Whether They Did It or Not, St. Petersburg Times, May 2, 1999, at D6. In another case, an 11-year-old confessed to murdering a toddler at her grandparents' day care center. Evidence subsequently suggested that the toddler was battered by her mother's boyfriend prior to arriving at the day care center. In re L.M., 933 S.W.2d 276 (Tex. Ct. App. 1999). Also, in 1999 in San Diego, a 14-year-old boy confessed to killing his 12-year-old sister, who was stabbed to death in her bedroom. DNA evidence eventually linked a transient in the neighborhood to the slaying. See Nashiba F. Boyd, Comment, "I Didn't Do It, I Was Forced to Say That I Did": The Problem of Coerced Juvenile Confessions, and Proposed Federal Legislation to Prevent Them, 47 How. L.J. 395, 395-396 (2004). And in another famous incident, five juveniles were convicted of the rape of a female jogger in Central Park. The teens were convicted on the basis of their respective confessions after lengthy interrogations, despite the fact that neither blood nor semen at the crime scene matched any of the juveniles. Twelve years later, the convictions were overturned after a convicted rapist confessed to the crime and DNA evidence substantiated his guilt.

Psychological research substantiates juveniles' propensity for false confession under police pressure.[74] Data suggest that youths under age 16, particularly, are apt to make choices that result in their complying with adult authority figures, such as confessing to police, rather than remaining silent.[75] Children often fail to understand the long-term implications of their confessions, often thinking that if they confess they will be allowed to go home. Moreover, children are especially likely to confess falsely when they are confronted with police pressure in the form of tactics presenting false evidence of their guilt.[76]

In response to the problems of juvenile confessions, commentators have proposed various reforms. Some commentators suggest that parental presence is a

---

[74] Steven A. Drizin & Richard A. Leo, The Problem of False Confessions in the Post-DNA World, 82 N.C. L. Rev. 891, 947 (2004) (revealing a study in which approximately one-third of documented false confessions were by juveniles).

[75] Thomas Grisso & Laurence Steinberg, Juveniles' Competence to Stand Trial: A Comparison of Adolescents' and Adults' Capacities as Trial Defendants, 27 Law & Hum. Behav. 333, 353-356 (2003).

[76] Allison D. Redlich & Gail S. Goodman, Taking Responsibility for an Act Not Committed: The Influence of Age and Suggestibility, 27 Law & Hum. Behav. 141, 151-152 (2003).

necessary but not sufficient condition and that police should videotape custodial interrogations. See Lawrence Schlam, Police Interrogation of Children and State Constitutions: Why Not Videotape the MTV Generation?, 26 U. Tol. L. Rev. 901 (1995); Welsh S. White, False Confessions and the Constitution: Safeguards Against Untrustworthy Confessions, 32 Harv.-C.R.-C.L. L. Rev. 105, 153 (1997). Another commentator proposes federal legislation to create the role of "juvenile justice officer" to explain *Miranda* warnings to juveniles, alert the court about improper police tactics, and notify parents of custodial interrogations. What do you think of these suggestions?

Recently, the United States Supreme Court was presented with yet another occasion to review some of the issues surrounding juvenile confessions. Yarborough v. Alvarado, 541 U.S. 652 (2004) (discussed infra), reveals the extent of the Court's disagreement about the relevance of a suspect's age in determining the admissibility of a confession on *Miranda* grounds (discussed below).

6. Miranda *Rights*

In Miranda v. Arizona, 384 U.S. 436 (1966), the Supreme Court held that a person in custody must be informed that (1) he has a right to remain silent; (2) anything he says can be used against him; (3) he has the right to consult with an attorney and to have an attorney with him during an interrogation; and (4) an attorney will be appointed for him if he cannot afford one. When *Miranda* requirements are applied to juveniles in custody, special issues arise.

a. When Is a Juvenile in Custody in Order to Trigger *Miranda* Warnings?

The United States Supreme Court recently explored the requirements that trigger a pre-interrogation *Miranda* warning for a juvenile suspect. In a case focusing on the availability of federal habeas corpus relief, the Court had occasion to consider the relevance of age in the determination of whether a suspect is in "custody" for *Miranda* purposes. According to the traditional rule, all "custodial" interviews require a pre-interrogation *Miranda* warning. The determination of whether a suspect is in "custody" is an objective test considering the totality of the circumstances: how a reasonable person in the suspect's situation would perceive the circumstances.

In Yarborough v. Alvarado, 541 U.S. 652 (2004), a police detective asked the parents of 17-year-old Michael Alvarado to bring him to the police station for questioning. There, Alvarado confessed to his role in an attempted robbery and murder (i.e., his participation in the robbery and concealment of the gun) during an interrogation that was conducted without his being advised of his *Miranda* rights. The boy later claimed that his parents had asked to be present during the two-hour interview that led to his confession, but police refused. At trial, Alvarado was convicted after unsuccessfully attempting to suppress his statement on *Miranda* grounds.

The appellate court affirmed the conviction, contending that Alvarado had not been in custody during the interview so that no *Miranda* warning was required. The state supreme court denied review, and Alvarado filed a petition for a writ of habeas corpus in federal court. The federal district court agreed with the state court that Alvarado had not been in custody for *Miranda* purposes. However, the Ninth Circuit Court of Appeals reversed. In holding that Alvarado should have received *Miranda* warnings because the interview was "custodial," the court took into account the factors of age and experience in the determination of whether an interrogation is "custodial." Alvarado v. Hickman, 316 F.3d 841 (9th Cir. 2002). The case was appealed to the United States Supreme Court.

Because *Alvarado* involved a plea for habeas corpus relief, federal law applied (i.e., the Antiterrorism and Effective Death Penalty Act of 1996 (AEDPA), Pub. L. No. 104-132, 110 Stat. 1214 (2000) (codified in scattered sections of 18 U.S.C. and 28 U.S.C.)). Under AEDPA, a federal court may grant an application for a writ of habeas corpus on behalf of a person held pursuant to a state-court judgment if the state-court adjudication resulted in a decision that was "contrary to, or involved an unreasonable application of, clearly established federal law, as determined by the Supreme Court." 28 U.S.C. §2254(d)(1) (2000). Although the Ninth Circuit ruled that the state court unreasonably applied clearly established law in holding that Alvarado was not in custody for *Miranda* purposes, the United States Supreme Court disagreed. The Supreme Court held that the California court's application of the law was reasonable because, in Justice Kennedy's words, "fair-minded jurists could disagree over whether Alvarado was in custody" (541 U.S. at 664). In so ruling, the Court did not establish guidelines regarding when a minor is in "custody" for purposes of *Miranda* warnings. Nonetheless, the *Yarborough* majority implied that a suspect's age and experience are irrelevant in the determination.

> [B]y labeling the test [for whether an interrogation is custodial] "objective" when it clearly contains a subjective element, the Court implied that a suspect's age is irrelevant in determining whether an interrogation is custodial. And it conclusively confirmed that a suspect's past experience with the police should never be a part of the equation. [Craig M. Bradley, Supreme Court Review on 'Custody,' 41 Trial 58, 59-60 (Feb. 2005).]

However, Justice Breyer in his dissent (and Justice O'Connor in her concurring opinion) asserts that age could be a relevant factor in the determination of whether an interrogation is "custodial" for *Miranda* purposes. Contending that a juvenile suspect in Alvarado's position would have believed that he was in "custody," Breyer argues:

> What reasonable person in the circumstances — brought to a police station by his parents at police request, put in a small interrogation room, questioned for a solid two hours, and confronted with claims that there is strong evidence that he participated in a serious crime, could have thought to himself, "Well, anytime I want to leave I can just get up and walk out"? If the person harbored any doubts, would he still think he might be free to leave once he recalls that the police officer has just refused to let his parents remain with him during questioning? Would he still think that he, rather than the officer, controls the situation? There is only one possible answer to these questions. . . .
>
> The fact that Alvarado was 17 helps to show that he was unlikely to have felt free to ignore his parents' request to come to the station. And a 17-year-old is more

likely than, say, a 35-year-old, to take a police officer's assertion of authority to keep parents outside the room as an assertion of authority to keep their child inside as well. . . .

Common sense, and an understanding of the law's basic purpose in this area, are enough to make clear that Alvarado's age — an objective, widely shared characteristic about which the police plainly knew — is also relevant to the inquiry. Unless one is prepared to pretend that Alvarado is someone he is not, a middle-aged gentleman, well-versed in police practices, it seems to me clear that the California courts made a serious mistake [in ruling that he was not in custody so that no *Miranda* warning was required. 541 U.S. at 670-671, 676.]

b. Parental Role

Miranda has been interpreted to mean that if either a child or the child's parents ask for a lawyer, questioning by officials must stop. What if the youth asks for his parents? Must questioning stop? See People v. Burton, 491 P.2d 793 (Cal. 1971):

> In this case we are called upon to decide whether a minor's request to see his parents "reasonably appears inconsistent with a present willingness on the part of the suspect to discuss his case freely and completely with police at that time." [People v. Randall, 464 P.2d 114 (Cal. 1970).] It appears to us most likely and most normal that a minor who wants help on how to conduct himself with the police and wishes to indicate that he does not want to proceed without such help would express such desire by requesting to see his parents. For adults, removed from the protective ambit of parental guidance, the desire for help naturally manifests in a request for an attorney. For minors, it would seem that the desire for help naturally manifests in a request for parents. It would certainly severely restrict the "protective devices" required by *Miranda* in cases where the suspects are minors if the only call for help which is to be deemed an invocation of the privilege is the call for an attorney. It is fatuous to assume that a minor in custody will be in a position to call an attorney for assistance and it is unrealistic to attribute no significance to his call for help from the only person to whom he normally looks — a parent or guardian. It is common knowledge that this is the normal reaction of a youthful suspect who finds himself in trouble with the law.

But see McIntyre v. State, 526 A.2d 30 (Md. 1987) (holding that a denial of a request to see his mother by a 15-year-old charged with rape did not constitute a violation of suspect's Fifth and Sixth Amendment rights).

Must a juvenile in custody be advised of a parent's presence? For an adult, the Supreme Court ruled in Moran v. Burbine, 475 U.S. 412 (1986), that an accused need not be advised of the presence of his or her attorney if the accused has not requested an attorney. However, some courts have held that juveniles must be so advised. See, e.g., In re Lucas F., 510 A.2d 270 (Md. 1986).

Are there situations in which a youth's request for an adult other than his parents should be treated as an invocation of his *Miranda* rights? Suppose the youth's parents are unavailable? Or the youth asks for another adult from fear of facing a parent as a result of his crime (for example, if the crime was patricide or matricide)?

In Fare v. Michael C., 442 U.S. 707 (1979), the Supreme Court considered whether a 16-year-old's request to see his probation officer was, in effect, a request for an attorney. The Court, in a 5-to-4 decision, held that it was not. Writing for the majority, Justice Blackmun noted:

> We . . . believe it clear that the probation officer is not in a position to offer the type of legal assistance necessary to protect the Fifth Amendment rights of an accused undergoing custodial interrogation that a lawyer can offer. The Court in *Miranda* recognized that "the attorney plays a vital role in the administration of criminal justice under our Constitution." [384 U.S. at 481.] It is this pivotal role of legal counsel that justifies the per se rule established in *Miranda*, and that distinguishes the request for counsel from the request for a probation officer, a clergyman, or a close friend. A probation officer simply is not necessary, in the way an attorney is, for the protection of the legal rights of the accused, juvenile or adult. He is significantly handicapped by the position he occupies in the juvenile system from serving as an effective protector of the rights of a juvenile suspected of a crime.
>
> The California Supreme Court, however, found that the close relationship between juveniles and their probation officers compelled the conclusion that a probation officer, for purposes of *Miranda*, was sufficiently like a lawyer to justify extension of the per se rule. . . . The fact that a relationship of trust and cooperation between a probation officer and a juvenile might exist, however, does not indicate that the probation officer is capable of rendering effective legal advice sufficient to protect the juvenile's rights during interrogation by the police, or of providing the other services rendered by a lawyer. [An extension of the per se rule to include requests for probation officers] would impose the burdens associated with the rule of *Miranda* on the juvenile justice system and the police without serving the interest that rule was designed simultaneously to protect. If it were otherwise, a juvenile's request for almost anyone he considered trustworthy enough to give him reliable advice would trigger the rigid rule *of Miranda*. [442 U.S. at 722-723.]

How explicit must be a juvenile's request to speak with a parent or a lawyer? Suppose that during a police interrogation, and after being advised of his *Miranda* rights, a 14-year-old asks the police officer, "Do I need a lawyer?" Is the youth's question an assertion of his right to counsel that would require questioning to stop? See In re Christopher K., 810 N.E.2d 145 (Ill. App. Ct. 2004) (upholding voluntariness of juvenile's confession to murder, reasoning that juvenile offender should have manifested a more positive assertion of his desire for an attorney to invoke his privilege against self-incrimination).

c. *Miranda* and the Possibility of Transfer to Adult Court

Must children be specifically advised that a confession may be used against them in an adult criminal proceeding if the juvenile court waives jurisdiction? Several courts, although a minority of those that have faced the issue, have held that such a warning is required. See, e.g., State v. Benoit, 490 A.2d 295 (N.H. 1985):

> Many juveniles are aware of the special mechanisms of the juvenile justice system. A child, in making a statement, may reasonably believe that the statement will

be used only in the protective and rehabilitative setting of juvenile court. The lack of knowledge on the part of a child concerning the possibility of felony criminal treatment of his offense cannot be allowed to induce the giving of a statement. Hence, to insure a truly knowing and intelligent waiver of the privilege against self-incrimination, the child must be advised of the possibility of prosecution in superior court as an adult.

Following *Benoit*, however, several states criticized its reasoning and declined to follow its lead. See State v. Perez, 591 A.2d 119, 124-125 (Conn. 1991); State v. Campbell, 691 A.2d 564, 567 (R.I. 1997). See also State v. Callahan, 979 S.W.2d 577 (Tenn. 1998) (holding that juvenile need not be informed of the possibility of waiver into adult court as a constitutional prerequisite to waiver of *Miranda* rights).

d. Additional *Miranda* Issues

What should be the specific style and content of the *Miranda* warning when juveniles are involved? In addition to the four basic *Miranda* warnings, should children be told that they have the right to stop the interrogator's questioning at any time? Compare State v. Nicholas, 444 A.2d 373 (Me. 1982) with Romans v. District Court, 633 P.2d 477 (Colo. 1981).

7. Waiver of a Juvenile's Rights

Should youths be able to waive their constitutional rights? For adults, *Miranda* made clear that accused persons may waive their rights so long as such "waiver is made voluntarily, knowingly, and intelligently." 384 U.S. at 444. Should the same standard be applicable to juveniles? Consider the approaches suggested by In re S.H. and the Juvenile Justice Standards.

In re S.H.
293 A.2d 181 (N.J. 1972)

PROCTOR, J.

A juvenile delinquency complaint in the Mercer County Juvenile and Domestic Relations Court charged that the appellant, S.H., age 10, caused the drowning of B.R., age 6, by pushing him into a canal. The court found that the appellant was a juvenile delinquent. However, it reserved decision as to whether the offense would be manslaughter or second degree murder had the act been committed by a person of the age of 18 or over until it received the report of the Menlo Park Diagnostic Center to which it committed S.H. for 90 days for examination. Upon receipt of the report the court determined the act would be second degree murder if done by an adult and committed S.H. to the State Home for Boys for an indeterminate period of time. S.H. appealed to the Appellate Division, and before argument there upon defendant's application the proceedings were certified to this Court.

... On March 17, 1970, three boys, E.J., age 7, W.W., age 8, and B.R. were returning to school in Trenton after lunch. A short distance from the school S.H. approached the boys, accused them of beating up his sister, and asked for some money. The boys denied beating up his sister and refused to give him any money. S.H. then punched W.W. in the face and took B.R. by the coat into an adjacent alley. The two other boys continued to school. B.R. did not return to school or to his home that evening.

The following day, March 18, the Trenton Police Department began a missing person's investigation of B.R. That morning Sergeant John Girman, along with two patrolmen, went to the school S.H. attended. At 11:00 A.M. in the presence of the vice-principal they spoke to S.H. He was not a suspect at this time, as the police did not know whether or not B.R. was the victim of foul play. S.H. was being questioned because the police had information that he was one of the last persons to see B.R. S.H. told the police that he had seen B.R. on Brunswick Avenue with W.W. and E.J. He said they were approached by a boy named Leroy who hit one or both of the older boys and took B.R. away with him. S.H. said he then went to school. After the questioning S.H. returned to class.

That same day, after speaking to W.W. and E.J., the police returned to S.H.'s school at 1:00 P.M. and asked to see the boy again. They questioned him as to the identity of Leroy. After describing Leroy, S.H. suddenly began to cry and said Leroy threw B.R. into the canal. He agreed to show the police the place where Leroy had thrown the boy. Shortly thereafter the police and fire departments along with S.H. went to the canal and he showed them the place where Leroy pushed B.R. into the water. He also told them B.R. floated down the canal, and he pointed out the spot where he last saw him go under. At 3:30 P.M. B.R.'s body was discovered about 300 feet from where S.H. said he saw Leroy push the boy into the water.

After the body was found, S.H. told the police he would take them to Leroy's house. They arrived at the address S.H. gave them about 4:45 P.M., where he identified a certain boy as Leroy. Investigation showed that the boy was not named Leroy, was in school at the time of the episode and was in no way involved.

Thereafter, at about 5:00 P.M., the police took S.H. to the first precinct Trenton Police Station. After discussing the matter with other policemen, Sergeant Girman concluded a homicide had occurred, and S.H. was a prime suspect.

When S.H. arrived at the police station, his father was already there. However, the police told Mr. H. he was not needed at that time, and he left the station and went home.

Sergeant Girman turned S.H. over to Detective Purdy of the Juvenile Bureau of the Trenton Police Department. The detective took the boy to a room on the second floor usually used to interrogate adults. Alone in the room with S.H., the detective read the boy his *Miranda* rights from a card, explaining what they meant as he went along. According to the detective, he spent about 10 minutes explaining the *Miranda* rights. The following colloquy adduced at the hearing shows the nature of the explanation and the extent of S.H.'s understanding of it:

> THE COURT: Well, what were his responses to your (explanation of the *Miranda* warnings)?
> MR. PURDY: And he would say yes and no to me in answer; along with the yes and no's he would also shake his head. And I would move on because I felt that he did know, what the answer was that he was giving me. When he said yes, I would move on. And when he said no, then I would explain to him further.

The entire interrogation lasted about 90 minutes.

About 6:30 P.M., after the interrogation was completed, the police picked Mr. H. up at his house and brought him to the station house. He was taken to a second floor room where he found four policemen. S.H. was brought in by Detective Purdy from the adjoining room where the questioning had taken place. The detective then asked S.H. to tell his father what he had told him during the interrogation. The boy complied.

At the hearing the State called Mr. H. and asked him what S.H. had told him in the presence of the police. Defense counsel objected to the State's use of the father to testify against his son. The objection was sustained. The State then put Detective Purdy back on the stand to relate what S.H. told his father. Purdy told the court that S.H. said, "I walked the boy down by the railroad crossing. And we got by the creek (canal) and, I mean by the water, and I pushed him in." . . . This testimony was admitted over defense counsel's objection.

The State rested, and after motions of defense counsel were heard and denied the defense rested without calling any witnesses.

On this appeal appellant contends his confession was the product of police coercion, and therefore its admission into evidence violated the due process clause of the Fourteenth Amendment. In a juvenile case where a serious offense is charged, before the confession of an accused can be received in evidence against him the State has the burden of establishing that the accused's will was not overborne and that the confession was the product of a free choice. We are not satisfied the State has borne its burden of proving that this confession was voluntarily made and that the fundamental fairness requirement of due process has been met.

The circumstances under which the station house interrogation was conducted showed a complete disregard for the well-being of the accused juvenile. Placing a young boy in the "frightening atmosphere" of a police station without the presence of his parents or someone to whom the boy can turn for support is likely to have harmful effects on his mind and will. Not only was S.H. interrogated in the police station, but he was isolated in a room with a detective for a period of 90 minutes. The State's proofs account for only 10 minutes of this period, that used to give and explain the *Miranda* warnings. There is nothing in the record to show what occurred during the remaining 80 minutes except Detective Purdy's testimony of what the boy told him about the episode (the same story which he told his father in the presence of the police). More significant is the action of the police in sending the father away from the police station before questioning the boy. We emphasize whenever possible and especially in the case of young children no child should be interviewed except in the presence of his parents or guardian. [In re Carlo, 225 A.2d 110 (N.J. 1966)]; Standards for Specialized Courts Dealing With Children (Children's Bureau, Department of Health, Education and Welfare, 1954) at 39. That the police allowed Mr. H. to be present immediately after the interrogation in order to secure a separate confession in no way detracts from our conclusion. This second confession was merely a reprise of what the boy told Detective Purdy when he was secluded alone with him in the room and at best was nothing more than the tainted product of the coercion which produced the first confession. See Wong Sun v. United States, 371 U.S. 471 (1963). The conduct of the police in sending Mr. H. home from the police station when he had appeared in the interest of his son without more may be sufficient to show that the confession was involuntary. In light of the other circumstances, however, we need not pursue this point.

In reaching our conclusion as to the voluntariness of the confession, we have taken into consideration that the police gave S.H. the *Miranda* warnings and that he purportedly waived his rights. We think this factor, however, was of little or no significance in the present case. Recitation of the *Miranda* warnings to a boy of 10 even when they are explained is undoubtedly meaningless. Such a boy certainly lacks the capability to fully understand the meaning of his rights. Thus, he cannot make a knowing and intelligent waiver of something he cannot understand. However, questioning may go forward even if it is obvious the boy does not understand his rights if the questioning is conducted with the utmost fairness and in accordance with the highest standards of due process and fundamental fairness. See State v. In the Interest of R.W., 115 N.J. Super. 286, 295-296, 279 A.2d 709 (App. Div. 1971), *aff'd o.b.*, 61 N.J. 118, 293 A.2d 186 (1972). Such was not the case here.

Upon a consideration of the totality of the circumstances under which the appellant's confession was obtained, we cannot say it convincingly appears that his confession was voluntarily made. In view of the appellant's age, the oppressive environment of the police station where the questioning was conducted, the lengthy period of interrogation (the nature of which is only partially explained) and the cavalier treatment of the father in sending him home when his boy most needed him, we cannot say the State has met its burden of proving the confession of appellant was obtained by methods consistent with due process. We therefore hold *[holding]* that his confession was improperly admitted in evidence.

A new trial, however, is not necessary. A juvenile hearing is not a criminal case; it is a civil proceeding, tried without a jury, and conducted in the interest of the juvenile and for the welfare of society. In such a case our Constitution and rules permit us to exercise such original jurisdiction as may be necessary to the complete determination of the cause on review. N.J. Const., Art. 6, Sec. 5, para. 3; R. 2:10-5; see State v. Taylor, 38 N.J. Super. 6, 21, 118 A.2d 36 (1955). In exercising that jurisdiction we have examined the undisputed evidence other than that contained in the inadmissible confession and find there from beyond a reasonable doubt that S.H. committed the act set forth in the charge and that he therefore requires rehabilitative treatment. . . .

A review of the admissible evidence completely satisfies us that S.H. pushed B.R. into the canal. S.H.'s description of Leroy's actions in stopping the three boys and taking B.R. away was shown, at the hearing, to be in reality the very actions of the appellant. S.H. was the only one who knew B.R.'s body was in the canal. He was the only one who knew the location of the body. And more significantly, he sought to place the blame on an innocent boy. These facts leave no doubt in our minds that the appellant caused the death of B.R.

We are not convinced, however, that appellant's act would constitute murder if committed by an adult rather than manslaughter. Malice differentiates murder from manslaughter. Ordinarily, proof of an intent to kill or to do grievous bodily harm is necessary to establish malice. We are not satisfied on the record before us that this 10-year-old boy had the intent to kill or to do grievous bodily harm. The diagnostic report later furnished the trial court in connection with the disposition of the juvenile discloses that S.H. had an I.Q. "within the mild defective range of intelligence," and that he was "functioning severely behind the norm for his chronological age." This report supports our doubt of the existence of the mens rea required for murder. It shows that S.H. was physically 10 but mentally much younger. Under the circumstances the finding should be that the homicide is involuntary manslaughter.

The judgment of the trial court is modified in accordance with this opinion.

ABA, Institute of Judicial Administration, Juvenile Justice Standards Project, Pretrial Court Proceedings (1980)

Part VI: Waiver of the Juvenile's Rights; The Role of Parents and Guardians ad Litem in the Delinquency Proceedings

Waiver of the Juvenile's Rights

6.1 Waiver of the juvenile's rights in general

A. Any right accorded to the respondent in a delinquency case by these standards or by federal, state, or local law may be waived in the manner described below. A juvenile's right to counsel may not be waived.

B. For purposes of this part:

1. A "mature respondent" is one who is capable of adequately comprehending and participating in the proceedings;

2. An "immature respondent" is one who is incapable of adequately comprehending and participating in the proceedings because of youth or inexperience. This part does not apply to determining a juvenile's incapacity to stand trial or otherwise participate in delinquency proceedings by reason of mental disease or defect.

C. Counsel for the juvenile bears primary responsibility for deciding whether the juvenile is mature or immature. If counsel believes the juvenile is immature, counsel should request the court to appoint a guardian ad litem for the juvenile.

D. A mature respondent should have the power to waive rights on his or her own behalf, in accordance with Standard 6.2. Subject to Standard 6.3, the rights of an immature respondent may be waived on his or her behalf by the guardian ad litem.

6.2 Waiver of the rights of mature respondents

A. A respondent considered by counsel to be mature should be permitted to act through counsel in the proceedings. However, the juvenile may not personally waive any right:

1. except in the presence of and after consultation with counsel; and

2. unless a parent has first been afforded a reasonable opportunity to consult with the juvenile and the juvenile's counsel regarding the decision. If the parent requires an interpreter for this purpose, the court should provide one.

B. The decision to waive a mature juvenile's privilege against self-incrimination; the right to be tried as a juvenile or as an adult where the respondent has that choice; the right to trial, with or without a jury; and the right to appeal or seek other post-adjudication relief should be made by the juvenile. Counsel may decide, after consulting with the juvenile, whether to waive other rights of the juvenile.

6.3 Waiver of the rights of immature respondents

A. A respondent considered by counsel to be immature should not be permitted to act through counsel, nor should a plea on behalf of an immature respondent admitting the allegations of the petition be accepted. The court may adjudicate an immature respondent delinquent only if the petition is proven at trial.

B. The decision to waive the following rights of an immature respondent should be made by the guardian ad litem, after consultation with the respondent and counsel: the privilege against self-incrimination; the right to be tried as a juvenile or as an adult, where the respondent has that choice; the right to a jury trial; and the right to appeal or seek other postadjudication relief. Subject to subsection A of this standard, other rights of an immature respondent should be waivable by counsel after consultation with the juvenile's guardian ad litem. . . .

The Role of Parents and Guardians ad Litem in the Delinquency
Proceedings

6.5 The role of parents

A. Except as provided in subsection B,

    1. the parent of a delinquency respondent should have the right to notice to be present, and to make representations to the court either pro se or through counsel at all stages of the proceedings;

    2. parents should be encouraged by counsel, the judge, and other officials to take an active interest in the juvenile's case. Their proper functions include consultation with the juvenile and the juvenile's counsel at all stages of the proceedings concerning decisions made by the juvenile or by counsel on the juvenile's behalf, presence at all hearings, and participation in the planning of dispositional alternatives. Subject to the consent of the mature juvenile, parents should have access to all records in the case. If the juvenile does not consent, the court should nevertheless grant the parent access to records if they are not otherwise privileged, and if the court determines, in camera, that disclosure is necessary to protect the parent's interests.

B. The court should have the power, in its discretion, to exclude or restrict the participation of a parent whose interests the court has determined are adverse to those of the respondent, if the court finds that the parent's presence or participation will adversely affect the interests of the respondent.

C. Parents should be provided with necessary interpreter services at all stages of the proceedings.

6.6 "Parent" defined

The term "parent" as used in this part includes:

A. the juvenile's natural or adoptive parents, unless their parental rights have been terminated;

B. if the juvenile is a ward of any person other than a parent, the guardian of the juvenile;

C. if the juvenile is in the custody of some person other than a parent, such custodian, unless the custodian's knowledge of or participation in the proceedings would be detrimental to the juvenile; and

D. separated and divorced parents, even if deprived by judicial decree of the respondent juvenile's custody.

6.7 Appointment of guardian ad litem

A. The court should appoint a guardian ad litem for a juvenile on the request of any party, a parent, or upon the court's own motion:

    1. if the juvenile is immature as defined in Standard 6.1 B.2;

    2. if no parent, guardian, or custodian appears with the juvenile;

    3. if a conflict of interest appears to exist between the juvenile and the parents; or

    4. if the juvenile's interests otherwise require it.

B. The appointment should be made at the earliest feasible time after it appears that representation by a guardian ad litem is necessary. At the time of appointment, the court should ensure that the guardian ad litem is advised of the responsibilities and powers contained in these standards.

C. The function of a guardian ad litem is to act toward the juvenile in the proceedings as would a concerned parent. If the juvenile is immature, the guardian ad litem should also instruct the juvenile's counsel in the conduct of the case, and may waive rights on behalf of the juvenile as provided in Standard 6.3. A guardian ad litem should have all the procedural rights accorded to parents under these standards.

D. The following persons should not be appointed as a guardian ad litem:

    1. the juvenile's parent, if the parent's interest and the juvenile's interest in the proceedings appear to conflict;

    2. the agent, counsel, or employee of a party to the proceedings, or of a public or private institution having custody or guardianship of the juvenile; and

    3. an employee of the court or of the intake agency.

E. Courts should experiment with the use of qualified and trained non-attorney guardians ad litem, recruited from concerned individuals and organizations in the community on a paid or volunteer basis.

6.8 The parent's right to counsel

A. A parent should receive notice of the right to counsel when he or she receives the petition or the summons and also, if the parent appears without counsel, at the start of all judicial hearings. The notice should state that the juvenile's counsel represents the juvenile rather than the parent, that if the parent wishes, he or she has a right to be advised and represented by his or her own counsel, to the extent permitted by Standard 6.5, and that a parent who is unable to pay for legal assistance may have it provided without cost.

B. A parent's counsel may be present at all delinquency proceedings but should have no greater right to participate than a parent does under Standard 6.5.

6.9 Appointment of counsel for parent unable to pay

A. The court should appoint counsel for a respondent's parent who does not waive that right and who is unable to obtain adequate representation without substantial hardship to the parent or family. . . .

6.10 Waiver of the parent's rights

A. Any right accorded to a parent by these standards or under federal, state or local law may be waived. A parent may effectively waive a right only if the parent is fully informed of the right and voluntarily and intelligently waives it. The failure of a parent who has the right to counsel to request counsel should not of itself be construed to constitute a waiver of that right.

---

a. Competence to Waive a Juvenile's Rights

Do you think it possible for a youth to "voluntarily, knowingly, and intelligently" waive a constitutional right? How likely is it that a 14-year-old, without parental advice or the advice of counsel, will know and understand his or her *Miranda* rights and the consequences of a waiver? Empirical studies suggest that while nearly all youths voluntarily waive their *Miranda* rights (in the sense of not having been coerced), a significant number fail to understand those rights and the consequences of a waiver.[77] Grisso summarizes his findings thus:

> [W]e saw in the study employing empirical measures of *Miranda* comprehension that about one-half of juveniles of ages 10-16 demonstrated inadequate understanding of at least one of the four *Miranda* warnings. Understanding of the *Miranda* warnings was significantly poorer among juveniles who were 14 years of age or younger than among 15-[to]16-year-old juveniles or adult offenders and nonoffenders. . . .
>
> Further deficiencies in juveniles' competence to waive rights were found in the study of their ability to understand the function and significance of the rights to silence and legal counsel. . . . Of special concern was that about one-third of the juveniles misperceived the intended nature of the attorney-client relationship. . . .[78]

[77] See A. Bruce Ferguson & Alan C. Douglas, A Study of Juvenile Waiver, 7 San Diego L. Rev. 39 (1970); Thomas Grisso, Juveniles' Waiver of Rights: Legal and Psychological Competence (1981); Richard A. Lawrence, The Role of Legal Counsel in Juveniles' Understanding of Their Rights, 34 Juv. & Fam. Ct.Q. J. 49 (1983-1984).

[78] Grisso, supra note [77], at 192.

If understanding of *Miranda* rights varies as a function of age, then Ferguson and Douglas' findings are illuminating: 96 percent of a sample of 14-year-olds failed to understand fully their *Miranda* rights and the consequences of a waiver.[79]

Should the court be required to assist a juvenile in understanding the consequences of a waiver in order for the waiver to be valid? Is the court under a greater responsibility to assist a juvenile in this regard than to assist an adult? See In re W.M.F., 349 S.E.2d 265 (Ga. Ct. App. 1986):

> [A]ppellant contends that she did not make a knowing and intelligent decision to proceed without counsel. We agree. Since the referee did not warn the appellant or her mother of the danger of proceeding without counsel or of the consequences of an affirmative finding or admission of the charge enumerated in the petition, we find that appellant and her mother did not stand before the court with open eyes, knowing the danger and consequences of proceeding without the benefit of legal representation. . . . This is reversible error.

See also In re Montrail M., 589 A.2d 1318 (Md. Ct. Spec. App. 1991) (court must admonish a juvenile who intends not to deny the state's allegations of the nature and possible consequences of such an action, even if the juvenile is represented by counsel).

Should evidence of previous occasions when a juvenile offender was given *Miranda* warnings be admissible to prove that the juvenile understood the *Miranda* warnings on the occasion in question? See State ex rel. Juvenile Dept. v. Charles, 779 P.2d 1075 (Or. Ct. App. 1989).

b. Applicable Standard

What standard should be applied to waivers by juveniles of such rights as the right to counsel and the right to remain silent? Should it be the standard articulated in *Miranda* — a knowing, intelligent, and voluntary waiver "under the totality of the circumstances"? Or, should it be another stricter standard — perhaps, a per se requirement that a juvenile waiver is invalid unless a parent or guardian is present and informed of the youth's rights? (Under the totality approach, the presence or absence of a parent or guardian is only one factor bearing on the validity of the juvenile's waiver.)

As explained above, the Supreme Court in Fare v. Michael C., 442 U.S. 707 (1979), adopted the "totality of the circumstances" test as the constitutional standard for determining the voluntariness of a juvenile waiver. The totality approach is currently employed in a majority of jurisdictions. Although the per se rule has received almost unanimous support from commentators,[80] it has been adopted in the form of "interested adult" rules in only a few jurisdictions.

[79] Ferguson & Douglas, supra note [77].

[80] See American Bar Association, Juvenile Justice Standards, Standards Relating to Counsel 98 (1980); Grisso, supra note [77], at 192; Paul Piersma et al., The Juvenile Court: Current Problems, Legislative Proposals, and a Model Act, 20 St. Louis U. L.J. 1, 30 (1975); President's Commission on Law Enforcement and Administration of Justice, Task Force Report: Juvenile Delinquency and Youth

Are there special reasons to apply the per se rule to mentally disabled juvenile suspects? See J.G. v. State, 883 So. 2d 915 (Fla. Ct. App. 2004) (holding that 13-year-old emotionally handicapped youth did not voluntarily waive his *Miranda* rights). See generally Kevin P. Weis, Note, Confessions of Mentally Retarded Juveniles and the Validity of *Miranda* Rights Waiver, 37 Brandeis L.J. 117 (1998-1999) (so arguing).

What constitutes a request for a parent to be present? In In re Shawn B.N., 497 N.W.2d 141 (Wis. Ct. App. 1992), a 13-year-old was accused of first-degree murder of a police officer. He was interrogated in a squad car by a policeman in plain clothes, who "removed Shawn's handcuffs, read him his *Miranda* rights and asked him if he understood." Id. at 148. The youth said that he did. When the waiver provisions were read to him, the youth did not reply, but assented in writing. In the course of the interrogation, Shawn asked whether he would ever be able to see his mother again. Subsequently, the appellate court, reasoning that Shawn had not asked to see his mother immediately, applied a totality of the circumstances test to hold that Shawn voluntarily waived his *Miranda* rights.

Should a parent or other interested adult be able to waive *Miranda* rights for the child? Compare In re Ewing, 350 S.E.2d 887 (N.C. Ct. App. 1986) ("[T]he finding that respondent's [a 10-year-old's] mother freely, understandingly, and knowingly waived respondent's juvenile rights is not equivalent to a finding that respondent knowingly and understandingly waived his rights.") with M.R. v. State, 605 N.E.2d 204, 207 (Ind. Ct. App. 1992) (although juvenile's mother brought him to the police station, she was considered merely "a loving parent, obviously concerned about her son and his future," without an interest adverse to the juvenile, and thus could lawfully waive the juvenile's constitutional rights).

Who may serve as an "interested adult"? Any relative, if the parents are unavailable? See Commonwealth v. Hogan, 688 N.E.2d 977 (Mass. 1998) (holding that grandmother could satisfy the role if both parents were unavailable). The Supreme Judicial Court of Massachusetts set forth a legal standard for determining whether the "interested-adult" standard was satisfied in Commonwealth v. Philip S., 611 N.E.2d 226 (Mass. 1993). The court explained that the situation must be viewed from the perspective of the officials conducting the interrogation as to whether the accompanying adult has the capacity to appreciate the situation and give advice or, instead, is antagonistic to the juvenile.

Does a parent's advice that the child confess interfere with a valid waiver? See Harden v. State, 576 N.E.2d 590 (Ind. 1991) (father's advice that son confess did not invalidate son's waiver).

With regard to waiver, is parental presence or concurrence an adequate safeguard? Two assumptions run through case law in terms of the value of parental presence: (1) parents' presence will be a mitigating force to reduce the likelihood of abusive coercion by officers or will reduce the pressures that are inherent in the status and power differences between the juvenile and the police, and (2) parents will be able to provide advice about matters that the juvenile may not be able to

---

Crime 24 (1967); Jan Kirby Byland, Comment, Louisiana Children's Code Article 808: A Positive Step on Behalf of Louisiana's Children, 52 La. L. Rev. 1141 (1992).

comprehend (such as waiver of constitutional rights and an understanding of the consequences of such waiver).[81] Are parents likely to be substantially more knowledgeable concerning the wisdom of waiver than the youth? Is it a safeguard at all when the parents want the child to plead guilty or confess? Consider the results of Grisso's study:

> The results of [our research] indicated that parents generally cannot be relied on to provide juveniles with explanations of the rights and their significance. In addition, a majority of the parents were negatively predisposed to juveniles' right to withhold information from police officers.
>
> In the discussion of these results, we concluded that the weight of the evidence from our studies clearly supported the [opinion] that "we cannot equate physical presence of a parent with meaningful representation." This conclusion has an important implication for judicial decisions concerning the validity of a juvenile's waiver of rights and the admissibility of a subsequent confession as evidence. Judges should not be influenced in their decisions by the mere fact that parents were present. They should weigh, in addition, the evidence concerning the parents' role in the preinterrogation waiver proceedings and evidence suggesting that the parents were or were not capable of providing the advice and protection which many juveniles need. Included in this deliberation should be a consideration of the parents' probable understanding of the rights and their potential significance, their attitudes toward these rights in juvenile cases, the parents' emotional and motivational states during the waiver proceedings, and the nature of the relationship between the parents and their child.[82]

See generally Kimberly Larson, Note, Improving the "Kangaroo Courts": A Proposal for Reform in Evaluating Juveniles' Waiver of *Miranda*, 48 Vill. L. Rev. 629 (2003) (suggesting that the law should reevaluate the safeguards afforded to juveniles during interrogations in order to take into account psychological research).

c. Incompetence as a Matter of Law

As mentioned above, virtually all courts treat age as one of several factors to be considered in analyzing a child's waiver. Should children below a certain age (what age?) *as a matter of law* be considered incapable of providing a knowing and intelligent waiver? Some state variations of the "per se" rule adopt this approach. Note how In re S.H., supra, and the ABA Standards deal with this question. On the basis of empirical research, Grisso concludes that special protections are necessary for youth aged 14 and younger. He writes:

> As a group, juveniles who were 14 years of age or younger consistently fell short of the research definitions of the legal standards for competence to waive rights. . . . We believe that the research results support the need for extraordinary protections

---

[81] Grisso, supra note [77], at 166.

[82] Id. at 199-200. See also Lawrence Schlam, Police Interrogation of Children and State Constitutions: Why Not Videotape the MTV Generation?, 26 U. Tol. L. Rev. 901, 919-921 (1995) (questioning protective functions of "interested adult" rule).

for juveniles at ages 14 and below. Legislation to provide blanket exclusion of confessions, or to provide automatically for effective counsel to these juveniles prior to police questioning, would afford the type of protection which our results suggest that these juveniles need.[83]

d. Mandatory Counsel

Is compliance with *Miranda* adequate to ensure that the juvenile has made a free and informed choice, particularly when the youth has waived counsel? Or when a confession in violation of *Miranda* is used for dispositional purposes alone? Should consultation with an attorney be a prerequisite to a valid waiver by a juvenile? Consider the following:

> If youths are considered more susceptible to pressure when the question is the voluntariness of a confession, then why does this conception not carry over to *Miranda* issues with the result, for example, that a juvenile may not waive the right to counsel unless first advised by counsel? Moreover, if it is important that juveniles act voluntarily and with knowledge of the possibly adverse consequences of giving preadjudication information, then why is it not equally important that the juvenile act similarly when giving information relevant to disposition? After adjudication, however, juveniles not only have no protection regarding interrogation relating to disposition — even questioning as to unadjudicated offenses — it is expected that they will cooperate. Given the fact that such information can influence the disposition, the juvenile's full awareness of the consequences must be equally important at this stage.[84]

Various commentators, as well as the ABA Standards, have recommended that the juvenile's right to counsel be nonwaivable.[85] Grisso, on the basis of his empirical research, concluded that the right to counsel be nonwaivable for some juveniles: "[c]ompared with that of adults, the comprehension of [the *Miranda*] rights of younger juveniles is so deficient as to mandate a per se exclusion of waivers made without legal counsel by these juveniles."[86] Few states go so far. However, some states insist on additional safeguards for a juvenile's waiver of the right to counsel. See, e.g., Ark. Code Ann. §9-27-317 (Michie 2003) (providing that juvenile's waiver of the right to counsel be accepted only if knowing and voluntary *and* the parent has agreed with the child's waiver of the right to counsel); Tex. Fam. Code Ann. §51.09 (Vernon 2005) (providing that waiver of right to counsel must be made ordinarily by the child and the attorney for the child).

[83] Grisso, supra note [77], at 202.
[84] J. Lawrence Schultz & Fred Cohen, Isolationism in Juvenile Court Jurisprudence, in Pursuing Justice for the Child 20, 26 (Margaret Kenney Rosenheim ed., 1976).
[85] See authorities cited supra note [77].
[86] Thomas Grisso, Juveniles' Capacities to Waive *Miranda* Rights: An Empirical Analysis, 68 Cal. L. Rev. 1134, 1166 (1980).

E.   THE ROLE OF THE LAWYER IN THE JUVENILE COURT PROCESS[87]

Is the role of a lawyer representing a juvenile accused of a delinquent act identical to that of a lawyer representing an adult accused of a crime? In an adult criminal proceeding, once the case is accepted by a lawyer, it is the attorney's responsibility "regardless of his personal opinion as to the guilt of the accused, . . . to invoke the basic rule that the crime must be proved beyond a reasonable doubt by competent evidence, to raise all valid defenses and, in the case of conviction, to present all proper grounds for probation or mitigation of punishment."[88] The lawyer is, of course, an "officer of the court." This imposes a duty of "candor and fairness," but it is generally assumed that the criminal defense attorney's responsibility to the client is in no way inconsistent with responsibility as an "officer of the court." The lawyer need not provide information suggesting the guilt of his client to the court and indeed is generally thought to have a duty to obtain an acquittal for the client, using all means short of fraud on the justice system. Is a juvenile delinquent proceeding any different?

Three issues are particularly important: (1) Do the possible inexperience and immaturity of the minor inevitably and appropriately require the lawyer to have a different role? (2) Should the often stated (if now somewhat tarnished) rehabilitative goal of the juvenile proceeding affect the lawyer's role? (3) What peculiar problems are created for the lawyer representing a juvenile client by reason of the child's parents and their desires for the child? The problem that follows offers an opportunity to explore these issues. Various perspectives are found in the subsequent materials.

PROBLEM

A delinquency petition has been filed against 16-year-old Ted Blanda, accusing him of armed robbery arising from a holdup of a gift shop. The only evidence against Ted consists of his identification by the shop owner. Based on a preliminary and incomplete description, the police arrested Ted and put him in a lineup, where he was identified by the victim. The lineup took place under circumstances that would violate the Supreme Court's decision in United States v. Wade, 388 U.S. 218 (1967), and Kirby v. Illinois, 406 U.S. 682 (1972), because it took place after a delinquency petition had been filed against Ted, and yet there had been no counsel present at

---

[87] See generally Mary Berkheiser, The Fiction of Juvenile Right to Counsel: Waiver in the Juvenile Courts, 54 Fla. L. Rev. 577 (2002); N. Lee Cooper et al., Fulfilling the Promise of In re Gault: Advancing the Role of Lawyers for Children, 33 Wake Forest L. Rev. 651 (1998); Jim Lewis, The Aftermath of the Lionel Tate Case: A Child and a Choice, 28 Nova L. Rev. 479 (2004) (discussing the attorney's role in representing a juvenile murder defendant who is offered a plea bargain); Robert E. Shepherd, Jr., Still Seeking the Promise of *Gault*: Juveniles and the Right to Counsel, 18 Crim. Just. 23 (Summer 2003); Suzanne M. Bookser, Comment, Making *Gault* Meaningful: Access to Counsel and Quality of Representation in Delinquency Proceedings for Indigent Youth, 3 Whittier J. Child & Fam. Advoc. 297 (2004).

[88] American College of Trial Lawyers, A Code of Trial Conduct, 36 N.D. L. Rev. 175, 176 (1960).

the lineup. While it appears likely that you will be able to exclude from evidence the lineup identification of the youth by the victim, the victim will nevertheless make an in-court identification. That testimony will be admissible so long as it is shown to be based on a recollection independent of the tainted lineup identification. Because the complaining witness is old and rather easily confused, however, it is your judgment that by very vigorous cross-examination, the victim's credibility might be sufficiently impeached to avoid an adjudication of delinquency.

While Ted has made no statement to the police, he did admit to you that he committed the offense. During your initial interview with Ted, he told you that he hates juvenile hall (where he has been detained for three weeks since his arrest) and that he is going crazy being locked up. He suggested that what he cares most about is being with his friends on the street.

From police records, you learn that Ted has been arrested 11 times before, mostly for purse snatching, petty theft, and minor property crimes. On nine of these occasions no juvenile court petition was filed. In the other two, a delinquency petition was filed and sustained, but Ted was put on probation. He lives with his mother, who is an alcoholic, in a chaotic home situation. His father is unknown. Neither the youth nor his 14-year-old brother nor 18-year-old sister go to school or work. Their three-room apartment is badly overcrowded and filthy, and the youth spends all his time on the street. When you interview the youth's mother, she tells you that the boy is a "pain in the ass" and that she wishes he would be "locked up" somewhere to get him out of her hair.

On further inquiry you learn that before Ted dropped out of school at age 15, his academic performance had been very bad. He tells you that because of headaches he was unable to concentrate in class. He suggests that he has had episodic ringing in his ears for the last two years. The probation report relating to one of his earlier arrests indicates that his performance on an I.Q. test was about 85 and that a psychiatric examination made six months ago had suggested that he had serious, but undefined emotional difficulties. The school district has no special program for a 16-year-old boy with your client's difficulties.

(1) Under the circumstances of this case, once your client tells you that he does not want to be adjudicated a delinquent but instead wants to go back to the street, must you pursue that goal? Suppose that it is your honest opinion that Ted might be better off if the court took jurisdiction, provided he were sent to a particular juvenile "ranch," where he would receive reasonable medical attention, live in a more structured environment, and possibly benefit from an educational program aimed at youth with severe reading difficulties.

(2) Do you have the responsibility to express to Ted what you think is best for him? To try to persuade him to your view? If he disagrees, should you resign from the case? May you act on what you believe is best for him despite his wishes? What are your social responsibilities? Suppose that you also believe that the juvenile's conduct has become increasingly violent and that it is probable that if he is sent back home, he will commit a more serious crime. Is this hunch relevant? Are your responsibilities different during the adjudicatory stage, as opposed to the dispositional stage of the proceedings?

(3) Suppose Ted's mother asks you whether Ted in fact robbed the shop. May you tell her that Ted confessed to you?

DISCUSSION

The *Gault* decision, supra p. 782, extended the Sixth Amendment guarantee of counsel to the delinquent juvenile. *Gault* mandated representation at the adjudicatory stage of a delinquency proceeding in which the juvenile faces a penalty of possible confinement in a juvenile institution. Although most states have now codified *Gault*'s guarantee of legal counsel,[89] empirical research suggests that a high percentage of juveniles charged with crimes still are not represented.[90]

Several questions arise in the wake of *Gault*. First, does the right to counsel attach at other stages in the proceedings? If not, should it? Second, does the presence of parents affect the right to counsel? And third, what should be the appropriate role of counsel for the minor in the delinquency proceeding?

(1) Stage at Which Right to Counsel Attaches.   *Gault* clearly specified that the right to counsel attaches only at that stage in the proceedings in which "a determination is made as to whether a juvenile is a 'delinquent' " [387 U.S. at 13]. The Court said, "we are not here concerned with the procedures or constitutional rights applicable to the pre-judicial stages of the juvenile process, nor do we direct our attention to the post-adjudicative or disposition process." Id. Nevertheless, many states have expanded the right to counsel beyond that contemplated by *Gault*. Legislation in these states typically directs that the right to counsel attaches at "every stage of the proceedings."[91] See, for instance, Cal. Welf. & Inst. Code §633 (West 2004). The Juvenile Delinquency Act, 18 U.S.C. §5034 (2000), requires counsel at "critical stages" of the proceedings. These statutes leave open the question of whether the right attaches, for example, during a custodial interrogation by the police (including the lineup in the Introductory Problem) and at an intake hearing.

According to the ABA Standards, the right should attach "as soon as the juvenile is taken into custody by an agent of the state, when a petition is filed against the juvenile, or when the juvenile appears personally at an intake conference, whichever comes first."[92] The Commentary to the Standards suggests that mandatory representation is necessary to protect the juvenile and to assist the court in handling cases efficiently. Early representation is intended to "relieve pressures on overcrowded detention facilities by speeding the release of juveniles whose continued incarceration there is unnecessary."[93] The Standards also require prompt communication to the juvenile of the right to counsel. They provide that as soon as the right to counsel attaches, authorities should advise the juvenile of the right and that counsel will be

---

[89] Andrea L. Martin, Note, Balancing State Budgets at a Cost to Fairness in Delinquency Proceedings, 88 Minn. L. Rev. 1638, 1645 (2004).

[90] See, e.g., Barry C. Feld, The Right to Counsel in Juvenile Court: An Empirical Study of When Lawyers Appear and the Difference They Make, 79 J. Crim. L. Criminology 1185, 1220 (1989) (reporting on the findings of a study of 17,195 juvenile delinquents and status offenders in Minnesota: "only 45.3% of juveniles in the state have lawyers").

[91] See Tory J. Caeti et al., Juvenile Right to Counsel: A National Comparison of State Legal Codes, 23 Am. J. Crim. L. 611, 628 (1996) (19 states include a statutory requirement that a juvenile has the right to counsel at "all stages" or "every stage" of the proceedings against them).

[92] American Bar Association, Juvenile Justice Standards: Standards Relating to Pretrial Court Proceedings, Rule 5.1, 89 (1990).

[93] Id. at 94.

retained if he or she, or the parents, are unable to pay. Notification should be in the juvenile's dominant language and, if necessary, an interpreter's services should be used to convey this message.[94]

A few jurisdictions significantly expand on *Gault*'s requirements. Courts in these jurisdictions have held that the right to counsel continues through various postadjudicative proceedings (e.g., restitution hearings, sentencing). One study of the right to counsel for juveniles concludes that (a) the right to counsel at intake is a rarity; (b) the right to counsel at detention hearings is becoming more widespread; (c) in most jurisdictions assigned counsel represents the child at both the adjudicatory and dispositional hearings; (d) few jurisdictions grant counsel at juvenile probation revocation proceedings; (e) few states assign counsel at placement review proceedings; and (f) many states fail to recognize a right to appointed counsel on appeal for juveniles. Ellen Marrus, Best Interests Equals Zealous Advocacy: A Not So Radical View of Holistic Representation for Children Accused of Crime, 62 Md. L. Rev. 288, 303-312 (2003).

(2) Parental Right. What effect does the presence of parents have? Do parents have a separate right to counsel? *Gault* specified that "the child and his parents must be notified of the *child's right* to be represented by counsel . . . . " 387 U.S. at 41 (emphasis added). This implies that the right to counsel is personal to the child. However, a few statutes do confer this right on parents. See, for example, Ill. Comp. Ann. Stat. ¶405/1-5(1) (West 2004). More often, statutes fail to address this issue. Statutes stating that a "party" to the proceeding is entitled to representation, e.g., N.D. Cent. Code §27-20-26 (2003), leave open the question as to whether representation is permitted for parents as well. See, e.g., In re L.A.J., 495 N.W.2d 128 (Iowa Ct. App. 1992) (examining legislative history of relevant statute and holding that parents do not have a right to counsel in delinquency proceedings).

The fact that parents are involved raises perplexing issues concerning payment of counsel fees. For adults to have court-appointed counsel, the defendant must be financially unable to retain counsel. When the client is a juvenile, the issue becomes more complicated. The Commentary to the ABA Standards raises several questions: Whose financial resources should be considered in evaluating a juvenile's eligibility — the juvenile's or the parents? If counsel is appointed, should the parent or juvenile be liable to reimburse the court for the costs? Suppose the parents are financially able to retain counsel but refuse to do so. Should the court appoint counsel and declare the parents liable to reimburse the court for the costs thereof?[95]

Finally, imagine a parent is financially able to and does retain counsel for the juvenile but that subsequently the parent's interests conflict with the

---

[94] Id. at 95.

[95] Juvenile Justice Standards, supra note [92], at 96. See State ex rel. Gordon v. Copeland, 803 S.W.2d 153 (Mo. Ct. App. 1991) (child is indigent if he has no funds, even though his parents may have funds; courts cannot require parents to hire a lawyer, and if parents in fact do not hire a lawyer, child is entitled to public defender). But see Fla. Stat. Ann. §938.29(2)(a)(2) (West 1997) (authorizing a lien to be entered against the parent of a minor who has been represented by a public defender). However, notice of the lien and an opportunity to contest it may be required. See Buiey v. State, 583 So. 2d 384 (Fla. Dist. Ct. App. 1991); In re L.A.D., 616 So. 2d 106 (Fla. Dist. Ct. App. 1993).

juvenile's interests. Since the parent is paying, to whom does counsel have a duty?[96]

(3) Appropriate Role for Counsel.   Although *Gault* extended a fundamental protection to juveniles in delinquency proceedings, it did not elaborate on the appropriate role for counsel in those proceedings. Three alternative models have been suggested for counsel: (a) the role of guardian, (b) the role of amicus curiae, and (c) the role of advocate. What duties do these roles encompass? Which role do you think is appropriate for the attorney representing a juvenile client accused of a criminal act?

The Commentary to the ABA Standards, infra p. 858, defines the roles of guardian and amicus curiae and also rejects those roles in favor of the role of advocate. On what basis does the Commentary reject those roles? Do you agree that the role of advocate is appropriate in light of the inexperience and immaturity of the client? In your determination, consider carefully the responsibilities of an advocate, especially taking into account the ABA Model Code of Professional Responsibility and the ABA Model Rules of Professional Conduct (infra pp. 857-858). The ABA House of Delegates adopted the Model Code of Professional Responsibility in 1969, and subsequently, in 1983, adopted the more recent statement of professional standards, the Model Rules of Professional Conduct. Currently, most jurisdictions follow the recent Model Rules; however, some jurisdictions still follow the earlier Model Code. How do the ABA's ethical responsibilities apply when the client is a minor?

The Code of Professional Responsibility dictates generally in Canon 7 that "a lawyer should represent a client zealously within the bounds of the law." American Bar Association, Code of Professional Responsibility 32 (1978). Two ethical considerations (EC 7-11 and EC 7-12) suggest that a lawyer has special responsibilities when the client is not fully competent.

ABA, Model Code of Professional Responsibility (1978)

EC 7-11

The responsibilities of a lawyer may vary according to the intelligence, experience, mental condition or age of a client, the obligation of a public officer, or the nature of a particular proceeding. Examples include the representation of an illiterate or an incompetent, service as a public prosecutor or other government lawyer, and appearances before administrative and legislative bodies.

EC 7-12

Any mental or physical condition of a client that renders him incapable of making a considered judgment on his own behalf casts additional responsibilities upon his lawyer. Where an incompetent is acting through a guardian or other legal

---

[96] Juvenile Justice Standards, Standard 5.3C, supra note [92], at 95.

representative, a lawyer must look to such representative for those decisions which are normally the prerogative of the client to make. If a client under disability has no legal representative, his lawyer may be compelled in court proceedings to make decisions on behalf of his client. If the client is capable of understanding the matter in question or of contributing to the advancement of his interests, regardless of whether he is legally disqualified from performing certain acts, the lawyer should obtain from him all possible aid. If the disability of a client and the lack of a legal representative compel the lawyer to make decisions for his client, the lawyer should consider all circumstances then prevailing and act with care to safeguard and advance the interests of his client. But obviously a lawyer cannot perform any act or make any decision which the law requires his client to perform or make, either acting for himself if competent, or by a duly constituted representative if legally incompetent.

Note that under EC 7-11, the responsibilities "may vary according to the intelligence, experience, mental condition or age of a client, . . . or the nature of a particular proceeding." Indeed, EC 7-12 suggests that the attorney may at times "be compelled in court proceedings to make decisions on behalf of the client"; EC 7-12 rather unhelpfully indicates that when the lawyer must act in behalf of the client, the lawyer should "consider all circumstances" and act to "safeguard and advance the interests of his client." How should a lawyer go about deciding whether the client's age, experience, or mental condition is such as to require broader and more active responsibility? Moreover, in such cases, how does the lawyer define the interests of the client? By what standards? Normally the lawyer asks the client what his or her interests are. Is this sufficient when the client is a juvenile?

ABA, Annotated Model Rules of Professional Conduct 215 (3d ed. 1996)

Client Under a Disability

Rule 1.14

(a) When a client's ability to make adequately considered decisions in connection with the representation is impaired, whether because of minority, mental disability or some other reason, the lawyer shall, as far as reasonably possible, maintain a normal client-lawyer relationship with the client. . . .

How is a lawyer supposed to "maintain a normal client-lawyer relationship" with a child? How is representation of a minor similar to that of a mentally disabled person? How is it different?

ABA, Institute of Judicial Administration, Juvenile Justice Standards, Standards Relating to Counsel for Private Parties 1-9 (1980)

Juvenile Representation and the Principle of Advocacy

There has always been sharp controversy regarding the propriety and role of counsel in juvenile court proceedings. Traditionally, cases involving children were considered "nonadversarial" with respect to both the relationship of the parties and the forms of procedure employed. The child's interest in the proceeding was assumed to be identical with that of the state, which claimed to seek only the child's welfare and not his or her punishment. There did not exist, accordingly, that adversity of interest among the parties which characterizes other civil or criminal proceedings. Given this premise, modes of trial and methods of protecting legal rights designed for cases involving frankly conflicting interests seemed inappropriate. Juvenile hearings were viewed not as a contentious process but as a therapeutic one. Informality and direct communication between judge and child replaced demonstration by ordinary rules of procedure and evidence as vehicles for eliciting needed information concerning the child's circumstances and, as well, for imparting to children, or sometimes their parents, a sense of social responsibility.

It is not surprising that, in such a forum, legal representation was thought unnecessary and even undesirable . . . Broad recognition of the importance of representation was not achieved until the Supreme Court in In re Gault, 387 U.S. 1 (1967), held it a matter of constitutional right for delinquency proceedings.

With *Gault*, however, expressions of good intention and references to parens patriae could no longer justify denial of access to counsel to juveniles. Legal assistance was necessary, the Court held, to allow the respondent to "cope with problems of law, to make skilled inquiry into the facts, to insist upon regularity of the proceedings, and to ascertain whether he has a defense and to prepare and submit it." No less than an adult faced with felony charges, "The child requires the guiding hand of counsel at every stage in the proceedings against him." Id. at 36. *Gault* thereby established the importance of legal representation in delinquency matters, while at the same time extending to juvenile respondents the privilege against self-incrimination and rights to notice of charges and confrontation of witnesses. The case did not, however, entirely clarify the nature of juvenile court proceedings nor the role of counsel participating in them. . . .

The post-*Gault* effort to accommodate traditional juvenile court theory and the requirement of counsel resulted, for some, in a fundamental redefinition of counsel's function. Many have suggested that attorneys for children abandon the sharply defined role of the advocate for a "guardianship" theory of representation. As a "guardian," counsel is primarily concerned with ascertaining and presenting the plea and program best calculated to serve the child's perceived welfare. E.g., Isaacs, The Role of Counsel in Representing Minors in the New Family Court, 12 Buffalo L. Rev. 501, 506-507 (1963). Others have urged an "amicus curiae" function, in which counsel acts largely as an intermediary between the participants and explains the significance of proceedings to the client. See Cayton, Relationship of the Probation Officer and the Defense Attorney After *Gault*, 34 Fed. Prob. 8, 10 (1970). See also Skoler & Tenney, Attorney Representation in Juvenile Court, 4 J. Fam. L. 77 (1964); [W. Stapleton & L. Teitelbaum, In Defense of Youth: A Study of the Role of Counsel in American Juvenile Courts 64-65 (1972).] It is apparent that both guardianship and amicus curiae approaches involved radical modification of the rules governing a lawyer's professional role. At the very least, either approach places on counsel responsibility for decisions ordinarily allocated to the client. For example, whether to admit or contest the charges may become a matter to be determined by the attorney, perhaps in consultation with probation staff and parents, rather than by the respondent. E.g., Edelstein, The Duties and Functions of the Law Guardian in the Family Court, 45 N.Y.S.B.J. 183, 184 (1973). Either of these approaches may also shift from client to counsel responsibility for the exercise of the privilege against self-incrimination, as suggested by the statement, "A sensitive lawyer, like a sensitive judge or a sensitive social worker, knows when confession is good for the soul." Coxe, Lawyers in Juvenile Court, 13 Crime & Delinq. 488, 490 (1967). Moreover, a lawyer who seeks to block presentation of complete and accurate information to the court through, for example, a motion to suppress illegally obtained evidence might be accused by proponents of this redefined role of frustrating the court's proper functioning. See Kay & Segal, The Role of the Attorney in Juvenile Court: A Non-Polar Approach, 61 Geo. L.J. 1401, 1412-1413 (1973). It has further been suggested that counsel is affirmatively required to disclose any information, including that derived from a confidential communication, which bears on the child's need for treatment. See NCCD, Procedure and Evidence in Juvenile Court 43 (1962); Steinfeldt, Kerper & Friel, The Impact of the *Gault* Decision in Texas, 20 Juv. Ct. Judges J. 154 (1969).

The standards set forth in this volume generally reject both guardianship and amicus curiae definitions of counsel's role and require instead that attorneys in juvenile court assume those responsibilities for advocacy and counseling which obtain in other areas of legal representation. Accordingly, counsel's principal function is a derivative one; it lies in furthering the "lawful objectives of his client through all reasonably available means permitted by law." ABA, Code of Professional Responsibility DR 7-101(A). Generally, determination of those objectives — whether to admit or deny, to press or abandon a claim, and the like — is the responsibility of the client whose interests will be affected by the proceeding. Attorneys may urge one course or another, but may not properly arrogate the final decision to themselves. Id. at EC 7-7, 7-8. Once the objective has been chosen by the client, the lawyer is bound by that choice, and must take care to conduct all phases of his or her professional activity, even those largely committed to counsel's discretion, in a manner consistent with the client's instructions in the matter. Id. at EC 7-9.

Reliance on the generally accepted standards of professional conduct in legal representation is justified and indeed demanded by the purposes for which those standards were created. The lawyer's role is defined by a set of rules for behavior which are thought desirable because they advance certain fundamental values or goals of the legal process. These goals are generally shared, with some variations, by all elements of the American justice system, including that of the juvenile court. . . .

The Relevance of the Client's Youth

It has sometimes been suggested that all or most of a juvenile court lawyer's clientele is not sufficiently mature to instruct counsel in any usual sense and that counsel must, therefore, usually act as guardian or amicus curiae. The proponents of this view often tend, however, to equate competence with capacity to weigh accurately all immediate and remote benefits or costs associated with the available options. In representing adults, wisdom of this kind is not required; it is ordinarily sufficient that clients understand the nature and purposes of the proceedings, and its general consequences, and be able to formulate their desires concerning the proceeding with some degree of clarity. Most adolescents can meet this standard, and more ought not be required of them. To do so would, in effect, reintroduce the identification of state and child by imposing on respondents an "objective" definition of their interests.

It is, of course, true that "the responsibilities of a lawyer may vary according to the intelligence, experience, mental condition or age of a client . . . or the nature of the particular proceeding." ABA, Code of Professional Responsibility EC 7-11. Attorneys will sometimes be required, by reason of their clients' youth and inexperience, to take special pains in explaining the nature and potential results of the action and to investigate formal and informal dispositional alternatives in their clients' interests. See, e.g., §§6.2, 8.1 and 9.3, infra. And, particularly where counsel represents a very young client (ordinarily but not always in connection with a child protection, custody or adoption matter), it will in some cases happen that the client is incapable of rational consideration regarding the proceeding. Where this is true, attorneys may be required to abandon their role as advocate. See §3.1(b), infra. However, the occasions for doing so are rare — particularly in delinquency and supervision cases — and may not properly be extended through manipulation of the general standard for competence.

The Lawyer as Counselor

Adoption of an advocacy role for purposes of juvenile court proceedings does not imply that lawyers should limit their concern or activity to the legal requirements of those proceedings. They not only may, but ordinarily should, be prepared to assume responsibility for counseling the client and, in some cases, the client's family with respect to legal and nonlegal matters independent of pending or contemplated litigation. The existence of such a role for an attorney has long been recognized in a variety of kinds of practice [e.g., commercial law, tax counseling and family law].

Recognition of the attorney's function as counselor seems particularly appropriate for juvenile court representation. In most instances, neither clients nor their families will be familiar with the juvenile court or its procedures, goals and powers. It will, ordinarily, fall to the lawyer to understand and allay their spoken and unspoken fears about the situation in which they find themselves. In addition to his or her capacity as interpreter of specific procedures and rules, the attorney may also become "the first law figure who has performed a helpful function" for the client. Paulsen, The Expanding Horizons of Legal Services: II, 67 W. Va. L. Rev. 267, 276 (1965). As such, counsel has a unique opportunity to explain legal and social propositions in an acceptable fashion to clients whose feelings are often colored by hostility to authoritarian figures and rules. Counsel should also attempt to ascertain whether nonlegal services are needed by the client and the client's family and to assist them in taking advantage of such services if they are available. Performance of these duties will not, it should be emphasized, involve compromise of the obligation to advocate the client's interests before the court, so long as the distinction between counseling and ultimate determination of interest in the matter is observed. See ABA, Code of Professional Responsibility EC 7-3.

Following *Gault*, several studies highlighted various shortcomings in the quality of representation for juvenile offenders (see discussion supra p. 852 note [87]). Congress addressed some of these concerns when it reauthorized the Juvenile Justice and Delinquency Prevention Act in 1992 by authorizing the Office of Juvenile Justice and Delinquency Prevention to fund a project to improve representation in delinquency proceedings. The ensuing report of the ABA Juvenile Justice Center called for representation by competent counsel who was knowledgeable about juvenile justice issues for every child accused of a crime. See ABA Juvenile Justice Center, A Call for Justice: An Assessment of Access to Counsel and Quality of Representation in Delinquency Proceedings (Dec. 1995). The report not only uncovered evidence of inadequate representation (e.g., frequent waiver of the right to counsel, high caseloads, inexperienced advocates, lack of representation before detention, scant pretrial preparation, rare appeals, and infrequent resort to other postdispositional remedies), but also made recommendations to improve the quality of legal services. Following that report, the ABA Juvenile Justice Center conducted additional state assessments of legal services to delinquents.

Subsequently, the ABA Juvenile Justice Center helped create the National Juvenile Defender Center (NJDC) in 1999 to improve the quality of representation for children in the justice system. NJDC separated from the American Bar Association in 2005 and became an independent organization. NJDC provides services to public defenders, appointed counsel, law school clinical programs and nonprofit law centers in urban, suburban, rural, and tribal areas. The organization offers services such as training, technical assistance, advocacy, and networking. NJDC also publishes reports, training guides, and practice-oriented fact sheets.

One commentator describes the impact of NJDC by pointing to their vision statement:

[NJDC's Web site] vision statement says:

> The National Juvenile Defender Center works to create an environment in which: children are treated with respect, dignity and fairness; juvenile courts are knowledgeable, sensitive and responsive to the needs of children; excellence is routine in juvenile defense; juvenile defenders have the capacity to fully protect children's rights, including adequate resources and compensation, manageable caseloads, and sufficient access to investigation, expert and other ancillary and administrative support; juvenile defenders have resources and pay parity with juvenile prosecutors; the representation of children is specialized and adequate opportunities exist for juvenile defenders to fully exercise and enhance their legal, political, organizational, research and advocacy skills. [See *www.abanet.org/crimjust/juvjus/jdc.html.*]

These statements clearly reinforce what the American Bar Association articulated more than two decades earlier in the IJA-ABA Juvenile Justice Standards on
Counsel for Private Parties.

> . . . [L]egal services in the juvenile courts must be backed up with interdis-
> ciplinary support services and particularized training in youth development and
> juvenile law, among other more generic trial advocacy and negotiation skills. There
> must be lower caseloads to allow for earlier representation of juveniles at deten-
> tion hearings and, in some instances, during intake, and to allow for more time to
> develop a well-thought-out dispositional plan, perhaps in conjunction with a dis-
> positional specialist. Attorneys need to spend more time with their youthful clients
> developing trust and simply explaining the legal process in developmentally appro-
> priate terms. The lawyer in juvenile court needs to develop expertise in the range
> of educational and mental health disabilities of young people, and the laws that
> define the special rights of those who are so disabled. These skills delineated are
> just the tip of the iceberg, but they may serve to illustrate that keeping the promise
> of *Gault* may go well beyond simply heeding the clarion call of *Gideon.* [Robert
> E. Shepherd, Jr., Still Seeking the Promise of *Gault*: Juveniles and the Right to
> Counsel, 18 Crim. Just. 23, 27 (2003).]

F.   THE FUTURE OF THE JUVENILE COURT

A heated debate concerning the future of the juvenile court has been in progress
for a number of years and has recently intensified.[97] The debate takes on added
significance at the hundredth anniversary of the juvenile court. Some commentators
argue for the abolition of the juvenile court. Consider the following excerpt in light
of the materials, supra, on the purposes of the juvenile justice system and the
procedural differences between the adult and juvenile justice systems.

Barry C. Feld, The Transformation of the Juvenile Court
75 Minn. L. Rev. 691, 723-724 (1991) (citations omitted)

. . . As juvenile courts converge procedurally and substantively with criminal
courts, is there any reason to maintain a separate court whose only distinctions are
procedures under which no adult would agree to be tried?

The juvenile court is at a philosophical crossroads that cannot be resolved
by simplistic formulations, such as treatment versus punishment. In reality, there
are no practical or operational differences between the two. Acknowledging that
juvenile courts punish, imposes an obligation to provide all criminal procedural

---

[97] See, e.g., Janet E. Ainsworth, Re-Imagining Childhood and Reconstructing the Legal Order:
The Case for Abolishing the Juvenile Court, 69 N.C. L. Rev. 1083 (1991); Barry C. Feld, The Juvenile
Court Meets the Principle of Offense: Punishment, Treatment, and the Difference It Makes, 68 B.U.
L. Rev. 821 (1988); Barry C. Feld, The Transformation of the Juvenile Court, 75 Minn. L. Rev. 691
(1991); Katherine Hunt Federle, The Abolition of the Juvenile Court: A Proposal for the Preservation
of Children's Legal Rights, 16 J. Contemp. L. 23 (1990); Irene Merker Rosenberg, Leaving Bad
Enough Alone: A Response to the Juvenile Court Abolitionists, 1993 Wis. L. Rev. 164.

safeguards because, in the words of *Gault*, "the condition of being a boy does not justify a kangaroo court." [387 U.S. 1, 28 (1967).] While procedural parity with adults may sound the death-knell of the juvenile court, to fail to do so perpetuates injustice. To treat similarly situated juveniles differently, to punish them in the name of treatment, and to deny them basic safeguards fosters a sense of injustice that thwarts any efforts to rehabilitate. Abolishing juvenile courts is desirable both for youths and society. After more than two decades of constitutional and legislative reform, juvenile courts continue to deflect, co-opt, ignore, or absorb ameliorative tinkering with minimal institutional change. Despite its transformation from a welfare agency to a criminal court, the juvenile court remains essentially unreformed. The quality of justice youths receive would be intolerable if it were adults facing incarceration. Public and political concerns about drugs and youth crime foster a "get tough" mentality to repress rather than rehabilitate young offenders. With fiscal constraints, budget deficits, and competition from other interest groups, there is little likelihood that treatment services for delinquents will expand. Coupling the emergence of punitive policies with our societal unwillingness to provide for the welfare of children in general, much less to those who commit crimes, there is simply no reason to believe that the juvenile court can be rehabilitated.

Without a juvenile court, an adult criminal court that administers justice for young offenders could provide children with all the procedural guarantees already available to adult defendants and additional enhanced protections because of the children's vulnerability and immaturity. The only virtue of the contemporary juvenile court is that juveniles convicted of serious crimes receive shorter sentences than do adults. Youthfulness, however, long has been recognized as a mitigating, even if not an excusing, condition at sentencing. The common law's infancy defense presumed that children below age fourteen lacked criminal capacity, emphasized their lack of fault, and made youthful irresponsibility explicit. Youths older than fourteen are mature enough to be responsible for their behavior, but immature enough as to not deserve punishment commensurate with adults. If shorter sentences for diminished responsibility is the rationale for punitive juvenile courts, then providing an explicit "youth discount" to reduce adult sentences can ensure an intermediate level of just punishment. Reduced adult sentences do not require young people to be incarcerated with adults; existing juvenile prisons allow the segregation of offenders by age.

Full procedural parity in criminal courts coupled with mechanisms to expunge records, restore civil rights, and the like can more adequately protect young people than does the current juvenile court. Abolishing juvenile courts, however, should not gloss over the many deficiencies of criminal courts such as excessive case loads, insufficient sentencing options, ineffective representation, and over-reliance on plea bargains. These are characteristics of juvenile courts as well. . . .

See also Barry C. Feld, Abolish the Juvenile Court: Youthfulness, Criminal Responsibility, and Sentencing Policy, 88 J. Crim. L. & Criminology 68, 96-136 (1997) (proposing abolishment of juvenile court and formal recognition of "youthfulness" as a mitigating factor in criminal sentencing, thus affording juveniles the same procedural protections and recognition of responsibility as adult defendants). Compare Irene Merker Rosenberg, Leaving Bad Enough Alone: A Response to Juvenile Court Abolitionists, 1993 Wis. L. Rev. 164, 183 ("if children are tried as adults, and convicted, they presumably will be subject to the jurisdiction of adult correctional authorities rather than youth services agencies, which are at least to some extent child-oriented").

How persuasive do you find Professor Feld's arguments? For additional proposals for reform of the juvenile court, see Thomas F. Geraghty, Justice for Children: How Do We Get There?, 88 J. Crim. L. & Criminology 190, 235-241 (1997) (arguing for retention of the current "child-centered" juvenile court system, but recommending greater financial and human resources to meet the changing needs of children); Gary B. Melton, Taking *Gault* Seriously: Toward a New Juvenile Court, 68 Neb. L. Rev. 146, 150 (1989) (arguing that the juvenile court should be maintained but noting that *"Gault* and its progeny, when examined in the light of empirical evidence, require a truly new juvenile court that relies on knowledge of psychological development in order not to treat juveniles, but to ensure protection of their right to due process"); Candace Zierdt, The Little Engine That Arrived at the Wrong Station: How to Get Juvenile Justice Back on the Right Track, 33 U.S.F. L. Rev. 401, 427-434 (1999) (arguing that early intervention and community treatment are more effective than incarceration in combating juvenile crime).

Table of Cases

Index